fundamentals of
investment management

THE MCGRAW-HILL/IRWIN SERIES IN FINANCE, INSURANCE AND REAL ESTATE

Stephen A. Ross
Franco Modigliani Professor of Finance and Economics
Sloan School of Management
Massachusetts Institute of Technology
Consulting Editor

Financial Management

Adair
Excel Applications for Corporate Finance
First Edition

Benninga and Sarig
Corporate Finance: A Valuation Approach

Block and Hirt
Foundations of Financial Management
Eleventh Edition

Brealey, Myers, and Allen
Principles of Corporate Finance
Eighth Edition

Brealey, Myers, and Marcus
Fundamentals of Corporate Finance
Fourth Edition

Brooks
FinGame Online 4.0

Bruner
Case Studies in Finance: Managing for Corporate Value Creation
Fourth Edition

Chew
The New Corporate Finance: Where Theory Meets Practice
Third Edition

Chew and Gillan
Corporate Governance at the Crossroads: A Book of Readings
First Edition

DeMello
Cases in Finance
Second Edition

Grinblatt and Titman
Financial Markets and Corporate Strategy
Second Edition

Helfert
Techniques of Financial Analysis: A Guide to Value Creation
Eleventh Edition

Higgins
Analysis for Financial Management
Seventh Edition

Kester, Ruback, and Tufano
Case Problems in Finance
Twelfth Edition

Ross, Westerfield, and Jaffe
Corporate Finance
Seventh Edition

Ross, Westerfield, and Jordan
Essentials of Corporate Finance
Fourth Edition

Ross, Westerfield, and Jordan
Fundamentals of Corporate Finance
Seventh Edition

Smith
The Modern Theory of Corporate Finance
Second Edition

White
Financial Analysis with an Electronic Calculator
Fifth Edition

Investments

Bodie, Kane, and Marcus
Essentials of Investments
Fifth Edition

Bodie, Kane, and Marcus
Investments
Sixth Edition

Cohen, Zinbarg, and Zeikel
Investment Analysis and Portfolio Management
Fifth Edition

Corrado and Jordan
Fundamentals of Investments: Valuation and Management
Third Edition

Farrell
Portfolio Management: Theory and Applications
Second Edition

Hirt and Block
Fundamentals of Investment Management
Eighth Edition

Financial Institutions and Markets

Cornett and Saunders
Fundamentals of Financial Institutions Management

Rose and Hudgins
Bank Management and Financial Services
Sixth Edition

Rose and Marquis
Money and Capital Markets: Financial Institutions and Instruments in a Global Marketplace
Ninth Edition

Santomero and Babbel
Financial Markets, Instruments, and Institutions
Second Edition

Saunders and Cornett
Financial Institutions Management: A Risk Management Approach
Fifth Edition

Saunders and Cornett
Financial Markets and Institutions: A Modern Perspective
Second Edition

International Finance

Beim and Calomiris
Emerging Financial Markets

Eun and Resnick
International Financial Management
Third Edition

Kuemmerle
Case Studies in International Entrepreneurship: Managing and Financing Ventures in the Global Economy
First Edition

Levich
International Financial Markets: Prices and Policies
Second Edition

Real Estate

Brueggeman and Fisher
Real Estate Finance and Investments
Twelfth Edition

Corgel, Ling, and Smith
Real Estate Perspectives: An Introduction to Real Estate
Fourth Edition

Ling and Archer
Real Estate Principles: A Value Approach
First Edition

Financial Planning and Insurance

Allen, Melone, Rosenbloom, and Mahoney
Pension Planning: Pension, Profit-Sharing, and Other Deferred Compensation Plans
Ninth Edition

Crawford
Life and Health Insurance Law
Eighth Edition (LOMA)

Harrington and Niehaus
Risk Management and Insurance
Second Edition

Hirsch
Casualty Claim Practice
Sixth Edition

Kapoor, Dlabay, and Hughes
Focus on Personal Finance: An Active Approach to Help You Develop Successful Financial Skills
First Edition

Kapoor, Dlabay, and Hughes
Personal Finance
Seventh Edition

Williams, Smith, and Young
Risk Management and Insurance
Eighth Edition

With the purchase of a New Book*

You Can Access the Real Financial Data that the Experts Use!

*If you purchased a used book, see other side for access information.

This card entitles the purchaser of a new textbook to six months of access to the Educational Version of Standard & Poor's Market Insight®, a rich online resource featuring hundreds of the most often researched companies in the Market Insight database.

For 1000 companies, this website provides you:

- Access to six years' worth of fundamental financial data from the renowned Standard & Poor's COMPUSTAT® database
- 12 Excel Analytics Reports, including balance sheets, income statements, ratio reports and cash flow statements; adjusted prices reports, and profitability; forecasted values and monthly valuation data reports
- Access to Financial Highlights Reports including key ratios
- S & P Stock Reports that offer fundamental, quantitative and technical analysis
- EDGAR reports updated throughout the day
- Industry Surveys, written by S & P's Equity analysts
- Charting, providing powerful, interactive JavaCharts with price and volume data, incorporating over 100 different technical studies, user-specific watch lists, easy to customize parameters and drawing tools. Delayed real time pricing available.
- News feeds (updated hourly) for companies and industries.

See other side for your unique site ID access code.

Welcome to the Educational Version of Market Insight!

www.mhhe.com/edumarketinsight

Check out your textbook's website for details on how this special offer enhances the value of your purchase!

1. To get started, use your web browser to go to
www.mhhe.com/edumarketinsight

2. Enter your site ID exactly as it appears below.

3. You may be prompted to enter the site ID for future use—please keep this card.

Your site ID is:

ad216321

ISBN# 0-07-111796-2

STANDARD & POOR'S

*If you purchased a used book, this site ID may have expired.
For new password purchase, please go to
www.mhhe.com/edumarketinsight.
Password activation is good for a 6 month duration.

fundamentals of investment management

eighth edition

Geoffrey A. Hirt
Professor of Finance
DePaul University

Stanley B. Block, CFA, CMM
Professor of Finance and Holder of the
Stan Block Endowed Chair in Finance
Texas Christian University

Boston   Burr Ridge, IL   Dubuque, IA   Madison, WI   New York   San Francisco   St. Louis
Bangkok   Bogotá   Caracas   Kuala Lumpur   Lisbon   London   Madrid   Mexico City
Milan   Montreal   New Delhi   Santiago   Seoul   Singapore   Sydney   Taipei   Toronto

To our former and current students in the Educational Investment Funds at DePaul University and Texas Christian University. It has been a great privilege to serve as your professor and advisor throughout the years.
—Geoffrey A. Hirt and Stanley B. Block

The McGraw·Hill Companies

FUNDAMENTALS OF INVESTMENT MANAGEMENT

Published by McGraw-Hill/Irwin, a business unit of The McGraw-Hill Companies, Inc., 1221 Avenue of the Americas, New York, NY 10020. Copyright © 2006, 2003, 1999, 1996, 1993, 1990, 1986, 1983 by The McGraw-Hill Companies, Inc. All rights reserved. No part of this publication may be reproduced or distributed in any form or by any means, or stored in a database or retrieval system, without the prior written consent of The McGraw-Hill Companies, Inc., including, but not limited to, in any network or other electronic storage or transmission, or broadcast for distance learning.

Some ancillaries, including electronic and print components, may not be available to customers outside the United States.

This book is printed on acid-free paper.

1 2 3 4 5 6 7 8 9 0 VNH/VNH 0 9 8 7 6 5 4

ISBN 0-07-111598-6

www.mhhe.com

about the authors

Geoffrey A. Hirt Dr. Hirt is currently Professor of Finance at DePaul University. He received his PhD in Finance from the University of Illinois at Champaign-Urbana, his MBA from Miami University of Ohio, and his BA from Ohio-Wesleyan University. Geoff directed the Chartered Financial Analysts Study program for the Investment Analysts Society of Chicago from 1987 to 2001.

From 1987 to 1997 he was Chairman of the Finance Department at DePaul University and teaches Investments and Managerial Finance. Dr. Hirt is past president of the Midwest Finance Association and former editor of the Journal of Financial Education. He is currently on the Board of Directors of the Investment Analysts Society of Chicago and on the editorial board of the Journal of Investment Consulting.

He plays tennis and golf, is a music lover, and enjoys traveling with his wife, Linda.

Stanley B. Block Professor Block teaches financial management and investments at Texas Christian University, where he received the Burlington Northern Outstanding Teaching Award and the M. J. Neeley School of Business Distinguished Teaching Award. His research interests include financial markets, mergers, and high-yield bonds. He has served as President of the Southwestern Finance Association and is a Chartered Financial Analyst and a Certified Cash Manager. He enjoys sports and has run the NY Marathon. Professor Block holds a BA from the University of Texas at Austin, an MBA from Cornell University, and a PhD from LSU.

In 2001, his former students established the Dr. Stan Block $1.5 million Endowed Chair in Finance at Texas Christian University. He is the first chairholder of the named chair.

preface

Many changes have taken place in the financial markets since the first edition of *Fundamentals of Investment Management* was published in the early 1980s. However, the one constant has been a sincere commitment to this text to capture the excitement and enthusiasm that we feel for the topic of investment management.

Throughout the book, we attempt to establish the appropriate theoretical base, while at the same time following through with real-world examples. Students ultimately will be able to translate what they have learned in the course to actual participation in the financial markets.

Key Updates in the Eighth Edition

Application Examples

This text now includes called-out examples to highlight key ideas and show them in action. This feature gives students a place to pause to make sure they understand the material covered in the chapter, and gives instructors a place to launch classroom discussion.

Excel Examples

This feature will help your students understand how to use Excel for key investment topics—whether you want them to turn in homework in Excel, or just to have a basic understanding of how it is used. The actual spreadsheets are located at www.mhhe.com/hirtblock8e for students to access. An Excel icon *eXcel* appears in the margin next to examples that are illustrated by these spreadsheets.

Standard & Poor's Educational Version of Market Insight and End-of-Chapter Problems

Every new copy of this text comes with a free semester of access to Compustat data for 600 copies in an easy-to-use Web-based format. There are end-of-chapter problems at the end of relevant chapters that tie to this data, giving students real-world insight on investments concepts. To access the Standard & Poor's Educational Version of Market Insight, go to www.mhhe.com/edumarketinsight, click on the link next to the 'Continue' arrow, type in your site ID which is printed on the card in the front of the book, and click 'Login'.

Real-World Emphasis

As with previous editions, a continuing theme throughout this edition is the use of real company examples throughout the text. The Real World of Investing boxes highlight concepts in the text, and companies like Coca-Cola and Johnson & Johnson are used throughout to highlight key issues.

The Potential of the Internet

This edition continues to highlight the Internet's role in investing. New advancements are recognized within the chapters. Updated relevant websites are listed in the Exploring the Web feature, and Web Exercises are included in the end-of-chapter material.

Please see the chart below for highlighted chapter revisions and benefits.

Chapter	New Content	Benefit to Students
1: The Investment Setting, and 3: Participating in the Market	Description of the Tax Relief Act of 2003, which now provides equal treatment of dividends and capital gains for tax purposes.	Students learn the most up-to-date investment strategies that this new act brings.
2: Security Markets: Present and Future	Coverage of ECNs (electronic communication networks) as a new way of trading in the market. Also includes after-hours trading.	Students learn the very latest in market technology.
4: Sources of Investment Information	Reconstruction of information sources with almost total coverage related to the Internet as opposed to hard-copy publications.	Students will have the best of financial information at their fingertips.
5: Economic Activity	Updated economic data and graphs.	Students have more current information and historical perspective.
6: Industry Analysis 7: Valuation of the Individual Firm 8: Financial Statement Analysis	The three chapters on fundamental analysis are now integrated around the drug industry and Johnson & Johnson.	Students see a coherent, integrative picture of how a company should be analyzed and are much better prepared for a term project.
10: Investments in Special Situations and Anomalies	The chapter is expanded to cover anomalies as well as special situations.	Students are able to observe "new" opportunities to make money in the market.
14: Convertible Securities and Warrants	Amazon.com convertible bonds are covered in extensive detail from issue to call.	Students understand the full dynamics of trading in convertible securities.
15: Put and Call Options	The International Securities Exchange's (ISE) role as an evolving member of the Options Clearing Corporation is described.	Students learn about the latest development in option trading.
18: Mutual Funds	Exchange traded funds (ETFs) are given new, expanded coverage. SPDRs, DIAMONDS, and so on, are discussed.	Students learn a new way to use mutual funds that did not exist a few years ago.
19: International Securities Markets	The world market is covered on a post 9/11 basis.	Students see the latest developments in international opportunities and risks.
22: Measuring Risks and Returns of Portfolio Managers	Extensive coverage of the effect of holding periods on returns over an 80-year time frame.	Students understand the extreme importance of holding periods in measuring returns.

Student Study Features

Application Examples

This text now includes called-out examples to highlight key ideas and show them in action. This feature gives students a place to pause to make sure they understand the material covered in the chapter and gives instructors a place to launch classroom discussion.

> **Application Example**
>
> 1.40 percent from December 31 (look at the last column to see the percentage change from the prior year) and that the Standard and Poor's 500 Stock Index is up 2.51 percent over a comparable time period. One might observe that this was a good period for market performance as further indicated in the 12-month percent change column. The average annual increase over the long term is 10 to 12 percent.
>
> The Standard & Poor's Indexes are **value-weighted indexes,** which means each company is weighted in the index by its own total market value as a percentage of the total market value for all firms. For example, in a value-weighted index comprising the following three firms, the weighting would be:
>
> | Stock | Shares | Price | Total Market Value | Weighting |
> |-------|--------|-------|--------------------|-----------|
> | A | 150 | $10 | $ 1,500 | 12.0% |
> | B | 200 | 20 | 4,000 | 32.0 |
> | C | 500 | 14 | 7,000 | 56.0 |
> | | | | $12,500 | 100.0% |
>
> In each case, the weighting is determined by dividing the total market value of the stock by the total market value for all firms. In the case of stock A, that would be $1,500 divided by $12,500, or 12 percent. The same procedure is followed for stocks B and C.
>
> Even though stock C has only the second highest price, it makes up 56 percent of the average because of its high total market value based on 500 shares

> **Application Example** *eXcel*
>
> discount rate as the required rate of return. The required rate of return is intended to provide the investor with a minimum rate of return based on the stock's beta. Twelve percent is sufficient to fulfill that function in this example.
>
> Rather than project the dividends for an extremely long period and then discount them back to the present, we can reduce previously presented Formula 7–4 to a more usable form:
>
> $$P_0 = D_1/(K_e - g) \quad (7-5)$$
>
> This formula is appropriate as long as two conditions are met. The first is that the growth rate must be constant. For the ABC Corporation, we are assuming that to be the case. It is a constant 8 percent. Second, K_e (the required rate of return) must exceed g (the growth rate). Since K_e is 12 percent and g is 8 percent for the ABC Corporation, this condition is also met. Let's further assume D_1 (the expected dividend at the end of period 1) is $3.38.
>
> Using Formula 7–5, we determine a stock value of:
>
> $$P_0 = D_1/(K_e - g)$$
> $$= \$3.38/(0.12 - 0.08)$$
> $$= \$3.38/0.04$$
> $$= \$84.50$$
>
> This value, in theory, represents the present value of all future dividends. The meaning is further illustrated in Table 7–1, in which we take the present value of the first 20 years of dividends ($43.71) and then add in a figure of $40.79 to arrive at the present value of all future dividends of $84.50 as previously determined by Formula 7–5. The $40.79 value represents the present value of dividends occurring between 2025 and infinity (i.e., after 2025).[2]

Excel Examples

This feature will help your students understand how to use Excel for key investment topics—whether for homework, projects, or for basic understanding. The actual spreadsheets are located at www.mhhe.com/hirtblock8e for students to access. An Excel icon appears in the margin next to examples that are illustrated by these spreadsheets.

> **the real world of investing**
>
> **Institutional Investors: Michael Eisner, and the Disney Corporation**
>
> The smooth functioning of a company in the financial markets is dependent upon a good interaction between stockholders and the management of the firm. No person is more important to this relationship than the Chairman of the Board of Directors.
>
> In March 2004, Michael Eisner saw his title of Chairman of the Board of Walt Disney Co. stripped away from him. Over 3,000 stockholders attended the firm's annual meeting, some wearing Disney costumes and many more handing out anti-Eisner pamphlets. In total, two billion votes were cast by stockholders through the mail, on the Internet, and in person. Forty-three percent of the votes withheld support for Eisner to continue as Chairman of the Board. Normally, votes for continuation as Chairman of the Board carry 1 or 2 percent dissenting votes, so 43 percent was an astronomical figure of nonsupport.
>
> The attention that Disney's election drew is reflective of the new era of institutional investor involvement in assessing the performance of company executives. Large pension funds, endowments, mutual funds, and so on, are making their voices heard as never before and this is changing the nature of the financial markets and the way companies are run. CalPERS, the California Public Employees Retirement System, holding 9.9 million shares of Disney stock, was particularly adamant in insisting that Eisner step down. Their voice is often loud and not easily ignored in corporate governance issues.
>
> As a slight concession, Eisner was allowed to stay on as CEO, but George Mitchell, a former Senator from Maine, was installed as Chairman of the Board. More and more companies are splitting up the positions of Chairman of the Board and CEO. This reduces the likelihood of the Board of Directors merely acting as a rubber stamp for the CEO.
>
> In fairness to Eisner, it should be recognized that at one time he was the golden boy of the Disney empire. Recruited to Disney from Paramount in 1984, he rejuvenated the firm from the edge of disaster to the "darling of Wall Street" through his theme parks, marketing savvy, and successful movie ventures.
>
> However, in the last decade his micromanagement style has driven off top managers such as studio chief Jeffrey Katzenberg, and Disney has underperformed other media companies. The stock market value of the firm and its earnings performances were still at 1997 levels in the Spring of 2004 while earnings of others in the industry had surged ahead. Failure to consider a lucrative takeover offer for Disney by Comcast put Eisner further behind the eight ball, and his tenure as CEO is in doubt.

"Real World of Investing" Boxes

Timely and relevant, these boxes highlight topics of interest concerning corporations and investors. Aimed at bringing real life to the classroom, these boxes provide a link from the material learned in the student's investment class to the real business world.

The Wall Street Journal Projects

1. Under the "What's News" section of *The Wall Street Journal,* there is often a story related to the economy covered under "Business and Finance." Track this column into the future until you find three such stories. They can be about GDP, Federal Reserve policy, unemployment, interest rates, and so on.
2. Observe the behavior of the stock market related to the story. Normally the journal will report the announcement from the prior day so observe stock market movements for the prior day (which are also reported in the current

WSJ PROJECTS

Offered at the end of each chapter, each problem utilizes current information for *The Wall Street Journal* to help illustrate main points within the chapter. These projects are especially useful to faculty who require the *WSJ* to be used in conjunction with their courses. See Packaging Options for a special *WSJ* student rate with this text.

The Market Environment

The financial markets have changed dramatically during the last decade, and they continue to change at a rapid pace. This period has been one of deregulation, new laws, mergers, global consolidation, online (Internet) brokerage, and electronic communication networks (ECNs). These structural changes have been accompanied by 24-hour trading, decimalization of stock quotes, and intense global competition.

The last part of the 1990s was punctuated with mergers and consolidations, both global and domestic. The 1998 merger between Citicorp (the parent of CitiBank) and Travelers Insurance (including the Salomon Smith Barney division) created Citigroup. This merger caused a significant change in the way competitors thought about financial services. For the first time since the 1930s we had an institution that was able to sell insurance, underwrite securities, perform brokerage functions, and offer commercial banking under the same ownership. This had been prohibited by the Glass Steagall Act, which was enacted after the "Great Crash" of 1929 to keep one bank from being both a commercial bank and an investment bank. In 1999 the U.S. Congress passed the Gramm-Leach-Bliley Act allowing financial institutions to offer full financial services. Shortly after, Chase and JPMorgan merged and other commercial banks gobbled up smaller investment banks and brokerage firms. In 2004 JPMorgan Chase merged with Bank One to become a major competitor to Citigroup. Throughout this process, American financial institutions were starting to look more like European universal banks and would be able to compete more effectively around the globe during the 21st century.

On September 11, 2001, the World Trade Center in New York City and the Pentagon in Washington, D.C., were attacked by terrorists. In New York both towers and many surrounding buildings were destroyed, and thousands of lives

www.citicorp.com
www.citigroup.com

Global Coverage

A new global icon cues students to specific areas of the text that focus on world issues and also explain why students need to understand those markets.

"Exploring the Web" Boxes

At the end of each chapter, this box serves as a quick reference of pertinent chapter-related websites and short comments on what can be found at each site.

exploring the web

Website	Comment
www.mhhe.com/hirtblock8e	The McGraw-Hill website for this textbook provides valuable student resources.
www.aaii.com	A nonprofit website educating do-it-yourself investors
www.nasdaq.com	Provides information about Nasdaq stocks and market
www.nyse.com	Provides information about New York Stock Exchange, listings, and regulations
www.nareit.com	Provides information and data about real estate investment trusts
www.quicken.com	Provides understandable coverage of financial planning and investing
www.morningstar.com	Contains evaluations of and information about stocks and mutual funds
www.bondmarkets.com	Provides information about corporate and government bonds
www.amex.com	Provides information about stocks, options, and exchange trade funds on the American Stock Exchange
www.business.com	Provides a searchable database for links to sites by industry
www.investmentsclub.com	Provides information and education for investment club members
www.investopedia.com	Provides a general education site about stocks and investing
web.utk.edu/~jwachowi/part2.html	Site created by finance professor with links to information resources
www.investorwords.com	Provides links to finance sites and glossary of finance terminology
www.reuters.com	Contains business and financial market news for United States and other countries
www.inetats.com	
www.tradearca.com	
www.isld.com	These six websites all represent electronic communication networks (ECNs) and represent the different companies and markets competing with traditional floor-based markets such as the NYSE.
www.bloombergtradebook.com	
www.ebrut.com	
www.nextrade.org	

CFA Questions

Many chapters also include questions and solutions from CFA Level I study materials. The CFA problems are designed to show students the relevancy of what is learned in their investment course to what is expected of certified professional financial analysts.

CFA Material

The following material contains sample questions and solutions from a prior Level I CFA exam. While the terminology is slightly different from that in this text, you can still view the skills necessary for the CFA exam.

CFA Exam Question

3. As a firm operating in a mature industry, Arbot Industries is expected to maintain a constant dividend payout ratio and constant growth rate of earnings for the foreseeable future. Earnings were $4.50 per share in the recently completed fiscal year. The dividend payout ratio has been a constant 55 percent in recent years and is expected to remain so. Arbot's return on equity (ROE) is expected to remain at 10 percent in the future, and you require an 11 percent return on the stock.
   a. Using the constant growth dividend discount model, *calculate* the current value of Arbot common stock. *Show* your calculations.

   After an aggressive acquisition and marketing program, it now appears that Arbot's earnings per share and ROE will grow rapidly over the next two years. You are aware that the dividend discount model can be useful in estimating the value of common stock even when the assumption of constant growth does not apply.

Critical Thought Cases

Critical Thought Cases, which examine investor behaviors, appear at the end of most chapters. Cases that reveal ethical dilemmas have a "Focus on Ethics" label. Each case is concluded with 2–4 questions that guide students to dig deeper into the issues.

Critical Thought Case (A Classic Example)—Focus on Ethics

Gail Rosenberg still had her head in the clouds when she joined Salomon Brothers Inc. in June 1990. While she was proud of her newly awarded MBA from the Wharton School of Business at the University of Pennsylvania, she was even prouder of joining the most prestigious investment banking house on Wall Street, the famous Salomon Brothers. She had a received five job offers, but this was the one she wanted. Not only would she train with the best and brightest on Wall Street, but she also would be working for a firm in which 90 employees made more than $1 million a year. How many *Fortune* 500 companies, law firms, or other employers could claim such a record? She was pleased with her own starting salary of $110,000 a year and could see matters only getting better in the future.

After some general training and apprenticeship-type work, she was assigned to the government bond-trading unit in February 1991. Here she would help in the bidding and distributing of U.S. Treasury bills and notes. Salomon Brothers was the largest participant among investment banking houses in this field, so she knew she would quickly learn the ropes.

Her first major participation would be in the Treasury bill auction for May 1991. Salomon Brothers would bid on behalf of many of its clients and probably have some influence on the ultimate price and yield at which the Treasury bills were sold. As Gail got on her PC to help process orders, she noticed Salomon Brothers submitted bids for clients that did not exist. It was no surprise to Gail that Salomon Brothers captured 85 percent of the bidding and virtually controlled the pricing of the securities.

In a state of shock, Gail went to her immediate supervisor and reported what she had observed on her computer screen. She was told to calm down, that she was no longer in school, and she was witnessing a common practice on "The Street." She was further informed that John Gutfreund, chairman of the board of Salomon Brothers, and President Thomas Strauss implicitly approved of such practices. She felt a little like Oliver North in the Iran-Contra affair cover-up. She had worked very hard to get to this tender point in her career and was now disillusioned.

Question

1. What strategy or advice can you offer to Gail Rosenberg?

Web Exercises

Web Exercises at the end of each chapter highlight specific chapter topics by having the student search the Internet for data and then spend time analyzing that data to solve exercises. Exercises range in topics from focusing on specific companies, SEC, NYSE, government agencies, to commercial websites.

Web Exercise

In this exercise, we get a better feel for the major market indexes. Go to www.bloomberg.com.

1. Click on "Market Data" across the top. Record the value and change for the Dow Jones Industrial Average (DJIA), Nasdaq, and S&P 500.
2. Click on "Stocks" in the left margin.
3. Then click on "Dow." Scroll down and record the current price for 3M, Hewlett Packard, and Procter and Gamble.
4. Which of the 30 Dow stocks had the largest percentage upside movement? Which had the largest percentage downside movement?
5. If you were using a price-weighted index, which stock would have the greatest impact on the DJIA?
6. Return to the prior page. Click on "Nikkei" across the top. Scroll down and indicate which stock in the Nikkei 225 had the highest volume.

Note: From time to time, companies redesign their websites, and occasionally a topic we have listed may have been deleted, updated, or moved into a different location. Most websites have a "site map" or "site index" listed on a different page. If you click on the site map or site index you will be introduced to a table of contents that should aid you in finding the topic you are looking for.

Standard & Poor's Educational Version of Market Insight and End-of-Chapter Problems

Every new copy of this text comes with a free semester of access to Compustat data for 600 copies in an easy-to-use Web-based format. There are end-of-chapter problems at the end of relevant chapters that tie to this data, giving students real-world insight on investments concepts.

S&P Problems
www.mhhe.com/edumarkinsight

STANDARD &POOR'S

1. Log on to the McGraw-Hill website: www.mhhe.com/edumarketinsight (see page vi in the preface for instructions).
2. Click on Company, which is the first box below the Market Insight title.
3. Put the ticker symbol for Johnson & Johnson (JNJ) in the box, and click on go.
4. On the left margin, click on Excel Analytics to open the list of choices. Under Valuation Data, click on Monthly Valuation Data to open the Excel spreadsheet. Given the data for the last seven months, what has been happening to the Johnson & Johnson's beta, price earnings ratio, and dividend yield?
5. Comparing the P/E ratio of the company to that of the S&P 500, what has been the trend of the P/E relative to the S&P 500? Is Johnson & Johnson selling at a premium or discount to the S&P 500? You may use the second worksheet at the bottom of the spreadsheet labeled "% Change" and the third worksheet at the bottom of the spreadsheet labeled "Key Item Charts" to help answer this question.
6. Close the spreadsheet and return to the valuation section in the left margin and click on Forecasted Values. What is the price forecast for Johnson & Johnson one year from now? Do the earnings per share trends justify the estimate?
7. On the bottom of the spreadsheet, click on the third worksheet labeled "Key Item Charts" and exam the graphs. What can you say about Johnson & Johnson's predictability over the last several years? Does the trend in long-term debt and cash flow support the price projection you found in the previous question?

Additional Student Resources

Self-Study Software CD, enclosed free with every new book! This CD, written by the authors, is perfect for preparing for exams. The program has 50–75 questions per chapter that students can use as practice tests to find out just where more study time is needed. All questions are multiple-choice, and they test on concepts and key equations.

Student Edition of the Online Learning Center at www.mhhe.com/hirtblock8e
Students have free access to the text site and will find online quizzes, additional study material, links to PowerWeb investments articles, and Investments Online, an additional site with current events, exercises, and tutorials on key investment topics.

Instructor Supplements

Instructor's Resource CD (ISBN 0-07-296651-3)

Find all of your teaching resources here!

- *Instructor's Manual.* Includes detailed solutions for all text problems, as well as teaching strategies for each chapter. Also available in print format (ISBN 0-07-310724-7)
- *Test Bank.* These Word files contain over 1,000 questions, including true-false, multiple choice, matching quizzes, and many problems for select chapters that lend themselves to problem material. Also available in print format (ISBN 0-07-310725-5)
- *Computerized Test Bank.* The test bank questions are in a computerized test bank format utilizing McGraw-Hill's EZ Test testing software to quickly create customized exams. This user friendly program allows instructors to sort questions by format; edit existing questions or add new ones; and scramble questions for multiple versions of the same test.
- *PowerPoint Presentations.* Developed by Victor Abraham. This new PowerPoint presentation incorporates key learning objectives and concepts, examples, tables and figures, Excel spreadsheets, and key websites. Instructors can manipulate the slides to fit their own course organization.

Videos (ISBN 0-07-296652-1)

Updated videos contain segments focusing on investments-related issues and case studies, such as derivatives, bonds, and portfolio management.

Instructor's Edition of the Online Learning Center
www.mhhe.com/hirtblock8e

Most of the above supplements are also located on the text's website, password-protected for instructor use only. You will also find links to Investments Online, which includes current events assignments and additional investment topics for classroom discussion. Also, the Finance Around the World feature provides links to news sources around the world to incorporate more international current events into your course.

Packaging Options

The following packages are available with this text. Ask your McGraw-Hill/Irwin sales representative for ordering information.

Finance and Investments using *The Wall Street Journal,* by Peter R. Crabb

This supplement teaches students how to analyze articles and data in the *WSJ* by providing exercises using past reprints and then asking students to do similar exercises using a current edition. Perfect for students wanting to get the most out of their *Wall Street Journal* subscriptions!

The Wall Street Journal Subscription

Students can add a 15-week subscription to *The Wall Street Journal* (both print and online) to the textbook for $20.00 in addition to the price of the text. Students will receive a card packaged with their text that they can fill out and mail in to start their subscription. Once 10 students in an instructor's class sign up, the instructor will receive a year's subscription free.

BusinessWeek Subscription

Students can add a 10-week subscription to *BusinessWeek* (either print or online) to the textbook for $8.25 in addition to the price of the text. Students can complete a registration card, and instructors will receive a year's subscription free.

Financial Times Subscription

Students can add a 15-week subscription to *Financial Times* (both print and online) to the textbook for $10.00 in addition to the price of the text. Students can complete a registration card, and instructors will receive a year's subscription free.

Acknowledgments

We are grateful to the following individuals for their thoughtful reviews and suggestions for the eighth edition:

Kristen Beck, Steven Freund, Thomas Krueger, Cheryl McGaughey, Peter Naylor, Mike Nugent, Linda Ravelle, Mark Rosa, Philip Russell, George Troughton, Glenn Wood, Sheng Yang, Zhong-Guo Zhou.

For their prior reviews and helpful comments, we are grateful to Grace C. Allen, Omar Benkato, Carol J. Billingham, Laurence E. Blose, Gerald A. Blum, Keith E. Boles, Jerry D. Boswell, Paul Bolster, Lynn Brown, John A. Cole, Joe B. Copeland, Marcia M. Cornett, Don R. Cox, James P. D'Mello, Betty Driver, John Dunkelberg, Adrian C. Edwards, Jane H. Finley, Adam Gehr, Paul Grier, Richard Gritta, Arthur C. Gudikunst, Mahmoud Haddad, David Haraway, Gay B. Hatfield, David Heskel, Marcus Ingram, Joel R. Jankowski, Amir Jassim, Domingo Joaquin, Peppi Kenny, James Khule, Sheri Kole, Thomas M. Krueger, David Lawrence, Joe B. Lipscomb, David Louton, Carl Luft, John D. Markese, Kyle Mattson, Cheryl McGaughey, Mike Miller, Majed Muhtaseb, Majed R. Muhtaseb, Harold Mulherin, Jamal Munshie, Winford Naylor, Carl C. Nielsen, Raj A. Padmaraj, Roger R. Palmer, John W. Peavy III, Richard Ponarul, Dave Rand, Spuma Rao, Linda Ravelle, Arnold Redman, Linda L. Richardson, Tom S. Sale, Art Schwartz, Maneesh Sharma, Joseph F. Singer, Ira Smolowitz, Don Taylor, Frank N. Tiernan, George Troughton, Allan J. Twark, Howard E. Van Auken, Bismarck Williams, and Glen Wood.

We would especially like to thank Barbara Hari, Editorial Coordinator, for her outstanding editorial work on this project; Michele Janicek, Senior Sponsoring

Editor, and Steve Patterson, Publisher, for their continued editorial support of this product; Rhonda Seelinger and Jennifer Jelinski for their continued significant support in marketing; and the entire team at McGraw-Hill/Irwin for their outstanding help and guidance in developing the eighth edition.

We are grateful for the support and encouragement provided by DePaul University and Texas Christian University. We also thank Victor Abraham for creating the PowerPoint slides and checking the accuracy of the Standard & Poor's problems found in the end of chapter material. Finally, we thank Brian Hirt for developing the "Self-Study" software that can be found on the *Fundamentals of Investment Management,* 8e Online Learning Center.

Geoffrey A. Hirt

Stanley B. Block

brief contents

part one
Introduction to Investments

1. The Investment Setting 4
2. Security Markets: Present and Future 27
3. Participating in the Market 58
4. Sources of Investment Information 84

part two
Analysis and Valuation of Equity Securities

5. Economic Activity 114
6. Industry Analysis 142
7. Valuation of the Individual Firm 168
8. Financial Statement Analysis 200

part three
Issues in Efficient Markets

9. A Basic View of Technical Analysis and Market Efficiency 240
10. Investments in Special Situations and Anomalies 267

part four
Fixed-Income and Leveraged Securities

11. Bond and Fixed-Income Fundamental 290
12. Principles of Bond Valuation and Investment 326
13. Duration and Reinvestment Concepts 354
14. Convertible Securities and Warrants 380

part five
Derivative Products

15. Put and Call Options 410
16. Commodities and Financial Futures 443
17. Stock Index Futures and Options 467

part six
Broadening the Investment Perspective

18. Mutual Funds 494
19. International Securities Markets 527
20. Investments in Real Assets 557

part seven
Introduction to Portfolio Management

21. A Basic Look at Portfolio Management and Capital Market Theory 586
22. Measuring Risk and Return of Portfolio Managers 619

appendices

Appendix A: Compound Sum of $1   650

Appendix B: Compound Sum of an Annuity of $1   652

Appendix C: Present Value of $1   654

Appendix D: Present Value of an Annuity of $1   656

Appendix E: Time Value of Money and Investment Applications   658

Appendix F: Using Calculators for Financial Analysis   667

glossary   676

index   695

contents

part one
Introduction to Investments

chapter 1. The Investment Setting   4

Forms of Investment   5
The Setting of Investment Objectives   7
   Risk and Safety of Principal   7
   Current Income versus Capital Appreciation   8
   Liquidity Considerations   8
   Short-Term versus Long-Term Orientation   9
   Tax Factors   9
   Ease of Management   10
   Retirement and Estate Planning Considerations   11
Measures of Risk and Return   12
   Risk   12
Actual Consideration of Required Returns   14
   Real Rate of Return   14
   Anticipated Inflation Factor   14
   Risk Premium   15
What You Will Learn   19

Appendix 1A: Career Opportunities in Investments   24

chapter 2. Security Markets: Present and Future   27

The Market Environment   28
Market Functions   29
   Market Efficiency and Liquidity   29
   Competition and Allocation of Capital   30
   Secondary Markets   30
   Primary Markets   30
Organization of the Primary Markets: The Investment Banker   30
   Underwriting Function   31
   Distribution   31
   Investment Banking Competition   34
Organization of the Secondary Markets   37
   Organized Exchanges   37
   Consolidated Tape   37
   Listing Requirements for Firms   38
   Membership for Market Participants   40

Other Organized Exchanges   43
   The American Stock Exchange   43
   The Chicago Board Options Exchange   43
   Futures Markets   43
Over-the-Counter Markets—Electronic Markets   44
   Nasdaq Stock Market   44
   Debt Securities Traded Over-the-Counter   45
Electronic Communication Networks (ECNs)   46
Institutional Trading   47
Regulation of the Security Markets   48
   Securities Act of 1933   48
   Securities Exchange Act of 1934   49
   The Securities Acts Amendments of 1975   50
   Other Legislation   50
   Insider Trading   51
   Program Trading and Market Price Limits   51

chapter 3. Participating in the Market   58

Measures of Price Performance: Market Indexes   58
Indexes and Averages   59
   Dow Jones Average   59
   Standard & Poor's Indexes   61
   Value Line Average   63
   Other Market Indexes   63
Buying and Selling in the Market   68
   Cash or Margin Account   68
   Long or Short?—That Is the Question   70
Types of Orders   71
Cost of Trading   71
Taxes and the 2003 Tax Act   74
   Capital Gains and Dividends   750

chapter 4. Sources of Investment Information   84

Aggregate Economic Data   85
   Federal Reserve Bulletin   85
   Federal Reserve Banks   86
   Survey of Current Business   89
   Websites and Economic Data   91
   Other Sources of Economic Data   91
Investment Advisory Resources   92
   Mergent (Moody's)   92

Standard & Poor's 93
Value Line 94
Morningstar 98
Other Investment Resources 98
SEC Filings, Periodicals, and Journals 99
Securities and Exchange Commission Filings 99
Periodicals and Newspapers 100
Journals 105
Databases 105
The Internet and Investment Information 107
Additional Websites 107
Class Project Websites 109

part two
Analysis and Valuation of Equity Securities

chapter 5. Economic Activity 114

Economic Activity and the Business Cycle 115
Federal Government Economic Policy 116
Fiscal Policy 118
Monetary Policy 122
Government Policy, Real Growth, and Inflation 124
Business Cycle and Cyclical Indicators 126
Economic Indicators 130
Stock Prices and Economic Variables 130
Money Supply 130
Gross Domestic Product 132
Industrial Production and Manufacturing 133
Business Cycles and Industry Relationships 135

chapter 6. Industry Analysis 142

Industry Life Cycles 143
Development—Stage I 144
Growth—Stage II 144
Expansion—Stage III 145
Maturity—Stage IV 146
Decline—Stage V 148
Growth in Nongrowth Industries 149
Industry Structure 149
Economic Structure 150
Competitive Structure 151
Pharmaceutical Industry—An Example 153
Life-Cycle Analysis 154

Government Regulation 154
Research and Development 157
Product Diversity 158
Patents and Generic Drugs 159
Demographics and Managed Care 159
Industry Groups and Rotational Investing 160

Appendix 6A: Sustainable Growth Model 165

chapter 7. Valuation of the Individual Firm 168

Basic Valuation Concepts 169
Review of Risk and Required Rate of Return Concepts 169
Dividend Valuation Models 171
General Dividend Model 171
Constant Growth Model 171
A Nonconstant Growth Model 174
Earnings Valuation Models 175
The Combined Earnings and Dividend Model 176
The Price-Earnings Ratio 177
The P/E Ratio for Individual Stocks 180
The Pure, Short-Term Earnings Model 182
Relating an Individual Stock's P/E Ratio to the Market 182
Other Valuation Models Using Average Price Ratios and 10-Year Averages 183
Forecasting Earnings per Share 185
Least Squares Trendline 186
The Income Statement Method 187
Growth Stocks and Growth Companies 188
Assets as a Source of Stock Value 189
Natural Resources 189

chapter 8. Financial Statement Analysis 200

The Major Financial Statements 201
Income Statement 201
Balance Sheet 202
Statement of Case Flows 204
Key Financial Ratios for the Security Analyst 207
Ratio Analysis 208
Bankruptcy Studies 208
Classification System 209
Uses of Ratios 217
Comparing Long-Term Trends 220

Deficiencies of Financial Statements 223
   Inflation Effects 223
   Inventory Valuation 224
   Extraordinary Gains and Losses 226
   Pension Fund Liabilities 226
   Foreign Exchange Transactions 226
   Other Distortions 226

part three
Issues in Efficient Markets

chapter 9. A Basic View of Technical Analysis and Market Efficiency 240

Technical Analysis 241
The Use of Charting 242
   Essential Elements of the Dow Theory 242
   Support and Resistance Levels 243
   Volume 244
   Types of Charts 244
Key Indicator Series 248
   Contrary Opinion Rules 248
   Smart Money Rules 251
   Overall Market Rules 253
Efficient Market Hypothesis 255
Weak Form of the Efficient Market Hypothesis 256
   Tests of Independence 256
   Trading Rule Tests 257
   Implications for Technical Analysis 257
Semistrong Form of the Efficient Market Hypothesis 258
   Implications for Fundamental Analysis 259
Strong Form of the Efficient Market Hypothesis 260

chapter 10. Investments in Special Situations and Anomalies 267

Mergers and Acquisitions 268
   Premiums for Acquired Company 268
   Acquiring Company Performance 270
   Form of Payment 271
New Stock Issues 271
   Performance of Investment Bankers 272
Exchange Listings 273
Stock Repurchase 275
   Reasons for Repurchase 275
   Actual Market Effect 275

The Small-Firm and Low-P/E Ratio Effect 277
The Book Value to Market Value Effect 280
Other Stock-Related Anomalies 281
Truly Superior Returns or Mismeasurement? 284

part four
Fixed-Income and Leveraged Securities

chapter 11. Bond and Fixed-Income Fundamentals 290

The Bond Contract 291
Secured and Unsecured Bonds 292
The Composition of the Bond Market 293
   U.S. Government Securities 293
   Federally Sponsored Credit Agency Issues 297
   State and Local Government Securities 298
   Corporate Securities 300
Bond Market Investors 302
Distribution Procedures 303
   Private Placement 303
Bond Ratings 303
   Actual Rating System 305
Junk Bonds or High-Yield Bonds 306
Bond Quotes 307
   Quotes on Government Securities 309
Bond Markets, Capital Market Theory, and Efficiency 310
The Global Bond Market 313
   Dollar-Denominated Bonds 313
   Foreign-Pay Bonds 314
Other Forms of Fixed-Income Securities 314
Preferred Stock as an Alternative to Debt 316
   Features of Preferred Stock 316

chapter 12. Principles of Bond Valuation and Investment 326

Fundamentals of the Bond Valuation Process 327
Rates of Return 329
   Current Yield 329
   Yield to Maturity 330
   Yield to Call 333
   Anticipated Realized Yield 334
   Reinvestment Assumption 334

The Movement of Interest Rates 335
    Term Structure of Interest Rates 336
Investment Strategy: Interest-Rate Considerations 339
    Bond-Pricing Rules 341
    Example of Interest-Rate Change 341
    Deep Discount versus Par Bonds 342
    Yield Spread Considerations 342
Bond Swaps 344

Appendix 12A: Interpolating to Find Yield to Maturity 353

chapter 13. Duration and Reinvestment Concepts 354

Review of Basic Bond Valuation Concepts 355
Duration 356
Duration and Price Sensitivity 359
    Duration and Market Rates 362
    Duration and Coupon Rates 363
Bringing Together the Influences on Duration 364
Duration and Zero-Coupon Bonds 365
The Uses of Duration 366
Bond Reinvestment Assumptions and Terminal Wealth Analysis 367
    Reinvestment Assumptions 367
    Terminal Wealth Analysis 368
    Zero-Coupon Bonds and Terminal Wealth 370

Appendix 13A: Modified Duration and Convexity 377

chapter 14. Convertible Securities and Warrants 380

Convertible Securities 381
Conversion Price and Conversion Ratio 382
    Value of the Convertible Bond 382
    Bond Price and Premiums 384
    Comparing the Convertible Bond with Common Stock Purchase 387
    Disadvantages of Convertibles 391
    When to Convert into Common Stock 391
Advantages and Disadvantages to the Issuing Corporation 392
Accounting Considerations with Convertibles 394

Speculating Through Warrants 395
    Valuation of Warrants 397
    Further Explanation of Intrinsic Value 398
    Use of Warrants by Corporations 399
Accounting Considerations with Warrants 400

part five
Derivative Products

chapter 15. Put and Call Options 410

Options Markets 411
    Listed Options Exchanges 411
The Options Clearing Corporation 414
    Option Premiums 414
    Intrinsic Value 415
    Speculative Premium (Time Value) 416
Basic Option Strategies 419
    Buying Call Options 420
    Writing Call Options 423
    Buying Put Options 425
Using Options in Combinations 426
    Spreads 426
    Straddles 426
Other Option Considerations 426

Appendix 15A: The Black-Scholes Option Pricing Model 432

Appendix 15B: The Use of Option Spreads and Straddles 438

chapter 16. Commodities and Financial Futures 443

Types of Commodities and Exchanges 445
    Types of Commodities Contracts 447
Actual Commodities Contract 447
    Margin Requirements 448
    Market Conditions 448
    Gains and Losses 449
    Price Movement Limitations 450
Reading Market Quotes 451
The Cash Market and the Futures Market 452
The Futures Market for Financial Instruments 452
Currency Futures 453

Interest-Rate Futures 454
    Hedging with Interest-Rate Futures 456
    An Actual Example 457
Options as Well as Futures 458
Interest-Rate Swaps 459

chapter 17. Stock Index Futures and Options 467

The Concept of Derivative Products 468
Trading Stock Index Futures 469
    Trading Cycle 471
    Margin Requirement 471
    Cash Settlement 472
    Basis 473
    Overall Features 473
Use of Stock Index Futures 473
    Speculation 474
    Hedging 476
    Arbitraging 479
Trading Stock Index Options 479
    Actual Trade in the S&P 100 Index 481
Hedging with Stock Index Options 482
Options on Stock Index Futures 482

part six — Broadening the Investment Perspective

chapter 18. Mutual Funds 494

Advantages and Disadvantages of Mutual Funds 496
Closed-End versus Open-End Funds 498
    Exchange Traded Funds 501
Investing in Open-End Funds 501
    Load versus No-Load Funds 502
    No-Load Funds 502
Information on Mutual Funds 506
Differing Objectives and the Diversity of Mutual Funds 506
    Matching Investment Objectives with Fund Types 511
The Prospectus 512
Distribution and Taxation 513
    Tax Differences between Mutual Funds and Individual Stock Portfolios 514

Shareholder Services 514
Investment Funds, Long-Term Planning, and Dollar-Cost Averaging 515
Evaluating Fund Performance 516
    Lipper Mutual Fund Performance Averages 517
    Computing Total Return on Your Investment 517

Appendix 18A: Unit Investment Trusts (UITs) 525

chapter 19. International Securities Markets 527

The World Equity Market 528
Diversification Benefits 532
Return Potential in International Markets 536
    Current Quotations of Foreign Market Performance 539
    Other Market Differences 539
Currency Fluctuation and Rates of Return 541
Other Obstacles to International Investments 545
    Political Risks 546
    Tax Problems 546
    Lack of Market Efficiency 546
    Administrative Problems 546
    Information Difficulties 547
Methods of Participating in Foreign Investments 547
    Direct Investments 548
    Indirect Investments 548

chapter 20. Investments in Real Assets 557

Advantages and Disadvantages of Real Assets 558
Real Estate as an Investment 559
    Real Estate in the Last Decade and the Future Outlook 559
Valuation of Real Estate 561
    The Cost Approach 561
    Comparative Sales Value 561
    The Income Approach 561
    Combination of the Three Approaches 562
A More Comprehensive Analysis 562
Financing of Real Estate 567
    Types of Mortgages 568
Forms of Real Estate Ownership 569
    Individual or Regular Partnership 569
    Syndicate or Limited Partnership 570
    Real Estate Investment Trust 571

Gold and Silver 571
   Gold 572
   Silver 575
Precious Gems 575
Other Collectibles 577

part seven
Introduction to Portfolio Management

chapter 21. A Basic Look at Portfolio Management and the Capital Market Theory 586

Formal Measurement of Risk 587
   Expected Value 587
   Standard Deviation 588
Portfolio Effect 589
   Standard Deviation for a Two-Asset Portfolio 590
Developing an Efficient Portfolio 593
   Risk-Return Indifference Curves 594
   Optimum Portfolio 596
Capital Asset Pricing Model 597
   Capital Market Line 599
Return on an Individual Security 600
   Systematic and Unsystematic Risk 602
   Security Market Line 603
Assumptions of the Capital Pricing Model 604

Appendix 21A: The Correlation Coefficient 612

Appendix 21B: Least Squares Regression Analysis 613

Appendix 21C: Derivation of the Security Market Line (SML) 614

Appendix 21D: Arbitrage Pricing Theory 615

chapter 22. Measuring Risks and Returns of Portfolio Managers 619

Learning from Historical Trends 620
   Holding Period 621

Stated Objectives and Risk 624
Measurement of Return in Relation to Risk 625
   Sharpe Approach 626
   Treynor Approach 626
   Jensen Approach 627
   Adequacy of Performance 628
Diversification 631
Other Assets as Well as Stocks 634
A Specific Example—Asset Allocation 635
The Makeup of Institutional Investors 639
   Investment Companies (Including Mutual Funds) 639
   Other Institutional Investors 639

appendices

Appendix A: Compound Sum of $1 650

Appendix B: Compound Sum of an Annuity of $1 652

Appendix C: Present Value of $1 654

Appendix D: Present Value of an Annuity of $1 656

Appendix E: Time Value of Money and Investment Applications 658

Appendix F: Using Calculators for Financial Analysis 667

glossary 676

index 695

list of selected real world examples

CHAPTER 1
IBM 5
Price of Gold 5
The Tax Act of 2003 9
Impact of 6 Percent Inflation 10
Estate Planning 11
Annual Total Returns 17
Compound Annual Rates of Return—
 Ibbotson Associates 18
Career Opportunities in Investments—
 Appendix 1A 24
30 Largest Brokerage Houses—
 Appendix 1A 25

CHAPTER 2
Citigroup and Travelers 28
World Trade Center, September 11, 2001 28
Sprint, JP Morgan Chase, Merrill Lynch,
 UBS Warburg 31
Sprint Corporation Stock Offering 32
Top Ten Underwriters of U.S. Debt and
 Equity 34
Data on Trading Volume NYSE Stocks 38
Consolidated Reported Trades on all
 Markets 39
Intel, Microsoft, Oracle, Sun Microsystems 45
Electronic Communications Networks 46
Michael Eisner and Disney 47
The "See Through" Wall between Security
 Analysts and Investment Bankers 52

CHAPTER 3
Indexes and Averages Found in
 the Wall Street Journal 60
IBM, ExxonMobil, Wendy's, Mattel 63
Value Line Average 63
Bond Indexes 66
Lipper Mutual Fund Performance Indexes 67
Selling Eli Lilly Short 70
Examples of Commissions on Stock Trades 73
Taxes and the 2003 Tax Act 74
Who Cheats on Their Income Taxes? 76

CHAPTER 4
List of Federal Reserve Banks 86
National Economic Trends, St. Louis Federal
 Reserve 87
Websites and Economic Data 91
Johnson & Johnson 95
Morningstar 98
Commodity Futures Prices 102
Samples of *Barron's* Market Laboratory 104
Websites 107

CHAPTER 5
Downsizing at IBM, AT&T, General Motors 117
Federal Budget Seasonally Adjusted 119
Exports and Imports 121
Breakdown of Gross Domestic Product 125
Business Cycle Expansions and
 Contractions 127
Composite Indexes (Leading, Lagging,
 Coincident) 130
Automobile Industry and Impact on
 Other Industries 136
Microsoft, Intel, Cisco, Oracle, Sun
 Microsystems and the Business Cycle 137

CHAPTER 6
Steven Jobs, Apple Computer and the
 Computer Industry 144
Automobile Industry versus
 Gross Domestic Product 147
Wal-Mart & McDonald's as Powerful
 Customers 152
Leading Pharmaceutical Companies 153
Dow Jones Industry Groups 161

CHAPTER 7
Johnson & Johnson Combined Dividends
 and Earnings Valuation 176
EVA at Coca Cola, AT&T, Eli Lilly, Merrill Lynch
 and Monsanto 178
Inflation and Price-Earnings Ratios 179
P/E Ratios 180

Valuation of Johnson & Johnson   182
International Paper's Hidden Resources   189

CHAPTER 8
Johnson & Johnson Analysis Throughout Chapter
Ratio Analysis and Bankruptcy—Chrysler and Lockheed   208
Price-Earnings Ratios for Selected U.S. Corporations   216
Texas Instruments, Cyclical Industries and Price Earnings Ratios   216
Ratio Comparisons for the Pharmaceutical Industry   218
Questionable Accounting Practices in the Real World: How IBM Met Its Earnings Goal   227

CHAPTER 9
Sample of Bar Chart for the Dow Jones Industrial Average   245
Investor Sentiment Readings   250
Barron's Confidence Index   252
Behavioral Finance—The New Finance   255

CHAPTER 10
Premiums Paid in Mergers and Acquisitions   269
Time Warner, Pillsbury, Wachovia Bank Corp.   269
Stock Movement of Potential Acquirees in Canceled Mergers   270
New Issues Markets—Netscape, Microsoft, Genetech, & Apple   272
New York Stock Exchange Listing Requirements   274
Special Situation: Is Bad News Sometimes Good News for Investors   276
Performance of Value Line Groups   282
Criminal Activity and Stock Valuation   283

CHAPTER 11
Inflation Indexed Treasury Securities   295
Fannie Mae, Ginnie Mae and Federal Home Loan Banks   297
Yield on Long-Term Municipals versus Taxable Corporates   300

Comparative Yields Between Industrial and Utility Aa Bonds   301
Standard & Poor's and Moody's Bond Ratings   306
Example of Ford Motor Credit Bond   307
Quotes on Government Issues   311
Yields on Corporate Bonds and High Grade Preferred Stock   317

CHAPTER 12
The Origination of 50 Year Bonds by Boeing, Conrail, Ford Motor and TVA   335
Volatility of Short-Term and Long-Term Interest Rates   339
Yield Spread Differentials on Long-Term Bonds   343

CHAPTER 13
International Bond Managers—Managing Interest Rate Risk   358
Zero-Coupon Bonds' Price Swings Jolt Investors Looking for Security   365

CHAPTER 14
Amazon.com Percent Convertible Bond Example   381
Selected Convertible Bonds and Convertible Preferred Stock   389
The Convertible Craze of 2000–2001—Mirant & Household International   393
Redback's Warrant Example   395
Selected Warrants—June 4, 2004   396

CHAPTER 15
Options Data, Options Clearing Corporation   412
Speculative Premiums   418
Speculative Premiums Related to Betas and Dividend Yields   418
Example of Leverage Play   420
Call Options Instead of Stock   422
Writing a Naked Call   423

CHAPTER 16
Can Derivatives Be Dangerous?—Procter & Gamble and Bank One   445

Introduction to Investments

part one

chapter 1
THE INVESTMENT SETTING

chapter 2
SECURITY MARKETS: PRESENT AND FUTURE

chapter 3
PARTICIPATING IN THE MARKET

chapter 4
SOURCES OF INVESTMENT INFORMATION

IN THE FOLLOWING FOUR CHAPTERS we establish the investment setting, including investment goals and the risk-return decisions investors have to make when managing their portfolios of assets. Additionally, we present the organization of the security markets, including how to participate in these markets and where to find information pertaining to investments. In all of these areas Charles Schwab, chairman of the board of the firm carrying his name, has been one of the innovative investment thinkers of the last 30 years.

Charles Schwab founded The Charles Schwab Corporation (**www.schwab.com**) in 1974 with a new approach to investing. He started the first discount brokerage firm that emphasized low commissions, access to investment information and trading tools, and a focus on the individual investor. His motto was and still is "Ethical Service at a Fair Price." Over the years the Schwab model has become more sophisticated and has been imitated by others. Schwab offered the first telephone trading system and once the Internet took off, the firm made that medium available to its clients also.

If imitation is the highest form of flattery, then Mr. Schwab should be well pleased. His model has been imitated and enhanced by companies such as E*TRADE, Ameritrade, Scottrade, Harrisdirect, and many other financial service firms. Unfortunately, the competition has made it more difficult for Charles Schwab Corporation to make the profits it is used to, and the board of directors recalled him from retirement in the summer of 2004 to resume his role as chief executive officer. How long it will take him to get the company back to its previous position of profitability is anyone's guess.

Schwab Corporation offers research on over 3,000 common stocks for companies headquartered in the United States and rates these stocks A to F, with an A indicating a buy with high expectations of outperforming the market and an F indicating a sell with expectations of seriously underperforming the market. Students should have no trouble understanding

Charles R. Schwab
AP Photo/John Todd.

the rating scale. No one wants to hold a stock with an F rating. To enhance its research capabilities, Schwab acquired SoundView Capital Markets in 2004.

Employing 16,000 professionals with over 8 million customers and revenues of almost $4.5 billion, Schwab ranks as one of the biggest brokerage and financial services firms in the country. Its clients now include high wealth investors through its U.S. Trust Corporation subsidiary as well as international and domestic individual investors, independent investment managers, financial institutions, broker-dealers, and 401(k) plan sponsors. It provides full-service investing through the Internet, and has multilingual domestic and international offices. Having enlarged its client focus, Schwab now goes head to head with major firms such as SmithBarney, Merrill Lynch, and Morgan Stanley.

Charles Schwab started investing in 1957 when he was 20 years old and got hooked on the market. He graduated from Stanford University with a BA in Economics in 1959 and earned an MBA from the Stanford Graduate School of Business in 1961. It was 13 years later that he started Charles Schwab Corporation. He has five children and lives with his wife Helen in San Francisco. He has written several books including *You're Fifty—Now What?*, published in 2001, and *Guide to Independence* in 1998, as well as his latest book coauthored with his daughter Carrie Schwab Pomerantz, *It Pays to Talk*.

chapter one

The Investment Setting

objectives

1. Understand the difference between financial and real assets.

2. Discuss the key considerations in setting investment objectives.

3. Appreciate the potential change in investment strategy caused by the tax law revisions.

4. Describe the relationship of risk and return.

5. Explain the three factors that comprise the required rate of return for an investor.

6. Understand the career opportunities that are open to students in the field of investments.

Forms of Investment
The Setting of Investment Objectives
    Risk and Safety of Principal
    Current Income versus Capital Appreciation
    Liquidity Considerations
    Short-Term versus Long-Term Orientation
    Tax Factors
    Ease of Management
    Retirement and Estate Planning Considerations
Measures of Risk and Return
    Risk
Actual Consideration of Required Returns
    Real Rate of Return
    Anticipated Inflation Factor
    Risk Premium
What You Will Learn
Appendix 1A: Career Opportunities in Investments

There is nothing more exciting than waking up in the morning and racing for the newspaper or computer screen to get the latest stock quotes. Everything that happens during the day affects your portfolio whether it's a snowstorm in the Midwest, congressional testimony by Alan Greenspan, or a surprise earnings announcement by a Fortune 500 company. There is no "free space" when your money is in play. You are always on real time with events in the United States, Europe, and the rest of the world.

These factors make investing very challenging where winners can become losers, and losers transformed into winners. Take the case of IBM. The stock price of this renowned computer manufacturer reached a high of 175⅞ per share in 1987. At the time, security analysts thought that "Big Blue" could go up forever with its dominance in the traditional mainframe computer market and its emergence as the leader in the rapidly growing personal computer market. Such was not to be. With the conversion of most computer applications from mainframes to microcomputers and the cloning of IBM products by its competitors, IBM rapidly lost market share and began to actually lose money in the early 1990s. This was in stark contrast to the $6 billion per year annual profits it had averaged for the prior decade. By mid-1993, the stock had fallen to 40⅝. Many investors threw up their hands in disgust and bailed out. A decade later, by the winter of 2004, the firm was once again consistently showing a profit after massive layoffs of employees and restructuring of operations, and the stock price was *up* to the equivalent of $200 (the actual stock price was $100, but there was a two-for-one stock split during this time period).

www.ibm.com

Common stocks are not the only volatile investment. In the past two decades, silver has gone from $5 an ounce to $50 and back again to $5. Gold has moved from $35 an ounce to $875 and back to $350 in 2004. The same can be said of investments in oil, real estate, and a number of other items. Commercial real estate lost more than 30 percent of its value in the late 1980s and then fully recovered by 2004. Other examples are constantly occurring both on the upside and downside as fortunes are made and lost.

How does one develop an investment strategy in such an environment? Suggestions come from all directions. The investor is told how to benefit from the coming monetary disaster as well as how to grow rich in a new era of prosperity. The intent of this text is to help the investor sort out the various investments that are available and to develop analytical skills that suggest what securities and assets might be most appropriate for a given **portfolio.**

We shall define an **investment** as the commitment of current funds in anticipation of receiving a larger future flow of funds. The investor hopes to be compensated for forgoing immediate consumption, for the effects of inflation, and for taking a risk. Investments may take the form of stocks, bonds, real estate, and even rare paintings or old baseball cards.

Forms of Investment

In the text, we break down investment alternatives between financial and real assets. A **financial asset** represents a financial claim on an asset that is usually documented by some form of legal representation. An example would be a share of stock or a bond. A **real asset** represents an actual tangible asset that may be seen, felt, held, or collected. An example would be real estate or gold. Table 1–1 on page 6 lists the various forms of financial and real assets.

As indicated in the left column of Table 1–1, financial assets may be broken down into five categories. **Direct equity claims** represent ownership interests and include common stock as well as other instruments that can be used to purchase common stock, such as warrants and options. Warrants and options allow the holder to buy a stipulated number of shares in the future at a given price. Warrants usually convert to one share and are long term, whereas options are generally based on 100 share units and are short term in nature.

Indirect equity can be acquired through placing funds in investment companies (such as a mutual fund). The investment company pools the resources of

TABLE 1–1 Overview of Investment Alternatives

Financial Assets	Real Assets

1. Equity claims—direct
    Common stock
    Warrants
    Options
2. Equity claims—indirect
    Investment company shares (mutual funds)
    Pension funds
    Whole life insurance
    Retirement accounts
3. Creditor claims
    Savings account
    Money market funds
    Commercial paper
    Treasury bills, notes, bonds
    Municipal notes, bonds
    Corporate bonds (straight and convertible to common stock)
4. Preferred stock (straight and convertible to common stock)
5. Commodity futures
	1. Real estate
	    Office buildings
	    Apartments
	    Shopping centers
	    Personal residences
	2. Precious metals
	    Gold
	    Silver
	3. Precious gems
	    Diamonds
	    Rubies
	    Sapphires
	4. Collectibles
	    Art
	    Antiques
	    Stamps
	    Coins
	    Rare books
	5. Other
	    Cattle
	    Oil
	    Common metals

many investors and reinvests them in common stock (or other investments). The individual enjoys the advantages of diversification and professional management (though not necessarily higher returns).

Financial assets may also take the form of **creditor claims** as represented by debt instruments offered by financial institutions, industrial corporations, or the government. The rate of return is often initially fixed, though the actual return may vary with changing market conditions. Other forms of financial assets are **preferred stock,** which is a hybrid form of security combining some of the elements of equity ownership and creditor claims, and **commodity futures,** which represent a contract to buy or sell a commodity in the future at a given price. Commodities may include wheat, corn, copper, or even such financial instruments as Treasury bonds or foreign exchange.

As shown in the right column of Table 1–1, there are also numerous categories of real assets. The most widely recognized investment in this category is *real estate,* either commercial property or one's own residence. For greater risk, *precious metals* or *precious gems* can be considered, and for those seeking psychic pleasure as well as monetary gain, *collectibles* are an investment outlet. Finally, the *other (all-inclusive)* category includes cattle, oil, and other items that stretch as far as the imagination will go.

Throughout the text, each form of financial and real asset is considered. What assets the investor ultimately selects will depend on investment objectives as well as the economic outlook. For example, the investor who believes inflation will be relatively strong may prefer real assets that have a replacement value reflecting increasing prices. In a more moderate inflationary environment, stocks and bonds are preferred. The latter has certainly been the case in the last 15 years.

The Setting of Investment Objectives

The setting of investment objectives may be as important as the selection of the investment. In actuality, they tend to go together. A number of key areas should be considered.

Risk and Safety of Principal

The first factor investors must consider is the amount of risk they are prepared to assume. In a relatively efficient and informed capital market environment, risk tends to be closely correlated with return. Most of the literature of finance would suggest that those who consistently demonstrate high returns of perhaps 20 percent or more are greater-than-normal risk takers. While some clever investors are able to prosper on their wits alone, most high returns may be perceived as compensation for risk.

And there is not only the risk of losing invested capital directly (a dry hole perhaps) but also the danger of a loss in purchasing power. At 6 percent inflation (compounded annually), a stock that is held for four years without a gain in value would represent a 26 percent loss in purchasing power.

Investors who wish to assume low risks will probably confine a large portion of their portfolios to short-term debt instruments in which the party responsible for payment is the government or a major bank or corporation. Some conservative investors may choose to invest in money market funds in which the funds of numerous investors are pooled and reinvested in high-yielding, short-term instruments. More aggressive investors may look toward longer-term debt instruments and common stock. Real assets, such as gold, silver, or valued art, might also be included in an aggressive portfolio.

It is not only the inherent risk in an asset that must be considered but also the extent to which that risk is being diversified away in a portfolio. Although an investment in gold might be considered risky, such might not be fully the case if it is combined into a portfolio of common stocks. Gold thrives on bad news, while common stocks generally do well in a positive economic environment. An oil embargo or foreign war may drive down the value of stocks while gold is advancing, and vice versa.

The age and economic circumstances of an investor are important variables in determining an appropriate level of risk. Young, upwardly mobile people are generally in a better position to absorb risk than are elderly couples on a fixed income. Nevertheless, each of us, regardless of our plight in life, has different risk-taking desires. Because of an unwillingness to assume risk, a surgeon earning $300,000 a year may be more averse to accepting a $2,000 loss on a stock than an aging taxicab driver.

One cruel lesson of investing is that conservative investments do not always end up being what you thought they were when you bought them. This was true of IBM as described at the beginning of the chapter. This has also been true of many other firms. Classic examples can be found in the drug industry where leading firms such as Merck and Pfizer, who have reputations for developing outstanding products for the cure of cardiovascular and other diseases, saw their stock values fall by 30 percent when a strong movement for health care regulation and cost containment began in the mid-1990s. Much crueler lessons were provided to dot-com investors in the late 1990s as "can't miss" first-mover $100 stocks became $2 disasters. The same could be said for investors in the energy company Enron, which shrank from $90 to 50¢ in 2001. Even short-term risk-averse investors in U.S. Treasury bills saw their income stream decline from 12 percent to 1 percent over a decade as interest rates plummeted. This declining cash flow can be a shock to your system if you are living on interest income.

Current Income versus Capital Appreciation

A second consideration in setting investment objectives is a decision on the desire for current income versus capital appreciation. Although this decision is closely tied to an evaluation of risk, it is separate.

In purchasing stocks, the investor with a need for current income may opt for high-yielding, mature firms in such industries as public utilities, chemicals, or apparel. Those searching for price gains may look toward smaller, emerging firms in high technology, energy, or electronics. The latter firms may pay no cash dividend, but the investor hopes for an increase in value to provide the desired return.

The investor needs to understand there is generally a trade-off between growth and income. Finding both in one type of investment is unlikely. If you go for high-yielding utilities, you can expect slow growth in earnings and stock price. If you opt for high growth with a biotechnology firm, you can expect no cash flow from the dividend.

Liquidity Considerations

Liquidity is measured by the ability of the investor to convert an investment into cash within a relatively short time at its fair market value or with a minimum capital loss on the transaction.

Most financial assets provide a high degree of liquidity. Stocks and bonds can generally be sold within a matter of seconds at a price reasonably close to the last traded value. Such may not be the case for real estate. Almost everyone has seen a house or piece of commercial real estate sit on the market for weeks, months, or years.

Liquidity can also be measured indirectly by the transaction costs or commissions involved in the transfer of ownership. Financial assets generally trade on a relatively low commission basis (perhaps ½ or 1 percent), whereas many real assets have transaction costs that run from 5 percent to 25 percent or more.

In many cases, the lack of immediate liquidity can be justified if there are unusual opportunities for gain. An investment in real estate or precious gems may provide sufficient return to more than compensate for the added transaction costs. Of course, a bad investment will be all the more difficult to unload.

Investors must carefully assess their own situation to determine the need for liquidity. If you are investing funds to be used for the next house payment or the coming semester's tuition, then immediate liquidity will be essential, and financial assets will be preferred. If funds can be tied up for long periods, bargain-buying opportunities of an unusual nature can also be evaluated.

Short-Term versus Long-Term Orientation

In setting investment objectives, you must decide whether you will assume a short-term or long-term orientation in managing the funds and evaluating performance. You do not always have a choice. People who manage funds for others may be put under tremendous pressure to show a given level of performance in the short run. Those applying pressure may be a concerned relative or a large pension fund that has placed funds with a bank trust department. Even though you are convinced your latest investment will double in the next three years, the fact that it is currently down 15 percent may provide discomfort to those around you.

Market strategies may also be short term or long term in scope. Those who attempt to engage in short-term market tactics are termed *traders*. They may buy a stock at 15 and hope to liquidate if it goes to 20. To help reach decisions, short-term traders often use technical analysis, which is based on evaluating market indicator series and charting. Those who take a longer-term perspective try to identify fundamentally sound companies for a buy-and-hold approach. A long-term investor does not necessarily anticipate being able to buy right at the bottom or sell at the exact peak.

Research has shown it is difficult to beat the market on a risk-adjusted basis. Given that the short-term trader encounters more commissions than the long-term investor because of more active trading, short-term trading as a rule is not a strategy endorsed by the authors.

Tax Factors

Investors in high tax brackets have different investment objectives than those in lower brackets or tax-exempt charities, foundations, or similar organizations. An investor in a high tax bracket may prefer municipal bonds (interest is not taxable), real estate (with its depreciation and interest write-offs), or investments that provide tax credits or tax shelters.

The Tax Relief Act of 2003 changed tax considerations related to investments substantially, and you should be aware of these changes and their impact on portfolio strategy. Prior to the passage of the act, dividends were taxed as ordinary income (the same as salary, for example) and the maximum tax rate on dividends was 38.8 percent. However, long-term capital gains, that is, gains on securities held for over a year, were only taxed at a maximum rate of 20 percent.

For high-income, high-tax-bracket investors this made stocks with large capital gains potential much more desirable. They looked to companies such as Home Depot or eBay that paid little or no dividends, but used their funds instead to generate growth and hopefully capital gains for investors. Companies that paid high dividends such as Duke Energy or AT&T were often shunned by wealthy investors because of the tax consequences of owning these stocks.

However, the Tax Relief Act of 2003 put dividends and long-term capital gains on an equal footing. They both are now taxed at a maximum rate of 15 percent. This means that high-income investors may now seriously consider

the real world of investing

Inflation—Why Should I Worry?

Inflation has been very tame from the mid-1980s through the early 2000s, with prices growing at 1 to 3 percent per year. This is a far cry from the double-digit inflation of 11.4 percent in 1979 and 13.4 percent in 1980. Even these rates would have to be considered mild compared with the triple-digit (100+ percent) inflation witnessed during the 1980s in such developing countries as Brazil, Israel, and Mexico.

As you plan your future, you might ask, "What effect could inflation have on my well-being?" If inflation is at 3 to 4 percent, the impact is not great. But observe in the table the effect of 6 percent sustained inflation over a 20-year time period. These values indicate why the Federal Reserve remains ever vigilant in trying to hold down the rate of inflation.

Impact of 6 Percent Inflation Over 20 Years

	2004 Price	20 Years Later
Average automobile	$ 18,000	$ 57,726
Mercedes	42,000	134,694
Typical three-bedroom house	130,000	416,910
BBA starting salary	42,000	142,590
MBA starting salary	85,000	272,595
Average private college annual tuition	17,000	57,715
Ivy League annual tuition	32,000	102,624
Poverty level (family of four)	36,000	115,452

stocks with high dividends such as Bristol-Myers, Squibb, Bank of America, or General Motors for their portfolios.

Ease of Management

Another consideration in establishing an investment program is ease of management. The investor must determine the amount of time and effort that can be devoted to an investment portfolio and act accordingly. In the stock market, this may determine whether you want to be a daily trader or assume a longer-term perspective. In real estate, it may mean the difference between personally owning and managing a handful of rental houses or going in with 10 other investors to form a limited partnership in which a general partner takes full management responsibility and the limited partners merely put up the capital.

Of course, a minimum amount of time must be committed to any investment program. Even when investment advisers or general partners are in charge, their activities must be monitored and evaluated.

In managing a personal portfolio, the investor should consider opportunity costs. If a lawyer can work for $200 per hour or manage his financial portfolio, a fair question would be, "How much extra return can I get from managing my portfolio, or can I add more value to my portfolio by working and investing more money?" Unless the lawyer is an excellent investor, it is probable that more money can be made by working.

Assume an investor can add a 2 percent extra return to his portfolio but it takes 5 hours per week (260 hours per year) to do so. If his opportunity cost is $40 per hour, he would have to add more than $10,400 ($40 × 260 hours) to his portfolio to make personal management attractive. If we assume a 2 percent excess return can be gained over the professional manager, the investor would need a portfolio of $520,000 before personal management would make sense under these assumptions. This example may explain why many high-income individuals choose to have professionals manage their assets.

the real world of investing

Estate Planning: The Only Two Sure Things Are Death and Taxes!! Maybe?

We know the first is not going to go away (not even Elvis got out alive), but what about the second (taxes)? In this case, we are especially talking about the estate tax, or the taxes paid on your assets at time of death.

Fewer than 100,000 people pay the estate tax. The primary reason is that starting in 2002, you had to have an estate of at least $1 million to owe the tax (there is a $1 million exemption). Also, there are tax planning devices that help you avoid part of the tax (lifetime gifts, trusts, the marital deduction, etc.). Nevertheless, for those who pay the estate tax, it is indeed an onerous burden.

During his or her lifetime, a successful person tends to pay 50 percent of every dollar earned in federal and state income taxes, local property taxes, state sales taxes, and excise taxes on foreign imports, alcoholic beverages, etc.

Then when he or she dies, an estate tax of up to 50 percent may be extracted. This double taxation may mean this person and his or her heirs may only get to keep 25 cents of each dollar earned; 75¢ could go to the government. Most people do not like that ratio.

To rectify this situation, the Bush Administration and Congress decided to eliminate the estate tax as one of the provisions of the newly enacted Economic Growth and Tax Reconciliation Act of 2001.

But wait a minute. Don't rush out to die just because of the legislation. First of all, the elimination is a slow process and is enacted by progressively larger estate tax exemptions. The tax table reads like this:

Years	Exemptions
2002–03	$1.0 million
2004–05	1.5 million
2006–08	2.0 million
2009	3.5 million
2010	Total exemption

Thus, a person who died in 2004 got a $1.5 million exemption and a death in 2006 will qualify for a $2 million exemption. The number goes up to $3.5 million in 2009, and finally there is no estate tax for those who die in 2010. If Bill Gates were to die in 2010 with an estate of $400 billion dollars, there would be no estate tax!

For those who wish to avoid the estate tax, this is all the good news. Now for the bad news. The Economic Growth and Tax Reconciliation Act of 2001 is automatically rescinded on January 1, 2011. This means the estate tax and all other provisions of the 2001 law are null and void unless a new Congress and president decide to re-pass it. We do not know what the politicians will do from one minute to the next, much less a decade from now.

For estate tax planning purposes, you need to take care of business by 2010 (apply your own interpretation) or pay the consequences.

Decisions such as these may also depend on your trade-off between work and leisure. An investor may truly find it satisfying and intellectually stimulating to manage a portfolio and may receive psychic income from mastering the nuances of investing. However, if you would rather ski, play tennis, or enjoy some other leisure activity, the choice of professional management may make more sense than a do-it-yourself approach.

Retirement and Estate Planning Considerations

Even the relatively young must begin to consider the effect of their investment decisions on their retirement and the estates they will someday pass along to their "potential families." Those who wish to remain single will still be called on to advise others as to the appropriateness of a given investment strategy for their family needs.

Most good retirement questions should not be asked at "retirement" but 40 or 45 years before because that's the period with the greatest impact. One of the first questions a person is often asked after taking a job on graduation is whether he or she wishes to set up an IRA. An IRA allows a qualifying taxpayer to deduct an allowable amount from taxable income and invest the funds at a brokerage house, mutual fund, bank, or other financial institution. The funds are normally placed in common stocks or other securities or in interest bearing instruments, such as a certificate of deposit. The income earned on the funds is allowed to grow tax-free until withdrawn at retirement. As an example, if a person places $3,000 a year in an IRA for 45 consecutive years and the funds earn 10 percent over that time, $2,156,715 will have been accumulated.

Measures of Risk and Return

Application Example

Now that you have some basic familiarity with the different forms of investments and the setting of investment goals, we are ready to look at concepts of measuring the return from an investment and the associated risk. The return you receive from any investment (stocks, bonds, real estate) has two primary components: capital gains or losses and current income. The rate of return from an investment can be measured as:

$$\text{Rate of return} = \frac{(\text{Ending value} - \text{Beginning value}) + \text{Income}}{\text{Beginning value}} \quad (1\text{--}1)$$

Thus, if a share of stock goes from $20 to $22 in one year and also pays a dollar in dividends during the year, the total return is 15 percent. Using Formula 1–1:

$$\frac{(\$22 - \$20) + \$1}{\$20} = \frac{\$2 + \$1}{\$20} = \frac{\$3}{\$20} = 15\%$$

Where the formula is being specifically applied to stocks, it is written as:

$$\text{Rate of return} = \frac{(P_1 - P_0) + D_1}{P_0} \quad (1\text{--}2)$$

where:

P_1 = Price at the end of the period.
P_0 = Price at the beginning of the period.
D_1 = Dividend income.

Risk

The risk for an investment is related to the uncertainty associated with the outcomes from an investment. For example, an investment that has an absolutely certain return of 10 percent is said to be riskless. Another investment that has a likely or expected return of 12 percent, but also has the possibility of minus 10 percent in hard economic times and plus 30 percent under optimum circumstances, is said to be risky. An example of three investments with progressively greater risk is presented in Figure 1–1. Based on our definition of risk, investment C is clearly the riskiest because of the large uncertainty (wide dispersion) of possible outcomes.

In the study of investments, you will soon observe that the desired or required rate of return for a given investment is generally related to the risk

FIGURE 1–1 Examples of Risk

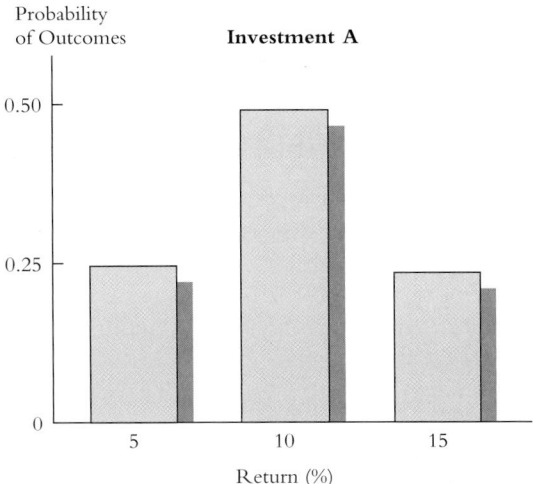
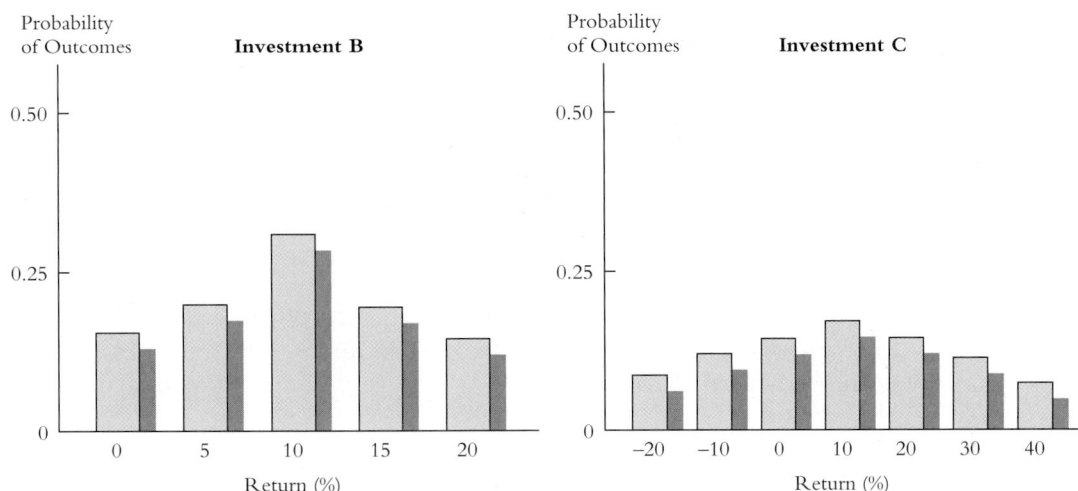

associated with that investment. Because most investors do not like risk, they will require a higher rate of return for a more risky investment. That is not to say the investors are unwilling to take risks—they simply wish to be compensated for taking the risk. For this reason, an investment in common stocks (which inevitably carries some amount of risk) may require an anticipated return 6 or 7 percent higher than a certificate of deposit in a commercial bank. This 6 or 7 percent represents a risk premium. You never know whether you will get the returns you anticipate, but at least your initial requirements will be higher to justify the risk you are taking.

There is another measure of risk also used in the investment community, and that is the **beta.** The beta measures the risk of a security relative to the market (the market measure is normally the Standard & Poor's 500 Stock Index). Stocks with betas greater than 1.00 have more risk than the market, and stocks with betas less than 1.00 have less risk than the market. You will become proficient in computing betas when you get to the section on portfolio management.

You will also learn, at that point, that beta represents **systematic risk** that cannot be diversified away in a portfolio of stocks and so it has special importance to the investor.

Actual Consideration of Required Returns

Let's consider how return requirements are determined in the financial markets. Although the following discussion starts out on a theoretical "what if" basis, you will eventually see empirical evidence that different types of investments do provide different types of returns.

Basically, three components make up the required return from an investment:

1. The real rate of return.
2. The anticipated inflation factor.
3. The risk premium.

Real Rate of Return

The **real rate of return** is the return investors require for allowing others to use their money for a given time period. This is the return investors demand for passing up immediate consumption and allowing others to use their savings until the funds are returned. Because the term *real* is employed, this means it is a value determined before inflation is included in the calculation. The real rate of return is also determined before considering any specific risk for the investment.

Historically, the real rate of return in the U.S. economy has been from 2 to 3 percent. During much of the 1980s and early 1990s, it was somewhat higher (4 to 6 percent), but in the last decade the real rate of return came back to its normal level of 2 to 3 percent, which is probably a reasonable long-term expectation.

Because an investor is concerned with using a real rate of return as a component of a required rate of return, the past is not always a good predictor for any one year's real rate of return. The problem comes from being able to measure the real rate of return only after the fact by subtracting inflation from the nominal interest rate. Unfortunately, expectations and occurrence do not always match. The real rate of return is highly variable (for seven years in the 1970s and early 1980s, it was even negative). One of the problems investors face in determining required rates of return is the forecasting errors involving interest rates and inflation. These forecasting errors are more pronounced in short-run returns than in long-run returns. Let us continue with our example and bring inflation into the discussion.

Anticipated Inflation Factor

The anticipated inflation factor must be added to the real rate of return. For example, if there is a 2 percent real-rate-of-return requirement and the **anticipated rate of inflation** is 3 percent, we combine the two to arrive at an approximate 5 percent required return factor. Combining the real rate of return and inflationary considerations gives us the required return on an investment before explicitly considering risk. For this reason, it is called the risk-free required rate of return or, simply, **risk-free rate (R_F).**

We can define the risk-free rate as:

$$\text{Risk-free rate} = (1 + \text{Real rate})(1 + \text{Expected rate of inflation}) - 1 \quad \textbf{(1–3)}$$

Plugging in numerical values, we would show:

$$\text{Risk-free rate} = (1.02)(1.03) - 1 = 1.0506 - 1 = 0.0506 \text{ or } 5.06\%$$

The answer is approximately 5 percent. You can simply add the real rate of return (2 percent) to the anticipated inflation rate (3 percent) to get a 5 percent answer or go through the more theoretically correct process of Formula 1–3 to arrive at 5.06 percent. Either approach is frequently used.

The risk-free rate (R_F) of approximately 5 percent applies to any investment as the minimum required rate of return to provide a 2 percent *real return* after inflation. Of course, if the investor actually receives a lower return, the real rate of return may be quite low or negative. For example, if the investor receives a 2 percent return in a 4 percent inflationary environment, there is a negative real return of 2 percent. The investor will have 2 percent less purchasing power than before he started. He would have been better off to spend the money *now* rather than save at a 2 percent rate in a 4 percent inflationary economy. In effect, he is *paying* the borrower to use his money. Of course, real rates of return and inflationary expectations change from time to time, so the risk-free required rate (R_F) also changes.

We now have examined the two components that make up the minimum risk-free rate of return that apply to investments (stock, bonds, real estate, etc.). We now consider the third component, the risk premium. The relationship is depicted in Figure 1–2 on page 16.

Risk Premium

Application Example

The **risk premium** will be different for each investment. For example, for a federally insured certificate of deposit at a bank or for a U.S. Treasury bill, the risk premium approaches zero. All the return to the investor will be at the risk-free rate of return (the real rate of return plus inflationary expectations). For common stock, the investor's required return may carry a 6 or 7 percent risk premium in addition to the risk-free rate of return. If the risk-free rate were 5 percent, the investor might have an overall required return of 11 to 12 percent on common stock.

+ Real rate	2%
+ Anticipated inflation	3%
= Risk-free rate	5%
+ Risk premium	6% or 7%
= Required rate of return	11% to 12%

Corporate bonds fall somewhere between short-term government obligations (virtually no risk) and common stock in terms of risk. Thus, the risk premium may be 3 to 4 percent. Like the real rate of return and the inflation rate,

16 Part 1 Introduction to Investments

FIGURE 1-2 The Components of Required Rate of Return

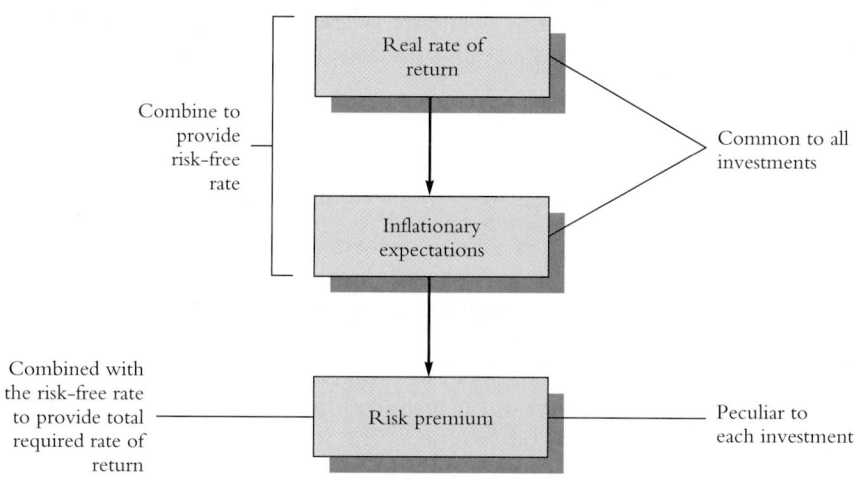

FIGURE 1-3 Risk-Return Characteristics

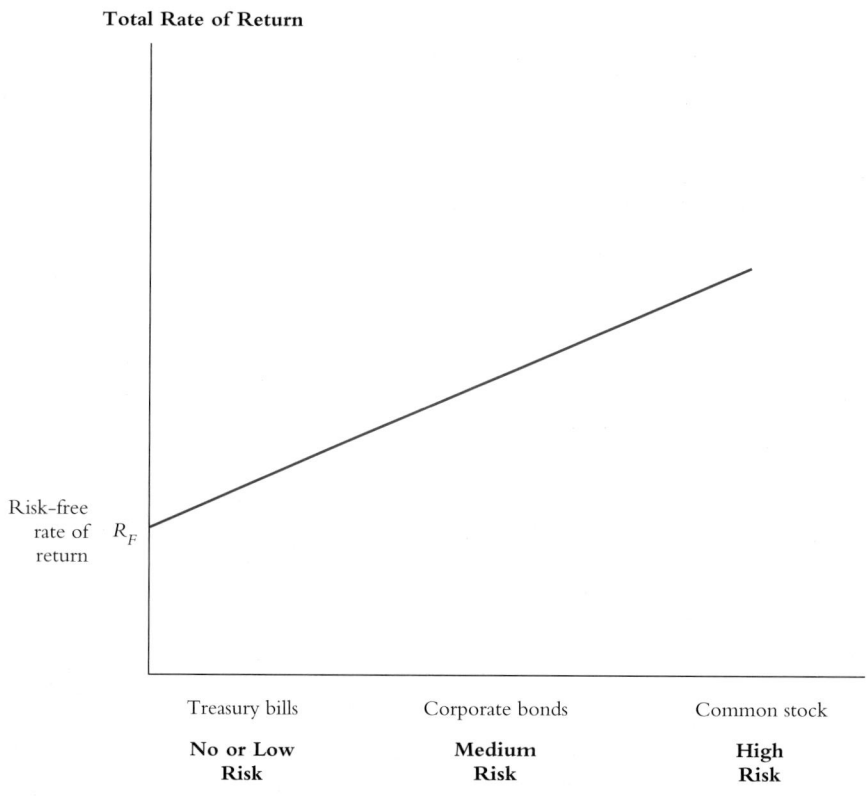

the risk premium is not a constant but may change from time to time. If investors are very fearful about the economic outlook, the risk premium may be 8 to 10 percent as it was for junk bonds in 1990 and 1991.

The normal relationship between selected investments and their rates of return is depicted in Figure 1–3.

Chapter 1 The Investment Setting 17

FIGURE 1–4 Basic Series: Summary Statistics of Annual Total Returns from 1926–2003

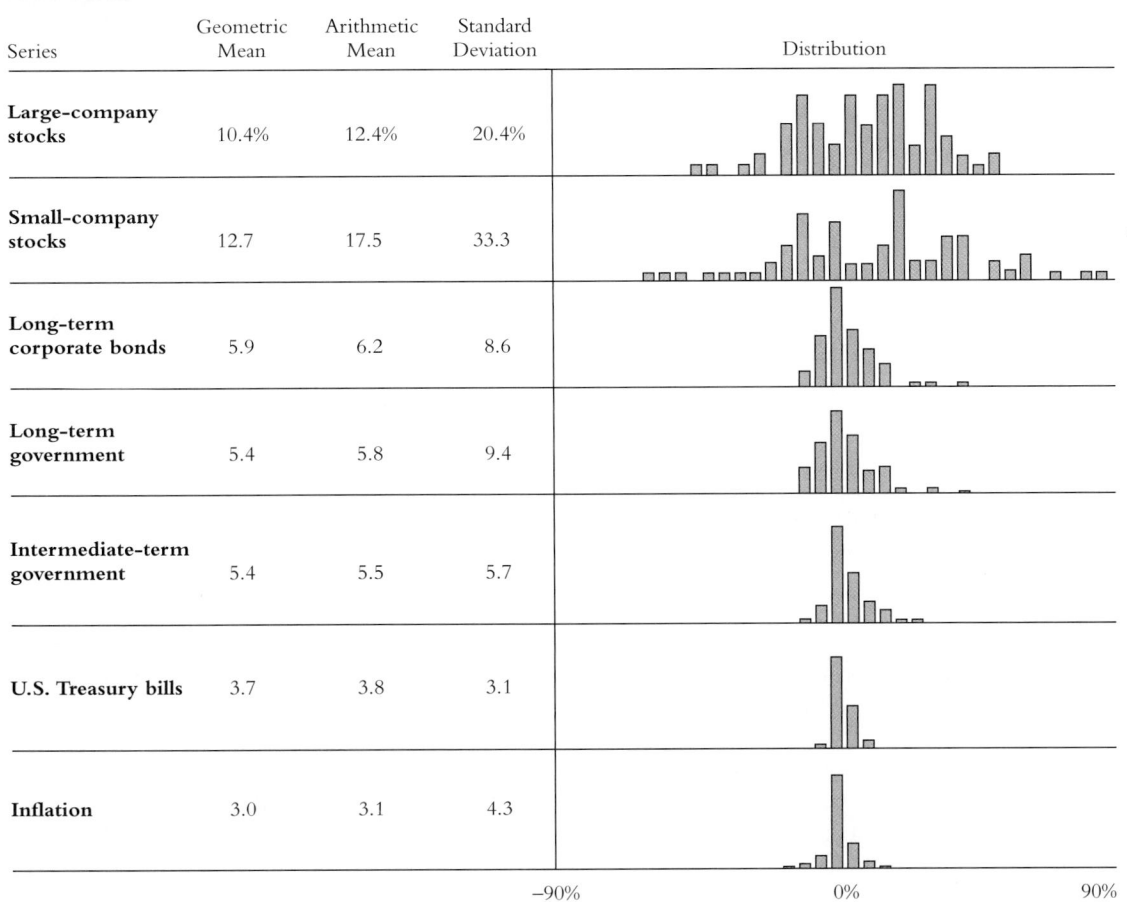

Source: *Stocks, Bonds, Bills and Inflation® 2004 Yearbook*, © 2004 Ibbotson Associates, Inc. Based on copyrighted works by Ibbotson and Sinquefield. All rights reserved. Used with permissions.

A number of empirical studies tend to support the risk-return relationships shown in Figure 1–3 over a long period. Perhaps the most widely cited is the Ibbotson and Associates data presented in Figure 1–4, which covers data from 1926 to 2003. Note that the high-to-low return scale is in line with expectations based on risk. Risk is measured by the standard deviation, which appears to the right of each security type. This distribution of returns indicates which security has the biggest risk. Figure 1–4 shows in practice what we discussed in theory earlier in the chapter; higher returns are normally associated with higher risk.

Of particular interest is the difference between the geometric mean return and the arithmetic mean return. The geometric mean is the compound annual rate of return while the arithmetic mean is a simple average of the yearly returns. The arithmetic mean is biased on the upside because it treats negative returns the same as positive returns. This is *not* true in reality. If you start with $1.00 and lose 50 percent, you now have 50 cents. To get back to your original investment, you need a 100 percent increase from 50 cents to $1.00.

Because the Ibbotson study in Figure 1–4 covered 78 years (including a decade of depression), the rates of return may be somewhat lower than those

| TABLE 1–2 | Compound Annual Rates of Return by Decade (in percent) |

	1920s*	1930s	1940s	1950s	1960s	1970s	1980s	1990s	2000s†	1994–03
Large company	19.2	−0.1	9.2	19.4	7.8	5.9	17.5	18.2	−5.3	11.1
Small company	−4.5	1.4	20.7	16.9	15.5	11.5	15.8	15.1	13.3	14.8
Long-term corporate	5.2	6.9	2.7	1.0	1.7	6.2	13.0	8.4	11.2	8.0
Long-term government	5.0	4.9	3.2	−0.1	1.4	5.5	12.6	8.8	10.8	8.0
Intermediate-term government	4.2	4.6	1.8	1.3	3.5	7.0	11.9	7.2	8.8	6.4
Treasury bills	3.7	0.6	0.4	1.9	3.9	6.3	8.9	4.9	3.1	4.2
Inflation	−1.1	−2.0	5.4	2.2	2.5	7.4	5.1	2.9	2.3	2.4

*Based on the period 1926–1929.
†Based on the period 2000–2003.
Source: *Stocks, Bonds, Bills and Inflation® 2004 Yearbook,* © 2004 Ibbotson Associates, Inc. Based on copyrighted works by Ibbotson and Sinquefield. All rights reserved. Used with permissions.

www.citigroup.com

currently available. This is particularly true for the bonds and Treasury bills. Table 1–2, from the *Stocks, Bonds, Bills and Inflation 2004 Yearbook,* shows returns for nine different periods.

The returns just discussed primarily apply to financial assets (stocks, bonds, and so forth). Salomon Brothers Inc., an investment banking firm and a subsidiary of Citigroup, tracks the performance of real assets as well as financial assets. Over long periods of time, common stocks generally tend to perform at approximately the same level as real assets such as real estate, coins, stamps, and so forth, with each tending to show a different type of performance in a different economic environment.[1] Real assets tend to do best in inflationary environments, while moderate inflation favors financial assets. In 1991, the best long-term performers in the Salomon Study were Old Master paintings, Chinese ceramics, gold, diamonds, and stamps. After 10 years of moderate inflation, stocks and bonds had risen to the top in 2000. No category was much of a winner for the next three years. No doubt the pattern will shift back and forth many times in the future, although in the euphoric stock market environment of the last decade many would question this statement. More will be said about the impact of inflation and disinflation on investments later in the text.

---

[1] Examples of other longer-term studies on comparative returns between real and financial assets are: Roger G. Ibbotson and Carol F. Fall, "The United States Wealth Portfolio," *The Journal of Portfolio Management,* Fall 1982, pp. 82–92; Roger G. Ibbotson and Lawrence B. Siegel, "The World Market Wealth Portfolio," *The Journal of Portfolio Management,* Winter 1983, pp. 5–17; and Alexander A. Robichek, Richard A. Cohn, and John J. Pringle, "Returns on Alternative Media and Implications for Portfolio Construction," *Journal of Business,* July 1972, pp. 427–43. (While Ibbotson and Siegel showed superior returns for metals between 1960 and 1980, metals have greatly underperformed other assets in the 1980s and 1990s.)

We have attempted to demonstrate the importance of risk in determining the required rate of return for an investment. As previously discussed, it is the third key component that is added to the risk-free rate (composed of the real rate of return and the inflation premium) to determine the total required rate of return.

What You Will Learn

The first part of the book covers the general framework for investing. You will look at an overview of the security markets (New York Stock Exchange, Chicago Board Options Exchange, and so on). Then you will examine the basics for participating in the market, such as opening an account, executing an order, investing individually or through a mutual fund, and so forth. Also in the first section of the book, you will become familiar with sources of important investment information so you can begin to make your university or public library as well as your computer valuable assets.

You will then go through the classic process of analyzing and valuing a security. You will start with examining the economy, then move to the industry level, and finally move to the actual company. The authors go through the process of putting a value on a stock. There is also heavy emphasis on financial analysis. Section two provides an in-depth analysis of the Johnson & Johnson Company to demonstrate procedures for identifying the strengths and weaknesses of a company. For enthusiasts of charting and other forms of technical analysis, we examine the advantages and disadvantages of such approaches.

You will then move from stocks to bonds. Your level of interest should not diminish because bonds also offer an opportunity for income and, surprisingly, for large gains or losses. Because an emphasis of the book is to present the student with a wide investment horizon from which to choose, we then consider a variety of other investment alternatives. These include convertible securities and warrants, put and call options, commodities and financial futures, stock index futures and options, and real assets such as real estate and precious metals. We realize some of these terms may have little meaning to you now, but they soon will.

You will also study mutual funds and international securities in depth. In the latter part of the book, we also consider the concepts of portfolio theory and how to put together the most desirable package of investments in terms of risk and return. We also consider the consequences of investing in a reasonably efficient stock market environment, one in which information is acted on very quickly. Can superior return be achieved in such a setting?

Many students taking an investments course are not sure of their ultimate career goals. We hope this course can be equally valuable to a future banker, CPA, insurance executive, marketing manager, or anyone else. However, for those specifically considering a career in investments, the authors present a brief summary of career opportunities in Appendix 1A at the back of this chapter.

exploring the web

Website	Comment
www.mhhe.com/hirtblock8e	The McGraw-Hill website for this textbook provides valuable student resources.
www.aaii.com	A nonprofit website educating do-it-yourself investors
www.nasdaq.com	Provides information about Nasdaq stocks and market
www.nyse.com	Provides information about New York Stock Exchange, listings, and regulations
www.nareit.com	Provides information and data about real estate investment trusts
www.quicken.com	Provides understandable coverage of financial planning and investing
www.morningstar.com	Contains evaluations of and information about stocks and mutual funds
www.bondmarkets.com	Provides information about corporate and government bonds
www.amex.com	Provides information about stocks, options, and exchange trade funds on the American Stock Exchange
www.business.com	Provides a searchable database for links to sites by industry
www.investmentsclub.com	Provides information and education for investment club members
www.investopedia.com	Provides a general education site about stocks and investing
web.utk.edu/~jwachowi/part2.html	Site created by finance professor with links to information resources
www.investorwords.com	Provides links to finance sites and glossary of finance terminology
www.reuters.com	Contains business and financial market news for United States and other countries
www.inetats.com www.tradearca.com www.isld.com www.bloombergtradebook.com www.ebrut.com www.nextrade.org	These six websites all represent electronic communication networks (ECNs) and represent the different companies and markets competing with traditional floor-based markets such as the NYSE.

Key Words and Concepts

anticipated rate of inflation 14
beta 13
commodity futures 6
creditor claims 6
direct equity claims 5
financial asset 5
indirect equity 5
investment 5

liquidity 8	real asset 5	risk premium 15
preferred stock 6	real rate of return 14	systematic risk 14
portfolio 5	risk-free rate (R_F) 15	

Discussion Questions

1. How is an investment defined?
2. What are the differences between financial and real assets?
3. List some key areas relating to investment objectives.
4. Explain the concepts of direct equity and indirect equity.
5. How are equity and creditor claims different?
6. Do those wishing to assume low risks tend to invest long-term or short-term? Why?
7. How is liquidity measured?
8. Explain why conservative investors who tend to buy short-term assets differ from short-term traders.
9. How does the Tax Relief Act of 2003 affect the relative attractiveness of long-term capital gains versus dividend income? (A general statement will suffice.)
10. Why is there a minimum amount of time that must be committed to any investment program?
11. In a highly inflationary environment, would an investor tend to favor real or financial assets? Why?
12. What two primary components are used to measure the rate of return achieved from an investment?
13. Many people think of risk as the danger of losing money. Is this the same way that risk is defined in finance?
14. What are the three elements that determine the return an investor should require from an investment?
15. Explain how an investor receiving a 2 or 3 percent quoted return in an inflationary environment may actually experience a negative real rate of return.
16. In Figure 1–4, what has been the highest return investment category over the 78-year period? What has been the lowest? Assuming risk is measured by the standard deviation, what can you say about the relationship of risk to return in Figure 1–4?

Problems

Rate of Return
1. The stock of Dynamo Corporation went from $25 to $28 last year. The firm also paid 50 cents in dividends. Compute the rate of return.

Rate of Return
2. In the following year, the dividend was raised to 70 cents. However, a bear market developed toward the end of the year, and the stock price declined from $28 to $22. Compute the rate of return or (loss) to stockholders.

Risk-free rate and required return
3. Assume the real rate of return in the economy is 2.5 percent, the expected rate of inflation is 4 percent, and the risk premium is 5.9 percent. Compute the risk-free rate and required rate of return.

Web Exercise

Assume you want to see how the market is doing on a given day as well as get additional perspective on a given stock. There are literally hundreds of options. We will merely suggest one for now.

Go to **www.quicken.com**

1. Note the changes in the Dow Jones (DJIA), Nasdaq, and S&P 500 Index. Write a brief comment on whether they all moved in the same direction or not.

2. On the upper left-hand portion of the home page, you will see "Enter Symbol." Put in the symbol for any stock and click on "Go." If you do not have a preference, use IBM.

3. Write down the last trade value, the change, the previous close, the 52-week range, the P/E ratio, and the dividend yield. All these terms will take on greater meaning as you progress through the text.

4. At the middle of the left column you will see "Chart." Click on this item. Describe when the stock hit its approximate high point (month and value) and its approximate low point (month and value). Based on the overall appearance of the chart, does the stock appear to have upward or downward momentum?

5. Click on "Compare to Industry" along the left margin. Indicate how the company compares to three other companies in the industry in terms of market capitalization (total market value). Write down the total values.

Note: From time to time, companies redesign their websites and occasionally a topic we have listed may have been deleted, updated, or moved into a different location. Most websites have a "site map" or "site index" listed on a different page. If you click on the site map or site index you will be introduced to a table of contents which should aid you in finding the topic you are looking for.

S&P Problems

www.mhhe.com/edumarketinsight

STANDARD &POOR'S

1. Log on to the McGraw-Hill website: **www.mhhe.com/edumarketinsight** (see page vi in the preface for instructions).

2. Click on Company, which is the first box below the Market Insight title.

3. Type Johnson & Johnson's ticker symbol JNJ in the box, and click on go.

4. Scroll down the left margin, and click on "Charting by Prophet" listed in blue. A chart will appear, and under Johnson & Johnson you will see capital letters that may be self-explanatory but just in case these letters D-O-H-L-C-R don't make sense, they stand for Date-Opening Price-High Price-Low Price-Closing Price and Range.

5. Now scroll across the top to the third box with the 1yr inside, and click on the arrow. Choose All at the bottom of the list. Now you will have a long-term trend of Johnson & Johnson's price.

6. Notice that as you move the cursor a vertical red line moves across the chart. Place the cursor on January 1, 1995, and record the closing price. Repeat this and record the closing price for December 31, 2004. Now calculate the percentage change in stock price over this ten-year period.

7. Using time value of money techniques (Present Value, Future Value, Number of Periods, etc.) and ignoring dividends, calculate the annual rate of return for the change in price.

8. Assuming that Johnson & Johnson had a dividend yield of 2 percent per year over this time period, what would be the total annual rate of return including dividend yield and price change?

The Wall Street Journal Project

1. In this chapter, a distinction is made between financial assets and real assets as well as between direct and indirect equity investments. Using *The Wall Street Journal,* bring your knowledge up to date by searching Section C for prices of the following assets (investments).
    a. Financial Assets
       General Electric (GE) Common Stock. General Electric is listed in the New York Stock Exchange section. You should look up the Last (closing price).
       Babson Group Growth (GWTH) Mutual Fund. It is listed in the "Mutual Funds" section. You should look up the NAV (net asset value), which is the same as the closing price.
    b. Real Assets
       Gold-Engelhard Industrial Bullion. It is listed in the "Cash Prices" section on the "Futures Prices" page. Go to "Commodities" in the index to find this material. You should look up the value in the first column, which is the same as the closing price.
       Silver-Engelhard Industrial Bullion. It is listed in the same section as gold. You should look it up in the same way.

Selected References

Rates and Return

Ibbotson, Roger G., and Paul D. Kaplen. Does Asset Allocation Policy Explain 40, 90, or 100 Percent of Performance?" *Financial Analysts Journal,* January–February 2000, pp. 26–32.

Malkiel, Burton G., and Yexiao Xu. "Risk and Return Revisited." *The Journal of Portfolio Management,* Spring 1997, pp. 9–14.

Modigliani, Franco, and Leah Modigliani. "Risk-Adjusted Performance." *The Journal of Portfolio Management,* Winter 1997, p. 54.

Renshaw, Edward. "Will Stocks Continue to Outperform Bonds in the Future?" *Financial Analysts Journal,* March–April 1997, pp. 67–73.

Stocks, Bonds, Bills and Inflation, 2001 Yearbook. Chicago: R. G. Ibbotson and Associates, Inc., 2001.

Setting Objectives

Bernstein, Peter L. "Points of Inflection: Investment Management Tomorrow." *Financial Analysts Journal,* July–August 2003, pp. 18–23.

Fox, Justin. "Can You Trust Anyone to Manage Your Money?" *Fortune,* December 29, 2003, pp. 109–112.

Ibbotson, Roger G., and Mark Riepe. "Growth vs. Value Investing: And the Winner is . . ." *Journal of Financial Planning,* June 1997, pp. 64–71.

Lamont, Owen A. "Investment Plans and Stock Returns." *Journal of Finance,* December 2000, pp. 2719–43.

Lezner, Robert. "The Case for Hard Assets." *Forbes,* June 20, 1994, pp. 146–51.

Paré, Terrence P. "How to Find a Financial Planner." *Fortune,* May 16, 1994, pp. 103–6.

Revell, Janice. "Ten Questions You Should Ask before Purchasing a Stock." *Fortune,* December 29, 2003, pp. 122–32.

Salomon, R. S. "Why I Like Financial Assets." *Forbes,* June 20, 1994, p. 262–63.

Appendix 1A

CAREER OPPORTUNITIES IN INVESTMENTS

Career opportunities in the investment field include positions as stockbroker, security analyst, portfolio manager, investment banker, or financial planner.

Stockbroker

A stockbroker (an account executive) generally works with the public in advising and executing orders for individual or institutional accounts. Although the broker may have a salary base to cushion against bad times, most of the compensation is in the form of commissions. Successful brokers do quite well financially.

Most brokerage houses look for people who have effective selling skills as well as an interest in finance. In hiring, some brokerage houses require prior business experience and a mature appearance. Table 1A–1 lists the 30 largest brokerage houses. Further information on these firms (as well as others not included on the list) can be found in the *Securities Industry Yearbook* published by the Securities Industry Association, 10 Broad Street, New York, N.Y. 10005.

Security Analyst or Portfolio Manager

Security analysts study various industries and companies and provide research reports to their clientele. Security analysts might work for a brokerage house, a bank trust department, or other type of institutional investor and often specialize in certain industries. They are expected to have an in-depth knowledge of overall financial analysis as well as the variables that influence their industry.

The role of the financial analyst has been upgraded over the years through a certifying program in which you can become a chartered financial analyst (CFA). There are approximately 40,000 CFAs in the United States and Canada. Achieving this designation calls for a three-year minimum appropriate-experience requirement and extensive testing over a three-year period. Each of the annual exams is six hours long and costs approximately $250 (the fee changes from year to year). There is also an initial, one-time registration fee (currently, $500). You can actually begin taking the exams while still in school (you can complete your experience requirement later).

Topics covered in the three years of exams are shown in Table 1A–2. An undergraduate or graduate degree in business with a major in finance or accounting or an economics degree is quite beneficial to the exam process (although other degrees are also acceptable). Of course, educational background must be supplemented with additional study prescribed by the Institute of Chartered Financial Analysts. The address for more information is: CFA Institute, P.O. Box 3668, Charlottesville, Virginia 22903 (phone 434-951-5499).

www.aimr.com

While many security analysts are not CFAs, those who carry this designation tend to enjoy higher salaries and prestige. Really top analysts are in strong demand, and six-figure to seven-figure salaries for top analysts are common. The magazine *Institutional Investor* picks an all-American team of security analysts, the best in energy, banking, and so on.

Portfolio managers are responsible for managing large pools of funds, and they are generally employed by insurance companies, mutual funds, bank trust

TABLE 1A–1 30 Largest U.S. Brokerage Houses

Rank 2003	Rank 2002	Firm	Total Consolidated Capital ($ millions)
1	1	Merrill Lynch & Co.	$81,945.0
2	2	Morgan Stanley	65,936.0
3	3	Credit Suisse First Boston Corp.	60,806.0
4	4	Goldman, Sachs & Co.	57,714.0
5	5	Lehman Brothers Holdings	48,329.0
6	6	Salomon Smith Barney Holdings	44,860.0
7	7	Bear Stearns Cos.	30,626.0
8	8	UBS	12,076.0
9	9	Deutsche Bank Securities	5,497.0
10	12	Banc of America Securities	5,369.0
11	10	Charles Schwab & Co.	4,653.0
12	11	JP Morgan Securities	4,573.0
13	13	TD Waterhouse Group	2,639.0
14	19	Wachovia Securities	2,317.6
15	14	Prudential Securities	2,116.0
16	17	Legg Mason Wood Walker	1,994.0
17	16	ABN Amro	1,751.0
18	15	Shelby Cullom Davis & Co.	1,721.0
19	20	A.G. Edwards & Sons	1,668.0
20	24	RBS Greenwich Capital Markets	1,641.0
21	18	CIBC World Markets	1,584.0
22	22	Quick & Reilly/Fleet Securities	1,391.3
23	26	LaBranche & Co.	1,372.9
24	21	SG Cowen Securities Corp.	1,368.5
25	31	Interactive Brokers Group	1,268.6
26	28	TD Securities (USA)	1,248.0
27	44	Ameritrade Holding Corp.	1,169.6
28	33	Edward Jones	1,139.0
29	35	Jefferies Group	1,081.1
30	23	Instinet Corp.	1,022.0

Source: "The Institutional Investor Ranking," *Institutional Investor,* April 2003, p. 79.

departments, pension funds, and other institutional investors. They often rely on the help of security analysts and brokers in designing their portfolios. They not only must decide which stocks to buy or sell, but they also must determine the risk level with the optimum trade-off between the common stock and fixed-income components of a portfolio. Portfolio managers often rise through the ranks of stockbrokers and security analysts.

Investment Banker

Investment bankers primarily distribute securities from the issuing corporation to the public. Investment bankers also advise corporate clients on their financial strategy and may help to arrange mergers and acquisitions.

TABLE 1A–2 Topics Covered in CFA Exams

Ethical and Professional Standards

Applicable laws and regulations	Ethical conduct and professional obligations
Professional standards of practice	International ethical and professional considerations

Tools and Inputs for Investment Valuation and Management

Quantitative methods and statistics	Microeconomics
Macroeconomics	Financial standards and accounting

Investment (Asset) Valuation

Overview of the valuation process	Equity securities
Applying economic analysis in investment valuation	Fixed-income securities
Applying industry analysis in investment valuation	Other investments
Applying company analysis in investment valuation	Derivative securities

Portfolio Management

Capital market theory	Equity portfolio management
Portfolio policies	Real estate portfolio management
Expectational factors	Specialized asset portfolio management
Asset allocation	Implementing the investment process
Fixed-income portfolio management	Performance management

The investment banker is one of the most prestigious participants in the securities industry. Although the hiring of investment bankers was once closely confined to Ivy League graduates with the right family ties, such is no longer the case. Nevertheless, an MBA and top credentials are usually the first prerequisites.

Financial Planner

The field of financial planning is emerging to help solve the investment and tax problems of the individual investor. Financial planners may include specially trained representatives of the insurance industry, accountants, and certified financial planners (an individual may fall into more than one of these categories).

Certified financial planners (CFPs) are so designated by the College of Financial Planning, a division of the National Endowment for Financial Education. To qualify as a CFP, an applicant must demonstrate proficiency in the five following areas through extensive testing and training.

- Financial planning process and insurance.
- Investment planning.
- Income tax planning.
- Retirement planning and employee benefits.
- Estate planning.

Information on the CFP program can be obtained from the CFP Board, 4695 South Monaco Street, Denver, Colorado 80237-3403 (phone 303-220-4800) or from colleges or universities that sponsor CFP classes or programs.

chapter two

Security Markets: Present and Future

objectives

1. Understand the functions of the financial markets.
2. Explain the role that the investment banker plays in the distribution of securities.
3. Discuss the differences between organized exchanges and over-the-counter markets.
4. Understand the impact of electronic markets on the efficiency of the markets.
5. Discuss the future outlook for the capital markets.
6. Understand the important legislation that affects the operations of the capital markets.

The Market Environment
Market Functions
    Market Efficiency and Liquidity
    Competition and Allocation of Capital
    Secondary Markets
    Primary Markets
Organization of the Primary Markets:
The Investment Banker
    Underwriting Function
    Distribution
    Investment Banking Competition
Organization of the Secondary Markets
    Organized Exchanges
    Consolidated Tape
    Listing Requirements for Firms
    Membership for Market Participants
Other Organized Exchanges
    The American Stock Exchange
    The Chicago Board Options Exchange
    Futures Markets
Over-the-Counter Markets—Electronic Markets
    Nasdaq Stock Market
    Debt Securities Traded Over-the-Counter
Electronic Communication Networks (ECNs)
Institutional Trading
Regulation of the Security Markets
    Securities Acts: 1933, 1934, 1975
    Other Legislation
    Insider Trading
    Program Trading and Market Price Limits

The Market Environment

The financial markets have changed dramatically during the last decade, and they continue to change at a rapid pace. This period has been one of deregulation, new laws, mergers, global consolidation, online (Internet) brokerage, and electronic communication networks (ECNs). These structural changes have been accompanied by 24-hour trading, decimalization of stock quotes, and intense global competition.

www.citicorp.com

www.citigroup.com

The last part of the 1990s was punctuated with mergers and consolidations, both global and domestic. The 1998 merger between Citicorp (the parent of CitiBank) and Travelers Insurance (including the Salomon Smith Barney division) created Citigroup. This merger caused a significant change in the way competitors thought about financial services. For the first time since the 1930s we had an institution that was able to sell insurance, underwrite securities, perform brokerage functions, and offer commercial banking under the same ownership. This had been prohibited by the Glass Steagall Act, which was enacted after the "Great Crash" of 1929 to keep one bank from being both a commercial bank and an investment bank. In 1999 the U.S. Congress passed the Gramm-Leach-Bliley Act allowing financial institutions to offer full financial services. Shortly after, Chase and JPMorgan merged and other commercial banks gobbled up smaller investment banks and brokerage firms. In 2004 JPMorgan Chase merged with Bank One to become a major competitor to Citigroup. Throughout this process, American financial institutions were starting to look more like European universal banks and would be able to compete more effectively around the globe during the 21st century.

On September 11, 2001, the World Trade Center in New York City and the Pentagon in Washington, D.C., were attacked by terrorists. In New York both towers and many surrounding buildings were destroyed, and thousands of lives were lost. This act of terror caused significant physical damage to the financial system, but less than one week later the New York Stock Exchange opened with a record trading volume of more than 2.3 billion shares. Despite the significant decline in stock prices at the time, many thought that the ability to generate this much volume was an indication of the strength of our financial system. Trading occurred from satellite backup facilities in Connecticut, Midtown Manhattan, and Jersey City, New Jersey. The New York Board of Trade opened up in a backup facility in Brooklyn, trading pits and all. It is clear that the markets could not have accomplished this feat without the technological improvements that have characterized the last decade.

Unfortunately, the economy was already in a recession, and the devastation both psychological and physical was enough to eliminate any chance for the economy to generate positive economic growth in the third quarter of that year. The stock market had already declined significantly from its highs, with the Dow Jones Industrial Average falling from a high of 11,436 on May 21, 2001, to 8,376 on September 20, 2001, for a drop of 26.76 percent. At the same time the over-the-counter Nasdaq Composite Index dropped from 3,913 on September 20, 2000, to 1,451 one year later—a one-year drop of almost 63 percent (not including the fall from its high of over 5,000 in March 2000). The nature of these stock market indexes is more fully explored in Chapter 3.

During this period of great grief and turmoil, many e-mail messages, websites, and talk shows were asking Americans to buy common stock when the market opened on September 17, 2001. This would be the patriotic thing to do and would help the market from suffering declines. Most market professionals argued against this logic by stating that markets were here to reflect reality and expectations and that there was nothing that could be done artificially to keep markets from falling or rising if expectations were negative or positive. In fact the markets did fall. Some industry groups such as the airlines and hotels/motels plunged between 25 and 50 percent in one day. Other companies in the defense industry rose more than 50 percent. In the eyes of the market participants, the markets did their job in reflecting the new reality facing Americans and the rest of the civilized world. Markets have gone up and down throughout history, including periods of prosperity, recession, war and other catastrophic events. What are markets supposed to do?

Market Functions

Many times people will call their stockbroker and ask, "How's the market?" What they are referring to is usually the market for common stocks as measured by the Dow Jones Industrial Average, the New York Stock Exchange Index, or some other measure of common stock performance. The stock market is not the only market. There are markets for each different kind of investment that can be made.

A **market** is simply a way of exchanging assets, usually cash, for something of value. It could be a used car, a government bond, gold, or diamonds. There doesn't have to be a central place where this transaction is consummated. As long as there can be communication between buyers and sellers, the exchange can occur. The offering party does not have to own what he sells but can be an agent acting for the owner in the transaction. For example, in the sale of real estate, the owner usually employs a real estate broker/agent who advertises and sells the property for a percentage commission. Not all markets have the same procedures, but certain trading characteristics are desirable for most markets.

Market Efficiency and Liquidity

In general, an **efficient market** occurs when prices respond quickly to new information, when each successive trade is made at a price close to the preceding price, and when the market can absorb large amounts of securities or assets without changing the price significantly. The more efficient the market, the faster prices react to new information; the closer in price is each successive trade; and the greater the amount of securities that can be sold without changing the price.

For markets to be efficient in this context, they must be liquid. **Liquidity** is a measure of the speed with which an asset can be converted into cash at its fair market value. Liquid markets exist when continuous trading occurs, and as the number of participants in the market becomes larger, price continuity increases along with liquidity. Transaction costs also affect liquidity. The lower the cost of buying and selling, the more likely it is that people will be able to enter the market.

Competition and Allocation of Capital

An investor must realize that all markets compete for funds: stocks against bonds, mutual funds against real estate, government securities against corporate securities, and so on. The competitive comparisons are almost endless. Because markets set prices on assets, investors are able to compare the prices against their perceived risk and expected return and thereby choose assets that enable them to achieve their desired risk-return trade-offs. If the markets are efficient, prices adjust rapidly to new information, and this adjustment changes the expected rate of return and allows the investor to alter investment strategy. Without efficient and liquid markets, the investor would be unable to do this. This allocation of capital occurs on both secondary and primary markets.

Secondary Markets

Secondary markets are markets for existing assets that are currently traded between investors. These markets create prices and allow for liquidity. If secondary markets did not exist, investors would have no place to sell their assets. Without liquidity, many people would not invest at all. Would you like to own $10,000 of Microsoft common stock but be unable to convert it into cash if needed? If there were no secondary markets, investors would expect a higher return to compensate for the increased risk of illiquidity and the inability to adjust their portfolios to new information.

Primary Markets

Primary markets are distinguished by the flow of funds between the market participants. Instead of trading between investors as in the secondary markets, participants in the primary market buy their assets directly from the source of the asset. A common example would be a new issue of corporate bonds sold by AT&T. You would buy the bonds through a brokerage firm acting as an agent for AT&T's investment bankers. Your dollars would flow to AT&T rather than to another investor. The same would be true of buying a piece of art directly from the artist rather than from an art gallery.

Primary markets allow corporations, government units, and others to raise needed funds for expansion of their capital base. Once the assets or securities are sold in the primary market, they begin trading in the secondary market. Price competition in the secondary markets between different risk-return classes enables the primary markets to price new issues at fair prices to reflect existing risk-return relationships. So far, our discussion of markets has been quite general but applicable to most free markets. In the following sections, we will deal with the organization and structure of specific markets.

Organization of the Primary Markets: The Investment Banker

The most active participant in the primary market is the investment banker. Since corporations, states, and local governments do not sell new securities daily, monthly, or even annually, they usually rely on the expertise of the investment banker when selling securities.

Underwriting Function

The **investment banker** acts as a middleman in the process of raising funds and, in most cases, takes a risk by underwriting an issue of securities. **Underwriting** refers to the guarantee the investment banking firm gives the selling firm to purchase its securities at a fixed price, thereby eliminating the risk of not selling the whole issue of securities and having less cash than desired. The investment banker may also sell the issue on a **best-efforts** basis where the issuing firm assumes the risk and simply takes back any securities not sold after a fixed period. A very limited number of securities are **sold directly** by the corporation to the public. Of the three methods of distribution, underwriting is far and away the most widely used.

With underwriting, once the security is sold, the investment banker will usually make a market in the security, which means active buying and selling to ensure a continuously liquid market and wider distribution. In the case of best efforts and for direct offerings by the issuer, which are even smaller than best efforts, the firm assumes the risk of not raising enough capital and has no guarantees that a continuous market will be made in the company's securities.

Corporations may also choose to raise capital through private placements rather than through a public offering. With a private placement, the company may sell its own securities to a financial institution such as an insurance company, a pension fund, or a mutual fund, or it can engage an investment banker to find an institution willing to buy a large block of stock or bonds. Most private placements involve bonds (debt issues) instead of common stock. During the last decade, publicly offered bonds approximated 80 percent of the funds raised with private placements accounting for about 20 percent. Publicly offered bonds issued through underwriters as opposed to privately placed issues are by far the most popular method of raising debt capital.

Distribution

In a public offering, the distribution process is extremely important, and on some large issues, an investment banker does not undertake this alone. Investment banking firms will share the risk and the burden of distribution by forming a group called a **syndicate.** The larger the offering in dollar terms, the more participants there generally are in the syndicate. For example, the tombstone advertisement in Figure 2–1 on page 32 for the Sprint Corporation's $3.697 billion combined issue of PCS common stock (cell phone division) and Sprint Capital Corporation Equity Units illustrates the participation of investment banks in the syndicate and the globalization of the investment banking community.

www.sprint.com
www.jpmorgan.com
www.ml.com
www.ibb.ubs.com

JPMorgan was the lead managing underwriter and was joined by Merrill Lynch and UBS Warburg as major partners in the underwriting syndicate. Several foreign banks were part of the international syndicate. UBS Warburg and Credit Suisse First Boston are Swiss-owned investment banks, while ABN AMRO Rothschild LLC is a Dutch investment bank. These three international banks are both commercial banks and investment banks, and for years they have had the flexibility to compete against U.S. commercial banks and investment banks on unequal footing. As discussed earlier, the U.S. Congress passed the Gramm-Leach-Bliley Act in 1999, repealing the Glass Steagall Act, which prohibited banks from offering both investment banking services and commercial banking

FIGURE 2–1 Tombstone Advertisement

These announcements are neither an offer to sell nor a solicitation of an offer to buy any of these Securities. The offer is made only by the Prospectuses and the related Prospectus Supplements, which may be obtained in any State from only such of the undersigned as may legally offer these Securities in compliance with the securities laws of such State.

$3,697,250,000

Sprint PCS™

Sprint Corporation

80,500,000 Shares
PCS Common Stock, Series 1

Price $24.50 Per Share

Joint Book-Running Managers

JPMorgan   Merrill Lynch & Co.   UBS Warburg

ABN AMRO Rothschild LLC   **Banc of America Securities LLC**

Credit Suisse First Boston   **Lehman Brothers**

Dain Rauscher Wessels   First Union Securities, Inc.   Robertson Stephens   The Williams Capital Group, L.P.

Sprint Corporation
Sprint Capital Corporation

69,000,000 Equity Units

Price $25.00 Per Unit

Joint Book-Running Managers

JPMorgan   Merrill Lynch & Co.   UBS Warburg

ABN AMRO Rothschild LLC   **Banc of America Securities LLC**

Credit Suisse First Boston   **Lehman Brothers**

August 10, 2001

services. Now U.S. banks can offer commercial and investment banking services as well as insurance and retail brokerage service.

Firms are listed in the tombstone advertisement from the lead banker on the upper left, JPMorgan in this case, to the smallest banker in the bottom right. The firms at the top of the advertisement have agreed to underwrite the largest number of shares and the firms on the bottom have taken the smallest number of shares. The actual number of shares allocated to each investment banker is listed in the prospectus filed with the Securities and Exchange Commission (SEC). It should be noted that the investment bankers make a commitment to purchase (at a discount from the public price) and sell their allotted shares. If the PCS common stock price falls below the intended offering price of $24.50 while the shares are still being sold to the public, the investment bankers in the syndicate will not make their original estimated profit on the issue. If the stock price drops too much below $24.50, perhaps to $23.00, the investment bankers could lose money on the offering.

For most original offerings, the investment banker is extremely important as a link between the original issuer and the security markets. By taking much of the risk, the investment banker enables corporations and others to find needed capital and also allows investors an opportunity to participate in the ownership of securities through purchase in the secondary market. The Sprint Corporation lists 80.5 million shares for its PCS cell phone division and 69 million shares for its Sprint Capital Corporation division. The total raised by the sale of the common stock and equity units was $3.7 billion. The offering included more than 50 million shares of Sprint PCS held by Deutsche Telekom. After the issue was completed, Sprint was expected to keep about $2.5 billion.

The demand for the offering was strong for a stock market that was certainly in a bear market by most measures (August 2001). Sprint had originally intended to offer 70 million shares but had given the underwriters an additional 10.5 million shares as an overallotment option for the common stock. The bankers exercised all these extra shares, and the total soared to 80.5 million shares.

The passage of the Gramm-Leach-Bliley Act is expected to have a significant effect on the structure of the investment and commercial banking industries. One continuing trend of the act will be the increased willingness of large financial institutions to take more risk. To consider that in our Sprint example, only 11 investment banking firms were able to absorb $3.7 billion of risk is an indication of the trend. Ten years ago the number of bankers would have been more than triple that number, and the offering size would have been no more than $1 billion.

More mergers—creating firms such as Citigroup with its Travelers Insurance Division and its Salomon Smith Barney brokerage and investment banking business—will occur. Chase Bank and JPMorgan merged and in 2004 they combined with Bank One to become the second largest financial services company in the United States after Citigroup. The insurance industry is in the process of moving from mutual companies owned by their policyholders to stock companies owned by their stockholders. By moving to a stock company, the insurance companies will have the ability to merge with other financial companies through an exchange of stock. Expect continued mergers between insurance companies and other financial service companies over the next decade.

Another change that has affected the distribution and underwriting process is the increased use of shelf registration under SEC Rule 415. A shelf registration

TABLE 2–1 Top 10 Underwriters of Global Stocks and Bonds

U.S. Public, Rule 144a, Domestic and International Equity and Euromarket Issues, Ranked by 2003 Proceeds.

Manager	2003 Proceeds (billions)	No. of Issues	Market Share	2002 Proceeds (billions)	Rank
Citigroup	$ 542.7	1,872	10.2%	$ 440.0	1
Morgan Stanley	394.8	1,365	7.4	294.3	5
Merrill Lynch	380.3	1,914	7.1	339.0	2
Lehman Brothers	354.1	1,264	6.7	280.7	6
JPMorgan	353.9	1,417	6.6	294.9	4
Credit Suisse First Boston	338.7	1,248	6.4	322.6	3
Deutsche Bank	317.4	1,256	6.0	247.4	8
UBS	293.8	1,147	5.5	259.2	7
Goldman Sachs	293.3	807	5.5	244.7	9
Banc of America Securities	206.4	737	3.9	169.7	10
Top 10 Totals	**$3,475.6**	**13,027**	**65.3%**	**$2,892.6**	—
Industry Totals	**$5,326.0**	**19,585**	**100.0%**	**$4,256.5**	—

Source: *The Wall Street Journal,* January 7, 2004. Reprinted with permission of *The Wall Street Journal,* © 2004 by Dow Jones & Company, Inc. All Rights Reserved Worldwide.

allows issuing firms to register their securities with the SEC and then sell them at will as funds are needed in the future. Over time, this allows bankers to buy portions of the shelf issue and immediately resell the securities to institutional clients without forming the normal syndicate or tying up capital for several weeks. Shelf registration is more popular with bond offerings than common stock offerings, where the traditional syndicated offering tends to dominate.

Investment Banking Competition

Table 2–1 shows the top 10 underwriters of global debt and equity offerings for the years 2002 and 2003. The list of bankers remains relatively the same from year to year with some bankers moving up or down the list due to mergers and the fund-raising activities of their clients. In previous years the listing would have emphasized *U.S.* offerings of debt and equity but as more international and multinational companies raise capital around the world, the investment banking game has become *global.*

The total market share of the top 10 bankers has dropped from the late 1990s and early 2000s as the global recession and economic slowdown have reduced the need for companies to raise capital for expansion. This has allowed the smaller investment banks, specializing in medium-sized companies, to take some market share from the big players who are more dependent on large companies. In 2001 the top 10 investment bankers had accounted for over 83 percent of the market share, while in 2003 they only accounted for 65 percent.

While investment bankers want to be on the top 10 underwriters list, they are more concerned about underwriting fees than about the number of issues in which they were the lead underwriter. Table 2–2 shows a slightly different ranking when looking at fees rather than at gross proceeds from underwriting. The

TABLE 2–2 Top 10 Underwriters of Global Stocks and Bonds Disclosed Fees

Top Underwriters, by Fees, for Global Stock and Bond Underwriting in 2003

	Disclosed Fees (in millions)	
Manager	2003	2002
Citigroup	$ 1,760.2	$ 1,981.8
Morgan Stanley	1,195.4	1,228.1
JPMorgan	1,013.4	967.5
Goldman Sachs	1,002.6	1,040.1
Merrill Lynch	982.0	1,191.6
Credit Suisse F.B.	908.1	1,210.3
UBS	816.1	632.8
Lehman Brothers	636.7	708.2
Deutsche Bank	631.9	777.5
Nomura	574.3	430.2
Top 10 Totals	$ 9,520.7	$10,168.1
Industry Totals	$14,460.5	$14,762.4

Source: *The Wall Street Journal,* January 7, 2004. Reprinted with permission of *The Wall Street Journal,* © 2004 by Dow Jones & Company, Inc. All Rights Reserved Worldwide.

reason for this difference is that some underwriting business, such as the sale of common stock, has higher fees than the sale of debt. Investment banks such as Goldman Sachs, which specializes in common stocks, can make more money with a smaller number of offerings. This is why Goldman Sachs moved up from ninth position in Table 2–1 to fourth in Table 2–2. Lehman Brothers, which is more active in the bond market, moved from fourth place in Table 2–1 to eighth place in Table 2–2.

Bringing private companies public for the first time is called an **initial public offering (IPO),** and distribution costs to the selling company are much higher than offerings of additional stock by companies that are already public. Average fees from IPOs are usually between 1.5 and 2.0 percent higher than the fees for secondary offerings of publicly traded stock. The previously discussed Sprint Corporation offering in Figure 2–1 is called a secondary offering because the shares were already listed on the New York Stock Exchange. The fees for the Sprint offering were lower than if the offering had been an IPO.

Underwriting competition is like a decathlon; there are many events for each contestant. Table 2–3 on page 36 provides a list of the categories in which investment bankers compete and the number one ranked investment bank in each category. While Merrill Lynch used to be the dominant player in many categories it does not show up in first place in any of the categories. Citigroup dominates the overall global markets, while Goldman Sachs dominates the issuance of common stock. JPMorgan leads the convertible bond category as well as syndicated loans. Credit Suisse First Boston (CSFB) leads the high-yield debt (junk bond) market, and United Banks of Switzerland (UBS) leads in the mortgage-backed securities market. Each firm competes based on its expertise.

The worldwide market is becoming more important to all investment bankers. Table 2–4 on page 36 lists the biggest corporate financings of stocks

TABLE 2–3 Who's Number 1?

Leading Stock and Bond Underwriters, by 2003 Proceeds

Market Sector	No. 1 Ranked Manager	2003 Mkt. Share	Change from 2002 (% pts.)
Global debt, stock, & stock-related	**Citigroup**	10.2%	−0.10
U.S. debt, stock, & stock-related	**Citigroup**	12.0	0.10
Stocks			
Global common stock—U.S. issuers	**Goldman Sachs**	16.2	−0.20
U.S. stock & stock-related	**Goldman Sachs**	14.1	−2.40
U.S. initial public offerings	**Goldman Sachs**	17.6	3.20
U.S. convertible offerings	**JPMorgan**	14.2	6.10
Bonds			
U.S. asset-backed securities	**Citigroup**	11.2	0.40
U.S. investment grade corporate debt	**Citigroup**	20.5	−1.30
U.S. high-yield corporate debt	**CSFB**	15.9	−0.30
U.S. mortgage-backed securities	**UBS**	11.6	−1.60
Syndicated Loans			
U.S. syndicated loans	**JPMorgan**	28.3%	−6.50

Source: *The Wall Street Journal,* January 7, 2004. Reprinted with permission of *The Wall Street Journal,* © 2004 by Dow Jones & Company, Inc. All Rights Reserved Worldwide.

TABLE 2–4 Biggest Corporate Financings of 2003

Top 10 Global Stock Issues

Issuer	Date	Amount ($ billions)
Koninklijke Ahold NV	Dec. 11	**$3.6**
China Life Insurance	Dec. 12	3.0
Mitsubishi Tokyo Fin'l	March 3	2.7
ENEL	Oct. 30	2.5
Koninklijke KPN	Sept. 19	2.3
Yell Group	July 9	2.0
Accenture	Sept. 23	2.0
BOC Hong Kong (Hldg)	Dec. 15	1.9
NEC	Dec. 8	1.8
Fortis Group	April 24	1.7

Top 10 Global Debt Issues

Issuer	Date	Amount ($ billions)
France Telecom	Jan. 15	**$5.8**
General Motors	June 26	5.3
Hutchison Whampoa Intl.	Nov. 19	5.0
General Electric	Jan. 23	5.0
Telecom Italia Capital	Oct. 20	4.0
General Electric Capital	May 7	4.0
GMAC	June 26	3.4
Muenchener Re	April 9	3.2
Olivetti Intl. Finance	Jan. 13	3.2
Morgan Stanley	Feb. 20	3.2

Source: *The Wall Street Journal,* January 7, 2004. Reprinted with permission of *The Wall Street Journal,* © 2004 by Dow Jones & Company, Inc. All Rights Reserved Worldwide.

(equity) and bonds (debt) in 2003. If you know your companies, in the stock column on the left you will find a Dutch company at the top of the list, followed by a Chinese company, a Japanese company, an Italian company, and so on. There is only one U.S. firm on the list and that is Accenture. If we go to the debt column we find five U.S. companies and companies from France, Hong Kong, Germany, and two from Italy. These international companies will look for international investment bankers and because of that, global mergers in the investment banking market are likely to continue, as well as expansion of these banks into emerging markets such as China and India.

Organization of the Secondary Markets

Once the investment banker or the Federal Reserve (for U.S. government securities) has sold a new issue of securities, it begins trading in secondary markets that provide liquidity, efficiency, continuity, and competition. The **organized exchanges** fulfill this need in a central location where trading occurs between buyers and sellers. The **over-the-counter markets** also provide markets for exchange but not in a central location. A new type of market that has developed in the last several years is the **ECN** or **electronic communication network.** In the next sections we will present an overview of each market.

Organized Exchanges

Organized exchanges are either national or regional, but both are organized in a similar fashion. Exchanges have a central trading location where securities are bought and sold in an auction market by brokers acting as agents for the buyer and seller. Stocks usually trade at various trading posts on the floor of the exchange. Brokers are registered members of the exchanges, and their number is fixed by each exchange. The national exchanges are the New York Stock Exchange (NYSE) and the American Stock Exchange (AMEX).

The regional exchanges began their existence trading securities of local firms. As the firms grew, they became listed on the national exchanges, but they also continued to trade on the regionals. Many cities, such as Chicago, Cincinnati, Philadelphia, and Boston, have regional exchanges. Today, most of the trading on these exchanges is done in nationally known companies. Trading in the same companies is common between the NYSE and such regionals as the Chicago Stock Exchange and the smaller regionals. More than 90 percent of the companies traded on the Chicago Stock Exchange are also listed on the NYSE. This is referred to as dual trading.

October 20, 1987, the day after the crash of '87, was the busiest day in the history of the New York Stock Exchange until October 28, 1997, the day after the next crash. On October 27, 1997, the stock market moved down significantly and this day was ranked as one of the 10 worst days in market history. What did make history however, were the 1.2 billion shares traded on the New York Stock Exchange the next day. This compares to 685 million shares on October 27, 1987. Perhaps the greatest triumph however was the record number of shares traded on the first day the New York Stock Exchange opened after being closed for almost one week after the attacks on the World Trade Center. The 2.368 billion shares set a record for the NYSE. The other markets (such as Chicago, Nasdaq, and Boston) also showed significant increases in volume from the previous record days. This data can be examined in Table 2–5 on page 38.

Consolidated Tape

Although dual listing and trading have existed for some time, it was not until June 16, 1975, that a consolidated ticker tape was instituted. This allows brokers

TABLE 2–5 Data on Trading Volume (Breakdown of Trading in NYSE Stocks)

By Market	Monday 27-Oct-87	Monday 28-Oct-97	Monday 17-Sep-01
New York	685,496,330	1,195,836,620	2,368,326,910
Chicago	28,857,300	40,187,200	95,613,840
CBOE	56,600	74,000	6,300
Pacific	20,331,100	20,001,000	8,512,700
NASD/Nasdaq Intermarket	59,636,200	85,585,150	157,846,400
Philadelphia	9,009,600	10,619,700	14,530,700
Boston	10,793,100	13,995,100	43,359,000
Cincinnati	9,605,000	8,432,100	10,205,400
Composite	823,785,230	1,374,731,570	2,698,401,250

Source: Various issues of *The Wall Street Journal*.

on the floor of one exchange to see prices of transactions on other exchanges in the dually listed stocks. Any time a transaction is made on a regional exchange or over-the-counter in a security listed on the NYSE, this transaction and any made on the floor of the NYSE are displayed on the composite tape. The composite price data keep markets more efficient and prices more competitive between exchanges at all times.

The NYSE and AMEX are both national exchanges and for years did not allow dual listing of companies traded on their exchanges, but as of August 1976, securities were able to be dually listed between these exchanges. There doesn't seem to be any advantage to this since both are located in New York City, and traditionally, shares that trade on one exchange are not traded on the other.

Panel A of Table 2–6 displays the number of trades (not number of shares) on all markets participating in the consolidated tape. Trading volume has steadily increased from 1988 through 2003 with the New York Stock Exchange increasing its market share (Panel B) over this period from 69 percent to over 89 percent. Since the consolidated tape only reflects dually listed NYSE stocks, it does not reflect volume in NASDAQ traded companies.

Listing Requirements for Firms

Securities can be traded on an exchange only if they have met the listing requirements of the exchange and have been approved by the board of governors of that exchange. All exchanges have minimum requirements that must be met before trading can occur in a company's common stock. Since the NYSE is the biggest exchange and generates the most dollar volume in large, well-known companies, its listing requirements are the most restrictive.

Initial Listing Although each case is decided on its own merits, there are minimum requirements that are specified by the exchanges. These requirements set minimums for the net income of the firm, the market value of publicly held shares, the number of shares publicly held, and the number of stockholders owning at least a round lot of 100 shares. Other exchanges such as the Chicago

TABLE 2-6 Panel A—Consolidated Tape Trades by Market, by Year

Year	NYSE	PSE	CHX	PHLX	BSE	CSE	NASD	CBOE	Total
2003	721,354,767	5,231,735	15,893,927	1,638,608	11,070,829	3,934,842	44,123,219	0	803,247,927
2002	544,229,948	1,352,780	15,559,045	2,070,170	13,653,725	2,713,460	39,395,436	86	618,974,650
2001	338,097,835	1,834,977	14,664,576	2,538,291	9,419,755	5,003,102	28,053,473	658	399,612,667
2000	220,739,392	6,910,943	16,825,364	3,214,078	9,091,805	7,324,681	31,455,042	444	295,561,749
1999	169,405,684	8,279,262	13,758,573	2,692,976	7,323,563	4,437,849	26,994,867	629	232,893,403
1998	135,897,193	6,604,518	10,055,265	2,426,065	4,942,783	3,322,434	19,255,326	1,641	182,505,225
1997	102,601,803	5,712,875	6,375,353	2,392,148	2,850,194	3,443,128	14,463,766	2,388	137,841,655
1996	75,200,205	4,816,909	4,403,600	2,053,439	1,847,777	3,370,843	11,027,891	512	102,721,176
1995	58,630,094	4,443,064	4,281,216	1,784,669	2,096,402	3,263,961	8,994,455	0	83,493,861
1994	49,121,044	3,549,380	3,890,199	1,693,062	1,640,202	2,167,923	6,466,497	0	68,528,227
1993	46,476,295	3,806,226	4,050,348	1,851,256	1,687,649	1,704,590	6,351,196	0	65,929,861
1992	30,557,805	3,541,541	3,909,578	1,554,026	1,485,169	867,926	4,957,152	0	46,886,467
1991	27,167,350	3,274,499	3,240,894	1,147,522	1,361,572	298,665	3,847,067	0	40,349,111
1990	19,148,610	2,355,273	2,810,029	875,100	1,090,871	181,470	2,468,490	0	28,939,640
1989	19,727,062	2,378,200	2,970,627	965,448	900,529	125,215	1,419,914	0	28,494,789

Data after 1988 include rights and warrants.
MSE changed its name to CHX on July 8, 1993.
INST totals included in NASD.

Panel B—Market Share of Consolidated Tape Trades by Year

Year	NYSE	PSE	CHX	PHLX	BSE	CSE	NASD	CBOE	Total
2003	89.8%	0.7%	2.0%	0.2%	1.4%	0.5%	5.5%	0.0%	100.0%
2002	87.9	0.2	2.5	0.3	2.2	0.4	6.4	0.0	100.0
2001	84.6	0.5	3.7	0.6	2.4	1.3	7.0	0.0	100.0
2000	74.7	2.3	5.7	1.1	3.1	2.5	10.6	0.0	100.0
1999	72.7	3.6	5.9	1.2	3.1	1.9	11.6	0.0	100.0
1998	74.5	3.6	5.5	1.3	2.7	1.8	10.6	0.0	100.0
1997	74.4	4.1	4.6	1.7	2.1	2.5	10.5	0.0	100.0
1996	73.2	4.7	4.3	2.0	1.8	3.3	10.7	0.0	100.0
1995	70.2	5.3	5.1	2.1	2.5	3.9	10.8	0.0	100.0
1994	71.7	5.2	5.7	2.5	2.4	3.2	9.4	0.0	100.0
1993	70.5	5.8	6.1	2.8	2.6	2.6	9.6	0.0	100.0
1992	65.2	7.6	8.3	3.3	3.2	1.9	10.6	0.0	100.0
1991	67.3	8.1	8.0	2.8	3.4	0.7	9.6	0.0	100.0
1990	66.2	8.1	9.7	3.0	3.8	0.6	8.6	0.0	100.0
1989	69.2	8.4	10.4	3.4	3.2	0.4	5.0	0.0	100.0

Participating markets: NYSE, New York; AMEX, American; PSE, Pacific; CHX, Chicago; PHLX, Philadelphia; BSE, Boston; CSE, Cincinnati; CBOE, Chicago Board Options Exchange; NASD, National Association of Securities Dealers; http://www.nysedata.com/factbook/.
Source: © NYSE Inc. All Rights Reserved.

www.NYSE.com

Stock Exchange have similar requirements, but the amounts are smaller. We have a web exercise at the back of the chapter that takes you to the New York Stock Exchange website where you can look up the latest minimum standards for companies wanting to be listed on the NYSE.

Corporations desiring to be listed on exchanges have decided that public availability of the stock on an exchange will benefit their shareholders by providing liquidity to owners or by allowing the company a more viable means for raising external capital for growth and expansion. The company must pay annual listing fees to the exchange and additional fees based on the number of shares traded each year.

Delisting   The New York Stock Exchange also has the authority to remove (delist) a security from trading when the security fails to meet certain criteria. There is much latitude in these decisions, but generally, a company's security may be considered for delisting if there are fewer than 1,200 round-lot (100 shares) owners, 600,000 shares or fewer in public hands, and the total market value of the security is less than $5 million. A company that easily exceeded these standards on first being listed may fall below them during hard times.

Membership for Market Participants

We've talked about listing requirements for corporations on the exchange, but what about the investment houses or traders that service the listed firms or trade for their own account on the exchanges? These privileges are reserved for a select number of people. The NYSE has 1,366 members who own "seats," which may be leased or sold with the approval of the NYSE. Multiple seats are owned by many member firms such as Merrill Lynch, so the number of member organizations totals 1,192. In recent years, the price of NYSE seats ranged from a low of $35,000 in 1977 to a high of $2,650,000 in early 1999 and a decline to $1,500,000 in 2004. Prices fluctuate with market trends, going up in bull markets and down in bear markets. The members owning these seats can be divided into five distinct categories, each with a specific job.

Commission Brokers   The **commission brokers** represent commission houses such as Merrill Lynch that execute orders on the floor of the exchange for customers of that firm. Many of the larger retail brokerage houses have more than one commission broker on the floor of the exchange. If you call your account executive (stockbroker) and place an order to buy 100 shares of Exxon-Mobil, the account executive will send your order to the NYSE where it will be transmitted to one of the firm's commission brokers who will go to the appropriate trading post and execute the order.

Floor Brokers   You can imagine that commission brokers could get very busy running from post to post on a heavy volume day. In times like these, they will rely on some help from **floor brokers,** who are registered to trade on the exchange but are not employees of a member firm. Instead, floor brokers own their own seat and charge a small fee for services.

Registered Traders   The **registered traders** own their own seats and are not associated with a member firm (such as Merrill Lynch). They are registered to trade for their own accounts and do so with the objective of earning a profit. Because they are members, they don't have to pay commissions on these trades; but in so trading, they help to generate a continuous market and liquidity for the market in general. There is always the possibility that these traders could manipulate the market if they acted in mass, and for that reason, the exchanges have rules governing their behavior and limiting the number of registered traders at one specific trading post.

Odd-Lot Dealers Odd lots (less than 100 shares) are not traded on the main floor of the exchange, so if a customer wants to buy or sell 20 shares of AT&T, the order will end up being processed by an **odd-lot dealer.** Dealers own their own inventory of the particular security and buy and sell for their own accounts. If they accumulate 100 shares, they can sell them in the market. A few very large brokerage firms, such as Merrill Lynch, make their own odd-lot market in actively traded securities, and it is expected that this trend will become common at other large commission houses. Odd-lot trading on other exchanges is usually handled by the specialist in the particular stock.

Specialists The **specialists** are a very important segment of the exchange and make up about one-fourth of total membership. Each stock traded has a specialist assigned to it, and most specialists are responsible for more than one stock. Specialists have two basic duties with regard to the stocks they supervise. First, they must handle any special orders that commission brokers or floor brokers might give. For example, a special order could limit the price someone is willing to pay for Time Warner (TWX) stock to $15 per share for 100 shares. If the commission broker reaches the TWX trading post and TWX is selling at $16 per share, the broker will leave the order with the specialist to execute if and when the stock of TWX falls to $15 or less. The specialist puts these special limit orders in his "book" with the date and time entered so he can execute orders at the same price by the earliest time of receipt. A portion of the broker's commission is then paid to the specialist.

The second major function of specialists is to maintain continuous, liquid, and orderly markets in their assigned stocks. This is not a difficult function in actively traded securities, such as General Motors, Du Pont, and AT&T, but it becomes more difficult in those stocks where there are no large, active markets. For example, suppose you placed an order to buy 100 shares of Brush Engineering at the market price. If the commission broker reaches the Brush Engineering trading post and no seller is present, the broker can't wait for one to appear since he has other orders to execute. Fortunately, the broker can buy the shares from the specialist who acts as a dealer—in this case buying for and selling from his own inventory. To ensure ability to maintain continuous markets, the exchange requires a specialist to have $500,000 or enough capital to own 5,000 shares of the assigned stock, whichever is greater. At times, specialists are under tremendous pressure to make a market for securities. A classic case occurred when President Reagan was shot in the 1980s, and specialists stabilized the market by absorbing wave after wave of sell orders.

The New York Stock Exchange keeps statistics on specialists' performance and their ability to maintain price continuity, quotation spreads, market depth, and price stabilization. These data are given in Table 2–7 on page 42. Price continuity is measured by the size of the price variation in successive trades. Column 1 is the percentage of transactions with no change in price or a minimum change of 12 cents or less. Column 2 presents the percentage of the quotes

TABLE 2–7 Market Quality and Specialists' Stabilization

NYSE Market Quality and Specialists' Stabilization, 1999–2002

	Price Continuity	Quotation Spreads	Market Depth	Stabilization Rate
2002	98.9%	97.7%	87.4%	80.8%
2001	98.6	96.3	89.5	82.7
2000	97.2	92.4	91.7	81.1
1999	98.1	94.2	88.4	82.8
1998	97.4	92.2	85.3	82.7
1997	97.7	93.5	86.9	80.0
1996	98.2	93.6	90.0	75.0
1995	98.2	93.1	90.8	74.6
1994	97.4	90.8	88.6	76.3
1993	97.1	88.9	88.3	77.6
1992	96.4	86.4	87.1	78.3
1991	95.9	84.6	85.5	80.9
1990	95.8	84.5	84.4	83.1

where the bid and asked prices were equal to or less than 25 cents. Market depth (Column 3) is displayed as a percentage of the time that 1,000 to 3,000 shares of volume failed to move the price of the stock more than 12 cents. Finally, the NYSE expects specialists to stabilize the market by buying and selling from their own accounts against the prevailing trend. This is measured in Column 4 as the percentage of shares purchased below the last different price and the percentage of shares sold above the last different price.

While these statistics are not 100 percent, it would be quite unreasonable for us to expect specialists to maintain that kind of a record in all types of markets. However, some critics of the specialist system on the NYSE think these performance measures could be improved by having more than one specialist for each stock. Many market watchers believe competing dealers on the over-the-counter market provide more price stability and fluid markets than the NYSE specialist system.

Somewhat in response to these criticisms, the New York Stock Exchange created computer systems that help the specialists manage order inflows more efficiently. **Super Dot** (designated order transfer system) allows NYSE member firms to electronically transmit all market and limit orders directly to the specialist at the trading post or the member trading booth. This order routing system takes orders and communicates executions of the orders directly back to the member firm on the same electronic circuit.

As a part of Super Dot, specialists are informed through OARS (Opening Automated Report Service) of market orders received before the opening bell. Another feature of Super Dot that greatly aids the specialist is the **Electronic Book.** This database covers stocks listed on the NYSE and keeps track of limit orders and market orders for the specialist. You can imagine the great improvement in recording, reporting, and error elimination over the old manual entry in the "specialist's book."

Other Organized Exchanges

The American Stock Exchange

The American Stock Exchange trades in smaller companies than the NYSE, and except for one dually listed company on the NYSE in 1983, the stocks traded on the AMEX are different from those on any other exchange. Because many of the small companies on the AMEX do not meet the liquidity needs of large institutional investors, the AMEX has been primarily a market for individual investors.

In an attempt to differentiate itself from the NYSE, the AMEX traded warrants in companies for many years before the NYSE traded them. The AMEX is also one of the largest markets for put and call options on individual stocks and long-term equity options and options on indexes. In recent years the American Stock Exchange also has transformed itself into the central market for **exchange traded funds (ETFs).** These exchange traded funds are structured products that imitate an index such as the Standard & Poor's 500 (SPDRS) and the Dow Jones Industrial Average (DIAMONDS). Close to 100 exchange traded funds are listed on the AMEX. More detail about these products will be covered in later chapters. If you can't wait to learn what they are, go to **www.amex.com** for definitions of these products.

The Chicago Board Options Exchange

Trading in call options started on the Chicago Board Options Exchange (CBOE) in April 1973 and proved very successful. The number of call options listed grew from 16 in 1973 to more than 500 in 2003. A **call option** gives the owner the right to buy 100 shares of the underlying common stock at a set price for a certain period. The CBOE standardized call options into three-month, six-month, and nine-month expiration periods on a rotating monthly series. Other sequences have since been developed. The CBOE and the AMEX currently have many options that are dually listed, and the competition between them is fierce. The two exchanges also trade put options (options to sell). A number of smaller regional exchanges also provide for option trading.

A new wrinkle in the options game has been options on stock market indexes or industry groupings (called subindexes). The CBOE offers puts and calls on the Standard & Poor's 500 Index and the Dow Jones Industrial Average; the AMEX has options on the AMEX Market Value Index, and so on. More about these markets will be presented in Chapter 17.

Futures Markets

Futures markets have traditionally been associated with commodities and, more recently, also with financial instruments. Purchasers of commodity futures own the right to buy a certain amount of the commodity at a set price for a specified period. As the time runs out (expires), the futures contract normally is reversed (closed out) before expiration. Chicago is the center of the major futures market and the Chicago Board of Trade (CBOT) **www.cbot.com** and the Chicago Mercantile Exchange (CME) **www.cme.com** are two of the largest in the world.

There are significant changes in the structure of these markets. Futures exchanges are becoming publicly traded companies. The Chicago Mercantile Exchange listed shares on the New York Stock Exchange in December of 2002. Exchanges are also consolidating and becoming electronic. Euronext www.euronext.com, a leading electronic exchange, bought the London International Financial Futures Exchange (LIFFE) in 2002 and moved into the Chicago market to compete with the Chicago Mercantile Exchange. Eurex, www.eurexchange.com, another European electronic exchange, was approved by U.S. regulators to begin trading in Chicago and thus can offer its global customers competitive products listed on the CME. These markets are truly becoming global and low cost in nature. The entrance of two new foreign competitors in the United States has already caused the CBOT and the CME to lower their fees. Chapters 16 and 17 cover the products that are traded on these exchanges.

Over-the-Counter Markets—Electronic Markets

Unlike the organized exchanges, the over-the-counter (OTC) markets have no central location where securities are traded. Being traded over-the-counter implies the trade takes place by telephone or electronic device and dealers stand ready to buy or sell specific securities for their own accounts. These dealers will buy at a bid price and sell at an asked price that reflects the competitive market conditions. By contrast, brokers on the organized exchanges merely act as agents who process orders. The National Association of Securities Dealers (NASD), a self-policing organization of dealers, requires at least two market makers (dealers) for each security, but often there are 5 or 10 or even 20 for government securities. As previously mentioned, the multiple-dealer function in the over-the-counter market is an attractive feature for many companies in comparison to the single specialist arrangement on the NYSE and other organized exchanges.

OTC markets exist for stocks, corporate bonds, mutual funds, federal government securities, state and local bonds, commercial paper, negotiable certificates of deposits, and various other securities. These securities make the OTC the largest of all markets in the United States in dollar terms.

In the OTC market, the difference between the bid and asked price is the spread; it represents the profit the dealer earns by making a market. For example, if XYZ common stock is bid 10 and asked 10.50, this simply means the dealer will buy at least 100 shares at $10 per share or will sell 100 shares at $10.50 per share. If prices are too low, more buyers than sellers will appear, and the dealer will run out of inventory unless he raises prices to attract more sellers and balances the supply and demand. If his price is at equilibrium, he will match an equal number of shares bought and sold, and for his market-making activities, he will earn 50 cents per share traded.

Nasdaq Stock Market

The **Nasdaq Stock Market** is linked by computer networks and provides up-to-the-minute quotation on approximately 6,000 of the stocks traded on the Nasdaq system. There is no central marketplace. The Nasdaq stocks are divided between national market issues and small cap issues. Each is presented separately in *The Wall Street Journal* and other newspapers.[1]

As the name implies, the national market issues represent larger Nasdaq companies that must meet higher listing standards than the small cap market. The standards are not as high as those on the NYSE but cover most of the same areas: net tangible assets, net income, pretax income, public float (shares outstanding in the hands of the public), operating history, market value of the float, a minimum share price, the number of shareholders, and the number of market makers. The web exercise at the end of the chapter will take you through the actual listing requirements of both the NYSE and Nasdaq.

Because the listing requirements are lower than those of the NYSE, many small public companies begin trading on the Nasdaq and many decide to stay there even after they far exceed the requirements for the NYSE. Companies such as Intel, Microsoft, Oracle, and Sun Microsystems trade on the Nasdaq Stock Market; as the company names suggest, Nasdaq is very popular with technology companies. Perhaps that is because Nasdaq is the world's largest *electronic* market built on technology.

www.intel.com
www.microsoft.com
www.oracle.com
www.sun.com

Like many other markets, Nasdaq is a publicly traded company trading on the OTC Bulletin Board under the ticker symbol NDAQ. It is traded in this very small market segment not because it is a small company but because there are very few shares outstanding available for trading. Most shares are closely held or restricted for trading. Nasdaq prides itself on its corporate governance, efficiency, and surveillance systems that avoid conflicts of interest and market manipulation. Nasdaq states that it has 11,000 traders at 790 firms, trading at 1,000 locations. The combined effect of its system is that over 2 million users in 83 countries have access to computer screens with Nasdaq data. Nasdaq created SuperMontage, its most recent electronic trading system. This system integrates the process of trading with information about limit orders, time stamps for receipt of orders, multiple quotes, and more. It is Nasdaq's response to the competitive environment that has turned most stock markets around the world into electronic trading platforms rather than floor-based markets such as the NYSE.

Over the last decade, the Nasdaq Stock Market has taken its place in world equity markets based on its dollar volume of trading activity. The NYSE is first followed by Nasdaq, London, and then Tokyo. This is a dramatic change for a market that was in fifth place in 1990. The U.S. equity market for small-growth companies boomed in the 1990s, and this helped to increase Nasdaq's volume. Additionally, its multiple-dealer system, efficient computerized quotation systems, and enhanced reporting capability are other reasons for the increased competitive nature. To add to its worldwide status, Nasdaq has begun to create Nasdaq stock markets in foreign cities such as Hong Kong.

Debt Securities Traded Over-the-Counter

Debt securities also trade over-the-counter. Actually, government securities of the U.S. Treasury provide the largest dollar volume of transactions on the OTC and account for billions of dollars in trades each week. These securities are

---

[1] Publicly traded firms that are not listed on organized exchanges or by the Nasdaq are normally not quoted in newspapers but may be shown on special pink sheets put out by investment houses.

traded by government securities dealers who are often associated with a division of a large financial institution, such as a New York, Chicago, or West Coast money market bank or a large brokerage house such as Merrill Lynch. These dealers make markets in government securities, such as Treasury bills and Treasury bonds, or federal agency securities such as Federal National Mortgage Association issues.

Municipal bonds of state and local governments are traded by specialized municipal bond dealers who, in most cases, work for large commercial banks. Commercial paper, representing unsecured, short-term corporate debt, is traded directly by *finance* companies, but a large portion of commercial paper sold by *industrial* companies is handled by OTC dealers specializing in this market. Every security has its own set of dealers and its own distribution system. On markets where large dollar trades occur, the spread between the bid and asked price could be as little as $\frac{1}{16}$ or $\frac{1}{32}$ of $1 per $1,000 of securities.

Electronic Communication Networks (ECNs)

A new competitor on the block for the exchanges and Nasdaq are the electronic communication networks, or ECNs. These are electronic trading systems that automatically match buy and sell orders at specified prices. ECNs are also known as alternative trading systems (ATSs) and have been given SEC approval to be more fully integrated into the national market system by choosing to either act as a broker–dealer or as an exchange. An ECN's subscribers can include retail and institutional investors, market makers, and broker–dealers. If a subscriber wants to buy a stock through an ECN, but there are no sell orders to match the buy order, the order cannot be executed. The ECN can wait for a matching sell order to arrive, or if the order is received during normal trading hours, the order can be routed to another market for execution. Some ECNs will let their subscribers see their entire order books, and some will even make their order books available on the Web. ECNs bid and asked prices are included in Nasdaq's quotation montage with the best bid and asked price being shown. This helps create more efficient and transparent market prices and demonstrates how Nasdaq's open architecture allows firms with different computer technologies to compete in the same market.

Advantages of ECNs ECNs have integrated the markets and allowed anonymity in trading. This is very beneficial to large institutions such as hedge funds, mutual funds, and large institutional investors who do not want other market participants to know what they are buying and selling. They also lower the cost of trading by creating better executions, more price transparency, and the ability to trade after the markets are closed in what is known as "after-hours trading." Rule 390 of the New York Stock Exchange prohibited trading of NYSE-listed companies off the floor of the exchange. However, with the repeal of Rule 390, the NYSE has given the ECNs the ability to trade in exchange-listed securities and this facilitates more competition, smaller spreads, and longer trading hours. It could be that decimalization of stock quotes accelerated electronic trading as it is much more cost-effective than floor trading.

the real world of investing

Institutional Investors: Michael Eisner, and the Disney Corporation

The smooth functioning of a company in the financial markets is dependent upon a good interaction between stockholders and the management of the firm. No person is more important to this relationship than the Chairman of the Board of Directors.

In March 2004, Michael Eisner saw his title of Chairman of the Board of Walt Disney Co. stripped away from him. Over 3,000 stockholders attended the firm's annual meeting, some wearing Disney costumes and many more handing out anti-Eisner pamphlets. In total, two billion votes were cast by stockholders through the mail, on the Internet, and in person. Forty-three percent of the votes withheld support for Eisner to continue as Chairman of the Board. Normally, votes for continuation as Chairman of the Board carry 1 or 2 percent dissenting votes, so 43 percent was an astronomical figure of nonsupport.

The attention that Disney's election drew is reflective of the new era of institutional investor involvement in assessing the performance of company executives. Large pension funds, endowments, mutual funds, and so on, are making their voices heard as never before and this is changing the nature of the financial markets and the way companies are run. CalPERS, the California Public Employees Retirement System, holding 9.9 million shares of Disney stock, was particularly adamant in insisting that Eisner step down. Their voice is often loud and not easily ignored in corporate governance issues.

As a slight concession, Eisner was allowed to stay on as CEO, but George Mitchell, a former Senator from Maine, was installed as Chairman of the Board. More and more companies are splitting up the positions of Chairman of the Board and CEO. This reduces the likelihood of the Board of Directors merely acting as a rubber stamp for the CEO.

In fairness to Eisner, it should be recognized that at one time he was the golden boy of the Disney empire. Recruited to Disney from Paramount in 1984, he rejuvenated the firm from the edge of disaster to the "darling of Wall Street" through his theme parks, marketing savvy, and successful movie ventures.

However, in the last decade his micromanagement style has driven off top managers such as studio chief Jeffrey Katzenberg, and Disney has underperformed other media companies. The stock market value of the firm and its earnings performances were still at 1997 levels in the Spring of 2004 while earnings of others in the industry had surged ahead. Failure to consider a lucrative takeover offer for Disney by Comcast put Eisner further behind the eight ball, and his tenure as CEO is in doubt.

Institutional Trading

www.schwab.com
www.fidelity.com
www.etrade.com
www.ameritrade.com

Financial institutions, such as banks, pension funds, insurance companies, and investment companies (mutual funds), have always invested and traded in securities. Their importance can be seen in the fact that block trades of 10,000 shares or more carried out by financial institutions has averaged close to 50 percent of trades since 1984. As a contrast, block trades only accounted for 3.1 percent of total trades in 1965.

Individual investors have been putting their money into the market through intermediaries such as mutual funds, pension funds, profit-sharing plans, and individual retirement accounts (IRAs). Individuals who directly invest in the stock market have gone up and down with consumer sentiment and market returns. In 1987 the market crash scared many individual investors out of the market, but they came back during the bull market of the 1990s. This increased participation by the individual investor was made easier by the rise of electronic trading on the Internet with prices as low as $5 per trade. Brokerage firms such as Charles Schwab, Fidelity Investments, E-Trade, Ameritrade, and others offered small investors low-cost trades. This was a great benefit. As is always the case, bear

TABLE 2–8 Holdings of Corporate Equities in the United States (End of Period, Dollars in Billions)

Sector	1950	1970	1990	1995	2000	2001	Q3 2002
Private pension funds	$ 1.1	$ 67.1	$ 595.0	$1,289.2	$ 2,195.1	$ 1,925.8	$ 1,414.8
State & local pension funds	0.0	10.1	270.7	678.9	1,335.1	1,221.9	937.0
Life insurance companies	2.1	14.6	81.9	315.4	940.8	855.2	701.7
Other insurance companies	2.6	13.2	79.9	134.2	194.3	173.9	150.3
Mutual funds	2.9	39.7	233.2	1,024.9	3,226.9	2,836.1	2,005.0
Closed-end funds	1.6	4.3	16.2	38.2	35.3	30.3	27.1
Bank personal trusts	0.0	87.9	190.1	224.9	356.8	313.4	227.2
Foreign sector	2.9	27.2	243.8	527.6	1,625.5	1,533.8	1,192.9
Households & nonprofit organizations	128.7	572.5	1,806.5	4,160.9	7,408.0	6,024.1	4,021.4
Others	0.8	4.8	25.3	80.6	294.1	331.0	282.7
Total equities outstanding	142.7	841.4	3,542.6	8,474.8	17,611.9	15,245.5	10,960.1

Source: © NYSE Inc. All Rights Reserved. http://www.nysedata.com/factbook/viewer.

markets and recessions cause individuals to move to the sidelines, and 2000 and 2001 were no different. However, with the demographics of the baby boom generation reaching the high-income-savings years, it is expected that the individual investor will continue to have a significant place in our stock markets.

Table 2–8 shows the holdings of corporate equities (common stock) by institutions and individuals. In the third quarter of 2002, individual investors (households and nonprofit organizations) accounted for about $4 trillion of common stock or about 36 percent of total ownership. Remember that individuals account for most of the ownership of mutual funds, closed-end funds, bank personal trusts, and pension funds. So even if the money is invested by institutions, the final claim on the asset is the individual.

Regulation of the Security Markets

Organized securities markets are regulated by the **Securities and Exchange Commission (SEC)** and by the self-regulation of the exchanges. The OTC market is regulated by the National Association of Securities Dealers. Three major laws govern the sale and subsequent trading of securities. The **Securities Act of 1933** pertains to new issues of securities, while the **Securities Exchange Act of 1934** deals with trading in the securities markets. The **Securities Acts Amendments of 1975** is the last major piece of legislation, and its main emphasis is on a national securities market. The primary purpose of these laws was to protect unwary investors from fraud and manipulation and to make the markets more competitive and efficient.

Securities Act of 1933

The Securities Act of 1933 was enacted after congressional investigations of the abuses present in the securities markets during the 1929 crash and again in 1931. The act's primary purpose was to provide full disclosure of all pertinent investment information whenever a corporation sold a new issue of securities. It is sometimes referred to as the "truth in securities" act. The Securities Act has several important features:

1. All offerings except government bonds and bank stocks that are to be sold in more than one state must be registered with the SEC.[2]

2. The registration statement must be filed 20 days in advance of the date of sale and include detailed corporate information. If the SEC finds the information misleading, incomplete, or inaccurate, it will delay the offering until the registration statement is corrected. The SEC in no way certifies that the security is fairly priced but only that the information seems to be factual and accurate. Under certain circumstances, the previously mentioned shelf registration is being used to modify the 20-day waiting period concept.

3. All new issues of securities must be accompanied by a *prospectus,* a detailed summary of the registration statement. Included in the prospectus is usually a list of directors and officers; their salaries, stock options, and shareholdings; financial reports certified by a certified public accountant (CPA); a list of the underwriters; the purpose and use for the funds to be provided from the sale of securities; and any other reasonable information that investors may need to know before they can wisely invest their money. A preliminary prospectus may be distributed to potential buyers before the offering date, but it will not contain the offering price or underwriting fees. It is called a red herring because stamped on the front in red letters are the words "Preliminary Prospectus."

4. Officers of the company and other experts preparing the prospectus or registration statement can be sued for penalties and recovery of realized losses if any information presented was fraudulent or factually wrong or if relevant information was omitted.

Securities Exchange Act of 1934

This act created the Securities and Exchange Commission to enforce the securities laws. It was empowered to regulate the securities markets and those companies listed on the exchanges. Specifically, the major points of the 1934 act are as follows:

1. Guidelines for insider trading were established. Insiders must hold securities for at least six months before they can sell them. This is to prevent them from taking quick advantage of information that could result in a short-term profit. All short-term profits were payable to the corporation. Insiders were generally thought to be officers, directors, major stockholders, employees, or relatives of key employees. In the last two decades, the SEC widened its interpretation to include anyone having information that was not public knowledge. This could include security analysts, loan officers, large institutional holders, and many others who had business dealings with the firm.

---

[2] Actually, the SEC did not come into existence until 1934. The Federal Trade Commission had many of these responsibilities before the formation of the SEC.

2. The Federal Reserve Board of Governors became responsible for setting margin requirements to determine how much credit one had available to buy securities.
3. Manipulation of securities by conspiracies between investors was prohibited.
4. The SEC was given control over the proxy procedures of corporations (a proxy is an absent stockholder vote).
5. In its regulation of companies traded on the markets, it required certain reports to be filed periodically. Corporations must file quarterly financial statements with the SEC, send annual reports to the stockholders, and file 10–K reports with the SEC annually. The 10–K report has more financial data than the annual report and can be very useful to an investor or loan officer. Most companies will now send 10–K reports to stockholders on request. The SEC also has company filings available on the Internet under its retrieval system called EDGAR.
6. The act required all securities exchanges to register with the SEC. In this capacity, the SEC supervises and regulates many pertinent organizational aspects of exchanges such as listing and trading mechanics.

The Securities Acts Amendments of 1975

The major focus of the Securities Acts Amendments of 1975 was to direct the SEC to supervise the development of a national securities market. No exact structure was put forth, but the law did assume that any national market would make extensive use of computers and electronic communication devices. Additionally, the law prohibited fixed commissions on public transactions and also prohibited banks, insurance companies, and other financial institutions from buying stock exchange memberships to save commission costs for their own institutional transactions. This was a worthwhile addition to the securities laws since it fosters greater competition and more efficient prices.

Other Legislation

In addition to these three major pieces of legislation, a number of other acts deal directly with investor protection. For example, the Investment Advisor Act of 1940 is set up to protect the public from unethical investment advisers. Any adviser with more than 15 public clients (excluding tax accountants and lawyers) must register with the SEC and file semiannual reports. The Investment Company Act of 1940 provides similar oversight for mutual funds and investment companies dealing with small investors. The act was amended in 1970 and currently gives the NASD authority to supervise and limit commissions and investment advisory fees on certain types of mutual funds.

Another piece of legislation dealing directly with investor protection is the Securities Investor Protection Act of 1970. The **Securities Investor Protection Corporation (SIPC)** was established to oversee liquidation of brokerage firms and to insure investors' accounts to a maximum value of $500,000 in case of bankruptcy of a brokerage firm. It functions much the same as the Federal Deposit Insurance Corporation. SIPC resulted from the problems encountered on Wall Street from 1967 to 1970 when share volume surged to then all-time highs, and many firms were unable to process orders fast enough. A back-office paper crunch caused Wall Street to shorten the hours the exchanges were formally open for new business, but even this didn't help. Investors lost large sums, and for many months, they were unable to use or get possession of securities held in their names. Even though SIPC insures these accounts, it still does not cover market value losses suffered while waiting to get securities from a bankrupt brokerage firm.

Insider Trading

The Securities Exchange Act of 1934 established the initial restrictions on insider trading. However, over the years, these restrictions have often proved to be inadequate. As previously indicated, the definition of *insider* may go beyond officers, directors, and major stockholders to include anyone with special insider knowledge. Both the Congress and the SEC are attempting to grapple with the issue of making punitive measures severe enough to discourage the illegal use of nonpublic information for profits.[3] Current and future legislation is likely to include tougher civil penalties and stiffer criminal prosecution. Also, the penalties for improper action will expand beyond simple recovery of profits to a penalty three or more times the profits involved.

The 1980s saw a rash of insider trading scandals involving major investment banking houses, traders, analysts, and investors. Ivan Boesky and Dennis Levine were the first of the well-known investors to end up in jail, and Michael Milken was not far behind. These insider trading scandals have plagued Wall Street and tarnished its image as a place where investors can get a fair deal.

On balance, all the legislation we have discussed has tended to increase the confidence of the investing public. In an industry where public trust is so critical, some form of supervision, whether public or private, is necessary and generally accepted.

Program Trading and Market Price Limits

Program trading is identified by some market analysts as the primary culprit behind the 508-point market crash on October 19, 1987. **Program trading** simply means computer-based trigger points are established in which large volume trades are initiated by institutional investors. For example, if the Dow Jones Industrial Average (or some other market measure) hits a certain point, a large sale or purchase may automatically occur. When many institutional investors are using program trading simultaneously, this process can have a major cumulative effect on the market. This was thought to be the case not only in the 1987 crash but also for many other highly volatile days in the market.

Circuit Breakers In 1989 **circuit breakers** were put in place; circuit breakers shut down the market for a period of time if there is a dramatic drop in stock prices. Under the initial provisions implemented by the NYSE, the exchange agreed to initiate a 30-minute halt in trading if the Dow Jones Industrial Average

---

[3] Insiders, of course, may make proper long-term investments in a corporation.

the real world of investing
The "See-Through" Wall between Security Analysts and Investment Bankers

The SEC and other related regulatory agencies have some of the toughest laws in the United States. Companies and executives that falsely report data can expect to face heavy penalties and even prison time. Just ask famed billionaire Michael Milken, who served a number of years in a federal jail for fraud and illegal insider trading. Much of the tough legislation dates back to the unregulated securities market abuses prior to the Great Market Crash of 1929 and the subsequent passage of the Securities Act of 1933 and the Securities Exchange Act of 1934.

Before you get too satisfied with the thought that the stock market represents an appropriately regulated playing field, though, consider the fact that there is a new form of abuse that our legislative forefathers of the 1930s never even considered—the relationship between security analysts who supposedly analyze and evaluate companies and investment bankers who help sell stock to the public.

Whether it's at Merrill Lynch, Goldman Sachs, Lehman Brothers, or elsewhere, the security analysts who work for the firm are supposed to be free and independent of the investment bankers who also work for the firm.

What this basically means is that the security analyst's responsibility is to provide an unbiased appraisal of the firm's operations and future outlook. Investors have a right to expect that analysts take a hard-nosed approach in "telling it like it is" and "letting the chips fall where they may." If the company is employing questionable accounting practices or failing to divulge problems in meeting debt obligations, it is up to the security analyst to bring this information to the public's attention, much as an investigative reporter for a newspaper would.

The investor banker, on the other hand, is supposed to bring new business and revenues to the firm. They are intended to be "homers" who root for and support the firm's clients. They are somewhat analogous to a major law firm that represents an important client. One of the investment banker's most important functions is to do initial public offerings (IPOs) for clients in which firms sell their stock to the public for the first time. The investment banker puts the deal together and promotes the issue, including doing "road shows" with the client.

The abuse is that the security analyst has become more and more a part of the home team in promoting the new issue rather than analyzing the stock and giving an unbiased viewpoint. In the wild dot-com IPO market of the late 1990s, security analysts often went so far as to take a piece of the action, thereby dictating that a critical report on their part would put a hole in their own pocketbook.

In an August 1, 2001, story in *The Wall Street Journal,* Laura Unger, the SEC's acting chairwoman, was quoted as saying: "Brokerage firms repeatedly obscured the supposed line that separates analysts, who work on behalf of investors, from investment bankers, who work to woo corporate clients." She further said, "Analysts routinely got involved in possible mergers, acquisitions and corporate-finance deals, and participated in corporate road shows. The firms also told the SEC that analysts' pay is largely based on the profitability of the investment-banking unit, and seven firms said that investment bankers provide input into the bonuses analysts receive."[*]

While some reform has taken place in the early 2000s, this is still an area that will receive considerable attention in the future.

---

[*] Jeff D. Opdyke, "Many Analysts Found to Invest in Companies They Covered." *The Wall Street Journal,* August 1, 2001, pp. C1, C10.

---

went down by 250 points during a given day and a one-hour halt in case of a 400-point decline.

As the market continued to go up during the 1990s, the circuit breakers were raised in February 1997 to a 350-point decline for a 30-minute halt and a 550-point decline for a one-hour break. Both circuit breakers were triggered by the 500-point-plus decline on October 27, 1997. The SEC has informed the New York Stock Exchange that it expects the exchange to continually evaluate the size of the circuit breakers as market conditions change.

Other markets, such as the Nasdaq, the American Stock Exchange, and the Chicago Board of Trade (for stock index futures), have also agreed to discontinue trading if there is a halt on the NYSE.

exploring the web

Website Address	Comments
www.nyse.com	Provides information on regulations and market operations
www.nasdaq.com	Provides information about the Nasdaq market
www.cboe.com	Provides information about options traded on the Chicago Board Options Exchange
www.cbs.marketwatch.com/tools/ipo	Contains information about CBS initial public offerings

Summary

A smoothly functioning market is one that is efficient and provides liquidity to the investor. The success of a primary market, in which new issues are generally underwritten by investment bankers, is highly dependent on the presence of an active resale (secondary) market.

Secondary markets may be established in the form of an organized exchange or as an over-the-counter market. The predominant organized market is the New York Stock Exchange, but increasing attention is being directed to various other markets. The possibility of a true national market system looms as a consideration for the future, with the completed first step being the development of a consolidated tape among different markets. Nasdaq (National Association of Securities Dealers Automated Quotations system) has done much to improve the communications network in the over-the-counter market and bring competition to the organized exchanges. The creation of ECNs will continue to change the way investors trade.

The dominant role of the institutional investor has had an enormous impact on the markets with higher stock turnover and increasing market volatility. A major consolidation of market participants has also occurred on Wall Street.

The term *market* is broadening with different types of new investment outlets as witnessed by the expansion of options, futures contracts on stock indexes, options on futures, and many other commodity trading mechanisms. Of equal importance, the term *market* must be viewed from a global viewpoint with securities trading throughout the world on a 24-hour basis.

Finally, problems or imperfections in the marketplace during critical time periods have led to a wide array of securities legislation. The legislation in the 1930s regulated the securities markets and created the SEC. Subsequent laws have dealt with restructuring the market and investor protection.

Key Words and Concepts

- best efforts 31
- call options 43
- circuit breakers 51
- commission brokers 40
- efficient market 29
- Electronic Book 42
- electronic communication networks (ECNs) 37
- exchange traded funds (ETFs) 43
- floor brokers 40
- initial public offering (IPO) 35
- investment banker 31
- liquidity 29
- market 29
- Nasdaq Stock Market 44
- odd-lot dealer 41
- organized exchange 37
- over-the-counter markets 37
- primary markets 30
- program trading 51
- registered traders 40
- secondary markets 30
- Securities Act of 1933 48
- Securities Acts Amendments of 1975 48
- Securities and Exchange Commission (SEC) 48
- Securities Exchange Act of 1934 48
- Securities Investor Protection Corporation (SIPC) 50
- sold directly 31
- specialists 41
- Super Dot 42
- syndicate 31
- underwriting 31

Discussion Questions

1. What is a market?
2. What is an efficient market?
3. What is the difference between primary and secondary markets?
4. What is the difference between an investment banker providing an underwriting function and a "best-efforts" offering?
5. What is a private placement?
6. What generally determines how firms are listed in a tombstone advertisement?
7. Briefly describe the participants on an exchange.
8. How do critics think the specialist system on the NYSE might be improved?
9. How is the over-the-counter market different from the organized exchanges?
10. Briefly describe the Nasdaq Stock Market.
11. Define a block trade. What does the increase in block trades since 1965 tend to indicate about the nature of investors in the market?
12. Indicate the primary purpose of the Securities Act of 1933. Why was it enacted? Does the SEC certify that a security is fairly priced?
13. How has the definition of an insider (inside trader) expanded over the past two decades?
14. Explain the purpose of the Securities Investor Protection Corporation (SIPC).

Critical Thought Case

The Securities and Exchange Commission is a federal agency created by Congress through the Securities Exchange Acts of 1933 and 1934 to protect investors. The stock market crash of 1929 and the Great Depression led the U.S. Senate to investigate the regulations of the securities industry. The existing laws were found to be inadequate, thus the formation of the securities industry watchdog, the SEC.

One of the main provisions of the 1933 act was to ensure full disclosure of facts by companies offering securities for sale to the public. Companies must submit a registration statement to the SEC for approval before securities can be sold. These statements contain financial information essential to a complete analysis of the investment at hand. A company prospectus disclosing this information is made available to the public.

Recently, disclosure of this information has posed many problems. As the world markets become increasingly competitive, foreign companies have access to important financial information about U.S. companies. In many cases, this same financial information on foreign companies is not available to U.S. companies. But, if foreign companies want to sell stock in the United States, the SEC requires them to submit the same financial information as U.S. companies. Many foreign companies are reluctant to do this because they believe it would give away their competitive advantage.

With the globalization of the world's securities markets, the New York Stock Exchange feels very strongly that to remain the leader in the industry, foreign securities must be traded in the United States. The NYSE has been attempting to attract major foreign companies for listing on the exchange, but many of these companies do not want to comply with the stringent financial disclosure requirements. If action is not taken quickly to rectify the situation, the NYSE believes it may lose its competitive position as the world's largest stock exchange.

The NYSE has been trying for some time to persuade the SEC to reduce corporate financial disclosure requirements for foreign companies. Although the SEC agrees in principle that it would be advantageous to investors to have foreign stocks listed on the exchange, it is not willing to lessen the disclosure standards for foreign companies. Investors would be at risk if this were allowed.

Questions

1. Should the SEC, for the sake of maintaining U.S. competitiveness in the world markets, reduce the disclosure requirements for foreign companies?
2. If so, is this fair to U.S. companies and investors?
3. What are the consequences to the NYSE and New York City if the exchange is no longer the world leader it once was?

Web Exercise

This chapter on capital markets focuses on long-term financing and the various stock markets. Each stock market has its own listing requirements, and this exercise will look at the New York Stock Exchange and Nasdaq listing requirements for comparative purposes. First, go to the New York Stock Exchanges website at **www.nyse.com**.

1. Click on "Listed-Companies" on the upper left side.
2. Then, click on "Listing Standards" in the left margin.
3. Then, click on "U.S. Standards" across the top and answer the following questions in writing.
    a. How many round-lot holders are required to be listed?
    b. What is the required average monthly trading volume?
    c. What are the earnings requirements to be listed?
    d. What is the average global market capitalization requirement to be listed?
4. Now go to the Nasdaq website at **www.nasdaq.com**.
5. Scroll down the home page until you see "Nasdaq Market Center" along the right-hand margin.
6. Click on "Nasdaq Listed Company Rules and Compliance Information."
7. Click on "Listing Qualifications."
8. Click on "Initial Listing."
9. Click on "What are the Initial Listing Standards?"
10. Click on "Listing Requirements and Fees" at the top of the page.
11. Scroll down and answer the following questions for Standard 1 Initial Listing (first numerical column).
    a. How many round-lot shareholders are required?
    b. How many market makers are required?
    c. What is the requirement for income from continuing operations?
    d. What is the market value of publicly held shares requirement?*

Note: From time to time, companies redesign their websites, and occasionally a topic we have listed may have been deleted, updated, or moved into a different location. Most websites have a "site map" or "site index" listed on a different page. If you click on the site map or site index, you will be introduced to a table of contents that should aid you in finding the topic you are looking for.

Selected References

Security Exchanges

Boutchkova, Maria K., and William L. Megginson. "Privatization and the Rise of Global Capital Markets." *Financial Management,* Winter 2000, pp. 31–76.

Chatterjea, Arkadev; Joseph A. Cherian; and Robert A. Jarrow. "Market Manipulation and Corporate Finance: A New Perspective." *Financial Management,* Summer 1993, pp. 200–09.

Kadlec, Gregory B., and John J. McConnell. "The Effect of Market Segmentation on Asset Prices: Evidence from Exchange Listings." *Journal of Finance,* June 1994, pp. 611–36.

Sanger, Gary C., and John J. McConnell. "Stock Exchange Listings, Firm Value, and Security Market Efficiency: The Impact of NASDAQ." *Journal of Financial and Qualitative Analysis,* March 1986, pp. 1–25.

Tandon, Kishore, and Gwendolyn Webb. "Evidence and Implications of Increases in Trading Volume around Exchange Listings." *Financial Review,* May 2001, pp. 21–44.

Trading Patterns by Investors

Ballalio, Robert H. "Third Market Broker-Dealers Cost Competitors or Cream Skimmers." *Journal of Finance,* March 1997, pp. 341–52.

Loomis, Carol. "Anyone Heard from Greenspan Lately?" *Fortune,* February 9, 2004, pp. 19–24.

Oxelheim, Lars. "Macroeconomic Variables and Corporate Performance." *Financial Analysts Journal,* July–August 2003, pp. 36–50.

Roll, Richard. "A Simple Implicit Measure of the Effective Bid–Ask Spread in an Efficient Market." *Journal of Finance,* September 1984, pp. 1127–39.

Tarun, Chordia: Richard Roll; and Avanidhar Subrahmanyam. "Market Liquidity and Trading Activity." *Journal of Finance,* April 2001, pp. 401–30.

Regulation

Caccese, Michael S. "Insider Trading Laws and the Role of Security Analysts." *Financial Analysts Journal,* March–April 1997, pp. 9–12.

Carter, Martha L,; Sattar A. Mansi; and David M. Reeb. "Quasi-Private Information and Insider Trading." *Financial Analysts Journal,* May–June 2003, pp. 60–68.

Gastineau, Gary L., and Robert A. Jarrow. "Larger-Trader Impact and Market Regulation." *Financial Analysts Journal,* July–August 1991, pp. 40–51.

Treynor, Jack. "Securities Law and Public Policy." *Financial Analysts Journal,* May–June 1994, p. 10.

chapter three

Participating in the Market

objectives

1. Understand how to measure the performance of securities in various markets through the use of market indexes.

2. Describe how an investor goes through the process of buying and selling securities.

3. Explain the difference between cash and margin accounts.

4. Describe the types of trading orders that can be executed.

5. Explain the tax implications of various investing strategies.

Measures of Price Performance: Market Indexes
Indexes and Averages
    Dow Jones Averages
    Standard & Poor's Indexes
    Value Line Average
    Other Market Indexes
Buying and Selling in the Market
    Cash or Margin Account
    Long or Short?—That Is the Question
Types of Orders
Cost of Trading
Taxes and the 2003 Tax Act
    Capital Gains and Dividends

Either now or at some point in the future, you are likely to become an investor in the financial markets. You need to know how to use indexes to gauge market performance, the rules and mechanics of opening and trading in an account, and basic tax considerations for an investor. This chapter walks you through the many steps that are involved.

Measures of Price Performance: Market Indexes

We first look at tracking market performance for stocks and bonds. Each market has several market indexes published by Dow Jones, Standard & Poor's, Value Line, and other financial services. These indexes allow investors to measure the performance of their portfolios against an index that approximates their portfolio composition; thus, different investors prefer different indexes. While a professional pension fund manager might use the Standard & Poor's 500 Stock Index, a mutual fund specializing in small, over-the-counter stocks might prefer the Nasdaq (National Association of Securities Dealers Automated Quotations) Index, and a small investor might use the Value Line Average or Russell 2000 as the best approximation of a portfolio's performance.

Indexes and Averages

Dow Jones Averages

www.dj.com

Since there are many stock market indexes and averages, we will cover the most widely used ones. Dow Jones, publisher of *The Wall Street Journal* and *Barron's*, publishes several market averages of which the **Dow Jones Industrial Average (DJIA)** is the most popular. This average consists of 30 large industrial companies and is considered a "blue-chip" index (stocks of very high quality). Many people criticize the DJIA for being too selective and representing too few stocks. Nevertheless, the Dow Industrials do follow the general trend of the market, and these 30 common stocks comprise more than 25 percent of the market value of the 3,000 firms listed on the New York Stock Exchange. Figure 3–1 shows the price movements of the Dow Jones Industrial Average over a six-month period as well as naming the 30 stocks in the average.

FIGURE 3–1 Dow Jones Industrial Average January 16, 2004

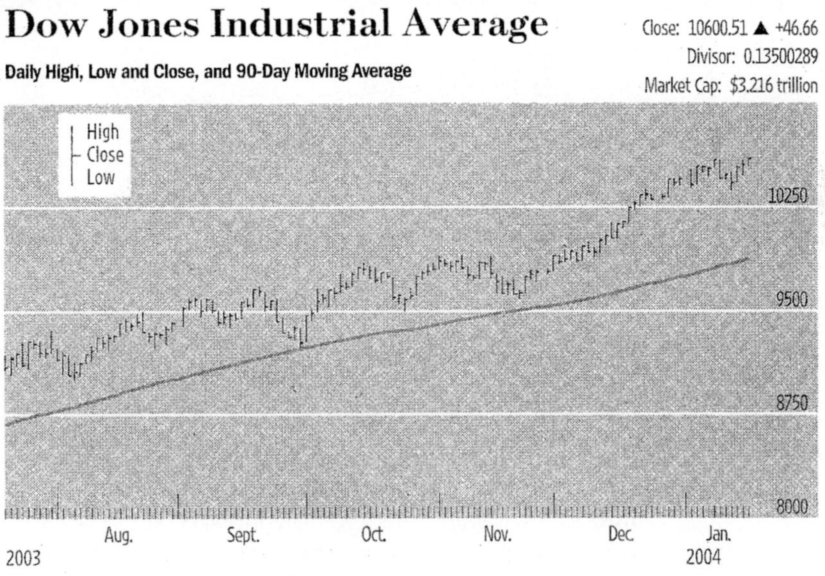

Dow Jones Industrial Average
Daily High, Low and Close, and 90-Day Moving Average

Close: 10600.51 ▲ +46.66
Divisor: 0.13500289
Market Cap: $3.216 trillion

Dow 30 Components Primary market net point change

AT&T	−0.12	Citigroup	unch	GenElec	+1.35	Intel*	−0.13	Microsoft*	+0.33
Alcoa	−0.43	CocaCola	+0.15	GenMotor	+0.07	IntPaper	−0.26	ProctGam	−0.51
AltriaGp	−0.57	Disney	+0.03	HewlettPk	+0.22	JohnsJohns	−1.39	SBC Comm	−0.27
AmExprss	+0.23	DuPont	−0.09	HomeDpt	−0.49	JPMorgChas	+0.36	3M	+1.18
Boeing	+0.97	EKodak	−0.07	Honeywell	+0.95	McDonalds	+0.16	UnitedTech	+2.10
Caterpillar	+0.76	ExxnMobl	+0.22	IBM	+1.30	Merck	+0.26	WalMart	−0.01

Source: *The Wall Street Journal*, January 19, 2004. p. C2. Reprinted by permission of *The Wall Street Journal*, © 2004 by Dow Jones & Company. All Rights Reserved Worldwide.

TABLE 3-1 Indexes and Averages Found in *The Wall Street Journal*

STOCK MARKET DATA BANK — 1/16/04

Major Stock Indexes

		DAILY				52-WEEK			YTD
Dow Jones Averages	HIGH	LOW	CLOSE	NET CHG	% CHG	HIGH	LOW	% CHG	% CHG
30 Industrials	10600.74	10542.52	10600.51	+46.66	+0.44	10600.51	7524.06	+23.45	+ 1.40
20 Transportations	3039.52	3020.13	3036.28	+17.80	+0.59	3038.15	1942.19	+29.50	+ 0.97
15 Utilities	267.32	266.06	266.81	+ 0.64	+0.24	268.27	190.22	+21.77	− 0.03
65 Composite	3031.66	3018.46	3031.64	+13.44	+0.45	3031.64	2108.95	+24.68	+ 1.03
Dow Jones Indexes									
US Total Market	270.10	268.04	270.06	+ 2.01	+0.75	270.06	186.43	+28.96	+ 2.81
US Large-Cap	247.18	245.57	247.18	+ 1.60	+0.65	247.18	176.51	+24.25	+ 2.39
US Mid-Cap	324.19	320.68	324.18	+ 3.51	+1.09	324.18	208.17	+40.38	+ 3.60
US Small-Cap	375.81	371.85	374.91	+ 3.06	+0.82	374.91	222.01	+49.69	+ 4.82
US Growth	1054.98	1046.15	1054.98	+ 8.77	+0.84	1054.98	722.86	+32.37	+ 3.27
US Value	1379.38	1370.17	1378.80	+ 8.63	+0.63	1378.80	969.45	+24.57	+ 2.17
Global Titans 50	188.15	186.95	188.13	+ 0.49	+0.26	189.83	134.92	+22.78	+ 1.81
Asian Titans 50	109.63	108.26	108.82	+ 0.54	+0.50	110.14	71.25	+27.62	+ 3.06
DJ STOXX 50	2738.58	2713.06	2734.86	+25.94	+0.96	2734.86	1909.05	+14.79	+ 2.80
Nasdaq Stock Market									
Composite	2140.47	2119.35	2140.46	+31.38	+1.49	2140.46	1271.47	+55.54	+ 6.84
Nasdaq 100	1553.64	1537.17	1553.62	+21.61	+1.41	1553.62	951.90	+52.68	+ 5.84
Biotech	774.32	761.53	774.32	+14.28	+1.88	799.73	467.46	+47.96	+ 6.93
Computer	1011.19	997.60	1011.19	+20.04	+2.02	1011.19	590.11	+58.13	+ 8.16
Telecommunications	204.20	200.97	203.83	+ 3.46	+1.73	203.83	108.04	+71.62	+11.04
Standard & Poor's Indexes									
500 Index	1139.83	1132.05	1139.83	+ 7.78	+0.69	1139.83	800.73	+26.40	+ 2.51
MidCap 400	594.05	589.44	593.76	+ 4.32	+0.73	593.76	385.18	+37.27	+ 3.08
SmallCap 600	281.47	279.40	280.15	+ 0.75	+0.27	280.15	173.60	+42.19	+ 3.60
SuperComp 1500	253.79	252.04	253.74	+ 1.70	+0.67	253.74	176.40	+27.78	+ 2.60
New York Stock Exchange									
Composite	6567.80	6539.67	6567.68	+17.64	+0.27	6569.32	4486.70	+28.56	+ 1.98
Financial	6849.63	6826.16	6842.91	+ 6.48	+0.09	6842.91	4415.12	+32.41	+ 2.49
Health Care	5954.48	5930.88	5949.75	+13.30	+0.22	6003.89	4647.25	+17.42	+ 0.40
Others									
Russell 2000	591.99	586.35	590.41	+ 4.05	+0.69	590.41	345.94	+52.13	+ 6.02
Wilshire 5000	11117.69	11036.77	11116.04	+79.26	+0.72	11116.04	7610.47	+30.31	+ 2.93
Value Line	379.22	375.96	378.72	+ 2.76	+0.73	378.72	230.94	+40.58	+ 4.43
Amex Composite	1187.12	1179.08	1183.74	− 2.19	−0.18	1202.33	803.54	+42.23	+ 0.37

Source: The *Wall Street Journal*, January 19, 2004, p. C2. Reprinted by permission of *The Wall Street Journal*, © 2004 by Dow Jones & Company. All Rights Reserved Worldwide.

Dow Jones also publishes an index of 20 transportation stocks and 15 utility stocks. At the top of Table 3–1 you see a listing of the daily changes for the three Dow Jones Averages on January 16, 2004. It also shows a Dow Jones 65-stock composite average that summarizes the performance of the Dow Jones industrial, transportation, and utility issues. Many other market averages are presented in the table, which we will discuss later.

For now, let's return to the Dow Jones Industrial Average of 30 stocks. The Dow Jones Industrial Average used to be a simple average of 30 stocks, but when a company splits its stock price, the average has to be adjusted. For the Dow Jones Industrials, the divisor in the formula has been adjusted downward from the original 30 to below 1. Each time a company splits its shares of stock (or provides a stock dividend), the divisor is reduced to maintain the average at the same level as before the stock split. If this were not done, the lower-priced stock after the split would reduce the average, giving the appearance that investors were worse off.

The Dow Jones Industrial Average is a **price-weighted average,** which means each stock in the average is weighted by its price. To simplify the meaning of price weighted: if you had three stocks in a price-weighted average that had values of 10, 40, and 100, you would add the prices and divide by three. In this case, you would get an average of 50 (150 divided by 3). A price-weighted average is similar to what you normally use in computing averages. Price-weighted averages tend to give a higher weighting bias to high-price stocks than to low-price stocks. For example, in the above analysis, if the $100 stock goes up by 10 percent, with all else the same, the average will go up over three points from 50 to 53.3. However, if the $10 stock goes up by 10 percent, with all else the same, the average will only go from 50 to 50.3.

In January of 2004 IBM was trading at 95 while Disney was at 24. Clearly, a 10 percent price movement up or down in IBM would have a greater impact on the Dow Jones Industrial Average than a 10 percent movement in Disney. Thus, we see the bias toward high-priced stocks in the Dow Jones Industrial Average.

Standard & Poor's Indexes

www.standardpoor.com

Standard & Poor's Corporation publishes a number of indexes. The best known is the **Standard & Poor's 500 Stock Index.** This index is widely followed by professional money managers and security market researchers as a measure of broad stock market activity. In 2004, the S&P 500 Stock Index included 373 industrial firms, plus 15 transportation firms, 47 utilities, and 65 financial firms. The Standard & Poor's 500 Index and other Standard and Poor's Indexes can be seen toward the bottom of Table 3–1. The stocks in the S&P 500 Stock Index are equivalent to approximately 75 percent of the total value of the 3,000 firms listed on the New York Stock Exchange.[1]

In the summer of 1991, Standard & Poor introduced its MidCap Index. The **Standard & Poor's 400 MidCap Index** is composed of 400 middle-sized firms that have total market values between $1.2 billion and $9 billion. The index was intended to answer the complaint that the S&P 500 Stock Index shows only the performance of larger firms. For example, Microsoft, which is part of the S&P 500 Index, had a total market value of more than $300 billion in January 2004. By creating an index of middle-sized firms, portfolio managers with comparable-sized holdings could more accurately track their performance against an appropriate measure. The same is true for the **Standard & Poor's 600 SmallCap Index,** which provides an opportunity for comparison of stocks that are smaller than the MidCap. The **Standard & Poor's 1500 Stock Index,** also shown in Table 3–1, combines the S&P 500, the S&P 400 MidCap, and the S&P Small-Cap 600.

Standard & Poor's also has other special purpose indexes, some of which are not shown in Table 3–1. For example, the **Standard & Poor's 100 Index** is

---

[1] Actually, some large Nasdaq firms are also in the S&P indexes, although the indexes are predominantly made up of NYSE firms.

composed of 100 blue-chip stocks on which the Chicago Board Options Exchange has individual option contracts. (This terminology will become clearer when we study options later in the text.) The S&P 100 Index closely mirrors the performance of the S&P 500 Stock Index.

All the S&P measures are true indexes in that they are linked to a base value. For the S&P 500 Stock Index, the base period is 1941–43. The base period price in 1941–43 was 10, so the S&P 500 Stock Index price of 1,139.83, on January 16, 2004, as previously shown in Table 3–1, represents an increase of 1,129.33 percent over this 60-year-plus period. For the newer indexes, the base period does not go back as far.

Regardless of the base period, the important consideration is how much the index changed over a given time period (such as a day, month, or year) rather than the absolute value. For example, looking back at Table 3–1 on page 60, you can see that the Dow Jones Industrial Average on January 16, 2004, is up 1.40 percent from December 31 (look at the last column to see the percentage change from the prior year) and that the Standard and Poor's 500 Stock Index is up 2.51 percent over a comparable time period. One might observe that this was a good period for market performance as further indicated in the 12-month percent change column. The average annual increase over the long term is 10 to 12 percent.

Application Example

The Standard & Poor's Indexes are **value-weighted indexes,** which means each company is weighted in the index by its own total market value as a percentage of the total market value for all firms. For example, in a value-weighted index comprising the following three firms, the weighting would be:

Stock	Shares	Price	Total Market Value	Weighting
A	150	$10	$ 1,500	12.0%
B	200	20	4,000	32.0
C	500	14	7,000	56.0
			$12,500	100.0%

In each case, the weighting is determined by dividing the total market value of the stock by the total market value for all firms. In the case of stock A, that would be $1,500 divided by $12,500, or 12 percent. The same procedure is followed for stocks B and C.

Even though stock C has only the second highest price, it makes up 56 percent of the average because of its high total market value based on 500 shares outstanding. This same basic effect carries through in the Standard & Poor's 500 Index, with large companies such as GE, Exxon, and AT&T having a greater impact on the index than smaller companies. Value-weighted indexes do not require special adjustments for stock splits because the increase in the number of shares automatically compensates for the decline in the stock value caused by the split.

Standard & Poor's also compiles value-weighted indexes for more than 100 different industries, and they are reported in the *Standard & Poor's Security Price Index Record.*

www.ge.com
www.exxon.com
www.att.com

the real world of investing

Babe Ruth Called Shot Home Run in the 1932 World Series Was the Equivalent of Ibbotson and Sinquefield Market Index Prediction in 1974

After taunting by the Chicago Cubs bench in the 1932 World Series, Babe Ruth bravely pointed his right finger to the grandstand and predicted he would hit a home run off Chicago Cubs Pitcher Charley Root. The legendary "Bambino" made good on his promise by taking two called strikes before sending a satellite shot into the bleachers at Wrigley Field in Chicago.

In 1974, when the Dow Jones Industrial Average was mired in a 10-year slump at a level of 800, financial researchers Ibbotson and Sinquefield stepped up to the plate and predicted that the Dow Jones Industrial Average would hit the seemingly astronomical level of 10,000 by November 1999. The mad "financial scientists" were only eight months off in their 25-year projection as the Dow Jones Industrial Average crashed through 10,000 on March 29, 1999. They used highly sophisticated statistical techniques and Monte Carlo analysis to make their prediction.

After such an incredible feat, one might assume the researchers would pack away their sophisticated crystal ball for posterity. After all, Babe Ruth never attempted another called shot home run.

But Roger Ibbotson of Ibbotson Associates stepped up to the plate again in 1998, and predicted the Dow Jones will hit a level of 100,000 by year-end 2025. Please stay tuned.

Value Line Average

www.valueline.com

The **Value Line Average** represents 1,700 companies from the New York and American stock exchanges and the Nasdaq market. Some individual investors use the Value Line Average because it more closely corresponds to the variety of stocks small investors may have in their portfolios.

Unlike the previously discussed price-weighted average (the Dow Jones Industrial Average) and value-weighted indexes (S&P 500), the Value Line Average is an **equal-weighted index.** This means each of the 1,700 stocks, regardless of market price or total market value, is weighted equally. It is as if there were $100 to be invested in each and every stock. In this case, IBM or ExxonMobil is weighted no more heavily than Wendy's International or Mattel Inc. This equal-weighting characteristic also more closely conforms to the portfolio of individual investors.

www.ibm.com
www.exxon.com
www.wendys.com
www.mattel.com

Other Market Indexes

www.nasdaq.com

Indexes are also computed and published by the New York Stock Exchange, American Stock Exchange, and the Nasdaq. Each index is intended to represent the performance of stocks traded in a particular exchange or market. As is seen in Table 3–1 on page 60, the NYSE publishes a composite index as well as other indexes. Each index represents the stocks of a broad group or type of company.

The Nasdaq also publishes a number of indexes, including the Nasdaq Composite, the Nasdaq 100, and other indexes that represent various sectors of the economy. The Nasdaq 100 is made up of the 100 largest firms in its market and is heavily populated by high-tech firms such as Microsoft, Intel, Oracle, and Cisco.

The Nasdaq Composite Index has become particularly popular in the last decade and is often featured along with the Dow Jones Industrial Average and the Standard and Poor's 500 Index on the nightly news.

The American Exchange (AMEX) Composite Index is composed of all stocks trading on the American Stock Exchange. This index is also shown in Table 3–1 in the "Others" category.

The indexes of the New York Stock Exchange, Nasdaq, and the American Stock Exchange are all value-weighted indexes.[2]

Another important index is the **Wilshire 5000 Equity Index** (shown under "Others"). It represents the *total dollar value* of 5,000 stocks, including all NYSE and AMEX issues and the most active Nasdaq issues. By the very fact of including total dollar value, it is value weighted. On January 16, 2004, the Wilshire Index had a value of $11,116.04 billion ($11.1 trillion). The index tells you the total value of virtually all important equities daily.

The Russell indexes have also become popular in recent times. There are three separate but overlapping value-weighted indexes provided by Frank Russell Company, a money management consulting firm in Tacoma, Washington.[3] While only one is shown in Table 3–1, we shall discuss all three. The **Russell 3000 Index** is comprised of 3,000 U.S. stocks as measured by market capitalization (market value times shares outstanding). The other two indexes allow you to see whether larger or smaller stocks are performing better. For example, the **Russell 1000 Index** includes only the largest 1,000 firms out of the Russell 3000, while the **Russell 2000** specifically includes the smallest 2,000 out of the Russell 3000. If the Russell 2000 is outperforming the Russell 1000, you can generally assume that smaller stocks are outperforming larger firms. The reverse would obviously be true if there is a superior performance by the Russell 1000.

International Stock Averages As the internationalization of investments has become progressively more important, so have international market indexes. *The Wall Street Journal* covers indexes throughout the world as shown in Table 3–2.

Of particular interest is the first item, the **Dow Jones World Index.** This index covers the performance of all the world's markets combined and is up 2.65 percent year-to-date as of January 16, 2004, as shown in the last column. During this time period, Argentina had the best performance (+12.71 percent) and Turkey the worst (−1.74 percent). Particularly closely watched is Japan's **Tokyo Nikkei 225** (the first of the three Japanese listed indexes). Although this fact is not shown in the table, the Nikkei is down over two-thirds from its glory days of 15 years ago.

Bond Market Indicators Performance in the bond market is not widely followed by an index or average but is usually gauged by interest-rate movements. Because rising interest rates mean falling bond prices and falling rates signal rising prices, investors can usually judge the bond market performance by yield-curve changes or interest-rate graphs. Nevertheless, there is still a wide menu to choose from in *The Wall Street Journal* when tracking the performance of bond prices as indicated in Table 3–3 on page 66. At the top of the table, yields are given for various maturities of Treasury and other issues. The indexes are then

---

[2] Until October 1973, the American Stock Exchange Index was price weighted.
[3] Frank Russell Company has other indexes as well.

TABLE 3–2 World Stock Market Average

January 16, 2004

International Stock Market Indexes

COUNTRY	INDEX	1/16/04 CLOSE	NET CHG	% CHG	YTD NET CHG	YTD % CHG
World	DJ World Index	191.91	+0.71	+0.37	+4.96	+2.65
Argentina	Merval	1208.18	+5.32	+0.44	+136.23	+12.71
Australia	All Ordinaries	3298.10	-r14.60	-0.44	-7.90	-0.24
Belgium	Bel-20	2381.64	+23.99	+1.02	+137.46	+6.13
Brazil	Sao Paulo Bovespa	23154.58	+192.88	+0.84	+918.19	+4.13
Canada	Toronto 300 Composite	8522.26	+98.32	+1.17	+301.37	+3.67
Chile	Santiago IPSA	1459.48	-15.61	-1.06	-25.32	-1.71
China	Dow Jones China 88	145.39	+1.08	+0.75	+9.66	+7.12
China	Dow Jones Shanghai	181.55	+1.80	+1.00	+12.14	+7.17
China	Dow Jones Shenzhen	165.08	+1.47	+0.90	+9.34	+6.00
Europe	DJ STOXX 600	237.78	+2.55	+1.08	+8.47	+3.69
Europe	DJ STOXX 50	2734.86	+25.94	+0.96	+74.49	+2.80
Euro Zone	DJ Euro STOXX	253.20	+2.41	+0.96	+9.99	+4.11
Euro Zone	DJ Euro STOXX 50	2865.96	+25.16	+0.89	+105.30	+3.81
France	Paris CAC 40	3671.80	+44.83	+1.24	+113.90	+3.20
Germany	Frankfurt Xetra DAX	4111.64	+42.89	+1.05	+146.48	+3.69
Hong Kong	Hang Seng	13167.76	-82.05	-0.62	+591.82	+4.71
India	Bombay Sensex	5946.19	-117.72	-1.94	+107.23	+1.84
Israel	Tel Aviv 25	520.17	Closed	...	+16.02	+3.18
Italy	Milan MIBtel	20610.00	+82.00	+0.40	+688.00	+3.45
Japan	Tokyo Nikkei 225	10857.20	+192.05	+1.80	+180.56	+1.69
Japan	Tokyo Nikkei 300	206.21	+3.21	+1.58	+2.67	+1.31
Japan	Tokyo Topix Index	1058.97	+14.40	+1.38	+15.28	+1.46
Mexico	I.P.C. All-Share	9193.81	+58.65	+0.64	+398.53	+4.53
Netherlands	Amsterdam AEX	357.55	+6.08	+1.73	+19.90	+5.89
Singapore	Straits Times	1836.87	+6.89	+0.38	+72.35	+4.10
South Africa	Johannesburg All Share	11009.46	+88.80	+0.81	+622.24	+5.99
South Korea	KOSPI	847.95	+2.29	+0.27	+37.24	+4.59
Spain	IBEX 35	7979.30	+22.00	+0.28	+242.10	+3.13
Sweden	SX All Share	204.88	+1.96	+0.97	+10.71	+5.52
Switzerland	Zurich Swiss Market	5694.50	+63.50	+1.13	+206.70	+3.77
Taiwan	Weighted	6269.71	+5.34	+0.09	+379.02	+6.43
Turkey	Istanbul National 100	18301.16	-651.06	-3.44	-323.86	-1.74
U.K.	London FTSE 100-share	4487.90	+31.80	+0.71	+11.00	+0.25
U.K	London FTSE 250-share	6108.10	+69.20	+1.15	+305.80	+5.27

r-Revised.

Source: *The Wall Street Journal*, January 19, 2004, p. C14. Reprinted by permission of *The Wall Street Journal*, © 2004 by Dow Jones & Company. All Rights Reserved Worldwide.

broken down by different types of bonds: Treasury securities, the broad market, U.S. corporate debt, mortgage-backed securities, and tax-exempt securities. (All of these securities are discussed in Part Four of the text.)

www.lipperweb.com

Mutual Fund Averages Lipper Analytical Services publishes the Lipper Mutual and Investment Performance Averages shown in Table 3–4 on page 67. It is interesting to observe the various categories that the funds are broken into to compute measures of performance. Also, observe in the next few columns of Table 3–4 that the starting point of the measurement period is very important in relation to relative performance.

Mutual funds and their performance have become progressively more important to investors in the United States and worldwide. Many of the 90 million investors in this country look to mutual funds to carry out their day-to-day investment activities. The authors feel that a thorough understanding of stocks and bonds is necessary before making a commitment to mutual funds; therefore,

TABLE 3–3 Bond Indexes

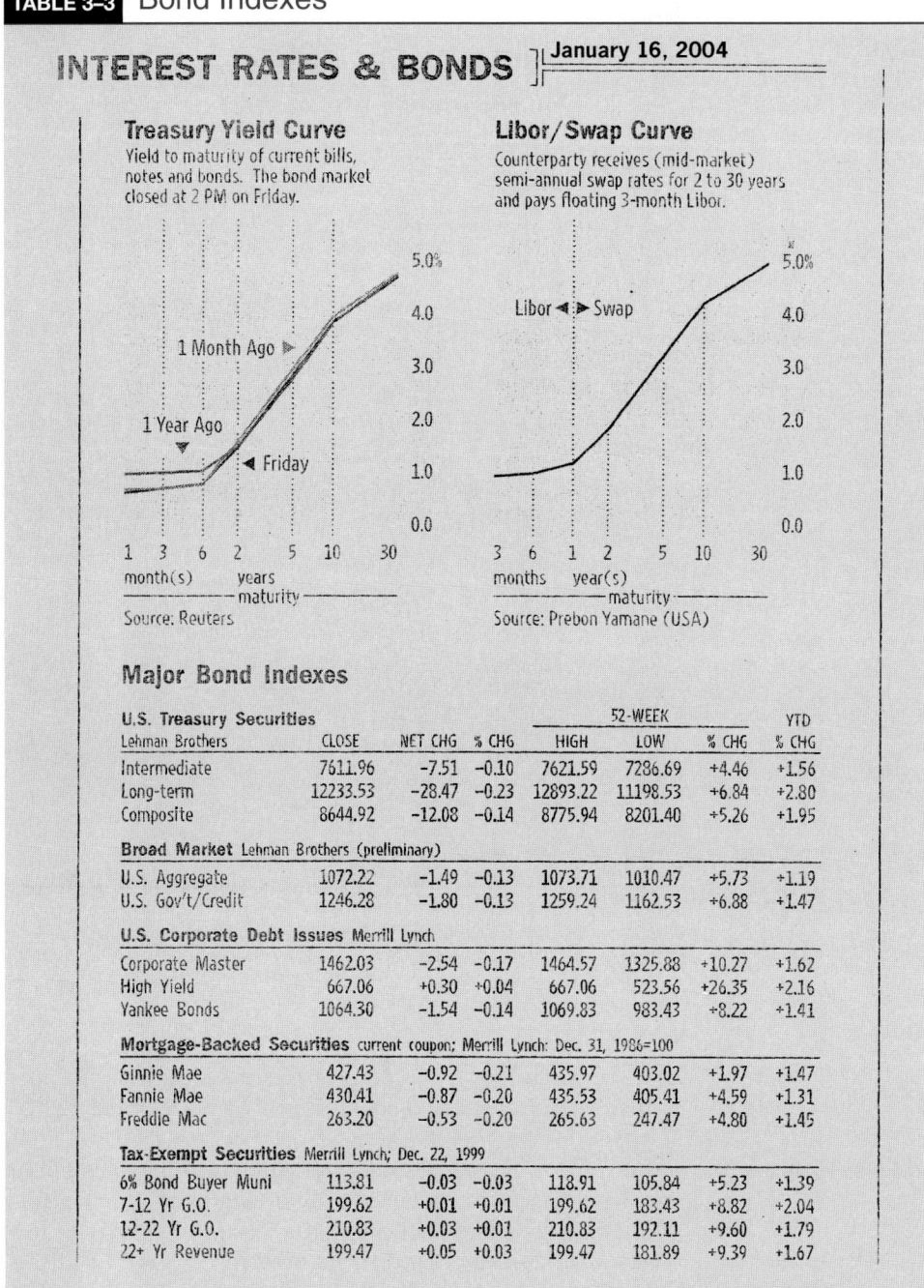

Source: *The Wall Street Journal*, January 19, 2004, p. C2. Reprinted by permission of *The Wall Street Journal*, © 2004 by Dow Jones & Company. All Rights Reserved Worldwide.

TABLE 3-4 Lipper Mutual Fund Performance Indexes

LIPPER MUTUAL FUND PERFORMANCE INDEXES
Weekly Summary Report: Thursday, 1/15/2004. Cumulative Performances With Dividends Reinvested

Current Value	No. Funds	Index	12/31/03-01/15/04	01/08/04-01/15/04	12/18/03-01/15/04	10/16/03-01/15/04	01/16/03-01/15/04
General Equity Indexes							
2,341.55	30	Capital Apprec Index	+ 2.87%	+ 0.47%	+ 4.84%	+ 7.62%	+ 29.57%
7,329.10	30	Growth Fund Index	+ 2.34	+ 0.19	+ 4.51	+ 6.89	+ 26.02
905.86	30	Mid Cap Fund Indx	+ 3.04	+ 0.63	+ 5.09	+ 8.49	+ 34.61
254.39	30	Micro Cap Fund IX	+ 5.69	+ 1.79	+ 8.28	+ 11.71	+ 60.28
860.87	30	Small Cap Fund Index	+ 3.76	+ 0.83	+ 5.84	+ 10.00	+ 42.53
7,563.86	30	Growth & Income Index	+ 1.57	+ 0.06	+ 3.70	+ 8.64	+ 25.28
433.88	10	S&P 500 Fund Indx	+ 1.85	+ 0.02	+ 4.02	+ 8.19	+ 25.57
4,109.62	30	Equity Income Index	+ 1.37	+ 0.10	+ 3.63	+ 9.11	+ 23.63
Specialized Equity Indexes							
335.34	10	Hlth/Biotch Fd IX	+ 2.23%	+ 0.69%	+ 4.18%	+ 8.26%	+ 29.11%
682.65	10	Sci & Tech Index	+ 7.41	+ 0.99	+ 10.30	+ 9.33	+ 50.77
330.41	30	Utility Fund Indx	+ 1.43	− 0.26	+ 3.67	+ 9.21	+ 19.98
580.87	10	Fincl Svs Fd Indx	+ 1.96	+ 1.27	+ 4.23	+ 7.50	+ 29.27
250.82	10	Real Estate Fd IX	+ 0.39	+ 0.82	+ 1.72	+ 5.82	+ 40.58
171.35	10	Gold Fund Index	− 7.06	− 8.43	− 2.64	+ 8.09	+ 42.55
735.68	30	Global Fund Index	+ 2.24	− 0.26	+ 5.28	+ 9.72	+ 31.13
778.09	30	International Index	+ 2.54	− 0.55	+ 6.04	+ 10.50	+ 35.96
316.25	10	European Fd Index	+ 3.22	− 0.26	+ 5.87	+ 15.43	+ 39.86
101.76	10	Pac Ex-Jpn Fd IX	+ 3.73	+ 0.48	+ 8.05	+ 11.16	+ 47.98
150.80	10	Pacific Reg Fd IX	+ 2.20	− 0.51	+ 6.71	+ 3.90	+ 40.18
105.98	30	Emerg Mkt Fd Indx	+ 3.53	− 0.90	+ 7.70	+ 13.23	+ 56.11
Other Equity Indexes							
397.53	30	Flex Port Fd Indx	+ 1.74%	+ 0.16%	+ 3.35%	+ 7.04%	+ 21.82%
282.16	10	Glbl Flx Fund IX	+ 2.83	+ 0.19	+ 4.33	+ 7.82	+ 25.76
4,994.21	30	Balanced Fund Index	+ 1.74	+ 0.46	+ 3.08	+ 6.62	+ 19.27
480.44	10	Conv Secur Index	+ 2.42	+ 0.37	+ 3.91	+ 8.10	+ 24.54
387.16	10	Income Fund index	+ 1.37	+ 0.52	+ 2.54	+ 5.70	+ 15.87
Fixed-Income Indexes							
194.60	10	Intl Inc Fd IX	+ 1.13%	− 0.23%	+ 2.29%	+ 6.86%	+ 17.67%
282.56	30	Global Inc Fd IX	+ 1.33	+ 0.31	+ 2.13	+ 5.66	+ 14.11
145.30	10	Ultra Short Fd Ix	+ 0.15	+ 0.11	+ 0.22	+ 0.46	+ 1.91
738.56	30	Gen Muni Dbt Indx	+ 1.19	+ 0.98	+ 1.24	+ 4.24	+ 7.51
401.63	30	Gen US Govt Fd IX	+ 1.22	+ 1.06	+ 0.93	+ 3.13	+ 3.66
435.24	10	GNMA Fund Index	+ 0.70	+ 0.38	+ 0.53	+ 2.35	+ 2.85
230.54	10	US Mortgage Fd IX	+ 0.76	+ 0.49	+ 0.70	+ 2.37	+ 3.54
1,082.63	30	A Rated Bnd Fd IX	+ 1.37	+ 1.08	+ 1.09	+ 3.59	+ 6.81
503.81	30	BBB Rated Fd IX	+ 1.64	+ 1.08	+ 1.61	+ 4.79	+ 11.36
269.00	10	Gen Bond Fd Index	+ 1.17	+ 0.76	+ 1.38	+ 3.72	+ 8.16
903.90	30	HI Yld Bond Fd IX	− 2.08	+ 0.58	+ 2.72	+ 6.38	+ 25.59
347.89	10	Ins Muni Fd Index	+ 1.29	+ 1.02	+ 1.25	+ 4.32	+ 7.24
335.21	10	HY Muni Dbt Fd IX	+ 1.17	+ 0.80	+ 1.35	+ 4.11	+ 8.50
145.39	10	Sh Muni Dbt Fd IX	+ 0.45	+ 0.28	+ 0.51	+ 0.92	+ 2.68
155.59	10	Sh-In Mun Dbt IX	+ 1.07	+ 0.77	+ 1.14	+ 2.53	+ 5.02
308.82	30	Intmdt Muni Fd IX	+ 1.32	+ 0.96	+ 1.35	+ 3.54	+ 6.42
254.24	10	Sht Inv Grd Fd IX	+ 0.43	+ 0.31	+ 0.47	+ 1.25	+ 3.14
232.08	30	Sh-In Inv Grd IX	+ 0.93	+ 0.77	+ 0.87	+ 2.42	+ 5.12
304.05	30	Intmdt Inv Grd IX	+ 1.29	+ 0.95	+ 1.12	+ 3.46	+ 6.92
222.24	10	Sh US Govt Fd IX	+ 0.30	+ 0.25	+ 0.35	+ 0.96	+ 1.88
266.24	30	Sh-In US Govt IX	+ 0.81	+ 0.66	+ 0.76	+ 2.00	+ 3.29
257.04	30	Intmdt US Govt IX	+ 1.02	+ 0.89	+ 0.84	+ 2.62	+ 3.92
164.86	10	CA Intmdt Muni IX	+ 1.34	+ 0.95	+ 1.41	+ 3.62	+ 5.61
416.55	30	CA Muni Dbt Fd IX	+ 1.37	+ 1.00	+ 1.36	+ 4.69	+ 7.12
203.48	10	FL Muni Dbt Fd IX	+ 1.15	+ 0.78	+ 1.22	+ 3.82	+ 6.55
184.38	10	MD Muni Dbt Fd IX	+ 1.14	+ 0.81	+ 1.14	+ 3.76	+ 6.29
300.75	10	MA Muni Dbt Fd IX	+ 1.41	+ 1.00	+ 1.46	+ 4.45	+ 7.42
225.28	10	MI Muni Dbt Fd IX	+ 1.07	+ 0.92	+ 1.10	+ 3.54	+ 6.33
289.17	10	MN Muni Dbt Fd IX	+ 1.21	+ 0.92	+ 1.23	+ 4.10	+ 7.16
227.73	10	NJ Muni Dbt Fd IX	+ 1.28	+ 0.88	+ 1.40	+ 4.08	+ 7.09
410.94	30	NY Muni Dbt Fd IX	+ 1.21	+ 0.96	+ 1.24	+ 4.18	+ 7.21
301.53	10	OH Muni Dbt Fd IX	+ 1.28	+ 0.94	+ 1.32	+ 4.33	+ 7.19
304.08	10	PA Muni Dbt Fd IX	+ 1.26	+ 0.89	+ 1.24	+ 4.03	+ 7.02
203.75	10	Muni Dbt VA Fd IX	+ 1.28	+ 0.91	+ 1.23	+ 4.20	+ 7.35

Source: *Barron's*, January 19, 2004, p. 15F. Reprinted by permission of *Barron's*, © 2004 by Dow Jones & Company. All Rights Reserved Worldwide.

mutual funds are discussed in Chapter 18 after you have covered the requisite background material.

Direction of Indexes   The direction of the indexes are closely related, but they do not necessarily move together. If a pension fund manager is trying to "outperform the market," then the choice of index may be crucial to whether the fund manager maintains his or her accounts. The important thing for you, as well as for a professional, when measuring success or failure of performance is to use an index that represents the risk characteristics of the portfolio being compared with the index.

Buying and Selling in the Market

Once you are generally familiar with the market and perhaps decide to invest directly in common stocks or other assets, you will need to set up an account with a retail brokerage house. Some of the largest and better-known retail brokers are Merrill Lynch, Smith Barney, and UBS, but there are many other good houses, both regional and national. When you set up your account, the account executive (often called stockbroker or financial consultant) will ask you to fill out a card listing your investment objectives, such as conservative, preservation of capital, income oriented, growth plus income, or growth. The account executive will also ask for your Social Security number for tax reporting, the level of your income, net worth, employer, and other information. Basically, the account executive needs to know your desire and ability to take risk in order to give good advice and proper management of your assets. Later in this section, we will also talk about discount brokers and online brokers, that is, brokers who charge very low commissions but give stripped-down service. These brokers are also very important, and a comparative analysis will be provided at that point in the chapter.

Cash or Margin Account

Your broker will need to know if you want a cash account or margin account. Either account allows you three business days to pay for any purchase. A cash account requires full payment, while a **margin account** allows the investor to borrow a percentage of the purchase price from the brokerage firm. The percentage of the total cost the investor must pay is called the margin and is set by the Federal Reserve Board. During the great crash in the 1920s, margin on stock was only 10 percent, but it was as high as 80 percent in 1968. It has been at 50 percent since January 1974. The margin percentage is used to control speculation. Historically, when the Board of Governors of the Federal Reserve System thinks markets are being pushed too high by speculative fervor, it raises the margin requirement, which means more cash must be put up. The Fed has been hesitant to take action in this area in recent times.

Application Example

Margin accounts are used mostly by traders and speculators or by investors who think their long-run return will be greater than the cost of borrowing. Most brokerage houses require a $2,000 minimum in an account before lending money, although many brokerage houses have higher limits. Here is how a margin account works. Assume you purchased 100 shares of General Motors at $60 per share on margin and that margin is 50 percent:

Purchase: 100 shares at $60 per share	$6,000
Borrow: Cost × (1 − margin percentage)	−3,000
Margin: Equity contributed (cash or securities)	$3,000

You can borrow $3,000 or the total cost times (1 − margin percentage). The cost of borrowing is generally 1 to 2 percent above the prime rate, depending on the size of the account. Rather than putting up $3,000 in cash, a customer could put $3,000 of other approved financial assets into the account to satisfy the margin. Not all stocks may be used for margin purchases. The Securities and Exchange Commission publishes a list of approved securities that may be borrowed against.

One reason people buy on margin is to leverage their returns. Assume that GM stock rises to $80 per share. The account would now have $8,000 in stock and an increase in equity from $3,000 to $5,000:

100 shares at $80	$8,000
Loan	−3,000
Equity (margin)	$5,000

This $2,000 increase in equity creates a 67 percent return on the initial $3,000 of equity. The 67 percent return was accomplished on the basis of only a 33 percent increase in the price of stock ($60 to $80). With the increased equity in the account, the customer could now purchase additional securities on margin.

Margin is a two-edged sword, however, and what works to your advantage in up markets works to your disadvantage in down markets. If GM stock had gone down to $40, your equity would decrease to $1,000:

100 shares at $40	$4,000
Borrowed	−3,000
Equity (margin)	$1,000

Minimum requirements for equity in a margin account are called *minimum maintenance standards* (usually 25 percent). Your equity would now be at minimum maintenance standards where the equity of $1,000 equals 25 percent of the current market value of $4,000. A fall below $1,000 would bring a margin call for more cash or equity. Many brokerage firms have maintenance requirements above 25 percent, and when margin calls are made, the equity often needs to be increased to 35 percent or more of the portfolio value. Normally, you must maintain a $2,000 minimum in your account, so you would have been called for more equity when the stock was at $50 even though the minimum maintenance requirement had not yet been reached.

One feature of a margin account is that margined securities may not be delivered to the customer. In this case, the GM stock would be kept registered in the street name of your retail brokerage house (e.g., Merrill Lynch), and your account would show a claim on 100 shares held as collateral for the loan. It is much like an automobile loan; you don't hold title to the car until you have made the last payment. In the use of margin, however, there is no due date on the loan. The use of margin increases risk and is not recommended for anyone who cannot afford large losses or who has no substantial experience in the market.

Long or Short?—That Is the Question

Once you have opened the account of your choice, you are ready to buy or sell. When investors establish a position in a security, they are said to have a **long position** if they purchase the security for their account. It is assumed the reason they purchased the security was to profit on an increase in price over time and/or to receive dividend income.

Sometimes investors anticipate that the price of a security may drop in value. If they are long in the stock, some may sell out their position. Those who have no position at all may wish to take a **short position** to profit from the expected decline. When you short a security, you are borrowing the security from the broker and selling it with the obligation to replace the security in the future. How you can sell something you don't own is an obvious question. Your broker will simply lend you the security from the brokerage house inventory. If your brokerage house doesn't have an inventory of the particular stock you want to short, the firm will borrow the stock from another broker.

Once you go short, you begin hoping and praying that the price of the security will go down so that you can buy it back and replace the security at a lower price. In a perverse way, bad news starts to become good news. When you read the morning paper, you look for signs of unemployment, high inflation, and rising interest rates in hopes of a stock market decline.

A short sale can only be made on a trade where the price of the stock advances (an uptick), or if there is no change in price, the prior trade must have been positive. These rules are intended to stop a snowballing decline in stock values caused by short sellers.

Application Example

A margin requirement is associated with short selling, and it is currently equal to 50 percent of the securities sold short. Thus, if you were to sell 100 shares of Eli Lilly short at $70 per share, you would be required to put up $3,500 in margin (50 percent of $7,000). In a short sale, the margin is considered to be good-faith money and obviously is not a down payment toward the purchase. The margin protects the brokerage house in case you start losing money on your account.

You would lose money on a short sales position if the stock you sold short starts going up. Assume Eli Lilly goes from $70 to $80. Since you initially sold 100 shares short at $70 per share, you have suffered a $1,000 paper loss. Your initial margin or equity position has been reduced from $3,500 to $2,500:

Initial margin (equity)	$3,500
Loss	−1,000
Current margin (equity)	$2,500

> We previously specified that there is a minimum 25 percent margin maintenance requirement in buying stock. A similar requirement exists in selling short. The equity position must equal at least 30 percent of the *current* value of the stock that has been sold short. In the present example, the equity position is equal to $2,500, and the current market value of Eli Lilly is $8,000 ($80 × 100). Your margin percentage is 31.25 percent ($2,500 ÷ $8,000) or slightly above the minimum requirement. However, if the stock goes up another point or two and your losses increase, you will be asked to put up more margin to increase your equity position.
>
> Of course, if the value of Eli Lilly stock goes down from its initial base of $70, you would be making profits off the bad news. A 20-point drop in Eli Lilly would mean a $2,000 profit on your 100 shares. Most market observers agree that it requires a "special breed of cat" to be an effective short seller. You often need nerves of steel and a contrarian outlook that cannot be easily shaken by good news.

One final point on selling short. In the last 10 or 15 years, some investors have chosen to use other ways to take a negative position in a security. These normally involve put and call options, which are discussed in Chapter 15. Both selling short and option transactions can be effectively utilized for strategic purposes.

Types of Orders

When an investor places an order to establish a position, he or she has many different kinds of orders from which to choose. When the order is placed with the broker on a NYSE-listed stock, it is sent electronically to the exchange where it is executed by the company's floor broker in an auction market. Each stock is traded at a specific trading post on the floor of the exchange, so the floor broker knows exactly where to go to find other brokers buying and selling the same company's shares.

Most orders placed will be straightforward market orders to buy or sell. The market order will be carried by the floor broker to the correct trading post and will usually trade close to the last price or within 0.10 of a point.[4] For example, if you want to sell 100 shares of AT&T at market, you would probably have no trouble finding a ready buyer since AT&T may be trading a few million shares per day. But if you wanted to sell 100 shares of Bemis, as few as 1,000 shares might be traded in a day, and no other broker would be waiting at the Bemis post to make a transaction with the floor broker. If the broker finds no one else wishing to buy the shares, he will transact the sale with the specialist who is always at the post ready to buy and sell 100-share round lots. If the broker wants to sell, the specialist will either buy the shares for her own account at 0.05 or 0.10 less than the last trade or will buy out of her book in which special orders of others are kept.

Two basic special orders are the limit order and the stop order. A **limit order** limits the price at which you are willing to buy or sell and ensures you will pay no more than the limit price on a buy or receive no less than the limit price on a sell. Assume you are trying to buy a thinly traded stock that fluctuates in value and you are afraid that with a market order you might risk paying more

---
[4] Since the NYSE has gone to decimals, the difference could be less.

than you want. So you would place a limit order to buy 100 shares of MedQuist Inc., as an example, at 16.50 or a better price. The order will go to the floor broker who goes to the post to check the price. The broker finds MedQuist trading at its high for the day of 16.80, and so he leaves the limit order with the specialist who records it in his book. The entry will record the price, date, time, and brokerage firm. There may be other orders in front of yours at 16.50, but once these are cleared, and assuming the stock stays in this range, your order will be executed at 16.50 or less. Limit orders are used by investors to buy or sell thinly traded stocks or to buy securities at prices thought to be at the low end of a price range and to sell securities at the high end of the price range. Investors who calculate fundamental values have a basic idea of what they think a stock is worth and will often set a limit to take advantage of what they view to be discrepancies in values.

Many traders are certain they want their order to be executed if a certain price is reached. A limit order does not guarantee execution if orders are time stamped ahead of you on the specialist's book. In cases where you want a guaranteed "fill" of the order, a stop order is placed. A **stop order** is a two-part mechanism. It is placed at a specific price like a limit order, but when the price is reached, the stop turns into a market order that will be executed at close to the stop price but not necessarily at the exact price specified. Often, many short-term traders will view a common stock price with optimism for a certain trading strategy. When the stock hits the price, it may pop up on an abundance of buy orders or decline sharply on a large volume of sell orders, and your "fill" could be several dollars away from the top price. Assume H. J. Heinz Corporation stock has been trading between $25 and $40 per share over the last six months, reaching both these prices three times. A trader may follow several strategies. One strategy would be to buy at $25 and sell at $40 using a stop buy and a stop sell order. Some traders may put in a stop buy at $41 thinking that if the stock breaks through its peak trading range it will go on to new highs, and finally some may put in a stop sell at $24 to either eliminate a long position or establish a short position with the assumption the stock has broken its support and will trend lower. When used to eliminate a long position, a stop order is often called a *stop-loss order*.

Limit orders and stop orders can be "day orders" that expire at the end of the day if not executed, or they can be GTC (good till canceled) orders. GTC orders will remain on the specialist's books until taken off by the brokerage house or executed. If the order remains unfilled for several months, most brokerage houses will send reminders that the order is still pending so that the client does not get caught buying stock for which he or she is unable to pay.

Cost of Trading

www.morganstanley.com

Nowhere has the field of investments changed more than in the means and cost of trading. A decade ago, the basic choice was between full-service brokerage firms such as Merrill Lynch, UBS, and Morgan Stanley and discount brokers such as Charles Schwab, Quick & Reilly, and Olde. The discount brokers provided bare bones service and generally charged 25 to 75 percent of the commissions charged by full-service brokers, who willingly provided research and stock analysis to clients, tax information, and help in establishing goals and objectives.

The nature of the landscape changed radically with the emergence of the Internet. Now, an investor can merely access an **online broker's** website to open an account, review the operating procedures and commission schedule, and initiate a trade. Confirmation of an electronic trade can take as little as 10 seconds and almost all trades are completed within a minute.

Application Example

www.ameritrade.com
www.etrade.com

Online brokers such as Ameritrade and E*TRADE have become household names—and why not? A recent study by the American Association of Individual Investors indicated that for a 100-share trade, the average online broker charged $15. In comparison, the average discount broker charged $42, while a full-service broker charged $100.

To examine the effect of the pricing differential, assume 100 shares are traded at $40 per share for a total value of $4,000. Note the difference in percentage costs between the three types of brokers.

Online broker	$15/$4,000 = 0.37%
Discount broker	$42/$4,000 = 1.05%
Full-service broker	$100/$4,000 = 2.50%

---

www.ml.com
www.schwab.com

Because of the intense competition provided by online brokers, in the late 1990s many full-service and deep discount brokers began offering their clients the alternative of online trading. Merrill Lynch was the first major full-service broker to go this route, and Charles Schwab led the way among discount brokers (over half of Schwab's trades are now online). All others in the industry have followed the same path, so the landscape is blurred between full-service and deep discount brokers that offer an online alternative and pure online brokers. Even banks and mutual funds offer online trading through brokerage subsidiaries.

While online trading is a very attractive trading alternative because of the low commission rate, it is not for everyone. For the less sophisticated investor or computer novice, full service (or even the discount broker) may be the way to go. The importance of explanations about long-term capital gains taxes, potential merger tender offers, retirement and estate planning, and so on, may outweigh savings in commissions. That is why most major traditional houses offer alternative ways to go. Nevertheless, for the sophisticated investor who knows his or her own mind, it is impractical to pay for additional unused and unnecessary services. While 25 to 30 percent of all trades are currently online, the number will undoubtedly double or triple in the next few years.

The Internet has not only influenced the way trades are executed, but has given the individual investor access to instant information that was once in the private domain of large institutional investors such as mutual funds or bank trust departments. Individual investors can download balance sheets, income statements, up-to-the-minute press releases, and so on. They can also participate with other investors in chat rooms and e-mail the company for immediate answers to questions.

All of these options certainly represent progress, with one caveat. The intoxication of it all has led to a new class of "day traders," who attempt to beat the market on an hourly or by-the-minute basis. While some with exceptional skill have profited by this activity, all too many others get badly hurt when the market makes unexpected moves. Surgeons and trial lawyers sometimes decide the market is not as easy a play toy as they once thought and return to their "day jobs."

Taxes and the 2003 Tax Act

In making many types of investments, an important consideration will be the tax consequences of your investment (taxes may be more significant than the brokerage commissions just discussed).

This section is intended only as a brief overview of tax consequences. For more information, consult a tax guide. Consultation with a CPA, CFP (Certified Financial Planner), or similar sources may also be advisable.

Before we specifically talk about the tax consequences of investment *gains and losses,* let's briefly look at the tax rates that were in place at year-end 2003. The rates are presented in Table 3–5. The values in the table will change very slightly each year for the rest of the decade.

TABLE 3–5 Tax Rates 2003

Taxable Income	Rate (%)
Single	
$0– 7,000	10%
$7,000– 28,400	15
$28,400– 68,800	25
$68,800–153,500	28
$153,500–311,950	33
Over 311,950	35
Married (joint return)	
$0– 14,000	10%
$14,000– 56,800	15
$56,800–114,650	25
$114,650–174,700	28
$174,700–311,950	33
Over 311,950	35

Application Example

Refer to Table 3–5 and assume you have appropriately computed your taxable income after all deductions as $34,000. Further assume you are single so that you fall into a bracket in the upper portion of the table. How much is your tax obligation? The answer is shown below:

	Amount	Rate	Tax
First	$ 7,000	10%	$ 700.00
Next	$21,400*	15	3,210.10
Next	5,600†	25	1,400.00
			$5,310.10

* $28,400 − 7,000
† $34,000 − 28,400

The total tax is $5,310.10. The rates of 10, 15, and 25 percent are referred to as marginal tax rates. The average tax is a slightly different concept. It is simply the amount of taxes paid divided by taxable income, or 15.62 percent in this case:

$$\frac{\text{Taxes paid}}{\text{Taxable income}} = \frac{\$5{,}310.10}{\$34{,}000} = 15.62\%$$

Capital Gains and Dividends

A **capital gain or loss** occurs when an asset held for investment purposes is sold. A long-term capital gain takes place when an asset is held for more than a year; and the maximum tax rate is 15 percent. The Tax Relief Act of 2003 made a radical shift in tax policy by lowering the maximum tax rate on dividends to 15 percent. Previously, dividends had been taxed the same as other forms of income at a maximum rate in the mid-to-high 30 percent range.[5] Thus, the tax rate on long-term capital gains and dividends is the same, and high-income investors have little tax preference between high dividend stocks and low dividend stocks that attempt to provide capital gains.[6] This is a major shift in strategic considerations since the Tax Relief Act of 2003.

However, if an asset is not held for more than 12 months, its sale represents a short-term capital gain or loss, and the tax treatment is exactly the same as ordinary income. This means it is taxed at the rates shown in Table 3–5. For example, if a person is in the 35 percent tax bracket and sells a stock owned for only six months, the tax on the gain would be 35 percent. If he or she had held the asset for 12 months, the long-term capital gains tax rate on the gain would have been only 15 percent.

Application Example

As you can see, there are some strong inducements to go for the longer-term capital gains treatment over short-term capital gains rate. Assume an investor is in a 35 percent tax bracket and sells a stock at a $10,000 profit. Note the different amounts of taxes owed based on the holding period:

Holding Period	Profit	Tax Rate	Taxes
6 months	$10,000	35%	$3,500
Over 12 months	10,000	15	1,500

For investors putting their money into tax-deferred investments (such as an IRA or 401k), these tax considerations during the holding period are not relevant. Furthermore, taxes are only one of the many variables that should influence an investment decision.

It should also be pointed out that when you have net investment losses in any one year, you can write off up to $3,000 of these losses against other taxable income (salary, interest income, etc.). Any unused balance can be carried

---

[5] The maximum tax rate of 15 percent does not apply to REIT and trusts.
[6] The one remaining advantage to long-term capital gains treatment is that the tax is deferred until the stock is sold, whereas the tax on dividends must be paid annually.

the real world of investing

Who Cheats on Their Income Taxes?

Each year the government loses 17 cents out of every dollar due on income taxes because of cheating by taxpayers. The cheating may take the form of not reporting income or taking nonexistent or unjustified deductions. The total loss to the government is more than $100 billion a year. This represents the unpaid taxes of otherwise honest Americans, not the additional tens of billions hidden by drug czars and other hardened criminals. If all taxes were properly collected, a portion of our federal deficit could be wiped out.

The most frequent offenders are the self-employed. A Government Accounting Office (GAO) study revealed that auto dealers, restaurateurs, and clothing store operators underreport their taxable income by nearly 40 percent. Doctors, lawyers, barbers, and *accountants* underpay (cheat?) on 20 percent of their revenues. The most proficient of the non-reporters are in the food-service industry. Collectively, waiters and waitresses fail to report 84 percent of their tips, according to the GAO.

Claiming deductions for dependent children that do not exist is another favorite approach. In 1987, the IRS began requiring taxpayers to report and verify the Social Security numbers of all dependents over five years of age. The following year 7 million fewer dependents were claimed as deductions. It seems that many people had been listing the same child two or three times and even claiming dogs, cats, and birds as tax-deductible dependents.

Of course, not all feel guilty about not paying their full share of taxes. A shipyard manager who did not report income from yacht repairs on the weekend told *Money* magazine, "The government squanders the money I already pay. Why give more?"

---

forward into the future to be written off against future capital gains from investments or other forms of income.[7]

---

[7] At this point the discussion can become progressively more complicated in terms of balancing short- and long-term gains and losses against each other. The authors have decided these topics are better left for a tax course.

exploring the web

Website Address	Comment
www.msci.com	Provides information on bond and stock indexes
www.barra.com	Provides information on various modified indexes
www.sec.gov	Provides access to SEC filings
www.quicken.com	Provides access to company SEC filings
finance.yahoo.com	Profile pages on stock quotes provide access to company SEC filings
www.standardandpoors.com	Contains information about S&P indexes and the markets
www.dowjones.com	Provides information about the Dow Jones indexes

Summary

The investor should have a basic understanding of measures of market performance, the rules and mechanics of opening and trading in an account, and tax considerations.

In gauging the movements in the market, the investor may view the Dow Jones Industrial Average, the Standard & Poor's 500 Stock Index, the Standard & Poor's MidCap Index, the Value Line Average of 1,700 companies, or the Nasdaq Averages (to name a few). To evaluate mutual funds, the investor may turn to the Lipper Mutual Fund Investment Performance Averages. There also are a number of bond indexes and averages for foreign trading. The investor will try to evaluate performance in light of an index that closely parallels the makeup of the investor's portfolio.

With some understanding of the various markets and the related means of measurements for those markets (such as the DJIA), the potential investor is now in a position to consider opening an account. The investor may establish either a cash or margin account and use the account to buy securities or to sell short (in which case a margin account is necessary). The investor can also execute a number of different types of orders such as a market order, a limit order, and a stop order. The latter two specify prices where the investor wishes to initiate transactions.

The investor must also consider the tax consequences of his or her actions. The Tax Relief Act of 2003 has caused many investors to rethink their investment strategy.

Key Words and Concepts

capital gain or loss 75
Dow Jones Industrial Average (DJIA) 59
Dow Jones World Index 64
equal-weighted index 63
limit order 71
long position 70
margin account 68
online broker 72
price-weighted average 61

Russell 1000 Index 64
Russell 2000 Index 64
Russell 3000 Index 64
short position 70
Standard & Poor's 100 Index 61
Standard & Poor's 400 MidCap Index 61
Standard & Poor's 500 Stock Index 61
Standard & Poor's 600 SmallCap Index 61

Standard & Poor's 1500 Stock Index 61
stop order 72
Tokyo Nikkei 225 Average 64
Value Line Average 63
value-weighted index 62
Wilshire 5000 Equity Index 64

Discussion Questions

1. Why is the Dow Jones Industrial Average considered a "blue-chip" measure of value?
2. How is the Dow Jones Industrial Average adjusted for stock splits?
3. What are the criticisms and a defense of the Dow Jones Industrial Average?
4. Explain the price-weighted average concept as applied to the Dow Jones Industrial Average.
5. What categories of stocks make up the Standard & Poor's 500 Stock Index?
6. Why was the Standard & Poor's MidCap Index created?

about the trucking industry, so you short-sell 300 shares of Ace Trucking Corporation at $75. Each transaction requires a 50 percent margin balance.

a. What is the initial equity in your account?

b. Assume the price of each stock is as follows for the next three months (month-end). Compute the equity balance in your account for each month:

Month	Scientific Resources	Ace Trucking
January	$68	$70
February	60	77
March	59	56

Commission percentages

9. Dr. Phil is considering buying 100 shares of the Psychological Testing Company. The price of the shares is $48. He has checked around with different types of brokers and has been given the following commission quotes for the trade: online broker, $16; discount broker, $45; full-service broker, $100.

a. Compute the percentage commission for all three categories.

b. How many times larger is the percentage commission of the full-service broker compared with the online broker? Round to two places to the right of the decimal point for this answer.

Computing tax obligation

10. Compute the tax obligation for the following using Table 3–5 on page 74:

a. An individual with taxable income of $38,400.

b. A married couple with taxable income of $110,000.

c. What is the average tax rate in part *b*?

Capital gains tax

11. Jennifer Franklin is in the 35 percent tax bracket. Her long-term capital gains tax rate is 15 percent. She makes $12,400 on a stock trade. Compute her tax obligation based on the following holding periods:

a. 6 months.

b. 14 months.

Critical Thought Case—Focus on Ethics

Elaine and Izzy Polanski have been happily married for the last 10 years. Elaine is a systems engineer for a major West Coast aerospace company, and Izzy is a pilot for a commuter airline flying out of Los Angeles International Airport. Together they anticipate a taxable income of $116,000.

Both Elaine and Izzy are concerned about their potential large tax obligation of $22,660. As the end of the year approached, they began to think of ways to reduce their anticipated taxable income. Izzy suggested they evaluate their stock portfolio to see if they might sell off a stock or two to create a deduction against taxable income. They have six stocks in their portfolio, and only one was trading at a loss from its original purchase price. They hold 500 shares of Atlantic Cellular Company, and the stock has fallen from $58 to $38 a share due to poor third-quarter earnings.

Before they made a decision to sell, Izzy and Elaine completed an intensive investigation of the company and found that the company was still fundamentally sound. It is their view that investors overreacted to the poor third-quarter earnings announcement and that prospects for the fourth quarter looked considerably better. Furthermore, they think that Atlantic Cellular Company has an excellent chance of wining a major contract with the U.S. Treasury Department on the installation and use of sophisticated telephone communication equipment. The other bidder on the contract is Atlas Corp., a firm in which Izzy and Elaine currently hold 1,000 shares. Since they purchased the stock of Atlas Corp. it has gone from $10 to $25.

To get a better feel for how the competition on the contract might turn out, Izzy told Elaine he might give Gordon Lewis a call. Lewis is currently the Vice President of Corporate Development at Atlantic Cellular Company and was Izzy's roommate in college. Elaine isn't sure this is such a good idea. Izzy countered with the argument that it is always best to be as fully informed as possible before making a decision and that Elaine, as a systems engineer, should know this better than anyone.

Questions

1. Do you think Izzy Polanski should call Gordon Lewis, his old college roommate, to get information on the contract bid?
2. Regardless of your answer to question 1, do you think the Polanskis should sell their stock in Atlantic Cellular Company? If they do sell the stock, what's the maximum deduction they can take from their taxable income this year?
3. What strategy do you recommend with their holdings in Atlas Corp.?

Web Exercise

In this exercise, we get a better feel for the major market indexes. Go to **www.bloomberg.com**.

1. Click on "Market Data" across the top. Record the value and change for the Dow Jones Industrial Average (DJIA), Nasdaq, and S&P 500.
2. Click on "Stocks" in the left margin.
3. Then click on "Dow." Scroll down and record the current price for 3M, Hewlett Packard, and Procter and Gamble.
4. Which of the 30 Dow stocks had the largest percentage upside movement? Which had the largest percentage downside movement?
5. If you were using a price-weighted index, which stock would have the greatest impact on the DJIA?
6. Return to the prior page. Click on "Nikkei" across the top. Scroll down and indicate which stock in the Nikkei 225 had the highest volume.

Note: From time to time, companies redesign their websites, and occasionally a topic we have listed may have been deleted, updated, or moved into a different location. Most websites have a "site map" or "site index" listed on a different page. If you click on the site map or site index you will be introduced to a table of contents that should aid you in finding the topic you are looking for.

S&P Problems

www.mhhe.com/edumarketinsight

STANDARD &POOR'S

1. Log on to the McGraw-Hill website: **www.mhhe.com/edumarketinsight** (see page vi in the preface for instructions).
2. Click on Company, which is the first box below the Market Insight title, and enter the ticker symbol.

3. Scroll down the left margin, and click on "Charting by Prophet" listed in blue/purple. If you haven't done the problem in Chapter 1, please return to that chapter and read through the directions to the problem before continuing.
4. When the chart appears, scroll down the left side to "Indices" and double-click on S&P500. The graph covers the last twelve months. What is the price at the beginning of this time period and the end of this time period? Calculate the percentage change in closing price.
5. Now scroll across the top to the third box with the 1yr inside, and click on the arrow. Choose "All" at the bottom of the list, and change the fourth box to "Y" for year. Calculate the percentage price change from January 1, 1995, to December 31, 1999. What is the total percentage price change?
6. Using time value of money techniques, what was the annual rate of return?
7. Now repeat this for the period of January 1, 2000, and ending December 31, 2004, and calculate the total percentage price change and the annual rate of return. Compare the results.
8. Return to the indices list and choose the NASDAQ index representing the over-the-counter market, and repeat steps 4, 5, 6, and 7 in this problem.
9. Now compare the S&P 500 index data to the NASDAQ data. What conclusions and explanations can you draw from your analysis?
10. As a final exercise, find the highest price for the NASDAQ and S&P 500 indexes, and compare them to the current indexes.

The Wall Street Journal Projects

1. A current picture of "The Dow Jones Industrial Averages" can be found in *The Wall Street Journal* in Section C. Please describe the recent market trend year to date.
2. *a.* A current update of Table 3–1, entitled "Major Stick Indices," is also available in *The Wall Street Journal* in Section C. Compare the performance of the various stock indexes over the last 12 months by looking at the 12-month percentage change. Which indexes are performing best? Worst?
   b. Are small stocks outperforming or underperforming large stocks? What indexes did you use to reach your conclusions?
   c. Are there some economic or market reasons for the difference in these performance measurements?
   d. When you compare the performance of the Dow Jones Industrial Average to the Standard & Poor's 500 Stock Index for the 12-month period, what accounts for the fact that these two indexes are not performing at the same percentage rates? Relate the last answer to weighting.

Selected References

Market Indexes

Denis, Diane; John J. McConnell; Alexei V. Ovtchinnikov; and Yun Yu. "S&P 500 Index Additions and Earnings Expectations." *Journal of Finance,* October 2003, pp. 1821–40.

Peters, Edgar E. "A Chaotic Attractor: The S&P 500." *Financial Analysts Journal,* March–April 1991, pp. 55–62.

Zwecher, Michael J. "The Relative Performance of Mid-Cap Stock Indexes." *The Journal of Investing.* Summer 1997, pp. 47–52.

Stock Trading

Angel, James A; Stephen E. Christopher; and Michael G. Ferri. "A Close Look at Short Selling on Nasdaq." *Financial Analysts Journal,* November–December 2003, pp. 66–74.

Berkin, Andrew L., and Jia Ye. "Tax Management, Loss Harvesting, and HIFO Accounting." *Financial Analysts Journal,* July–August 2003, pp. 91–102.

Berkowitz, Stephen A., and Dennis E. Logue. "Transaction Costs." *Journal of Portfolio Management,* Winter 2001, pp. 65–74.

Chan, Louis K. C., and Josef Lakonishok. "Institutional Trading Costs: NYSE Versus Nasdaq." *Journal of Finance,* June 1997, pp. 713–34.

Ferguson, Robert, and Dean Leisikow. "Valuing Active Managers, Fees, and Fund Discounts." *Financial Analysts Journal,* May–June 2001, pp. 52–62.

Jacobs, Bruce I., and Kenneth N. Levy. "The Long and Short on Long-Short." *The Journal of Investing.* Spring 1997, pp. 73–86.

Poterba, James M., and Scott J. Weisbenner. "Capital Gains Tax Rules, Tax-Loss Trading, and Turn-of-the-Year Returns." *Journal of Finance,* February 2001, pp. 353–68.

Brokerage Services

Brennan, Michael J., and Tarun Chordia. "Brokerage Commission Schedules." *Journal of Finance,* September 1993, pp. 1379–1402.

chapter four

Sources of Investment Information

objectives

1. Explain the major categories of financial information that are available to investors.

2. Discuss the major products that the investment advisory services provide.

3. Understand the key role of the Internet in investment research.

4. Identify important financially oriented websites on the Internet.

5. Explain significant filings that are made with the SEC.

6. Discuss key categories of information in *The Wall Street Journal* and in *Barron's*.

Aggregate Economic Data
    Federal Reserve Bulletin
    Federal Reserve Banks
    Survey of Current Business
    Websites and Economic Data
    Other Sources of Economic Data
Investment Advisory Resources
    Mergent (Moody's)
    Standard & Poor's
    Value Line
    Morningstar
    Other Investment Resources
SEC Filings, Periodicals, and Journals
    Securities and Exchange Commission Filings
    Periodicals and Newspapers
    Journals
Databases
The Internet and Investment Information
    Additional Websites
Class Project Websites

We are continually exposed to much information in this world of expanding and rapid communications. As the scope of investments has grown to include more than stocks and bonds, investment information has expanded to cover items such as gold and silver, diamonds, original art, antiques, stamps and coins, real estate, farmland, oil and gas, commodities, mutual funds, and other specialized assets. The problem investors are faced with is not only which investments to choose from the many available, but also where to find relevant and reliable investment information.

This chapter was coauthored by Celia A. Ross, Reference & Instruction Librarian and Finance Bibliographer at DePaul University.

First, the investor needs a basic knowledge of the economic environment. After determining the economic climate, the investor will proceed to a more detailed analysis of industries and unique variables affecting a specific investment. It is often said that the sign of an educated person is whether he or she knows where to find information to make an intelligent decision. The rest of this chapter will attempt to provide a list and descriptions of the basic information sources for some of the more common forms of investments as well as sources for general economic data.

Keep in mind that there is an enormous amount of investment information out there from both free and fee-based sources. As with any information source, maintain a critical eye and evaluate the data you find. Consider the source's accuracy, reliability, perspective and currency (e.g., "freshness"). And, especially when it comes to investment data, be on the lookout for consistently adjusted figures. Numbers from different sources may have been modified using different variables and formulas. In other words, Caveat researcher (Researcher beware).

You may want to refer to this chapter as you go through the chapters that follow. This chapter is not intended to be a guide for analysis—only an overview of what information is available. You may have heard the phrase "a picture is worth a thousand words." You will find that is certainly true of the tables and figures in this chapter. It is virtually impossible to discuss each and every variable found in them. As with any skill, navigating and exploiting these and other investment research resources will become easier for you with practice over time. To acquaint yourself more fully with information sources, we suggest you browse the Internet and visit your college and local libraries.

Aggregate Economic Data

Economic data are necessary for analyzing the past and predicting trends. The economic environment that exists today and the one expected in the future will bear heavily on the types of investments selected when creating or managing an investment portfolio. Information on inflation, wages, disposable income, interest rates, money supply, demographic trends, and so on are important economic data that will influence investor decisions. This information is available in many publications from the government, commercial banks, and periodicals. What follows is a brief description of some of the major sources of economic data.

Federal Reserve Bulletin

The *Federal Reserve Bulletin* is published monthly by the Board of Governors of the Federal Reserve System, Washington, D.C. It contains an abundance of monetary data such as money supply figures, interest rates, bank reserves, and various statistics on commercial banks. Fiscal variables such as U.S. budget receipts and outlays and federal debt figures are also found in the *Bulletin*. This publication also contains data on international exchange rates and U.S. dealings with foreigners and overseas banks.

A complete description of the *Federal Reserve Bulletin* is outside the scope of this chapter, but a partial listing of the table of contents will provide a better idea of what information it contains. Each heading may be divided into more detailed sections that provide information for the previous month, the current year on a monthly basis, and several years of historical annual data:

www.federalreserve.gov

Domestic Financial Statistics
Federal Reserve Banks
Monetary and Credit Aggregates
Commercial Banks
Financial Markets
Federal Finance
Securities Markets and Corporate Finance
Real Estate
Consumer Installment Credit
Domestic Nonfinancial Statistics
International Statistics
Securities Holdings and Transactions
Interest and Exchange Rates

Federal Reserve Banks

The 12 Federal Reserve banks in the Federal Reserve System represent different geographical areas (districts) of the United States. Each bank publishes its own monthly letter or review that includes economic data about its region and sometimes commentary on national issues or monetary policy. Eight times each year the 12 district banks publish "The Beige Book" on their region's economy. This report relies on anecdotal information on the regional economy collected by the banks from their directors, bankers, key business contacts, economists, and other professionals who understand the regional economy. The following list of Federal Reserve District banks includes their website addresses:

City/District	Address	Website
Atlanta/6	Atlanta, GA 30301	www.frbatlanta.org
Boston/1	Boston, MA 02106	www.bos.frb.org
Chicago/7	Chicago, IL 60690	www.chicago.fed.org
Cleveland/4	Cleveland, OH 44101	www.clevelandfed.org
Dallas/11	Dallas, TX 75222	www.dallasfed.org
Kansas City/10	Kansas City, KS 64198	www.kc.frb.org
Minneapolis/9	Minneapolis, MN 55380	www.minneapolisfed.org
New York/2	New York, NY 10045	www.newyorkfed.org
Philadelphia/3	Philadelphia, PA 19105	www.phil.frb.org
Richmond/5	Richmond, VA 23219	www.rich.frb.org
San Francisco/12	San Francisco, CA 94120	www.frbsf.org
St. Louis/8	St. Louis, MO 63166	www.stlouisfed.org

Information about the 12 Federal Reserve Banks in the United States is quick and easy to retrieve through their websites. Some of the banks' websites are linked to each other and in some cases, for example the San Francisco Fed, you can get directly to government economic data such as the BEA (Bureau of Economic Analysis). Each website is organized by subject headings followed by more specific choices. Most of the websites contain similar information pertaining to their geographical area. For instance, news on public announcements, banking, economic data, and education can be found at each site. Other information such as financial services, community affairs, and job opportunities are only found on some of the sites.

While all sites are interesting to visit, we will use examples from the St. Louis Federal Reserve Bank. One of our favorite databases is called FRED II and is maintained by the St. Louis Federal Reserve Bank. FRED stands for Federal Reserve Economic Data and contains historical financial and economic data on the United States. Information such as monthly reserves, interest rates, commercial banking data, gross domestic product (GDP), and regional economic data are available. Visit the website at **www.stls.frb.org**.

The Federal Reserve Bank of St. Louis publishes some of the most comprehensive economic statistics on a weekly and monthly basis. The following titles, which include tables and graphs, can be found on their website under "Publications."

- *U.S. Financial Data* (USFD), one of the St. Louis bank's products, is published weekly and includes data on the monetary base, bank reserves, money supply, a breakdown of time deposits and demand deposits, borrowing from the Federal Reserve banks, and business loans from the large commercial banks. The publication also includes yields and interest rates on a weekly basis on selected short-term and long-term securities.

- *Monetary Trends,* also published monthly by the Federal Reserve Bank of St. Louis, includes charts and tables of monthly data. The information is similar to that found in *U.S. Financial Data* but covers a longer time period. The tables provide compound annual rates of change, while the graphs include the raw data with trend changes over time. Additional data are available on the federal government debt and its composition by type of holder and on the receipts and expenditures of the government for both the National Income Account Budget and the High Employment Budget.

- *International Economic Trends* is published quarterly and is a compilation of data on the G7 countries and countries in the European Union. The information includes typical economic data such as output, inflation, interest rates, gross domestic product, labor markets, government budgets, and more. The St. Louis Fed also publishes an annual edition of *International Economic Trends,* which includes data from 1987 to the present.

- *National Economic Trends* is also published by the Federal Reserve Bank of St. Louis and presents monthly economic data on employment, unemployment rates, consumer and producer prices, industrial production, personal income, retail sales, productivity, compensation and labor costs. It also contains information on GDP, the implicit price deflator for the GDP, personal consumption expenditures, gross private domestic investment, government purchases of goods and services, disposable personal income, corporate profit after taxes, and inventories. This information is presented in graphic form and in tables showing the compounded annual rate of change on a monthly basis. If raw data are needed, other economic publications are required.

Figure 4–1 on page 88 features six graphs taken from the St. Louis Federal Reserve Bank's *National Economic Trends.* These graphs depict a snapshot of the economy showing real GDP (gross domestic product) growth, industrial

FIGURE 4–2 National Economic Trends—Long Term

Interest Rates

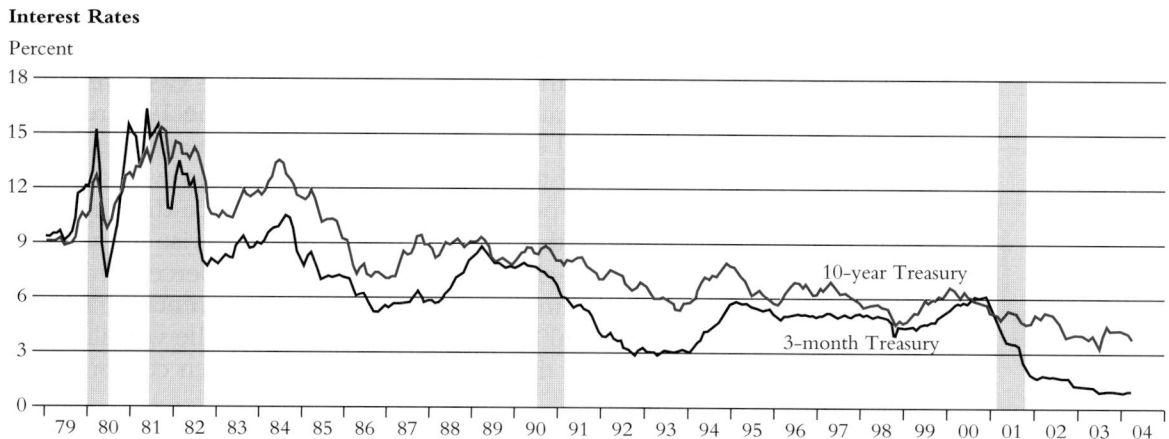

Corporate Profits

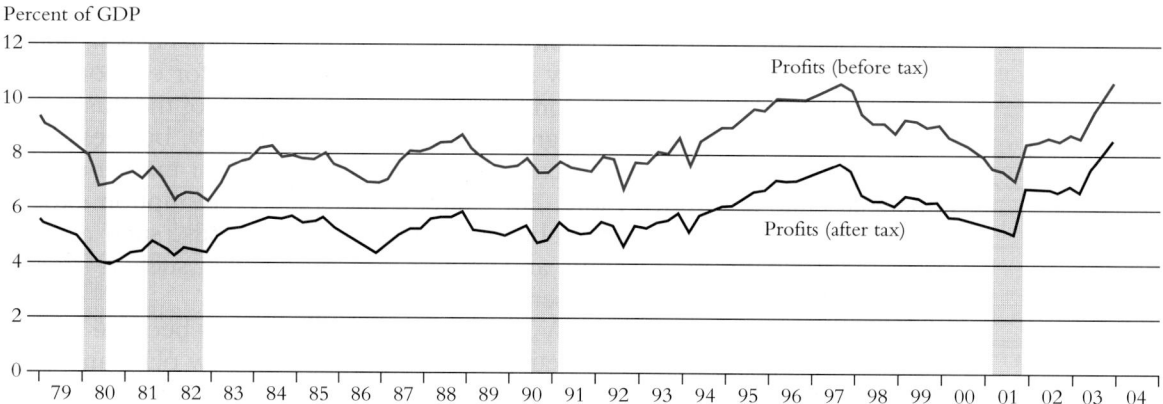

Standard and Poor's 500 Index with Reinvested Dividends

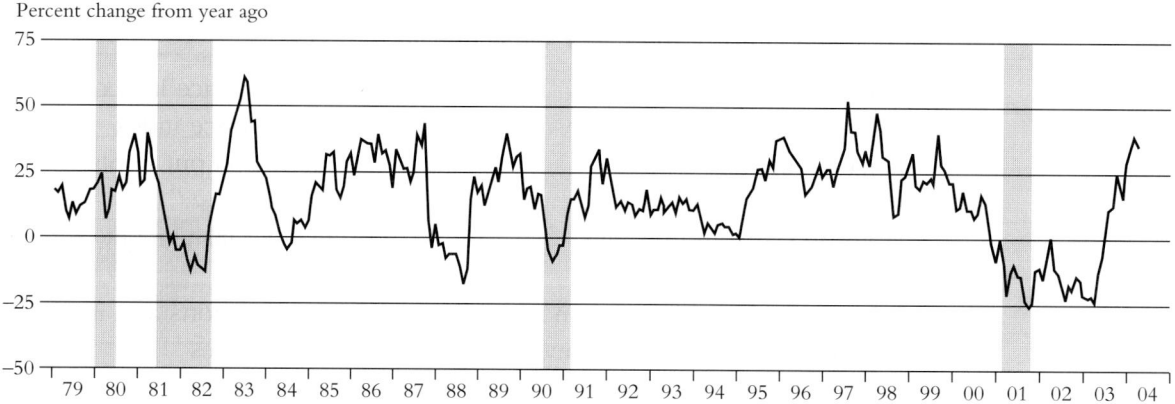

Source: Research Division, Federal Reserve Bank of St. Louis.

are now published by the Conference Board in the fee-based periodical publication, *Business Cycle Indicators*. Graphical presentations of economic time series data such as leading, lagging, and coincident indicators are in *Business Cycle Indicators*. Overall, these kinds of indicators can be very helpful in understanding past economic behavior and in forecasting future economic activity. Some examples of these indicators are graphically presented in Chapter 5.

In addition to the Bureau of Economic Analysis's (BEA) *Survey of Current Business,* there is a lot of data, economic and otherwise, produced by the U.S. government and available online. The BEA is an agency of the U.S. Department of Commerce (**www.commerce.gov**). The U.S. Census Bureau is another prolific aggregator of data. For some guidance in searching through the myriad of government agencies and all the data they produce, you can use the U.S. Government's Official Web portal, Firstgov (**www.firstgov.gov**) or the Government Printing Office website, GPO Access (**www.gpoaccess.gov**) as gateways for searching. And don't forget you can always ask for assistance at your college or local library.

Websites and Economic Data

There are many websites that provide economic data but this section will only highlight two of our favorites. The first is **www.economy.com**. Economy.com provides both free and fee-based economic, financial, country, and industry research. Please note that, like many websites that provide this kind of content, much of the material on **www.economy.com** requires an initial free registration and some requires that you be a paying subscriber. We will briefly discuss a few of Economy.com's products.

The Dismal Scientist (**www.economy.com/dismal**) offers comprehensive and timely analysis and data. The site covers over 180 economic indicators for 40 countries (again, much of this information requires a fee). The Dismal Scientist does provide a free listing of weekly releases of global economic data as well as discussions on the markets and business environment.

Another Economy.com product, Free Lunch (**www.economy.com/freelunch**), provides a free database of economic, industry, financial, and demographic data with more than 1 million time series available. Economy.com provides many other fee-based products, including a number of other databases and publications as well as consulting services.

Another useful economic website is **www.economagic.com**. As it describes itself, economagic.com is "meant to be a comprehensive site of free, easily available economic time series data useful for economic research, in particular economic forecasting." There are currently over 100,000 time series for which data, including charts, can be obtained. Their "Most Frequently Requested Series" page offers quick and easy access to a number of popular economic, market, and demographic data figures, including GDP, population, and the consumer price index. The "Economagic Reporter" feature provides a number of customizable reports. Economagic.com also offers subscription-based services and features, including access to data in Excel format.

Other Sources of Economic Data

So far, we have presented the basic sources of economic data. Many more sources are available. What is available to each investor may vary, so here are some brief notes on other sources of data.

Many universities have bureaus of business research that provide statistical data on a statewide or regional basis. Major banks, such as JP MorganChase, Citicorp, and Bank of America, publish monthly or weekly letters or economic reviews, including raw data and analysis. Several other government sources are available such as *Economic Indicators* prepared by the Council of Economic Advisors and the *Annual Economic Report of the President*. Additionally, many periodicals, such as *Business Week, Fortune,* and *Barron's,* contain raw data as well as economic commentary. Mergent and Standard & Poor's investment services (introduced in the following section) both publish economic data along with other market-related information.

www.gpoaccess.gov/indicators

www.gpoaccess.gov/eop/index.html

Investment Advisory Resources

Investment information and advice is available from many other sources—from corporate financial services to individuals writing investment letters. A look through such financial magazines as *Barron's, Forbes,* and *Financial World* will turn up hundreds of investment services charging fees large and small for the information they sell. Most public libraries and universities subscribe to several major publishers, such as Mergent (Moody's), Standard & Poor's, or Value Line.

Mergent (Moody's)

www.mergent.com

Mergent (Moody's) publishes several databases for bonds and stocks that were formerly called *Moody's Manuals*. These are widely used and present historical financial information on the companies listed, their officers, and the companies' general corporate condition. The *Manuals* are divided into several categories (Banks and Finance, Industrial, Municipals and Government, OTC Industrial, Public Utility, and Transportation). Each manual has a biweekly news supplement that updates quarterly earnings, dividend announcements, mergers, and other news of interest. *Mergent Manuals* are comprehensive, with each category taking up one or two volumes and several thousand pages.

Mergent Bond Record, a monthly publication, contains data on corporate, convertible, government and municipal bonds, and ratings on commercial paper and preferred stock. Corporate bond information includes the interest coupon, payment dates, call price, Moody's rating, and yield to maturity. The current price as well as the yearly and historical high-low prices are presented. The total amount of the bond issue outstanding is given with a designation for a sinking fund and the original issue date. Data on convertible bonds also include the conversion price, conversion value, and conversion period. Information on industrial revenue and municipal bonds is usually limited to the Moody's rating. *Mergent Bond Record* also contains historical yield graphs for various types of bonds over at least 30 years.

Mergent also publishes a weekly *Bond Survey* that reviews the week's activity in the bond market, rating changes, new issues, and bonds called for redemption. *Mergent Dividend Record* presents quarterly dividends and the date of declaration, date of record, date payable, and ex-dividend dates. This is an annual publication. *Mergent Handbook of Common Stock* is a quarterly reference guide that summarizes a company's 10-year historical financial data along with a discussion of corporate background, recent developments, and prospects. Approximately 1,000 companies are listed in the *Handbook*.

Only a brief description has been given for each Moody's publication, but enough has been presented for you to know whether a particular one may be worth looking at further.

Standard & Poor's

Another major source of investor information is Standard & Poor's Corporation, a subsidiary of McGraw-Hill. Standard & Poor's has very comprehensive coverage of company, industry, and market financial data. Not all of Standard & Poor's products will be discussed in this chapter, but we will highlight some of their notable publications and services. Nor will all Standard & Poor's products necessarily be available at a university library, due to the high cost associated with this kind of proprietary data and analysis. Often however, your public library will have some of these services and data. A listing of all of Standard & Poor's products, as well as free access to some of their data, is available on their website, **www.standardpoor.com**.

Among Standard & Poor's products are their *Corporation Records, Stock Reports, Industry Surveys, Outlook,* and the *Register of Public Companies* and the *Register of Private Companies*. Each is briefly described below.

Corporation Records provide detailed information on over 12,000 publicly held U.S., Canadian, and international companies. They feature full balance sheets and income statements, corporate profiles, subsidiary and division information, SEC reports, and news and press releases. *Stock Reports* provide an in-depth look at a company's market performance and include technical evaluation, insider activity, key stock statistics, analysts' consensus earnings estimates, and peer industry-group comparisons. *Standard & Poor's Industry Surveys* are packaged reports covering broad industry areas and contain ratios, statistics, trends, projections, and comparative company analysis for that industry as well as information on how to analyze companies in that area. The *Standard and Poor's Outlook* is their investment advisory newsletter. The *Registers* provide basic directory information, including executive names and industry classification. The *Register of Private Companies* is one of a small number of reference sources available about private companies and includes revenue estimates when available.

Standard and Poor's also covers corporate bonds and mutual funds with their *Bond Guide* publication and their *Mutual Fund Reports*. Many of the products discussed here are available electronically through their "single-source solution" product called NetAdvantage, a database that is available at many large business libraries. The Compustat, Compustat Global, and Research Insight products provide access to fundamental company and market financial data. Standard & Poor's publications can be useful when beginning research into a particular company or industry because they provide concise, comprehensive snapshot overviews.

The *Stock Guide* is a monthly publication that enables investors to take a preliminary look at the common and preferred stocks of several thousand companies and hundreds of mutual funds. The introduction to the *Stock Guide* presents name changes, new exchange listings, common stock rating changes, and a graph of Standard & Poor's stock price indexes.

The *Bond Guide* has the same format as the *Stock Guide*. A monthly publication in booklet form, it presents data on corporate and convertible bonds. The

Standard & Poor's rating for each bond is presented along with other information such as interest payment dates, maturity date, coupon, high-low annual prices, current price, current yield, yield to maturity and a few other facts for convertible bonds such as conversion ratios, conversion value, and conversion price.

Stock Reports were previously mentioned on page 93. Table 4–1 shows a copy of the print version of a *Standard & Poor's Stock Report* for Johnson & Johnson and provides a good example of what one can expect to find in such reports. Keep in mind that because much of this information is migrating to on-line formats, such as Standard & Poor's NetAdvantage product, the data can often be searched and sorted according to various criteria. For example, it is possible to do an advanced search in the *Stock Reports* section of NetAdvantage for stocks above a certain stock price per share, with a particular buy/sell ranking, within various subindustry groups, or within a range of total return values. Your search could even combine all of those criteria. To develop an appreciation for the myriad of Standard & Poor's publications and the additional functionality that online access to the data might provide, make a visit to your library, inquire about what is available, and do some investment research of your own.

Last, we should point out that McGraw-Hill has made a limited amount of data from NetAdvantage available for students through **www.mhhe.com/edumarketinsight**. These data come with a new edition of this book, and can also be purchased online at the aforementioned website. There are end-of-chapter assignments centered around the data available on this site.

Value Line

Value Line Investment Survey, a publication of Arnold Bernhard & Co., is one of the investment services most widely used by individuals, stockbrokers, and small bank trust departments. The *Value Line Investment Survey* follows 1,700 companies, and each common stock is covered in a one-page summary (see the one for Johnson & Johnson, in Table 4–2 on page 97). Value Line is noted for its comprehensive coverage, which can be seen by comparing Table 4–2 with Table 4–1. Raw financial data are available as well as trendline growth rates, price history patterns in graphic form, quarterly sales, earnings and dividends, and a breakdown of sales and profit margins by line of business. Value Line contains 13 sections divided into several industries each. The first few pages of an industry study are devoted to an overview of the industry, with the company summaries following. Each section is revised on a 13-week cycle.

Value Line has a unique evaluation system that is primarily dependent on historical relationships and regression analysis. From the valuation model, each company is rated 1 through 5, with 1 being the highest positive rating and 5 the lowest. Each company is rated on timeliness and safety. It should be noted that Value Line minimizes human judgment in making its evaluation.

Value Line publishes other products, including *Value Line Options,* which features put and call options and *Value Line Convertibles,* which features convertible bonds, convertible preferred stocks, and warrants. Value Line also offers some individual investor services in such areas as mutual funds and special situations.

Chapter 4 Sources of Investment Information   95

TABLE 4–1 Standard & Poor's Stock Reports

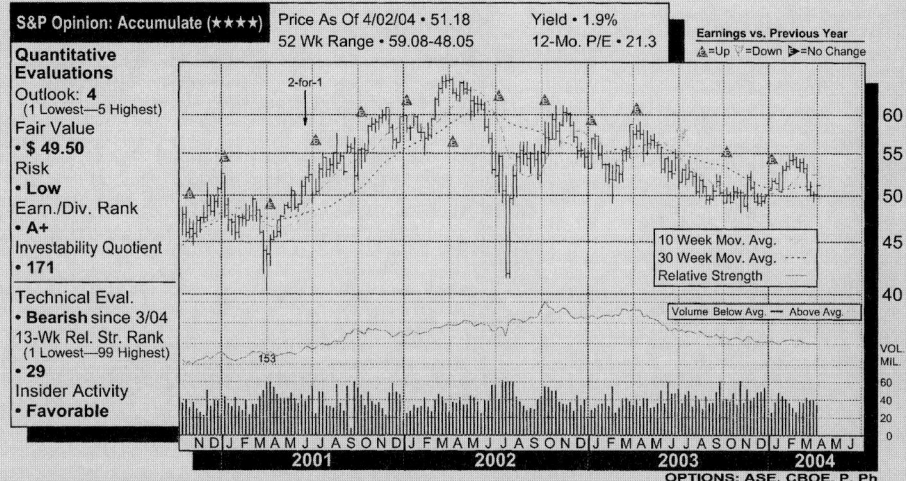

Overview - 29-MAR-04

We project 2004 revenue growth of nearly 11%, to $46.4 billion, including an expected 2% to 3% contribution from favorable foreign currency movements. Broken down by business segment, we are looking for an approximate 7% advance in the pharmaceutical segment, 16% to 17% growth in medical devices and diagnostics, and an 11% increase in sales of consumer products. In our view, the key risk elements to our revenue forecasts revolve around weakening sales of the Procrit/Eprex drugs, a possible loss of sales exclusivity on the Duragesic drug, and possible share inroads in drug-coated coronary stents by rival Boston Scientific (BSX: accumulate, $42). We project gross margins at 71.3%, and see R&D costs equal to 11.5% of sales, and SG&A expenses at 33.7% of sales. We project 2004 free cash flow of $8.9 billion. Our 2004 operating EPS estimate is $2.96, and our 2005 forecast is $3.27. For 2004, our Standard & Poor's Core Earnings estimate is $3.01 a share, as results should be aided by the reversal of prior year expenses associated with the company's pension plans.

Valuation - 29-MAR-04

We believe JNJ will continue to face a slowdown in sales of Procrit/Eprex in 2004, but anticipate that growth in medical devices and rising sales of Remicade, Risperdal and Levaquin will allow for currency-neutral revenue growth above the average of major pharmaceutical companies. We are not modeling significant gross or operating margin expansion in 2004, but JNJ believes it can reduce operating costs by $1.0 billion by the end of 2005, helping to sustain double digit earnings growth. The shares recently traded at a discount to the S&P 500 and our medical device group, and about in line with our pharmaceutical coverage universe, based on projected 2004 EPS. We believe the stock deserves a premium relative to the pharmaceutical group, reflecting what we view as a superior drug research pipeline and the company's exposure to the dynamic medical device segment. Based on a blend of DCF and relative valuation analyses, we have a 12-month target price of $57.

Key Stock Statistics

S&P EPS Oper. Est. '04	2.96	Tang. Bk. Value/Share	5.17
P/E on S&P Oper. Est. '04	17.3	Beta	0.26
S&P EPS Oper. Est. '05	3.27	Shareholders	187,708
Dividend Rate/Share	0.96	Market cap. (B)	$151.9
Shs. outstg. (M)	2967.8	Inst. holdings	61%
Avg. daily vol. (M)	7.557		

Value of $10,000 invested five years ago: $ 11,650

Fiscal Year Ending Dec. 31

	2003	2002	2001	2000	1999	1998
Revenues (Million $)						
1Q	9,821	8,743	7,791	7,319	6,638	5,783
2Q	10,332	9,073	8,342	7,508	6,854	5,783
3Q	10,455	9,079	8,238	7,204	6,749	5,724
4Q	11,254	9,403	8,403	7,108	6,877	6,367
Yr.	41,862	36,298	33,004	29,139	27,471	23,657
Earnings Per Share ($)						
1Q	0.69	0.59	0.53	0.47	0.41	0.36
2Q	0.40	0.54	0.48	0.47	0.42	0.37
3Q	0.69	0.57	0.49	0.45	0.40	0.35
4Q	0.62	0.46	0.36	0.32	0.27	0.03
Yr.	2.40	2.16	1.84	1.70	1.47	1.11

Next earnings report expected: mid April

Dividend Data (Dividends have been paid since 1944.)

Amount ($)	Date Decl.	Ex-Div. Date	Stock of Record	Payment Date
0.240	Apr. 24	May. 16	May. 20	Jun. 10 '03
0.240	Jul. 22	Aug. 15	Aug. 19	Sep. 09 '03
0.240	Oct. 16	Nov. 14	Nov. 18	Dec. 09 '03
0.240	Jan. 05	Feb. 12	Feb. 17	Mar. 09 '04

For important regulatory information, go to www.standardandpoors.com, "Regulatory Disclosures."

All of the views expressed in this research report accurately reflect the research analyst's personal views regarding any and all of the subject securities or issuers. No part of analyst compensation was, is, or will be, directly or indirectly, related to the specific recommendations or views expressed in this research report.

This report is for information purposes and should not be considered a solicitation to buy or sell any security. Neither S&P nor any other party guarantees its accuracy or makes warranties regarding results from its usage. Redistribution is prohibited without written permission. Copyright © 2004

(continued)

TABLE 4-1 Standard & Poor's Stock Reports *(concluded)*

STANDARD & POOR'S STOCK REPORTS

Johnson & Johnson

03-APR-04

Business Summary - 29-MAR-04

Well known for household names like Tylenol and Band-Aid adhesive bandages, Johnson & Johnson ranks among the world's largest and most diversified health care companies. JNJ traces its roots to James Johnson and Edward Mead Johnson, who formed the company more than 110 years ago. JNJ currently offers a broad list of prescription drugs, medical devices and health-related consumer products.

The pharmaceutical segment (47% of 2003 sales) focuses on the antifungal, anti-infective, cardiovascular, contraceptive, dermatology, gastrointestinal, hematology, immunology, neurology, oncology, pain management, central nervous system, and urology fields. The pharmaceutical division was enlarged in recent years through the acquisitions of ALZA, a leading drug delivery concern; and Centocor, a leading biotechnology company. In 2003, the company had seven products that each generated over $1 billion of sales, including Procrit/Eprex ($4.0 billion), Risperdal ($2.5 billion), Remicade ($1.7 billion), Duragesic ($1.6 billion), hormonal contraceptives ($1.2 billion), Levaquin/Floxin ($1.1 billion) and Topamax ($1.0 billion).

In April 2003, JNJ acquired Scios Inc., a biopharmaceutical company with a commercialized product for cardiovascular disease and research projects focused on autoimmune diseases, for net cash of $2.4 billion. In June 2003, the company entered into an agreement with Millenium Pharmaceuticals Inc. under which JNJ would have rights to sell Velcade, an FDA-approved protease inhibitor to treat multiple myeloma, in markets outside the U.S. if the compound gains regulatory approval in those markets.

The medical devices and diagnostics segment (35%) sells a wide range of products used by physicians, nurses, therapists, hospitals, diagnostic labs and clinics. These include Ethicon's wound care, surgical sports medicine and women's healthcare products; Cordis's circulatory disease management products; Lifescan's blood glucose monitoring products; Ortho-Clinical Diagnostic's professional diagnostic products; Depuy's orthopaedic joint reconstruction and spinal products; and Vistakon's disposable contact lenses.

In April 2003, JNJ received FDA approval to market the Cypher Sirolimus-eluting coronary stent, making it the first U.S. approved drug coated stent intended to help reduce restenosis, or the reblockage of a treated coronary artery. Shipments of the product began in the 2003 second quarter. The company believes that more than 350,000 U.S. patients received the device through the end of 2003.

The consumer segment (18%) primarily sells personal care products, including nonprescription drugs, adult skin and hair care products, baby care products, oral care products, first aid products, women's health products and nutritional products. Major brands include Band-Aid Brand Adhesive Bandages, Imodium A-D anti-diarrheal, Johnson's Baby line of products; Neutrogena skin and hair care products, and Tylenol pain reliever.

The company spent $4.7 billion (11.2% of sales) on R&D in 2003, up from $4.0 billion (10.9%) in 2002.

Per Share Data ($) (Year Ended Dec. 31)	2003	2002	2001	2000	1999	1998	1997	1996	1995	1994
Tangible Bk. Val.	5.17	4.53	4.97	4.15	3.11	2.38	3.38	2.90	2.35	1.84
Cash Flow	3.01	2.67	2.35	2.23	1.98	1.57	1.59	1.47	1.26	1.06
Earnings	2.40	2.16	1.84	1.70	1.47	1.11	1.21	1.08	0.93	0.78
S&P Core Earnings	2.31	1.99	1.66	NA	NA	NA	NA	NA	NA	NA
Dividends	0.93	0.80	0.70	0.62	0.55	0.49	0.43	0.37	0.32	0.28
Payout Ratio	39%	37%	38%	36%	37%	43%	35%	34%	34%	36%
Prices - High	59.08	65.89	60.97	52.96	53.43	44.87	33.65	27.00	23.09	14.12
- Low	48.05	41.40	40.25	33.06	38.50	31.68	24.31	20.78	13.40	9.00
P/E Ratio - High	25	31	33	31	36	40	28	25	25	18
- Low	20	19	22	19	26	28	20	19	14	12
Income Statement Analysis (Million $)										
Revs.	41,862	36,298	33,004	29,139	27,471	23,657	22,629	21,620	18,842	15,734
Oper. Inc.	12,740	11,340	9,490	7,992	7,370	6,291	5,689	5,312	6,002	3,531
Depr.	1,869	1,662	1,605	1,515	1,444	1,246	1,067	1,009	857	724
Int. Exp.	207	160	153	146	197	110	120	180	213	186
Pretax Inc.	10,308	9,291	7,898	6,622	5,753	4,269	4,576	4,033	3,317	2,681
Eff. Tax Rate	30.2%	29.0%	28.2%	27.5%	27.6%	28.3%	27.8%	28.4%	27.6%	25.2%
Net Inc.	7,197	6,597	5,668	4,800	4,167	3,059	3,303	2,887	2,403	2,006
S&P Core Earnings	6,927	6,052	5,090	NA	NA	NA	NA	NA	NA	NA
Balance Sheet & Other Fin. Data (Million $)										
Cash	9,523	7,596	8,941	6,013	4,320	2,994	2,753	2,136	1,364	704
Curr. Assets	22,995	19,266	18,473	15,450	13,200	11,132	10,563	9,370	7,938	6,680
Total Assets	48,263	40,556	38,488	31,321	29,163	26,211	21,453	20,010	17,873	15,668
Curr. Liab.	13,448	11,449	8,044	7,140	7,454	8,162	5,283	5,184	4,388	4,266
LT Debt	2,955	2,022	2,217	2,037	2,450	1,269	1,126	1,410	2,107	2,199
Common Equity	26,869	22,697	24,233	18,808	16,213	13,590	12,359	10,836	9,045	7,122
Total Cap.	30,604	25,362	26,943	21,100	18,950	15,437	13,660	12,416	11,308	9,451
Cap. Exp.	2,262	2,099	1,731	1,646	1,728	1,460	1,391	1,373	1,256	937
Cash Flow	9,066	8,259	7,273	6,315	5,611	4,305	4,370	3,896	3,260	2,730
Curr. Ratio	1.7	1.7	2.3	2.2	1.8	1.4	2.0	1.8	1.8	1.6
% LT Debt of Cap.	9.7	8.0	8.2	9.7	12.9	8.2	8.2	11.4	18.6	23.3
% Net Inc.of Revs.	17.2	18.2	17.2	16.5	15.2	12.9	14.6	13.3	12.8	12.7
% Ret. on Assets	16.2	16.7	15.6	15.9	14.8	12.8	15.9	15.2	14.3	14.4
% Ret. on Equity	29.0	28.1	25.4	27.4	27.5	23.6	28.5	29.0	29.7	31.6

Data as orig reptd.; bef. results of disc opers/spec. items. Per share data adj. for stk. divs. Bold denotes primary EPS - prior periods restated. E-Estimated. NA-Not Available. NM-Not Meaningful. NR-Not Ranked. UR-Under Review.

Office—One Johnson & Johnson Plaza, New Brunswick, NJ 08933. **Tel**—(732) 524-0400. **Website**—http://www.jnj.com **Chrmn & CEO**—W. C. Weldon. **Vice Chrmn & CFO**—R. J. Darretta. **Secy**—M. H. Ullmann. **Treas**—J. A. Papa. **Investor Contact**—Helen E. Short (800-950-5089). **Dirs**—G. N. Burrow, J. G. Cullen, R. J. Darretta, M. J. Folkman, A. D. Jordan, A. G. Langbo, S. L. Lindquist, L. F. Mullin, S. S. Reinemund, D. Satcher, H. B. Schacht, W. C. Weldon. **Transfer Agent & Registrar**—EquiServe Trust Co., Providence, RI. **Incorporated**—in New Jersey in 1887. **Empl**— 110,600. **S&P Analyst:** Robert M. Gold/PMW/BK

TABLE 4–2 Value Line Investment Survey

Morningstar

Morningstar offers products for everyone from investors to finance professionals. Some of their products include *Morningstar Mutual Funds, Morningstar No-Load Funds, Morningstar Investor, Morningstar Mutual Fund 500, Morningstar Variable Annuity/Life,* and *Performance Reports.* These publications, available in print and online, provide historical data on fund performance, expense information, asset allocation and breakdown, and a five-star ranking system (in which five stars is the highest ranking and one star the lowest).

Best known for their mutual fund coverage, Morningstar also covers other areas including stocks and exchange traded funds (ETFs) and has expanded to cover global markets. Morningstar also produces software products for financial users, such as *Morningstar Ascent,* a product for the individual investor who wants to create customized portfolios, and *Morningstar Principia* and *Principia-Plus,* which are designed specifically for the investment professional who wants to develop a complex portfolio system to track mutual funds, close-end funds, and variable annuities.

Visit Morningstar online at **www.morningstar.com** to examine their product offerings more fully and to look up stock quotes, mutual fund information, and other daily market happenings.

Other Investment Resources

Business ratios can provide you with some good data for comparison when analyzing a company against its industry peers. Dun & Bradstreet publishes a print volume called *Key Business Ratios.* This publication contains 14 significant ratios on 800 different lines of business listed by SIC code. Examples of ratios featured in *Key Business Ratios* are current assets to current debt, net profits on net sales, and total debt to tangible net worth.

Another good source of ratios is *RMA Annual Statement Studies,* published by Robert Morris Associates. Over 150 industry classifications are covered, comparing balance sheet and income statement data from companies of varying sizes.

Dun & Bradstreet also publishes the *Million Dollar Directory;* both print and online versions of this product exist. The print volumes list companies by name, location, and industry classification. The online version offers additional search and export capabilities. Both the print and online versions provide key directory information for public as well as private companies, including addresses, sales, and executives' names. This is a useful resource for identifying companies within the same industry or for generating contact lists.

Thomson Financial, a division of the Thomson Corporation, is another major producer of investment research resources, including their Thomson Research product which includes current and historical financials and filings and analyst reports for over 30,000 companies worldwide (much of this material was formerly referred to through the product name *Disclosure*). Another powerful product is their SDC Platinum database of merger and acquisition activity. Thomson's IRChannel is a product that includes access to First Call earnings estimates and offers buying and selling activity tracking capabilities, among other features.

Another source of investment information is through retail stockbrokers and analyst houses; these kinds of researchers and firms have long provided this information to their clients. The more the client can afford to pay and the bigger the account, generally the more research results they receive. Large brokers, like Merrill Lynch, Smith Barney, UBS, Prudential Securities, and so on, often provide their clients with industry and company analyses, bond market analysis, futures and commodities information, options advice, tax shelters in oil and gas and real estate, and so on. Today the brokerage industry provides ever more sophisticated and expanded information on investments, going beyond just the typical stock and bond coverage. This is due, in part, to a combination of the growing access to information available online and the increasing savvy of investors in finding this information, as well as the increasing numbers and complexity of alternative investments.

While not all investment research products and tools can be found in every library, it is important not to dismiss and/or overlook what you might be able to find in even a small library's business reference collection. You may not have access to all the proprietary and packaged information that retail stockbrokers may have at their fingertips, but take the time to ask a business librarian for assistance and you could be pointed towards a number of the resources discussed in this section and others.

SEC Filings, Periodicals, and Journals

Securities and Exchange Commission Filings

As discussed in Chapter 2, the Securities and Exchange Commission was established by the Securities Exchange Act of 1934 and has the power to regulate trading on the exchanges and to require corporate disclosure of information relevant to the stockholders of publicly traded companies. The SEC even has the power to dictate accounting conventions.

Information available through the SEC consists primarily of corporate income statements, balance sheets, detailed support of accounting information, and internal data not always found in a company's annual report. Public companies are required to file specific reports with the SEC. The annual 10–K report is perhaps the most widely known and can usually be obtained free directly from the company or from its website, rather than paying the SEC a copying charge. This report should be read in combination with the firm's annual report as it contains the same type of information but in greater detail. The 8–K report must be filed when the corporation undergoes some important event that stockholders would be interested in knowing about, such as changes in control, bankruptcy, resignation of officers or directors, and other material events. 10–Q statements are filed quarterly, no later than 45 days after the end of the quarter. This report includes quarterly financial statements, changes in stockholdings, legal proceedings, and other matters.

There are many other SEC reports. The most common are proxy statements that disclose information relevant to stockholders' votes; a prospectus, which must be issued whenever a new offering of securities is made to the public; and a registration trading statement, which is normally required for new issues by firms trading on an organized exchange or over-the-counter.

Corporate SEC filings can be found online through a number of portals. You can search for them through the Securities and Exchange Commission's website at **www.sec.gov** where you will find a section on "Filings & Forms (EDGAR)." The SEC's website provides information on numerous investor issues, including regulations, special studies, and any securities-related litigation. Access to descriptions of filing contents, blank forms, some historical filings, and an EDGAR tutorial is provided as well. EDGAR is the name of the SEC filings database and is an acronym for electronic data gathering, analysis, and retrieval.

In addition to websites like **www.10kwizard.com** and **www.freeedgar.com** and many finance portal sites like MSN/Money, Yahoo! Finance, and so on (which will be discussed later in the chapter), many company websites include links to their SEC filings as well as to their annual reports and any other relevant documentation, which is usually found under the heading of "Investor Relations."

Periodicals and Newspapers

Several of the most popular business periodicals are *Fortune, BusinessWeek, Forbes,* and *Financial World. Fortune* is published biweekly and is known for its coverage of industry problems and specific company analysis. *Fortune* has several regular features that make interesting reading. One, "Business Roundup," usually deals with a major business concern such as the federal budget, inflation, or productivity. Another feature, "Personal Investing," is always a thought-provoking article presenting ideas and analysis for the average investor.

Forbes is also a biweekly publication featuring several company-management interviews. This management-oriented approach points out various management styles and provides a look into the qualitative factors of security analysis. Several regular columnists discuss investment topics from a diversified perspective. *BusinessWeek* is somewhat more general than *Forbes*. It includes a weekly economic update on such economic variables as interest rates, electricity consumption, and market prices while also featuring articles on industries and companies. Many other periodicals, such as *Money,* are helpful to the financial manager or personal investor.

Newspapers in most major cities (Chicago, Dallas, and Cleveland, to name a few) have good financial sections. *The New York Times* has an exceptional financial page. However, the most widely circulated financial daily is *The Wall Street Journal,* published by Dow Jones & Company. It is read by millions of investors who want to keep up with the economy and business environment. Feature articles on labor, business, economics, personal investing, technology, and taxes appear regularly. Corporate announcements of all kinds are published. Also, the "Digest of Earnings Reports," is a daily feature that updates quarterly and annual earnings of firms.

New offerings of stocks and bonds are also advertised by investment bankers in *The Wall Street Journal*. Prices of actively traded securities are presented by the market in which they trade. Common and preferred stock prices are organized by exchange and over-the-counter markets. Table 4–3 is an example of common stock prices on the New York Stock Exchange.

Many other prices are printed in *The Wall Street Journal*. An investor will find prices of government Treasury bills, notes, and bonds; government agency securities; prices of mutual funds; put and call prices from the option exchanges; foreign market quotes and foreign exchange prices; and commodities futures prices. Table 4–4 on page 102 is an example of the commodity futures prices from *The Wall Street Journal*. The prices are listed by category and exchange. Because of the comprehensive price coverage on a daily basis and other features, it is hard to believe that an up-to-date intelligent investor would be able

TABLE 4-3 New York Stock Exchange Composite Transactions (Common stock prices)

Source: The Wall Street Journal, April 1, 2004. Reprinted by permission of The Wall Street Journal, © 2004 by Dow Jones & Company. All Rights Reserved Worldwide.

TABLE 4–4 Commodity Futures Prices

Source: The Wall Street Journal, April 1, 2004. Reprinted by permission of The Wall Street Journal, © 2004 by Dow Jones & Company. All Rights Reserved Worldwide.

TABLE 4–5 Barron's Table of Contents for Its "Market Week" Section

THE WEEK'S STATISTICS

THE MARKETS		THE INDICATORS		THE INDEXES	
American Stock Exchange	22	Adjustable Mortgage Base Rates	37	American Stock Exchange	32
Bonds	28	Advance/Decline	31	Arms Index	32
Closed-End Funds	F18	American Debt and Deficits	38	Bank New York ADR Indexes	32
Distributions & Offerings	35	Analysts' Meetings	39	Bond Buyers Muni Bond Index	36
Emerging Markets	34	Block Transaction Summary	32	CBOE Put/Call Ratio	35
Equity Financing	35	Bond Statistics, Rating Changes	36	Cambridge Associates Indexes	32
Exchange Traded Portfolios	21	Box Score	36	Dow Jones Averages	31
Foreign Exchange	27	Conference Call Calendar	35	Dow Jones Corporate Bond	36
Foreign Markets	26	Dividend Payment Dates	39	Dow Jones Specialty Indexes	32
Futures, Commodities & Financials	30	DJ U.S. Total Market Groups	33	Dow Jones U.S. Total Market	32
Global Stock Markets	26	Federal Reserve Statistics	37	Emerging Markets Bond Index	36
Guaranteed Investment Contracts	36	Gold & Silver Prices	37	Gold Mining Index	37
Hedge Fund Monthly	F4	Initial Public Offerings	35	Key Foreign Market Indexes	26
Hedge Fund Benchmark	F11	Investor Sentiment Readings	37	Lehman Bros T-Bond Index	36
Junk Bonds	36	Lipper Mutual Fund Averages	F19	Lehman Bros U.S. Credit Index	36
Late-Trading Snapshot	17	Money Fund Report	37	Lipper Mutual Fund Indexes	F19
Money Fund Top Yields	F8	Money Supply	37	Morgan Stanley Indexes	32
Money Rates, U.S. & Foreign	37	Multex Investment Ratings	T15	Nasdaq	32
Mortgage-Related Securities	37	New Corporate Listings	39	New York Stock Exchange	32
Mutual Funds	F10	New Highs & Lows	34	Overseas Government Bond	36
Nasdaq National Market	T6	NYSE Members Reports	21	P/Es & Yields	34
Nasdaq Small Cap Issues	T14	NYSE Odd-Lot Trading	21	Russell Indexes	32
N.Y. Stock Exchange	15	NYSE Program Trading	33	Standard & Poor's	32
Preferred Stock Listings	23	Pulse of the Economy	38	Value Line	32
Short Interest NASDAQ	24	Savings Deposit Yields	37	Value Line Convertible	36
Traders' Commitments	29	SEC Form 144 Filings	33	Wilshire Total Market Value	32
U.S. Regional Markets	27	Stock/Bond Yield Gap	36	Barron's Confidence Index	36
CHARTING THE MARKET	8	Stock Volume	32	Consensus Estimates Dow Indus	32
MARKET LAB	31	Trading Diary	31	Dow Jones Per Share Values	34
WINNERS & LOSERS/STOCKS	6	Week In Stocks	31		

Statistics: 609-520-4799
To subscribe, call 800-321-2871

Source: *Barron's*, March 1, 2004. Reprinted by permission of *Barron's*, © 2004 by Dow Jones & Company. All Rights Reserved Worldwide.

to function without *The Wall Street Journal*. Each fall, *The Wall Street Journal* publishes an educational edition that explains how to read *The Wall Street Journal* and interpret some of the data presented. There is also an online tutorial available at: **info.wsj.com/college/guidedtour**.

Barron's Business and Financial Weekly, published by Dow Jones every weekend, contains regular features on dividends, put and call options, international stock markets, commodities, a review of the stock market, and many pages of prices and financial statistics. *Barron's* takes a weekly perspective and summarizes the previous week's market behavior. It also has regular analyses of several companies in its section called "Investment News and Views."

Perhaps the best way to show the depth of information available in *Barron's* is to present a table of contents for the "Market Week" section. This is illustrated in Table 4–5 above. One unique feature of *Barron's* is the "Market Laboratory" covering nine pages of each issue. Weekly data on major stock and bond markets are presented with the week's statistics. Table 4–6 on page 104 includes information on price-to-earnings ratios (P/E) and yields of major indexes as well as consensus earnings forecasts for the Dow Jones Industrial companies. Being able to find the market price-to-earnings ratio will come in handy for any valuation work you do in Chapter 7 using relative P/E models.

TABLE 4-6 Market Laboratory—Stocks from *Barron's*

BARRON'S • Market Week
MARKET LABORATORY • STOCKS

BARRON'S 50-STOCK AVERAGE

This 50-stock index is an unweighted average of 50 leading issues with each stock given equal weight in determining the average. It offers comparisons to the projected quarterly and annual earnings which appear in the table. The earnings yield, which is the reciprocal of the Price/Earnings Ratio (1 divided by the P/E), can be compared to bond yields in the table. The dividend yield equals the dividend divided by the price of the average.

	Feb 26 2004	Feb 19 2004	Feb 2003
Average price index	3825	3853	2955
Projected quarterly earn	13.21	16.49	31.24
Annualized projected earn	52.84	65.97	124.95
Annualized projected P/E	72.4	58.4	23.7
Five-year average earn	157.07	157.73	162.33
Five-year average P/E	24.3	24.4	18.2
Year-end earn	141.28	144.56	126.99
Year-end P/E	27.1	26.7	23.3
Year-end earns yield, %	3.7	3.8	4.3
Best grade bond yields, %	5.71	5.70	5.98
Bond yields/stock ylds, %	1.55	1.52	1.39
Actual year-end divs	80.33	80.25	73.18
Actual yr-end divs yld, %	2.10	2.08	2.48

CONSENSUS OPERATING EARNINGS ESTIMATES FOR DOW INDUSTRIALS

Company	2003 EPS¹ 4 Wks Ago	Cur	2003 P/E²	2004 EPS¹ 4 Wks Ago	Cur	2004 P/E²
AT&T	2.35	2.36	8.5	1.38	1.34	15.0
Alcoa	1.16	1.10	33.8	1.84	1.95	19.1
Altria Group	4.60	4.62	12.3	4.88	4.85	11.8
Amer Express	2.30	2.33	22.9	2.64	2.64	20.2
Boeing	.96	1.00	42.4	1.85	1.86	22.8
Caterpillar	3.07	3.13	24.9	4.14	4.44	17.6
Citigroup Inc	3.41	3.42	14.6	3.84	3.85	13.0
Coca Cola	1.93	1.95	25.6	2.10	2.11	23.6
Disney	.66	.80	33.4	.90	.96	27.8
DuPont	1.61	1.66	27.1	2.10	2.15	21.0
Eastman Kodak	2.14	2.32	12.3	2.34	2.32	12.3
Exxon Mobil	2.45	2.56	16.5	2.24	2.34	18.1
Genl Electric	1.55	1.56	20.9	1.57	1.57	20.8
Genl Motors	5.37	5.62	8.5	6.20	6.23	7.7
Hewlett Packard	1.21	1.23	18.9	1.49	1.48	15.7
Home Depot	1.67	1.88	19.6	2.05	2.09	17.6
Honeywell	1.55	1.56	22.4	1.50	1.51	23.1
IBM	4.28	4.34	22.3	4.93	4.93	19.6
Intel Corp	.78	.85	34.7	1.26	1.25	23.6
Intl Paper	.75	.80	55.5	1.64	1.44	30.8
Johns & Johns	2.64	2.65	20.4	2.95	2.95	18.3
McDonald's	1.42	1.43	19.8	1.57	1.60	17.7
Merck	2.92	2.92	16.3	3.13	3.13	15.2
Microsoft	1.03	1.14	23.2	1.21	1.21	21.9
Morgan (J.P)	3.11	3.24	12.5	3.20	3.20	12.7
Proc & Gam	4.30	4.39	23.5	4.81	4.82	21.4
SBC Comm	1.55	1.55	15.6	1.45	1.36	17.7
3M	3.07	3.09	25.3	3.52	3.53	22.1
United Tech	4.66	4.69	19.2	5.22	5.21	17.3
Wal Mart	2.04	2.03	29.3	2.32	2.36	25.2
Median			21.6			18.7
DJ Industrials	522.52	534.96	19.8	594.59	597.63	17.7

¹ Earnings estimates are for calendar years.
² Based on latest earnings estimate.
Source: First Call/Thomson Financial (www.firstcall.com).

INDEXES' P/ES & YIELDS

DJ latest 52-week earnings and dividends adjusted by Dow Divisors at Friday's close. S&P Dec. 4-quarter's earnings as reported and indicated dividends based on Friday close. S&P 500 P/E ratios based on earnings as reported. For additional earnings series, please refer to www.spglobal.com/earnings.html. DJ latest available book values for FY 2002 and 2001, and S&P latest for 2002 and 2001.

	Last Week	Prev. Week	Year Ago Week
DJ Ind Avg	**10583.92**	**10619.03**	**7891.08**
P/E Ratio	20.23	20.33	20.50
Earns Yield %	4.94	4.92	4.88
Earns $	523.25	522.29	384.95
Divs Yield %	2.03	2.02	2.46
Divs $	214.33	214.25	194.08
Mkt to Book	4.63	4.64	3.20
Book Value $	2286.69	2286.69	2463.72
DJ Trans Avg	**2902.19**	**2892.18**	**2049.05**
P/E Ratio	37.95	37.82	Nil
Earns Yield %	2.64	2.64	Nil
Earns $	76.48	76.48	-90.06
Divs Yield %	1.16	1.16	1.45
Divs $	33.62	33.62	29.81
Mkt to Book	2.34	2.33	1.13
Book Value $	1241.65	1241.65	1809.28
DJ Utility Avg	**278.02**	**271.23**	**197.96**
P/E Ratio	24.63	36.51	43.63
Earns Yield %	4.06	2.74	2.29
Earns $	11.29	7.43	4.54
Divs Yield %	3.47	3.56	5.80
Divs $	9.66	9.66	11.48
Mkt to Book	1.96	1.91	1.18
Book Value $	141.77	141.77	167.48
S&P 500 Index	**1144.94**	**1144.11**	**841.15**
P/E Ratio	29.68	29.66	28.00
Earns Yield %	3.37	3.37	3.57
Earns $	38.58	38.58	30.04
Divs Yield %	1.63	1.63	1.93
Divs $	18.66	18.65	16.23
Mkt to Book	3.53	3.53	3.87
Book Value $	324.14	324.14	217.32
S&P Ind Index	**1301.96**	**1303.15**	**966.23**
P/E Ratio	36.89	36.93	37.49
Earns Yield %	2.71	2.71	2.67
Earns $	35.29	35.29	25.77
Divs Yield %	1.37	1.37	1.68
Divs $	17.84	17.85	16.23
Mkt to Book	4.15	4.16	4.72
Book Value $	313.56	313.56	204.54

PER SHARE VALUES OF STOCKS IN THE DOW JONES AVERAGES

This is a list of the Dow Jones trailing 52-week diluted share earnings, dividends and book values as reported by the company.

Industrial Stocks

	Earns	Divs.	Book Value		Earns	Divs.	Book Value
AT&T	2.34	0.85	15.68	Home Depot	1.88	0.26	8.55
Alcoa	1.14	0.60	11.64	Honeywell	1.56	0.75	10.44
Altria Group	4.52	2.64	9.39	IBM	4.32	0.64	13.23
Am Exp	2.31	0.38	10.47	Intel	0.85	0.10	5.24
Boeing	-0.86	0.68	9.15	Int Paper	0.66	1.00	15.32
Caterpillar	3.13	1.44	15.68	Johnson&John	2.40	0.96	7.52
Citigroup	3.42	1.30	16.28	JPMorgChase	3.24	1.36	20.71
Coca Cola	1.77	0.88	4.75	McDonalds	1.18	0.40	8.05
Disney Walt	0.83	0.21	11.57	Merck Co	3.03	1.46	8.10
Du Pont	0.99	1.40	8.88	Microsoft	0.82	0.24	10.50
East Kodak	0.92	1.15	9.68	Proc Gam	4.15	1.775	10.00
ExxonMobil	3.15	1.00	11.04	SBC Commun	1.80	1.41	10.09
Gen Elec	1.55	0.78	6.32	3M Co	3.02	1.35	15.03
GM	7.14	2.00	12.16	Utd Tech	4.69	1.24	17.32
HewlettPack	-0.90	0.32	11.91	Wal-mart	2.07	0.36	8.91

Source: *Barron's*, March 1, 2004. Reprinted by permission of *Barron's*, © 2004 by Dow Jones & Company. All Rights Reserved Worldwide.

Table 4–7 on page 106 includes prices for a list of bond indexes, *Barron's* confidence index, junk bond yields, and more. We have only included samples of two pages from *Barron's* due to space limitations. However, careful reading of *Barron's* will turn up useful data in a compact summary form not found in other weekly publications.

Other major papers are *Investor's Business Daily,* the *Wall Street Transcript* (weekly), and the *Commercial and Financial Chronicle* (weekly). Media General's *Industriscope* is a good source of fundamental and technical indicators for the professional manager.

Journals

Most journals are academic and, because of this, are more theoretical than investor oriented. However, there are exceptions, such as the *Financial Analysts Journal,* which is a publication of the CFA Institute. This journal has both academic and practitioner articles that deal mainly with analytical tools, new laws and regulations, and financial analysis. *The Journal of Portfolio Management* and the *Institutional Investor* are also widely read by the profession. The more scholarly, research-oriented academic journals would include the *Journal of Finance,* the *Journal of Financial Economics,* and the *Journal of Financial and Quantitative Analysis.* These journals include information on the development and testing of theories such as the random walk and efficient market hypothesis, the capital asset pricing model, arbitrage pricing theory, and much empirical research on a variety of financial topics. The *Journal of Financial Education* includes articles on classroom topics and computer applications.

Databases

Many of the resources discussed in this chapter are available in online format. As mentioned earlier this kind of online access can provide you with additional searching and/or data exporting functionality. The use of the term *database* can refer to these sorts of online or CDROM-based resources (for example, some databases will allow you to search through many journals and newspapers at once, while others will allow you to enter specific criteria to find and generate lists of companies). Or *database* can also refer to a resource that provides access to raw data, financial and otherwise, with even greater searching and exporting capabilities. These are the kinds of databases we will be referring to in this part of the chapter.

One database like this is Compustat. Published by Investors Management Science Company, a subsidiary of Standard & Poor's Corporation, Compustat is very comprehensive. Depending on the data package, Compustat contains over 20 years of fundamental annual and quarterly financial and market data for over 50,000 North American and global companies. Compustat data has been standardized to allow for comparisons over time, between industries and between companies, and also includes companies that are no longer active.

This kind of information is useful for analyzing large numbers of companies. Ratios can be created, analyzed, and compared. Trends and regression analysis can be performed. Searches can be implemented for specific kinds of companies. For example, one could screen for companies using the following criteria:

TABLE 4-7 Market Laboratory—Bonds from *Barron's*

BARRON'S • Market Week
MARKET LABORATORY • BONDS

DOW JONES CORPORATE BOND INDEX

Daily	2/23	2/24	2/25	2/26	2/27
Close	178.42	178.59	178.73	178.40	178.86
Change	0.45	0.17	0.14	-0.33	0.46

DJ WEEKLY CORPORATE BOND INDEX

	First	High	Low	Last	Chg.	%
CpBd	178.42	178.86	178.40	178.86	0.89	0.50

DJ CORPORATE BOND INDEX FOR 2004

	First	High	Low	Last	Chg.	%
CpBd	173.86	178.94	173.86	178.86	3.91	2.23

NEW YORK EXCHANGE BOND DIARY

	2/23	2/24	2/25	2/26	2/27
Total	81	92	82	73	77
Advances	35	40	39	24	35
Declines	29	34	31	29	27
Unchanged	17	18	12	20	15
NewHighs	2	5	3	2	4
NewLows	2	1	3	1	0

WEEKLY BARRON'S C.I./YIELD GAP

The weekly Barron's Confidence Index is a ratio of the average yield-to-maturity of the Best-Grade bond list compared to the average yield-to-maturity of the Intermediate Grade bond list. The ratio is higher and the bond yield spread narrower as the confidence index rises when investors are confident about the market. The ratio is lower when the intermediate grade average bond yield is rising faster, or at least, falling more slowly than the best-grade bonds. A falling confidence index reflects decreasing confidence in the market. The weekly yield gap reflects the spread between the Barron's Best Grade Bonds yield-to-maturity and the Dow Jones Industrial Average dividend yield.

Week Ended	Conf. Index	Intrm. Bonds	Best Grade	DJI Yield		Yield Gap
2004						
Feb 20	90.4	6.31	5.70	2.02	−	3.68
13	90.3	6.34	5.73	2.01	−	3.72
6	89.7	6.42	5.76	2.01	−	3.75
Jan 30	90.4	6.42	5.81	2.03	−	3.78
23	90.9	6.24	5.67	2.00	−	3.67
16	91.0	6.25	5.68	1.99	−	3.69
9	91.4	6.43	5.88	2.01	−	3.87
2	90.8	6.49	5.90	2.02	−	3.88
2003						
Dec 26	90.0	6.46	5.81	2.03	−	3.78
19	89.8	6.43	5.78	2.04	−	3.74
12	89.3	6.61	5.90	2.08	−	3.82
5	89.7	6.64	5.95	2.12	−	3.83
Nov 28	88.8	6.63	5.89	2.14	−	3.75
21	88.7	6.60	5.85	2.17	−	3.68
14	89.4	6.66	5.95	2.14	−	3.81

VALUE LINE CONVERTIBLE INDEXES

The Value Line Convertible Price Index is equally weighted, and measures the price performance of 612 convertibles (Bonds, Preferreds and Euro-Converts) followed in Value Line Convertibles. The Value Line Total Return Index includes an income component for issues making timely interest and dividend payments. The Value Line Warrant Index is equally weighted and measures price performance of 120 warrants followed in Value Line Convertibles. 3/1/82 = 100

Prices as of February 19, 2004

	Index Value	% Chg. 1 Week	% Chg. 12 Mo.	Cur. % Yld
Convertibles	194.43	+ 0.8	+ 19.3	3.20
Total Ret. (CVTS)	952.80	+ 0.9	+ 24.6	
Warrants	19674.17	+ 8.0	+ 339.0	

GUARANTEED INVESTMENT CONTRACTS

Week Ending: February 27, 2004

Rates	Three-Year Comp.	Simple	Five-Year Comp.	Simple	Seven-Year Comp.	Simple
$1 Million						
High	2.79	2.73	3.80	3.72	4.40	4.23
Average	2.52	2.50	3.55	3.47	4.10	3.99
Low	1.81	1.81	3.10	3.10	3.68	3.68
# Issuers	11	9	11	9	9	8
$5 Million						
High	2.84	2.82	3.85	3.77	4.40	4.26
Average	2.55	2.53	3.57	3.49	4.12	4.02
Low	1.93	1.93	3.22	3.05	3.80	3.55
# Issuers	17	14	17	14	15	13
$10 Million						
High	2.86	2.83	3.85	3.77	4.40	4.26
Average	2.56	2.54	3.57	3.49	4.14	4.04
Low	1.93	1.93	3.22	3.05	3.80	3.55
# Issuers	18	15	18	15	16	14
$25 Million						
High	2.80	2.76	3.76	3.63	4.40	4.24
Average	2.60	2.56	3.59	3.49	4.16	4.04
Low	2.26	2.25	3.30	3.05	3.83	3.55
# Issuers	11	10	11	10	10	10
Treasuries[1]		2.14		2.97		3.39

Treasuries-GIC/BIC Spreads[2]

$1 Million	0.65	0.59	0.83	0.75	1.01	0.84
$5 Million	0.70	0.68	0.88	0.80	1.01	0.87
$10 Million	0.72	0.69	0.88	0.80	1.01	0.87
$25 Million	0.66	0.62	0.79	0.66	1.01	0.85
Average	0.68	0.65	0.85	0.75	1.01	0.86

[1]Current Treasury quotes, as reported in the Wall Street Journal. Total issuers quoting: 37. [2]Spreads between GIC/BIC high and Treasury with the same maturity. All rates for non benefit responsive, investment only contracts, net of expenses, no commissions.
Source: Fiduciary Capital Management Inc., Woodbury, Conn.

PRICES & YIELDS OF ACTIVE JUNK-BOND ISSUES

Issuer	Cpn.	Maturity	Bid	Ask	Wk. Chg.	%Bid/Yld
Nextel Comm	9.375	11/15/09	108.750	109.250	0.125	3.29
Lyondell Petrochem	9.625	05/01/07	105.000	106.500	0.000	7.80
MGM Grand Inc	9.75	06/01/07	115.000	115.750	- 0.250	4.71
Charter Comm Hlds	8.625	04/01/09	82.500	86.250	- 1.000	13.49
HMH Properties Inc	7.875	08/01/08	103.000	104.000	- 0.500	6.51
Level 3 Comm	9.125	05/01/08	81.500	83.000	- 4.500	15.28
Six Flags Inc	9.625	06/01/14	105.000	106.000	- 0.250	8.76
Panamsat Corp	8.5	02/01/12	104.750	105.750	- 2.500	7.49

Source: Lehman Brothers

Source: *Barron's,* March 1, 2004. Reprinted by permission of *Barron's,* © 2004 by Dow Jones & Company. All Rights Reserved Worldwide.

1. Dividend yield greater than 4 percent.
2. Earnings growth greater than 15 percent per year.
3. Price-earnings ratio less than the Standard & Poor's 500 Stock Index.
4. Market price less than book value.

Other companies produce similar products to Compustat. For example, Interactive Data Corporation offers a product called FT Interactive that tracks equivalent kinds of financial data as Compustat. Another product is the CRSP database, created and maintained by the University of Chicago's Center for Research in Security Prices. CRSP data is oriented to earnings, dividends, stock prices, and dates of mergers, stock splits, stock dividends, and so on. They also produce a merged CRSP/Compustat database called CCM. CRSP data is extremely useful for historical research on stock performance (coverage began in 1926). It is widely used in academia for research on the efficient market hypothesis, the capital asset pricing model, and other investment questions.

Another powerful source of financial and market data is Bloomberg's Professional Financial Service. Bloomberg is renowned for its financial instruments and real-time market data access. In addition to data, Bloomberg provides current news and headlines, audio and television reports, and a multitude of proprietary analytical content.

The Internet and Investment Information

The Internet and online tools and resources have been referred to throughout the chapter. A distinction should be made here between information that is accessed *via the Internet* (e.g., using a proprietary online database), versus that which is accessed *on the Internet* (e.g., using a search engine or going to an openly available, free website). A subscription or fee-based online database will often provide you with a more streamlined, packaged form of data that has been selected and verified and processed in a way that will allow you greater functionality than data you may be able to track down on the open Internet. That said, using the open Internet with a critical eye and knowing how to search effectively using search engines and portals can provide you with an abundance of useful information.

As mentioned in the beginning of this chapter, it is imperative to be alert and wary when using data found online. Check your source and look for clues indicating how recent the data are and whether or not they have been adjusted.

Additional Websites

There are thousands of sites that offer finance and investment information and of course we cannot cover them all in this chapter or even in the whole book. In this section, we'll present a few that we use or that our students find interesting. First of all, let's not overlook the stock exchanges and other markets. They all have websites and quite a bit of information is available through them concerning listing requirements, volume, historical data, trading data, stock quotes, regulatory issues, and much more. Take a look at www.cbot.com, www.cboe.com, www.nasdaq.com, www.cme.com, www.nyse.com, www.amex.com and even the international exchanges such as the London Stock Exchange at

www.londonstockexchange.com. The World Federation of Exchanges site offers links to their members' sites and other information at **www.world-exchanges.org**.

Another category of websites is the news media. The networks all have websites that provide business information, stock quotes, breaking stories on mergers and acquisitions, and other economic news that investors find interesting. Take a look at **www.abc.com**, **www.cnbc.com**, **www.foxnews.com**, and **www.cbs.com**. You can also go to your local newspapers such as the *Chicago Tribune* and a more national newspaper such as *The New York Times,* which covers Wall Street. These two papers can be found at **www.chicagotribune.com** and **www.newyorktimes.com**. Besides getting scores for your favorite sports team, you can find out about companies headquartered in your city or companies that have a major economic impact on the region. CNN has a website called CNN Financial, which can be accessed by **www.cnnfn.com**. This website specializes in business news and is also a good source of information on foreign markets. In addition there are financial news organizations such as Bloomberg Financial News, **www.bloomberg.com**, and Reuters, **www.reuters.com**, that have excellent websites.

There are some websites such as **www.yahoo.com** and **www.msn.com** that allow investors to build a portfolio and keep track of their stocks. When you access your portfolio, the prices are always updated. Microsoft's **www.msn.com** has a money section that you can click on to get into stock prices and index performance. If you enter a stock ticker such as SUNW for Sun Microsystems, you will get stock price information, the ability to look at a graph, and a listing of news stories about Sun Microsystems that you can download or print.

It has been mentioned earlier, but we'll mention it here again because it is a source that is often overlooked: When researching a company, don't hesitate to go directly to their website. Most companies have websites, and if you find the investor relations part of the website you will usually have the ability to look at annual reports, quarterly reports, and, in many instances, direct links to the SEC filings for that company. In addition, many investor relations departments maintain the ability for stockholders to access prices on a specific day of the year. If, for example, you don't have the price of a stock on the day it was bought for tax purposes, this feature is very helpful and a time saver. The Coca Cola website, **www.coca-cola.com**, has ratios for the last several years calculated from its financial statements.

Another place to look for information is on the websites of brokers and financial service firms. Most have information available to their customers, and many have information available to the general public. Sometimes it is just good marketing to give away information free. Take a look at the websites for Merrill Lynch, Smith Barney, Prudential, Goldman Sachs, JPMorgan, your regional brokerage firms, and even the discount firms such as Fidelity, **www.fidelity.com**. If you don't know the web addresses, simply go to **www.google.com** and type in the name. Google will usually come up with their website on the first try.

There are other specialized investment research websites. If you are after stock price charts, one good place to look is www.bigcharts.com. This website allows a look at stock prices over many different time periods such as one day, daily prices over many months, and monthly prices over many years. You can also compare company prices to indices like the S&P 500. Many of the other general financial sites like Yahoo! Finance, and others, also offer some charting capabilities.

Other useful sites to check out are those from university business libraries or schools and other academic sources. Many business-related academic departments run special centers for research into various areas like real estate, financial economics, and so on. Check out sources like Harvard's Baker Library site at: **www.library.hbs.edu** for access to some research guides and other useful material. Much of the material found on sites like this may be restricted to current students and faculty of each institution, but you can often find good pointers to resources and/or websites that you may otherwise miss.

Another thing to watch out for when searching the open Internet (and even when dealing with the online interface of proprietary databases) is that the look and feel of a site can change without warning. Contents can be reorganized so that you have to dig around to find the same material you just found easily last week. Some content may become available to subscribers only or suddenly require a free registration. Your best bet is to become familiar with some of the databases discussed here as well as others that are out there and find which work best for you. Much of the content available through websites overlaps and you will find that you prefer one source over another to get the same type of information. Make sure to leverage whatever access you have to libraries and the content available through them.

Class Project Websites

Table 4–8 is a listing of websites that may be particularly helpful for class projects. As an example, the authors frequently send their students to

TABLE 4–8 Class Project Websites

Website	Comment
moneycentral.msn.com/investor	Information on investing, news, and financial data
money.cnn.com	Current information about markets and companies
www.bloomberg.com	Market news and data
www.freerealtime.com	News, information, and real-time quotes
finance.yahoo.com	Information about investing, companies, and markets
www.thestreet.com	Information and opinion about markets and companies
www.business.com	Business-specific search engine and business information
www.businessweek.com	News and business information—requires fee
www.wsj.com	*The Wall Street Journal* online—requires fee
www.financialtimes.com	*Financial Times* online—most articles require fee
www.forbes.com	*Forbes* online—some information requires fee
www.stocksandnews.com	News and commentary on stocks and markets
www.moneychimp.com	Stock analysis and educational information
www.economy.com	Various forms of economic information
www.stls.frb.org	St. Louis Federal Reserve Bank site—includes FRED (Federal Reserve Economic Data) with historical financial and economic data on the United States
www.sec.gov	Company filings and other securities information
www.bigcharts.com	Create stock price charts
www.financewise.com	Finance-only search engine
www.economagic.com	Directory site of economic data collections
www.investorlinks.com	Directory site of finance-related websites

finance.yahoo.com as a starting point for research on an individual stock. If you do not know the company's stock symbol, click on "Symbol Lookup" at the top of the home page.

After using this source, the student may wish to go to the company's website (such as **www.pfizer.com**), which includes extensive company information and normally recent annual reports (under the "Investor Relations" link).

Summary

Information is easy and yet difficult to find. The problem beginners have is knowing where to look and what to look for, and this chapter has attempted to provide some guidance and sample data. The problem advanced investors have is knowing what information is usable. This may also haunt beginners once they find the sources. To become proficient in finding data, spend a day in your library looking through the volumes. Also, determine what software packages are available for your personal computer. This process will increase your awareness of the types of information available.

S&P Problems

www.mhhe.com/edumarketinsight

STANDARD & POOR'S

1. Log on to the McGraw-Hill website: **www.mhhe.com/edumarketinsight** (see page vi in the preface for instructions).
2. Click on Company, which is the first box below the Market Insight title.
3. In this chapter, we just want to familiarize you with the feature of Market Insight so that you are prepared for the problems in the following chapters. We will continue to use Johnson & Johnson as our example.
4. Notice that across the top line you can choose Company, Industry, Commentary, and Home, and down the left margin you can choose from a selection of Compustat Reports, S&P Stock Reports, Excel Analytics, Recent News, and more.
5. Type Johnson & Johnson's ticker symbol JNJ in the box, and click on Company Profile in the left margin, then "Financial Hlts." (Financial Highlights) and finally "Long Bus. Desc." (Long Business Description).
6. Next click on S&P Stock Reports to open the list, and click through the list to see the information available. What is the S&P recommendation on Johnson & Johnson, and how does this compare with the Wall Street Consensus?
7. Next click on EDGAR to open the list of reports filed with the SEC. Notice that these reports cover annual filings, quarterly filings, current filings, tenders and acquisitions, proxy statements, prospectuses, registrations, and other filings. Choose an annual 10K statement, open it up, and examine the information available.
8. Next click on Excel Analytics to open the list of reports available. Notice that there are reports for annual and quarterly income statements, balance sheets, statements of cash flow, and ratios. There are also a market price data on a monthly basis and valuation spreadsheets. Please select one report from each file to see what information is available.

9. Now return to the top and click on "Industry." Under industry there is a drop-down menu where you can select an industry. Click on the arrow to open the industry list. Scroll down the industry list to "Pharmaceuticals" and click on go. You will find a list of industry reports listed in the left margin. Scroll down to S&P Industry Surveys, and click on Healthcare: Pharmaceuticals with the Adobe PDF symbol in front of it. Scan through the industry report to familiarize yourself with the information available. You may open any other file in the list out of curiosity.

10. Finally return to the top of the page and click on "Commentary." You will find two major titles in the left margin: "IPC Notes" (Investment Policy Committee Notes) and "Trends and Projections." Notice in both cases there are historical material that is archived.

11. Open the IPC Notes and read the document. What are the current policy recommendations of the committee?

12. Open the Trends and Projections, and scan through the available information. You need go no further because we will return to this document in the next chapter.

Analysis and Valuation of Equity Securities

part two

2

chapter 5
ECONOMIC ACTIVITY

chapter 6
INDUSTRY ANALYSIS

chapter 7
VALUATION OF THE INDIVIDUAL FIRM

chapter 8
FINANCIAL STATEMENT ANALYSIS

tHE SECOND SECTION OF THE TEXT presents the fundamental analysis approach to the valuation of common stocks and highlights the valuation methods most commonly used by security analysts. By starting with an analysis of the economy, moving to the industry, and then the company, we employ what is called a top down approach—starting with the big picture and moving to the individual company. Other fundamental analysts may use the bottom-up approach, doing the analysis in reverse order. These analysts are called stock pickers. Both types are value investors, trying to find undervalued stocks that they can buy and patiently hold until the price rises enough above the estimated fair market values so that the stocks can be sold at an above-average profit. Investors are usually optimists and normally choose one of the approaches that they think will find undervalued stocks.

There is another way to make profits in the stock market and that is to sell high and buy low. In other words you can be a short seller. Short sellers are pessimists. They look for companies that are overvalued and likely to decline in price. They sell borrowed stock and expect to purchase the stock at a lower price and replace the borrowed stock. Thus they sell high, buy low, and make a profit if the stock goes down. David Tice, president of the Prudent Bear Fund is such a short seller although he has said, "I consider myself more of an accounting critic." In the interest of full disclosure, David Tice was a student of both authors of this text in 1976 and 1977 at Texas Christian University and a participant in the Educational Investment Fund.

David W. Tice is a CFA (Chartered Financial Analyst) and a CPA (Certified Public Accountant), and he has applied both those skills in finding overvalued companies. David W. Tice & Associates, LLC, located in Dallas, Texas, is the investment advisor to the Prudent Bear Mutual Fund and the Prudent Global Income Fund. His firm also publishes *Behind the Numbers*, an institutional research service that provides quality of earnings analysis to more than 200 money managers. The annual subscription fee of $15,000 is costly but professionals pay for respected research. While the firm only employs 10 full-time analysts, some would say that the company is one of the strongest independent research boutiques in the country.

Tice was the first to call into question the accounting practices of Mercury Finance and Sunbeam. He also hammered on Tyco for years and eventually was proven right. He even took on General Electric's accounting practices at one time.

When David Tice appeared before a congressional financial services subcommittee on June 13, 2001, he pointed out the conflicts of interest between analysts' recommendations and the investment banking business. He also testified that these conflicts encouraged speculation in the stock market and contributed to a misallocation of capital toward Internet and telecom companies at the expense of other industries. By 2004, he was proved right and many Wall Street firms paid fines of billions of dollars and agreed to separate their research functions from their investment banking functions. Additionally, as part of their settlement with the SEC, these firms agreed to make independent research available to their clients.

Now while we both admire our former student, we can't always agree with his predictions and one forecast that we hope will be wrong is his forecast of a Dow Jones Industrial Average of 3,000 before the bear market is done. This forecast was made in November 2002 and given David's penchant for sticking to his guns and often being proven right several years later, maybe we should put some of our assets in the Prudent Bear Fund.

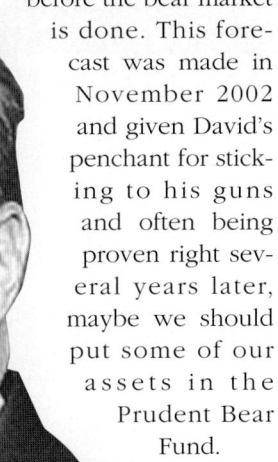

David W. Tice
Photo provided by David W. Tice & Associates, Inc.

www.mhhe.com/hirtblock8e

chapter five

Economic Activity

objectives

1. Explain the concept of a top-down valuation process.

2. Discuss the role of the federal government in influencing economic policy.

3. Distinguish between the effects of fiscal policy and monetary policy.

4. Explain how inflation and trade policy influence the economy.

5. Describe the business cycle and how it relates to cyclical indicators.

6. Explain the relationship of the business cycle to various industries.

Economic Activity and the Business Cycle
    Federal Government Economic Policy
    Fiscal Policy
    Monetary Policy
    Government Policy, Real Growth, and Inflation
Business Cycles and Cyclical Indicators
    Economic Indicators
Stock Prices and Economic Variables
    Money Supply
    Gross Domestic Product
    Industrial Production and Manufacturing
Business Cycles and Industry Relationships

To determine the value of the firm, fundamental analysis relies on long-run forecasts of the economy, the industry, and the company's financial prospects. Short-run changes in business conditions are also important in that they influence investors' required rates of return and expectations of corporate earnings and dividends. This chapter presents the basic information for analysis of the economy, while other chapters in this section focus on industry analysis and the individual firm.

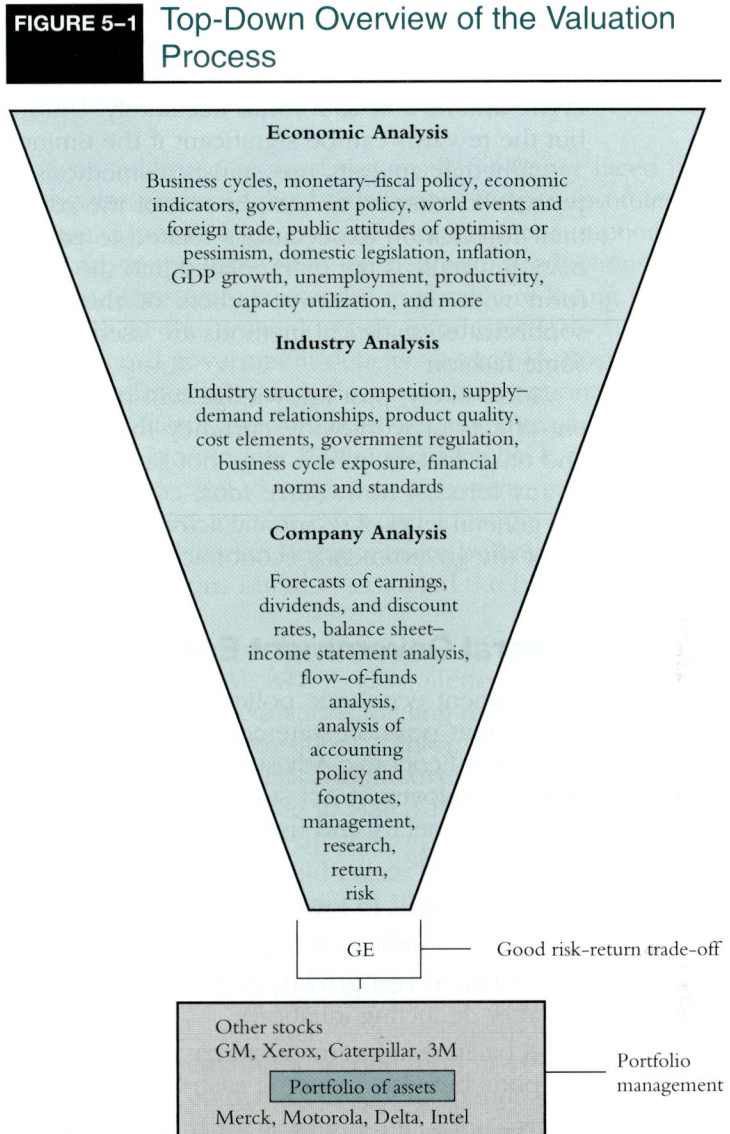

FIGURE 5–1 Top-Down Overview of the Valuation Process

Figure 5–1 presents an overview of the top-down valuation process as an inverted triangle. The process starts with a macroanalysis of the economy and then moves into industry variables. Next, common stocks are individually screened according to expected risk-return characteristics, and finally the surviving stocks are combined into portfolios of assets. This figure is not inclusive of all variables considered by an analyst, but is intended to indicate representative areas applicable to most industries and companies.

Economic Activity and the Business Cycle

An investor begins the valuation process with an economic analysis. The hope is that an accurate forecast and examination of economic activity will provide the basis for accurate stock market predictions and indicate which industries

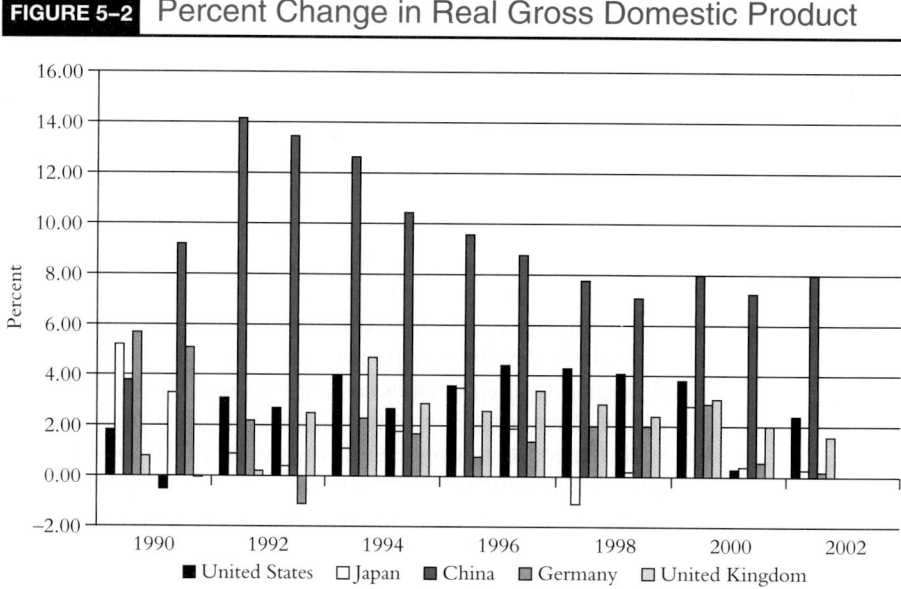

FIGURE 5–2 Percent Change in Real Gross Domestic Product

September 11th terrorist attack, generated a negative growth rate and the National Bureau of Economic Research declared a recession with a starting date of March 2001 and the end in November 2001. The economy picked up steam and managed reasonable growth in 2002 and 2003. However, President Bush's tax cuts coupled with large expenditures on the Iraqi war and homeland security, put the United States on course to have a $550 billion deficit for the fiscal year 2004.

The international landscape is changing rapidly, and this includes economic changes in North America, South America, Europe, and Asia. As we enter this new era of the global economy, we cannot always rely on the past for indications about the future. The new European economy now includes the euro as its currency and by the end of the decade the European Union will include about 20 countries, as many countries such as Poland, Hungary, and the Czech Republic join the EU. China's emergence as an economic power and world trade agreements will change the way the world's political and economic systems interact. The knowledge of economic theory and its applications will increase in importance to investors pursuing international strategies or to U.S. companies making foreign investments. The ability to interpret these events could have significant financial implications on investment returns for both investors and companies. Figure 5–2 shows some examples of the real GDP growth patterns of the United States' major trading partners. It is clear that China is at the head of the list for growth, while the developed countries are growing between 2 and 4 percent with the United States leading most of the other developed economies.

Fiscal Policy

Fiscal policy can be described as the government's taxing and spending policies. These policies can have a great impact on the direction of economic activity. One must realize at the outset that fiscal policy is cumbersome. It has a long implementation lag and is often motivated by political rather than economic

FIGURE 5-3 | Panel A: Federal Budget Receipts and Expenditures

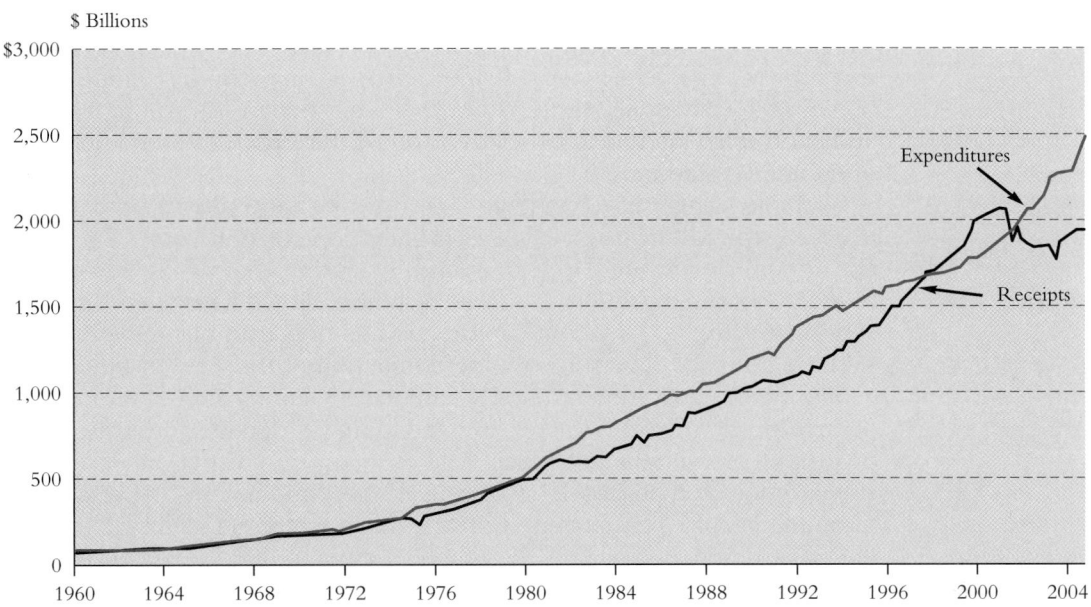

Panel B: Federal Deficit and Surplus

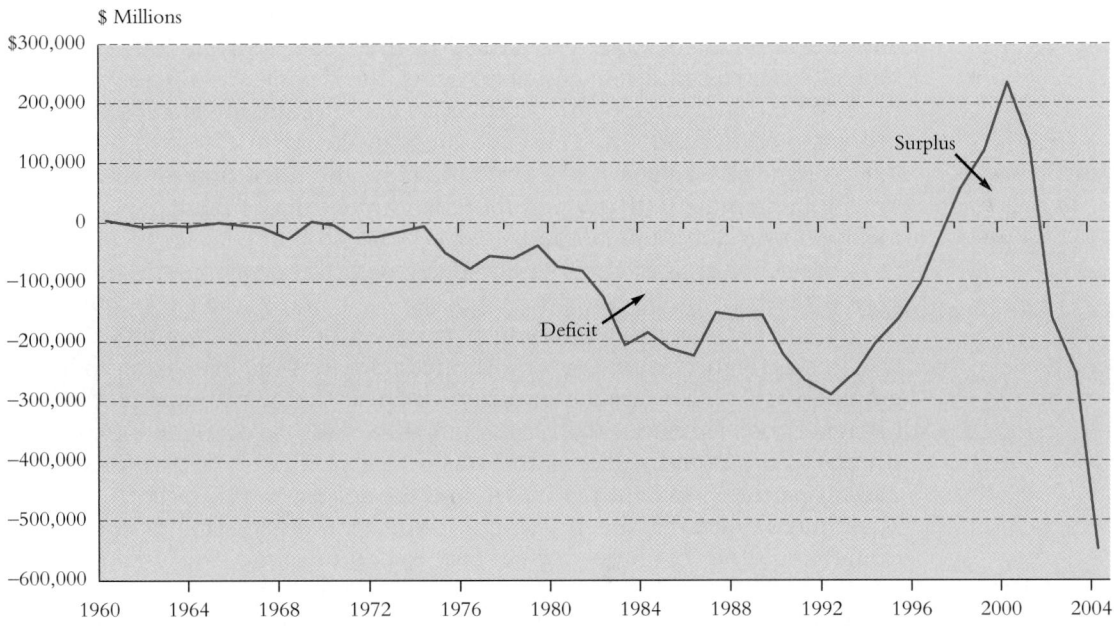

considerations since Congress must approve budgets and develop tax laws. Figure 5–3 presents a historical picture of government income and expenditures. When the government spends more than it receives, it runs a **deficit** that must be financed by the Treasury.

A forecaster must pay attention to the size of the deficit and how it is financed to measure its expected impact on the economy. If the deficit is financed by the Treasury selling securities to the Federal Reserve, it is very expansive. The money supply will increase without having any significant short-run effects on interest rates. If the deficit is financed by selling securities to banks and individuals, there is not the same expansion in the money supply, and short-term interest rates will rise unless the Federal Reserve intervenes with open-market trading.

A look at Figure 5–3 on page 119 shows that **surpluses,** in which revenues exceed expenditures, have been virtually nonexistent from 1966 to 1997, and the annual deficit increased dramatically during the 1980s. Surpluses tend to reduce economic growth as the government slows its demand for goods and services relative to its income. In an analysis of fiscal policy, the important consideration for the investor is the determination of the flow of funds. In a deficit economy, the government usually stimulates GDP by spending on socially productive programs or by increasing spending on defense, education, highways, or other government programs. The Reagan administration instituted budget cuts in education and social programs at the same time it reduced tax revenues through tax cuts. This strategy was one that attempted to shift GDP growth from the government sector into the private sector. In the George H. Bush administration, there was inconsistent fiscal policy. Clinton made it clear with his new tax increases that he would use fiscal policy to increase tax revenues to help shrink the fiscal deficit. He instituted a more progressive tax policy in 1993 by raising rates and reducing deductions for high-income people. His hope was that the wealthy would not slow down their spending and that the increased tax revenues would help decrease the fiscal deficit. He was right. Although Clinton and the Republican Congress passed further legislation in 1997 to reduce the deficit, cut taxes, and reduce entitlements, the deficit was already well in check by then (and moving toward a surplus) because of greatly increased tax revenue in a prospering economy. The increasing surplus from 1997 to 2001 is quite visible in Panel B of Figure 5–3. Unfortunately, the government expenditures following September 11th pushed the government into a deficit spending budget for fiscal year 2002 and beyond.

One other area of fiscal policy deals with the government's ability to levy import taxes or tariffs on foreign goods. As a free market economy, we have fought for years with our trading partners to open their countries' markets to U.S. goods. Figure 5–4 depicts the annual trade deficits that started piling up beginning in 1982. This deficit occurred because U.S. consumers purchased more foreign goods (imports) than U.S. companies sold to foreigners (exports). This occurred for several reasons; one was a lack of free markets with some of our trading partners, specifically Japan, and the robust health of the U.S. economy. The United States has been trying to open markets for U.S. goods with Japan, China, and other countries for the last several decades. The World Trade Organization (WTO) and its round of tariff negotiations have been instrumental in breaking down trade barriers during the last half of the 1990s, and in 2001 China was approved for membership in the WTO, which should have long-term positive effects on world trade.

Countries can create trade barriers by either setting up import tariffs or taxes that raise the price of foreign goods and make them less competitive with domestic goods. This is a common way to protect domestic industries. The WTO

FIGURE 5-4 Exports and Imports

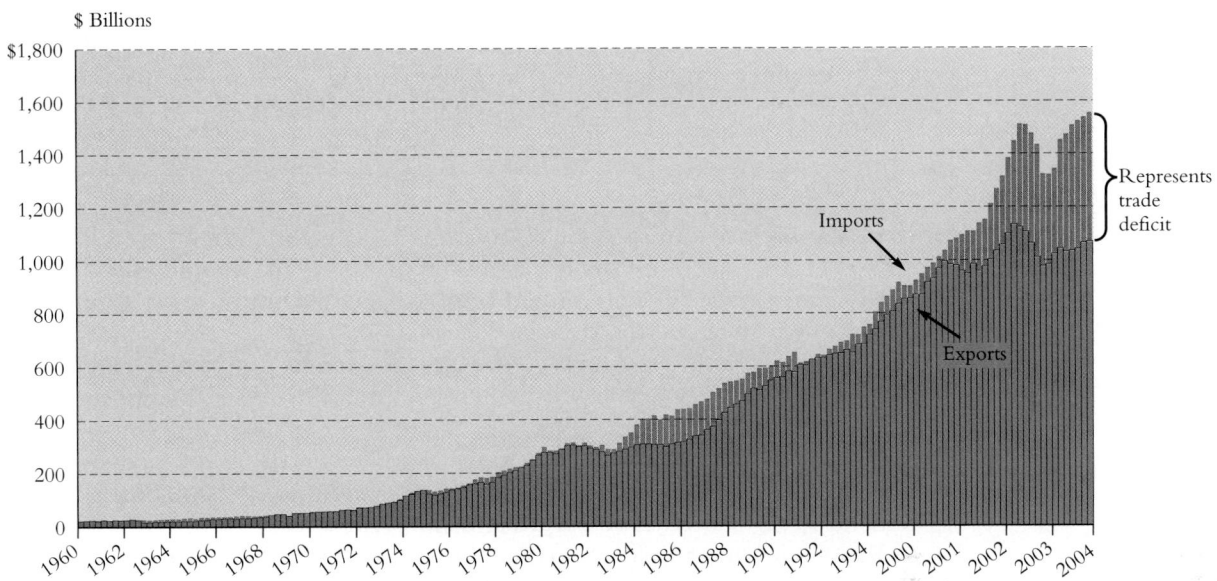

Source: St. Louis Federal Reserve Bank, FREDII.

deals with these issues through negotiations and if necessary through a world court to arbitrate complaints from one country against another.

As Figure 5–4 shows, the U.S. trade deficit increased quite rapidly from 1996 to 2004, rising from a negative $89.4 billion in 1997 to a negative $480 billion in 2004. The United States had the largest trading deficit with China, followed by Japan in second place.

The rising trade deficit during most of this time period was a function of the healthy U.S. economy and a strong dollar. When a country's economy is healthy with high employment and income, its citizens spend more in general and import more goods (especially high-priced luxury goods) from other countries. When there is a recession, people spend less, look for less expensive items, and import fewer goods. The second factor is the exchange rate between two currencies. For example, if the U.S. dollar rises against the British pound, U.S. goods become more expensive for British citizens, and British goods become less expensive for U.S. citizens. If the dollar exchange rate stays high or continues to rise, eventually British citizens change their buying habits and buy fewer U.S. goods, and U.S. citizens buy more British goods. This effect can also be seen in the U.S.–Japanese automobile market. As the Japanese yen rose against the dollar, in the early 1990s, Americans bought fewer Japanese cars and more U.S. domestic cars. The Japanese consumer did the opposite.

Since late 2002 the Bush administration has been following a weak dollar policy as a way of curbing U.S. imports and raising U.S. exports. The euro has risen against the U.S. dollar by over 50 percent from its low to its peak, but unfortunately the United States' biggest trading deficit is with China and the Chinese renmimbi has remained pegged to the dollar.

Short-term swings in exchange rates have little effect on imports and exports, but changes in long-term currency relationships eventually change import-export balances between countries. It usually takes more than a year before the effects of exchange rates on prices show up at the retail level and influence the buying patterns of consumers. As world trade increases, exchange rates and economic trends around the world become more important. While exchange rates and economic activity are influenced by fiscal policy, they are also affected by monetary policy, as discussed in the next section.

Monetary Policy

Monetary policy determines the "appropriate" levels for the money supply and interest rates that accomplish the economic goals of the Employment Act of 1946. Monetary policy is determined by the Federal Open Market Committee (FOMC), which includes the Federal Reserve Board of Governors and the 12 Federal Reserve bank presidents. Monetary policy can be implemented very quickly to reinforce fiscal policy or, when necessary, to offset the effects of fiscal policy.

The Federal Reserve has several ways to influence economic activity. First, it can raise or lower the reserve requirements on commercial bank time deposits or demand deposits. **Reserve requirements** represent the percent of total deposits that a bank must hold as cash in its vault or as deposits in Federal Reserve banks. An increase in reserve requirements contracts the money supply. The banking system has to hold larger reserves for each dollar deposited and is not able to lend as much money on the same deposit base. A reduction in reserve requirements has the opposite effect. The Fed also changes the discount rate periodically to reflect its attitude toward the economy. This **discount rate** is the interest rate the Federal Reserve charges commercial banks on very short-term loans. The Fed does not make a practice of lending funds to a single commercial bank for more than two or three weeks, and so this charge can influence an individual bank's willingness to borrow money for expansionary loans to industry. The Fed can also influence bank behavior by issuing policy statements, or jawboning.

Beyond these monetary measures, the tool most widely used is **open-market operations** in which the Fed buys and sells U.S. government securities for its own portfolio. When the Fed sells securities in the open market, purchasers write checks to pay for their securities, and demand deposits fall, causing a contraction in the money supply. At the same time, the increase in the supply of Treasury bills sold by the Fed forces prices down and interest rates up to entice buyers to part with their money. The Fed usually accomplishes its adjustments by selling securities to commercial banks, government securities dealers, or individuals.

If the Fed buys securities, the opposite occurs; the money supply increases, and interest rates go down. This tends to encourage economic expansion. As you will see in Chapter 7, the interest rate is extremely important in determining the required rate of return, or discount rate for a stock.

Figure 5–5 summarizes the four policy goals set by the Employment Act of 1946 and the monetary policy actions that help achieve these goals. The problem with monetary policy is that the four goals are not complementary, and so the Federal Reserve has to choose which goals it will focus upon given the state of the economy. If the economy is sluggish or contracting it will lower rates to stimulate the economy and employment. However, lowering rates will increase

Application Example

FIGURE 5-5 Economic Policy Goals and Monetary Policy

Goals	Raise Rates	Lower Rates
1. Sustainable Growth in Real GDP	Reduces economic growth	Stimulates economic growth
2. High Rates of Employment (low unemployment)	Reduces Employment	Stimulates employment
3. Balance of International Payments	Strengthens domestic currency	Decreases domestic currency
a) Balance of Trade	Over time high rates will cause imports to go up, and exports down if the currency stays strong	Over time low rates will cause imports to go down and exports to go up if the currency stays weak
b) Cash Flows between Countries	Increases foreign Investment Inflows	Increases foreign investment outflows
4. Maintain Stable Prices (low inflation rate)	Reduces inflationary impact	Increases inflationary impact

Monetary Tools	To Raise Rates	To Lower Rates
Bank Reserve Requirements	Raise reserve requirements—Takes money out of banking system—Creates less loanable funds	Lower reserve requirements—Puts money into banking system—Creates more loanable funds
Discount Rate	An increase in the discount rate reduces banks willingness to borrow from the Federal Reserve and contracts the economy	A decrease in the discount rate increases banks' willingness to borrow from the Federal Reserve and expands the economy.
Federal Open Market Committee Activity	Sells Treasury securities—Lowers prices and raises rates—Takes money out of economy	Buys Treasury securities—Raises prices and lowers rates—Puts money into economy
Jawboning (The art of the Chairman of the Federal Reserve or governors of the Fed talking rates up or down in markets)	Say good things about GDP	Say bad things about GDP

the outflow of foreign funds from the United States and as the economy expands, inflation may increase. The early years of the millennium (2000–2004) demonstrate this goal conflict. The Federal Reserve was able to keep rates low to stimulate the economy, and excess capacity in the manufacturing sector allowed the economy to expand without creating too much inflation. Once the economy expands enough to reach capacity constraints, prices will start rising, and the Federal Reserve will have to raise rates which will slow the economy.

In a sense, the Federal Reserve is always prioritizing the four goals, and by watching the Federal Reserve's monetary policy actions, an investor may be able to anticipate potential profitable investments. Analysts are continually playing chess with the Federal Reserve, trying to guess the next move, and Alan Greenspan, Chairman of the Federal Reserve, is adept at not disclosing what his next move will be. In a perfect world, monetary and fiscal policy would create a balanced economy achieving all four goals. Unfortunately the economy has a tendency to move in cycles with changing demand and consumer behavior, international trade and the hundreds of other factors making a perfect balance impossible.

Government Policy, Real Growth, and Inflation

In November 1991, the U.S. Commerce Department's Economic Bureau of Analysis shifted from gross national product to gross domestic product as the measure of economic activity for the U.S. economy. The **gross domestic product (GDP)** measurement makes us more compatible with the rest of the world and measures only output from U.S. factories and consumption within the United States. Gross domestic product does not include products made by U.S. companies in foreign countries, but gross national product did. Other U.S. economic measures such as employment, production, and capacity are also measured within the boundaries of the United States, and, with the switch to GDP, we now measure economic output consistently with these other variables.

Twenty-one years (84 quarters) of real gross domestic product (GDP) and inflation are shown in Figure 5–6. Real GDP reflects gross domestic product in constant dollars, which eliminates the effects of inflation form GDP. Real GDP measures output in physical terms rather than in dollars that are inflated by price increases. One common measure of inflation that most Americans are familiar with is the consumer price index, which is a basket of goods consumed by the

FIGURE 5–6 Real Growth and Inflation (quarterly % changes at annual rates)

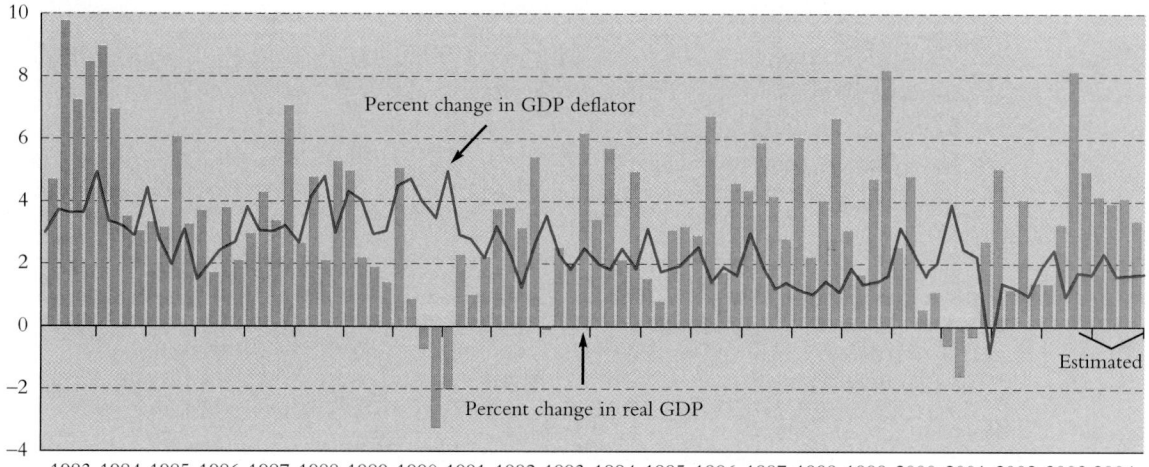

Source: "Trends & Projections," Standard & Poor's. © January 22, 2004, The McGraw-Hill Companies.

average person. The GDP price deflator is a broader measure of inflation and is used in Figure 5–6.

Notice the relationship between real GDP and inflation. The change in real GDP is inversely related to the rate of inflation. Notice that the healthy economy in the mid-1980s caused inflation to move upward from 1985 to 1990. However by 1989, the real GDP growth declined and a recession occurred in 1990 and early 1991. Inflation came down (with a lagged effect) and by 1992 bottomed out. Inflation stayed relatively tame throughout most of the 1990s, but again in 2001 the economy went into a recession. The United States had one quarter of deflation in the fourth quarter of 2001 before the economy recovered in the third quarter of 2003 with an 8.2 percent growth in real GDP. Because real GDP is the measure of economic output in real physical terms, it does no good to stimulate the economy only to have all the gains eroded by inflation.

To understand the major sectors of the economy and the relative influence of each sector, we divide gross domestic product into its four basic areas: personal consumption expenditures, government purchases, gross private investment, and net exports. Figure 5–7 shows the contribution of each one to the total GDP over the past four decades. It becomes clear from Figure 5–7 that personal consumption is growing faster than the other sectors and is the driving force behind economic growth. In fact consumer spending accounts for more than 60 percent of GDP. For this reason economic forecasters pay close attention to the mood of the consumer.

The University of Michigan surveys consumer expectations on a monthly basis and reports whether consumers are becoming more or less optimistic. Consumer expectation are a leading indicator of economic activity—when consumer confidence increases, this bodes well for spending; when consumer confidence decreases, this indicates a possible contraction in spending. Figure 5–8 on page

FIGURE 5–7 Breakdown of GDP in Current Dollars

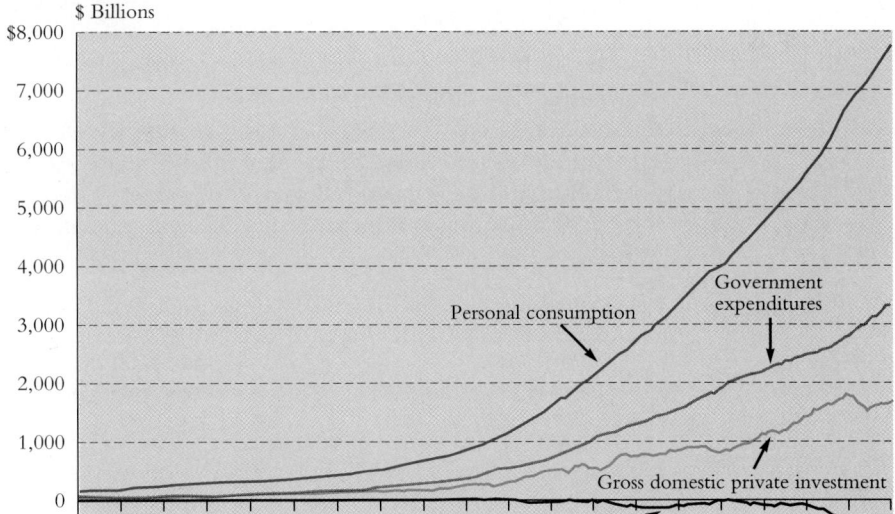

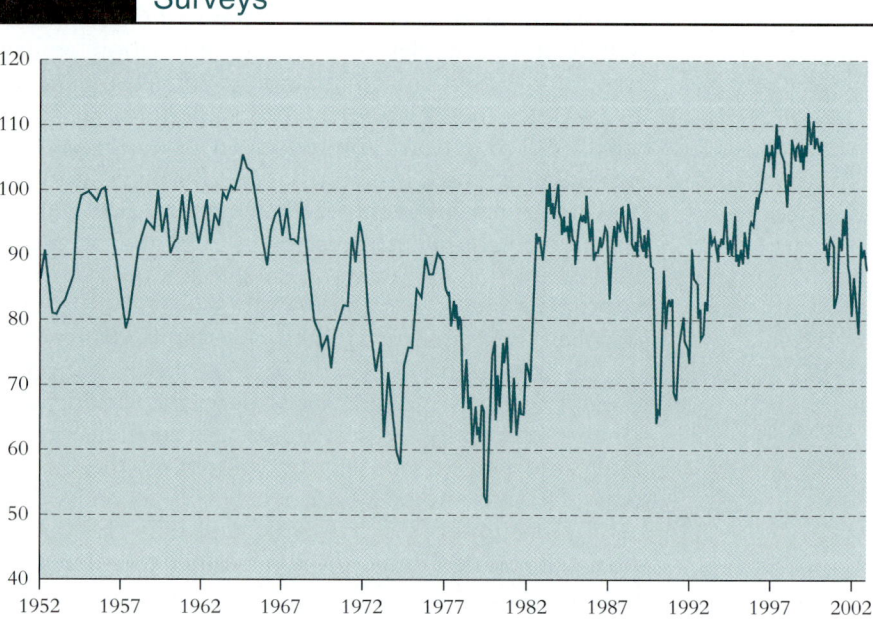

FIGURE 5–8 Consumer Expectations, University of Michigan Surveys

126 presents a historical view of the index of consumer expectation. It is easy to spot the recessions of 1973–75, 1980–81, and 1990–91. In all cases consumer expectations turned down before the recession began. In looking at the period 1990–2001, we can see the large rise in confidence with many short-term reversals on the downside. In the next section we look at the cyclical nature of gross domestic product.

Business Cycles and Cyclical Indicators

The economy expands and contracts through a **business cycle** process. By measuring GDP and other economic data, we can develop a statistical picture of the economic growth pattern. Traditionally, the definition of a recession is two or more consecutive quarters of negative real GDP growth. However, the National Bureau of Economic Research (NBER) is the final authority in documenting cyclical turning points and they have amended their definition of a recession as follows:

> The NBER does not define a recession in terms of two consecutive quarters of decline in real GDP. Rather, a recession is a significant decline in economic activity spread across the economy, lasting more than a few months, normally visible in real GDP, real income, employment, industrial production, and wholesales-retail sales.

Table 5–1 presents a historical picture of business cycle expansions and contractions in the United States. While the modern-day data may be more relevant, it is interesting to see that economic cycles have existed and been defined for 150 years.

Table 5–1 measures each contraction and expansion and then presents summary data at the bottom of the table for all business cycles and for cycles in

TABLE 5–1 Business Cycle Expansions and Contractions in the United States

Contractions (Recessions) Start at the Peak of a Business Cycle and End at the Trough.

Business Cycle Reference Dates		Duration in Months			
Peak	Trough	Contraction	Expansion	Cycle	
		Peak to Trough	Previous Trough to This Peak	Trough from Previous Trough	Peak from Previous Peak
	(Quarterly dates are in parentheses)				
—	December 1854 (IV)	—	—	—	—
June 1857 (II)	December 1858 (IV)	18	30	48	—
October 1860 (III)	June 1861 (III)	8	22	30	40
April 1865 (I)	December 1867 (I)	**32**	**46**	**78**	**54**
June 1869 (II)	December 1870 (IV)	18	18	36	50
October 1873 (III)	March 1879 (I)	65	34	99	52
March 1882 (I)	May 1885 (II)	38	36	74	101
March 1887 (II)	April 1888 (I)	13	22	35	60
June 1890 (III)	May 1891 (II)	10	27	37	40
January 1893 (I)	June 1894 (II)	17	20	37	30
December 1895 (IV)	June 1897 (II)	18	18	36	35
June 1899 (III)	December 1900 (IV)	18	24	42	42
September 1902 (IV)	August 1904 (III)	23	21	44	39
May 1907 (II)	June 1908 (II)	13	33	46	56
January 1910 (I)	January 1912 (IV)	24	19	43	32
January 1913 (I)	December 1914 (IV)	23	12	35	36
August 1918 (III)	March 1919 (I)	**7**	**44**	**51**	**67**
January 1920 (I)	July 1921 (III)	18	10	28	17
May 1923 (II)	July 1924 (III)	14	22	36	40
October 1926 (III)	November 1927 (IV)	13	27	40	41
August 1929 (III)	March 1933 (I)	43	21	64	34
May 1937 (II)	June 1938 (II)	13	50	63	93
February 1945 (I)	October 1945 (IV)	**8**	**80**	**88**	**93**
November 1948 (IV)	October 1949 (IV)	11	37	48	45
July 1953 (II)	May 1954 (II)	**10**	**45**	**55**	**56**
August 1957 (III)	April 1958 (II)	8	39	47	49
April 1960 (II)	February 1961 (I)	10	24	34	32
December 1969 (IV)	November 1970 (IV)	**11**	**106**	**117**	**116**
November 1973 (IV)	March 1975 (I)	16	36	52	47
January 1980 (I)	July 1980 (III)	6	58	64	74
July 1981 (III)	November 1982 (IV)	16	12	28	18
July 1990 (III)	March 1991 (I)	8	92	100	108
March 2001 (I)	November 2001 (IV)	8	120	128	128
Average, All Cycles:					
1854–2001 (32 cycles)		17	38	55	56[a]
1854–1919 (16 cycles)		22	27	48	49[b]
1919–1945 (6 cycles)		18	35	53	53
1945–2001 (10 cycles)		10	57	67	67
Average, Peacetime Cycles:					
1854–2001 (27 cycles)		18	33	51	52[c]
1854–1919 (14 cycles)		22	24	46	47[d]
1919–1945 (5 cycles)		20	26	46	45
1945–2001 (8 cycles)		10	52	63	63

[a] 31 cycles

[b] 15 cycles

[c] 26 cycles

[d] 13 cycles

Note: Figures printed in **bold** are the wartime expansions (Civil War, World Wars I and II, Korean War, and Vietnam War); the wartime contractions; and the full cycles that include the wartime expansions.

Sources: NBER; the U.S. Department of Commerce, *Survey of Current Business,* October 1994, Table C–51. From Public Information Office, National Bureau of Economic Research, Inc., 1050 Massachusetts Avenue, Cambridge, MA 02138, 617-868-3900. http://www.nber.com/cycles/cyclesmain.html.

peacetime only. A **trough** represents the end of a recession and the beginning of an expansion, and a **peak** represents the end of an expansion and the beginning of a recession. In general, we see on the last line of Table 5–1 that during eight peacetime cycles between 1945 and 2001, contractions (recessions) lasted an average of 10 months, while expansions averaged 52 months. Thus, one *complete* business cycle during modern *peacetimes* lasts 63 months or five and one-quarter years. The NBER declared that March 2001 was the beginning of a recession and the end of a 10-year expansion. This unusual dating of the recession occurred without two quarters of negative real GDP growth, but in the face of months of declining manufacturing output, declining employment, and sagging consumer confidence. The NBER dated the end of the recession as November 2001.

Predicting business cycles is easier said than done. It is important to realize that each business cycle is unique; no two cycles are alike. Some cycles are related to monetary policy; some are demand related; some are inventory induced. The length and depth of each is also different—some are shallow, and others deep; some are short, while others are long.

Additionally, not all industries or segments of the economy are equally affected by business cycles. However, if investors can make some forecast concerning the beginning and ending of the business cycle, they will be better able to choose which types of investments to hold over the various phases of the cycle.

So far, we have discussed the government's impact on the economy. Fiscal policy and monetary policy both provide important clues to the direction and magnitude of economic expansions and contractions. Other measures are used to evaluate the direction of the business cycle. These measures, called economic indicators, are divided into leading, lagging, and roughly coincident indicators. The NBER classifies indicators relative to their performance at economic peaks and troughs. **Leading indicators** change direction in advance of general business conditions and are of prime importance to the investor who wants to anticipate rising corporate profits and possible price increases in the stock market. **Coincident indicators** move approximately with the general economy, and **lagging indicators** usually change directions after business conditions have turned around.

The leading, lagging, and coincident indicators of economic activity are published by the Conference Board in its publication called *Business Cycle Indicators*. This publication includes moving averages, turning dates for recessions and expansions, cyclical indicators, composite indexes and their components, diffusion indexes,[1] and information on rates of change. Many of the series are seasonally adjusted and are maintained on a monthly or quarterly basis. This information is also available on its website **www.conference-board.org** for a fee.

Table 5–2 presents a summary of cyclical indicators by cyclical timing with Part A of the table presenting timing at business cycle peaks and Part B showing timing at business cycle troughs. Thus, in the first part, we see the leading, coincident, and lagging indicators for business cycle peaks, and in the second part, similar indicators for the bottoming out of business cycles (troughs). While

---

[1] A diffusion index shows the pervasiveness of a given movement in a series. If 100 units are reported in a series, the diffusion index indicates what percentage followed a given pattern.

TABLE 5-2 Cross Classification of Cyclical Indicators by Economic Process and Cyclical Timing

A. Timing at Business Cycle Peaks

Cyclical Timing \ Economic Process	I. Employment and Unemployment (15 series)	II. Production and Income (10 series)	III. Consumption, Trade Orders, and Deliveries (13 series)	IV. Fixed Capital Investment (19 series)	V. Inventories and Inventory Investment (9 series)	VI. Price, Costs, and Profits (18 series)	VII. Money and Credit (28 series)
Leading (L) Indicators (61 series)	Marginal employment adjustments (3 series) Job vacancies (2 series) Comprehensive employment (1 series) Comprehensive unemployment (3 series)	Capacity utilization (2 series)	Orders and deliveries (6 series) Consumption and trade (2 series)	Formation of business enterprises (2 series) Business investment commitments (5 series) Residential construction (3 series)	Inventory investment (4 series) Inventories on hand and on order (1 series)	Stock prices (1 series) Sensitive commodity prices (2 series) Prices and profit margins (7 series) Cash flows (2 series)	Money (5 series) Credit flows (5 series) Credit difficulties (2 series) Bank reserves (2 series) Interest rates (1 series)
Roughly Coincident (C) Indicators (24 series)	Comprehensive employment (1 series)	Comprehensive output and income (4 series) Industrial production (4 series)		Consumption and trade commitments (1 series) Business investment expenditures (6 series)	Business investment (4 series)		Velocity of money (2 series) Interest rate (2 series)
Lagging (Lg) indicators (19 series)	Comprehensive unemployment (2 series)			Business investment expenditures (1 series)	Inventories on hand and on order (4 series)	Unit labor costs and labor share (4 series)	Interest rate (4 series) Outstanding debt (4 series)
Timing Unclassified (U) (8 series)	Comprehensive unemployment (3 series)		Consumption and trade (1 series)	Business investment commitments (1 series)		Sensitive commodity prices (1 series) Profit and profit margins (1 series)	Interest rates (1 series)

B. Timing at Business Cycle Troughs

Cyclical Timing \ Economic Process	I.	II.	III.	IV.	V.	VI.	VII.
Leading (L) indicators (47 series)	Marginal employment adjustments (1 series)	Industrial production (1 series)	Orders and deliveries (5 series) Consumption and trade (4 series)	Formation of business enterprises (2 series) Business investment commitments (4 series) Residential construction (3 series)	Inventory investment (4 series)	Stock prices (1 series) Sensitive commodity prices (3 series) Profit and profit margins (6 series) Cash flows (2 series)	Money (4 series) Credit flows (5 series) Credit difficulties (2 series)
Roughly Coincident (C) Indicators (23 series)	Marginal employment adjustments (2 series) Comprehensive employment (4 series)	Comprehensive output and income (4 series) Industrial production (3 series) Capacity utilization (2 series)	Consumption and trade (3 series)	Business investment commitments (1 series)		Profits and profit margins (2 series)	Money (1 Series) Velocity of money (1 series)
Lagging (Lg) indicators (41 series)	Job vacancies (2 series) Comprehensive employment (1 series) Comprehensive unemployment (5 series)		Orders and deliveries (1 series)	Business investment commitments (2 series) Business investment expenditures (7 series)	Inventories on hand and on order (5 series)	Unit labor costs and labor share (4 series)	Velocity of money (1 series) Bank reserves (1 series) Interest rates (8 series) Outstanding debt (4 series)
Timing Unclassified (U) (1 series)							Bank reserves (1 series)

Source: *Business Conditions Digest* (U.S. Department of Commerce Bureau of Economic Analysis, July 1988).

we would not expect you to study or learn all the leading or lagging indicators for a cyclical peak or trough, it is important that you know they are relied on by economists and financial analysts. Let's look more specifically at how they are used.

Economic Indicators

Of the 108 leading indicators shown in Parts A and B of Table 5–2, 61 lead at peaks and 47 lead at troughs. Of these, 10 basic indicators have been reasonably consistent in their relationship to the business cycle and are considered most important. These 10 leading indicators have been standardized and used to compute a composite index that is widely followed. It is a much smoother curve than each individual component since erratic changes in one indicator are offset by movements in other indicators. The same can be said for a similar index of four coincident indicators and six lagging indicators.

Figure 5–9 shows the performance of the composite index of leading, lagging, and coincident indicators over several past business cycles. The shaded areas are recessions as defined by the NBER. The numbers at the top of the graph give the year and month for the beginning and end of the recession (the shaded area).

While the composite index of leading indicators (top of Figure 5–9) has been a better predictor than any single indicator, it has varied widely over time. Table 5–3 on page 132 presents the components for the 10 leading, 4 roughly coincident, and 7 lagging indicators.

Studies have found that the 10 leading indicators do not exhibit the same notice at peaks as they do at troughs. The notice before peaks is quite long, but the warning before troughs is very short, which means it is very easy to miss a turnaround to the upside, but on the downside you can be more patient waiting for confirmation from other indicators. Indicators occasionally give false signals. Sometimes the indicators give no clear signal, and with the large variability of leads and lags versus the average lead time, an investor is lucky to get close to predicting economic activity within three or four months of peaks and troughs. Despite economic indicators and forecasting methods, investors cannot escape uncertainty in an attempt to manage their portfolios.

One very important fact is that the stock market is the most reliable and accurate of the 10 leading indicators. This presents a very real problem for us because our initial objective is to forecast (as well as we are able) changes in common stock prices. To do this, we are constrained by the fact that the stock market is anticipatory and, in fact, has worked on a lead time of nine months at peaks and five months at troughs.

Stock Prices and Economic Variables

Money Supply

One variable that has been historically popular as an indicator of the stock market is the money supply. The money supply is supposed to influence stock prices in several ways. Studies of economic growth and the money supply by

FIGURE 5-9 | U.S. Composite Indexes (1996=100)

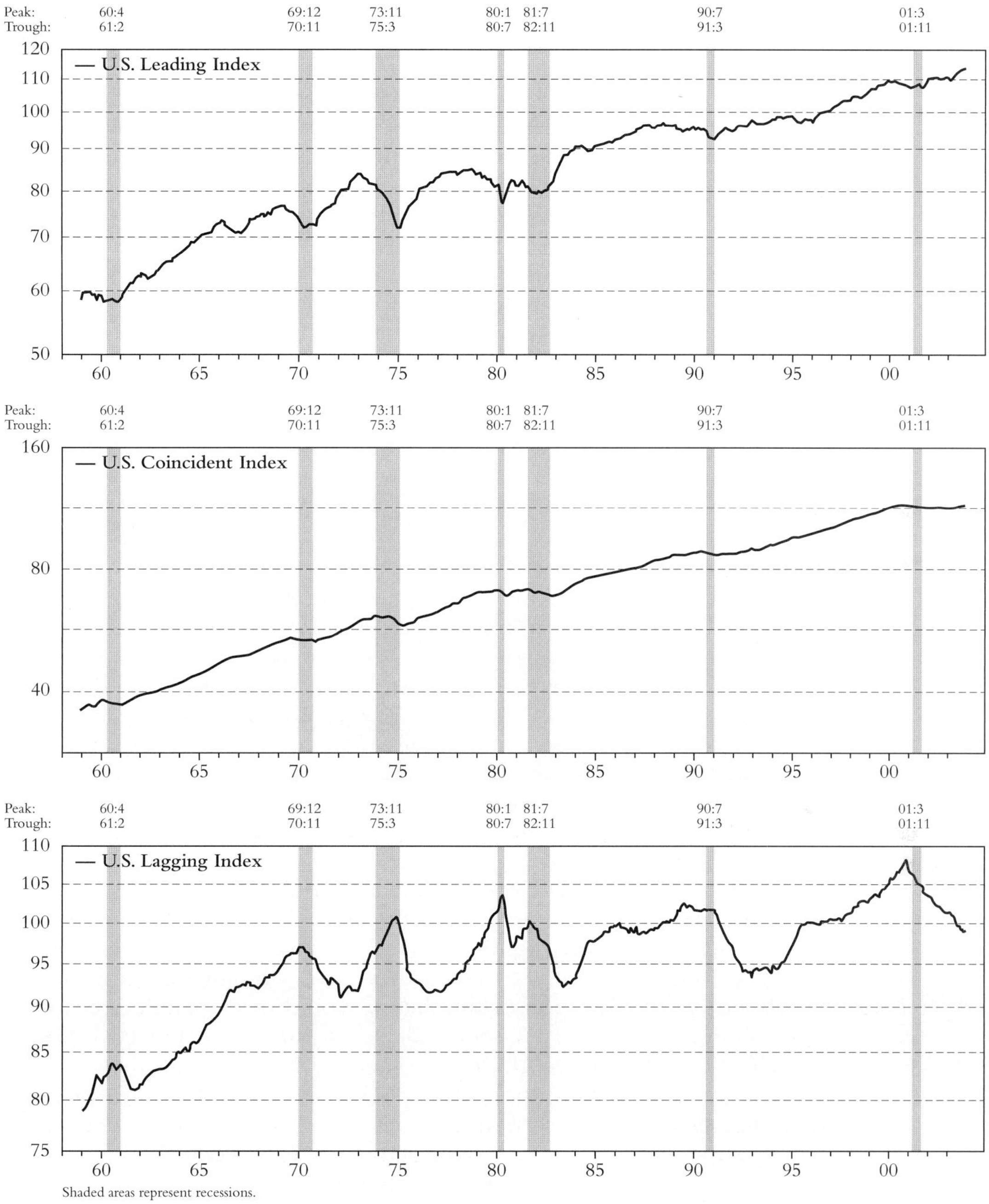

Shaded areas represent recessions.

Source: The Conference Board.

Milton Friedman and Anna Schwartz found a long-term relationship between these two variables.[2]

---

[2] Milton J. Friedman and Anna J. Schwartz, "Money and Business Cycles," *Review of Economics and Statistics,* Supplement, February 1963.

Application Example

TABLE 5–3 Components of the Leading, Coincident, and Lagging Indicators

Leading Index:
1. Average weekly hours, manufacturing
2. Average weekly initial claims for unemployment insurance
3. Manufacturers' new orders, consumer goods and materials
4. Vendor performance, slower deliveries diffusion index
5. Manufacturers' new orders, nondefense capital goods
6. Building permits, new private housing units
7. Stock prices, 500 common stocks
8. Money supply, M2
9. Interest rate spread, 10-year Treasury bonds less federal funds
10. Index of consumer expectations

Coincident Index:
1. Employees on nonagricultural payrolls
2. Personal income less transfer payments
3. Industrial production
4. Manufacturing and trade sales

Lagging Index:
1. Average duration of unemployment, weeks
2. Inventories to sales ratio, manufacturing and trade
3. Labor cost per unit of output, manufacturing
4. Average prime rate
5. Commercial and industrial loans
6. Consumer installment credit to personal income ratio
7. Consumer price index for services

Source: The Conference Board, February 2004.

Why does money matter? If you are a **monetarist,** money explains much of economic behavior. The quantity theory of money holds that as the supply of money increases relative to the demand for money, people will make adjustments in their portfolios of assets. If they have too much money, they will first buy bonds (a modification of the theory would now include Treasury bills or other short-term monetary assets), stocks, and finally, real assets. This is the direct effect of money on stock prices sometimes referred to as the *liquidity effect*.

The indirect effect of money on stock prices would be its impact on gross domestic product and corporate profits. As an increase or decrease in the money supply influences economic activity, it will eventually impact corporate earnings, dividends, and returns to investors.

Gross Domestic Product

There is a strong relationship with the long-run movement of the stock market and overall economic activity as measured by gross domestic product (GDP). This relationship appears in Figure 5–10, which plots the total return of the S&P

| FIGURE 5–10 | The S&P 500 and GDP |

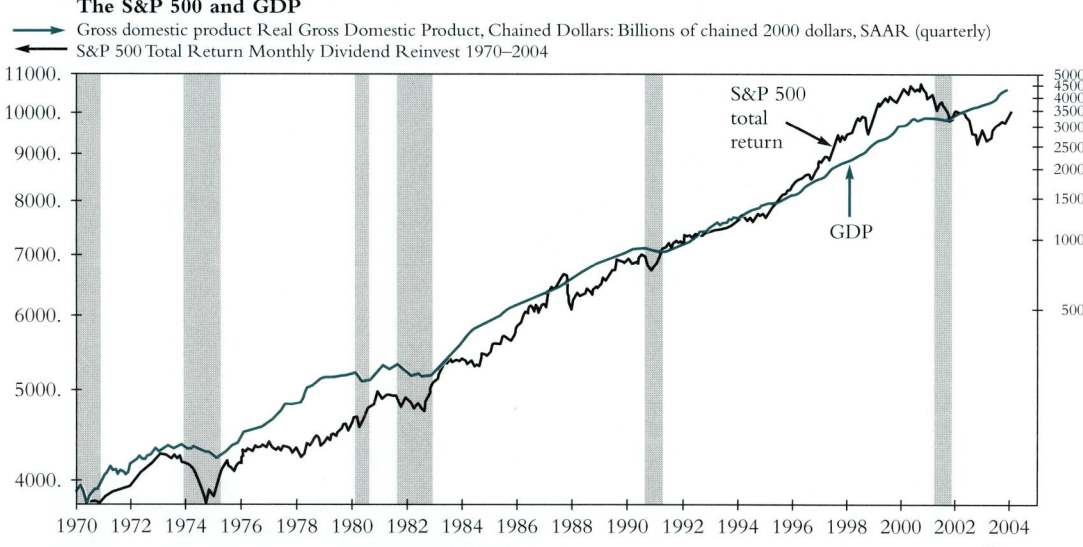

Source: http://www.economagic.com/em-cgi/PW_MChartOmni.exe/form.

500 Index with GDP from 1970 to 2004. The data are plotted on a log scale so that we can see the relationship between them a little better because of the size differences in their values. GDP is plotted on the left-hand scale and S&P 500 cumulative returns are plotted on the right scale. A careful inspection of the relationship between the two variables shows that the stock market was quite undervalued during most of the 1970s and quite a bit overvalued in the late 1990s. After the fact, it is always easier to see relationships than while an event is occurring. Another point worth reiterating is that the stock market usually turns down before recessions and up before the recession is over. This has been true except for the latest recession in 2001. While the recession ended in November 2001, the stock market didn't start its upward move until April 2003. This most likely is because corporate earnings took a long time to recover from the excesses of the late 1990s and the recession. Good earnings announcements started occurring in the third quarter of 2003, and so in some sense the stock market did anticipate these improved earnings about 6 to 9 months in advance.

Industrial Production and Manufacturing

Even though manufacturing in the United States accounts for only about 20 percent of the U.S. GDP, it is still a very important sector and employs a large number of people. There are several very important relationships shown in Figure 5–11 on page 134. First this figure with its series of three graphs shows the percentage change from a period of the past. This is different than Figure 5–10 which showed total values over time.

Notice in the first graph of the percentage changes for the Standard & Poor's 500 Index that the stock market provides positive returns much more often than negative returns. Between 1978 and 2000 there were only a few periods with

FIGURE 5–11 Stock Prices and Manufacturing Activity

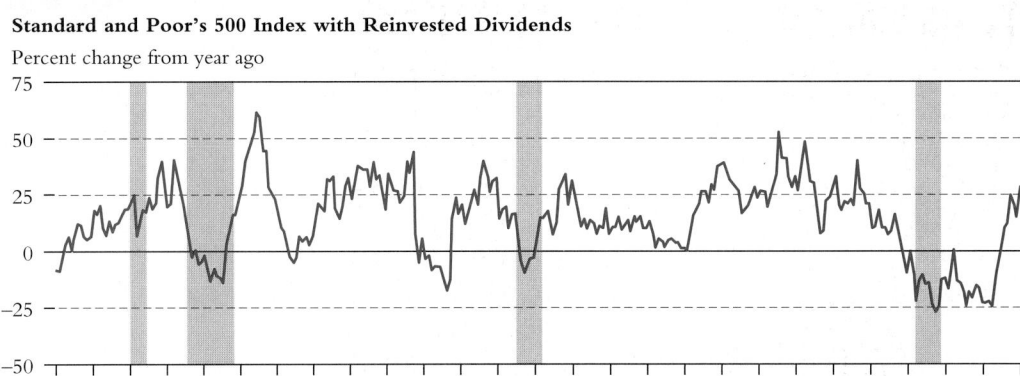

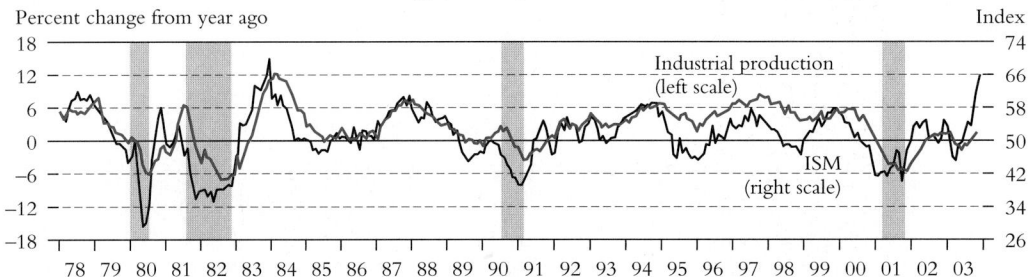

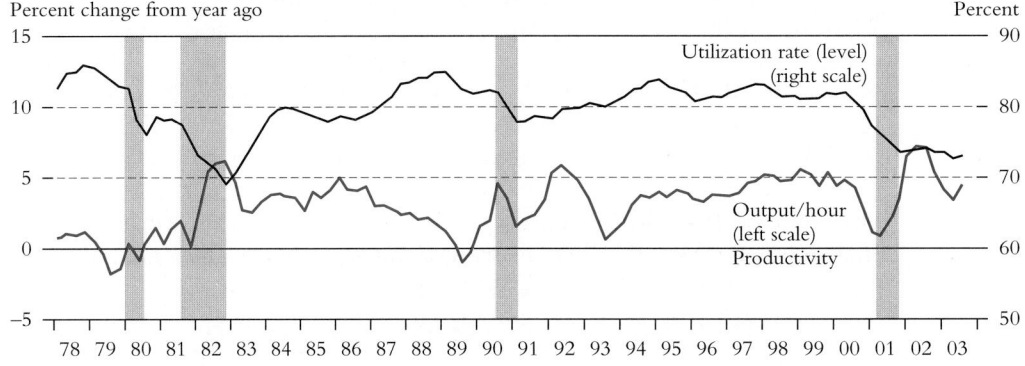

Source: Research Division, *National Economic Trends,* Federal Reserve Bank of St. Louis, January 2004.

negative returns. However the three-year period during 2000 to 2003 was the worst during the time shown and is one of the three or four worst three-year periods since the Great Depression of 1930s. The annual percentage change is given on the left axis and there were many periods when returns were above 25 percent and in a few cases above 50 percent. In fact when the market recovered in 2003, the return reached 25 percent for the year.

In the second panel we have industrial production as a percentage change from the period of the past year and the Institute for Supply Management Index (ISM) which is listed on the right scale. When the ISM is above 50, manufacturing is expanding and when it is below 50, manufacturing is contracting. The last reading in the table for ISM is 66 which is as strong as it has been since 1983. In deciding the last recession the NBER gave significant weight to the continuous decline in manufacturing that started at the end of 1997 and continued throughout 2001 before reversing.

The last panel shows output per hour and capacity utilization and is important in helping an analyst forecast inflation and interest rates. One very important change in the economy is that worker productivity (measured on the left axis) has been rising since the mid-1990s, which reversed the downward trend of the late 1980s. Corporate America's investment in technology has started to pay off for the economy. Since bottoming out during the last recession, productivity has hit a new peak and continues to remain positive. Increases in productivity reduce the costs of production and keep a lid on the prices of manufactured products. The ability of management to continuously modernize their company's plant and equipment is central in a firm's maintaining a competitive position in the worldwide market.

Capacity utilization (right axis at the bottom of Figure 5–10) measures current manufacturing output against potential output. When the capacity utilization rate is low, companies use their most productive and efficient plant and equipment, but as demand for goods increases, less efficient plant and equipment is brought online. The less efficient equipment is more costly, and as profit margins are reduced, companies raise prices. This inflationary effect is generally thought to begin occurring when capacity utilization moves past 80 percent. At the end of 2003, capacity utilization was about 73 percent. This means that there is excess capacity and as demand increases, prices won't necessarily have to rise because manufacturers can meet demand without any shortages that could lead to price increases. When manufacturers have excess capacity, price competition also abounds, and when you couple this with international competition and increased worker productivity, inflation doesn't seem to be on the horizon during the early part of 2004. Without inflation imminent, interest rates are likely to remain low for a while. One of the best games on Wall Street is predicting when Alan Greenspan and the Federal Reserve Board will raise interest rates. By the time you read this chapter you will probably have the answer.

Business Cycles and Industry Relationships

Each industry may be affected by the business cycle differently. Industries where the underlying demand for the product is consumer oriented will quite likely be sensitive to short-term swings in the business cycle. These industries would include durable goods such as washers and dryers, refrigerators, electric and gas ranges, and automobiles. Changes in the automobile industry will also be felt in the tire and rubber industry as well as by auto glass and other automobile component suppliers.

Table 5–4 on page 136, which appeared in the *Chicago Tribune*, demonstrates the impact of this ripple effect through many industries. The automobile industry purchases 77 percent of the output from the natural rubber industry

TABLE 5–4 Automobile Industry and Its Impact on Other Industries

The automotive industry purchases these percentages of the output of other U.S. industries.[a]		What's in a Car — A typical American car includes:[b]
Natural rubber	77%	1,774 pounds of steel
Lead	67	460 pounds of iron
Malleable iron	63	222 pounds of plastic
Synthetic rubber	50	183 pounds of fluids
Platinum	39	146 pounds of aluminum
Zinc	23	135 pounds of rubber
Aluminum	18	86 pounds of glass
Steel	12	25 pounds of copper
Copper	10	24 pounds of lead
		18 pounds of zinc

[a] Motor Vehicle Manufacturers Association.
[b] *World Book Encyclopedia.*

(tires and bumpers), 67 percent of the output from the lead industry (batteries), and so on to 10 percent of the copper output (electrical and tubing). Additionally, the automobile industry accounts for more than 4 percent of the GDP. The U.S. automobile industry employs 800,000 people, and one in seven workers (15 million) in America has a job in an industry somewhat dependent on the automobile industry.

Not all industries are so closely related to the business cycle. Necessity-oriented industries, such as food and pharmaceuticals, are consistent performers since people have to eat, and illness is not dependent on the economy. Industries that have products with low price elasticities that are habitual in nature, such as cigarettes and alcohol, do not seem to be much affected by business cycles either. In fact, some industries do better during a recession. The movie industry traditionally prospers during a recession as more people substitute low-cost entertainment for more expensive forms. This is one pattern that may not remain the same, however. As cable television, VCRs, and DVDs continue to come into their own, people may find it even more convenient to stay at home than to go to the movies when money is tight. This is one thing that makes investments exciting, the ever-changing environment.

Housing is another example of an industry that historically has done well in recessionary environments. As the economy comes to a standstill, interest rates tend to come down, and prospective home purchasers are once again able to afford mortgage rates on a home. After the period of extremely high mortgage rates in the early 1980s, a precipitous drop in mortgage rates helped to stimulate growth in the housing market. The Federal Reserve followed such a policy again in the early 1990s by pushing interest rates down to their lowest level in decades. This happened again in 2001. Sales of existing housing units picked up, and people refinanced their mortgages at lower rates, giving them more disposable income. As mortgage costs came down, housing became more affordable to more people. For example, if interest rates declined 3 percentage points on a $120,000 loan, the same priced house would now cost $300 per month less in interest expense. Low mortgage rates through the early 2000s stimulated the housing market to record levels and demand stayed strong into 2004.

the real world of investing

The New Economy: Going from Gain to Pain

According to some economists, there was supposed to be very little pain in the new economy. After a decade of uninterrupted growth in the 1990s, some went so far as to suggest the business cycle had been repealed. The reasoning was that ever-increasing productivity fueled by technology in the new economy would increase output per man(woman)-hour to the point where growth could continue indefinitely.

But the 3 to 4 percent annual growth in GDP came to a halt in the new century, and so did the decade-long bull market. Many popular market indexes fell between 20 percent (S&P 500 Stock Index) and 60 percent (Nasdaq).

Among those to feel the greatest pain from the stock market decline were entrepreneurs and CEOs in the Internet/technology area. *Fortune* magazine actually listed "The Billion Dollar Losers Club" in its June 11, 2001, edition.* Among the 20 unhappy participants, the top five losers were:

1. Michael Saylor, chair and CEO, MicroStrategy; lost $13.53 billion.
2. Jeffrey Bezos, chairman and CEO, Amazon.com; lost $10.80 billion.
3. David Filo, cofounder and chief, Yahoo; lost $10.31 billion.
4. Navaan Jain, chair and CEO, IntoSpace; lost $10.13 billion.
5. Jay Walker, founder, Pipeline.com; lost $7.51 billion.

Can you feel their pain?

---
*Julia Boorstein and Mathew Boyle, "The Billion Dollar Losers Club," *Forbes,* July 11, 2001, pp. 127–28.

Sensitivity to the business cycle may also be evident in industries that produce *capital* goods for other business firms (rather than consumer goods). Examples would be manufacturers of business plant and equipment, machine tools, or pollution-control equipment. A lag often exists between the recovery from a recession and the increased purchase of capital goods, so recoveries within these industries may be delayed.

Service industries have also become extremely important in our economy. While service-oriented business firms (doctors, lawyers, accountants) are generally less susceptible to the business cycle, there are exceptions. Examples of cyclically oriented service providers include architects, civil engineers, and auto repair shops.

One industry that has taken on increased importance is high technology. Companies in high technology generally include computer hardware and software producers; information technology, networking, database management firms; and other related fields. Examples of firms in these areas are Microsoft, Intel, CISCO, Oracle, IBM, and Sun Microsystems. These firms are also somewhat cyclical in that they depend on a high volume of business activity to continue an ever-expanding need for their products. Many of the newer high-tech firms were tested in the economic slowdown of the early 2000s, but the ones that survived came out stronger with better business models. Amazon.com finally made a profit and e-Bay continues to be the star of the group.

www.microsoft.com
www.intel.com
www.cisco.com

As a general statement, we do not mean to imply that cyclical industries are bad investments or that they should be avoided. We merely point out the cyclical influence of the economy. Often cyclical industries are excellent buys in the stock market because the market does not look far enough ahead to see a recovery and its impact on cyclical profits. We develop these ideas more completely in the next chapter.

exploring the web

Website Address	Comments
www.economy.com	Provides access to economic data—some sources are fee based
finance.yahoo.com	Provides information about companies, markets, and the economy
www.dismal.com	Contains articles on economies and tracks information from U.S. and global sources
www.fedstats.gov	Has links to economic data
www.freelunch.com	Has links to other economic sites, has listings of economic reports and news events, and provides access to economic data
www.smartmoney.com	Has information and news about U.S. economy
www.bea.doc.gov	Provides links to sources of U.S. government economic data
www.ny.frb.org	Contains links to New York Federal Reserve Bank analyses and data
www.stls.frb.org/fred	Contains historical interest rate, bond and economic data—site is free
www.mworld.com	Provides industry and economic data as well as data on money flows into stock funds
www.stat-usa.gov	Provides general information about the U.S. economy
www.bos.frb.org	Home page of the Federal Reserve of Boston providing economic information
www.ita.doc.gov	Provides access to U.S. government reports on international trade with reports being fee-based

Summary

The primary purpose of this chapter is to provide you with a process of valuation and an appreciation of some of the variables that should be considered. The valuation process is based on fundamental analysis of the economy, industry, and company. This method assumes decisions are made based on economic concepts of value over the long-term trend of the stock market. The purpose of the process is to eliminate losers from consideration in your portfolio and to thereby provide you with a good opportunity to build a sound portfolio.

The first step in the valuation process is an analysis of the economy and long-term economic trends. The difficulties of attaining government policy goals are discussed as trade-offs between conflicting objectives (high growth versus low inflation). Fiscal and monetary policy are discussed as the primary tools used to stimulate economic activity. Interest rates are influenced by inflation, with the end result being a higher required rate of return for the investor.

Business cycles are short-term swings in economic activity; they affect stock prices because they change investor expectations of risk and return. To forecast economic activity, cyclical indicators are presented as leading, lagging, and coincident indexes. The one index potentially most valuable to an investor is the composite index of 10 leading indicators.

The sensitivity of various types of industries to the business cycle is also examined. Firms in consumer durable goods (automobiles), as well as those in heavy capital goods manufacturing (plant and equipment) are perhaps most vulnerable to the business cycle.

Key Words and Concepts

business cycle 126
coincident indicators 128
deficit 119
discount rate 122
fiscal policy 118
gross domestic product (GDP) 124
lagging indicators 128
leading indicators 128
monetarist 132
monetary policy 122
open-market operations 122
peak 128
reserve requirements 122
surpluses 120
trough 128

Discussion Questions

1. As depicted in Figure 5–1 on page 115, what are the three elements in the valuation process?
2. As shown in Figure 5–5 on page 123, what are the four goals under the Employment Act of 1946?
3. What is fiscal policy? A one-sentence definition will suffice.
4. What is monetary policy?
5. How, specifically, can the Fed influence economic activity? Name three ways.
6. In regard to Federal Reserve open-market activity, if the Fed buys securities, what is the likely impact on the money supply? Is this likely to encourage expansion or contraction of economic activity?
7. What is the historical relationship between real GDP and inflation? What lesson might be learned from observing this relationship?
8. In terms of the business cycle, distinguish between a trough and a peak.
9. What are the four basic areas that make up gross domestic product? Over the past three decades, what area has been growing most rapidly?
10. What is the advantage of using a composite of indicators (such as the 10 leading indicators) over simply using an individual indicator?
11. Do leading indicators tend to give longer warnings before peaks or before troughs? What is the implication for the investor?
12. Comment on whether each of the following three industries is sensitive to the business cycle. If it is sensitive, does it do better in a boom period or a recession?
    a. Automobiles
    b. Pharmaceuticals
    c. Housing
13. Observe the performance of the 10 leading indicators for the next month. Compare this with changes in stock prices and interest rates.

Web Exercise

The Federal Reserve Board plays an important role in analyzing and regulating the economy. In this exercise, we will look at a couple of important reports that it provides. Go to **www.federalreserve.gov/**.

1. Click on "Monetary Policy" along the left margin.
2. Now click on "Beige Book" in the middle of the page. This book represents an important report that the Fed puts out describing economic conditions in various parts of the country. It is taken very seriously by stock and bond market investors.
3. Click on the latest report on the calendar.
4. Next, click on the area of the country (Federal Reserve district) that covers your hometown.
5. Write a three-paragraph report on your area of the country.

Note: From time to time, companies redesign their websites, and occasionally a topic we have listed may have been deleted, updated, or moved into a different location. Most websites have a "site map" or "site index" listed on a different page. If you click on the site map or site index you will be introduced to a table of contents that should aid you in finding the topic you are looking for.

S&P Problems

www.mhhe.com/edumarketinsight

STANDARD &POOR'S

1. Log on to the McGraw-Hill website: **www.mhhe.com/edumarketinsight** (see page vi in the preface for instructions).
2. Click on Commentary, which is the third box below the Market Insight title.
3. Click on the blue Trends and Projections in the left margin, under the bold heading. Trends and Projections is Standard & Poor's monthly economic update. Please read the entire document, and examine the charts and graphs.
4. What is the trend for real GDP and inflation?
5. What is the trend for short-term and long-term interest rates?
6. What is the trend for common stock prices and consumer confidence? Do you notice any relationship between the graphical patterns of these two graphs?
7. Be prepared to discuss employment trends, capital spending, manufacturing, imports and exports, and corporate profits.
8. On the last page of trends and projections, you will find an economic forecast. What is Standard & Poor's prediction for future economic activity?

The Wall Street Journal Projects

1. Under the "What's News" section of *The Wall Street Journal*, there is often a story related to the economy covered under "Business and Finance." Track this column into the future until you find three such stories. They can be about GDP, Federal Reserve policy, unemployment, interest rates, and so on.
2. Observe the behavior of the stock market related to the story. Normally the journal will report the announcement from the prior day so observe stock market movements for the prior day (which are also reported in the current

day's journal in which the story appears). Pay particular attention to the Dow Jones Industrial Average, the S&P 500 Stock Index, and the Nasdaq Composite Index. Does the direction of the market appear to react to the content of the story?

Selected References

Business-Cycle Analysis

Cohen, Marilyn. "How to Fight Inflation." *Fortune,* January 12, 2004, p. 206.

Durham, J. Benson. "Monetary Policy and Stock Price Returns." *Financial Analysts Journal,* July–August 2003, pp. 26–35.

Fisher, Kenneth L. "Bears, Bush and Greenspan." *Forbes,* April 16, 2001, p. 361.

Fleming, Jeff; Chris Kirby; and Barbara Ostdiek. "The Economic Value of Volatility Timing." *Journal of Finance,* February 2001, pp. 329–52.

Moore, Geoffrey H.; John P. Cullity; and Beth W. Taubman. "New Signals of Recession and Recovery." *Business Economics,* October 1995, pp. 41–44.

Santa-Clara, Pedro, and Rossen Valkanov. "The Presidential Puzzle: Political Cycles and the Stock Market." *Journal of Finance,* October 2003, pp. 1841–72.

Ulan, Michael. "Is the Current Business Cycle Different? Does How We Measure Matter?" *Business Economist,* April 1994, pp. 41–47.

Forecasting

Cho, Doug W. "Forecast Accuracy: Are Some Business Economists Consistently Better Than Others?" *Business Economics,* October 1996, pp 45–49.

Koretz, Gene. "Inflation Detectives Are Rounding Up the Wrong Suspects." *BusinessWeek,* August 8, 1994, p. 16.

Lim, Terrence. "Rationality and Analysts' Forecast Bias." *Journal of Finance,* February 2001, pp. 369–85.

Renshaw, Edward. "Modeling the Stock Market for Forecasting Purposes." *The Journal of Portfolio Management,* Fall 1993, pp. 76–81.

chapter six

Industry Analysis

objectives

1. Explain the phases of the industry life cycle.

2. Relate dividend policy to the life cycle.

3. Describe the various economic structures of industries.

4. Explain the effect that government regulation can have on an industry.

5. Describe how to compare the performance of many companies within the same industry.

6. Explain the concept of rotational investing in which the investor shifts emphasis among industries during various phases of the business cycle.

Industry Life Cycles
    Development—Stage I
    Growth—Stage II
    Expansion—Stage III
    Maturity—Stage IV
    Decline—Stage V
    Growth in Nongrowth Industries
Industry Structure
    Economic Structure
    Competitive Structure
Pharmaceutical Industry: An Example
    Life Cycle Analysis
    Government Regulation
    Research and Development
    Product Diversity
    Patents and Generic Drugs
    Demographics and Managed Care
Industry Groups and Rotational Investing
Appendix 6A: Sustainable Growth Model

We saw in Chapter 5 that *economic analysis* is the first step in the valuation process. Figure 5–1 (back on page 115) is funnel shaped and leads from the economy to industry analysis and then to company analysis. This method of choosing common stocks is called the **top-down approach** because it goes from the macroeconomic viewpoint to the individual company. The opposite approach is the **bottom-up approach,** which starts with picking individual companies and then looks at the industry and economy to see if there is any reason an investment in the company should not be made. People who follow the bottom-up approach are sometimes referred to as **stock pickers,** as opposed to industry analysts.

Industry analysis is the second step in the top-down approach used in this text, and it focuses on industry life cycles and industry structure. Industries can be affected by government regulation, foreign and domestic competition, and the economic business cycle. As we shall also see, industry competition is affected by product quality, the cost structures within the industry, and the competitive strategies among companies in the industry. A starting point for industry analysis is determining where an industry's current position is in its industry life cycle.

Industry Life Cycles

Industry life cycles are created because of economic growth, competition, availability of resources, and the resultant market saturation by the particular goods and services offered. Life-cycle growth influences many variables considered in the valuation process. The particular phase in the life cycle of an industry or company determines the growth of earnings, dividends, capital expenditures, and market demand for products.

An analysis of industry financial data helps place an industry on the life-cycle curve and, in turn, guides the analyst toward decisions on industry growth, the duration of growth, profitability, and potential rates of return. The analyst can determine whether all companies in the industry are in the same stage of the life cycle and translate company differences into various assumptions that will affect their individual valuations.

Figure 6–1 shows a five-stage industry life cycle (although it could very well be a company life cycle) and the corresponding dividend policy most likely to be found at each stage. The vertical scale on this graph is logarithmic, which means that a straight line on this scale represents a constant growth rate. The

FIGURE 6–1 Industry Life Cycle

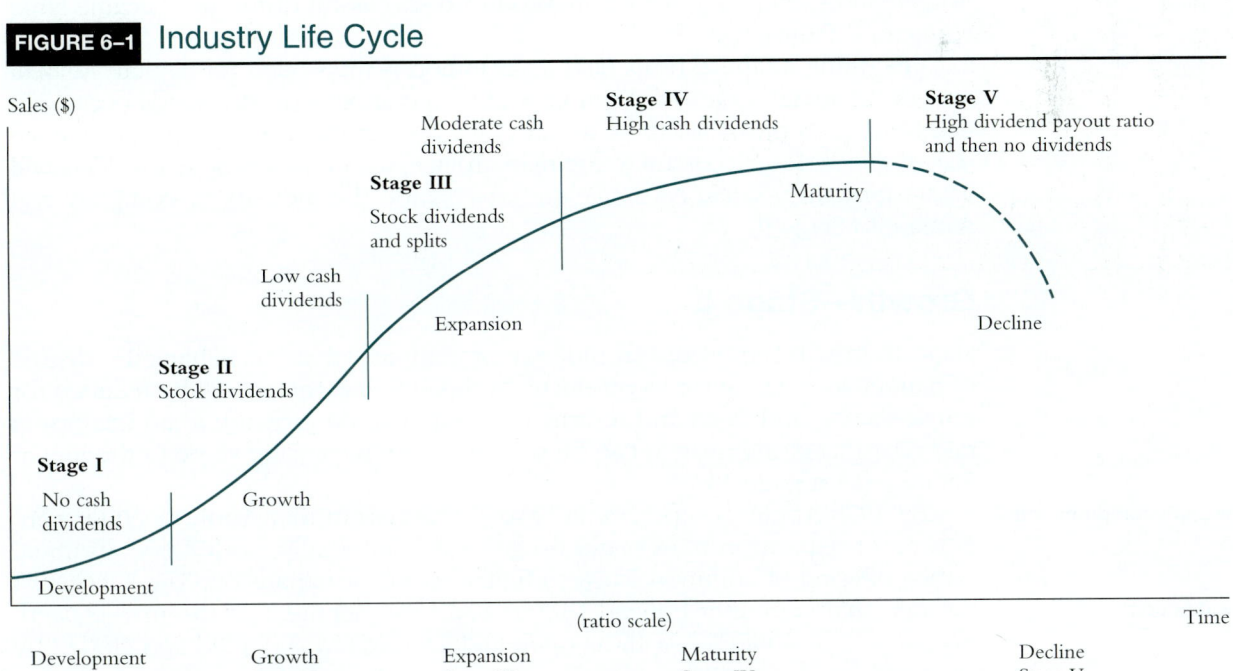

steeper the line, the faster the growth rate, and the flatter the line, the smaller the growth rate. The slope of the line in the life-cycle curve and how it changes over time is very important in the analysis of growth and its duration. We will examine each stage separately and learn why the dividend policy is important in placing an industry or company in a particular stage.

Development—Stage I

The development stage includes companies that are getting started in business with a new idea, product, or production technique that makes them unique. Firms in this stage are usually privately owned and are financed with the owner's money as well as with capital from friends, family, and a bank. If the company has some success, there is a probability that outside money from a venture capital group may increase the financing available to the company. In this stage, the company is also the industry or a subset of an existing industry. For example, when Steve Jobs started Apple Computer in the early 1970s, it was a development startup company that created an entirely new industry. In the beginning, Apple was certainly not taken seriously by IBM, but by the early 2000s the personal computer (PC) industry and its related software products represented a sizable multibillion dollar industry much bigger than the old mainframe business of IBM and others.

The pharmaceutical industry has been around for a long time, but in the 1970s and 1980s many small biotechnology firms were founded that created drugs using different production and research techniques. Hundreds of small biotech firms using genetic techniques were created by entrepreneurs in medical research. This focus on medical research created a subset of the pharmaceutical industry, and, eventually, large companies such as Merck and Eli Lilly created joint partnerships with these companies. Some biotech firms such as Amgen and Genentech eventually produced successful drugs and became large companies themselves.

One thing all these firms have in common is their need for capital. A small firm in the initial stages of development (Stage I) pays no dividends because it needs all of its profits (if there are any) for reinvestment in new productive assets. If the firm is successful in the marketplace, the demand for its products will create growth in sales, earnings, and assets, and the industry or company will move into Stage II.

Growth—Stage II

Stage II growth represents an industry or company that has achieved a degree of market acceptance for its products. At this stage, earnings will be retained for reinvestment, and sales and returns on assets will be growing at an increasing rate. The increasing growth can be seen from the increasing slope of the line in Figure 6–1 on page 143.

www.applecomputer.com

www.ibm.com

By 1978 Apple Computer's PC was so successful that Apple needed more capital for expansion than could be generated internally, so it made an initial public offering of common stock to finance a major expansion. The success of the personal computer enticed IBM to enter this segment of the market, and, eventually, the IBM PC—with its open architecture—was copied and cloned by companies such as Compaq (acquired by Hewlett Packard), Gateway, and Dell. All these firms are now publicly traded in U.S. markets and control more than 90 percent of the PC market.

Companies such as IBM entered the developing PC industry with a small amount of their total assets targeted at this market and were able to fund the move into this market with internal sources of capital. However, the other companies entering this market were "pure plays"; in other words, all they did was make personal computers. These companies were in the early part of Stage II, and they still needed to reinvest their cash flow back into research and development and into new plant and equipment.

In general, companies in Stage II become profitable, and, in their early stage of growth, they want to acknowledge to their shareholders that they have achieved profitability. Because they still need their internal capital, they often pay stock dividends (distributions of additional shares). A stock dividend preserves capital but often signals to the market that the firm made a profit. In the latter part of Stage II, low cash dividends may be paid out when the need for new capital declines as new sources of capital appear. A cash dividend policy is sometimes necessary to attract institutional investors to the company stock since some institutions cannot own companies that pay no dividends.

Obviously, industries in Stage I or early Stage II are very risky, and the investor does not really know if growth objectives will be met or if dividends will ever be paid. But if you want to have a chance to make an investment (after careful research) in a high-growth industry with large potential returns, then Stage I or II industries will provide you with opportunities for large gains. Since actual dividends are irrelevant in these stages, an investor will be purchasing shares for capital gains based on expected growth rather than on current income.

Expansion—Stage III

In Stage III, sales expansion and earnings continue but at a decreasing rate. As the industry crosses from the growth stage to the expansion stage, the slope of the line in Figure 6–1 becomes less steep, signaling slower growth. It is this crossover point that is important to the analyst who will also be evaluating declining returns on investment as more competition enters the market and attempts to take away market share from existing firms. The industry has grown to the point where asset expansion slows in line with production needs, and the firms in the industry are more capable of paying cash dividends. Stock dividends and stock splits are still common in Stage III, and the dividend payout ratio usually increases from a low level of 5 to 15 percent of earnings to a moderate level of 25 to 30 percent of earnings by Stage III.

Because industries and companies do not grow in a nice smooth line, it is often difficult to tell when the industry or company has crossed from Stage II growth to Stage III expansion. Determining the crossover point is extremely important to investors who choose to invest in growth companies. Once investors recognize that the past growth rate will not be extrapolated and, instead, is in decline, stock prices can take a sizable tumble as price-earnings ratios collapse because of slower growth expectations. Figure 6–2 on the following page demonstrates this relationship.

FIGURE 6–2   The Crossover Point

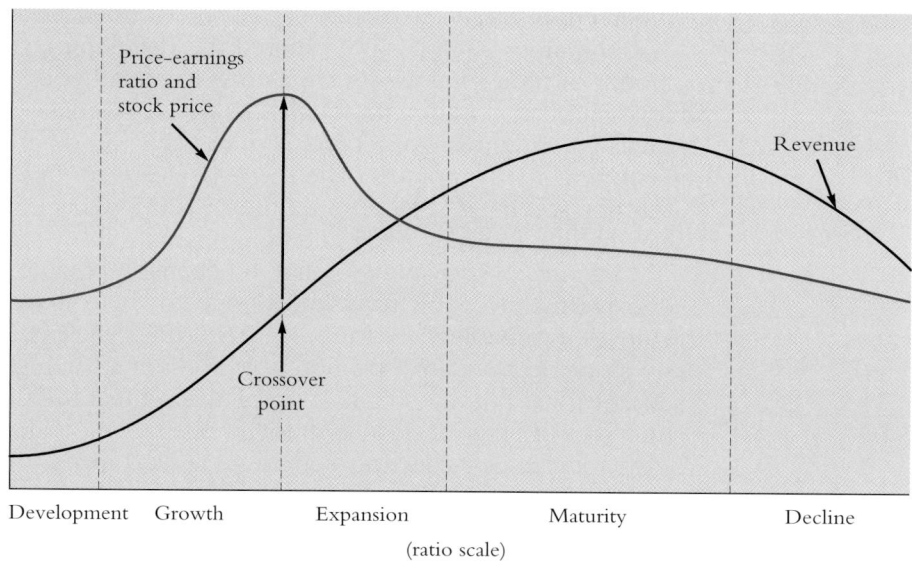

FIGURE 6–3   S&P Industrials versus GDP

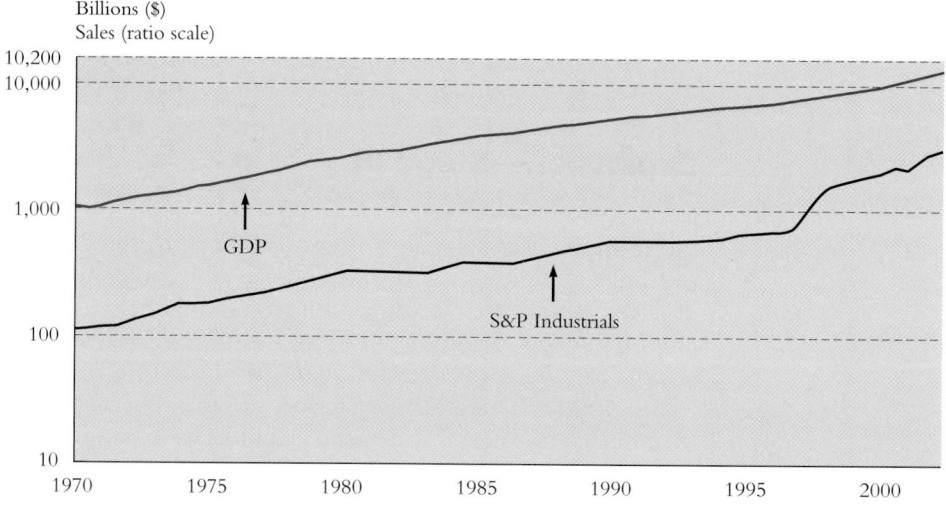

Maturity—Stage IV

Maturity occurs when industry sales grow at a rate equal to the economy as measured by the long-term trend in gross domestic product (GDP). Some analysts like to use the growth rate of the Standard & Poor's 500 Index for comparison because the growth rate of these 500 large companies sets the norm for mature companies. Figure 6–3 graphs sales for the S&P Industrials and the GDP using a logarithmic graph. The use of a logarithmic graph (sometimes called a ratio scale) allows a comparison of growth rates between trend lines since a

FIGURE 6–4 Automobile Industry versus GDP

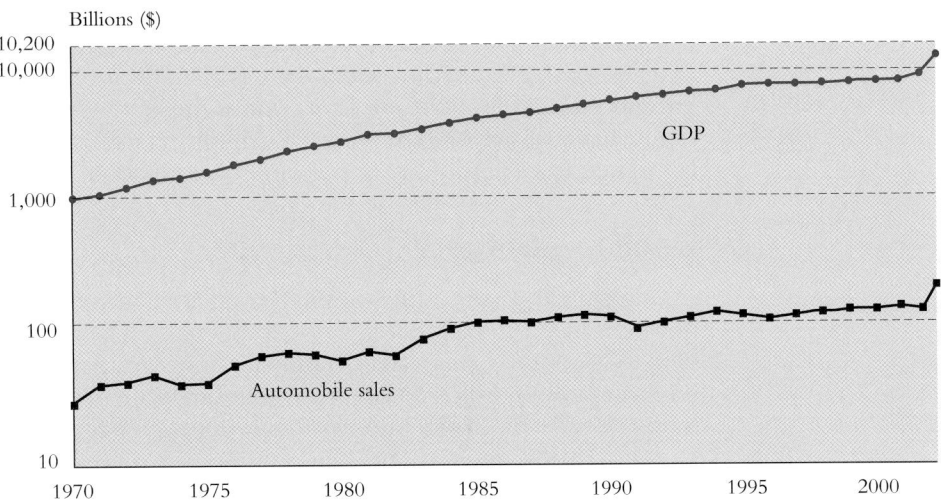

FIGURE 6–5 S&P Industrials Sales versus GDP, 1970–2002

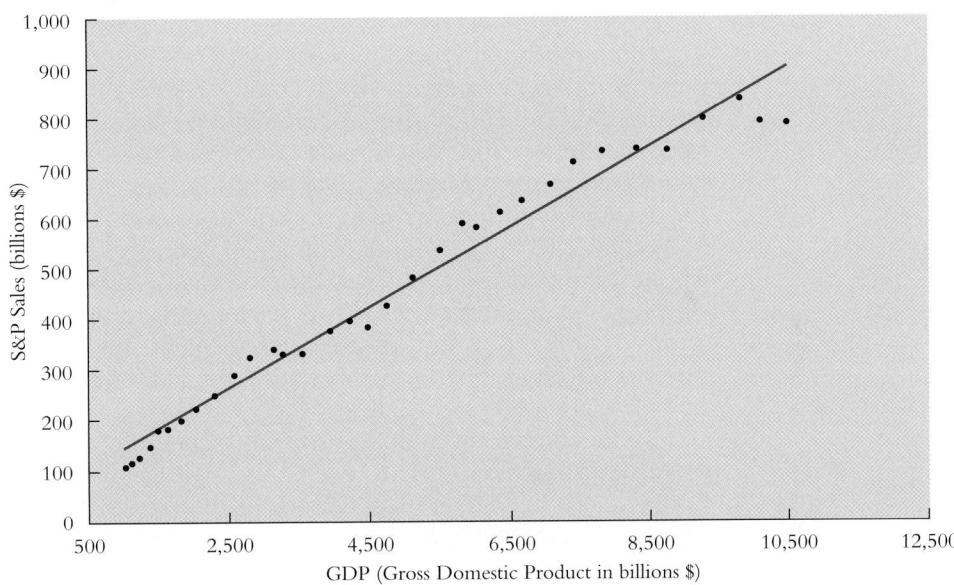

straight line on a vertical logarithmic scale represents a constant growth rate. The steeper the slope of the line, the faster the growth rate. Notice that on the graph, the S&P Industrials' sales and GDP seem to have similar long-term growth rates (slope).

Automobiles are a good example of a mature industry. You may remember that, in Chapter 5, we looked at the automobile industry as it related to the business cycle. Figure 6–4 shows the relationship between sales of the automobile industry and GDP in current dollars. While automobile sales do not have the relatively smooth line of GDP, the slope of the two lines appears similar. Figure 6–5 plots sales for the S&P 500 Industrials against the GDP for the years 1970 through 2002. The scatter diagram again depicts the cyclical nature of industrial sales and a close relationship to that of GDP.

By the time an industry or firm reaches maturity, plant and equipment are in place, financing alternatives are available domestically and internationally, and the cash flow from operations is usually more than enough to meet the growth requirements of the firm. Under these conditions, dividends will usually range from 45 to 50 percent of earnings. These percentages will be different from industry to industry, depending on individual characteristics.

Decline—Stage V

In unfortunate cases, industries suffer declines in sales if product innovation has not increased the product base over the years. Declining industries may be specific to a country; passenger trains are such an example. In Europe, passenger trains are common forms of transportation, while in the United States, passenger trains have been in decline for many decades because competition from automobiles, buses, and airplanes has cut into the market. Besides the famous buggy whip example, black-and-white television, vacuum tubes, and transistor radios are examples of products within an industry that have been in decline. In some cases, the companies producing these products repositioned their resources into growth-oriented products, and, in other cases, the companies went out of business.

Often it is not a whole industry that goes into decline but the weakest company in the industry that cannot compete. Currently, industries such as banks, airlines, and breweries are undergoing consolidation. The number of banks has been declining, and this trend is expected to accelerate as national banking takes hold in the United States. The airline industry has been in consolidation for decades with famous names such as Braniff, Eastern, and Pan Am defunct and others such as TWA and Continental continually on the brink of bankruptcy. Apple Computer represents an extreme case of a leading company in the early stages of development that fell on hard times during the later stages because of intense competition and its inability to meet that competition in pricing and product development. Only time will tell whether its alliance with Microsoft will help save the company.

Dividend payout ratios of firms in decline often rise to 100 percent or more of earnings. Often, the firm does not want to signal stockholders that it is in trouble, so it maintains its dividends in the face of falling earnings. This causes the payout ratio to soar until management realizes that the firm is bleeding to death and needs to conserve cash. Then either drastic dividend cuts follow, or there is an elimination of dividends entirely.

Dividend Policy and the Life-Cycle Curve   The dividend payout ratio has an important effect on company growth. As previously pointed out, the more funds a firm retains—and, thus, the lower the dividend payout—the greater the opportunity for growth. The dividend policy followed by management often provides the analyst with management's view of the company's ability to grow and some indication of where the company is on the life-cycle curve. For example, a firm paying out 50 percent of earnings in dividends is probably not in Phase I, II, or

III of the life-cycle curve. This relationship is further demonstrated in Appendix 6A with a discussion of the sustainable growth model.

Growth in Nongrowth Industries

It is also important to realize that growth companies can exist in a mature industry and that not all companies within an industry experience the same growth path in sales, earnings, and dividends. Some companies are simply better managed, have better people, have more efficient assets, and have put more money into productive research and development that has created new or improved products.

www.cocacola.com
www.mcDonalds.com

Many U.S. companies, such as Coca-Cola and McDonald's, have found growth by expansion abroad. While their domestic markets are saturated and growing at the rate of GDP or less, the international demand for their products in Asia, Europe, Eastern Europe, Russia, and China has allowed these two companies to maintain double-digit growth rates. This may also be true of other marketing-oriented companies with global trademarks such as Sony, Pepsi, Heineken, and Nike.

Electric utilities are generally considered mature, but utilities in states such as Florida, Arizona, and the Carolinas, which have undergone rapid population explosions over the last decade, would still have higher growth rates than the industry in general.

Computer companies such as IBM were fast approaching maturity until technical innovations created new markets. Unfortunately for IBM, demand for its mainframe computers declined worldwide as personal computers and local area networks increased in flexibility and power. To combat this decline in its major product line, IBM restructured in an effort to revive growth from its personal computer, software, and service divisions. Some analysts would place the PC industry in the expansion stage, but IBM as the dominant player in the computer industry is playing catch-up to other PC makers like Dell who dominate the growth segments.

The warning to the investor is not to become enamored with a company just because it is in a "growth industry." Its time of glory may have passed. Other investors improperly ignore companies that are in the process of revitalization. More will be said about growth stocks in Chapter 7.

Industry Structure

The structure of the industry is another area of importance for the analyst. Industry structure determines whether the companies in the industry are profitable, whether there are special considerations such as government regulations that positively or negatively affect the industry, and whether cost advantages and product quality create a dominant company within the industry.

A financial analyst may want to evaluate other significant factors for a given industry. For example, is the industry structure monopolistic like a regulated utility, oligopolistic like the automobile industry, partially competitive like the pharmaceutical industry, or very competitive like the industry for farm commodities? Questions of industry structure are very important in analyzing pricing structures and price elasticities that exist because of competition or the lack of it.

Economic Structure

We often look at the economic structure of an industry to determine how companies compete within the industry. **Monopolies** are generally not common in the United States because of our antitrust laws, but they have existed by government permission in the area of public utilities. In return for the monopoly, the government has the right to regulate rates of return on equity and assets and to approve customer fees. This sets the limits of growth and profitability and creates minimums and maximums for the analyst. Monopolies are almost always in mature industries, although the government may occasionally grant a monopoly on emerging technologies and even offer subsidies for the development of new technologies, especially in the defense industry.

Oligopolies have few competitors and are quite common in large mature U.S. industries such as automobiles, steel, oil, airlines, and aluminum to name a few. The competition between companies in an oligopoly can be intense, and profitability can suffer as a result of price wars and battles over market share. Increasingly, oligopolistic industries are facing international competition, which has altered their competitive strategies. Note that many of the industries mentioned above have competition from other industrial countries such as Japan, Germany, the Netherlands, Britain, and France.

Pure competition in manufacturing is not widely found in the United States. The food processing industry may be the closest example of this economic form. Generally, companies in pure competition do not have a differentiated product such as corn, soybeans, and other commodities. Firms will often compete by trying to create perceived differences in product quality or service.

Other Economic Factors to Consider Questions of supply and demand relationships are very important because they affect the price structure of the industry and its ability to produce quality products at a reasonable cost. The cost variable can be affected by many factors. For example, high relative hourly wages in basic industries such as steel, autos, and rubber are somewhat responsible for the inability of the United States to compete in the world markets for these products. Availability of raw material is also an important cost factor. Industries such as aluminum and glass need to have an abundance of low-cost bauxite and silicon to produce their products. Unfortunately, the aluminum industry uses very large amounts of electricity in the production process, so the low cost of bauxite may be offset by the high cost of energy. Energy costs are of concern to all industries, but the availability of reasonably priced energy sources is particularly important to the airline and trucking industries. The list could go on and on, but as analysts become familiar with a specific industry, they learn the crucial variables.

Government Regulation Most industries are also affected by government regulation. This applies to the automobile industry where safety and exhaust emissions are regulated and to all industries where air, water, and noise pollution are of concern. Many industries engaged in interstate commerce—such as utilities, railroads, and telephone companies—have been strongly regulated by the government, but even these have begun to feel the effects of deregulation and competition. The telephone companies have begun a global expansion with international partners that is changing the face of competition for long-distance calling worldwide. Industries such as airlines, trucking, and natural gas production have been deregulated and are still undergoing structural changes within the industry as new competitive forces emerge. Most industries are affected by government expenditures; this is especially true for industries involved in defense, education, health care, and transportation.

These are but a few examples to alert you to the importance of having a thorough understanding of your industry. This is why in many large investment firms, trust departments, and insurance companies, analysts are assigned to only one industry or to several related industries so that they may concentrate their attention on a given set of significant factors. Perhaps one of the most important aspects of industry analysis is the competitive structure of the industry.

Competitive Structure

Industries consist of competing firms; some industries have many firms, others have few. Nevertheless, the existing firms compete with each other and employ different strategies for success. Increasingly, the competition is among large international companies where cultural values and production processes are different. It becomes important for the investment analyst to know the attractiveness of industries for long-term profitability and what factors determine an industry's long-term outlook.

As we discussed previously, just because an industry as a whole is in a certain life-cycle stage, all companies within that industry may not be in the same position. An individual company within the industry may have chosen a poor competitive position or an excellent competitive position. While the industry outlook is important, a company may be able to create a competitive position that shapes the industry environment. There are profitable firms in poor industries and unprofitable firms in good industries.

Perhaps one of the most efficient ways to indicate competitive issues is to consider Michael Porter's elements of industry structure.[1]

Porter divides the competitive structure of an industry into five basic competitive forces: (1) threat of entry by new competitors, (2) threat of substitute goods, (3) bargaining power of buyers, (4) bargaining power of suppliers, and (5) rivalry among existing competitors. All affect price and profitability. The first is the threat of entry by new competitors. If competitors can easily enter the market, firms may have to construct barriers to entry that raise the cost to the firm. This threat places a limit on prices that can be charged and affects profitability. A second force, as we know from economics, is the threat of substitute goods. If we can easily substitute one good for another, this will again affect the price that can be charged and profit margins. An example of this would be in the beverage industry. We can drink water (tap or bottled), beer, soft drinks, fruit juice, and so on. If not for the tremendous advertising expenditures from companies trying to get us to drink their beverages, the cost would be considerably lower.

---

[1] Professor Porter is a leading business strategist at Harvard University. See the Selected References at the end of the chapter.

the real world of investing

In Analyzing an Industry or Company, What's a Brand Name Worth?

In our modern economy, a brand name is often worth as much as brick or mortar. In recognizing this fact, in August 2001, *BusinessWeek* began publishing its ranking of the 100 most valuable brand names in the world and their value.*

The first question is, "How do you establish the value?" For this purpose, *BusinessWeek* engaged the services of Interbrand Corp., a pioneering brand consulting firm in New York. The value is based on the power to increase sales and earnings and is quantified through taking the present value of the future impact on these variables. While intangible assets such as brand name recognition are normally not quantified in the United States because of rulings by the Financial Accounting Standards Board, financial analysts recognize their essential nature in valuing a firm. The lack of inclusion of intangible assets on the balance sheet (with the exception of postmerger goodwill) is one reason firms in the S&P 500 Stock Index, on average trade at five times their accounting determined book value. For companies in Great Britain and Australia, brand name value *must* be included on the balance sheet.

Having said all this, which U.S. company had the most valuable brand name recognition? The envelope please. And the answer is Coca-Cola with a value of $68.9 billion. The top 10 in the *BusinessWeek* survey are:

	(in billions)		(in billions)
Coca-Cola	$70.4	Nokia	$29.4
Microsoft	65.2	Disney	28.0
IBM	51.8	McDonald's	24.7
GE	42.3	Marlboro	22.1
Intel	31.1	Mercedes	21.3

Because this chapter is on industry analysis, we also show the top-ranked brand names in two industries where brand recognition is particularly important:

Automotive	(in billions)	Technology	(in billions)
Mercedes	$21.3	IBM	$51.8
Toyota	20.8	Intel	31.1
Ford	17.1	H-P	19.9
Honda	15.6	Cisco	15.8
BMW	15.1	Oracle	11.3

The story is not positive for all companies. According to the survey, due to unfortunate events or poor performance, Xerox lost 38 percent of its brand name value in 2001, and Yahoo! and Amazon.com each lost 31 percent.

---
* "The Best Global Brands," *BusinessWeek,* August 6, 2001, pp. 50–55.

www.cocacola.com   www.ford.com   www.ibm.com

www.walmart.com

Two other competitive forces are the bargaining power of buyers and the bargaining power of suppliers. A large buyer of goods (Wal-Mart) can influence the price suppliers can charge for their goods. Firms such as McDonald's have stringent requirements for their suppliers, and, because it is a powerful buyer, McDonald's expects and gets cost-efficient service and quality control from its suppliers. This behavior restricts the prices that suppliers can charge. On the other hand, there are many powerful suppliers, such as the Middle East oil cartel or DeBeers, the company that controls more than 70 percent of the worldwide diamond market. These suppliers control the cost of raw materials to their customers, and their behavior determines a major part of their customers' profitability.

The last competitive force is the rivalry among existing competitors. The extent of the rivalry affects the costs of competition—from the investment in plant and equipment, to advertising and product development. The automobile industry is a reasonable example of intense rivalry that eventually caused Japanese auto manufacturers, for political reasons, to limit their exports to the United States and instead start producing automobiles in the United States. Because the threat of entry was thought to be small, U.S. automobile companies were complacent for years and did not modernize their production processes with new technology or work flow techniques. Once the Japanese took a large market share, the rivalry intensified and caused a restructuring of the whole U.S. automobile industry. The impact of intense rivalry, therefore, has the same effect as the threat of new entrants.

These five forces vary from industry to industry and directly affect the return on assets and return on equity. The importance of each factor is a function of industry structure or the economic and technical characteristics of an industry. These forces affect prices, costs, and investment in plants, equipment, advertising, and research and development. While each industry has a set of competitive forces that are most important to it in terms of long-run profitability, competitors will devise strategies that may change the industry structure. Strategies that change the environment may improve or destroy the industry structure and profitability. Sometimes it takes several years to see the impact of competitive strategies.

Pharmaceutical Industry—An Example

Every industry has its own unique issues that arise from the economic and competitive structure of the industry. As we discussed on the previous pages, there is a lot to consider when analyzing an industry. For example the pharmaceutical industry is a global industry and barriers to entry are high because it is not easy or cheap to develop new drugs. Additionally, drugs have predictable life cycles as they go through the development process, the approval process, and then the remainder of their life under patent protection, which may last no more that 10 years as a practical matter. Table 6–1 presents the leading pharmaceutical companies at the end of 2002 listed by sales.

Table 6–1 demonstrates the global nature of this industry. Pfizer is the largest company and even though it is a U.S. company, it has a worldwide presence through its recent merger with the Italian firm Pharmacia (second from the

TABLE 6–1 Leading Pharmaceutical Companies, 2002

Company	Sales ($ billions)
Pfizer	28.28
GlaxoSmithKline	28.20
Merck	21.63
AstraZeneca	17.84
Aventis	17.25
Johnson & Johnson	17.20
Novartis	15.36
Bristol-Myers Squibb	14.70
Pharmacia	12.03
Wyeth	11.70

Sources: *Pharmaceutical Executive.* Standard & Poor's Industry Survey, December 11, 2003, p. 7.

bottom of the list). In second place is the large British firm of GlaxoSmithKline, another company created through global mergers. Aventis is French, Novartis is Swiss, and AstraZeneca is German. Foreign sales account for close to 40 percent of pharmaceutical companies' sales listed in the table.

Life-Cycle Analysis

These large companies are for the most part somewhere in the expansion stage of their life cycle. While each new drug will go through a product life cycle, the portfolio of products for these companies is quite diversified with each in a different phase of the cycle. Overall, the industry is growing faster than the economy and the Standard and Poor's 500 Index, but growth is decelerating rather than accelerating. Each company could be on a different part of the expansion curve. Table 6–2 depicts a comparative company analysis of pharmaceutical companies. Panel A on page 155 shows the operating revenues of a selected group with their corresponding 1-year, 5-year and 10-year growth rates, while panel B on page 156 displays the net income and growth rates for these companies.

As you analyze the growth rates in operating revenues for each company, you can see the variability from company to company. While many of the very large companies like Merck could be in the expansion stage of their life cycle, many of the smaller or medium-size firms such as Barr Laboratories could be in the growth phase. Some companies such as Wyeth have not been successful in developing new products and demonstrate stagnant growth. So while we can generalize about an industry, it is very difficult to assume all companies in the same industry are in the same phase of the life cycle. You might also notice that revenue growth does not always translate into growth in net income. For example, Pfizer's growth in net income surpasses its revenue growth because of the economies of scale achieved through merger activity and rising profit margins from the development of new drugs.

Government Regulation

These firms sell their drugs throughout the world and are regulated by many governments. It is quite possible for a drug to be approved in five European countries but not approved for sale in the United States. The U.S. Food and Drug Administration (FDA) is considered to be one of the most risk-averse and strict enforcement agencies in the world, and it is not unusual for drugs to be approved for use in other countries before receiving approval from the FDA. This is a controversial issue for people with a disease that needs to be treated with drugs not yet available in the United States. The FDA would respond that it is better to err on the side of peoples' health than to take the risk of fatal side effects with an unproven drug.

Table 6–3 on page 157 presents the annual number of drugs submitted to the FDA between 1992 and 2002. The number has been close to 2,000 per year and it can take up to ten years of research and development for each drug before submission. Notice that the number of new drugs approved is a very small percentage of the total submitted. For example in 2002, there were 2,374 drugs submitted and only 78 approved, for a 3.3 percent approval rate.

TABLE 6-2 Comparative Company Analysis—Health Care: Pharmaceuticals—Panel A

			Operating Revenues ($ millions)						Compound Growth Rate (%)		
Ticker	Company	Yr-End	2002	2001	2000	1999	1998	1997	1992	10-Yr.	5-Yr.	1-Yr.
Pharmaceuticals[‡]												
ABT	Abbot Laboratories	DEC	17,684.7	16,285.2	13,745.9	13,177.6	12,477.8	11,883.5	7,851.9	8.5	8.3	8.6
AGN	Allergan Inc.	DEC	1,425.3	1,745.5	1,625.5	1,452.4	1,296.1	1,149.0	897.7	4.7	4.4	−18.3
ALO	Alpharma Inc.—CLA	DEC	1,238.0	975.0	900.8	732.4	604.6	500.3	295.1	15.4	19.9	27.0
BRL	Barr Laboratories, Inc	JUN	1,189.0	509.7	482.3	444.0	377.3	257.4	100.8	28.0	35.8	133.3
BMY	Bristol-Myers Squibb	DEC	18,119.0	18,213.0	18,216.0	20,222.0	18,284.0	16,701.0	11,156.0	5.0	1.6	−0.5
CIMA	Cima Labs Inc.	DEC	46.6	32.0	23.9	13.4	7.2	4.9	NA	NA	56.9	45.6
FRX	Forest Laboratories—CLA	MAR	2,206.7	1,566.6	1,174.5	872.8	546.3	427.1	285.4	22.7	38.9	40.9
ICN	ICN Pharmaceuticals Inc	DEC	737.1	858.1	800.3	747.4	838.1	476.1	NA	4.5	−0.4	−14.1
IVX	IVAX Corp	DEC	1,197.2	1,215.4	793.4	656.3	637.9	602.1	451.0	10.3	14.7	−1.5
JNJ	Johnson & Johnson	DEC	36,298.0	33,004.0	29,139.0	27,471.0	23,657.0	22,629.0	13,753.0	10.2	9.9	10.0
KG	King Pharmaceuticals Inc	DEC	1,128.3	872.3	620.2	348.3	163.5	47.9	NA	NA	88.1	29.4
LLY	Lilly (Eli) & Co.	DEC	11,077.5	11,542.5	10,862.2	9,912.9	9,236.8	8,517.6	6,167.3	6.0	5.4	−4.0
MRX	Medicis Pharmaceut CP—CLA	JUN	212.8	167.8	139.1	116.9	77.6	41.2	9.0	37.2	38.9	26.8
MRK	Merck & Co.	DEC	51,790.3	47,715.7	40,363.2	32,714.0	26,898.2	23,636.9	9,662.5	18.3	17.0	8.5
MOGN	MGI Pharma Inc.	DEC	28.2	33.0	25.2	24.7	16.8	12.4	3.1	24.5	17.8	−14.4
MYL	Mylan Laboratories	MAR	1,269.2	1,104.1	846.7	790.1	721.1	555.4	212.0	19.6	18.0	15.0
NOVN	Noven Pharmaceuticals Inc	DEC	55.4	45.9	42.9	31.6	16.2	14.3	1.9	39.9	31.2	20.5
PRGO	Perrigo Co	JUN	826.3	753.5	738.6	877.6	902.6	844.6	409.8	7.3	−0.4	9.7
PFE	Pfizer Inc	DEC	32,373.0	32,084.0	29,574.0	16,204.0	13,544.0	12,504.0	7,230.2	16.2	21.0	0.9
PRX	Pharmaceutical Res Inc	DEC	381.6	271.0	85.0	80.3	60.4	53.2	52.5	21.9	48.3	40.8
SGP	Schering-Plough	DEC	10,180.0	9,802.0	9,815.0	9,176.0	8,077.0	6,778.0	4,055.7	9.6	8.5	3.9
SEPR	Sepracor Inc	DEC	239.0	152.1	85.2	22.7	17.4	15.3	17.6	29.8	73.2	57.1
SCRI	Sicor Inc	DEC	456.0	369.8	293.8	229.0	178.5	149.7	30.8	30.9	25.0	23.3
WPI	Watson Pharmaceuticals Inc	DEC	1,223.2	1,160.7	811.5	689.2	556.1	338.3	34.7	42.8	29.3	5.4
WYE	Wyeth	DEC	14,587.0	14,128.5	13,262.8	13,550.2	13,462.7	14,196.0	7,873.7	6.4	0.5	3.2

Note: Data as originally reported.
[‡] S&P Index group.

(continued)

TABLE 6-2 Comparative Company Analysis—Health Care: Pharmaceuticals—Panel B

Net Income ($ millions)

Ticker	Company	Yr-End	2002	2001	2000	1999	1998	1997	1992	10-Yr.	5-Yr.	1-Yr.
Pharmaceuticals‡												
ABT	*Abbot Laboratories	DEC	2,793.7	1,550.4	2,786.0	2,445.8	2,333.2	2,094.5	1,239.1	8.5	5.9	80.2
AGN	*Allergan Inc.	DEC	64.0	226.7	215.1	188.2	-90.2	128.3	105.8	-4.9	-13.0	-71.8
ALO	§Alpharma Inc.—CLA	DEC	-97.7	-35.7	55.5	37.0	24.2	17.4	11.4	NM	NM	NM
BRL	†Barr Laboratories, Inc	JUN	212.4	62.5	42.3	49.3	33.5	19.4	-1.9	NM	61.3	239.9
BMY	*Bristol-Myers Squibb	DEC	2,034.0	2,034.0	4,096.0	4,167.0	3,141.0	3,205.0	1,538.0	2.8	-8.7	-0.4
CIMA	§Cima Labs Inc.	DEC	18.6	15.0	4.8	-1.3	-3.2	-5.8	NA	NA	NM	24.2
FRX	*Forest Laboratories—CLA	#MAR	622.0	338.0	215.1	112.7	77.2	36.7	64.3	25.5	76.1	87.0
ICN	†ICN Pharmaceuticals Inc	DEC	84.2	85.2	93.4	118.6	-352.1	113.9	34.5	9.3	-5.9	-1.1
IVX	†IVAX Corp	DEC	118.6	236.1	139.8	69.5	24.6	-219.5	44.6	10.3	NM	-49.8
JNJ	*Johnson & Johnson	DEC	6,597.0	5,668.0	4,800.0	4,167.0	3,059.0	3,303.0	1,625.0	15.0	14.8	16.4
KG	*King Pharmaceuticals Inc	DEC	182.5	232.9	104.6	45.7	25.3	6.6	NA	NA	94.2	-21.6
LLY	*Lilly (Eli) & Co.	DEC	2,707.9	2,809.4	3,057.8	2,546.7	2,096.3	-385.1	827.6	12.6	NM	-3.6
MRX	§Medicis Pharmaceut CP—CLA	JUN	50.0	40.4	43.0	41.4	-12.4	17.3	-6.9	NM	23.6	23.8
MRK	*Merck & Co.	DEC	7,149.5	7,281.8	6,821.7	5,890.5	5,248.2	4,614.1	2,446.6	11.3	9.2	-1.8
MOGN	§MGI Pharma Inc.	DEC	-36.1	-34.8	-10.1	4.7	0.4	-1.8	-9.2	NM	NM	NM
MYL	†Mylan Laboratories	#MAR	272.4	260.3	37.1	154.2	115.4	100.8	70.6	14.5	22.0	4.7
NOVN	§Noven Pharmaceuticals Inc	DEC	13.9	12.1	19.6	10.5	-4.1	-9.6	-3.0	NM	NM	14.8
PRGO	†Perrigo Co	JUN	50.2	27.7	19.3	1.5	-51.6	45.0	28.6	5.8	2.2	81.5
PFE	*Pfizer Inc	DEC	9,181.0	7,752.0	3,718.0	3,199.0	1,950.0	2,213.0	1,093.5	23.7	32.9	18.4
PRX	†Pharmaceutical Res Inc	DEC	79.5	53.9	-0.9	-1.8	-9.6	-8.9	4.1	34.5	NM	47.3
SGP	*Schering-Plough	DEC	1,974.0	1,943.0	2,423.0	2,110.0	1,756.0	1,444.0	720.0	10.6	6.5	1.6
SEPR	†Sepracor Inc	DEC	-276.5	-224.0	-204.0	-182.7	-93.3	-26.1	-10.5	NM	NM	NM
SCRI	†Sicor Inc	DEC	128.3	79.3	38.5	11.7	-18.6	-76.7	-37.9	NM	NM	61.9
WPI	*Watson Pharmaceuticals Inc	DEC	175.8	116.4	170.7	178.9	120.8	90.2	3.6	47.6	14.3	51.1
WYE	*Wyeth	DEC	4,447.2	2,285.3	-901.0	-1,227.1	2,474.3	2,043.1	1,150.7	14.5	16.8	94.6

Note: Data as originally reported.
‡ S&P Index group.
* Company included in the S&P 500.
† Company included in the S&P MidCap.
§ Company included in the S&P SmallCap.
# Of the following calendar year.

Source: Health Care: Pharmaceuticals Industry Survey, December 11, 2003.

TABLE 6-3 New Drug Filings with the Food & Drug Administration

Year	INDs Submitted	Approved	New Molecular Entities	NME Mean Approval Time (months) Priority	Standard
2002	2,374	78	17	13.8	15.9
2001	1,872	66	24	6.0	19.0
2000	1,815	98	27	6.0	19.9
1999	1,763	83	35	6.3	16.3
1998	2,419	90	30	6.2	13.4
1997	1,996	121	39	6.4	15.0
1996	1,831	131	53	7.7	15.1
1995	1,924	82	28	6.0	17.8
1994	2,156	62	22	15.0	23.7
1993	2,323	70	25	13.9	27.2
1992	2,578	91	26	NA	NA

IND—Investigational new drug. NME—New molecular entity. NA—Not available.

Sources: FDA Center for Drug Evaluation and Research; *Standard & Poor's Industry Survey*, December 11, 1003, p. 11.

Research and Development

One of the unique and extremely important areas for the pharmaceutical industry is the large amount of money invested in research and development. A very important ratio in this industry is the amount spent on research and development as a percentage of sales. Small companies are often at a disadvantage because they may only have enough money to work on a few drugs, while large companies like Pfizer can work on many chemical compounds and perhaps have a higher success rate. With only a 3.3 percent success rate in passing FDA approval, a great deal of research and development money is spent on failures. Table 6–4 demonstrates the research and development expenditures in this

TABLE 6-4 Research and Development Expenditures

Company	2000 ($ mil.)	% of Sales	2001 ($ mil.)	% of Sales	2002 ($ mil.)	% of Sales
Abbott	1,351	10	1,578	10	1,562	9
Bristol-Myers Squibb	1,878	11	2,183	12	2,218	12
Eli Lilly	2,018	19	2,235	19	2,149	19
Johnson & Johnson	3,105	11	3,591	16	3,957	11
Merck	2,344	6	2,456	5	2,677	5
Pfizer	4,374	17	4,776	16	4,045	12
Pharmacia	2,165	17	2,361	17	2,359	17
Schering-Plough	1,333	14	1,312	13	1,425	14
Wyeth	1,687	13	1,870	13	2,080	14

Sources: Company reports; *Standard & Poor's Industry Survey*, December 11, 1003, p 23.

TABLE 6–5 Top Prescription Drugs of 2002—Global Market

Drug Company	Use	2002 Sales ($ billions)
Lipitor (Pfizer)	Cholesterol reducer	7.97
Zocor (Merck)	Cholesterol reducer	5.60
Prilosec (AstraZeneca-Merck)	Antiulcer	4.62
Procrit (Johnson & Johnson)	Antianemia	4.30
Norvasc (Pfizer)	Antihypertensive	3.84
Zyprexa (Lilly)	Antipsychotic	3.69
Paxil (GlaxoSmithKline)	Antidepressant	3.22
Prevacid (TAP Pharma-Abbott)	Antiulcer	3.14
Celebrex (Pfizer)	Antiarthritic	3.05
Zoloft (Pfizer)	Antidepressant	2.74

Sources: *Standard & Poor's Industry Survey,* December 11, 2003, p. 9.

industry and shows that most companies on the list were spending over $2 billion on R&D in 2002, with Pfizer leading the pack at over $4 billion.

In recent years, companies like Pfizer have merged with others to create very large companies that can pool their research resources to develop new drugs and achieve economies of scale. Mergers can also result from lack of research productivity. Large firms that have been unsuccessful at research may buy smaller companies with only one popular drug as a way of filling their product line. An analyst has to be careful in judging the research and development expense as a percentage of sales. Just because a company spends a large percentage of money on drug research doesn't mean they will be successful. What counts is how many successful drugs that can be developed through the FDA approval process, and the percentage of the drugs under development that actually improve the treatment of the targeted diseases.

A successful drug can reap large profits for a firm. Lipitor, the top selling drug for 2002, is Pfizer's drug to reduce cholesterol and it accounted for $7.97 billion of Pfizer's $28.3 billion sales in 2002. Table 6–5 presents the top prescription drugs in the global market for 2002, and if you count the winners you will see that Pfizer has four of the top 10 drugs.

The pharmaceutical industry lives and dies by its ability to create new chemical compounds that combat disease. The more effective the companies are in developing new drugs, the more profitable they will be and the more good they will do society. Advances in technology that allow researchers to analyze human genes have enabled scientists to better understand how genetic defects can cause many of our common diseases such as Alzheimer's disease, muscular dystrophy, and others. Many hope that new discoveries concerning genetics will allow researchers to move faster in solving some of the world's more puzzling medical problems.

Product Diversity

The pharmaceutical industry is more complex than it might seem at first glance. Companies sell diagnostic and hospital supplies, nutritional supplements, human health products, animal health products, agricultural products, prescription pharmaceuticals, consumer products, and over-the-counter products such as aspirin and Tylenol. There are large and small companies, and even within the industry, companies concentrate their research efforts on targeted areas such as coronary, infectious, central nervous system, or pulmonary diseases. Even within the industry there is not a lot of direct competition.

For example, it is unusual to find more than three drugs with high market shares treating the same problem. Usually one or two drugs dominate a market. Examining the product categories in Table 6–5, there are two cholesterol-reducing drugs in first and second place, two antiulcer drugs and two antidepressants in the top 10, with the other four leaders used for treating other aliments. Perhaps more important to the investor than a company's drugs currently in the market is the probability that its research laboratory is full of potential blockbuster drugs. Often stock prices are more influenced by a promising research pipeline than the current drugs that may come off patent in the next few years.

Patents and Generic Drugs

Drugs receive patent protection from the U.S. patent office and are protected from competition for a limited number of years. When a drug comes off patent protection, other companies are finally allowed to compete. Since the chemical makeup is available through the patent license, imitating some other company's chemical cocktail is not that difficult. Drugs imitated by other companies after a patent runs out are called generics, since they are copies. Once a generic duplicate hits the market, the profit on the original drug will shrink. Eli Lilly's Prozac is a case in point. This antidepressant generated close to $3 billion worth of sales for Lilly but when it became available in generic form, Lilly lost approximately 80 percent of its Prozac sales. Of course, this is positive for consumers as they can buy the pills at a reduced price. Most pharmaceutical companies would like longer patent protection to insure that the profits from their discoveries can be reinvested in new research. (The normal protection period is now effectively 10 years.) In spite of complaints about inadequate patent protection, pharmaceutical companies generate high profit margins relative to many other industries.

Because this is a global industry, worldwide patent protection is a big issue. Many countries violate or don't enforce international patent protection. A company only needs to buy a pill and analyze it to determine its chemical formula and then manufacture the drug. This is usually easy for another pharmaceutical company to do. Patent violations and counterfeiting have been prevalent more in developing countries, especially Africa, where the AIDs epidemic is a serious problem. These violations have also occurred in India where many people can't afford the prices charged by the major global manufacturers. In recent years, companies have begun working with these governments to reduce the price of their drugs in exchange for more rigorous enforcement of the companies' patents.

Demographics and Managed Care

Other issues that have a large effect on the pharmaceutical industry are demographics. As the world population ages, the demand for drugs will grow. Europe and Japan have relatively old populations and the United States is rapidly aging.

As the baby boomers age, their demand for drugs to treat all kinds of disease will increase. According to the *Standard and Poor's Industry Survey,* global demographics are bullish for the pharmaceutical industry. The drive to restrain rising drug prices through managed care and government programs will put downward pressure on company profit margins. The new Medicare coverage for drugs, while keeping a lid on prices, could create enough of an increased demand for drugs to overshadow any pricing constraints imposed on the pharmaceutical industry.

To keep yourself up to date on this industry or any other industry you are interested in analyzing, please refer to *Standard & Poor's Industry Surveys.* They are available online and accompany this book through McGraw-Hill's S&P Market Insight website **www.mhhe.com/edumarketinsight**. Most likely your library has a print copy.

Industry Groups and Rotational Investing

One strategy of investment used by institutional investors and occasionally by individual investors is the concept of **rotational investing.** Rotational investing refers to the practice of moving in and out of various industries over the business cycle. As the business cycle moves from a trough to a peak, different industries benefit from the economic changes that accompany the cycle. Table 6–6 lists 10 Dow Jones Industry Groups; industries are classified into groups that are related in some form and that may exhibit similar behavior during different phases of the business cycle.

For example, as interest rates bottom out, houses become more easily financed and cost less per month to purchase. Because of this, housing stocks, home builders, lumber, and housing-related industries such as household durable goods benefit from the lower interest rates. Earnings of companies in these fields are expected to rise, and investors start buying the common stocks of these companies before any profits are actually visible. The same could be said for the automobile industry because of the effect of low-cost financing.

Once an economic recovery is under way, the unemployment rate declines, personal income starts growing, and consumers start spending more. It may take six quarters or more of growth from the recessionary trough, but investors usually anticipate when the consumer will start spending again and bid prices of consumer cyclical stocks up before earnings increases appear. While automobile sales are affected by the lower interest rates, they also get a second boost from healthier and more affluent consumers.

When interest rates begin to rise, this is not good news for utility stocks. Utilities generate high dividend payouts and usually sell based on their dividend yield. As interest rates rise, utility stock prices fall along with prices of bonds. Another group that eventually loses favor after rates have risen somewhat from their bottom and are expected to continue rising is the banking sector. Rising rates eventually reduce bank lending and squeeze bank margins, which are small anyway.

Investors fearful of rising rates and a potential economic slowdown will often retreat into consumer noncyclical goods such as food, pharmaceuticals, beverages, and tobacco. A move into these industries is often considered defensive because the industries are not much influenced by economic downturns, so their earnings do not suffer nearly as much as cyclical industries.

TABLE 6–6 Dow Jones Industry Groups

Basic Materials	Distillers and brewers	**Industrial**
Chemicals	Food products	Aerospace and defense
Chemicals, commodity	Soft drinks	Building materials
Chemicals, specialty	Food retailers and wholesalers	Heavy construction
Forest products	Consumer products	Containers and packaging
Paper products	Household products, durables	Industrial diversified
Aluminum	Household products, nondurables	Industrial equipment
Mining, diversified	Tobacco	Advanced industrial equipment
Other nonferrous (e.g., aluminum)		Electrical components and equipment
Precious metals	**Energy**	Factory equipment
Steel	Coal	Heavy machinery
	Oil and gas	Industrial services
Consumer, Cyclical	Oil, drilling	Pollution control and waste management
Advertising	Oil, integrated majors	Industrial transportation
Broadcasting	Oil, secondary	Air freight and couriers
Publishing	Oilfield equipment and services	Marine transportation
Auto manufacturers	Pipelines	Railroads
Auto parts		Trucking
Casinos	**Financial**	Transportation equipment
Entertainment	Banks	
Recreation products and services	Insurance, composite	**Technology**
Restaurants	Insurance, full line	Hardware and equipment
Toys	Insurance, life	Communications technology
Home construction	Insurance, property and casualty	Computers
Furnishings	Specialty finance	Office equipment
Retailers	Real estate investment	Semiconductor and related
Retailers, apparel	Financial services, diversified	Software
Retailers, broadline	Savings and loans	
Retailers, drug-based	Securities brokers	**Telecommunications**
Retailers, specialty (e.g., drug and apparel)		Fixed line communications
	Health Care	Wireless communications
Clothing and fabrics	Health care providers	
Footwear	Medical products	**Utilities**
Airlines	Advanced medical devices	Electric
Lodging	Medical supplies	Gas
	Pharmaceutical and biotech	Water
Consumer, Noncyclical	Biotechnology	
Consumer services	Pharmaceuticals	
Cosmetics and personal care		

Eventually, as the economy moves through its business cycle, inflation fears return as demand for products pushes up prices of goods. One possible move is into basic materials and energy. The pricing pressures in the economy spill over into rising prices for these commodities and rising profits for aluminum, oil, steel, and other companies in these industries. A move into these industry groups usually occurs later in the business cycle.

While we do not necessarily endorse buying and selling common stocks in a rotational manner throughout the business cycle, many investors follow this approach, and you should be well aware of this strategy.

exploring the web

Website Address	Comments
www.hoovers.com	Provides limited free information about sectors and industries
cbs.marketwatch.com	Contains news and industry performance on daily basis
www.smartmoney.com	Provides sector and market performance—feature is map of market
www.wsj.com	Provides limited information about industry data; has searchable archive on articles about companies and industries—most content requires subscription to access.
www.corporateinformation.com	Provides links to information on industries and by country—requires free registration
www.ita.doc.gov	Provides access to industry reports that are fee-based
www.investorguide.com	Has links to sites providing sector and industry information

Summary

The preceding chapter presented a three-step model for stock valuation in Figure 5–1. Industry analysis as presented in this chapter is the second step in the top-down valuation process we use in the text. One of the most crucial issues in valuing a firm is its potential growth rate in sales, earnings, and cash flow. In order to have some idea of how fast a company can grow, we look at the underlying industry growth characteristics, especially its position on the life-cycle curve.

The industry life-cycle approach includes five stages: development, growth, expansion, maturity, and decline. The life-cycle process is depicted in Figures 6–1 and 6–2.

In addition to life-cycle analysis, the analyst must understand the importance of industry structure. Every industry has an economic structure, for example, monopoly, oligopoly, pure competition, or some other form of competition. The economic structure affects product pricing and returns. Government regulation is another issue that affects many industries. The government regulates profits (utilities), product quality (U.S. Food and Drug Administration), energy consumption (automobile efficiency), and many other areas of commerce such as transportation and education. Other areas that need to be examined are international competition, supply and demand relationships, availability of raw materials, energy costs, and so on. The pharmaceutical industry was given special attention in this chapter because of its significance to people of all ages and the many social issues associated with this industry.

Key Words and Concepts

bottom-up approach 142	pure competition 150	sustainable growth model 165
industry life cycles 143	retention ratio 166	top-down approach 142
monopolies 150	rotational investing 160	
oligopolies 150	stock pickers 142	

Discussion Questions

1. Distinguish between a "top-down approach" and a "bottom-up approach" to selecting stocks.
2. List the five stages of the industry life cycle. How does the pattern of cash dividend payments change over the cycle? (A general statement is all that is required.)
3. Why might a firm begin paying stock dividends in the growth stage?
4. If the investor does not correctly identify the crossover point between growth and expansion, what might happen to the price of the stock?
5. Suggest two companies that have continued to grow in nongrowth industries, and explain why.
6. Why are monopolies not common in the United States?
7. How would you describe the nature of competition in oligopolies, and what is the potential effect on profitability? How has international competition affected oligopolies?
8. What are the five competitive forces that affect prices and profitability in an industry?
9. As a follow up to question 8, give two examples of powerful suppliers.
10. In the pharmaceutical industry, is government regulation tougher in the United States than in foreign countries?
11. Who has the greater advantage for research and development in the pharmaceutical industry, large drug companies or smaller ones?
12. What is meant by the concept of rotational investing?
13. Explain why low interest rates make housing stocks and other related stocks attractive.
14. If an investor fears higher inflation, what possible industries might he or she choose for investment?

Web Exercise

Merck is one of the drug firms discussed in the chapter. We will now do further analysis. Click on **www.bloomberg.com**.

1. Enter MRK for Merck under "Stock Quotes" across the top and click.
2. Scroll down the right-hand margin and record earnings (estimated earnings per share).
3. Record the latest reported dividend and multiply by four.
4. Some have suggested Merck is not an expanding firm as depicted in Figure 6–1 on page 143 of the chapter. The typical expanding firm does not pay out more than 25 to 30 percent of earnings in the form of dividends. How does Merck fare in this regard? Divide your answer to question three

by your answer to question two. Does Merck qualify as an expanding firm in terms of dividend policy? Write a one sentence answer.

Note: From time to time, companies redesign their websites, and occasionally a topic we have listed may have been deleted, updated, or moved into a different location. Most websites have a "site map" or "site index" listed on a different page. If you click on the site map or site index, you will be introduced to a table of contents that should aid you in finding the topic you are looking for.

S&P Problems

www.mhhe.com/edumarketinsight

1. Log on to the McGraw-Hill website: **www.mhhe.com/edumarketinsight** (see page vi in the preface for instructions).
2. Click on Industry, which is the second box below the Market Insight title. Under industry there is a line to select an industry. Click on the arrow to open the industry list. Scroll down the industry list to "Pharmaceuticals" and click on Go!
3. Under GICS Sub-Industry Financial Highlights, click on S&P 500. How many pharmaceutical companies are in the S&P 500 index, and what weight does the pharmaceutical industry have as a percentage of the S&P 500 index?
4. Return to the left margin and go to S&P Industry Surveys, and click on Healthcare: Pharmaceuticals with the Adobe PDF symbol in front. This is a fairly long report but it summarizes the critical issues faced by the industry. Name five of the most important current issues facing this industry.
5. What are the long-term favorable and unfavorable issues that face the pharmaceutical industry?
6. Go to the last section under comparative company analysis, and under the pharmaceutical grouping, identify the company with the highest and lowest ten-year growth rate in operating revenues and net income.
7. Which company(ies) has/have the lowest debt to capital ratio?
8. Examine the price earnings ratios, dividend yield, and dividend payout ratio of the companies you have chosen in questions 6 and 7, and determine if there is a rational relationship between these variables and those in questions 6 and 7.

The Wall Street Journal Project

The Wall Street Journal publishes the "Dow Jones Global Sector Titans" in the "Markets Scoreboard" section of Part C. Approximately 18 industries' performances are tracked daily. For a five-day period, track the three best and three worst performing industries (ignore the companies). Is there any consistency in performance?

Selected References

Industry Analysis

Akhigbe, Aigbe; Stephen F. Borde; and Ann Marie Whyte. "The Source of Gains to Targets and Their Industry Rivals: Evidence Based on Terminated Merger Proposals." *Financial Management,* Winter 2000, pp. 101–18.

Cavaglia, Stefano; Christopher Brightman; and Michael Aked. "The Increasing Importance of Industry Factors." *Financial Analysts Journal,* September–October 2000, pp. 41–54.

Dreman, David. "Tech Value." *Forbes,* March 5, 2001, p. 186.

Hesseldahl, Arik. "The McDonald's of Computers." *Forbes,* November 24, 2003, pp. 170–172.

Lord, Richard A., and W. Ken Farr. "Collusion and Financial Leverage: An Analysis of the Integrated Steel Industry." *Financial Management,* Spring 2003, pp. 127–48.

Nocera, Joseph. "How to Invest in Today's Growth Companies." *Fortune,* October 14, 1996, pp. 72–73.

Norton, Rob. "Exploding the Myths about Growth." *Fortune,* November 25, 1996, pp. 76–77.

Porter, Michael E., *Competitive Advantage: Creating and Sustaining Superior Performance*. New York: The Free Press, 1985.

Sellers, Patricia. "How Coke Is Kicking Pepsi's Can." *Fortune,* October 28, 1996, pp. 70–84.

Simons, John. "Five Drug Stocks to Buy Now." *Fortune,* December 29, 2003, pp. 134–38.

Appendix 6A

SUSTAINABLE GROWTH MODEL

The **sustainable growth model** looks at how much growth a firm can generate by maintaining the same financial relationships as the year before. The process of generating earnings using the sustainable growth model provides many insights into the financial interactions that produce earnings. This method requires an understanding of several ratios—we will examine the return on equity and the retention ratios.

The return on equity can take several forms. First, let's define equity to equal (1) assets − liabilities, (2) net worth, or (3) book value. These are all equal even though we call them by different names. We will use the term *book value* to equal the equity of the firm. The return on equity (ROE) is equal to:

$$\text{ROE} = \frac{\text{Net income or After-tax earnings}}{\text{Book value}} \qquad \textbf{(6A–1)}$$

We can also express earnings and book value on a per share basis and the formula becomes:

$$\text{ROE} = \frac{\text{Earnings per share (EPS)}}{\text{Book value per share (BVPS)}} \qquad \textbf{(6A–2)}$$

Because we are using the sustainable growth model, we want to know what the return on equity was, based on the book value at the beginning of the year. This makes sense because it is the book value at the beginning of the year that is in place to generate earnings. Assume the following:

$$\text{ROE} = \frac{\$1.20_{2005}(\text{full year})}{\$6.44_{2004}(\text{year end})^*}$$
$$= 18.63\%$$

---

*We use year-end 2004 (beginning of 2005) BVPS to measure return on equity for 2005.

Because we want to forecast earnings per share, we will look at the process of growth on a per share basis. We can rearrange Formula 6A–2 by multiplying both sides by the book value per share (BVPS) and we end up with:

$$EPS = ROE \times BVPS \qquad (6A-3)$$

Using this information, we will examine how earnings per share can grow if the financial relationships stay the same from year to year. Let's say BVPS was $6.44 in 2004 (year-end) and return on equity was 18.63 percent, which we already computed. Substituting these numbers into Formula 6A–3 gives us:

$$EPS = ROE \times BVPS$$
$$\$1.20 = 18.63\% \times \$6.44$$

This is the value of earnings per share for 2005. Future growth in earnings comes from the firm reinvesting in new plant and equipment and thus being able to generate more income for next year. In this case, the firm paid out a dividend of $0.38 in 2005 and retained $0.82 ($1.20 − $0.38). The $0.82 gets added to the beginning book value per share to get ending book value of $7.26 ($6.44 + $0.82) for 2005.

If the firm can continue to earn 18.63 percent on its equity, it will earn $1.35 per share for 2006. This can be computed as follows:

$$EPS_{2003} = ROE \times BVPS_{\text{year end 2005}}$$
$$= 18.63\% \times \$7.26$$
$$= \$1.353$$

The growth rate in earnings per share using this model can be calculated by taking the increased earnings of $0.153 and dividing by beginning earnings of $1.20. This produces an earnings per share growth rate of 12.7 percent.

One of the conditions of growth is that the firms must retain some earnings. If the firm paid out all its earnings in dividends, it would start 2006 with the same book value and would experience no growth. The more earnings retained, the higher the growth rate would be. In this case, it retained $0.82 out of $1.20 in earnings. This is called the **retention ratio,** which is sometimes denoted by B to keep it from being confused with a rate of return symbol.

$$\text{Retention ratio (B)} = \frac{\text{Earnings per share} - \text{Dividends per share}}{\text{Earnings per share}} \qquad (6A-4)$$
$$= (\$1.20 - \$.38)/\$1.20$$
$$= 0.6833 \text{ or } 68.33\%$$

The outcome of this analysis is that the growth in earnings per share is a function of the return on equity and the retention ratio. We can calculate growth in EPS as follows:

$$\text{Growth } (g) = \text{Return on equity} \times \text{Retention ratio}$$
$$= ROE \times B \qquad (6A-5)$$

Using our example, we have:

$$g_{eps} = 18.63\% \times 68.33\%$$
$$= 12.7\%$$

The sustainable growth model would predict a 12.7 percent growth rate for 2006 based on dividend policy and return on equity. This rate will continue into the future as long as the firm maintains its return on equity and its retention ratio.

Discussion Questions

1. Do you think the sustainable growth model would be appropriate for a highly cyclical firm?
2. Based on the sustainable growth model, if a firm increases the dividend payout ratio (1 − the retention ratio), will this increase or decrease the growth in earnings per share in the future?

Problems

Sustainable growth model

1. The Bolten Corporation had earnings per share of $2.60 in 2005, and book value per share at the end of 2004 (beginning of 2005) was $13.
   a. What was the firm's return on equity (book value) in 2005?
   b. If the firm pays out $0.78 in dividends per share, what is the retention ratio? How much will book value per share be at the end of 2002? Add retained earnings per share for 2005 to book value per share at the beginning of 2005.
   c. Assume the same rate of return on book value for 2006 as you computed in part *a* for 2005. What will earnings per share be for 2006? Multiply rate of return on book value (part *a*) by book value at the end of 2005 (second portion of part *b*).
   d. What is the growth rate in earnings per share between 2005 and 2006?
   e. If the firm continues to earn the same rate of return on book value and maintains the same earnings retention ratio, what will the sustainable growth rate be for the foreseeable future?

chapter seven

Valuation of the Individual Firm

objectives

1. Understand the basic valuation process as it relates to earnings and dividends.
2. Explain the related concepts of risk and return.
3. Be able to use various present value–oriented valuation models.
4. Describe the role of the price-earnings ratio in determining value.
5. Explain how an individual stock's price-earnings ratio is related to the market.
6. Explain techniques for forecasting earnings per share.

Basic Valuation Concepts
Review of Risk and Required Return Concepts
Dividend Valuation Models
    General Dividend Model
    Constant Growth Model
    A Nonconstant Growth Model
Earnings Valuation Models
    The Combined Earnings and Dividend Model
The Price-Earnings Ratio
    The P/E Ratio for Individual Stocks
    The Pure, Short-Term Earnings Model
    Relating an Individual Stock's P/E Ratio to the Market
Other Valuation Models Using Average Price Ratios and 10-Year Averages
Forecasting Earnings per Share
    Least Squares Trendline
    The Income Statement Method
Growth Stocks and Growth Companies
Assets as a Source of Stock Value
    Natural Resources

We have been building the foundation for the valuation of the individual firm, depicted in Figure 5–1 on page 115. **Valuation** is based on economic factors, industry variables, an analysis of the financial statements, and the outlook for the individual firm. Valuation determines the long-run fundamental economic value of a company's common stock. In the process, we try to determine whether a common stock is undervalued, overvalued, or fairly valued relative to its market price. The orientation in this chapter is mostly toward long-run concepts of valuation rather than toward determining short-term market pricing factors. The valuation concepts we develop in this chapter should be valuable to you in eventually developing your own portfolio.

Basic Valuation Concepts

The valuation of common stock can be approached in several ways. Some models rely solely on dividends expected to be received during the future, and these are usually referred to as **dividend valuation models.** A variation on the dividend model is the **earnings valuation model,** which substitutes earnings as the main income stream for valuation. Earnings valuation models may also call for the determination of a price-earnings ratio, or multiplier of earnings, to determine value. Some models rely on long-run historical relationships between market price and sales per share, or market price and book value per share. Other methods may include the market value of assets, such as cash and liquid assets, replacement value of plant and equipment, and other hidden assets such as undervalued timber holdings. For the first part of our discussion, we develop the dividend valuation model and then go to earnings-related approaches.

Review of Risk and Required Return Concepts

Application Example

As we move to the valuation models, it is helpful to review and consolidate the concepts of risk and required return presented in Chapter 1. Calculation of the required rate of return is extremely important because it is the rate at which future cash flows are discounted to reach a valuation. An investor needs to know the required rate of return on the various risk classes of assets to reach intelligent decisions to buy or sell.

Chapter 1 examined rates of returns for various assets and returns based on Ibbotson Associates data and explained how the risk-free rate is a function of both the real rate of return and an inflation premium. The required return was a function of the risk-free rate plus a risk premium for a specific investment.

In this section, we develop a simple methodology based on the capital asset pricing model for determining a required rate of return when valuing common stocks in a diversified portfolio. First, we determine the risk-free rate. The **risk-free rate** (R_F) is a function of the real rate of return and the expected rate of inflation. Some analysts express the risk-free rate as simply the addition of the real rate of return and the expected rate of inflation, while a more accurate answer is found as follows:

$$R_F \text{ (risk-free rate)} = (1 + \text{Real rate})(1 + \text{Expected rate of inflation}) - 1 \quad (7\text{–}1)$$

We now add a risk component to the risk-free rate to determine K_e, the total **required rate of return.** We show the following relationships.

$$K_e = R_F + b(K_M - R_F) \quad (7\text{–}2)$$

where:

K_e = Required rate of return
R_F = Risk-free rate
b = Beta coefficient
K_M = Expected return for common stocks in the market
$(K_M - R_F)$ = Equity risk premium (ERP)

The risk-free rate, in practice, is normally assumed to be the return on U.S. Treasury securities. **Beta** measures individual company risk against the market risk (usually the S&P 500 Stock Index). Companies with betas greater than 1.00 have more risk than the market; companies with betas less than 1.00 have less risk than the market; and companies with betas equal to 1.00 have the same risk as the market. It stands to reason then that high beta stocks ($b > 1.00$) would have higher required returns than the market.

The last term ($K_M - R_F$) in Formula 7–2, the **equity risk premium** (ERP), is not observable from current market information because it is based on investor expectations. The equity risk premium represents the extra return or premium the stock market must provide compared with the rate of return an investor can earn on U.S. Government Treasury securities. Between 1926 and the first quarter of 2004, the mean return of large company stocks was 11.4 percent and for government bonds 5 percent. It is clear that stocks outperformed long-term government bonds by 6.4 percent. If we use large-company stocks (the S&P 500) for our K_M and long-term government bonds for our R_F, then we have an equity risk premium of 6.4 percent.

In early finance courses K_M and R_F are usually given. In the real world they are thought of as one number, and called the equity risk premium or ERP for short. The equity risk premium represents the premium an investor would expect to receive for buying a more risky equity asset such as common stock compared to the return an investor could expect to receive for a risk-free asset, namely a U.S. government security. In this case, history would create an expectation that the ERP would equal ($K_M - R_F$) or ($11.4\% - 5\%$) or 6.4 percent. An equity risk premium could be computed in a similar calculation for short-term Treasury bills, intermediate government securities, or long-term corporate bonds. We could also compute an equity risk premium for small stocks using the return on small stocks for our K_M. If an analyst were analyzing a small company, a small stock equity risk premium would be more appropriate than using a large-stock equity risk premium.

Application Example

Having discussed the beta and the equity risk premium (the second term in Formula 7–2), what is the appropriate value for the first term, the risk-free rate (R_F)?

$$K_e = \underset{\text{risk-free rate}}{R_F} + \underset{\text{beta}}{b}(\underset{\text{equity risk premium}}{K_M - R_F}) \qquad \text{(7–2) reproduced.}$$

In previous editions of this book we have used the one-year Treasury bill for our R_F. In this edition we have switched to long-term government bonds for our R_F. There are several reasons for this switch: First the U.S. Treasury stopped issuing one-year Treasury bills, and second, short-term rates can be more volatile than long-term bond rates. By using the long-term government bond rate for our equity risk premium calculation we have matched the long-term nature of common stocks with the long-term returns generated by 20-year government bonds. For example, if the current long-term government bond has a yield of 4.6 percent return, our ERP is 6.4 percent, and the beta for the market by definition is 1.00, then our required return for the stock market would be as follows:

$$K_e = R_F + b(K_M - R_F)$$
$$= 4.6\% + 1.00(6.4\%)$$
$$= 11.00\%$$

Now, K_e, the required rate of return, can be used as a discount rate for future cash flows from an investment. If the company we are valuing has a beta different from 1.00, then the required return will reflect either a higher or lower return for a company with higher or lower risk. This methodology will be helpful as you work through the dividend valuation models and other valuation models for common stock.

Dividend Valuation Models

The value of a share of stock may be interpreted by the shareholder as the present value of an expected stream of future dividends. Although in the short run, stockholders may be influenced by a change in earnings or other variables, the ultimate value of any holding rests with the distribution of earnings in the form of dividend payments. Although the stockholder may benefit from the retention and reinvestment of earnings by the corporation, at some point, the earnings must generally be translated into cash flow for the stockholder.[1] While dividend valuation models are theoretical in nature and subject to many limitations, they are the most frequently used models in the literature of finance. Perhaps this is because they demonstrate so well the relationship between the major variables affecting common stock prices.

General Dividend Model

A generalized stock valuation model based on future expected dividends can be stated as follows:

$$P_0 = \frac{D_1}{(1+K_e)^1} + \frac{D_2}{(1+K_e)^2} + \frac{D_3}{(1+K_e)^3} + \ldots + \frac{D_\infty}{(1+K_e)^\infty} \quad (7\text{--}3)$$

where:

P_0 = Present value of the stock price
D_i = Dividend for each year, for example, 1, 2, 3 . . . ∞
K_e = Required rate of return (discount rate)

This model is very general and assumes the investor can determine the right dividend for each and every year as well as the annualized rate of return an investor requires.

Constant Growth Model

Rather than predict the actual dividend each year, a more widely used model includes an estimate of the growth rate in dividends. This model assumes a constant growth rate in dividends to infinity.

---

[1] Some exceptions to this principle are noted later in the chapter.

172   Part 2   Analysis and Valuation of Equity Securities

If a constant growth rate in dividends is assumed, Formula 7–3 can be rewritten as:

$$P_0 = \frac{D_0(1+g)^1}{(1+K_e)^1} + \frac{D_0(1+g)^2}{(1+K_e)^2} + \frac{D_0(1+g)^3}{(1+K_e)^3} + \cdots + \frac{D_0(1+g)^\infty}{(1+K_e)^\infty} \quad (7\text{–}4)$$

where:

$D_0(1+g)^1 = D_1 =$ Dividends in the initial year
$D_0(1+g)^2 = D_2 =$ Dividends in year 2, and so on
$g =$ Constant growth rate in the dividend

The current price of the stock should equal the present value of the expected stream of dividends. If we can correctly predict the growth of future dividends and determine the discount rate, we can estimate the true value of the stock.

For example, assume we wanted to determine the present value of ABC Corporation common stock based on this model. We shall assume ABC anticipates an 8 percent growth rate in dividends per share, and we use a 12 percent discount rate as the required rate of return. The required rate of return is intended to provide the investor with a minimum rate of return based on the stock's beta. Twelve percent is sufficient to fulfill that function in this example.

Application Example

eXcel

Rather than project the dividends for an extremely long period and then discount them back to the present, we can reduce previously presented Formula 7–4 to a more usable form:

$$P_0 = D_1/(K_e - g) \quad (7\text{–}5)$$

This formula is appropriate as long as two conditions are met. The first is that the growth rate must be constant. For the ABC Corporation, we are assuming that to be the case. It is a constant 8 percent. Second, K_e (the required rate of return) must exceed g (the growth rate). Since K_e is 12 percent and g is 8 percent for the ABC Corporation, this condition is also met. Let's further assume D_1 (the expected dividend at the end of period 1) is $3.38.

Using Formula 7–5, we determine a stock value of:

$$P_0 = D_1/(K_e - g)$$
$$= \$3.38/(0.12 - 0.08)$$
$$= \$3.38/0.04$$
$$= \$84.50$$

This value, in theory, represents the present value of all future dividends. The meaning is further illustrated in Table 7–1, in which we take the present value of the first 20 years of dividends ($43.71) and then add in a figure of $40.79 to arrive at the present value of all future dividends of $84.50 as previously determined by Formula 7–5. The $40.79 value represents the present value of dividends occurring between 2025 and infinity (i.e., after 2025).[2]

---

[2] If you need to brush up on your present value calculations please refer to Appendix E called "Time Value of Money and Investment Applications."

TABLE 7–1 Present Value Analysis of ABC Corporation

Year	Expected Dividends $g = 8\%$	Present Value Factor $K_e = 12\%$[a]	Present Value of Dividends
2005	$ 3.38	0.893	$ 3.02
2006	3.65	0.797	2.91
2007	3.94	0.712	2.81
2008	4.26	0.636	2.71
2009	4.60	0.567	2.61
2010	4.97	0.507	2.52
2011	5.37	0.452	2.43
2012	5.80	0.404	2.34
2013	6.26	0.361	2.26
2014	6.76	0.322	2.18
2015	7.30	0.287	2.10
2016	7.88	0.257	2.03
2017	8.51	0.229	1.95
2018	9.19	0.205	1.87
2019	9.93	0.183	1.81
2020	10.72	0.163	1.75
2021	11.58	0.146	1.69
2022	12.51	0.130	1.63
2023	13.51	0.116	1.57
2024	$14.59	0.104	1.52
PV of dividends for years 2005–2024			$43.71
PV of dividends for years 2025 to infinity			40.79
Total present value of ABC common stock			$84.50[b]

[a] Figures are taken from Appendix C at the end of this book.
[b] Notice that this value is the same as that found on the previous page using Formula 7–5.

We must be aware that several things could be wrong with our analysis. First, our expectations of dividend growth may be too high for an infinite period. Perhaps 6 percent is a more realistic estimate of expected dividend growth. If we substitute our new estimate into Formula 7–5, we can measure the price effect as dividend growth changes from an 8 percent rate to a 6 percent rate:

$$P_0 = \$3.38/(0.12 - 0.06)$$
$$= \$3.38/0.06$$
$$= \$56.33$$

A 6 percent growth rate (a 2 percent change) cuts the price down substantially from the prior value of $84.50.

We could also misjudge our required rate of return, K_e, which could be higher or lower. A lower K_e would increase the present value of ABC Corporation, whereas a higher K_e would reduce its value. We have made these points to show how sensitive stock prices are to the basic assumptions of the model.

Even though you may go through the calculations, the final value is only as accurate as your inputs. This is where a security analyst's judgment and expertise are important—in justifying the growth rate and required rate of return.

A Nonconstant Growth Model

Many analysts do not accept the premise of a constant growth rate in dividends or earnings. As we examined in Chapter 6, industries go through a life cycle in which growth is nonlinear. Growth is usually highest in the infancy and early phases of the life cycle, and as expansion is reached, the growth rate slows until the industry reaches maturity. At maturity, a constant, long-term growth rate that approximates the long-term growth of the macro economy may be appropriate for a particular industry.

Some companies in an industry may not behave like the industry in general. Companies constantly try to avoid maturity or decline, and so they strive to develop new products and markets to maintain growth.

In situations where the analyst wants to value a company without the constant-growth assumption, a variation of the constant-growth model is possible. Growth is simply divided into several periods with each period having a present value. The present value of each period is summed to attain the total value of the firm's share price. An example of a two-period model may illustrate the concept. Assume that JAYCAR Corporation is expected to have the growth pattern shown in Figure 7–1.

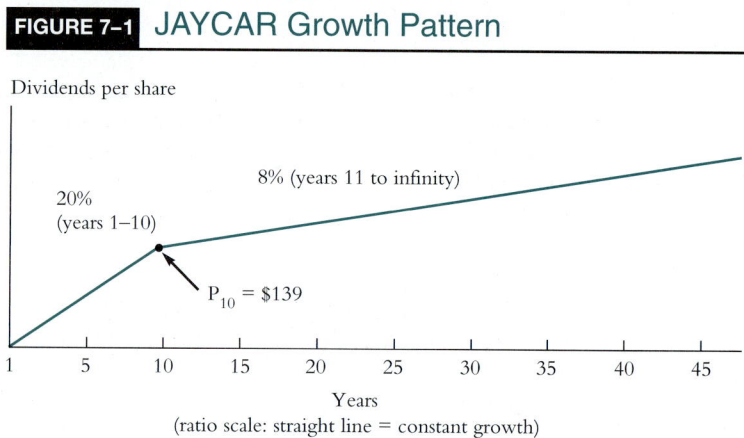

FIGURE 7–1 JAYCAR Growth Pattern

Application Example

It is assumed that JAYCAR will have a dividend growth rate of 20 percent for the next 10 years and an 8 percent perpetual growth rate after that. JAYCAR's dividend is expected to be $1 at the end of year one, and the appropriate required rate of return (discount rate) is 12 percent. Taking the present value for the first 10 years of dividends and then applying the constant dividend growth model for years 11 through infinity, we can arrive at an answer. First, we find the present value of the initial 10 years of dividends:

Year	Dividends (20% growth)	PV Factor (12%)[a]	Present Value of Dividends First 10 Years
1	$1.00	0.893	$ 0.89
2	1.20	0.797	0.96
3	1.44	0.712	1.03
4	1.73	0.636	1.10
5	2.07	0.567	1.17
6	2.48	0.507	1.26
7	2.98	0.452	1.35
8	3.58	0.404	1.45
9	4.29	0.361	1.55
10	5.15	0.322	1.66
			$12.42

[a] Present value factors are taken from Appendix C at the end of this book.

We then determine the present value of dividends after the 10th year. The dividend in year 11 is expected to be $5.56, or $5.15 (for year 10) compounded at the new, lower 8 percent growth rate ($5.15 × 1.08). Because the rest of the dividend stream will be infinite, Formula 7–5 can provide the value of JAYCAR at the end of year 10, based on a discount rate of 12 percent and an expected growth rate of 8 percent.

$$P_{10} = D_{11}/(K_e - g)$$
$$= \$5.56/(0.12 - 0.08)$$
$$= \$5.56/0.04$$
$$= \$139$$

An investor would pay $139 at the end of the 10th year for the future stream of dividends from year 11 to infinity. To get the present value of the 10th year price, the $139 must be discounted back to the present by the 10-year PV factor for 12 percent from Appendix C (0.322). This part of the answer is $139.00 × 0.322, or $44.76. The two parts of this analysis can be combined to get the current valuation per share of $57.18.

Present value of the dividends from years 1 to 10	$12.42
Present value of 10th year price ($139.00 × 0.322)	44.76
Total present value of JAYCAR common stock	$57.18

Earnings Valuation Models

Dividend valuation models are best suited for companies in the expansion or maturity life-cycle phase. Dividends of these companies are more predictable and usually make up a larger percentage of the total return than capital gains. Earnings-per-share models are also used for valuation. For example, the investor may take the present value of all future earnings to determine a value. This might be appropriate where the firm pays no cash dividend and has no immediate intention of paying one.

The Combined Earnings and Dividend Model

Application Example

www.johnsonand
johnson.com

Another, more comprehensive valuation model relies on earnings per share (EPS) and a price-earnings (P/E) ratio (earnings multiplier) combined with a finite dividend model. The value of common stock can be viewed as a dividend stream plus a market price at the end of the dividend stream. We have selected Johnson & Johnson from the health care and pharmaceutical industry as our sample company for the valuation models that follow. Assuming that we start our valuation at the beginning of 2004, we develop a present value for the common stock listed on the New York Stock Exchange. The numbers are shown in Table 7–2.

TABLE 7–2 Johnson & Johnson Combined Dividend and Earnings Present Value Analysis

Part A: Present Value of Dividends for 5 Years.

Year	(1) Estimated Earnings Per Share[a]	(2) Estimated Payout Ratio	(3) Estimated Dividends Per Share	(4) Present Value Factor at $K_e = 12.00\%$[b]	(5) Present Value of the Cash Flows
2004	$3.00	32.00%	$0.96	0.893	$ 0.86
2005	3.30	32.00	1.06	0.797	0.84
2006	3.63	32.00	1.16	0.712	0.83
2007	3.99	32.00	1.28	0.636	0.81
2008	4.39	32.00	1.40	0.567	0.79
				PV of estimated dividends	$ 4.13

Part B: Present Value of Johnson & Johnson's 2008 Common Stock Price

	EPS	P/E Ratio	Price$_{2008}$	PV Factor	
2008	$4.39	22.00	$96.58	0.567	$54.76
Part A + Part B = the total present value of Johnson & Johnson at beginning of 2004					$58.89

[a] The growth rate for earnings per share is expected to be 10 percent through 2008.
[b] $K_e = R_F + b(K_M - R_F)$ $R_F = 5.3\%$ $b = 1.05$ $(K_M - R_F) = 6.4\%$
   $K_e = 5.3\% + 1.05(6.4\%) = 5.3\% + 6.7\% = 12\%$

The present value of the common stock for Johnson & Johnson is shown at the bottom of Table 7–2 to be $58.89. Note that Part A of Table 7–2 calculates the present value of the future dividends, while Part B is used to determine the present value of the future stock price at the end of 2008. These are assumed to be the two variables that determine the current stock price under this model.

In Part A, earnings per share are first projected for the next five years. Johnson & Johnson's payout ratio fluctuated between 30 and 35 percent from 1994 to 2003, and we estimate the payout ratio will average 32 percent over the next five years. The earnings are then multiplied by the company's estimated payout ratio of 32 percent to determine anticipated dividends per share for those five years (as indicated in column 3).

What about the 12 percent discount rate (as shown in column 4)? At the time of the analysis, Johnson & Johnson had a beta of 1.05, long-term interest rates had a 5.3 percent yield, and we used an equity risk premium ($K_M - R_F$) of 6.4 percent. The total required rate of return (K_e) is 12 percent, and this is shown in footnote b at the bottom of Table 7–2. Twelve percent is the rate that will be used to discount all future values to the present.

The present value of dividends from 2004 through 2008 is shown in column 5 of Part A of Table 7–2 to equal $4.13.

In Part B, we multiply estimated 2008 earnings per share of $4.39 by the P/E ratio (earnings multiplier) of 22 to arrive at an anticipated price of $96.58 five years into the future. The P/E ratio used to determine the price is the average P/E ratio for Johnson & Johnson over the last 10 years. Of course, the future P/E ratio could be affected by higher or lower expected growth of earnings, the risk characteristics of the stock in 2008, and other variables. In any event, the price of $96.58 is then discounted back for five years at 12 percent to arrive at a present value of $54.76. The total present value of the stock is equal to the present value of the dividend stream for five years ($4.13) plus the present value of the future stock price of $54.76 for a total present value at the beginning of 2004 of $58.89. This is the estimated value of the stock based on future expectations. This is slightly above the actual stock price for Johnson & Johnson of $53 at the beginning of 2004.

The Price-Earnings Ratio

Mathematically, the **price-earnings ratio** (P/E) is simply the price per share divided by earnings per share, and it is ultimately set by investors in the market as they bid the price of a stock up or down in relation to its earnings. Price-earnings ratios are often expressed in the financial press as historical numbers using today's price divided by the latest 12-month earnings.

For companies with cyclical earnings, a P/E using the latest 12-month earnings might be misleading because these earnings could be high. If investors expect earnings to fall back to a normal level, they will not bid the price up in relation to this short-term cyclical swing in earnings per share, and the P/E ratio will appear to be low. But if earnings are severely depressed, investors will expect a return to normal higher earnings, and the price will not fall an equal percentage with earnings, and the P/E will appear to be high.

In the Johnson & Johnson example in Table 7–2, we used a P/E of 22.00 in 2008. The P/E ratio is determined by historical analysis and by other factors such as expected growth in earnings per share. The P/E of a company is also affected by overall conditions in the stock market.

Even though the current P/E ratio for a stock is known, investors may not agree it is appropriate. Stock analysts and investors probably spend more time examining P/E ratios and assessing their appropriate level than any other variable. Although the use of P/E ratios in valuation approaches lacks the theoretical underpinning of the present value-based valuation models previously discussed in the chapter, P/E ratios are equally important. The well-informed student of investments should have a basic understanding of both the theoretically based present value approach and the more pragmatic, frequently used P/E ratio approach.

the real world of investing

EVA: Economic Value Added: Why Is It Important?

There is a valuation concept that has garnered attention at leading U.S. corporations such as Coca-Cola, AT&T, Eli Lilly, Merrill Lynch, and Monsanto. These firms are not nearly so interested at generating earnings per share as they are in maximizing economic value added (EVA).

Economic value added is based on the concept that decisions should be made or projects accepted only if net operating profit after taxes (NOPAT) exceeds the capital costs to finance the investment. If this rule is followed, then economic value will be added. To many readers, this may sound like the capital budgeting principle you learned in the first course in corporate finance, warmed over and served again as a hot new idea.

Not so, say the founders of the EVA concept at Stern Stewart & Co. (www.sternstewart.com) in New York.* EVA is an overriding concept that is intended to be applied to every decision the corporation makes, from investing overseas to adding three more widgets in the stock room. The question repeatedly asked is, "Is the firm earning an adequate return on the money investors entrusted to it?" Even at the lowest levels of the organization, this question cannot be escaped.

Proponents of EVA say that all too often chief financial officers evaluate projects based on net present value, but they modify recommendations to meet earnings growth targets of the firm. Business unit evaluations may not be based on either parameter but rather on return on assets or some other unrelated profit goal set by top management. Bonuses for operating managers may be linked to demand–supply conditions within an industry. New-product introductions may be based on gross profit margin. Furthermore, the analysis for some decisions may be based on cash flow, while other decisions are linked to earnings per share. There is no coherent theme or goal, and stockholder wealth may be harmed in the process.

With EVA, the firm is assumed to always be working for the stockholder's benefit. Under the EVA concept, the firm will not accept a project or idea that does not earn back the cost of funds the stockholder provided. Economic value added is also intended to lead to market value added (MVA). MVA is another hot new topic and represents the total market value of the firm minus the total capital provided since day one (including the retained earnings). MVA requires a company's top managers to justify what they did with the money that was given to them. Did they increase the value and thereby produce a positive MVA as expected, or did they destroy contributed capital and generate a negative MVA?

MVA is thought to be linked to EVA because, according to Stern Stewart & Co., the way MVA increases is by consistently increasing EVA. In fact, MVA is intended to be the present value of all future EVAs.

Annual data on MVA and EVA for the 1,000 largest companies can be acquired directly from Stern Stewart & Co. of New York. *Fortune* magazine also publishes Stern Stewart & Co. data on the 200 top MVA creators toward the end of each year. (However, not all of these companies formally use EVA and MVA.)

Detractors of the EVA-MVA emphasis say it is not widely enough followed to truly affect value. They suggest that earnings per share is still the "king" on Wall Street. In spite of EVA, it is still quarterly earnings estimates that drive investors crazy. Only time will tell whether this hot new concept can permanently compete. Today, there are 300 to 350 firms that use EVA in their strategic development.

---

* EVA, The Real Key to Creating Wealth (New York: Stern Stewart & Co., 1996–97).

What determines whether a stock should have a high or low P/E ratio? Let's first talk about the market for stocks in general, and then we will look at individual securities.

Stocks generally trade at a relatively high P/E ratio (perhaps 20 or greater) when there are strong growth prospects in the economy. However, inflation also plays a key role in determining P/E ratios for the overall market.

Chapter 7 Valuation of the Individual Firm 179

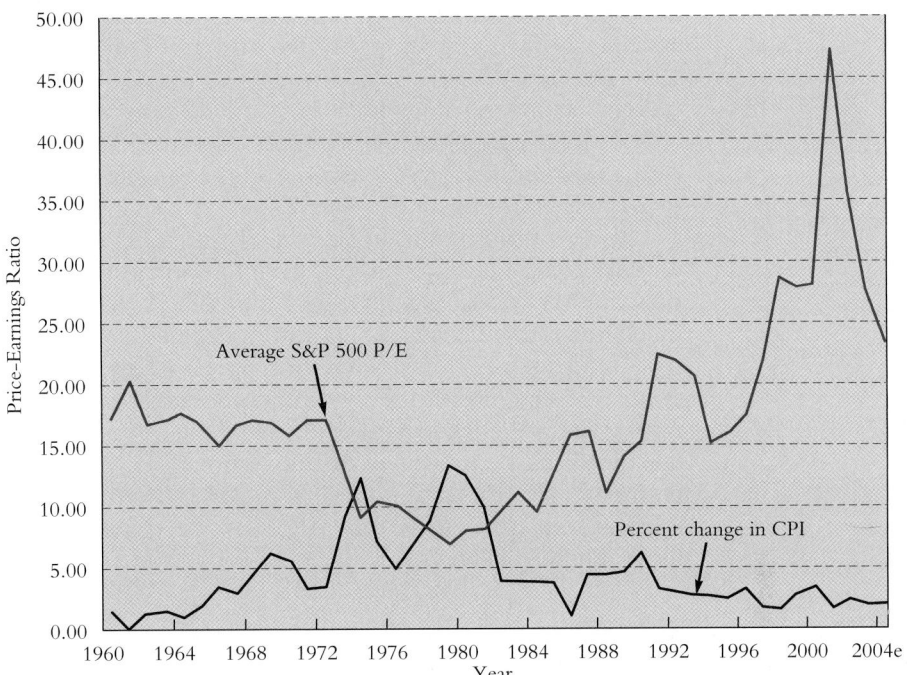

FIGURE 7–2 Inflation and Price-Earnings Ratios

To illustrate the latter point, Figure 7–2 presents the relationship between the year-end Standard & Poor's 500 composite P/E ratio and the annual rate of inflation measured by the change in the consumer price index (CPI). The graphical relationship between these two variables shows they are inversely related. The price-earnings ratio goes down when the change in the CPI goes up, and the reverse is also true.

The dramatic drop in the P/E ratio in 1973–74 can be attributed in large measure to the rate of inflation increasing from 3.4 percent in 1972 to 12.2 percent in 1974, or a change of more than three times its former level. For a brief period in 1976, inflation decreased to an annual rate of less than 5 percent, only to soar to 13.3 percent by 1979. The average rate of inflation for 1982 was reduced to 3.8 percent, and the market responded by paying higher share prices for one dollar of earnings (that is, higher P/E ratios).

From 1983 through 1985, the consumer price index hovered around 3 to 4 percent, but in 1986, inflation subsided to 1.1 percent, and the S&P price-earnings ratio soared. In 1987, the S&P 500 P/E ratio remained high until the crash of October 1987 brought stock prices down to lower levels. During the sobering and risk-averse period after the crash, market prices were fairly stable.

As fears of higher inflation rose during 1989, the S&P 500 P/E ratio came back to the low-midrange of its 40-year history shown in Figure 7–2. The higher price-earnings ratios in 1991–93 reflect both the impact of falling inflationary expectations and depressed earnings suffered by corporations during the recessionary period of 1990–91 and the slow recovery in 1992 and 1993. As earnings grew quickly in 1994, 1995, and 1996, the Standard & Poor's 500 P/E ratio fell below 20 again. The economy in 1997 saw low inflation, strong economic growth, low unemployment, and reduced government deficits. This economy was described as a dream economy, one that was perfectly balanced with GDP growth of 3.8 percent and inflation of 1.8 percent. In response, P/E ratios again soared above 21 times earnings, and the raging bull market, lasting through 1999, pushed P/E ratios over 30.

Collapsing earnings from 2000 to 2002 caused the S&P price-earnings ratio to soar to over 45, but with an earnings rebound in 2003, the P/E started to return to a more reasonable level. At the beginning of 2004 the S&P 500 had a P/E of 23 times earnings.

As was pointed out in Chapter 1, required rates of return are directly influenced by the rate of inflation. As inflation changes, the required rate of return on common stock, K_e, changes, and prices go up or down. This is the basic mechanism that causes inflation to influence P/E ratios.

Other factors besides inflationary considerations and growth factors influence the P/E ratio for the market in general. Federal Reserve policy and interest rates, federal deficits, the government's leading indicators, the political climate, the mood and confidence of the population, international considerations, and many other factors affect the P/E ratio for the overall market. The astute analyst is constantly studying a multitude of variables that could cause P/E ratios to move higher or lower.

The P/E Ratio for Individual Stocks

Although the overall market P/E ratio is the collective average of individual P/Es, those factors that influence the market P/E do not necessarily affect P/E ratios of individual companies consistently from one industry to another. An individual firm's P/E ratio is heavily influenced by its growth prospects and the risk associated with its future performance. Table 7–3 shows examples of growth rates and P/E ratios for different industries and firms.

TABLE 7–3 P/E and Expected Growth in EPS

(1) Industry	(2) Company	(3) 10-Year Past Growth Rate in EPS	(4) Expected 5-Yr.[b] Growth in EPS	(5) P/E January 2004
Retail department stores	Sears	8.50%	6.00%	9.3
Banks	Bank of America	13.50	9.00	11.1
Electric utility	Dominion Resources	5.00	9.00	15.4
Retail special lines	Best Buy	39.00	18.50	19.5
Entertainment technology	Electronic Arts	18.00	27.00	26.0
Computer software	Microsoft Corp.[a]	28.50	8.50	30.9
Computer and peripherals	Dell Computer[a]	40.50	13.00	31.1
Computer software	Novell	−15.00	22.00	58.3
Internet	Yahoo	NA	35.00	95.0

[a] Some companies like Microsoft and Dell sell at high P/E ratios because the market thinks they will grow at their historical growth rate.

[b] All growth rates are from *Value Line Investment Survey*.

Generally the higher the expected growth rate (column 4) the higher the P/E ratio (column 5). Some companies like Dell and Microsoft have high P/E ratios even after their expected growth rates decline because they maintain an aura of quality and growth.

In addition to the future growth of the firm and the risk associated with that growth, investors and analysts also consider a number of other factors that influence a firm's P/E ratio. These cannot be easily quantified, but they affect a broad range of stocks. Included in this category are the debt-to-equity ratio and the dividend policy of the firm. All things being equal, the less debt a firm has, the more likely it is to be highly valued in the marketplace.

The dividend policy is more elusive. For firms that show superior internal reinvestment opportunities, low cash dividends may be desired. But maturing companies may be expected to pay a high cash dividend. For the latter group, a reduction in cash dividends may be associated with a lower P/E ratio if the dividend cut signals falling earnings per share.

Certain industries also traditionally command higher P/E ratios than others. Investors seem to prefer industries that have a high technology and research emphasis. Thus, firms in computers, medical research and health care, and sophisticated telecommunications often have higher P/E ratios than the market in general. This does not mean firms in these industries represent superior investments, but merely that investors value their earnings more highly.[3] Also, fads and other factors can cause a shift in industry popularity. For example, because Ronald Reagan emphasized military strength, defense-oriented stocks were popular during his administration. Jimmy Carter stressed the need for environmental control, and stocks dealing in air and water pollution control traded at high P/E ratios during his tenure. Bill Clinton's health care proposals lowered P/Es of pharmaceutical stocks dramatically until a Republican Congress killed his proposals. Tobacco and defense stocks rallied under George W. Bush.

The quality of management as perceived by those in the marketplace also influences a firm's P/E ratio. If management is viewed as being highly capable, clever, or innovative, the firm may carry a higher P/E ratio. Investors may look to magazines such as *Forbes* or *BusinessWeek,* which highlight management strategies by various companies.

Not only is the quality of management important to investors in determining the firm's P/E ratio, but the quality of earnings is also important. There are many interpretations of a dollar's worth of earnings. Some companies choose to use very conservative accounting practices so their reported earnings can be interpreted as being very solid by investors (they may even be understated). Other companies use more liberal accounting interpretations to report maximum earnings to their shareholders, and they, at times, overstate their true performance. It is easy to see that a dollar's worth of conservatively reported earnings (high quality earnings) may be valued at a P/E ratio of 20 to 25 times, whereas a dollar's worth of liberally reported earnings (low quality earnings) should be valued at a much lower multiple.

All of these factors affect a firm's P/E ratio. Thus, investors will consider growth in sales and earnings, future risk, the debt position, the dividend policy,

---

[3] William Kittrell, Geoffrey A. Hirt, and Roger Potter, "Price-Earnings Multiples, Investors' Expectations, and Rates of Return: Some Analytical and Empirical Findings" (Paper presented at the 1984 Financial Management Association meeting).

the quality of management and earnings, and a multitude of other factors in arriving at the P/E ratio. The P/E ratio, like the price of the stock, is set by the interaction of the forces of demand and supply. Those firms that are expected to provide returns greater than the overall economy, with equal or less risk, generally have superior P/E ratios.

The Pure, Short-Term Earnings Model

Often investors/speculators take a very short-term view of the market and ignore present value analysis with its associated long-term forecasts of dividends and earnings per share. Instead, they only use earnings per share and apply an appropriate multiplier to compute the estimated value.

Application Example

If we look at Johnson & Johnson's five-year high and low P/E ratios we get a high average P/E of 27.99 and a low average P/E of 19.19 which gives us an average of 23.54. From Table 7–2 on page 176 we estimated Johnson & Johnson's 2004 earnings per share to be $3.00. Using this data, we can come up with a high, low and average value for the beginning of 2004.

$$\text{Price} = \text{EPS}_{2004} \times \text{P/E}_{\text{10-year high, average, low}}$$

$$\text{High price} = \$3.00 \times 27.99 = \$83.97$$
$$\text{Average price} = \$3.00 \times 23.54 = \$70.62$$
$$\text{Low price} = \$3.00 \times 19.19 = \$57.57$$

Given that Johnson & Johnson was selling at about $53.00 per share at the time of this valuation, we could assume that it appears to be undervalued based on past history. Even at the low P/E, it is undervalued. Every valuation method has its limitations. Although this method is simplified by ignoring dividends and present value calculations, earnings need to be correctly estimated, and the appropriate price-earnings multiplier must be applied. Since the P/E is also a function of expected growth rates the analyst has to consider whether the future growth will be higher or lower than past growth and thereby adjust the P/E appropriately. Unfortunately, even if you have the correct forecast for EPS, there is no assurance that the market will agree with your forecast or your price-earnings ratio. You may have to wait for the price to adjust until the market comes to see things through your eyes.

Relating an Individual Stock's P/E Ratio to the Market

Johnson & Johnson is the leading producer of health care products and pharmaceuticals. Everyone has probably used a least one of their products, such as Band-Aids, Q-tips, baby oil, or Tylenol, but you may not be familiar with the financial data presented in Table 7–4. This table provides an historical summary and an estimate of sales per share (SPS), dividends per share (DPS), earnings per share (EPS), cash flow per share (CFPS), and book value per share (BVPS). It also indicates Johnson & Johnson's high and low stock prices and the high and low P/E ratios for the company and the Standard & Poor's 500 index.

In the last three double columns, the high and low P/E ratios for Johnson & Johnson are compared with the high and low P/E ratios for the S&P 500. We calculate a relative price-earnings ratio as follows:

TABLE 7–4 Johnson & Johnson

Year	Sales per Share (SPS)	Dividends per Share (DPS)	Cash Flow per Share (CFPS)	Book Value per Share (BVPS)	Stock Price High	Stock Price Low	P/E Ratio High	P/E Ratio Low	S&P 500 P/E Ratio High	S&P 500 P/E Ratio Low	Relative P/E Ratios High	Relative P/E Ratios Low
1994	$ 6.12	$0.28	$1.06	$ 2.77	$14.10	$19.00	18.08	11.54	15.78	14.24	1.15	0.81
1995	7.27	0.32	1.26	3.49	23.10	13.40	24.84	14.41	18.34	13.46	1.35	1.07
1996	8.11	0.37	1.46	4.07	27.00	20.80	24.77	19.08	19.68	15.42	1.26	1.24
1997	8.41	0.43	1.62	4.59	33.70	24.30	27.85	20.08	24.83	18.37	1.12	1.09
1998	8.80	0.49	1.83	5.06	44.90	31.70	33.51	23.66	33.01	24.21	1.02	0.98
1999	9.88	0.55	2.03	5.83	53.40	38.50	35.84	25.84	30.58	25.03	1.17	1.03
2000	10.47	0.62	2.27	6.76	53.00	33.10	31.18	19.47	31.06	25.08	1.00	0.78
2001	10.83	0.70	2.46	7.95	61.00	40.30	31.94	21.10	56.03	38.26	0.57	0.55
2002	12.23	0.80	2.85	7.65	65.90	41.40	29.55	18.57	42.66	27.86	0.69	0.67
2003	13.95	0.93	3.35	9.10	59.10	48.10	22.30	18.15	30.73	24.85	0.73	0.73
10-year average	$ 9.61	$0.55	$2.02	$ 5.73	$43.52	$30.06	27.99	19.19	23.70	18.46	1.01	0.89
2004 estimates	$15.12	$1.06	$3.78	$10.33	$36.79 10-year average stock price for 1994–2003							

$$\text{Relative P/E} = \frac{\text{Company P/E}}{\text{S\&P 500 P/E}}$$

This market relative model compares the company P/E to the market P/E and tells us whether the company's stock has historically sold at a discount or premium to the market P/E.

For example in the first row for 1994, Johnson & Johnson's high P/E ratio was 18.08 and the S&P 500 high P/E was 15.78. When Johnson & Johnson's high P/E is divided by the S&P 500 high P/E, a relative P/E of 1.15 is calculated in the high relative P/E column. This indicates that Johnson & Johnson's high P/E ratio was at 115 percent of the market or selling at a 15 percent premium to the S&P 500 index. Over the 10 years listed we can see that Johnson & Johnson's high P/E relative to the S&P 500 sold as high as a 35 percent premium in 1995 (shown as 1.35) and as low as a 43 percent discount in 2001 when it sold at only 57 percent of the index.

For each year, a high and low relative was calculated for Johnson & Johnson with the 10-year average of the high and low shown on the last line. Over this time period, Johnson & Johnson's high relative P/E averaged 1.01 (a 1 percent premium to the market's high P/E) and its low relative P/E averages 0.89 (an 11 percent discount to the market's low P/E). When we add the high and low and divide by 2, we get an average of 95, which indicates that Johnson & Johnson historically sells at 95 percent of the S&P 500 P/E ratio.

Other Valuation Models Using Average Price Ratios and 10-Year Averages

Application Example

Notice that Table 7–4 also gives us estimates for sales per share (SPS), dividends per share (DPS), cash flow per share (CFPS), and book value per share (BVPS). Using the 10-year averages for price and per share data from Table 7–4 (bottom line), we can use

TABLE 7–5 Other Valuation Models Using Average Price Ratios and 10-Year Averages

A. Price to Sales per Share

Average Price	÷	Average Sales per Share	=	Price-to-SPS Ratio	×	Estimated 2004 SPS	=	Projected 2004 Price
$36.79		$9.61		3.83		$15.12		$57.91

B. Price to Dividend per Share

Average Price	÷	Average Dividends per Share	=	Price-to-DPS Ratio	×	Estimated 2004 DPS	=	Projected 2004 Price
$36.79		$ .55		66.89		$ 1.06		$70.90

C. Price to Cash Flow per Share

Average Price	÷	Average Cash Flow per Share	=	Price-to-CFPS Ratio	×	Estimated 2004 CFPS	=	Projected 2004 Price
$36.79		$2.02		18.21		$ 3.78		$68.83

D. Price to Book Value per Share

Average Price	÷	Average Book Value per Share	=	Price-to-BVPS Ratio	×	Estimated 2004 BVPS	=	Projected 2004 Price
$36.79		$5.73		6.42		$10.33		$66.31

the average price of $36.79 to determine the historical relationships. These models will simply determine whether the current stock price is selling above or below its historical valuation. It is up to the analyst to determine if the results are warranted by expectations.

Using the data in Table 7–4 on the previous page we develop the four models in Table 7–5. In each case in Table 7–5, we calculate the historical price ratios and multiply the result times the value estimated for 2004. The answer provides an estimated value of the common stock based on history. For example in Part A of Table 7–5, Johnson & Johnson exhibits a price-to-sales ratio of 3.83, which indicates that over the 10 years covered, Johnson & Johnson stock sold at 383 percent of its sales per share. Multiplying this ratio times estimated sales per share of $15.12 for 2004 produces a value of $57.91. This is around the current market price of $53. The other models indicate a higher value.

The analyst needs to look at the results of these models as information. In the case of Johnson & Johnson, all the models show that the current stock price of $53 is below fair value. The models in the chapter indicate that the company could be undervalued by as much as $20. It is the analyst's job to make a judgment based on experience, expectations, and an in-depth knowledge of the company. These models do not provide foolproof values, only information that can be used to make a financial judgment.

the real world of investing

Valuing Companies without Earnings: EBITDA and Free Cash Flow

In the high-tech, "new economy" era of the late 1990s and early 2000s, many popular companies did not achieve consistent earnings (or earnings at all). Examples include eBay, WorldCom, Oracle, and virtually every high-tech or telecommunications startup firm.

For a firm with negative earnings per share, the concept of a price-earnings ratio is hardly applicable. For example, a company that has a loss of $0.75 a share and is assigned a P/E ratio of 20 by analysts would have a negative value of $15. No such concept exists in finance. For that reason, analysts looked for other values to track besides earnings. Some developed stock price to revenue, stock price to website hits, stock price to actual website sales (as opposed to just hits), and so on. All of these were done on a per share basis. While these new "metrics" were popular, sophisticated analysts looked for greater depth in their analysis.

The term EBITDA fits the bill. **EBITDA** stands for earnings before interest, taxes, depreciation, and amortization. Companies that have negative earnings may well have a positive EBITDA.

An example of computing EBITDA is shown here for a company with reported negative earnings of $5 million and 1 million shares outstanding:

Earnings	−$5,000,000
+ Amortization	1,000,000
+ Depreciation	6,000,000
+ Taxes	0
+ Interest	2,000,000
Earnings before interest, taxes, depreciation, and amortization (EBITDA)	$4,000,000
− Shares outstanding	1,000,000
EBITDA per share	$4.00

Amortization (line 2) usually represents the write-off of intangible assets (perhaps goodwill), while depreciation represents the write-off of physical assets (such as plant and equipment). The other terms are self-explanatory. EBITDA per share is very close to the concept of cash flow per share, but in addition to depreciation and amortization, taxes and interest are added back to earnings. What the analyst ends up with is operating income per share. In other words, this tells the analyst how much the company is making purely from its operations out in the plant before financing charges and taxes as well as noncash charges. While the latter items are important in a traditional sense, the analyst needs to get a handle on something, and what better than how the company is doing on its actual day-to-day operations.

Once EBITDA is determined for a firm in a given industry, analysts look to other companies in the same industry to determine their stock price to EBITDA multiplier. Because this often is not commonly available data, the analyst may have to do the work on his or her own. Assume in this example that the industry average stock price/EBITDA ratio was 12×, then the firm with $4 in EBITDA per share might be valued at $48. If the firm has unusually bright prospects, it might be higher and the opposite would also be true.

Analysts may also use a slightly different concept of **free cash flow** per share by adding depreciation and amortization to earnings and subtracting out necessary capital expenditures and dividends (and dividing by the number of shares outstanding). Once again, an industry multiplier of stock price to free cash flow is developed and applied to free cash flow per share.

Forecasting Earnings Per Share

The other side of choosing an appropriate P/E ratio is forecasting the earnings per share of a company with the proper growth rate. Investors can get earnings forecasts in several ways. They can rely on professional brokerage house research, investment advisory firms such as Value Line or Standard & Poor's, or financial magazines such as *Forbes, BusinessWeek, Worth,* or *Money,* or they can do it themselves.

Least Squares Trendline

One of the most common ways of forecasting earnings per share is to use regression or **least squares trend analysis.** The technique involves a statistical method whereby a trendline is fitted to a time series of historical earnings. This trendline, by definition, is a straight line that minimizes the distance of the individual observations from the line. Figure 7–3 depicts a scattergram for the earnings per share of XYZ Corporation. The earnings of this company have been fairly consistent, and so we get a good trendline with a minimum of variation. The compounded growth rate for the whole 10-year period was 16.5 percent, with 9.8 percent for the first 5 years and 20.4 percent for the second 5 years. This shows up in Figure 7–3 as two distinct five-year trendlines. There are many statistical programs on PCs and mainframes that run regression analysis, and even handheld calculators have the ability to compute a growth rate from raw data.

Whenever a mechanical forecast is made, subjectivity still enters the decision in choosing the data that will be considered in the regression plot. If we compare two companies, one with consistent growth and one with cyclical growth, we find that the cyclical companies (e.g., autos, chemicals, airlines, forest products) are much more difficult to forecast than the consistent growth companies (e.g., pharmaceuticals, food, beverages). Cyclical companies are much more sensitive to swings in the economy and are likely to be in industries with high-priced durable goods where consumers can postpone purchases or where the economy has a direct effect on their products. Do not confuse cyclical with seasonal. Seasonal companies show earnings variability because their products have seasonal demand, such as fuel oil for winter heating and electricity for summer air conditioning or snowmobiles for winter. Cyclical companies have earnings related to the economy and exhibit variability over many years rather than three-month seasons.

FIGURE 7–3 Least Squares Trendline for EPS of XYZ Corporation

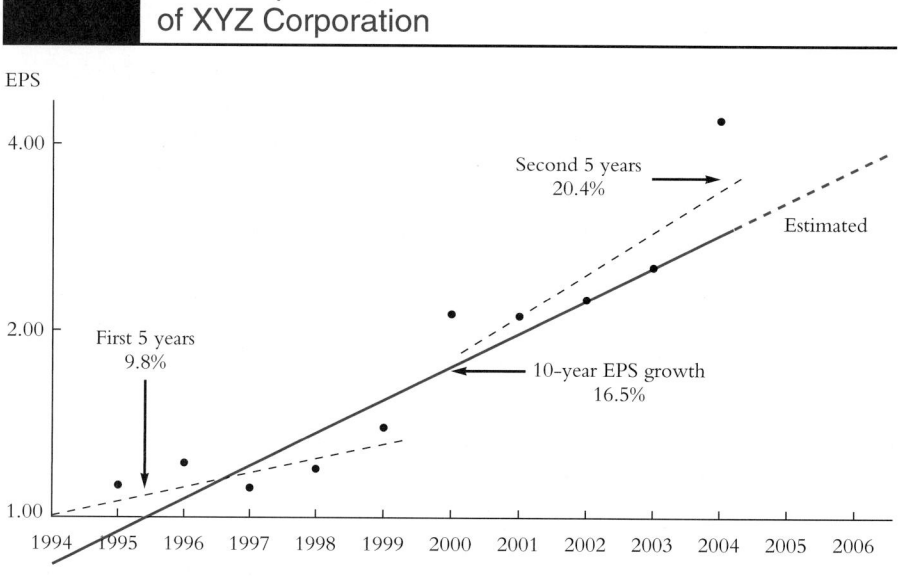

(ratio scale: straight line = constant growth)

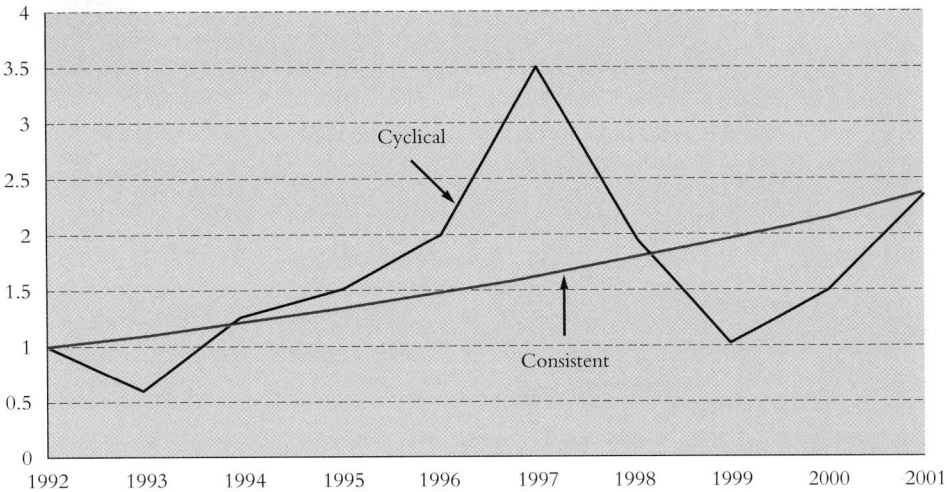

FIGURE 7–4 Trendlines for Cyclical and Consistent Growth Companies

Consistently growing companies often have higher P/E ratios on average than cyclical companies because investors are more confident in their future earnings. We compare two growth trends in Figure 7–4.

With cyclical companies you have to be careful not to start your forecast at a peak or trough period because you will get either biased-downward or -upward forecasts. Instead it is important to forecast cyclical companies throughout several business cycles with several peaks and troughs. Often the forecast for cyclical firms will cover 10 to 15 years of historical data, while the forecast for consistently growing firms might be based on five years of data.

The Income Statement Method

A more process-oriented method of forecasting earnings per share is to start with a sales forecast and create a standardized set of financial statements based on historical relationships. The sales forecast must be accurate if the earnings estimates are to have any significance. This method can be involved and provides a student with a very integrated understanding of the relationships that go into the creation of earnings.

Several important factors are included in this method of forecasting. The analyst is forced to examine profitability and the resultant fluctuations in profit margins before and after taxes. The impact of short-term interest expense and any new bond financing can be factored into the analysis as well as any increase in shares of common stock from new equity financing.

Application Example

Some analysts use an abbreviated method of forecasting earnings per share. They use a sales forecast combined with after-tax profit margins. For example, let us assume the Hutchins Corporation has a sales and profit margin history as set forth in Table 7–6 on page 188. The sales have been growing at a 10 percent growth rate, so the forecast is a simple extrapolation. However, the profit margin has fluctuated between 6.7 and 9.1 percent, with 8.2 percent being the average. Common stock

TABLE 7-6 Abbreviated Income Statement Method—Hutchins Corporation

Year	Sales ($000s)	×	After-Tax Profit Margin	=	Earnings ($000s)	−	Shares (000s)	=	Earnings per Share
1999	$1,250,000		7.9%		$ 98,750		30,000		$3.29
2000	1,375,000		9.1		125,125		31,500		3.97
2001	1,512,500		8.5		128,562		33,200		3.87
2002	1,663,750		6.7		111,471		35,000		3.18
2003	1,830,125		8.3		151,900		35,200		4.31
2004	2,013,137		8.5		171,117		37,000		4.62
2005e	2,214,452		8.2		181,585		38,400		4.73
2006e	2,435,896		9.0		219,230		39,800		5.50

e = Estimated.

outstanding has also grown by an average of 1.4 million shares per year. Given the cyclical nature of the profit margin, 8.2 percent was used for 2005, which is expected to be an average year. Nine percent was used for 2006, a year expected to be economically more robust for the firm. Multiplying the profit margin times the estimated sales produced an estimate of earnings that was divided by the number of shares outstanding to find the earnings per share. Once the EPS is found, it still must be plugged into an earnings valuation model to determine an appropriate value.

Growth Stocks and Growth Companies

In assessing the worth of an investment, stockholders, analysts, and investors often make reference to such terms as growth stock and growth companies. As part of the process of improving your overall valuation skills, you should have some familiarity with these terms.

A **growth stock** may be defined as the common stock of a company generally growing faster than the economy or market norm. These companies are usually predictable in their earnings growth. Many of the more popular growth stocks, such as Disney, Coca-Cola, and McDonald's, are really in the middle-to-late stages of the expansion phase. They tend to be fully valued and recognized in the marketplace.

Growth companies, on the other hand, are those companies that exhibit rising returns on assets each year and sales that are growing at an increasing rate (growth phase of the life cycle curve). Growth companies are found in stage 1 and 2 of the life cycle curve discussed in Chapter 6. Growth companies may not be as well-known or recognized as growth stocks. Companies that may be considered to be growth companies might be in such industries as computer networking, cable television, cellular telephones, biotechnology, medical electronics, and so on. These companies are growing very rapidly, and extrapolations of growth trends can be very dangerous if you guess incorrectly. Growth companies have many things in common. Usually, they have developed a proprietary product that is patented and protected from competition like the original Xerox process. This market protection allows a high rate of return and generates cash for new-product development.

There are also other indicators of growth potential. Companies should have sales growth greater than the economy by a reasonable margin. Increasing sales should be translated into similar earnings growth, which means consistently stable and high profit margins. Additionally, the earnings growth should show up in earnings per share growth (no dilution of earnings through unproductive stock offers). The firm should have a low labor cost as a percentage of total cost since wages are prone to be inflexible on the downside but difficult to control on the upside.

The biggest error made in searching for growth-oriented companies is that the price may already be too high. By the time you identify the company, so has everyone else, and the price is probably inflated. If the company has one quarter where earnings do not keep up with expectations, the stock price could tumble. The trick is to find growth companies before they are generally recognized in the market, and this requires taking more risk in small companies trading over-the-counter.

Assets as a Source of Stock Value

Until now, our emphasis has been primarily on earnings and dividends as the sources of value. However, in certain industries, asset values may have considerable importance. These assets may take many forms—cash and marketable securities, buildings, land, timber, old movies, oil, and other natural resources. At times, any one of these assets may dominate a firm's value. Furthermore, companies with heavy cash positions are attractive merger and acquisition candidates because of the possibility that a firm with highly liquid assets could be taken over and its own cash used to pay back debt incurred in the takeover.

In the last two decades, natural resources also had an important influence on value. Let's briefly examine this topic.

Natural Resources

Natural resources such as timber, copper, gold, and oil often give a company value even if the assets are not producing an income stream. This is because of the present value of the future income stream that is expected as these resources are used up. Companies such as International Paper, Weyerhaeuser, and other forest product companies have timberlands with market values far in excess of their book values and, in some cases, in excess of their common stock prices.

Oil companies with large supplies of oil in the ground may have to wait 20 years before some of it is pumped, but there may be substantial value there. In the case of natural gas pipeline companies, increasing reserves have changed the way these companies are viewed by the market. They were previously considered similar to utilities because of their natural gas transmission systems, but now they are also being valued based on their hidden assets (energy reserves). The term **hidden assets** refers to assets that are not readily apparent to investors in a traditional sense but that add substantial value to the firm.

Investors should not overlook hidden assets because of naive extrapolation of past data or failure to understand an industry or company. Furthermore, assets do not always show up on the books of a company. They may be fully depreciated, like the movies *Sound of Music, 101 Dalmatians,* or *Star Wars,* but still have substantial value in the television, VCR, or DVD market.

exploring the web

Website Address	Comments
my.yahoo.com	**Provides portfolio and stock tracking and screening—requires free registration**
cbs.marketwatch.com	**Provides stock information, screening, and evaluation**
www.quicken.com	**Provides stock screening and analysis; has intrinsic value calculator**
www.valuepro.net	**Has free intrinsic value calculator—other services fee-based**
www.morningstar.com	**Provides stock screening and detailed evaluation with Quick Quotes**
www.fool.com	**Contains stock evaluation and information from Motley Fool**
www.wsj.com	**Provides company information along with news—Most content requires subscription to access**
www.finportfolio.com	**Has portfolio tracker—requires free registration**
www.moneycentral.msn.com	**Has portfolio tracker, company information, investment information**
www.valuengine.com	**Provides stock analyses and forecasts, mainly fee-based—requires free registration**
www.bestsignals.com	**Provides stock research; has interactive research tools**
www.pcquote.com	**Provides stock quotes, portfolio tracking, and news**
www.validea.com	**Provides fee-based valuation of stocks**
www.stockworm.com	**Provides stock analysis and screening**
www.zacks.com	**Provides consensus earnings forecasts**

Summary

This chapter presents several common stock valuation models that rely on dividends and earnings per share. For the valuation to be accurate, the forecast of earnings and dividends needs to be correct.

Firms can be valued in many ways, and an analyst may use several methods to substantiate estimates. Valuation models based primarily on dividends look at future projections of dividends and the associated present values of the dividends. Assumptions must be made as to whether the dividend growth pattern is constant, accelerating, or decreasing.

Valuation using the earnings method requires that a price-earnings ratio be used as a multiplier of EPS. Price-earnings ratios are influenced by many variables such as growth, risk, capital structure, dividend policy, level of the market in general, industry factors, and more. A careful study of each situation must be concluded before choosing the appropriate P/E. The price-earnings ratio is a function of two fluctuating variables—earnings and price. The two variables combine to form a ratio that is primarily future oriented. High price-earnings ratios usually indicate positive expectations of the future, whereas low price-earnings ratios connote negative expectations.

To choose a P/E that is reasonable, the analyst must have some idea about the expected growth rate in earnings per share. Investors may find earnings estimates in investment advisory services, in statistical forecasts by brokerage houses, through their own time series statistical regression analysis, or by using the income statement method. Growth stocks were discussed more with the view of alerting the student to what to look for when trying to identify a growth stock or company than with the concept of valuation. The previously developed methods of valuation can be used on growth stocks as long as care is taken to evaluate the duration and level of growth.

We also presented some basic ideas about the value of companies based not on their earnings or dividend stream but on their assets such as cash or natural resources.

Key Words and Concepts

beta 170
dividend valuation models 169
earnings valuation model 169
EBITDA 185
equity risk premium (ERP) 170
free cash flow 185
growth companies 188
growth stock 188
hidden assets 189
least squares trend analysis 186
price-earnings ratio 177
required rate of return 169
risk-free rate 169
valuation 168

Discussion Questions

1. To determine the required rate of return, K_e, what factor is added to the risk-free rate? (Use Formula 7–2 on page 169).
2. What does beta represent?
3. What does the equity risk premium (ERP) represent?
4. How is value interpreted under the dividend valuation model?
5. What two conditions are necessary to use Formula 7–5 on page 172?
6. How can companies with non-constant growth be analyzed?
7. In considering P/E ratios for the overall market, what has been the relationship between price-earnings ratios and inflation?
8. What factors besides inflationary considerations and growth factors influence P/E ratios for the general market?
9. For cyclical companies, why might the current P/E ratio be misleading?
10. What two factors are probably most important in influencing the P/E ratio for an *individual stock?* Suggest a number of other factors as well.
11. What type of industries tend to carry the highest P/E ratios?
12. What is the essential characteristic of a least squares trendline?
13. What two elements go into an abbreviated income statement method of forecasting?

Problems

Required rate of return

1. If $R_F = 6$ percent, $b = 1.2$, and the ERP $= 6.5$ percent, compute K_e (the required rate of return).

Beta

2. If in problem 1 the beta (b) were 1.8 and the other values remained the same, what is the new value of K_e? What is the relationship between a higher beta and the required rate of return (K_e)?

Equity risk premium

3. Assume the same facts as in problem 1, but with an ERP of 10 percent. What is the new value for K_e? What does this tell you about investors' feelings toward risk based on the new ERP?

Constant growth dividend model

4. Assume $D_1 = \$1.80$, $K_e = 13$ percent, and $g = 9$ percent. Using Formula 7–5 on page 172 for the constant growth dividend valuation model, compute P_0.

Constant growth dividend model

5. Using the data from problem 4:
   a. If D_1 and K_e remain the same, but g goes up to 10 percent, what will the new stock price be? Briefly explain the reason for the change.
   b. If D_1 and g retain their original value ($\$1.80$ and 9 percent), but K_e goes up to 15 percent, what will the new stock price be? Briefly explain the reason for the change.

Proof of constant growth dividend model

6. Using the original data from problem 4, find P_0 by following the steps described below:
   a. Project dividends for years 1 through 3 (the first year is already given). Round all values that you compute to two places to the right of the decimal point throughout this problem.
   b. Find the present value of the dividends in part a using a discount rate of 13 percent.
   c. Project the dividend for the fourth year (D_4).
   d. Use Formula 7–5 to find the value of all future dividends, beginning with the fourth year's dividend. The present value you find will be at the end of the third year (the equivalent of the beginning of the fourth year).
   e. Discount back the value found in part d for three years at 13 percent.
   f. Observe that in part b you determined the percent value of dividends for the first three years and, in part e, the present value of an infinite stream after the first three years. Now add these together to get the total present value of the stock.
   g. Compare your answers in part f to your answer to problem 4. Comment on the relationship.

Appropriate use of constant dividend growth model

7. If $D_1 = \$2.50$, $K_e = 12$ percent, and $g = 7$ percent, can Formula 7–5 on page 172 be used to find P_0? Explain the reasoning behind your answer.

Appropriate use of constant growth dividend model

8. If $D_1 = \$2.50$, $K_e = 12$ percent, and $g = 15$ percent, can Formula 7–5 on page 172 be used to find P_0? Explain the reasoning behind your answer.

Nonconstant growth dividend model

9. The Haltom Corporation anticipates a nonconstant growth pattern for dividends. Dividends at the end of year 1 are $2.40 per share and are expected to grow by 15 percent per year until the end of year 5 (that's four years of growth). After year 5, dividends are expected to grow at 5 percent as far as the company can see into the future. All dividends are to be discounted back to the present at a 9 percent rate (K_e = 9 percent).
   a. Project dividends for years 1 through 5 (the first year is already given). Round all values that you compute to two places to the right of the decimal point throughout this problem.
   b. Find the present value of the dividends in part *a*.
   c. Project the dividend for the sixth year (D_6).
   d. Use Formula 7–5 on page 172 to find the present value of all future dividends, beginning with the sixth year's dividend. The present value you find will be at the end of the fifth year. Use Formula 7–5 as follows: $P_5 = D_6/(K_e - g)$.
   e. Discount back the value found in part *d* for five years at 9 percent.
   f. Add together the values from parts *b* and *e* to determine the present value of the stock.
   g. Explain how the two elements in part *f* go together to provide the present value of the stock.

Nonconstant growth dividend model

10. Rework problem 9 with a new assumption, that dividends at the end of the first year are $1.60 and that they will grow at 18 percent per year until the end of the fifth year, at which point they will grow at 6 percent per year for the foreseeable future. Use a discount rate of 12 percent throughout your analysis. Round all values that you compute to two places to the right of the decimal point.

Combined earnings and dividend model

11. R. L. Lynch investment bankers will use a combined earnings and dividend model to determine the value of the Pierce Corporation. The approach they take is basically the same as that in Table 7–2 on page 176. Estimated earnings per share for the next five years are:

    | 2004 | $4.00 |
    | 2005 | 4.40 |
    | 2006 | 4.84 |
    | 2007 | 5.32 |
    | 2008 | 5.85 |

   a. If 35 percent of earnings are paid out in dividends and the discount rate is 14 percent, determine the present value of dividends. Round all values you compute to two places to the right of the decimal point throughout this problem.
   b. If it is anticipated that the stock will trade at a P/E of 17 times 2008 earnings, determine the stock's price at that point in time and discount back the stock price for five years at 14 percent.
   c. Add together parts *a* and *b* to determine the stock price under this combined earnings and dividend model.

P/E ratio analysis

12. Mr. Sanders of Prime Time Investment Company is evaluating the P/E ratio of Delta Consumer Electronics (DCE). The firm's P/E is currently 20. With earning per share of $2, the stock price is $40.

The average P/E ratio in the consumer electronic industry is presently 19. However, DCE has an anticipated growth rate of 15 percent versus 10 percent for the industry norm, so 2 will be added to the industry P/E by Mr. Sanders. Also, the operating risk associated with DCE is less than that for the industry because of its long-term contract with Sears. For this reason, Mr. Sanders will add a factor of 1 to the industry P/E ratio.

The debt-to-total-assets ratio is not as encouraging. It is 50 percent, while the industry ratio is 40 percent. In doing his evaluation, Mr. Sanders decides to subtract a factor of 0.5 from the industry P/E ratio. Other ratios, including dividend payout, appear to be in line with the industry, so Mr. Sanders will make no further adjustment along these lines.

However, he is somewhat distressed by the fact that the firm only spent 3 percent of sales on R&D last year, when the industry norm is 5 percent. For this reason he will subtract a factor of 1 from the industry P/E ratio.

Despite the relatively low research budget, Mr. Sanders observes that the firm has just hired two of the top executives from a competitor in the industry. He decided to add a factor of 0.5 to the industry P/E ratio because of this.

a. Determine the P/E ratio for DCE based on Mr. Sanders' analysis.

b. Multiply this times earnings per share and comment on whether you think the stock might possibly be under- or overvalued in the marketplace at its current P/E and price.

P/E ratio analysis

13. Refer to Table 7–4 on page 183. Assume that because of unusually bright long-term prospects, analysts determine that Johnson & Johnson's P/E ratio in 2004 should be 20 percent above the average high S&P 500 P/E ratio for the last 10 years. (Carry your calculation of the P/E ratio two places to the right of the decimal point in this problem.) What would the stock price be, based on estimated earnings per share of $3.00 (for 2004)?

P/E ratio analysis

14. Refer to problem 13, and assume new circumstances cause the analysts to reduce the anticipated P/E in 2004 to 10 percent below the average low S&P 500 P/E for the last 10 years as shown in Table 7–4. Furthermore, projected earnings per share are reduced to $2.50. What would the stock price be?

Income statement method of forecasting

15. Security analysts following Wolfson Corporation use a simplified income statement method of forecasting as shown in Table 7–6 on page 188. Assume that 2004 sales are $20 million and are expected to grow by 12 percent in 2005 and 2006. The after-tax profit margin is projected at 6.1 percent in 2005 and 5.9 percent in 2006. The number of shares outstanding is anticipated to be 500,000 in 2005 and 510,000 in 2006. Project earnings per share for 2005 and 2006.

P/E ratio and price

16. The average price-earnings ratio for the industry that Wolfson Corporation is in is 16. If the company has a P/E ratio 20 percent higher than the industry ratio of 16 in 2005 and 25 percent higher than the industry ratio also of 16 in 2006:

a. Indicate the appropriate P/Es for the firm in 2005 and 2006.

b. Combine this with the earnings per share data in problem 15 to determine the anticipated stock price for 2005 and 2006.

P/E ratio and price

17. Relating to problems 15 and 16, assume you wish to determine the probable price range in 2006 if the P/E ratio is between 18 and 22. What is the price range?

Web Exercise

Given that the valuation models in Chapter 7 focused on Johnson & Johnson, it seems only appropriate to continue the analysis using more current data from Johnson & Johnson's website. Go to **www.jnj.com**.

Click on the "Investor Relations" tab on the front page and then click on "Dividend History."

1. Look at the quarterly listing of dividends paid, and comment on the growth in dividends and the pattern of payment. What are your expectations for future growth of dividends?
2. Go back to "Investor Relations" and click on "Common Stock," then click on "Historical Price Lookup" on the right-hand of the screen.
3. Go to the "Year" and go back 10 years. Then click on "Update Price." By what percent has the price of Johnson & Johnson changed over the last 10 years?
4. Click on "Stock Chart" on the right-hand portion of the screen. Select a "Period" of five years. Click on "Update Graph." How has Johnson & Johnson performed compared to the Dow Jones Industrial Average? The Dow is shown in red and Johnson & Johnson in blue.
5. Click on "Trading Statistics" on the upper right-hand part of the screen. Find "Percent of Shares Outstanding Held by Institutional Investors." Anything over 50 percent is considered high. How does Johnson & Johnson fare on this statistic?

Note: From time to time, companies redesign their websites and occasionally a topic we have listed may have been deleted, updated, or moved into a different location. Most websites have a "site map" or "site index" listed on a different page. If you click on the site map or site index you will be introduced to a table of contents which should aid you in finding the topic you are looking for.

CFA Material

The following material contains sample questions and solutions from a prior Level I CFA exam. While the terminology is slightly different from that in this text, you can still view the skills necessary for the CFA exam.

CFA Exam Question

3. As a firm operating in a mature industry, Arbot Industries is expected to maintain a constant dividend payout ratio and constant growth rate of earnings for the foreseeable future. Earnings were $4.50 per share in the recently completed fiscal year. The dividend payout ratio has been a constant 55 percent in recent years and is expected to remain so. Arbot's return on equity (ROE) is expected to remain at 10 percent in the future, and you require an 11 percent return on the stock.

    a. Using the constant growth dividend discount model, *calculate* the current value of Arbot common stock. *Show* your calculations.

    After an aggressive acquisition and marketing program, it now appears that Arbot's earnings per share and ROE will grow rapidly over the next two years. You are aware that the dividend discount model can be useful in estimating the value of common stock even when the assumption of constant growth does not apply.

b. *Calculate* the current value of Arbot's common stock using the dividend discount model assuming Arbot's dividend will grow at a 15 percent rate for the next two years, returning in the third year to the historical growth rate and continuing to grow at the historical rate for the foreseeable future. *Show* your calculations.

Solution: Question 3—Morning Session (I–91) (15 points)

a. Constant growth (single-stage) dividend discount model:

$$\text{Value}_0 = \frac{D_1}{K - g}$$

where:

D_1 = Next year's dividend
K = Required rate of return
g = Constant growth rate
D_1 = $(EPS_0)(1 + g)(P/O) = (4.50)(1.045)(0.55) = \$2.59$
K = given at 11% or 0.11
g = $(ROE)(1 - P/O) = (0.10)(1 - 0.55) = 0.045$

$$\text{Value}_0 = \frac{\$2.59}{11 - 0.045} = \frac{\$2.59}{0.065} = \$39.85$$

b. Multistage dividend discount model (where $g_1 = 0.15$ and g_2 is 0.045):

$$\text{Value}_0 = \frac{D_1}{1 + K} + \frac{D_2}{(1 + K)^2} + \frac{D_3/(K - g_2)}{(1 + K)^2}$$

D_1 = $(EPS_0)(1 + g_1)(P/O) = (4.50)(1.15)(0.55) = \$2.85$
D_2 = $(D_1)(1 + g_1) = (\$2.85)(1.15) = \$3.27$
K = given at 11% or 0.11
g_2 = 0.045
D_3 = $(D_2)(1 + g_2) = (\$3.27)(1.045) = \$3.42$

$$\text{Value}_0 = \frac{\$2.85}{(1.11)} + \frac{\$3.27}{(1.11)^2} + \frac{\$3.42/(0.11 - 0.045)}{(1.11)^2}$$

$$= \frac{\$2.85}{(1.11)} + \frac{\$3.27}{(1.11)^2} + \frac{\$52.62}{(1.11)^2}$$

$$= \$2.56 + \$2.65 + \$42.71$$

$$= \$47.92$$

CFA Exam Question

7. The constant growth dividend discount model can be used both for the valuation of companies and for the estimation of the long-term total return of a stock.

Assume: $20 = Price of a stock today
8% = Expected growth rate of dividends
$0.60 = Annual dividend one year forward

a. Using *only* the above data, *compute* the expected long-term total return on the stock using the constant growth dividend discount model. *Show* calculations.
b. *Briefly discuss three* disadvantages of the constant growth dividend discount model in its application to investment analysis.
c. *Identify three* alternative methods to the dividend discount model for the valuation of companies.

Solution: Question 7—Morning Session (I–90)(10 points)
(Reading reference: Cohen, Zinbarg, & Ziekel, Chapter 10)

a. The dividend discount model is: $P = \dfrac{d}{k - g}$

where:
- P = Value of the stock today
- d = Annual dividend one year forward
- k = Discount rate
- g = Constant dividend growth rate

Solving for k: $(k - g) = \dfrac{d}{p}$; then $k = \dfrac{d}{p} + g$

So k becomes the estimate for the long-term return of the stock.

$$k = \dfrac{\$0.60}{\$20.00} + 8\% = 3\% + 8\% = 11\%$$

b. Many professional investors shy away from the dividend discount framework analysis due to its many inherent complexities.
   (1) The model cannot be used where companies pay very small or no dividends and speculation on the level of future dividends could be futile. (Dividend policy may be arbitrary.)
   (2) The model presumes one can accurately forecast long-term growth of earnings (dividends) of a company. Such forecasts become quite tenuous beyond two years out. (A short-term valuation may be more pertinent.)
   (3) For the variable growth models, small differences in g for the first several years produce large differences in the valuations.
   (4) The correct k or the discount rate is difficult to estimate for a specific company as an infinite number of factors affect it that are themselves difficult to forecast, e.g., inflation, riskless rate of return, risk premium on stocks, and other uncertainties.
   (5) The model is not definable when $g > k$ as with growth companies, so it is not applicable to a large number of companies.
   (6) Where a company has low or negative earnings per share or has a poor balance sheet, the ability to continue the dividend is questionable.
   (7) The components of income can differ substantially, reducing comparability.

c. Three alternative methods of valuation would include: (1) price-earnings ratios; (2) price-asset value ratios (including market and book asset values); (3) price-sales ratios; (4) liquidation or breakup value; and (5) price–cash flow ratios.

S&P Problems

www.mhhe.com/edumarkinsight

1. Log on to the McGraw-Hill website: www.mhhe.com/edumarketinsight (see page vi in the preface for instructions).
2. Click on Company, which is the first box below the Market Insight title.
3. Put the ticker symbol for Johnson & Johnson (JNJ) in the box, and click on go.
4. On the left margin, click on Excel Analytics to open the list of choices. Under Valuation Data, click on Monthly Valuation Data to open the Excel spreadsheet. Given the data for the last seven months, what has been happening to the Johnson & Johnson's beta, price earnings ratio, and dividend yield?
5. Comparing the P/E ratio of the company to that of the S&P 500, what has been the trend of the P/E relative to the S&P 500? Is Johnson & Johnson selling at a premium or discount to the S&P 500? You may use the second worksheet at the bottom of the spreadsheet labeled "% Change" and the third worksheet at the bottom of the spreadsheet labeled "Key Item Charts" to help answer this question.
6. Close the spreadsheet and return to the valuation section in the left margin and click on Forecasted Values. What is the price forecast for Johnson & Johnson one year from now? Do the earnings per share trends justify the estimate?
7. On the bottom of the spreadsheet, click on the third worksheet labeled "Key Item Charts" and exam the graphs. What can you say about Johnson & Johnson's predictability over the last several years? Does the trend in long-term debt and cash flow support the price projection you found in the previous question?

The Wall Street Journal Project

Chapter 7 presents the required rate of return K_e for an individual common stock as follows:

$$K_e = R_F + b(\text{ERP})$$

What would be the required return for Bristol-Myers Squibb? As a first step, find R_F. Use the 20-year Treasury bond yield for this value. To get the yield, go to "Treasury, Bonds, Notes and Bills" in Section C (found under "Treasury/Agency Issues") in the index.

Once you are on the page, go to "Government Bonds and Notes." Read under the "Maturity–Mo/Yr" column until you are 20 years in the future and as close to the current month as possible. In reading the table, August 2025 would read as August 25. Once you've gotten to the right place in the table, write down the value in the last column (Ask Yield). This will be R_F.

Now assume the beta (b) is 1.15 and ERP (equity risk premium) is 6.4 percent. What is the required rate of return (K_e) for Bristol-Myers Squibb?

Selected References

Considerations in Valuing Securities

Bauman, W. Scott, and Robert E. Miller. "Investor Expectations and Value Stocks versus Growth Stocks." *The Journal of Portfolio Management,* Spring 1997, pp. 57–68.

Bierman, Harold, Jr. "Accounting for Valuation and Evaluation." *The Journal of Portfolio Management,* Spring 1994, pp. 64–67.

Connell, Bradford, and Wayne R. Landsman. "Accounting Valuation: Is Earnings Quality an Issue? *Financial Analysts Journal,* November–December 2003, pp. 20–28.

Der Horanesian, Mara. "If You're Missing Dividend Stocks, You're Missing Out." *BusinessWeek,* December 29, 2003.

Doukas, John A.; Charson Kim; and Christos Pantzalis. "Security Analysis, Agency Costs, and Company Characteristics." *Financial Analysts Journal,* November–December 2000, pp. 54–63.

EVA: The Real Key to Creating Wealth. New York: Stern Stewart & Co., 1996–97.

Ferguson, Robert. "Making the Discount Valuation Model Relevant for Financial Analysts." *The Journal of Investing,* Summer 1997, pp. 53–64.

Kirilenko, Andrei. "Valuation and Control in Venture Capital." *Journal of Finance,* April 2001, pp. 565–87.

O'Bryne, Stephen F. "EVA and Market Value." *Journal of Applied Corporate Finance,* Spring 1996, pp. 116–25.

Pastor, Lubos, and Pietro Verones. "Stock Valuation and Learning about Profitability." *Journal of Finance,* October 2003, pp. 1749–89.

Price-Earnings Ratio Considerations

Leibowitz, Martin L., and Stanley Kogelman. "The Growth Illusion: The P/E Cost of Earnings Growth." *Financial Analysts Journal,* March–April 1994, pp. 36–48.

White, Barry C. "What P/E Will the U.S. Market Support?" *Financial Analysts Journal,* November–December 2000, pp. 30–38.

Earnings Forecast

Moses, O. Douglas. "Cash Flow Signals and Analysts' Earnings Forecast Revisions." *Journal of Business, Finance and Accounting,* November 1991, pp. 807–32.

Growth Stocks

Ibbotson, Roger G., and Mark Riepe. "Growth vs. Value Investing and the Winner Is . . ." *Journal of Financial Planning,* June 1997, pp. 64–71.

8
chapter eight

Financial Statement Analysis

objectives

1. Understand the relationship between the income statement, balance sheet, and statement of cash flows.

2. Be able to break down and analyze ratios in six major categories.

3. Explain how the ratios can be applied to a specific company.

4. Be able to do long-term trend analysis based on the ratios.

5. Explain potential deficiencies that are often part of the published financial statements of companies.

The Major Financial Statements
    Income Statement
    Balance Sheet
    Statement of Cash Flows
Key Financial Ratios for the Security Analyst
    Ratio Analysis
    Bankruptcy Studies
    Classification System
Uses of Ratios
Comparing Long-Term Trends
Deficiencies of Financial Statements
    Inflation Effects
    Inventory Valuation
    Extraordinary Gains and Losses
    Pension Fund Liabilities
    Foreign Exchange Transactions
    Other Distortions

www.freeedgar.com

Financial statements present a numerical picture of a company's financial and operating health. Since each company is different, an analyst needs to examine the financial statements for industry characteristics as well as for differences in accounting methods. The major financial statements are the balance sheet, the income statement, and the statement of cash flows. A very helpful long-term financial overview also is provided by a 5- or 10-year summary statement found in the corporate annual report. One must further remember that the footnotes to these statements are an integral part of the statements and provide a wealth of in-depth explanatory information. More depth can often be found in additional reports such as the 10–K filed with the Securities and Exchange Commission and obtainable on request (free) from most companies or the SEC's Edgar website.

Fundamental analysis depends on variables internal to the company, and the corporate financial statements are one way of measuring fundamental value and risk. Financial statement analysis should be combined with economic and industry analysis before a final judgment is made to purchase or sell a specific security. Chapter 7 presented methods of valuation that used forecasts of dividends and earnings per share. Earnings per share combined with an estimated price-earnings ratio was also used to get a future price. Careful study of financial statements provides the analyst with much of the necessary information to forecast earnings and dividends, to judge the quality of earnings, and to determine financial and operating risk.

The Major Financial Statements

In the first part of this chapter, we examine the three basic types of financial statements—the income statement, the balance sheet, and the statement of cash flows—with particular attention paid to the interrelationships among these three measurement devices. In the rest of the chapter, ratio analysis is presented in detail, and deficiencies of financial statements are discussed along with the role of the security analyst in interpreting financial statements.

Income Statement

The **income statement** is the major device for measuring the profitability of a firm over a period of time. An example of the income statement is presented in Table 8–1 for Johnson & Johnson, the company used in the previous chapter for valuation models. Johnson & Johnson calls their income statement the

TABLE 8–1 Consolidated Statements of Earnings

Johnson & Johnson and Subsidiaries
(dollars in millions except per share figures)

	2003	2002	2001
Sales to customers	$41,862	36,298	32,317
Cost of products sold	12,176	10,447	9,581
Gross profit	29,686	25,851	22,736
Selling, marketing and administrative expenses	14,131	12,216	11,260
Research expense	4,684	3,957	3,591
Purchased in-process research and development	918	189	105
Interest income	(177)	(256)	(456)
Interest expense, net of portion capitalized	207	160	153
Other (income) expense, net	(385)	294	185
	19,378	16,560	14,838
Earnings before provision for taxes on income	10,308	9,291	7,898
Provision for taxes on income	3,111	2,694	2,230
Net earnings	**$ 7,197**	**6,597**	**5,668**
Basic net earnings per share	**$ 2.42**	**2.20**	**1.87**
Diluted net earnings per share	**$ 2.40**	**2.16**	**1.84**

"Consolidated Statement of Earnings" which reflects that they have consolidated the activities of all their subsidiaries into this one statement. Note that an income statement is for a defined period, whether it is for one month, three months, or in this case one year. The statement is presented in a stair-step fashion so that we can examine the profit after each type of expense item is deducted.

For 2003, Johnson & Johnson had sales of almost $42 billion. After subtracting the cost of goods (products) sold, their gross profit was $29.6 billion. From gross profit they subtracted other expenses related to operations, such as selling, marketing, and administrative expenses; research expense; purchased in-process research and development; interest expense, and other expenses. Notice that there is also interest income of $177 million which is almost equal to their interest expense of $207 million. The interest income is generated by their marketable securities found on the balance sheet. After subtracting expenses of $19.378 billion we arrive at earnings before taxes of $10.308 billion. After Johnson & Johnson pays taxes of $3.111 billion they have net earnings (earnings after taxes) of $7.197 billion.

When net earnings are divided by the number of shares outstanding we have basic net earnings per share of $2.42. Diluted earnings per share of $2.40 are two cents lower than basic net earnings per share because the number of shares used in the denominator includes new shares that might be created by the exercise of stock options or securities convertible into common stock. An examination of the two preceding years indicates that basic earnings are consistently diluted by three or four cents per share, indicating that dilution of earnings by the issuance of new shares is not a serious problem for Johnson & Johnson. Additionally, net earnings show a steady increase from $5.668 billion in 2001, to $6.597 in 2002, and finally $7.197 in 2003. Is this a good or bad income statement? As we shall see later, the analyst's interpretation of the numbers will depend on historical figures, on industry data, and on the relationship of income to balance sheet items such as assets and net worth.

Balance Sheet

The **balance sheet** indicates what the firm owns and how these assets are financed in the form of liabilities or ownership interest. While the income statement purports to show the profitability of the firm, the balance sheet delineates the firm's holdings and obligations. Together, these statements are intended to answer two questions: How much did the firm make or lose, and what is a measure of its worth? A balance sheet for Johnson & Johnson is presented in Table 8–2.

Johnson & Johnson was chosen for analysis because of its international scope and its well-known products such as Band-Aids, Tylenol, Neutrogena skin care products, ORTHO contraceptives, baby products, and its many drugs that treat schizophrenia and bipolar mania, and anti-infective and immune disorders.

Note that the balance sheet is dated at the end of the year 2003. It does not represent the result of transactions for a specific month, quarter, or year but rather is a cumulative chronicle of all transactions that have affected the corporation since its inception. This is in contrast to the income statement, which measures results only over a short, quantifiable period. Generally, balance sheet items are stated on an original cost basis rather than at market value.

The balance sheet is divided into two basic parts: Assets, and Liabilities and Stockholders' Equity. Assets and Liabilities are separated into current and

TABLE 8-2 Consolidated Balance Sheets

Johnson & Johnson and Subsidiaries
At December 28, 2003 and December 29, 2002 (dollars in millions except share and per share data)

	2003	2002
Assets		
Current assets		
Cash and cash equivalents	$ 5,377	2,894
Marketable securities	4,146	4,581
Accounts receivable trade, less allowances for doubtful accounts $192 (2002, $191)	6,574	5,399
Inventories	3,588	3,303
Deferred taxes on income	1,526	1,419
Prepaid expenses and other receivables	1,784	1,670
Total current assets	**22,995**	**19,266**
Marketable securities, noncurrent	84	121
Property, plant and equipment, net	9,846	8,710
Intangible assets	11,539	9,246
Deferred taxes on income	692	236
Other assets	3,107	2,977
Total assets	**$48,263**	**40,556**
Liabilities and Shareowners' Equity		
Current liabilities		
Loans and notes payable	$ 1,139	2,117
Accounts payable	4,966	3,621
Accrued liabilities	2,639	2,059
Accrued rebates, returns and promotions	2,308	1,761
Accrued salaries, wages and commissions	1,452	1,181
Accrued taxes on income	944	710
Total current liabilities	**13,448**	**11,449**
Long-term debt	2,955	2,022
Deferred tax liability	780	643
Employee-related obligations	2,262	1,967
Other liabilities	1,949	1,778
Shareowners' equity		
Preferred stock—without par value (authorized and unissued 2,000,000 shares)	—	—
Common stock—par value $1.00 per share (authorized 4,320,000,000 shares; issued 3,119,842,000 shares)	3,120	3,120
Note receivable from employee stock ownership plan	(18)	(25)
Accumulated other comprehensive income	(590)	(842)
Retained earnings	30,503	26,571
	33,015	28,824
Less common stock held in treasury, at cost (151,869,000 and 151,547,000)	6,146	6,127
Total shareholders' equity	**26,869**	**22,697**
Total liabilities and shareholders' equity	**$48,263**	**40,556**

Ratio Analysis

Ratios are used in much of our daily life. We buy cars based on miles per gallon, we evaluate baseball players by their earned run averages and batting averages and basketball players by field goal and foul shooting percentages, and so on. These are all ratios constructed to judge comparative performance. Financial ratios serve a similar purpose, but you must know what is being measured to construct a ratio and to understand the significance of the resultant number.

Financial ratios are used to weigh and evaluate the operating performance and capital structure of the firm. While an absolute value such as earnings of $50,000 or accounts receivable of $100,000 may appear satisfactory, its acceptability can be measured only in relation to other values.

For example, are earnings of $50,000 actually good? If a company earned $50,000 on $500,000 of sales (10 percent profit-margin ratio), that might be quite satisfactory, whereas earnings of $50,000 on $5 million could be disappointing (a meager 1 percent return). After we have computed the appropriate ratio, we must compare our firm's results to the achievement of similar firms in the industry as well as to our own firm's past performance. Even then, this "number-crunching" process is not always adequate because we are forced to supplement our financial findings with an evaluation of company management, physical facilities, and numerous other factors.

Ratio analysis will not uncover "gold mines" for the analyst. It is more like a physical exam at the doctor's office. You hope you are all right, but if not, you may be content to know what is wrong and what to do about it. Just as with medical illness where some diseases are easier to cure than others, the same is true of financial illness. The analyst is the doctor. He or she determines the illness and keeps track of management to see if they can administer the cure. Sometimes ailing companies can be very good values. Penn-Central went into bankruptcy, and its common stock could have been purchased at $2 per share for several years. In the 1990s, Penn-Central traded in the $17 to $27 range after a three-for-two stock split in 1982 and a two-for-one stock split in 1988. Chrysler (now DaimlerChrysler) and Lockheed (now Lockheed Martin) were both on the brink of bankruptcy in the 1970s until the government made guaranteed loans available. Both Chrysler and Lockheed could have been bought at less than $3 per share. After recovering and generating higher stock prices, they both split their common stock. These were all sick companies that returned to health, and any investor willing to take such great risk as to buy their stocks would have been well rewarded.

www.daimlerchrysler.com

www.lockheedmartin.com

Bankruptcy Studies

In a sense, ratio analysis protects an investor from picking continual losers more than it guarantees picking winners. Several studies have used ratios as predictors of financial failure. The most notable studies are by William Beaver and Edward Altman. Beaver found that ratios of failing firms signal failure as much as five years ahead of bankruptcy, and as bankruptcy approaches, the ratios deteriorate more rapidly, with the greatest deterioration in the last year. The Beaver studies also found (a) "Investors recognize and adjust to the new solvency positions of failing firms," and (b) "The price changes of the common stocks act as if investors rely upon ratios as a basis for their assessments, and impound the ratio information in the market prices."[1]

The first Altman research study indicated that five ratios combined were 95 percent accurate in predicting failure one year ahead of bankruptcy and were 72 percent accurate two years ahead of failure, with the average lead time for the ratio signal being 20 months.[2] Altman developed a Z score that was an index developed through multiple discriminate analysis that could predict failure. Altman modified and improved his model's accuracy even further by increasing the number of ratios to seven.[3] This service is currently sold to institutional investors by Zeta Services Inc. The Z (zeta) score relies on the following variables:

1. Retained earnings/total assets (cumulative profitability).
2. Standard deviation of operating income/total assets (measure of earnings stability during the last 10 years).
3. Earnings before interest and taxes/total assets (productivity of operating assets).
4. Earnings before interest and taxes/interest (leverage ratio, interest coverage).
5. Current assets/current liabilities (liquidity ratio).
6. Market value of common stock/book value of equity (a leverage ratio).
7. Total assets (proxy for size of the firm).

The greater the firm's bankruptcy potential, the lower its Z score. The ratios are not equally significant, but together they separate the companies into a correct bankruptcy group and nonbankruptcy group a high percentage of the time. Retained earnings/total assets has the heaviest weight in the analysis, and leverage is also very important. In the next section, we present six classifications of ratios that are helpful to the analyst. Many more would be used, but these represent the most widely used measures.

Classification System

We divide 20 significant ratios into six primary groupings:

A. Profitability ratios:
    1. Gross profit margin.
    2. After-tax profit margin.
    3. Return on assets.
    4. Return on equity.

B. Asset-utilization ratios:
    5. Receivables turnover.
    6. Inventory turnover.
    7. Fixed-asset turnover.
    8. Total asset turnover.

---

[1] William H. Beaver, "Market Prices, Financial Ratios, and the Prediction of Failure," *Journal of Accounting Research*, Autumn 1968, p. 192.

[2] Edward I. Altman, "Financial Ratios, Discriminant Analysis, and the Prediction of Corporate Bankruptcy," *Journal of Finance*, September 1968, pp. 589–609.

[3] Edward I. Altman, *Corporate Financial Distress* (New York: John Wiley & Sons, 1983).

C. Liquidity ratios:
   9. Current ratio.
   10. Quick ratio.
   11. Net working capital to total assets.
D. Debt-utilization ratios:
   12. Long-term debt to equity.
   13. Total debt to total assets.
   14. Times interest earned.
   15. Fixed charge coverage.
E. Price ratios:
   16. Price to earnings.
   17. Price to book value.
   18. Dividends to price (dividend yield).
F. Other ratios:
   19. Average tax rate.
   20. Dividend payout.

The users of financial statements will attach different degrees of importance to the six categories of ratios. To the potential investor, the critical consideration is profitability and debt utilization. For the banker or trade creditor, the emphasis shifts to the firm's current ability to meet debt obligations. The bondholder, in turn, may be primarily influenced by debt to total assets—while also eyeing the profitability of the firm in terms of its ability to cover interest payments in the short term and principal payments in the long term. Of course, the shrewd analyst looks at all the ratios, with different degrees of attention.

A. Profitability Ratios The **profitability ratios** allow the analyst to measure the ability of the firm to earn an adequate return on sales, total assets, and invested capital. The profit-margin ratios (1, 2) relate to income statement items, while the two return ratios (3, 4) relate the income statement (numerator) to the balance sheet (denominator). Many of the problems related to profitability can be explained, in whole or in part, by the firm's ability to effectively employ its resources. We shall apply these ratios to Johnson & Johnson's income statement and balance sheet for 2003, which were previously presented in Tables 8–1 and 8–2.

Application Example

Profitability ratios (Johnson & Johnson, 2003—in millions)

1. Gross profit margin $= \dfrac{\text{Gross profit}}{\text{Sales (revenue)}} = \dfrac{\$29{,}686}{\$41{,}862} = 70.91\%$

2. After-tax profit margin $= \dfrac{\text{Net income}}{\text{Sales}} = \dfrac{\$7{,}197}{\$41{,}862} = 17.19\%$

3. Return on assets

   (a) $\dfrac{\text{Net income}}{\text{Total assets}} = \dfrac{\$7{,}197}{\$48{,}263} = 14.91\%$

   (b) $\dfrac{\text{Net income}}{\text{Sales}} \times \dfrac{\text{Sales}}{\text{Total assets}}$

   $\dfrac{\$7{,}197}{\$41{,}862} \times \dfrac{\$41{,}862}{\$48{,}263}$ $17.19\% \times .8674 = 14.91\%$

4. Return on equity

(a) $\dfrac{\text{Net income}}{\text{Stockholders' equity}^4} = \dfrac{\$7{,}197}{\$26{,}869} = 26.79\%$

(b) $\dfrac{\text{Return on assets}}{(1 - \text{Debt/Assets})^5} = \dfrac{14.91\%}{(1 - .44)}$ or

$\dfrac{14.91\%}{(.56)} = 26.79\%$

The profitability ratios indicate that J&J is quite profitable, but the analysis of its return on equity using 4(b) indicates that its high return on stockholders' equity is partially a result of a fairly level total debt to assets. The disparity between return on assets and return on equity is the result of financing 44 percent of assets with debt.

Du Pont Analysis Notice that the return on assets and return on equity have parts (a) and (b), or two ways to determine the ratio. The methods employed in (b), which arise from the Du Pont Company's financial system, help the analyst see the relationship between the income statement and the balance sheet. The return on assets is generated by multiplying the after-tax profit margin (income statement) by the asset-turnover ratio (combination income statement–balance sheet ratio).

www.dupont.com

The Du Pont Company was a forerunner in stressing that satisfactory return on assets may be achieved through high profit margins or rapid turnover of assets, or a combination of both. The Du Pont system causes the analyst to examine the sources of a company's profitability. Since the profit margin is an income statement ratio, a high profit margin indicates good cost control, whereas a high asset turnover ratio demonstrates efficient use of the assets on the balance sheet. Different industries have different operating and financial structures. For example, in the heavy capital goods industry (machinery and equipment), the emphasis is on a high profit margin with a low asset turnover, while in food processing, the profit margin is low, and the key to satisfactory returns on total assets is a rapid turnover of assets.

Du Pont analysis further stresses that the return on equity stems from the return on assets adjusted for the amount of financial leverage by using the total debt-to-asset ratio. About 44 percent of the Johnson & Johnson's assets are financed by debt, and the return on equity reflects a fairly high level of debt financing because the return on equity of 26.79 percent is almost twice as large as return on assets of 14.91 percent. As a detective, the financial analyst can judge how much debt a company employs by comparing these two measures of return. Of course, you will want to check this clue with the debt-utilization

---

[4] A working definition of stockholders' equity is the preferred and common stock accounts plus retained earnings. Johnson & Johnson also has a few other adjustments. The total can be found on the second line from the bottom at the end of Table 8–2.

[5] Debt represents total debt on the balance sheet and is often given. In the case of Johnson & Johnson, it is not. However, it can easily be computed as total current liabilities of $13,448 (million) plus the four items under it for a total of $21,394 (million). This number divided by total assets of $48,263 (million) give a Debt/Assets Value of .44 ($21,394/$48,263 = .44).

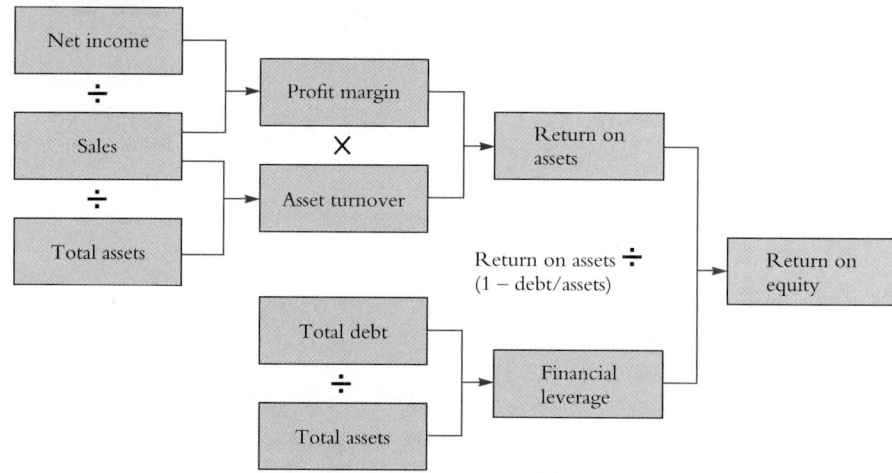

FIGURE 8-2 Du Pont Analysis

ratios. The total relationship between return on assets and return on equity under the Du Pont system is depicted in Figure 8–2.

In computing return on assets and equity, the analyst must also be sensitive to the age of the assets. Plant and equipment purchased 15 years ago may be carried on the books far below its replacement value. A 20 percent return on assets that were purchased in the late 1980s may be inferior to a 15 percent return on newly purchased assets.

B. Asset-Utilization Ratios With **asset-utilization ratios,** we measure the speed at which the firm is turning over accounts receivable, inventory, and longer-term assets. In other words, asset-utilization ratios measure how many times per year a company sells its inventory or collects its accounts receivable. For long-term assets, the utilization ratio tells us how productive the fixed assets are in terms of sales generation.

Application Example

Asset-utilization ratios (Johnson & Johnson, 2003—in millions)

5. Receivables turnover $= \dfrac{\text{Sales}}{\text{Receivables}} = \dfrac{\$41{,}862}{\$6{,}574} = 6.37\times$

6. Inventory turnover $= \dfrac{\text{Sales}^6}{\text{Inventory}} = \dfrac{\$41{,}862}{\$3{,}588} = 11.67\times$

7. Fixed-assets turnover $= \dfrac{\text{Sales}}{\text{Fixed assets}^7} = \dfrac{\$41{,}862}{\$9{,}846} = 4.25\times$

8. Total asset turnover $= \dfrac{\text{Sales}}{\text{Total assets}} = \dfrac{\$41{,}862}{\$48{,}263} = 0.87\times$

---

[6] Some may prefer to use cost of goods sold in the numerator for theoretical reasons. We use sales to be consistent with Dun & Bradstreet, the well-known credit rating bureau.

[7] The fixed-asset value is equal to property, plant and equipment, net on the balance sheet.

The asset-utilization ratios relate sales on the income statement (numerator) to the various assets on the balance sheet. Given that Johnson & Johnson's products are a combination of household products and pharmaceuticals, the repeat nature of purchases creates a receivables turnover of 6.37× which indicates that J&J gets paid close to every 60 days. The inventory turnover is very high at 11.67× which shows that there is about a one-month inventory cycle, which certainly makes sense for the pharmaceutical side of the business.

The fixed-asset turnover ratio is relatively high at 4.25× because in the long-term asset area, J&J has a relatively small dollar amount invested in fixed assets (plant and equipment). The amount is only $9.8 billion. The nature of the business allows J&J to generate high margin products with a small investment in plant and equipment but requires a large investment in research and development.

The total asset turnover ratio of .87× is not so positive. There are many other assets causing this low turnover. Productive investment in research and development of $11.5 billion ends up under the intangible category in the long-term asset section because patents on new drugs can have a life of up to 14 years. The other variable that makes the asset turnover ratio low is that J&J has about $9.5 billion in cash, cash equivalents, and marketable securities on their balance sheet. This is almost equal to the $9.8 billion they have invested in plant and equipment.

C. Liquidity Ratios

The primary emphasis of the **liquidity ratios** is a determination of the firm's ability to pay off short-term obligations as they come due. These ratios can be related to receivables and inventory turnover in that a faster turnover creates a more rapid movement of cash through the company and improves liquidity. Again remember that each industry will be different. A jewelry store chain will have much different ratios from a grocery store chain.

Application Example
eXcel

Liquidity ratios (Johnson & Johnson, 2003—in millions)

9. Current ratio

$$\frac{\text{Current assets}}{\text{Current liabilities}} = \frac{\$22{,}995}{\$13{,}448} = 1.71\times$$

10. Quick ratio

$$\frac{\text{Current assets} - \text{Inventory}}{\text{Current liabilities}} = \frac{\$22{,}995 - \$3{,}588}{\$13{,}448} = 1.44\times$$

11. Net working capital to total assets

$$\frac{\text{Current assets} - \text{Current liabilities}}{\text{Total assets}} = \frac{\$22{,}995 - \$13{,}448}{\$48{,}263} = 0.20\times$$

The first two ratios (current and quick) indicate whether the firm can pay off its short-term debt in an emergency by liquidating its current assets. The quick ratio looks only at the most liquid assets, which include cash, marketable securities, and receivables. Cash and securities are already liquid, but receivables usually will be turned into cash during the collection period. If there is concern about the firm's liquidity, the analyst will want to cross-check the liquidity ratios with receivables and inventory turnover to determine how fast the current assets are turned into cash during an ordinary cycle.

The last liquidity ratio is a measure of the percentage of current assets (after short-term debt has been paid) to total assets. This indicates the liquidity of the assets of the firm. The higher the ratio, the greater the short-term assets relative to fixed assets, and the safer a creditor is. In this example, the ratio of .20× is small, but indicates no problem given the solid current and quick ratios, which are both well over 1.

D. Debt-Utilization Ratios The **debt-utilization ratios** provide an indication of the way the firm is financed between debt (lenders) and equity (owners) and therefore helps the analyst determine the amount of financial risk present in the firm. Too much debt cannot only impair liquidity with heavy interest payments but can also damage profitability and the health of the firm during an economic recession or industry slowdown.

Application Example

eXcel

Debt-utilization ratios (Johnson & Johnson, 2003—in millions)

12. Long-term debt to equity $= \dfrac{\text{Long-term debt}}{\text{Stockholders' equity}} = \dfrac{\$2{,}955}{\$26{,}869} = 11.00\%$

13. Total debt to total assets $= \dfrac{\text{Total debt}}{\text{Total assets}} = \dfrac{\$21{,}394}{\$48{,}263} = 44.33\%$

14. Times interest earned $= \dfrac{\text{Income before interest and taxes}[8]}{\text{Interest}} = \dfrac{\$10{,}308 + 207}{\$207} = 50.80$

15. Fixed-charge coverage $= \dfrac{\text{Income before fixed charges and taxes}[9]}{\text{Fixed charges}[10]} = \dfrac{\$10{,}308 + 207}{\$207} = 50.80$

We have already discussed the impact of financial leverage on return on equity, and the first two ratios in this category indicate to the analyst how much financial leverage is being used by the firm. The more debt, the greater the interest payments and the more volatile the impact on the firm's earnings. Companies with stable sales and earnings such as utilities can afford to employ more debt than those in cyclical industries such as automobiles or airlines. Ratio 12, long-term debt to equity, provides information concerning the long-term capital structure of the firm. In the case of J&J, long-term liabilities represent only 11.00 percent of the stockholders' equity base provided by the owners of the firm. Ratio 13, total debt to total assets, looks at the total assets and the use of debt. Each firm must consider its optimum capital structure, and the analyst should be aware of industry fluctuations in assessing the firm's proper use of leverage. J&J seems safe, given that its business is not subject to large swings in sales.

The last two debt-utilization ratios indicate the firm's ability to meet its cash payments due on fixed obligations such as interest, leases, licensing fees, or

---

[8] Income before interest and taxes equals earnings before provision for taxes on income of $10,308 million plus the interest expense of $207 million as shown in Table 8–1.

[9] Because there are no other fixed charges besides interest, the numerators are the same in Formulas 14 and 15.

[10] The denominators are also the same in Formulas 14 and 15.

sinking-fund charges. The higher these ratios, the more protected the creditor's position. Use of the fixed-charge coverage is more conservative than interest earned since it includes all fixed charges. Now that most leases are capitalized and show up on the balance sheet, it is easier to understand that lease payments are similar in importance to interest expense. Charges after taxes such as sinking-fund payments must be adjusted to before-tax income. For example, if a firm is in the 40 percent tax bracket and must make a $60,000 sinking-fund payment, the firm would have had to generate $100,000 in before-tax income to meet that obligation. The adjustment would be as follows:

$$\text{Before-tax income required} = \frac{\text{After-tax payment}}{1 - \text{Tax rate}}$$

$$= \frac{\$60,000}{1 - 0.40} = \$100,000$$

Johnson & Johnson's fixed-charge coverage is the same as its interest-earned ratio because it has no fixed charges other than interest expense. Both ratios are very strong.

E. *Price Ratios* The **price ratios** relate the internal performance of the firm to the external judgment of the marketplace in terms of value. What is the firm's end result in market value? The price ratios indicate the expectations of the market relative to other companies. For example, a firm with a high price-to-earnings ratio has a higher market price relative to $1 of earnings than a company with a lower ratio.

Price ratios (Johnson & Johnson, 2003)

16. Price to earnings $= \dfrac{\text{Common stock price}[11]}{\text{Earnings per share}} = \dfrac{\$53.00}{\$2.42} = 21.90\times$

17. Price to book value $= \dfrac{\text{Common stock price}}{\text{Book value per share}[12]} = \dfrac{\$53.00}{\$8.61} = 6.16\times$

18. Dividends to price (Dividend yield) $= \dfrac{\text{Dividends per share}}{\text{Common stock price}} = \dfrac{\$0.96}{\$53.00} = 1.81\%$

J&J's price-earnings ratio indicates that the firm's stock price represents $21.9 for every $1 of earnings. This number can be compared with that of other companies in the pharmaceutical industry and/or related industries. As indicated in Chapter 7, the price-earnings ratio (or P/E ratio) is influenced by the earnings and the sales growth of the firm and also by the risk (or volatility in performance), the debt-equity structure of the firm, the dividend-payment policy, the quality of management, and a number of other factors. The P/E ratio indicates expectations about the future of a company. Firms that are expected to provide greater returns than those for the market in general, with equal or less risk, often have P/E ratios higher than the overall market P/E ratio.

---

[11] Stock price is 2003 year-end price.

[12] Book value per share $= \dfrac{\text{Stockholders' equity}}{\text{Number of shares}} = \dfrac{\$26,869}{3,119} = \$8.61$

TABLE 8–4 Price-Earnings Ratios for Selected U.S. Corporations

Corporation	Industry	P/E Ratio[a] 12/31/81	10/24/88	8/13/97	4/2/04
Exxon	International oil	5	12	19	15
Bank America	Banking	7	9	17	11
Halliburton	Oil service	11	26	30	21
Winn-Dixie	Retail	8	15	21	NMF[c]
IBM	Computers	9	14	20	19
McDonald's	Restaurant franchise	10	15	22	18
Texas Instruments	Semiconductors	15	13	cc[b]	36
S&P 500	Market index	8	13	21	23

[a] P/E ratio is calculated by taking the market price and dividing by the previous 12 months' earnings per share.
[b] cc indicates that the P/E ratio is 100 or more.
[c] NMF indicates that earnings are either negative or too small to create a meaningful ratio.
Source: *Value Line Investment Survey.*

Expectations of returns and P/E ratios do change over time, as Table 8–4 illustrates. Price-earnings ratios for a selected list of U.S. firms in 1981, 1988, 1997, and 2004 show that during this 23-year period, price-earnings ratios generally rose between 1981 and 2004.

The P/E ratios are more complicated than they may appear at first glance. The level of the market was higher in 2004, but not all companies exhibited higher P/E ratios. A high P/E ratio can result from many sets of assumptions. P/E ratios can be high because of high expected growth in earnings per share. For a company in a cyclical industry, the P/E ratio can be high because of low earnings, and a stock price that has not declined as rapidly as earnings. This is true of Texas Instruments in 2004.

www.texasinstruments.com

The price-to-book-value ratio relates the market value of the company to the historical accounting value of the firm. In a company that has old assets, this ratio may be quite high, but in one with new, undepreciated fixed assets, the ratio might be lower. This information needs to be combined with a knowledge of the company's assets and of industry norms.

The **dividend yield** is part of the total return that an investor receives along with capital gains or losses. It is usually calculated by annualizing the current quarterly dividend since that is the cash value a current investor is likely to receive over the next year.

The price-to-earnings and price-to-book-value ratios are often used in computing stock values. The simple view of these ratios is that when they are relatively low compared with a market index or company history, the stock is a good buy. In the case of the dividend yield, the opposite is true. When dividend yields are relatively high compared with the company's historical data, the stock may be undervalued. Of course, the application of these simple models is much more complicated. The analyst has to determine if the company is performing the same as it was when the ratios were at what the analyst considers a normal level.

F. Other Ratios The other ratios are presented in category F to help the analyst spot special tax situations that affect the profitability of an industry or company and to determine what percentage of earnings are being paid to the stockholder and what is being reinvested for internal growth.

> **Application Example**
> eXcel
>
> **Other ratios** (Johnson & Johnson, 2003)
>
> 19. Average tax rate $= \dfrac{\text{Income tax}}{\text{Taxable income}} = \dfrac{\$3{,}111}{\$10{,}308} = 30.18\%$
>
> 20. Dividend payout $= \dfrac{\text{Dividends per share}}{\text{Earnings per share}} = \dfrac{\$0.96}{\$2.42} = 39.67\%$

These other ratios are calculated to provide the analyst with information that may indicate unusual tax treatment or reinvestment policies. For example, the tax ratio for forest products companies will be low because of the special tax treatment given timber cuttings. A company's tax rate may also decline in a given year as a result of special tax credits. Thus, earnings per share may rise, but we need to know if it is from operations or favorable tax treatment. If it is from operations, we will be more sure of next year's forecast, but if it is from tax benefits, we cannot normally count on the benefits being continued into the future.

The **dividend-payout ratio** provides data concerning the firm's reinvestment strategies. It represents dividends per share divided by earnings per share. A high payout ratio tells the analyst that the stockholder is receiving a large part of the earnings and that the company is not retaining much income for investment in new plant and equipment. High payouts are usually found in industries that do not have great growth potential, while low payout ratios are associated with firms in growth industries.

Johnson & Johnson's tax rate is slightly below the statutory rate of 35 percent, which can be attributed to its operations outside of the United States, which may have more favorable tax rates. The dividend payout ratio of almost 40 percent would indicate that J&J is somewhere between the expansion and maturity stages of its life cycle. Given Johnson & Johnson's record of increased earnings, it can be expected that the payout ratio will stay relatively constant and dividends will rise with earnings per share.

Uses of Ratios

The previous section presented 20 ratios that may be helpful to the analyst when evaluating a firm. How can we further use the data gathered to check the health of companies we are interested in analyzing?

One way is to compare the company with the industry. This is becoming more difficult as companies diversify into several industries. Twenty years ago, many firms competed in only one industry, and ratio comparisons were more reliable. Now companies have a wide range of products and markets.

Let us see how Johnson & Johnson compares to its industry competitors based on selected ratios. The companies chosen for comparison include Abbott Laboratories, Aventis, GlaxoSmithKline, and Novartis. Several large U.S. companies such as Merck and Pfizer were excluded because data are no longer meaningful due to mergers or divestitures.

Application Example

The ratios presented in Table 8–5 can be found in the *Standard and Poor's Industry Surveys* available in most libraries either on line or in print format.

TABLE 8–5 Comparative Data for Year Ending 2002

	Abbott Laboratories	Aventis (Franco-German)	GlaxoSmithKline (British)	J & J	Novartis AG (Swiss)
Operating revenues 2002 (in billions of dollars)	$17.7	$22.8	$34.2	$36.2	$23.4
5-yr. ann. growth of revenues	8.30%	8.80%	20.60%	9.90%	1.90%
5-yr. ann. growth of net income	5.90%	NM	15.90%	14.80%	8.20%
Profit margin	15.20%	10.00%	18.50%	18.20%	22.60%
Return on assets	11.70%	6.50%	18.60%	16.70%	12.30%
Return on equity	28.30%	21.00%	58.60%	28.10%	19.50%
Current ratio	1.3×	0.9×	1.2×	1.7×	2.5×
Debt to capital	28.50%	12.80%	27.60%	8.00%	8.10%
Dividend payout ratio	51%	20%	61%	36%	26%
Dividend yield (average)	2.35%	0.90%	3.30%	1.55%	1.40%
Price-earnings ratio (average)	24.5	22	19.5	24.5	18.5

Source: *Standard & Poor's Industry Survey, Healthcare: Pharmaceuticals,* www.mhhe.com/edumarketinsight.

    The companies chosen, with the exception of Merck & Pfizer, are five of the biggest pharmaceutical companies in the world. In comparing growth rates for the five years 1998 through 2002, we see that GlaxoSmithKline has the highest growth rate in revenues and net income with Johnson & Johnson in second place. It should be pointed out that even though Johnson & Johnson's sales growth of 9.9 percent is less than half of GlaxoSmithKline's 20.6 percent, its growth of net income is only about 1 percent less than GlaxoSmithKline's 15.9 percent.

    In comparing the profitability ratios of profit margin, return on assets, and return on equity, it is evident GlaxoSmithKline is still the leader with J&J close behind. Overall, except for Aventis, the industry has high profitability. While GlaxoSmithKline has the highest return on equity, both GlaxoSmithKline and Abbott Labs leverage their return on equity through the use of more debt to capital than the other companies listed in the table. As for liquidity measures, Novartis has a relatively high current ratio of 2.5 times followed by Johnson & Johnson's current ratio of 1.7 times.

    In general all companies presented are in good financial shape, with some differences evident in the numbers. There is a wide variation in both payout ratios and dividend yields. GlaxoSmithKline has the highest payout ratio at 61 percent and highest dividend yield at 3.30 percent. It should be pointed out that British investors expect higher dividend yields than U.S. investors and the

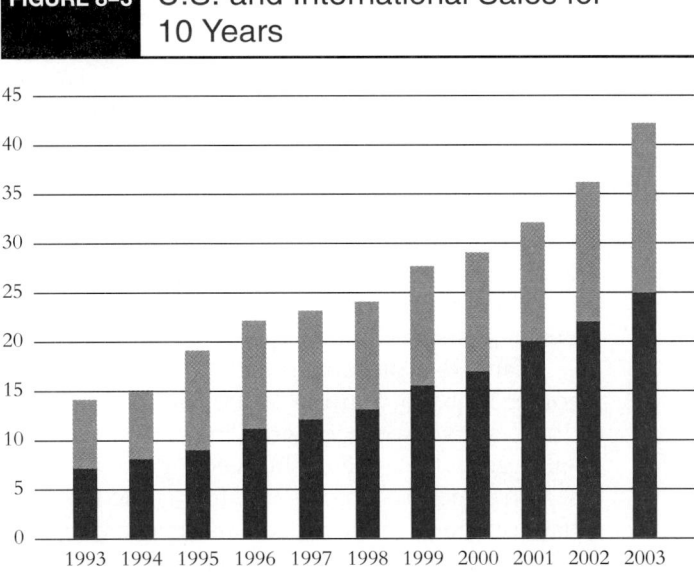

FIGURE 8–3 U.S. and International Sales for 10 Years

Source: *Johnson & Johnson's 2003 Annual Report.*

spread between GlaxoSmithKline's dividend yield compared to others can be chalked up to cultural differences in the marketplace.

When it comes to valuation, Abbott Labs and Johnson exhibit the highest price-earnings ratios of 24.5 for this particular year. In Abbott Labs case the P/E is perhaps a function of the market's expectation that earnings have a higher future growth potential than the past growth rates. It is important to understand that growth rates for these companies are quite dependent on the introduction of new drugs. Introducing a new drug is expensive because advertising costs are high, and the costs of research and development are being amortized. After several years, the new drug may become profitable as it gains market share. The point is, past growth rates are not a good predictor of future growth rates. Rather, the analyst looks at the "pipeline" of new drugs that are in clinical trials. Companies that are good at developing new drugs have higher growth rates and higher price-earnings ratios. In the case of Johnson & Johnson, the high P/E is also an indication of low financial risk and consistent growth and profitability.

Johnson & Johnson's consistent growth is demonstrated in Figure 8–3 for the years 1993 through 2003. The graph shows both domestic and international sales. International sales account for approximately 40 percent of Johnson & Johnson's revenues.

Because J&J is an international company, it may be affected by political and economic events abroad. Foreign price controls on pharmaceuticals are common. Earnings are affected by currency exchange rates and the fact that poor countries in the Third World are clamoring for drugs they can't afford. In 2004 Johnson & Johnson gave the rights to its very promising AIDS drug to a non-profit medical foundation to develop, test, and if successful, distribute to countries in Africa. Johnson & Johnson retained the rights to sell the drug in the developed world.

For now we have just compared Johnson & Johnson to four competitors looking at ratios for a one-year period. Long-term trend analysis is also important because one year of data doesn't really tell an analyst much about the direction of the company's performance. Trend analysis can focus on increasing or decreasing performance as well as the volatility of the results.

Comparing Long-Term Trends

Over the course of the business cycle, sales and profitability may expand and contract, and ratio analysis for any one year may not present an accurate picture of the firm. Therefore, we look at **trend analysis** of performance over a number of years to examine long-term performance.

Table 8–6 presents the 10-year summary of selected financial data for Johnson & Johnson. Starting at the top, we can see that both domestic and international sales have been growing over the 10-year period, but that international sales growth stagnated between 1996 and 2000 before it picked up again. Research expense, which some feel is the lifeblood of the pharmaceutical industry, has continued to grow each and every year with a total of $4.684 billion spent in 2003. Just eyeballing the research expenditures compared to total sales, it looks as if J&J spends between 10 and 12 percent of its sales on research and development.

In the middle of the page we see a category called Percent increase over previous year. In this category we can look at diluted net earnings per share growth and see that between 1993 and 1999 growth was between 0 and 85.3 percent. In short, it was unpredictable. However growth of earnings per share since 2000 has been relatively stable—between 11.1 and 17.4 percent.

At the bottom of the table, Johnson & Johnson presents common stock information. We can see that it has increased its dividend every year since 1993. This provides valuable information to the potential investor. The average stock price tends to move in fits and starts and has been relatively stable between 1999 and 2003, even though sales and earnings have grown quite a bit since 1999. We can also see that the number of shares outstanding has remained relatively stable between 1996 and 2003, which tells us that Johnson & Johnson is not repurchasing shares on a consistent basis or selling new shares. The variation in shares that does exist comes from the exercise of employee stock options with J&J occasionally entering the market to repurchase an equal number of shares to avoid dilution of earnings over time. In general the 10-year data look good and have become more stable over the last five years.

If we take a look at selected ratios and data over the last five years compared to competitors, how does Johnson & Johnson look? Figure 8–4 on page 222 provides some partial answers. On a comparative basis, we can see that Johnson & Johnson has stable and high returns on assets. While GlaxoSmithKline has higher returns on assets, they are more volatile, as are those of Abbott Labs. In the case of GlaxoSmithKline the volatility comes from merging with another company. The merger created initial costs but after absorbing the other company GlaxoSmithKline was able to eliminate duplicate areas and its returns recovered. In Abbott's case, the volatility stemmed from production problems and a plant closure by the Food and Drug Administration. Both firms are working hard to reach their former levels of profitability. In the debt to capital area, Johnson & Johnson and Novartis are the least leveraged while Abbott and GlaxoSmithKline ended up 2002 about equal at close to 30 percent.

TABLE 8-6 Summary of Operations and Statistical Data 1993–2003[a]

Johnson & Johnson and Subsidiaries
(dollars in millions except for share figures)

	2003	2002	2001	2000	1999	1998	1997	1996	1995	1994	1993
Sales to customers—Domestic	$25,274	22,455	19,825	17,316	15,532	12,901	11,814	10,851	9,065	7,731	7,121
Sales to customers—International	16,588	13,843	12,492	11,856	11,825	10,910	10,708	10,536	9,472	7,723	6,756
Total sales	**41,862**	**36,298**	**32,317**	**29,172**	**27,357**	**23,811**	**22,522**	**21,387**	**18,537**	**15,454**	**13,877**
Cost of products sold	12,176	10,447	9,581	8,957	8,539	7,700	7,350	7,185	6,352	5,393	4,908
Selling, marketing, and administrative expenses	14,131	12,216	11,260	10,495	10,065	8,525	8,185	7,848	6,950	5,901	5,364
Research expense	4,684	3,957	3,591	3,105	2,768	2,506	2,373	2,109	1,788	1,416	1,296
Purchased in-process research and development	918	189	105	66	—	298	108	—	—	37	—
Interest income	(177)	(256)	(456)	(429)	(266)	(302)	(263)	(196)	(151)	(85)	(104)
Interest expense, net of portion capitalized	207	160	153	204	255	186	179	176	184	182	165
Other (income) expense, net	(385)	294	185	(94)	119	565	248	122	70	(5)	(71)
	31,554	27,007	24,419	22,304	21,480	19,478	18,180	17,244	15,193	12,839	11,558
Earnings before provision for taxes on income	10,308	9,291	7,898	6,868	5,877	4,333	4,342	4,143	3,344	2,615	2,319
Provision for taxes on income	3,111	2,694	2,230	1,915	1,604	1,232	1,237	1,185	926	654	533
Net earnings	**7,197**	**6,597**	**5,668**	**4,953**	**4,273**	**3,101**	**3,105**	**2,958**	**2,418**	**1,961**	**1,786**
Percent of sales to customers	17.2	18.2	17.5	17.0	15.6	13.0	13.8	13.8	13.0	12.7	12.9
Diluted net earnings per share of common stock*	2.40	2.16	1.84	1.61	1.39	1.02	1.02	.98	.84	.69	.63
Percent return on average shareholders' equity	29.0	28.1	25.4	26.5	27.0	22.2	24.6	27.2	27.6	28.4	30.1
Percent increase over previous year:											
Sales to customers	15.3	12.3	10.8	6.6	14.9	5.7	5.3	15.4	19.9	11.4	2.0
Diluted net earnings per share	11.1	17.4	14.3	15.8	36.3	0.0	4.1	16.7	21.7	9.5	85.3
Supplementary expense data:											
Cost of materials and services[b]	18,568	16,540	15,333	14,113	13,922	11,779	11,702	11,341	9,984	8,104	7,168
Total employment costs	10,005	8,450	7,749	7,085	6,537	5,908	5,586	5,447	4,849	4,401	4,181
Depreciation and amortization	1,869	1,662	1,605	1,592	1,510	1,335	1,117	1,047	886	754	649
Maintenance and repairs[c]	395	360	372	327	322	286	270	285	257	222	205
Total tax expense[d]	4,078	3,497	2,995	2,619	2,271	1,881	1,824	1,753	1,458	1,132	957
Supplementary balance sheet data:											
Property, plant and equipment, net	9,846	8,710	7,719	7,409	7,155	6,767	6,204	6,025	5,544	5,230	4,717
Additions to property, plant and equipment	2,262	2,099	1,731	1,689	1,822	1,610	1,454	1,427	1,307	979	1,001
Total assets	48,263	40,556	38,488	34,245	31,064	28,966	23,615	22,248	19,355	17,027	13,372
Long-term debt	2,955	2,022	2,217	3,163	3,429	2,652	2,084	2,347	2,702	2,776	1,761
Operating cash flow	10,595	8,176	8,864	6,903	5,920	5,106	4,210	4,001	3,436	2,984	2,202
Common stock information*											
Dividends paid per share	.925	.795	.70	.62	.55	.49	.425	.368	.32	.283	.253
Shareholders' equity per share	9.05	7.65	7.95	6.77	5.70	4.93	4.51	4.07	3.46	2.76	2.16
Market price per share	50.62	53.11	59.86	52.53	46.63	41.94	32.44	25.25	21.38	13.69	11.19
Average shares outstanding (millions)—basic	2,968.1	2,998.3	3,033.8	2,993.5	2,978.2	2,973.6	2,951.9	2,938.0	2,820.1	2,796.9	2,816.6
—diluted	3,008.1	3,054.1	3,099.3	3,099.2	3,100.4	3,082.7	3,073.0	3,046.2	2,890.0	2,843.2	2,840.8
Employees (thousands)	**110.6**	**108.3**	**101.8**	**100.9**	**99.8**	**96.1**	**92.6**	**91.5**	**84.2**	**83.4**	**83.2**

* Adjusted to reflect the 2001 two-for-one stock split.
[a] All periods have been adjusted to include the effects of the ALZA merger.
[b] Net of interest and other income.
[c] Also included in cost of materials and services category.
[d] Includes taxes on income, payroll, property and other business taxes.

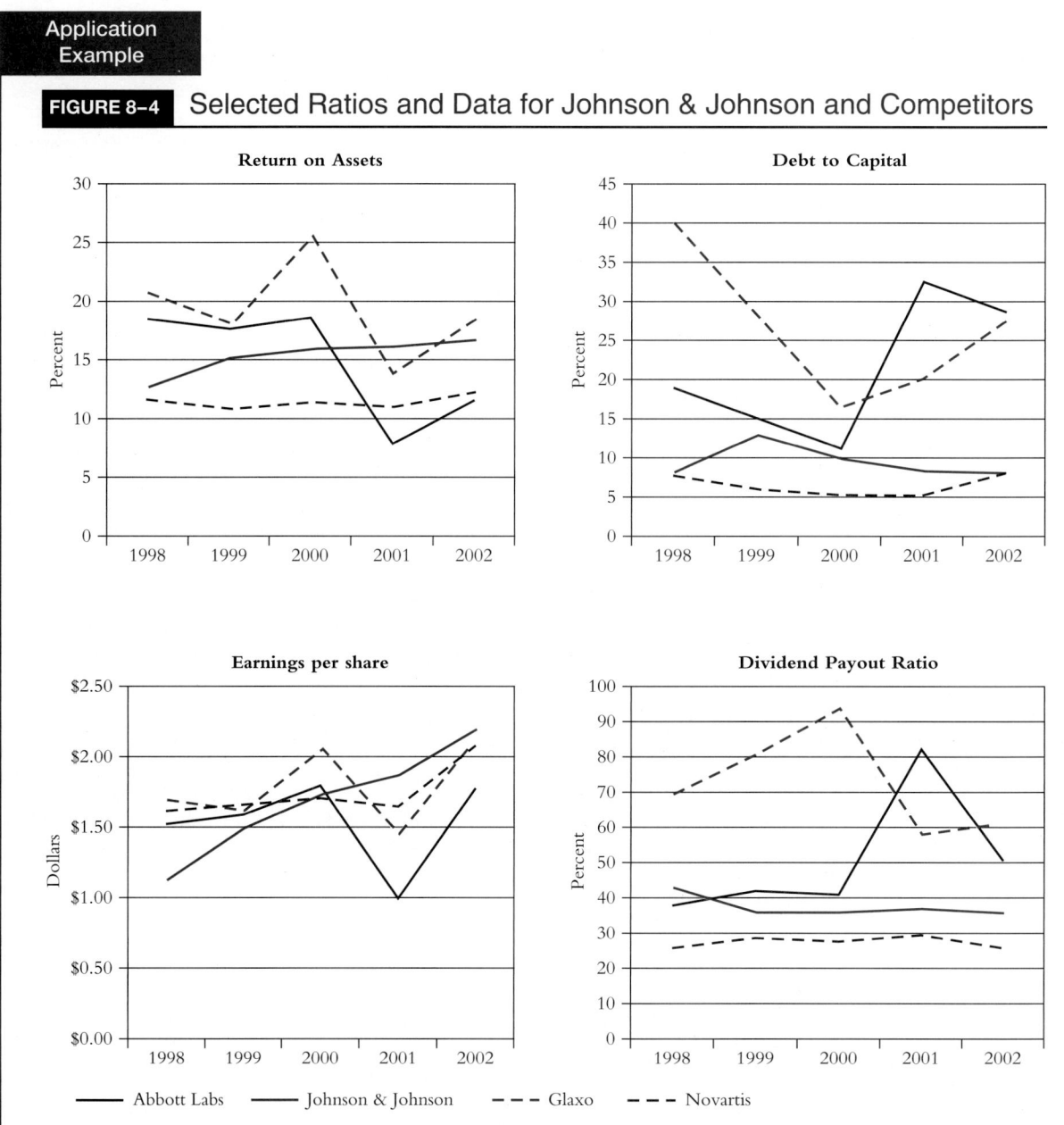

FIGURE 8-4 Selected Ratios and Data for Johnson & Johnson and Competitors

As far as earnings per share, the trend for all of the companies is up, with Abbott and GlaxoSmithKline having the most volatile earnings per share trend line and Johnson & Johnson having the most stable trend line. Moving to the dividend payout ratio, again Johnson & Johnson and Novartis are very consistent with the payout ratios. Even this brief look provides a picture of Johnson & Johnson as one of the stronger competitors and having low risk.

Deficiencies of Financial Statements

Several differences occur between companies and industries, and, at times, inflation has additionally clouded the clarity of accounting statements. Some of the more important difficulties occur in the area of inflation-adjusted accounting statements, inventory valuation, depreciation methods, pension fund liabilities, research and development, deferred taxes, and foreign exchange accounting. We do not have space to cover all of them, but we will touch on the most important ones.

Inflation Effects

While inflation has been extremely mild in the last decade, the student who is preparing for a long-term career in finance should be aware of its potential effects for the future.

Inflation causes phantom sources of profit that may mislead even the most alert analyst. Revenue is almost always stated in current dollars, whereas plant and equipment or inventory may have been purchased at lower price levels. Thus, profit may be more a function of increasing prices than of satisfactory performance.

Distortion of inflation also shows up on the balance sheet since most of the values on the balance sheet are stated on a historical or original-cost basis. This may be particularly troublesome in the case of plant and equipment and inventory, which may now be worth two or three times the original cost or—from a negative viewpoint—may require many times the original cost for replacement.

The accounting profession has been groping with this problem for decades, and the discussion becomes particularly intense each time inflation rears its ugly head. In October 1979, the Financial Accounting Standards Board (FASB) issued a ruling that required about 1,300 large companies to disclose **inflation-adjusted accounting** data in their annual reports. This information shows the effects of inflation on the financial statements of the firm. The ruling on inflation adjustment was extended for five more years in 1984 but was later made optional. As inflation temporarily slowed, many companies chose not to disclose inflation-adjusted statements in addition to the historical cost statements.

From a study of 10 chemical firms and 8 drug companies using current-cost (replacement-cost) data found in the financial 10–K statements these companies filed with the SEC, it was found that the changes shown in Table 8–7 on page 224 occurred in their assets, income, and other selected ratios. The impact of these changes is important as an example of the changes that take place on ratio analysis during periods of high inflation.

The comparison of replacement-cost and historical-cost accounting methods in Table 8–7 shows that replacement cost increases assets but at the same time reduces income. This increase in assets lowers the debt-to-assets ratio since debt is a monetary asset that is not revalued because it is paid back in current dollars.

The decreased debt-to-assets ratio would indicate that the financial leverage of the firm decreased, but a look at the interest-coverage ratio tells a different story. Because the interest-coverage ratio measures the operating income available to cover interest expense, the declining income penalizes the ratio, and the firm shows a decreased ability to cover its interest cost.

TABLE 8–7 Comparison of Replacement-Cost Accounting to Historical-Cost Accounting

	10 Chemical Companies		8 Drug Companies	
	Replacement Cost	Historical Cost	Replacement Cost	Historical Cost
Increase in assets	28.4%	—	15.4%	—
Decrease in net income before taxes	(45.8)	—	(19.3)	—
Return on assets	2.8	6.2%	8.3	11.4%
Return on equity	4.9	13.5	12.8	19.6
Debt-to-assets ratio	34.3	43.8	30.3	35.2
Interest-coverage ratio (times interest earned)	7.1×	8.4×	15.4×	16.7×

Note: Replacement cost is but one form of current cost. Nevertheless, it is widely used as a measure of current cost.
Source: Jeff Garnett and Geoffrey A. Hirt, "Replacement Cost Data: A Study of the Chemical and Drug Industry for Years 1976 through 1978."

As long as prices continue to rise in an inflationary environment, profits appear to feed on themselves. The main objection is that when prices do level off, management and unsuspecting stockholders have a rude awakening as expensive inventory is charged against softening retail prices. A 15 to 20 percent growth rate in earnings may be little more than an "inflationary illusion." Industries most sensitive to inflation-induced profits are those with cyclical products, such as lumber, copper, rubber, and food products, as well as those in which inventory is a significant percentage of sales and profits. Reported profits for the lumber industry have been influenced as much as 50 percent by inventory pricing, and profits of a number of other industries have been influenced by 15 to 20 percent.

Inventory Valuation

Application Example

The income statement can show considerable differences in earnings, depending on the method of inventory valuation. The two basic methods are FIFO (first-in, first-out) and LIFO (last-in, first-out). In an inflationary economy, a firm could be reporting increased profits even though no actual increase in physical output occurred. The example of the Rhoades Company will illustrate this point. We first observe its income statement for 2004 in Table 8–8. It sold 1,000 units for $20,000 and shows earnings after taxes of $4,200 and an operating margin and after-tax margin of 35 percent and 21 percent, respectively.

Assume that in 2005 the number of units sold remains constant at 1,000 units. However, inflation causes a 10 percent increase in price, from $20 to $22 per unit as shown in Table 8–9. Total sales will go up to $22,000, but with no actual increase in physical volume. Further assume the firm uses FIFO inventory pricing so that inventory first purchased will be written off against current sales. We will assume that 1,000 units of 2004 inventory at a cost of $10 per unit are written off against 2005 sales revenue. If Rhoades used LIFO inventory and if the cost of goods sold went up 10 percent also, to $11 per unit, income will be less than under FIFO. Table 8–9 shows the 2005 income statement of Rhoades under both inventory methods.

The table demonstrates the difference between FIFO and LIFO. Under FIFO, Rhoades Corporation shows higher profit margins and more income even though no

TABLE 8-8 Rhoades Corporation Income Statement

RHOADES CORPORATION
First-Year Income Statement
Net Income for 2004

Sales	$20,000 (1,000 units at $20)
Cost of goods sold	10,000 (1,000 units at $10)
Gross profit	10,000
Selling and administrative expense	2,000
Depreciation	1,000
Operating profit	7,000
Taxes (40 percent)	2,800
Earnings after taxes	$ 4,200
Operating margin	$7,000/$20,000 = 35%
After-tax margin	$4,200/$20,000 = 21%

TABLE 8-9 Rhoades Corporation Income Statement

RHOADES CORPORATION
Second-Year Income Statement Using FIFO and LIFO
Net Income for 2005

	FIFO	LIFO
Sales	$22,000 (1,000 at $22)	$22,000 (1,000 at $22)
Cost of goods sold	10,000 (1,000 at $10)	11,000 (1,000 at $11)
Gross profit	12,000	11,000
Selling and administrative expense	2,200 (10% of sales)	2,200 (10% of sales)
Depreciation	1,000	1,000
Operating profit	8,800	7,800
Taxes (40 percent)	3,520	3,120
Earnings after taxes	$ 5,280	$ 4,680
Operating margin	$ 8,800/$22,000 = 40%	$ 7,800/$22,000 = 35.4%
After-tax margin	$ 5,280/$22,000 = 24%	$ 4,680/$22,000 = 21.2%

physical increase in sales occurs. This is because FIFO costing lags behind current prices, and the company generates "phantom profits" due to gains on inventory. Unfortunately, this inventory will need to be replaced next period at higher costs. When and if prices turn lower in a recessionary environment, FIFO will have the opposite effect and drag down earnings. LIFO inventory costing, on the other hand, relates current costs to current prices, and although profits rise in dollar terms from 2004, the margins stay basically the same. The only problem with LIFO inventory accounting is that low-cost layers of inventory build up on the balance sheet of the company and understate inventory. This will cause inventory turnover to appear higher than under FIFO.

> While many companies shifted to LIFO accounting in the past, FIFO inventory valuation still exists in some industries, and the analyst must be alert to the consequences of both methods.

Extraordinary Gains and Losses

Extraordinary gains and losses may occur from the sale of corporate fixed assets, lawsuits, or similar events that would not be expected to occur often, if ever, again. Some analysts argue that such extraordinary events should be included in computing the current income of the firm, while others would leave them off when assessing operating performance. The choice can have a big impact on ratios that rely on earnings or earnings per share. Extraordinary gains can inflate returns and lower payout ratios if they are included in earnings. The analyst concerned about forecasting should include only those earnings from continuing operations; otherwise, the forecast will be seriously off its mark. Unfortunately, there is some inconsistency in the manner in which nonrecurring losses are treated despite determined attempts by the accounting profession to ensure uniformity.

Pension Fund Liabilities

One area of increasing concern among financial analysts is the unfunded liabilities of corporate pension funds. These funds eventually will have to pay workers their retirement income from the pension fund earnings and assets. If the money is not available from the pension fund, the company is liable to make the payments. These unfunded pensions may have to come out of earnings in future years, which would penalize shareholders and limit the corporation's ability to reinvest in new assets.

Foreign Exchange Transactions

Foreign currency fluctuations have a major impact on the earnings of those companies heavily involved in international trade. The drug industry is significantly affected, as well as firms like Coca-Cola, with more than 70 percent of operating income coming from foreign operations. Coca-Cola is a prime example of a company affected by swings in the currency markets. For example, when the dollar declines relative to foreign currencies as it has between 2001 and 2004, earnings from foreign subsidiaries get translated into more U.S. dollars and help the earnings of U.S. companies such as Coca-Cola. The opposite is true when the dollar increases in value. Coca-Cola's foreign exchange currency transactions had a negative effect of $140 million in 2000. Because Coca-Cola is available in almost 200 countries, the firm has a diversification effect with some currencies rising and others falling. However, a major change in a given part of the world could cause this diversification effect to lose its impact.

Other Distortions

Other problems exist in accounting statements and methods of reporting earnings. A mention of some of them might provide you with areas that require

the real world of investing

Questionable Accounting Practices in the Real World: How IBM Met Its Earnings Goal

The stock market is tough on companies that, in the parlance of Wall Street, "don't make their numbers." If your parents expect you to make an A in investments and you make a C, you're likely to hear about it. The same type of discipline exists on Wall Street.

Just ask a couple of IBM's competitors (www.ibm.com). In the year 2000, Compaq (www.compaq.com) and Unisys (www.unisys.com) issued warnings about not meeting their earnings goals, and their stocks plummeted 50 to 75 percent.

IBM fortunately did not have to issue such negative news to investors, but many question the firm's very aggressive financial reporting techniques. For the year 2000, IBM reported $8.1 billion in earnings, which translated into earnings per share of $4.44. That represented a 5 percent increase in EPS over the prior year that, on the surface, looked very good for a firm in the computer industry, which was going through a minirecession of its own during this period.

But how did IBM get such commendable numbers? Bradley Rexford, a financial analyst at the Center for Financial Research and Analysis, implies IBM took the low road.*

He says $1.02 should be backed out of IBM's 2000 reported earnings per share of $4.44 to arrive at a more realistic value of $3.42 for IBM's earning power for the year. While there is no specific contention that IBM violated accounting or SEC rules, there is no question that IBM employed "a very aggressive offense" in reporting its numbers.

Rexford says that among IBM's questionable techniques was a gain in its pension fund value. Because the stock market had been steadily increasing for the last decade and also because of other related pension fund policy changes, IBM was able to claim $0.43 in pension funds gains. This represented almost 10 percent of IBM's entire earnings per share of $4.44. Of course, the pension fund gains had absolutely nothing to do with IBM's ability to manufacture and sell computer hardware, software, or related service.

IBM also posted a $0.15 gain by reversing prior reserve accounts entries for accounts receivable, inventory, and a reserve related to the sale of its Micrus semiconductor business. Reserves or changes against income are sometimes set up in good times and then reversed to bolster income during bad times. This so-called dipping into the cookie jar can be used to smooth out income.

A further $0.28 boost to IBM's earnings came from an assumption of a lower tax rate for the year 2000. In 1999, income was taxed at 34.4 percent, while in 2000, the rate was 29.9 percent.

Other minor items, related to share repurchases and capitalizing rather than expensing website expenses, added $0.16 more to earnings per share. Once again, none of these items had anything to do with IBM's ability to generate profit from its basic computer business. As stipulated earlier, all the cited transactions added $1.02 to IBM's reported earnings per share and allowed the firm to make its numbers.

The question to you as a future financial analyst is, "How much credit do you want to give to IBM for increasing earnings per share?" A firm that uses more conservative accounting practices might not have shown an increase in earnings per share, but you might have more confidence in valuing the earnings and in computing the profitability ratios. IBM is now in the position of having to use very aggressive accounting practices in the future to match prior earnings, which were based on a similar premise. Once you get started, it is hard to stop. You can also ask the former top officers of Enron about this principle.

---
*"Recurring Gains," *Forbes*, May 14, 2001, pp. 86–88.

further investigation. Additional areas for detective work are in accounting methods for the following: off balance sheet financing (e.g., Enron), research and development expenditures, deferred taxes, tax credits, merger accounting, intangible drilling and development costs, and percentage depletion allowances. As you can see, many issues cause analysts to dig further and to be cautious about accepting bottom-line earnings per share.

exploring the web

Website Address	Comments
www.zacks.com	**Provides detailed company financial information and ratios—mostly free**
www.investor.reuters	**Provides detailed financial information, including ratios and statements**
www.morningstar.com	**Provides financial information and ratios for free, some information fee-based**
www.investors.com	**From *Investor's Business Daily,* provides investment related charts and tools**
www.valueline.com	**Is a Web version of print information source**
www.investopedia.com	**Provides tutorials on financial ratios**
www.ventureline.com	**Allows access to financial ratios and other analytics, requires registration for access, and is fee-based**

Summary

Chapter 8 presents the basics of accounting statements and ratio analysis. After going through an income statement, a balance sheet, and the statement of cash flows, ratios are presented that help tie together these statements.

Ratio analysis is used to evaluate the operating performance and capital structure of a firm. Ratios will not help to find a gold mine, but they can help to avoid buying sick companies. Using ratio analysis, a brief description of two bankruptcy studies was given that emphasized the ability of ratios to spot troubled firms with a potential for failure.

Twenty ratios were classified into six categories that measured profitability, asset utilization, liquidity, debt utilization, relative prices, and taxes and dividend policy. Johnson & Johnson was used as an example as we computed each ratio. The Du Pont method was presented to demonstrate the relationship between assets, sales, income, and debt for creating returns on assets and equity.

Ratios are best used when compared with industry norms, company trends, and economic and industry cycles. It is becoming more difficult to use ratio analysis on an industry basis as firms become more integrated and diversified into several industries.

Finally, the deficiencies of financial statements were discussed. The effect on ratios was examined for replacement cost versus historical cost data. Other distortions were discussed such as extraordinary gains and losses and pension fund liabilities.

Financial analysis is a science as well as an art, and experience certainly sharpens the skills. It would be unrealistic for someone to pick up all the complex relationships involved in ratio analysis immediately. This is why analysts are assigned industries they learn inside and out. After much practice, the analytical work is easier, and the true picture of financial performance becomes focused.

Key Words and Concepts

- asset-utilization ratios 212
- balance sheet 202
- debt-utilization ratios 214
- dividend-payout ratio 217
- dividend yield 216
- extraordinary gains and losses 226
- income statement 201
- inflation-adjusted accounting 223
- liquidity ratios 213
- price ratios 215
- profitability ratios 210
- statement of cash flows 204
- trend analysis 220

Discussion Questions

1. Does a balance sheet that is dated year-end 2004 reflect only transactions for that year?
2. Explain why the statement of cash flows is particularly relevant in light of the fact that the accrual method of accounting is used in the income statement and balance sheet.
3. Can we automatically assume that a firm that has an operating loss on the income statement has reduced the cash flows for the firm during the period?
4. What ratios are likely to be of greatest interest to the banker or trade creditor? To the bondholder?
5. If a firm's operating margin and after-tax margin are almost the same (an unusual case), what can we say about the firm?
6. Comment on the heavy capital goods industry and the food-processing industry in terms of performance under the Du Pont system of analysis.
7. In computing return on assets, how does the age of the assets influence the interpretation of the values?
8. If a firm's return on equity is substantially higher than the firm's return on assets, what can the analyst infer about the firm?
9. How do the asset-utilization ratios relate to the liquidity ratios?
10. Can public utility firms better justify the use of high debt than firms in the automobile or airline industry? Comment.
11. Why will the fixed-charge-coverage ratio always be equal to or *less* than times interest earned?
12. What might a high dividend-payout ratio suggest to an analyst about a company's growth prospects?
13. Explain the probable impact of replacement-cost accounting on the ratios of return on assets, debt to total assets, and times interest earned for a firm that has substantial old fixed assets.

Problems

Du Pont analysis

1. Given the following financial data: net income/sales = 5 percent; sales/total assets = 2.5; debt/total assets = 60 percent; compute:
   a. Return on assets.
   b. Return on equity.

Du Pont analysis

2. Explain in problem 1 why return on equity was so much higher than return on assets.

Du Pont analysis

3. A firm has assets of $1,200,000 and turns over its assets two times per year. Return on assets is 15 percent. What is its profit margin (return on sales)?

Du Pont analysis

4. A firm has assets of $1,800,000 and turns over its assets 1.5 times per year. Return on assets is 25 percent. What is its profit margin (return on sales)?

Du Pont analysis

5. A firm has a return on assets of 10 percent and a return on equity of 15 percent. What is the debt-to-total-assets ratio?

Du Pont analysis

eXcel

6. In the year 2004, the average firm in the S&P 500 Index had a total market value of fives times stockholders' equity (book value). Assume a firm had total assets of $15 million, total debt of $9 million, and net income of $900,000.
   a. What is the percent return on equity?
   b. What is the percent return on total market value? Does this appear to be an adequate return on the actual market value of the firm?

General ratio analysis

eXcel

7. A firm has the following financial data:

Current assets	$900,000
Fixed assets	500,000
Current liabilities	400,000
Inventory	150,000

If inventory increases by $200,000, what will be the impact on the current ratio, the quick ratio, and the net working capital to total assets ratio? Show the ratios before and after the changes.

General ratio analysis

eXcel

8. Given the following financial data:

Assets:	
Cash	$ 1,000
Accounts receivable	3,500
Inventory	1,500
Fixed assets	4,000
Total assets	$10,000
Liabilities and stockholders' equity:	
Short-term debt	$ 2,000
Long-term debt	1,000
Stockholders' equity	7,000
Total liabilities and stockholders' equity	$10,000
Income before fixed charges and taxes	$ 3,000
Interest payments	500
Lease payment	700
Taxes (35% tax rate)	630
Net income (after-taxes)	$ 1,170

Compute:
   a. Return on equity.   c. Long-term debt to equity.
   b. Quick ratio.   d. Fixed-charge coverage.

Coverage of sinking fund

9. Assume in part *d* of problem 8 that the firm had a sinking fund payment obligation of $100. How much before-tax income is required to cover the sinking fund obligation? Would higher tax rates increase or decrease the before-tax income required to cover the sinking fund?

Return on equity

10. In problem 8, if total debt were increased to 50 percent of assets and interest payments went up by $200, what would be the new value for return on equity?

Stock price ratios

11. Assume the following financial data:

Short-term assets	$200,000
Long-term assets	350,000
Total assets	$550,000
Short-term debt	$100,000
Long-term debt	50,000
Total liabilities	150,000
Common stock	150,000
Retained earnings	250,000
Total liabilities and stockholders' equity	$550,000
Total earnings (after-tax)	$ 48,000
Dividends per share	$ 1.10
Stock price	$ 54
Shares outstanding	16,000

a. Compute the P/E ratio (stock price to earnings per share).
b. Compute the ratio of stock price to book value per share (note that book value equals stockholders' equity).
c. Compute the dividend yield.
d. Compute the payout ratio.

Tax considerations and financial analysis

12. Referring to problem 11:
a. If the tax rate were 40 percent, what could you infer the value of before-tax income was? (Hint: Divide after-tax income by (1 − tax rate).
b. Compute after-tax return on equity. This is not affected by the answer to part *a*.
c. Now assume the same before-tax income computed in part *a*, but a tax rate of 25 percent; recompute after-tax return on equity (using the simplifying assumption that equity remains constant).
d. Assume the taxes in part *c* were reduced largely as a result of one-time, nonrecurring tax credits. Would you expect the stock value to go up substantially as a result of the higher return on equity?

Divisional analysis

13. The Diversified Corporation has three different operating divisions. Financial information for each is as follows:

	Bowling	Machine Tools	Toys
Sales	$2,000,000	$10,000,000	$16,000,000
Operating income	220,000	800,000	2,000,000
Net income (A/T)	100,000	600,000	900,000
Assets	1,000,000	8,000,000	6,000,000

a. Which division provides the highest operating margin?
  b. Which division provides the lowest after-tax profit margin?
  c. Which division has the lowest after-tax return on assets?
  d. Compute net income (after-tax) to sales for the entire corporation.
  e. Compute net income (after-tax) to assets for the entire corporation.
  f. The vice president of finance suggests the assets in the Machine Tool division be sold off for $8,000,000 and redeployed in Toys. The new $8,000,000 in Toys will produce the same after-tax return on assets as the current $6,000,000 in that division. Recompute net income to total assets for the entire corporation assuming the previously suggested change.
  g. Explain why Toys, which has a lower return on sales than Machine Tools, has such a positive effect on return on assets. Try to use numbers to support your answer.

Approaches to security evaluation

14. Security Analyst A thinks the Oliver Corporation is worth 16 times current earnings. Security Analyst B has a different approach. She assumes 30 percent of earnings (per share) will be paid out in dividends and the stock should provide a 2 percent current dividend yield. Assume total earnings are $10,000,000 and that there are 5,000,000 shares outstanding.
    a. Compute the value of the stock based on Security Analyst A's approach.
    b. Compute the value of the stock based on Security Analyst B's approach.
    c. Security Analyst C uses the constant-dividend-valuation model approach presented in Chapter 7 as Formula 7–5 on page 172. He uses Security Analyst B's assumption about dividends (per share), and assigns a growth rate, (g) of 9 percent and a required rate of return (K_e) of 12 percent. Is his value higher or lower than that of the other security analysts?

Critical Thought Case–Focus on Ethics

Barry Minkow founded ZZZZ Best Co., a carpet-cleaning firm, when he was 15 years old. He ran the business from his family's garage in Reseda, California. The company became one of the biggest carpet-cleaning firms in California, and Minkow was a millionaire by age 18. Minkow took his company public by selling its stock when he was 21, and his personal worth was estimated at close to $10 million. At that time ZZZZ Best ("Zee Best") had 1,300 employees and 1986 sales of $4.8 million. Minkow boldly predicted that 1987 revenues would exceed $50 million.

In July 1990, ZZZZ Best management filed for bankruptcy protection and sued Minkow for misappropriating $21 million in company funds. In addition, several customers accused ZZZZ Best of overcharging them in a credit card scam. Minkow publicly admitted the overcharges but blamed them on subcontractors and employees. He also said he had fired those responsible and had personally repaid the charges.

The Securities and Exchange Commission (SEC) and other law enforcement agencies began investigating Minkow and his company. It became apparent that ZZZZ Best was built on a foundation of lies, dishonesty, and inconsistent accounting practices. The company had submitted phony credit card charges and had issued press releases claiming millions of dollars in bogus contracts, sending the price of the company's stock even higher. The SEC investigated other charges, including possible phony receivables, bogus financial accounting statements, organized-crime connections, and securities law violations by Minkow and other executives. The SEC placed an independent trustee in charge of the company until its accounting records could be examined.

The Los Angeles Police Department investigated charges that ZZZZ Best was a money-laundering operation for organized crime. The investigation linked Minkow and ZZZZ Best with drug dealings and organized crime members.

These allegations ultimately led Minkow to resign from ZZZZ Best for "health reasons." But his resignation was not the end of his troubles. ZZZZ Best's new management sued Minkow for embezzling $3 million of the company's funds for his personal use and misappropriating $18 million to perform fictitious insurance restoration work. The suit charged that Minkow actually diverted this money to an associate's refurbishing business, which was part of an elaborate scheme designed to allow Minkow to take corporate funds for his own and others' personal use. According to the suit, these discrepancies in the company's accounting practices were the reasons behind the bankruptcy filing. As a result ZZZZ Best's accounting firm quit.

Questions

1. Given the extent of fraud in this case, should ZZZZ Best's accounting firm be held responsible for not discovering the fraudulent activities?
2. What are the responsibilities of the broker and financial analyst in recommending the company to investors? To what extent are they responsible for their investment recommendations?

Web Exercise

We will look at Eli Lilly, a prominent member of the pharmaceutical industry. Go to **www.lilly.com**.

1. Click on "Investor" along the upper-right part of the screen.
2. Then click on "Financial Reports."
3. Next select "Financial Ratios."
4. Assume Lilly had the following targets for each of the financial ratios listed below. Write a one-sentence description (for each) of how the firm did against the target and the implications.
    a. Yield   3%
       Does the comparison enhance or restrict Lilly's growth potential?
    b. Total debt/equity   40%
       Does the comparison enhance or restrict Lilly's return on equity?
    c. Price/book   7×
       Does the comparison indicate that Lilly is likely to be overpriced or underpriced?
    d. Gross margin   81%
       Profit margin   22.5%
       How is Lilly doing in terms of its profitability ratios?
    e. Quick ratio   .70
       Current ratio   1.75
       In comparing these two ratios to the targets, what might you infer about the level of inventory Lilly carries?

Note: From time to time, companies redesign their websites, and occasionally a topic we have listed may have been deleted, updated, or moved into a different location. Most websites have a "site map" or "site index" listed on a different page. If you click on the site map or site index you will be introduced to a table of contents that should aid you in finding the topic you are looking for.

CFA Material

The following material contains sample questions and solutions from a prior Level I CFA exam. While the terminology is slightly different from that in this text, you can still view the skills necessary for the CFA exam.

CFA Exam Question

Question 1 is composed of two parts, for a total of 15 minutes.

1. As shown in Table I, Tennant's operating results have been less favorable during the 1980s than the 1970s based on three representative years, 1975, 1981, and 1987. To develop an explanation, you decide to examine Tennant's operating history employing the industrial life-cycle model, which recognizes four stages as follows:

   I. Early development.   II. Rapid expansion.   III. Mature growth.

TABLE I Tennant Company

**Selected Historic Operating and Balance Sheet Data
As of December 31, 1975, 1981, and 1987
(in thousands)**

	1975	1981	1987
Net sales	$47,909	$109,333	$166,924
Cost of goods sold	27,395	62,373	95,015
Gross profits	20,514	46,960	71,909
Selling, general, and administrative expenses	11,895	29,649	54,151
Earnings before interest and taxes	8,619	17,311	17,758
Interest on long-term debt	0	53	248
Pretax income	8,619	17,258	17,510
Income taxes	4,190	7,655	7,692
After-tax income	$ 4,429	$ 9,603	$ 9,818
Total assets	$33,848	$ 63,555	$106,098
Total common stockholders' equity	25,722	46,593	69,516
Long-term debt	6	532	2,480
Total common shares outstanding	5,654	5,402	5,320
Earnings per share	$ 0.78	$ 1.78	$ 1.85
Dividends per share	0.28	0.72	0.96
Book value per share	4.55	8.63	13.07

   IV. Stabilization or decline.
   a. Describe the behavior of revenues, profit margins, and total profits as a company passes through *each* of the *four* stages of the industrial life cycle.
   b. Using 1975, 1981, and 1987 results as representative, discuss Tennant's operating record from 1975 through 1987 in terms of the industrial life-cycle record. (*15 minutes*)

Solution: Question 1—Morning Section (I–88) (15 points)

   a. During the early development stage, revenue growth is rapid. However, profit margins are negative until revenues reach a critical mass. From that point forward, rapidly improving margins combine with continued strong revenue growth to create extremely rapid earnings progress.

Profit margins continue to expand during the rapid expansion phase but level out during the mature growth phase. Despite gradual tapering of profit margins, earnings continue to rise during the mature growth phase due to continuing revenue growth. However, earnings progress is significantly slower than during the rapid expansion phase.

The final stage of earnings stabilization or decline is characterized by a continuing moderation in the rate of sales growth and deteriorating profit margins. In the extreme, declining revenues in combination with decreasing profit margins lead to significant earnings declines.

b. Tennant appeared to be in the rapid expansion to the mature growth stage between 1975 and 1981. Although pretax margins weakened, the company was able to double pretax earnings, while sales revenues increased even more rapidly. However, a sharp change occurred after 1981. Sales growth moderated, and profit margins declined sharply. On this basis, Tennant clearly entered the mature growth stage between 1981 and 1987. Based on profit trends, it could be argued that the company had progressed to Stage IV, stabilization and decline. However, a continuation of reasonably strong revenue growth suggests this is not the case.

(Good answers to this question will recognize that the life cycle of a corporation is identified primarily by trends in revenue growth and profit margins. An ideal answer might include simple calculations along the line shown below.)

	1975	1981	1987
Sales	$47,909	$109,333	$166,924
Percent change during prior 6 years	N.A.	128.2%	52.7%
Pretax earnings	$ 8,619	$ 17,311	$ 17,758
Percent change during prior 6 years	N.A.	100.8%	2.6%
Pretax margins	18.0%	15.8%	10.6%

Question 2 is composed of two parts, for a total of 25 minutes.

2. The director of research suggests that you use the Du Pont model to analyze the components of Tennant's return on equity during 1981 and 1987 to explain the change that has occurred in the company's return on equity. She asks you to work with the five factors listed below.
   I. EBIT margin.
   II. Asset turnover.
   III. Interest burden.
   IV. Financial leverage.
   V. Tax retention rate.
   a. Compute 1981 and 1987 values of *each* of these *five* factors. (*15 minutes*)
   b. Identify the individual component that had the greatest influence on the change in return on equity from 1981 and 1987, and briefly explain the possible reasons for the changes in the value of this component between the two years. (*10 minutes*)

Solution: Question 2—Morning Section (I–88) (25 points)

a.

Tennant Equity Return Components	Value 1981	1987
I. EBIT margins	15.8%	10.6%
II. Asset turnover	1.72×	1.57×
III. Interest burden	0.1%	0.2%
IV. Financial leverage	1.36×	1.53×
V. Tax retention rate	55.6%	56.1%

b. Increases in financial leverage and the tax retention rate acted to increase return on equity between 1981 and 1987. Declining EBIT margins, a decline in asset turnover, and an increase in interest burden tended to reduce profitability.

The dominant factor was the 33 percent decline in EBIT margins. This is due to the increase in SG&A and Tennant's entering mature growth. Interest burden was a relatively trivial factor, and the tax-retention rate changed only nominally. The decrease in asset turnover and increase in financial leverage were more meaningful but tended to cancel each other.

S&P Problems

STANDARD & POOR'S

www.mhhe.com/edumarketinsight

1. Log on to the McGraw-Hill website: **www.mhhe.com/edumarketinsight** (see page vi in the preface for instructions).
2. Click on Company, which is the first box below the Market Insight title.
3. Put the ticker symbol for Johnson & Johnson (JNJ) in the box, and click on go.
4. In the left margin, click on Excel Analytics to open the list of choices. Click on "Annual Ratio Report." You will get an Excel spreadsheet with six years of data covering 32 ratios. Some of these ratios will be similar to those covered in this chapter and others will be the same but will have different titles. Since there are only twenty ratios calculated in this chapter, there are extra ratios available for your analysis.
5. Analyze the liquidity of Johnson & Johnson. Do you see any problems or trends that are important?
6. Analyze the activity and performance ratios (Asset Utilization Ratios), and determine how well the company is managing its assets.
7. Looking at the profitability ratios, what trends do you see and are they favorable or unfavorable?
8. Given the leverage ratios (Debt Utilization Ratios) found in the table, would you say that Johnson & Johnson is highly leveraged and risky or slightly leveraged and not risky?
9. Looking at the "Key Item Charts" in the third worksheet on the bottom of the spreadsheet, how would you sum up the position of Johnson & Johnson?
10. Finally, compare Johnson & Johnson's effective tax rate (under profitability ratios) with the statutory tax rate for corporations, and discuss the difference between the two. Can you think of any reason why they should be different?

11. Go back to the left margin, and under quarterly, click on the quarterly ratio report and repeat the analysis above. Do you notice any difference between the long-term trends and trends over the last six quarters? In other words, are the quarterly trends consistent with the long-term trends, or are there changes that might affect the price of the stock?

The Wall Street Journal Projects

1. Chapter 8 features Johnson & Johnson as the sample company under analysis. Locate the stock price, price-earnings ratio (P/E), and dividends from *The Wall Street Journal* in Section C. Also use *The Value Line Investment Survey* to find the book value.
    a. Calculate the dividends-to-price (dividend yield).
    b. Calculate the price-to-book value.
2. Examine the companies listed in Table 8–4 on page 216, and compare their current price-earnings (P/E) ratios from Section C in *The Wall Street Journal* to those in the table. Do stock prices on a relative P/E basis seem to be higher or lower than they were?

Selected References

Financial Reporting

Bailey, Warren; Haitao Li; Connie X. Mao; and Rui Zhong. "Regulation Fair Disclosure and Earnings Information: Market, Analyst, and Corporate Responses." *Journal of Financial and Quantitative Analysis,* December 2003, pp. 2487–2514.

Bernasek, Anna. "By the Numbers." *Fortune,* January 26, 2004, p. 26.

Carty, Lea V. "Corporate Credit Risk Dynamics." *Financial Analysts Journal,* July–August 2000, pp. 67–81.

Denis, David J., and Atulya Sarin. "Is the Market Surprised by Poor Earnings Realizations Following Seasoned Equity Offerings?" *Journal of Financial and Quantitative Analysis,* June 2001, pp. 169–93.

Devero, Amie. "Corporate Values: Stimulus to the Bottom Line." *Financial Executive,* May 2003, pp. 20–23.

Frankel, Micah, and Robert Trezevant. "The Year-End LIFO Inventory Purchasing Decision: An Empirical Test." *The Accounting Review,* April 1994, pp. 382–98.

Warshawsky, Mark J.; H. Fred Mittelstaedt; and Carrie Cristea. "Recognizing Retiree Health Benefits: The Effect of SFA 106." *Financial Management,* Summer 1993, pp. 188–99.

The Use of Ratios

Bacidore, Jeffrey M.; John A. Boquist; Todd M. Milbourn; and Anjan V. Thakor. "The Search for the Best Financial Performance Measure." *Financial Analysts Journal,* May–June 2001, pp. 11–20.

Distortions in Reported Data

Choi, Frederick D. S., and Richard M. Levich. "International Accounting Diversity: Does It Affect Market Participants?" *Financial Analysts Journal,* July–August 1991, pp. 73–82.

MacDonald, Elizabeth. "Numbers Game. Recurring Gains." *Forbes,* May 14, 2001, pp. 86–88.

Issues in Efficient Markets

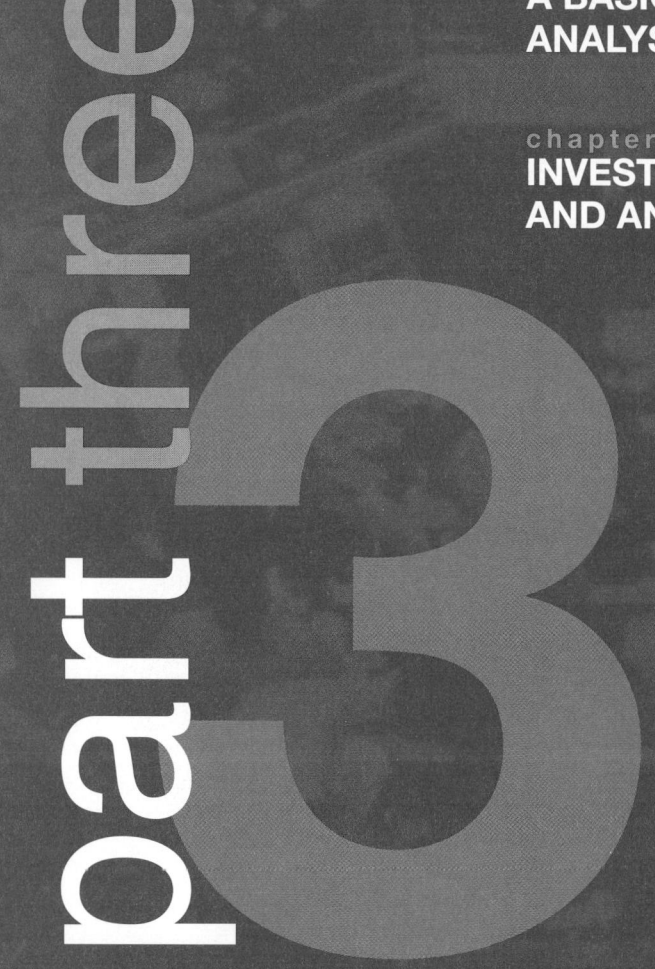

chapter 9
A BASIC VIEW OF TECHNICAL ANALYSIS AND MARKET EFFICIENCY

chapter 10
INVESTMENTS IN SPECIAL SITUATIONS AND ANOMALIES

part three
3

CHAPTER 9 FOCUSES ON the use of technical analysis and Chapter 10 looks at the so-called anomalies of the efficient market. In other words, what is the evidence that shows an investor can outperform a buy and hold strategy of owning a portfolio structured to equal the composition of a benchmark index such as the Standard & Poor's 500 Index or the Russell 2000 small stock index? Well, there is evidence that one can outperform the index using public data, but may have to accept more risk. Academics have published numerous articles testing various portfolio strategies that will lead to better than average performance. One investor that isn't a value investor and has a track record of out performing his benchmarks is Richard Driehaus, chairman of Driehaus Capital of Chicago, a company with over 100 employees and $2.7 billion of assets under management.

Richard Driehaus makes a statement that students should take to heart. "Everyone wants to be rich, but few want to work for it." Richard was raised by his Irish mother and attended St. Ignatius High School and DePaul University, but as he said in a *Chicago Sun Times* article, "I credit more of my success to what the nuns taught me at St. Margaret's. The sisters told us that you're responsible for your own actions."

Richard took this to heart and worked hard as a boy delivering newspapers. At age 13 when he had saved enough money from his paper route, he bought his first common stock. After graduation from DePaul University with a BSC. and MBA, Richard went to work for A.G. Becker as a research analyst. After working at several other Wall Street firms, he founded Driehaus Securities Corporation in 1979 and Driehaus Capital Management in 1982.

Driehaus Capital Management manages individual portfolios for institutional investors and wealthy individuals and manages a family of no-load funds which you can check out on his website **www.driehaus.com**. The website sums up the Driehaus investment strategy as follows:

Richard Driehaus
Courtesy of Driehaus Capital Management, Inc.

"Our portfolios are diversified among our best investment ideas, rather than stocks selected to mimic a particular investment index. Because we focus on stocks demonstrating the best growth fundamentals as evidenced by strong price and volume movements, our portfolios are concentrated in companies displaying strong fundamental and technical characteristics. We try to remain fully invested at all times, without making asset allocation decisions between equities and cash."

The Driehaus focus is on companies with accelerating sales and positive earnings surprises as well as technical indicators such as a stock's relative strength, daily price, and volume chart. The firm also looks at sectors, economic conditions affecting those sectors, and recovering companies with earnings surprises. Driehaus says the income statement is more interesting than the balance sheet. He is an active investor with high turnover rates of 200 to 300 percent per year and so we are not talking about a value oriented buy-and-hold investor. The strategy is to cut losses short and consider no stock a core holding unable to be sold.

Like all investors featured in these part openers, Richard Driehaus has been active in his community and a very generous benefactor to charities including Mercy Home for Boys and Girls, DePaul University, and many other organizations. He has already given $25 million in charitable gifts and says one of his goals is to give $100 million to worthy causes before he dies. The DePaul Finance Department is the beneficiary of the Richard Driehaus Endowed Chair and Center in Behavior Finance. Thanks, Richard.

9 chapter nine

A Basic View of Technical Analysis and Market Efficiency

objectives

1. Understand the difference between fundamental and technical analysis.

2. Appreciate how technical analysis is related to patterns of stock price movement.

3. Explain the types of charting that are used in technical analysis.

4. Describe the use of key indicator series in attempting to track the direction of the market.

5. Explain the efficient market hypothesis and the various forms it can take.

6. Relate the efficient market hypothesis to fundamental and technical analysis.

Technical Analysis
The Use of Charting
    Essential Elements of the Dow Theory
    Support and Resistance Levels
    Volume
    Types of Charts
Key Indicator Series
    Contrary Opinion Rules
    Smart Money Rules
    Overall Market Rules
Efficient Market Hypothesis
Weak Form of the Efficient Market Hypothesis
    Tests of Independence
    Trading Rule Tests
    Implications for Technical Analysis
Semistrong Form of the Efficient Market Hypothesis
    Implications for Fundamental Analysis
Strong Form of the Efficient Market Hypothesis

In the preceding four chapters, we followed a fundamental approach to security analysis. That is, we examined the fundamental factors that influence the business cycle, the performance of various industries, and the operations of the individual firms. We further examined the financial statements and tools of measurement that are available to the security analyst. In following a fundamental approach, one attempts to evaluate the appropriate worth of a security and perhaps ascertain whether it is under- or overpriced.

In this chapter, we examine a technical approach to investment timing. In this approach, analysts and market technicians examine prior price and volume data, as well as other market-related indicators, to determine past trends in the belief that they will help forecast future ones. Technical analysts place much more emphasis on charts and graphs of *internal market data* than on such fundamental factors as earnings reports, management capabilities, or new-product development. They believe that even when important fundamental information is uncovered, it may not lead to profitable trading because of timing considerations and market imperfections.

We also devote much time and attention in this chapter to the concept of market efficiency; that is, the ability of the market to adjust very rapidly to the supply of new information in valuing a security. This area of study has led to the efficient market hypothesis, which states that all securities are correctly priced at any point.

At the outset, be aware there are many disagreements and contradictions in the various areas we examine. As previously implied, advocates of technical analysis do not place much emphasis on fundamental analysis, and vice versa. Even more significant, proponents of the efficient market hypothesis would suggest that neither works.

In light of the various disagreements that exist, we believe it is important that the student be exposed to many schools of thought. For example, we devote the first part of the chapter to technical analysis and then later offer research findings that relate to the value of the technical approach as well as the fundamental approach. Our philosophy throughout the chapter is to recognize that there sometimes is a gap between practices utilized by brokerage houses (and on Wall Street) and beliefs held in the academic community, yet the student should be exposed to both.

Technical Analysis

Technical analysis is based on a number of basic assumptions:

1. Market value is determined solely by the interaction of demand and supply.
2. It is assumed that though there are minor fluctuations in the market, stock prices tend to move in trends that persist for long periods.
3. Reversals of trends are caused by shifts in demand and supply.
4. Shifts in demand and supply can be detected sooner or later in charts.
5. Many chart patterns tend to repeat themselves.

For our purposes, the most significant items to note are the assumptions that stock prices tend to move in trends that persist for long periods, and these trends can be detected in charts. The basic premise is that past trends in market movements can be used to forecast or understand the future. The market technician generally assumes there is a lag between the time he perceives a change in the value of a security and when the investing public ultimately assesses this change.

In developing the tools of technical analysis, we shall divide our discussion between (a) the use of charting and (b) the key indicator series to project future market movements.

The Use of Charting

Charting is often linked to the development of the Dow theory in the late 1890s by Charles Dow. He was the founder of the Dow Jones Company and editor of *The Wall Street Journal*. Many of his early precepts were further refined by other market technicians, and it is generally believed the Dow theory was successful in signaling the market crash of 1929.

Essential Elements of the Dow Theory

The **Dow theory** maintains that there are three major movements in the market: daily fluctuations, secondary movements, and primary trends. According to the theory, daily fluctuations and secondary movements (covering two weeks to a month) are only important to the extent they reflect on the long-term primary trend in the market. Primary trends may be characterized as either bullish or bearish in nature.

In Figure 9–1, we look at the use of the Dow theory to analyze a market trend. Note that the primary movement in the market is positive despite two secondary movements that are downward. The important facet of the secondary movements is that each low is higher than the previous low and each high is higher than the previous high. This tends to confirm the primary trend, which is bullish.

Under the Dow theory, it is assumed that this pattern will continue for a long period, and the analyst should not be confused by secondary movements. However, the upward pattern must ultimately end. This is indicated by a new pattern in which a recovery fails to exceed the previous high (abortive recovery) and a new low penetrates a previous low as indicated in Figure 9–2. For a true turn in the market to occur, the new pattern of movement in the Dow Jones Industrial Average must also be confirmed by a subsequent movement in the Dow Jones Transportation Average as indicated on the bottom part of Figure 9–2.

A change from a bear to a bull market would require similar patterns of confirmation. While the Dow theory has proved helpful to market technicians, there is always the problem of false signals. For example, not every abortive recovery

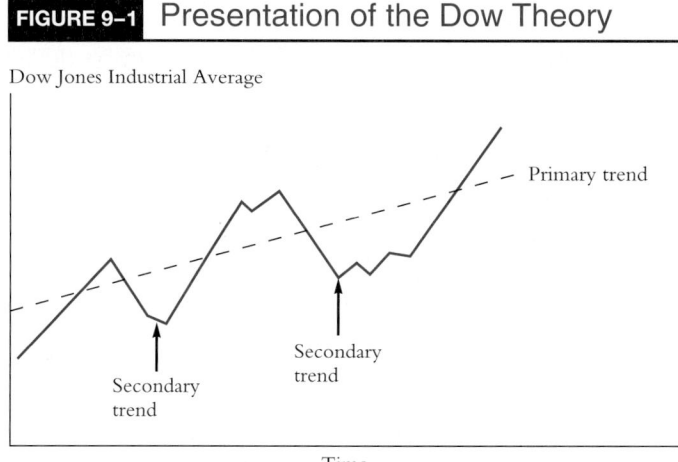

FIGURE 9–1 Presentation of the Dow Theory

FIGURE 9–2 Market Reversal and Confirmation

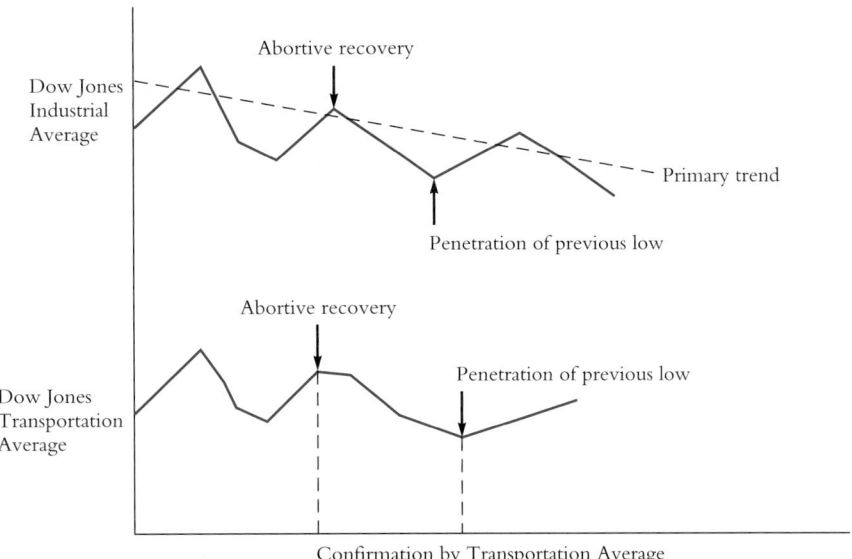

is certain to signal the end of a bull market. Furthermore, the investor may have to wait a long time to get full confirmation of a change in a primary trend. By the time the transportation average confirms the pattern in the industrial average, important market movements may have already occurred.

Support and Resistance Levels

Chartists attempt to define trading levels for individual securities (or the market) where there is a likelihood that price movements will be challenged. Thus, in the daily financial press or on television, the statement is often made that the next barrier to the current market move is at 11,000 (or some other level). This assumes the existence of support and resistance levels. As indicated in Figure 9–3, a support level is associated with the lower end of a trading range and a resistance level with the upper end.

Support may develop each time a stock goes down to a lower level of trading because investors who previously passed up a purchase opportunity may now choose to act. It is a signal that new demand is coming into the market. When a stock reaches the high side of the normal trading range, **resistance** may develop because some investors who bought in on a previous wave of enthusiasm (on an earlier high) may now view this as a chance to get even. Others may simply see this as an opportunity to take a profit.

A breakout above a resistance point (as indicated in Figure 9–3 on page 244) or below a support level is considered significant. The stock is assumed to be trading in a new range, and higher (lower) trading values may now be expected.

A good example of support and resistance levels can be found in the trading pattern of IBM in the 1990s. After trading in the $150 to $170 range in the early 1990s, the stock hit rock bottom in mid-1993 at $40 per share. Part of the decline was due to a loss in EPS in 1993 for the first time in decades. However,

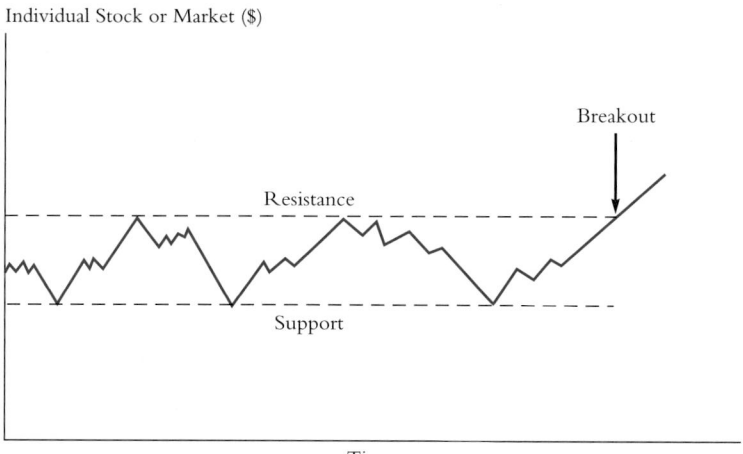

FIGURE 9-3 Support and Resistance

the stock did find support at $40 per share as investors began to purchase the stock in anticipation of a possible comeback. Lou Gerstner, Jr., a highly respected executive, had come on board as chairman and CEO. He immediately began eliminating redundant operations as well as implementing a strategic pattern for future growth. By 1996, the stock was in the $90s range and made a number of attempts to break through a resistance point of 100. After several tries, the stock finally crossed the 100 resistance barrier and then made an almost uninterrupted run up to $200 in mid-1997. The stock then split two for one. By September 2004 it was still in the post-split $100 range. IBM will undoubtedly continue to face new support and resistance levels in the future.

Volume

The amount of volume supporting a given market movement is also considered significant. For example, if a stock (or the market in general) makes a new high on heavy trading volume, this is considered to be bullish. Conversely, a new high on light volume may indicate a temporary move that is likely to be reversed.

A new low on light volume is considered somewhat positive because of the lack of investor participation. When a new low is established on the basis of heavy trading volume, this is considered to be very bearish.

In early 2004, the New York Stock Exchange averaged a volume of 1.3 to 1.5 billion shares daily. When the volume jumped to 2.0 billion shares, analysts took a very strong interest in the trading pattern of the market.

For an individual stock, the same principles also apply. In 2004, Intel normally traded 50 to 60 million shares daily. However, movements on volumes of 80 to 100 million shares or more were considered significant.

Types of Charts

Until now, we have been using typical line charts to indicate market patterns. Technicians also use bar charts and point and figure charts. We shall examine each.

Chapter 9 A Basic View of Technical Analysis and Market Efficiency 245

Bar Chart   A bar chart shows the high and low price for a stock with a horizontal dash along the line to indicate the closing price. An example is shown in Figure 9–4 below.

We see on November 12 the stock traded between a high of 41 and a low of 38 and closed at 40. Daily information on the Dow Jones Industrial Average is usually presented in the form of a bar chart, with daily volume shown at the bottom as indicated in Figure 9–5.

FIGURE 9–4   Bar Chart

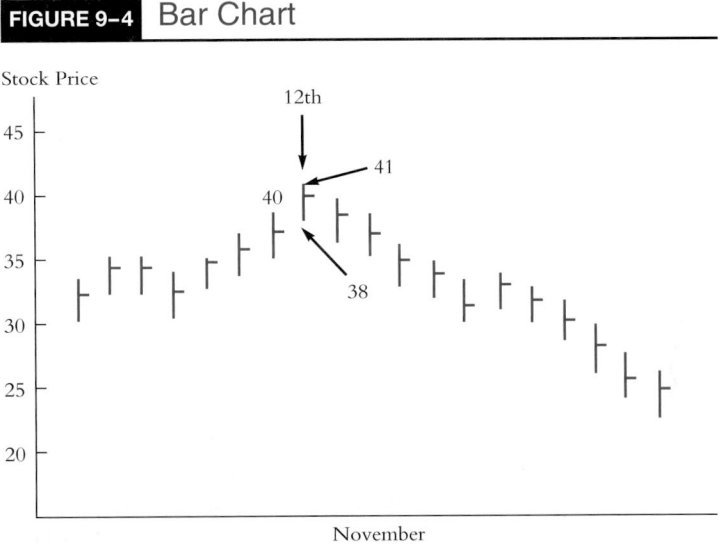

FIGURE 9–5   Bar Chart of Market Average

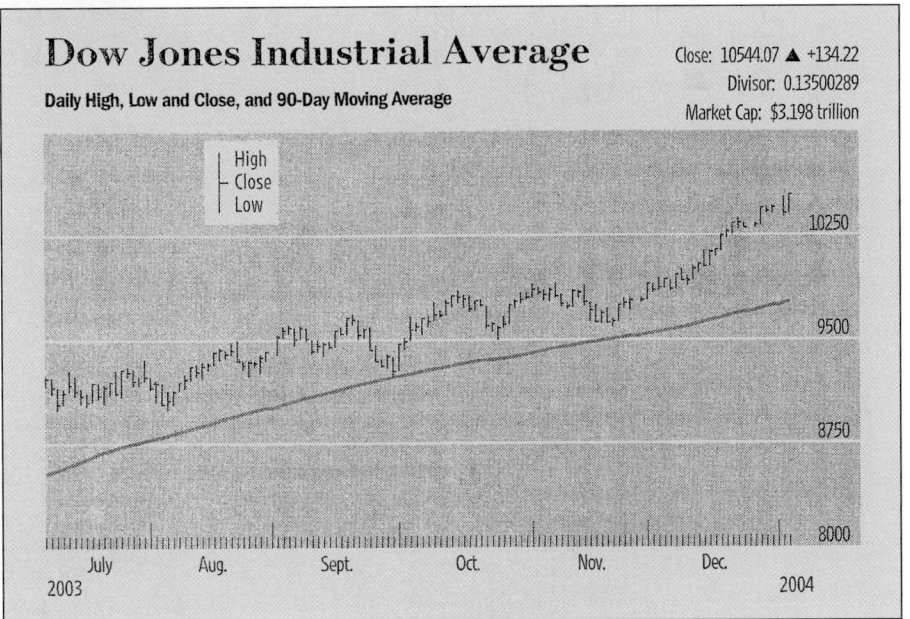

Source: *The Wall Street Journal,* January 6, 2004, p. C2. Reprinted by permission of *The Wall Street Journal.* © 2003 by Dow Jones & Company, Inc. All Rights Reserved Worldwide.

Trendline, published through a division of Standard & Poor's, provides excellent charting information on a variety of securities traded on the major exchanges and is available at many libraries and brokerage houses. Market technicians carefully evaluate the charts, looking for what they perceive to be significant patterns of movement. For example, the pattern in Figure 9–4 on the previous page might be interpreted as a head-and-shoulder pattern (note the head in the middle) with a lower penetration of the neckline to the right indicating a sell signal. In Figure 9–6 we show a series of the price-movement patterns presumably indicating market bottoms and tops.

FIGURE 9–6 Chart Representation of Market Bottoms and Tops

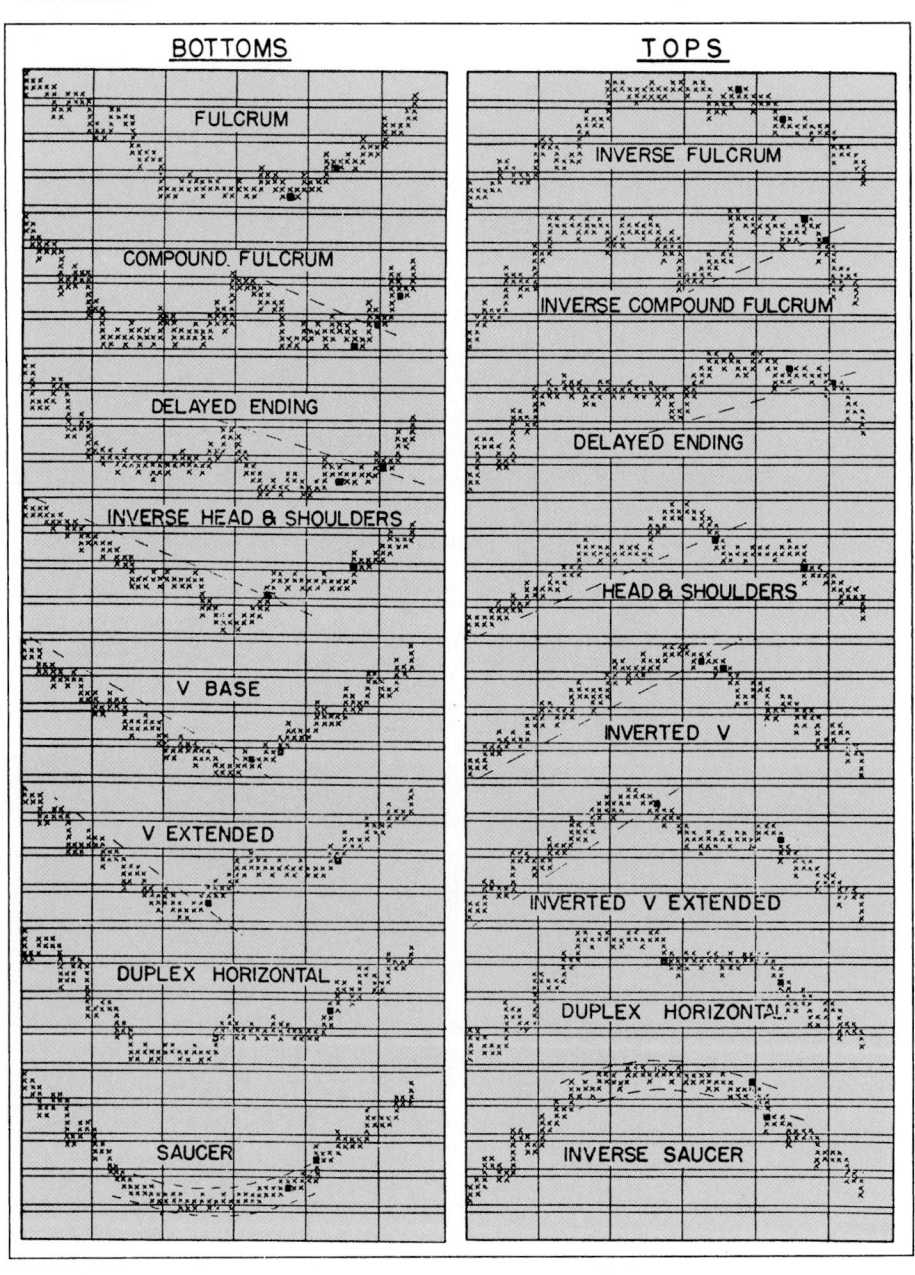

Although it is beyond the scope of this book to go into interpretation of chart formations in great detail, special books on the subject are suggested at the end of our discussion of charting.

Point and Figure Chart A point and figure chart (PFC) emphasizes significant price changes and the reversal of significant price changes. Unlike a line or bar chart, it has no time dimension. An example of a point and figure chart is presented in Figure 9–7.

The assumption is that the stock starts at 30. Only moves of two points or greater are plotted on the graph (some may prefer to use one point). Advances are indicated by Xs, and declines are shown by Os. A reversal from an advance to a decline or vice versa calls for a shift in columns. Thus, the stock initially goes from 30 to 42 and then shifts columns in its subsequent decline to 36 before moving up again in column 3. A similar pattern persists throughout the chart.

Chartists carefully read point and figure charts to observe market patterns (where there is support, resistance, breakouts, congestion, and so on). Students with a strong interest in charting may consult such books as Colby and Meyers, *The Encyclopedia of Technical Market Indicators*,[1] and DeMark, *The New Science of Technical Analysis*.[2] The problem in reading charts has always been to analyze patterns in such a fashion that they truly predict stock market movements before they unfold. To justify the effort, one must assume there are discernible trends over the long term.

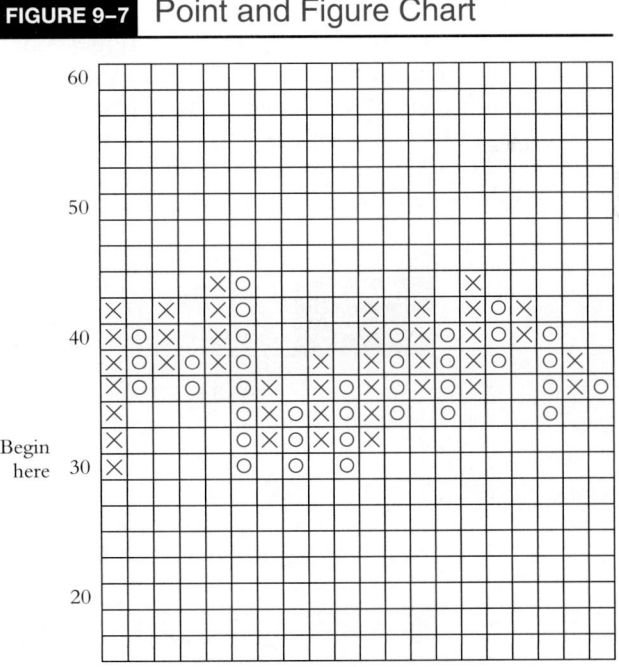

FIGURE 9–7 Point and Figure Chart

---

[1] Robert W. Colby and Thomas A. Meyers, *The Encyclopedia of Technical Market Indicators* (Homewood, IL: Business One Irwin, 1988).
[2] Thomas R. DeMark, *The New Science of Technical Analysis* (New York: John Wiley & Sons, 1994).

Key Indicator Series

In the former television series *Wall Street Week,* host Louis Rukeyser traditionally watched a number of indicators on a weekly basis and compared the bullish and bearish indicators to determine what the next direction of the market might be.

In this section, we examine bullish and bearish technical indicator series. We first look at contrary opinion rules, then smart money rules, and finally, overall market indicators.

Contrary Opinion Rules

The essence of a **contrary opinion rule** is that it is easier to figure out who is wrong than who is right. If you know your neighbor has a terrible sense of direction and you spot him taking a left at the intersection, you automatically take a right. In the stock market there are similar guidelines.

Odd-Lot Theory   An odd-lot trade is one of less than 100 shares, and only small investors tend to engage in odd-lot transactions. The odd-lot theory suggests you watch very closely what the small investor is doing and then do the opposite. The weekly edition of *Barron's* breaks down odd-lot trading on a daily basis in its "Market Laboratory—Stocks" section. It is a simple matter to construct a ratio of odd-lot purchases to odd-lot sales. For example, on May 7, 2004, 6,173,600 odd-lot shares were purchased, and 7,322,200 shares were sold, indicating a ratio of 0.843. The ratio has historically fluctuated between 0.50 and 1.45.

The odd-lot theory actually suggests that the small trader does all right most of the time but badly misses on key market turns. As indicated in Figure 9–8, the odd-lot trader is on the correct path as the market is going up; that is, selling off part of the portfolio in an up market (the name of the game is to buy low and sell high). This net selling posture is reflected by a declining odd-lot index (purchase-to-sales ratio). However, as the market continues upward, the odd-lot

www.barrons.com

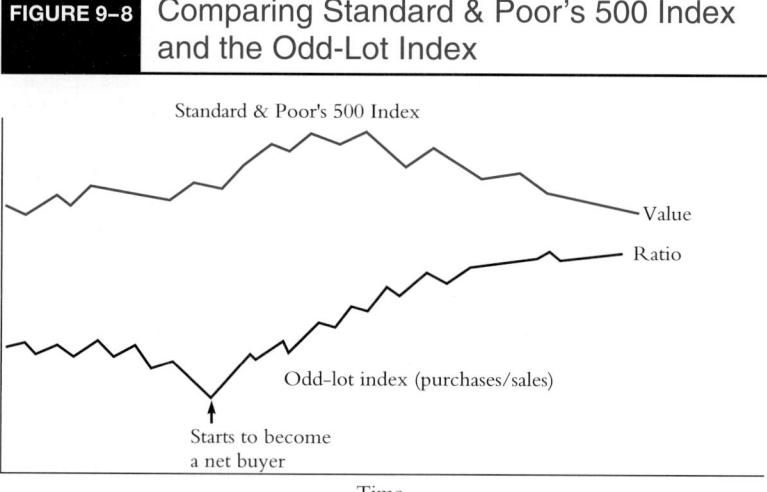

FIGURE 9-8 Comparing Standard & Poor's 500 Index and the Odd-Lot Index

the real world of investing

Ask Your Professor for Six Hours of Credit: Three Hours in Finance and Three Hours of Psychology

In addition to all the financial theories discussed in this chapter, there is a new branch of finance called **behavioral finance.** This school of thought is an offshoot of cognitive psychology, which suggests that people are not consistent in how they view or "frame" equivalent events if they are presented in different contexts. For example, the color of blue may appear different to two people (who are not color blind) if they are viewing it in radically different contexts.

They may also view or frame economically equivalent events differently even after adjusting for risk and all other rational considerations. It is an irrational behavior phenomenon. Suppose you bought an Alex Rodriguez baseball card at a baseball card show for $10. On the way out the door you discovered you have lost the card and after a thorough search, you cannot find it. You are totally disgusted with your careless behavior associated with the card and may not buy another Alex Rodriguez card.

In a similar incident, assume you lost a $10 bill on the way to a baseball card show. When you get to the show, you see an Alex Rodriguez card for sale for $10, and you decide to buy it. While it's true you are unhappy with yourself for losing the $10 bill, your displeasure is not related to the Alex Rodriguez card.

But keep in mind under either scenario, if you buy an Alex Rodriguez card at the show (for the first or second time), the economic consequences are the same. You have $20 less than when you left the house and one Alex Rodriguez baseball card. You have merely "framed" or viewed economically equivalent events differently.

The same type of scenario can be transposed to the stock market. Suppose you previously lost $10 per share on an investment in CISCO Systems and made $10 a share on a prior investment in Intel. It is now six months later, and you view either stock as having an equally favorable payoff after adjusting for risk and other variables. Rational analysis should indicate you are totally indifferent between the investment alternatives. But in the jargon of cognitive psychology, you may "frame" the alternatives differently, and opt to go with Intel. You may pick Intel even if its prospects are slightly less favorable.

Similarly, financial behaviorists suggest that people overreact to good and bad news, and the reaction goes beyond any rational assessment. Such a description may well portray the high-tech fervor and debacle of the last decade. The key message that behavioral finance seems to impart is that one should spend a bit less time computing expected values, standard deviations, and betas and spend a bit more time examining the "irrational" human being making the decisions.

At the lower end of the boundary, it would appear that mutual funds are fully invested and can provide little in the way of additional purchasing power. As their cash position goes to 15 percent or higher, market technicians assess this as representing significant purchasing power that may help to trigger a market upturn. While the overall premise is valid, there are problems in identifying just what is a significant cash position for mutual funds in a given market cycle. It may change in extreme market environments.

Efficient Market Hypothesis

We shift our attention from technical analysis to that of examining market efficiency. As indicated at the beginning of the chapter, we now view any contradictions between the assumptions of fundamental or technical analysis and findings of the **efficient market hypothesis (EMH).**

Earlier in the text, we said that an efficient market is one in which new information is very rapidly processed so that securities are properly priced at any given time.[7] An important premise of an efficient market is that a large number of profit-maximizing participants are concerned with the analysis and valuation of securities. This would seem to describe the security market environment in the United States. Any news on IBM, AT&T, an oil embargo, or tax legislation is likely to be absorbed and acted on very rapidly by profit-maximizing individuals. For this reason, the efficient market hypothesis assumes that no stock price can be in disequilibrium or improperly priced for long. There is almost instantaneous adjustment to new information. The EMH applies most directly to large firms trading on the major security exchanges.

The efficient market hypothesis further assumes that information travels in a random, independent fashion and that prices are an unbiased reflection of all currently available information.

More generally, the efficient market hypothesis is stated and tested in three different forms: the weak form, the semistrong form, and the strong form. We shall examine each of these and the related implications for technical and fundamental analysis.

Weak Form of the Efficient Market Hypothesis

The **weak form of the efficient market hypothesis** suggests there is no relationship between past and future prices of securities. They are presumed to be independent over time. Because the efficient market hypothesis maintains that current prices reflect all available information and information travels in a random fashion, it is assumed that there is little or nothing to be gained from studying past stock prices.

The weak form of the efficient market hypothesis has been tested in two different ways—tests of independence and trading rule tests.

Tests of Independence

Tests of independence have examined the degree of correlation between stock prices over time and have found the correlation to be consistently small (between +0.10 and −0.10) and not statistically significant. This indicates that stock price changes are independent.[8] A further test is based on the frequency and extent of runs in stock price data. A run occurs when there is no difference in direction between two or more price changes. An example of a series of data and some runs is presented below:

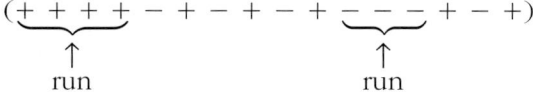

---

[7] A slightly more precise definition is that securities are priced in an unbiased fashion at any given time. Because information is assumed to travel in a random, independent fashion, there is no consistent upside or downside pricing bias mechanism. Although the price adjustment is not always perfect, it is unbiased and cannot be anticipated in advance.

[8] Sidney S. Alexander, "Price Movements in Speculative Markets: Trends or Random Walks," *Industrial Management Review,* May 1961, pp. 26; and Eugene F. Fama, "The Behavior of Stock Market Prices," *Journal of Business,* January 1965, pp. 34–105.

Runs can be expected in any series of data through chance factors, but an independent data series should not produce an unusual amount of runs. Statistical tests have indicated that security prices generally do not produce any more runs than would be expected through the process of random number generation.[9] This also tends to indicate that stock price movements are independent over time.[10]

Trading Rule Tests

A second method of testing the weak form of the efficient market hypothesis (that past trends in stock prices are not helpful in predicting the future) is through trading rule tests. Because practicing market technicians maintain that tests of independence (correlation studies and runs) are too rigid to test the assumptions of the weak form of the efficient market hypothesis, additional tests by academic researchers have been developed. These are known as trading rule or filter tests. These tests determine whether a given trading rule based on past price data, volume figures, and so forth can be used to beat a naive buy-and-hold approach. The intent is to simulate the conditions under which a given trading rule is used and then determine if superior returns were produced after considering transaction costs and the risks involved.

As an example of a trading rule, if a stock moves up 5 percent or more, the rule might be to purchase it. The assumption is that this represents a breakout and should be considered bullish. Similarly, a 5 percent downward movement would be considered bearish and call for a sell strategy (rather than a buy-low/sell-high strategy, this is a follow-the-market-trend strategy). Other trading rule tests might be based on advance-decline patterns, short sales figures, and similar technical patterns. Research results have indicated that in a limited number of cases, trading rules may produce slightly positive returns, but after commission costs are considered, the results are neutral and sometimes negative in comparison to a naive buy-and-hold approach.[11]

Implications for Technical Analysis

The results of the *tests of independence* and *trading rules* would seem to uphold the weak form of the efficient market hypothesis. Security prices do appear to be independent over time or, more specifically, move in the pattern of a random walk.

Some challenge the research on the basis that academic research in this area does not capture the personal judgment an experienced technician brings forward in reading charts. There is also the fact that there are an infinite number of trading rules, and not all of them can or have been tested. Nevertheless, research on the weak form of the EMH still seems to suggest that prices move

---

[9] Ibid.

[10] A possible exception to this rule was found in small stocks. A sample study is Jennifer Conrad and Gantam Kaul, "Time Variation and Expected Returns," *Journal of Business,* October 1988, pp. 409–25.

[11] Eugene F. Fama and Marshall Blume, "Filter Rules and Stock Market Trading Profits," *Journal of Business,* supplement, January 1966, pp. 226–41; and George Pinches, "The Random Walk Hypothesis and Technical Analysis," *Financial Analysts Journal,* March–April 1970, pp. 104–10.

independently over time, that past trends cannot be used to easily predict the future, and that charting and technical analysis may have limited value.

Semistrong Form of the Efficient Market Hypothesis

The **semistrong form of the efficient market hypothesis** maintains that all public information is already impounded into the value of a security, and therefore, one cannot use fundamental analysis to determine whether a stock is undervalued or overvalued.

Basically, the semistrong form of the efficient market hypothesis supports the notion that there is no learning lag in the distribution of public information. When a company makes an announcement, investors across the country assess the information with equal speed. Also, a major firm listed on the New York Stock Exchange could hardly hope to utilize some questionable accounting practice that deceptively leads to higher reported profits and not expect sophisticated analysts to pick it up. (This may not be equally true for a lesser known firm that trades over-the-counter and enjoys little investor attention.)

Researchers have tested the semistrong form of the EMH by determining whether investors who acted on the basis of newly released public information have been able to enjoy superior returns. If the market is efficient in a semistrong sense, this information is almost immediately impounded in the value of the security, and little or no trading profits would be available. The implications are that one could not garner superior returns by trading on public information about stock splits, earnings reports, or other similar items.

Tests on the semistrong form of the efficient market hypothesis have generally been on the basis of risk-adjusted returns. Thus, the return from a given investment strategy must be compared with the performance of popular market indicators with appropriate risk adjustments. As will be described in Chapter 21, the risk measurement variable is usually the beta. After such adjustments are made, the question becomes: Are there abnormal returns that go beyond explanations associated with risk? If the answer is yes and can be shown to be statistically significant, then the investment strategy may be thought to refute the semistrong form of the efficient market hypothesis. The investor must also cover transaction costs in determining that a given strategy is superior.

For example, assume a stock goes up 15 percent. The security is 20 percent riskier than the market. Further assume the overall market goes up by 10 percent. On a risk-adjusted basis, the security would need to go up in excess of 12 percent (the 10 percent market return $\times$ 1.2 risk factor) to beat the market. In the above case, the stock with the 15 percent gain beat the market on a risk-adjusted basis.

Tests examining the impact of such events as stock splits and stock dividends, corporate announcements, and changes in accounting policy indicate that the market is generally efficient in a semistrong sense. For example, a study by Fama, Fisher, Jensen, and Roll indicated that almost all of the market impact of a stock split occurs before a public announcement.[12] There is little to be gained from acting on the announcement.

According to the semistrong form of the efficient market hypothesis, investors not only digest information very quickly, but they also are able to see

---

[12] Eugene F. Fama, Lawrence Fisher, Michael G. Jensen, and Richard Roll, "The Adjustment of Stock Prices to New Information," *International Economic Review*, February 1969, pp. 2–21.

through mere changes in accounting information that do not have economic consequences. For example, the switching from accelerated depreciation to straight-line depreciation for financial reporting purposes (but not tax purposes) tends to make earnings per share look higher but provides no economic benefit for the firm. Research studies indicate this has no positive impact on valuation.[13]

Similarly, investors are not deceived by mere accounting changes related to inventory policy, reserve accounts, exchange translations, or other items that appear to have no economic benefits. The corporate treasurer who switches from LIFO to FIFO accounting to make earnings look better in an inflationary economy will probably not see the firm's stock price rise because investors look at the economic consequences of higher taxes associated with the action and disregard the mere financial accounting consequences of higher reported profits.[14] Under this circumstance, the effect on stocks may be neutral or negative.

Implications for Fundamental Analysis

If stock values are already based on the analysis of all available public information, it may be assumed that little is to be gained from additional fundamental analysis. Under the semistrong form of the efficient market hypothesis, if General Motors is trading at $55, the assumption is that every shred of public information about GM has been collected and evaluated by thousands of investors, and they have determined an equilibrium price of $55. The assumption is that anything you read in *The Wall Street Journal* or Standard & Poor's publications has already been considered many times over by others and is currently impounded in the value of the stock. If you were to say you think GM is really worth $57 because of some great new product, proponents of the semistrong form of the efficient market hypothesis would suggest that your judgment cannot be better than the collective wisdom of the marketplace in which everyone is trying desperately to come out ahead.

www.gm.com

Ironically, although many suggest that fundamental analysis may not lead to superior profits in an efficient market environment, it is fundamental analysis itself that makes the market efficient. Because everyone is doing fundamental analysis, there is little in the way of unabsorbed or undigested information. Therefore, one extra person doing fundamental analysis is unlikely to achieve superior insight.

Although the semistrong form of the efficient market hypothesis has research support, there are exceptions. These are referred to as **anomalies** or deviations from the basic proposition that the market is efficient. For example, Basu has found that stocks with low P/E ratios consistently provide better returns than stocks with high P/E ratios on both a non-risk-adjusted and risk-adjusted basis.[15] Because a P/E ratio is publicly available information that may be used to generate superior returns, this flies in the face of the more

---

[13] T. Ross Archibald, "Stock Market Reaction to Depreciation Switch-Back," *Accounting Review*, January 1972, pp. 22–30; and Robert S. Kaplan and Richard Roll, "Investor Evaluation of Accounting Information: Some Empirical Evidence," *Journal of Business*, April 1972, pp. 225–57.

[14] Shyam Sunder, "Stock Price and Risk Related to Accounting Changes in Inventory Valuation," *Accounting Review*, April 1975, pp. 305–15.

[15] S. Basu, "Investment Performance of Common Stocks in Relation to Their Price-Earnings Ratios: A Test of the Efficient Market Hypothesis," *Journal of Finance*, June 1977, pp. 663–82. Also, S. Basu, "The Information Content of Price-Earnings Ratios," *Financial Management*, Summer 1975, pp. 53–64.

common conclusions on the semistrong form of the efficient market hypothesis. Banz's[16] and Reinganum's[17] research indicates that small firms tend to provide higher returns than larger firms even after considering risk. Perhaps fewer institutional investors in smaller firms make for a less-efficient market and superior potential opportunities.

Additional evidence of this nature continues to accumulate, and in Chapter 10 covering special situations and anomalies, we present an extended discussion of some of these items and other possible contradictions to the acceptance of the semistrong version of the efficient market hypothesis. We also comment on measurement problems in that chapter.

Thus, even if the semistrong form of the efficient market hypothesis appears to be generally valid, exceptions can be noted. Also, it is possible that while most analysts may not be able to add additional insight through fundamental analysis, there are exceptions to every rule. It can be assumed that some analysts have such *extraordinary* insight and capability in analyzing publicly available information that they can perceive what others cannot. Also, if you take a very long-term perspective, the fact that a stock's value is in short-term equilibrium may not discourage you from taking a long-term position or attempting to find long-term value.

Before we move on, it is also appropriate to point out that there is not only debate about whether the market is efficient in a semistrong sense but also over whether market researchers are appropriately testing for efficiency. For example, if risk is not properly measured, then conclusions about research studies can be questioned. This is an issue that cannot be easily settled and is discussed again at the end of Chapter 10.

Strong Form of the Efficient Market Hypothesis

The **strong form of the efficient market hypothesis** goes beyond the semistrong form to state that stock prices reflect not only all public information but *all* information. Thus, it is hypothesized that insider information is also immediately impounded into the value of a security. In a sense, we go beyond the concept of a market that is highly efficient to one that is perfect.

The assumption is that no group of market participants or investors has monopolistic access to information. If this is the case, then no group of investors can be expected to show superior risk-adjusted returns under any circumstances.

Unlike the weak and semistrong forms of the efficient market hypothesis, major test results are not supportive of the strong form of the hypothesis. For example, specialists on security exchanges have been able to earn superior rates of return on invested capital. The book they keep on unfilled limit orders appears to provide monopolistic access to information. An SEC study actually found that specialists typically sell above their latest purchase 83 percent of the time and buy below their latest sell 81 percent of the time.[18] This implies

---

[16] Rolf W. Banz, "The Relationship between Returns and Market Value of Common Stocks," *Journal of Financial Economics,* March 1981, pp. 3–18.

[17] Marc R. Reinganum, "Misspecification of Capital Asset Pricing—Empirical Anomalies Based on Earnings Yield and Market Values," *Journal of Financial Economics,* March 1981, pp. 19–46.

[18] Securities and Exchange Commission, *Report of the Special Study of the Security Markets,* part 2 (Washington, DC: U.S. Government Printing Office).

www.sec.gov

wisdom that greatly exceeds that available in a perfect capital market environment. Likewise, an institutional investor study, also sponsored by the SEC, indicated that specialists' average return on capital was more than 100 percent.[19] While these returns have decreased somewhat recently in a more competitive environment, specialists still appear to outperform the market.

Another group that appears to use nonpublic information to garner superior returns is corporate insiders. As previously described, an insider is considered to be a corporate officer, member of the board of directors, or substantial stockholder. The SEC requires that insiders report their transactions to that regulatory body. A few weeks after reporting to the SEC, the information becomes public. Researchers can then go back and determine whether investment decisions made by insiders appeared, on balance, to be wise. Did heavy purchases by insiders precede strong upward price movements, and did sell-offs precede poor market performance? The answer appears to be yes. Research studies indicate insiders consistently achieve higher returns than would be expected in a perfect capital market.[20] Although insiders are not allowed to engage in short-term trades (of six months or less) or illegal transactions to generate trading profits, they are allowed to take longer-term positions, which may prove to be profitable. It has even been demonstrated that investors who follow the direction of inside traders after information on their activity becomes public may enjoy superior returns.[21] (This, of course, represents contrary evidence to the semistrong form of the efficient market hypothesis as well.)

Even though there is evidence on the activity of specialists and insiders that would cause one to reject the strong form of the efficient market hypothesis (or at least not to accept it), the range of participants with access to superior information is not large. For example, tests on the performance of mutual fund managers have consistently indicated they are not able to beat the market averages over the long term.[22] Although mutual fund managers may get the first call when news is breaking, that is not fast enough to generate superior returns.

While the strong form of the efficient market hypothesis suggests more opportunity for superior returns than the weak or semistrong forms, the premium is related to monopolistic access to information rather than other factors.

It should also be pointed out that those who act *illegally* with insider information may initially achieve superior returns from their special access to information, but the price of their actions may be high. For example, Ivan Boesky and Michael Milken, convicted users of illegal insider information in the late 1980s, were forced to give up their gains, pay heavy fines, and serve jail sentences. In their particular cases, they traded on insider information about mergers well before the public was informed. Although they were not officers of the companies or on the boards, they had special fiduciary responsibilities as money managers that they violated.

---

[19] Securities and Exchange Commission, *Institutional Investor Study Report* (Washington, DC: U.S. Government Printing Office).

[20] For an overview, see Alexandra Peers, "Insiders Reap Big Gains from Big Trades," *The Wall Street Journal*, September 23, 1992, pp. C1, C12.

[21] Michael S. Rozeff and Mir. A. Zaman, "Market Efficiency and Insider Trading: New Evidence," *Journal of Business*, January 1988, pp. 24–25.

[22] Richard A. Ippolito, "On Studies of Mutual Fund Performance," 1962–1991, *Financial Analysts Journal*, January–February 1993, pp. 42–50.

exploring the web

Website Address	Comments
www.bigcharts.com	Provides data, charts, and technical indicators, free
cbs.marketwatch.com	Has technical charts and information
www.quicken.com	Contains some technical analytical data and charts
www.stockworm.com	Has technical charts
www.stockcharts.com	Provides free technical charts and education on technical analysis
www.investopedia.com	Has primer on technical analysis
www.stocksites.com	Contains links to technical analysis sites and related finance sites

Summary

Following the discussion of fundamental analysis in Chapters 5 through 8, we examined technical analysis in this chapter and, more significantly, the impact of the efficient market hypothesis (EMH) on both fundamental and technical analysis.

While fundamental analysis deals with financial analysis and determinants of valuation, technical analysis is based on the study of past price and volume data as well as associated market trends to predict future price movements. Technical analysis relies heavily on charting and the use of key market indicators to make forecasts.

Technical analysts also observe support and resistance levels in the market as well as data on volume. Line, bar, and point and figure charts are used to determine turns in the market.

Market technicians also follow a number of key indicator series to predict the stock market—contrary opinion indicators, smart money indicators, and general market indicators.

Although there have been traditional arguments about whether fundamental or technical analysis is more important, a great deal of current attention is directed to the efficient market hypothesis and its implications for all types of analysis.

The efficient market hypothesis maintains that the market adjusts very rapidly to the supply of new information, and because of this, securities tend to be correctly priced at any given time (or very rapidly approaching this equilibrium value).

The efficient market hypothesis has been stated and tested in three different forms.

1. The weak form states there is no relationship between past and future prices (they are independent over time).
2. The semistrong form suggests all public information is currently impounded in the price of a stock.
3. The strong form suggests *all* information, public or otherwise, is included in the value of a security.

Research tends to support the weak form of the efficient market hypothesis, which causes many researchers to seriously question the overall value of technical analysis. However, many on Wall Street would vigorously debate this position. The semistrong form of the efficient market hypothesis is also reasonably supported by research, and this fact would tend to question the value of fundamental analysis by the individual investor. (It is, however, the collective wisdom of all fundamental analysis that leads to the efficient market hypothesis in the first place.) There are some contradictions to the semistrong form of the efficient market hypothesis, and much research is aimed at supplying additional contradictory data.

The strong form of the efficient market hypothesis is not generally accepted.

Key Words and Concepts

anomalies 259
Barron's Confidence Index 251
behavioral finance 255
contrary opinion rule 248
Dow theory 242
efficient market hypothesis (EMH) 255
resistance 243
semistrong form of the efficient market hypothesis 258
strong form of the efficient market hypothesis 260
support 243
technical analysis 241
weak form of the efficient market hypothesis 256

Discussion Questions

1. What is technical analysis?
2. What are the views of technical analysts toward fundamental analysis?
3. Outline the basic assumptions of technical analysis.
4. Under the Dow theory, if a recovery fails to exceed the previous high and a new low penetrates a previous low, what does this tell us about the market?
5. Also under the Dow theory, what other average is used to confirm movements in the Dow Jones Industrial Average?
6. What is meant by a support level for a stock or a market average? When might a support level exist?
7. In examining Figure 9–7 on page 247, if the next price movement is to 34, will a shift to a new column be indicated? (Assume the current price is 36.)
8. What is the logic behind the odd-lot theory? If the odd-lot index starts to move higher in an up market, what does the odd-lot theory indicate the next movement in the market will be?
9. If the Investors Intelligence Service has a bearish sentiment of 70 percent, would you generally want to be a buyer or seller?
10. What is the logic behind *Barron's* Confidence Index?
11. If the advance-decline movement in the market is weak (more declines than advances) while the DJIA is going up, what might this indicate to a technician about the market?
12. Categorize the following as either contrary opinion or smart money indicators (as viewed by technicians):
    a. Short sales by specialists.
    b. Odd-lot positions.
    c. Short sales positions.
    d. *Barron's* Confidence Index.
    e. Investment advisory recommendations.
    f. Put-call ratio.
13. Under the efficient market hypothesis, what is the assumption about the processing of new information, and what effect does this have on security pricing?
14. What does the weak form of the efficient market hypothesis

suggest? What are the two major ways in which it has been tested?

15. Would low correlation coefficients over time between stock prices tend to prove or disprove the weak form of the efficient market hypothesis?

16. Under the semistrong form of the efficient market hypothesis, is there anything to be gained from a corporate treasurer changing accounting methods to increase earnings per share when there is no associated economic benefit or gain?

17. Why does fundamental analysis tend to make the market efficient?

18. Suggest some studies that would indicate the market is not completely efficient in the semistrong form.

19. What does the strong form of the efficient market hypothesis suggest? Are major test results generally supportive of the strong form?

20. How do specialists, insiders, and mutual fund managers fare in terms of having access to superior information to generate large returns? (Comment on each separately.)

Web Exercise

Assume you want to see how much momentum a stock has going forward (a form of technical analysis). Go to **www.quicken.com**.

1. In the left margin, put in the symbol for any stock and click on "Go." If you do not have a preference, use pg (Procter & Gamble).
2. Click on "Chart" in the left column. Looking at the entire graph, has the overall momentum generally been up or down? Write a one- to two-sentence answer for this and the following questions.
3. If you were to draw a straight line of best fit through the data, what stock price would you be projecting for the future?
4. Have the peaks generally been associated with high or low volumes? What about the lows?
5. Click on "Analysts Ratings." Has the consensus rating gone up or down over the last three months? Is this consistent with the future outlook line you constructed in Part 3?
6. Add some fundamental analysis to this study by clicking on "One-Click Scoreboard." Now click on question 5, "Is the stock currently undervalued?" Write down a brief answer and continue to question 7.
7. Does the fundamental analysis in question 6 match expectations of the prior technical analysis? Do not be surprised if it does not. Many different parameters are being used.

Note: From time to time, companies redesign their websites, and occasionally a topic we have listed may have been deleted, updated, or moved into a different location. Most websites have a "site map" or "site index" listed on a different page. If you click on the site map or site index, you will be introduced to a table of contents that should aid you in finding the topic you are looking for.

S&P Problems

www.mhhe.com/edumarketinsight

STANDARD &POOR'S

Problem 1
1. Log on to the McGraw-Hill website: **www.mhhe.com/edumarketinsight** (see page vi in the preface for instructions).
2. Click on Company, which is the first box below the Market Insight title.

3. Put the ticker symbol for Johnson & Johnson (JNJ) in the box, and click on go.
4. Scroll down the left margin, and click on "Charting by Prophet" listed in blue. In the Symbol box, type in the ticker symbol for Standard & Poor's 500 index ($SPX). A chart will appear, and under S&P 500 Index you will see capital letters that may be self-explanatory but just in case these letters D-O-H-L-C-R don't make sense, they stand for Date, Opening Price, High Price, Low Price, Closing Price, and Range. Your first graph will cover 1 year.
5. Go to the box with 1 yr at the top of the graph, and change the time period to 20 years. Does the market decline of the early 2000s take on a different meaning if you are a young student with a 40-year time horizon ahead of you? Now change the time period to 5 years and ten years. How does your perspective change if you are 70 years old and retired? Before moving to the next question, reset the time period to 1 year.
6. Return to the left margin, and click on the plus (+) sign in front of Technical Studies, and then click on the plus sign in front of All Studies. You will find an alphabetical list of technical indicators, many of which are not covered in this chapter. Scroll down to Advancing-Declining Issues (it will be the first listing above ADX) and double click. At the bottom of the chart you see an up-and-down blue line. Can you see any patterns of predictability?
7. Go back to the left margin, and scroll down to Intraday Momentum and double click. Do you see any relationship between the momentum pattern and the stock price pattern?
8. Go back to the left margin, and scroll down to New Highs and New Lows and double click. What relationships do you see?
9. Go back to the left margin, and scroll down to Standard Dev. Channel and double click. Given the high and low lines defining the channel and the mean value between the two, what observations can you make about the market?
10. The point of this exercise was to expose you to the many ways technical analysts construct methods to analyze trends in the market. Since most academics believe in a less than efficient market system, don't expect your professor to believe in the power of all these methods or even be able to explain them since for the most part, most professors don't pay attention to technical analysis.

Problem 2

1. Log on to the McGraw-Hill website, **www.mhhe.com/edumarketinsight**
2. Click on Company, which is the first box below the Market Insight title.
3. Put the ticker symbol for Johnson & Johnson (JNJ) in the box, and click on go.
4. Scroll down the left margin, and click on "Charting by Prophet" listed in blue. Your first graph will cover 1 year.
5. Go to tools which is the last box on the top line, and click on the arrow. Go to studies and another box will come up. Click on the last item comparison chart. A box will come up with a list of indexes. Scroll down the list to the bottom, and highlight S&P 500. Click on "Add" next to the list and then close the box.
6. How does Johnson & Johnson compare with the S&P 500 over the last year?
7. Change the years to 5 years, and repeat the comparison.

8. Change the number of years to 10 years, and repeat the comparison.
9. If history is any indicator of how Johnson & Johnson will perform, based on the three charts, would you say that Johnson & Johnson is undervalued or overvalued?

The Wall Street Journal Projects

1. Section C of *The Wall Street Journal* carries the "Market Scorecard." In this section, the "Diaries" table gives data on advances and declines for NYSE, Nasdaq, and AMEX stocks. It also includes data for these markets on new highs and new lows, advancing volume and declining volume, and block trades.

   Use this data to create a table similar to Table 9–1 on page 254. For this assignment, use the advances and declines on the NYSE and also use the Dow Jones Industrial Average (DJIA). Track the pattern for 10 market days. Do you see any pattern evolving?

2. Find the graph in Section C of *The Wall Street Journal* similar to Figure 9–5 on page 245. Make a determination about the support and resistance level you see in the market.

Selected References

Technical Analysis

Benning, Carl J. "Prediction Skills of Real-World Market Timers." *The Journal of Portfolio Management,* Winter 1997, pp. 55–65.

Blume, Lawrence; David Easley; and Maureen O'Hara. "Market Statistics and Technical Analysis: The Role of Volume." *Journal of Finance,* March 1994, pp. 153–81.

DeMark, Thomas R. *The New Science of Technical Analysis.* New York: John Wiley & Sons, 1994.

Lo, Andrew W.; Harry Mamaysky; and Jiang Wang. "Fundamentals of Technical Analysis, Computational Algorithms, Statistical Inference, and Empirical Investigation." *Journal of Finance,* August 2000, pp. 1705–65.

Fundamental Analysis

Brennan, Michael J., and Patricia J. Hughes. "Stock Prices and the Supply of Information." *Journal of Finance,* December 1991, pp. 1665–91.

Mott, Claudia E., and Daniel P. Coker. "Earnings Surprise in the Small-Cap World." *Journal of Portfolio Management,* Fall 1993, pp. 64–93.

Efficient Markets

Constantinou, Constantina; William P. Forbes; and Len Skeratt. "Analyst Underreaction in the United Kingdom." *Financial Management,* Summer 2003, pp. 93–106.

Coy, Peter. "Investors Are Bullish All Over Again. It's Not Just Irrational Exuberance." *BusinessWeek,* December 20, 2003, pp. 76–77.

Fama, Eugene F. "Efficient Capital Markets: II." *Journal of Finance,* December 1991, pp. 1575–1617.

Hirschey, Mark, and Vernon J. Richardson. "Investor Underreaction to Goodwill Write-Offs." *Financial Analysts Journal,* November–December 2003, pp. 75–84.

Rubinstein, Mark. "Rational Markets: Yes or No? The Affirmative Case." *Financial Analysts Journal,* May–June 2001, pp. 15–28.

Saunders, Edward M. "Testing the Efficient Market Hypothesis without Assumptions." *Journal of Portfolio Management,* Summer 1994, pp. 28–30.

chapter ten

Investments in Special Situations and Anomalies

objectives

1. Understand the potential for abnormal returns in special investment situations.

2. Explain how abnormal returns might occur in mergers, new public issues, exchange listings, stock repurchases, and other investment opportunities.

3. Explain the controversy related to the small-firm and low-P/E ratio effects on stock market returns.

4. Be familiar with the latest theories about the relationship of book value to superior stock market returns.

5. Explain timing effects such as the January effect or the weekend effect on stock market returns.

6. Discuss the problem of distinguishing between superior returns and incorrect measurement of returns.

Mergers and Acquisitions
    Premiums for Acquired Company
    Acquiring Company Performance
    Form of Payment
New Stock Issues
    Performance of Investment Bankers
Exchange Listings
Stock Repurchase
    Reasons for Repurchase
    Actual Market Effect
The Small-Firm and Low-P/E-Ratio Effect
The Book Value to Market Value Effect
Other Stock-Related Anomalies
Truly Superior Returns or Mismeasurement?

In most instances, special or **abnormal returns** refer to gains beyond what the market would normally provide after adjustment for risk. This is also referred to as an **anomaly.** Transactions cost must also be covered to qualify as an anomaly. In this chapter, we explore such topics as market movements associated with mergers and acquisitions, the underpricing of new stock issues, the effect of an exchange listing on a stock's valuation, the stock market impact of a firm repurchasing its own shares, and the small-firm and low-P/E effects. Many qualify as anomalies. By identifying and understanding anomalies, the reader may be able to find opportunities for stock market gains.

Mergers and Acquisitions

Many stocks that were leaders in daily volume and price movement in the last decade represented firms that were merger candidates—that is, companies that were being acquired or anticipated being acquired by other firms. The stocks of these acquisition candidates often increased by 40–60 percent or more over a relatively short period. The list of acquired companies includes such well-known names as Duracell, Turner Broadcasting, Chemical Bank, and Quaker Oats.

www.duracell.com
www.turner.com
www.quakeroats.com

Premiums for Acquired Company

The primary reason for the upward market movement in the value of the acquisition candidate is the high premium that is offered over current market value in a merger or acquisition. The **merger price premium** represents the difference between the offering price per share and the market price per share for the candidate (before the impact of the offer). For example, a firm that is selling for $25 per share may attract a purchase price of $37.50 per share. Quite naturally, the stock goes up in response to the offer and the anticipated consummation of the merger.

As expected, researchers have consistently found that there are abnormal returns for acquisition candidates.[1] A study has indicated the average premium paid in a recent time period was approximately 40 to 60 percent, and there was an associated upward price movement of a similar magnitude.[2] The premium was based on the difference between the price paid and the value of the acquisition candidate's stock *three months* before announcement of the merger. Some examples of premiums paid during the last decade are presented in Table 10–1.

The only problem from an investment viewpoint is that approximately two-thirds of the price gain related to large premiums occurs before public announcement. It is clear that people close to the situation are trading on information leaks. The highly prestigious investment banking house of Morgan Stanley was embarrassed by charges brought by the U.S. Attorney's Office that

www.morganstanley.com

---

[1] Gershon Mandelker, "Risk and Return: The Case of Merging Firms," *Journal of Financial Economics,* December 1974, pp. 303–35; Donald R. Kummer and J. Ronald Hoffmeister, "Valuation Consequences of Cash Tender Offers," *Journal of Finance,* May 1978, pp. 505–6; Peter Dodd, "Merger Proposals, Management Discretion and Stockholder Wealth," *Journal of Financial Economics,* December 1980, pp. 105–38; and Steven Kaplan, "The Effect of Management Buyouts on Operating Performance and Value," *Journal of Financial Economics,* October 1989, pp. 217–54.

[2] Henry Oppenheimer and Stanley Block, "An Examination of Premiums and Exchange Ratios Associated with Merger Activity during the 1975–78 Period" (Financial Management Association Meeting, 1980).

TABLE 10–1 Premiums Paid in Mergers and Acquisitions

Acquiring Firm	Acquired Firm	Price Paid for Acquired Company's Stock	Value of Acquired Firm Three Months before Announcement	Premium Paid (percent)
Roche	Syntex	$24.00	$15.25	57.38%
Beatrice Food Co.	Harmon International Inc.	35.25	20.00	76.25
Parker Pen Co.	Manpower, Inc.	15.20	11.50	32.18
Colt Industries	Menaso Manufacturing	26.60	15.00	77.33
PepsiCo, Inc.	Pizza Hut, Inc.	38.00	22.375	69.83
Walter Kidde & Co.	Victor Comptometer	11.75	7.375	59.32
Dana Corporation	Weatherford Co.	14.00	9.375	49.33
Allis Chalmers Corporation	American Air Filter	34.00	19.50	74.36
Time, Inc.	Inland Containers	35.00	20.75	68.67
J.P. Morgan Chase	Bank One	46.25	32.50	42.31

two of its former merger and acquisition specialists were conspiring to use privileged information on takeovers to make profits on secret trading accounts.[3]

Those who attempt to legitimately profit by investing in mergers and acquisitions can follow a number of routes. First, some investors try to identify merger candidates before public announcement to capture maximum profits. This is difficult. While researchers have attempted to identify financial and operating characteristics of acquisition candidates, the information is often contradictory and may even change over time.[4] In prior time periods, acquisition candidates were often firms with sluggish records of performance, whereas many of the recent acquirees are high-quality companies that have unusually good records of performance (e.g., Time Warner, Cellular Communications, Pillsbury, and Wachovia Bank Corp.).

www.time.com
www.pillsbury.com
www.wachovia.com

Some alert analysts keep a close eye on securities undergoing unusual volume or pricing patterns (this could be for any number of reasons). Other investors identify industries where companies are being quickly absorbed and attempt to guess which firm will be the next to be acquired. Prime examples of such industries in recent times were banking, telecommunications, pharmaceuticals, and energy.

While trying to guess an acquisition candidate before public announcement can be potentially profitable, it requires that an investor tie up large blocks of capital in betting on an event that may never come to pass. Others prefer to invest at the time of announcement of a merger or acquisition. A gain of the magnitude of 15 percent or more may still be available (over a few months' time period). Perhaps a stock that was $25 before any consideration of merger moves

---

[3] "Two Former Morgan Stanley Executives Accused of Plot Involving Takeover Data," *The Wall Street Journal,* February 4, 1981, p. 2.

[4] Robert J. Monroe and Michael A. Simkowitz, "Investment Characteristics of Conglomerate Targets: A Discriminant Analysis," *Southern Journal of Business,* November 1971, pp. 1–15; and Donald J. Stevens, "Financial Characteristics of Merger Firms: A Multivariate Analysis," *Journal of Financial and Quantitative Analysis,* March 1973, pp. 149–58.

TABLE 10–2 Stock Movement of Potential Acquirees in Canceled Mergers

Acquirer–Potential Acquiree	Preannouncement	One Day after Announcement	One Day after Cancellation
Mead Corporation–Occidental Petroleum	20⅜	33¼	23¼
Olin Corp.–Celanese	16	23¾	16¾
Chicago Rivet–MITE	20¾	28⅛	20¾

up to $33 on announcement. If the acquisition price is $37.50, there may still be a nice profit to be made. The only danger is that the announced merger may be called off, in which case the stock may sharply retreat in value. Examples of other price drops associated with merger cancellations are shown in Table 10–2.

The wise investor must carefully assess the likelihood of cancellation. Special attention must be given to such factors as the possibility of antitrust action, the attitude of the target company's management toward the merger, the possibility of unhappy stockholder's suits, and the likelihood of poor earnings reports or other negative events. In a reasonably efficient market environment, the potential price gain that exists at announcement may be well correlated with the likelihood of the merger being successfully consummated. That is to say, if it appears the merger is almost certain to go through, the stock may be up to $36.50 at announcement based on an anticipated purchase price of $37.50. If a serious question remains, the stock may only be at $32. When a merger becomes reasonably certain, arbitrageurs come in and attempt to lock in profits by buying the acquisition candidate at a small spread from the purchase price.

One of the most interesting features of the latest merger movement was the heavy incidence of **unfriendly takeovers,** that is, the bidding of one company for another against its will. Such events often lead to the appearance of a third company on the scene, referred to as a **white knight,** whose function is to save the target company by buying it out, thus thwarting the undesired suitor. The new suitor is generally deemed to be friendly to the interests of the target company and may be invited by it to partake in the process. Examples of white knights occurred when Gulf Oil thwarted an offer from Mesa Petroleum and joined with Standard Oil of California (renamed Chevron). Similarly, Marathon Oil rejected an offer from Mobil to merge with U.S. Steel.

www.chevron.com
www.ussteel.com

As one might guess, these multiple-suitor bidding wars often lead to unusually attractive offers. A 40 to 60 percent premium may ultimately parlay into an 80 to 100 percent gain or more. For example, the bidding for Gulf Oil sent the stock from 38 to 80.

Acquiring Company Performance

What about the acquiring company's stock in the merger and acquisition process? Is this a special situation; that is, does this stock also show abnormal market gains associated with the event? A study by Mandelker indicated that it did not.[5] Long-term economic studies indicate that many of the anticipated re-

---

[5] Mandelker, "Risk and Return," pp. 303–35. Also see Anup Agrawal, Jeffrey F. Jaffe, and Gershon Mandelker, "The Post-Merger Performance of Acquiring Firms," *Journal of Finance*, September 22, 1992, pp. 1605–21.

sults from mergers may be difficult to achieve.[6] There is often an initial feeling of optimism that is not borne out in reality. The **synergy,** or "2 + 2 = 5," effect associated with broadening product lines or eliminating overlapping functions may be offset by the inability of management to mesh divergent philosophies. Sometimes, there is also a fear that a too high a price may have been paid.

A good example of the reaction to a merger announcement for the acquiring company was presented in October 2003 when Bank of America announced it was going to acquire Fleet Boston Financial. On the day of the announcement of the merger, Bank of America shares fell by 10 percent from $82 per share to $73.80. Analysts claimed the banking giant was paying too high a price for the Northeast bank holding company (the premium was approximately 40 percent over the then current market value of Fleet). Bank of America tried to explain the merger to investors on the premise that it would give Bank of America even greater power as a retail banker and a foothold in the lucrative Northeast. At least initially, investors weren't convinced. Of course, the shareholders in Fleet Boston Financial were quite pleased as their stock climbed from $31.80 to $39.20 on the day of the announced merger (a gain of approximately 23 percent).

Form of Payment

Another consideration in a merger is the form of payment. Cash offers usually carry a slightly higher premium than stock offers because of the immediate tax consequences to the acquired firm's shareholders. When stock is offered, the tax obligation may be deferred by the acquired company's stockholders until the stock of the acquiring firm is actually sold. This may occur relatively soon or many years in the future.

While cash was the popular medium of payment a decade or two ago, this is no longer the case. Acquiring firms have shown a strong preference for trading their shares for that of the merger candidate.[7] Example of recent mergers in which stock-for-stock trades took place include the Gillette acquisition of Duracell and the J. P. Morgan-Chase Manhattan merger.

New Stock Issues

Another form of a special situation is the initial issuance of stock by a corporation. There is a belief in the investment community that securities may be underpriced when they are issued to the public for the first time. That is to say, when a company **goes public** by selling formerly privately held shares to new investors in an initial public offering, the price may not fully reflect the value of the security.

Why does this so-called underpricing occur, and what is the significance to the investor? The underpricing may be the result of the investment banker's firm

---

[6] T. Hogarty, "The Profitability of Corporate Managers," *Journal of Business,* July 1970, pp. 317–27. For a contrary opinion, see Paul M. Healy, Krisha G. Paleps, and Richard S. Ruback, "Does Corporate Performance Improve after Mergers?" *Journal of Financial Economics,* April 1992, pp. 132–65.

[7] For further justification of type of payment, see Kenneth J. Martin, "The Method of Payment in Corporate Acquisitions, Investment Opportunities and Management Ownership," *Journal of Finance,* September 1996, pp. 1227–46.

commitment to buy the shares when distributing the issue. That is, the investment banker normally agrees to buy the stock from Company A at a set price and then resells it to the public (along with other investment bankers, dealers, and brokers). The investment banker must be certain the issue will be fully subscribed to at the initial public market price or the banker (and others) will absorb losses or build up unwanted inventory. To protect his position, the investment banker may underprice the issue by 5 to 10 percent to ensure adequate demand.

Studies by Miller and Reilly;[8] Ibbotson, Sindelar, and Ritter;[9] Muscarella and Vetsuypens;[10] and others have indicated positive **excess returns** are related to the issue of the stock. Miller and Reilly, for example, observed positive excess returns of 9.9 percent one week after issue. However, the efficiency of the market comes into play after the stock is actively trading on a regular basis, and any excess returns begin to quickly disappear. Excess returns represent gains above the market averages after adjusting for the relative risk of the investment. The lesson to be learned is that, on average, the best time to buy a new, unseasoned issue is on initial distribution from the underwriting syndicate (investment bankers, dealers, brokers), and the best time to sell is shortly after. These new issues may actually underperform the market over the long term.[11]

The point has been strongly made by recent research by Barry and Jennings.[12] They calculated positive excess returns of 8.69 percent on the first date of trading for new issues but discovered that 90 percent of that gain occurred on the opening transaction.

Participating in the distribution of a new issue is not always as easy as it sounds. A really hot new issue may be initially oversubscribed, and only good customers of a brokerage house may be allocated shares. Such was the case in the feverish atmosphere that surrounded the initial public trading of NexGen, Netscape, Microsoft, Apple Computer, and Genentech. Genentech actually went from $35 to $89 in the first 20 minutes of trading (only to quickly come back down). For the most part, customers with a regular brokerage account and a desire to participate in the new-issues market can find adequate opportunities for investment, though perhaps in less spectacular opportunities than those described above.

www.netscape.com
www.microsoft.com
www.applecomputer.com
www.genentech.com

Performance of Investment Bankers

Research studies indicate that large, prestigious investment banking houses do not generally provide the highest initial returns to investors in the new issues

---

[8] Robert E. Miller and Frank K. Reilly, "An Examination of Mispricing Returns, and Uncertainty for Initial Public Offerings," *Financial Management*, Winter 1987, pp. 33–38.

[9] Roger G. Ibbotson, J. Sindelar, and Jay R. Ritter, "Initial Public Offerings," *Journal of Applied Corporate Finance*, Fall 1988, pp. 37–45.

[10] Chris Muscarella and Mike Vetsuypens, "A Simple Test of *Barron's* Model of IPO Underpricing," *Journal of Financial Economics*, September 1989, pp. 125–35.

[11] Jay Ritter, "The Long-Term Performance of Initial Public Offerings," *Journal of Finance*, March 1991, pp. 3–27.

[12] Christopher B. Barry and Robert H. Jennings, "The Opening Performance of Initial Offerings of Common Stock," *Financial Management*, Spring 1993, pp. 54–63.

they underwrite.[13] The reason for this is that the upper-tier investment bankers tend to underwrite the issues of the strongest firms coming into the market. Less uncertainty is associated with these strong firms.[14] These firms generally shop around among the many investment bankers interested in their business and eventually negotiate terms that would allow for very little underpricing when they reach the market. (They want most of the benefits to go to the corporation, not to the initial stockholders.)

Exchange Listings

A special situation of some interest to investors is an **exchange listing,** in which a firm trading over-the-counter now lists its shares on an exchange (such as the American or New York Stock Exchange). Another version of a listing is for a firm to step up from an American Stock Exchange listing to a New York Stock Exchange listing.

An exchange listing may generate interest in a security (particularly when a company moves from the over-the-counter market to an organized exchange). The issue will now be assigned a specialist who has responsibility for maintaining a continuous and orderly market.[15] An exchange listing may also make the issue more acceptable for margin trading and short selling. Large institutional investors and foreign investors may also consider a listed security more appropriate for inclusion in their portfolios.

Listed firms must meet certain size and performance criteria provided in Table 10–3 (and previously mentioned in Chapter 2 for the NYSE). Although the criteria are not highly restrictive, meeting these standards may still signal a favorable message to investors.

A number of research studies have examined the stock market impact of exchange listings. As might be expected, a strong upward movement is associated with securities that are to be listed, but there is also a strong sell-off after the event has occurred. Research by Van Horne,[16] Fabozzi,[17] and others[18] indicates

---

[13] Brian M. Neuberger and Carl T. Hammond, "A Study of Underwriters' Experience with Unseasoned New Issues," *Journal of Financial and Quantitative Analysis,* March 1974, pp. 165–74. Also, see Dennis E. Logue, "On the Pricing of Unseasoned New Issues, 1965–1969," *Journal of Financial and Quantitative Analysis,* January 1973, pp. 91–103; and Brian M. Neuberger and Chris A. La Chapelle, "Unseasoned New Issue Price Performance on Three Tiers: 1976–1980," *Financial Management,* Autumn 1983, pp. 23–28.

[14] Richard Carter and Steven Manaster, "Initial Public Offerings and Underwriter Reputation," *Journal of Finance,* September 1990, pp. 1045–67.

[15] This is not always a superior arrangement to having multiple market makers in the over-the-counter market. It depends on how dedicated the specialist is to maintaining the market. Some banks and smaller industrial firms may choose the competitive dealer system in the over-the-counter market in preference to the assigned specialist. For a truly extensive overview of research on stock listings, see H. Kent Baker and Sue E. Meeks, "Research on Exchange Listings and Delistings: A Review and Synthesis," *Financial Practice and Education,* Spring 1991, pp. 57–71.

[16] James C. Van Horne, "New Listings and Their Price Behavior," *Journal of Finance,* September 1970, pp. 783–94.

[17] Frank J. Fabozzi, "Does Listing on the AMEX Increase the Value of Equity?" *Financial Management,* Spring 1981, pp. 43–50.

[18] Richard W. Furst, "Does Listing Increase the Market Value of Common Stock?" *Journal of Business,* April 1970, pp. 174–80; and Waldemar M. Goulet, "Price Changes, Managerial Accounting and Insider Trading at the Time of Listing," *Financial Management,* Spring 1974, pp. 303–6.

www.nyse.com

TABLE 10–3 Minimum Requirements for NYSE* Listing

Round-lot holders (number of holders of a unit of trading—generally 100 shares)	2,000 U.S.
or:	
Total shareholders	2,200
. . . together with:	
Average Monthly Trading Volume (for the most recent six months)	100,000 shares
or:	
Total shareholders	500
. . . together with:	
Average Monthly Trading Volume (for the most recent 12 months)	1,000,000 shares
Public shares	1,100,000 outstanding
Market value of public shares	
Public companies	$100,000,000
IPOs, spin-offs, carve-outs	$60,000,000
Minimum Quantitative Standards: Financial Criteria	
Earnings	
Aggregate pretax earnings (D) over the last three years	$10,000,000
Minimum in each of the two most recent years (must be positive amount in the third year)	$2,000,000
or:	
Valuation with Cash Flow	
For companies with not less than $500 million in global market capitalization and $200 million in revenues in the last 12 months:	
Aggregate for the three years operating cash flow (each year must report a positive amount)	$25,000,000
Global Market Capitalization	
Revenues for the last fiscal year	$75,000,000
Average global market capitalization	$750,000,000
REITs (less than 3 years operating history) stockholders' equity	$60,000,000
Funds (less than 3 years operating history) Net assets	$60,000,000

*www.nyse.com.

that the total effect may be neutral. Research by Ying, Lewellen, Schlarbaum, and Lease (YLSL) would tend to indicate an overall gain.[19]

The really significant factor is that regardless of whether a stock has a higher net value a few months after listing as opposed to a few months before listing, there still may be profits to be made. This would be true if the investor simply bought the stock four to six weeks before listing and sold it on listing. Because an application approval for listing is published in the weekly bulletin of the New York Stock Exchange well before the actual date of listing, a profit is often possible. The study by YLSL, cited above, indicates there may be an opportunity for abnormal returns on a risk-adjusted basis in the many weeks between

---

[19] Louis K. W. Ying, Wilbur G. Lewellen, Gary G. Schlarbaum, and Ronald C. Lease, "Stock Exchange Listing and Securities Returns," *Journal of Financial and Quantitative Analysis,* September 1977, pp. 415–32.

announcement of listing and actual listing (between 4.40 and 16.26 percent over normal market returns, depending on the time period). In this case, YLSL actually reject the semistrong form of the efficient market hypothesis by suggesting there are substantial profits to be made even after announcement of a new listing. The wise investor may wish to sell on the eventual date of listing because sometimes a loss in value may occur at that point.

The reader should also be aware of the potential impact of delisting on a security, that is, the formal removal from a New York Stock Exchange or American Stock Exchange listing, and a resumption of trading over-the-counter. This may occur because the firm has fallen substantially below the requirements of the exchange. As you would expect, this has a large negative effect on the security. Merjos found that 48 of the 50 firms in her study declined between the last day of trading on an exchange and the resumption of trading over-the-counter.[20] The average decline was 17 percent. While the value was not risk adjusted, it is large enough to indicate the clear significance of the event. Other studies have found similar results.[21]

Stock Repurchase

The **repurchase** by a firm of its own shares provides for an interesting special situation. The purchase tends to increase the demand for the shares while decreasing the effective supply. Before we examine the stock market effects of a repurchase, we briefly examine the reasons behind the corporate decision.

Reasons for Repurchase

In some cases, management believes the stock is undervalued in the market. Prior research studies indicated that repurchased securities generally underperformed the popular market averages before announcement of repurchase.[22] Thus, management or the board of directors may perceive this to be an excellent opportunity because of depressed prices. Others, however, might see the repurchase as a sign that management is not creative or that it lacks investment opportunities for the normal redeployment of capital.[23] Past empirical studies indicated that firms that engage in repurchase transactions often have lower sales and earnings growth and lower return on net worth than other, comparable firms.[24] However, in the bull market of the 1990s, many of the firms repurchasing their own shares were among the strongest and most respected on Wall Street. Examples include Exxon, GE, IBM, Merck, and Monsanto.

Actual Market Effect

From the viewpoint of an anomaly, the key question is, What is the stock market impact of the repurchase? Is there money to be made here or not? Much of

---

[20] Anna Merjos, "Stricken Securities," *Barron's,* March 4, 1963, p. 9.

[21] Gary C. Sanger and James D. Paterson, "An Empirical Analysis of Common Stock Delistings," *Journal of Financial and Quantitative Analysis,* June 1990, pp. 261–72.

[22] Richard Norgaard and Connie Norgaard, "A Critical Evaluation of Share Repurchase," *Financial Management,* Spring 1974, pp. 44–50; and Larry Y. Dann, "Common Stock Repurchases: An Analysis of Returns to Bondholders and Stockholders," *Journal of Financial Economics,* June 1981, pp. 113–38.

[23] Charles D. Ellis and Allen E. Young, *The Repurchase of Common Stock* (New York: The Ronald Press, 1971), p. 61.

[24] Norgaard and Norgaard, "A Critical Evaluation."

the real world of investing

Special Situation: Is Bad News Sometimes Good News for Investors?

Event	Reaction Dates	DJIA % Gain/ Loss During Reaction Dates[a]	DJIA Percentage Gain Days After Reaction Dates 22	63	126
Fall of France	05/09/1940–06/22/1940	(17.1)	(−0.5)	8.4	7.0
Pearl Harbor	12/06/1941–12/10/1941	(6.5)	3.8	(2.9)	(9.6)
Truman upset victory	11/02/1948–11/10/1948	(4.9)	1.6	3.5	1.9
Korean War	06/23/1950–07/13/1950	(12.0)	9.1	15.3	19.2
Eisenhower heart attack	09/23/1955–09/26/1955	(6.5)	0.0	6.6	11.7
Sputnik	10/03/1957–10/22/1957	(9.9)	5.5	6.7	7.2
Cuban missile crisis	08/23/1962–10/23/1962	(9.4)	15.1	21.3	28.7
JFK assassination	11/21/1963–11/22/1963	(2.9)	7.2	12.4	15.1
U.S. bombs Cambodia	04/29/1970–05/26/1970	(14.4)	9.9	20.3	20.7
Kent State shootings	05/04/1970–05/14/1970	(4.2)	0.4	3.8	13.5
Arab oil embargo	10/18/1973–12/05/1973	(17.9)	9.3	10.2	7.2
Nixon resigns	08/09/1974–08/29/1974	(15.5)	(7.9)	5.7	12.5
U.S.S.R. in Afghanistan	12/24/1979–01/03/1980	(2.2)	6.7	4.0	6.8
Hunt silver crisis	02/13/1980–03/27/1980	(15.9)	6.7	16.2	25.8
Falkland Islands war	04/01/1982–05/07/1982	4.3	(8.5)	(9.8)	20.8
U.S. invades Grenada	10/24/1983–11/07/1983	(2.7)	3.9	(2.8)	(3.2)
U.S. bombs Libya	04/15/1986–04/21/1986	2.6	(4.3)	(4.1)	(1.0)
Financial panic '87	10/02/1987–10/19/1987	(34.2)	11.5	11.4	15.0
Invasion of Panama	12/15/1989–12/20/1989	(1.9)	(2.7)	0.3	8.0
Gulf War ultimatum	12/24/1990–01/16/1991	(4.3)	17.0	19.8	18.7
Gorbachev coup	08/16/1991–08/19/1991	(2.4)	4.4	1.6	11.3
ERM U.K. currency crisis	09/14/1992–10/16/1992	(6.0)	0.6	3.2	9.2
World Trade Center bombing	02/26/1993–02/27/1993	(0.5)	2.4	5.1	8.5
Russia, Mexico, Orange County	10/11/1994–12/20/1994	(2.8)	2.7	8.4	20.7
Oklahoma City bombing	04/19/1995–04/20/1995	0.6	3.9	9.7	12.9
Asian stock market crisis	10/07/1997–10/27/1997	(12.4)	6.8	10.5	25.0
Russian LTCM crisis	08/18/1998–10/08/1998	(11.3)	15.1	24.7	33.7
Terrorist Attack– World Trade Center, Pentagon	09/11/2001–09/17/2001	(7.1)	5.7	6.1	10.5

[a] Losses are given in parentheses.

the earlier research said no.[25] A number of studies based on data from the 1970s and 1980s took a more positive viewpoint.[26] Recent research, published in 1995,

---

[25] A good example is Ellis and Young, *The Repurchase of Common Stock,* p. 156.

[26] Terry E. Dielman, Timothy J. Nantell, and Roger L. Wright, "Price Effects of Stock Repurchasing: A Random Coefficient Regression Approach," *Journal of Financial and Quantitative Analysis,* March 1980, pp. 175–89; Larry Y. Dann, "Common Stock Repurchases: An Analysis of Returns to Bondholders and Stockholders," *Journal of Financial Economics,* June 1981, pp. 113–38; Theo Vermaelen, "Common Stock Repurchases and Market Signaling: An Empirical Study," *Journal of Financial Economics,* June 1981, pp. 139–83; and R. W. Masulis, "Stock Repurchase by Tender Offer: An Analysis of the Causes of Common Stock Price Changes," *Journal of Finance,* May 1980, pp. 305–19.

by Ikenberry, Lakonishok, and Vermaelen (ILV) gives only a conditionally positive response.[27]

The researchers found that the immediate reaction to share repurchase announcements was only minimal. For the 1,239 repurchases included in the study, the average gain was only 3.5 percent. One reason for the small increase might be the skepticism with which share repurchases are often viewed. Approximately 90 percent of stock repurchases are announced as future intentions to make open market purchases rather than firm commitments (so-called tender offers). Many analysts are hesitant to accept the premise that there will be a follow-through. A 50 million share repurchase program might be announced, but only 15 million shares might actually be repurchased over time.

Nevertheless, in this latest study, the researchers did find large positive returns over a long period of time following a stock repurchase announcement, even though the initial reaction was muted. Over a four-year time period following the month of announcement, the stocks in the study had an average abnormal return of 12.1 percent (return over and above comparable firms with equal risk).

While there was undoubtedly skepticism about follow-through at time of announcement, the most important factor influencing future market performance was the type of stock involved in the repurchase. For value-oriented stocks with solid fundamentals, the average abnormal return was 45.3 percent over the four-year time horizon.[28] For high-flying "glamour stocks," the returns were neutral to slightly negative (in comparison to similar firms).

The predominant argument for the beneficial effects of the repurchase is that management knows what it is doing when it purchases its *own* shares. In effect, management is acting as an insider for the benefit of the corporation, and we previously observed in Chapter 9 that insiders tend to be correct in their investment decisions. This factor may provide positive investment results. Of course, these are merely average results over many transactions, and not all tender offers will prove to be beneficial events. The investor must carefully examine the number of shares to be repurchased, the reasons for repurchase, and the future impact on earnings and dividends per share.

The Small-Firm and Low-P/E-Ratio Effect

Two University of Chicago doctoral studies in the early 1980s contended that the true key to superior risk-adjusted rates of return rests with investing in firms with small **market capitalizations.** (Market capitalization refers to shares outstanding times stock price.) In a study of New York Stock Exchange firms, covering from 1936 to 1975, Banz indicates that the lowest quintile (bottom 20 percent) of firms in terms of market capitalization provide the highest returns even after adjusting for risk. Banz suggests, "On average, small NYSE firms have had significantly larger risk-adjusted returns than larger NYSE firms over a 40-year period."[29]

---

[27] David Ikenberry, Josef Lakonishok, and Theo Vermaelen, "Market Underreaction to Open Market Share Repurchases," *Journal of Financial Economics,* October 1995, pp. 181–208.

[28] The most important valuation measure used by Ikenberry, Lakonishok, and Vermaelen was book-to-market value, a topic covered in a later section of the chapter.

[29] Rolf W. Banz, "The Relationship between Returns and Market Value of Common Stocks," *Journal of Financial Economics,* March 1981, pp. 3–18.

Some criticized Banz for using only NYSE firms in his analysis and for using a time period that included the effects of both a depression and a major war. Small firms had incredibly high returns following the Depression. A similar type study, produced by Reinganum[30] at about the same time, overcame these criticisms. Reinganum examined 2,000 firms that were traded on the New York Stock Exchange or the American Stock Exchange between 1963 and 1980. He annually divided the 2,000 firms into 10 groupings based on size, with the smallest category representing less than $5 million in market capitalization and the largest grouping representing a billion dollars or more.

A synopsis of the results from the Reinganum study is presented in Table 10–4.

Column 2 indicates the median value of the market capitalization for the firms in each group. Column 3 is the median stock price for firms in each group, while column 4 indicates average annual return associated with that category.

As observed in column 4, the smallest capitalization group (MV 1) outperformed the largest capitalization group (MV 10) by more than 23 percentage points per year. Although not included in the table, in 14 out of the 18 years under study, the MV 1 group showed superior returns to the MV 10 group. In another similar analysis, Reinganum found that $1 invested in the smallest capitalization group would have grown to $46 between 1963 and 1980, while the same dollar invested in the largest capitalization group would have only grown to $4. As did Banz, Reinganum adjusted his returns for risk and continued to show superior risk-adjusted returns.

Such superior return evidence drew criticisms from different quarters. Roll suggested that small-capitalization studies underestimate the risk measure (beta)

TABLE 10–4 Synopsis of Results—Reinganum Study

(1) Grouping[a]	(2) Median Market Value (Capitalization, in millions)	(3) Median Share Price	(4) Average Annual Return
MV 1	$ 4.6	$ 5.24	32.77%
MV 2	10.8	9.52	23.51
MV 3	19.3	12.89	22.98
MV 4	30.7	16.19	20.24
MV 5	47.2	19.22	19.08
MV 6	74.2	22.59	18.30
MV 7	119.1	26.44	15.64
MV 8	209.1	30.83	14.24
MV 9	434.6	34.43	13.00
MV 10	1,102.6	44.94	9.47

[a] MV = Market value.

Source: Marc R. Reinganum, "Portfolio Strategies Based on Market Capitalization," *Journal of Portfolio Management,* Winter 1983, pp. 29–36.

---

[30] Marc R. Reinganum, "Misspecification of Capital Asset Pricing—Empirical Anomalies Based on Earnings Yield and Market Values," *Journal of Financial Economics,* March 1981, pp. 19–46. Also, "A Direct Test of Roll's Conjecture on the Firm Size Effect," *Journal of Finance,* March 1982, pp. 27–35; and "Portfolio Strategies Based on Market Capitalization," *Journal of Portfolio Management,* Winter 1983, pp. 29–36.

by failing to account for the infrequent and irregular trading patterns of stocks of smaller firms.[31] Stoll and Whaley maintained that transaction costs associated with dealing in smaller capitalization firms might severely cut into profit potential.[32] They indicated the average buy-sell spread on small-capitalized, low-priced stocks might be four or five times that of large-capitalization firms. Reinganum has maintained that even after accounting for these criticisms, small-capitalization firms continue to demonstrate superior risk-adjusted returns.[33]

Given that there might be advantages to investing in smaller firms, why haven't professional money managers picked up on the strategy? This, in part, is a catch-22. Part of the reason for the inefficiency in this segment of the market that allows for superior returns is the absence of institutional traders. This absence means less information is generated on the smaller firms, and the information that is generated is reacted to in a less immediate fashion. Studies suggest an important linkage between the absence of organized information and superior return potential.[34]

Advocates of the small-firm effect argue that it is this phenomenon alone, rather than others, such as the low-P/E-ratio effect, that leads to superior risk-adjusted returns. Peavy and Goodman argued that the low-P/E-ratio effect is also important.[35] In following up on the earlier work of Basu[36] on the importance of P/E ratios, they compensated for other factors that may have resulted in superior returns, such as the small size of the firm, the infrequent trading of stock, and the overall performance of an industry. They did this by using firms that had a market capitalization of at least $100 million, that had an active monthly trading volume of at least 250,000 shares, and that were in the same industry. Thus, none of these factors was allowed to be an intervening variable in the relationship between returns and the level of P/E ratios.

After following these parameters, Peavy and Goodman showed a significant relationship between the firm's P/E ratios and risk-adjusted returns. Firms were broken down into quintiles based on the size of their P/E ratios. Quintile 1 contained firms with the lowest P/E ratios, quintile 2 had the next lowest P/E ratios, and so on up the scale. A portion of their results is presented in Table 10–5 on the next page.

Note that lower P/E stocks have higher risk-adjusted returns. While Table 10–5 shows data only for the electronics industry, a similar pattern was found for other industries.

In summarizing this section, some researchers such as Banz and Reinganum argue that small size is the primary variable leading to superior returns, while others argue that it is the low-P/E-ratio effect.

---

[31] Richard Roll, "A Possible Explanation of the Small Firm Effect," *Journal of Finance,* September 1981, pp. 879–88.

[32] H. A. Stoll and R. E. Whaley, "Transaction Costs and the Small Firm Effect," *Journal of Financial Economics,* March 1985, pp. 121–43.

[33] Reinganum, "Misspecification of Capital Asset Pricing," pp. 19–46.

[34] Avner Arbel and Paul Strebel, "Pay Attention to Neglected Firms," *Journal of Portfolio Management,* Winter 1983, pp. 37–42.

[35] John W. Peavy III and David A. Goodman, "The Significance of P/Es for Portfolio Returns," *Journal of Portfolio Management,* Winter 1983, pp. 43–47.

[36] S. Basu, "Investment Performance of Common Stocks in Relation to Their Price-Earnings Ratios: A Test of the Efficient Market Hypothesis," *Journal of Finance,* June 1977, pp. 663–82.

TABLE 10–5 P/E Ratios and Performance: The Electronics Industry (1970–1980)

Quintile	Average P/E	Average Quarterly Return (risk-adjusted)	Average Beta
1	7.1	8.53	1.15
2	10.3	4.71	1.12
3	13.4	4.34	1.13
4	17.4	2.53	1.19
5	25.5	1.86	1.29

Source: John W. Peavy III and David A. Goodman, "The Significance of P/Es for Portfolio Returns," *Journal of Portfolio Management,* Winter 1983, pp. 43–47.

The Book Value to Market Value Effect

Just to make sure that finance professors and their students do not sleep too soundly at night, we have another theory to explain why certain stocks outperform the market. Professors Fama and French maintain that the ratio of book value to market value and size are more important than P/E ratios, leverage, or other variables in explaining stock market performance. Since we've already discussed size, let's concentrate on book value to market value. The Fama-French study says that the higher the ratio of book value to market value (lower the ratio of market value to book value) the higher the potential return on the stock.[37]

This conclusion is somewhat surprising to students who have been taught that book value, which is based on historical cost rather than current replacement value, is not an important variable. The newer logic is that stocks that have a book value that approaches market value are more likely to be undervalued than stocks that have book values that are perhaps only 20 percent of market value. The latter figure implies that the stock is trading at five times its book value (or net worth) as shown on the corporate books:

$$\frac{\text{Book value}}{\text{Market value}} \leftrightarrow \frac{\text{Market value}}{\text{Book value}}$$
$$0.20 \leftrightarrow 5\times$$

The high ratio of 5× means the company may be due for a correction as opposed to a stock that is trading at very close to book value.

With this third theory in mind, the investor may wish to keep his or her eye on stocks that meet some or all of the attributes previously discussed, that is, small size, low P/E ratios, and a high book-to-market value ratio.

---

[37] Eugene F. Fama and Kenneth R. French, "The Cross Section of Stock Returns," *Journal of Finance,* June 1992, pp. 427–65. The Fama and French study dealt with nonfinancial firms. A similar study with financial firms produced the same type of results. See Brad M. Barber and John D. Lyon, "Firm Size, Book-to-Market Ratio, and Security Returns: A Holdout Sample of Financial Firms," *Journal of Finance,* June 1997, pp. 875–83.

Other Stock-Related Anomalies

Although the authors have attempted to highlight the major special situations related to stocks in the preceding pages, there are other opportunities as well. While only brief mention will be made in this section, the student may choose to follow up the footnoted references for additional information.

The January Effect Because stockholders may sell off their losers in late December to establish tax losses, these stocks are often depressed in value in early January and may represent bargains and an opportunity for high returns.[38] In fact, the January effect and the potential for high returns has attracted so much attention that it often is used as a variable to explain other phenomena as well as itself. For example, Keim has found that roughly half the small-firm effect for the year occurs in January.[39] Actually, as more and more investors begin anticipating and playing the January effect, it has moved up in time (everyone wants to be the first one to arrive). Part of the January effect may be viewed in December now.

The Weekend Effect Research evidence indicates that stocks tend to peak in value on Friday and generally decline in value on Monday. Thus, the theory is that the time to buy is on late Monday and the time to sell is on late Friday. While over many decades this observation is valid,[40] generally the price movement is too small to profitably cover transaction costs. However, if you *know* you are going to sell a stock that you have held for a long time, you may prefer to do so later in the week rather than early in the week.

The Value Line Ranking Effect

> **Application Example**
>
> www.valueline.com

The *Value Line Investment Survey* contains information on approximately 1,700 stocks. Using a valuation model, each company is rated from 1 through 5 for profitable market performance over the next 12 months. One is the highest possible rating, and 5 is the lowest. One hundred stocks are always in category 1. Researchers have generally indicated that category 1 stocks provide superior risk-adjusted returns over the other four categories and the market in general.[41] Of course, frequent trading may rapidly cut into these profits. Table 10–6 on the next page presents the strong performance of the Value Line Group 1 category compared with the other four categories.

---

[38] Ben Branch and J. Ryan, "Tax-Loss Trading: An Inefficiency Too Large to Ignore," *Financial Review,* Winter 1980, pp. 20–29.

[39] Donald B. Keim, "Size-Related Anomalies and Stock Return Seasonality," *Journal of Financial Economics,* March 1983, pp. 13–32. Also see Richard Roll, "Vas ist das? The Turn of the Year Effect and the Return Premium of Small Firms," *Journal of Portfolio Management,* Winter 1983, pp. 18–28.

[40] Frank Cross, "The Behavior of Stock Prices on Fridays and Mondays," *Financial Analysts Journal,* November–December 1973, pp. 67–69; Kenneth R. French, "Stock Returns and the Weekend Effect," *Journal of Financial Economics,* March 1980, pp. 55–69; and Lawrence Harris, "A Transaction Data Study of Weekly and Interdaily Patterns in Stock Returns," *Journal of Financial Economics,* May 1986, pp. 99–117.

[41] Fisher Black, "*Yes,* Virginia, There Is Hope: Test of the Value Line Ranking System," *Financial Analysts Journal,* September–October 1973, pp. 10–14; Clark Holloway, "A Note on Testing an Aggressive Strategy Using Value Line Ranks," *Journal of Finance,* June 1981, pp. 711–19; and Scott E. Stickel, "The Effect of *Value Line Investment Survey* Rank Changes on Common Stock Prices," *Journal of Financial Economics,* March 1985, pp. 121–43.

TABLE 10-6 Performance of Value Line Groups

Record of Value Line Rankings for Timeliness (allowing for changes in rank each week)

Group	'65	'66	'67	'68	'69	'70	'71	'72	'73	'74	'75	'76	'77	'78	'79	'80	'81	'82	'83	'84
1	28.8%	−5.5%	53.4%	37.1%	−10.4%	7.3%	30.6%	12.6%	−19.1%	−11.1%	75.6%	54.0%	26.6%	32.6%	54.7%	52.6%	13.6%	50.6%	40.9%	−2.1%
2	18.5	−6.2	36.1	26.9	−17.5	−3.2	13.7	7.4	−28.9	−29.5	47.4	31.2	13.4	18.3	38.0	35.6	1.8	31.0	19.1	−0.8
3	6.7	−13.9	27.1	24.0	−23.8	−8.0	9.3	3.5	−33.6	−34.1	40.7	29.0	1.3	3.0	20.7	15.4	−3.3	17.9	20.2	−5.6
4	−0.4	−15.7	23.8	20.9	−33.3	−16.3	8.4	−7.1	−37.9	−40.6	39.3	28.8	−6.9	−3.8	12.8	7.4	−8.7	5.1	25.0	−17.4
5	−3.2	−18.2	21.5	11.8	−44.9	−23.3	−5.5	−13.4	−43.8	−55.7	−40.9	26.7	−17.6	−3.2	10.4	2.9	−21.4	−10.9	19.0	−31.0

Group	'85	'86	'87	'88	'89	'90	'91	'92	'93	'94	'95	'96	'97	'98	'99	'00	'01	'02	'03	'65 to 2003
1	47.0%	22.9%	5.4%	9.5%	27.9%	−10.4%	55.4%	10.0%	13.4%	−2.6%	22.8%	20.4%	11.3%	8.2%	24.1%	−10.4%	−20.3%	−27.2%	33.8%	45,605%
2	30.7	14.4	−2.4	20.4	26.5	−10.2	34.1	14.3	12.4	−2.2	28.1	19.0	24.0	0.1	−0.5	−4.4	−3.8	−28.8	38.2	4,020
3	22.8	7.7	−12.6	16.1	13.7	−24.4	18.9	11.0	9.8	−6.9	16.6	12.3	21.5	−3.9	−3.3	−3.2	−0.8	−27.1	38.2	284
4	11.4	−6.8	−15.8	17.6	2.6	−33.7	16.7	6.2	8.5	−9.9	17.1	7.1	14.5	−11.0	−7.5	−3.7	5.9	−26.7	34.2	−50
5	−5.6	−19.6	−28.0	11.4	−19.2	−45.5	25.5	15.4	0.3	−15.2	5.2	7.5	16.6	−11.5	−1.3	−19.7	−7.2	−15.7	52.2	−97

Source: *Value Line Selection and Opinion*, January 23, 2004. Copyright by Value Line Publishing, Inc.

the real world of investing

Special Situation: Would Jesse James Have Been a Momentum Play?

Martha Stewart was found guilty of lying to the SEC and federal investigators in her March 2004 trial. As you might recall, she sold her ImClone stock based on a tip from her Merrill Lynch broker that the company's founder, Sam Waksal, was selling his stock because the firm was not going to get FDA approval for its new blockbuster drug. All this transpired before public announcement of the negative news of the FDA decision. Not only did Martha Stewart personally suffer, but her public company, Martha Stewart Living Omnimedia, lost hundreds of millions of dollars in market value. It seems Martha failed to follow a cardinal rule of business, "You need to know when to buy, when to sell, and when to bake."

But you should not necessarily be down on all executives or companies that are under federal investigation. Just ask the fund managers at the Guardian Life Insurance Company who in 2003 created the "Feds Index." This is an index of the market performance of firms that are under investigation by the federal government (Feds) or the SEC, for possible wrongdoing.

In 2003, the equally weighted index consisted of such troubled firms as Tyco, HealthSouth, El Paso, Quest, Symbol Technologies, and Computer Associates. How did the index do in its first year? In a banner year for the S&P 500 Index (26.4 percent return), the Feds Index more than double that performance with a gain of 58.8 percent.

Many of the firms in the index had been battered down so badly they had nowhere to go but up. Take HealthSouth as an example. By March 2003, HealthSouth had lost 98 percent of its value. It was down to 8.5 cents per share. However, it registered a gain of 5,365 percent for the rest of the year to end up 9 percent ahead.* Other stocks in the index followed a similar pattern.

The question becomes, "Can the performance of the Feds Index be continued into the future?" The jury is still out, not only on the firms, but on the index as well.

*Bethany McLean, "When Bad Companies Go Up," *Fortune*, February 23, 2004, p. 156.

The Surprise-Earnings Effect As indicated in Chapter 9 in the discussion of efficient markets, accounting information tends to be quickly impounded in the value of a stock, and there appears to be little opportunity to garner superior returns from this data. Even if a firm reports a 20 percent increase in earnings, there is likely to be little market reaction to the announcement if the gain was generally anticipated. However, an exception to this rule may relate to truly *unexpected* earnings announcements.[42] If they are very positive, the stock may go up for a number of days after the announcement and thus provide a superior investment opportunity. The opposite would be true of a totally unexpected negative announcement.

The latter factor was particularly evident in the momentum market of the mid- to late 1990s. Stocks that had superior market performance, such as Microsoft, Intel, and Hewlett-Packard, were expected to produce ever-increasing earnings to justify their high valuation. If they did not, the punishment was swift and strong. For example, when Intel announced that its earnings would be below predictions for the second quarter of 1997, its stock dropped 25 points in the first hour of trading.

---

[42] Richard Rendleman, Charles Jones, and Henry A. Latane, "Empirical Anomalies Based on Unexpected Earnings and the Importance of Risk Adjustments," *Journal of Financial Economics*, November 1982, pp. 269–87.

Truly Superior Returns or Mismeasurement?

In our discussions in the previous chapter and in this chapter, we pointed out the possibility that high returns may be the result of a superior strategy in a less than efficient capital market or an anomaly. It also may be the result of mismeasurement thus showing that you got a superior risk-adjusted return when you did not. You simply misspecified the extent of the risk (beta) component or used the wrong model. If all risk-adjusted superior return studies were the result of misspecification, we could then once again assume the market is perfectly efficient.

The predominant view is that while there is some mismeasurement, many opportunities truly reflect market inefficiencies. There are "special situations" that if properly analyzed provide an opportunity for abnormally high risk-adjusted returns. The most literal and unbending interpretations of efficient markets no longer carry the weight they did two decades ago.[43]

---

[43] Eugene F. Fama, "Efficient Capital Markets: II," *Journal of Finance,* December 1991, pp. 1575–1617.

exploring the web

Website Address	Comments
cbs.marketwatch.com/tools/ipo	CBS's Marketwatch IPO Section
www.redherring.com	Provides free information on public offerings and links to related sites
www.thehfa.com	Website for the hedge fund association providing information about the industry
www.hedgefundcenter.com	Education site on hedge funds

Summary

In this chapter, we examined various forms of special situations and anomalies. Perhaps none has received more attention than the great wave of mergers and acquisitions of the last decade. Because of the premiums paid by the acquiring companies, there is substantial upward potential in the stocks of the acquired firms.

Next, we observe the price patterns of firms going public (selling their stock to the general public for the first time). There appear to be abnormal returns after issue, and then the efficiency of the market comes strongly into play.

Exchange listings may or may not provide higher values for the securities involved; the research is somewhat contradictory in this regard. However, the interesting feature suggested by the Ying, Lewellen, Schlarbaum, and Lease research is that there may be excess returns between the point of announcement and listing (regardless of whether there is a sell-off after listing). This is at variance with the semistrong form of the efficient market hypothesis.

There is also conflicting evidence on the impact of a firm's repurchase of its own shares in the marketplace.

Recent research, however, indicates that while there may not be an immediate positive effect, over the longer term the results are positive.

Studies of the small-firm effect indicate there may be superior return potential in investing in smaller capitalization firms. Others suggest it is the low P/E ratios or high book value to market value of many of these firms that leads to superior returns.

Finally, researchers have indicated some special opportunities for profits related to seasonality, unexpected earnings reports, and the Value Line ranking system.

Key Words and Concepts

abnormal returns 268
anomaly 268
excess returns 272
exchange listing 273
going public (initial public offering) 271
market capitalizations 277
merger price premium 268
repurchase 275
synergy 271
unfriendly takeovers 270
white knights 270

Discussion Questions

1. Define special or abnormal returns.
2. What is the basis for upward movement in the stock of an acquisition candidate?
3. What is an unfriendly takeover?
4. What is the primary danger in investing in merger and acquisition candidates?
5. What factor(s) determine the extent of upward price potential for an acquisition candidate at the time of a merger announcement?
6. Do the stocks of acquiring companies tend to show strong upward market movement as a result of the merger process? Comment on the reasoning behind your answer.
7. Why do cash tender offers frequently carry a higher premium than stock offers?
8. Why does abnormal return potential sometimes exist in the new-issues market?
9. What are some factors to consider before buying a new issue?
10. Why might firms that are underwritten by large, prestigious investment banking houses not necessarily provide the highest initial returns to investors in the new-issues market?
11. What are some reasons a firm may wish to have its security listed on an exchange?
12. What was the major finding of the Ying, Lewellen, Schlarbaum, and Lease study? How does this relate to the semistrong form of the efficient market hypothesis?
13. What are some reasons a firm may repurchase its own stock?
14. What is likely to be the immediate market reaction to the announcement of a share repurchase program? Does this change over the long term?
15. According to researchers such as Banz and Reinganum, what is the general performance of small firms relative to larger firms?
16. What does the term *market capitalization* mean?

17. What criticisms of the small-firm effect were offered by Roll, and Stoll and Whaley? Were these considered valid by Reinganum?
18. What problem does an institutional investor have when he or she tries to purchase shares of a small firm?
19. Advocates of the small-firm effect argue that it is this factor *alone* that leads to superior risk-adjusted returns. Does the Peavy and Goodman study support this position?
20. What does Table 10–5 on page 280 indicate about the relationship between a firm's P/E ratio and its average quarterly return?
21. What does the research by Fama and French indicate about the importance of the ratio of book value to market value? If a stock has a book value that is 20 percent of market value, is it thought to possibly be undervalued or overvalued (due for a correction)?
22. Why might the first week in January be a good time to purchase stocks that were losers in the prior year? What do we mean when we say the January effect may be moving up in time?
23. If a corporation has an anticipated large positive earnings report, is that a good time to buy? What if the positive report were unexpected?
24. What is meant by the statement that "mismeasurement or misspecification of risk could give the false appearance of superior returns"?

Web Exercise

IPOs (initial public offerings) were discussed in the chapter as having superior short-term performance. We will examine some recent IPOs. Go to **www.moneycentral.msn.com**.

1. Click on "Investing" near the top.
2. Then click on "Markets" near the top.
3. Click on "IPO Center" along the left margin.
4. Click on "View IPOs" near the top.
5. Then one at a time, click on the company name and write down the company name, the offer price, the first-day opening price, and the first-day closing price.
6. Write a one- or two-sentence description comparing the offer prices to the first-day closing prices. Is there a pattern present? Generally speaking, did those who bought in at the offer price come out ahead or behind?

Note: From time to time, companies redesign their websites, and occasionally a topic we have listed may have been deleted, updated, or moved into a different location. Most websites have a "site map" or "site index" listed on a different page. If you click on the site map or site index you will be introduced to a table of contents which should aid you in finding the topic you are looking for.

The Wall Street Journal Projects

Go to the "Lipper Indexes" in Section C of *The Wall Street Journal*. This can be found on the page that has the "Major Stock Indexes." It is shown under "Mutual Funds." Compare the change since December 31 of the "Small-Cap Value Funds" to the "Large-Cap Value Funds." Does the evidence tend to confirm or refute the small-firm effect?

Selected References

Market Inefficiency

Beebower, G. L., and A. P. Varikooty. "Measuring Market Timing Strategies." *Financial Analysts Journal,* November–December 1991, pp. 78–84.

Fama, Eugene F. "Efficient Capital Markets: II." *Journal of Finance,* December 1991, pp 1575–1617.

Mergers and Acquisitions

Agrawal, Anup; Jeffrey F. Jaffe; and Gershon Mandelker. "The Post-Merger Performance of Acquiring Firms." *Journal of Finance,* September 22, 1992, pp. 1605–21.

DeLong, Gayla L. "Does Long-Term Performance of Mergers Match Market Expectations? Evidence form the U.S. Banking Industry." *Financial Management,* Summer 2003, pp. 5–25.

Healy, Paul M.; Krisha G. Paleps; and Richard S. Ruback. "Does Corporate Performance Improve after Mergers?" *Journal of Financial Economics,* April 1992, pp. 132–65.

Martin, Kenneth J. "The Method of Payment in Corporate Acquisitions, Investment Opportunities, and Management Ownership." *Journal of Finance,* September 1996, pp. 1227–46.

New Stock Issues (Initial Public Offerings)

Baker, Malcomb, and Jeffrey Wurgler. "The Equity Share in New Issues and Aggregate Stock Returns." *Journal of Finance,* October 2000, pp. 2219–57.

Barry, Christopher B., and Robert H. Jennings. "The Opening Performance of Initial Offerings of Common Stock." *Financial Management,* Spring 1993, pp. 54–63.

Barry, Christopher B.; Chris J. Muscarella; and Michael R. Vetsuypens. "Underwriter Warrants, Underwriter Compensation and Cost of Going Public." *Journal of Financial Economics,* March 1991, pp. 113–35.

Carter, Richard, and Steven Manaster. "Initial Public Offering and Underwriter Reputation." *Journal of Finance,* September 1990, pp. 1045–67.

Corwin, Shane A., and Jeffrey H. Harris. "The Initial Listing Decisions of Firms That Go Public." *Financial Management,* Spring 2001, pp. 35–55.

Rajan, Raghuram, and Henri Servaes. "Analyst Following of Initial Public Offerings." *Journal of Finance,* June 1997, pp. 507–29.

Ritter, Jay. "The Long-Term Performance of Initial Public Offerings." *Journal of Finance,* March 1991, pp. 3–27.

Exchange Listings Effect

Sanger, Gary C., and James D. Peterson. "An Empirical Analysis of Common Stock Delistings." *Journal of Financial and Quantitative Analysis,* June 1990, pp. 261–72.

Stock Repurchases

Jagannathan, Murale, and Clifford Stephens. "Motives for Multiple Open-Market Repurchase Programs." *Financial Management,* Summer 2003, pp. 71–91.

The Value Line Effect

Stickel, Scott E. "The Effect of *Value Line Investment Survey* Rank Changes on Common Stock Prices." *Journal of Financial Economics,* March 1985, pp. 121–43.

The Earnings Effect

Brown, Lawrence D. "Earnings Surprise Research: Synthesis and Perspective." *Financial Analysts Journal,* March–April, 1997, pp. 13–19.

The January Effect

Eleling, Ashlea. "The January Effect." *Forbes,* January 12, 2004, p. 2000.

Fixed-Income and Leveraged Securities

part four

chapter 11
BOND AND FIXED-INCOME FUNDAMENTALS

chapter 12
PRINCIPLES OF BOND VALUATION AND INVESTMENT

chapter 13
DURATION AND REINVESTMENT CONCEPTS

chapter 14
CONVERTIBLE SECURITIES AND WARRANTS

tHERE ARE SEVERAL THINGS that make bonds an important asset class to individual investors as well as to the U.S. government and corporations. Government bonds set the minimum lending rates for all other forms of debt. As investors or borrowers move from risk-free government debt to risky forms of debt like corporate debt, they pay a higher rate of interest. The interest rate on corporate debt is dependent on the debt rating given to the individual bond by the rating agencies Moody's, Standard & Poor's, and Fitch, Duff & Phelps. A company with a triple A (AAA) rating from Standard and Poor's will pay the lowest interest rate, and as the rating moves down to AA, A, BBB, BB, and so on, the interest rate will rise. The financial statements of the company are very important in the analysis of bonds and stock for the determination of the company's risk.

There are a wide variety of generally accepted accounting principles that are used across industries and the very nature of these accounting statements is affected by the accounting methodology. The rating services use detailed ratio analysis, industry variables, the state of the economy, and the firm's competitive position as the major determining factors in assessing risk. As students you have all had accounting and should understand its use in finance. The Financial Accounting Standards Board plays a big role in how accounting statement are presented. Robert H. Herz, the current Chairman of FASB, has many issues on his agenda as the accounting industry deals with the aftermath of the accounting scandals of the early part of the decade. One very significant issue is how to account for employee stock options. Expensing the options reduces earnings immediately when the options are given and will have a significant effect on many high-tech companies that have used stock options as a form of compensation. FASB is a significant force in dealing with these issues.

Before becoming the Chairman of FASB in July 2002, Robert Herz was a senior partner with PricewaterhouseCoopers in charge of its North America Professional, Technical, Risk & Quality division.

Robert H. Herz
Photo provided by the FASB.

Robert Herz lived in Argentina and England during a portion of his childhood and earned a Bachelor of Arts degree in Economics from the University of Manchester in England. Mr. Herz is both a Certified Public Accountant (United States) and a Chartered Accountant (United Kingdom). Mr. Herz is widely regarded in the accounting profession and with 30 years in the accounting field has served as an audit partner for major clients in the financial services, telecommunications, and manufacturing industries.

Robert Herz has chaired the AICPA SEC Regulations Committee and the Transnational Auditors Committee of the International Federation of Accountants. He has served as a member of the Emerging Issues Task Force, the FASB Financial Instruments Task Force, the American Accounting Association's Financial Accounting Standards Committee, and the SEC Practice Section Executive Committee of the AICPA.

When Mr. Herz became Chairman of FASB, he gave up his board seat on the International Accounting Standards Board, but his international experience will come in handy as international accounting standards and U.S. accounting standards become more consistent in our global economy. One of the tasks at hand for the board is to achieve a consistent set of high quality international accounting standards. Another area of interest is the quarterly earnings games played by Wall Street. Mr. Herz coauthored a book called the *Value Reporting Revolution: Moving Beyond the Earnings Game.*

chapter eleven

Bond and Fixed-Income Fundamentals

objectives

1. Explain the fundamental characteristics of a bond issue.

2. Describe the differences among bonds offered by the U.S. government, state and local governments, and corporations.

3. Explain the difference between a private placement and public distribution of a bond.

4. Explain the meaning and impact of bond ratings.

5. Understand how to read bond quotes in the financial press.

6. Describe the characteristics of other forms of fixed-income securities such as preferred stock, money market funds, etc.

The Bond Contract
Secured and Unsecured Bonds
The Composition of the Bond Market
    U.S. Government Securities
    Federally Sponsored Credit Agency Issues
    State and Local Government Securities
    Corporate Securities
Bond Market Investors
Distribution Procedures
    Private Placement
Bond Ratings
    Actual Rating System
Junk Bonds or High-Yield Bonds
Bond Quotes
    Quotes on Government Securities
Bond Markets, Capital Market Theory, and Efficiency
The Global Bond Market
    Dollar-Denominated Bonds
    Foreign-Pay Bonds
Other Forms of Fixed-Income Securities
Preferred Stock as an Alternative to Debt
    Features of Preferred Stock

As the reader will observe in various sections of this chapter, bonds actually represent a more substantial portion of new offerings in the capital markets than common stock. Some of the most financially rewarding jobs on Wall Street go to sophisticated analysts and dealers in the bond market. If you are to be a player in this market, you must understand the terms and financial ramifications of bond trading.

In this chapter, we examine the fundamentals of the bond instrument for both corporate and government issuers, with an emphasis on the debt contract and security provisions. We also look at the overall structure of the bond market and the ways in which bonds are rated. The question of bond market efficiency is also considered. While most of the chapter deals with corporate and government bonds, other forms of fixed-income securities also receive attention. Thus, there is a brief discussion of short-term, fixed-income investments (such as certificates of deposit and commercial paper) as well as preferred stock.

In Chapter 12, we shift the emphasis to actually evaluating fixed-income investments and devising strategies that attempt to capture profitable opportunities in the market. In Chapter 13, we look at the interesting concept of *duration*. We begin our discussion by considering the key elements that go into a bond contract.

The Bond Contract

A bond normally represents a long-term contractual obligation of the firm to pay interest to the bondholder as well as the face value of the bond at maturity. The major provisions in a bond agreement are spelled out in the **bond indenture,** a complicated legal document often more than 100 pages long, administered by an independent trustee (usually a commercial bank). We shall examine some important terms and concepts associated with a bond issue.

The **par value** represents the face value of a bond. Most corporate bonds are traded in $1,000 units, while many federal, state, and local issues trade in units of $5,000 or $10,000.

Coupon rate refers to the actual interest rate on the bond, usually payable in semiannual installments. To the extent that interest rates in the market go above or below the coupon rate after the bond is issued, the market price of the bond will change from the par value. A bond initially issued at a rate of 8 percent will sell at a substantial discount from par value when 12 percent is the currently demanded rate of return. We will eventually examine how the investor makes and loses large amounts of money in the bond market with the swings in interest rates. A few corporate bonds are termed **variable-rate notes** or **floating-rate notes,** meaning the coupon rate is fixed for only a short period and then varies with a stipulated short-term rate such as the rate on U.S. Treasury bills. In this instance, the interest payment rather than the price of the bond varies up and down. In recent times, zero-coupon bonds have also been issued at values substantially below maturity value. With **zero-coupon bonds,** the investor receives return in the form of capital appreciation over the life of the bond since no semiannual cash interest payments are received.

The **maturity date** is the date on which final payment is due at the stipulated par value.

Methods of bond repayment can occur under many different arrangements. Some bonds are never paid off, such as selected **perpetual bonds** issued by the Canadian and British governments, and have no maturity dates. A more normal procedure would simply call for a single-sum lump payment at the end of the obligation. Thus, the issuer may make 40 semiannual interest payments over the next 20 years plus one lump-sum payment of the par value of the bond at maturity. There are also other significant means of repayment.

The first is the **serial payment** in which bonds are paid off in installments over the life of the issue. Each serial bond has its own predetermined date of maturity and receives interest only to that point. Although the total bond issue may span more than 20 years, 15 to 20 maturity dates are assigned. Municipal bonds are often issued on this basis. Second, there may be a **sinking-fund provision** in which semiannual or annual contributions are made by a corporation into a fund administered by a trustee for purposes of debt retirement. The trustee takes the proceeds and goes into the market to purchase bonds from willing sellers. If no sellers are available, a lottery system may be used to repurchase the required number of bonds from among outstanding bondholders.

Third, debt may also be retired under a call provision. A **call provision** allows the corporation to call or force in all of the debt issue prior to maturity. The corporation usually pays a 3 to 5 percent premium over par value as part of the call provision arrangement. The ability to call is often *deferred* for the first 5 or 10 years of an issue (it can only occur after this time period).

The opposite side of the coin for a bond investor is a put provision. The **put provision** enables the bondholder to have an option to sell a long-term bond back to the corporation at par value after a relatively short period (such as three to five years). This privilege can be particularly valuable if interest rates have gone up since the initial issuance and if the bond is currently trading at 75 to 80 percent of par. A put bond generally carries a lower interest rate than conventional bonds (perhaps 1 to 2 percent lower) because of this protective put privilege. If one buys a put bond and interest rates go down and bond prices up (perhaps to $1,200), the privilege is unnecessary and is merely ignored.

Secured and Unsecured Bonds

We have discussed some of the important features related to interest payments and retirement of outstanding issues. At least of equal importance is the nature of the security provision for the issue. Bond market participants have a long-standing practice of describing certain issues by the nature of asset claims in liquidation. In actuality, pledged assets are sold and the proceeds distributed to bondholders only infrequently. Typically, the defaulting corporation is reorganized, and existing claims are partially satisfied by issuing new securities to the participating parties. Of course, the stronger and *better secured* the initial claim, the higher the quality of the security to be received in a reorganization.

A number of terms are used to denote **secured debt,** that is, debt backed by collateral. Under a **mortgage** agreement, real property (plant and equipment) is pledged as security for a loan. A mortgage may be senior or junior in nature, with the former requiring satisfaction of claims before payment is given to the latter. Bondholders may also attach an **after-acquired property clause** requiring that any new property be placed under the original mortgage.

A very special form of a mortgage or collateralized debt instrument is the **equipment trust certificate** used by firms in the transportation industry (railroads, airlines, etc.). Proceeds from the sale of the certificate are used to purchase new equipment, and this new equipment serves as collateral for the trust certificate.

Not all bond issues are secured or collateralized by assets. Most federal, state, and local government issues are unsecured. A wide range of corporate issues also are unsecured. There is a set of terminology referring to these unsecured issues. A corporate debt issue that is unsecured is referred to as a **debenture.** Even though the debenture is not secured by a specific pledge of assets, there may be priorities of claims among debenture holders. Thus, there are senior debentures and junior or subordinated debentures.

If liquidation becomes necessary because all other avenues for survival have failed, secured creditors are paid off first out of the disposition of the secured assets. The proceeds from the sale of the balance of the assets are then distributed among unsecured creditors, with those holding a senior ranking being satisfied before those holding a subordinate position (subordinated debenture holders).[1]

Unsecured corporate debt may provide slightly higher yields because of the greater suggested risk. However, this is partially offset by the fact that many unsecured debt issuers have such strong financial statements that security pledges may not be necessary.

Companies with less favorable prospects may issue income bonds. **Income bonds** specify that interest is to be paid only to the extent that it is earned as current income. There is no legally binding requirement to pay interest on a regular basis, and failure to make interest payments cannot trigger bankruptcy proceedings. These issues appear to offer the corporation the unusual advantage of paying interest as a tax-deductible expense (as opposed to dividends) combined with freedom from the binding contractual obligation of most debt issues. But any initial enthusiasm for these issues is quickly reduced by recognizing that they have very limited appeal to investors. The issuance of income bonds is usually restricted to circumstances where new corporate debt is issued to old bondholders or preferred stockholders to avoid bankruptcy or where a troubled corporation is being reorganized.

The Composition of the Bond Market

Having established some of the basic terminology relating to the bond instrument, we are now in a position to take a more comprehensive look at the bond market. Corporate issues must vie with offerings from the U.S. Treasury, federally sponsored credit agencies, and state and local governments (municipal offerings). The relative importance of the four types of issues is indicated in Figure 11–1 on page 294.

Over the 24-year period presented in Figure 11–1, the two fastest growing users of funds (borrowers) were the U.S. government and corporations. The former's needs can be attributed to persistent federal deficits that must be financed by increased borrowing.

In the case of corporations, strong growth combined with the need to finance mergers and leveraged buyouts has led to increased borrowing requirements. State and local governments have been active participants with municipal bond issues used to finance local growth and cover local deficits. Finally, federally sponsored credit agencies must call on the long-term funds market. Please observe the explosive growth in long-term borrowing by all sectors of the economy since 1980.

U.S. Government Securities

U.S. government securities take the form of Treasury bills, Treasury notes, and Treasury bonds (only the latter two are considered in Figure 11–1). The

---

[1] Those secured creditors who are not fully satisfied by the disposition of secured assets may also participate with the unsecured creditors in the remaining assets.

294 Part 4 Fixed-Income and Leveraged Securities

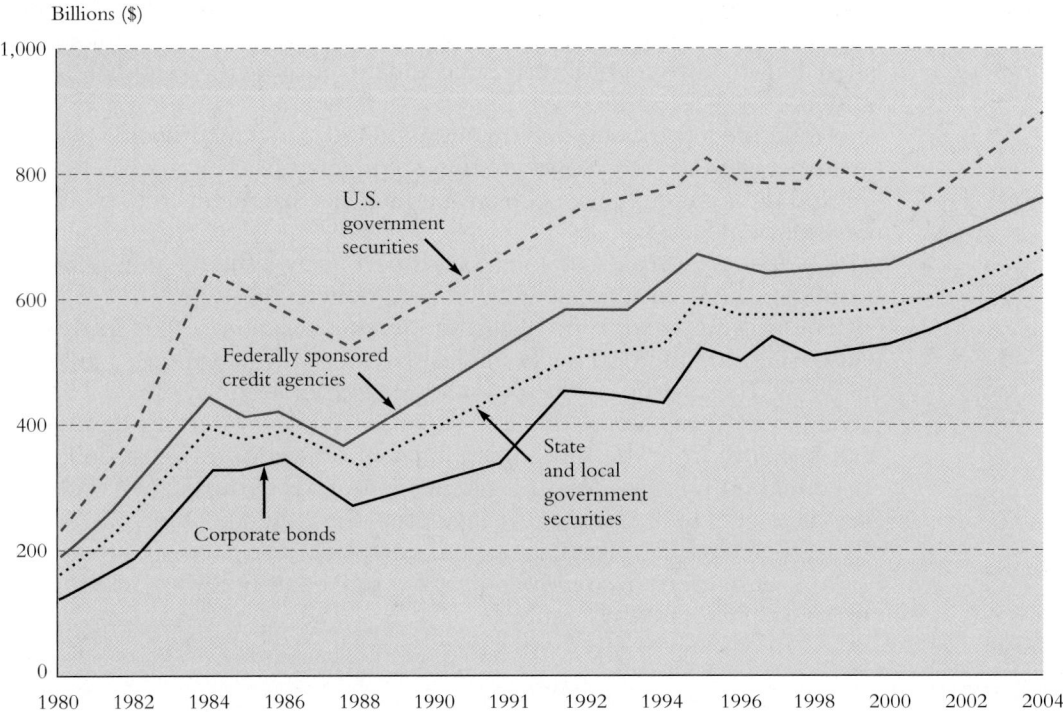

FIGURE 11–1 Long-Term Funds Raised by Business and Government

distinction among the three categories relates to the life of the obligation. A fourth category, termed Treasury strips, has other attributes and is also discussed.

Treasury bills (T-bills) have maturities of 91 and 182 days. Treasury bills trade on a discount basis, meaning the yield the investor receives occurs as a result of the difference between the price paid and the maturity value (and no actual interest is paid). A further discussion of this is presented later in the chapter.

Treasury bills trade in minimum units of $1,000, and there is an extremely active secondary, or resale, market for these securities. Thus, an investor buying a Treasury bill from the government with an initial life of approximately six months would have no difficulty selling it to another investor after two or three weeks. Because the T-bill now has a shorter time to run, its market value would be a bit closer to par.

A second type of U.S. government security is the **Treasury note,** which is considered to be of intermediate term and generally has a maturity of 1 to 10 years. Finally, **Treasury bonds** are long term in nature and mature in 10 to 30 years. Unlike Treasury bills, Treasury notes and bonds provide direct interest and trade in units of $1,000 and higher. Because there is no risk of default (unless the government stops printing money or the ultimate bomb explodes), U.S. government securities provide lower returns than other forms of credit obligations. Interest on U.S. government issues is fully taxable for IRS purposes but is exempt from state and local taxes.

Treasury securities may also trade in the form of **Treasury strips** (strip-T's). Treasury strips pay no interest, and all returns to the investor come in the form of increases in the value of the investment (as is true of Treasury bills also). Treasury strips are referred to as zero-coupon securities because of the absence of interest payments.

As an example, 25-year Treasury strips might initially sell for 19 percent of par value. You could buy a 25-year, $10,000 Treasury strip for $2,950.[2] All your return would come in the form of an increase in value. Of course, you could sell at the going market price before maturity should you so desire.

Actually the U.S. Treasury does not offer Treasury strips directly. It allows government security dealers to strip off the interest payments and principal payment from regular Treasury notes and bonds and repackage them as Treasury strips. For example, on a 25-year Treasury bond, there would be 50 semiannual interest payments and one final principal payment. Each of these 51 payments could be stripped off and sold as a zero-coupon strip.[3] Those who desired short-term Treasury strips would buy into the early payments. The opposite would be true for an investor with a long-term orientation.

The Internal Revenue Service taxes zero-coupon bonds, such as Treasury strips, as if interest were paid annually even though no cash flow is received until maturity. The tax is based on amortizing the built-in gain over the life of the instrument. For tax reasons, zero coupons are usually only appropriate for tax-deferred accounts such as individual retirement accounts, 401(k) plans, or other nontaxable pension funds.

Inflation-Indexed Treasury Securities In January 1997, the U.S. Treasury began offering 10-year notes that were intended to protect investors against the effects of inflation. The maturities were later expanded to include longer terms to maturity.

Here's how these inflation-indexed Treasury notes work. The investor receives two forms of return as a result of owning the security. The first is annual interest that is paid out semiannually, and the second is an automatic increase in the initial value of principal to account for inflation.

These securities are formally called **Treasury Inflation Protection Securities (TIPS).** TIPS might pay 3.5 percent in annual interest and, assuming a 3 percent rate of inflation, an additional 3 percent to compensate for inflation. As implied in the preceding paragraph, the 3 percent inflation adjustment is not paid in cash but is added on to the principal value of the bond. Assume the bond had an initial par value of $1,000. At the end of the first year, the principal value would go up to $1,030. Thus, during the first year, the investor would receive $35 (3.5 percent) in cash as interest payments, plus enjoy a $30 increase in principal. On a 10-year indexed Treasury security, this procedure continues for each of the remaining nine years and at maturity, the security is redeemed at the indexed value of the principal by the Treasury. If the investor needs to sell before the maturity date, he or she can sell it in the secondary market to other investors at a value approximating the appreciated principal value.[4]

---

[2] The yield is approximately 5 percent. Zero-coupon securities are also offered by corporations and are discussed more fully in Chapter 13.

[3] Any one payment, such as the first, may be stripped from many hundreds of Treasury bonds at one time to provide a $10,000 Treasury strip.

[4] Other factors can come into play in pricing this security, but they unnecessarily complicate this basic example.

the real world of investing

TIPS—Flood Insurance During a Drought?

Treasury Inflation Protection Securities (TIPS) are discussed in the main body of the chapter, so the basics will not be restated here. As the name implies, TIPS are a protection against the ravages of inflation, but absolutely no one was worried about inflation at the time they were introduced in January 1997. The years 1996–97 represented some of the lowest levels of inflation (about 2 percent) in the post–World War II period. As the title of this box implies, introducing TIPS at that point in time was like selling flood insurance to farmers who are suffering through a six-month rain drought.

It's unlikely that private sector investment bankers such as Goldman Sachs or C.S. First Boston would have come out with a similar product at such an inopportune time, but keep in mind we are talking about the federal government. In fairness, it should also be pointed out that the majority of TIPS have an initial 10-year life, so even though there is no immediate threat of inflation, they could well prove to be important during the time period they are outstanding.

Furthermore, those who advocate the purchase of TIPS for a portfolio generally suggest that they represent a relatively small percentage of total holdings. The message is, "Bet on low inflation with 80 to 90 percent of your investments, but put the balance in inflation-protected securities."

Surprisingly, the first auction of TIPS went relatively well in January 1997, although subsequent auctions have seen less enthusiasm. This general lack of enthusiasm has continued into 2004. However, among the more enthusiastic investors are foreigners from countries such as Great Britain, Canada, and Sweden, where inflation-indexed securities are more widely accepted. Eighteen percent of British government debt is actually financed by securities whose returns are tied to inflation.

The advantage to the federal government of offering TIPS is that they can be sold to the public at a slightly lower yield than conventional fixed-rate Treasury securities because the government is taking the risk of inflation going up (the amount the government will have to pay to redeem the securities will go up sharply if there is high inflation). In return for the government taking this risk, investors accept a slightly lower return.

The reader should be aware that the base against which the 3.5 percent annual interest is paid is the inflation-adjusted value of the security. Thus, in the second year, the interest payment would be $36.05 (3.5% × $1,030). In each subsequent year, there is a similar adjustment depending on the prior year's rate of inflation.

Assuming inflation remains at 3 percent over the 10-year time period, the inflation-adjusted value of the principal will increase to $1,344 (10 periods compounded at 3 percent). The investor is effectively getting a return of 6.5 percent in the form of interest and appreciation of principal. Of course, if inflation averages 6 percent over the life of the investment, the investor will get a return of 9.5 percent. The interest payment (real return) will remain at 3.5 percent, but the inflation adjustment will supply the extra return.

Through inflation-indexed Treasury notes, the investor is protected against the effect of inflation. This may be quite a benefit if inflation is high, but the security can provide an inferior return compared with other investments in a low-inflation environment (the reader may wish to see the related box above for further discussion of this point).

Also, the investor should be aware that the annual adjustment in principal is treated as taxable income each year even though no cash is received until redemption at maturity. For this reason, inflation-indexed Treasury securities are more appropriate for tax-deferred or nontaxable accounts.

Federally Sponsored Credit Agency Issues

www.fanniemae.com
www.fhlbanks.com

Referring back to Figure 11–1 on page 294, the second category represents securities issued by federal agencies. The issues represent obligations of various agencies of the government such as the Federal National Mortgage Association and the Federal Home Loan Bank. Although these issues are authorized by an act of Congress and are used to finance federal projects, they are not direct obligations of the Treasury but rather of the agency itself.

While the issues are essentially free of risk (there is always the implicit standby power of the government behind the issues), they carry a slightly higher yield than U.S. government securities simply because they are not directly issued by the Treasury. Agency issues have been particularly active as a support mechanism for the housing industry. The issues generally trade in denominations of $5,000 and up and have varying maturities of from 1 to 40 years, with an average life of approximately 15 years. Examples of some agency issues are presented below:

	Minimum Denomination	Life of Issue
Federal Home Loan Bank	$10,000	12–25 years
Federal Intermediate Credit Banks	5,000	Up to 4 years
Federal Farm Credit Bank	50,000	1–10 years
Export-Import Bank	5,000	Up to 7 years

Interest on agency issues is fully taxable for IRS purposes and is generally taxable for state and local purposes although there are exceptions. (For example, interest on obligations issued by the Federal Farm Credit Bank are subject to state and local taxes, but those of the Federal Home Loan Bank are not.)

www.ginniemae.gov

One agency issue that is of particular interest to the investor because of its unique features is the **GNMA (Ginnie Mae) pass-through certificate.** These certificates represent an undivided interest in a pool of federally insured mortgages. Actually, GNMA, the Government National Mortgage Association, buys a pool of mortgages from various lenders at a discount and then issues securities to the public against these mortgages. Security holders in GNMA certificates receive monthly payments that essentially represent a pass-through of interest and principal payments on the mortgages. These securities come in minimum denominations of $25,000, are long term, and are fully taxable for federal, state, and local income tax purposes. A major consideration in this investment is that the investor has fully consumed his or her capital at the end of the investment. (Not only has interest been received monthly but also all principal has been returned over the life of the certificate, and therefore, there is no lump-sum payment at maturity.)

Because mortgages that are part of GNMA pass-through certificates are often paid off early as a result of the sale of a home or refinancing at lower interest rates, the true life of a GNMA certificate tends to be much less than the quoted life. For example, a 25-year GNMA certificate may actually be paid off in 12 years. This feature can be a negative consideration because GNMA certificates are particularly likely to be paid off early when interest rates are going down and homeowners are refinancing. The investor in the GNMA certificate is then forced to reinvest the proceeds in a low interest rate environment.

State and Local Government Securities

Debt securities issued by state and local governments are referred to as **municipal bonds.** Examples of issuing agencies include states, cities, school districts, toll roads, or any other type of political subdivision. The most important feature of a municipal bond is the tax-exempt nature of the interest payment. Dating back to the U.S. Supreme Court opinion of 1819 in *McCullough v. Maryland,* it was ruled that the federal government and state and local governments do not possess the power to tax each other. An eventual by-product of the judicial ruling was that income from municipal bonds cannot be taxed by the IRS. Furthermore, income from municipal bonds is also exempt from state and local taxes if bought within the locality in which one resides. Thus, a Californian buying municipal bonds in that state would pay no state income tax on the issue. However, the same Californian would have to pay state or local income taxes if the originating agency were in Texas or New York.

We cannot overemphasize the importance of the federal tax exemption that municipal bonds enjoy. The consequences are twofold. First, individuals in high tax brackets may find highly attractive investment opportunities in municipal bonds.[5] The formula used to equate interest on municipal bonds to other taxable investments is:

Application Example

$$Y = \frac{i}{(1 - T)} \quad (11\text{--}1)$$

where:
- Y = Equivalent before-tax yield on a taxable investment
- i = Yield on the municipal obligation
- T = Marginal tax rate of the investor

If an investor has a marginal tax rate of 35 percent and is evaluating a municipal bond paying 6 percent interest, the equivalent before-tax yield on a taxable investment would be:

$$\frac{6\%}{(1 - 0.35)} = \frac{6\%}{0.65} = 9.23\%$$

Thus, the investor could choose between a *non*-tax-exempt investment paying 9.23 percent and a tax-exempt municipal bond paying 6 percent and be indifferent between the two. Table 11–1 presents examples of trade-offs between tax-exempt and non-tax-exempt (taxable) investments at various interest rates and marginal tax rates. Clearly, the higher the marginal tax rate, the greater the advantage of tax-exempt municipal bonds.

---

[5] It should be noted that any capital gain on a municipal bond is taxable as would be the case with any investment.

TABLE 11–1 Marginal Tax Rates and Return Equivalents

Yield on Municipal	27% Bracket	35% Bracket	38.6% Bracket
5%	6.85%	7.69%	8.14%
6	8.22	9.23	9.77
7	9.59	10.77	11.40
8	10.96	12.31	13.03
9	12.32	13.85	14.66
10	13.70	15.38	16.28

A second significant feature of municipal bonds is that the yield the issuing agency pays on municipal bonds is lower than the yield on taxable instruments. Of course, a municipal bond paying 6 percent may be quite competitive with taxable instruments paying more. Average differentials are presented in Table 11–2 (on the next page). You should notice in Table 11–2 that the yield differences between municipal bonds and corporate bonds was normally 1 to 4 percentage points. A major distinction that is also important to the bond issuer and investor is whether the bond is of a general obligation or revenue nature.

General Obligation versus Revenue Bonds A **general obligation issue** is backed by the full faith, credit, and "taxing power" of the governmental unit. For a **revenue bond,** on the other hand, the repayment of the issue is fully dependent on the revenue-generating capability of a specific project or venture, such as a toll road, bridge, or municipal colosseum.

Because of the taxing power behind most general obligation (GO) issues, they tend to be of extremely high quality. Approximately three-fourths of all municipal bond issues are of the general obligation variety, and very few failures have occurred in the post–World War II era. Revenue bonds tend to be of more uneven quality, and the economic soundness of the underlying revenue-generating project must be carefully examined (though most projects are quite worthwhile).

Municipal Bond Guarantee A growing factor in the municipal bond market is the third-party guarantee. Whether dealing with a general obligation or revenue bond, a fee may be paid by the originating governmental body to a third-party insurer to guarantee that all interest and principal payments will be made. There are four private insurance firms that guarantee municipal bonds, the largest of which are the Municipal Bond Investors Assurance (MBIA) and the American Municipal Bond Assurance Corporation (AMBAC). Municipal bonds that are guaranteed carry the highest rating possible (AAA) because all the guaranteeing insurance companies are rated AAA. Approximately 30 percent of municipal bond issues are guaranteed.

A municipal bond that is guaranteed will carry a lower yield and have a better secondary or resale market. This may be important because municipal bonds, in general, do not provide as strong a secondary market as U.S. government issues. The market for a given municipal issue is often small and fragmented, and high indirect costs are associated with reselling the issue.

TABLE 11–2 Comparable Yields on Long-Term Municipals and Taxable Corporates (Yearly Averages)

Year	Municipals Aa	Corporates Aa	Yield Difference
2004	4.88%	6.04%	1.16%
2003	4.84	5.95	1.11
2002	5.64	6.93	1.29
2001	5.80	7.14	1.34
2000	6.01	7.80	1.79
1999	5.48	7.36	1.88
1998	5.13	6.80	1.67
1997	5.52	7.48	1.96
1996	5.90	7.72	1.82
1995	5.60	7.55	1.95
1994	6.40	8.60	2.20
1993	5.51	7.40	1.89
1992	6.30	8.46	2.16
1991	6.80	9.09	2.29
1990	7.15	9.56	2.41
1989	7.51	9.46	1.95
1988	8.38	9.66	1.28
1987	8.50	9.68	1.18
1986	7.35	9.47	2.12
1985	8.81	11.82	3.01
1984	9.95	12.25	2.30
1983	9.20	12.42	3.22
1982	11.39	14.41	3.02
1981	10.89	14.75	3.86
1980	8.06	12.50	4.44

Source: *Moody's Municipal & Government Manual, Moody's Industrial Manual,* and *Mergent Bond Record* (published by Mergent, Inc., New York, NY), selected issues.

Corporate Securities

Corporate bonds are the dominant source of new financing for the U.S. corporation.

Bonds normally supply 80 to 85 percent of firms' external financial needs. Even during the great bull stock market of the 1990s, corporations looked as heavily as ever to the debt markets to provide financing (this was justified by the decreasing interest rates during this period).

The corporate market may be divided into a number of subunits, including *industrials, public utilities, rails and transportation,* and *financial issues* (banks, finance companies, etc.). The industrials are a catchall category that includes everything from high-technology companies to discount chain stores. Public utilities represent the largest segment of the market and have issues that run up to 40 years in maturity. Because public utilities are in constant need of funds to meet ever-expanding requirements for power generation, telephone services, and other essential services, they are always in the bond market to raise new funds. The needs associated with rails and transportation as well as financial issues tend to be less than those associated with public utilities or industrials. Table 11–3 shows comparative yields for the two main categories.[6]

The higher yields on public utility issues represent a supply-demand phenomenon more than anything else. A constant stream of new issues to the market can only be absorbed by a higher yield pattern. In other cases, the higher required return may also be associated with quality deterioration as measured by profitability and interest coverage. During 1983–84, the default of the Washington State Power Authority on bonds issued to construct power-generating facilities sent waves through the bond market. Again in 1984, when Public Service of Indiana canceled construction of a partially complete nuclear power plant, nuclear utility issues (both stocks and bonds) suffered severe price erosion, and the bond market demanded high risk premiums on bonds of almost all nuclear utilities. In 2001, the public utility bond market was once again "spooked" by the energy crisis and blackouts in northern California.

TABLE 11–3 Comparative Yields on Aa Bonds among Corporate Issuers

Year	Industrial	Public Utility
2004	6.04%	6.47%
2003	5.94	6.41
2002	6.93	7.34
2001	7.14	7.89
2000	7.80	8.05
1999	7.36	7.92
1998	6.80	7.12
1997	7.48	8.00
1996	7.55	7.70
1995	7.72	7.84
1994	8.41	8.74
1993	7.05	7.19
1992	8.24	8.65
1991	9.01	9.25
1990	9.41	9.65
1989	9.35	9.55
1988	9.41	10.20
1987	9.73	9.83
1986	9.49	9.44
1985	11.57	12.02
1984	12.39	13.02
1983	11.94	12.74
1982	15.01	16.48
1981	13.01	14.03
1980	11.16	11.95

Source: *Mergent Bond Record* (published by Mergent, Inc., New York, NY), selected issues.

---

[6] Financial and transportation issues are generally not broken out of the published data.

Corporate bonds of all types generally trade in units of $1,000, and this is a particularly attractive feature to the smaller investor who does not wish to purchase in units of $5,000 to $10,000 (which is necessary for many Treasury and federally sponsored credit agency issues). Because of higher risk relative to government issues, the investor will generally receive higher yields on corporates as well. All income from corporates is taxable for federal, state, and local purposes. Finally, corporate issues have the disadvantage of being subject to calls. When buying a bond during a period of high interest rates, the call provision must be considered a negative feature because the high-yielding bonds may be called in for early retirement as interest rates go down.

Bond Market Investors

Having considered the issuer or supply side of the market, we now comment on the investor or demand side. The bond market is dominated by large institutional investors (insurance companies, banks, pension funds, mutual funds) even more than the stock market. Institutional investors account for 80 to 85 percent of the trading in key segments of the bond market. However, the presence of the individual investor is partially felt in the corporate and municipal bond market where the incentives of low denomination ($1,000) corporate bonds or tax-free municipal bonds have some attraction. Furthermore, in the last decade individual investors have made their presence felt in the bond market through buying mutual funds that specialize in bond portfolios. The activities of individuals in mutual funds are covered in detail in Chapter 19, so for now we concentrate on institutional investors.

Institutional investors' preferences for various sectors of the bond market are influenced by their tax status as well as by the nature of their obligations or liabilities to depositors, investors, or clients. For example, banks traditionally have been strong participants in the municipal bond market because of their substantial tax obligations. Their investments tend to be in short- to intermediate-term assets because of the short-term nature of their deposit obligations (the funds supplied to the banks). One problem that banks find in their bond portfolios is that such investments are often preferred over loans to customers when the economy is weak and loan demand is sluggish. Not so coincidentally, this happens to be the time period when interest rates are low. When the economy improves, interest rates go up, and so does loan demand. To meet the loan demand of valued customers, banks liquidate portions of their bond portfolios. The problem with this recurring process is that banks are buying bonds when interest rates are *low* and selling them when interest rates are *high*. This can cause losses in the value of the bank portfolio.

The bond investor must be prepared to deal in a relatively strong primary market (new issues market) and a relatively weak secondary market (resale market). While the secondary market is active for many types of Treasury and agency issues, such is not the case for corporate and municipal issues. Thus, the investor must look well beyond the yield, maturity, and rating to determine if a purchase is acceptable. The question that must be considered is: How close to the going market price can I dispose of the issue if that should be necessary? If a 5 or 10 percent discount is involved, that might be unacceptable. Unlike the stock market, the secondary market in bonds tends to be dominated by over-the-counter transactions (although listed bonds are traded as well).

A significant development in the last decade has been the heavy participation of foreign investors in U.S. bond markets. Foreign investors now bankroll between 10 to 15 percent of the U.S. government's debt. While these investors have helped to finance the U.S. government's deficits, they can be a disruptive factor in the market when they decide to partially withdraw their funds. This happened in the mid-1990s when the declining value of the dollar and fear of inflation in the United States caused many foreign investors to temporarily cash in their investments. Because the U.S. government fears the flight of funds provided by foreign investors, it is sensitive to their needs and desires.

Distribution Procedures

In February 1982, the Securities and Exchange Commission began allowing a process called shelf registration under SEC Rule 415. **Shelf registration** permits large companies to file one comprehensive registration statement that outlines the firm's plans for future long-term financing. Then, when market conditions seem appropriate, the firm can issue the securities through an investment banker without further SEC approval. Future issues are said to be sitting on the shelf, waiting for the most advantageous time to appear. An issue may be on the shelf for up to two years.

Approximately half of the new public bond issues are distributed through the shelf registration process. The rest are issued under more traditional procedures in which the bonds are issued shortly after registration by a large syndicate of investment bankers in a highly structured process.

Private Placement

A number of bond offerings are sold to investors as a **private placement;** that is, they are sold privately to investors rather than through the public markets. Private placements are most popular with investors such as insurance companies and pension funds, and they are primarily offered in the corporate sector by industrial firms rather than public utilities. The lender can generally expect to receive a slightly higher yield than on public issues to compensate for the extremely limited or nonexistent secondary market and the generally smaller size of the borrowing firm in a private placement.

Bond Ratings

Bond investors tend to place much more emphasis on independent analysis of quality than do common stock investors. For this reason, both corporate financial management and institutional portfolio managers keep a close eye on bond rating procedures. The difference between an AA and an A rating may mean the corporation will have to pay ¼ point more interest on the bond issue (perhaps 8½ percent rather than 8¼ percent). On a $100 million, 20-year issue, this represents $250,000 per year (before tax), or a total of $5 million over the life of the bond.

www.moodys.com
www.standardandpoors.com

The two major bond-rating agencies are Moody's Investors Service and Standard & Poor's (a subsidiary of McGraw-Hill, Inc.). They rank thousands of corporate and municipal issues as well as a limited number of private placements, commercial paper, preferred stock issues, and offerings of foreign companies and governments. U.S. government issues tend to be free of risk and therefore are given no attention by the bond-rating agencies. Moody's, founded in 1909, is the older of the two bond-rating agencies and covers twice as many securities as Standard & Poor's (particularly in the municipal bond area). Fitch Investors Service, Inc., acquired Duff & Phelps, another rating agency, in an attempt to diversify and expand its rating coverage.

The bond ratings, generally ranging from an AAA to a D category, are decided on a committee basis at both Moody's and Standard & Poor's. There are no fast and firm quantitative measures that specify the rating a new issue will receive. Nevertheless, measures pertaining to cash flow and earnings generation in relationship to debt obligations are given strong consideration. Of particular interest are coverage ratios that show the number of times interest payments, as well as all annual contractual obligations, are covered by earnings. A coverage of 2 or 3 may contribute to a low rating, while a ratio of 5 to 10 may indicate the possibility of a strong rating. Operating margins, return on invested capital, and returns on total assets are also evaluated along with debt-to-equity ratios.[7] Financial ratio analysis makes up perhaps 50 percent of the evaluation. Other factors of importance are the nature of the industry in which the firm operates, the relative position of the firm within the industry, the pricing clout the firm has, and the quality of management. Decisions are not made in a sterile, isolated environment. Thus, it is not unusual for corporate management or the mayor to make a presentation to the rating agency, and on-site visitations to plants or cities may occur.

The overall quality of the work done by the bond-rating agencies may be judged by the agencies' acceptance in the business and academic community. Their work is very well received. Although UBS and some other investment houses have established their own analysts to shadow the activities of the bond-rating agencies and look for imprecisions in their classifications (and thus potential profits), the opportunities are not great. Academic researchers have generally found that accounting and financial data were well considered in the bond ratings and that rational evaluation appeared to exist.[8]

One item lending credibility to the bond-rating process is the frequency with which the two major rating agencies arrive at the same grade for a given issue (this occurs well over 50 percent of the time). When "split ratings" do occur (different ratings by different agencies), they are invariably of a small magnitude. A typical case might be AAA versus AA rather than AAA versus BBB. While one can question whether one agency is looking over the other's shoulder or "copying its homework," this is probably not the case in this skilled industry.

Nevertheless, there is room for criticism. While initial evaluations are quite thorough and rational, the monitoring process may not be wholly satisfactory. Subsequent changes in corporate or municipal government events may not trigger a rating change quickly enough. One sure way a corporation or municipal

www.
financialservicesinc.
ubs.com

---

[7] Similar appropriate measures can be applied to municipal bonds, such as debt per capita or income per capita within a governmental jurisdiction.

[8] James O. Horrigan, "The Determination of Long-Term Credit Standing with Financial Ratios," *Empirical Research in Accounting: Selected Studies,* supplement to *Journal of Accounting Research* 4 (1966), pp. 44–62; Thomas F. Pogue and Robert M. Soldofsky, "What's in a Bond Rating?" *Journal of Financial and Quantitative Analysis,* June 1969, pp. 201–8; and George E. Pinches and Kent A. Mingo, "A Multivariate Analysis of Industrial Bond Ratings," *Journal of Finance,* March 1973, pp. 1–18.

the real world of investing

The Bond Rating Game: Who Really Runs the Corporation?

When Shell Canada (www.shellcanada.com), an integrated oil company with many U.S. investors, decided to sell its coal business, it called Moody's and Standard & Poor's first. Although its own financial analysis indicated the move was appropriate, it would not have made the decision without the blessings of the two major U.S. bond-rating agencies as well as similar rating agencies in Canada. The sell-off provided a $120 million write-off that could have caused a downgrading of Shell Canada's double-A rating, and the firm was not about to take a chance.

The firm's concern was well justified. Its action was taken in June 1991 (a recession year). During the first six months of 1991, 422 corporations suffered a downgrading in ratings while only 88 had an increase. In the prior decade, the big causes for downgradings were the effects of acquisitions or attempts by corporations to defend themselves against takeovers. In the 1990s, these factors were less important, and the major concern was poor earnings performance.

Three good rules for firms to follow in dealing with bond-rating agencies is never surprise the agencies, tell all, and show good intent. A number of years ago, Manville Corporation (www.jm.com) was severely downgraded not for poor performance, but because it took Chapter 11 bankruptcy protection as a way to face asbestos damage litigation. The decision may have been right at the time, but the firm did not have the blessings of the bond-rating agencies.

---

government will get a reevaluation is for them to come out with a new issue. This tends to generate a review of all existing issues.

Actual Rating System

Table 11–4 on the next page shows an actual listing of the designations used by Moody's and Standard & Poor's. Note that Moody's combines capital letters and small *a*'s, and Standard & Poor's uses all capital letters.

The first four categories are assumed to represent investment-grade quality. Large institutional investors (insurance companies, banks, pension funds) generally confine their activities to these four categories. Moody's also modifies its basic ratings with numerical values for categories Aa through B. The highest in a category is 1, 2 is the midrange, and 3 is the lowest. A rating of Aa2 means the bond is in the midrange of Aa. Standard & Poor's has a similar modification process with pluses and minuses applied. Thus, AA+ would be on the high end of an AA rating, AA would be in the middle, and AA− would be on the low end.

It is also possible for a corporation to have issues outstanding in more than one category. For example, highly secured mortgage bonds of a corporation may be rated AA, while unsecured issues carry an A rating.

The level of interest payment on a bond is inverse to the quality rating. If a bond rated AAA by Standard & Poor's pays 6.5 percent, an A quality bond might pay 7.0 percent; a BB, 8.0 percent; and so on. The spread between these yields changes from time to time and is watched closely by the financial community as a barometer of future movements in the financial markets. A relatively small spread between two rating categories would indicate that investors generally have confidence in the economy. As the yield spread widens between higher and lower rating categories, this may indicate loss of confidence. Investors are demanding increasingly higher yields for lower rated bonds. Their loss of confidence indicates they will demand progressively higher returns for taking risks.

TABLE 11–4 Description of Bond Ratings

Quality	Moody's	Standard & Poor's	Description
High grade	Aaa	AAA	Bonds that are judged to be of the best quality. They carry the smallest degree of investment risk and are generally referred to as "gilt edge." Interest payments are protected by a large or exceptionally stable margin, and principal is secure.
	Aa	AA	Bonds that are judged to be of high quality by all standards. Together with the first group, they comprise what are generally known as high-grade bonds. They are rated lower than the best bonds because margins of protection may not be as large.
Medium grade	A	A	Bonds that possess many favorable investment attributes and are to be considered as upper-medium-grade obligations. Factors giving security to principal and interest are considered adequate.
	Baa	BBB	Bonds that are considered as medium-grade obligations—they are neither highly protected nor poorly secured.
Speculative	Ba	BB	Bonds that are judged to have speculative elements; their future cannot be considered as well assured. Often the protection of interest and principal payments may be very moderate.
	B	B	Bonds that generally lack characteristics of the desirable investment. Assurance of interest and principal payments or of maintenance of other terms of the contract over any long period may be small.
Default	Caa	CCC	Bonds that are of poor standing. Such issues may be in default, or there may be elements of danger present with respect to principal or interest.
	Ca	CC	Bonds that represent obligations that are speculative to a high degree. Such issues are often in default or have other marked shortcomings.
	C		The lowest-rated class in Moody's designation. These bonds can be regarded as having extremely poor prospects of attaining any real investment standing.
		C	Rating given to income bonds on which interest is not currently being paid.
		D	Issues in default with arrears in interest and/or principal payments.

Sources: *Mergent Bond Record* (published by Mergent, Inc., New York, NY) and *Bond Guide* (Standard & Poor's).

This logic was previously covered in Chapter 9 as part of the discussion of the *Barron's* Confidence Index.

Junk Bonds or High-Yield Bonds

Lower quality bonds are sometimes referred to as **junk bonds** or high-yield bonds. Any bond that is not considered to be of investment quality by Wall Street analysts is put in the junk bond category. As previously indicated, investment quality means the bond falls into one of the four top investment-grade categories established by Moody's and Standard & Poor's. This indicates investment-grade bonds extend down to Baa in Moody's and BBB in Standard & Poor's (Table 11–4). A wide range of quality is associated with junk bonds. Some are very close to investment quality (such as the Ba and BB bonds), while others carry ratings in the C and D categories.

Bonds tend to fall into the junk bond category for a number of reasons. First are the so-called fallen angel bonds issued by companies that once had high credit rankings but now face hard times. Second are emerging growth companies or small firms that have not yet established an adequate record to justify an investment-quality rating. Finally, a major part of the junk bond market is made of companies undergoing a restructuring either as a result of a leveraged buyout or as part of fending off an unfriendly takeover offer. In both these cases, equity capital tends to be replaced with debt and a lower rating is assigned.

Many junk bonds behave more like common stock than bonds and rally on good news, actual interest payments, or improving business conditions. Several institutions such as Merrill Lynch and Fidelity Investments manage mutual funds with a junk bond emphasis.

The main appeal of junk bonds historically is that they provided yields 300 to 800 basis points higher than that for AAA corporate bonds or U.S. Treasury securities. Also, until the recession of 1990–91, there were relatively few defaults by junk bond issuers. Thus, the investor got a substantially higher yield with only a small increase in risk.

However, in the 1990–91 recession, junk bond prices tumbled by 20 to 30 percent, while other bond values stayed firm. Examples of junk bond issues that dropped sharply in value included those issued by Rapid-American Corporation, Revco, Campeau Corporation, and Resorts International. Many of these declines were due to poor business conditions. However, the fall of Drexel Burnham Lambert, the leading underwriter of junk bond issues, also contributed to the difficulties in the market. That problem was further compounded when Michael Milken, the guru of junk bond dealers, was sentenced to 10 years in prison for illegal insider trading.

As the economy came out of the recession of 1990–91, junk bonds once again gained in popularity. Many of these issues had their prices battered down so low that they appeared to be bargains. As a result, junk bonds recovered and continued to perform exceptionally well throughout the 1990s—so much so that the spread between the yield on junk bonds and U.S. Treasury securities was half of its historical spread in 1997. While these securities took a hit in 2001 as the economy slowed down, they rallied strongly as the economy improved in 2003 (they were up 25 percent). These securities appear to have a place in the portfolio of investors with a higher than average risk tolerance. This is particularly true for bonds that are in the low- to mid-B rating categories.

Bond Quotes

Application Example

www.fordmotorcredit.com

The Wall Street Journal and a number of other sources publish bond values on a daily basis. Table 11–5 provides an excerpt from the daily quote sheet for corporate bonds.

Starting in the first column, the company name is followed by the annual coupon rate and maturity date. For example, the table shows Ford Motor Credit bonds with a coupon rate of 7 percent maturing in 2033. The "Last Price" is 106.538. The quote does not represent actual dollars, but percent of par value because corporate bonds trade in units of $1,000.

The 106.538 represents $1,065.38 ($1,000 × 106.538 percent). The next item of interest in the table is "Last Yield." This is the true rate of return the bond investor is receiving and is 6.097 percent. More formally, this is referred to as yield to maturity and is covered in the next chapter on "Principles of Bond Valuation and Investments."

TABLE 11-5 Daily Quotes on Corporate Bonds

Corporate Bonds

Tuesday, January 6, 2004

Forty most active fixed-coupon corporate bonds

COMPANY (TICKER)	COUPON	MATURITY	LAST PRICE	LAST YIELD
Sprint Capital (FON)	8.375	Mar 15, 2012	118.229	5.569
Ford Motor Credit (F)	7.000	Oct 01, 2013	106.538	6.097
Sprint Capital (FON)	8.750	Mar 15, 2032	120.626	7.053
Ford Motor (F)	7.450	Jul 16, 2031	102.694	7.223
General Motors (GM)	8.375	Jul 15, 2033	117.715	6.954
Goldman Sachs Group (GS)	5.250	Oct 15, 2013	100.759	5.149
Ford Motor Credit (F)	6.700	Jul 16, 2004	102.557	1.278
Duke Energy (DUK)-c	1.750	May 15, 2023	103.188	0.698
Wyeth (WYE)	5.500	Feb 01, 2014	101.296	5.330
Ford Motor Credit (F)	5.625	Oct 01, 2008	103.025	4.898
General Motors Acceptance (GMAC)	8.000	Nov 01, 2031	113.531	6.898
Goldman Sachs Group (GS)	4.125	Jan 15, 2008	102.379	3.485
Sprint Capital (FON)	7.625	Jan 30, 2011	113.519	5.303
Household Finance (HSBC)	6.500	Jan 24, 2006	108.100	2.410
Citigroup (C)	3.500	Feb 01, 2008	100.359	3.404
Verizon New Jersey (VZ)	5.875	Jan 17, 2012	106.256	4.921
General Electric Capital (GE)	5.450	Jan 15, 2013	104.376	4.845
Household Finance (HSBC)	8.000	May 09, 2005	108.213	1.739
Ford Motor Credit (F)	7.375	Feb 01, 2011	109.919	5.651
Goldman Sachs Group (GS)	4.750	Jul 15, 2013	97.246	5.119
Ford Motor Credit (F)	7.375	Oct 28, 2009	110.501	5.250
Ford Motor Credit (F)	7.875	Jun 15, 2010	112.251	5.581
Bank One (ONE)	3.700	Jan 15, 2008	101.207	3.376
Albertson's (ABS)	7.500	Feb 15, 2011	114.697	5.013
Verizon New York (VZ)	7.375	Apr 01, 2032	111.725	6.465
Altria Group (MO)	7.000	Nov 04, 2013	107.905	5.925
DaimlerChrysler North America Holding (DCX)	8.500	Jan 18, 2031	120.030	6.861
Ford Motor (F)	6.375	Feb 01, 2029	90.450	7.203
Bank of America (BAC)	5.125	Nov 15, 2014	99.395	5.198
Wachovia (WB)	4.950	Nov 01, 2006	106.003	2.716
J.P. Morgan Chase (JPM)	3.125	Dec 11, 2006	100.744	2.857
Walt Disney (DIS)-c	2.125	Apr 15, 2023	107.313	0.395
AT&T Wireless Services (AWE)	8.125	May 01, 2012	117.940	5.414
Morgan Stanley (MWD)	6.100	Apr 15, 2006	107.973	2.443
Credit Suisse First Boston (USA) (CRDSUI)	5.500	Aug 15, 2013	102.925	5.110
Comcast Cable Communications Holdings (CMCSA)	8.375	Mar 15, 2013	122.716	5.227
Ford Motor Credit (F)	6.875	Feb 01, 2006	106.936	3.362
Verizon Global Funding (VZ)	7.750	Dec 01, 2030	118.313	6.324
Boeing Capital (BA)	5.800	Jan 15, 2013	105.307	5.060
Goldman Sachs Group (GS)	6.600	Jan 15, 2012	111.585	4.839
Sprint Capital (FON)	6.125	Nov 15, 2008	107.007	4.499

Source: *The Wall Street Journal,* January 7, 2004, p. C14. Reprinted by permission of *The Wall Street Journal,* © 2004 by Dow Jones & Company. All Rights Reserved Worldwide.

A student interested in further information on a bond could proceed to *Mergent Bond Record* published by Mergent, Inc., or the *Bond Guide,* published by Standard & Poor's. For example, using *Mergent Bond Record,* as shown in Table 11–6, the reader could determine information about a firm. Let's look at Anheuser-Busch Cos.' 7.125 issue of 2017. The code designation in the left margin indicates the industry classification of the firm. Also, the firm has a Moody's bond rating of A1 and a call price of 103.03 percent of par or $1,030.30 ($1,000 × 103.03%). The *Mergent Bond Record* further indicates that interest is payable on J&J (January and July 1) of each year ("Interest Dates" column). The current price of the bond is $1,139.20 ($1,000 × 113.92%).

TABLE 11-6 Background Data on Bond Issues

CUSIP	ISSUE	MOODY'S RATING	INTEREST DATES	CURRENT CALL PRICE	CALL DATE	SINK FUND PROV	CURRENT PRICE		YIELD TO MAT.	2003 HIGH	2003 LOW	AMT. OUTST. MIL. $	ISSUED	ISSUED PRICE	ISS. YLD.
035229CK	Anheuser-Busch Cos., Inc. nt 5.60 2006	A1	J&J 6	N.C.	—		107.53	bid	5.21	110.72	107.41	50.0	7-6-01	0.00	0.00
035229BM	nt 7.10 2007	A1 r	J&D 6	100.00 fr	6-15-04		103.25	bid	6.88	105.95	103.25	250	6-6-97	99.90	0.00
035229BR	nt 5.65 2008	A1	M&S 15	N.C.	—		109.10	bid	5.18	111.90	108.66	100	9-15-98	99.66	0.00
035229CA	nt 5.375 2008	A1	M&S 15	N.C.	—		106.49	bid	5.05	109.44	106.05	100	9-21-98	99.52	0.00
035229CB	nt 5.125 2008	A1	A&O 1	N.C.	—		106.43	bid	4.82	111.08	105.99	100	10-1-98	99.48	0.00
035229AL	nt 9.00 2009[1]	A1 r	J&D 1	N.C.	—		123.53	bid	7.29	126.05	123.30	350	12-6-89	99.80	9.00
035229CD	nt 5.75 2010[2]	A1	A&O 1	100.00	—		108.32	bid	5.31	115.22	107.89	150	4-9-99	99.56	0.00
035229CC	bd 5.75 2011	A1	J&J 15	100.00 fr	1-15-06		105.30	bid	5.46	107.33	105.18	150	1-13-99	99.82	0.00
035229CH	nt 6.00 2011	A1	A&O 15	100.00 to	4-15-11		109.17	bid	5.50	117.53	109.17	250	4-10-01	99.38	0.00
035229CE	nt 7.50 2012	A1	M&S 15	100.00 to	3-15-12		119.74	bid	6.26	123.81	117.52	200	3-6-00	99.37	0.00
035229CP	nt 4.375 2013	A1	J&J 15	100.00 to	1-15-13		97.34	bid	4.49	104.60	96.65	300	10-10-02	99.70	0.00
035229CU	nt 4.95 2014	A1	J&J 15	100.00 to	1-15-14		100.67	bid	4.92	101.89	99.22	300	9-9-03	99.73	0.00
035229BG	nt 7.25 2015	A1	M&S 15	—	—		110.08	bid	6.59	115.14	110.08	150	9-6-95	99.90	7.30
035229CR	nt 4.625 2015	A1	F&A 1	100.00 to	2-1-15		95.56	bid	4.84	101.31	95.47	200	1-22-03	99.44	0.00
035229CV	nt 5.05 2016	A1	A&O 15	100.00 to	10-15-16		98.39	bid	5.13	101.26	97.77	400	10-8-03	99.44	0.00
035229BN	deb 7.125 2017	A1 r	J&J 1	103.03 fr	7-1-07		113.92	bid	6.25	117.50	113.66	250	7-7-97	98.93	0.00
035229CS	nt 4.50 2018	A1 r	A&O 1	100.00 to	4-1-18		93.31	bid	4.82	101.18	90.62	200	3-6-03	98.99	0.00
035229AX	deb 7.375 2023	A1 r	J&J 1	102.95 fr	7-1-04		—	bid	7.02	—	—	200	6-22-93	99.20	7.40
035229CT	nt 5.35 2023	A1	F&A 15	100.00 fr	5-15-07		97.91	bid	5.46	100.17	91.89	180	5-1-03	100.00	0.00
035229BH	deb 7.00 2025	A1 r	J&D 1	103.34 fr	12-1-05 No		109.47	bid	6.39	110.28	107.58	200	11-30-95	99.70	0.00
035229BP	deb 6.75 2027	A1	J&D 15	100.00 to	12-15-27		110.93	bid	6.09	112.81	107.78	100	12-11-97	99.77	0.00
035229BQ	deb 6.50 2028	A1 r	J&J 1	100.00	—		106.94	bid	6.08	108.77	92.00	100	1-7-98	99.76	0.00
035229CF	deb 7.55 2030	A1	A&O 1	100.00 to	10-1-30		121.82	bid	6.20	129.18	120.09	200	10-2-00	99.99	0.00
035229CG	deb 6.80 2031	A1	J&J 15	100.00 to	1-15-31		112.73	bid	6.03	126.26	110.70	200	12-14-00	99.42	0.00
035229CJ	deb 6.80 2032	A1	F&A 1	100.00 to	8-20-32		113.84	bid	5.97	118.97	110.30	300	6-19-01	99.87	0.00
035229CQ	deb 5.95 2033	A1	J&J 15	100.00 to	1-15-33		103.09	bid	5.77	106.54	99.09	300	10-28-02	99.29	0.00
035229CL	deb 6.00 2041	A1	M&N 1	100.00 to	11-1-41		101.69	bid	5.90	106.29	97.70	250	11-1-01	99.01	0.00
035229CM	deb 6.50 2042	A1	M&N 1	100.00 to	5-1-42		108.39	bid	6.00	122.39	105.09	250	5-2-02	98.71	0.00
035229CN	deb 6.50 2043	A1	F&A 1	100.00 to	2-1-43		104.37	bid	6.23	114.47	102.66	300	6-24-02	99.75	0.00
001814AT	ANR Pipeline Co. sr nt 1.18577E263	B1		—	—		—	bid	—	—	—	300	0-0-00	0.00	0.00
001814AR	deb 9.625 2021	B1 r	M&N 1	N.C.	— No		115.77	bid	8.31	117.36	99.50	300	10-24-91	99.40	9.70
001814AQ	deb 7.375 2024	B1	F&A 15	N.C.	—		93.67	bid	7.87	95.05	—	125	2-14-94	99.30	7.40
001814AS	deb 7.00 2025[3]	B1 r	J&D 1	N.C.	— No		89.72	bid	7.80	100.00	84.00	75.0	5-24-95	100.00	7.00
036734AC	Anthem Insurance Cos., Inc. surplus nt 9.125 2010[4]	Baa1		—	—		116.64	bid	7.82	122.69	116.25	300	1-31-00	0.00	0.00
036734AA	surplus nt 9.00 2027[4]	Baa1 r	A&O 1	N.C.	—		121.04	bid	7.44	130.15	119.56	200	3-26-97	99.60	0.00
03674BAB	Anthem, Inc. nt 4.875 2005	Baa1 r	F&A 1	N.C.	—		102.35	bid	4.76	106.20	102.35	150	7-26-02	99.80	0.00
03674BAC	nt 6.80 2012	Baa1 r	F&A 1	N.C.	—		101.86	bid	6.68	113.87	101.24	800	7-26-02	99.46	0.00
036778AB	Anthony Crane Rental LP / Ant gtd sr nt 10.375 2008[5]	C	F&A 1	—	—		—	bid	103.75	—	—	155	7-15-98	100.00	0.00
	Anthracite Rated Investments prin protect nt ser 12 1.20 2013	Aaa	A&O 26	—	—		—	bid	—	—	—	54.04	4-25-03	0.00	0.00
	prin protect nt ser 12 1.20 2013	Aaa	A&O 26	—	—		—	bid	—	—	—	20.0	4-25-03	0.00	0.00

Source: *Mergent Bond Record* (published by Mergent, Inc. New York, NY), December, 2003, p. 75.

Quotes on Government Securities

Application Example

Table 11–7 on page 311 features quotes on U.S. government securities. Treasury notes and bonds are traded as a percentage of par value, similar to corporate bonds. Historically, price changes in the market have been rather small, and bonds are quoted in $1/32$ of a percentage point. For example, the price for the 5.625 Treasury note due May 2008 is quoted as 110.22 bid and 110.23 asked.[9] These prices translate into $110^{22}/_{32}$ and $110^{23}/_{32}$ percent of $1,000.

The bid price on a $1,000 note would be 110.6875 percent × $1,000 or $1,106.875:

$$110.6875\% \text{ (Same as } 110^{22}/_{32}\text{)}$$
$$\times \$1,000$$
$$\$1,106.875$$

---

[9] The bid price is the value at which the bond can be sold, and the asked price is the value at which it can be bought.

The asking price is 110.7188 percent × $1,000 or $1,107.188:

$$110.7188\% \text{ (Same as } 110^{23}/_{32}\text{)}$$
$$\times \$1,000$$
$$\$1,107.188$$

The spread between the bid and asked price is $3.13:

Bid price	$1,106.875
Asked price	1,107.188
Spread	$.313

While Treasury notes and bonds are quoted on the basis of price, Treasury bills are quoted on the basis of yield. Look at the Treasury bills on the right side of Table 11–7 on page 311. These yields (ask. yld.) represent the return to the Treasury bill investor. How is the yield determined? First, you must understand that the interest on a Treasury bill is treated on a discount basis; that is, it is subtracted from the $1,000 face value to get the purchase price. On a six-month, $1,000 Treasury bill, paying 1 percent interest, the actual yield is 1.005 percent. Let's see how we arrive at this number:

Interest = 1% × $1,000 × ½ year = $10 × ½ = $5.

We multiply $10 by ½ in the second part of the above line to arrive at $5 because the Treasury bill is for half a year.

The amount to be paid for the Treasury bill is $995 ($1,000 − $5).

The true yield is $5/$995 × 2 = .5025% × 2 = 1.005%

The reason .5025% is multiplied by 2 is to translate a six-month return into an annual return.

The actual rate (1.005 percent in this case) is always higher than the quoted rate (1 percent) because you do not have to pay the full face value ($1,000), but rather a discounted value ($995).

Examples of Treasury strip quotes are shown in Table 11–8 on page 312. Note the May 2014 strip is selling at 61.31 bid and 62.03 asked. The yield is 4.66 percent. What this means is that on January 8, 2004 (the date of the table), you could buy a Treasury strip maturing in May 2014 at slightly over 62 percent of par value and that would provide you with a yield of 4.66 percent. In the Type column (second column), there is a "ci." This means you are buying stripped coupon interest. An "np" also appears in the Type column, indicating you are purchasing stripped principal.

Bond Markets, Capital Market Theory, and Efficiency

In many respects, the bond market appears to demonstrate a high degree of rationality in recognition of risk and return. Corporate issues promise a higher yield than government issues to compensate for risk, and furthermore, federally sponsored credit agencies pay a higher return than Treasury issues for the same

TABLE 11-7 Quotes on Government Issues— Treasury Bonds, Notes, and Bills

Government Bonds & Notes

RATE	MATURITY MO/YR	BID	ASKED	CHG	ASK YLD
3.000	Jan 04n	100:03	100:04	-1	0.83
4.750	Feb 04n	100:12	100:13	-1	0.75
5.875	Feb 04n	100:16	100:17	...	0.84
3.000	Feb 04n	100:09	100:10	...	0.84
3.625	Mar 04n	100:19	100:20	...	0.89
3.375	Apr 04n	100:23	100:24	-1	0.92
5.250	May 04n	101:15	101:16	-1	0.95
7.250	May 04n	102:06	102:07	...	0.96
12.375	May 04	104:00	104:01	-2	0.90
3.250	May 04n	100:28	100:29	...	0.95
2.875	Jun 04n	100:28	100:29	...	0.98
2.250	Jul 04n	100:21	100:22	...	1.00
2.125	Aug 04n	100:21	100:22	1	1.05
6.000	Aug 04n	102:30	102:31	...	1.04
7.250	Aug 04n	103:23	103:24	1	1.02
13.750	Aug 04	107:18	107:19	-1	1.11
1.875	Sep 04n	100:17	100:18	...	1.08
2.125	Oct 04n	100:24	100:25	1	1.14
5.875	Nov 04n	103:30	103:31	1	1.19
7.875	Nov 04n	105:20	105:21	1	1.20
11.625	Nov 04	108:25	108:26	...	1.20
2.000	Nov 04n	100:22	100:23	2	1.19
1.750	Dec 04n	100:16	100:17	2	1.20
1.625	Jan 05n	100:13	100:14	2	1.21
7.500	Feb 05n	106:26	106:27	2	1.23
1.500	Feb 05n	100:08	100:09	3	1.25
1.625	Mar 05n	100:11	100:12	3	1.32
1.625	Apr 05n	100:09	100:10	3	1.37
6.500	May 05n	106:26	106:27	3	1.38
6.750	May 05n	107:04	107:05	3	1.38
12.000	May 05	114:08	114:09	3	1.31
1.250	May 05n	99:24	99:25	4	1.41
1.125	Jun 05n	99:15	99:16	4	1.46
1.500	Jul 05n	99:30	99:31	5	1.52
6.500	Aug 05n	107:26	107:27	4	1.54
10.750	Aug 05	114:16	114:17	4	1.55
2.000	Aug 05n	100:20	100:21	4	1.58
1.625	Sep 05n	99:30	99:31	4	1.63
1.625	Oct 05n	99:27	99:28	5	1.69
5.750	Nov 05n	107:10	107:11	5	1.70
5.875	Nov 05n	107:18	107:19	6	1.70
1.875	Nov 05n	100:06	100:07	5	1.75
1.875	Dec 05n	100:02	100:03	6	1.83
5.625	Feb 06n	107:23	107:24	6	1.85
9.375	Feb 06	115:14	115:15	7	1.85
2.000	May 06n	100:01	100:02	8	1.97
4.625	May 06n	105:30	105:31	7	2.01
6.875	May 06n	111:03	111:04	7	2.01
7.000	Jul 06n	111:30	111:31	8	2.10
2.375	Aug 06n	100:17	100:18	8	2.15
6.500	Oct 06n	111:10	111:11	9	2.25
2.625	Nov 06n	100:27	100:28	9	2.30
3.500	Nov 06n	103:09	103:10	8	2.29
3.375	Jan 07i	108:13	108:14	8	0.55
6.250	Feb 07n	111:13	111:14	10	2.41
6.625	May 07n	113:03	113:04	11	2.52
4.375	May 07n	105:26	105:27	10	2.55
3.250	Aug 07n	102:00	102:00	12	2.66
6.125	Aug 07n	111:27	111:28	12	2.65
3.000	Nov 07n	100:25	100:26	12	2.78
3.625	Jan 08i	110:20	110:21	10	0.92
3.000	Feb 08n	100:12	100:13	12	2.89
5.500	Feb 08n	110:05	110:06	14	2.85
2.625	May 08n	98:14	98:15	13	3.00
5.625	May 08n	110:22	110:23	14	2.98
3.250	Aug 08n	100:18	100:19	15	3.11
3.125	Sep 08n	99:27	99:28	14	3.15
3.125	Oct 08n	99:23	99:24	14	3.18
3.375	Nov 08n	100:23	100:24	15	3.20
4.750	Nov 08n	107:00	107:00	16	3.18

Treasury Bills

MATURITY	DAYS TO MAT	BID	ASKED	CHG	ASK YLD
Jan 08 04	1	0.86	0.85	0.05	0.86
Jan 15 04	8	0.91	0.90	0.01	0.91
Jan 22 04	15	0.85	0.84	0.03	0.85
Jan 29 04	22	0.88	0.87	0.02	0.88
Feb 05 04	29	0.85	0.84	0.01	0.85
Feb 12 04	36	0.83	0.82	...	0.83
Feb 19 04	43	0.82	0.81	0.01	0.82
Feb 26 04	50	0.83	0.82	-0.01	0.83
Mar 04 04	57	0.83	0.82	-0.02	0.83
Mar 11 04	64	0.84	0.83	...	0.84
Mar 18 04	71	0.84	0.83	-0.01	0.84
Mar 25 04	78	0.87	0.86	-0.01	0.87
Apr 01 04	85	0.90	0.89	-0.01	0.90
Apr 08 04	92	0.91	0.90	...	0.91
Apr 15 04	99	0.91	0.90	...	0.91
Apr 22 04	106	0.90	0.89	-0.01	0.90
Apr 29 04	113	0.90	0.89	-0.02	0.90
May 06 04	120	0.91	0.90	-0.01	0.92
May 13 04	127	0.91	0.90	...	0.92
May 20 04	134	0.91	0.90	-0.01	0.92
May 27 04	141	0.89	0.88	-0.02	0.90
Jun 03 04	148	0.92	0.91	-0.02	0.93
Jun 10 04	155	0.94	0.93	...	0.95
Jun 17 04	162	0.93	0.92	-0.01	0.94
Jun 24 04	169	0.97	0.96	-0.01	0.98
Jul 01 04	176	0.99	0.98	-0.01	1.00
Jul 08 04	183	1.01	1.00	...	1.02

Source: *The Wall Street Journal*, January 7, 2004, C13. Reprinted by permission of *The Wall Street Journal,* © 2004 by Dow Jones & Company. All Rights Reserved Worldwide.

TABLE 11-8 Quotes on Treasury Strips

MATURITY	TYPE	BID	ASKED	CHG	ASK YLD
May 06	ci	95:12	95:14	1	2.00
May 06	np	95:10	95:12	1	2.03
Jul 06	ci	95:18	95:19	1	1.80
Jul 06	np	94:25	94:27	1	2.12
Aug 06	ci	94:18	94:20	2	2.14
Oct 06	np	93:29	93:30	3	2.27
Nov 06	ci	93:21	93:23	2	2.30
Nov 06	np	93:22	93:23	2	2.29
Feb 07	ci	92:19	92:21	3	2.48
Feb 07	np	92:24	92:25	3	2.43
May 07	ci	91:25	91:27	3	2.56
May 07	np	91:26	91:28	3	2.55
Aug 07	np	90:26	90:28	3	2.68
Aug 07	ci	90:21	90:23	3	2.72
Aug 07	np	90:25	90:28	3	2.68
Nov 07	ci	89:29	90:00	4	2.76
Nov 07	np	89:29	89:31	4	2.77
Feb 08	ci	88:20	88:22	4	2.95
Feb 08	np	88:27	88:29	4	2.89
May 08	ci	87:16	87:18	4	3.08
May 08	np	87:21	87:23	4	3.03
Aug 08	ci	86:22	86:25	4	3.11
Nov 08	ci	85:14	85:17	4	3.25
Nov 08	np	85:18	85:21	4	3.22
Feb 09	ci	84:05	84:08	4	3.39
May 09	ci	83:03	83:06	5	3.47
May 09	np	83:31	84:02	5	3.27
Aug 09	ci	82:05	82:08	5	3.52
Aug 09	np	82:13	82:16	5	3.47
Nov 09	ci	81:14	81:17	5	3.52
Nov 09	bp	80:22	80:25	6	3.68
Feb 10	ci	79:23	79:27	5	3.73
Feb 10	np	80:05	80:08	5	3.64
May 10	ci	78:23	78:26	5	3.79
Aug 10	ci	77:23	77:26	6	3.84
Aug 10	np	78:00	78:03	6	3.78
Nov 10	ci	77:02	77:05	6	3.82
Feb 11	ci	75:11	75:15	7	4.01
Feb 11	np	75:29	76:00	7	3.90
May 11	ci	74:10	74:13	7	4.06
Aug 11	ci	73:13	73:17	7	4.09
Aug 11	np	73:24	73:27	7	4.03
Nov 11	ci	72:17	72:21	7	4.11
Feb 12	ci	71:03	71:07	6	4.23
Feb 12	np	71:20	71:23	6	4.14
May 12	ci	69:31	70:03	6	4.30
Aug 12	ci	69:00	69:04	7	4.34
Aug 12	np	69:26	69:29	6	4.20
Nov 12	ci	68:00	68:04	7	4.38
Nov 12	np	68:29	69:01	7	4.23
Feb 13	ci	66:31	67:03	7	4.43
May 13	ci	66:00	66:04	7	4.47
Aug 13	ci	65:01	65:05	7	4.51
Nov 13	ci	64:00	64:04	7	4.56
Feb 14	ci	63:00	63:04	7	4.61
May 14	ci	61:31	62:03	7	4.66
Aug 14	ci	61:01	61:05	7	4.69
Nov 14	ci	60:01	60:05	7	4.74

Source: *The Wall Street Journal,* January 8, 2004, p. C7. Reprinted by permission of *The Wall Street Journal,* © 2004 by Dow Jones & Company. All Rights Reserved Worldwide.

reason. Also, lower rated bonds consistently trade at larger yields than higher quality bonds to provide a risk premium.

Taking this logic one step further, bonds should generally pay a lower return than equity investments since the equity holder is in a riskier position because of the absence of a contractual obligation to receive payment. As was pointed out in Chapter 1, researchers have attributed superior returns to equity investments relative to debt over the long term.

A number of studies have also investigated the efficiency of the bond market. A primary item under investigation was the extent of a price change that was associated with a change in a bond rating. If the bond market is efficient, much of the information that led to the rating change was already known to the public and should have been impounded into the value of the bond before the rating change. Thus, the rating change should not have led to major price movements. Major research has generally been supportive of this hypothesis.[10] Nevertheless, there is evidence that the bond market may still be less efficient than the stock market (as viewed in terms of short-term trading profits.)[11] The reason behind this belief is that the stock market is heavily weighted toward being a secondary market in which *existing* issues are constantly traded between investors. The bond market is more of a primary market, with the emphasis on new issues. Thus, bond investors are not constantly changing their portfolios with each new action of the corporation. Many institutional investors, such as insurance companies, are not active bond traders in existing issues but, instead, buy and hold bonds to maturity.

The Global Bond Market

The global bond market is in excess of $40 trillion. The United States makes up approximately 49 percent of the market, with no one else even close. Japan has a 19 percent market position, followed by Germany at 12 percent, and Italy at 5 percent.

The astute U.S. investor may wish to scout the entire world bond market for investments. In certain years, foreign bonds perform better than U.S. bonds. For example, in 1996, the total return in the U.S. bond market was 1.4 percent, whereas it was 30.4 percent in Italy and 17.8 percent in the United Kingdom (these latter two values represent returns translated to U.S. dollars). Going back further to 1994, there was a negative return of 7.8 percent in the United States, while the return in Germany was 9.1 percent and 8.5 percent in Japan (once again the two latter returns are translated to U.S. dollars). The high foreign returns can be related to more favorable interest rate conditions (declining rates) and/or an increasing value of the currency against the dollar.

Of course, in many years the U.S. bond market is the best-performing market in the world. The U.S. investor must carefully assess world market conditions, but there are potential benefits to international diversification as explained in Chapter 19.

Dollar-Denominated Bonds

There are key terms associated with the international bond investments. **Dollar-denominated bonds** are bonds in which the payment is in dollars, and these may take the form of **Yankee bonds** or **Eurodollar bonds.** Examples of dollar denominated Yankee and Eurodollar bonds and foreign-pay bonds are presented in Table 11–9 on page 314. Yankee bonds are issued by foreign

---

[10] Steven Katz, "The Price Adjustment Process of Bonds to Rating Classifications: A Test of Bond Market Efficiency," *Journal of Finance,* May 1974, pp. 551–59; and George W. Hettenhouse and William S. Sartoris, "An Analysis of the Informational Content of Bond Rating Changes," *Quarterly Review of Economics and Business,* Summer 1976, pp. 65–78.

[11] George E. Pinches and Clay Singleton, "The Adjustment of Stock Prices to Bond Rating Changes," *Journal of Finance,* March 1978, pp. 29–44.

TABLE 11–9 Global Bonds

Issuer	Type	Maturity	Rating	Currency Denomination
Italy (Republic of)	Yankee	2005	Aa3	U.S. dollar
Petro-Canada	Yankee	2021	Baa1	U.S. dollar
Bank America Corp.	Eurodollar	2009	Aa2	U.S. dollar
North American Holdings	Eurodollar	2013	Baa3	U.S. dollar
Nippon Credit Bank	Foreign-pay	2009	Baa3	Yen
Robo Securities (European firm)	Foreign-pay	2008	Aaa	Euro

Source: *Mergent Bond Record* (published by Mergent, Inc., New York, NY), January 2004.

governments, corporations, or major agencies (such as the World Bank) and are traded in the United States and denominated (payable) in U.S. dollars. To the U.S. investor, they appear the same as any other domestically traded bond.

Eurodollar bonds are also denominated in dollars, but they are issued and traded outside the United States. The issuing firm is normally a major U.S. corporation raising money overseas. Even though the term *euro* is used in the title Eurodollar, it could be issued in any country outside the United States.

Foreign-Pay Bonds

Foreign-pay bonds are issued in a foreign country and payable in that country's currency. For example, a Japanese government bond payable in yen would represent a foreign-pay bond. There is currency exposure to a U.S. investor in a foreign-pay bond in that the yen (or some other currency) may go up or down against the dollar.

Other Forms of Fixed-Income Securities

Our interest so far in this chapter has been on fixed-income securities, primarily in the form of bonds issued by corporations and various sectors of the government. There are other significant forms of debt instruments from which the investor may choose, and they are primarily short term in nature.

Certificates of Deposit (CDs) The **certificates of deposit (CDs)** are provided by commercial banks and savings and loans (or other thrift institutions) and have traditionally been issued in small amounts such as $1,000 or $10,000, or large amounts such as $100,000. The investor provides the funds and receives an interest-bearing certificate in return. The smaller CDs usually have a maturity of anywhere from six months to eight years, and the large $100,000 CDs, 30 to 90 days.

The large CDs are usually sold to corporate investors, money market funds, pension funds, and so on, while the small CDs are sold to individual investors. One main difference between the two CDs, besides the dollar amount, is that there may be a secondary market for the large CDs, which allows these investors to maintain their liquidity without suffering an interest penalty. Investors in the small CDs have no such liquidity. Their only option when needing the money before maturity is to redeem the certificate to the borrowing institution and suffer an interest loss penalty.

Small CDs have been traditionally regulated by the government, with federal regulatory agencies specifying the maximum interest rate that can be paid and the life of the CD. In 1986, all such interest-rate regulations and ceilings were phased out, and the free market now determines return. Any financial institution is able to offer whatever it desires. Almost all CDs are federally insured for up to $100,000 in the event of the collapse of the financial institution offering the instrument. This feature became particularly important in the late 1980s and early 1990s as a result of the problems in the savings and loan and banking industries.

Commercial Paper Another form of a short-term credit instrument is **commercial paper,** which is issued by large corporations to the public. Commercial paper usually comes in minimum denominations of $25,000 and represents an unsecured promissory note. Commercial paper carries a higher yield than small CDs or government Treasury bills and is in line with the yield on large CDs. The maturity is usually 30, 60, or 90 days (though up to six months is possible).

Bankers' Acceptance This instrument often arises from foreign trade. A **bankers' acceptance** is a draft drawn on a bank for approval for future payment and is subsequently presented to the bank for payment. The investor buys the bankers' acceptance from an exporter (or other third party) at a discount with the intention of presenting it to the bank at face value at a future date. Bankers' acceptances provide yields comparable to commercial paper and large CDs and have an active secondary or resale market.

Money Market Funds **Money market funds** represent a vehicle to buy short-term fixed-income securities through a mutual fund arrangement.[12] An individual with a small amount to invest may pool funds with others to buy higher-yielding large CDs and other similar instruments indirectly through the fund. There is a great deal of flexibility in withdrawing funds through check-writing privileges.

Money Market Accounts **Money market accounts** are similar to money market funds but are offered by financial institutions rather than mutual funds. Financial institutions introduced money market accounts in the 1980s to compete with money market funds. These accounts pay rates generally competitive with money market funds and normally allow up to three withdrawals (checks) a month without penalty. One advantage of a money market account over a money market fund is that it is normally insured by the federal government for up to $100,000. However, because of the high quality of investments of money market funds, this advantage is not particularly important in most cases.

---

[12] Most brokerage houses also offer money market fund options.

Both money market funds and money market accounts normally have minimum balance requirements of $500 to $1,000. Minimum withdrawal provisions may also exist. Each fund or account must be examined for its rules. In any event, both provide much more flexibility than a certificate of deposit in terms of access to funds with only a slightly lower yield.

Preferred Stock as an Alternative to Debt

Finally, we look at preferred stock as an alternative to debt because some investors may elect to purchase preferred stock to satisfy their fixed-income needs. **Preferred stock** pays a stipulated annual dividend but does not include an ownership interest in the corporation. A $50 par value preferred stock issue paying $4.40 in annual dividends would provide an annual yield of 8.8 percent.

Preferred stock as an investment falls somewhere between bonds and common stock as far as protective provisions for the investor. In the case of debt, the bondholders have a contractual claim against the corporation and may force bankruptcy proceedings if interest payments are not forthcoming. Common stockholders have no such claim but are the ultimate owners of the firm and may receive dividends and other distributions after all prior claims have been satisfied. Preferred stockholders, on the other hand, are entitled to receive a stipulated dividend and must receive the dividend before any payment to common stockholders. However, the payment of preferred stock dividends is not compelling to the corporation as is true in the case of debt. In bad times, preferred stock dividends may be omitted by the corporation.

While preferred stock dividends are not tax deductible to the corporation, as would be true with interest on bonds, they do offer certain investors unique tax advantages. The tax law provides that any corporation that receives preferred or common stock dividends from another corporation must add only 30 percent of such dividends to its taxable income. Thus, if a $5 dividend is received, only 30 percent of the $5, or $1.50, would be taxable to the corporate recipient.[13]

Because of this tax feature, preferred stock may carry a slightly lower yield than corporate bond issues of similar quality as indicated in Table 11–10 on top of the next page.

Features of Preferred Stock

Preferred stock may carry a number of features that are similar to a debt issue. For example, a preferred stock issue may be *convertible* into common stock. Also, preferred stock may be *callable* by the corporation at a stipulated price, generally slightly above par. The call feature of a preferred stock issue may be of particular interest in that preferred stock has no maturity date as such. If the corporation wishes to take preferred stock off the books, it must call in the issue or purchase the shares in the open market at the going market price.

An important feature of preferred stock is that the dividend payments are usually *cumulative* in nature. That is, if preferred stock dividends are not paid

---

[13] An individual investor does not enjoy the same tax benefit.

TABLE 11-10 Yields on Corporate Bonds and High-Grade Preferred Stock

Year	(1) High-Grade Bonds	(2) High-Grade Preferred Stock	(2) − (1) Spread
2004	6.04%	5.40%	−0.64%
2003	5.97	5.39	−0.58
2002	6.92	6.30	−0.62
2001	7.07	6.42	−0.65
2000	7.72	7.19	−0.53
1999	7.31	6.44	−0.87
1998	6.71	6.09	−0.62
1997	7.40	6.70	−0.70
1996	7.55	6.91	−0.64
1995	7.72	7.01	−0.71
1994	8.50	7.75	−0.75
1993	7.40	6.89	−0.51
1992	8.46	7.46	−1.00
1991	8.97	8.55	−0.42
1990	9.40	9.14	−0.26
1989	9.33	9.08	−0.25
1988	9.75	9.05	−0.70
1987	9.68	8.37	−1.31
1986	9.47	8.76	−0.71
1985	11.82	10.49	−1.33
1984	13.31	11.59	−1.72
1983	12.42	10.55	−1.87
1982	14.41	11.68	−2.73
1981	14.75	11.64	−3.11
1980	12.50	10.11	−2.39

in any one year, they accumulate and must be paid before common stockholders can receive any cash dividends. If preferred stock carries an $8 dividend and dividends are not paid for three years, the full $24 must be paid before any dividends go to common stockholders. This provides a strong incentive for the corporation to meet preferred stock dividend obligations on an annual basis even though preferred stock does not have a fixed, contractual obligation as do bonds. If the corporation gets behind in preferred stock dividends, it may create a situation that is difficult to get out of in the future. Being behind or in arrears on preferred stock dividends can make it almost impossible to sell new common stock because of the preclusion of common stock dividends until the preferred stockholders are satisfied.

Examples of existing preferred stock issues are presented in Table 11–11 on top of the next page. The issues are listed in *Standard & Poor's Security Owners Stock Guide,* and the daily price quotes may be found in the NYSE Composite Stock Transactions section of *The Wall Street Journal* or other newspapers.

TABLE 11-11 Examples of Outstanding Preferred Stock Issues, January 2004

Issuer	S&P Rating	Par Value	Call Price	Market Price	Yield
Consolidated Edison (www.coned.com) 5% cumulative preferred stock	A−	100	105	$76.45	6.54%
PPL Electric Utilities (www.pplweb.com) 4.40% cumulative preferred stock	BBB	100	102	$64.71	6.80
Texaco Corp. (www.texaco.com) 6.875% cumulative preferred stock	A−	25	25	$27.15	6.33

exploring the web

Websites	Comments
www.bondmarkets.com	Provides bond information and trading
www.moodys.com	Provides bond information; some is fee-based
www.bondsonline.com	Provides bond information
www.smartmoney.com	Provides information on bond yields, bond investing, and related topics
www.briefing.com	Provides some bond trading information and general information about bonds
www.teachmefinance.com	Education site pertaining to finance and bonds
www.investorguide.com	Links to sites provide information on government and corporate bonds

Summary

Debt continues to play an important role in our economy from both the issuer's and investor's viewpoints. The primary fund raisers in the bond market are the U.S. Treasury, federally sponsored credit agencies, state and local governments, and corporations.

Bond instruments are evaluated on the basis of many factors, including yield, maturity, method of repayment, security provisions, and tax treatment. The greater the protection and privileges accorded the bondholder, the lower the yield.

A significant feature for a bond issue is the rating received by Moody's Investors Service or Standard & Poor's. The ratings generally range from AAA to D and determine the required yield to sell a security in the marketplace. Although there are no firm and fast rules to determine a rating, strong attention is given to such factors as cash flow and earnings generation in relation to interest and other obligations (coverage ratios) as well as to operating margins and return on invested capital and total assets. Qualitative factors are also considered.

The bond market appears to be reasonably efficient in terms of absorbing new information into the price of existing issues. Some researchers have suggested that the bond market may be slightly less efficient than the stock market in pricing outstanding issues because of the lack of a highly active secondary, or resale, market for certain issues. Insurance companies, pension funds, and bank trust departments are not normally active traders in their bond portfolios.

Short-term investors with a need for fixed income may look to certificates of deposit, commercial paper, bankers' acceptances, money market funds, money market accounts, and the previously discussed government securities as sources of investment. Such factors as maturity, yield, and minimum amount must be considered.

Finally, preferred stock may also be thought of as an alternative form of a fixed-income security. Although dividends on preferred stock do not represent a contractual obligation to the firm as would be true of interest on debt, they must be paid before common stockholders can receive any payment.

Key Words and Concepts

after-acquired property clause 292	general obligation issue 299	put provision 292
bankers' acceptance 315	GNMA (Ginnie Mae) pass-through certificates 297	revenue bond 299
bond indenture 291		secured debt 292
call provision 292		serial payment 291
certificates of deposit (CDs) 314	income bonds 293	shelf registration 303
	junk bonds 306	sinking-fund provision 292
commercial paper 315	maturity date 291	Treasury bills 294
coupon rate 291	money market accounts 315	Treasury bonds 294
debenture 292		Treasury Inflation Protection Securities (TIPS) 295
dollar-denominated bonds 313	money market funds 315	
	mortgage 292	
equipment trust certificate 292	municipal bonds 298	Treasury note 294
	par value 291	Treasury strips 294
Eurodollar bonds 313	perpetual bonds 291	variable-rate notes 291
floating-rate notes 291	preferred stock 316	Yankee bonds 313
foreign-pay bonds 314	private placement 303	zero-coupon bonds 291

Discussion Questions

1. What are some of the major provisions found in the bond indenture?
2. Does a serial bond normally have only one maturity date? What types of bonds are normally issued on this basis?
3. Explain how a sinking fund works.
4. Why do you think the right to call a bond is often deferred for a time?
5. What is the nature of a mortgage agreement?
6. What is a senior security?
7. Discuss the statement, "A debenture may not be more risky than a secured bond."
8. How do zero-coupon securities, such as Treasury strips, provide returns to investors? How are the returns taxed?

9. What are the two forms of returns associated with inflation-indexed Treasury securities?
10. What is an agency issue? Are they direct obligations of the U.S. Treasury?
11. What tax advantages are associated with municipal bonds?
12. Distinguish between general obligation and revenue bonds.
13. How might an investor reduce the credit risk in buying a municipal bond issue?
14. What is an industrial bond?
15. What is shelf registration?
16. What is meant by the private placement of a bond issue?
17. What is a split bond rating?
18. What is meant by the term *junk bond*? What quality rating does it fail to meet?
19. What does a bond quote of 72¼ represent in dollar terms?
20. Why might the bond market be considered less efficient than the stock market?
21. What is the advantage of a money market fund? How does it differ from a money market account?
22. Why would a corporate investor consider preferred stock over a bond? What is meant by the cumulative feature of preferred stock issues?

Problems

Municipal bond

1. If an investor is in a 33 percent marginal tax bracket and can purchase a municipal bond paying 6.25 percent, what would the equivalent before-tax return from a nonmunicipal bond have to be to equate the two?

Municipal bond

2. If an investor is in a 30 percent marginal tax bracket and can purchase a straight (nonmunicipal bond) at 8.20 percent and a municipal bond at 5.95 percent, which should he or she choose?

Bond quotes

3. Using the data in Table 11–6 on page 309, indicate the closing *dollar* value of the Goldman Sachs Group bonds that pay 4.750 percent interest and mature July 15, 2113. There are a number of Goldman Sachs bonds in the table, so be sure to select the correct one. State your answer in terms of dollars based on a $1,000 par value bond.

Interest payments

4. Using the data in Table 11–6 on page 309, indicate the semiannual interest payment dates for the Anheuser-Busch Cos. bonds that mature in 2043. (For the item in question, look under "Interest Payment Dates.") How much will the semiannual payments be?

Bond quotes

5. Using the data in Table 11–7 on page 311, indicate the asking price for the 5.500 percent government note maturing in February 2008 (08). The ask price is the purchase price for the note. State your answer based on a $1,000 par value.

Treasury bill

6. Assume a $1,000 Treasury bill is quoted to pay 4 percent interest over a six-month period.
   a. How much interest would the investor receive?
   b. What will be the price of the Treasury bill?
   c. What will be the effective yield?

Treasury bill

7. In problem 6, if the Treasury bill had only three months to maturity,
   a. How much interest would the investor receive?
   b. What will be the price of the Treasury bill?
   c. What will be the effective yield?

Treasury strip

8. The price of a Treasury strip note or bond can be found using Appendix C toward the back of the text. It is simply the present value factor from the table times the maturity (par) value of the Treasury strip. Assume you are considering a $10,000 par value Treasury strip that matures in 30 years. The discount rate is 6 percent. What is the price (present value) of the investment?

Treasury Inflation Protection Securities (TIPS)

9. You buy a $1,000 inflation-indexed Treasury security that pays 4 percent annual interest. Assume inflation is 6 percent in the first two years you own the security.
   a. What is the inflation-adjusted value of the security after two years?
   b. How much interest will be paid in the third year? The basis for computing interest is the inflation-adjusted value after year two.

Treasury Inflation Protection Securities (TIPS)

10. You buy a 10-year, $1,000 inflation-indexed Treasury security that pays 3 percent annual interest. Assume inflation is 2 percent for the first five years and 5 percent for the last five years. What will be the value of the bond after 10 years? (Use Appendix A to help you in your calculations.) Disregard the 3 percent annual interest.

Comparative after-tax returns

11. A corporation buys $100 par value preferred stock of another corporation. The dividend payment is 7.2 percent of par. The corporation is in a 35 percent tax bracket.
    a. What will be the after-tax return on the dividend payment? (Show the answer in dollars and percent.) Fill in the table below.

Par value	_____
Dividend payment (%)	_____
Actual dividend	_____
Taxable income (30% of dividend)	_____
Taxes (35% of taxable income)	_____
After-tax return (Actual dividend − Taxes)	_____
Percent return = $\dfrac{\text{After-tax return}}{\text{Par value}}$	_____

   b. Assume a second investment in a $1,000 par value corporate bond pays 8.3 percent interest. What will be the after-tax return on the interest payment? (Show answers in dollars and percent.) Fill in the table below.

Par value	_____
Interest payment (percent)	_____
Actual interest	_____
Taxes (35 percent of interest)	_____
After-tax return (Actual interest − Taxes)	_____
Percent return = $\dfrac{\text{After-tax return}}{\text{Par value}}$	_____

   c. Should the corporation choose the corporate bond over the preferred stock because it has a higher quoted yield (8.3 percent versus 7.2 percent)?

Critical Thought Case (A Classic Example)—Focus on Ethics

Gail Rosenberg still had her head in the clouds when she joined Salomon Brothers Inc. in June 1990. While she was proud of her newly awarded MBA from the Wharton School of Business at the University of Pennsylvania, she was even prouder of joining the most prestigious investment banking house on Wall Street, the famous Salomon Brothers. She had a received five job offers, but this was the one she wanted. Not only would she train with the best and brightest on Wall Street, but she also would be working for a firm in which 90 employees made more than $1 million a year. How many *Fortune* 500 companies, law firms, or other employers could claim such a record? She was pleased with her own starting salary of $110,000 a year and could see matters only getting better in the future.

After some general training and apprenticeship-type work, she was assigned to the government bond-trading unit in February 1991. Here she would help in the bidding and distributing of U.S. Treasury bills and notes. Salomon Brothers was the largest participant among investment banking houses in this field, so she knew she would quickly learn the ropes.

Her first major participation would be in the Treasury bill auction for May 1991. Salomon Brothers would bid on behalf of many of its clients and probably have some influence on the ultimate price and yield at which the Treasury bills were sold. As Gail got on her PC to help process orders, she noticed Salomon Brothers submitted bids for clients that did not exist. It was no surprise to Gail that Salomon Brothers captured 85 percent of the bidding and virtually controlled the pricing of the securities.

In a state of shock, Gail went to her immediate supervisor and reported what she had observed on her computer screen. She was told to calm down, that she was no longer in school, and she was witnessing a common practice on "The Street." She was further informed that John Gutfreund, chairman of the board of Salomon Brothers, and President Thomas Strauss implicitly approved of such practices. She felt a little like Oliver North in the Iran-Contra affair cover-up. She had worked very hard to get to this tender point in her career and was now disillusioned.

Question
1. What strategy or advice can you offer to Gail Rosenberg?

Web Exercise

In this exercise, we will examine how the yield on municipal bonds relates to the yield on taxable bonds and also how bond ratings affect the yield that a bond pays. Go to **www.bondsonline.com**.

1. Click on "Composite Bond Yield" along the left margin. Under the Municipal Bonds column, write down the yield on 20-year, AAA-rated bonds. Divide this value by (1 − 0.35). The value 0.35 is assumed to represent the investor's marginal tax bracket. The answer you get is intended to represent the equivalent before-tax yield on a taxable investment.

   Now compare this value to the yield on the 20-year, AAA-rated corporate bond (which represents the yield on a before-tax basis of a taxable investment). What is the difference between this value and the value you just computed? Of course, they will never be the same because of the inefficiencies in the market and different tax rates for investors.

2. Bond ratings and yields were discussed in the chapter. Click on "Corporate Bond Spreads" along the left margin. These spreads represent the difference in yields between a given rated bond and a risk-free Treasury bond. We will work with 10-year issues (across the top). As an example, a Aaa/AAA industrial bond pays 50 to 100 basis points (percentage points) more than a Treasury bond. The AAA industrial is very low risk, but it is still riskier than a Treasury bond issued by the U.S. government.

3. What is the yield spread for a 10-year, A3/A− industrial bond? How many basis points is it greater than a 10-year, Aaa/AAA industrial bond?

4. What is the yield spread on the highest rated junk bond (10-year column)? Look up Ba1/BB+.

5. What is the yield spread of the lowest rated junk bond (10-year column)? Look up Caa/ccc.

6. Generally speaking, what happens to the yield spread as the maturity period increases from 1 year to 30 years for all different categories of bond ratings?

Note: From time to time, companies redesign their websites, and occasionally a topic we have listed may have been deleted, updated, or moved into a different location. Most websites have a "site map" or "site index" listed on a different page. If you click on the site map or site index, you will be introduced to a table of contents that should aid you in finding the topic you are looking for.

CFA Material

The following material contains sample questions and solutions from a prior Level I CFA exam. While the terminology is slightly different from that in this text, you can still view the skills that are necessary for the CFA exam.

CFA Exam Question
The investment manager of a corporate pension fund has purchased a U.S. Treasury bill with 180 days to maturity at a price of $9,600 per $10,000 face value. He has computed the discount yield at 8 percent.

a. *Calculate* the bond equivalent yield for the Treasury bill. *Show* calculations. (*3 minutes*)

b. *Briefly state two* reasons why a Treasury bill's bond equivalent yield is always different from the discount yield. (*2 minutes*)

Solution: Morning Section (I–86) (5 points)
a. $\text{BEY} = \frac{(F - P)}{P} \times \frac{365}{N}$

where:

BEY = Bond equivalent yield
F = Face value
P = Price
N = Days to maturity

$\text{BEY} = \frac{(\$100 - \$96)}{\$96} \times \frac{365}{180} = 8.45\%$

    b. (1) The bond equivalent yield is computed using the actual purchase price of the instrument in the denominator, while the discount yield is calculated using the face value.

    (2) The bond equivalent yield is based on a 365-day year, whereas the discount yield is computed using a 360-day year.

The Wall Street Journal Projects

Look for "Treasury/Agency Issues" in the index at the bottom of the first page of Section C of *The Wall Street Journal*. On the designated page, you will find prices for government agency securities (these are the same as federally sponsored credit agencies). Write down the current bid and ask prices and yield for the following securities:

   a. Fannie Mae—rate of 6.63 and maturity of September 2009 (9-09).
   b. Freddie Mac—rate of 6.38 and maturity of June 2009 (6-09).
   c. Federal Home Loan Bank—rate of 5.80 and maturity of September 2008 (9-08).
   d. Compare the yields with a U.S. government note due in May of 2009 carrying a coupon rate of 5½ percent. This bond is found on the same page under "Treasury Bonds, Notes, and Bills." Explain the differences in yields between the agency issues and the U.S. government bonds.
   e. What can you say about the relative risk of agency securities compared to Treasury securities as reflected in the yields?

Selected References

General Bond Information

Kao, Duen-Li. "Estimating and Pricing Credit Risk: An Overview." *Financial Analysts Journal,* July–August 2000, pp. 50–66.

Kuhn, Susan E. "For Safety and Income, Buy Bonds." *Fortune,* December 23, 1996, pp. 123–4.

Moeller, Thomas, and Carlos A. Molina. "Survival and Default of Original Issue High-Yield Bonds." *Financial Management,* Spring 2003, pp. 83–107.

Park, Cheol. "Monitoring and Structure of Debt Contracts." *Journal of Finance,* October 2000, pp. 2157–95.

Sweeney, Richard J.; Arthur D. Warga; and Drew Winters. "The Market Value of Debt, Market versus Book Value of Debt, and Returns to Assets." *Financial Management,* Spring 1997, pp. 5–21.

Municipal and U.S. Government Bonds

Kihn, John. "The Financial Performance of Low-Grade Municipal Bond Funds." *Financial Management,* Summer 1996, pp. 52–73.

Bond Management Strategies

Elton, Edwin J.; Merlin J. Gruber; Deepak Agrawal; and Christopher Mam. "Explaining the Rate Spread on Corporate Bonds." *Journal of Finance,* February 2001, pp. 247–77.

Research on Bond Ratings

Carty, Lea V. "Corporate Credit Risk Dynamics." *Financial Analysts Journal,* July–August 2003, pp. 67–81.

Crabbe, Leland, and Mitchell A. Post. "The Effect of a Rating Downgrade on Outstanding Commercial Paper." *Journal of Finance,* March 1994, pp. 39–56.

Hite, Gailen, and Arthur Warga. "The Effect of Bond Rating Changes on Bond Price Performance." *Financial Analysts Journal,* May–June 1997, pp. 35–51.

Kealhofer, Stephen. "Quantifying Credit Risk II: Debt Valuation." *Financial Analysts Journal,* May–June 2003, pp. 78–92.

12

chapter twelve

Principles of Bond Valuation and Investment

objectives

1. Describe how the valuation of a bond is based on present value techniques.

2. Explain the differences among various concepts of yield such as yield to maturity, yield to call, and anticipated realized yield.

3. Describe the techniques for anticipating changes in interest rates.

4. Develop an investment strategy for investing in bonds.

5. Describe how bond swaps may be used to increase after-tax returns.

Fundamentals of the Bond Valuation Process
Rates of Return
    Current Yield
    Yield to Maturity
    Yield to Call
    Anticipated Realized Yield
    Reinvestment Assumption
The Movement of Interest Rates
    Term Structure of Interest Rates
Investment Strategy: Interest-Rate Considerations
    Bond-Pricing Rules
    Example of Interest-Rate Change
    Deep Discount versus Par Bonds
    Yield Spread Considerations
Bond Swaps
Appendix 12A: Interpolating to Find Yield to Maturity

The old notion that a bond represents an inherently conservative investment can be quickly dispelled. A $1,000, 10 percent coupon rate bond with 25 years to maturity could rise $214.80 or fall $157.60 in response to a 2 percent change in interest rates in the marketplace. Investors enjoyed a total return of 43.79 percent on long-term high-grade corporate bonds in 1982 and 25.37 percent in 1985. However, the same bond investors would have had a negative total return in 13 of the 35 years between 1968 and 2004. Losses were as high as 10 percent.

This type of movement in the market creates opportunities for an investor. As a student of finance, you should not view bonds as a place where you temporarily park funds while waiting to make stock market investments. Investors in the bond markets are often richly rewarded or harshly punished based on their ability to predict interest rates and the future movement of bond prices.

Perhaps the investment banking team of Goldman Sachs is the most aggressive of the high prestige investment houses when it comes to bond trading. For five straight years, it showed large gains in its own proprietary bond trading portfolio. However, in the third quarter of 2003, it failed to hedge its large mortgage bond portfolio and when interest rates went up, its bond portfolio went down. When the poor bond trading performance of this heavy hitter on Wall Street was announced after the third quarter, its stock went down by 5.9 percent in one day.

In this chapter, we examine the valuation process for bonds, the relationship of interest-rate changes to the business cycle, and various investment and speculative strategies related to bond maturity, quality, and pricing.

Fundamentals of the Bond Valuation Process

Application Example

The price of a bond at any given time represents the present value of future interest payments plus the present value of the par value of the bond at maturity. We say that:

$$V = \sum_{t=1}^{n} \frac{C_t}{(1+i)^t} + \frac{P_n}{(1+i)^n} \tag{12-1}$$

where:

- V = Market value or price of the bond
- n = Number of periods
- t = Each period
- C_t = Coupon or interest payment for each period, t
- P_n = Par or maturity value
- i = Interest rate in the market

We can use logarithms and various mathematical calculations to find the value of a bond or simply use Tables 12–1 and 12–2 on page 328 to determine the present value of C_t and P_n and add the two. (Expanded versions of these two tables are presented in appendixes at the end of the text.)[1]

Assume a bond pays 10 percent interest or $100 ($C_t$) for 20 years ($n$) and has a par ($P_n$) or maturity value of $1,000. The interest rate (i) in the marketplace is assumed to be 12 percent. The present value of the bond, using annual compounding, is shown to be $850.90 as follows:

eXcel

Present Value of Coupon Payments (C_t) (from Table 12–1 or Appendix D)	Present Value of Maturity Value (P_n) (from Table 12–2 or Appendix C)
$n = 20, i = 12\%$	$n = 20, i = 12\%$
$100 × 7.469 = $746.90	$1,000 × 0.104 = $104.00
Present value of coupon payments	= $746.90
Present value of maturity value	= 104.00
Value of bond	= $850.90

---

[1] Students who have difficulty with the time value of money may wish to review Appendix E.

TABLE 12–1 Present Value of an Annuity of $1 (Coupon payments, C_t)

Number of periods (n)	4 Percent	5 Percent	6 Percent	8 Percent	9 Percent	10 Percent	12 Percent
1	0.962	0.952	0.943	0.926	0.917	0.909	0.893
2	1.886	1.859	1.833	1.783	1.759	1.736	1.690
3	2.775	2.723	2.673	2.577	2.531	2.487	2.402
4	3.630	3.546	3.465	3.312	3.240	3.170	3.037
5	4.452	4.329	4.212	3.993	3.890	3.791	3.605
10	8.111	7.722	7.360	6.710	6.418	6.145	5.650
15	11.118	10.380	9.712	8.559	8.061	7.606	6.811
20	13.590	12.462	11.470	9.818	9.129	8.514	7.469
30	17.292	15.372	13.765	11.258	10.274	9.427	8.055
40	19.793	17.160	15.046	11.925	10.757	9.779	8.244

Interest Rate (i)

TABLE 12–2 Present Value of a Single Amount of $1 (Par or maturity value, P_n)

Number of periods (n)	4 Percent	5 Percent	6 Percent	8 Percent	9 Percent	10 Percent	12 Percent
1	0.962	0.952	0.943	0.926	0.917	0.909	0.893
2	0.925	0.907	0.890	0.857	0.842	0.826	0.797
3	0.889	0.864	0.840	0.794	0.772	0.751	0.712
4	0.855	0.823	0.792	0.735	0.708	0.683	0.636
5	0.822	0.784	0.747	0.681	0.650	0.621	0.567
10	0.676	0.614	0.558	0.463	0.422	0.386	0.322
15	0.555	0.481	0.417	0.315	0.275	0.239	0.183
20	0.456	0.377	0.312	0.215	0.178	0.149	0.104
30	0.308	0.231	0.174	0.099	0.075	0.057	0.033
40	0.208	0.142	0.097	0.046	0.032	0.022	0.011

Interest Rate (i)

Application Example

Because the bond pays 10 percent of the par value when the competitive market rate of interest is 12 percent, investors will pay only $850.90 for the issue. This bond is said to be selling at a discount of $149.10 from the $1,000 par value. The discount is determined by several factors, such as the years to maturity, spread between the coupon and market rates, and the level of the coupon payment. While the $850.90 price was calculated using annual compounding, coupon payments on most bonds are paid semiannually. To adjust for this, we *divide* the annual coupon payment and required interest rate in the market by two and *multiply* the number of periods by two. Using the same example as before but with the appropriate adjustments for semiannual compounding, we show a slightly lower price of $849.30 as follows:

Present Value of Coupon Payments (C_t) (from Table 12–1 or Appendix D)	Present Value of Maturity Value (P_n) (from Table 12–2 or Appendix C)
$n = 40, i = 6\%$	$n = 40, i = 6\%$
$\$50 \times 15.046 = \$752.30$	$\$1,000 \times 0.097 = \$97.00$
Present value of coupon payments	= $752.30
Present value of maturity value	= 97.00
Value of bond	= $849.30

We see a minor adjustment in price as a result of using the more exacting process. To check our answer, Table 12–3 presents an excerpt from a bond table indicating prices for 10 percent and 12 percent annual coupon rate bonds at various market rates of interest (yields to maturity) and time periods. Although the values are quoted on an annual basis, the assumption is that semiannual discounting, such as that shown in our second example, was utilized. Note that for a bond with a 10 percent coupon rate, a 12 percent market rate (yield to maturity), and 20 years to run, the value in the table is 84.93. This is assumed to represent 84.93 percent of par value. Since the par value of the bond in our example was $1,000, the answer would be $849.30 ($1,000 × 84.93%). This is the answer we got in our second example. A typical modern bond table may be 1,000 pages long and cover time periods up to 30 years and interest rates from ¼ to 30 percent. For professionals working with bonds on a continual basis, financial calculators and computers are quite common and have a quicker response time.

TABLE 12–3 Excerpts from Bond Value Table

Yield to Maturity (percent)	Coupon Rate (10 percent)				Coupon Rate (12 percent)				Yield to Maturity (percent)
	1 Year	5 Years	10 Years	20 Years	1 Year	5 Years	10 Years	20 Years	
8%	101.89%	108.11%	113.50%	119.79%	103.77%	116.22%	127.18%	139.59%	8%
9	100.94	103.96	106.50	109.20	102.81	111.87	119.51	127.60	9
10	100.00	100.00	100.00	100.00	101.86	107.72	112.46	117.16	10
11	99.08	96.23	94.02	91.98	100.92	103.77	105.98	108.02	11
12	98.17	92.64	88.53	84.93	100.00	100.00	100.00	100.00	12
13	97.27	89.22	83.47	78.78	99.09	96.41	94.49	92.93	13
14	96.38	85.95	78.81	73.34	98.19	92.98	89.41	86.67	14

Rates of Return

Bonds are evaluated on a number of different types of returns, including current yield, yield to maturity, yield to call, and anticipated realized yield.

Current Yield

The **current yield,** which is shown in *The Wall Street Journal* and many daily newspapers, is the annual interest payment divided by the price of the bond. An example might be a 10 percent coupon rate $1,000 par value bond selling for $950. The current yield would be:

$$\frac{\$100}{\$950} = 10.53\%$$

The 10.53 percent indicates the annual cash rate of return an investor would receive in interest payments on the $950 investment but does not include any adjustments for capital gains or losses as bond prices change in response to new market interest rates. Another problem with current yield is that it does not take into consideration the maturity date of a debt instrument. A bond with 1 year to run and another with 20 years to run would have the same current yield quote if interest payments were $100 and the price were $950. Clearly, the one-year bond would be preferable under this circumstance because the investor would not only get $100 in interest but also a $50 gain in value ($1,000 − $950) within a *one-year* period, as the price goes to its $1,000 maturity value.

Yield to Maturity

Yield to maturity is a measure of return that considers the annual interest received, the difference between the current bond price and its maturity value, and the number of years to maturity. More importantly, **yield to maturity** is the same concept as the internal rate of return or true yield on an investment. That is, it is the interest rate (i) at which you can discount the future coupon payments (C_t) and maturity value (P_n) to arrive at a known current value (V) of the bond. Now, we are assuming that you know the current value (price) of the bond (perhaps from *The Wall Street Journal*), the coupon payments, the maturity value, and the number of periods to maturity and that you want to know what the true yield to maturity is on the bond.

Restating Formula 12–1 below, the unknown is now assumed to be i, the interest rate in the market. The interest rate in the market is always going to be the same as the yield to maturity (the bond will yield what the market dictates):

$$V = \sum_{t=1}^{n} \frac{C_t}{(1+i)^t} + \frac{C_t}{(1+i)^n}$$

$$\underset{\text{Unknown}}{\nwarrow \quad \nearrow}$$

Let us compute the value of i. We will use annual analysis to facilitate the calculations. First, we do an easy problem to demonstrate the process, and then we extend the analysis to a more involved calculation.

Assume V (market value or price of the bond) is $850.90, C_t (coupon or interest payment for each period) is $100, P_n (par or maturity value) is $1,000, and n (number of periods) is 20. What i will force the future cash inflows to equal $850.90? Let's use 12 percent, and prove that it works:

Present Value of Coupon Payments (C_t) (from Table 12–1 or Appendix D)	Present Value of Maturity Value (P_n) (from Table 12–2 or Appendix C)
$n = 20, i = 12\%$	$n = 20, i = 12\%$
$100 × 7.469 = $746.90	$1,000 × 0.104 = $104.00
Present value of coupon payments	= $746.90
Present value of maturity value	= 104.00
Value of bond	= $850.90

An i of 12 percent gave us the $850.90 we desired because we used the same *12 percent* we employed earlier in the chapter to get $850.90. (We turned the problem around.) Thus, 12 percent is the yield to maturity.

Let us now go to a situation where we presumably do not know the answer in advance. It should be mentioned at this point that if you have a financial calculator, you may wish to follow the recommended steps for the calculator (such as those shown in Appendix F for the Texas Instruments BA-35 or the Hewlett-Packard 12C) to find yield to maturity. Because the authors cannot assume this is the case, we will introduce you to a trial-and-error method of solution. Please feel free to use the approach that is best for you.

Application Example

Assume a bond is paying a 7 percent coupon rate (C_t), has 15 periods to maturity (n), is selling for $839.27 ($V$), and has a par maturity value (P_n) of $1,000. What is the value of i? Using a trial-and-error process, we will need to make a first guess at the value of i and try it out. Because the bond is selling for less than par value ($1,000), we can assume that the interest rate is greater than 7 percent. Why? Anytime a bond is trading at an interest rate (i) greater than the coupon rate, it will sell for less than par value, and that is the case in this example. Of course, if the coupon rate were greater than the interest rate (i), the bond would sell for more than par value. It would be paying more than the market is demanding and would sell at a premium rather than a discount.

Remember that our first trial-and-error calculation in this example must be at an interest rate (i) greater than 7 percent. Let's try 8 percent for the 15 periods to maturity:

Present Value of Coupon Payments (C_t) (from Table 12–1 or Appendix D)	Present Value of Maturity Value (P_n) (from Table 12–2 or Appendix C)
$n = 15, i = 8\%$	$n = 15, i = 8\%$
$70 × 8.559 = $599.13	$1,000 × 0.315 = $315
Present value of coupon payments	= $599.13
Present value of maturity value	= 315.00
Value of bond	= $914.13

The answer of $914.13 is higher than our desired answer of $839.27. To bring the answer down, we use a higher interest rate. The next try is at 9 percent:

Present Value of Coupon Payments (C_t) (from Table 12–1 or Appendix D)	Present Value of Maturity Value (P_n) (from Table 12–2 or Appendix C)
$n = 15, i = 9\%$	$n = 15, i = 9\%$
$70 × 8.061 = $564.27	$1,000 × 0.275 = $275
Present value of coupon payments	= $564.27
Present value of maturity value	= 275.00
Value of bond	= $839.27

Obviously, 9 percent is the interest rate that equates the future coupon payments (C_t) and maturity value (P_n) to the bond value of $839.27. Thus, we say that 9 percent is the yield to maturity.

Interpolation We cannot always assume that the value we derive from the interest rates in the tables will allow us to arrive at exactly the current value for the bond. Therefore, we may wish to interpolate between two values derived from the table. Using a calculator will provide an exact answer.

Actually, interpolation represents a lot of tedious work and does not convey enough new knowledge to warrant extensive discussion. However, an example of the use of interpolation is presented in Appendix 12A for those who wish to pursue the calculation.

The Formula for Approximate Yield to Maturity

Most textbooks present a formula for *approximate* yield to maturity, and we shall also. Although the formula gives a less precise answer than that determined by financial calculators, computers, or the trial-and-error method, it is an appropriate tool for getting an approximation for the yield on a bond.

The formula is:[2]

$$Y' = \frac{C_t + \frac{P_n - V}{n}}{(0.6)V + (0.4)P_n} \qquad (12\text{--}2)$$

Plugging values into the formula on an annual basis, we find:

Y' = Approximate yield to maturity
C_t = Coupon payment = $100
P_n = Par or maturity value = $1,000
V = Market value = $850.90
n = Number of periods = 20

$$Y' = \frac{\$100 + \frac{\$1,000 - \$850.90}{20}}{(0.6)\$850.90 + (0.4)\$1,000}$$

$$= \frac{\$100 + \frac{\$149.10}{20}}{\$510.54 + \$400}$$

$$= \frac{\$100 + 7.45}{910.54}$$

$$= \frac{\$107.45}{\$910.54} = 11.80\%$$

Actually, the true yield to maturity is 12.00 percent, so the approximate yield to maturity of 11.80 percent is 0.20 percent below the actual yield. In the jargon of bond trading, each 1/100 of 1 percent is referred to as a **basis point,** so the difference is 20 basis points. The approximate yield to maturity method tends to understate exact yield to maturity for issues trading at a discount (in this case, the bond is priced at $850.90). The opposite effect occurs for bonds trading at a premium (above par value).[3]

---

[2] This formula is recommended by Gabriel A. Hawawini and Ashok Vora, "Yield Approximations: A Historical Perspective," *Journal of Finance,* March 1982, pp. 145–56. It tends to provide the best approximation.

[3] In all our bond problems, we assume we buy the bond at the beginning of an interest payment period. To the extent there is accrued interest, we would have to modify our calculations slightly.

Yield to Call

As discussed in the preceding chapter on bond fundamentals, not all fixed-income securities are held to maturity. To the extent a debt instrument may be called in before maturity, a separate calculation is necessary to determine yield to the call date. The answer is termed the **yield to call.** Assume a 20-year bond was initially issued at 11.5 percent interest rate, and after two years, rates have dropped. Let us assume the bond is currently selling for $1,180, and the yield to maturity on the bond is 9.48 percent. However, the investor who purchases the bond for $1,180 may not be able to hold the bond for the remaining 18 years because the issue can be called. Under these circumstances, yield to maturity may not be the appropriate measure of return over the expected holding period.

In the present case, we assume the bond can be called at $1,090 five years after issue. Thus, the investor who buys the bond two years after issue can have his bond called back after three more years at $1,090. To compute yield to call, we determine the approximate interest rate that will equate a $1,180 investment today with $115 (11.5 percent) per year for the next three years plus a payoff or call price value of $1,090 at the end of three years. We can adjust Formula 12–2 (approximate yield to maturity) to Formula 12–3 (approximate yield to call):

$$Y'_c = \frac{C_t + \frac{P_c - V}{n_c}}{(0.6)V + (0.4)P_c} \qquad (12\text{–}3)$$

On an annual basis, we show:

Y'_c = Approximate yield to call
C_t = Coupon payment = $115
P_c = Call price = $1,090
V = Market value = $1,180
n_c = Number of periods to call = 3

$$Y'_c = \frac{\$115 + \frac{\$1{,}090 - \$1{,}180}{3}}{(0.6)\$1{,}180 + (0.4)\$1{,}090}$$

$$= \frac{\$115 + \frac{-\$90}{3}}{\$708 + \$436}$$

$$= \frac{\$115 - \$30}{\$1{,}144}$$

$$= \frac{\$85}{\$1{,}144}$$

$$= 7.43\%$$

The yield to call figure of 7.43 percent is 205 basis points less than the yield to maturity figure of 9.48 percent cited above. Clearly, the investor needs to be aware of the differential, which represents the decrease in yield the investor would receive if the bond is called. Generally, any time the market price of a bond is equal to or greater than the call price, the investor should do a separate calculation for yield to call.[4]

In the case where market interest rates are much lower than the coupon, there is always the chance the company will call the bond. Because of this possibility, the call price often serves as an upper price limit, and further reductions in market interest rates will not cause this callable bond to increase in price. In other words, investors' capital gain potentials may be quite limited with bonds subject to a call.

Anticipated Realized Yield

Finally, we have the case where the investor purchases the bond with the intention of holding the bond for a period that is different from either the call date or the maturity date. Under this circumstance, we examine the **anticipated realized yield.** This represents the return over the holding period.

Assume an investor buys a 12.5 percent coupon bond for $900. Based on her forecasts of lower interest rates, she anticipates the bond will go to $1,050 in three years. The formula for the approximate realized yield is:

$$Y'_r = \frac{C_t + \frac{P_r - V}{n_r}}{(0.6)V + (0.4)P_r} \qquad (12\text{--}4)$$

The terms are:

Y'_r = Anticipated realized yield
C_t = Coupon payment = $125
P_r = Realized price = $1,050
V = Market price = $900
n_r = Number of periods to realization = 3

$$Y'_r = \frac{\$125 + \frac{\$1{,}050 - \$900}{3}}{(0.6)\$900 + (0.40)\$1{,}050}$$

$$= \frac{\$125 + \frac{\$150}{3}}{\$540 + \$420}$$

$$= \frac{\$175}{\$960}$$

$$= 18.23\%$$

The anticipated return of 18.23 percent would not be unusual in periods of falling interest rates.

Reinvestment Assumption

Throughout our analysis, when we have talked about yield to maturity, yield to call, and anticipated realized yield, we have assumed that the determined rate

---

[4] Bond tables may also be used to find the exact value for yield to call. A source is *Thorndike Encyclopedia of Banking and Financial Tables* (Boston: Warren, Gorham & Lamont, 1981).

the real world of investing

So You Want a Long Maturity—How about 1,000 Years?

That's right—bonds of Canadian Pacific Limited have a 1,000-year maturity. By then the cost of a postage stamp should be a few million dollars.

On a more serious note, five major corporations recently offered 50-year bonds, the longest maturities in U.S. history. The following firms participated:

TVA (www.tva.com)	$1 billion
Boeing (www.boeing.com)	$275 million
Conrail (www.conrail.com)	$250 million
Ford Motor (www.ford.com)	$200 million

All were issued at about ¼ percent above comparable 30-year issues of the same firm. Because long-term interest rates were considered low at the time for highly rated corporate bonds (approximately 7½ percent), one can clearly see the motivation to the issuing firm.

What about the investor? Half a century is a long time to be tied in to an investment. Look back 50 years ago; we didn't know about computers, space shots to the moon, or artificial heart transplants. What new events will transpire during the next 50 years?

Nevertheless, approximately $2 billion of these 50-year issues were absorbed in the marketplace. Some investors were motivated by the fact that the maturity of the issues matched their liabilities. An example would be insurance companies with long-term policy commitments. Others recognized that the price sensitivity of a 50-year bond is not much greater than a 30-year bond. Although bond price sensitivity increases with maturity, it increases at a greatly decreasing rate with long maturity obligations. For example, an interest rate increase of 2 percent on a 30-year, 8 percent, $1,000 par value bond will cause a price decline to $811.16. On a 50-year bond, the same 2 percent increase will cause a price decline to $802.20—only about a $9 difference. The extra ¼ percent interest on the 50-year bonds apparently justified accepting the slightly greater price sensitivity exposure.

Also keep in mind that if interest rates fall below the initial issue rate any time over the next 50 years, the investor may have the opportunity for capital appreciation. Fifty years is a long opportunity to wait for a depression, a stock market crash, or other type of event that might drive down interest rates.

An added feature was that the issuers were all in the A to AAA category so that the threat of bankruptcy was thought to be relatively small. However, keep in mind that a lot can happen over a 50-year period. By that time, there may not even be conventional airplanes, automobiles, or gasoline, the primary products of many of the issuers.

---

also represents an appropriate rate for reinvestment of funds. If yield to maturity is 11 or 12 percent, then it is assumed that coupon payments, as they come in, can also be reinvested at that rate. To the extent that this is an unrealistic assumption, investors will wish to temper their thinking. For example, if it is anticipated that returns can be reinvested at a higher rate in the future, this increases true yield, and the opposite effect would be present for a decline in interest rates. The reinvestment topic is more fully developed in Chapter 13.

The Movement of Interest Rates

In developing our discussion of bond valuation and investments, we observed that lower interest rates bring higher bond prices and profits. A glance back at Table 12–3 on page 329 (right-hand portion) indicates a 12 percent coupon rate, 20-year bond will sell for $1,171.60 if yields to maturity on competitive bonds decline to 10 percent and for $1,276.00 when yields decline to 9 percent. The maturity of the bond is also important, with the impact on price being greater for longer-term obligations.

The investor who wishes to make a substantial profit in the bond market must try to anticipate the turns and directions of interest rates. While much of the literature on efficient markets indicates that this is extremely difficult,[5] Wall Street economists, bank economists, and many others rely on interest-rate forecasts to formulate financial strategies. The fact that short-term and long-term rates do not necessarily move in the same direction or move with the same magnitude makes the task even more formidable. Nevertheless, some historical analysis and knowledge of interest-rate patterns over the business cycle are useful in making investment decisions.

Interest rates have long been viewed as a coincident indicator in our economy; that is to say, they are thought to move in concert with industrial production, gross domestic product, and similar measures of general economic health. This is generally true, although in the last five recessions, the change in interest rates has actually lagged behind the decline in industrial production.

While inflationary expectations have the greatest influence on long-term rates, a number of other factors also influence overall interest rates. The demand for funds by individuals, businesses, and the government represents one side of the equation, with the desire for savings and Federal Reserve policy influencing the supply side.

Term Structure of Interest Rates

Of general importance to understanding the level of interest rates is the development of an appreciation for the relationship between the level of interest rates and the maturity of the debt obligation. There is no one single interest rate but, rather, a whole series of interest rates associated with the given maturity of bonds.

The **term structure of interest rates** depicts the relationship between maturity and interest rates. It is sometimes called a yield curve because yields on existing securities having maturities from three months to 30 years are plotted on a graph to develop the curve. To eliminate any business risk consideration, the securities analyzed are usually U.S. Treasury issues. Examples of four different types of term structures are presented in Figure 12–1.

In panel *a*, we see an ascending term structure pattern in which interest rates increase with the lengthening of the maturity dates. When the term structure is in this posture, it is a general signal that interest rates will rise in the future. In panel *b*, we see a descending pattern of interest rates, with this pattern generally predictive of lower interest rates. Panel *c* is a variation of panel *b*, with the hump representing intermediate-term interest rates. This particular configuration is an even stronger indicator that interest rates may be declining in the future. Finally, in panel *d*, we see a flat-term structure indicating investor indifference between debt instrument maturity. This generally indicates that there is no discernible pattern for the future of interest rates. Several theories of interest rates are used to explain the particular shape of the yield curve. We review three of these theories.

---

[5] Michael J. Prell, "How Well Do the Experts Forecast Interest Rates?" *Federal Reserve Bank of Kansas City, Monthly Review,* September–October 1973, pp. 3–13; Oswald D. Bowlin and John D. Martin, "Extrapolations of Yields over the Short Run: Forecast or Folly?" *Journal of Monetary Economics,* 1975, pp. 275–88; and Richard Roll, *The Behavior of Interest Rates* (New York: Basic Books, 1970).

FIGURE 12–1 Term Structure of Interest Rates

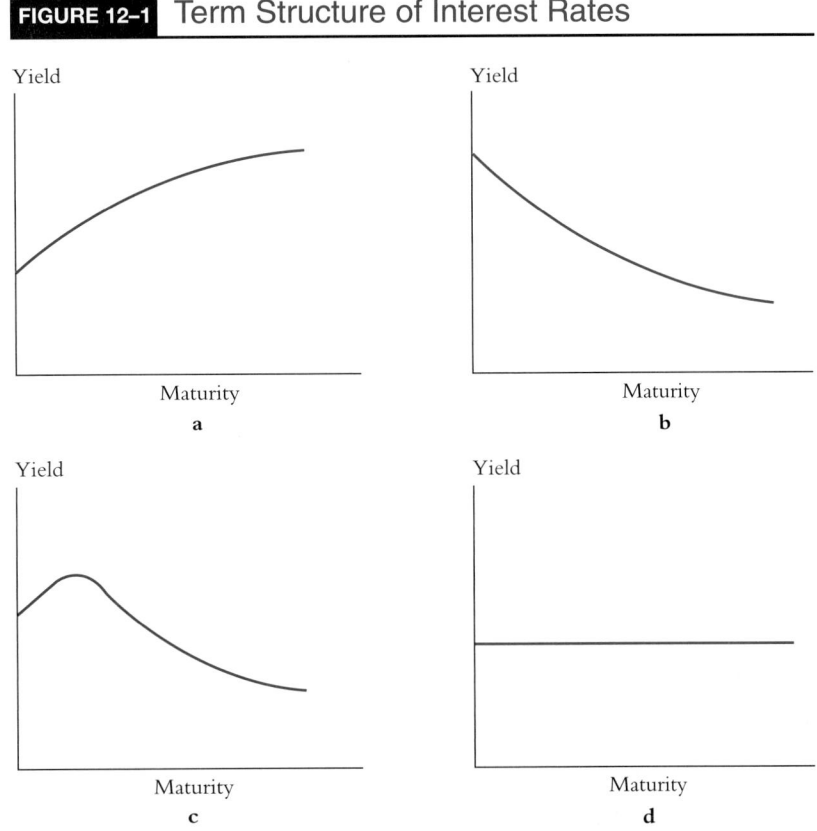

Expectations Hypothesis The dominant rationale for the shape of the term structure of interest rates rests on a phenomenon called the **expectations hypothesis.** The hypothesis is that any long-term rate is an average of the expectations of future short-term rates over the applicable time horizon. Thus, if lenders expect short-term rates to be continually increasing, they will demand higher long-term rates. Conversely, if they anticipate short-term rates to be declining, they will accept lower long-term rates. An example may be helpful. Suppose the interest rate on a one-year Treasury security is 6 percent, and that after one year, it is assumed that a new one-year Treasury security may be bought to yield 8 percent. At the end of year 2, it is assumed that a third one-year Treasury security may be bought to yield 10 percent. In other words, the investor can buy (this is sometimes called roll over) three one-year Treasury securities in yearly succession, each with an expected one-year return.

But what about investors who buy one-, two-, or three-year securities today? The yield they will require will be based on expectations about the future. For the one-year security, there is no problem. The 6 percent return will be acceptable. But investors who buy a two-year security now will want the average of the 6 percent they could expect in the first year and the 8 percent expected in the second year, or 7 percent.[6] An investor who buys a three-year security will

---

[6] The expectations hypothesis actually uses the geometric mean (compound growth rate) rather than the arithmetic mean (simple average) used in the example. For a short number of years, the two means would be quite similar.

demand an average of 6, 8, and 10 percent, or an 8 percent return. Higher expected interest rates in the future will mean that longer maturities will carry higher yields than will shorter maturities. The reverse would be true if interest rates were expected to go down.

The expectations hypothesis tends to be reinforced by lender/borrower strategies. If investors (lenders) expect interest rates to increase in the future, they will attempt to lend short-term and avoid long-term obligations so as to diminish losses on long maturity obligations when interest rates go up. Borrowers have exactly the opposite incentive. When interest rates are expected to go up, they will attempt to borrow long term now to lock in the lower rates. Thus, the desire of lenders to lend short term (and avoid long term) and the desire of borrowers to borrow long term (and avoid short term) accentuates the expected pattern of rising interest rates. The opposite motivations are in effect when interest rates are expected to decline.

Liquidity Preference Theory The second theory used to explain the term structure of interest rates is called the **liquidity preference theory,** which states that the shape of the term structure curve tends to be upward sloping more than any other pattern. This reflects a recognition of the fact that long maturity obligations are subject to greater price-change movements when interest rates change. Because of the increased risk of holding longer-term maturities, investors demand a higher return to hold long-term securities relative to short-term securities. This is called the liquidity preference theory of interest rates. Since short-term securities are more easily turned into cash without the risk of large price changes, investors pay a higher price for short-term securities and thus receive a lower yield.

Market Segmentation Theory The third theory related to the term structure of interest rates is called the **market segmentation theory** and focuses on the demand side of the market. The theory is that there are several large institutional participants in the bond market, each with its own maturity preference. Banks tend to prefer short-term liquid securities to match the nature of their deposits, whereas life insurance companies prefer long-term bonds to match their long-run obligations. The behavior of these two institutions, as well as that of savings and loans, often creates pressure on short-term or long-term rates but very little in the intermediate market of five- to seven-year maturities. This theory helps to focus on the accumulation or liquidation of securities by institutions during the different phases of the business cycle and the resultant impact on the yield curve.

We have now covered all three explanations of the term structure of interest rates. As stated earlier, the expectations hypothesis is probably the most dominant theory, but all three theories have some part in the creation of the term structure of interest rates.

The question being asked in the first part of this decade was, What would be the next major movement in the term structure of interest rates? Would inflation rear its ugly head, causing a shift up in all levels of interest rates, or could the economy continue to grow at a relatively slow pace with no significant evidence of inflation? Of course, a recession is always a possibility as well.

Before concluding our discussion of the term structure of interest rates and proceeding to the development of investment strategies, one final observation is

Chapter 12 Principles of Bond Valuation and Investment 339

| FIGURE 12–2 | Relative Volatility of Short-Term and Long-Term Interest Rates |

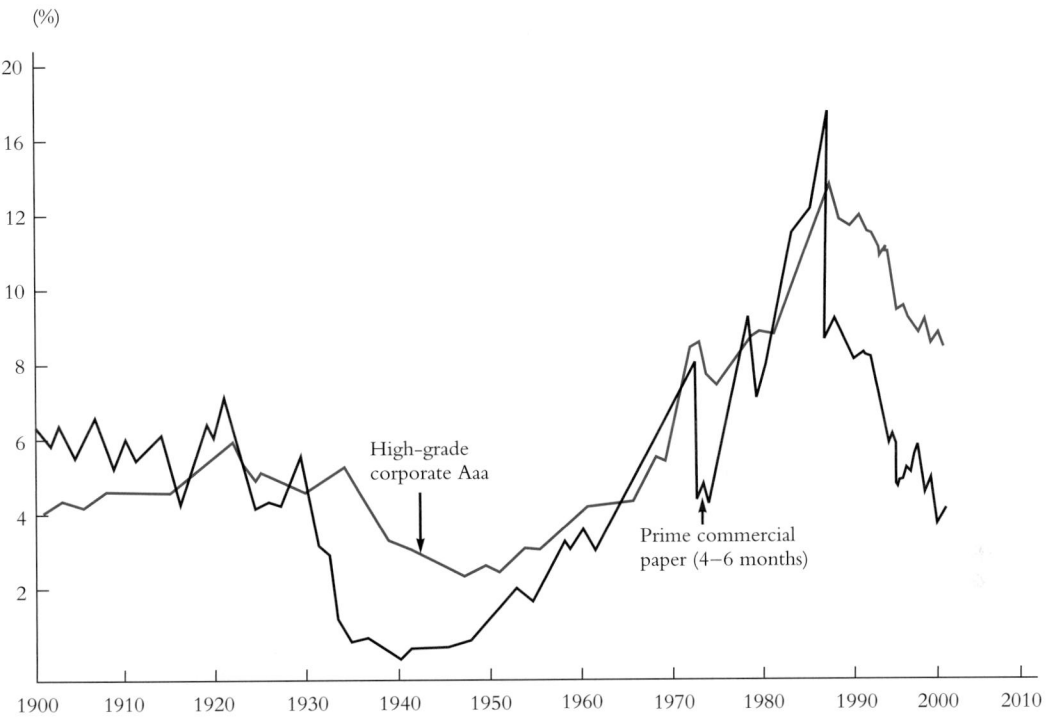

Source: *Federal Reserve Bulletin* (Washington, D.C.: Federal Reserve Board of Governors).

significant. Short-term rates, which are most influenced by Federal Reserve policy in attempting to regulate the money supply and economy, are much more volatile than long-term rates. An examination of Figure 12–2 indicates that *short-term* prime commercial paper rates move much more widely than *long-term,* high-grade corporate bond rates.

Investment Strategy: Interest-Rate Considerations

Thus far in this chapter, we have examined the different valuation procedures for determining the price or yield on a bond and the methods for evaluating the future course of interest rates. We now bring this knowledge together in the form of various investment strategies.

When the bond investor believes interest rates are going to fall, he will take a bullish position in the market by buying long-term bonds and try to maximize the price movement pattern associated with a change in interest rates. The investor can do this by considering the *maturity, coupon rate,* and *quality* of the issue.

Because the impact of an interest-rate change is much greater on long-term securities, the investor generally looks for extended maturities. The impact of various changes in yields on bond prices for a 12 and a 6 percent coupon rate bond can be examined in Table 12–4 on the next page. For example, looking at the −2% line for the 12 percent coupon bond in the upper part of the table, we

TABLE 12–4 Change in Market Prices of Bonds for Shifts in Yields to Maturity

12 Percent Coupon Rate

Yield Change	Maturity (Years)				
	1	5	10	20	30
+3%	−2.69%	−10.30%	−15.29%	−18.89%	−19.74%
+2	−1.81	−7.02	−10.59	−13.33	−14.04
+1	−0.91	−3.57	−5.01	−7.08	−7.52
−1	+0.92	+3.77	+5.98	+8.02	+8.72
−2	+1.86	+7.72	+12.46	+17.16	+18.93
−3	+2.81	+11.87	+19.51	+27.60	+30.96

6 Percent Coupon Rate

Yield Change	Maturity (Years)				
	1	5	10	20	30
+3%	−2.75%	−11.67%	−19.25%	−27.39%	−30.82%
+2	−1.85	−7.99	−13.42	−19.64	−22.52
+1	−0.94	−4.10	−7.02	−10.60	−12.41
−1	+0.95	+4.33	+7.72	+12.46	+15.37
−2	+1.92	+8.90	+16.22	+27.18	+34.59
−3	+2.91	+13.74	+25.59	+44.63	+58.80

see a 2 percent drop in competitive yields would cause a 1.86 percent increase in value for a bond with 1 year to maturity but an 18.93 percent increase in value for a bond with 30 years to maturity. For the same 2 percent drop in rates, the 6 percent coupon bond would increase 1.92 percent (1 year to maturity) and 34.59 percent (30 years to maturity). The relationship between these two bonds further shows that the lower 6 percent coupon bond is more price sensitive than the higher 12 percent coupon bond.

We can also observe that the effect of interest-rate changes is not symmetrical. Drops in interest rates cause proportionally greater gains than increases in interest rates cause losses, particularly as we lengthen the maturity. An evaluation of the 30-year column in Table 12–4 confirms that both bonds are more price sensitive to a decline in yields than to a rise in yields.[7]

Although we have emphasized the need for long maturities in maximizing price movement, the alert student will recall that short-term interest rates generally move up and down more than long-term interest rates as was indicated in

---

[7] A sophisticated investor would also consider the concept of *duration*. Duration is defined as the weighted average time to recover interest and principal. For a bond that pays interest (which includes most cases except zero-coupon bonds), duration will be shorter than maturity in that interest payments start almost immediately. Portfolio strategy may call for maximizing duration rather than maturity in order to achieve maximum movement. A complete discussion of this topic is presented in Chapter 13.

Figure 12–2 on page 339. What if short-term rates are more volatile—even though long-term rates have a greater price impact—which do we choose then? The answer is fairly direct. The mathematical impact of long maturities on price changes far outweighs the more volatile feature of short-term interest rates. A 1-year, 12 percent debt instrument would need to have an interest-rate *change* of almost 9 *percent* to have the equivalent impact of a 1 percent change in a 30-year debt obligation.

Bond-Pricing Rules

The relationships we presented in this section can be summarized in a set of bond-pricing rules. Prices of existing bonds have a relationship to maturities, coupons, and market yields for bonds of equal risk. These relationships are evident from an examination of previously presented Table 12–4. If you look at the change in bond prices in Table 12–4, you may be able to describe many of the relationships presented in the following list:

1. Bond prices and interest rates are inversely related.
2. Prices of long-term bonds are more sensitive to a change in yields to maturity than short-term bonds.
3. Bond price sensitivity increases at a decreasing rate as maturity increases.
4. Bond prices are more sensitive to a decline in market yields to maturity than to a rise in market yields to maturity.
5. Prices of low-coupon bonds are more sensitive to a change in yields to maturity than high-coupon bonds.
6. Bond prices are more sensitive when yields to maturity are low than when yields to maturity are high.

Understanding these six bond-pricing relationships is at the heart of creating bond trading and investment strategies. The next chapter on duration provides a more comprehensive analysis of price sensitivity, coupon rates, maturity, market rates, and their combined impact on bond prices.

Application Example

Example of Interest-Rate Change

Assume we buy 20-year, $1,000 Aaa bonds at par providing a 12 percent coupon rate. Further assume interest rates on these bonds in the market fall to 10 percent. Based on Table 12–5 on page 342, the new price on the bonds would be $1,171.60 ($1,000 × 117.16).

Although we could assume the gain in price from $1,000 to $1,171.60 occurred very quickly, even if the time horizon were one year, the gain is still 17.16 percent. This is only part of the picture. An integral part of many bond-interest-rate strategies is the use of margin or borrowed funds. For government securities, it is possible to use margin as low as 5 percent, and on high-quality utility or corporate bonds, the requirement is generally 30 percent. In the preceding case, if we had put down 30 percent cash and borrowed the balance, the rate of return on invested capital would have been 57.2 percent:

$$\frac{\text{Return}}{\text{Investment}} = \frac{\$171.60}{\$300.00} = 57.2\%$$

TABLE 12-5 Bond Value Table

	Coupon Rate 12 percent		
	Number of Years		
Yield to Maturity	10	20	30
8%	127.18%	139.59%	145.25%
10	112.46	117.16	118.93
12	100.00	100.00	100.00
14	89.41	86.55	85.96

Source: Reprinted by permission from the *Thorndike Encyclopedia of Banking and Financial Tables,* 1981. Copyright © 1981, Warren, Gorham and Lamont Inc., 210 South Street, Boston, MA. All rights reserved.

Although we have to pay interest on the $700 we borrowed, the interest on the bonds (which belongs to the borrower/investor) would have partially or fully covered this expense. Also, if interest rates drop further to 8 percent, our leveraged return could be over 100 percent on our original investment.

Lest the overanxious student sell all his or her worldly possessions to participate in this impressive gain, there are many admonitions. Even though we think interest rates are going down, they may do the opposite. A 2 percent *increase* in interest rates would cause a $133.30 loss or a negative return on a leveraged investment of $300 or a 44.4 percent loss. At the very time it appears that interest rates should be falling due to an anticipated or actual recession, the Federal Reserve may generate the opposite effect by tightening the money supply as an anti-inflation weapon as it did in 1974, 1979, 1981, 1994, and 2001.

Deep Discount versus Par Bonds

Another feature in analyzing a bond is the current pricing of the bond in regard to its par value. Bonds that were previously issued at interest rates significantly lower than current market levels may trade at deep discounts from par. These are referred to as **deep discount bonds.** As an example, the Missouri Pacific 4¾ percent bonds due to mature in 2020 were selling at $695 in January 2004. Their bond rating was Baa2, and the yield to maturity was 7.99 percent.

Deep discount bonds generally trade at a lower yield to maturity than bonds selling at close to par. There are two reasons for this. First, a deep discount bond has almost no chance to be called away. Even if prices go up because of falling interest rates, the price is still likely to be below par value. Because of this protection against a call, the investor in deep discount bonds accepts a lower yield. Second, investors in deep discount bonds have the potential for higher percentage price increases (because of the low price base at which the investment is made).

Yield Spread Considerations

As discussed in the previous chapter, different types or grades of bonds provide different yields. For example, the yield on Baa corporate bonds is always above

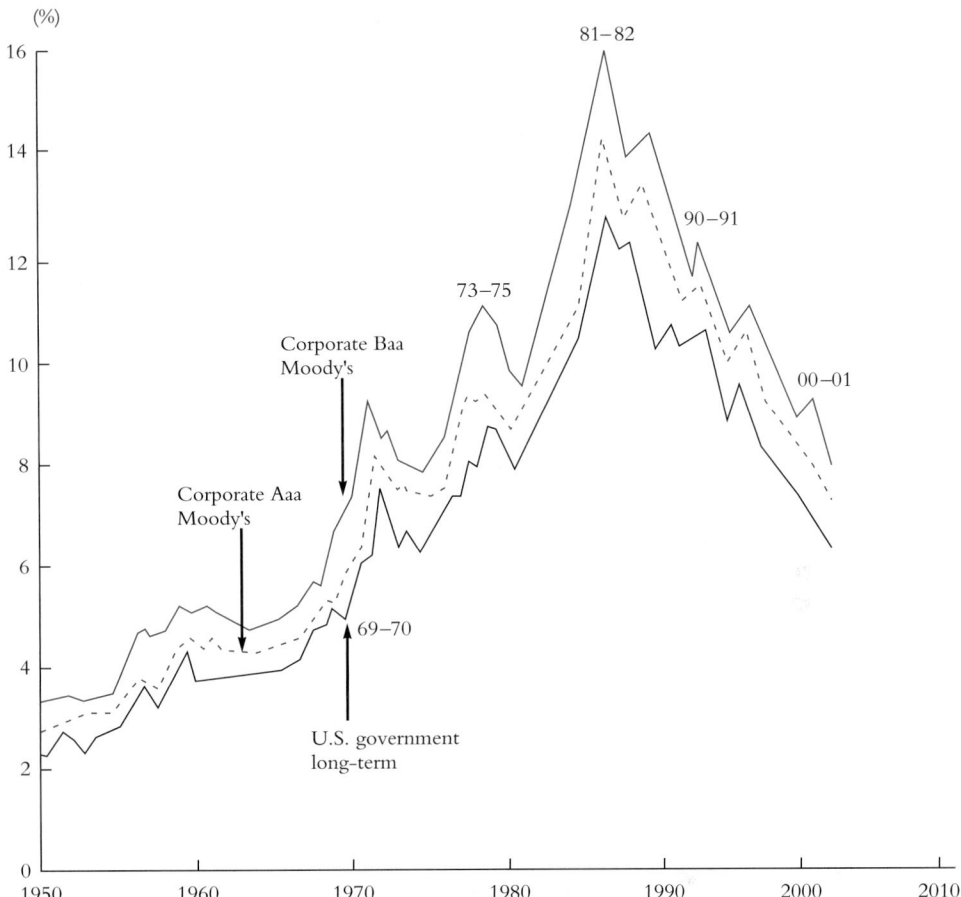

FIGURE 12-3 Yield Spread Differentials on Long-Term Bonds

Source: *Federal Reserve Bulletins* (Washington, DC: Federal Reserve Board of Governors).

that of corporate Aaa obligations to compensate for risk. Similarly, Aaa corporates pay a higher yield than long-term government obligations. In Figure 12–3, we observe the actual yield spread between Moody's corporate Baa's, Moody's corporate Aaa's, and long-term government securities.

Let's direct our attention to total spread between corporate Baa bonds and government securities (corporate Aaa's fall somewhere in between). Over the long term, the spread appears to be between 75 and 100 basis points.[8] Nevertheless, at certain phases of the business cycle, the yield spread changes. For example, in the early phases of a recession, confidence tends to be at a low ebb, and as a consequence, investors attempt to shift out of lower grade

---

[8] The concept of higher yields on Baa bonds should not be confused with that of junk bonds. In the latter case, the yield is substantially higher, but so is the risk of default.

securities into stronger instruments. The impact on the yield spreads can be observed in the recessions of 1969–70, 1973–75, 1981–82, 1990–91, and 2000–01. In all cases, the yield spread between corporate Baa's and government securities went over 150 basis points, only to narrow again during the recovery. Remember that in Chapter 9, on technical analysis, one of the market indicators was the *Barron's* Confidence Index, which measured the ratio of high-grade bonds to medium-grade bonds. The closer the confidence index is to 1.00, the smaller the spread between rates and the more optimistic investors are about the economy. The further the index is below 1.00, the greater the spread in yields and the less the confidence.

Investors must determine how the yield spread affects their strategy. If they do not need to increase the quality of the portfolio during the low-confidence periods of a recession, they can enjoy unusually high returns on lower-grade instruments relative to higher grades.

Bond Swaps

The term **bond swap** refers to selling out of a given bond position and immediately buying into another one with similar attributes in an attempt to improve overall portfolio return or performance.[9]

Often there are bonds that appear to be comparable in every respect with the exception of one characteristic. For example, *newly issued bonds* that are the equivalent in every sense to outstanding issues generally trade at a slightly higher yield.

Swaps may also be utilized for tax-adjustment purposes and are very popular at the end of the year. Assume you own a single A rated AT&T bond that you bought five months ago, and you are currently sitting on a 20 percent capital loss because of rising interest rates. You can sell the bond and claim the loss (up to $3,000) against other income.[10] This will save you taxes equal to the loss times your marginal tax rate. You can then take the proceeds from the sale and reinvest in a bond of equal risk, and you will have increased your total cash returns because of tax benefits.

Another common swap is the **pure pickup yield swap** in which a bond owner thinks he can increase the yield to maturity by selling a bond and buying a different bond of equal risk. The key to this swap is that the bond price of one or both bonds has to be in disequilibrium. This assumes that the market is less than totally efficient. By selling the bond that is overpriced and purchasing the bond that is underpriced, the investor is increasing the yield on the investment. If by chance the true quality and risk of the two bonds are different, the bond trader may have swapped for nothing or may even end up losing on the trade. Other types of swaps exist for arbitrages associated with interest-payment dates, call transactions, conversion privileges, or any quickly changing factor in the market.

---

[9] Interest rate swaps are a somewhat different concept and will be discussed in Chapter 16.
[10] Losses greater than $3,000 can be carried forward to future years.

exploring the web

Website Address	Comments
www.smartmoney.com	Provides some bond information; unique feature is living yield curve
www.bondsonline.com	Provides trading, yield curve data
www.stls.frb.org	The St. Louis Federal Reserve Board website has a wealth of interest rate data.

Summary

The price of a bond is based on the concept of the present value of future interest payments plus the present value of a single-sum payment at maturity. The true return on a bond investment may be measured by yield to maturity, yield to call, or anticipated realized yield. A study of interest rates in the business cycle indicates that while interest rates were at one time a coincident indicator, their movement has tended to lag behind the drop in business activity during recent recessions.

The term structure of interest rates depicts the relationship between maturity and interest rates over a long time horizon. The slope of the curve gives some indication as to future movements, with an ascending pattern generally followed by higher interest rates and a descending pattern associated with a possible decline in the future. While these movements hold true in the long run, it is somewhat difficult to project interest movements in the short run.

An investor who wishes to capture maximum gains from an anticipated interest-rate decline should maximize the length of the portfolio while investing in low-coupon, interest-sensitive securities. Deep discount bonds also offer some protection from call provisions.

A complete analysis of a bond portfolio will also include a consideration of the yield spreads between low- and high-quality issues. The spread between long-term U.S. government bonds and corporate Baa's has been as high as 150 basis points or more during certain periods in the 1970s, 1980s, 1990s, and 2000s. This factor can have a strong influence on bond portfolio construction.

Key Words and Concepts

anticipated realized yield 334
basis point 332
bond swap 344
current yield 329
deep discount bonds 342
expectations hypothesis 337
liquidity preference theory 338
market segmentation theory 338
pure pickup yield swap 344
term structure of interest rates 336
yield to call 333
yield to maturity 330

Discussion Questions

1. Why are bonds not necessarily a conservative investment?
2. How can the market price of a bond be described in terms of present value?
3. Why does a bond price change when interest rates change?
4. Why is current yield not a good indicator of bond returns? (Relate your answer to maturity considerations.)
5. Describe how yield to maturity is the same concept as the internal rate of return (or true yield) on an investment.
6. What is the significance of the yield-to-call calculation?
7. What is the bond reinvestment assumption? Is this necessarily correct?
8. What is the meaning of term structure of interest rates?
9. What does an ascending term structure pattern tend to indicate?
10. Explain the general meaning of the expectations hypothesis as it relates to the term structure of interest rates.
11. Explain the liquidity preference theory as it relates to the term structure of interest rates.
12. How might the market segmentation theory help to explain why short-term rates on government securities increase when bank loan demand becomes high?
13. Under what circumstances would the yield spread on different classes of debt obligations tend to be largest?
14. List the six principles associated with bond-pricing relationships.
15. How do margin requirements affect investor strategy for bonds?
16. Explain the benefits derived from investing in deep discount bonds.
17. What is a bond swap investment strategy? Explain how it might relate to tax planning.

Problems

Bond price

1. Given a 15-year bond that sold for $1,000 with an 11 percent coupon rate, what would be the price of the bond if interest rates in the marketplace on similar bonds are now 12 percent? Interest is paid semiannually. Assume a 15-year time period.

Bond price

2. Given the facts in problem 1, what would be the price if interest rates go down to 8 percent? (Once again, do a semiannual analysis for 15 years).

Use of bond table

3. Using Table 12–3 on page 329, determine the price of a
   a. 10 percent coupon rate bond, with 20 years to maturity and an 11 percent yield to maturity.
   b. 12 percent coupon rate bond with 10 years to maturity and a 9 percent yield to maturity.

Use of bond table

4. Using Table 12–3 on page 329:
   Assume you bought a bond with a 10 percent coupon rate with 20 years to maturity at a yield to maturity of 13 percent. Assume 10 years later the yield to maturity is 8 percent.

Chapter 12 Principles of Bond Valuation and Investment

Determine the price of the bond that you initially paid and the bond price with 10 years remaining to maturity. Also, compute the dollar and percentage profit related to the bond over the 10-year holding period.

Current yield

5. What is the current yield of an 8 percent coupon rate bond priced at $830.12?

Yield to maturity

excel

6. What is the yield to maturity for the data in problem 5? Assume there are 20 years left to maturity. It is a $1,000 par value bond. Use the trial-and-error approach with annual analysis. [*Hint:* Because the bond is trading for less than par value, you can assume the interest rate (*i*) for which you are solving is greater than the coupon rate of 8 percent.]

Yield to maturity

7. What is the yield to maturity for a 9 percent coupon rate bond priced at $1,040.37? Assume there are five years left to maturity. It is a $1,000 par value bond. Use the trial-and-error approach with annual analysis. (*Hint:* Since the bond is trading at a price above par value, first decide whether your initial calculation should be at an interest rate above or below the coupon rate.)

Comparison of yields

8. What is the current yield in problem 7? Why is it slightly higher than the yield to maturity?

Approximate yield to maturity

excel

9. What is the approximate yield to maturity of a 13 percent coupon rate, $1,000 par value bond priced at $1,150 if it has 15 years to maturity? Use Formula 12–2 on page 332.

Yield to call

10. *a.* Using the facts given in problem 9, what would be the yield to call if the call can be made in four years at a price of $1,070? Use Formula 12–3 on page 333.
    b. Explain why the answer is lower in part *a* than in problem 9.
    c. Given a call value of $1,070 in four years, is it likely that the bond price would actually get to $1,150?

Anticipated realized yield

11. *a.* Using the facts given in problem 9, what would be the anticipated realized yield if the forecast is that the bond can be sold in three years for $1,270? Use Formula 12–4 on page 334. Continue to assume the bond has a 13 percent coupon rate ($130) and a current price of $1,150.
    b. Now break down the anticipated realized yield between current yield and capital appreciation. (*Hint:* Compute current yield and subtract this from anticipated realized yield to determine capital appreciation.)

Use of bond table

12. An investor places $900,000 in 20-year bonds (12 percent coupon rate), and interest rates decline by 3 percent. Use Table 12–4 on page 340 to determine the current value of the portfolio.

Use of bond table

13. Use Table 12–4 on page 340 to describe the worst possible scenario for a $1,000 bond based on yield change, years to maturity, and coupon rate. What would be the price of the bond?

Expectations hypothesis

14. The following pattern for one-year Treasury bills is expected over the next four years:

Year 1	6%
Year 2	7
Year 3	9
Year 4	11

a. What return would be necessary to induce an investor to buy a two-year security?
b. What return would be necessary to induce an investor to buy a three-year security?
c. What return would be necessary to induce an investor to buy a four-year security?
d. Diagram the term structure of interest rates for years 1 through 4.

Margin purchase

15. a. Assume an investor purchases a 20-year, $1,000 bond with a coupon rate of 10 percent. The market rate falls to 8 percent. What would be the return on the investment if the buyer borrowed part of the funds with a 25 percent margin requirement? Assume the interest payments on the bond cover the interest expense on the borrowed funds. (You can use Table 12–3 on page 329 to determine the new value of the bond in this problem.)
b. Assume the same 20-year bond in part *a* is purchased with 25 percent margin, but market rates go up to 12 percent from 10 percent instead of going down to 8 percent. You can once again use Table 12–3 on page 329 to determine the price of the bond. What is the percentage loss on the cash investment?

Deep discount bond

16. Assume an investor is trying to choose between purchasing a deep discount bond or a par value bond. The deep discount bond pays 5 percent interest, has 20 years to maturity, and is currently trading at $571 with a 10 percent yield to maturity. It is callable at $1,050.

The second bond is selling at its par value of $1,000. It pays 12 percent interest and has 20 years to maturity. Its yield to maturity is also 12 percent. The bond is callable at $1,080.

a. If the yield to maturity on the deep discount bond goes down by 2 percent to 8 percent, what will the new price of the bond be? Do semiannual analysis.
b. If the yield to maturity on the par value bond goes down by 2 percent to 10 percent, what will the new price of the bond be? Do semiannual analysis.
c. Based on the facts in the problem and your answers to parts *a* and *b*, which bond appears to be the better purchase? (Consider the call feature as well as capital appreciation.)

Tax swap

17. Mr. Williams bought $10,000 in bonds four months ago. The bonds were purchased at par with a 10 percent coupon rate. Now interest rates in the market are 14 percent for similar obligations with 10 years to maturity. The rapid rise in interest rates was caused by an unexpected increase in inflation.

a. Determine the current value of Mr. Williams's portfolio. Use Table 12–3 on page 329 to help accomplish this.
b. How large a deduction from other income can Mr. Williams take if he sells the bonds?
c. If he is in a 28 percent tax bracket, what is the tax write-off worth to him in terms of tax shield benefits?
d. Assume he will replace the old 10 percent bonds with 11.2 percent bonds selling at $875. Based on your answer in part *a*, how many new bonds can be purchased? Round to the nearest whole number.

Web Exercise

In this exercise, we will demonstrate how you can get information on the term structure of interest rates and relate yields spreads to the economic outlook. Go to **www.bondsonline.com**.

1. Click on "Composite Bond Yield" along the left margin. Write down the yields under "U.S. Treasury Rates" for three months through 30 years. Plot out the data.
2. Based on the expectations hypothesis, would you expect the future movement in interest rates to be up or down?
3. What is the yield on 30-year U.S. Treasuries? What is the yield on 30-year AAA-rated corporate bonds? Compute the differences between the two to get the so-called "spread." The normal spread between the two is 75 to 100 basis points, but it expands to 125 to 150 basis points when people become concerned about the economy (they want an increasingly higher yield to take a risk). Based on the number you just computed, what does it appear bond investors are telling us about their outlook for the economy?

Note: From time to time, companies redesign their websites, and occasionally a topic we have listed may have been deleted, updated, or moved into a different location. Most websites have a "site map" or "site index" listed on a different page. If you click on the site map or site index, you will be introduced to a table of contents that should aid you in finding the topic you are looking for.

CFA Material

The following material contains sample questions and solutions from a prior Level I CFA Exam. While the terminology is slightly different from that in this text, you can still view the skills that are necessary for the CFA exam.

CFA Exam Question

4. *a.* *Briefly explain* why bonds of different maturities have different yields in terms of the (1) expectations, (2) liquidity, and (3) segmentation hypotheses. (*5 minutes*)
   b. Briefly describe the implications of each of the three hypotheses when the yield curve is (1) upward sloping, and (2) downward sloping. (*5 minutes*)

Solution: Question 4—Morning Section (I–86) (10 points)

a. (1) The expectations hypothesis maintains that the current long-term rate should equal the average of current and expected future short-term rates. Unless the current and expected future rates are all equal, the averages will be different for different maturities.

(2) The liquidity hypothesis maintains that since longer securities have greater risk, interest rates should increase with maturity as a compensation to investors.

(3) The segmentation hypothesis maintains that individual borrowers are constrained to particular segments of the maturity spectrum. The interest rate for a given maturity will thus depend on the supply and demand for funds in each segment.

b. *Upward sloping yield curve:*
   (1) Expectations—short-term interest rates are expected to be higher in the future.
   (2) Liquidity—as predicted, longer-term securities have higher return to compensate for risk.
   (3) Segmentation—signifies relatively less demand for long-term bonds than short-term bonds.

   Downward sloping yield curve:
   (1) Expectations—short-term interest rates are expected to be lower in the future.
   (2) Liquidity—this is inconsistent with the liquidity hypothesis. When liquidity plus expectations is considered, a decrease in future short-term rates that is larger than the liquidity premium is indicated.
   (3) Segmentation—signifies relatively higher demand for long-term bonds than for short-term bonds.

CFA Exam Question

5. You are considering the purchase of a 10 percent, 10-year bond with a par value of $1,000.
   a. Using Tables I and II, *compute* the price you should pay for this bond assuming semiannual interest payments and 8 percent yield to maturity. (*2 minutes*)
   b. A year from now, you expect that the yield to maturity for this bond will be 6 percent. Using Tables I and II, *compute* the realized compound yield during the year, assuming a reinvestment rate of 5 percent and semiannual interest payments. *Identify* and *comment* on the significance of each of the components of the calculated realized compound yield. (*7 minutes*)

Solution: Question 5—Morning Section (I–87) (10 points)

a. $50 × 13.5903 (4% − 20 periods) = $ 679.52
   $1,000 × 0.4564   =   456.40
   Value   = $1,135.92

b. $50 × 13.7535 (3% − 18 periods) = $ 687.68
   $1,000 × 0.5874   =   587.40
   Value of bond 1 year from now = $1,275.08

TABLE I Present Value of $1

Periods	3 Percent	4 Percent	5 Percent	6 Percent	7 Percent	8 Percent
4	0.8885	0.8548	0.8227	0.7921	0.7629	0.7350
6	0.8375	0.7903	0.7462	0.7050	0.6663	0.6302
8	0.7874	0.7307	0.6768	0.6274	0.5820	0.5403
10	0.7441	0.6756	0.6139	0.5584	0.5083	0.4632
12	0.7014	0.6246	0.5568	0.4970	0.4440	0.3971
14	0.6611	0.5775	0.5051	0.4423	0.3878	0.3405
16	0.6232	0.5339	0.4581	0.3936	0.3387	0.2919
18	0.5874	0.4936	0.4155	0.3503	0.2959	0.2502
19	0.5703	0.4746	0.3957	0.3305	0.2765	0.2317
20	0.5537	0.4564	0.3769	0.3118	0.2584	0.2145

TABLE II Present Value of $1 Annuity

Periods	3 Percent	4 Percent	5 Percent	6 Percent	7 Percent	8 Percent
4	3.7171	3.6299	3.5460	3.4651	3.3872	3.3121
5	5.4172	5.2421	5.0757	4.9173	4.7665	4.6229
8	7.0197	6.7327	6.4632	6.2098	5.9713	5.7466
10	8.5302	8.1109	7.7217	7.3601	7.0236	6.7101
12	9.9540	9.3851	8.8633	8.3838	7.9427	7.5361
14	11.2961	10.5631	9.8986	9.2950	8.7455	8.2442
16	12.5611	11.6523	10.8378	10.1059	9.4466	8.8514
18	13.7535	12.6593	11.6896	10.8276	10.0591	9.3719
19	14.3238	13.1339	12.0853	11.1581	10.3356	9.6036
20	14.8775	13.5903	12.4622	11.4699	10.5940	9.8181

Realized compound yield:
Ending wealth value:

$1,275.08—ending price of bond
50.00—interest at end of year
50.00—mid-year interest payment
1.25—5% interest on interest for ½ year
───────
$1,276.33

$$\text{Realized compound yield} = \frac{\$1,376.33}{\$1,135.92} - 1 = 1.2116 - 1$$
$$= 21.16\%$$

There are three components of the realized compound yield calculated above: price appreciation due to decline in rates from 8 percent to 6 percent, coupon interest, and interest on interest.

The total return in dollars for the year was $240.41. Of that total return, $139.16, or about 58 percent, was due to price appreciation; $100, or about 42 percent, was due to coupon interest; and about 0.5 percent was due to interest on interest.

Because the realized compound yield is calculated over only one year in which rates have fallen, the interest-on-interest component will be very small, and the appreciation component is the largest. Had the coupon been smaller than 10 percent, the appreciation component would have been even larger.

S&P Problems

STANDARD &POOR'S

www.mhhe.com/edumarketinsight

1. Log on to the McGraw-Hill website: www.mhhe.com/edumarketinsight (see page vi in the preface for instructions).
2. Click on Commentary, which is the third box below the Market Insight title.
3. Click on the blue Trends and Projections in the left margin, under the bold heading. Trends and Projections is Standard & Poor's monthly economic update.

4. Scroll through the article until you find the long-term interest rate chart showing the 10-year treasury note, the 3-month treasury bill, and the real treasury note rate. Using this chart, forecast next year's interest rates. Will interest rates move up, down, or remain flat? Why and on what basis do you make your recommendation?
5. Now go to the last page showing economic indicators. Halfway down the page, under prices and interest rates, you will find interest rate forecasts for treasury bills, 10-year notes, and 30-year bonds. What are the interest rate projections for each of these over the next four quarters?
6. If Standard & Poor's is right in their forecast, what are your expectations for bond prices? Explain your rationale.
7. What bond strategy would you pursue if you were managing a bond portfolio? Why?

The Wall Street Journal Projects

Look up "Treasury Bonds, Notes & Bills" in Section C of *The Wall Street Journal*. This can be found in the index under "Treasury/Agency Securities." Use this information to plot the term structure of interest rates as illustrated in Figure 12–1 on page 337. Follow these steps:

a. Find the Ask Yld. (yield) on a Treasury bill that matures approximately six months in the future.

b. Find the Ask Yld. under the "Government Bonds & Notes" subheading on a security that matures approximately five years into the future. Follow this same procedure for a security maturing approximately 10, 20, and 30 years in the future. Exact dates are not critical.

c. Plot the dates on the horizontal axis.

d. Plot the yields on the vertical axis.

e. Which of the four patterns in Figure 12–1 does your term structure most resemble?

Selected References

Investment Strategies with Bonds

Brick, Ivan E., and S. Abraham Ravid. "Interest Rate Uncertainty and the Optimal Debt Maturity Structure." *Journal of Financial and Quantitative Analysis,* March 1991, pp. 63–81.

Cao, Melanie, and Jason Wei. "Vulnerable Options, Risky Corporate Bonds, and Credit Spread." *The Journal of Futures Markets,* April 2001, pp. 301–27.

Farnsworth, Heber, and Richard Bass. "The Term Structure and Semi-credible Targeting." *Journal of Finance,* April 2003, pp. 839–65.

Gutner, Toddi. "How to Pick Bonds That Won't Wither If Interest Rates Go Up." *BusinessWeek,* December 29, 2003, pp. 110–11.

McAdams, Lloyd, and Evangelos Karagiannis. "Using Yield Curve Shapes to Manage Bond Portfolios." *Financial Analysts Journal,* May–June 1994, pp. 57–59.

Bond Yields

Campbell, John Y., and Glen B. Takslar. "Equity Trading and Corporate Bond Yields." *Journal of Finance,* December 2003, pp. 2285–2320.

Heynen, Ronald; Angelien Kemna; and Tom Vorst. "Analysis of the Term Structure of Implied Volatilities." *Journal of Financial and Quantitative Analysis,* March 1994, pp. 31–56.

Santa-Clara, Pedro. "The Dynamics of Forward Interest Rate Curves with Stochastic String Shocks." *Review of Financial Studies,* Spring 2001, pp. 149–85.

Empirical Studies

Clark, Timothy; F. Crack; and Sanjay K. Nawalkha. "Interest Rate Sensitivities of Bond Risk Measures." *Financial Analysts Journal,* January–February 2000, pp. 34–43.

Wilson, Jack W., and Charles P. Jones. "Long-Term Returns and Risk for Bonds." *The Journal of Portfolio Management,* Spring 1997, pp. 15–28.

APPENDIX 12A

INTERPOLATING TO FIND YIELD TO MATURITY

Interpolation allows you to find a more exact answer to a bond yield problem.

Assume a bond has a coupon rate of 7 percent ($70), has 15 years to maturity (n), and is selling at $875.00.

We will assume that at an interest rate of 8 percent, you got a bond price of $914.13, and at 9 percent, the value was $839.27. Thus, the interest rate associated with $875.00 must fall between 8 and 9 percent. Using interpolation, we find the yield y* as follows:

Interest Rate	Bond Price		
8%	$914.13 ⎤	$39.13	
y*	875.00 ⎦	↑	$74.86
9%	839.27	Difference between upper and middle value	↑ Difference between upper and lower value

$$8\% + \frac{\$39.13}{74.86}(1\%) = 8\% + 0.52\% = 8.52\%$$

The interpolated answer between 8 and 9 percent is 8.52 percent.

13

chapter thirteen

Duration and Reinvestment Concepts

objectives

1. Understand that duration is a better measure of the life of a bond than maturity.

2. Be able to use present value techniques to compute duration.

3. Explain the effect that duration has on bond price sensitivity to interest rates changes.

4. Describe the uses of duration in protecting the value of a portfolio.

5. Relate zero-coupon bonds to the concept of duration.

6. Explain how the reinvestment rate for inflows may materially affect the final value of an investment.

Review of Basic Bond Valuation Concepts
Duration
Duration and Price Sensitivity
    Duration and Market Rates
    Duration and Coupon Rates
Bringing Together the Influences on Duration
Duration and Zero-Coupon Bonds
The Uses of Duration
Bond Reinvestment Assumptions and Terminal Wealth Analysis
    Reinvestment Assumptions
    Terminal Wealth Analysis
    Zero-Coupon Bonds and Terminal Wealth
Appendix 13A: Modified Duration and Convexity

Review of Basic Bond Valuation Concepts

In Chapter 12, we discussed the principles of bond valuation. The value of a bond was established in Formula 12–1 on page 327 as follows:

$$V = \sum_{t=1}^{n} \frac{C_t}{(1=i)^t} + \frac{P_n}{(1+i)^n}$$

where:

V = Market value or price of the bond
n = Number of periods
t = Each period
C_t = Coupon or interest payment for each period, t
P_n = Par or maturity value
i = Interest rate in the market

Based on this equation, as interest rates in the market rise, the price of the bond will decline because the present value of the cash flows is worth less at a higher discount rate. The opposite is true if interest rates decline. We also demonstrated in Table 12–4 that bonds with long-term maturities were generally more sensitive to changes in interest rates than were short-term bonds. Reproduction of part of Table 12–4 below shows that a 30-year bond exhibits larger price changes in response to a change in yield than do shorter-term obligations. For example, a 2 percent drop in interest rates would cause a 1.86 percent increase in value for a bond with one year to maturity, but an 18.93 percent price change for a bond with 30 years to maturity. Given the relationship between the life of a bond and the price sensitivity just described, it is particularly important that we have an appropriate definition of the life or term of a bond.

(Reproduction of Table 12–4) Change in Market Prices of Bonds for Shifts in Yields to Maturity (12 percent coupon rate)

Yield Change	\multicolumn{5}{c}{Maturity (Years)}
	1	5	10	20	30
+3%	−2.69%	−10.30%	−15.29%	−18.89%	−19.74%
+2	−1.81	−7.02	−10.59	−13.33	−14.04
+1	−0.91	−3.57	−5.01	−7.08	−7.52
−1	+0.92	+3.77	+5.98	+8.02	+8.72
−2	+1.86	+7.72	+12.46	+17.16	+18.93
−3	+2.81	+11.87	+19.51	+27.60	+30.96

The first inclination is to say that the term of a bond is an easily determined matter. One supposedly merely needs to look up the maturity date (such as 2010 or 2020) in a bond book, and the matter is settled. However, the notion of effective life of a bond is more complicated than this. The situation is somewhat analogous to the quoted coupon rate on the bond not really conveying the true yield on the obligation. Similarly, the maturity date on a bond may not convey all important information about the life of a bond.

shown in column (5), is determined by dividing $63.76 by $855.40 to arrive at 0.0745. In column (6), each year is multiplied by the weights developed in column (5). For example, year 1 is multiplied by 0.0835 to arrive at 0.0835 in column (6). Year 2 is multiplied by 0.0745 to arrive at 0.1490. This procedure is followed for each year, and the values are then summed.

The final answer for duration (the weighted average life based on present value) is 4.2498. This 4.2498 duration is referred to as **Macaulay duration,** named after Frederick Macaulay who developed this concept more than 100 years ago. Duration, once determined, is the most representative value for effective bond life and the measure against which bond price sensitivity should be evaluated.

The formula for duration can be formally stated as:

$$\text{Macaulay duration (D)} = \underbrace{\frac{CF\ PV}{V}}_{\text{Weight}} \underbrace{(1)}_{\text{Year}} + \underbrace{\frac{CF\ PV}{V}}_{\text{Weight}} \underbrace{(2)}_{\text{Year}} + \underbrace{\frac{CF\ PV}{V}}_{\text{Weight}} \underbrace{(3)}_{\text{Year}} + \ldots + \underbrace{\frac{CF\ PV}{V}}_{\text{Weight}} \underbrace{(n)}_{\text{Year}} \quad \text{(13–1)}$$

where:

CF = Yearly cash flow for each time period

PV = Present value factor for each time period (from Appendix C at the end of the book)

V = Total present value or market price of the bond

n = Number of periods to maturity[1]

In Table 13–3 on page 360, we observe durations for an 8 percent coupon rate bond with maturities of 1, 5, and 10 years. The discount rate is 12 percent. The procedure used to compute duration in Table 13–3 is the same as that employed in Table 13–2. Although many calculations are involved, you should primarily direct your attention to the last value presented in column (6) for each of the three bonds. This value represents the duration of the issue.

We see in Table 13–3 that the duration for a one-year bond is 1.0. Since all cash flows are paid at the end of year 1, duration equals the maturity.[2] As maturity increases (to 5 and 10 years), duration increases but less than the maturity of the bond. With a 5-year bond, duration is 4.2498, and with a 10-year bond, duration is 6.8381. Duration is increasing at a decreasing rate because the principal repayment in the last year becomes a smaller percentage of the total

---

[1] Using the symbols from Formula 12–1, duration can also be stated as:

$$\text{Duration} = \sum_{t=1}^{n} \frac{C_t \frac{1}{(1+i)^t}}{V}(t) + \frac{P_n \frac{1}{(1+i)^n}}{V}(n)$$

If semiannual analysis is used throughout the calculation, the answer should be divided by two to convert the figure to annual terms.

[2] If semiannual analysis were used, the duration would be slightly less than the maturity in the first year.

the real world of investing

International Bond Managers—Changing Interest Rates and Bond Prices

International bond managers have their hands full managing interest rate risk around the globe. In addition to changing interest rates, these managers also have to pay attention to currency fluctuations, local economies, and government intervention into the money markets. During the last half of 2003, long-term interest rates in the world's large economies all declined. Between June and December long-term U.S. Treasuries fell from 5.5 percent to 5.0 percent and similar patterns were present for the British gilts, German bonds, and other securities.

It is difficult to forecast changes in interest rates, and most bankers admit that any forecast of interest rates more than three months into the future is hazardous. There are always unexpected changes in inflation, GDP, central bank policy, and so on.

All these factors can impact world bond prices and create price fluctuations. Given the sophistication of these international bond managers, let's give them the benefit of the doubt and assume they can actually forecast changing interest rates over the next three months. Let's also assume they can make money by shorting bonds whose prices will fall as interest rates rise and buying long those bonds whose prices will rise as interest rates fall.

How does a bond manager know whether an increase in rates by ¼ percent on a 1.8 percent Japanese bond will change the price more or less than a ½ percent increase on a 5.5 percent German bond? They will most likely have to use the concept of *duration* to calculate which bond is most price sensitive to a change in interest rates. Given that all international bonds will not have the same maturity may appear to complicate the decision, but duration measures bond price sensitivity and considers the current market interest rate, the maturity of the bond and the bond's coupon rate. This is just what the international trader needs to make decisions in this fast moving world of international interest rate movements.

present value of cash flow, and the annual coupon payments become more important.[3]

Duration and Price Sensitivity

Once duration is computed, its most important use is in determining the price sensitivity of a bond. In Table 13–4 on page 361, we consider the maturity, duration, and percentage price change for an 8 percent coupon rate bond based on a 2 percent decrease and on a 2 percent increase in interest rates. The *market* rate of interest for computing duration in Table 13–4 is 8 percent. Duration is related not only to maturity but also to coupon rate and market rate of interest. For example, in Table 13–3, the coupon rate of interest was 8 percent, and the market rate of interest was 12 percent. In the calculations in Table 13–4, the coupon rate is 8 percent, and the initial market rate of interest is assumed to be 8 percent. Because of the different market rates of interest in Tables 13–3 and 13–4, the duration for a given maturity (such as 5 or 10 years) will be different. The point just discussed will be further clarified later in the chapter, so even if you do not fully understand it, you should still continue to read on.

We see in Table 13–4 that the longer the maturity or duration, the greater the impact of a 2 percent change in interest rates on price. However, we shall also

---

[3] A sinking-fund provision can also have an effect on duration, causing the weighted average life of the bond to be shorter.

TABLE 13–3 Duration for 8 Percent Coupon Rate Bonds with Maturities of 1, 5, and 10 Years Discounted at 12 Percent

1-Year Bond

(1) Year, t	(2) Cash Flow (CF)	(3) PV Factor at 12 Percent	(4) PV of Cash Flow (CF)	(5) PV of Annual Cash Flow (4) ÷ by Total PV of Cash Flows	(6) Year × Weight (1) × (5)
1	$ 80	0.893	$ 71.44	0.0741	0.0741
1	1,000	0.893	893.00	0.9259	0.9259
			Total PV of → $964.44 cash flows	1.0000	1.0000 ↑ Duration

5-Year Bond

1	$ 80	0.893	$ 71.44	0.0835	0.0835
2	80	0.797	63.76	0.0745	0.1490
3	80	0.712	56.96	0.0666	0.1998
4	80	0.636	50.88	0.0595	0.2380
5	80	0.567	45.36	0.0530	0.2650
5	1,000	0.567	567.00	0.6629	3.3145
			Total PV of → $855.40 cash flows	1.0000	4.2498 ↑ Duration

10-Year Bond

1	$ 80	0.893	$ 71.44	0.0923	0.0923
2	80	0.797	63.76	0.0824	0.1648
3	80	0.712	56.96	0.0736	0.2208
4	80	0.636	50.88	0.0657	0.2628
5	80	0.567	45.36	0.0586	0.2930
6	80	0.507	40.56	0.0524	0.3144
7	80	0.452	36.16	0.0467	0.3269
8	80	0.404	32.32	0.0418	0.3344
9	80	0.361	28.88	0.0373	0.3357
10	80	0.322	25.76	0.0330	0.3330
10	$1,000	0.322	322.00	0.4160	4.1600
			Total PV of → $774.08 cash flows	1.0000	6.8381 ↑ Duration

observe how much more closely the percentage change in price parallels the change in duration as compared with maturity. For example, between 25 and 50 years, duration increases very slowly [column (2)], and the same can be said for the increase in the percentage impact that a 2 percent decline in interest rates has on price [column (3)]. This is true despite the fact that the maturity period has increased by 100 percent, from 25 to 50 years.

TABLE 13–4 Duration and Price Sensitivity (8 Percent Coupon Rate Bond)

(1) Maturity	(2) Duration	(3) Impact of a 2% Decline in Interest Rates on Price	(4) Impact of a 2% Increase in Interest Rates on Price
1	1.0000	+1.89%	−1.81%
5	4.3121	+8.42	−7.58
10	7.2470	+14.72	−12.29
20	10.6038	+22.93	−17.03
25	11.5290	+25.57	−18.50
30	12.1585	+27.53	−18.85
40	12.8787	+30.09	−19.55
50	13.2123	+31.15	−19.83

Application Example

As a rough measure of price sensitivity, one can multiply duration times the change in interest rates to determine the percentage change in the value of a bond.

$$\text{Percentage change in the value of a bond approximately equals} \rightarrow \text{Duration} \times \text{Change in interest rates} \quad (13\text{–}2)$$

The sign in the final answer is reversed because interest-rate changes and bond prices move in opposite directions. For example, if a bond has a duration of 7.2470 years, and interest rates go down by 2 percent, a rough measure of bond value appreciation is +14.494 percent (7.2470 × 2). Columns (2) and (3) in Table 13–4, across from 10 years maturity, indicate this is a good approximation. That is, when duration was 7.2470, a 2 percent drop in interest rates actually produced a 14.72 percent increase in bond prices (not too many basis points away from our formula value of +14.494 percent).[4] The approximation gets progressively less accurate as the term of the bond is extended. It is also a less valid measure for interest-rate increases (and the associated price decline). Even with these qualifications, one can observe a more useful relationship between price changes and duration than between price changes and maturity.

It is for this reason that the analyst must have a reasonable feel for the factors that influence duration. The length of the bond affects duration, but as previously mentioned, it is not the only variable. Duration is also influenced by market rate of interest and the coupon rate on the bond. It is theoretically possible for these two factors to outweigh maturity in determining duration. That is to say, it is possible that a bond with a shorter maturity than another bond may actually have a longer duration and be more price sensitive to interest rate changes.

---

[4] The approximation can be slightly improved by using modified duration instead of actual duration. Modified duration is explained in Appendix 13A as is convexity. This is not required reading to understand the material in the chapter, but it may prove interesting to the more advanced student.

Duration and Market Rates

Market rates of interest (yield to maturity) and duration are inversely related. The higher the market rate of interest, the lower the duration. This is because of the present-value effect that is part of duration. Higher market rates of interest mean lower present values. For example, in Table 13–2 on page 357, if the market rate of interest in column (3) had been 16 percent instead of 12 percent, the final answer for duration would have been 4.1859. The new value is computed in Table 13–5. Clearly, it is less than the 4.2498 duration value in Table 13–2.

To expand our analysis, in Table 13–6 we see the duration values for an 8 percent coupon rate bond at different market rates of interest. As market rates of interest increase, duration decreases. This can be easily seen in the 20-year row (reading across). At a 4 percent market rate of interest, duration for the 8 percent coupon rate bond is 12.3995. At 8 percent, it is 10.6038, and at 12 percent, 8.9390.

TABLE 13–5 Duration of an 8 Percent Coupon Rate Bond with a 16 Percent Market Rate of Interest

(1) Year, t	(2) Cash Flow (CF)	(3) PV Factor at 16 Percent	(4) PV of Cash Flow (CF)	(5) PV of Annual Cash Flow (4) ÷ by Total PV of Cash Flows	(6) Year × Weight (1) × (5)
1	$ 80	0.862	$ 68.96	0.0935	0.0935
2	80	0.743	59.44	0.0806	0.1612
3	80	0.641	51.28	0.0695	0.2085
4	80	0.552	44.16	0.0598	0.2392
5	80	0.476	38.08	0.0516	0.2580
5	$1,000	0.476	476.00	0.6451	3.2255
			Total PV of → $737.92 cash flows	1.0000	4.1859 ↑ Duration

TABLE 13–6 Duration Values at Varying Market Rates of Interest (Based on 8 Percent Coupon Rate Bond)

	Market Rates of Interest				
Maturity (Years)	4 Percent	6 Percent	8 Percent	10 Percent	12 Percent
1	1.0000	1.0000	1.0000	1.0000	1.0000
5	4.3717	4.3423	4.3121	4.2814	4.2498
10	7.6372	7.4450	7.2470	7.0439	6.8381
20	12.3995	11.4950	10.6038	9.7460	8.9390
25	14.2265	12.8425	11.5290	10.3229	9.2475
30	15.7935	13.8893	12.1585	10.6472	9.3662
40	18.3274	15.3498	12.8787	10.9176	9.3972
50	20.2481	16.2494	13.2123	10.9896	9.3716

Also note in Table 13–6 that an equal change in market rates of interest will have a bigger impact on duration when rates move down than when they move up. For example, in the 50-year row, a 4 percentage point decrease in market rates of interest (say, from 8 percent to 4 percent) causes duration to increase by 7.0358 years, from 13.2123 to 20.2481 years. A similar increase from 8 percent to 12 percent would cause duration to decrease by only 3.8407 years, from 13.2123 to 9.3716 years.

Duration and Coupon Rates

In the previous section, we learned that duration is inversely related to the market rate of interest. We now look at the relationship between duration and the coupon rate on a bond. As the coupon rate rises, duration decreases. Why? The answer is that high coupon rate bonds tend to produce higher annual cash flows before maturity and thus tend to weight duration toward the earlier to middle years. On the other hand, low coupon rate bonds produce less annual cash flows before maturity and have less influence on duration. Duration is weighted more heavily toward the final payment at maturity, and duration tends to be somewhat closer to the actual maturity on the bond. At the extreme, a zero-coupon bond has the same maturity and duration.

The relationship between duration and coupon rates can be seen in Table 13–7. Here three different coupon rate bonds are presented. Each bond is assumed to have a maturity of 25 years. The best way to read the table is to pick a market rate of interest in the first column and then read across the table to determine the duration at various coupon rates. For example, at an 8 percent market rate of interest, duration is 13.2459 at a 4 percent coupon rate, 11.5290 at an 8 percent coupon rate, and 10.8396 at a 12 percent coupon rate. Clearly, the higher the coupon rate, the lower the duration (and vice versa).

The impact of coupon rates on duration is also demonstrated in Figure 13–1 on page 364. Note that with a zero-coupon bond, the line is at a 45-degree angle; that is, duration and years to maturity are always the same value. There is only one payment, and it is at maturity.

You can also observe in Figure 13–1 that progressively higher coupon rates lead to a lower duration. As an example, go to point N on the horizontal axis and observe duration for 4 percent, 8 percent, and 12 percent interest. Clearly the higher the coupon rate, the lower the duration value.

TABLE 13–7 Duration and Coupon Rates (25-Year Bonds)

Market Rate of Interest	4 Percent	8 Percent	12 Percent
4%	16.2470	14.2265	13.3278
6	14.7455	12.8425	12.0407
8	13.2459	11.5290	10.8396
10	11.8112	10.3229	9.7501
12	10.4912	9.2475	8.7844

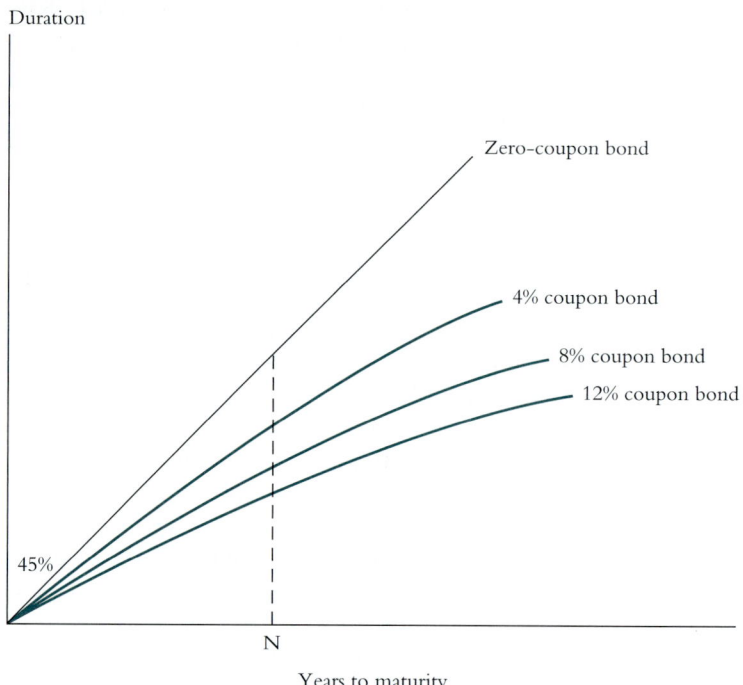

FIGURE 13-1 The Effect of Coupon Rates on Duration

Because the higher the duration, the greater the price sensitivity, it follows that an investor desiring maximum price movements will look toward lower coupon rate bonds. As previously demonstrated, low coupon rate and high duration go together, and high duration leads to maximum price sensitivity. The relationship of low coupon rates to price sensitivity was briefly discussed in Chapter 12 under investment strategy. We now see that the unnamed explanatory variable at that point was duration.

Bringing Together the Influences on Duration

The three factors that determine the value of duration are the maturity of the bond, the market rate of interest, and the coupon rate. Duration is positively correlated with maturity but moves in the opposite direction of market rates of interest and coupon rates; that is, the higher the market rate of interest or the coupon rate, the lower the duration. Earlier in this chapter, you were asked to consider whether you should invest in an 8 percent coupon rate, 20-year bond or a 12 percent coupon rate, 25-year bond. Since we were assuming interest rates were going to go down, you were looking for maximum price volatility. Had you not studied duration, you probably would have selected the bond with the longer maturity. This would generally be a valid assumption as indicated in Chapter 12. However, the primary emphasis to the sophisticated bond investor when assessing price volatility, or sensitivity, is duration.

Note that the bond with the longer maturity (25 years versus 20 years) also has a higher coupon rate (12 percent versus 8 percent). The first factor (longer maturity) would indicate higher duration, but the second factor (higher coupon rate) would indicate a lower duration. What is the net effect? The answer can be found in earlier tables in this chapter. Let's assume that the *market rate* of interest is 12 percent for both bonds. Table 13–6 on page 362 presented information on 8 percent coupon rate bonds for varying maturities and market rates of interest. To determine the duration on the 8 percent coupon rate, 20-year bond, assuming a 12 percent market rate of interest, we read across the 20-year row to the last column in the table and see the answer is 8.9390. (Note that all bonds in Table 13–6 have an 8 percent coupon rate, so we must identify the value associated with 20 years and a 12 percent market rate of interest.)

To determine the duration for the 12 percent coupon rate, 25-year bond with a 12 percent market rate of interest, we must go to Table 13–7 on page 363. Note that all bonds in this table have a 25-year maturity, so read down to a market rate of interest of 12 percent and across to a coupon rate of 12 percent. The value for duration on this bond is 8.7844.

Based on this analysis, the answer to the question posed earlier in the chapter is that the bond with the shorter maturity (8 percent coupon rate for 20 years) has a higher duration than the bond with the greater maturity (12 percent for 25 years) and thus is the most price sensitive.[5]

Bond	Duration
8%, 20 years	8.9390 ← greater price sensitivity
12%, 25 years	8.7844

In actuality, if interest rates went down by 2 percent, the 8 percent, 20-year bond would go up by 18.5 percent, while the 12 percent, 25-year bond would increase by only 17.9 percent.

Duration and Zero-Coupon Bonds

Characteristics of zero-coupon bonds were briefly described in Chapter 11. As previously mentioned, Figure 13–1 depicts the duration of zero-coupon bonds as a 45-degree line relative to years to maturity. This graphically indicates that the duration of a zero-coupon bond equals the number of years it has to maturity. For all bonds of equal risk and maturity, the zero-coupon bond has the greatest duration and therefore the greatest price sensitivity. This price risk is one that is often lost in the image of safety that zero-coupons have when backed by U.S. government securities.

A classic headline in *The Wall Street Journal* on June 1, 1984, appeared as follows: "Zero-Coupon Bonds' Price Swings Jolt Investors Looking for Security."[6] It was reported that between March 31, 1983 and March 31, 1984, Salomon Brothers' 30-year CATs declined 25 percent in price, while returns on conventional 30-year government bonds declined only a few percentage points. The article cited one client buying $100,000 of zero-coupons, thinking they were similar to short-term Treasury bill investments, only to find out four weeks later that his zero-coupon bonds had declined in value by $24,000.

---

[5] As previously indicated, if we vary the market rate of interest, we can also influence the outcome to our question.

[6] Randall Smith, "Zero-Coupon Bonds' Price Swings Jolt Investors Looking for Security," *The Wall Street Journal*, June 1, 1984, p. 19.

TABLE 13–8 Duration of Zero-Coupon versus 8 Percent Coupon Bonds (Market Rate of Interest Is 12 Percent)

(1) Years to Maturity	(2) Duration of Zero-Coupon Bond	(3) Duration of 8 Percent Coupon Bond	(4) Relative Duration of Zero-Coupon to 8 Percent Coupon Bonds (2) ÷ (3)
10	10	6.8374	1.4625
20	20	8.9390	2.2374
30	30	9.3662	3.2030
40	40	9.3972	4.2566
50	50	9.3716	5.3353

To put the volatility of a zero-coupon bond into better perspective, we compare the duration of a zero-coupon bond to that of an 8 percent coupon bond for several maturities in Table 13–8.

The far right column in Table 13–8 indicates the ratio of duration between zero-coupon and 8 percent coupon rate bonds. As stressed throughout the chapter, duration represents a measure of price sensitivity. Thus, for a 10-year maturity period, a zero-coupon bond is almost 1½ times as price sensitive as an 8 percent coupon rate bond (the ratio in the last column is 1.4625). For a 20-year maturity period, it is over two times more price sensitive (2.2374), and for 50 years the price sensitivity ratio is over five times greater (5.3353). This might explain why zero-coupons were much more sensitive to rising interest rates during 1983–84 as described in the story in *The Wall Street Journal*. Of course, tremendous profits can be made in zero-coupon bonds when there is a sharp drop in interest rates as in early 1985 and again in 1997 and early 2003.

The Uses of Duration

Duration is primarily used as a measure to judge bond price sensitivity to interest-rate changes. Because duration includes information on several variables (maturity, coupon rate, and market rate of interest), it captures more information than any one of them. It therefore allows more accurate decisions for complex bond strategies. One such strategy involves the timing of investment inflows to provide a needed cash outlay at a known future date. Perhaps $1 million is needed after five years. Everything is tailored to this five-year time horizon. If interest rates go up, there will be a decline in the value of the portfolio but a higher reinvestment rate opportunity for inflows. Similarly, if interest rates go down, there will be capital appreciation for the portfolio but a lower reinvestment rate opportunity. By tying all the investment decisions to a duration period, the portfolio manager can take advantage of these counter forces to ensure a necessary outcome. This strategy is called **immunization** and is used by insurance companies, pension funds, and other institutional money managers to protect their portfolios against swings in interest rates. For a more comprehensive discussion of immunization strategies, an article by Fisher and Weil is an appropriate source.[7] For an excellent criticism of duration and immunization

---
[7] Lawrence Fisher and Roman L. Weil, "Coping with Risk of Interest Rate Fluctuations: Returns to Bondholders from Naive and Optimal Strategies," *Journal of Business*, October 1971, pp. 408–31.

strategy, see Yawitz and Marshall.[8] One of the problems with duration analysis is that it often assumes a parallel shift in yield curves. Although long-duration bonds are clearly more price sensitive than shorter-duration bonds, there is no assurance that long- and short-term interest rates will move by equal amounts.

Bond Reinvestment Assumptions and Terminal Wealth Analysis

Reinvestment Assumptions

As indicated in the previous section, one concern an investor may have when purchasing bonds is that the interest income will not be reinvested to earn the same return the coupon payment represents. This may not be a problem for an individual consuming the interest payments, but it could be a serious concern for individuals building a retirement portfolio or a pension fund manager accumulating funds for future payout to retirees. The crucial issue is the amount of money accumulated at the time the retirement fund will be used to cover living expenses. One major determinant of the ending value of a retirement fund is the rate of return on coupon payments as they are reinvested.

Since the middle 1970s, interest rates have generally been more volatile than during previous periods. This has caused more emphasis on the management of fixed-income securities, not only in the selection of maturity but also in the switching from short- to long-term securities. These volatile rates have caused more emphasis on concepts such as duration to measure bond price sensitivity and on total return as a measure of bond management success. Given that interest rates change daily and by large amounts over a year, what impact would a lower or higher **reinvestment assumption** have on the outcome of your retirement nest egg?

First, let us look at a partial reproduction of Appendix A at the back of the text (reproduced in Table 13–9). The material covers the compound sum of $1. Appendix A assumes all interest is reinvested at the stated rate in order to find the ending value of $1 invested to maturity. For our current analysis, we are assuming annual interest (though the answer changes only slightly if we use semiannual interest).

The table values are given in $1 amounts, so for a $1,000 bond we would just move the decimal three places to the right. A $1,000 bond having a 12 percent

TABLE 13–9 Compound Sum of $1.00 (from Appendix A)

Period	7 Percent	8 Percent	9 Percent	10 Percent	11 Percent	12 Percent
10	$ 1.967	$ 2.159	$ 2.367	$ 2.594	$ 2.839	$ 3.106
20	3.870	4.661	5.604	6.727	8.062	9.646
30	7.612	10.063	13.268	17.449	22.892	29.960
40	14.974	21.725	31.409	45.259	65.001	93.051

---

[8] Jess B. Yawitz and William J. Marshall, "The Shortcomings of Duration as a Risk Measure for Bonds," *Journal of Financial Research,* Summer 1981, pp. 91–101.

coupon rate with interest being reinvested at 12 percent would compound to $93,051 over 40 years, while a 7 percent coupon bond reinvested at 7 percent would compound to only $14,974 over a similar period. A difference of 5 points in the rates creates a total difference of $78,077. This is quite a large difference. Notice that the longer the compounding period, the larger the amount. From further inspection of Table 13–9, other comparisons can be made between years and total ending values.

The importance of the reinvestment assumption can also be viewed from the perspective of its contribution to total wealth. For example, an investor owning a 40-year bond with a 12 percent coupon rate and an assumed reinvestment rate of 12 percent will have an accumulated value of $93,051. In terms of payout, $4,800 (40 × $120) comes directly from 40 years of 12 percent interest payments, $1,000 comes from principal, and the balance of $87,251 comes from interest that is earned on the annual interest payments. In this case, interest on interest represents 93.8 percent of the overall return ($87,251/$93,051).

Terminal Wealth Analysis

Application Example

Now, we will assume a reinvestment assumption different from the coupon rate. Take the two extreme values from Table 13–9 on page 367 of 12 percent and 7 percent. Assume you buy a bond having a 12 percent coupon rate, but the interest can only be reinvested at 7 percent. To find the ending value of this investment, we will need to use a **terminal wealth table**.

Table 13–10 is called a terminal wealth table because it generates the ending value of the investment at the end of each year, assuming the bond has a *maturity* date corresponding to that year. Let's use 10 years as an example in examining Table 13–10. If the bond matures in 10 years, the $1,000 principal in column (2) will be recovered. Also the investor will receive $120 in annual interest (12 percent of $1,000) in year 10 as indicated in column (3). In column (4), the accumulated interest up to the *beginning* of year 10 is shown. The reinvestment rate on this previously accumulated interest is a mere 7 percent as indicated in column (5). The interest on the previously accumulated interest is $100.62 (0.07 × $1,437.38). Finally, the total interest for year 10 is shown in column (7). This consists of the coupon interest of $120 and the interest on interest of $100.62 and totals to $220.62. The total ending value of the portfolio is shown in column (8). The ending value consists of the recovered principal of $1,000 plus the accumulated interest of $1,437.38 up to the beginning of year 10 plus the total interest paid in year 10 of $220.62. The ending wealth value (portfolio sum) thus shown in column (8) is $2,658.00. The value is summarized below:

Recovered principal	$1,000.00	Column (2)
Accumulated interest (beginning of year 10)	1,437.38	Column (4)
Total annual interest (during year 10)	220.62	Column (7)
Ending wealth value (portfolio sum)	$2,658.00	Column (8)

A $1,000 investment that grows to $2,658.00 after 10 years is the equivalent of a $1 investment that grows to 2.65800 as indicated in column (9). The annual percentage return for a $1 investment that grows to 2.65800 after 10 years is 10.26 percent as indicated in column (10).

TABLE 13–10 Terminal Wealth Table (12 Percent Coupon with 7 Percent Reinvestment Rate on Interest)

(1) Years to Maturity	(2) Principal	(3) Annual Coupon Interest	(4) Accumulated Interest[a]	(5) Reinvestment Rate on Interest	(6) Interest on Interest	(7) Total Annual Interest	(8) Portfolio Sum	(9) Compound Sum Factor	(10) Annual Percentage Return
0.0	$1,000.00								
1.0	1,000.00	$120.00	$ 0.00			$ 120.00	$ 1,120.00	1.12000	12.00%
2.0	1,000.00	120.00	120.00	0.07	$ 8.40	128.40	1,248.40	1.24840	11.73
3.0	1,000.00	120.00	248.40	0.07	17.39	137.39	1,385.79	1.38579	11.48
4.0	1,000.00	120.00	385.79	0.07	27.01	147.01	1,532.80	1.53280	11.26
5.0	1,000.00	120.00	532.80	0.07	37.30	157.30	1,690.10	1.69010	11.06
6.0	1,000.00	120.00	690.10	0.07	48.31	168.31	1,858.41	1.85841	10.86
7.0	1,000.00	120.00	858.41	0.07	60.90	180.09	2,038.50	2.03850	10.71
8.0	1,000.00	120.00	1,038.50	0.07	72.70	192.70	2,231.20	2.23120	10.55
9.0	1,000.00	120.00	1,231.20	0.07	86.18	206.18	2,437.38	2.43738	10.40
10.0	1,000.00	120.00	1,437.38	0.07	100.62	220.62	2,658.00	2.65800	10.26
11.0	1,000.00	120.00	1,658.00	0.07	116.06	236.06	2,894.06	2.89406	10.14
12.0	1,000.00	120.00	1,894.06	0.07	132.58	252.58	3,146.64	3.14664	10.02
13.0	1,000.00	120.00	2,146.64	0.07	150.26	270.26	3,416.90	3.41690	9.91
14.0	1,000.00	120.00	2,416.90	0.07	169.18	289.18	3,706.08	3.70608	9.80
15.0	1,000.00	120.00	2,706.08	0.07	189.43	309.43	4,015.51	4.01551	9.71
16.0	1,000.00	120.00	3,015.51	0.07	211.09	331.09	4,346.60	4.34660	9.61
17.0	1,000.00	120.00	3,346.60	0.07	234.26	354.26	4,700.86	4.70086	9.54
18.0	1,000.00	120.00	3,700.86	0.07	259.06	379.06	5,079.92	5.07992	9.44
19.0	1,000.00	120.00	4,079.92	0.07	285.59	405.59	5,485.51	5.48551	9.37
20.0	1,000.00	120.00	4,485.51	0.07	313.99	433.99	5,919.50	5.91950	9.29
21.0	1,000.00	120.00	4,919.50	0.07	344.37	464.37	6,383.87	6.38387	9.22
22.0	1,000.00	120.00	5,383.87	0.07	376.87	496.87	6,880.74	6.88074	9.16
23.0	1,000.00	120.00	5,880.74	0.07	411.65	531.65	7,412.39	7.41239	9.09
24.0	1,000.00	120.00	6,412.39	0.07	448.87	568.87	7,981.26	7.98126	9.04
25.0	1,000.00	120.00	6,981.26	0.07	488.69	608.69	8,589.95	8.58995	8.98
26.0	1,000.00	120.00	7,589.95	0.07	531.30	651.30	9,241.25	9.24125	8.92
27.0	1,000.00	120.00	8,241.25	0.07	576.89	696.89	9,938.14	9.93814	8.87
28.0	1,000.00	120.00	8,938.14	0.07	625.67	745.67	10,683.81	10.68381	8.82
29.0	1,000.00	120.00	9,683.81	0.07	677.87	797.87	11,481.68	11.48168	8.78
30.0	1,000.00	120.00	10,481.68	0.07	733.72	853.72	12,335.40	12.33540	8.73
31.0	1,000.00	120.00	11,335.40	0.07	793.48	913.48	13,248.88	13.24888	8.69
32.0	1,000.00	120.00	12,248.88	0.07	857.42	977.42	14,226.30	14.22630	8.65
33.0	1,000.00	120.00	13,226.30	0.07	925.84	1,045.84	15,272.14	15.27214	8.61
34.0	1,000.00	120.00	14,272.14	0.07	999.05	1,119.05	16,391.19	16.39119	8.57
35.0	1,000.00	120.00	15,391.19	0.07	1,077.38	1,197.38	17,588.57	17.58857	8.53
36.0	1,000.00	120.00	16,588.57	0.07	1,161.20	1,281.20	18,869.77	18.86977	8.50
37.0	1,000.00	120.00	17,869.77	0.07	1,250.88	1,370.88	20,240.65	20.24065	8.46
38.0	1,000.00	120.00	19,240.65	0.07	1,346.85	1,466.85	21,707.50	21.70750	8.43
39.0	1,000.00	120.00	20,707.50	0.07	1,449.53	1,569.53	23,277.03	23.27703	8.40
40.0	1,000.00	120.00	22,277.03	0.07	1,559.39	1,679.39	24,956.42	24.95642	8.37

[a] At beginning of year.

A similar analysis can be done for all other maturity periods running from 1 to 40 years. One thing to notice from Table 13–10 is that the longer the maturity period of the bond, the greater the effect the low 7 percent reinvestment rate has on the bond. For 5 years, the annual percentage return [column (10)] is 11.06 percent; for 15 years, 9.71 percent; and for 40 years, 8.37 percent.

What is the actual difference between the ending value for a 40-year, 12 percent coupon rate bond assuming a *12 percent* reinvestment rate and the 40-year, *7 percent* reinvestment rate just presented in Table 13–10? Earlier in this section, Table 13–9 demonstrated that a 12 percent coupon rate bond with an assumed 12 percent reinvestment rate for 40 years would grow to $93,051. In Table 13–10, we see that a 12 percent coupon rate bond with a 7 percent reinvestment rate will grow to only $24,956.42 after 40 years. It should be evident that it is not only the coupon rate that matters but the reinvestment rate as well.

If the bond were not held to maturity in our analysis, then we would have to rely on the realized rate of return analysis developed in Chapter 12. The realized rate of return approach would assume that the bond is not held to maturity and that it is sold at either a gain or a loss. In the case of the bond analyzed in the terminal wealth table (Table 13–10), we know that since interest rates are assumed to decline, any sale of the bond before maturity should result in a capital gain. How large that capital gain would be will be dependent on its duration. Terminal wealth analysis is a way of analyzing the reinvestment assumption when bonds are held to maturity, while the realized yield approach assumes bonds are actively traded to take advantage of interest-rate swings.

Zero-Coupon Bonds and Terminal Wealth

One of the benefits of zero-coupon bonds is that they lock in a compound rate of return (or reinvestment rate) for the life of the bond *if held to maturity*. There are no coupon payments during the life of the bond to be reinvested, so the originally quoted rate holds throughout if held to maturity. If a $1,000 par value, 15-year zero-coupon bond is quoted at a price of $183 to yield 12 percent, you truly have locked in a 12 percent reinvestment rate. Some would say you have not only locked in 12 percent but have thrown away the key. In any event, zero-coupon bonds allow you to predetermine your reinvestment rate.

Of course, if a zero-coupon bond is sold before maturity, there could be large swings in the sales price of the bond because of its high duration characteristics. Under this circumstance, the locked-in reinvestment concept for the zero-coupon bond loses much of its meaning. It is valid only when the zero-coupon bond is held to maturity.

Summary

In Chapter 13, we have taken the concepts developed in Chapter 12 and expanded on the principles of bond price volatility and total return. We developed the concept of duration so that the student has a basic understanding of its meaning and some of its applications. In general, we have shown that duration is the number of years, on a present-value basis, that it takes to recover an initial investment in a bond. More specifically, each year is weighted by the present value of the cash flow as a proportion of the present value of the bond and then summed. The higher the duration, the more sensitive the bond price is to a change in interest rates. Duration as one number captures the three variables—maturity, coupon rate, and market rate of interest—to indicate the price sensitivities of bonds with unequal characteristics. Generally, bond duration increases with the increase in number of years to maturity. Duration also increases as coupon rates decline to zero, and finally, duration declines as market interest rates increase.

Zero-coupon bonds are highlighted as the most price sensitive of bonds to a change in market interest rates, and comparisons are made between zero-coupon bonds and coupon bonds. Duration's primary use is in explaining price volatility, but it also has applications in the insurance industry and other areas of investments where interest-rate risk can be reduced by matching duration with predictable cash outflows in a process called immunization.

An important concept has to do with the reinvestment of interest at rates other than the coupon rate. The method used to explain the effect on the total return is terminal wealth analysis, which assumes that the investment is held to maturity and that all proceeds over the life of the bond are reinvested at the reinvestment rate. In general, the longer the maturity, the more total annualized return approaches the reinvestment rate. If the reinvestment rate is significantly different from the coupon rate, the annualized return can differ greatly from the coupon rate in as little as five years.

Key Words and Concepts

duration 357
immunization 366
Macaulay duration 358
modified duration 377
reinvestment assumption 367
terminal wealth table 368
weighted average life 356

Discussion Questions

1. Why is the weighted average life of a bond less than the maturity date?
2. Define duration.
3. How can duration be used to determine a rough measure of the percentage change in the price of a bond as a result of interest-rate changes?
4. Comment on the statement, "It is possible that a bond with a shorter maturity than another bond may actually have a longer duration and be more price sensitive to interest-rate changes." Explain why a bond with a shorter maturity than another bond could have a longer duration.
5. As market rates of interest become higher, what impact does this have on duration?
6. What happens to duration as the coupon rate on a bond issue declines from 12 percent to 0 percent with the maturity date remaining constant?
7. Why are the maturity date and duration the same for a zero-coupon bond?
8. Should an investor who thinks interest rates are going down seek low or high coupon rate bonds?

Relate your answer to duration and price sensitivity.

9. Why are zero-coupon bonds the most price sensitive of any type of bond issue?

10. Why is the reinvestment rate assumption critical to bond portfolio management?

11. What is a terminal wealth table? How is terminal wealth analysis different from the realized yield approach in Chapter 12?

12. Why is it said that zero-coupon bonds lock in the reinvestment rate?

13. Is the locked-in reinvestment assumption valid for zero-coupon bonds if they are sold before maturity? Explain.

Problems

Weighted average life

1. Compute the simple weighted average life for the following data. Use an approach similar to that in Table 13–1 on page 356.

Year	Cash Flow
1	$ 65
2	65
3	65
4	65
4	1,000

Weighted average life

2. Compute the simple weighted average life for the following data. Use an approach similar to that in Table 13–1 on page 356.

Year	Cash Flow
1	$ 115
2	115
3	115
4	115
5	115
5	1,000

Duration

3. Compute the duration for the data in problem 2. Use an approach similar to that in Table 13–2 on page 357. A discount rate of 14 percent should be applied.

Price sensitivity

4. As part of your answer to problem 3, you computed the price of the bond (column 4). This is the same as the *PV* of cash flows.
   a. Recompute the price of a bond based on a 12 percent discount rate (market rate of interest).
   b. What is the percentage change in the price of the bond as interest rates decline from 14 percent to 12 percent?
   c. Approximate this same value by multiplying the duration computed in problem 3 times the change in interest rates (2 percent). The answer in part *c* should come reasonably close to the answer in part *b* (about .60% difference).

Comparative duration
eXcel

5. *a.* Compute the duration for the following data. Use a discount rate of 14 percent.

Year	Cash Flow
1	$ 60
2	60
3	60
4	60
5	60
5	1,000

  b. Explain why the answer to 5*a* is higher than the answer to problem 3.
  c. If in part 5*a* the discount rate were 10 instead of 14 percent, would duration be longer or shorter? You do not need to actually compute a value; merely indicate an answer based on the discussion material in the text.

Comparative duration

6. You are considering the purchase of two $1,000 bonds, both issued by Levitt Incorporated. Your expectation is that interest rates will drop, and you want to buy the bond that provides the maximum capital gains potential. The first Levitt bond has a coupon rate of 5 percent with four years to maturity, while the second has a coupon rate of 14 percent and comes due six years from now. The market rate of interest (discount rate) is 10 percent. Which bond has the best price movement potential? Use duration to answer the question.

Comparative duration

7. Dr. Foresight thinks that recent Federal Reserve policy is going to push interest rates up. He is considering keeping only one of the three bonds in his portfolio. He knows that bond A has a duration of 3.1727, bond B has a duration of 4.6125, and bond C has the following characteristics:

Par Value	$1,000
Life	4 years
Coupon rate	5 percent
Discount rate	10 percent

Which one of the three bonds should he keep?

Comparative duration

8. Assume you desire maximum duration to take advantage of anticipated interest rate declines. Answer the following questions based on information taken from Tables 13–6 on page 362 and 13–7 on page 363.
  a. Would you prefer an 8 percent coupon rate bond with a 20-year maturity or a 4 percent coupon rate bond with a 25-year maturity? The market rate of interest is 10 percent.
  b. Would you prefer an 8 percent coupon rate bond with a 20-year maturity or a 12 percent coupon rate bond with a 25-year maturity? The market rate of interest is 12 percent.
  c. Would you prefer an 8 percent coupon rate bond with a 20-year maturity or a 12 percent coupon rate bond with a 25-year maturity? The market rate of interest is 6 percent.

Zero-coupon bond and duration

9. A 25-year, $1,000 par value zero-coupon bond provides a yield of 12 percent.
   a. Compute the current price of the zero-coupon bond. (*Hint:* Simply take the present value of the ending $1,000 payment).
   b. What is the duration of the bond?
   c. Does the bond have a longer or shorter duration than a 50-year, 8 percent coupon rate bond, where the duration on the latter bond is based on a 10 percent market rate of interest (consult Table 13–6 on page 362).
   d. Assume you were going to put the zero-coupon bond(s) in a nontaxable IRA. If you wish to have $30,000 after 25 years, how much would you need to invest today?
   e. If a $1,000 par value zero-coupon rate bond had a 40-year maturity and provided a yield of 12 percent, what would be the current price of the zero-coupon bond?

Return on zero-coupon bond

10. Assume you buy a 15-year, $1,000 par value zero-coupon bond that provides a 12 percent yield. Almost immediately after you buy the bond, yields go down to 11 percent. What will be your gain on the investment?

Reinvestment assumption

eXcel

11. You have invested $1,000 in a 14 percent coupon bond that matures in five years. This bond is held in your individual retirement account, and you are not concerned about tax consequences. You are investing the interest income in a fund earning 9 percent. At the end of five years, what will be your portfolio sum? Follow the procedure in Table 13–10 on page 369 (first eight columns).

Annual return with reinvestment assumption

12. In problem 11, what is the annual percentage return? Use Appendix A at the end of the book to help you find the answer. An approximation will be sufficient.

Web Exercise

To maximize your understanding of duration, it is helpful to calculate the duration on an actual bond issue. Go to **www.investinginbonds.com**.

1. Click on "Trade Information Reports" on the right-hand portion of the screen.
2. Then click "Go" after "Show Most Active Bonds (last 7 days)." Wait a few seconds and you will see a listing of bonds.
3. Scroll down the bond listings until you find a bond maturing in approximately five years. You are going to use the techniques in Table 13–2 on page 357 to calculate the duration of the bond. You will need a calculator for ease of computation. Examining Table 13–2 of the chapter:
   a. Set up column (1) as running from 1–5. Even if the bond you have selected does not end in exactly five years, treat it as if it does. Don't be concerned about partial years. Simply use 1, 2, 3, 4, 5.
   b. Use the coupon rate on the screen and multiply it times $1,000 to get cash flow.
   c. To get the discount rate in column (3), round the yield value on the screen to the nearest whole number.
   d. Compute the present value of the cash flows for each year, and sum them as is shown in column (4).

These securities have been used as financing alternatives by corporations in periods of high interest rates or tight money. Also, convertibles have been utilized as a medium of exchange for acquiring other companies' stock in mergers and acquisitions. Convertibles and warrants have advantages to the corporation and to the owner of the security. It is important to realize as we go through this chapter that what is an advantage to the corporation is often a disadvantage to the investor, and vice versa. These securities involve trade-offs between the buyer and the corporation that are considered in the pricing of each security.

Convertible Securities

A **convertible security** is a bond or share of preferred stock that can be converted into common stock at the option of the holder. Thus, the owner has a fixed-income security that can be transferred to common stock if and when the performance of the firm indicates such a conversion is desirable.

As an example of a convertible security, we use the Amazon.com 4.75 percent convertible subordinated debenture maturing on February 1, 2009. Amazon.com is a familiar name; the company started its corporate life in 1995 selling books online. It later added CDs and DVDs, video games and now, if you go on their website www.amazon.com, you will find a virtual warehouse of goods to buy, including shoes, computers, software, cell phones, toys, and so on.

Amazon is the biggest online retailer and has had meteoric growth since its beginning. Its sales rose from $15.7 million in 1996 to $1.6 billion in 1999. While the growth rate has not been the same as in the early years, the sales dollars keep climbing. In 2001 Amazon.com made its first operating profit of $35.1 million on sales of $3.12 billion and finally in 2003 made its first after-tax profit of $35.3 million on sales of $5.26 billion. Obviously Amazon.com has very small operating margins and hasn't been able to use much internally generated cash to finance the expansion of its business. In 1999 the firm sold the 4.75 percent convertible bonds to raise $1.250 billion. This allowed it to pay off bank debt, buy computers to enhance its infrastructure, and finance the current assets needed in the business.

In 2003 Amazon.com retired $200 million of its convertible debt and still had $1.4 billion cash at year-end. Sales of $6.5 billion were forecast for 2004 with operating income of $450 million. In January 2004 the board of directors authorized the repurchase of $500 million more of the convertible debt, which will leave about $550 million outstanding.

In general, the best time for an investor to buy convertible securities is when interest rates are high (bond and preferred prices are depressed) and when stock prices are relatively low. A purchase in this environment increases the probability of a successful investment because rising stock prices and falling interest rates both exert upward pressure on the price of a convertible security. This will become more apparent as we proceed through the discussions in the chapter. Table 14–1 on page 382 shows the details of the Amazon.com convertible bond with the data taken from the company's annual report and from Standard & Poor's. We will rely on this information as we go through the various calculations required to understand convertible bonds.

> **TABLE 14–1** Amazon.com 4.75 Percent Convertible Subordinated Notes: Due February 1, 2009
>
> Convertible at $78.03 into 12.81558 shares subject to adjustment for stock splits and stock dividends.
>
> $23.75 Semiannual interest payable on February 1 and August 1.
>
> Regular calls beginning February 1, 2005 through each of the following years.
>
> **Call Price**
>
> $1,019.00 February 1, 2005–January 31, 2006
> $1,014.25 February 1, 2006–January 31, 2007
> $1,009.50 February 1, 2007–January 31, 2008
> $1,000.00 After January 31, 2008

Conversion Price and Conversion Ratio

Table 14–1 shows that the Amazon.com convertible bond is convertible at $78.03 into 12.81558 shares of common stock. The $78.03 is called the **conversion price** and the 12.81558 is called the **conversion ratio.** Normally you will find only one of these pieces of information and have to calculate the other. If you find the conversion price stated in the annual report or another financial source, divide the conversion price into the par value of $1,000 to find how many shares you will receive. The conversion ratio is shown in Formula 14–1.

$$\text{Conversion ratio} = \frac{\text{Face value or Par value}}{\text{Conversion price}} \quad (14\text{–}1)$$

If we go through the calculation for the Amazon.com bond, it would be as follows:

$$\frac{\$1{,}000 \text{ (Face value or Par value)}}{\$78.03 \text{ per share (Conversion price)}} = 12.81558 \text{ shares}$$

Value of the Convertible Bond

The Amazon.com convertible bond was originally sold at its par value of $1,000 but the stock was highly speculative and very volatile. Even the common stock price around the day of the convertible bond offering was volatile. On February 1, 1999, Amazon's common stock sold at $57.9375 per share. The next day it fell to $55.125 and on February 3 it rose to $62.875. Clearly Amazon is part of the Internet bubble story of the 1999–2000 period.

Application Example

A convertible bond has two calculated values, a **pure bond value,** which is the value of the bond if it trades without any conversion features, and a **conversion value,** which is the value of the bond based on the common stock price and the number of shares the bondholder could receive based on the conversion ratio. What would be the conversion value of the Amazon.com bond based on the common stock price on February 1, 1999, the day of the offering, and the two days after? We can find this by multiplying the conversion ratio by the market price per share of the common stock.

Conversion ratio × Common stock price = **Conversion value** (14–2)
12.81558 shares × $57.9375 = $742.50 February 1, 1999
12.81558 shares × $55.125 = $706.46 February 2, 1999
12.81558 shares × $62.875 = $805.78 February 3, 1999

The amount of $742.50 indicates the value of the underlying shares of common stock each bond represents on the day of the offering, but we can also see how the conversion value changes with the stock price. Two days after the offering the conversion value was up over $60 to $805.78.

How do we calculate the pure bond value? In the case of Amazon.com assume that a similar bond without the conversion privilege carries a yield to maturity of 6 percent. We use the same techniques that we applied in Chapter 12 to value a bond. We would take the semiannual coupon of $23.75, the number of periods to maturity would be 20 six-month periods, and we would use the 3 percent yield, which is one-half of the annual yield to maturity of 6 percent. The pure bond value would be as follows:

$23.75 × 14.877 (*PV* interest factor for an annuity) = $353.33
$1,000.00 × .554 (*PV* interest factor for a single amount) = $554.00
Pure bond value $907.33

The pure bond value is considered the **floor value,** or minimum price at which the bond will sell in the market. The conversion value and pure bond value for the Amazon.com convertible bond are graphed in Figure 14–1. You should be aware that it is possible for the pure bond value to change if interest rates change. In other word, the pure bond value will follow the bond pricing rules

FIGURE 14–1 Amazon.com Convertible Bond on Day of Issue (February 1, 1999)

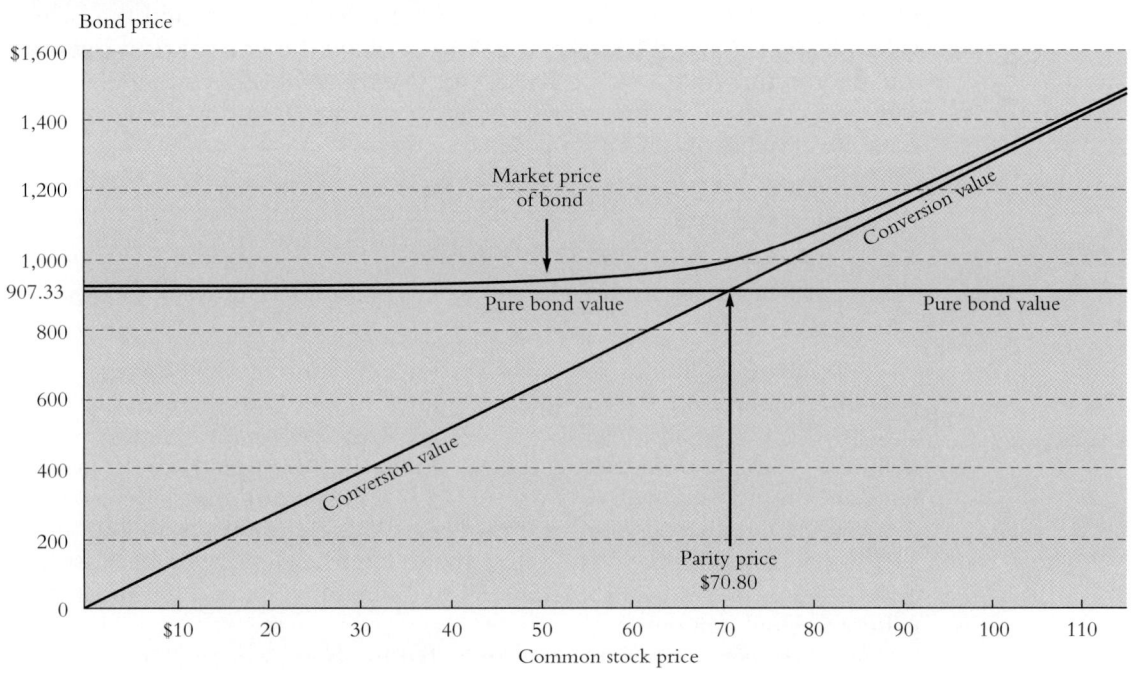

presented in Chapter 12, and bond prices will be inversely related to interest rates. We could see this relationship if we recalculated the pure bond value at an 8 percent yield to maturity. Following the same method as in the 6 percent example we would find a pure bond value of $778.76 at an 8 percent yield to maturity. This would cause the pure bond value line to move down in Figure 14–1 on the previous page.

In examining Figure 14–1, realize that the investor will always take the higher of the two values between the pure bond value and the conversion value. When the stock price is low and the conversion value is less than the pure bond value, the bond will have a minimum price of at least the pure bond value of $907.33. This makes sense because the bond has a value based on its guaranteed interest payment and par value at maturity. When the conversion value is higher than the pure bond value, the price of the bond will sell at least at the conversion value, because the investor could convert to stock and have the higher market value created by a high stock price.

The point where the conversion value and pure bond value are equal is called the **parity price** and the stock price at that point is currently $70.80. To find this parity point we simply divide the $907.33 pure bond value by the conversion ratio of 12.81558 shares. The important issue here is that when the stock is selling at less than $70.80, the pure bond value will create a minimum or floor price, and when the common stock is selling at more than $70.80, the conversion value will be higher than the pure bond value and determine the minimum value an investor would pay.

Bond Price and Premiums

Why is the market price line higher than both the pure bond value and the conversion value? You may wonder why the market price is $1,000 while the pure bond value is $907.35 and the conversion value is $742.50 on the first day of trading. The difference between the market price of $1,000 and the conversion value of $742.50 is $257.50. This $257.50 is called the **conversion premium** or the amount that investors are willing to pay above and beyond the value of the 12.81558 shares of common stock they would receive upon conversion. In this case the conversion premium is 34.68 percent:

$$\text{Conversion premium} = \frac{\text{Market price of bond} - \text{Conversion value}}{\text{Conversion value}} \quad (14\text{–}3)$$

$$\frac{\$1,000 - 742.50}{\$742.50} = \$257.50/\$742.50 = 34.68\%$$

People are willing to pay a conversion premium for several reasons. In the case of Amazon.com, the premium is slightly higher than the usual 20 to 25 percent paid on new offerings. One reason for the premium is that Amazon.com common stock paid no dividend at all while the bond paid $47.50 per year. At that rate the investor will recover the $257.50 premium in a little over 5 years' time. While the analysis of dividends versus interest is always an important consideration, you also have to realize that a bond is less risky because it has a higher claim on assets and income than common stock and the income is a legal contractual agreement.

Another reason for the premium is that the bond price will rise as the stock price rises because of the option of converting the bond to 12.81558 shares of stock. If the common stock price rises, the convertible bond investor benefits while an investor in a nonconvertible bond of the same company would not benefit. Also the pure bond value places a floor value under the investment to make the convertible bond less volatile than the underlying common stock. This floor value creates a **downside limit** if the common stock should fall below the parity price. One way to compute this downside protection is to calculate the difference between the market price of the bond and pure bond value as a percentage of the market price. We call this measure the **downside risk.**

$$\text{Downside risk} = \frac{\text{Market price of bond} - \text{Pure bond value}}{\text{Market price of bond}} \quad (14\text{--}4)$$

$$= \frac{\$1{,}000 - 907.33}{\$1{,}000} = \frac{\$92.67}{\$1{,}000} = 9.267\%$$

The Amazon.com downside risk is only 9.267 percent, which means that even if the common stock fell to $50 per share and had a $641 conversion value, the bond would have a minimum value of $907.33. The market price will slowly approach the pure bond value as the common stock price falls and it will slowly approach the conversion value as the common stock price rises. In fact, you should notice that the conversion premium is the largest at the parity price, because this is the price at which the risk-return trade-offs to the investor are the highest. At the parity point, there is no downside risk if the stock price should fall, and if the stock price should rise, the investor will benefit from the increase in conversion value.

The conversion premium is also affected by several other variables. The more volatile the stock price as measured by beta or standard deviation of returns, the higher the conversion premium. In the case of Amazon.com that is true. This higher premium occurs because the potential for capital gains is larger than on less volatile stocks. The longer the term to maturity, the higher the premium—because there is a greater chance that the stock price could rise, making the bond more valuable.

Figure 14–2 on the next page presents two graphs of the Amazon.com convertible bond and depicts the conversion premium in Panel (a) and the downside risk in Panel (b). Note in the Panel (a) that as the stock price gets higher, the conversion premium declines. This is because the investor is getting almost no downside protection. This is confirmed by the presence of large downside risk at high stock prices in Panel (b).

You can track the actual performance of the Amazon.com convertible bond since the offering in 1999 in Table 14–2 on page 387. We have presented the high and low prices for the market price of the bond, the common stock price, the conversion value, and the conversion premium that arises from these price fluctuations. Table 14–2 demonstrates the point made in the previous paragraph; in 1999 when the highest Amazon.com stock price was $113, the conversion value was $1,448 and the conversion premium was 3.36 percent. On the other hand, when the stock price hit its low of $5.51 in 2001, the conversion value fell to $70.61 and the conversion premium went up to 395.65 percent.

Another important point is the ability of the company to call the bond for redemption. In most cases the companies who issue convertible bonds are hoping that the stock price rises and thus creates a conversion value that is higher than the par value or call value. If you return to Table 14–1 on page 382, you will find the call prices for 2005 through 2009. For example, if the Amazon.com

386 **Part 4** Fixed-Income and Leveraged Securities

FIGURE 14–2 Amazon.com Convertible Bond—Conversion Premium and Downside Risk

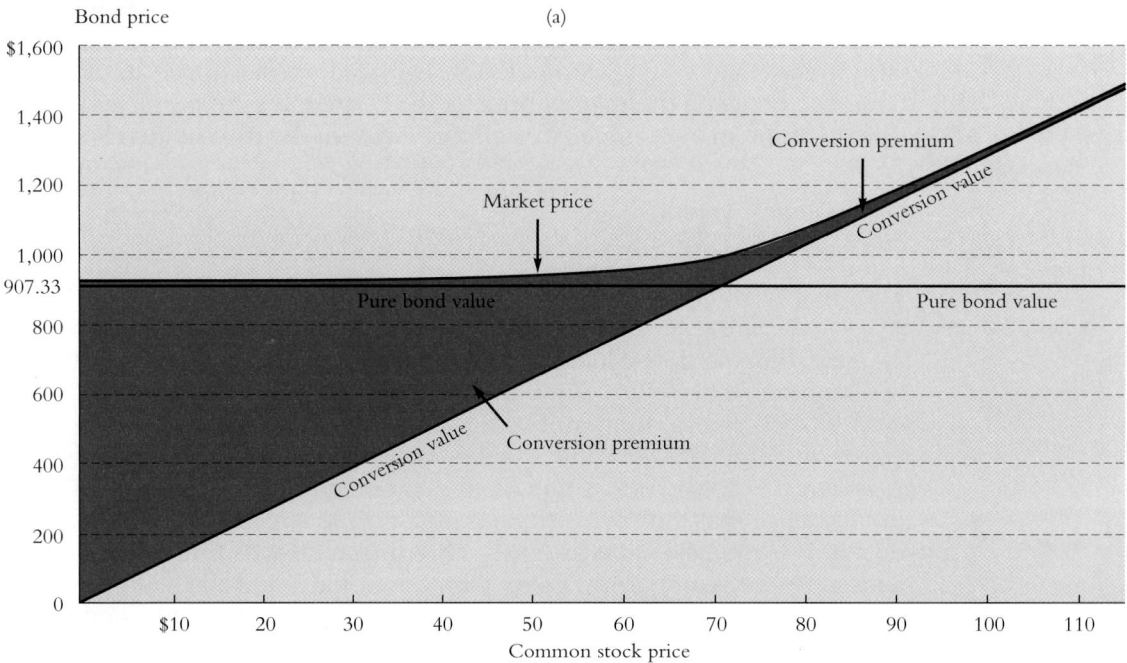

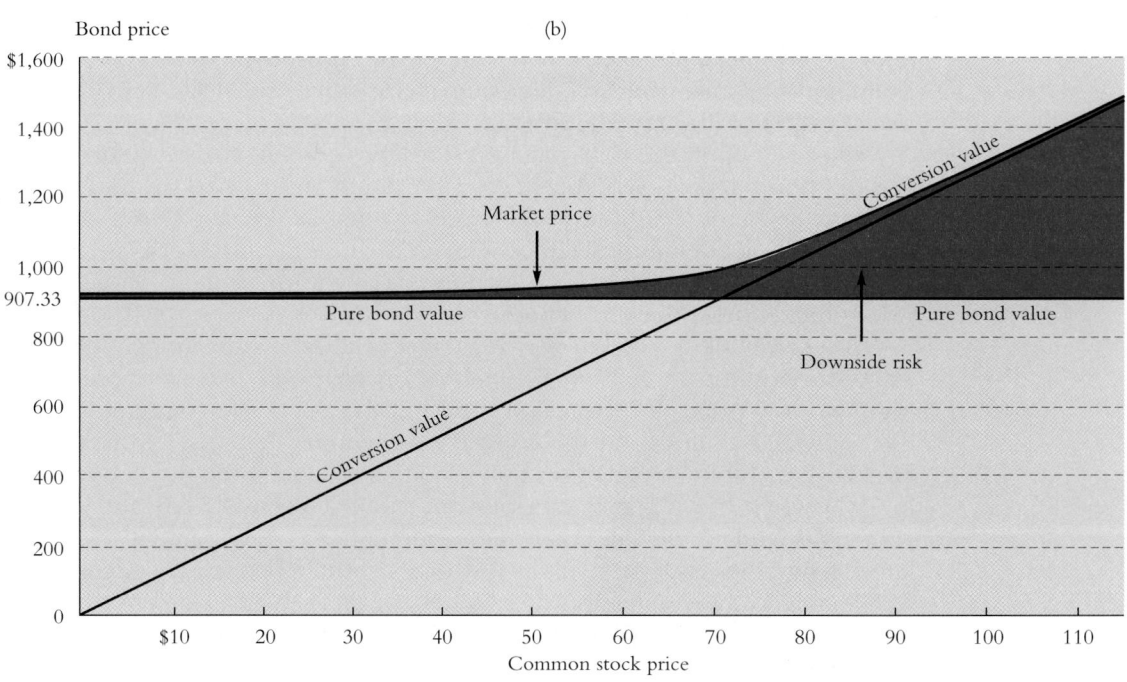

| TABLE 14–2 | Amazon.com Bond Prices, Stock Prices, Conversion Values, and Conversion Premiums |

	Bond Price		Stock Price		Conversion Value		Conversion Premium at High and Low Stock Price	
Year	High	Low	High	Low	High	Low	High	Low
2003	$1,011.25	$733.75	$61.15	$18.55	$783.67	$237.73	29.04%	208.65%
2002	765.00	493.75	25.00	9.03	320.39	115.72	138.77	326.66
2001	545.00	350.00	22.37	5.51	286.68	70.61	90.10	395.65
2000	1,173.75	370.00	91.50	14.88	1,172.63	190.63	0.10	94.09
1999	1,512.50	760.00	113.00	57.38	1,448.16	735.29	4.44	3.36

convertible bond should have a conversion value of $1,100 in the first call period, Amazon could call the bonds and the investors would have a choice between the call price of $1,019 and 12.81558 shares of common stock worth $1,100. The rational bondholders would convert and take the higher value of the shares. This is known as **forced conversion.** There are two advantages to the corporation of forced conversion. First, the company doesn't have to pay off the debt with cash, and secondly, they most likely will reduce their cash outflows for interest expense. Since the majority of companies selling convertible securities do not pay a dividend on their common stock, the elimination of interest is a cash flow benefit. This may not always be the case—some companies sell convertibles in their growth stages and by the time the bonds mature or are called, the common dividend can actually be a higher cash outflow on an after-tax basis than the interest savings.

Comparing the Convertible Bond with Common Stock Purchase

Application Example

Would you have been better off putting $1,000 into Amazon.com common stock on February 1, 1999 or $1,000 into the convertible bond? The answer depends largely on whether the common stock went up in price, and whether it went up fast enough to outpace the income you may have received from the bond. If the common stock price went down, then the answer is pretty clear, you would be better off owning the convertible bond. On June 4, 2004, Amazon.com stock closed at a price of $50.95, which was lower than the $57.95 price on the day of the bond offering. All the data used in this example have been adjusted for the 2-for-1 stock split that occurred in August 1999. During this time period (1999–2004) Amazon.com paid no dividends on its common stock. Table 14–3 on page 388 demonstrates the analysis that we used to answer the question we posed in the first sentence above.

The trade-off the investor makes in the stock versus the convertible security investment decision is whether to buy stock and receive more shares and a lower cash flow or to buy the convertible bond with fewer shares (because of the premium) but higher cash flow from interest. In this case, the stock price declined about $7 and the bond price stayed fairly close to its par value of $l,000 on the day of the initial offering. The investor who bought stock was able to buy 4.444 more shares because no

TABLE 14–3 Comparing Returns between Purchasing Amazon.com Common Stock or Convertible Bond

	Amount Invested Feb. 1, 1999	Amazon.com Shares Purchased or Controlled	Stock Price June 4, 2004	Ending Stock or Bond Value	Total Dividends or Interest	Total Value
Stock	$1,000	17.25625*	$50.95	$879.21	$ 0.00	$ 879.21
Bond	1,000	12.81558	50.95	995.30	253.33	1,248.63

*The initial stock price was $57.95.

premium was paid. This gave them $226.42 in extra stock value on June 4, 2004 (4.444 × $50.95). The convertible bond investor received 10 semiannual interest payments and accrued three months' interest through June 1 for a total interest payment of $253.33. This example ignores interest on interest but clearly the bond investor would have reinvested the cash flow to earn a little extra income. The total advantage to the bondholder was $369.42 (the difference between the last two entries in Table 14–3).

Table 14–4 presents a selection of convertible bonds and helps illustrate basic concepts. While an occasional bond such as Medtronic Inc. carries a bond rating of Aa, most bonds are low-end investment grade Baa, or high yield junk bonds with ratings of Ba or less. We have divided up the bonds into four categories: Bonds selling at a discount to par value, bonds selling at close to par value, bonds selling at a premium to par value, and zero-coupon bonds that include all of the three previous categories. Looking at the dividend yields in Column (11), we can see that most of the underlying common stocks pay no or small dividends. Also in Column (13), we see the notation NCB, which means not a callable bond. This may mean that the call date has not yet arrived or that the bond is noncallable throughout its life.

Looking at the bonds by categories, we can make some generalizations that are more often true than false, although we are sure there are exceptions to the general rules. First when you look at the bonds selling at a discount you can see that the conversion premiums in Column (9) are relatively high compared to the bonds selling at a premium. The bonds selling at a premium are so far past the parity price that the advantages to investors have mostly evaporated and so has the premium. The bonds selling close to par have bond prices that are relatively close to their pure bond values. For the most part, except for Barnes & Noble, these bond prices are being supported by their pure bond values rather than their conversion values based on the underlying stock price. In the case of the bonds selling at premiums, their bond prices are all well beyond their pure bond values and are very close to their conversion values. In this case, the bond price is being supported by the underlying common stock price.

Convertible preferred stock selections are presented in Table 14–5 on page 390 and exhibit the same type of characteristics as convertible bonds, except

TABLE 14–4 Selected Convertible Bonds

Convertible Bond Issues	(1) Coupon	(2) Maturity	(3) Moody's Bond Rating	(4) Bond Price	(5) Conversion Price	(6) Conversion Ratio	(7) Common Stock Price	(8) Conversion Value	(9) Conversion Premium	(10) Pure Bond Value	(11) Stock Dividend Yield	(12) Bond Current Yield	(13) Call Price
Bonds Selling at a Discount													
American Airlines	4.50%	2024	Ca	$ 757.70	$ 22.05	45.352	$10.10	$ 458.06	65%	$830.00	0%	5.90%	NCB
CV Therapeutics	2.00	2023	Caa	748.20	47.58	21.017	12.95	272.17	175	710.00	0	2.70	NCB
Nortel Networks	4.25	2008	Caa	888.40	10.00	100.00	3.26	326.00	173	860.00	0	4.80	NCB
Bonds Selling at Close to Par													
Amazon.com	4.75%	2009	Ca	$ 995.30	$ 78.03	12.816	$42.08	$ 539.28	85%	$840.00	0%	4.80%	$1,023.75
American Tower	5.00	2010	Ca	1,001.40	51.50	19.418	12.66	245.83	307	910.00	0	5.00	NCB
Barnes & Noble	5.25	2009	B	1,033.40	32.51	30.758	28.65	881.22	17	900.00	0	5.10	$1,030.00
Disney (Walt)	2.125	2023	Baa	1,038.50	29.46	33.944	22.90	777.32	34	870.00	0.90	2.00	NCB
Medtronic Inc.	1.250	2021	Aa	1,033.10	61.80	16.180	49.30	797.67	30	990.00	0.50	1.20	NCB
Bonds Selling at a Premium													
Elan Corp.	6.50%	2008	C	$3,132.50	$ 7.42	134.771	$22.04	$2,970.35	5%	$810.00	0%	2.10%	$1,000.00
Ligand Pharmaceuticals	6.00	2007	Caa	2,983.80	6.17	161.991	17.77	2,878.58	4	940.00	0	2.00	NCB
Nextel Partners	1.50	2008	Ca	1,979.60	7.58	131.909	14.08	1,857.28	7	730.00	0	0.80	NCB
OSI Pharmaceuticals	4.00	2009	C	1,672.40	50.00	20.00	80.35	1,607.00	4	710.00	0	2.40	$1,000.00
Sierra Health Services	2.25	2023	Caa	2,225.90	18.29	54.675	39.40	2,154.20	3	810.00	0	1.00	NCB
Zero-Coupon Bonds													
Anadarko Petroleum	0%	2021	Baa	$ 987.50	$100.72	9.929	$55.38	$ 549.87	80%	$900.00	0.50%	0.00%	NCB
Biogen (Idec Pharm.)	0	2019	Caa	2,354.50	24.75	40.404	58.15	2,349.49	0	440.00	0	0.00	$ 443.14
International Paper	0	2021	Baa	542.60	105.14	9.511	40.04	380.82	42	530.00	2.50	0.00	NCB
Masco Corp.	0	2031	Baa	453.00	78.59	12.724	27.79	353.60	28	420.00	1.90	0.00	$ 475.11
Yahoo Corp.	0	2008	Caa	1,449.40	20.50	48.78	27.02	1,318.04	10	74.00	0.00	0.00	NCB

TABLE 14-5 Selected Convertible Preferred Stocks

Convertible Preferred Issues	(1) Dividend	(2) Call Price	(3) Preferred Stock Price	(4) Common Stock Price	(5) Conversion Ratio	(6) Conversion Value	(7) Conversion Premium	(8) Pure Value	(9) Common Dividend Yield	(10) Preferred Dividend Yield
Chesapeake Energy	$3.375	$50.00	$88.80	$13.58	6.494	$88.19	1%	$38.00	1%	3.80%
Citizens Utilities	2.500	50.00	52.46	12.76	3.760	47.98	9	32.00	0	4.80
Continental Airlines	3.000	51.50	22.38	9.30	0.833	7.75	189	24.00	0	13.40
Emmis Communications	3.125	51.34	50.50	21.06	1.280	26.96	87	43.00	0	6.20
Ford Capital Trust II	3.250	NCB	52.53	14.27	2.825	40.31	30	41.00	2.80	6.20
IndyMac Bancorp	3.000	50.00	53.00	22.92	1.597	36.60	42	36.00	0	5.70
Philippine Long Distance Tel.	3.500	0.00	42.70	17.23	1.713	29.51	45	39.00	0.50	3.20

that most of the preferred stocks were issued at $50 per share and not the $1,000 par of the bonds. The dividend yield of the preferred stock (Column 10) is higher than the current yield on the bonds in Table 14–4 on page 389 (Column 12). Additionally, convertible preferreds are favorite financing vehicles for companies with a high percentage of debt in their capital structures. These would include utilities, banks, real estate investment trusts, and other companies with a more stable income stream.

Disadvantages of Convertibles

It has been said that everything has a price, and purchasing convertible securities at the wrong price can eliminate one of their main advantages. For example, once convertible bonds begin rising in value, or the pure bond value declines substantially due to higher interest rates, the downside protection becomes meaningless. In the case of Elan Corp. in Table 14–4 on page 389 under "Bonds Selling at a Premium," the market price of the bond is $3,132.50 (Column 4) and the pure bond value is $810 (Column 10). Purchasing any of the five bonds in the premium category would provide almost no downside protection at all because if the stock price declines, the bond price will follow the stock price down.

Another drawback for the purchaser of convertible bonds is that they pay lower yields than "straight" nonconvertible bonds. Therefore, convertible bondholders accept below-market yields in the hope of price appreciation through common stock performance. The interest rate on convertible bonds is generally one-third or more below that for bonds in a similar risk class. For example, while a straight bond might pay 6 percent, a convertible bond for the same company could pay 4 percent or less.

From an institutional investor's standpoint, many convertible securities lack liquidity because of small trading volume or because they are small in dollar size. In general, institutional investors would like to own convertible issues when the size of the total bond issue is $200 million or more.

When to Convert into Common Stock

Convertible securities generally have a call provision, which gives the corporation the option of redeeming the bond at a specified price before maturity. The call price is usually at a premium over par value ($1,000) in the early years of callability, and it generally declines over time to par value. We know that as the price of the common stock goes up, the convertible security will rise along with the stock so the investor has no incentive to convert bonds into stock. However, the corporation may use the call privilege to force conversion before maturity. Companies usually force conversion when the conversion value is well above the call price. Investors will take the shares rather than the call price since the shares are worth more. This enables the company to turn debt into equity on its balance sheet and makes new debt issues a better risk for future lenders because of higher interest coverage and a lower debt-to-equity ratio.

Corporations may also encourage voluntary conversion by using a step-up in the conversion price over time. When the bond is issued, the contract may specify the following conversion provisions.

	Conversion Price	Conversion Ratio
First five years	$40	25.0 shares
Next three years	45	22.2 shares
Next two years	50	20.0 shares
Next five years	55	18.2 shares

At the end of each time period, there is a strong inducement to convert rather than accept an adjustment to a higher conversion price and a lower conversion ratio. This is especially true if the bond's conversion value is the dominating influence on the market price of the bond. In the case where the conversion value is below the pure bond value and where the interest income is greater than the dividend income, an investor will most likely not be induced to convert through the step-up feature.

About the only other reason for voluntarily converting in the case stated above is if the dividend income received on the common stock is greater than the interest income on the bond. Even in this case, risk-averse investors may want to hold the bond because interest payments are legally required whereas dividends may be reduced.

Advantages and Disadvantages to the Issuing Corporation

Having established the fundamental characteristics of the convertible security from the investor's viewpoint, let us now examine the factors a corporate financial officer must consider in weighing the advisability of a convertible offer for the firm.

It has been stated that the interest rate paid on convertible issues is normally lower than that paid on a straight debt instrument. Also, the convertible feature may be the only device for allowing smaller corporations access to the bond market.

Convertible bonds are also attractive to a corporation that believes its stock is undervalued. For example, assume a corporation's $1,000 bonds are convertible into 20 shares of common stock at a conversion price of $50. Also assume the company's common stock has a current price of $45, and new shares of stock might be sold at only $44.[1] Thus, the corporation will effectively receive $6 over current market price, assuming future conversion. Of course, one can also argue that if the firm had delayed the issuance of common stock or convertibles for a year or two, the stock might have gone up from $45 to $60 or $65, and new common stock might have been sold at this lofty price.

To translate this to overall numbers for the firm, if a corporation needs $10 million in funds and offers straight stock now at a new price of $44, it must issue 227,272 shares ($10 million/$44 per share). With convertibles, the number of shares potentially issued is only 200,000 shares ($10 million/$50 per share). Finally, if no stock or convertible bonds are issued now and the stock goes up to a level at which new shares can be offered at a price of $60, only 166,667 will be required ($10 million/$60).

---

[1] There is always a bit of underpricing to ensure the success of a new offering.

the real world of investing

The Convertible Craze of 2000–2001 and Its Aftermath

It seems that convertible bonds have been the most popular source of funds for many companies during the market downturn of 2000–2001. Suzanne McGee of *The Wall Street Journal* profiles the frenzy in this market in two articles. During the spring of 2000 there was a string of new zero-coupon convertibles. With companies trying to preserve their cash, what makes better sense than to sell zero-coupon bonds? In addition, with interest rates falling and stock prices off their highs of late 1999 and early 2000, many investors were willing to load up on convertibles to play the drop-in-interest-rates game and to take advantage of a potential rebound in stock prices. Both effects would cause convertible bonds to rise. Remember from Chapter 13 that zero-coupon bonds are the most price sensitive to changes in interest rates.

Some mutual fund managers and professional investors complained that Wall Street was pricing these issues at premiums that were too large. In fact, conversion premiums in many of these deals were between 40 and 45 percent, quite a bit higher than the more normal 20 to 25 percent. One advantage of convertible bonds to the issuing corporation is that they have coupons lower than straight bonds, and many of the convertibles that were sold in 2000–2001 had annual yields to maturity of 2 to 3 percent.

Traditionally, convertible bonds have usually been small issues of less than $100 million sold by smaller, more risky growth companies, but this new round included well-known quality companies selling issues of $500 million and larger. Investment bankers were more than eager to sell these large issues because they generate larger fees. During normal markets, convertible securities may generate 10 percent of the equity-based underwriting fees, but in the first seven months of 2001 these convertible issues accounted for more than 50 percent of equity-based underwriting fees.

Investment bankers were so hungry for these convertible issues that some companies have had an auction to choose the best deal from among investment bankers. One company, Mirant of Atlanta, Georgia (**www.mirant.com**), chose Salomon Smith Barney as the winner of its auction. The firm offered Mirant a conversion premium of 51 percent, twice the rate in normal times. The market eventually lost its appetite for convertibles priced this high, and some professionals on the street think that Salomon Smith Barney took a loss on the deal. A loss occurs when the banker can't sell the bonds to investors at a price that covers costs plus the price paid to the company. What happens is that they lose their underwriting fee and more.

In perhaps the largest deal to date, Household International (**www.household.com**) sold $1 billion zero-coupon convertibles in July 2001 through Morgan Stanley (**www.morganstanley.com**). The issue was priced at $81.914, but traders indicate that almost a third of the deal was sold at a discounted price of $80.75. Traders say that when the liquidity in the aftermarket is small, it indicates that the investment bankers probably ate some of their fees and maybe more. Bankers are very competitive in this market and are always looking for ways to charge new fees. What they are doing is taking bigger risks in pricing issues than they did in the raging bull market of the late 1990s.

As a postlude to the Mirant story, we should point out that being able to sell bonds is one thing, but being able to pay them off is another. Mirant was affected by the energy fallout caused by Enron's collapse and was forced to file for Chapter 11 bankruptcy protection in mid-July 2003.

Sources: Suzanne McGee, "Zero Interest: Investors Balk at Some Convertibles' Prices," *The Wall Street Journal*, July 27, 2000, and Suzanne McGee, "A Frenzy of Big Deals; A String of Losses," *The Wall Street Journal*, August 17, 2001.

Another matter of concern to the corporation is the accounting treatment accorded to convertibles. In the funny-money days of the 1960s' conglomerate merger movement, corporate management often chose convertible securities over common stock because the convertibles had a nondilutive effect on earnings per share. As indicated in the following section on reporting earnings for convertibles, the rules were changed.

Accounting Considerations with Convertibles

Before 1969, the full impact of the conversion privilege as it applied to convertible securities, warrants (long-term options to buy stock), and other dilutive securities was not adequately reflected in reported earnings per share. Because all of these securities may generate additional common stock in the future, the potential effect of this **dilution** (the addition of new shares to the capital structure) should be considered. The accounting profession has applied many different measures to earnings per share over the years, most recently replacing the concepts of primary earnings per share and fully diluted earnings per share with **basic earnings per share** and **diluted earnings per share.** In 1997, the Financial Accounting Standards Board issued "Earnings per Share" *Statement of Financial Accounting Standards No. 128* that covered the adjustments that must be made when reporting earnings per share.

If we examine the financial statements of the XYZ Corporation in Table 14–6 we find that the earnings per share reported are not adjusted for convertible securities and are referred to as basic earnings per share.

Diluted earnings per share adjusts for all potential dilution from the issuance of any new shares of common stock arising from convertible bonds, convertible preferred stock, warrants, or any other options outstanding. The comparison of basic and diluted earnings per share give the analyst or investor a measure of the potential effects of these securities.

We get diluted earnings per share for the XYZ Corporation by assuming that 400,000 new shares will be created from potential conversion, while at the same time, allowing for the reduction in interest payments that would occur as a result of the conversion of the debt to common stock. Since before-tax interest payments on the convertibles are $450,000, the after-tax interest cost ($270,000) will be saved and can be added back to income. After-tax interest cost is determined by multiplying interest payments by one minus the tax rate

TABLE 14–6 XYZ Corporation

1. Capital section of balance sheet:

Common stock (1 million shares at $10 par)	$10,000,000
4.5% convertible debentures (10,000 debentures of $1,000; convertible into 40 shares per bond, or a total of 400,000 shares)	10,000,000
Retained earnings	20,000,000
Net worth	$40,000,000

2. Condensed income statement:

Earnings before interest and taxes	$ 2,950,000
Interest (4.5% of $10 million of convertibles)	450,000
Earnings before taxes	$ 2,500,000
Taxes (40%)	1,000,000
Earnings after taxes	$ 1,500,000

3. Basic earnings per share:

$$\frac{\text{Earnings after taxes}}{\text{Shares of common stock}} = \frac{\$1,500,000}{1,000,000} = \$1.50$$

$(1 - 0.4)$ times $\$450,000 = \$270,000$. Making the appropriate adjustments to the numerator and denominator, we show diluted earnings per share as $1.26 in Formula 14–5.

$$\begin{aligned} \text{Diluted earnings per share} &= \frac{\text{Adjusted earnings after taxes}}{\text{Shares outstanding} + \text{All convertible securities}} \\ &= \frac{\$1,500,000 \text{ (Reported earnings)} + \$270,000 \text{ (Interest savings)}}{1,000,000 + 400,000} \\ &= \frac{\$1,770,000}{1,400,000} \\ &= \$1.26 \end{aligned} \qquad (14\text{–}5)$$

We see a $0.24 reduction from the basic earnings per share figure of $1.50 in Table 14–6. The new figure is the value that a sophisticated security analyst would utilize.

Speculating Through Warrants

A **warrant** is an option to buy a stated number of shares of stock from the issuing company at a specified price over a given time period. Warrants can trade between investors, but at the expiration of the warrant, the final owner of the warrant will have to decide whether to exercise the option to purchase stock or to let the warrant expire without exercising the option. For example, if a warrant entitles the holder to purchase one share at the exercise price of $20 per share and the stock is trading at $30 per share, the investor will give the company $20 per share and have stock worth $30 for a $10 gain. If the stock price is less than $20 at expiration, then the warrant expires worthless.

The warrants listed in Table 14–7 on page 396 demonstrate the relationships discussed above. Redback Networks, a casualty of the Internet bubble, emerged from Chapter 11 bankruptcy proceedings on January 2, 2004. The company provides advanced telecommunications networking equipment that enables telephone companies and service providers to give high-speed Internet access to corporate networks. The warrants listed in Table 14–7 were part of Redback's bankruptcy refinancing package. They were given to former investors with the hope that if the company recovers and does well, the stock will rise and the former stockholders may be able to recover a portion of their losses. The common stock was selling at $5.17 per share (Column 2) and the exercise price for the warrant was $5.00 per share (Column 3). Since the warrant allows the holder to buy one share of stock for each warrant held, the warrant has a value of $.17 (Column 4) since you can buy stock for $5.00 and sell it for $5.17. However, because the warrant is actually selling for $5.00 (Column 1) instead of the $.17 it is worth, it is selling above its true value by $4.83 (Column 5). The warrant has about six and one-half years before expiration and speculators may be willing to gamble on the potential increase in price of the common stock. Since Redback emerged from bankruptcy, its stock has traded as high as $13. If this price would be reached again, the warrant would be worth at least $8 ($13 market price minus the $5.00 exercise price in Column 3).

TABLE 14–7 Selected Warrants as of June 4, 2004

Company Name	Common Stock Exchange Listing & Warrant Ticker Symbol	(1) Warrant Price	(2) Per Share Stock Price	(3) Per Share Exercise Price	(4) Intrinsic Value [(2) − (3)]*(6)	(5) Speculative Premium (1) − (4)	(6) Shares Per Warrant	(7) Due Date
Chiquita Brands Intl.	NYSE, CQB WS	$ 4.70	$18.07	$19.23	−$1.16	$ 5.86	1.00	3/19/2009
Forest Oil	NYSE, FTYLL	13.00	24.41	12.50	9.53	3.47	0.80	3/15/2010
InterActive Corp.	OTC, IACIZ	35.31	30.27	6.92	45.25	−9.94	1.938	2/4/2009
Redback Networks	OTC, RBAKW	5.00	5.17	5.00	0.17	4.83	1.00	1/5/2011
SpectraSite	OTC, SPCSW	52.00	40.91	32.00	8.91	43.09	1.00	2/10/2010
XO Communications	OTC, XOCML	0.73	3.93	10.00	−6.07	6.80	1.00	1/16/2010

Most warrants allow the holder to buy one share of common stock per warrant on the date of issue, but if the common stock performs well and stock splits occur, the warrant gets adjusted to reflect the stock splits. In Column (6) of Table 14–7, InterActive Corp. has a warrant with a claim on more than one share while Forest Oil has a warrant with a claim to eight-tenths of a share.

Forest Oil, a domestic oil producer, has common stock traded on the New York Stock Exchange. During the last 52 weeks Forest's common stock traded between a high price of $29.60 and a low price of $19.80. Forest has a warrant listed in Table 14–7 that allows the holder to buy one share of stock for $12.50 per share (Column 3) until March 15, 2010. The common stock is selling at $24.41 (Column 2) which is above the $12.50 exercise price by $11.91. Since the warrant holder is entitled to 0.8 (eight-tenths) of a share of common stock, the $11.91 has to be multiplied by 0.8 to arrive at its true value of $9.53 shown in Column (4). Because there is almost six years left before the warrant expires, investors are willing to pay more than the warrant is worth on the chance that the stock price will rise and push the warrant price up. For example if Forest Oil would rise to $50 per share over the next five years, the warrant would be worth ($50 − 12.50) × 0.8 or $30.00.

Warrants are usually issued as a sweetener to a bond offering, and they may enable the firm to issue debt when this would not be feasible otherwise. The warrants allow the bond issue to carry a lower coupon rate and are usually detachable from the bond after the issue date. After being separated from the bond, warrants have their own market price and may trade on a different market from the common stock. After the warrants are exercised, the initial debt with which they were sold remains in existence.

www.prufn.com

The Bache Group, a financial company (now Prudential Securities), had a bond offering October 30, 1980. It offered 35,000 units of $1,000 debentures due in the year 2000 with a coupon interest rate of 14 percent. To each bond, 30 warrants were attached. Each warrant allowed the holder to buy one share of stock at $18.50 until November 1, 1985. At the time of issue, the warrant had no true value since the common stock was selling below $18.50. During 1981, however, the stock went up as several merger offers were made for retail brokerage companies. On May 29, 1981, Bache common stock was selling at 31½, and each warrant traded at 13⅝. The 30 warrants received with each bond were now worth $408.75 and provided the sweetener every bondholder had hoped for.

Because a warrant is dependent on the market movement of the underlying common stock and has no "security value" as such, it is highly speculative. If the common stock of the firm is volatile, the value of the warrants may change dramatically.

Valuation of Warrants

Because the value of a warrant is closely tied to the underlying stock price, we can develop a formula for the minimum or intrinsic value of a warrant:

$$I = (M - EP) \times N \qquad (14\text{--}6)$$

where:

I = The intrinsic or minimum value of the warrant
M = The market value of the common stock
EP = The option or exercise price of the warrant
N = The number of shares each warrant entitles the holder to purchase

Assume that the common stock of the Graham Corporation is $25 per share and that each warrant carries an option to purchase one share at $20 over the next 10 years. The purchase price stipulated in the warrant is the **option** or **exercise price.** Using Formula 14–6, the intrinsic value is $5 or [($25 − 20) × 1]. The **intrinsic value** in this case is equal to the market price of the common stock minus the option price of the warrant times the number of shares each warrant represents. Because the warrant has 10 more years before it expires and is an effective vehicle for speculative trading, it may well trade for over $5. If the warrant were selling for $9, we would say it had an intrinsic value of $5 and a speculative premium of $4. The **speculative premium** is equal to the price of the warrant, minus the intrinsic value when the warrant entitles the holder to purchase one share. When the number of shares is different than one, the calculation of the speculative premium has to be modified as shown in Formula 14–7.

$$SP = (W - I) \times N \qquad (14\text{--}7)$$

where:

SP = The speculative premium
W = The warrant price
I = The intrinsic value of the warrant
N = The number of shares each warrant represents

The speculative premium represents the amount that the stock price must rise by its expiration date for you to break even on the purchase of the warrant. In the example of Graham Corporation, if you pay $9 for the warrant when the intrinsic value is only $5, the stock would have to rise by $4 for you to recover the premium you paid. On the exercise date there is no speculative premium because you have run out of time to speculate.

As long as there is time to expiration left, investors can gamble on a rise in the stock price and be willing to pay a speculative premium. Even if the stock were trading at less than $20 (the exercise price), the warrant might still have some value in the market. Speculators might purchase the warrant with the hope that the common stock price would increase sufficiently to make the warrant valuable. If the common stock were selling for $15 per share, thus giving the warrant a negative intrinsic value, the warrant might still command a value of $1 or $2 in anticipation of increased common stock value.

Further Explanation of Intrinsic Value

The typical relationship between the market price and the intrinsic value of a warrant is depicted in Figure 14–3. We assume the warrant entitles the holder to purchase one new share of common stock at $20.

Although the intrinsic value of the warrant is theoretically negative at a common stock price between 0 and $20, the warrant still carries some value in the market. Also, observe that the difference between the market price of the warrant and its intrinsic value is diminished at the upper ranges of value. Two reasons may be offered for this declining premium.

First, the speculator loses the ability to use leverage to generate high returns as the price of the stock goes up. When the price of the stock is relatively low, say, $25, and the warrant is in the $5 to $10 range, a 10-point movement in the stock could mean a 200 percent gain in the value of the warrant, as indicated in part A of Table 14–8. At the upper levels of stock value, much of this leverage is lost, as indicated in part B of the table. At a stock value of $50 and a warrant value of approximately $30, a 10-point movement in the stock would produce only a 33 percent gain in the warrant.

FIGURE 14–3 Market Price Relationships for a Warrant

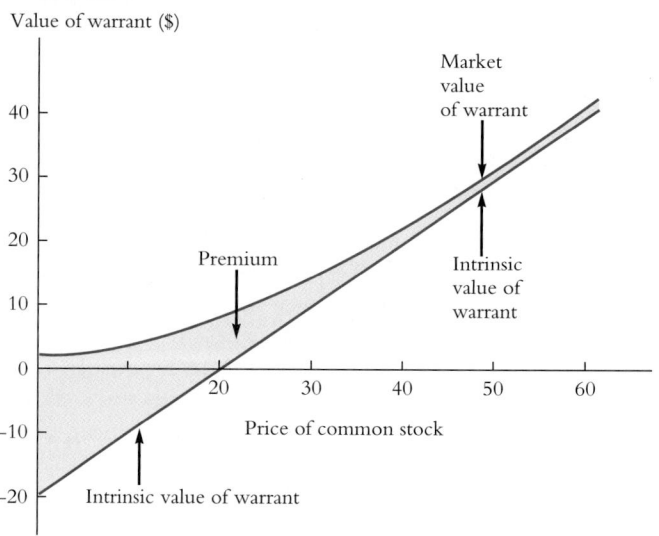

TABLE 14–8 Leverage in Valuing Warrants

(A)	(B)
Stock price = $25; warrant price = $5ᵃ + 10-point movement in stock price New warrant price = $15 (10-point gain) Percentage gain in warrant = $\frac{\$10}{\$5} \times 100 = 200\%$	Stock price = $50; warrant price = $30 + 10-point movement in stock price. New warrant price = $40 (10-point gain) Percentage gain in warrant = $\frac{\$10}{\$30} \times 100 = 33\%$

ᵃ The warrant price would, of course, be greater than $5 because of a premium. Nevertheless, we use $5 for ease of computation.

Another reason speculators pay a very low premium at higher stock prices is that there is less downside protection. A warrant selling at $30 when the stock price is $50 is more vulnerable to downside movement than is a $5 to $10 warrant when the stock is between $20 and $30.

Warrant premiums are also influenced by the same factors that affect convertible bond premiums. More volatile common stocks will have greater potential to create short-run profits for warrant speculators, so the higher the price volatility, the greater the premium. Also, the longer the option has before expiration, the higher the premium will be. This "time premium" is worth more the longer the common stock has to reach and surpass the option price of the warrant.

Use of Warrants by Corporations

As previously indicated, warrants may allow for the issuance of debt under difficult circumstances. While a straight debt issue may not be acceptable or may be accepted only at extremely high rates, the same security may be well received because detachable warrants are included. Warrants may also be included as an add-on in a merger or acquisition agreement. A firm might offer $20 million in cash plus 10,000 warrants in exchange for all the outstanding shares of the acquisition candidate.

The use of warrants has traditionally been associated with such aggressive, "high-flying" firms as biotechs, airlines, and conglomerates.

As a financing device for creating new common stock, warrants may not be as desirable as convertible securities. A corporation with convertible bonds outstanding may force the conversion of debt to common stock through a call, while no similar device is available to the firm with warrants. The only possible inducement might be a step-up in the option price—whereby the warrant holder must pay a progressively higher option price if he does not exercise by a given date.

The capital structure of the firm after the exercise of a warrant also is somewhat different from that created after the conversion of a debenture. In the case of a warrant, the original debt outstanding remains in existence after the detachable warrant is exercised, whereas the conversion of a debenture extinguishes the former debt obligation.

the real world of investing

Venture Capitalists Love Convertibles and Warrants

Venture capital is normally raised in the early stages of growth for a firm, well before the company has "gone public" (sold its shares in the public market).

Even successful, rapidly developing young companies often have needs for capital that far outstrip their profit generating capability, their ability to borrow, or the resources of their owners. This is where the venture capitalist comes in. He or she provides funding (seed capital) with the hope that his or her capital will eventually be harvested in the form of a successful public offering of stock at some point in the future.

Venture capitalists are normally overwhelmed with potential proposals for funding. The acceptance rate is lower than 1 out of 100. When the Basses of Fort Worth, the Pritzkers of Chicago, or other venture capitalists see a deal, they always have their eye out for the next Microsoft or Intel. The odds are long, but the potential payout is great. Not only do venture capitalists provide funding, but they also may share their expertise in management, marketing, finance, and so on. Some venture capitalists even specialize in certain areas such as biotechnology or computer software. Often, the financing takes place in sequential stages. This means that additional funding after the original funding will only take place if certain goals are met. These goals may relate to profitability ratios, new product development, market penetration, and so on.

The venture capitalist often provides relatively low-cost debt financing, but with the understanding that the funding carries with it the potential to participate in a major way in any successful public offering of stock in the future. While the venture capitalist may not care about owning a direct equity interest in the company while it is private, he or she wants to participate in ownership when there is a public distribution of shares.

Convertibles and warrants fit very well into these investment parameters. With convertibles the venture capitalist is able to receive interest income and enjoy a relatively high priority of claims among other suppliers of capital. At the time an equity position becomes desirable, he or she can merely convert the debt to common stock.

Another alternative is to provide the venture capitalist with warrants as part of the compensation package for extending debt financing. As incentive, the exercise price on the warrants may be set at one-fifth to one-tenth of the anticipated potential price for a public offering.

When convertibles or warrants are used in early-stage financing, one can think of the interest payments on the related debt as providing singles or doubles to the venture capitalist. What he or she is really hoping for is a grand slam home run in the form of a successful public offering that is fully subscribed to and one in which the stock continues to go up in value after the offering.

Accounting Considerations with Warrants

As with convertible securities, the potential dilutive effect of warrants must be considered. In calculating the earnings per share resulting from conversion of warrants, accountants use the treasury stock method. Under this method the accountant must compute the number of new shares that could be created by the exercise of all warrants, with the provision that the total can be reduced by the assumed use of the cash proceeds to purchase a partially offsetting amount of shares at the market price. Assume that warrants to purchase 10,000 shares at $20 are outstanding and the current price of the stock is $50. We show the following:

1. New shares created	10,000
2. Reduction of shares from cash proceeds (computed below)	4,000
Cash proceeds—10,000 shares at $20 = $200,000	
Current price of stock—$50	
Assumed reduction in shares outstanding from cash proceeds = $200,000/$50 = 4,000	
3. Assumed net increase in shares from exercise of warrants (10,000 − 4,000)	6,000

In computing earnings per share, we will add 6,000 shares to the denominator with no adjustment to the numerator, which will lower earnings per share. If earnings per share had previously been $1 based on $100,000 in earnings and 100,000 shares outstanding, EPS would now be reduced to $0.943:

$$\frac{\text{Earnings}}{\text{Shares}} = \frac{\$100,000}{106,000} = \$0.943$$

With warrants included in computing diluted earnings per share, their impact on reported earnings is important from both the investor and corporate viewpoints.

exploring the web

Website Address	Comment
www.convertbond.com	Fee-based source of information on convertible bond issues
www.numa.com	Provides calculator for convertible bonds
cbs.marketwatch.com	Personal finance section contains general information on convertible bonds
www.bondsonline.com	Provides information about convertible bonds

Summary

Convertible securities and warrants offer the investor an opportunity for participating in increased common stock values without owning common stock directly. Convertible securities may be in the form of debt or preferred stock, though most of our examples refer to debt.

Convertible securities provide a guaranteed income stream and a floor value based on required yield on the investment. At the same time, they have an established conversion ratio to common stock (par value/conversion price). The conversion value of an issue is equal to the conversion ratio times the current value of a share of common stock. The conversion value is generally less than the current market price of the convertible issue. Actually, the difference between the market price of the convertible issue and the conversion value is referred to as the conversion premium. The conversion premium is influenced by the volatility of the underlying common stock, the time to maturity, the dividend payment on common stock relative to the interest rate on the convertibles, and other lesser factors. Generally, when the common stock price has risen well above the conversion price (and the convertible is trading well above par), the conversion premium will be quite small, as indicated in Panel (a) of Figure 14–2 on page 386. The small premium is attributed to the fact that the investor no longer enjoys significant downside protection.

A warrant is an option to buy a stated number of shares of stock (usually one) at a specified price over a given time period. Warrants are often issued as a sweetener to a bond issue and may allow the firm to issue debt where it would not normally be feasible. The warrants are generally detachable from the bond issue. Thus, if the warrants are exercised, the bond issue still remains in existence (this is clearly different from a convertible security).

Key Words and Concepts

basic earnings per share 394
conversion premium 384
conversion price 382
conversion ratio 382
conversion value 382
convertible security 381
diluted earnings per share 394
dilution 394
downside limit 385
downside risk 385
exercise price (of warrant) 397
floor value 383
forced conversion 387
intrinsic value (of warrant) 397
option price (of warrant) 397
parity price 384
pure bond value 382
speculative premium 397
warrant 395

Discussion Questions

1. Why would an investor be interested in convertible securities? (What do they offer to the investor?)
2. What are the disadvantages of investing in convertible securities?
3. When is the best time to buy convertible bonds?
4. How can you determine the conversion ratio from the conversion price?
5. How do you determine the conversion value?
6. What is meant by the pure bond value?
7. For bonds that have conversion premiums in excess of 100 percent, what can you generally infer about the stock price?
8. How does the volatility of a stock influence the conversion premium?
9. How might a step-up in the conversion price force conversion?
10. Why do corporations use convertible bonds?
11. What is meant by the dilutive effect of convertible securities?
12. What is a warrant?
13. For what reasons do firms issue warrants?
14. Please explain why warrants are highly speculative.

15. Why do investors tend to pay a smaller premium for a warrant as the price of the stock goes up?
16. If warrants were initially a detachable part of a bond issue, will the amount of debt be reduced if the warrants are eventually exercised? Contrast this with a convertible security.
17. What type of firm generally issues warrants?

Problems

Conversion terms

1. A convertible bond has a face value of $1,000, and the conversion price is $40 per share. The stock is selling at $33 per share. The bond pays $70 per year interest and is selling in the market for $960. It matures in 10 years. Market rates are 12 percent per year.
   a. What is the conversion ratio?
   b. What is the conversion value?
   c. What is the conversion premium (in dollars and percent)?
   d. What is the floor value or pure bond value? (You may wish to review material in Chapter 12 for computing bond values.)

Downside risk

2. Compute the downside risk as a percentage in problem 1. What does this mean?

Downside risk

3. Under what circumstances might the downside risk increase? Relate your answer to interest rates in the market.

Conversion premium

4. Alvin Motor Corporation has a $1,000 face value convertible bond outstanding that has a market value of $1,030. It has a coupon rate of 6 percent and matures in five years. The conversion price is $50. The common stock currently is selling for $44.
   a. What is the conversion premium (in percent)?
   b. At what price does the common stock need to sell for the conversion value to be equal to the current bond price?

Pure bond value

5. In problem 4, market rates of interest for comparable bonds are 10 percent and the pure bond value is $845.66. What will happen to the pure bond value if market rates of interest go to 12 percent? (Once again, you may wish to consult Chapter 12 for computing bond values.)

Comparative analysis of stock and convertible bond

6. Assume you bought a convertible bond two years ago for $900. The bond has a conversion ratio of 32. When the bond was purchased, the stock was selling for $25 per share. The bond pays $75 in annual interest. The stock pays no cash dividend. Assume after two years the stock price rises to $35 and the firm forces investors to convert to common stock by calling the bond (there is no conversion premium at this point).
   Would you have been better off if you (a) had bought the stock directly or (b) bought the convertible bond and eventually converted it to common stock? Assume you would have invested $900 in either case. Disregard taxes, commissions, etc. *Hint:* Consider appreciation in value plus any annual income received. See Table 14–3 on page 388 for an example.

EPS and convertibles

7. Given the following data, compute diluted earnings per share.

Common stock (500,000 shares at $5 par) =	$2,500,000
Eight percent convertible debentures (5,000 bonds at $1,000 each; convertible into 50 shares per bond)	5,000,000
Retained earnings	5,000,000
Earnings before interest and taxes	2,800,000
Interest	400,000
Earnings before taxes	$2,400,000
Earnings after taxes (50 percent)	$1,200,000

Valuing warrants

8. Assume a firm has warrants outstanding that permit the holder to buy one new share of stock at $30 per share. The market price of the stock is now $36.
   a. What is the intrinsic value of the warrant?
   b. Why might the warrant sell for $2 in the market even if the stock price is $28?

Valuing warrants

9. Morgan Donuts has warrants outstanding that allow the holder to purchase 1.85 shares per warrant at $18 per share (option price). The common stock is currently selling for $21. The warrant has a market value of $7.
   a. What is the intrinsic value of the warrant?
   b. If the stock sold for $16.50, how large would the negative intrinsic value be?

Comparative analysis of stock and warrants

10. A firm has warrants outstanding that allow the holder to buy one share of stock at $30 per share. The stock is selling for $35 per share, and the warrants are now selling for $7 per warrant (this, of course, is above intrinsic value). You can invest $1,000 in the stock or the warrants (for purposes of the computation, round to two places to the right of the decimal point). Assume the stock goes to $42, and the warrants trade at their intrinsic value when the stock goes to $42. Would you have a larger total dollar profit by initially investing in the stock or the warrants?

EPS and warrants

11. Assume a corporation has $300,000 in earnings and 150,000 shares outstanding ($2 in earnings per share). Also assume there are warrants outstanding to purchase 25,000 shares at $30 per share. The stock is currently selling at $50 per share. In considering the effect of the warrants outstanding, what would revised earnings per share be?

Web Exercise

Scholastic Corp. is a major publisher of children's books, including the Harry Potter series. To get more information on Scholastic Corp. go to **www.bloomberg.com**.

1. On the home page, enter the ticker symbol for Scholastic Corp. (SCHL) after "ticker symbol" on the left-hand corner of the page, and click enter.
2. You will see Scholastic Corp. in the middle of the page.
3. Write down the volume traded for the day and the P/E ratio (trailing).
4. Now record the stock price.

5. Scholastic has convertible securities outstanding. Based on the conversion ratio of 26.022, what is the current conversion value of Scholastic Corp.?
6. Assume the convertible bond is presently trading at 90 points above the conversion value. What is the conversion premium? You may refer to Formula 14–3 on page 384 in the text to help you with this calculation.

Note: From time to time, companies redesign their websites, and occasionally a topic we have listed may have been deleted, updated, or moved into a different location. Most websites have a "site map" or "site index" listed on a different page. If you click on the site map or site index, you will be introduced to a table of contents that should aid you in finding the topic you are looking for.

CFA Material

The following material contains a sample question and solution from a prior Level I CFA exam. While the terminology is slightly different from that in this text, you can still view the skills that are necessary for the CFA exam.

CFA Exam Question

6. In examining a company's straight debentures and subordinated convertible debentures, both issued at the same time with the same maturity and at par, you note that the coupon and yield for the subordinated convertible debenture are lower than for the straight debenture. *Discuss* the return potential for the convertible bond in an environment of stable interest rates and rising stock prices that would explain its lower coupon and yield. (*5 minutes*)

Solution: Question 6—Morning Section (5 points)

The reason for the lower coupon and yield is that convertible bonds and preferred stock have the ability to act like common stock on the upside and be valued as a straight bond on the downside. This is demonstrated by the graph in Figure 14–4.

As shown, it has the upside potential of common stock and the downside protection of a bond. Thus, it could have a rate of return approaching common stock with substantially lower risk because it is protected on the downside. Also, the convertible bond has an income advantage relative to common stock until the point at which parity value drives the current yield below the dividend yield.

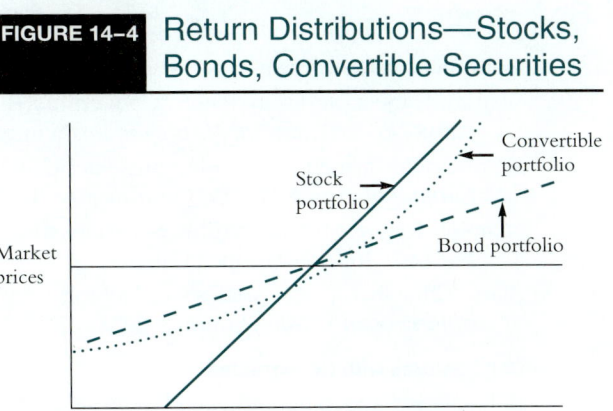

FIGURE 14–4 Return Distributions—Stocks, Bonds, Convertible Securities

S&P Problems

www.mhhe.com/edumarketinsight

1. Log on to the McGraw-Hill website: www.mhhe.com/edumarketinsight (see page vi in the preface for instructions).
2. Click on Company, which is the first box below the Market Insight title.
3. Put the ticker symbol for Amazon.com (AMZN) in the box, and click on go.
4. In the left margin, click on Excel Analytics to open the list and then click on monthly adjusted prices under market data. You will get a spreadsheet with about four years of price data.
5. Given the convertible bond example in Chapter 14 for Amazon, on pages 382–387, compute the current conversion value for Amazon given the most recent closing price. Assume the conversion rate is 12.81558.
6. Compute the conversion value using the price one year ago and two years ago. Are the convertible bond investors better off today than they were in the two previous years?
7. Notice the cumulative adjustment factor in the last column. This indicates whether there is a stock split or not. If the number is greater than 1.00, you will have to adjust the conversion ratio given in the chapter.

The Wall Street Journal Projects

You will work with the convertible bonds of Automatic Data Processing.

1. Using a conversion ratio of 25.884, compute the current conversion value. You need to multiply the conversion ratio by the price of the common stock as currently shown in the "New York Stock Exchange Composite Transactions" in Section C of *The Wall Street Journal*.
2. Compute the conversion premium. The appropriate equation to use is Formula 14–3, which is restated below. The answer should be shown as a percentage:

$$\text{Conversion Premium} = \frac{\text{Market price of bond} - \text{Conversion value}}{\text{Conversion value}}$$

Assume the market price of the bond is $180 over conversion value.

Selected References

Innovations in Convertible-Type Securities

Bhabra, Harjeet, and Ajay Patel. "Convertible Bond Financing: Are Some Issues Mimickers?" *Financial Management,* Winter 1996, pp. 67–77.

Hovakimian, Armen; Tim Opler; and Sheridan Titman. "The Debt-Equity Choice." *Journal of Financial and Quantitative Analysis,* March 2001, pp. 1–24.

Schmidt, Klause M. "Convertible Securities and Venture Capital Finance" *The Journal of Finance,* June 2003, pp. 1139–66.

Zhou, Chunsheng. "An Analysis of Default Correlations and Multiple Defaults." *Review of Financial Studies,* Summer 2001, pp. 555, 576.

Call Features with Convertibles

Billingsley, Randall S., and David M. Smith. "Why Do Firms Issue Convertible Debt?" *Financial Management,* Summer 1996, pp. 93–99.

Calamos, John P. "Convertible Securities as an Asset Class for the 1990s." *The Journal of Investing,* Spring 1994, pp. 63–65.

Ederington, Louis H.; Gary L. Caton; and Cynthia J. Campbell. "To Call or Not to Call Convertible Debt." *Financial Management,* Spring 1997, pp. 22–31.

Emery, Douglas R.; Mai E. Iskandar; and Johg-Chul Rhim. "Capital Structure Management as a Motivation for Calling Convertible Debt." *The Journal of Financial Research,* Spring 1994, pp. 91–116.

Kerins, Francis J. Jr., "Do Nonrefunding Provisions Constrain Corporate Behavior?" *Financial Management,* Spring 2001, pp. 57–83.

Korkeamaki, Timo P., and William T. Moore. "Convertible Bond Design and Capital Investment: The Role of Call Provisions." *The Journal of Finance,* February 2004, pp. 391–405.

Singh, Ajai; Arnold R. Cowan; and Nandkumer Nayar. "Underwritten Calls of Convertible Bonds." *Journal of Financial Economics,* March 1991, pp 173–96.

Accounting Issues and Convertibles

Hagler, J. L., and P. B. Thomas, "Should FASB 84-Induced Conversions of Convertible Debt Apply to Convertible Preferred Stock?" *CPA Journal,* May 1986, pp. 86–88.

King, T. E. and A. K. Ortegren. "Accounting for Hybrid Securities: The Case of Adjustable-Rate Convertible Notes." *The Accounting Review,* July 1988, pp. 522–35.

Derivative Products

part five

chapter 15
PUT AND CALL OPTIONS

chapter 16
COMMODITIES AND FINANCIAL FUTURES

chapter 17
STOCK INDEX FUTURES AND OPTIONS

dERIVATIVES HAVE BECOME a very important part of the financial landscape and in many cases have been at the center of some high-risk strategies. In fact, high-risk financial strategies using derivatives played a part in the collapse of Long-Term Capital Management in the 1990s and more recently, Enron. While derivatives can be used to reduce risk, it seems that they only bring public attention when they are used for speculative purposes or when they "blow up" because of too much leverage or misuse. The employee stock options mentioned in the fourth introductory section are also derivatives and if the employee is compensated with options, he or she takes the risk that there will actually be something there of value in the future, based on the increasing price of the company's common stock. This section provides an overview of equity options, commodities and financial futures, and stock index futures and options.

On January 1, 2004, Craig S. Donohue became chief executive officer of the Chicago Mercantile Exchange (CME), the largest futures exchange in the United States and one of the world's leading futures exchanges. The common stock of the Chicago Mercantile Exchange is traded on the New York Stock Exchange and is included in the Russell 1000 Index. Mr. Donohue joined the CME as an attorney in 1989 and advanced in the organization through teamwork and commitment. Mr. Donohue has held many positions at the CME including vice president and associate general counsel; vice president, Division of Market Regulation; senior vice president and general counsel, and chief administrative officer of CME Holding.

Managing a global financial company that is regulated by the Commodities Futures Trading Commission requires not only an understanding of finance and management, but also the regulatory environment. To position himself for his current leadership role at the CME, Craig Donohue acquired a diverse set of educational skills. Not only does he have a Master of Management degree from Northwestern University's Kellogg Graduate School of Management, but also a Juris Doctor from John Marshall Law School in Chicago. He also holds a Master of Laws degree in Financial Services Regulation from IIT Chicago Kent College of Law and a Bachelor of Arts degree from Drake University. At the age of 41, Mr. Donohue has a job that many finance majors might dream about, so take note and see what you need to do to make it to the top.

Craig Donohue has worked hard to maintain the CME's competitiveness in the world markets. He has helped implement a competitive tiered pricing program for the Eurodollar contract as well as a new pricing program aimed at attracting more large-scale European business. He has also introduced changes in the CME corporate governance that he felt were compatible with a public company. The corporate governance issues were considerable given that the Chicago Mercantile Exchange transformed itself from a member-owned private institution to a publicly traded company.

One of Mr. Donohue's social service interests is the National Council on Economic Education (NCEE) where he is currently on the board of directors. He is committed to financial and economic education and in a press release from NCEE, he is quoted as saying "As a parent and having worked in financial markets over the last 15 years, I see evidence every day of the importance of economic education."

Craig S. Donohue
Photo provided by the Chicago Mercantile Exchange.

15

chapter fifteen

Put and Call Options

objectives

1. Understand the basic concept of an option.

2. Distinguish between put and call options.

3. Define strike price, intrinsic value, and speculative premium.

4. Describe speculative and hedging strategies with options.

5. Explain how option contracts are closed out at expiration.

6. Be aware of the tax and commission factors associated with options.

Options Markets
    Listed Options Exchanges
The Options Clearing Corporation
    Option Premiums
    Intrinsic Value
    Speculative Premium (Time Value)
Basic Option Strategies
    Buying Call Options
    Writing Call Options
    Buying Put Options
Using Options in Combinations
    Spreads
    Straddles
Other Option Considerations
Appendix 15A: The Black-Scholes Option Pricing Model
Appendix 15B: The Use of Option Spreads and Straddles

The word **option** has many different meanings, but most of them include the ability or right to choose a certain alternative. One definition provided by *Webster's* is "the right, acquired for a consideration, to buy or sell something at a fixed price within a specified period of time." This definition is very general and applies to puts, calls, warrants, real estate options, or any other contract entered into between two parties where a choice of action or decision can be put off for a limited time at a cost. The person acquiring the option pays an agreed-upon sum to the person providing the option. For example, someone may want to buy your house for its sale price of $100,000. The buyer does not have the money but will give you $2,000 in cash if you give him the right to buy the house at $100,000 for the next 60 days. If you accept, you have given the buyer an option and have agreed not to sell the house to anyone else for the next 60 days. If the buyer raises $100,000 within the 60-day limit, he may buy the house, giving you the $100,000. Perhaps he gets the $100,000 but also finds another house he likes better for $95,000. He will not buy your house, but you have a $2,000 option premium and must now find someone else to buy your house. By selling the option, you tied up the sale of your house for 60 days, and if the option is not exercised, you have forgone an opportunity to sell the house to someone else.

The most widely known options are puts and calls on common stock. A **put** is an option to sell 100 shares of common stock at a specified price for a given period. **Calls** are the opposite of puts and allow the owner the right to buy 100 shares of common stock from the option seller (writer). Contracts on listed puts and calls have been standardized and can be bought on several different exchanges.

Options Markets

Before the days of options trading on exchanges, puts and calls were traded over-the-counter by the Put and Call Dealers Association. These dealers would buy and sell puts and calls for their own accounts for stocks traded on the New York Stock Exchange and then try to find an investor, hedger, or speculator to take the other side of the option. For example, if you owned 1,000 shares of GE and you wanted to write a call option giving the buyer the right to buy 1,000 shares of GE at $30 per share for six months, the dealer might buy the calls and look for someone who would be willing to buy them from him.

This system had several disadvantages. Dealers had to have contact with the buyers and sellers, and the financial stability of the option writer had to be endorsed (guaranteed) by a brokerage house. The option writer either had to keep the shares on deposit with the brokerage firm or put up a cash margin. Options in the same stock could exist in the market at various strike prices (price at which the option could be exercised) and scattered expiration dates. This meant that when an option buyer wanted to exercise or terminate the contract before expiration, he or she would have to deal directly with the option writer. This does not make for an efficient, liquid market. Unlisted options also reduced the striking price of a call by any dividends paid during the option period, which did not benefit the writer of the call.

Listed Options Exchanges

www.cboe.com

The Chicago Board Options Exchange was established in 1973 as the first exchange for call options. The market response was overwhelming, and within three years, the American, Pacific, and Philadelphia exchanges were also trading call options. By 2004, there were over 2,000 individual equity options traded on the options exchanges. The securities traded have expanded from individual common stocks to include options on stock indexes such as the Nasdaq 100 and the Standard & Poor's 500 indexes. The ability to buy and sell options on indexes provides a good hedging strategy for portfolio managers and it allows individual traders to speculate on market movements. The details of these strategies are covered in Chapter 17, while this chapter concentrates on options for individual common stocks.

Option markets thrive under volatile pricing conditions and uncertainty. The period 2000 through 2004 has provided ample volatility in the markets, and average daily trading volume of 3.6 million contracts set an annual record in 2003. For the first five months of 2004, average daily volume for equity contracts was poised to set another record at 4.4 million contracts per day.

Table 15–1, from the Options Clearing Corporation's website (www.optionsclearing.com), shows the growth in options trading since 1973. The Options Clearing Corporation is equally owned by its major trading exchanges, which include the American Exchange (AMEX), the Philadelphia Exchange (PHLX), the

TABLE 15–1 Options Data, Options Clearing Corporation—Yearly Contract Volume Statistics

	Equity Volume	Nonequity Volume	Futures Volume	Total Volume	Average Daily Volume	Futures Average Daily Volume	Year-End Equity Open Interest	Futures Open Interest	Number of Equity Issues
2003	830,308,227	77,550,428	2,592,193	910,450,848	3,612,900	10,286	128,509,275	197,822	2,227
2002	709,784,014	70,673,329	310,299	780,767,642	3,098,283	8,693	98,475,772	50,952	2,306
2001	722,680,249	58,581,686		781,261,935	3,150,250		86,024,850		2,261
2000	672,871,757	53,856,182		726,727,939	2,883,841		71,249,929		2,364
1999	444,765,224	63,126,259		507,891,483	2,015,442		56,907,365		2,579
1998	329,641,875	76,701,323		406,343,198	1,612,473		36,285,828		2,724
1997	272,998,701	80,824,417		353,823,118	1,398,510		28,677,748		2,400
1996	199,117,729	95,679,973		294,797,702	1,160,621		21,252,103		2,080
1995	174,380,236	112,916,673		287,296,909	1,140,068		18,836,632		1,720
1994	149,932,665	131,449,737		281,382,402	1,116,597		16,030,910		1,512
1993	131,726,101	100,935,994		232,662,095	919,614		14,778,179		1,294
1992	106,484,452	95,511,305		201,995,757	795,259		11,612,580		1,104
1991	104,850,686	93,950,914		198,801,600	785,777		9,311,298		937
1990	111,425,744	98,497,004		209,922,748	829,734		7,295,008		808
1989	141,839,748	85,176,912		227,016,660	900,860		9,013,121		701
1988	114,927,723	81,020,868		195,948,591	774,501		7,648,262		641
1987	164,431,851	140,737,084		305,168,935	1,206,201		8,073,498		590
1986	141,930,945	147,280,190		289,211,135	1,143,127		10,039,591		490
1985	118,555,989	114,354,558		232,910,547	924,248		10,443,038		462
1984	118,925,239	77,512,122		196,437,361	776,432		7,984,602		395
1983	135,658,976	14,397,099		150,056,075	593,107		12,499,329		936
1982	137,264,816	41,389		137,306,205	543,394		9,802,070		375
1981	109,405,782	0		109,405,782	432,434		9,495,497		354
1980	96,728,546	0		96,728,546	382,326		5,865,776		241
1979	64,264,863	0		64,264,863	254,011		4,199,696		220
1978	57,231,018	0		57,231,018	227,107		3,636,918		217
1977	39,637,328	0		39,637,328	157,291		3,343,185		222
1976	32,373,925	0		32,373,925	127,960		2,746,882		202
1975	18,103,018	0		18,103,018	71,553		1,109,227		44
1974	5,682,907	0		5,682,907	22,462		380,840		40
1973	1,119,245	0		1,119,245	6,470		242,825		32

Source: http://www.optionsclearing.com/market/vol_data/main/yearly_volume.xls, June 6, 2004.

Pacific Exchange, the Chicago Board Options Exchange (CBOE), and the International Securities Exchange.

The International Securities Exchange (ISE) is the "new kid on the block." The ISE traded its first option on May 26, 2000, and since then it has grown to be the leading member of the Options Clearing Corporation, accounting for 32 percent of the trades during the first five months of 2004. The International Securities Exchange is an electronic communications network (ECN), providing electronic trading in options. The move to electronic trading in the equity markets, which was covered in Chapter 2, has made its way to the options markets. Before the ISE started, the Chicago Board Options Exchange accounted for 45.5 percent of the trading volume in 2000, but by 2004 its market share had dropped to 25.6 percent. Obviously the ISE has taken a bite out of the CBOE. Notice that in addition to clearing options, the Options Clearing Corporation started clearing futures trades in 2002 for an electronic communication network specializing in futures trades so Table 15–1 includes two years of futures volume.

There are several reasons the listed options markets are so desirable compared with the previous method of over-the-counter trading for options before 1973. The contract period was standardized with three-, six-, and nine-month expiration dates on three calendar cycles:

Cycle 1: January/April/July/October.

Cycle 2: February/May/August/November.

Cycle 3: March/June/September/December.

The use of three cycles spread out the expiration dates for the options so that not all contracts came due on the same day.[1] Each contract expires at 11:59 p.m. Eastern time on the Saturday immediately following the third Friday of the expiration month. For all practical purposes, any closing out of positions must be done on that last Friday while the markets are open.

In an attempt to satisfy demand for longer-term options, **long-term equity anticipation securities (LEAPS)** were added and provided options with up to two years of expiration. LEAPS have generally been limited to blue-chip stocks such as Coca-Cola, Dow Chemical, General Electric, IBM, and others. LEAPS have the same characteristics as the short-term options, but because of their long-term nature, they have higher prices.

Another important feature of option trading is the standardized **exercise price** (strike price). This is the price the contract specifies for a buy or sell. For all stocks over $25 per share, the striking price normally changes by $5 intervals, and for stocks selling under $25 per share, the strike price usually changes by $2.50 a share. As the underlying stocks change prices in the market, options with new striking prices are added. For example, a stock selling at $30 per share when the January option is added will have a striking price of 30, but if the stock gets to 32.50 (halfway to the next striking price), the exchange may add another option (to the class of options) with a 35 strike price or even a 32.50 strike price.

This standardization of expiration dates and strike prices creates more certainty when buying and selling options in a changing market and allows more efficient trading strategies because of better coordination between stock prices,

---

[1] Additional cycles have also been added.

strike prices, and expiration dates. Dividends no longer affect the option contract as they did in the unlisted market. Transactions occur at arm's length between the buyer and seller without any direct matchmaking needed on the part of the broker. The ultimate result of these changes in the option market is a highly liquid, efficient market where speculators, hedgers, and arbitrageurs all operate together.

SINGLE Systems (a hypothetical company) call and put options are presented in Table 15–2 on page 415 as an example of different strike prices (15, 17.50, 20, 22.50, 25) and expiration months of December, January, and April. Calls represent options to buy stock and puts represent options to sell stocks. SINGLE Systems common stock closed at $18.93 on November 8, but during the last 52 weeks its price had fallen from a high of $57.63 to as low as $11.06. The values within Table 15–2, such as 4.20 and 4.50, reflect the prices of the various options contracts. This information will take on greater meaning as we go through the chapter.

The Options Clearing Corporation

Much of the liquidity and ease of operation of the option exchanges is due to the role of the **Options Clearing Corporation,** which functions as the issuer of all options listed on the five exchanges—the CBOE, the AMEX, the Philadelphia Exchange, the International Securities Exchange, and the Pacific Coast Exchange. Investors who want to trade puts and calls need to have an approved account with a member brokerage firm; on opening an account, they receive a prospectus from the Options Clearing Corporation detailing all aspects of option trading.

Options are bought and sold through a member broker the same as other securities. The exchanges allow special orders, such as limit, market, and stop orders, as well as orders used specifically in options trading, such as spread orders and straddle orders. The order process originates with the broker and is transacted on the floor of the exchange. Remember that for every order there must be a buyer and seller (writer) so that the orders can be "matched." Once the orders are matched, they are filed with the Options Clearing Corporation, which then issues the necessary options or closes the position.[2]

Option Premiums

Before investors or speculators can understand various option strategies, they must be able to comprehend what creates option premiums (prices). In Table 15–2, using SINGLE Systems as an example, we can see that the common stock closed at $18.93 per share and that calls and puts are available at a variety of strike prices ranging from $15 to $25. Calls (left-hand side) allow the option holder to buy the stock at the strike price. The January 17.50 calls closed at 2.80 ($280 for one call on 100 shares), while the January 20 call closed at 1.50. The 15 and 17.50 call options are said to be **in-the-money** because the market price of $18.93 is above the **strike** (or purchase) **price** of 15 and 17.50. The 20, 22.50

---

[2] In a transaction, holders and writers of options are not contractually linked but are committed to the Options Clearing Corporation.

TABLE 15–2 SINGLE Systems Prices on November 8

Closing Stock Price	Strike Price	Calls—Last December	Calls—Last January	Calls—Last April	Puts—Last December	Puts—Last January	Puts—Last April
$18.93	$15.00	$4.20	$4.50	n/a	$0.40	$0.65	n/a
18.93	17.50	2.40	2.80	n/a	1.05	1.40	n/a
18.93	20.00	1.10	1.50	$2.50	2.20	2.60	$3.40
18.93	22.50	0.40	0.70	1.60	3.70	4.20	5.00
18.93	25.00	n/a	0.30	1.10	n/a	6.30	7.10

Note: n/a indicates that the put or call was either not traded on that day or that the option was not offered.

and 25 calls are **out-of-the-money** because the strike price is above the market price. If SINGLE Systems common were trading at 20, the calls with a strike price of 20 would be **at the money** because the stock price and the strike price are equal. In this example, the stock price of $18.93 is 1.07 away from the January 20 put and call. Puts (right-hand side) are the opposite of calls. Because the put allows the holder to sell the stock at the strike price, in-the-money puts would have strike prices greater than $18.93 and out-of-the-money puts would have strike prices less than $18.93.

Application Example

Intrinsic Value

In-the-money *call* options have an **intrinsic value** equal to the market price minus the strike price. In the case of the SINGLE Systems January 17.50 call, the intrinsic value is 1.43 as indicated by Formula 15–1:

$$\text{Intrinsic value (call)} = \text{Market price} - \text{Strike price} \qquad (15\text{–}1)$$
$$= \$18.93 - \$17.50$$
$$= \$1.43 \text{ (SINGLE Systems January 17.50 call)}$$

Options that are out-of-the-money have no positive intrinsic value. If we use Formula 15–1 for the SINGLE Systems January 20 call, we calculate a negative intrinsic value of 1.07. When the market price minus the strike price is negative, the negative value represents the amount the stock price must increase to have the option at-the-money where the strike price and market price are equal. In actual practice, an option cannot have a negative value.

The intrinsic value for the in-the-money put options equals the strike price minus the market price. In the case of the SINGLE Systems January 20 put, the intrinsic value is 1.07 as indicated by the Formula 15–2. Notice that this in-the-money put has a value in the opposite direction from the call:

$$\text{Intrinsic value (put)} = \text{Strike price} - \text{Market price} \qquad (15\text{–}2)$$
$$= \$20.00 - \$18.93$$
$$= \$1.07 \text{ (SINGLE Systems January 20.00 put)}$$

Because puts allow the owner to sell stock at the strike price, in-the-money put options exist where the strike price is above the market price of the stock. Out-of-the-money puts have market prices for common stock above the strike price.

Speculative Premium (Time Value)[3]

Application Example

Returning to the SINGLE Systems January 17.50 call, we see in Table 15–2 on the previous page that the total premium is 2.80, while the previously computed intrinsic value is 1.43. This call option has an additional **speculative premium** of 1.37 due to other factors. The total premium (option price) is a combination of the intrinsic value plus a speculative premium. This relationship is indicated in Formula 15–3 and shown in Figure 15–1:

$$\text{Total premium} = \text{Intrinsic value} + \text{Speculative premium} \quad (15\text{–}3)$$
$$= 1.43 + 1.37$$
$$= 2.80$$

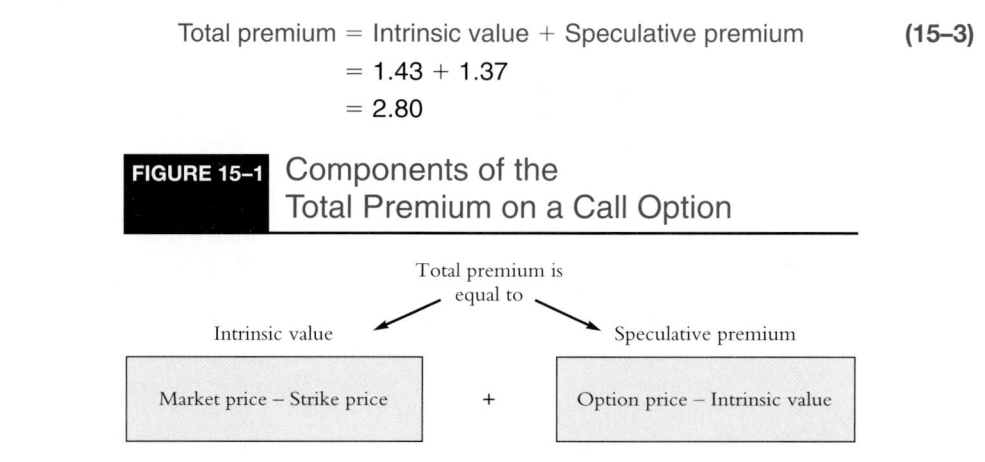

FIGURE 15–1 Components of the Total Premium on a Call Option

Generally, the higher the volatility of the common stock—as measured by the stock price's standard deviation or by its beta—and the lower the dividend yield, the greater the speculative premium. The longer the exercise period, the higher the speculative premium, especially if market expectations over the duration of the option are positive. Finally, the deeper the option is in the money, the smaller the leverage potential and therefore the smaller the speculative premium. Most often, we examine the speculative premium separately to see if it is a reasonable premium to pay for the possible benefits.

The speculative premium can be expressed in dollars or as a percentage of the common stock price. A speculative premium expressed in percent indicates the increase in the stock price needed for the purchaser of a call option to break even on the expiration date. Table 15–3 shows this point.[4] Notice that the SINGLE Systems January 15 call option, which is deep in the money, has the lowest speculative premium, while the 25 call option has the highest. Realize that the 25 call option has a cash value of only 0.30 (the total premium), and the other 6.07 represents the required increase in the stock price for the market price and the strike price to be equal. The 33.65 percent speculative premium for the January 25 call option represents the percentage movement in stock price by the expiration date for a break-even position. At expiration, there will be no speculative premium. The option will reflect only the intrinsic value and possibly even a discount because of commission expenses incurred on exercise.

---

[3] People often refer to the speculative premium as time value because time may be the overriding factor affecting the speculative premium.

[4] As applied to put options, the speculative premium indicates the decrease in stock price needed for the purchaser of a put option to break even on the expiration date.

TABLE 15–3 Speculative Premiums on November 8 for SINGLE Systems January Options

Market Price on November 8	Strike Price	Total Premium	− Intrinsic Value	= Speculative Premium	Speculative Premium as a Percentage of Stock Price
$18.93	$15.00 Jan Call	$4.50	$3.93	$0.57	3.01%
18.93	17.50 Jan Call	2.80	1.43	1.37	7.24
18.93	20.00 Jan Call	1.50	−1.07	2.57	13.58
18.93	22.50 Jan Call	0.70	−3.57	4.27	22.56
18.93	25.00 Jan Call	0.30	−6.07	6.37	33.65

Speculative Premiums and the Time Factor Table 15–4 provides a look at premiums for the in-the-money and out-of-the-money call options with varying times to expiration. Since the quotes are as of November, the December options will expire first, then the January options, and finally the April options. The option premiums increase with more time to expiration.

SINGLE Systems' speculative premiums in Table 15–4 demonstrate that percentage speculative premiums increase with time across all series of strike prices. The speculative premiums are lowest with the in-the-money 15 and 17.50 calls because of the low leverage potential and the downside risk if the stock declines. The 25 call option has a high speculative premium, but an option writer (seller) *would not reap much cash inflow.* Generally, out-of-the-money call options have high speculative premiums, but little of the premium may be in the form of cash. As previously indicated in Table 15–3, the January 25 call has a total premium of 0.30. The fact that the cash premium is only $0.30 ($30 on 100 shares) is an important consideration for an option writer. Commissions would eat up a good portion of the cash inflow.

TABLE 15–4 Speculative Premiums over Time (SINGLE Systems Call Options, November 8)

Market Price	Strike Price	December Total Premium (Option Price)	Speculative Dollars	Premium Percent	January Total Premium (Option Price)	Speculative Dollars	Premium Percent	April Total Premium (Option Price)	Speculative Dollars	Premium Percent
$18.93	$15.00	$4.20	$0.27	1.43%	$4.50	$0.57	3.01%	n/a	n/a	n/a
18.93	17.50	2.40	0.97	5.12	2.80	1.37	7.24	n/a	n/a	n/a
18.93	20.00	1.10	2.17	11.46	1.50	2.57	13.58	$2.50	$3.57	18.86%
18.93	22.50	0.40	3.97	20.97	0.70	4.27	22.56	1.60	5.17	27.31
18.93	25.00	n/a	n/a	n/a	0.30	6.37	33.65	1.10	7.17	37.88

SINGLE System's 52 Week High = 57.63; low 11.06.

TABLE 15–5 Speculative Premiums Related to Betas and Dividend Yields (In-the-Money Call Options)

Company Name	January 04 2005 Strike Price	June 04 2004 Market Price	Percent above Strike	Intrinsic Value	Option Premium Asked	Speculative Premium (Time Value) Dollars	Speculative Premium (Time Value) Percent	Beta	Expected Dividend Yield
Amazon.com	$50.00	$52.21	4.42%	$2.21	$7.60	$5.39	10.32%	1.49	0.00%
Texas Instruments	25.00	25.95	3.80	0.95	3.70	2.75	10.60	1.60	0.34
Intel	27.50	28.50	3.64	1.00	3.40	2.40	8.42	1.57	0.57
Vodafone Group	22.50	23.36	3.82	0.86	2.55	1.69	7.23	1.18	1.69
Pfizer Inc.	35.00	35.98	2.80	0.98	3.00	2.02	5.61	0.81	1.91
Johnson & Johnson	55.00	56.32	2.40	1.32	3.90	2.58	4.58	0.67	2.02

Source: Merrill-Lynch On-Line, June 7, 2004.

Speculative Premiums, Betas, and Dividend Yields Table 15–5 demonstrates the relationship of betas and dividend yields to the speculative premium. Each of the six options is in-the-money and the price of their common stock is between 2.4 percent and 4.42 percent above their strike price, which makes them relatively comparable. While the relationships in this table don't hold for all options, we have structured this example to make two points. Although the betas in this example don't decline in rank order, it is clear that the high-beta stocks have the highest speculative premiums. High-beta stocks have a greater probability of participating in a market upturn, and so speculators will pay a higher speculative premium on a call option for the chance to participate in an up market. A beta is usually calculated over a five-year period and is only one measure of risk. Shorter-term volatility measures such as six-month or one-year standard deviations may influence a trader's willingness to pay a high or low speculative premium as well.

Also, stocks with low dividend yield are more likely to have a high speculative premium than high-dividend-yield stocks. In this table the dividend yields and premiums are inversely related. High-dividend-yield stocks are the ones favored by call writers, and therefore, the speculative premiums are lower because there is a larger number of speculators willing to write calls for these stocks.

Dividends and betas are only two variables that affect speculative premiums. Other factors, such as market conditions or individual company conditions, can also have a strong bearing on speculative premiums. If interest rates are increasing, interest-sensitive stocks may suffer and the speculative premiums on puts might rise while the speculative premiums on calls decline. As always, future expectations for a company will dominate historical information if that information is now considered irrelevant by the market.

Speculative Premiums per Day Speculative premiums can be deceiving. The novice may attempt to write the options with the highest total premium or speculative premium, while the buyer may think the smallest dollar investment provides the greatest advantage. These notions are not usually true if we look at speculative premiums on a per day basis. For example, the previously discussed SINGLE Systems calls have the following speculative premiums per day. The information is based on a strike price of 20 and expiration months of December, January, and April. Note that the speculative premium is divided by the number of days to expiration to arrive at the speculative premium per day:

Month	Strike Price	Speculative Premium	Days to Expiration	Speculative Premium per Day
December	$20	11.46%	43	0.267%
January	20	13.58	71	0.191
April	20	18.86	162	0.116

An examination of daily premiums suggests that call writers should write short-lived calls on a continuous basis to get a maximum return. In this case, the December calls give the maximum premium per day. On the other hand, call buyers get more time for less premium per day by purchasing the April calls.

Understanding option premiums is important if the investor is to make sense out of option strategies. Various strategies involving calls and puts are covered in the next section. Appendix 15A presents the Black-Scholes option pricing model, a much more sophisticated way of analyzing option prices and their time premiums and speculative premiums. This appendix is primarily designed for those who wish to achieve a more advanced understanding of the theoretical basis for option pricing; it is not essential for the standard reading of the text.

Basic Option Strategies

Option strategies can be very aggressive and risky, or they can be quite conservative and used as a means of reducing risk. Option buyers and writers both attempt to take advantage of the option premiums discussed in the preceding section. In theory, many option strategies can be created, but in practice, the market must be liquid enough to execute these strategies. After a decade of explosive growth, option volume on individual common stocks has not expanded as much in the recent decades as in the first years of the Chicago Board Options Exchange. Although volume on the underlying common stock has continued to increase, much of the option activity has been absorbed by options on the Standard & Poor's 100 and 500 Stock Indexes, where large institutional investors can transact portfolio strategies on the market rather than on individual stocks.

A reduction of individual option trading reduces the ability to create workable strategies for specific companies. For example, the lack of a liquid market can keep institutional investors from executing hedging strategies involving several hundred thousand shares. Even with these limitations in mind, the average investor can still find many opportunities for option strategies. In this section, we discuss the possible uses of calls and puts to achieve different investment goals. Table 15–6 on the next page provides option quotes as of three different dates for our examples. All the options expire in November. We ignored commissions in most examples, but commissions can be a significant hidden cost in some types of option strategies.

TABLE 15-6 November Call Option Quotes over Three Months

Company Name	Expiration Month	Strike Price	September 28 49 Days to Expiration Option Price	September 28 49 Days to Expiration Common Stock Price	October 19 28 Days to Expiration Option Price	October 19 28 Days to Expiration Common Stock Price	November 2 14 Days to Expiration Option Price	November 2 14 Days to Expiration Common Stock Price
American Travel	November	$30.00	n/a	$33.10	$2.80	$31.17	$2.85	$32.01
American Travel	November	32.50	n/a	33.10	1.60	31.17	1.35	32.01
American Travel	November	35.00	$1.95	33.10	0.75	31.17	0.35	32.01
American Travel	November	40.00	0.55	33.10	0.15	31.17	n/a	32.01
Bow Wing Inc.	November	35.00	2.00	33.50	1.25	33.45	0.95	34.35
SINGLE Systems	November	15.00	0.40	12.18	2.35	16.72	2.50	17.26
SINGLE Systems	November	17.50	0.15	12.18	1.00	16.72	0.90	17.26
SINGLE Systems	November	20.00	n/a	n/a	0.30	16.72	0.25	17.26
Deli USA	November	20.00	2.40	18.53	1.60	24.05	n/a	24.92
Deli USA	November	22.50	1.25	18.53	2.65	24.05	n/a	24.92
Deli USA	November	25.00	1.05	21.55	1.35	24.05	1.05	24.92
Howard & David	November	17.50	2.00	18.08	1.30	18.29	0.50	16.92
Home Delivery	November	40.00	2.10	38.37	2.40	40.41	1.60	40.32
Home Delivery	November	45.00	n/a	n/a	n/a	40.41	0.20	40.32
International Optics	November	100.00	2.40	91.72	5.80	102.65	n/a	109.50
International Optics	November	110.00	1.25	91.72	1.50	102.65	2.45	109.50
Intelligent Systems	November	20.00	2.60	20.39	n/a	24.15	6.50	26.30
Intelligent Systems	November	25.00	0.45	20.39	1.15	24.15	2.05	26.30
Orisis Gaming	November	12.50	1.35	12.58	n/a	14.54	2.05	14.45
Orisis Gaming	November	15.00	0.45	12.58	0.95	14.54	0.45	14.45
World Airways	November	15.00	1.20	15.04	0.30	13.17	0.15	13.48

Note: n/a indicates that the quote was not available because the option did not trade on that date or was not yet listed because the stock price was too far below the strike price.

Buying Call Options

The Leverage Strategy Leverage is a very common reason for buying call options when the market is expected to rise during the exercise period. The use of calls in this way is similar to warrants discussed in Chapter 14, but calls have shorter lives. The call option is priced much lower than common stock, and the leverage is derived from a small percentage change in the price of the call option. For example, for our hypothetical company, SINGLE Systems, on September 28 common stock closed at $12.18 per share and the November 15 call option closed at $0.40 (see Table 15–6).

About three weeks later on October 19, the stock closed at $16.72 for a $4.54 gain on the stock or 37.27 percent ($4.54/$12.18). The November 15 call option closed at $2.35 on October 19, for a $1.95 gain of 487.5 percent ($1.95/$0.40). The call option increased by 13.1 times the percentage move of the common stock over this three-week span. The relationship is indicated at the top of the next page.

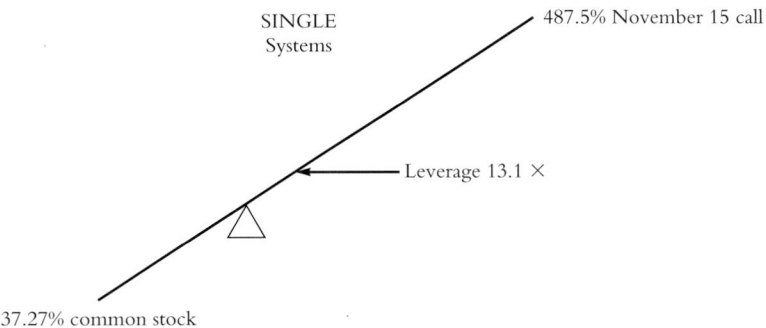

Figure 15–2 depicts the relationship between profit and loss opportunities for the SINGLE Systems November 15 call option, assuming the option is held until the day of expiration (no speculative premium exists at expiration).

As long as the common stock closes under 15, the call buyer loses the whole premium of $0.40 (100 × $0.40 = $40). At a price of $15.40 the call buyer breaks even because the option is worth an intrinsic value of $0.40. As the stock increases past $15.40, the profit starts accumulating. At a price of $19.40, the profit equals $400 at expiration. If the option is sold before expiration, a speculative premium may increase the profit potential.

An investor striving for maximum leverage generally buys options that are out-of-the-money or slightly in-the-money. Buying high-priced options for $10 or $15 that are well in-the-money limits the potential for leverage. You may have to invest almost as much in the options as you would in the stock.

Playing the leverage game doesn't always work. Let's once again look at Table 15–6. If, on September 28, a speculator assumed that Howard & David would go up and bought the November 17.50 call option for $2.00, approximately one month later, on November 2, the Howard & David call option would have been worth $0.50 per share. A $1.50 loss occurred in the option price. The

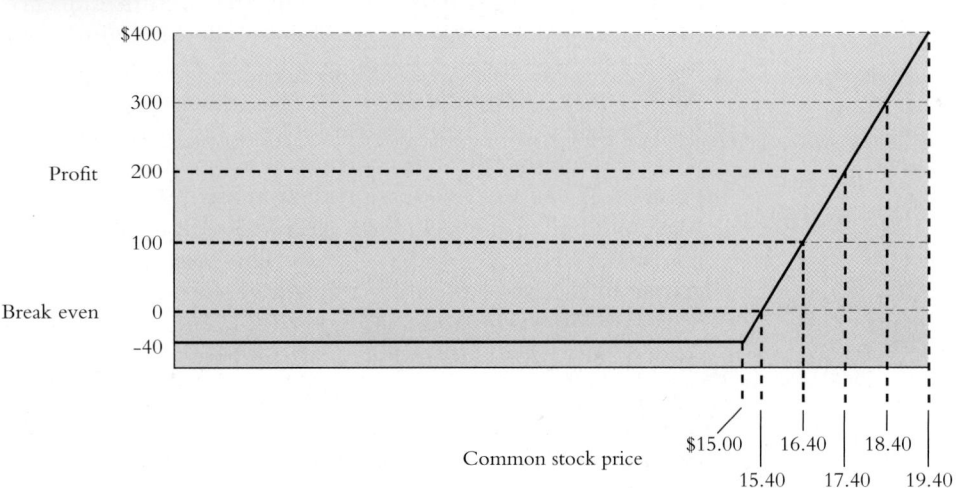

decline in Howard & David stock from $18.08 to $16.92 was only $1.16, or a 6.4 percent loss, while at the same time the option lost 75 percent of its value, going from $2.00 to $0.50. A loss of $1.50 per share would equal a $150 loss on one call option. If the stock price stays below $17.50 until expiration, the owner of the November 17.50 call can expect to lose the current call premium of $0.50. It is not hard to lose all your money under these circumstances—leverage works in reverse, too.

Call Options Instead of Stock Many people do not like to risk large amounts of money and view call options as a way of controlling 100 shares of stock without a large dollar commitment. For example, assume you could buy 100 shares of common stock for $40 per share ($4,000) or a call option with a strike price of 40 at a cost of $4 or $400. You choose to spend the $400 and invest the $3,600 difference ($4,000 − $400) in short-term money market securities at 4 percent. The call option has six months to expiration. During the six months your common stock falls from $40 per share to $30 per share, and your call option is worthless at expiration. During this time your short-term money market securities generated $72 of interest income[5] which helps offset your $400 loss on your call option. Your total loss on your call investment was $328 ($400 − $72) but if you had bought the common stock, you would have lost $1,000, or $10 per share on 100 shares. When stock prices are falling, this strategy can reduce an investor's losses. This strategy works to the investor's advantage because in the end the loss is less for owning the call option than it would have been for owning 100 shares of stock outright.[6] This will not always be the case.

Had your stock only declined in value by 1¢ to $39.99, you still would have lost $328 on your call option. If you had bought the stock you would have only lost $1.00 (1¢ × 100 shares). One thing to remember is that the purchaser of the call option cannot lose more than the initial purchase price of $400. This will be slightly offset by the $72 of interest earned. Of course, there is the possibility that the stock rises to $50 per share and both the stock purchaser and the option purchaser will show profits. Paying commissions to buy and sell will reduce profits.

Protecting a Short Position Calls are often used to cover a short sale against the risk of rising stock prices. This is called hedging your position. By purchasing a call, the short seller guarantees a loss of no more than a fixed amount while at the same time reducing any potential profit by the total premium paid for the call. Again refer to Table 15–6 on page 420, and assume you sold 100 shares of Intelligent Systems short at $20.39 on September 28, and bought a November 25 call for $0.45 as protection against a rise in the price of the stock. By November 2, the stock rises to $26.30 for a $591 loss on the short position [($26.30 − $20.39) × 100 shares]. This loss has been partially offset by an increase in the November 25 call option price from $0.45 to $2.05, or a $160 gain [($2.05 − $0.45) × 100 shares = $160]. The loss on the short sale has been cut from $591 to $431, or reduced by the $160 profit on the call option.

---

[5] The approximate calculation is $3,600 × 4% × 180/360 = $72.

[6] It should be pointed out we are talking about absolute dollar losses. On a percentage basis, the options would be the bigger losers.

Reconsider the initial $0.45 call premium. If the stock goes up, the call limits your loss, but if the stock goes down as expected, your profit on the short position may be reduced by the call premium. If Intelligent Systems had declined to $18 and generated a profit of $2.39 ($20.39 − $18) per share, this gain would have been reduced by the loss of $0.45 on the call option. Writing a call to protect a short sale is equivalent to buying an insurance policy that you hope you won't need.

Guaranteed Price Often, an investor thinks a stock will rise over the long term but does not have cash currently available to purchase the stock. The important point for this strategy is that the investor wants to own this stock eventually but does not want to miss out on a good buying opportunity (based on expectations). Perhaps the oil stocks are depressed, or semiconductors have hit bottom. A call option can be utilized. The investor could be anticipating a cash inflow in the future when he or she plans to exercise the call option with a tax refund, a book royalty check, or even the annual bonus.

Please refer back to Table 15–6 on page 420. On September 28, assume an investor buys an Orisis Gaming November 12.50 call option for $1.35. The intrinsic value for the November 12.50 call option is $0.08 because the stock is selling for $12.58 per share. The speculative premium is equal to the option price of $1.35 minus the intrinsic value of $0.08, or $1.27. By November 2, she has received her $1,250 royalty check and exercises the option to buy the stock at $12.50 when the stock is selling at $14.45. For tax purposes the cost or basis of these 100 shares of Orisis is the strike price of $12.50 plus the option premium of $1.35, or a total cost of $13.85 per share. If she had waited until November 2 to buy the stock, she would have paid an extra $0.60 per share above $13.85, or $14.45. Her strategy locked in a guaranteed price just as it was supposed to. There is always the possibility that the stock price declines to below your strike price; in that case, you buy the stock in the market directly and consider your option premium an insurance policy.

Writing Call Options

Writers of call options take the opposite side of the market from buyers. The writer is similar to a short seller in that he or she expects the stock to decline or stay the same. For short sellers to profit, prices must decline, but because writers of call options receive a premium, they can make a profit if prices stay the same or even rise less than the speculative premium. Option writers can write **covered options,** meaning they own the underlying common stock, or they can write **naked options,** meaning they do not own the underlying stock.

Writing covered call options is often considered a hedged position because if the stock price declines, the writer's loss on the stock is partially offset by the option premium. A potential writer of a covered call must decide if he is willing to sell the underlying stock if it closes above the strike price. If not, the writer must repurchase the call option before the option is exercised by the owner.

Returning to Table 15–6 for another set of option quotes, find the Bow Wing November 35 call options on September 28. The market price of the common stock is $33.50 and the writer for a November 35 call option will receive $2.00 per share.

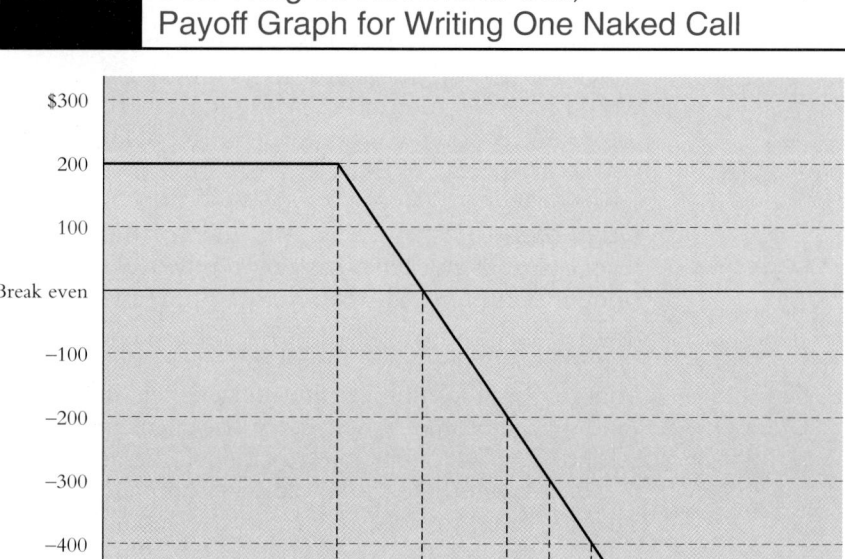

FIGURE 15–3 Bow Wing 35 November Call, Payoff Graph for Writing One Naked Call

Remember, the writer agrees to sell 100 shares at the 35 strike price as the consideration for the premium. The 35 call option would be a good write if the stock closed at $35 per share or less because the call would not get exercised and the writer would keep the $2.00 premium. If the stock closed at $35 or higher, then the call could get exercised, and the writer would have to deliver 100 shares at $35. More likely, the option writer would buy back the option for its price in the market to avoid having the option exercised. If the ending value of the stock were 40, the option writer could buy back the 35 call for 5. The purchase at $5 would be offset by the initial receipt of the $2 premium and the total loss before commissions would be $3. Figure 15–3 shows this relationship between profit and loss and the common stock price in writing a naked option.

Let's now go to covered call options. Assume an investor bought 100 shares of Bow Wing at $33.50 on September 28. He also sold a November 35 call option for $2. If the stock ends up at $35, he will make a total profit of $350, a $150 capital gain on the stock (100 shares × $1.50) plus the $200 option premium (100 × $2). Of course, if the stock really goes up in value, the covered call option writer will wish he had not written the call option. The increased cost to buy back the option will severely cut into the profit on the long position in the stock.

Application Example

Let's look at what actually happened with Bow Wing. By November 2, Bow Wing stock closed at $34.35, and at that point, the cover call writer would make money, and a naked call writer would also make money. The covered call writer is assumed to have bought 100 shares at $33.50 per share at the time he or she wrote the option for $2.00 on September 28. The naked option writer merely sold the option for $2.00. It is further assumed the covered option writer would receive a $17 dividend during the period. Also note that the November 35 option is only worth $0.95 on November 2. The analysis is presented at the top of the next page:

Bow Wing Example			
Covered Writer		**Naked Writer**	
− Initial investment (100 × 33.50)	−$3,350.00	− Margin (30% × $3,350)	−$1,005.00
+ Option premium (100 × 2.00)	200.00	+ Option premium	200.00
+ Dividend	17.00	(no dividends received)	
+ Ending stock value (100 × 34.35)	3,435.00	+ Ending value margin	1,005.00
Gain	302.00	Gain	200.00
Investment = $3,350 − $200.00	$3,150.00	Investment	$1,005.00
Percent return on initial investment	9.6%	Return on investment	19.9%

Because the stock price ended at less than the strike price, neither the covered writer nor the naked writer needed to buy back their option as of November 2. They both had profits—with the covered writer ahead of the naked writer by $102 with $17 from the dividend and $85 from the capital gain on the stock, while the naked writer was ahead in percentage terms (19.9 percent versus 9.6 percent) because of a smaller initial investment. The naked writer was required to put up a margin on 30 percent of the value of the stock to ensure the ability to close out the option write if the stock should rise significantly. The capital was returned to the naked call writer when it was no longer needed as collateral. If the stock price had risen, the naked writer was exposed to unlimited risk because he either had to close out the position at a loss or purchase the stock above the strike price and deliver it at a loss. The covered writer had limited risk because she owned the stock and could deliver it or close out the position before it was called.

Another critical decision for a call writer is the choice of months. In the section on option premiums, we examined percentage premiums per day and found that the shortest expiration dates usually provided the highest daily speculative premium. In most cases, the call writer chooses the short-term options and as they expire, writes another short-term option. Annualized returns of 12 to 15 percent are not uncommon for continuously covered writing strategies.

Buying Put Options

The owner (buyer) of a put may sell 100 shares of stock to the put writer at the strike price. The strategy behind a put is similar to selling short or writing a call except losses are limited to the total investment (premium), and no more risk exposure is possible if the stock rises. Buying a put in anticipation of a price decline is one method of speculating on market price changes. The same factors influencing call premiums also apply to put premiums except that expectations for the direction for the market are the opposite.

Let's assume that the New Age Internet Co. was selling at $50 per share in July 2004, already down from its all-time high of $200 per share. You expected it to decline and possibly collapse as many other "new economy" companies had already done. You decided to buy a put rather than sell the stock short because you did not want to take the risk of unlimited loss if the stock should reverse and go back to $200. You found an at-the-money 50 put with an expiration date of April 2005 for an option premium of $7. This was a high premium, but New Age had been a quite volatile stock and often moved $4 or $5 per share in one day.

You bought the put for $700 and hoped that the stock price declined. By April 2005, the company was almost bankrupt and the stock was selling at $5 per share, and at expiration your put option had an intrinsic value of $45 per share. For your $700 investment you received $4,500 when you sold the put for a profit of $3,800 on a $700 investment. That's a good conclusion; but, of course, it doesn't always happen that way.

Puts can also help you offset a potential decline in the price of common stock that you continue to hold for tax purposes. For example, assume you own ABZ Company at a gain and you would like to defer taking a profit until next year. You can protect yourself from a decline in the stock price by buying a put. If the stock falls, the put will make money as the stock loses money. In this case the put becomes an insurance policy against the potential decline in the stock. You can hold the put along with your stock and keep buying new puts if necessary until you are ready to sell your stock.

Using Options in Combinations

Spreads

Now that you have studied puts and calls from both the buyer's and writer's perspectives, we briefly proceed with a discussion of spreads. Most combinations of options are called **spreads** and consist of buying one option (going long) and writing an option (going short) on the same underlying stock. Spreads are for the sophisticated investor and involve many variations on a theme. For an in-depth discussion of spreads, the reader may wish to consult Appendix 15B.

Straddles

A **straddle** is a combination of a put and call on the same stock with the same strike price and expiration date. It is used to play wide fluctuations in stock prices and is usually applied to individual stocks with high betas and a history of large, short-term fluctuations in price. The speculator using a straddle may be unsure of the direction of the price movement but may be able to make a large enough profit on one side of the straddle to cover the cost of both options even if one option expires worthless.

For example, assume a put and a call can be bought for $5 apiece on ABC October 50s when ABC Corporation is selling at 50 with six months to expiration. The total investment is 10 ($1,000). If the stock should rise from 50 to 65 at expiration, the call would provide a profit of 10 (15 value − 5 cost), and the put would be left to expire worthless for a loss of 5. This would provide a net gain of 5, or $500. The same type of example can be drawn if the price goes way down. Some who engage in spreads or straddles might attempt to close out one position before the other. This expands the profit potential but also increases the risk.

Other Option Considerations

Many factors have not been covered in detail because of their changing nature over time. Tax laws relating to options are constantly changing, and some items, such as capital gains, have been revised several times in the last few years. We do know that the tax laws have a significant impact on spread positions and also on the tax treatment where put options are involved. The recognition of the year in which a gain or loss is declared can still be affected by option strategies in combination with stock positions. The best advice we can give is to check the tax consequences of any option strategy with your accountant or stockbroker.

Commissions vary among brokerage houses and are not easy to pinpoint for option transactions since quantity discounts exist. Because many option positions involve small dollar investment outlays, commissions of $25 to $50 for buying and selling can significantly alter your returns and even create losses. Commissions on acquiring common stock through options are higher than the transaction costs of options, and this is a motivating force in closing out option transactions before expiration. Overall, commissions on options tend to be more significant than commissions on commodities or other highly leveraged investments.

exploring the web

Website Address	Comment
www.cboe.com	Chicago Board Options Exchange website. A good source of education and data.
www.amex.com	American Stock Exchange trades options and has a website section on options.

Summary

Put and call options are an exciting area of investment and speculation. We have discussed the past history of over-the-counter options trading and more recent trading of options on the listed options exchanges, such as the CBOE. The markets are more efficient, and the standardized practices of the listed exchanges have made options more usable for many investors and widened the number of option strategies that can be employed.

Option premiums (option prices) are affected by many variables such as time, market expectations, stock price volatility, dividend yields, and in-the-money/out-of-the-money relationships. The total premium consists of an intrinsic value plus a speculative premium that declines to zero by the expiration date. Calls are options to buy 100 shares of stock, while puts are options to sell 100 shares of stock.

Understanding the benefits and risks of trading options is complicated. Options can be risky or used to reduce risk. Calls can be bought for leverage, to cover a short position, or as an alternative to investing in the underlying common stock while buying time to purchase the stock (waiting for the financial resources to exercise the call). Calls are written either as a hedge on a long position in the underlying stock or to speculate on a price decline. Puts are bought to hedge a long position against a price decline or as an alternative to selling short. A writer of a put may speculate on a price increase or use the write as a hedge against a short position (if

430 Part 5 Derivative Products

Leverage strategy

6. Assume High Tech, Inc., is trading at $39 and its October call option is $1.75. If the stock ends up at $50 and the option at $10, what is the leverage factor?

Naked call options

7. Assume an investor writes a call option for 100 shares at a strike price of 40 for a premium of 6½. This is a naked option.
    a. What would the gain or loss be if the stock closed at 35?
    b. What would the break-even point be in terms of the closing price of the stock?

Covered call options

eXcel

8. Assume you purchase 100 shares of stock at $73 per share and wish to hedge your position by writing a 100-share call option on your holdings. The option has a $70 strike price and a premium of $8. If the stock is selling at $68 at the time of expiration, what will be the overall dollar gain or loss on this covered option play? (Consider the change in stock value as well as the gain or loss on the option.) Note that the stock does not pay a cash dividend.

Covered call options

9. In problem 8, what would be the overall gain or loss if the stock ended up at (a) $70, (b) $48, (c) $85, (d) $100. (Disregard the stock being called away in (a) and (c).)

Commission considerations

10. Though commissions are not explicitly considered in problems 7 through 9, might they be significant?

Put options

11. Assume a 40 July put option is purchased for $5.50 on a stock selling at $36 per share. If the stock ends up on expiration at $29.50, what will be the value of the put option?

Put options

12. In problem 11, at what ending stock price would the investor break even?

Protecting a short position with options

13. Assume you sell 100 shares of Larson Corporation short at $61. You also buy a 60 call option for $3.50 to protect against the stock price going up.
    a. If the stock ends up at $80, what will be your overall gain or loss?
    b. If the stock ends up at $40, what will be your overall gain or loss?
    c. What is the most you can lose under this short sale–call option plan?
    d. If you have an unprotected short sale position (no call option), what is the most you could lose?

Web Exercise

This exercise will give you an opportunity to view online data on options. Go to **www.cboe.com**.

1. Click on "Market Data" across the top of the screen.
2. Then click on "Most Actives" near the top of the screen.
3. Pick a stock on the most active list by its stock symbol. Normally, the most likely candidates are:
    MSFT (Microsoft)
    CSCO (CISCO)
    IBM (IBM)
    MRK (Merck)
4. Write down the option under the "High Series" column. Then write down the price under the "Last Sale" column.
5. Now go to **www.bloomberg.com**.

6. Type in the stock symbol in the "Enter Symbol" box. Write down the stock price shown in the first box "Price."
7. Compute the intrinsic value and speculative premium for the option.
8. Repeat this process for two other stocks.

Note: From time to time, companies redesign their websites, and occasionally a topic we have listed may have been deleted, updated, or moved into a different location. Most websites have a "site map" or "site index" listed on a different page. If you click on the site map or site index, you will be introduced to a table of contents that should aid you in finding the topic you are looking for.

The Wall Street Journal Projects

Go to the "Index/Listed Options" page in Section C of *The Wall Street Journal*. On that page, find the "Most Active Listed Options." Find the first company call option as opposed to an index option. The company option will be listed by the company name (such as CISCO, Intel, etc.). You can tell if it's a call option by the absence of the "p" symbol in the third column.

Write down the month, strike price (second column), and "last" traded price for the option. Also write down the closing price for the stock (second column from the right).

If the price of the common stock goes up by 20 percent at the expiration of the option, what will be your dollar profit or loss on the option? Assume you close out your option position at its intrinsic value.

Selected References

Option Trading Strategy

Bliss, Robert R., and Nikolaos Panigirtzoglou. "Options—Implied Risk Aversion Estimates." *The Journal of Finance,* February 2004, pp. 407–46.

Bodnar, Gordon M.; Gregory S. Hayt; and Richard C. Marston. "1995 Wharton Survey of Derivatives Usage by US Non-Financial Firms." *Financial Management,* Winter 1996, pp. 113–34.

Easton, Stephen A. "Put-Call Parity with Futures-Style Margining." *The Journal of Futures Markets,* April 1997, pp. 215–27.

Finucane, Thomas J. "Put-Call Parity and Expected Returns." *Journal of Financial and Quantitative Analysis,* December 1991, pp. 445–57.

Hauser, R. J., and J. S. Eales. "On Marketing Strategies with Options: A Technique to Measure Risk and Return." *Journal of Futures Markets,* Summer 1986, pp. 273–78.

Mayhew, Stewart, and Vissol Mihov. "How Do Exchanges Select Stocks for Option Listing?" *The Journal of Finance,* February 2004, pp. 447–71.

Naik, Vasanttilak. "Option Valuation and Hedging Strategies with Jumps in the Volatility of Asset Returns." *Journal of Finance,* December 1993, pp. 1969–84.

Valuing Options

Black, Fischer, and Myron Scholes. "The Valuation of Option Contracts and a Test of Market Efficiency." *Journal of Finance,* May 1972, pp. 399–417.

———. "The Pricing of Options and Corporate Liabilities." *Journal of Political Economy,* May–June 1973, pp. 637–54.

Brenner, Michael; Rafi Eldor; and Shmuel Hauser. "The Price of Options Illiquidity." *Journal of Finance,* April 2001, pp. 789–805.

Buraschi, Andrea, and Jens Jackworth. "The Price of a Smile: Hedging and Spanning in Options Markets." *Review of Financial Studies,* Summer 2001, pp. 495–529.

Carr, Peter, and Liuren Wu. "What Type of Process Underlies Options? A Simple Robust Test." *The Journal of Finance,* December 2003, pp. 2581–2610.

Longstaff, Francis A., and Eduardo S. Schwartz. "Valuing American Options by Simulation: A Simple Least Squares Approach." *Review of Financial Studies,* Spring 2001, pp. 113–47.

Milonas, Nikolaos, and Stavros B. Thomadakis. "Convenience Yields on Call Options: An Empirical Analysis." *The Journal of Futures Markets,* February 1997, pp. 1–15.

Appendix 15A

THE BLACK-SCHOLES OPTION PRICING MODEL*

Theory

In 1973, Fischer Black and Myron Scholes published their derivation of a theoretical option pricing model. They started with three securities: riskless bonds, shares of common stock, and call options. The shares of common stock and call options were combined to form a riskless hedge that, by definition, had to duplicate the return of a discount bond with the same maturity length as the option. Using the riskless-hedge concept as a basis, Black and Scholes then proceeded with their model derivation.

Black and Scholes made the following assumptions:

1. Markets are frictionless. This means there are no taxes or transactions costs; all securities are infinitely divisible; all market participants may borrow and lend at the known and constant riskless rate of interest; there are no penalties for short selling.
2. Stock prices are lognormally distributed, with a constant variance for the underlying returns.
3. The stock neither pays dividends nor makes any other distributions.
4. The option may be exercised only at maturity.

Given the above assumptions and the riskless hedging strategy, Black and Scholes derived a call option pricing model that may be expressed as:

$$c = (S)[N(d_1)] - (X)(e^{-rt})[N(d_2)] \qquad (15A\text{–}1)$$

where:

$$d_1 = \frac{\ln(S/X) + [r + (\sigma^2/2)](T)}{(\sigma)(\sqrt{T})} \qquad (15A\text{–}2)$$

$$d_2 = d_1 - (\sigma)/(\sqrt{T}) \qquad (15A\text{–}3)$$

The terms are defined as follows:

- c = Price of the call option
- S = Prevailing market price of a share of common stock on the date the call option is written

---

*This appendix was developed by Professor Carl Luft of DePaul University in consultation with the authors.

X = Call option's striking price (exercise price)
r = Annualized prevailing short-term riskless rate of interest
T = Length of the option's life expressed in annual terms
σ^2 = Annualized variance associated with the underlying security's price changes
$N(\cdot)$ = Cumulative normal density function

At maturity ($T = 0$), the call option must sell for either its intrinsic value or zero, whichever is greater. This boundary condition may be expressed mathematically as:

$$c = \text{Max}(0, S - X) \tag{15A–4}$$

It can be shown that given a put option and a call option, with the same striking price, and one share of the underlying stock, one can form a portfolio that will earn an amount equal to the option's striking price no matter what value the stock takes at expiration. From this relationship, the value of a put option can be determined mathematically as:

$$p = (X)(e^{-rt}) - S + c \tag{15A–5}$$

with the boundary condition,

$$p = \text{Max}(0, X - S) \tag{15A–6}$$

Formula 15A–5 is known as the put-call parity relationship, and Formula 15A–6 shows that at maturity the put must sell for either its intrinsic value or zero.

Inspection of Formulas 15A–1 through 15A–6 reveals that both the call and put option prices are a function of only five variables: S, the underlying stock's market price; X, the striking price; T, the length of the option's life; σ^2, the volatility of the stock price changes; and r, the riskless rate of interest. All of these variables are easily observed or estimated. Previously developed option pricing models relied on variables that were based on individual investor risk preferences or on expected values of the stock price. Since the Black-Scholes model does not rely on such variables, it is superior to prior models.

To understand the behavior of options, it is necessary to examine the relationship of the option price to each of the five inputs. For call options, the price is positively related to the stock's price, the riskless rate of interest, the volatility, and the time to maturity; whereas an inverse relationship exists between the call option price and the striking price. Put options exhibit positive relationships with the striking price and volatility, negative relationships with the underlying stock price and riskless rate, and either a positive or negative relationship with time.

These relationships are easy to grasp if one realizes that options will not be exercised unless they have an intrinsic value. Consider first the price of the underlying stock. As it increases, calls go in the money and gain intrinsic value while puts fall out of the money and lose intrinsic value. If the stock price declines, then the reverse is true. This explains the positive relationship between the call price and the stock price and the inverse relationship between the put price and the stock price. Higher striking prices cause lower intrinsic values for call options but result in greater intrinsic values for put options. In this case, the loss of intrinsic value causes the inverse relationship between the call option and striking price, while the gain in intrinsic value causes the positive relationship between the put price and the striking price. The positive relationship of both put and call prices to the volatility can be explained by the fact that options written on higher volatility stocks have a relatively better chance of being in-the-money at expiration than do options written on lower volatility stocks. The positive relationship of the call price to the risk-free rate reflects the fact that the intrinsic value increases because the present value of the exercise price decreases as the risk-free rate rises. For put options, such rate increases and declining present values of exercise prices cause a loss of intrinsic value and account for the inverse relationship between the put option price and risk-free rate. Finally, the positive relationship of the call price to time is caused by an increasing intrinsic value due to lower present values of the exercise price for longer time periods. A more complex relationship exists for put options.

Intuitively, one might expect a strictly positive relationship between the put option price and time. Such a relationship will occur if the put is at the money or out of the money, while a negative relationship can exist for deep in-the-money puts. The reason for this inverse relationship lies embedded in the stock's price behavior. Since stock prices cannot be less than zero, the put option has a maximum value that equals the strike price. Investors who own deep in-the-money put options that are close to their maximum value because of extremely low stock prices are prohibited from exercising these options by assumption 4. Thus, time is working against these investors since they run the risk of losing intrinsic value if the stock price rises before expiration.

After deriving the model, Black and Scholes subjected it to empirical testing. They implemented the riskless-hedging strategy by combining options and stock in proportions dictated by the model and comparing these hedged returns to observed Treasury bill returns. They hypothesized that if the model provided equilibrium, or fair option prices, then the hedged returns should equal the returns generated by the investment in riskless securities. In effect, they attempted to create a synthetic Treasury bill by combining options and stock. If the returns from the option-stock hedge were not equal to the Treasury bill return, it meant the model was unable to provide equilibrium option prices. On the other hand, if there was no significant difference between the hedge and Treasury bill returns, then it could be concluded that the model provided equilibrium prices. The results of the Black-Scholes empirical test showed no significant difference between the option-stock hedged returns and the Treasury bill returns. Thus, Black and Scholes concluded the model did provide equilibrium prices.

The theoretical derivation and empirical justification of an option pricing model by Black and Scholes was an extremely important accomplishment with far-reaching implications. Basically, it meant that model-generated prices could be considered as the equilibrium, or correct, prices. Thus, an investor could use the model to determine whether the market had mispriced an option. Mispriced options spawn arbitrage opportunities. Given such an opportunity, the most obvious way to benefit is to form a riskless hedge by combining options and stock and then maintaining the hedge until the option's market price adjusts to the equilibrium model price. This strategy will provide arbitrage profits since the level of risk that is being assumed equals that of a Treasury bill, but the profits earned when the mispriced option adjusts to the equilibrium, or model price, will exceed the profits earned from investing in a Treasury bill.

TABLE 15A–1 Illustrative Data for Black-Scholes Option Model

(1) Stock Symbol	(2) (S) Stock Price	(3) (X) Strike Price	(4) (T) Days to Maturity Dividend by Days in Year	(5) (r) Risk-Free Rate	(6) (σ) Standard Deviation of Returns	(7) (σ²) Variance of Stock Returns
CFL	33	35	180/365	0.09	0.20	0.04
GAH	42	40	50/365	0.10	0.23	0.0529

Application

The data in Table 15A–1 illustrate the mechanics of the Black-Scholes option pricing model.

Column 1 simply denotes the stock's ticker symbol, while Columns 2 through 7 provide the required inputs for the model. Notice that the option maturity is expressed in calendar days and the volatility is given as the standard deviation of returns. The call and put option prices (for both stocks) implied by the data will not be computed.

When the values from Table 15A–1 for CFL stock are used in Formulas 15A–2 and 15A–3, we obtain the following answers for d_1 and d_2:

$$d_1 = \frac{\ln(33/35) + [0.09 + (0.04/2)][(0.4932)]}{(0.2)(\sqrt{0.4932})}$$

$$= \frac{-0.0588 + 0.0543}{0.1405}$$

$$= -0.032$$

$$d_2 = -0.032 - 0.1405$$

$$= -0.1725$$

To obtain values for $N(d_1)$ and $N(d_2)$, the Standard Normal Distribution Function Table (Table 15A–2) on page 436 must be used. The $N(d_1)$ and $N(d_2)$ values are found by first locating the row and column entries in the table that correspond to the computed d_1 and d_2 values. For CFL stock, the row entry is −0.0, and the column entry is 3. This value of −0.03 approximates the computed d_1 value of −0.032. For d_2, the row entry is −0.1, and the column entry is 7, yielding a value of −0.17, approximating the computed value of −0.1725 for d_2.

Locating the d_1 and d_2 values yield the table entries that define the values of $N(d_1)$ and $N(d_2)$. For CFL stock, the $N(d_1)$ value is 0.4880, while the $N(d_2)$ value is 0.4325. In this example, these values are only approximations, since −0.03 and −0.17 are approximations. If one desires more precise $N(d_1)$ and $N(d_2)$ values, they can be obtained through interpolation. For these examples, the approximations are sufficient.

At this point, all the necessary values for computing the option price have been found. Determining the options' prices via Formulas 15A–1 and 15A–5 is all that remains to be done. Thus, the CFL call option price is:

TABLE 15A–2 Standard Normal Distribution Function

t	0	1	2	3	4	5	6	7	8	9
−3.0	.0013									
−2.9	.0019	.0018	.0017	.0017	.0016	.0016	.0015	.0015	.0014	.0014
−2.8	.0026	.0025	.0024	.0023	.0023	.0022	.0021	.0021	.0020	.0019
−2.7	.0035	.0034	.0033	.0032	.0031	.0030	.0029	.0028	.0027	.0026
−2.6	.0047	.0045	.0044	.0043	.0041	.0040	.0039	.0038	.0037	.0036
−2.5	.0062	.0060	.0059	.0057	.0055	.0054	.0052	.0051	.0049	.0048
−2.4	.0082	.0080	.0078	.0075	.0073	.0071	.0069	.0068	.0066	.0064
−2.3	.0107	.0104	.0102	.0099	.0096	.0094	.0091	.0089	.0087	.0084
−2.2	.0139	.0136	.0132	.0129	.0125	.0122	.0119	.0116	.0113	.0110
−2.1	.0179	.0174	.0170	.0166	.0162	.0158	.0154	.0150	.0146	.0143
−2.0	.0227	.0222	.0217	.0212	.0207	.0202	.0197	.0192	.0188	.0183
−1.9	.0287	.0281	.0274	.0268	.0262	.0256	.0250	.0244	.0239	.0233
−1.8	.0359	.0351	.0344	.0336	.0329	.0322	.0314	.0307	.0300	.0294
−1.7	.0446	.0436	.0427	.0418	.0409	.0401	.0392	.0384	.0375	.0367
−1.6	.0548	.0537	.0526	.0516	.0505	.0495	.0485	.0475	.0465	.0455
−1.5	.0668	.0655	.0643	.0630	.0618	.0606	.0594	.0582	.0571	.0559
−1.4	.0808	.0793	.0778	.0764	.0749	.0735	.0721	.0708	.0694	.0681
−1.3	.0968	.0951	.0934	.0918	.0901	.0885	.0869	.0853	.0838	.0823
−1.2	.1151	.1131	.1112	.1093	.1075	.1056	.1038	.1020	.1003	.0985
−1.1	.1357	.1335	.1314	.1292	.1271	.1251	.1230	.1210	.1190	.1170
−1.0	.1587	.1562	.1539	.1515	.1492	.1469	.1446	.1423	.1401	.1379
−0.9	.1841	.1814	.1788	.1762	.1736	.1711	.1685	.1660	.1635	.1611
−0.8	.2119	.2090	.2061	.2033	.2005	.1977	.1949	.1921	.1894	.1867
−0.7	.2420	.2389	.2358	.2326	.2297	.2266	.2236	.2206	.2177	.2148
−0.6	.2743	.2709	.2676	.2643	.2611	.2578	.2546	.2514	.2483	.2451
−0.5	.3085	.3050	.3015	.2981	.2946	.2912	.2877	.2843	.2810	.2776
−0.4	.3446	.3409	.3372	.3336	.3300	.3264	.3228	.3192	.3156	.3121
−0.3	.3821	.3783	.3745	.3707	.3669	.3632	.3594	.3557	.3520	.3483
−0.2	.4207	.4168	.4129	.4090	.4052	.4013	.3974	.3936	.3897	.3859
−0.1	.4602	.4562	.4522	.4483	.4443	.4404	.4364	.4325	.4286	.4247
−0.0	.5000	.4960	.4920	.4880	.4840	.4801	.4761	.4721	.4681	.4641

$$c = (33)(0.4880) - (35)[e^{-(0.09)(0.4932)}](0.4325)$$
$$= 16.1040 - (35)(0.9566)(0.4325)$$
$$= 16.1040 - 14.4805$$
$$= 1.6235$$

and the CFL put option price is:

$$p = (35)[e^{-(0.09)(0.4932)}] - 33 + 1.6235$$
$$= (35)(0.9566) - 33 + 1.6235$$
$$= 2.1045$$

Since each option controls 100 shares of stock, the theoretical call price is $162.35, while the put's theoretical price is $210.45.

TABLE 15A–2 Standard Normal Distribution Function—(Concluded)

t	0	1	2	3	4	5	6	7	8	9
0.0	.5000	.5040	.5080	.5120	.5160	.5199	.5239	.5279	.5319	.5359
0.1	.5398	.5438	.5478	.5517	.5557	.5596	.5636	.5675	.5714	.5753
0.2	.5793	.5832	.5871	.5910	.5948	.5987	.6026	.6064	.6103	.6141
0.3	.6179	.6217	.6255	.6293	.6331	.6368	.6406	.6443	.6480	.6517
0.4	.6554	.6591	.6628	.6664	.6700	.6736	.6772	.6808	.6844	.6879
0.5	.6915	.6950	.6985	.7019	.7054	.7088	.7123	.7157	.7190	.7224
0.6	.7257	.7291	.7324	.7357	.7389	.7422	.7454	.7486	.7517	.7549
0.7	.7580	.7611	.7642	.7673	.7704	.7734	.7764	.7794	.7823	.7852
0.8	.7881	.7910	.7939	.7967	.7995	.8023	.8051	.8079	.8106	.8133
0.9	.8159	.8186	.8212	.8238	.8264	.8289	.8315	.8340	.8365	.8189
1.0	.8413	.8438	.8461	.8485	.8508	.8531	.8554	.8577	.8599	.8621
1.1	.8643	.8665	.8686	.8708	.8729	.8749	.8770	.8790	.8810	.8830
1.2	.8849	.8869	.8888	.8907	.8925	.8944	.8962	.8980	.8997	.9015
1.3	.9032	.9049	.9066	.9082	.9099	.9115	.9131	.9147	.9162	.9177
1.4	.9192	.9207	.9222	.9236	.9251	.9265	.9279	.9292	.9306	.9319
1.5	.9332	.9345	.9357	.9370	.9382	.9394	.9406	.9418	.9429	.9441
1.6	.9452	.9463	.9474	.9484	.9495	.9505	.9515	.9525	.9535	.9545
1.7	.9554	.9564	.9573	.9582	.9591	.9599	.9608	.9616	.9625	.9633
1.8	.9641	.9649	.9656	.9664	.9671	.9678	.9686	.9693	.9700	.9706
1.9	.9713	.9719	.9726	.9732	.9738	.9744	.9750	.9756	.9761	.9767
2.0	.9773	.9778	.9783	.9788	.9793	.9798	.9803	.9808	.9812	.9817
2.1	.9821	.9826	.9830	.9834	.9838	.9842	.9846	.9850	.9854	.9857
2.2	.9861	.9864	.9868	.9871	.9875	.9878	.9881	.9884	.9887	.9890
2.3	.9893	.9896	.9898	.9901	.9904	.9906	.9909	.9911	.9913	.9916
2.4	.9918	.9920	.9922	.9925	.9927	.9929	.9931	.9932	.9934	.9936
2.5	.9938	.9940	.9941	.9943	.9945	.9946	.9948	.9949	.9951	.9952
2.6	.9953	.9955	.9956	.9957	.9959	.9960	.9961	.9962	.9963	.9964
2.7	.9965	.9966	.9967	.9968	.9969	.9970	.9971	.9972	.9973	.9974
2.8	.9974	.9975	.9976	.9977	.9977	.9978	.9979	.9979	.9980	.9981
2.9	.9981	.9982	.9982	.9983	.9984	.9984	.9985	.9985	.9986	.9986
3.0	.9987									

A second example (using GAH stock) again uses the variables from Table 15A–1 and substitutes them into Formulas 15A–2 and 15A–3 to derive d_1 and d_2 as follows:

$$d_1 = \frac{\ln(42/40) + [0.10 + (0.0529/2)](0.1370)}{(0.23)(\sqrt{0.1370})}$$

$$= \frac{0.0488 + 0.0173}{0.0851}$$

$$= 0.7767$$

$$d_2 = 0.7767 - 0.0851$$

$$= 0.6916$$

The $N(d_1)$ and $N(d_2)$ values from the standard normal distribution table (Table 15A–2) are 0.7823 and 0.7549, respectively. As mentioned in the previous example, greater precision is possible through interpolation.

Given the above values, the GAH call and put prices are computed as:

$$c = (42)(0.7823) - (40)[e^{-(0.10)(0.1370)}](0.7549)$$
$$= 32.8566 - (40)(0.9864)(0.7549)$$
$$= 32.8566 - 29.7853$$
$$= 3.0713$$
$$p = (40)[e^{-(0.10)(0.1370)}] - 42 + 3.0713$$
$$= (40)(0.9864) - 42 + 3.0713$$
$$= 0.5273$$

These calculations indicate the theoretically correct price (for 100 shares) for the call is $307.13 and that $52.73 is the theoretically correct price for the put.

Suppose the market had priced the GAH call at $262.50. How would you be able to earn arbitrage profits? According to Black and Scholes, you would buy the undervalued calls at $262.50 and sell shares of GAH stock at $42 per share to form a riskless hedge and thus obtain arbitrage profits when equilibrium is established. However, to implement such a strategy, an investor must know how many shares to combine with each option to form the riskless hedge. This information is provided by $N(d_1)$ and is known as the hedge ratio or delta.

Since each option controls 100 shares of stock, the appropriate arbitrage activity in this example is to sell 0.7823 shares of GAH stock for every option purchased. Practically speaking, one cannot buy and sell fractional shares. Thus, 78 shares should be sold for each option that is purchased. If the market had overpriced the option, then the arbitrageur would sell options and purchase 78 shares for each option sold. In either case, the hedge's risk level will equal that of a Treasury bill, but the hedge's returns will exceed the Treasury bill's return, thus generating arbitrage profits.

Appendix 15B

THE USE OF OPTION SPREADS AND STRADDLES

We will look at two primary types of option spreads: vertical spreads and horizontal spreads. Vertical spreads involve buying and writing two contracts at different striking prices with the same month of expiration. Horizontal spreads consist of buying and writing two options with the same strike price but different months, and a diagonal spread is a combination of the vertical and horizontal spreads. Table 15B–1 presents an example of XYZ Corporation demonstrating the options, months, and strike prices involved in each type of spread. There are more complicated spreads than these, such as the butterfly spread, variable spread, and domino spread. We cannot attempt to explain all of these spreads in the space available, so we will concentrate on vertical bull spreads and vertical bear spreads.

Because spreads require the purchase of one option and the sale of another option, a speculator's account will have either a debit or credit balance. If the cost of the long option position is greater than the revenue from the short

TABLE 15B–1 Spreads (Call Options)

Vertical Spread

	Market Price	Strike Price	October	January	April
XYZ	36⅜	35	4	6	6½
	36⅜	40	2	3⅜	4
	36⅜	45	11/16	1½	6

Horizontal Spread

	Market Price	Strike Price	October	January	April
XYZ	36⅜	35	4	6	6½
	36⅜	40	2	3⅜	4
	36⅜	45	11/16	1½	6

Diagonal Spread

	Market Price	Strike Price	October	January	April
XYZ	36⅜	35	4	6	6½
	36⅜	40	2	3⅜	4
	36⅜	45	11/16	1½	6

option position, the speculator has a net cash outflow and a debit in his account. When your spread is put on with a debit, it is said you have "bought the spread." You have "sold the spread" if the receipt from writing the short option position is greater than the cost of buying the long option position and you have a credit balance. For example, the difference between the option prices for a vertical spread on XYZ Corporation in Table 15B–1 with October strike prices of 35 and 40 is $2 ($4 − $2). The $2 difference between these two option prices could be either a debit or credit, depending on whether a bull or bear spread is used. In either case, the profit or loss from a spread position results in the change between the two option prices over time as the price of the underlying stock goes up or down.

Vertical Bull Spread

In a bull spread, the expectation is that the common stock price will rise. The speculator can buy the common stock outright, or if he wants to profit from an expected price increase but reduce his risk of loss, he can enter into a bull spread. Vertical bull spreads limit both the maximum gain and maximum loss available. They are usually debit positions because the spreader buys the higher-priced, in-the-money option and shorts (writes) an inexpensive, out-of-the-money option. Using Table 15B–1 for an XYZ October vertical bull spread, we would buy the October 35 at 4 and sell the October 40 at 2 for a debit of 2 (price spread). This represents a $200 investment. Assume that three weeks later, XYZ stock rises from 36⅜ to 42 with the October 35 selling at 7½ (previously purchased at 4) and the October 40 at 4½ (previously sold at 2). Table 15B–2 on the next page shows the result of closing out the spread.

TABLE 15B–2 Profit on Vertical Bull Spread

XYZ October 35		XYZ October 40		Price Spread
Bought at	4	Sold at	2	2
Sold at	7½	Bought at	4½	3
Gain	3½	(Loss)	(2½)	1
		Net gain	$100	
		Investment	$200	
		Return	50%	

TABLE 15B–3 XYZ Vertical Bull Spread

XYZ Stock Price at Expiration 35				XYZ Stock Price at Expiration 40				XYZ Stock Price at Expiration 45			
October 35		October 40		October 35		October 40		October 35		October 40	
Bought at	4	Sold at	2	Bought at	4	Sold at	2	Bought at	4	Sold at	2
Expired at[a]	0	Expired at[a]	0	Sold at[a]	5	Expired at[a]	0	Sold at[a]	10	Bought at[a]	5
(Loss)	(4)	Gain	2	Gain	1	Gain	2	Gain	6	Loss	(3)
(Net loss) (2)				Net gain 3				Net gain 3			
($200) = 100 percent loss				$300 = 150 percent gain				$300 = 150 percent gain			

[a] All call options on date of expiration equal their intrinsic value.

Because the investment was only $200, the total return of $100 provided a 50 percent return. However, returns on spreads can be greatly altered by commissions. If the following spread incurred commissions of $25 in and $25 out, the percentage return could be cut in half to 25 percent.

The maximum profit at expiration is equal to the difference in strike prices ($5 in this case) minus the initial price spread ($2 in this case). For the XYZ vertical bull spread, the maximum profit is $300, and the maximum loss is the original debit of $200. At expiration, all speculative premiums are gone, and each option sells at its intrinsic value. Table 15B–3 shows maximum profit and loss at various closing market prices at expiration. Remember, our initial investment is $200.

As Table 15B–3 indicates, profit does not increase after the stock moves through the 40 price range. Every dollar of increased profit on the long position is offset by $1 of loss on the short position after the stock passes a price of 40. One of the important but difficult aspects of spreading is forecasting a range of prices rather than just the direction prices will move. If a speculator is bullish, he or she may buy a call instead of spreading. The potential loss is higher with the call but still limited, while the possible gain is unlimited. The relationship between long calls and bull spreads starts in the *bottom* of Figure 15B–1. Note the maximum loss with the bull spread is $200 and $400 with a long call. The break-even point is also $2 less for the bull spread ($37 versus $39). However, the long call has unlimited profit potential, and the bull spread is locked in at $300 at a stock price of $40 or higher. The spread position lowers the break-even point by $2 per share but also limits potential returns—a classic case of risk-return trade-off.

Vertical Bear Spread

The speculator enters a bear spread anticipating a decline in stock prices. Instead of selling short or writing a call with both having unlimited risk, he spreads by selling short the call with the lower strike price (highest premium) and covers the upside risk with the purchase of a call having a higher strike price. This creates a credit balance. In a sense, the bear spread does the opposite of the vertical bull spread as seen in Table 15B–4 on page 442 in which we show profits and losses from the strategy if XYZ ends up at 35 or at 40. With a bear spread, the price spread of 2 is the maximum gain if the stock closes at 35 or less at expiration, while the maximum loss equals 3, the difference between the exercise prices minus the price spread. The relationship between bear spreads and writing a call option is also demonstrated in Figure 15B–1 (the comparison starts at the *top* of the figure).

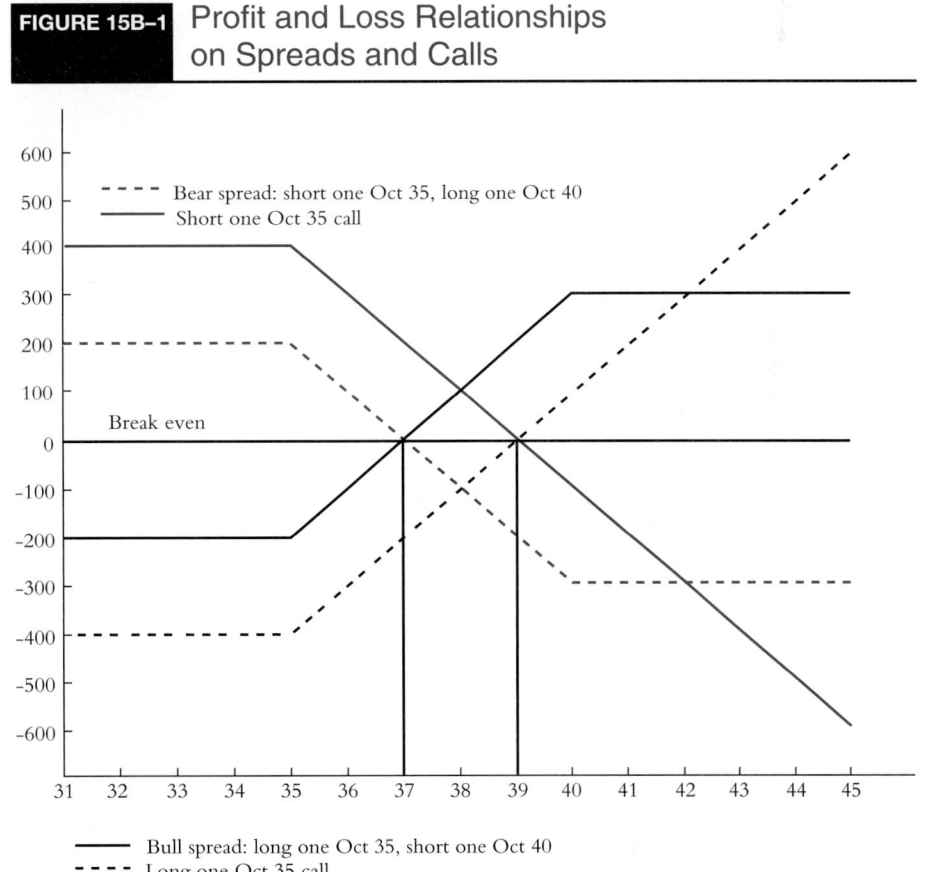

FIGURE 15B–1 Profit and Loss Relationships on Spreads and Calls

TABLE 15B–4 XYZ Vertical Bear Spread

XYZ Stock Price at Expiration 35				XYZ Stock Price at Expiration 40			
October 35		**October 40**		**October 35**		**October 40**	
Sold at	4	Bought at	2	Sold at	4	Bought at	2
Expired at	0	Expired at	0	Bought at	5	Expired at	0
Gain	4	(Loss)	(2)	(Loss)	1	(Loss)	2
	Net gain 2				Net loss (3)		
	$200				$(300)		

16
chapter sixteen

Commodities and Financial Futures

objectives

1. Explain how commodities and financial futures can be used for speculation or for hedging.

2. Describe the different types of commodities and financial futures contracts that are available.

3. Explain how margin is used in the futures markets to magnify gains (or losses).

4. Explain the difference between the cash and the futures markets.

5. Describe how currency futures and interest rate futures are currently utilized in a business environment.

6. Explain the role of interest rate swaps as an alternative to futures.

Types of Commodities and Exchanges
    Types of Commodities Contracts
Actual Commodities Contract
    Margin Requirements
    Market Conditions
    Gains and Losses
    Price Movement Limitations
Reading Market Quotes
The Cash Market and the Futures Market
The Futures Market for Financial Instruments
Currency Futures
Interest-Rate Futures
    Hedging with Interest-Rate Futures
    An Actual Example
Options as Well as Futures
Interest-Rate Swaps

What do pork bellies, soybeans, Japanese yen, and Treasury bills have in common? They are all items on which contracts may be traded in the commodities and financial futures markets. While numerous examples are given in this chapter of the use of futures contracts by people who are in the commodities business (farmers, millers, etc.), keep in mind that commodities and futures contracts can be used by others as well. In early 2004, the euro and Japanese yen were skyrocketing in value against the U.S. dollar. By betting for or against this trend continuing, you could make or lose a lot of money. The same could be said about betting for or against the continued decline in beef prices due to the threat of "mad cow disease" in January 2004.

A **futures contract** is an agreement that provides for the delivery of a specific amount of a commodity at a designated time in the future at a given price. An example might be a contract to deliver 5,000 bushels of corn next September at $2.40 per bushel. The person who sells the contract does not need to have actual possession of the corn, nor does the purchaser of the contract need to plan on taking possession of the corn. Almost all commodities futures contracts are closed out or reversed before the actual transaction is to occur. Thus, the seller of a futures contract for the delivery of 5,000 bushels of corn may simply later buy back a similar contract for the purchase of 5,000 bushels and close out his position. The initial buyer also reverses his position. More than 99 percent of all contracts are closed out in this fashion rather than through actual delivery. The commodities futures market is similar to the options market in that there is a tremendous volume of activity, but very few actual items ever change hands.

The futures markets were originally set up to allow grain and livestock producers and processors to **hedge** (protect) their positions in a given commodity. For example, a wheat producer might have a five-month lead time between the planting of his crop and the actual harvesting and delivery to the market. While the current price of wheat might be $3.50 a bushel, there is a tremendous risk that the price might change before delivery to the market. The wheat farmer can hedge his position by offering to sell futures contracts for the delivery of wheat. Even though he will probably close out or reverse these futures contracts before the call for actual delivery, he will still have effectively hedged his position. Let's see how this works. If the price of wheat goes down, he will have to sell his crop for less than he anticipated when he planted the wheat, but he will make up the difference on the wheat futures contracts. That is, he will be able to buy back the contracts for less than he sold them. Of course, if the price of the wheat goes up, the extra profit he makes on the crop will be lost on the futures contracts as he now has to buy back the contracts at a higher price.[1]

A miller who uses wheat as part of his processing faces the opposite dilemma in terms of pricing. The miller is afraid the price of wheat might go up and ultimately cut into his profit margin when he takes actual delivery of his product. He can hedge his position by buying futures contracts in wheat. If the actual price of wheat does go up, the extra cost of producing his product will be offset by the profits he makes on his futures contracts.

The commodities market allows the many parties in need of hedging opportunities to acquire contracts. Although some of this could be accomplished on a private basis (one party in Kansas City calls another party in Chicago on the advice of his banker), this would be virtually impossible to handle on a large-scale basis. Liquid, fluid markets such as those provided by the commodity exchanges are necessary to accomplish this function.

While the hedgers are the backbone and basic reason for the existence of commodity exchanges, they are not the only significant participants. We also have the speculators who take purely long or short positions without any intent

---

[1] The hedger not only reduces risk of loss but also eliminates additional profit opportunities. This may be appropriate for farmers since they are not in the risk-taking business but rather in agriculture.

the real world of investing

Can Derivatives Be Dangerous?

Derivatives such as futures, options, swaps, caps, floors, and collars keep making headlines. While derivatives are basically neutral instruments, their misuse or overindulgence by investors may not be. Not only are derivatives growing into a multitrillion dollar market, but they are spreading worldwide. Congressional committees and governmental organizations such as the Federal Reserve and U.S. Treasury Department are calling for increased regulation.

Why? The answer may be that many derivatives intended for use in a neutral or defensive way are being utilized in a speculative, highly risky fashion. One can compare the misuse of a derivative with driving an automobile in an irresponsible manner. Although the automobile is basically sound, if it is driven at 95 miles per hour in a rainstorm down a steep hill, it can indeed be a danger to society.

Corporate treasurers at such firms as Procter & Gamble (www.pg.com) and Bank One Corporation (www.bankone.com) found themselves behind the "eight ball" when they went from using derivatives to protect against interest-rate exposure to attempting to generate huge profits from guessing the next move in interest rates. They had unprotected, exposed positions that became very costly when they guessed wrong. (Both firms have since corrected the situation.)

Because derivatives can be used in a highly sophisticated fashion, derivatives trading is not easily understood by many corporate auditors. The derivatives trader may take positions that move in five directions on financial markets throughout the world, which the auditor may not have the expertise to follow and analyze. For that reason, it is particularly important that the board of directors and top management of a corporation have clearly stated policies and boundaries on the trading of derivatives. They also must implement adequate monitoring policies to ensure that their directions are being followed.

to hedge actual ownership. Thus, there is the speculator in wheat or silver who believes that the next major price move can be predicted to such an extent that a substantial profit can be made. Because commodities are purchased on the basis of a small investment in the form of margin (usually running 2 to 10 percent of the value of the contract), there is substantial leverage on the investment, and percentage returns and losses are greatly magnified. The typical commodities trader often suffers many losses with the anticipation of a few very substantial gains. Commodities speculation, as opposed to hedging, represents somewhat of a gamble, and stories have been told of reformed commodities speculators who gave up the chase to spend the rest of their days merely playing the slot machines. Nevertheless, commodity speculators are quite important to the liquidity of the market.

Types of Commodities and Exchanges

Commodities and financial futures can be broken down into a number of categories based on their essential characteristics. As indicated in Table 16–1 on page 446, there are five primary categories. In each case, we show representative items that fall under the category.

The first four categories represent traditional commodities, but category five came into prominence in the 1970s and 1980s—with foreign exchange futures originating in 1972, interest rate futures beginning in 1975, and stock index futures in 1982. Because foreign exchange and interest rate financial futures have tremendous implications for financial managers, we will give them special

TABLE 16–1 Categories of Commodities and Financial Futures

(1) Grains and oilseeds:	(2) Livestock and meat:	(3) Food and fiber:
Corn	Cattle—feeder	Cocoa
Oats	Cattle—live	Coffee
Soybeans	Hogs—live	Cotton
Wheat	Pork bellies	Orange juice
Barley	Turkeys	Potatoes
Rye	Broilers	Sugar
		Rice
		Butter

(4) Metals and petroleum:
- Copper
- Gold
- Platinum
- Silver
- Mercury
- Heating oil no. 2

(5) Financial futures:
- a. Foreign exchange:
  - Euro, yen, peso, etc.
- b. Interest rate futures:
  - Treasury bonds
  - Treasury bills
  - Municipal bonds
  - Eurodollars
- c. Stock index futures:
  - S&P 500
  - Value Line
  - Dow Jones Industrial Average

TABLE 16–2 Major United States and Canadian Commodity Exchanges

American Commodities Exchange (ACE)
Chicago Board of Trade (CBT)
Chicago Mercantile Exchange (CME)
   Also controls International Monetary Market (IMM)
Commodity Exchange (CMX)
Kansas City Board of Trade (KC)
Minneapolis Grain Exchange (MPLS)
New Orleans Commodity Exchange
New York Coffee, Sugar, and Cocoa Exchange (CSCE)
New York Cotton Exchange (CTN)
New York Futures Exchange (NYFE)
   Subsidiary of the New York Stock Exchange
New York Mercantile Exchange (NYM)
Pacific Commodities Exchange (PCE)
Winnipeg Grain Exchange (WPG)

attention later in this chapter. We will defer discussion of stock index futures to Chapter 17 so that they can be given *complete coverage* as a separate topic.

The commodities listed in Table 16–1 trade on various commodity exchanges in the United States and Canada (see Table 16–2). While the exchanges are well organized and efficient in their operation, they are still run by an open auction complete with outcries of bids and various hand-signal displays.

www.cbt.com

The largest commodity exchange is the Chicago Board of Trade (CBT). While some exchanges are highly specialized, such as the New York Cotton Exchange, most exchanges trade in a number of securities. For example, the Chicago Board of Trade deals in such diverse products as corn, oats, soybeans, wheat, silver, and Treasury bonds.

www.cftc.gov

The activities of the commodity exchanges are primarily regulated by the Commodity Futures Trading Commission (CFTC), a federal regulatory agency established by Congress in 1975. The CFTC has had a number of jurisdictional disputes with the SEC over the regulation of financial futures.

Types of Commodities Contracts

The commodity contract lists the type of commodity and the denomination in which it is traded (bushels, pounds, troy ounces, metric tons, percentage points, etc.). The contract will also specify the standardized unit for trade (5,000 bushels, 30,000 pounds, etc.). A further designation will indicate the month in which the contract ends, with most commodities having a whole range of months from which to choose. Typically, contracts run as long as a year into the future, but some interest rate futures contracts extend as far as three years.

Examples of the sizes of futures contracts are presented in Table 16–3. Be aware that there may be many different forms of the same commodity (such as spring wheat or amber/durum wheat).

TABLE 16–3 Size of Commodity Contracts

Contract	Trading Units	Size of Contract Based on Winter 2004 Prices (in dollars)
Corn	5,000 bushels	$ 12,000
Oats	5,000 bushels	8,150
Wheat	5,000 bushels	17,400
Pork bellies	38,000 pounds	31,600
Coffee	37,500 pounds	33,725
Cotton	50,000 pounds	34,360
Sugar	112,000 pounds	22,312
Copper	25,000 pounds	26,000
Gold	100 troy ounces	43,186
Silver	5,000 troy ounces	30,250
Treasury bonds	$100,000	102,000
Treasury bills	$1,000,000	97,500

Actual Commodities Contract

To examine the potential gain or loss in a commodities contract, let's go through a hypothetical investment. Assume we are considering the purchase of a December wheat contract (it is now May 1). The price on the futures contract is $3.50 per bushel. Since wheat trades in units of 5,000 bushels, the total price is

$17,500. As we go through our example, we will examine many important features associated with commodity trading—beginning with margin requirements.

Margin Requirements

Commodity trading is based on the use of margin rather than on actual cash dollars. Margin requirements are typically 2 to 10 percent of the value of the contract and may vary over time or even among exchanges for a given commodity. For our example, we will assume a $600 margin requirement on the $17,500 wheat contract.[2] That was the specified margin in 2004. The $600 would represent 3.4 percent of the value of the contract ($17,500).

Margin requirements on commodities contracts are much lower than those on common stock transactions, where 50 percent of the purchase price has been the requirement since 1974. Furthermore, in the commodities market, the margin payment is merely considered to be a good-faith payment against losses. There is no actual borrowing or interest to be paid.[3]

In addition to the initial margin requirements, **margin maintenance requirements** (minimum maintenance standards) run 60 to 80 percent of the value of the initial margin. In the case of the wheat contract, the margin maintenance requirement might be $400 (67% × $600). If our initial margin of $600 is reduced by $200 due to losses on our contract, we will be required to replace the $200 to cover our margin position. If we do not do so, our position will be closed out, and we will take our losses.

The margin requirement, relative to size, is even less for financial futures. For example, on a $1 million Treasury bill contract, the investor must post only an initial margin of $675. Similar requirements exist for other types of financial futures.

Note that the high risk inherent in a commodities contract is not so much a function of volatile price movements as it is the impact of high leverage made possible by the low initial margin requirements. A 5 percent price move may equal or exceed the size of our initial investment in the form of the margin deposit. This is similar to the type of leverage utilized in the options market as described in Chapter 15. However, the action in the commodities market is much quicker. You can be asked to put up additional margin within hours after you establish your initial position.

Market Conditions

Because the price of every commodity moves in response to market conditions, each investor must determine the key market variables that influence the value of his or her contract. In the case of wheat, the investor may be particularly concerned about such factors as weather and crop conditions in the Midwest, the price of corn as a substitute product, the carryover of wheat supply from the previous year, and potential wheat sales to other countries.

---

[2] The amount of margin required also differs between speculative and hedging activities. For example, $600 represents the margin for speculation. The margin for hedging is $400 in this case.

[3] It should also be pointed out that a customer may need a minimum account balance of $5,000 or greater to open a commodity account.

Gains and Losses

Application Example

In the present example, assume we guessed right in our analysis of the wheat market; we purchased a December futures contract for $3.50 per bushel, and the price goes to $3.62 per bushel (recall that the contract was for 5,000 bushels). With a $0.12 increase per bushel, we have established a dollar gain of $600 (5,000 bushels × $0.12 per bushel profit). With an initial margin requirement of $600, we have made a percentage profit of 100 percent as indicated in the following formula:[4]

$$\frac{\text{Dollar gain}}{\text{Amount of margin deposit}} = \frac{\$600}{\$600} \times 100 = 100\%$$

If this transaction occurred over one month, the annualized gain would be 1,200 percent (100% × 12 = 1,200%). Note that this was all accomplished by a $0.12 movement in the price of a December wheat contract from $3.50 to $3.62.

Actually, we may choose to close out the contract or attempt to let the profits run. We also may use the profits to establish the basis for margin on additional futures contracts. A paper gain of $600 is enough to provide the $600 margin on a second wheat contract.

We are now in a position to use an inverse pyramid to expand our position. With two contracts outstanding, a mere $0.06 price change will provide $600 in profits:

$0.06 Price change
× 10,000 Bushels (two contracts)
$600 Profits (can be applied to third contract)

The new $600 in profits can be used to purchase a third contract, and now with 15,000 bushels under control, a $0.04 price change will generate enough profits for a fourth contract:

$0.04 Price change
× 15,000 Bushels (three contracts)
$600 Profits (can be applied to fourth contract)

Inverse pyramiding begins to sound astounding since eventually a 1¢ or ½¢ change in the price of wheat will trigger enough profits for a new contract. Of course, great risks are associated with such a process. It is like building a house with playing cards. If one tumbles, the whole house comes down. The investor can become so highly leveraged that any slight reversal in price can trigger margin calls. While it is often wise to let profits run and perhaps do some amount of pyramiding, prudence must be exercised.

Our primary attention up to this point has been on contracts that are making money. What are the implications if there is an immediate price reversal after we have purchased our December wheat contract? You will recall there was a margin maintenance requirement of $400 based on our initial margin of $600. In this case, a $200 loss would call for an additional deposit to bring our margin position up to $600. How much would the price of wheat have to

---

[4] This does not include commissions, which are generally less than $100 for a complete transaction (buy and sell).

decline for us to get this margin call to increase our deposit? With a 5,000-bushel contract, we are talking about a mere decline of $0.04 per bushel:

$$\frac{\$200 \text{ loss}}{5{,}000 \text{ bushels}} = \$0.04 \text{ per bushel}$$

This could happen in a matter of minutes or hours after our initial purchase. When we get the margin call, we can either elect to put up the additional $200 and continue with the contract or tell our commodities broker to close out our contract and take our losses. If we put up the $200, our broker could still be on the phone a few minutes later asking for more margin because the price has shown further deterioration. Because investors often buy multiple contracts, such as 10 December wheat contracts, the process can be all the more intense. In the commodities market, the old adage of "cut your losses short and let your profits run" probably has its greatest significance. Even a seasoned commodities trader might determine that he is willing to lose 80 percent of the time and win only 20 percent of the time, but those victories will represent home runs and the losses mere outs.

Price Movement Limitations

Because of the enormous opportunities for gains and losses in the commodities markets, the commodity exchanges do limit maximum daily price movements in a commodity. Some examples are shown in Table 16–4.

These daily trading limits obviously must affect the efficiency of the market somewhat. If market conditions indicate that the price of wheat should decline by $0.30 and the daily limit is $0.20, then obviously the price of wheat is not in equilibrium as it opens the following morning. However, the desire to stop market panics tends to override the desire for total market efficiency in the commodity markets. Nevertheless, the potential intraday trading range is still large. Recall, for example, that a $0.20 change in the price of wheat, which is the daily limit, is more than enough to place tremendous pressure on the investor to repeatedly increase his margin position. On the typical 5,000-bushel contract, this would represent a daily loss of $1,000.

TABLE 16–4 Maximum Daily Price Changes

Commodity	Exchange[a]	Normal Price Range	Maximum Daily Price Change (from Previous Close)[b]
Corn	CBT	$2.00–$3.00	$0.10 per bushel
Oats	CBT	$1.00–$1.75	$0.10 per bushel
Wheat	CBT	$2.50–$4.50	$0.20 per bushel
Pork bellies	CBT	$0.40–$0.80	$0.02 per pound
Copper	CMX	$0.70–$1.40	$0.03 per pound
Silver	CBT	$4.00–$7.50	$1.00 per ounce
Treasury bills	IMM of CME	85% of par and up	No limit

[a] CBT (Chicago Board of Trade), CMX (Commodity Exchange), IMM (International Monetary Market), CME (Chicago Mercantile Exchange).

[b] These values may change slightly from exchange to exchange and are often temporarily altered in response to rampant speculation.

Reading Market Quotes

We turn our attention to interpreting market quotes in the daily newspaper. Table 16–5 shows an excerpt from the January 5, 2004, edition of *The Wall Street*

TABLE 16–5 Examples of Price Quotes on Commodity Futures

Monday, January 5, 2004

Grain and Oilseed Futures

	OPEN	HIGH	LOW	SETTLE	CHG	LIFETIME HIGH	LIFETIME LOW	OPEN INT
Corn (CBT)-5,000 bu.; cents per bu.								
Mar	252.00	256.00	250.50	253.00	−.25	264.00	219.00	276,673
May	255.00	259.00	253.75	256.25	.25	260.25	224.50	65,646
July	257.00	260.50	256.00	259.00	.50	264.50	227.75	43,171
Sept	254.50	257.50	254.00	255.00	...	257.50	229.75	8,985
Dec	250.00	254.50	249.50	253.00	−.50	260.00	232.50	43,222
Mr05	255.00	258.00	255.00	257.00	−.50	258.50	239.00	2,828
Dec	248.25	248.25	248.00	248.00	.50	248.25	235.00	797
Est vol 56,423; vol Fri 92,825; open int 442,006, +16,077.								
Oats (CBT)-5,000 bu.; cents per bu.								
Mar	152.00	154.75	148.50	154.50	2.50	157.75	131.00	4,500
May	154.50	155.25	151.00	155.25	2.00	158.50	135.00	582
Est vol 2,669; vol Fri 1,857; open int 5,208, +7.								
Soybeans (CBT)-5,000 bu.; cents per bu.								
Jan	790.00	802.00	786.00	796.75	4.25	805.50	507.00	8,295
Mar	798.00	806.00	790.00	800.50	2.25	808.00	508.00	123,356
May	794.00	802.00	787.00	796.50	1.25	802.50	515.50	55,896
July	783.50	792.00	778.00	785.25	1.25	792.00	520.00	28,909
Aug	760.00	764.00	756.00	758.00	−1.00	764.00	521.00	5,906
Sept	709.00	711.00	705.00	705.00	−2.00	711.00	528.00	2,758
Nov	640.00	645.00	639.00	642.00	3.75	645.00	483.00	17,351
Est vol 45,893; vol Fri 54,738; open int 242,638, +4,045.								
Soybean Meal (CBT)-100 tons; $ per ton.								
Jan	246.00	246.00	239.80	242.20	.40	255.00	151.00	4,999
Mar	245.70	247.30	242.00	245.30	−.40	251.00	152.50	65,219
May	245.00	246.50	241.00	244.30	−1.00	249.50	153.00	48,718
July	241.70	241.70	236.70	239.40	−1.00	243.50	152.50	28,007
Aug	232.50	232.50	228.50	230.80	−.70	234.50	154.00	6,931
Sept	219.50	221.00	216.70	217.80	−1.60	222.00	154.00	5,099
Oct	197.50	197.50	193.80	193.80	−2.30	197.50	150.50	5,615
Dec	193.30	194.00	190.50	190.80	−1.90	194.00	150.00	12,037
Est vol 19,721; vol Fri 21,118; open int 177,534, −1,346.								
Soybean Oil (CBT)-60,000 lbs.; cents per lb.								
Jan	28.10	28.88	27.87	28.52	.48	28.88	18.92	7,507
Mar	28.11	28.78	27.75	28.49	.58	28.78	19.00	74,860
May	27.78	28.60	27.65	28.32	.56	28.60	19.01	46,313
July	27.55	28.28	27.40	28.02	.54	28.28	19.01	37,437
Aug	27.25	27.85	27.25	27.55	.52	27.85	19.05	4,094
Sept	26.40	26.85	26.40	26.75	.57	26.85	19.01	3,562
Oct	25.30	25.35	25.25	25.35	.65	25.35	19.00	3,405
Dec	24.05	24.70	24.00	24.70	.60	24.70	18.98	9,716
Est vol 22,577; vol Fri 12,879; open int 187,584, −940.								
Rough Rice (CBT)-2,000 cwt.; cents per cwt.								
Jan	871.00	878.00	865.00	875.50	5.50	888.00	584.00	674
Mar	891.00	894.00	880.00	893.00	4.50	903.00	680.00	5,823
July	911.00	911.00	906.00	909.00	7.00	911.00	761.00	482
Est vol 635; vol Fri 994; open int 7,983, −8.								
Wheat (CBT)-5,000 bu.; cents per bu.								
Mar	402.75	405.50	397.00	398.50	−7.25	421.50	301.50	79,732
May	401.50	405.00	398.00	401.00	−2.25	413.00	290.00	11,057
July	385.00	385.00	381.00	383.50	−3.00	391.75	298.00	15,638
Sept	386.00	388.00	384.00	386.50	−3.50	390.50	326.00	656
Dec	394.50	395.00	393.00	394.50	−6.00	401.00	330.00	1,185
Est vol 25,777; vol Fri 40,090; open int 108,349, +937.								
Wheat (KC)-5,000 bu.; cents per bu.								
Mar	406.00	407.00	400.00	403.75	−5.25	416.00	314.00	48,713
May	403.00	404.50	397.50	401.25	−8.25	411.00	315.00	5,616
July	389.50	389.50	384.00	386.00	−4.75	392.00	313.00	5,724
Sept	390.50	390.50	387.00	389.00	−7.25	397.00	330.50	512
Dec	395.00	397.00	393.50	397.00	.50	398.00	341.00	515
Est vol 12,062; vol Fri 15,332; open int 61,082, +3,157.								
Wheat (MPLS)-5,000 bu.; cents per bu.								
Mar	413.00	413.75	407.50	408.50	−7.25	423.75	343.75	22,748
May	408.00	409.00	402.50	404.25	−8.75	420.00	349.50	4,211
July	399.00	400.00	394.00	394.00	−6.00	405.50	352.00	1,032
Sept	388.00	391.00	386.50	389.00	...	394.00	346.00	1,042
Dec	390.00	395.00	390.00	393.00	−1.00	397.00	355.00	302
Est vol 3,998; vol Fri 5,899; open int 29,335, +1,215.								

Source: *The Wall Street Journal*, January 6, 2004, p. C12. Reprinted by permission of *The Wall Street Journal*, © 2004 by Dow Jones & Company, Inc. All Rights Reserved Worldwide.

Journal covering nine different types of contracts (this represents about 30 percent of the contracts reported for that day).

In each case, we see a wide choice of months for which a contract may be purchased. For example, corn, which trades on the Chicago Board of Trade (CBT), has futures contracts for March, May, July, and September. Some commodities offer a contract for virtually every month. To directly examine some of the terms in the table, we produce a part of the corn contract (CBT) in Table 16–6.

TABLE 16–6 Price Quotes for Corn Contracts

	Open	High	Low	Settle	Change	Lifetime High	Lifetime Low	Open Interest
Corn (CBT)—5,000 bushel; cents per bushel								
March	252.00	256.00	250.50	253.00	−.25	264.00	219.00	276,673
May	255.00	259.00	253.75	256.25	.25	260.25	224.50	65,646
July	257.00	260.50	256.00	259.00	.50	264.50	227.75	43,171
Sept	254.50	257.50	254.00	255.00	—	257.50	229.75	8,985

Source: *The Wall Street Journal*, January 6, 2004, p. C12. Reprinted by permission of *The Wall Street Journal*, © 2004 by Dow Jones & Company, Inc. All Rights Reserved Worldwide.

The first line in the table indicates that we are dealing in corn traded on the CBT. We then note that corn is traded in 5,000-bushel units and quoted in cents per bushel. Quotations in cents per bushel require some mental adjustment. For example, 200 cents per bushel would actually represent $2 per bushel. We generally move the decimal point two places to the left and read the quote in terms of dollars. For example, the March 2004 opening price was $2.5200 per bushel.

Across the top of the table we observe that we are given information on the open, high, low, settle (close), and change from the previous day's close as well as the lifetime high and low for that particular contract. The last column represents the open interest, or the number of actual contracts presently outstanding for that delivery month.

The Cash Market and the Futures Market

Many commodity futures exchanges provide areas where buyers and sellers can negotiate **cash** (or **spot**) **prices.** The cash price is the actual dollar value paid for the immediate transfer of a commodity. Unlike a futures contract, there must be a transfer of the physical possession of the goods. Prices in the cash market are somewhat dependent on prices in the futures market. Thus, it is said that the futures markets provide an important service as a price discovery mechanism. By cataloging price trends in everything from corn to cattle, the producers, processors, and handlers of more than 50 commodities are able to observe price trends in categories of interest.

The Futures Market for Financial Instruments

The major event in the commodities markets for the last three decades has been the development of financial futures contracts. With the great volatility in the foreign exchange markets and in interest rates, corporate treasurers, investors, and others have felt a great need to hedge their positions. Financial futures also appeal to speculators because of their low margin requirements and wide swings in value.

Financial futures may be broken down into three major categories: currency futures, interest-rate futures, and stock index futures (the latter is covered in depth in Chapter 17). Trading in currency futures began in May 1972 on the International Monetary Market (part of the Chicago Mercantile Exchange). Interest-rate futures started trading on the Chicago Board of Trade in October 1975 with the GNMA certificate. Trading in financial futures, regardless of whether they are currency or interest-rate futures, is very similar to trading in traditional commodities such as corn, wheat, copper, or pork bellies. There is a stipulated contract size, month of delivery, margin requirement, and so on. We will first look at currency futures and then shift our attention to interest-rate futures.

Currency Futures

Futures are available in the currencies listed below:

Euro	Japanese yen
Australian dollar	Mexican peso
Canadian dollar	Russian ruble

The futures market in currencies provides many of the same functions as the older and less formalized market in foreign exchange operated by banks and specialized brokers, who maintain communication networks throughout the world. In either case, one can speculate or hedge. The currency futures market, however, is different in that it provides standardized contracts and a strong secondary market.

Application Example

Let's examine how the currency futures market works. Assume you wish to purchase a currency futures contract in Mexican pesos. The standardized contract is 500,000 pesos. The value of the contract is quoted in cents per peso. Assume you purchase a December futures contract in May, and the price on the contract is $0.08860 per peso. The total value of the contract is $44,300 (500,000 × $0.08860). The typical margin on a peso contract is $1,500.

We also assume the peso strengthens relative to the dollar. This might happen because of decreasing U.S. interest rates, declining inflation in Mexico, or any number of other reasons. Under these circumstances, the currency might rise to $0.09010 (the peso is worth more cents than it was previously). The value of the contract has now risen to $45,050 (500,000 × $0.09010). This represents an increase in value of $750:

$45,050 Current value
−44,300 Original value
$750 Gain

With an original margin requirement of $1,500, this represents a return of 50 percent:

$$\frac{\$750}{\$1,500} \times 100 = 50\%$$

On an annualized basis, it could even be higher. Of course, the contract could produce a loss if the peso weakens against the dollar as a result of higher interest rates in the United States or increasing inflation in Mexico. With a normal margin maintenance requirement of $1,500, a $300 loss on the contract will call for additional margin.

Corporate treasurers often try to hedge an exposed position in their foreign exchange dealings through the currency futures market. Assume a treasurer closes a deal today to receive payment in two months in Japanese yen. If the yen goes down relative to the dollar, he will have less value than he anticipated. One solution would be to sell a yen futures contract (go short). If the value of the yen goes down, he will make money on his futures contract that will offset the loss on the receipt of the Japanese yen in two months.

Table 16–7 lists the typical size of contracts for four other foreign currencies that trade on the International Monetary Market.

TABLE 16–7 Contracts in Currency Futures

Currency	Trading Units	Size of Contract Based on Winter 2004 Prices
Euro	125,000	$155,000
Canadian dollar	100,000	76,090
British pound	62,500	110,060
Japanese yen	12,500,000	116,815

Interest-Rate Futures

Since the inception of the interest-rate futures contract with GNMA certificates in October 1975, the market has been greatly expanded to include Treasury notes, Treasury bills, municipal bonds, federal funds, and Eurodollars. There is almost unlimited potential for futures contracts on interest-related items.

Interest-rate futures trade on a number of major exchanges, including the Chicago Board of Trade, the International Monetary Market of the Chicago Mercantile Exchange, and the New York Futures Exchange. There is strong competition between Chicago and New York City for dominance in this business, with Chicago being not only the historical leader but also the current leader.

Table 16–8 shows examples of quotes on interest-rate futures. Direct your attention to the first category, Treasury bonds (CBT), trading on the Chicago Board of Trade.

The bonds trade in units of $100,000, and the quotes are in percent of par value taken to 32nds of a percentage point. Although it is not shown in these data, the bonds on which the futures are based are assumed to be new, 15-year Treasury instruments paying 4 percent interest. In the first column for the March contract for Treasury bonds, we see an opening price of 107-31. This indicates a value of $107^{31}/_{32}$ percent times stated (par) value. We thus have a contract value

TABLE 16–8 Examples of Price Quotes on Interest-Rate Futures

	OPEN	HIGH	LOW	SETTLE	CHG	LIFETIME HIGH	LIFETIME LOW	OPEN INT

Interest Rate Futures

Treasury Bonds (CBT)-$100,000; pts 32nds of 100%
Mar	107-31	108-03	107-08	107-28	−1	116-23	101-05	422,344
June	106-13	106-20	105-27	106-14	−1	116-15	104-00	10,190
Sept	104-06	104-06	104-06	105-03	−1	104-06	101-25	228

Est vol 129,942; vol Fri 99,431; open int 432,944, +6,894.

Treasury Notes (CBT)-$100,000; pts 32nds of 100%
| Mar | 111-09 | 11-145 | 111-01 | 111-10 | −1.0 | 116-10 | 106-29 | 961,239 |
| June | 109-17 | 09-255 | 109-17 | 109-23 | −2.0 | 111-15 | 107-13 | 319 |

Est vol 366,886; vol Fri 232,863; open int 961,558, +22,183.

10 Yr. Agency Notes (CBT)-$100,000; pts 32nds of 100%
| Mar | ... | ... | ... | na | ... | 0 | 0 | 0 |

Est vol 0; vol Fri 0; open int 0, unch.

5 Yr. Treasury Notes (CBT)-$100,000; pts 32nds of 100%
| Mar | 111-00 | 11-055 | 10-265 | 111-02 | ... | 19-215 | 09-145 | 799,550 |

Est vol 155,344; vol Fri 95,444; open int 799,572, +1,516.

2 Yr. Treasury Notes (CBT)-$200,000; pts 32nds of 100%
| Mar | 06-267 | 06-285 | 06-245 | 06-272 | .2 | 07-037 | 106-02 | 160,420 |

Est vol 11,353; vol Fri 14,025; open int 160,420, +3,823.

30 Day Federal Funds (CBT)-$5,000,000; 100 − daily avg.
Jan	98.995	99.000	98.990	98.995	...	99.240	98.660	52,133
Feb	99.00	99.00	99.00	98.99	...	99.22	98.70	76,999
Mar	98.98	98.98	98.98	98.98	...	99.16	98.74	50,800
Apr	98.96	98.96	98.96	98.96	...	99.17	89.96	62,691
May	98.88	98.88	98.87	98.88	.01	99.79	98.40	30,728
July	98.73	98.73	98.71	98.72	.01	98.89	98.20	15,665

Est vol 8,545; vol Fri 9,560; open int 352,494, +1,655.

10 Yr. Interest Rate Swaps (CBT)-$100,000; pts 32nds of 100%
| Mar | 108-26 | 108-26 | 108-16 | 108-24 | ... | 111-00 | 107-20 | 36,955 |

Est vol 216; vol Fri 169; open int 36,956, +55.

10 Yr. Muni Note Index (CBT)-$1,000 x index
| Mar | 101-19 | 101-27 | 101-14 | 101-25 | 3 | 103-14 | 99-21 | 1,881 |

Est vol 123; vol Fri 408; open int 1,881, −77.
Index: Close 103-08; Yield 4.59.

	OPEN	HIGH	LOW	SETTLE	CHG	YIELD	CHG	OPEN INT

13 Week Treasury Bills (CME)-$1,000,000; pts of 100%
| Jan | ... | ... | ... | n.a. | ... | ... | ... | 0 |

Est vol n.a.; vol Fri 0; open int 0, unch.

1 Month Libor (CME)-$3,000,000; pts of 100%
Jan	98.87	98.88	98.87	98.88	...	1.12	...	19,862
Feb	98.87	98.87	98.86	98.87	...	1.13	...	32,964
Mar	98.83	98.83	98.83	98.83	...	1.17	...	7,080
Apr	98.78	98.78	98.78	98.78	...	1.22	...	5,454

Est vol 3,021; vol Fri 4,847; open int 77,163, +1,489.

Eurodollar (CME)-$1,000,000; pts of 100%
Jan	98.83	98.83	98.83	98.83	...	1.17	...	107,160
Feb	98.81	98.82	98.81	98.82	.02	1.18	−.02	23,423
Mar	98.77	98.77	98.76	98.76	...	1.24	...	818,026
Apr	98.70	98.70	98.69	98.70	...	1.30	...	14,122
June	98.50	98.53	98.50	98.52	.02	1.48	−.02	716,029
Sept	98.13	98.16	98.12	98.14	.02	1.86	−.02	594,366
Dec	97.69	97.72	97.66	97.69	.01	2.31	−.01	529,503
Mr05	97.26	97.29	97.22	97.26	...	2.74	...	361,496
June	96.87	96.89	96.81	96.85	...	3.15	...	287,136
Sept	96.53	96.55	96.46	96.51	...	3.49	...	217,422
Dec	96.24	96.24	96.16	96.21	...	3.79	...	174,464
Mr06	96.01	96.01	95.93	95.97	−.01	4.03	.01	145,125
June	95.74	95.75	95.69	95.73	−.01	4.27	.01	127,129
Sept	95.53	95.55	95.48	95.52	−.02	4.48	.02	104,382
Dec	95.32	95.33	95.26	95.30	−.02	4.70	.02	101,394
Mr07	95.15	95.15	95.08	95.13	−.02	4.87	.02	75,900
June	94.97	94.98	94.90	94.95	−.02	5.05	.02	66,788
Sept	94.81	94.81	94.74	94.79	−.02	5.21	.02	63,544
Dec	94.60	94.65	94.57	94.63	−.01	5.37	.01	52,584
Mr08	94.45	94.52	94.44	94.50	−.02	5.50	.02	47,904
June	94.41	94.41	94.32	94.38	−.02	5.62	.02	47,990
Sept	94.22	94.30	94.22	94.27	−.02	5.73	.02	31,745
Dec	94.13	94.21	94.12	94.17	−.03	5.83	.03	19,200
Mr09	94.03	94.11	94.03	94.08	−.04	5.92	.04	14,157
June	94.02	94.05	93.97	94.02	−.04	5.98	.04	9,084
Dec	93.88	93.92	93.86	93.89	−.04	6.11	.04	5,417

Est vol 709,503; vol Fri 522,968; open int 4,811,749, +41,106.

Source: *The Wall Street Journal,* January 6, 2004, p. C12. Reprinted by permission of *The Wall Street Journal,* © 2004 by Dow Jones & Company, Inc. All Rights Reserved Worldwide.

of $107,968.75$ ($107^{31}/_{32}$ × $100,000$). This represents the opening value. The entire line in Table 16–8 reads as follows:

	Open	High	Low	Settle	Change	Lifetime High	Lifetime Low	Open Interest
Mar	$107^{31}/_{32}$	$108^{3}/_{32}$	$107^{9}/_{32}$	$107^{28}/_{32}$	−1	$116^{23}/_{32}$	$101^{5}/_{32}$	422,344

The **settle price**, or closing price is $107^{28}/_{32}$, which represents a negative change of 1 or $^{32}/_{32}$nds from the close of the previous day. The close for the previous day is not always the same as the open for the current day.[5] Since the value of the futures went down, we can assume interest rates increased. We can also observe the lifetime high and low for this contract. Finally, we see an open interest of 422,344, indicating the number of contracts outstanding for March.

Application Example

Assume we buy a futures contract for $107^{28}/_{32}$ or $107,875 ($107^{28}/_{32}$ × $100,000$). The margin requirement on the Chicago Board of Trade is $2,565 with a $1,900 margin maintenance requirement. In this case, it may be that we bought the futures contract because we anticipate easier monetary policy by the Federal Reserve, which will trigger a decline in interest rates and an increase in bond prices. If interest rates decline by 0.6 percent (60 basis points), Treasury bond prices will increase by approximately $1^{17}/_{32}$.[6] On a $100,000 par value futures contract, this would represent a gain of $1,531.25 as indicated below:

$$\begin{aligned} \$100,000 \\ \times\ 1^{17}/_{32}\%\ (1.53125\%) \\ \hline \$1,531.25 \end{aligned}$$

With a $2,565 initial margin, the $1,531.25 profit represents an attractive return on our original $2,565 investment of 59.7 percent:

$$\frac{\$1,531.25}{\$2,565.00} = 59.70\%$$

Note, however, that if interest rates go up by even a small amount, our Treasury bond futures contract value will fall, and there may be a margin call.

As is true of other commodities, when we trade in interest rate futures, we do not take actual title or possession of the commodity unless we fail to reverse our initial position. The contract merely represents a bet or hedge on the direction of future interest rates and bond prices.

Hedging with Interest-Rate Futures

Interest-rate futures have opened up opportunities for hedging that can only be compared with the development of the agricultural commodities market more

---

[5] A number of overnight events can cause the difference. In this case, we can assume the close for the previous day was $108^{28}/_{32}$.

[6] This is derived from a standard bond table and not explicitly calculated in the example.

than a century ago. Consider the following potential hedges against interest-rate risks.

1. A corporate treasurer is awaiting a new debt issue that will occur in 60 days. The underwriters are still putting the final details together. The great fear is that interest rates will rise between now and then. The treasurer could hedge his or her position in the futures market by selling a Treasury bond or other similar security short. If interest rates go up, the price to buy back the interest-rate futures will be lower, and a profit will be made on the short position. This will partially or fully offset the higher interest costs on the new debt issue.

2. A corporate treasurer is continually reissuing commercial paper at new interest rates or borrowing under a floating prime agreement at the bank. He or she fears that interest rates will go up and make a big dent in projected profits. By selling (going short) interest-rate futures, the corporate treasurer can make enough profit on interest-rate futures if interest rates go up to compensate for the higher costs of money.

3. A mortgage banker has made a forward commitment to provide a loan at a set interest rate one month in the future. If interest rates go up, the resale value of the mortgage in the secondary market will go down. He or she can hedge the position by selling or going short on an interest rate futures contract.

4. A pension fund manager has been receiving a steady return of 6 percent on his short-term portfolio in 90-day Treasury bills. He is afraid interest rates will go down and he will have to adjust to receiving lower returns on the managed funds. His strategy might be to buy (go long on) a Treasury bill futures contract. If interest rates go down, he will make a profit on his futures contract that will partially or fully offset his decline in interest income for one period. Of course, if he is heavily invested in long-term securities and fearful of an interest-rate rise, a sell or short position that would provide profits on an interest-rate rise would be advisable. This would offset part of the loss in the portfolio value due to increasing interest rates.

5. A commercial banker has most of her loans on a floating prime basis, meaning the rate she charges will change with the cost of funds. However, some of the loans have a fixed rate associated with them. If the cost of funds goes up, the fixed-rate loans will become unprofitable. By selling or going short on interest-rate futures, the danger of higher interest rates can be hedged away by the profits she will make on the interest-rate futures. Similarly, a banker may make a commitment to pay a set amount of interest on certificates of deposit for the next six months. If interest rates go down, the banker may have to lend the funds at a lower rate than she is currently paying. If she buys a futures contract, then lower interest rates will increase the value of the contract and provide a profit. This will offset the possible negative profitability spread described earlier.

An Actual Example

Application Example

Assume an industrial corporation has a $10 million, 15-year bond to be issued in 60 days. Long-term rates for such an issue are currently 9.75 percent, and there is concern that interest rates will go up to 10 percent by the time of the issue. The corporate

> treasurer has figured out that the extra ¼ point would have a present value cost of $190,150 over the life of the issue (on a before-tax basis):
>
> | | | |
> |---:|---:|---|
> | $10,000,000 | | |
> | × ¼% | | |
> | $ 25,000 | | |
> | × 7.606 | | Present value factor for 15 years at 10 percent (Appendix D) |
> | $ 190,150 | | Present value of future costs |
>
> To establish a hedge position, he sells 97 Treasury bond futures short. We assume they are currently selling at 104 (104% × $100,000), equaling $104,000 each. The total value of the hedge would be $10,088,000 (97 Treasury bond contracts × $104,000). This is roughly equivalent to the $10 million size of the corporate bond issue. If interest rates go up by ¼ point, the profit on the Treasury bond futures contract (due to falling prices with a short position) will probably offset the present value of the increased cost of the corporate bond issue.

Of course, we do not suggest that both rates (on Treasury bonds and corporate bonds) would move exactly together. However, the general thrust of the example should be apparent. We are actually establishing a **cross-hedging** pattern by using one form of security (Treasury bonds) to hedge another form of security (corporate bonds). This is often necessary. Even when the same security is used, there may be differences in maturity dates so that a perfect hedge is difficult to establish.

Many financial managers prefer **partial hedges** to complete hedges. They are willing to take away part of the risk but not all of it. Others prefer no hedge at all because it locks in their position. While a hedge ensures them against loss, it precludes the possibility of an abnormal gain.

Nevertheless, in a risk-averse financial market environment, most financial managers can gain by hedging their position as described in the many examples in this section. Companies such as Burlington Northern, Eastman Kodak, and McDonald's have established reputations for just such actions. Others have not yet joined the movement because of a lack of appreciation or understanding of the highly innovative financial futures market. Much of this will change with the passage of time.

Options as Well as Futures

www.cboe.com

In late 1982, many exchanges began offering options on financial instruments and commodities. For example, the Chicago Board Options Exchange began listing put and call options on Treasury bonds. Also, the American Stock Exchange started trading options on Treasury bills and Treasury notes, and the Philadelphia Exchange offered foreign currency options. The Chicago Board of Trade, the Chicago Mercantile Exchange, and other exchanges have also added options. The relationship, similarities, and dissimilarities between option contracts and futures contracts are given much greater attention in the following chapter. For now it suffices to say that the futures contract requires an initial margin, which can be parlayed into large profits or immediately wiped out, whereas an option requires the payment of an option premium, which represents the full extent of an option purchaser's liability. In Chapter 17 we also see there are options to purchase futures, which combine the elements of both types of contracts.

Interest-Rate Swaps

No chapter relating to hedging interest-rate risk would be complete without a discussion of the latest instrument, the **interest-rate swap.**

The basic premise of interest-rate swaps is that one party is able to trade one type of risk exposure to another party, and both parties are able to rebalance their portfolios with less risk. For example, Bank A may be obligated to pay a fixed rate on a $100,000 certificate of deposit (CD) for the next five years. The bank is fearful that rates may go down and that it will be paying more on the CD than it will be receiving on loans. Under these circumstances, Bank A may try to find a "counterparty" who has the opposite type of problem. Perhaps Company B is borrowing money from a finance company at a variable rate and is fearful that rates will go up. Assume it has a $100,000 loan that is also due over the next five years.

Under these circumstances, Bank A will agree to pay Company B a variable rate on a hypothetical $100,000 of principal (referred to as notational principal).[7] In return, Company B will agree to pay Bank A a fixed rate on the same hypothetical principal. Both parties have used this swap agreement to eliminate their risk. Let's see how.

Because Bank A is paying a variable rate and receiving a fixed rate, if rates go down (its original fear), it will come out ahead on the swap agreement. Let's say rates start out at 8 percent (fixed and variable), but variable rates go down to 5 percent. Bank A will receive a net payment of $3,000 from Company B on the hypothetical principal:

$100,000 Hypothetical Principal	
Bank A pays variable (5%)	$5,000
Company B pays fixed (8%)	8,000
Net payment of B to A	$3,000

The swap agreement has effectively protected Bank A against lower interest-rate exposure that it has with the customer who owns the $100,000 CD. It has achieved this through an entirely unrelated interest-rate swap agreement with Company B.

At the same time, Company B has protected itself against its original fear that interest rates will go up. For example, if interest rates go from 8 percent to 11 percent, it will make $3,000 on the interest-rate swap with Bank A:

$100,000 Hypothetical Principal	
Bank A pays variable (11%)	$11,000
Company B pays fixed (8%)	8,000
Net payment of A to B	$ 3,000

---

[7] There is no principal actually put up. The $100,000 is merely used to keep score on who owes whom and is referred to as "notational principal."

This $3,000 profit will offset the exposure that company B has on its loan with the finance company. It has also achieved its goal through an interest-rate swap agreement with Bank A.

We have presented the most basic type of swap agreement (although you may not think so!). The point is that interest-rate swap agreements are not, initially, as structured as are futures and options contracts (contract months, strike prices, etc.). The counterparties can start out with a blank piece of paper and put together any kind of deal they desire. Major financial institutions such as Goldman Sachs, JPMorgan Chase, and CS/First Boston often serve as facilitators or dealers in bringing parties together for a transaction.

exploring the web

Website	Comment
www.cme.com	Chicago Mercantile Exchange
www.cbot.com	Chicago Board of Trade
www.liffe.com	London International Financial Futures and Options Exchange
www.kcbt.com	Kansas City Board of Trade
www.mgex.com	Minneapolis Grain Exchange
www.nyce.com	New York Board of Trade

Summary

In this chapter, we broke down the commodities futures market into traditional commodities (such as grains, livestock, and meat) and financial futures primarily in currencies and interest rates.

A commodities futures contract is an agreement that provides for the delivery of a specific amount of a commodity at a designated time in the future. It is not intended that the purchaser of a contract take actual possession of the goods but, rather, that he or she reverse or close out the contract before delivery is due. The same is true for the seller.

Primary participants in the commodities market include both speculators and hedgers. We first examine speculators. A speculator buys a commodities contract (goes long) or sells a commodities contract (goes short) because he believes he can anticipate the direction in which the market is going to move. A hedger buys or sells a commodities futures contract to protect an underlying position he or she might have in the actual commodity.

Many commodity futures exchanges provide areas where buyers and sellers can negotiate cash (spot) prices. The cash price is the actual dollar paid for the immediate delivery of the goods. Near-term futures prices and cash prices tend to approximate each other.

Currency and interest rate futures represent important financial futures. Although these markets only came into existence in the 1970s, they have seen explosive growth. The contract on financial futures is very similar to that on basic, traditional commodities; only the items traded and units of measurement are different.

Currency futures relate to many different currencies and enable financial managers to hedge their position in foreign markets. There is also active participation by speculators.

Interest-rate futures cover Treasury bonds, Treasury bills, Treasury notes, certificates of deposit, and similar items.

In the current environment of volatile interest rates, interest-rate futures offer an excellent opportunity to hedge dangerous interest-rate risks. Possible hedgers include corporate financial officers, pension fund managers, mortgage bankers, and commercial bankers.

Key Words and Concepts

cash or spot prices 452
cross hedge 458
financial futures 453
futures contract 444
hedge 444
interest-rate swap 459
margin maintenance requirements 448
partial hedges 458
settle price 456

Discussion Questions

1. What is a futures contract?
2. Do you have to take delivery or deliver the commodity if you are a party to a futures contract?
3. Explain what hedging is.
4. Why is there substantial leverage in commodity investments?
5. What are the basic categories of items traded on the commodity exchanges?
6. What group has primary regulatory responsibility for the activities of the commodity exchanges?
7. How does the concept of margin on a commodities contract differ from that of margin on a stock purchase?
8. Indicate some factors that might influence the price of wheat in the commodities market.
9. What is meant by a daily trading limit on a commodities contract?
10. Refer to Table 16–5 on page 451, and explain the quotation for July 2004 corn on the Chicago Board of Trade (CBT).
11. How does the cash market differ from the futures market for commodities?
12. What are the three main categories of financial futures? Which two are discussed in this chapter?
13. How does the currency futures market differ from the foreign exchange market?
14. Describe the Treasury bonds that are part of the futures contract that trades on the Chicago Board of Trade (size of units, maturity, assumed initial interest rate).
15. How can using the financial futures markets for interest rates and foreign exchange help financial managers through hedging? Briefly explain, and give one example of each.
16. Explain how interest-rate swaps can reduce risks for the counterparties.

Problems

Gain on commodities contract

1. You purchase a 5,000-bushel contract for corn at $2.40 per bushel with an initial margin requirement of 8 percent. The price goes up to $2.49 in one month. What are your percentage of profit and the annualized gain?

Gain on commodities contract

2. An investor purchases a 25,000-pound contract for copper at $1.10 per pound with an initial margin requirement of 6 percent. The price goes up to $1.14 in three months. What are the percentage of profit and the annualized gain?

Loss on commodities contract

3. An investor purchases a 50,000-pound contract for cotton at $0.68 per pound with an initial margin requirement of 6 percent. The price goes down to $0.65 after a year. What are the dollar and percent losses?

Gain or loss on commodities contract

4. Alex Rodriguez purchases a 5,000 troy ounce contract on silver at $6.00 an ounce. At the same time he purchases a 112,000 pound sugar contract at .191 cents a pound. If the price of silver goes down to $5.94 at the same time the price of sugar goes up to .196 cents, will Alex have an overall net gain or loss?

Hedging

5. Farmer William Cropley anticipates taking 100,000 bushels of oats to the market in four months. The current cash price for oats is $1.29. He can sell a four-month futures contract for oats at $1.33. He decides to sell ten 5,000-bushel futures contracts at that price. Assume in four months when Farmer Cropley takes the oats to market and also closes out the futures contracts (buys them back), the price of oats has tumbled to $1.15.
   a. What is his total loss in value over the four months on the actual oats he produced and took to market?
   b. How much did his hedge in the futures market generate in gains?
   c. What is his overall net loss considering the answer in part *a* and the partial hedge in part *b*?

Hedging

eXcel

6. The Midwestern Grain Miller's Corporation anticipates the need to purchase 70,000 bushels of wheat in six months to use in its products. The current cash price for wheat is $2.80 a bushel. A six-month futures contract for wheat can be purchased at $2.84.
   a. Explain why Midwestern Grain Miller's Corporation might need to purchase futures contracts to hedge their position.
   b. To attempt to completely hedge their exposure, how many contracts will they need to purchase? (Consult Table 16–3 on page 447 for the size of the trading units in a contract.)
   c. If the price of wheat ends up at $3.06 per bushel after six months, by how much will the actual cost of 70,000 bushels of wheat have gone up?
   d. After the futures contracts are closed out (sold) at $3.06 also, what will be the gain on the futures contracts?
   e. Considering the answers to parts *c* and *d,* what is Midwestern Grain Miller's net position?
   f. Given the number of wheat futures contracts Midwestern controls, what is the most it can lose in the futures markets on any given day? You may want to consult Table 16–4 on page 450 for part of the answer.

Margin maintenance

7. With a 5,000-bushel contract for $15,000, assume the margin requirement is $1,000 and the maintenance margin is 70 percent of the margin requirement. How much would the price per bushel have to fall before additional margin is required?

Chapter 16 Commodities and Financial Futures

Generating margin

8. If contracts are written on a 5,000-bushel basis requiring $1,000 of margin and you control four contracts, how much would the price per bushel have to change to generate enough profit to purchase an additional contract?

Pyramiding

9. Referring to problem 8, how many contracts would need to be controlled to generate enough profit for a new margin contract if the price changed by only 1 cent per bushel?

Currency futures

10. You purchase a futures contract in euros for $157,000. The trading unit is 125,000 euros.
    a. What is the ratio of cents to euros in this contract? (Divide the dollar contract size by the size of the trading unit.)
    b. Assume you are required to put up $3,900 in margin and the euro increases by 3 cents (per euro). What will be your return as a percentage of margin?

Treasury bond futures

11. Boone Securities buys a $100,000 par value, June Treasury bond contract on the Chicago Board of Trade (CBT) at the quoted settle price in Table 16–8 on page 455.
    a. What is the dollar value of the contract? Use the settle price in your calculation.
    b. There is an initial margin requirement of $2,565 and a margin maintenance requirement of $1,900. If an interest-rate increase causes the bond contract to go down by 0.9 percent of par value, will Boone be called on to put up more margin?
    c. If an interest-rate decrease causes the bond contract to go up by 0.7 percent of par value, what will be the percent return on margin?

Hedging by corporate treasurer

12. The treasurer of the Atlas Corporation, Wanda Zinke, is going to bring a $10 million issue to the market in 45 days. It will be a 25-year issue. The interest-rate environment is highly volatile, and even though interest rates are currently 10¼ percent, there is a fear that interest rates will be up to 11 percent by the time the bonds get to the market.
    a. If interest rates go up by ¾ point, what is the present value of the extra interest this increase will cost the corporation? Use an 11 percent discount rate and disregard tax considerations.
    b. Assume the corporation is going to short September Treasury bonds as quoted at the top of Table 16–8 on page 455. Based on the settle price, how many contracts must the corporation sell to equal the $10 million exposed position? Round to the nearest whole number of contracts.
    c. Based on your answer in part b, if Treasury bond prices increase by 2.8 percent of par value in each contract in response to an unexpected ½ point decline in interest rates over the next 45 days, what will be the total dollar loss on the futures contracts?

Hedging by corporate treasurer

13. Should the treasurer of the Atlas Corporation think she has failed in her tasks if the circumstance in part c of problem 12 occurs?

Critical Thought Case—Focus on Ethics

Milt Samuals joined Garrett Construction Company in 1998 in the budgeting section of the corporate treasurer's office. He worked with a team of two accountants and a senior vice president of finance to provide pro forma budgets and financial statements. Although his undergraduate degree was in finance with an emphasis on investments, he still felt he was acquiring experience with his budgeting work. Nevertheless, he was quite excited when he learned that he was being shifted to a new department in the treasurer's office in which he would share responsibility for managing the excess funds of the corporation as well as participate in the hedging function that the corporation undertook to offset interest-rate exposure.

By 2003, he had moved to the top position in the hedging area. Samuals had the major responsibility for hedging against interest-rate increases that might take place from the time Garrett Construction Company agreed to undertake a project until the time it was completed. The period often ran from 6 to 12 months. Samuals used financial derivatives such as interest-rate futures and swaps to accomplish his purpose. Most often, he employed Treasury bond futures. He would sell (short) them to protect against interest-rate increases. If interest rates went up, the market value of the bonds covered under the contract would go down, and he could close out or cover his position at a profit. As he explained it, he would establish the sales price at approximately $100,000, and if interest rates went up, he could buy them back at perhaps $95,000. The $5,000 profit he made on the derivatives would help cover the added interest expense that Garrett Construction Company experienced on its loan at the bank as a result of increasing interest rates. Of course, if interest rates went down, he would lose money on the futures contract, but that would be offset by the lower interest the company would pay. Basically, he was neutralizing the company's position regardless of what happened to interest rates. If the company had a large amount of interest rate exposure, Samuals might engage in 10 or 20 contracts at one time.

Although Samuals was acquiring expertise in his hedging function, he eventually found himself becoming somewhat bored with his normal hedging activities. While he continued to hedge the company's interest-rate exposure, he also began speculating on interest-rate movements for the company. These contracts had nothing to do with the company's interest-rate exposure. For example, if he thought interest rates were going down, he would buy Treasury bond futures contracts. If rates did go down, the value of the bonds covered under the contract would go up, and he would sell (cover) his position at a nice profit. Because only a small amount of margin (cash) was involved, he could really use leverage to establish spectacular gains (though sometimes there were losses).

For the most part, Samuals was doing well, and he could not wait to tell Roger Garrett, the president of the company, about the new activity he had decided to undertake and how well he was doing for the company. He felt certain an added bonus was coming.

Question

1. If you were Roger Garrett, would you be inclined to reward Milt Samuals with an added bonus?

Web Exercise

We will examine the futures contracts for a typical commodity. Go to **www.cbot.com**.

1. Click on "Soybeans."
2. Click on "Settlement."
3. Write down the settle prices for the first six contracts listed on the left. Remember to move the decimal point two places to the left to go from dollars to cents.

4. Do the pattern of settle prices appear to be upward or downward with the passage of time? What might this tell you about anticipated future price movements for soybeans?
5. Under the "Product News" column on the same page, see if you can find a story that validates the pattern shown in question 4. If you can, write a one-sentence summary. If not, bypass this question. (Appropriate news stories are not always available.)

Note: From time to time, companies redesign their websites, and occasionally a topic we have listed may have been deleted, updated, or moved into a different location. Most websites have a "site map" or "site index" listed on a different page. If you click on the site map or site index, you will be introduced to a table of contents that should aid you in finding the topic you are looking for.

The Wall Street Journal Project

Using *The Wall Street Journal,* find the settle (closing) price for the nearest term contract (the one listed first) for the following commodities and financial futures. To find the placement of the quotes, go to "Commodities" in Section C and look up the values under "Futures." When you are writing down the prices of the commodities in group A, move the decimal price two places to the left; that is, 132½ would translate to $1.3250.

Group A*
1. Wheat (CBT)
2. Pork bellies (CME)
3. Coffee (CSCE)
4. Copper—high (CMX)
5. Gold (CMX)

After you have written down the quote for the nearest term contract, indicate whether contracts in the future have a higher or lower value for each commodity. What might this tell you about investor expectations concerning the future price of the commodity?

Group B
Once again write down the settle (closing) price for the nearest term contract. For the financial futures in this group, you do *not* need to move the decimal point two places to the left. However, for the Treasury bonds, use the procedures in the chapter shown under "Interest-Rate Futures" to properly state the quote.

1. Euro/US Dollar (CME)
2. British pound (CME)
3. Treasury bonds (CBT)

After you have written down the quote for the nearest term contract, indicate whether contracts in the future have a higher or lower value. Indicate what this might tell you about investor expectations for each contract.

---

*The item in parentheses is the exchange the commodity trades on. The full name of the exchange can be found at the bottom of the "Commodities" page in the "Exchange Abbreviation" box in the upper left corner.

Selected References

Trading Strategy and Hedging

Fan, Rong; Anurag Gupta; and Peter Ritchen. "Hedging in the Possible Presence of Unspanned Stochastic Volatility: Evidence from Swaption Markets." *The Journal of Finance,* October 2003, pp. 2219–48.

Foreign Currency Futures

Nesbitt, Stephen L. "Currency Hedging Plans for Plan Sponsors." *Financial Analysts Journal,* March–April 1991, pp. 73–81.

Interest-Rate Swaps

Filler, R. "Credit Risks and Costs in Interest-Rate Swaps." *Journal of Cash Management,* January–February 1993, pp. 38–41.

Kim, S. H., and G. D. Koppenhaver. "An Empirical Analysis of Bank Interest-Rate Swaps." *Journal of Financial Services Research,* February 1993, pp. 57–72.

Usmen, Nilufer. "Currency Swaps, Financial Arbitrage, and Default Risk." *Financial Management,* Summer 1994, pp. 43–56.

Returns on Futures

Fabozzi, Frank J.; Christopher K. Ma; and James E. Briley. "Holiday Trading in Futures Markets." *Journal of Finance,* March 1994, pp. 307–24.

Commodity Futures

Crain, Susan J., and Jae Ha Lee. "Volatility in Wheat Spot and Futures Markets, 1950–1993: Government Farm Programs, Seasonality and Causality." *The Journal of Finance,* March 1996, pp. 325–43.

Géczy, Christopher; Bernadette A. Minton; and Catherine Schrand. "Why Firms Use Currency Derivatives." *The Journal of Finance,* September 2001, pp. 1323–54.

Jobman, Darrell. "Grains Depend on Weather and a Whole Lot More." *Futures,* June 2001, pp. 26–29.

Treasury Futures

Haushalter, David. "Why Hedge? Some Evidence from Oil and Gas Producers." *Journal of Applied Corporate Finance,* Winter 2001, pp. 87–92.

Murphy, Austin. "Hedging Fixed-Rate Preferred Stock Investments." *Journal of Applied Corporate Finance,* Spring 2001, pp. 80–89.

Shefrin, Hersh, and Meir Statman. "Behavioral Aspects of the Design of Financial Products." *Financial Management,* Summer 1993, pp. 123–34.

chapter seventeen

Stock Index Futures and Options

objectives

1. Understand the difference between derivatives on stock indexes and individual stocks.

2. Appreciate the role of derivatives in hedging and speculation.

3. Distinguish between futures and options and the consequences of using each.

4. Describe the importance of derivatives in forecasting future stock movements.

5. Explain how to design a hedge based on the volatility of a portfolio.

6. Describe specific examples of stock index hedging.

The Concept of Derivative Products
Trading Stock Index Futures
    Trading Cycle
    Margin Requirement
    Cash Settlement
    Basis
    Overall Features
Use of Stock Index Futures
    Speculation
    Hedging
    Arbitraging
Trading Stock Index Options
    Actual Trade in the S&P 100 Index
Hedging with Stock Index Options
Options on Stock Index Futures

Back in Chapter 15, you learned about the use of put and call options to speculate or hedge positions in individual stocks. But for those who have multiple stocks in their portfolio, this can be an expensive and time-consuming process. Wouldn't it be easier for you just to speculate or hedge using a market index such as the Standard and Poor's 500 Stock Index? That way you could take a major position with just one transaction. How did all this get started?

In February 1982, the Kansas City Board of Trade began trading futures on a stock index, the Value Line Index. This event ushered in a new era of futures and options trading related to equities.

TABLE 17–1 Stock Index Futures (January 6, 2004)

```
                                                    LIFETIME     OPEN
         OPEN    HIGH    LOW   SETTLE   CHG    HIGH    LOW      INT
Index Futures
DJ Industrial Average (CBT)-$10 x index
Mar     10521   10530   10480  10514    -6    10530   8580    32,295
Est vol 5,421; vol Mon 7,756; open int 32,648, +317.
Idx prl: Hi 10549.18; Lo 10499.85; Close 10538.66, -5.41.
Mini DJ Industrial Average (CBT)-$5 x index
Mar     10522   10528   10479  10514    -6    10528   9069    33,854
Vol Tue 55,297; open int 34,665, +1,136.
DJ-AIG Commodity Index (CBT)-$100 x index
Jan     447.4   447.4   447.1  446.1   -0.9   447.4   418.7    2,581
Est vol 2; vol Mon 104; open int 2,581, +76.
Idx prl: Hi 142.693; Lo 139.932; Close 140.078, -.342.
S&P 500 Index (CME)-$250 x index
Mar    111970  112340  111580 112200   200   123950  77700   589,757
June   111850  112220  111700 112120   200   112220  78000    10,778
Est vol 41,109; vol Mon 46,766; open int 603,263, +386.
Idx prl: Hi 1124.46; Lo 1118.44; Close 1123.67, +1.45.
Mini S&P 500 (CME)-$50 x index
Mar    111975  112350  111550 112200   200   112350  98650   414,061
Vol Tue 609,689; open int 414,474, +38,013.
S&P Midcap 400 (CME)-$500 x index
Mar     581.00  583.00  579.10 581.50   .50   583.00  559.75   15,860
Est vol 610; vol Mon 838; open int 15,861, +57.
Idx prl: Hi 582.95; Lo 579.71; Close 581.86, +1.25.
Nasdaq 100 (CME)-$100 x index
Mar    149500  150800  148950 150450   900   150800 148950   75,709
Est vol 9,540; vol Mon 12,414; open int 75,759, +2,468.
Idx prl: Hi 1504.47; Lo 1486.59; Close 1501.26, +4.68.
Mini Nasdaq 100 (CME)-$20 x index
Mar     1494.5  1508.0  1489.0 1504.5   9.0   1508.0  1307.0  187,298
Vol Tue 272,004; open int 187,731, +23,117.
```

Source: *The Wall Street Journal*, January 7, 2004, p. C15. Reprinted by permission of *The Wall Street Journal*, © 2004 by Dow Jones & Company, Inc. All Rights Reserved Worldwide.

TABLE 17–2 Value of Contracts

	March Settle Price	Multiplier	Contract Value
Dow Jones Industrial Average	10,514.00	10	$105,140
Mini Dow Jones Industrial Average	10,514.00	5	52,570
S&P 500 Index	1,122.00	250	280,050
Mini S&P 500 Index	1,122.00	50	56,100
S&P MidCap 400	581.50	500	290,750
Nasdaq 100	1,504.50	100	150,450
Mini Nasdaq 100	1,504.50	20	30,090

If the investor thinks the market is going up, he will purchase a futures contract. If he thinks the market is going down, he will sell a futures contract and hope the market will decline so that the contract can be closed out (repurchased) at a lower value than the sales price. Selling futures contracts can also be used to hedge a large stock portfolio. If the market goes down, what you lose on your portfolio you recoup in your futures contract.

In the example in Table 17–2, the investor has seven contracts from which to choose. Although not covered here, there are also futures contracts on the Russell 2000, the Nikkei 225, and other indexes.

We shall direct our attention for now to the S&P 500 Index futures contract (although the same basic principles would apply to other contracts).

Part of the material from Table 17–1 that pertains to the S&P 500 Index futures contract is reproduced in Table 17–3 so we can examine a number of key features related to the contract.

TABLE 17–3 S&P Index Futures Contract (CME), 500 Multiplier (January 6, 2004)

	Open	High	Low	Settle	Change
March	1,119.70*	1,123.40	1,115.80	1,122.00	2.00
June	1,118.50	1,122.20	1,117.00	1,122.20	2.00
September	—	—	—	—	—
December	—	—	—	—	—

Value of S&P 500 Stock Index (January 6, 2004), 1,123.67.

* Note the "assumed" decimal point in previously presented Table 17–1 for the S&P 500 Index is moved two places to the left.

Trading Cycle

The trading cycle in the table is made up of the four months of March, June, September, and December. The last day of trading for a contract is the third Thursday of the ending month.

Margin Requirement

Application Example

www.cme.com

As previously mentioned, the basic margin requirement for buying or selling an S&P 500 futures contract on the Chicago Mercantile Exchange was $20,000 in 2004. Based on the March 2004 contract value (found on the third line in Table 17–2) this represents a margin requirement of 7.14 percent ($20,000/$280,050).

There is also a margin maintenance requirement of $16,000. Thus, if the initial margin or equity in the account falls to this level, the investor will be required to supply sufficient cash or securities to bring the account back up to $20,000. A drop from $20,000 to $16,000 represents $4,000. Because the contract trades at 250 times the index, a decline of 16 points in the S&P contract value would cause a loss of $4,000. The investor would be asked to put up that amount in new funds.

If the investor can prove he is hedging a long position, the margin requirement will be less. For example, if an investor owns a portfolio of stocks that roughly equals the value of the index futures contract ($280,000 in this case), the initial margin requirement is reduced. Since a hedged position is not as risky as a speculative position, less initial margin is required.[7]

---

[7] It should be mentioned that on a hedged position, the margin maintenance requirement is the same as the original margin.

the real world of investing

The S&P Is Not Your Father's Index

Just as Buick and Chevrolet claim their latest models are not to be confused with "your father's car," similar claims are made for the Standard & Poor's 500 Index. This is of potential interest because the S&P 500 Index is the most popular venue on which to trade futures contracts.

Thomas McManus, U.S. investment strategist at NatWest Securities, was quoted in *The Wall Street Journal* as saying, "The S&P 500 is higher growth, more global, less cyclical, and more diversified than it has ever been and therefore deserves a higher (price-to-earnings) multiple."* While the last point about higher multiple is subject to debate, the changing characteristics of the Index are not.

The biggest change has been the inclusion of more technology and financial firms, industries that have shown a particularly strong performance during the 1990s. Between 1989 and 2003, the two industries combined have grown from 14 percent of the S&P 500 Index to 34 percent. While much of the growth can be attributed to market value gains that have outstripped the rest of the market, this is not the only explanation. For example, the number of financial firms represented in the S&P 500 has grown from 40 in the late 1980s to 72 in 2004. Furthermore, Microsoft was not added to the S&P 500 Index until 1994, but in mid-2004 represented 2.5 percent of the value of the index.

The changes are not only in technology and finance, but in many other areas as well. Eighty-two changes in the Index have taken place since 1995. There has been a deemphasis on public utilities, energy, steel, and old-style retail establishments and a renewed emphasis on health care, multinationals, entertainment, as well as technology and finance.

The S&P 500 Index represents a shinier, faster (in terms of growth) model than it was in your father's day. The same can also be said of the Dow Jones Industrial Average, which in early 2001 dropped Woolworth, Bethlehem Steel, Texaco, and Westinghouse Electric in favor of more widely traded stocks as represented by Hewlett-Packard, Johnson & Johnson, Travelers Group, and Wal-Mart stores.

*Greg Ip, "S&P 500 Is Not Your Father's Index," *The Wall Street Journal*, July 29, 1997, pp. C1, C29.

Cash Settlement

In traditional commodity futures markets, the potential for physical delivery exists. One who is trading in wheat could actually decide to deliver the commodity to close out the contract. As discussed in Chapter 16, this happens only a very small percentage of the time, but it is possible. The stock index futures market, on the other hand, is purely a **cash-settlement** market. There is never the implied potential for future delivery of the Standard & Poor's 500 Stock Index. An investor simply closes out (or reverses) his position before the settlement date. If he does not, his account is automatically credited with his gains or debited with his losses, and the transaction is completed.[8]

One of the advantages of a cash-settlement arrangement is that it makes it impossible for a "short squeeze" to develop. A short squeeze occurs when an investor attempts to corner a market in a commodity, such as silver, so that it is not possible for those who have short positions to make physical delivery. Clearly, with a cash-settlement position, this can never happen.

---

[8] Actually, the account is adjusted daily to reflect the gains and losses. This is known as marking the customer's position to market.

Basis

The term **basis** represents the difference between the stock index futures price and the value of the actual underlying index.[9] Assume the following for the S&P 500 contract for September and December of a given year. (This is a hypothetical example.)

	September	December
Stock index futures price	1125.10	1137.60
Actual underlying index	1120.00	1130.00
Basis	5.10	7.60

In this example, the basis indicates that a premium is being paid over the actual value, and furthermore, the premium expands with the passage of time. This is generally thought to be a positive sign. If the index futures price is below the actual underlying index, there is a negative basis.

An excellent discussion of the ability of stock index futures to forecast the actual underlying index is presented in an article by Zeckhauser and Niederhoffer in the *Financial Analysts Journal*.[10] A part of their thesis is that futures contracts move instantaneously to reflect market conditions, whereas the actual underlying index moves more slowly. If the market makes an important move, some of the stocks that are part of the actual underlying index will not yet have reacted. Thus, initial, significant, and potentially predictive information may be found in the futures market quotes.

Also, at times, futures or options markets stay open later or begin trading earlier than the actual underlying stock markets. This can be very beneficial not only in providing lead time information on market movements, but also in giving the trader an opportunity to take a position before the opening or after the closing of the stock market.

Overall Features

Many of the important features related to stock index futures on the various exchanges are presented in Table 17–4 on the next page. This table can serve as a ready reference guide to trading commodities in various markets.

Use of Stock Index Futures

There are a number of actual and potential users of stock index futures. As is true of most futures contracts, the motivation may be either speculation or the opportunity to hedge.

---

[9] The same concept can be applied to other types of futures contracts.
[10] Richard Zeckhauser and Victor Niederhoffer, "The Performance of Market Index Futures Contracts," *Financial Analysts Journal,* January–February 1983, pp. 59–65.

TABLE 17-4 Specifications for Stock Index Futures Contracts

Index and Exchange	Index	Contract Size and Value (in dollars)	Contract Months
Dow Jones Industrial Average Chicago Board of Trade (CBOT)	Value of 30 stocks in DJIA	10 × DJIA	March June September December
S&P 500 Index Index & Options Market (IOM) of Chicago Mercantile Exchange (CME)	Value of 500 selected stocks on NYSE, AMEX, and Nasdaq, weighted to reflect market value of issues	250 × S&P 500	March June September December
Mini S&P 500 Index Index & Options Market (IOM) of Chicago Mercantile Exchange (CME)	Same as above	50 × S&P 500 Index	March June September December
S&P MidCap 400 Index & Options Market (IOM) of Chicago Mercantile Exchange (CME)	Index of 400 medium-sized stocks with values from $1.2 to $9 billion, weighted to reflect market value of issues	50 × S&P MidCap 400	March June September December
Nikkei 225 Stock Average Index and Options Market (IOM) of Chicago Mercantile Exchange (CME)	Index of 225 Japanese stocks, weighted to reflect market value of issues	5 × Nikkei Stock Average	March June September December
Nasdaq 100 Stock Index Index and Options Market (IOM) of Chicago Mercantile Exchange (CME)	Index for the 100 largest stocks on the Nasdaq, weighted to reflect market value of issues	100 × Nasdaq 100 Stock Index	March June September December
Mini Nasdaq 100 Stock Index Index and Options Market (IOM) of Chicago Mercantile Exchange (CME)	Index for the 100 largest stocks on the Nasdaq, weighted to reflect market value of issues	20 × Nasdaq 100 Stock Index	March June September December

Speculation

The speculator may use stock index futures in an attempt to profit from major movements in the market. He or she may have developed a conviction about the next move in the market through fundamental or technical analysis. For example, those who utilize fundamental analysis may determine that P/E ratios are relatively low or that earnings performance should be extremely good in the next two quarters, so they wish to bet on the market moving upward. Market technicians might observe that a resistance or support position in the market is being penetrated and that it is time to take a position based on the anticipated consequences of that penetration.

While the market participant could put his or her money in individual stocks, it might be more efficient and less time consuming to simply invest in stock index futures. In buying futures on the S&P 500 Index, the investor is capturing the performance of 500 securities; with the S&P MidCap, 400 securities, and so on.

Two types of risks are associated with investments: systematic or market-related risks, and unsystematic or firm-related risks. Because many believe only systematic risk is assumed to be rewarded in an efficient capital market environment (unsystematic risk can be diversified away), the investor may wish to be exposed only to systematic risk. Stock index futures represent an efficient approach to only taking systematic, market-related risk.

Another advantage of stock index futures is that there is less manipulative action and insider trading than with individual securities. While it is possible (though not legal) for "informed" insider trading to cause an individual stock to move dramatically in the short term, such activity is not as likely for an entire index. This advantage, however, should not be overstated. Unusual trading activity of stock index futures comes under the scrutiny of federal regulators from time to time.

Stock index futures also offer leverage potential. A $280,050 S&P futures contract can be established for $20,000 in margin and with no interest on the balance.[11] If you were investing $280,050 in actual stocks through margin, you would have to put up a minimum of $140,025 (50 percent) in margin and pay interest on the balance. The margin requirement is still considerably lower than that on an outright stock purchase. Also, the commissions on a stock index futures contract are minuscule in comparison with commissions on securities of comparable value.

Application Example

Volatility and Profits or Losses Before the market crash of 1987, the average daily move on the S&P 500 Index was approximately 0.50 (one-half point per day). It has been moving up ever since. In the late 1990s and early 2000s, the daily move has been in the seven-point range. A seven-point upward move in an S&P 500 futures contract (say, from 1120 to 1127) means a daily gain of $1,750 (recall the contract has a multiplier of 250). With a margin requirement of $20,000, that is an 8.75 percent, one-day return on your money:

$$\begin{array}{rl} \$7 & \text{Gain on futures contract} \\ \times\ 250 & \text{Multiplier} \\ \hline \$\ 1{,}750 & \text{Dollar gain} \\ \$20{,}000 & \text{Margin} \\ 8.75\% & \text{Percent gain} \end{array}$$

This translates into a 3,193.75 percent annualized return (8.75% × 365). By contrast, if the $20,000 were invested in a 5 percent certificate of deposit, only $2.74 in interest would accrue on a daily basis. The difference here, of course, is that the $1,750 average daily movement related to the index may be up or down, whereas the $2.74 is only up.

When a stock index futures contract starts to run against an investor, he or she can bail out and cut losses. If the contract value is going down rapidly, the investor will be continually called on to put up more margin as the margin position is being depleted. That puts tremendous pressure on the investor. He or

---

[11] As mentioned in Chapter 16, margin on futures contracts merely represents good-faith money, and there is never any interest on the balance.

she must decide whether to put up more margin and hold the position in hopes of a comeback or close out the position and take a loss.

Not all speculation in stock index futures must necessarily be based on the market going up. You can also speculate that the market will go down. You simply sell a contract with the anticipation of repurchasing it at a lower price later. Margin requirements are similar, and gains come from a declining market and losses from an increasing market. If the index goes up rapidly, the investor will be called on to put up more margin.[12]

Hedging

Up to now our discussion of stock index futures has mainly related to speculating (or anticipating the next major move in the market). Perhaps the most important use of stock index futures is for hedging purposes. An investor who has a large diversified portfolio may think the market is about to decline. A portfolio manager who suffers a 20 percent decline in his or her portfolio actually requires a 25 percent gain from the new lower base to break even.

A portfolio manager faced with the belief that a declining market is imminent may be inclined to sell part or all of the portfolio. The question becomes, is this realistic? First, large transaction costs are associated with selling part or all of a portfolio and then repurchasing it later. Second, it may be difficult to liquidate a position in certain securities that are thinly traded. For example, a mutual fund or pension fund that tries to sell 10,000 shares of a small over-the-counter stock may initially find a price quote of $25 but only be able to close out its relatively large position at $23.50. A $15,000 loss would be suffered. Furthermore, the fund might find the same type of problem in reacquiring the stock after the overall market decline is over. This problem could be multiplied by 25 or 50 times, depending on the number of securities in the portfolio. Although larger, more liquid holdings would be easier to trade, significant transactions costs are still involved.

A more easily executed defensive strategy would be to sell one or more stock index futures as a hedge against the portfolio. If the stock market does go down, the loss on the portfolio will be partially or fully offset by the profit on the stock index futures contract(s) because they are bought back at a lower price than the initial sales price.

As an example, assume a corporate pension fund has $20 million in stock holdings. The investment committee for the fund is very bearish in its outlook, fearing that the overall market could go down by 20 percent in the next few months and a $4 million loss would be suffered. The pension fund decides to fully hedge its position.

The fund is going to use S&P 500 Index futures for the hedge. We shall assume the futures can be sold for 1,120, with a settlement date in three months. Before the number of contracts for execution is determined, the portfolio manager must consider the relative volatility of his portfolio. If the portfolio is more volatile than the market, this must be factored into the decision-making process. As discussed in Chapter 7, the beta coefficient indicates how volatile a stock is relative to the market. If a stock has a beta of 1.20, it is 20 percent more volatile than the market. We shall assume the $20 million portfolio discussed above has

---

[12] The margin maintenance requirements are similar to those on a long position.

a weighted average beta of 1.15 (that is, the portfolio is 15 percent more volatile than the market).

To determine the number of contracts necessary to hedge the position, we use the following formula:

$$\frac{\$ \text{ Value of portfolio}}{\$ \text{ Value of contract}} \times \frac{\text{Weighted beta}}{\text{of portfolio}} = \frac{\text{Number of}}{\text{contracts}} \quad (17\text{–}1)$$

In the example under discussion, we would show:

$$\frac{\$20,000,000}{1,120 \times 250} \times 1.15 = \text{Number of contracts}$$

In the first term of the formula, the numerator is the size of the portfolio being hedged. The denominator is the size of each contract and, in this example, is found by multiplying the S&P futures contract value of 1,120 by 250. The first term is then multiplied by the weighted beta value of 1.15. The answer works out as:

$$\frac{\$20,000,000}{\$280,000} \times 1.15 = 71.42 \times 1.15 = 82 \text{ contracts (rounded)}$$

The portfolio can be effectively hedged with 82 contracts.

Assume the market does go down but only by 10 percent instead of the 20 percent originally anticipated. Let's demonstrate that the hedge has worked. Since the portfolio has a beta of 1.15, its decline would be 11.5 percent (10% × 1.15). With a $20 million portfolio, the loss would be $2.3 million. To offset this loss, we will have a gain on 82 contracts. The gain is shown as follows:

    1,120.00 S&P Index futures contract (sales price)
  − 112.00 Decline in price on the futures contract (10% × 1,120.00)
    1,008.00 Ending value (purchase price)

The 112.00 point decline on the index futures contract indicates the profit made on each contract.[13] They were sold for 1,120.00 and repurchased for 1,008.00. With 82 contracts, the profit on the stock index futures contracts was $2,296,000.

    $ 28,000 Profit per contract (112.00 × $250)
        × 82 Number of contracts
    $2,296,000 Total profit

The gain of approximately $2.3 million on the stock index futures contracts offsets the loss of $2.3 million on the portfolio. The small difference between the two values represents the fact that we rounded values. Actually, executing a perfect hedge may be further complicated by a number of other factors such as the lack of an appropriate index to match against the portfolio and the change in basis over time. Also, the portfolio may not move exactly in accordance with the beta. No doubt, many real-world factors can complicate any hedge.

While a stock index futures hedge offers the advantage of protecting against losses, it takes away the upside potential. If the market goes up by 10 percent instead of down, the gain on the portfolio may be wiped out by the loss on

---

[13] Note that the futures contract is assumed to move on a one-to-one basis with the market. The actual relationship may not be this precise.

the stock index futures contracts. The investor could be forced to buy back the futures contract for 10 percent more than the selling price. Because some portfolio managers are afraid of losing all their upside potential in a hedged position, they may wish to hedge less than 100 percent of their portfolio.

While the hedging procedure just described can be potentially beneficial to portfolio managers, it can be potentially detrimental to the market in general if overused. Actually, protecting a large portfolio against declines is sometimes referred to as **portfolio insurance.** It is potentially a good strategy, but what if many investors initiate their portfolio-insurance strategies at the same time? Perhaps they are worried because there has been an increase in the prime rate or a bad report on inflation. An overload of stock index futures sales hitting the market at the same time drives down not only stock index futures prices but the stocks in the indexes as well (such as those in the S&P 500 Stock Index). An overall panic can result. The chain reaction is that a whole new round of portfolio-insurance-induced sales is triggered.

Other Uses of Hedging   Hedging with stock index futures has a number of other uses besides attempting to protect the position of a long-term investment portfolio. These include the following.

Underwriter Hedge   As described in Chapter 10, the investment banker (underwriter) has a risk exposure from buying stock from the issuing corporation with the intention of reselling it in the public markets. If there is weakness during the distribution period, the potential resale price could fall below the purchase price, and the underwriter's profit would be wiped out. To protect against this market risk, the underwriter could sell stock index futures contracts. If the market goes down, presumably, the loss on the stock will be compensated for by the gain on the stock index futures contract as a result of being able to repurchase it at a lower price. This, of course, is not a perfect hedge. It is possible that the individual stock could go down while the market is going up, and losses on both the stock and stock index futures contract would occur (writing options directly against the stock might be more efficient, but in many cases such options are not available).

Specialist or Dealer Hedge   As indicated in Chapter 2, a specialist on an exchange or a dealer in the over-the-counter market buys and sells stocks for his own inventory for temporary holding. He may, at times, assume a larger temporary holding than desired, with all the risks associated with that exposure. Stock index futures can reduce the market (or systematic) risk, although the use of futures cannot reduce the specific risk associated with a security.

Retirement or Estate Hedge   As we move into the next two or three decades, large retirement funds will be accumulated from voluntary retirement plans. A retirement plan participant who has accumulated a large sum in an equity fund may feel a need to hedge his or her position in certain time periods in the economy (where liquidation is neither tax advantageous or possible). A futures contract may provide that hedge. Also, a person with responsibility for an estate may be locked into a portfolio during the period of probate (validation of the will process) and wish to hedge his or her position with a stock index futures contract.

Tax Hedge An investor may have accumulated a large return on a diversified portfolio in a given year. To maintain the profitable position but defer the taxable gains until the next year, futures contracts may be employed.

Arbitraging

While stock index futures started out as a major tool for speculating and hedging, they are now also widely used for arbitraging. Basically, an **arbitrage** is set up when a simultaneous trade (a buy and a sell) occurs in two different markets and a profit is locked in. Assume the S&P 500 Stock Index has a value of 1,120 based on the market value of all the stocks in the index. Also, assume the S&P 500 Stock Index futures contract, due to expire in two months, is selling for 1,125. There is a five-point positive basis between the futures contract and the underlying index. A sophisticated institutional investor may decide to arbitrage based on this difference. He or she will simultaneously sell a futures contract for 1,125 and buy a basket of stocks that matches[14] the S&P 500 Stock Index for 1,120. Because at expiration, the futures contract and underlying index will have the same value, a five-point profit is locked in at the time of arbitraging. For example, if at expiration, the S&P 500 Stock Index has a value of 1,118, a gain of seven will occur on the sale, and a loss of two will be associated with the purchase for a net profit of five. If thousands of such contracts are involved, the profits can be substantial, and the potential for losses in a true arbitrage is nonexistent.

As you might assume, index arbitraging is in the exclusive providence of wealthy, sophisticated investors. For this reason, many smaller investors are somewhat resentful of the process and claim it tends to disrupt the normal operations of the marketplace. While there is nothing inherently wrong with arbitraging and it may even make the markets more efficient, it is sometimes a target for criticism by regulators. This is because it involves the process of program trading, discussed earlier in the chapter.

Trading Stock Index Options

Stock index options also allow the market participant to speculate or hedge against major market movements, although there is no opportunity for arbitraging. Stock index options are similar in many respects to the standard put and call options on individual stocks discussed in Chapter 15. The purchaser of an option pays an initial premium and then closes out the option at a given price in the future. One essential difference between stock index options and options on individual securities is that in the former case, there is only a cash settlement of the position, whereas in the latter case (individual securities), you can force the option writer to deliver the securities.

There are stock index options on the Dow Jones Industrial Average, the S&P 500, Nasdaq 100, Russell 2000, and other indexes. They all trade on the Chicago

---

[14] Actually, arbitraging has become sufficiently sophisticated through mathematics and computer analysis that all 500 stocks do not actually have to be purchased. Perhaps 10 or 15 key stocks bought in large quantities will be sufficient to adequately represent the S&P 500 Index. Commissions on such transactions tend to be extremely small. Mutual funds and exchange traded funds that replicate the S&P 500 index can also be purchased.

Part 5 Derivative Products

TABLE 17–5 S&P 500 Stock Index Options (January 6, 2004 Closing Index = 1123.67)

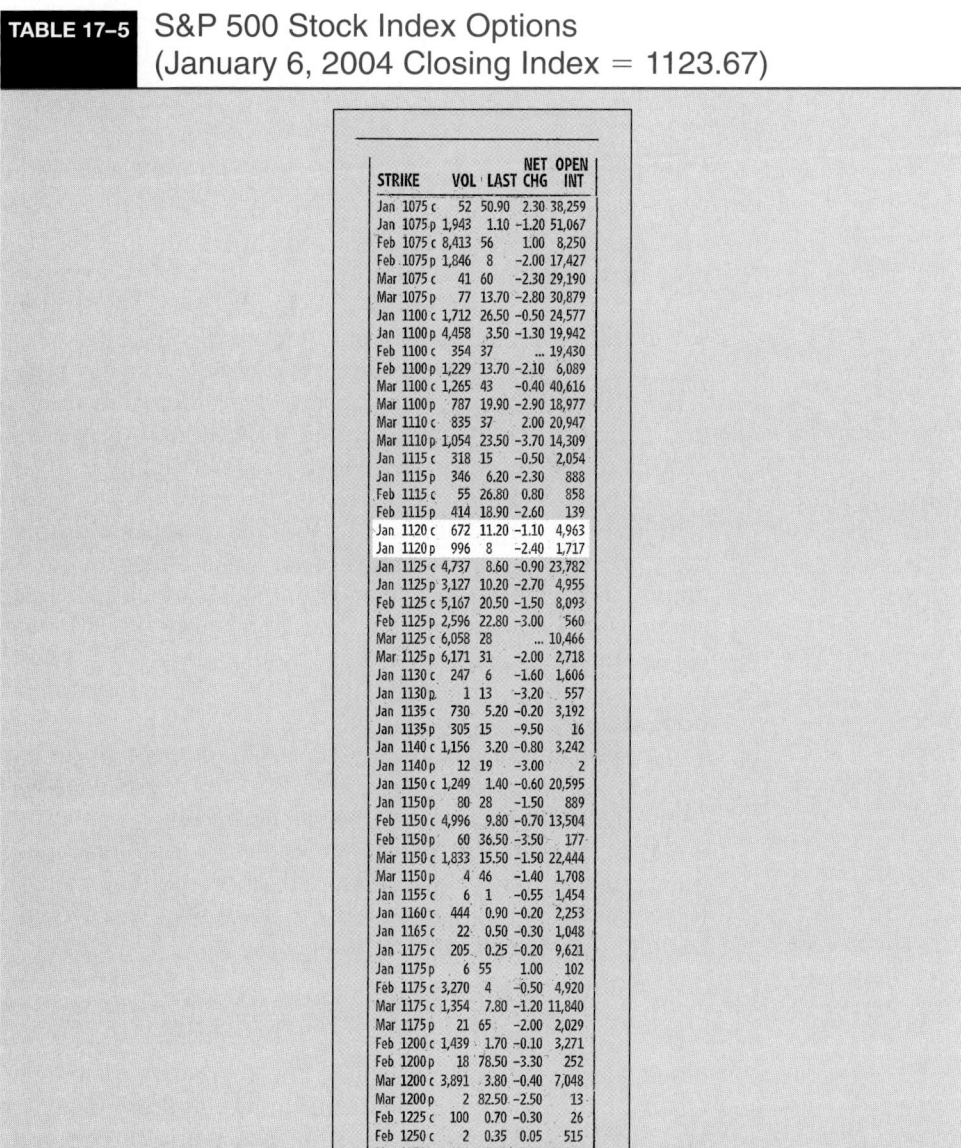

Source: *The Wall Street Journal,* January 7, 2004, p. C11. Reprinted by permission of *The Wall Street Journal,* © 2004 by Dow Jones & Company, Inc. All Rights Reserved Worldwide.

Board Options Exchange. Examples of stock index options for the S&P Index are presented in Table 17–5.

In reading Table 17–5, you need to distinguish between put and call options. Read down to the Jan 1120c and Jan 1120p rows. The "c" after the strike price indicates it is a call option, while the "p" after the stock price indicates it is a put option.

Actual Trade in the S&P 500 Index

Application Example

We reproduce part of data covering the S&P 500 Index options in Table 17–6. For ease of presentation, we will reconstruct the data in columns for calls and columns for puts.

Note in the footnote of Table 17–6 that the S&P 500 Index closed at 1123.67. With this value in mind, we can examine the strike prices and premiums for the various contracts. The premium in each case is multiplied by 100 to determine the total cash value involved. Let's look at the 1115 strike price and across to the February call option. The premium is 26.80.

TABLE 17–6 S&P 500 Index Options (January 6, 2004)

Strike Price	Calls Jan	Calls Feb	Calls Mar	Puts Jan	Puts Feb	Puts Mar
1115	15.00	26.80	—	6.20	18.90	—
1120	11.20	—	—	8.00	—	—
1125	8.60	20.50	28.00	10.20	22.80	31.00
1130	6.00	—	—	13.00	—	—

The multiplier times the premium is 100.
Value of the S&P 500 Index (January 7, 2004) = 1123.67.

Assume an investor bought a February 1115 contract for a premium of 26.80 on January 6, 2004, and that when the February contract expired, the S&P 500 Index was 1165 under an optimistic assumption and 1065 under a pessimistic assumption. At an index value of 1165, the option value is 50 (1165 − 1115). The ending or expiration price is 50 points higher than the strike price. Also, keep in mind the option cost is 26.80. The profit is shown to be $2,320.

At an ending value of $1,065 (pessimistic assumption), the option is worthless and there is a loss of $2,680. Remember these are 1,115 calls.

We have been working with 1115 call options. Let's shift our attention to put options. If a February 1115 put option (the option to sell at 1115 rather than buy at 1115) had been acquired on January 6, 2004, we can see in Table 17–6 (put column) that the price of our put option would be 18.90. Let's assume that when the February put option expired, the S&P 500 Index was 1165 under what is now the pessimistic assumption and 1065 under what is now the optimistic assumption.

At an index value of 1165, no value is associated with a put option that allows you to sell at 1115. No one would want to use the option to sell at 1115 if the index value were 1165. Because the put option cost is 18.90, there is a loss of $1,890. At a final value of 1065, the put option to sell at 1115 has a value of 50. With a cost of 18.90, a profit of 31.10 occurs. The profit and losses are indicated below.

	1165 Optimistic Assumption	1065 Pessimistic Assumption
Final value (100 × 50)	$5,000	$ 0
Purchase price (100 × 26.80)	−2,680	−2,680
Profit or loss	$2,320	−$2,680

	1165 Pessimistic Assumption	1065 Optimistic Assumption
Final value (100 × 50)	$ 0	$5,000
Purchase price (100 × 18.90)	1,890	1,890
Profit or loss	−$1,890	$3,110

Hedging with Stock Index Options

The discussion of stock index options thus far has pertained to speculation about market moves. Stock index options can also be used for hedging. Like stock index futures, stock index options can be utilized to protect a portfolio or for special purposes by underwriters, specialists, dealers, tax planners, and others.

At times, options may offer a hedging advantage over futures to investors who are limited by law from purchasing futures contracts. On the other hand, futures generally allow for a more efficient hedge than options. If the market goes down by 20 or 25 percent, chances are good that a completely hedged short futures position (selling futures contracts) will compensate for losses in a portfolio. An option write, used to hedge a portfolio, may be inadequate. Perhaps the option premium income represents 10 percent of the portfolio, but the market goes down by 25 percent. Fifteen percent of the loss will be unprotected. Buying a put option may overcome this problem, but the cash outflow to purchase the put option could involve substantial funds. Clearly, both futures and options have their advantages and disadvantages.

There are also options on industry indexes that can be used for hedging or speculation. For example, the American Stock Exchange has index options on high-tech and pharmaceutical companies, and the Philadelphia Exchange covers gold/silver, oil services, semiconductors, and public utilities. The trading in industry options is basically the same as trading in overall market options.

Options on Stock Index Futures

We have discussed *stock index futures* and *stock index options,* so a natural extension of our discussion is to consider the third form of stock index trading, *options on stock index futures*. The three forms of index trading are listed below for reference.

1. Stock index futures.
2. Stock index options.
3. Options on stock index futures.

An option on stock index futures (item 3 above) gives the holder the right to purchase the stock index *futures contract* at a specified price over a given period. This is slightly different from the stock index option (item 2) that gives the holder the right to purchase the *underlying index* at a specified price over a given time period.[15]

The primary topic for discussion in this section is represented by the left-hand column in Figure 17–1, an option on a stock index futures contract. The value of an option to purchase a stock index futures contract will depend on the outlook for the futures contract. Quotes on options to purchase stock index futures are shown in Table 17–7 on page 484.

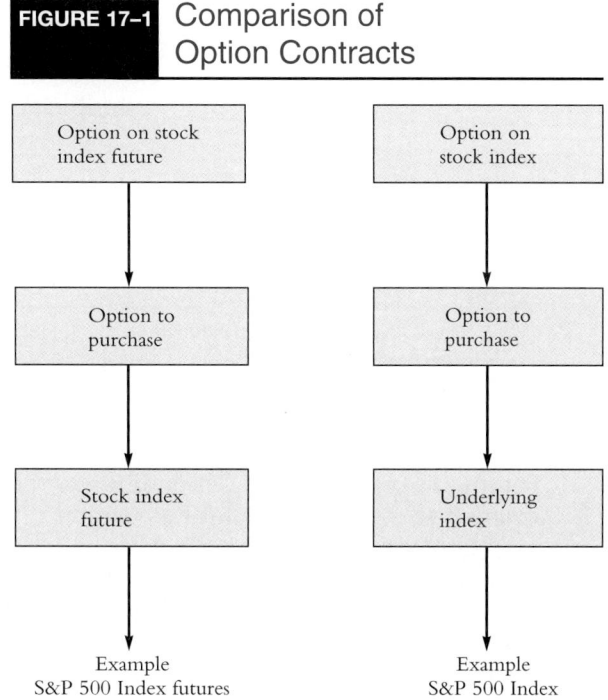

FIGURE 17–1 Comparison of Option Contracts

As indicated in Table 17–7, options on stock index futures are available for the Dow Jones Industrial Average and the S&P 500 Stock Index. For both indexes, call options are shown in the first three columns and put options in the next three columns.

A call option to buy a January DJIA futures contract at a strike price of 104 (representing 1040) has a premium of 16.50. On these option contracts, the premium is multiplied by 100 to get the value of the contract. Thus, the cost of the contract is $1,650 (100 × 16.50).

In examining Table 17–7, note that the premiums on the call options increase substantially with the passage of time from January to March. This gain in value is not only a function of the extended time period associated with the option but is also due to the fact that the DJIA futures contract normally has a higher value with the passage of time.[16] Thus, options on stock index futures

---

[15] Because of cash-settlement procedures, the actual index will never actually be purchased, and the gain or loss will be settled for cash.

[16] Of course, if the market outlook were highly pessimistic, there would be a decline in the S&P futures contract with the passage of time.

TABLE 17–7 Options on Stock Index Futures (January 6, 2004)

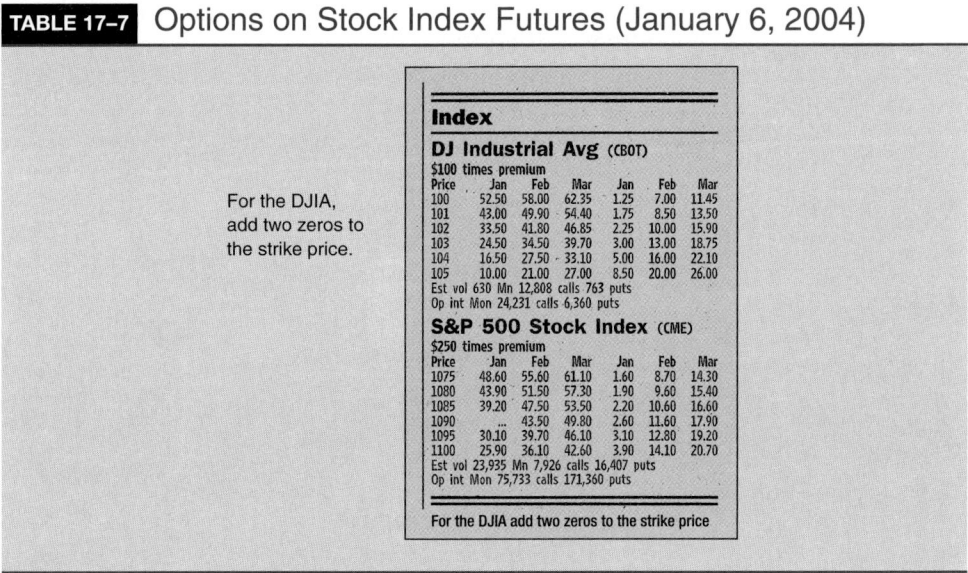

For the DJIA, add two zeros to the strike price.

Value of the DJIA (January 6, 2004) is 10,538.66; the S&P 500 is 1123.67.

Source: *The Wall Street Journal,* January 7, 2004, p. C15. Reprinted by permission of *The Wall Street Journal,* © 2004 by Dow Jones & Company, Inc. All Rights Reserved Worldwide.

not only have a time premium (all options do) but may also have an additional premium (or discount) depending on the relationship of the far-term futures market to the near-term futures market.

Options on stock index futures may be settled on a cash basis, or the holder of a call option may exercise the option and force the option writer to produce a specified futures contract. There are also puts for options on stock index futures.

exploring the web

Website Address	Comments
www.cboe.com	Website for major options exchange
www.schaeffersresearch.com	Offers technical analysis for options
www.cbs.marketwatch.com	Contains some information and tracking on stock options
www.888options.com	Educational site on options
www.cbot.com	Website for the Chicago Board of Trade providing information, quotes, and educational features
www.pcquote.com	Provides research and quotes on options and commodities
www.liffe.com	Home site for the London International Financial Futures and Options market
www.cme.com	Home site for the Chicago Mercantile Exchange containing quotes and information about futures
www.cftc.gov	Home site for the future market regulator Commodities Futures Trading Commission

Summary

For the investor who wishes to trade in stock indexes, there are three basic types of securities: stock index futures, stock index options, and options on stock index futures.

Stock index futures and options offer the potential for speculation as well as for hedging. With stock index futures, the margin is relatively low, which allows for a strong leverage potential. In hedging a portfolio position, the investor should consider the beta of his or her portfolio and adjust the number of contracts accordingly. Basis in the futures market represents the difference between the stock index futures price and the value of the actual underlying index. Basis may present the investor with a potential clue about the future direction of the market. The stock index futures market and the stock index option market trade on a cash-settlement basis. No securities ever change hands as the settlement is always in cash.

Investors in stock index futures may also engage in arbitraging procedures in which a simultaneous trade (a buy and a sell) occurs in the stock index futures contract and in the underlying securities in the index. This allows the investor to lock in a profit. The use of arbitraging, portfolio insurance, and program trading has been blamed by some for the market crash in October 1987 and the subsequent volatility in the market after the crash.

The stock index option contract is generally similar to the option contract on individual securities. The investor has an opportunity to buy puts and calls, and the premium is related to the future prospects for the index.

The third form of stock index contracts, an option on stock index futures, combines the option concept with the futures market. Instead of an option on an actual index, you have an option on a stock index futures contract. The contract may be settled either with cash or with securities.

Key Words and Concepts

arbitrage 479
basis 473
cash settlement 472
derivative products 468
futures contract on a stock market index 468
options to purchase futures 468
portfolio insurance 478
program trading 469
stock index options 468

Discussion Questions

1. Why are stock index futures and options sometimes referred to as derivative products? Why do some investors believe derivative products make the markets more volatile?
2. Why does a hedging position require less initial margin than a speculative position?
3. What is meant by the concept of cash settlement?
4. What does the term *basis* mean in the futures market? If there is a premium and it expands with the passage of time, what is the general implication?
5. Why does a down market put tremendous pressure on a speculator if he or she is the purchaser of a contract in anticipation of a market increase? Relate this answer directly to margin.

6. Why is it unrealistic for a portfolio manager to sell a large portion of his portfolio if he thinks the market is about to decline?
7. How does the beta of a portfolio influence the number of contracts that must be used in the hedging process?
8. What are some complicating factors in attempting to hedge a portfolio?
9. Why might the overuse of portfolio insurance be dangerous to the market?
10. What is an arbitrage position?
11. What is an essential difference between stock index options and options on individual securities in terms of settlement procedures?
12. Under what circumstance might a portfolio manager be more likely to use index option contracts instead of futures contracts to hedge a portfolio? What is the counter argument for futures contracts over index options?
13. Explain the difference between a stock index option and an option on stock index futures.
14. Suggest two reasons an option on a stock index futures contract that has a distant expiration date might have a high premium.

Problems

Stock index futures

1. Based on the information in Table 17–1 on page 470, what is the total value of the S&P 500 Index futures contract for June? Use the settle price (moving the decimal point two places to the left) and the appropriate multiplier. Also, if the required margin is $20,000, what percentage of the contract value does the margin represent?

Gain on S&P futures

2. In problem 1, if the S&P Index futures contract goes up to 1136.20, what will be the total dollar profit on the contract? What is the percent return on the initial margin? If this price change occurred over four months, what is the annualized return? (Multiply by 12/4.)

Loss on S&P futures and margin

3. Return to problem 1 and assume that margin must be maintained at a minimum level of $16,000. If the S&P Index futures contract goes from its initial value down to 1103.10, will there be a call for more margin?

Computing settle price

4. Based on the information in Table 17–1 on page 470, assume you buy a Dow Jones (DJ) Industrial Average March contract at the settle price. You hold the contract for six months and enjoy a gain in value of $12,000. What was the settle price after six months?

Computing basis

5. Examine Table 17–3 on page 471. Using settle prices, what is the value of the basis for March and June contracts?

Hedging and basis

6. Haltom Electric Company has a $16 million stock portfolio. The company is very aggressive, and the portfolio has a weighted beta of 1.25.
   a. Assume the company uses S&P 500 Index futures contracts to hedge the portfolio for the next 90 days and the contracts can be sold at 1125. The contracts have a multiplier of 250. With the appropriate beta adjustment factor, how many contracts should be sold? Round the final answer to the nearest whole number.
   b. If Dow Jones (DJ) Industrial Average contracts selling at 10,650 were used instead, how many contracts should be sold? These contracts have

Hedging and betas

7. The Pennsylvania Midcap Pension Fund decides to hedge its $50 million stock portfolio on January 1. The portfolio has a beta of 1.10. It will use S&P Midcap 400 futures contracts selling at 595 to hedge. These contracts have a multiplier of 500.
   a. With the appropriate beta adjustment factor, and rounding the final answer to the nearest whole number, how many contracts should be sold?
   b. Assuming that by March 1 the market has gone down by 20 percent, and the stock portfolio moves in accordance with its beta, what will be the total dollar decline in the portfolio?
   c. Assume the S&P Midcap Index futures contracts decline by 20 percent from 595. What will be the total dollar gain on futures contracts? How does the total dollar gain on the futures contracts compare with the portfolio loss in part b?
   d. Now assume that because of changing basis, the stock index futures contract does not move parallel to the market. Although the market goes down by 20 percent, the stock index futures decline by only 15 percent. What will be the gain on the futures contracts? How does this compare with the loss in portfolio value in part b?

a multiplier of 10. Once again, consider the appropriate beta adjustment factor and round your final answer to the nearest whole number.

S&P 500 call options
eXcel

8. The following problem relates to data in Table 17–6 on page 481. Assume you purchase a Jan 1115 (strike price) S&P 500 call option. Compute your total dollar profit or loss if the index has the following values at expiration:
   a. 1150
   b. 1127
   c. 1108

S&P 500 call options

9. Using data from Table 17–6 on page 481, assume you purchase a Jan 1125 (strike price) S&P 500 put option. Compute your total dollar profit or loss if the index has the following values at expiration:
   a. 1140
   b. 1100
   c. 1060

Hedging with the S&P 500 options

10. The Fleer Company has a $1 million funded pension plan for its employees. The portfolio beta is equal to 1.14. Assume the company sells (writes) 35 March 1125 (strike price) call option contracts on the S&P 500 Index as shown in Table 17–6 on page 481. Each contract trades in units of 100. At the time the options were written, the index had a value of 1123.67.
    a. What are the proceeds from the sale of the call options?
    b. Assume the market goes down by 15 percent. Considering the portfolio beta, what will be the total dollar decline in the portfolio?
    c. Assume the S&P 500 Index shown at the bottom of Table 17–6 also goes down by 15 percent at expiration. What will be the value of the index at that time?
    d. Based on your answer to part c, what will be your profit on the option writes?
    e. Considering your answers to parts b and d, what is your net gain or loss?

Using puts to hedge

11. Assume that in problem 10 the firm had purchased 15 March 1125 put option contracts on the S&P 500 Index listed in Table 17–6 on page 481 instead

of selling the call options. If the S&P 500 Index goes down by 15 percent at expiration,

a. What will be your profit on the puts? Comparing that to your loss on the stock portfolio in problem 10*b*, what is your net overall gain or loss?

b. Compare the protection afforded by the call-writing hedge in problem 10 with the protection afforded by the put purchase in this problem.

c. Suggest any modifications to the call writing or put purchase strategy that would allow you to increase your protection even more. A general statement is all that is required.

Using calls and puts to hedge

12. The New Century Fund is in charge of a $40 million portfolio. Its beta is equal to the market. To hedge its position, it sells (writes) 200 March 1125 call option contracts on the S&P 500 Stock Index as shown in Table 17–6 on page 481. It also buys 350 March 1125 put option contracts on the same index shown in Table 17–6. Instead of going down, the market goes up by 10 percent (as does the portfolio), and the S&P 500 Stock Index ends at 1240.

    Consider the change in the portfolio value and the gains or losses on the call and put options. Each option contract trades in units of 100. What is the overall net gain or loss of the New Century Fund as a result of the change in the market?

Options on stock index futures

13. The Teachers Pension Fund purchases a call on a stock option futures contract. The quote can be found in Table 17–7 on page 484. The option is on the S&P 500 Stock Index. It has a strike price of 1100 for March.

    a. What is the quoted option premium (price)?
    b. Referring to Table 17–1 on page 470, what is the quote for the March (futures) contract for the S&P 500 Stock Index? (Use the settle price.)
    c. Also referring to Table 17–1, what was the actual quote (value) for the S&P Stock Index? (Use the closing price at the bottom of the S&P 500 Stock Index data. It can be found on the line above the Mini S&P 500.)
    d. By how much does the futures quote (part *b*) exceed or trail the actual index quote (part *c*)? That is, how much is the basis?
    e. By how much does the quoted option premium calculated in part *a* exceed the basis calculated in part *d*?
    f. If the basis were to suddenly go to zero and the option changed by a similar amount, what would the new option premium be?

Web Exercise

In the chapter, we examined a number of stock index futures and options index contracts. To further our understanding of such trading mechanisms, we will expand our analysis to another index, the Russell 1000 (which is obviously different from the Russell 2000). It trades on the New York Board of Trade (NYBOT) and other exchanges. Go to **www.nybot.com**.

1. Click on "Market Information" on the left-hand margin.
2. Under "NYBOT Product Markets," click on "Russell Indexes"
3. Under "NYBOT Publications," click on "Russell 1000 Brochure," then wait a few seconds.
4. Scroll down to find the "Top 10 Holdings" in the left column of Table 1. Write the companies' names down. Only two are on the Nasdaq. Which two are they? (Use a best guess.)
5. Now click "X" on the upper right-hand portion of the screen. You will be returned to the prior page.
6. Under "Other Market Data," click on "R1000 Price Data." Looking at the "Last" column, has the pattern of movement been up or down?
7. Return to the prior page. Click on "Contract Specs" (specifications).
8. On the next page, click on "Russell 1000 Index." If the Russell 1000 Index is currently trading at 700, what is the size of the contract?
9. If you have $10,000 invested in a contract (margin) and the minimum margin requirement is $9,000, how many points could the Index fall before you needed to put up more margin? As you can see on the screen, the multiplier is 50.

Note: From time to time, companies redesign their websites, and occasionally a topic we have listed may have been deleted, updated, or moved into a different location. Most websites have a "site map" or "site index" listed on a different page. If you click on the site map or site index, you will be introduced to a table of contents that should aid you in finding the topic you are looking for.

The Wall Street Journal Project

Assume you are working for a bank trust department that wishes to hedge to protect a $15 million portfolio for one of its clients. The portfolio has a beta of 1.25 and is made up primarily of S&P 500 Index stocks.

Go to the "Commodities" pages of Section C of *The Wall Street Journal* and under "Futures" find the S&P 500 Index (under "Index Futures"). Use the nearest term settle (closing) price in doing the rest of the assignment.

You are asked to determine how many futures contracts the bank trust department customer needs to protect her position.

Use Formula 17–1 on page 477 from the chapter plus information from *The Wall Street Journal* to determine your answer.

Apply Formula 17–1 by dividing the dollar value of the portfolio by the dollar value of the contract and multiplying by the weighted beta of the portfolio of 1.25. The dollar value of the contract is equal to 250 times the settle price of the S&P 500 Index futures contract. Round your answer to a whole number.

Selected References

Use of Stock Index Futures and Options

Bharadwaj, Anu, and James B. Wiggins. "Box Spread and Put-Call Parity Tests for the S&P 500 Index LEAPS Market," *Journal of Derivatives,* Summer 2001, pp. 62–71.

Bodner, Gordon M.; Gregory S. Hayt; and Richard C. Marston, "The Wharton Study of Derivatives Usage by US Non-Financial Firms." *Financial Management,* Winter 1996, pp. 113–27.

Castelino, Mark G.; Jack C. Francis; and Avner Wolf. "Cross Hedging: Basis Risk and Choice of the Optimal Hedging Vehicle." *Financial Review,* May 1991, pp. 179–210.

Comára, António. "A Generalization of the Brennan-Rubinstein Approach for the Pricing of Derivatives." *The Journal of Finance,* April 2003, pp. 805–19.

Copeland, Laurence; Kim Lam; and Sally-Ann Jones. "The Index Futures Markets: Is Screen Trading More Efficient?" *The Journal of Finance,* February 2004, pp. 337–57.

Franchette, Darren L. "The Demand for Hedging with Futures and Options." *The Journal of Futures Markets,* August 2001, pp. 693–712.

Fung, Hung-Gay Fung; Wai-Chung Lo; and John E. Peterson. "Examining the Dependency in Intraday Stock Index Futures." *The Journal of Futures Markets,* June 1994, pp. 405–19.

Holden, Craig W. "Index Arbitrage and the Media." *Financial Analysts Journal,* September–October 1991, pp. 8–9.

Moster, James T. "A Note on the Crash and Participation in Stock Index Futures." *The Journal of Futures Markets,* February 1994, pp. 117–19.

Valuation of Stock Index Futures and Options

Marchard, Patrick H.; James T. Lindley; and Richard A. Followill. "Further Evidence on Parity Relationships in Options on S&P 500 Index Futures." *The Journal of Futures Markets,* September 1994, pp. 757–71.

Simon, David P. "The Nasdaq Volatility Index during and after the Bubble." *The Journal of Derivatives,* Winter 2003, pp. 1–24.

Simon, David P., and Roy A. Wiggins III. "S&P Futures Returns and Contrary Sentiment Indicators." *The Journal of Futures Markets,* May 2001, pp. 447–62.

Broadening the Investment Perspective

chapter **18**
MUTUAL FUNDS

chapter **19**
INTERNATIONAL SECURITIES MARKETS

chapter **20**
INVESTMENTS IN REAL ASSETS

part six

PART SIX COVERS alternative investments and includes mutual funds, international investing, and real assets. Through the use of mutual funds, an investor can own just about any asset class from bonds to stocks, sometimes originating from international countries or regions, and even real estate through real estate investment trusts. Perhaps no one is more closely associated with international investing and mutual funds than Mark Mobius, who has been the president of Templeton Emerging Markets Fund Incorporated in Hong Kong since 1987. Dr. Mobius, who holds a PhD from Massachusetts Institute of Technology in economics and political science, and bachelor and master degrees from Boston University, is responsible for all of Templeton's emerging market funds.

In all, Mobius covers 11 countries and is president of seven mutual funds for Templeton as well as a managing director of Templeton Asset Management Ltd. Mark Mobius has had a distinguished career and has won so many awards for outstanding performance we can't list them all here. However, as an indicator of his success, Mobius was awarded the "Emerging Markets Equity Manager of the Year 2001" by International Money Marketing in London, and in 1999 he was one of the "Ten Top Money Managers of the 20th Century" in a survey conducted by the Carson Group, a leading global capital markets intelligence consulting firm.

Mark Mobius is a bottom-up value investor who manages over $14 billion in international assets. He follows a strict methodology of finding undervalued stocks. His database covers 14,000 emerging market companies and includes information from local analysts and is continuously updated. For about 1,000 of these companies there are in-depth analyses that are available to all Templeton international fund managers. He relies on traditional valuation metrics such as price-earnings ratios, debt ratios, price-to-book value ratios, and dividend yields. With emerging market companies the structure of the company is important and Mobius also considers ownership structure and the corporate governance issues before investing.

In his book, *Passport to Profits,* Mobius gives us some contrary opinion advice. He suggests several rules such as: Mobius Rule No. 57: When everyone else is dying to get in, get out; Mobius Rule No. 58: When everyone else is screaming to get out, get in; and Mobius Rule No. 78: If the whole world is down on a country for exaggerated, short-term reasons, shift it from a hold to a buy.

The life of an emerging market investor is not always rosy. Economies can sputter, currencies can rise or fall dramatically, and stock markets can be extremely volatile and sensitive to small amounts of capital inflows and outflows. While Dr. Mobius spends hundreds of days a year in his private jet to research his companies and countries, he has not always hit the jackpot. In 1997 he started the Thailand Fund 12 days before the Thai baht collapsed and signaled the beginning of the Asian currency crisis. Nine months later the fund was down 53 percent. However when Mobius makes investments, he intends to hold them for five years, and he thinks investors in emerging market funds should have the same time horizon, and that patience will be rewarded in the long run if one buys good companies in rapidly growing healthy emerging markets.

A look at the Franklin Templeton website **www.franklintempleton.co.uk** will provide you with the opportunity to examine the performance of the mutual funds Dr. Mobius manages. These are load funds with a 5 percent commission on the front end and fairly high annual expense ratios of around 1.5 percent per year. You will find generally that the funds have lower volatility than the benchmark index, but the returns vary from period to period. Even the best don't always win in every time period.

Mark Mobius
© Ron McMillan/Getty Images.

18
chapter eighteen

Mutual Funds

objectives

1. Understand the concept of a mutual fund.
2. Distinguish between closed-end and open-end funds.
3. Explain the difference between load and no-load funds.
4. Compute the net asset value of a fund.
5. Identify the key information sources for mutual funds.
6. Explain how to evaluate the performance of a mutual fund.

Advantages and Disadvantages of Mutual Funds
Closed-End versus Open-End Funds
    Exchange Traded Funds
Investing in Open-End Funds
    Load versus No-Load Funds
    No-Load Funds
Information on Mutual Funds
Differing Objectives and the Diversity of Mutual Funds
    Matching Investment Objectives with Fund Types
The Prospectus
Distribution and Taxation
    Tax Differences between Mutual Funds and Individual Stock Portfolios
Shareholder Services
Investment Funds, Long-Term Planning, and Dollar-Cost Averaging
Evaluating Fund Performance
    Lipper Mutual Fund Performance Averages
    Computing Total Return on Your Investment
Appendix 18A: Unit Investment Trusts (UITs)

Mutual funds have become a very important part of investing. Owning them is an excellent way of getting a broad-based portfolio of assets that would be virtually impossible for most individual investors. According to the Investment Company Institute (www.ici.org), at the end of 2003 mutual funds were owned by 53.3 million U.S. households, an increase from 25.8 million households at the end of 1992. Not only had the number of households owning mutual funds doubled during this time, but the dollars invested had gone from $1 trillion to $7.4 trillion at the end of 2003. Figure 18–1 shows both the number and percentage of U.S. households owning mutual funds between 1980 and 2003.

FIGURE 18-1 U.S. Households Owning Mutual Funds, 1980–2001

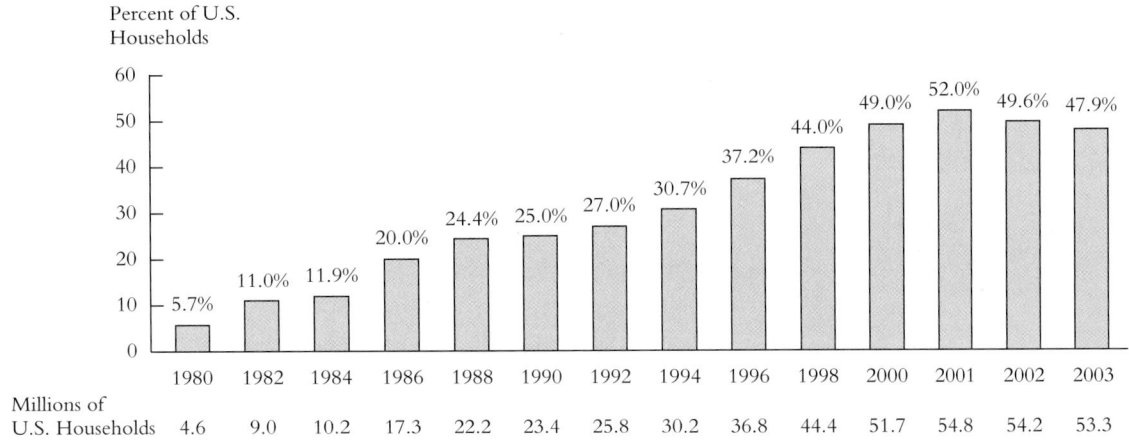

Source: *Fundamentals,* "U.S. Household Ownership of Mutual Funds in 2003" (www.ici.org/pdf/fm-v12n4.pdf).

At year-end 2003, mutual funds accounted for $2.7 trillion of U.S. retirement assets, or 22.5 percent of the $12.0 trillion families had earmarked for retirement. The other $9.3 trillion were held in accounts at insurance companies, brokerage firms, banks, and pension funds. Because many investors use mutual funds as investment vehicles for retirement or educational savings, they are long-term investors and not likely to abandon mutual funds in down markets.

However, as Figure 18–1 demonstrates, there is some sensitivity to market returns. The percentage of households owning mutual funds peaked in 2001, the year after the stock market bubble burst. Even though the stock market recovered and recorded over a 25 percent return in 2003, ownership declined to 47.9 percent of U.S. households, a drop of a little over 4 percent in two years.

The concept of a mutual fund is best understood by an example. Suppose you and your friends are too busy to develop the expertise needed to manage your own assets. One of your neighbors, however, has had years of hands-on experience as a trustee of his company's pension fund. You and your friends decide to pool your money and have this experienced investor act as your investment advisor. He will be compensated by receiving a small percentage of the average amount of assets under his management during the forthcoming year.

By common agreement, the pooled money is to be invested in the common stock of large, stable companies with the objective of capital appreciation and moderate dividend income; funds not so invested are to be placed in short-term T-bills to earn interest. Group members collectively contribute $100,000 and decide to issue shares in the fund at a rate of one share for each $10 contributed—a total of 10,000 shares. Since you put in $10,000, you receive 1,000 shares of the fund—or 10 percent of the fund's shares. Over the next few weeks, your investment advisor uses $90,000 to purchase common stock in a number of companies representing several different industries and puts $10,000 in T-bills. The portfolio is shown in Table 18–1 on the next page.

TABLE 18–1 Companies Grouped by Different Industries to Get Some Diversification:

Industries	Companies
Automobiles	General Motors
Banking	Citigroup
Chemicals	Du Pont
Computers	Dell
Financial services	Merrill Lynch
Oil	ExxonMobil
Pharmaceuticals	Eli Lilly
Semiconductors	Texas Instruments
Telecommunications	SBC
Treasury bills: $10,000	

Since you own 10 percent of this portfolio, you are entitled to 10 percent of all income paid out to shareholders and 10 percent of all realized capital gains or losses.

The initial value of the portfolio is $100,000, or $10 per share. Assume your investment manager picked some winning stocks, and the portfolio rises to $115,000. Now each share is worth $11.50.

Your group of investors has many characteristics of a mutual fund: ownership interest represented by shares, professional management, stated investment objectives, and a diversified portfolio of assets. A multibillion dollar mutual fund would operate with many of the same concepts and principles—only the magnitude of the operation would be thousands of times larger.

Advantages and Disadvantages of Mutual Funds

Diversification The traditional way to think about diversification is to make sure you have securities from different industries in your portfolio. You want to invest in a variety of industries so that the economy does not affect all the companies equally. To help you achieve this diversification we have structured a portfolio as indicated in Table 18–1. Another way of diversifying a portfolio is to include different kinds of assets such as bonds, preferred stock, convertible securities, international securities, and real estate. Generally these asset classes are not highly correlated. The highest correlation would be +1.00 which would mean that the returns of two assets would go up and down together 100 percent of the time. If the correlation is −1.00, the returns on two assets would do the opposite, if one went up 10 percent the other would go down 10 percent.

It is extremely difficult to find assets that are negatively correlated but it is easy to find assets that have a correlation of less than +1.00. When we combine assets together with correlations of less than +1.00, we help diversify a portfolio and reduce our risk. Mutual funds offer an efficient way to diversify your investments. For many small investors, diversification may be difficult to achieve. To have a properly diversified portfolio, it is suggested that the portfolio contain at least 20 stocks and that also assumes the investor employs some risk-reduction optimization techniques. With the normal trading unit for listed stocks being 100 shares (called a round lot), accumulating a portfolio of 20 stocks could take $40,000 if we assume the average price per share was $20.

Investors can buy different types of mutual funds to achieve diversification. For example, they can buy a corporate or U.S. government bond fund, a domestic equity fund, an international equity fund, a real estate investment trust, a municipal bond fund, or a short-term money market fund, all of which have a correlation of less than +1.00 with each other. As we move into the next chapter, you will realize that international investing is a good way to diversify a portion of your portfolio.

Professional Management With a mutual fund you are also buying the expertise of the fund manager. In many cases, fund managers have a long history of investment experience and may be specialists in certain areas such as international securities, gold stocks, or municipal bonds. By entrusting your funds to a professional investor, you should get a diversified portfolio that meets your investment objectives. However, a careful investor should not assume that all professional investment managers generate above-average returns. You should select a manager with great care and study. Look at long-term returns of the fund for 3 to 5 and 10-year time periods. Don't be swayed by last year's results. Look at the longevity of the manager so that you know whether the performance numbers were generated by this investment manager or someone else. Research your choice thoroughly before choosing a manager. Our advice would be to use no-load (no commission) funds, with an eye on the above caveats, plus an eye for low expenses.

Time Savings For many people, managing money is a chore and can be very time consuming. By letting a professional manage their money they free time for leisure or more work. For example, if a lawyer or doctor was capable of making $200 or $300 per hour, why would they spend four hours per week managing a portfolio when they could make an extra $800 or $1,200 per week working. Over the course of a year they could work an additional 200 hours making an extra $40,000 to $60,000. However, you have to consider whether this doctor or lawyer could actually outperform a professional manager. On a million dollar portfolio, they would have to outperform the market by 4 to 6 percent just to recover the lost revenue they could have generated by working instead of managing their money. In most cases, the law of competitive advantage is true. Make your money doing what you do best. For many, golf, travel, fishing, sporting events, and myriad of other leisure activities beats managing your money. However, it should be pointed out that for some professionals, managing their own money may be a form of leisurely escape.

Performance Having stated some of the advantages of mutual funds, let's look at the drawbacks. First, mutual funds, on average, do not outperform the market. That is to say that over long periods, they do no better than the Standard & Poor's 500 Stock Index, the Dow Jones Industrial Average, and other benchmark indexes to which they are compared. Nevertheless, mutual funds do provide an efficient means for diversifying a portfolio. Also, only a minority of funds have had exceptional returns over time. This is why we suggest careful research before committing your money to a fund manager.

In regard to performance results, a mutual fund investor must also be sensitive to the excessive claims sometimes made by mutual fund salespeople. Often potential returns to the investor are emphasized without detailing the offsetting risk. The fact that a fund made 20 to 25 percent last year in no way ensures such a return in the future. In addition, returns have to be compared against proper benchmarks. You can't fairly compare the return on a large capitalization mutual fund against a small capitalization mutual fund because their risk is not the same.

Expenses Mutual funds have several types of expenses. You can incur sales commissions, management fees, and other costs. These fees will be discussed in more depth later in the chapter, but suffice it to say that the investor should be aware of all fees involved in the purchase and management of any mutual fund.

Selection Problems A final potential drawback to mutual funds is actually a reverse view of an advantage. With more than 8,100 mutual funds from which to choose, an investor has as much of a problem in selecting a mutual fund as a stock. For example, there are approximately 3,000 stocks on the New York Stock Exchange, considerably less than the number of mutual funds in existence. Nevertheless, if you sharpen your goals and objectives, you will be able to focus on a handful of funds that truly meet your needs.

Having discussed the general nature of mutual funds and some of their potential advantages and disadvantages, we now examine their actual mechanics. In the remainder of this chapter, we shall discuss closed-end versus open-end funds, load versus no-load funds, fund objectives, considerations in selecting a fund, and measuring the return on a fund. There is also a brief description of unit investment trusts (UITs) in Appendix 19A. UITs have some attributes similar to mutual funds.

Closed-End versus Open-End Funds

There are basically two types of investment funds, the closed-end fund and the open-end fund. We shall briefly discuss the closed-end fund and then move on to the much more important type of arrangement, the open-end fund.

Actually, these terms refer to the manner in which shares are distributed and redeemed. A **closed-end fund** has a fixed number of shares, and purchasers and sellers of shares must trade with each other. You cannot buy the shares directly from the fund (except at the inception of the fund) because of the limitation on shares outstanding. Furthermore, the fund does not stand ready to buy the shares back from you.

As we shall eventually see, an open-end fund represents exactly the opposite concept. The **open-end fund** stands ready at all times to sell you new shares or buy back your old shares. Having made this distinction, let's stay with the closed-end fund for now. The shares of closed-end funds trade on security exchanges or over-the-counter just as any other stock might; but when you look for their prices in *Barron's,* you will find closed-end funds listed under a separate heading as illustrated in Table 18–2. This makes them more easily identifiable, but you still buy and sell them through a broker and pay a commission.

TABLE 18–2 Closed-End Funds

Fund Name (Symbol)	Stock Exch	NAV	Market Price	Prem/Disc	52 Week Market Return
Friday, May 21, 2004					
General Equity Funds					
Adams Express (ADX)	♣N	14.06	12.07 −	14.2	14.7
AdvMSFI (N/A)	z	24.58	NA	NA	NA
Alliance All-Mkt (AMO)	N	13.67	14.54 +	6.4	12.1
Blue Chip Value Fd (BLU)	♣N	5.35	6.00 +	12.1	29.0
Boulder Growth & Income (BIF)-h	N	6.93	5.57 −	19.6	17.2
Boulder Tot Rtn (BTF)	N	18.64	15.36 −	17.6	18.5
Brantley Cap Corp (BBDC)	O	NA	10.76	NA	26.8
Central Secs (CET)	A	NA	20.48	NA	22.7
Cornerstone Str Val (CLM)	A	6.34	8.79 +	38.6	57.6
Cornerstone Total Return (CRF)	A	12.77	15.67 +	22.7	43.0
DrmnClayDivInco (DCS)	♣N	17.38	17.00 −	2.2	N
EV Tax Div Inc (EVT)-a	N	19.77	18.80 −	4.9	N
Engex (EGX)	A	8.68	9.30 +	7.1	7.8
Equus II (EQS)	♣N	10.67	7.49 −	29.8	8.2
FstTrVal100Fd (FVL)	A	15.88	15.10 −	4.9	N
FstTrValLineDiv (FVD)	A	15.61	13.59 −	12.9	N
First Tr VI Ibbotson (FVI)	A	18.49	16.80 −	9.1	N
Recov Adv (N/A)	z	11.62	NA	NA	N
GabelliDiv&IncTr (GDV)	N	18.68	17.80 −	·4.7	N
Gabelli Equity Tr (GAB)	N	7.74	8.23 +	6.3	22.5
General American (GAM)	♣N	32.59	29.56 −	9.3	16.3
Investors First Fund (MGC)	N	9.99	12.00 +	20.1	60.6
JHancockTaxAdvDiv (HTD)-a	N	17.56	16.10 −	8.3	N
Librty AllStr Eq (USA)-g	♣N	8.62	9.42 +	9.3	35.8
Librty AllStr Gr (ASG)	♣N	6.02	6.48 +	7.6	25.3
MFS Special Value (MFV)	N	9.79	10.94 +	11.7	25.6
NAIC Growth (GRF)-c	C	10.46	9.20 −	12.0	8.3
NuvTaxAdvTRStrat (JTA)	N	18.34	16.70 −	8.9	N
ProgressiveReturn (PGF)	A	20.54	27.95 +	36.1	54.2
Ren Cap G&I III (RENNE)	O	18.39	15.05 −	18.2	109.5
Royce Focus Trust (FUND)	O	9.17	8.51 −	7.2	60.2
Royce Micro-Cap Tr (RMT)	N	13.36	12.20 −	8.7	47.1
Royce Value Trust (RVT)	N	16.90	16.10 −	4.7	21.9
S&P 500 Protected Eq (PEFX)	N	9.60	8.82 −	8.1 −	0.8
SalomonSBF (SBF)	N	13.73	11.62 −	15.4	18.1
Source Capital (SOR)	N	56.59	60.50 +	6.9	31.1
Tri-Continental (TY)	♣N	19.47	16.18 −	16.9	15.2
Zweig (ZF)	♣N	5.56	4.80 −	13.7	0.0
Specialized Equity Funds					
AEW Real Est Inc (RIF)	♣A	17.40	15.79 −	9.3	13.2
AIM Sel Real Est (RRE)-a	♣N	16.21	14.95 −	7.8	12.4
ASA Limited (ASA)-c	♣N	39.45	36.45 −	7.6 −	2.8
Centrl Fd Canada (CEF)-cl	♣A	4.61	5.30 +	15.0	23.2
CohenStrsAdvIncRlty (RLF)	♣N	17.24	16.45 −	4.6	12.5
CohenStrsPremIncReal (RPF)	♣N	17.77	16.91 −	4.8	19.9
Cohen&SteersQualInc (RQI)	♣N	16.74	16.16 −	3.5	15.6
CohenStrsREITUtls (RTU)	♣N	16.85	15.88 −	5.8	NS
ChnStrSelctUtl (UTF)	♣N	17.90	16.80 −	6.1	NS
Cohen&Steers TotRet (RFI)	♣N	16.02	15.90 −	0.7	8.4
Evergreen Util & Hi Inc (ERH)	A	18.38	20.00 +	8.8	NS
First Financial (FF)	N	18.73	17.11 −	8.6	35.6
Foxby Corp (FXX)	A	2.54	2.17 −	14.6 −	3.5
Gabelli Gl MltiMed (GGT)	N	10.39	8.78 −	15.5	22.2
Gabelli Utility (GUT)-h	N	6.38	8.82 +	38.2	11.7
H&Q Health Inv (HQH)-a	♣N	19.60	21.00 +	7.1	39.8
H&Q Life Sci Inv (HQL)-a	♣N	16.75	16.93 +	1.1	27.2
J Han Bank (BTO)	♣N	10.45	9.33 −	10.7	32.2
ING ClrnGlbRlEst (IGR)-a	A	12.42	12.65 +	1.9	NS
ING ClrnRlEst (IIA)-a	A	13.98	12.98 −	7.2	NS
JHnck Finl Trnds (JHFT)	♣O	17.42	14.75 −	15.3	21.3
Munder @Vantage (N/A)	z	8.02	NA	NA	NA
MVC Capital (MVC)	N	8.87	8.95 +	0.9	11.8
NubrgrRlEstSec (NRO)	A	13.15	12.32 −	6.3	NS
NeubrgrBrmREI (NRL)	N	18.34	16.61 −	9.4	10.7
Neuberger Realty Inc (NRI)	N	16.49	15.25 −	7.5	9.2
Nuv Real Est (JRS)	♣A	17.16	16.12 −	6.1	5.3
Petroleum & Res (PEO)	♣N	24.27	22.56 −	7.0	14.1
Real Estate Inc (RIT)-a	N	16.71	15.36 −	8.1	13.6
ReavesUtilityIncome (UTG)	A	16.87	16.90 +	0.2	NS
RMR HospRlEstFd (RHR)	A	19.05	19.30 +	1.3	NS
RMRRealEstate Fd (RMR)-a	A	12.79	12.52 −	2.1	NS
Scudder RREEF R Est (SRQ)	♣A	19.05	17.39 −	8.7	20.8
Scudder RREEF (SRO)	♣A	14.02	13.21 −	5.8	NS
Seligman New Tech (N/A)	z	4.28	NA	NA	NA

Source: *Barron's,* Market Week, May 24, 2004, p. MW26.

the real world of investing

How Naive Can Investors Be?

It is assumed that the stock market is reasonably efficient; that is, information is quickly absorbed by investors and impounded into the value of securities. An associated feature of market efficiency is that stocks tend to be correctly priced at any point in time. Forget it! While IBM and General Motors might be correctly priced, such is not the case with closed-end investment companies. Clearly, the true value per share of a closed-end investment company is the total current value of the stock holdings (less any liabilities) divided by the number of shares outstanding. If a fund has a net asset value of $10, but is selling at a 15 percent discount for $8.50, all the fund management has to do is liquidate the assets of the fund and give each stockholder $10 per share. Forget about whether the fund is popular or not; its assets still have an immediate liquidation value of $10.

It is indeed surprising that 80 to 90 percent of closed-end funds sell at a discount from actual value (normally 10 to 20 percent below). The discount tends to be well in excess of the relatively small costs to liquidate the fund or simply convert it into an open-end fund (where it immediately trades at full net asset value).

Even more surprising is the fact that closed-end funds are almost always initially issued at a premium above net asset value. Then, within the first couple of weeks of trading, they slip to a discount. Why would anyone buy a fund with such a high probability of a loss? To directly quote *Forbes* magazine, "How Dumb Can Investors Be?"* If an investor wants to invest in a closed-end fund, why not buy an existing one at a discount and hope for a liquidation? Why pay the initial premium and then wait to take a beating?

The most plausible answer, according to *Forbes* and other sources, is that this is the least sophisticated part of the investment community. Naive investors engage in a mass misunderstanding about their own self-interest when they buy into an initial distribution of a closed-end fund. Rest assured there are very few institutional investors or enlightened finance majors playing this game.

*Mark Fadiman, "Muni Mystery," *Forbes*, September 3, 1990, p. 174, updated 2003.

Application Example

One of the most important considerations in purchasing a closed-end fund is whether it is trading at a discount or premium from net asset value. First, let's look at the formula for net asset value.

$$\text{Net asset value (NAV)} = \frac{\text{Total value of securities} - \text{Liabilities}}{\text{Shares outstanding}} \quad (18\text{--}1)$$

The **net asset value (NAV)** is equal to the current value of the securities owned by the fund minus any liabilities divided by the number of shares outstanding. For example, assume a fund has securities worth $140 million, liabilities of $5 million, and 10 million shares outstanding. The NAV is $13.50:

$$\text{NAV} = \frac{\$140 \text{ million} - \$5 \text{ million}}{10 \text{ million shares}} = \frac{\$135 \text{ million}}{10 \text{ million}} = \$13.50$$

The NAV is computed at the end of each day for a fund.

Intuitively, one would expect a closed-end fund to sell at its net asset value, but that is not the case. Many funds trade at a discount from NAV because they have a poor record of prior performance, are heavily invested in an unpopular industry, or are thinly traded (illiquid). A few trade at a premium because of the known quality of their management, the nature of their investments, or the fact they have holdings in nonpublicly traded securities that are believed to be undervalued on their books. Note in Table 18–2 on page 499 (second column from the right), the predominance of common stock funds trading at discounts from NAV in May 2004. This has normally been the case over the last decade. Some researchers even use the fact that closed-end funds do not sell for what they are worth (in terms of their holdings) as evidence that the market is something less than truly efficient in valuing securities.

Exchange Traded Funds

A new wrinkle in closed-end mutual funds is the concept of **exchange traded funds (ETFs).** These are investment company shares that trade on stock exchanges (most commonly the American Stock Exchange). The market determines the price of ETFs, and investors buy and sell them through brokers just like common stock. Exchange traded funds began in 1993 and, according to the Investment Company Institute, there were 134 ETFs by April 2004. Of these, 87 were domestic equity funds, 41 were global/international funds, and 6 were bond funds. Together these exchange traded funds had a total value of $162 billion in assets. This is a small percentage of total mutual fund assets but one that has shown rapid growth over the last several years and is expected to continue to grow.

Exchange traded funds are essentially index-based mutual funds that imitate a market index such as the S&P 500 Index (called SPDRs for Standard and Poor's Depository Receipts) or the Dow Jones Index (called DIAMONDS). Of the 87 domestic equity ETFs, 50 of them use broad-based market indexes and the other 37 use industry or sector indexes. The 41 global and international ETFs will be discussed more fully in the next chapter. The major advantage of ETFs is that they allow the investor to buy "the market" or "an industry" just like you would buy a common stock.

Investing in Open-End Funds

As previously indicated, an open-end fund stands ready at all times to sell new shares or buy back old shares from investors at net asset value. More than 95 percent of the investment funds in the United States are open-ended. Actually, the term *mutual fund* applies specifically to *open-end* investment companies, although closed-end funds are sometimes loosely labeled as mutual funds as well. We shall be careful to make the distinction where appropriate.

Transactions with open-end funds are made at the net asset value as described in Formula 18–1 on page 500 (though there may be an added commission). If the fund has 100 million shares outstanding at an NAV of $10 per share ($1 billion) and sells 20 million more shares at $10 per share, the new funds ($200 million) are redeployed in investments worth $200 million, and the NAV remains unchanged. The only factor that changes the NAV is the up and down movement of the securities in the fund's portfolio. The primary distinctions between closed-end and open-end funds are presented in Table 18–3 on the next page. All of our subsequent discussion will be about open-end (mutual) funds. These include such established names as Fidelity, Dreyfus, Vanguard, IDS, T. Rowe Price, and Templeton.

TABLE 18–3 Distinction between Closed-End and Open-End Funds

	Method of Purchase	Number of Shares Outstanding	Shares Traded at Net Asset Value
Closed-end fund	Stock exchange or over-the-counter	Fixed	No—there may be a discount or premium from NAV; there will be a commission.
Open-end fund Load fund	Usually through a full-line retail brokerage firm	Fluctuates	Yes—but there may be a high commission to buy the shares.
No-load fund	Direct from fund or through a discount or online broker	Fluctuates	Yes—no commission if bought direct from fund.

Load versus No-Load Funds

Some funds have established selling agreements with stockbrokers, financial planners, insurance agents, and others licensed to sell securities. These selling agents receive a commission for selling the funds. The funds are termed **load funds** because there is a commission associated with the purchase of the fund shares. The commission may run to 7.25 percent or higher.

Several stock funds are referred to as **low-load funds** because their sales charges are 2 to 3 percent instead of 7.25 percent. A number of funds also have a back-end load provision. While there may or may not be a front-end load in buying such a fund, there is an exit fee in selling a fund with a **back-end load** provision. The fee may be 2 to 3 percent of the selling price, but typically declines with the passage of time.

No-Load Funds

No-load funds do not charge commissions and are sold directly by the investment company through advertisements, prospectuses, and 800-number telephone orders.[1] As of 2003, no-load funds made up about 50 percent of all mutual fund assets and accounted for 50 percent of new sales. Some wonder how no-load funds justify their existence since they charge no front-end commission to purchase their shares. The answer is because of the fee they charge to manage the assets in the fund. This management fee plus expenses normally average 0.75 to 1.25 percent. On a billion dollar fund, this represents approximately $10 million a year and can be more than adequate to compensate the fund managers. It should also be pointed out that load funds also have similar management fees.

The question then becomes, why pay the load (commission)? Studies indicate there is no significant statistical difference in the investment performance of load and no-load funds. Consequently, most astute investors shop around for a no-load fund to fit their needs rather than pay a commission. This statement

---

[1] Some of these funds may have a small back-end load that declines to zero with the passage of time.

is not intended to dismiss the possibility that apprehensive or uncomfortable investors may benefit from the consultation and advice of a competent mutual fund salesman or financial advisor, and thus receive a commensurate service from paying the commission. Also, some specialized funds may exist only in the form of load funds. However, whenever possible, investors are better off using the commission toward the purchase of new shares rather than the payment of a sales fee.

> **Application Example**
>
> If you invest $1,000 in a load mutual fund and pay a 7.25 percent commission, only 92.75 percent will go toward purchasing your shares. A $1,000 investment will immediately translate into a holding of $927.50. This means the fund must go up by $72.50 or 7.82 percent, just for you to break even:
>
> $$\frac{\$72.50}{\$927.50} = 7.82\%$$
>
> It used to be simple to figure out which funds charged a load and which ones were no-load funds. You could look in *The Wall Street Journal* or *Barron's* to find both the price and the NAV. If the price and the NAV were equal, there was no load (commission) and if the price was higher than the NAV, there was a load and the percentage could be calculated.
>
> Let's assume that the net asset value of the Hirt Block Fund is $13.32 and the offer price is $13.98. This means the fund has a net asset value of $13.32 per share but is offered to the public for $13.98. The difference between $13.32 and $13.98 of $0.66 represents the commission:
>
> | | |
> |---|---|
> | $13.98 | Offer price |
> | 13.32 | NAV (net asset value) |
> | $ 0.66 | Commission |
>
> In this case, the commission represents 4.72 percent of the offer price ($0.66/$13.98 = 4.72%). You will buy a fund valued at $13.32 for $13.98 because of the sales charge.

In an effort to save space, *The Wall Street Journal* has reduced the amount of information on mutual fund quotations to those found in Table 18–4 on page 504. This trimmed-down version shows the net asset value (NAV), the net change (NET CHG) the year-to-date percent return and the three-year percent return.

Now perhaps the best way to determine whether a mutual fund is load or no-load is to consult the *Morningstar Mutual Fund Survey* if you are only interested in no-load or low-load funds, or consult the annual publication of the American Association of Individual Investors, "Individual Investor's Guide to Low-Load Mutual Funds."

www.morningstar.com

Over the last 20 years no-load funds have made steady inroads into what was once the market of the load fund. In 1984 load funds counted for about 70 percent of all equity mutual funds, and no-load funds accounted for the remaining 30 percent. By 2003 no-load funds had a slight edge. These relationships can be seen in Figure 18–2 on page 505 taken from the *Investment Company Institute 2004 Fact Book*.

Since load funds are sold by retail brokers, these changes indicate that investors are buying their mutual funds differently than in the past. There are

TABLE 18–4 Mutual Funds

Source: The Wall Street Journal, May 25, 2004, p. D6.

FIGURE 18-2 Load and No-Load Fund Assets as a Share of Fund Assets, 1984–2003

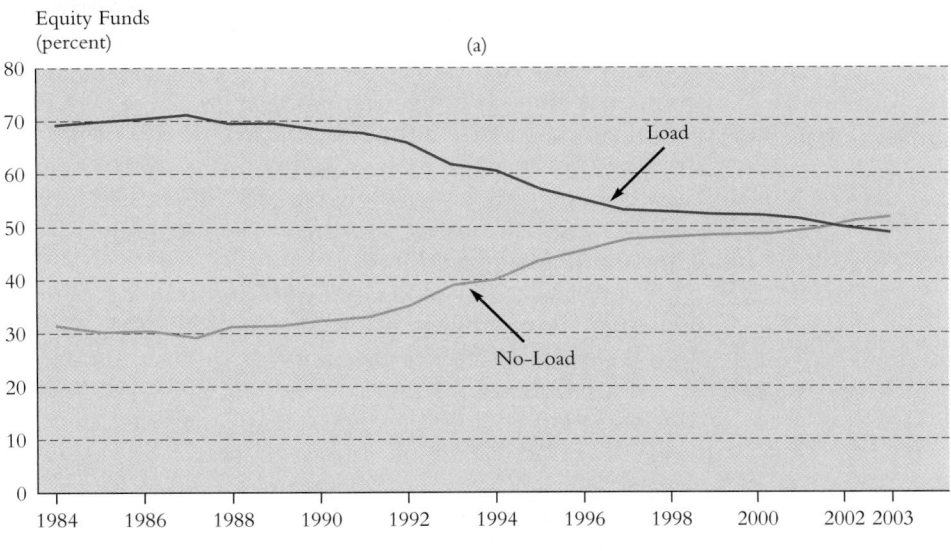

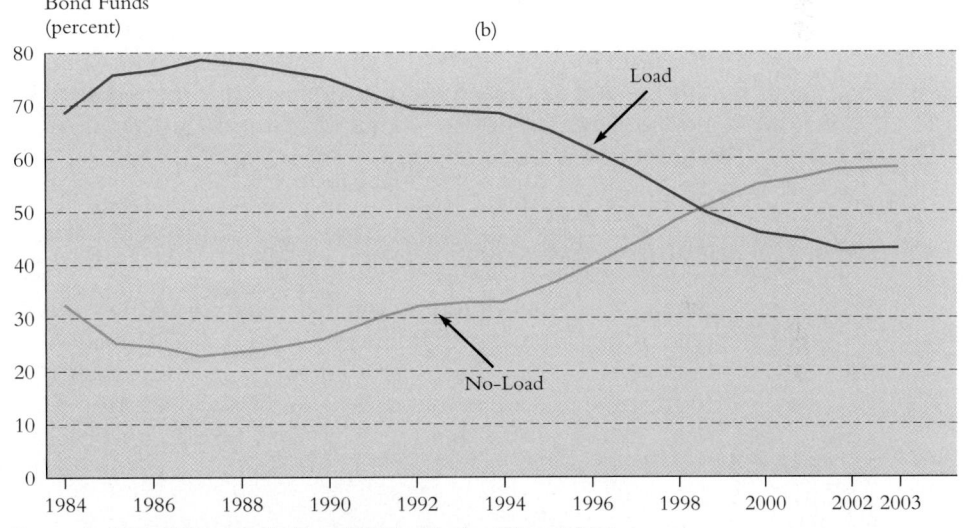

Source: *Investment Company Institute 2004 Fact Book*, p. 70, www.ici.org.

several reasons for this change. First, many employers are using mutual fund supermarkets to provide pension plans for their employees. Plan participants buy directly from the fund through paycheck withdrawals and don't pay brokerage fees. Second, more investors are using discount brokers such as Charles Schwab, Harrisdirect, Ameritrade, and other online brokers. These brokers generally sell no-load funds to their clients for a small brokerage fee of $10 to $25 per trade.

Information on Mutual Funds

www.troweprice.com

Figure 18–3 illustrates the one-page analysis on the T. Rowe Price European Stock Fund from the *Morningstar Mutual Fund Survey*. This has become the information source of choice for mutual fund investors who want to track their holdings on a quarterly basis. Morningstar ranks each mutual fund in their universe on a one-star to five-star rating system. T. Rowe Price European Stock fund is ranked three stars in the box toward the top of the page. As you look at the top line on the page, you will also see its ticker symbol and that it does not carry a load. The data in the table are self-explanatory but notice that the table includes annual returns, tax analysis, risk analysis, country exposure, major company holdings, and more.

There are other good sources of information, and *Forbes* publishes an annual mutual fund review every August. While this is only a once-a-year publication, it is very helpful for investors looking for mutual funds or evaluating their funds. It lists funds by mutual fund category—stock funds, balanced funds, index funds, global funds, foreign funds, European funds, Pacific Funds, and bond funds. The full listing of Forbes' mutual funds is available on its website at **www.forbes.com/fundsurvey**. *Forbes* ranks mutual funds in up and down markets much like a professor, with an A for great performance and F for failing performance. Additionally it provides five-year returns, asset size, annual expenses per $100, the minimum initial investment, and a few other items.

If you see a fund that interests you after reviewing either the *Morningstar Mutual Fund Survey* or the *Forbes* website, you can request a prospectus. If the fund is a load fund, you can request the prospectus from your broker; if it is a no-load fund you can contact the fund directly through their 800 telephone number or website address.

Differing Objectives and the Diversity of Mutual Funds

Recognizing that different investors have different objectives and sensitivities to risk, the mutual fund industry offers a large group of funds from which to choose. In 2001, there were more than 8,100 mutual funds, each unique in terms of stated objectives, investment policies, and current portfolio. To make some sense out of this much variety, funds can be classified in terms of their stated objectives, which are described in the following material.

Money Market Funds **Money market funds** have had strong growth in the last two decades. (*Forbes* Mutual Fund Survey provides a helpful list of funds.) Money market mutual funds invest in short-term securities, such as U.S. Treasury bills and Eurodollar deposits, commercial paper, jumbo bank certificates of deposit (CDs), and repurchase agreements.

Money market funds are no-load, and most require minimum deposits of $500 to $1,000. Most have check-writing privileges, but usually the checks must be written for at least $250 to $500.

Because the maturities of assets held in money market portfolios generally range from 20 to 50 days, the yields of these funds closely track short-term market interest rates. Money market funds give small investors an opportunity to invest in securities that were once out of reach.

FIGURE 18–3 One-Page Analysis of T. Rowe Price European Stock Fund

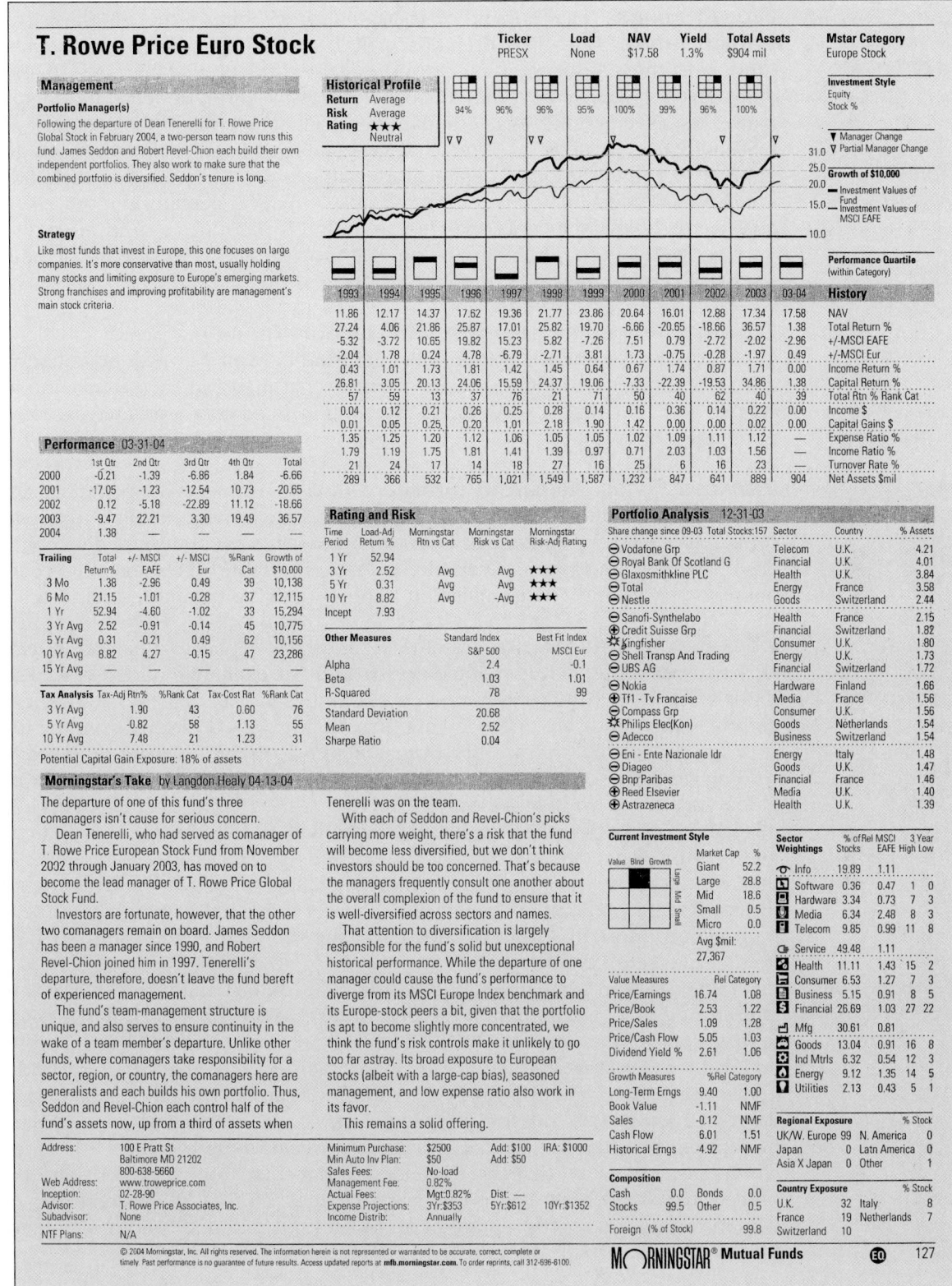

Growth Funds The pursuit of capital appreciation is the emphasis with **growth funds.** This class of funds includes those called aggressive growth funds and those concentrating on more stable and predictable growth. Both types invest primarily in common stock. Aggressive funds concentrate on speculative issues, emerging small companies, and "hot" sectors of the economy and frequently use financial leverage to magnify returns. Regular growth funds generally invest in common stocks of more stable firms. They are less inclined to stay fully invested in stocks during periods of market decline, seldom use aggressive techniques such as leverage, and tend to be long term in orientation.

The best way to determine the type of growth fund is to carefully examine the fund's prospectus and current portfolio.

Growth with Income **Growth with income funds** pay steady dividends. Their stocks are attractive to investors interested in capital growth potential with a base of dividend or interest income. Funds that invest in such stocks are less volatile and risky than growth funds investing in small companies paying low or no dividends.

Balanced Funds **Balanced funds** combine investments in common stock and bonds and often preferred stock. They try to provide income plus some capital appreciation. Funds that invest in convertible securities are also considered balanced since the convertible security is a hybrid fixed-income security with the opportunity for appreciation if the underlying common stock rises.

Index Funds **Index funds** are mutual funds that replicate a market index as closely as possible. It was pointed out earlier that exchange traded closed-end funds were index funds that traded on exchanges just like common stock. Conversely, index funds are open-end and may be purchased directly from the fund sponsor. As you may remember from Chapter 3, there are many indexes, including stock market indexes and bond market indexes as well as foreign and global indexes. If an investor truly believes that the market is efficient and that it is hard to outperform the market, he or she will try to reduce transaction costs and attempt to imitate the market. Index funds arose because of the efficient market hypothesis (presented in Chapter 9). Quite a bit of academic research indicates that it is difficult to outperform a market index unless you have superior information. Most investors do not have superior information and so index funds make sense.

www.vanguard.com

Table 18–5 presents the Vanguard Idx: 500 Idx index fund, which was the largest fund at $75.32 billion at the end of 2003. This fund replicates the Standard & Poor's 500 Composite Index. The S&P 500 Index is considered a growth and value index; this fund competes with other funds in that category, and its performance is compared against the category returns. The table is taken from the AAII's "Individual Investor's Guide to Low-Load Mutual Funds" and provides quite a bit of valuable information. The fund has a beta equal to 1.00 as you would expect. Notice that the expense ratio averages between 0.18 and 0.20 percent (18 to 20 basis points) versus a normal .75 to 1.25 percent, and this demonstrates the low-cost nature of an index fund that needs no research analysts or huge databases.

Bond Funds Income-oriented investors have always been attracted to bonds. Because bonds represent a contractual obligation on the part of the issuer to the

TABLE 18-5 Sample Page for the Vanguard Idx: 500 Idx

Vanguard Idx: 500 Idx
(VFINX)
Growth & Income

800-635-1511, 610-669-1000
www.vanguard.com

PERFORMANCE   fund inception date: 8/31/76

	3yr Annual	5yr Annual	10yr Annual	Bull	Bear
Return (%)	12.2	18.3	17.3	56.3	-11.5
Differ from Category (+/-)	3.3 high	4.0 high	2.4 high	22.8 high	-11.4 blw av

Standard Deviation	Category Risk Index	Beta
17.6%—av	1.02—abv av	1.00

	2000	1999	1998	1997	1996	1995	1994	1993	1992	1991
Return (%)	-9.0	21.0	28.6	33.2	22.8	37.4	1.1	9.8	7.4	30.2
Differ from Category (+/-)	-14.7	10.2	15.8	6.3	3.1	7.9	1.6	-4.0	-4.2	2.1
Return, Tax-Adjusted (%)	-9.3	20.3	27.9	32.2	21.7	36.1	0.0	8.6	6.4	28.9

PER SHARE DATA

	2000	1999	1998	1997	1996	1995	1994	1993	1992	1991
Dividends, Net Income ($)	1.30	1.41	1.33	1.32	1.28	1.22	1.17	1.13	1.12	1.15
Distrib'ns, Cap Gain ($)	0.00	0.99	0.42	0.59	0.25	0.13	0.20	0.03	0.10	0.12
Net Asset Value ($)	121.86	135.33	113.95	90.07	69.16	57.60	42.97	43.83	40.97	39.32
Expense Ratio (%)	na	0.18	0.18	0.19	0.20	0.20	0.19	0.19	0.19	0.20
Yield (%)	1.06	1.03	1.16	1.45	1.84	2.11	2.71	2.57	2.72	2.91
Portfolio Turnover (%)	na	6	6	5	5	4	6	6	4	5
Total Assets (Millions $)	89,393	104,652	74,228	49,357	30,331	17,371	9,356	8,272	6,547	4,345

PORTFOLIO (as of 6/30/00)

Portfolio Manager: committee, George Sauter - 1987

Investm't Category: Growth & Income
✔ Domestic   ✔ Index
  Foreign   Sector
  Asset Allocation State Specific

Investment Style
✔ Large Cap   Mid Cap   Small Cap
  Growth   ✔ Grth/Val   Value

Portfolio
4.0% cash   0.0% corp bonds
96.0% stocks   0.0% gov't bonds
0.0% pref/conv't pref 0.0% muni bonds

SHAREHOLDER INFORMATION

Minimum Investment
Initial: $3,000   Subsequent: $100

Minimum IRA Investment
Initial: $1,000   Subsequent: $100

Maximum Fees
Load: none   12b-1: none
Other: none

Services
✔ IRA
✔ Keogh
✔ Telephone Exchange

Source: "Individual Investor's Guide to Low-Load Mutual Funds" (American Association of Individual Investors, 2004), p. 125.

bondholder, they normally offer a certain return. But as pointed out in Chapter 12, rising interest rates can undercut the market value of all classes of fixed-income securities. During the early 1980s and early 1990s, times of intense interest-rate fluctuations, many bondholders watched the principal value of even their "safe" government bonds drop to 75 percent of face value. Bonds held in **bond mutual funds** were affected by the same market forces. Returns from bonds are historically lower than those from stocks, and bond funds are no exception.

Bond mutual funds can be roughly subdivided into corporate, government, and municipal funds.

Some corporate bond funds are particularly targeted to low-rated, high-yielding bonds. These funds are termed *junk bond funds* or *high yield bond funds*. They may have a yield of 3 or 4 percent over the typical corporate bond fund but also possess greater risk in terms of potential default by the securities in the bond portfolio. Just how much greater that risk is was discovered in the fall of 1989 when a number of low-rated bonds in these funds defaulted on their interest payments and prices for all junk bonds fell.

Because municipal bond funds buy only tax-exempt securities, interest income to shareholders is free of federal tax. Special tax-exempt funds also have been established for the benefit of investors in states with high state and local income taxes. For example, fund managers of New York municipal bond funds establish portfolios of tax-exempt securities issued within the boundaries of that state. Under current tax law, interest income from these funds is exempt from federal, state, and local taxes for New York residents—a very appealing feature to high-bracket taxpayers.

Sector Funds Special funds have been created to invest in specific sectors of the economy. **Sector funds** exist for such areas as energy, medical technology, computer technology, leisure, and defense.

Because stock performance of companies within a particular industry, or sector, tends to be positively correlated, these funds offer investors less diversification potential.

Investors should be cautious with regard to the initial offering of new sector funds. An initial offering usually occurs after the sector has already been the subject of intense interest based on recent spectacular performance. As a result, stocks in that sector are often fully priced or overpriced.

Foreign Funds As will be noted in Chapter 19, investors seeking participation in foreign markets and foreign securities confront a number of obstacles, but the rewards can be remarkable. The mutual fund industry has made overseas investing convenient by establishing **foreign funds** whose policies mandate investing on an international basis (Templeton World Fund), within the markets of a particular locale (Canadian Fund, Inc.), or within a region (Merrill Lynch Pacific). Some funds even specialize in Third World countries.

A listing of various types of international funds is presented in Table 18–6. The mutual fund industry distinguishes between global and international funds. Global funds have foreign stocks plus U.S. stocks, while international have only foreign stocks.

www.sbs.gov.uk/phoenix

www.calvertgroup.com

www.usfunds.com

Specialty Funds Some mutual funds have specialized approaches that do not fit neatly into any of the preceding categories and so are called **specialty funds.** Their names are often indicative of their investment objectives or policies: the Phoenix Fund (rising from the ashes?), the Calvert Social Investment Fund, and United Services Gold Shares, to name just a few.

TABLE 18–6 Internationally Oriented Funds

Name of Fund	Open- or Closed-End	Load (L) or No-Load (NL)	Where Invested
Dean Witter European Growth B	Open	5%	Europe
Central European Community	Closed	—	Europe
Invesco European	Open	None	Europe
France Growth	Closed	—	France
Mexico Equity and Income	Closed	—	Mexico
Latin American Discovery	Closed	—	Latin America
Chile Fund	Closed	—	Chile
Argentina Fund	Closed	—	Argentina
Scudder International Fund	Open	None	Mexico and Central America
Morgan Stanley Latin American A	Open	5.75%	Latin America
GT Latin America Growth A	Open	4.75%	Latin America
Fidelity Europe Capital Appreciation	Open	3.00%	Europe
Putnam Europe Growth A	Open	5.75%	Europe

There is even a "fund of funds" (FundTrust) that manages a portfolio of different mutual fund shares.

Hedge Funds **Hedge funds** are products of the 1990s and have become very popular in the current decade. Actually the name is somewhat misleading in that hedge funds do not restrict their activities to hedging or reducing risk. Rather the term is a generic name for funds that engage in a wide range of activities at one time in an attempt to generate a superior return. They normally are neither bullish nor bearish, but engage in buying, short selling, and transacting in puts and calls at the same time in the attempt to gain an edge. They tend to be highly leveraged and are usually in the form of a limited partnership. Hedge funds normally charge management fees only on profits (the industry norm is 20 percent).

Finally, funds are sometimes distinguished by the size of the market value (capitalization) of the firms in which they invest. Examples might be small-cap funds, which invest in firms with market values up to $1 billion; mid-cap funds, which invest in firms with market values up to $9 billion, and so on.[2]

Matching Investment Objectives with Fund Types

Investors must consider how much volatility of return they can tolerate. Investors who require safety of principal with very little deviation of returns should choose money market funds first and intermediate-term bond funds second. They should also expect to receive lower returns based on historical evidence. While aggressive growth stock funds provide the highest return, they also have the biggest risk.

Liquidity objectives are met by all mutual funds since redemption can occur any time. If investors need income, bond funds provide the highest annual

---

[2] The market value limitation for the small- or mid-cap fund designation varies from fund to fund.

current yield, while aggressive growth funds provide the least. Growth-income and balanced funds are most appropriate for investors who want growth of principal with moderate current income.

Many investors diversify by fund type. For example, at one stage in the business cycle, an investor may want to have 50 percent of assets in U.S. common stocks, 35 percent in bonds, 10 percent in money market funds, and 5 percent in an international stock fund. These percentages could change as market conditions change. If interest rates are expected to decline, it would be better to have a higher percentage of bonds and fewer money market securities since bond prices will rise as rates decline. Investing with a "family of funds" allows the investor a choice of many different types of funds and the privilege of switching between funds at no or low cost. Some of the larger families of funds are managed by American Capital, Dreyfus Group, Federated Funds, Fidelity Investments, T. Rowe Price Funds, and the Vanguard Group. In addition, most major retail brokerage firms, such as Merrill Lynch, Dean Witter, and Salomon Smith Barney, have families of mutual funds.

Each mutual fund has a unique history and management team. There is no guarantee that past performance will be repeated. Investors should check on a fund's longevity of management, historical returns, trading history, and management expenses. A very key instrument in providing information in this regard is the fund prospectus.

The Prospectus

The Investment Companies Act of 1940, which established the standard of practice for all investment companies, requires that the purchaser of fund shares be provided with a current prospectus. The **prospectus** contains information deemed essential by the SEC in providing "full disclosure" to potential investors regarding the fund's investment objectives and policies, risks, management, and expenses. The prospectus also provides information on how shares can be purchased and redeemed, sales and redemption charges (if any), and shareholders' services. Other fund documents are available to the public on request including the Statement of Additional Information and the fund's annual and quarterly reports.

While it is beyond the scope of this chapter to provide a complete discourse on interpreting a prospectus, investors need to understand the following essentials.

Investment Objectives and Policies This section is always found in the beginning of the prospectus. It usually describes the fund's basic objectives such as:

> The Fund will invest only in securities backed by the full faith and credit of the U.S. Government. At least 70 percent of the Fund's assets will be invested in certificates issued by the Government National Mortgage Association (GNMA). It may also purchase other securities issued by the U.S. Government, its agencies, or instrumentalities as long as these securities are backed by the full faith and credit of the U.S. Government.

The prospectus normally goes on to detail investment management policies under which it intends to operate—typically with regard to the use of borrowed money, lending of securities, or something like the following:

The Fund may, under certain circumstances, sell covered call options against securities it is holding for the purpose of generating additional income.

Portfolio (or "Investment Holdings") This section of the prospectus lists the securities held by the fund as of the date indicated. Since investment companies are only required to publish their prospectuses every 14 months, the information is probably dated. Still, the portfolio should be compared with the stated objectives of the fund to see if they are consistent.

Management Fees and Expenses Besides sales and redemption charges, the prospectus also provides information and figures on fund managers' reimbursement and the fund's housekeeping expenses. Annual fees for the investment advisor are expressed as a percentage of the average daily net assets during the year (usually 0.50 percent). Other expenses include legal and auditing fees, the cost of preparing and distributing annual reports and proxy statements, directors' fees, and transaction expenses. When lumped together with investment advisory fees, a fund's total yearly expenses typically range from 0.75 to 1.25 percent of fund assets. Experienced mutual fund investors cast a jaundiced eye on funds with expense ratios that exceed this figure. It is required that all expenses appear on one page in a table format.

A controversial SEC ruling—Rule 12b-1—allows mutual funds to use fund assets for marketing expenses, which are included in the expense ratio. Since marketing expenses have nothing to do with advancing shareholders' interests and everything to do with increasing the managers' fees, investors should be alert to this in the prospectus.

Turnover Rate A number of mutual funds trade aggressively in pursuit of profits; others do just the opposite. In one year, the Fidelity Contrafund had a 243 percent turnover rate; the rate for the Oppenheimer Special Fund was 9 percent.

In reality, transaction costs amount to more than just commissions, and they are not accounted for in the expense ratio. When fund assets are traded over-the-counter, the dealer's spread between the bid and asked price is not considered. Nor is the fact that large block trades—the kind mutual funds usually deal in—are made at less favorable prices than are smaller volume transactions.

The prospectus also contains audited data on the turnover rate, the expense ratio, and other important data in the section on per share income and capital changes. In 1998 the SEC ordered mutual funds to provide shortened forms of the prospectus to investors who do not want to be overwhelmed with data.

Distribution and Taxation

The selling of securities by a mutual fund manager results in capital losses or gains for the fund. After netting losses against gains, mutual funds distribute net capital gains to shareholders annually.

Funds with securities that pay dividends or interest also have a source of investment income. The fund, in turn, distributes such income to shareholders either quarterly or annually.

A fund that distributes at least 90 percent of its net investment income and capital gains is not subject, as an entity, to federal income tax. It is simply acting as a "conduit" in channeling taxable sources of income from securities held in the portfolio to the fund's shareholders. Most funds operate this way. But while the mutual fund may not be subject to taxation, its shareholders are.

At the end of every calendar year, each fund shareholder receives a Form 1099-DIV. This document notifies the shareholder of the amount and tax status of his or her distributions.

When the investor actually sells (redeems) shares in a mutual fund, another form of taxable event occurs. It is precisely the same as if stocks, bonds, or other securities were sold. The investor must consider the cost basis, the selling price, and any gain or loss and appropriately report the tax consequences on his or her tax form.

Tax Differences between Mutual Funds and Individual Stock Portfolios

When you manage your own portfolio of common stocks, you can choose when to sell a specific stock, and by having that choice, you control when you pay capital gains taxes. When you own a mutual fund, the manager decides when to buy and sell, so you end up with a capital gain or loss at the manager's discretion. This difference might not seem significant, but if you receive a bonus this year, you might want to take losses this year to offset some of the bonus income and wait until next year to take your gains. You might also want to wait until the gain is long term and taxed at a lower rate.

The initial purchase of a common stock sets the cost basis; if the stock goes up you have a gain, and if it goes down you have a loss. At least if the stock stays the same you have no gain or loss. This is not so with a mutual fund. When you buy fund shares, a portfolio of stocks already exists, and these stocks are either held at a gain or loss. In rapidly rising bull markets, you may be buying into mutual funds that have large accumulated gains; if the manager decides to take those gains, you will have to pay the capital gains tax—even though the net asset value of your shares did not change. This would leave you with a negative return even though the price did not fall. This particular tax issue is what keeps more sophisticated investors from buying mutual funds during the last several months of the year.

Shareholder Services

Most mutual funds offer a number of services to their shareholders. Some can be used in the investor's strategy. Common services include the following:

Automatic reinvestment. The fund reinvests all distributions (usually without sales charge). Shares and fractional shares are purchased at the net asset value. Purchases are noted on annual and periodic account statements.

Safekeeping. While shareholders are entitled to receive certificates for all whole shares, it is often convenient to let the fund's transfer agent hold the shares.

Exchange privilege. Many large management companies sponsor a family of funds. They may have five or more funds, each dedicated to a different investment objective. Within certain limits, shareholders are free to move their money between the different funds in the family on a net asset value basis. Transfers can often be done by telephone; a minimal charge is common to cover paperwork. These exchanges are taxable events.

Preauthorized check plan. Many people lack the discipline to save or invest regularly. Those who recognize this trait in themselves can authorize a management company to charge their bank account for predetermined amounts on a regular basis. The amounts withdrawn are used to purchase new shares.

Systematic withdrawal plan. Every shareholder plans to convert shares into cash at some time. The investor who wants to receive a regular amount of cash each month or quarter can do so by arranging for such a plan. The fund sells enough shares on a periodic basis to meet the shareholder's cash requirement.

Checking privileges. Most money market mutual funds furnish shareholders with checks that can be drawn against the account, provided that the account balance is above a minimum amount (usually $1,000). A per-check minimum of $250 to $500 is common.

Investment Funds, Long-Term Planning, and Dollar-Cost Averaging

Perhaps more than anything else, the liquidity and conveniences inherent in mutual funds lend themselves best to financial planning activities. The most important of these is the gradual accumulation of capital assets.

Using the preauthorized check plan, investors can have fixed amounts regularly withdrawn from their checking accounts to purchase fund shares. Just as savers can have their banks channel a specific amount from their paychecks into savings accounts, so too can investors make regular, lump-sum fund share purchases on an "out of sight, out of mind" basis. Reinvestment of distributions enhances this strategy.

What distinguishes the mutual fund from the bank savings strategy is the fact that fund shares are purchased at different prices. The investor can even use a passive strategy known as dollar-cost averaging. Under **dollar-cost averaging,** the investor buys a fixed dollar's worth of a given security at regular intervals regardless of the security's price or the current market outlook. By using such a strategy, investors concede they cannot outsmart the market. The intent of dollar-cost averaging is to avoid the common practice of buying high and selling low. In fact, investors are forced to do the opposite. Why? They commit a fixed-dollar amount each month (or year) and buy shares at the current market price. When the price is high, they are buying relatively fewer shares; when the price is low, they are accumulating more shares. An example is presented in Table 18–7 on page 516. Suppose we use the preauthorized check plan to channel $200 per month into a mutual fund. The price ranges from a low of $12 to a high of $19.

Note that when the share price is relatively low, such as in January, we purchased a larger number of shares than when the share prices were high, as in April. In this case, the share price ended in June at the same price it was in January ($12).

What would happen if the price merely ended up at the average price over the six-month period? The values in Column (3) total $88, so the average price over six months is $14.67 ($88/6). Actually, we would still make money under

TABLE 18–7 Dollar-Cost Averaging

(1) Month	(2) Investment	(3) Share Price	(4) Shares Purchased
January	$ 200	$12	16.66
February	200	14	14.28
March	200	16	12.50
April	200	19	10.52
May	200	15	13.33
June	200	12	16.66
Totals	$1,200	$88	83.95 total shares
		Average price $14.67	Average cost $14.29

this assumption because the average *cost* is less than this amount. Consider that we invested $1,200 and purchased 83.95 shares. This translates to an average cost of only $14.29:

$$\frac{\text{Investment}}{\text{Shares purchased}} = \frac{\$1,200}{83.95} = \$14.29$$

The average cost ($14.29) is less than the average price ($14.67) because we bought relatively more shares at the lower price levels, and they weighed more heavily in our calculations. Thus, under dollar-cost averaging, investors can come out ahead over a period of investing fixed amounts, even if the share price ends up less than the average price paid on each transaction.[3]

The only time investors lose money is if the eventual price falls below the average cost ($14.29) and they sell at that point. While dollar-cost averaging has its advantages, it is not without criticism. Clearly, if the share price continues to go down over a long period, it is hard to make a case for continued purchases. However, the long-term performance of most diversified mutual funds has been positive, and long-term investors may find this strategy useful in accumulating capital assets for retirement, children's education funds, or other purposes.

Evaluating Fund Performance

Throughout this chapter, we referred to mutual fund performance. Let's return to Figure 18–3 on page 507 to further discuss the topic.

In the case of the *Morningstar Mutual Fund Survey* in Figure 18–3, the T. Rowe Price European Stock fund is compared against market indexes. This can be seen on the left side on the middle of the page under "Performance 03-31-04." In the second box under performance, we see a comparison for 3 months, 6 months, 1 year, 3 years, 5 years, 10 years, and 15 years against the MSCI[4] EAFE and MSCI Europe indexes. Because this is an international European fund, it makes sense to use these European indexes as a benchmark for comparison purposes, and we find that on a 1-year basis, the T. Rowe Price

---

[3] This does not consider any sales charges or commissions, which could be important but can generally be avoided.

[4] MSCI represents Morgan Stanley Capital International, headquartered in Geneva, Switzerland.

European Stock fund underperformed both indexes. Other time periods tended to show mixed results.

Performance should always be measured against an appropriate benchmark. One common benchmark is the average performance of all competing mutual funds in the same fund category. Another and more rigorous performance comparison is against an index that measures the performance of a stock portfolio that matches the fund's investment objectives. That is why we compared the T. Rowe Price European Stock fund against the European indexes.

One warning: Past performance in no way guarantees future performance. A fund that did well in the past may do poorly in the future and vice versa.[5] Nevertheless, all things being equal, investors generally prefer funds that have a prior record of good performance. Investors do not know whether the funds can reproduce the performance, but at least the funds have indicated the capacity for good returns in the past. The same cannot be said for underperformers.

Lipper Mutual Fund Performance Averages

As you can see in Table 18–8 on page 518, mutual fund performance can also be broken down by type of fund. This type of information was previously presented in Chapter 3 under the discussion of stock market indexes and averages but now takes on greater meaning in the current context of mutual fund evaluation. You can observe that certain types of funds did better or worse and how their performance changed with differing periods for measurement. The Lipper Mutual Fund Performance Averages shown in Table 18–8 are published weekly in *Barron's*.

Computing Total Return on Your Investment

Application Example

Assume you own a fund for a year and want to determine the total return on your investment. There are three potential sources of return:

Change in net asset value (NAV).
Dividends distributed.
Capital gains distributed.[6]

Assume the following:

	$14.05	Beginning NAV
	15.10	Ending NAV
	1.05	Change in NAV (+)
0.72	{ 0.40	Dividends distributed
	0.32	Capital gains distributed
	$ 1.77	Total return

---

[5] The factor is covered more fully in Chapter 22.

[6] This represents net capital gains that the fund actually had as a result of selling securities. They are distributed to shareholders.

TABLE 18-8 Lipper Mutual Fund Performance Averages

LIPPER MUTUAL FUND PERFORMANCE AVERAGES

Weekly Summary Report: Thursday, 5/20/2004
Cumulative Performances With Dividends Reinvested

NTA Mil.$	No. Funds		12/31/03-05/20/04	05/13/04-05/20/04	04/22/04-05/20/04	02/19/04-05/20/04	05/22/03-05/20/04
General Equity Funds							
473,629.0	1,065	Large-Cap Core Funds	− 2.56%	− 0.75%	− 4.74%	− 5.33%	+ 15.53%
245,166.5	636	Large-Cap Growth Funds	− 2.46	− 1.02	− 5.25	− 5.04	+ 14.84
286,005.2	439	Large-Cap Value Funds	− 1.74	− 0.48	− 4.65	− 5.19	+ 18.97
271,043.2	674	Multi-Cap Core Funds	− 2.04	− 0.62	− 5.60	− 5.52	+ 19.11
268,795.9	457	Multi-Cap Growth Funds	− 2.72	− 1.12	− 7.18	− 5.86	+ 19.68
210,064.5	516	Multi-Cap Value Funds	− 1.39	− 0.51	− 5.22	− 5.22	+ 20.70
115,919.0	330	Mid-Cap Core Funds	− 1.80	− 0.81	− 7.02	− 5.75	+ 24.82
85,838.9	524	Mid-Cap Growth Funds	− 2.73	− 1.29	− 8.36	− 6.49	+ 21.41
92,072.8	213	Mid-Cap Value Funds	− 0.76	− 0.70	− 6.73	− 4.97	+ 28.40
123,410.6	554	Small-Cap Core Funds	− 1.58	− 0.96	− 8.09	− 5.70	+ 32.27
67,220.1	522	Small-Cap Growth Funds	− 4.71	− 1.58	− 9.71	− 8.64	+ 27.41
54,441.6	229	Small-Cap Value Funds	− 0.72	− 0.58	− 7.58	− 4.68	+ 32.92
7,677.9	94	Specialty Dvsfd Eq Funds	+ 0.10	+ 0.33	+ 1.05	+ 0.60	− 2.88
280,236.3	172	S&P 500 Funds	− 1.64	− 0.63	− 4.31	− 4.77	+ 18.16
117,199.0	237	Equity Income Funds	− 1.79	− 0.34	− 4.49	− 4.68	+ 18.06
2,698,720.5	6,662	Gen. Equity Funds Avg.	− 2.22	− 0.84	− 6.20	− 5.59	+ 20.97
Other Equity Funds							
47,109.2	197	Health/Biotechnology	+ 2.94%	− 1.86%	− 6.13%	− 2.70%	+ 20.50%
12,421.7	85	Natural Resources	+ 0.50	− 0.47	− 6.59	− 2.79	+ 24.01
44,982.9	324	Science & Technol.	− 6.78	− 1.78	− 8.75	− 10.95	+ 25.31
2,512.3	30	Telecommunication Funds	+ 0.35	− 0.66	− 7.62	− 9.97	+ 26.94
12,627.3	88	Utility Funds	− 1.31	+ 0.44	− 3.94	− 4.51	+ 12.38
13,701.0	112	Financial Services	− 1.76	+ 0.23	− 3.88	− 7.33	+ 21.94
30,017.1	215	Real Estate Fund	− 3.21	+ 3.23	− 1.93	− 7.93	+ 18.15
10,062.9	80	Specialty/Misc.	− 0.02	− 0.45	− 5.47	− 2.83	+ 23.98
5,757.2	49	Gold Oriented Funds	− 22.69	+ 5.70	− 8.71	− 19.61	+ 23.87
140,273.1	340	Global Funds	− 2.38	− 0.07	− 6.04	− 6.80	+ 22.74
19,260.8	56	Global Small Cap Funds	− 1.58	− 0.44	− 7.88	− 7.03	+ 33.43
279,590.0	901	International Funds	− 2.44	+ 0.64	− 6.34	− 7.78	+ 26.66
18,342.7	100	Int'l Small Cap Funds	+ 0.30	+ 0.03	− 7.96	− 7.07	+ 39.57
18,939.8	148	European Region Fds	− 1.81	+ 0.52	− 4.01	− 9.28	+ 26.36
5,722.0	42	Pacific Region Funds	− 3.57	+ 0.20	− 11.50	− 7.73	+ 36.69
9,195.0	52	Japanese Funds	− 0.52	+ 1.49	− 11.49	− 0.11	+ 44.24
6,439.4	61	Pacific Ex Japan Funds	− 7.22	− 2.19	− 13.96	− 14.85	+ 36.60
2,131.7	22	China Region Funds	− 9.81	− 1.80	− 10.78	− 17.74	+ 37.02
52,325.6	182	Emerging Markets Funds	− 6.02	− 1.11	− 13.04	− 12.74	+ 37.77
1,386.4	26	Latin American Funds	− 9.56	− 0.78	− 13.02	− 13.80	+ 25.87
559,363.7	1,979	World Equity Funds Avg.	− 3.36	+ 0.29	− 7.53	− 8.63	+ 28.90
3,431,518.6	9,772	All Equity Funds Avg.	− 2.46	− 0.54	− 6.42	− 6.36	+ 22.68
Other Funds							
63,539.4	358	Flexible Portfolio	− 2.04%	− 0.14%	− 4.05%	− 4.56%	+ 12.43%
25,602.0	94	Global Flex Port.	− 1.77	+ 0.08	− 4.60	− 5.24	+ 17.16
252,131.0	615	Balanced Funds	− 1.74	− 0.18	− 3.77	− 4.26	+ 11.00
6,847.2	81	Balanced Target	− 2.10	+ 0.11	− 2.57	− 3.70	+ 0.12
10,716.8	76	Conv. Securities	− 1.46	− 0.11	− 4.83	− 4.81	+ 13.87
119,640.8	201	Income Funds	− 1.45	+ 0.21	− 2.80	− 3.53	+ 8.82
28,498.5	204	World Income Funds	− 3.66	+ 0.93	− 2.50	− 4.78	+ 1.61
787,179.3	2,648	Fixed Income Funds	− 0.94	+ 0.55	− 1.56	− 2.14	+ 1.36
4,725,673.7	14,049	Long-Term Average	− 2.12	− 0.27	− 5.17	− 5.33	+ 17.24
N/A		Long-Term Median	− 1.78	− 0.34	− 4.96	− 5.00	+ 17.64
N/A		Funds with a % Change	+ 13,749	+ 13,601	+ 13,907	+ 13,907	+ 13,108
Securities Market Indexes							
Value		**U.S. Equities**					
6,277.12		NYSE Composite P	− 2.89	− 0.28	− 5.37	− 6.52	+ 19.03
1,247.38		S&P Industrials	− 1.68	− 0.91	− 4.64	− 4.50	+ 17.23
1,089.19		S&P 500 P	− 2.04	− 0.66	− 4.45	− 5.05	+ 16.88
9,937.64		Dow Jones Ind. Avg. P	− 4.94	− 0.73	− 5.00	− 6.82	+ 15.63
		International Equities					
10,862.04		Nikkei 225 Average P	+ 1.74	+ 0.34	− 9.33	+ 1.01	+ 34.90
4,428.70		FT S-E 100 Index	− 1.08	− 0.56	− 3.13	− 1.92	+ 10.98
3,839.32		DAX Index	− 3.17	+ 0.38	− 5.42	− 7.30	+ 34.00
Fund Management Companies							
Value							
5,573.51		Stock-price Index	− 4.56%	− 0.03%	− 7.07%	− 14.38%	+ 21.36%

P-Price only index. Calculated without reinvestment of dividends.   Source: Lipper

Source: *Barron's*, May 24, 2004, p. F15.

In this instance, there is a total return of $1.77. Based on a beginning NAV of $14.05, the return is 12.60 percent:

$$\frac{\text{Total return}}{\text{Beginning NAV}} = \frac{\$1.77}{\$14.05} = 12.60\%$$

As a further consideration, assume that instead of taking dividends and capital gains income in cash, you decide to automatically reinvest the proceeds to purchase new mutual fund shares. To compute the percentage return in this instance, you must compare the total value of your ending shares to the total value of your beginning shares. Assume you owned 100 shares to start, and you received $0.72 in dividends plus capital gains per share (see prior example). This would allow you to reinvest $72 (100 shares × $0.72 per share). Further assume you bought new shares at an average price of $14.40 per share. This would provide you with five new shares.[7]

$$\frac{\text{Dividends and capital gains allocated to the account}}{\text{Average purchase price of new shares}} = \frac{\$72}{\$14.40} = 5 \text{ new shares}$$

In comparing the ending and beginning value of the investment based on the example in this section, we show the following:

$$\text{Total return} = \frac{\begin{pmatrix}\text{Number of}\\ \text{ending shares}\\ \times \text{ Ending price}\end{pmatrix} - \begin{pmatrix}\text{Number of}\\ \text{beginning shares}\\ \times \text{ Beginning price}\end{pmatrix}}{\text{Number of beginning shares} \times \text{Beginning price}} \quad (18\text{–}2)$$

$$= \frac{(105 \times \$15.10) - (100 \times \$14.05)}{(100 \times \$14.05)}$$

$$= \frac{\$1,585.50 - \$1,405}{\$1,405}$$

$$= \frac{\$180.50}{\$1,405} = 12.85\%$$

In determining whether the returns computed in this section are adequate, you must compare your returns with the popular market averages and with the returns on other mutual funds. While the returns might be considered quite good for a conservative fund, such might not be the case for an aggressive, growth-oriented fund. You must also consider the amount of risk you are taking in the form of volatility of returns. These factors of risk and return are more fully developed in the chapters on portfolio management, in Chapters 21 and 22.

---

[7] In this case, the number of new shares came out to be a whole number. It is also possible to buy fractional shares in a mutual fund.

exploring the web

Website Address	Comments
www.morningstar.com	Basic site containing detailed information about mutual funds, portfolio tracking, and analysis
www.quicken.com	Provides mutual fund data and quotes along with portfolio tracking and financial planning information
www.my.yahoo.com	Permits tracking of mutual funds in portfolios
moneycentral.msn.com	Provides information about mutual funds

Summary

Investment funds allow investors to pool their resources under the guidance of professional managers. Some funds are closed-end, which means there is a *fixed* number of shares, and purchasers and sellers of shares must deal with each other (via brokers). They normally cannot buy new shares from the fund. Much more important is the open-end fund, which stands ready at all times to sell new shares or buy back old shares. Actually, it is the open-end investment fund that technically represents the term *mutual fund*.

An important consideration with an open-end fund is whether it is a load fund or a no-load fund. The former requires a commission that may run as high as 7.25 percent, while the latter has no such charge. Because there is no proof that load funds deliver better performance than no-load funds, the investor should think long and hard before paying a commission.

Mutual funds may take many different forms such as those emphasizing money market management, growth in common stocks, bond portfolio management, special sectors of the economy (such as energy or computers), or foreign investments. The funds with an international orientation have enjoyed strong popularity in the last decade.

Through examining a fund's prospectus, the investor can become familiar with the fund's investment objectives and policies, its portfolio holdings, its turnover rate, and the fund's management fees. The investor can also become aware of whether the fund offers such special services as automatic reinvestment of distributions (when desired), exchange privileges among different funds, systematic withdrawal plans, and check-writing privileges.

Return to fund holders may come in the form of capital appreciation or yield. Over the long term, mutual funds have not outperformed the popular market averages. However, they do offer an opportunity for low-cost, efficient diversification, and they normally have experienced management. Also, a minority of funds have turned in above-average performances.

Key Words and Concepts

back-end load 502	growth funds 508	net asset value (NAV) 500
balanced funds 508	growth with income funds 508	no-load funds 502
bond mutual funds 510		open-end fund 498
closed-end fund 498	hedge funds 511	prospectus 512
dollar-cost averaging 515	index funds 508	sector funds 510
exchange traded funds (ETFs) 501	load funds 502	specialty funds 510
	low-load funds 502	unit investment trusts (UITs) 525
foreign funds 510	money market funds 506	

Discussion Questions

1. Do mutual funds, on average, outperform the market?
2. Do mutual funds generally provide efficient diversification?
3. Explain why the vast array of mutual funds available to the investor may be a partial drawback and not always an advantage.
4. What is the basic difference between a closed-end fund and an open-end fund?
5. Define net asset value. Do closed-end funds normally trade at their net asset value? What about open-end funds?
6. Is it mandatory that you pay a load fee when purchasing an open-end mutual fund? What is a low-load fund?
7. Should you get better performance from a load fund in comparison to a no-load fund?
8. If there is a difference between the net asset value (NAV) and the offer price for a mutual fund, what does that tell us about the fund?
9. How can you distinguish between regular growth funds and aggressive growth funds?
10. What type of fund is likely to invest in convertible securities?
11. Why might there be some potential danger in investing in sector funds?
12. What does Rule 12b-1 enable mutual funds to do? Is this normally beneficial to current mutual fund shareholders?
13. Are earnings of mutual funds normally taxed at the fund level or the shareholder level?
14. What is the advantage of investing in a mutual fund that offers an exchange privilege?
15. What is dollar-cost averaging? If you were a particularly astute investor at timing moves in the market, would you want to use dollar-cost averaging?
16. From the viewpoint of an individual investor, what is the potential tax disadvantage of investing in a mutual fund?

Problems

Net asset value

1. The New Frontier closed-end fund has $420 million in securities, $6 million in liabilities, and 20 million shares outstanding. It trades at a 10 percent discount from net asset value (NAV).
   a. What is the net asset value of the fund?
   b. What is the current price of the fund?

c. Suggest two reasons why the fund may be trading at a discount from net asset value.

Net asset value

2. The Scientific American closed-end fund has $625 million in securities, $10 million in liabilities, and 10 million shares outstanding. It trades at a 6 percent premium above its net asset value (NAV).
   a. What is the net asset value of the fund?
   b. What is the current price of the fund?
   c. Why might a fund trade at a premium above its net asset value?

Net asset value

3. In problem 2, if Scientific American converted to an open-end fund trading at net asset value with a four percent load (commission), what would its purchase price be?

Load funds

4. An open-end fund is set up to charge a load. Its net asset value is $11.80, and its offer price is $12.40.
   a. What is the dollar value of the load (commission)?
   b. What percent of the offer price does the load represent?
   c. What percent of the net asset value does the load represent?
   d. Do load funds necessarily outperform no-load funds?
   e. How do no-load funds earn a return if they do not charge a commission?

Load funds

5. In problem 4, assume the fund increased in value by 20 cents the first month after you purchased 200 shares.
   a. What is your total dollar gain or loss? (Compare the total current value with the total purchase amount.)
   b. By what percentage would the net asset value of the shares have to increase for you to break even?

Comparative fund performance and loads

6. a. If you purchased a low-load fund at $10.30 and it had a net asset value of $10.00, what is the percent load?
   b. If the fund's net asset value went up by 33.72 percent, what would its new net asset value be?
   c. What is your dollar profit or loss per share based on your purchase price?
   d. What is your percentage return on your purchase price?

Total returns to a fund

7. An investor buys shares in the no-load Atlas World Fund on January 1 at a net asset value of $22.10. At the end of the year, the price is $26.50. Also, the investor receives 60 cents in dividends and 30 cents in capital gains distributions. What is the total percent return on the beginning net asset value? (Round to two places to the right of the decimal point.)

Total returns to a fund

8. Dale Hansen purchases shares in the no-load 21st Century Fund at a net asset value of $12.20. During the year, he receives 55 cents in dividends and 17 cents in capital gains distributions. At the end of the year, the fund's price is $11.80. What is the total percent return or loss on the beginning net asset value? (Round to two places to the right of the decimal point.)

Total returns with reinvestment

9. Anna Gomez had 200 shares of the Discovery Fund on January 1. The shares had a value of $12.60. During the year she received $80 in dividends and $206 in capital gains distributions. She used the new funds to purchase shares at an average price of $13 per share. By the end of the year, the shares were up to $13.40. What is her percent total return? Use Formula 18–2 on page 519, and round to two places to the right of the decimal point. Recall you first must determine the number of new shares.

Dollar-cost averaging

10. Under dollar-cost averaging, an investor will purchase $9,000 worth of stock each year for three years. The stock price is $60 in year 1, $45 in year 2, and $75 in year 3.
    a. Compute the average price per share.
    b. Compute the average cost per share.
    c. Explain why the average cost is less than the average price.

Critical Thought Case—Focus on Ethics

Al Harris was particularly glad to have an opportunity to visit with Mildred Frazier. Al had been selling mutual funds for the last five years, and he believed he was about to make his best sale of the year.

Mildred, age 70, had inherited $500,000 on the death of her husband four months ago. Her husband had been a successful businessman and had managed their financial affairs up to the time of his death. Although their home mortgage had been paid, Mildred had the inherited $500,000 in CDs, money market funds, and widely diversified stocks and bonds to manage. Her first inclination had been to turn over the assets to the trust department of the largest bank in town and let it manage the funds for a 1½ percent fee.

When she mentioned this plan to Al at a church gathering, he responded that bank trust departments were so conservative in their management policies that she probably would not get a return high enough to keep up with inflation.

He suggested she put her $500,000 in the New Era Science and Technology fund. He emphasized that the fund had enjoyed an increase in net asset value of 20 percent per year over the past five years for a total compounded gain of 148.8 percent. He suggested a $500,000 investment could easily be worth $1,244,000 five years from now as the same pattern was likely to persist.

When Mildred asked if there were any expenses involved in buying the fund, Al said there was a courtesy commission of 7¼ percent at the time of purchase. Also, there was a back-end fee of 5 percent if she decided to sell the fund. He stressed that the 7¼ percent commission was insignificant when one considered the enormous return potential. Furthermore, he said, the 5 percent back-end sales commission would be reduced by 1 percent each year and would be eliminated after five years. Mildred was excited about the information Al had given her and promised to consider it very carefully.

Question
1. Comment on the practices used by Al Harris.

Web Exercise

Many large mutual fund sponsors have a large family of funds under management. One example of this is the Fidelity fund group. Go to **www.fidelity.com**.

1. Click on "Mutual Funds" along the right-hand side.
2. On the next page, click on "Learn about Fidelity Funds." Then on the following page, click on "Browse Our Funds" toward the middle of the page.
3. Then click on "Growth" toward the middle of the next page.
4. On the screen before you, you will see a list of approximately 30 Fidelity growth funds.

5. One of the most famous of the Fidelity funds is the Magellan fund, so click on that.
6. Record the following information for the Magellan fund as you scroll down the page.
   a. Lipper ranking over 1, 5, and 10 years (scroll down for this).
   b. Morningstar rating overall and after 3, 5, and 10 years.
   c. Its "Annual Total Returns" compared to The S&P 500 Index for 1, 3, 5, and 10 years.
   d. The "Major Market Sector" in which it has its three largest holdings and what the most recent percentages are.
   e. Its "Asset Allocation" between "Equity" and "Cash & Other" in percentages (most recent value).
   f. Its expense ratio.
   g. The minimum investment required.
7. Start over and go to the page with the 30 funds listed. Pick the fund that had the largest percentage change in NAV for the prior day. Click on that fund. Without writing down the information, scroll down the page, and observe and compare the variables that you recorded for Magellan. How does the firm compare?

Note: From time to time, companies redesign their websites, and occasionally a topic we have listed may have been deleted, updated, or moved into a different location. Most websites have a "site map" or "site index" listed on a different page. If you click on the site map or site index, you will be introduced to a table of contents that should aid you in finding the topic you are looking for.

The Wall Street Journal Projects

1. Go to the "Mutual Funds" section of *The Wall Street Journal*. Select any four different families of funds that have at least five funds listed under them.
2. For each family of funds, pick the individual fund that has the best and the one that has the worst performance YTD (year-to-date). Do the same for the three years column.
3. Does any individual fund show up more than once?

Selected References

Investment Strategy

Detamore-Rodman, Crystal. "Hidden Hedge Fund Risks Jeopardize Unknowing Investors." *CFA Magazine,* May–June 2003, pp. 52–44.

Healy, Thomas J., and Donald J. Hardy. "Alternative Investments Grow Rapidly at Tax Exempt Funds." *Journal of Investing,* Spring 1994, pp. 12–18.

Ruth, Simon. "Why Good Brokers Sell Bad Funds." *Money,* July 1991, pp. 94–99.

Mutual Fund Performance

Baks, Klaas; Andrew Metrick; and Jessica Wachter. "Should Investors Avoid All Actively Managed Mutual Funds? A Study in Bayesian Performance Evaluation." *Journal of Finance,* February 2001, pp. 45–85.

Bekaert, Geert, and Michael S. Urias. "Diversification, Integration and Emerging Market Closed-End Funds." *Journal of Finance,* July 1996, pp. 835–69.

Carhart, Mark M. "On Persistence in Mutual Fund Performance." *Journal of Finance,* March 1997, pp. 57–82.

Daniel, Kent; Mark Grinblatt; Sheridan Titman; and Russ Wermers. "Measuring Mutual Fund Performance and Characteristic-Based Benchmarks." *Journal of Finance,* July 1997, pp. 1035–58.

Ferguson, Robert, and Dean Leisikow. "Valuing Active Managers, Fees, and Fund Discounts." *Financial Analysis Journal,* May–June 2001, pp. 52–62.

Ferson, Wayne E., and Rudi W. Schadt. "Measuring Fund Strategy and Performance in Changing Economic Conditions." *Journal of Finance,* June 1996, pp. 425–61.

Goetzmann, William N., and Roger G. Ibbotson. "Do Winners Repeat?" *Journal of Portfolio Management,* Winter 1994, pp. 9–18.

Ippolito, Richard A. "On Studies of Mutual Fund Performance, 1962–1991." *Financial Analysts Journal,* January–February 1993, pp. 42–50.

Lynch, Anthony W., and David K. Musto. "How Investors Interpret Past Fund Returns?" *The Journal of Finance,* October 2003, pp. 2033–58.

O'Neal Edward S. "Industry Momentum and Sector Mutual Funds." *Financial Analysts Journal,* July–August 2000, pp. 37–49.

Mutual Fund Guides and Surveys

"A Guide to Mutual Funds." *Consumer Reports* (published annually).

"Individual Investor's Guide to Low-Load Mutual Funds." American Association of Individual Investors (published annually).

"Morningstar Mutual Funds." Morningstar Inc. (published every other week).

"Tallying the Totals: Mutual Fund Scorecard." *Financial World* (published annually).

"The Money Ranking of Mutual Funds." *Money* (published annually).

Appendix 18A

UNIT INVESTMENT TRUSTS (UITS)

Unit investment trusts (UITs) are investment companies organized for the purpose of purchasing a pool of securities—usually tax-exempt municipal bonds. UITs issue units to investors, representing a proportionate interest in the assets of the trust. Investors also receive a proportionate share in the interest or dividends received by the trust.

According to the Investment Company Institute, by the end of 2003 there were a total of 10,263 unit trusts with a market value of $85.24 billion. While this is not a lot of money compared with mutual funds, unit trusts do meet a market niche for specialized investors. Of the 10,000 trusts, more than 8,000 were tax-free bond trusts. While equity trusts only accounted for slightly more than 1,500 trusts, they made up the lion's share of the value with $60 billion.

Unit investment trusts are passive investments. They normally purchase assets and hold them for the benefit of owners for a specified period.

To understand UITs better, consider the following hypothetical example. Nuveen, Inc.—a prominent firm in this field—announces the formation of the next in its series of tax-exempt unit trusts: Nuveen Series 200. Through advertising and selling agents, Nuveen will raise $4 million; investors will pay approximately $1,000 per unit. After deducting 2 to 3 percent for sales commissions, Nuveen will use the remaining cash to purchase large blocks of municipal securities from 10 to 20 different issuers. Once this diversified pool of bonds is acquired, Nuveen will play a passive role. It will collect and pass on to unit holders all interest payments received and all principal repayments resulting from maturing or recalled bonds. While UITs usually hold bonds until maturity, the trust custodian may sell off bonds whose future ability to pay interest and principal is altered by events.

Often, trusts are formed to purchase tax-exempt securities from issuers in specific, high-tax states, such as New York, Massachusetts, and Minnesota. Unit holders residing in these states expect to receive a stream of income exempt from federal, state, and local taxation.

Even unit investment trusts dedicated to tax-exempt bonds have different investment objectives. Some deal strictly in long-term, high-rated issues. Others seek higher yields by purchasing issues with low ratings.

Units of a trust are redeemable under terms set forth in the prospectus. In most cases, this means a unit holder can sell units back to the trust at their net asset value, which is the current market value of each trust unit.

A secondary market for unit trusts is evolving among broker-dealers. Investors seeking to acquire or sell units can sometimes find a better deal in this market. However, most investors in UITs do not intend to redeem early.

Investors in UITs benefit by professional selection of securities, by diversification, and by avoiding the housekeeping chores of collecting coupon payments. As a large buyer, a UIT can usually purchase securities at a better price than the individual who buys in small lots.

Essential Difference between a Unit Investment Trust and a Mutual Fund

There is an important difference between UITs and mutual funds. UITs are formed with the intention of keeping all the initially purchased assets until maturity. The investment strategy, as described above, is strictly passive. A UIT of $4 million with a 10-year life will draw interest over that time period, while only cashing in bonds as they mature and returning the funds to the investors. The UIT will cease to exist after 10 years. Because of the features just described, there is very little interest-rate risk associated with UITs. Since all bonds are intended to be held until maturity, the investor can be reasonably well assured of recovering his initial investment (plus interest). The fact that interest rates and bond prices are changing at any point in time during the life of the UIT makes little difference.[1]

A bond-oriented mutual fund has no such assurance of recovering the initial investment. First, mutual funds have no stipulated life. Second, the bonds in the portfolio are actively managed and frequently sold off before their maturity dates at large profits or losses. Thus, the purchaser of a bond-oriented mutual fund may experience large capital gains or losses as well as receiving interest income.

The message is that if preservation of capital is of paramount importance to the investor, the UIT may be a better investment than a mutual fund. Of course, if one thinks interest rates are going down and bond prices up, the bond-oriented mutual fund would be a better investment.

---

[1] Of course, if the investor needs to redeem shares before the end of the life of the trust, there will be fluctuations in value.

19

chapter nineteen

International Securities Markets

objectives

1. Describe the diversification benefits of international investments.

2. Explain the difference between market performance in developed countries versus emerging countries.

3. Describe the return potential in foreign markets versus that in the United States.

4. Explain the effect of currency fluctuations on rates of return.

5. Understand the various methods of participating in foreign investments.

6. Describe the risks and obstacles associated with foreign investments.

The World Equity Market
Diversification Benefits
Return Potential in International Markets
    Current Quotations on Foreign Market Performance
    Other Market Differences
Currency Fluctuations and Rates of Return
Other Obstacles to International Investments
    Political Risks
    Tax Problems
    Lack of Market Efficiency
    Administrative Problems
    Information Difficulties
Methods of Participating in Foreign Investments
    Direct Investments
    Indirect Investments

In Chapter 1, we discussed the advantage of diversification in terms of risk reduction. To reduce risk exposure, the investor may desire a broad spectrum of securities from which to choose. An investor who lives in California would hardly be expected to limit all his investments to that geographic boundary. The same might be said for an investor living in the United States or Germany or Japan. The advantages of crossing international boundaries may be substantial in terms of diversification benefits.

Companies operating in different countries will be affected differently by international events such as crop failures, energy prices, wars, tariffs, trade between countries, and the value of local currencies relative to other currencies, especially the U.S. dollar. Furthermore, despite the up and down markets in the United States, there is almost certain to be a bull market somewhere in the world for the investor who likes to keep his chips on the table at all times.

Of course, there are some disadvantages to investing in international securities. The main drawback would appear to be the more complicated nature of the investment. Currently, one cannot simply pick up the phone and ask a broker to buy 100 shares of any stock listed on a foreign exchange. Some foreign markets have very low liquidity or require citizenship for ownership, or U.S. brokers may be restricted from dealing in these securities.

The primary focus of this chapter is international equities, although investments may certainly include fixed-income securities and real assets. We shall examine the composition of world equity markets, the diversification and return benefits that can be derived from foreign investments, the obstacles that are present, and finally, the methods of participating in foreign investments directly and indirectly.

The World Equity Market

The world equity markets grew rapidly from 1992 to 1999 and then went into reverse. At the peak of the stock market bubble at year-end 1999, the market capitalization (value) of the developed countries' stock markets was $33 trillion. Three years later, as you can see in the middle of Table 19–1, the total capitalization decreased to about $20.9 trillion. This is a lot of money to evaporate in three years time. Fortunately, markets fluctuate with economic activity and over time they recover with the economy. As you will see in Table 19–4 later in the chapter, world markets had a strong recovery in 2003. To some extent Japan demonstrates the economic truth that stock market growth is related to the overall growth in a country's economy. As Japan's economy stagnated and profits declined, so did the Nikkei 225 Index representing the Tokyo stock market.

While market capitalization in the world declined, the relative percentages by geographical area stayed relatively the same, as shown in Figure 19–1, with North America (United States, Canada, and Mexico) increasing their share of the world market by 2 percent to 55 percent, Europe increasing its share by 1 percent to 30 percent, and Asia giving up 3 percent to 15 percent.

Returning to Table 19–1, you may be surprised by some of the countries listed as developed countries. The International Monetary Fund defines developed countries by per capita income not by the size of GDP or the population. That is why several small countries like Bermuda and Iceland with small stock markets, small economies, and small populations are included in the table.

While the developed world securities markets continue to expand, major growth in securities markets has also occurred in the "emerging" markets such as Argentina, Brazil, China, Taiwan, and Mexico. Additionally, the Eastern European countries of Poland, Hungary, The Czech Republic, Slovakia, and Slovenia have developed fledgling stock markets, with Poland leading the group with a market value of $28.75 billion, constituting over 1 percent of the total emerging market. Table 19–2 on page 530 lists the market capitalizations of the emerging markets. The total value in 1996 was $2.2 trillion, which grew to $2.4 trillion by 2002. The emerging markets grew much more slowly than the developed markets during this time period, but with $2.4 trillion, emerging markets (in total) would rank in second place among developed countries, just edging out the

TABLE 19–1 Market Capitalization of Developed Countries (in millions of U.S. dollars)

Country	Year-End 1996	Percent of Total	Year-End 2002	Percent of Total	Percent Change between 1996–2002
Australia	$ 311,981	1.73%	$ 380,969	1.82%	18.1%
Austria	33,953	0.19	31,664	0.15	−7.2
Belgium	119,831	0.67	127,556	0.61	6.1
Bermuda	0	0.00	2,175	0.01	100.0
Canada	486,268	2.70	575,316	2.75	15.5
Cyprus	2,355	0.01	1,489	0.01	−58.2
Denmark	71,688	0.40	76,788	0.37	6.6
Finland	63,078	0.35	138,833	0.66	54.6
France	591,123	3.29	966,962	4.61	38.9
Germany	670,997	3.73	685,970	3.27	2.2
Greece	24,178	0.13	68,741	0.33	64.8
Hong Kong	449,381	2.50	463,108	2.21	3.0
Iceland	1,210	0.01	6,318	0.03	80.8
Ireland	12,242	0.07	59,938	0.29	79.6
Italy	258,160	1.44	477,075	2.28	45.9
Japan	3,088,850	17.18	2,126,075	10.15	−45.3
Luxembourg	32,692	0.18	22,587	0.11	−44.7
Netherlands	378,721	2.11	401,465	1.92	5.7
New Zealand	38,641	0.21	21,745	0.10	−77.7
Norway	57,423	0.32	67,300	0.32	14.7
Portugal	24,660	0.14	42,846	0.20	42.4
Singapore	150,215	0.84	101,900	0.49	−47.4
Spain	242,779	1.35	461,559	2.20	47.4
Sweden	247,217	1.37	177,065	0.84	−39.6
Switzerland	402,104	2.24	553,758	2.64	27.4
United Kingdom	1,740,246	9.68	1,864,134	8.90	6.6
United States	8,484,433	47.18	11,052,403	52.74	23.2
	$17,984,426		$20,955,739		14.2%

Source: *Global Stock Markets Factbook, 2003,* Standard & Poor's, 2004, p. 25.

FIGURE 19–1 Developed Markets by Geographical Area, 2002

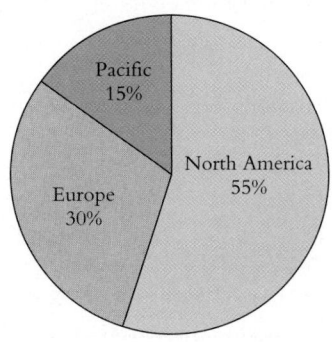

Source: *Global Stock Markets Factbook, 2003,* Standard & Poor's, 2004, p. 25.

TABLE 19–2 Market Capitalization of Emerging Markets Greater Than 500 Million in Capitalization (in millions of U.S. dollars)

Country	Year-End 1996	Percent of Total	Year-End 2002	Percent of Total
Argentina	$ 44,679	2.01%	$ 103,434	4.27%
Bahrain	0	0.00	6,855	0.28
Bangladesh	4,551	0.20	1,193	0.05
Barbados	766	0.03	3,441	0.14
Brazil	216,990	9.77	123,807	5.11
Chile	65,940	2.94	47,584	1.96
China	**113,755**	**5.12**	**463,080**	**19.10**
Colombia	17,137	0.77	9,664	0.40
Cote d'Ivoire	914	0.04	1,328	0.05
Croatia	2,975	0.13	3,796	0.16
Czech Republic	18,077	0.81	15,893	0.66
Ecuador	1,946	0.09	1,750	0.07
Egypt	14,173	0.64	26,094	1.08
El Salvador	452	0.02	2,704	0.11
Estonia	0	0.00	2,430	0.10
Ghana	1,492	0.07	740	0.03
Hungary	5,273	0.24	13,110	0.54
India	122,605	5.52	131,011	5.40
Indonesia	91,016	4.10	29,991	1.24
Iran	17,008	0.77	14,344	0.59
Israel	35,935	1.62	45,371	1.87
Jamaica	1,887	0.08	5,838	0.24
Jordan	4,551	0.20	7,087	0.29
Kazakhstan	0	0.00	1,341	0.06
Kenya	1,846	0.08	1,423	0.06
Korea	**138,817**	**6.25**	**249,639**	**10.30**
Lebanon	0	0.00	1,401	0.06
Lithuania	900	0.04	1,463	0.06
Malaysia	307,179	13.84	123,872	5.11
Mauritius	1,676	0.08	1,328	0.05
Mexico	106,540	4.80	103,137	4.25
Morocco	8,705	0.39	8,591	0.35
Nigeria	3,560	0.16	5,740	0.24
Oman	2,673	0.12	3,997	0.16
Pakistan	10,639	0.48	10,200	0.42
Panama	1,279	0.06	2,950	0.12
Peru	12,291	0.55	13,363	0.55
Philippines	80,649	3.63	39,021	1.61
Poland	8,390	0.38	28,750	1.19
Russia	**37,230**	**1.68**	**124,198**	**5.12**
Saudi Arabia	45,861	2.07	74,855	3.09
South Africa	241,571	10.88	184,622	7.61
Slovakia	2,182	0.10	1,904	0.08
Slovenia	663	0.03	4,606	0.19
Sri Lanka	1,848	0.08	1,681	0.07
Taiwan	273,608	12.32	261,474	10.78
Thailand	99,828	4.50	46,084	1.90
Trinidad and Tobago	1,405	0.06	6,506	0.27
Tunisia	4,263	0.19	2,131	0.09
Turkey	30,020	1.35	33,958	1.40
Ukraine	0	0.00	3,119	0.13
Venezuela	10,055	0.45	3,962	0.16
Yugoslavia	0	0.00	734	0.03
Zimbabwe	3,635	0.16	15,632	0.64
Total (in $ millions)	$2,220,217		$2,424,530	

Source: *Global Stock Markets Factbook, 2003,* Standard & Poor's, 2004, p. 24, 25.

United Kingdom and Japan. Some of the emerging markets, such as Korea ($249 billion) and China ($463 billion), are bigger than markets in developed countries, but because these countries have a low per capita GDP, they are listed with the emerging markets.

China, Korea, and Russia are highlighted because they have had the biggest increase in value. China's story is well known. It is an emerging giant that entered into the World Trade Organization in 2003. It boasts one of the highest GDP growth rates in the world and is fast becoming an economic power. It has embraced a limited form of capitalism and created an active stock market. Korea is slightly different because the country had a near economic collapse during the 1997–1998 currency crises and had the fastest recovery of any of the Asian countries suffering through that period. Russia on the other hand is interesting because as the former giant among communist countries, its fledgling stock market has increased 3.3 times in the six-year period shown in Table 19–2.

One way to keep emerging markets in perspective is to compare their size with some well-known U.S. companies. For example, in June 2004, General Electric had a market capitalization of $324 billion and would rank second behind China's market value. Microsoft had a market value of $295 billion and ExxonMobil $288 billion. They would be in third and fourth place on the emerging market list.

The small size of some emerging markets explains the low liquidity of these markets and also explains why small capital flows in and out of these markets can create wide price swings. When U.S. investors suddenly decide they want to own stocks in emerging market countries, money managers of mutual funds specializing in these countries have a difficult time placing all the funds without driving prices up dramatically.

Investors often equate emerging markets to high growth, and there is some truth in this. Between 1992 and 2002 the developed countries increased in market capitalization from $9.9 trillion to $20.9 trillion, a 111 percent increase. The emerging markets increased in size from $882 billion to $2.4 trillion, an increase of 172 percent. While this is higher than the developed countries, many individual emerging market countries increased at much higher growth rates than the average. China increased 2,472 percent over this time, from $18 billion to $463 billion. During this time period, several other countries increased their market value by more than 500 percent, which far outdistanced growth among the developed countries.

A geographical breakdown of the emerging markets for 1996 and 2002 is depicted in Figure 19–2 on the next page. The relationships among the emerging countries have changed dramatically over this time period. Primarily, the currency meltdown in South Asia caused a big decrease in the value of South Asian countries' market values from $631 billion to $341 billion. At the same time East Asia's markets grew from $651 billion to $1.146 trillion. The South Asian countries lost one-half of their market share declining from 28 percent to 14 percent. East Asia was the big gainer going from 29 percent to 47 percent, while Europe, Latin America, and the Mideast/Africa gained or lost a few percentage points.

As emerging markets have grown, there are more opportunities to own equity positions in emerging markets. It is useful to look at the different market structures and institutional characteristics of these and other markets.

532 Part 6 Broadening the Investment Perspective

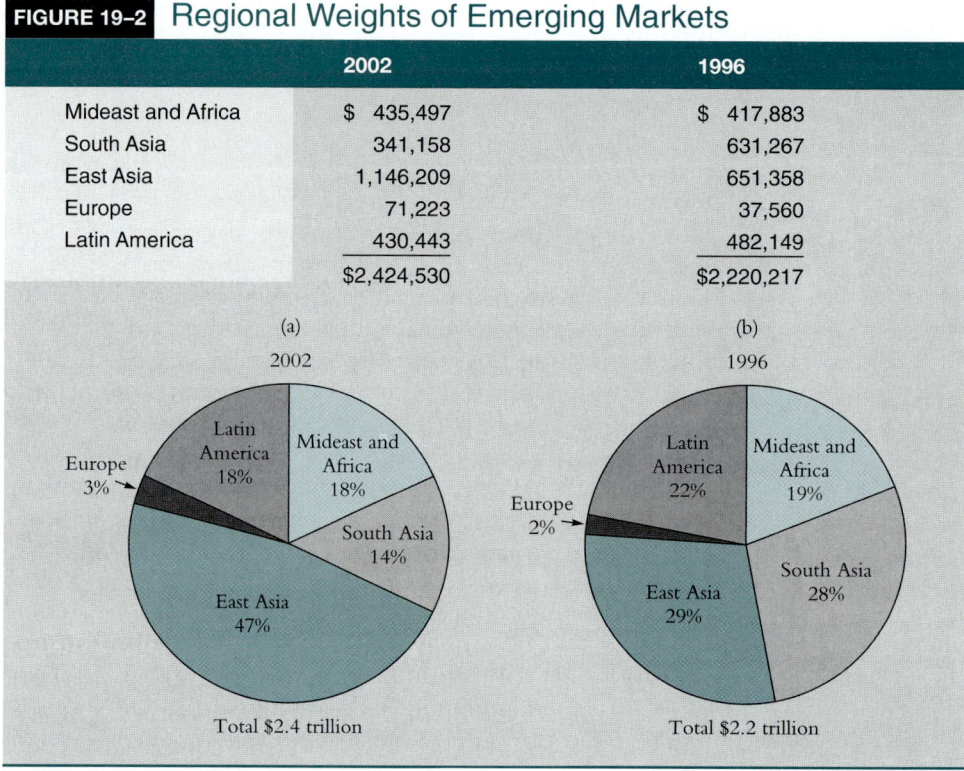

FIGURE 19-2 Regional Weights of Emerging Markets

Markets are structured quite differently. For example, continuous auction markets are the standard in countries such as the United States, Japan, United Kingdom, Germany, Canada, Hong Kong, and others. In many smaller emerging markets, there is not enough continuous buying and selling of securities to create the liquid markets necessary for continuous auction markets; instead, exchanges may trade shares once or twice per day. Some markets have specialists, automated trading, and computer-directed trading, while others do not. Even in the developed markets, most exchanges do not allow trading in options and futures on the stock exchanges. While most exchanges do not have limits on price movements, some exchanges limit prices within a band of 5 or 10 percent on a daily basis. Transaction taxes can be significant on foreign exchanges, ranging from 0 percent in Mexico to 2.4 percent in the Netherlands. Taxes at very high levels can reduce trading, liquidity, and potential returns. Many exchanges use some form of margin, which allows investors to purchase securities with a percentage of borrowed money, and some do not allow this practice at all. In some countries such as Korea, foreign investors may not be allowed to buy shares of companies at all. The moral is, do not assume that foreign markets function like those in the United States. Foreign markets usually have higher transactions costs, less liquidity, and are generally less efficient. Institutional practices around the world can have significant impacts on your rates of return.

Diversification Benefits

One of the benefits of foreign investing is that not all foreign markets move in the same direction at any point in time, so a diversified portfolio consisting of stocks from many countries will have less volatility than a purely domestic portfolio of stocks and could even have a higher rate of return. This benefit has not always been perfect, and in the 1987 market crash, 19 of 23 markets declined more than 20 percent. This is unusual given the low degree of correlation between the historical returns of different countries. An article by Richard Roll[1] pointed out that the most significant factor relating to the size of the market decline in each country was the beta of that market to the world market index.

In Table 19–3 on page 534, we see the stock market movements for a number of key countries over 28 years. Each year there is a wide range of performance numbers among these eight countries; the highest and lowest yearly returns are highlighted. There are several issues worth noting. No country continually outperforms the others on an annual basis. Hong Kong has the highest returns 8 out of 28 years and Japan had the lowest returns 9 out of 28 years. Canada has never had the highest return. In 20 of these years one of these countries had a loss.

Table 19–3 further shows that the developed markets in 2000, 2001, and 2002 were mostly in negative territory except for Switzerland and Canada in 2000. When markets move in the same direction, you sometimes hear that international markets don't provide any risk reduction. Occasionally markets move together because of some global economic force. In 1989 and 1997 during the October collapses of the U.S. markets and right after the September 11, 2001, attacks on New York's World Trade Center and the Pentagon in Washington, D.C., markets around the world reacted together as they fell in sympathy with the U.S. markets. International events that cause markets to move in unison have caused many market analysts to surmise that markets are more connected than they used to be for several reasons:

1. We have a global economy where international companies do business across borders. This phenomenon will cause economies across these geographical regions to become more intertwined and less diverse.

2. We have a new European Monetary Union with 11 countries (perhaps more by the time you read this) adopting the euro as the single currency. With the European Central Bank harmonizing monetary policy across the region, these European markets will behave more in line with each other.

While all these stories make sense, and even if they are true, we should recognize that over the long run, the world economies and their markets do not move directly with the U.S. economy on a consistent basis.

Let us look at a U.S. investor based on the data in Table 19–3. In 1976, a 23.8 percent return could be earned in the United States, while a 12.7 percent loss occurred in the United Kingdom. In 1977, this situation was reversed with a 7.2 percent loss in the United States and a 58 percent return in the United Kingdom. If an investor had held equal positions in both countries, returns would have been less volatile (risky), and a U.S. investor would have had a greater total return. Diversification reduces portfolio volatility and at the same time offers opportunities for higher returns than a single country portfolio.

One way to consider **diversification benefits** is to measure the extent of correlation of stock movements. The **correlation coefficient** measures the

---

[1] Richard Roll, "The International Crash of 1987," *Financial Analysts Journal,* September–October 1988, pp. 19–35.

TABLE 19–3 The Best Performing Equity Markets, 1976–2001 (in U.S. dollars)

	Germany	Switzerland	United Kingdom	Australia	Hong Kong	Japan	Canada	United States
1976	6.6	10.5	*(12.70)*	(10.2)	**40.7**	25.6	9.7	23.8
1977	25.8	28.7	**58.0**	11.9	*(11.20)*	15.9	(2.1)	(7.2)
1978	26.9	21.9	14.6	21.8	18.5	**53.3**	20.4	6.5
1979	(2.2)	12.1	22.1	43.6	**83.5**	*(11.9)*	51.8	18.5
1980	*(9.1)*	(7.3)	41.1	55.3	**72.7**	30.3	22.6	32.4
1981	(8.2)	(9.5)	(10.6)	*(23.9)*	(15.8)	15.8	(10.7)	(4.9)
1982	12.3	3.4	9.2	(22.6)	*(44.5)*	(0.5)	2.4	**21.5**
1983	25.9	19.3	17.2	**56.0**	*(3.0)*	24.9	33.4	22.2
1984	(3.8)	(11.1)	5.4	*(12.6)*	**46.8**	17.1	(7.6)	6.2
1985	**139.2**	107.4	52.8	20.9	51.6	43.4	15.9	31.6
1986	37.2	34.3	27.1	43.8	56.0	**99.7**	*10.7*	18.2
1987	*(23.4)*	(8.8)	36.5	10.3	(4.1)	**43.2**	14.6	5.2
1988	23.1	*7.1*	*7.1*	**38.0**	28.0	35.5	18.0	16.5
1989	**48.8**	27.1	23.1	10.8	8.3	*1.8*	25.2	31.4
1990	(10.8)	(7.8)	**6.0**	(21.0)	3.7	*(36.4)*	(15.3)	(5.6)
1991	8.7	13.6	12.0	n.a.	**43.4**	6.5	8.7	30.3
1992	(13.2)	13.3	(6.2)	(16.2)	**28.3**	*(23.1)*	(15.7)	2.8
1993	33.7	47.5	*3.2*	36.3	**107.7**	25.3	17.0	9.0
1994	3.3	2.4	(4.7)	2.9	*(31.0)*	**20.7**	(4.9)	(0.9)
1995	14.8	**42.4**	17.2	8.3	18.2	*0.0*	16.1	34.7
1996	12.1	1.2	23.3	13.4	**28.9**	*(16.0)*	26.4	21.4
1997	23.3	**43.2**	19.1	(12.6)	*(28.8)*	(24.2)	11.2	31.7
1998	28.2	22.6	14.8	3.8	*(7.6)*	4.3	(7.4)	**28.8**
1999	18.7	*(7.8)*	9.7	15.2	54.9	**60.6**	51.8	20.9
2000	(16.5)	**4.9**	(13.6)	(12.0)	(17.0)	*(28.5)*	4.4	(13.6)
2001	(23.5)	(21.9)	(16.1)	**(0.6)**	(21.2)	*(29.9)*	(21.4)	(13.2)
2002	*(34.8)*	(11.4)	(17.3)	**(3.9)**	(19.0)	(9.9)	(11.1)	(22.8)
2003	**64.5**	32.7	28.2	47.1	34.6	38.7	51.0	26.1
2004 (5 months)	*(5.5)*	1.7	1.6	(1.1)	(0.5)	**4.7**	(4.7)	0.5

Note: n.a.—not sufficient information.
Numbers represent total return, assuming reinvestment of dividends in U.S. dollars of the Morgan Stanley Capital International.
For 2002 and 2003, country specific exchange traded fund prices were used.
Index for each country. (Bold color numbers represent lowest returns and bold black numbers represent highest returns.)
Sources: Templeton International; Morgan Stanley Capital International Perspective, Geneva, located in *Barron's* January issues; Year-end issues of *The Wall Street Journal,* local index returns in U.S. dollars.

movement of one series of data over time to another series of data, in this case stock market returns. The correlation coefficient can be between −1 and +1. A coefficient of +1 indicates a perfect positive relationship as the two variables move together up and down. A coefficient of −1 indicates a perfect negative relationship as the two variables move opposite of each other. A zero coefficient describes a series that has no relationship. Any time you can diversify into assets that have a correlation coefficient of less than +1, you reduce the amount of risk assumed. Such a measure is presented in Table 19–4, in which stock movements for a number of developed countries are compared with those of the United States.

TABLE 19–4 Correlations of Foreign Stock Movements with U.S. Stock Movements

Country	Correlation 1960–1980	Rank	Correlation June 1981–Sept. 1987	Rank	Correlation July 1991–July 1996	Rank	Correlation Dec. 1997–Dec. 2002	Rank
United States	1.00		1.00		1.00		1.00	
Netherlands	0.73	(1)	0.47	(4)	0.32	(5)	0.72	(5)
Canada	0.71	(2)	0.72	(1)	0.70	(1)	0.81	(2)
Australia	0.70	(3)	0.33	(7)	0.17	(9)	0.64	(7)
United Kingdom	0.62	(4)	0.51	(2)	0.32	(6)	0.82	(1)
Switzerland	0.45	(5)	0.50	(3)	0.18	(8)	0.58	(9)
Sweden	0.40	(6)	0.28	(9)	0.29	(7)	0.72	(5)
Belgium	0.39	(7)	0.25	(10)	0.34	(3)	0.56	(10)
Denmark	0.24	(8)	0.35	(6)	0.08	(11)	0.62	(8)
Japan	0.22	(9)	0.33	(8)	0.08	(12)	0.51	(12)
France	0.21	(10)	0.39	(5)	0.36	(2)	0.77	(3)
Germany	0.21	(11)	0.21	(12)	0.14	(10)	0.76	(4)
Italy	0.21	(12)	0.22	(11)	0.33	(4)	0.54	(11)
Average Correlation	**0.47**		**0.43**		**0.33**		**0.70**	

Sources: Roger G. Ibbotson, Richard C. Carr, and Anthony W. Robinson, "International Equity and Bond Returns," *Financial Analysts Journal*, July–August 1982, p. 71; Richard Roll, "The International Crash of 1987," *Financial Analysts Journal*, September–October 1988, pp. 20–21; J.P. Morgan Correlation Calculator, www.jpmorgan.com; *Global Stock Markets Factbook, 2003*, Standard & Poor's, 2004, p. 55.

Four sets of correlation coefficients are presented: one long-term set from 1960 to 1980, and three short-term sets from June 1981 through September 1987, from July 1991 through July 1996, and from December 1997 through December 2002. The countries are listed from the highest correlation to the lowest based on 1960 to 1980 data. By comparing the four sets of correlations, we can see there is not a great amount of stability among the time periods, with some countries such as Italy going from 12th to 11th place to 4th place and back to 11th place in the latest period. Canada, because of its close ties with the U.S. economy, is highly correlated with the U.S. markets.

The best risk-reduction benefits can be found by combining U.S. securities with those from countries having low correlations such as Switzerland and Japan. Countries with high correlations provide the least benefit from diversification. According to one researcher, Bruno Solnik, a well-diversified international portfolio can achieve the same risk-reduction benefits as a pure U.S. portfolio that is twice the size in terms of securities.[2]

The last period presented does show some interesting changes from all the previous periods. First, the correlations are higher for almost all countries. Second, the average correlation coefficient is 0.70 versus 0.33 for the previous period. We could find some causal effects. Many of these countries are now in the European Monetary Union with a common currency. Their economies have begun to work together with a European Central Bank to coordinate monetary policy and it is possible that these countries have become more highly correlated among themselves. It is also possible that the United States has been the

---

[2] Bruno H. Solnik, "Why Not Diversify Internationally Rather than Domestically?" *Financial Analysts Journal*, July–August 1974, pp. 48–54.

engine of growth for a lagging Europe and Japan and that as the U.S. economy slowed down, it affected the rest of the world. However we should be forewarned that just as correlations can rise, they can also fall in the next period. The moral of this story is that you can still reap strong diversification benefits even with 70 percent correlations. Perhaps you can't achieve them as easily as with correlations of 43 and 33 percent, but nevertheless, they are still good reasons to include foreign stocks in your portfolio.

In Table 19–4, we examined the correlation between developed countries' market returns and the U.S. Standard & Poor's 500 Index. Using Table 19–5 on the previous page, we look at similar data for emerging markets from December 1997 through December 2002. Looking down the last column of numbers gives each country's correlation coefficient against the U.S. market as measured by the Standard & Poor's 500 Index. Three countries have a negative correlation with the United States but they are such small markets (Jordan, Morocco, and Oman) that it would be impossible for any investor of size to use these markets to take advantage of the negative correlation to reduce their portfolio risk. Sixteen countries have correlations of less than 30 percent.

Many countries have correlations with the United States of around 50 percent with the highest being Mexico at 66 percent. This makes sense since Mexico is a NAFTA trading partner with Canada and the United States. Notice that each region has a correlation with the United States that is higher than most individual country correlations in the region. The combination of markets into a regional index provides between 52 percent correlation in Mideast/Africa and 67 percent in Latin America. It would appear that emerging market countries provide better diversification benefits than developed countries, but we must remember that the annual returns on these markets must also be considered whenever diversifying a portfolio to achieve a risk-return benefit.

Return Potential in International Markets

Actually, risk reduction through effective international diversification is only part of the story. Not only does the investor have less risk exposure, but there is also the potential for higher returns in many foreign markets. Why? A number of countries have had long-term growth rates superior to those of the United States in terms of real GDP. These would include Norway, Singapore, and China. Second, many countries have become highly competitive in traditional U.S. products such as automobiles, steel, and consumer electronics. Third, many nations (Germany, Japan, France, Canada) enjoy higher individual savings rates than the United States, and this leads to capital formation and potential investment opportunity. This is not to imply that the United States does not have the strongest and best regulated securities markets in the world. It clearly does. However, it is a more mature market than many others, and there may be abundant opportunities for high returns in a number of foreign markets.

We have already presented the annual returns for eight developed countries in Table 19–3 on page 534. However, we now present five different international indexes of investment performance in Figure 19–3 on page 538, showing the wealth that would have accumulated by the end of 2001 from an investment of $1 in each index at the beginning of 1969. The Pacific region is more volatile than the other regions; it peaked in 1989 and 1999 and then took a dive. Europe on the other hand is ahead in the race because they have had smaller negative

TABLE 19-5 Statistics of the S&P/IFCG Price Indexes (US$, December 1997–December 2002)

Market	Number of Months	Mean of Percent Change	Standard Deviation	Annualized Mean	Annualized Standard Deviation	Correlation with S&P 500
S&P 500	60	−0.01	5.45	−0.12	18.88	1.00
Latin America	60	−0.38	9.53	−1.8	33.01	0.67
Argentina	60	−1.41	13.33	−16.92	46.18	0.36
Brazil	60	−0.21	14.63	−2.53	50.68	0.58
Chile	60	−0.41	7.52	−4.92	26.05	0.56
Colombia	60	−1.38	9.02	−16.56	31.25	0.20
Mexico	60	0.14	9.55	1.68	33.08	0.66
Peru	60	−0.16	7.07	−1.92	24.49	0.21
Venezuela	60	−1.27	13.09	−15.24	45.35	0.23
Asia	60	0.06	8.21	0.72	28.44	0.64
China	60	−0.05	7.66	−0.60	26.54	0.27
India	60	0.15	8.11	1.80	28.09	0.27
Indonesia	60	0.89	18.82	10.68	65.19	0.31
Korea	60	3.17	17.07	38.04	59.13	0.51
Malaysia	60	1.01	13.59	12.12	47.08	0.43
Pakistan	60	0.37	14.09	4.44	48.81	0.03
Philippines	60	−0.73	11.65	−8.76	40.36	0.47
Sri Lanka	60	0.12	9.71	1.44	33.64	0.07
Taiwan	60	−0.51	11.09	−6.12	38.42	0.51
Thailand	60	1.44	16.04	17.28	55.56	0.52
Europe	60	0.21	9.91	2.52	34.33	0.61
Czech Republic	60	0.37	8.81	4.44	30.52	0.31
Hungary	60	0.38	10.43	4.56	36.13	0.52
Poland	60	0.26	11.04	3.12	38.24	0.54
Russia	60	1.78	20.96	21.36	72.61	0.48
Slovakia	60	−0.71	8.09	−8.52	28.02	0.09
Turkey	60	0.45	20.95	5.40	72.57	0.49
Mideast/Africa	60	0.19	6.37	2.28	22.07	0.52
Bahrain	48	−0.26	3.68	−3.12	0.16	0.29
Egypt	60	−2.03	6.58	−24.36	22.79	0.25
Israel	60	0.19	8.01	2.28	27.75	0.34
Jordan	60	0.13	3.62	1.56	12.54	−0.05
Morocco	60	−0.43	4.69	−5.16	16.25	−0.01
Nigeria	60	0.74	7.62	8.88	26.40	0.20
Oman	48	−0.09	6.75	−1.08	23.38	−0.09
Saudi Arabia	60	0.48	4.53	5.76	15.69	0.11
South Africa	60	0.52	9.72	6.24	33.67	0.49
Zimbabwe	60	3.30	15.00	39.60	51.96	0.04

returns when they occurred while North America, consisting of the United States and Canada, ended up in the middle. Despite strong performances in 1995 through 1999, the market downturns in 2000 and 2001 took their toll on the final

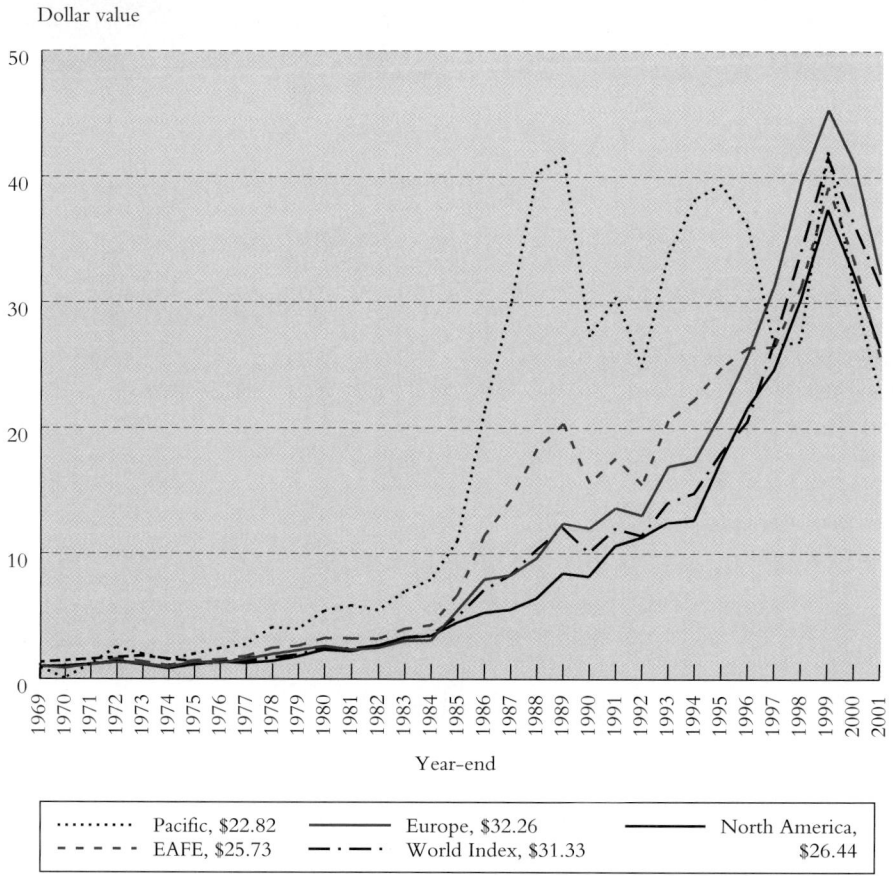

FIGURE 19-3 U.S. Dollar-Adjusted Cumulative Wealth Indexes of World Equities, 1969–2001

·········· Pacific, $22.82   ——— Europe, $32.26   ——— North America, $26.44
- - - - EAFE, $25.73   —·—· World Index, $31.33

wealth numbers. The annualized rates of return for each index over this 32-year period are as follows:

Region	Annualized Rates of Return
Pacific	10.27%
EAFE[a]	10.68
Europe	11.47
World Index	11.37
North America	10.77

[a] Europe, Australia, and the Far East.

Figure 19–3 represents a long-term perspective. There are of course, time periods when the United States outperforms foreign markets and foreign markets in turn outperform the U.S. markets.

Current Quotations of Foreign Market Performance

www.msci.com

To track the current performance of selected world markets, the most comprehensive quotations come from Morgan Stanley Capital International (MSCI). Their website www.msci.com provides daily quotes on international equity indexes and bond indexes. Quotes on the developed equity markets are presented in Table 19–6 on the next page. The table has been abbreviated here to show the last quote and year-to-date returns. The full table at **www.msci.com** will have more data.

The quotes are presented in local currencies as well as in U.S. dollars. For a U.S. investor, the returns in U.S. dollars are the best comparative measure against an investment in the U.S. stock market. Table 19–6 presents regional indexes, world indexes excluding countries, and individual country indexes. One thing that stands out is the large difference between returns in local currencies and U.S. dollars. For example, the first index EAFE (Europe, Australia, and Far East) shows a return of 2.57 percent in local currency and only a 0.91 percent return in dollars. Because the dollar has risen slightly against the euro over this five-month period, the results are not equal. If you look at the individual country examples toward the bottom of Table 19–6, almost all returns are higher in local currencies than in U.S. dollars. This would not have been true during the 2002–2003 period when the dollar fell against most other world currencies. 2004 has seen only a slight recovery of the dollar.

Notice the **World Index** (the last index in the first grouping) which is priced at 1,041.85 in U.S. dollars. This is a value-weighted index of the performance in 22 major countries. Of course, as with all indexes the analyst has to look at it over time to make sense out of the numbers. In November 2001, the World Index was quoted at 988.7 in U.S. dollars and in May of 2004 it was quoted at 1,041.85. The index moved 53 points or a little more than 5 percent over two and one-half years. Obviously, the world stock markets weren't providing very high returns during this time period. There are also many other differences between countries besides currencies.

Other Market Differences

There are large differences among cultures, including willingness to take risk, desire for dividend income versus growth in share value, the number and type of companies available to stockholders, and bureaucratic differences such as accounting conventions and government regulation of markets. In a book of this type, we do not intend to cover each issue but simply bring them to your attention. Table 19–7 on page 542 presents differences in price-earnings ratios, price-to-book value ratios, and dividend yield from the *Global Stock Markets Factbook, 2003,* published by Standard & Poor's Corporation.

The ratios for the developing countries can be compared to the world benchmarks given at the bottom of the table on page 543. For example the data can be compared to Japan, the United Kingdom, the United States, and the Citigroup's Global index (CGEI). In many cases the price-earnings ratios are high because of low earnings or in some cases they are calculated as negative to show deficit earnings. The problem with comparing price-earnings ratios is that earnings are calculated differently according to local or regional accounting

TABLE 19-7 Comparative Valuations of Emerging Countries

Comparative Valuations of the S&P/IFCG Price Indexes

Market	Price-Earnings Ratio End 2002	Relative to MSCI World	End 2001	Price-Book Value Ratio End 2002	Relative to MSCI World	End 2001	Dividend Yield End 2002	Relative to MSCI World	End 2001
Latin America									
Argentina	−1.37	−0.06	32.64	0.76	0.40	0.60	0.51	0.21	7.83
Brazil	13.45	0.60	8.84	1.25	0.65	1.24	4.36	1.77	6.61
Chile	16.26	0.72	16.16	1.31	0.69	1.40	2.97	1.20	8.23
Colombia	−44.80	−1.99	20.93	0.78	0.41	0.64	4.70	1.90	5.22
Mexico	15.40	0.68	13.72	1.54	0.81	1.67	1.76	0.71	3.04
Peru	12.78	0.57	21.27	1.16	0.61	1.36	2.37	0.96	4.25
Venezuela	−11.85	−0.53	−347.60	0.53	0.28	0.48	8.39	3.40	10.75
Asia									
China	21.55	0.96	22.18	1.87	0.98	2.33	1.43	0.58	1.35
India	15.03	0.67	12.84	2.00	1.05	1.92	2.96	1.20	2.39
Indonesia	22.01	0.98	−7.72	0.95	0.50	1.70	3.14	1.27	2.68
Korea	21.63	0.96	28.65	1.12	0.59	1.24	1.61	0.65	1.77
Malaysia	21.32	0.95	50.61	1.32	0.69	1.21	3.15	1.28	3.27
Pakistan	10.01	0.44	7.50	1.90	0.99	0.93	9.20	3.72	12.50
Philippines	21.80	0.97	45.92	0.77	0.40	0.92	2.34	0.95	1.37
Sri Lanka	15.60	0.69	14.38	1.08	0.57	0.87	3.09	1.25	6.22
Taiwan	19.95	0.88	29.43	1.63	0.85	2.80	1.21	0.49	1.14
Thailand	16.36	0.73	163.79	1.49	0.78	1.27	2.21	0.89	2.56
Europe									
Czech Republic	11.17	0.50	5.80	0.77	0.40	0.75	1.82	0.74	10.48
Hungary	14.57	0.65	13.40	1.83	0.96	1.76	1.65	0.67	1.63
Poland	88.55	3.93	6.09	1.28	0.67	1.39	1.42	0.57	2.56
Russia	12.37	0.55	5.60	0.86	0.45	1.12	2.43	0.98	1.04
Slovakia	3.07	0.14	7.80	0.39	0.20	0.42	5.10	2.06	35.31
Turkey	37.88	1.68	72.53	2.77	1.45	3.81	0.73	0.31	1.06
ME & Africa									
Bahrain	20.50	0.91	34.50	1.19	0.62	0.97	5.24	2.12	7.19
Egypt	5.60	0.25	6.50	1.01	0.53	1.02	10.30	4.17	7.72
Israel	79.95	3.54	−81.50	1.80	0.94	2.08	0.72	0.29	1.32
Jordan	11.40	0.51	18.77	1.31	0.69	1.46	2.79	1.13	2.75
Morocco	9.54	0.42	11.71	1.61	0.84	1.95	5.27	2.13	4.54
Nigeria	16.43	0.73	12.60	3.96	2.07	3.67	5.41	2.19	5.27
Oman	52.65	2.33	24.41	1.13	0.59	0.78	3.04	1.23	9.21
Saudi Arabia	23.43	1.04	22.19	2.75	1.44	2.42	3.94	1.60	3.94
South Africa	10.14	0.45	11.67	1.90	0.99	2.06	3.61	1.46	5.08
Zimbabwe	9.44	0.42	10.99	4.10	2.15	4.29	3.01	1.22	2.46

(continued)

TABLE 19–7 Comparative Valuations of Emerging Countries *(concluded)*

Comparative Valuations of the S&P/IFCG Price Indexes

Market	Price-Earnings Ratio End 2002	Relative to MSCI World	End 2001	Price-Book Value Ratio End 2002	Relative to MSCI World	End 2001	Dividend Yield End 2002	Relative to MSCI World	End 2001
Regions									
Composite	17.94	0.80	17.83	1.42	0.74	1.62	2.27	0.92	2.81
Latin America	19.21	0.85	11.78	1.29	0.68	1.30	3.63	1.47	5.57
Asia	20.00	0.89	26.77	1.42	0.74	1.69	1.76	0.71	1.68
Europe	15.28	0.68	7.94	1.04	0.54	1.42	2.02	0.82	1.69
ME & Africa	14.02	0.62	19.37	2.01	1.05	2.05	3.06	1.24	4.75
World Benchmarks									
Japan, Nikkei 225	27.09	1.20	31.22	1.38	0.72	1.65	1.08	0.44	0.95
U.K., FTSE 100	17.73	0.79	20.29	—	—	—	3.55	1.44	2.59
U.S., S&P 500	29.00	1.29	46.49	2.64	1.38	3.34	1.81	0.73	1.23
CGEI BMI Global	22.56	1.00	21.17	1.91	1.00	2.55	2.47	1.00	1.82

Source: *Global Stock Markets Factbook, 2003,* Standard & Poor's.

assume an investment in Switzerland produces a 10 percent return. But suppose at the same time the Swiss franc declines in value by 5 percent against the U.S. dollar. The Swiss franc profits are thus worth less in dollars. In the present case, the gain on the investment would be shown as follows:

	110%	(Investment with 10% profit)
		(Adjusted value of Swiss franc relative to U.S. dollar)
×	0.95	(1.00 − 0.05 decline in currency)
	104.5%	Percent of original investment

The actual return in U.S. dollars would be 4.5 instead of 10 percent. Of course, if the Swiss franc appreciated by 5 percent against the dollar, the Swiss franc profits converted to dollars would be worth considerably more than 10 percent. The values are indicated below:

	110%	(Investment with 10% profit)
		(Adjusted value of Swiss franc relative to U.S. dollar)
×	1.05	(1.00 − 0.05 decline in currency)
	115.5%	Percent of original investment

The 10 percent gain in the Swiss franc investment has produced a 15.5 percent gain in U.S. dollars. A U.S. investor in foreign securities must consider not only the potential trend of security prices but also the trend of foreign currencies against the dollar.

This point will become more apparent as we look at Table 19–8 on page 544, which depicts rates of return on the JP Morgan Overseas Government Bond Index for 12 developed countries from January 1, 2001, through November 12,

TABLE 19–8 Bond Returns in Local Currency and U.S. Dollars (January 1 to November 12, 2001)

	J.P. MORGAN OVERSEAS				GOVERNMENT BOND INDEX		
	Local Currency				U.S. Dollar		
Country	Index	Wkly Chg	YTD Chg	Devaluation Against U.S. $	Index	Wkly Chg	YTD Chg
Australia	454.23	0.89	8.25	7.36%	323.88	1.96	0.28
Belgium	315.19	0.60	9.09	4.96%	229.85	− 0.97	3.68
Canada	371.87	0.46	9.72	5.92%	302.71	0.08	3.22
Denmark	364.29	0.28	8.11	4.77%	264.86	− 1.31	2.95
France	341.29	0.57	8.28	4.96%	246.86	− 1.00	2.91
Germany	256.66	− 0.04	7.95	4.96%	183.70	− 1.60	2.60
Italy	507.39	0.60	9.08	4.95%	271.06	− 0.97	3.68
Japan	213.15	0.05	3.79	5.45%	213.60	0.78	− 1.87
Netherlands	273.26	− 0.03	8.13	4.96%	195.28	− 1.58	2.77
Spain	450.39	0.62	8.70	4.96%	259.16	− 0.95	3.31
Sweden	405.65	0.21	4.58	10.41%	222.62	0.50	− 6.31
U.K.	394.78	0.40	7.09	2.58%	304.62	− 0.10	4.33
U.S.	312.36	− 0.11	10.77	0.00%	312.36	− 0.11	10.77
Non-U.S.	295.16	0.26	6.50	5.06%	218.04	− 0.27	1.11
Global	304.12	0.16	7.66	3.85%	252.56	− 0.23	3.78

YTD-Year to date. Yields-Semi-annual. Dec. 31, 1987=100. Source: J.P. Morgan Government Bond Index

Source: *Barron's*, November 12, 2001, p. MW 60.

2001. During this period, the U.S. dollar was relatively strong against the rest of the world. This can be seen by comparing the return in local currency against the return in U.S. dollars (YTD change column). In every case, the return in U.S. dollars is lower than the returns in local currencies.

Let's examine the currency effects in Sweden year to date (YTD). In this instance, the return in the local currency was 4.58 percent (third column) while the return in U.S. dollars was −6.31 percent (seventh column). The change in the dollar versus the kroner caused a positive return in local currency to become a negative return in U.S. currency. If you were Swedish this would not have a negative effect on your return, but if you were an international investor translating returns to U.S. dollars, the negative return would definitely reduce your wealth. We would compute the returns as follows:

    104.58%   (Investment with 4.58% profit)
               (Adjusted value of the Swedish kroner to the U.S. dollar)
  × 0.896   (1.000 − 0.104 decline in currency)
     93.7%   Percent of original investment

The ending value of 93.7 indicates a loss of approximately 6.31 percent from the initial value of 100 percent.[3] If we were merely to subtract the foreign

---
[3] Due to rounding and other statistical adjustments, not all values adjusted to U.S. dollars come out as precisely as this.

currency loss of 10.4 percent from the 4.58 percent profit, the answer would be a loss of 5.82 percent, but this is not the correct procedure. The gain of 4.58 percent was on an initial base of 100 percent, but the foreign currency loss of 10.4 percent was on an ending value of 104.58 percent. The resulting loss in U.S. dollar terms is the 6.3 percent, which leaves investors with 93.7 percent of their original investment.

You can see that several countries had their currency fall against the dollar by 4.96 percent (middle column). These countries are all in the Monetary Union and have their currencies pegged to the euro. Those countries that are not in the Monetary Union, such as Australia, Canada, Japan, Sweden, and the United Kingdom all had different percent devaluations against the U.S. dollar.

Those who track the performance in foreign markets usually make adjustments so that the reported returns are in U.S. dollars that have already been adjusted for **foreign currency effects.** For example, most of the returns in prior tables of this chapter have already been adjusted for the foreign currency effect.

One might justifiably ask, how important is the foreign currency effect in relation to the overall return performance in the foreign currency? Do events in foreign exchange markets tend to overpower actual returns achieved in specific investments in foreign countries? Normally, the foreign currency effect is only about 10 to 20 percent as significant as the actual return performance in the foreign currency.[4] However, when the dollar is rising or falling rapidly over a short period, the impact can be much greater. For example, the returns to U.S. investors in Japanese securities between 1985 and 1988 were increased by 50 percent from the gain in the yen against the dollar.

In a well-diversified international portfolio, the changes in foreign currency values in one part of the world normally tend to cancel changes in other parts of the world. Also, those who do not wish to have foreign currency exposure of any sort may use forward exchange contracts, futures market contracts, or put options on foreign currency to hedge away the risk. Finally, there are those who believe in parity theories that suggest one should get additional compensation in local returns to make up for potential losses in foreign currency values. This latter point is a purely theoretical matter that provides little comfort in the short run.

The authors would suggest that those considering international investments be sensitive to the foreign currency effect, but not be overly discouraged by it. The superior return potentials from foreign investments previously shown in Figure 19–3 on page 538 (and most other places in this chapter) are constructed *after* considering the foreign exchange effect on U.S. dollar returns. While foreign currency swings have been *wider* in recent times, they are still not a major deterrent to an internationally diversified portfolio.

Other Obstacles to International Investments

Other problems are peculiar to international investments. Let us consider some of them.

---

[4] Bertrand Jacquillat and Bruno Solnik, "Multinationals Are Poor Tools for Diversification," *Journal of Portfolio Management,* Winter 1978, pp. 8–12.

Political Risks

Many firms operate in foreign political climates that are more volatile than that of the United States. There is the danger of nationalization of foreign firms or the restriction of capital flows to investors. There also may be the danger of a violent overthrow of the political party in power. Furthermore, many countries have been unable to meet their foreign debt obligations, and this has important political implications.

The informed investor must have some feel for the political/economic climate of the foreign country in which he or she invests. Of course, problems sometimes create opportunities. Local investors may overreact to political changes occurring in their environment. Because all their eggs are in one basket, they may engage in an oversell in regard to political changes. A less impassioned outside investor may identify an opportunity for profit.

Nevertheless, political risk represents a potential deterrent to foreign investment. The best solution for the investor is to be sufficiently diversified around the world so that a political or economic development in one foreign country does not have a major impact on his or her portfolio (this can be accomplished through a mutual fund or through other means discussed later in the chapter).

Tax Problems

Many major foreign countries may impose a 15 to 30 percent withholding tax against the dividends or interest paid to nonresident holders of equity or debt securities. However, it is often possible for *tax-exempt* U.S. investors to secure an exemption or rebate on part or all of the withholding tax. Also, taxable U.S. investors can normally claim a U.S. tax credit for taxes paid in foreign countries. The problem is more likely to be one of inconvenience and paper shuffling rather than loss of funds.

Lack of Market Efficiency

U.S. capital markets tend to be the most liquid and efficient in the world. Therefore, an investor who is accustomed to trading on the New York Stock Exchange may have some difficulties adjusting to foreign markets. A larger spread between the bid (sell) and asked (buy) price in foreign countries is likely. Also, an investor may have more difficulty executing a large transaction (the seller may have to absorb a larger discount in executing the trade). Furthermore, as a general rule, commission rates are higher in foreign markets than in the United States.

Administrative Problems

There can also be administrative problems in dealing in foreign markets in terms of adjusting to the various local systems. For example, in the Hong Kong, Swiss, and Mexican stock markets, you must settle your account one day after the transaction; in London, there is a two-week settlement procedure; and in France, there are different settlement dates for cash and forward markets. The different administrative procedures of foreign countries simply add up to an extra dimension of difficulty in executing trades. (As implied throughout this section, there are ways to avoid most of these difficulties by going through mutual funds and other investment outlets.)

Information Difficulties

The U.S. securities markets are the best in the world at providing investment information. The Securities and Exchange Commission, with its rigorous requirements for full disclosure, is the toughest national regulator of investment information. Also, the United States has the Financial Accounting Standards Board (FASB) continually providing pronouncements on generally accepted accounting principles for financial reporting. Publicly traded companies are required to provide stockholders with fully audited annual reports. In the United States, we are further spoiled by the excellent evaluative reports and ratings generated by Moody's, Standard & Poor's, Value Line, and other firms. We also have extensive economic data provided by governmental sources such as the Department of Commerce and the Federal Reserve System.

Many international firms, trading in less sophisticated foreign markets, simply do not provide the same quantity or quality of data. This would be particularly true of firms trading in some of the smaller foreign markets. Even when the information is available, there may be language problems for the analyst who does not speak German, French, Portuguese, and so on.

Also, the analyst must be prepared to analyze the firm in light of the standards that are generally accepted in the foreign market in which the company operates. For example, Japanese companies often have much higher debt ratios than U.S. firms. A debt-to-equity ratio of three times is not unusual in Japan, whereas in the United States, the standard is closer to 1:1. The analyst may be inclined to "mark down" the Japanese firm for high debt unless he or she realizes the different features at play in the Japanese economy. For example, in Japan there are normally very close relationships between the lending bank and the borrower, with the lender perhaps having an equity position in the borrower and with interlocking boards between the two. This diminishes the likelihood of the lender calling in the loan in difficult economic periods. Also, the Japanese make extensive use of reserve accounts that tend to give the appearance of a smaller asset or equity base than actually exists. This pattern of understatement is further aided by a strict adherence to historical cost valuation. When appropriate adjustments are made for these effects on financial reporting, a Japanese debt-to-equity ratio of 3:1 may not be a matter of any greater concern than a U.S. debt-to-equity ratio of 1:1.

Methods of Participating in Foreign Investments

The avenues to international investment include investing in firms in their own foreign markets, purchasing the shares of foreign firms trading in the United States, investing in mutual funds and closed-end funds with a global orientation, buying the shares of multinational corporations, and entrusting funds to private money managers who specialize in international equities. We shall examine each of these alternatives.

Direct Investments

The most obvious but least likely alternative would be to directly purchase the shares of a firm in its own foreign market through a foreign broker or an overseas branch of a U.S. broker. The investor might consider such firms as Toshiba or Fanuc on the Tokyo Stock Exchange, Consolidated Rutile on the Sydney Stock Exchange, or Hoechst on the Frankfurt Stock Exchange. This approach is hampered by all the difficulties and administrative problems associated with international investments. There could be information-gathering problems, tax problems, stock-delivery problems, capital-transfer problems, and communication difficulties in executing orders. Only the most sophisticated money manager would probably follow this approach (although this may change somewhat in the future as foreign markets become better coordinated).

A more likely route to direct investment would be to purchase the shares of foreign firms that actually trade in U.S. securities markets. Hundreds of foreign firms actively trade their securities in the United States on the New York Stock Exchange.

www.alcan.com

www.nortel.com

Firms such as Alcan Aluminum, Ltd., Campbell Resources, Inc., and Nortel Networks Corporation (all Canadian firms) trade their stocks *directly* on the New York Stock Exchange. Most of the other foreign firms trade their shares in the United States through **American depository receipts (ADRs).** The ADRs represent the ownership interest in a foreign company's common stock. If you go to the New York Stock Exchange website **www.nyse.com** and click on International, then on non–U.S. listed companies, you will be able to access the entire list of foreign companies traded on the NYSE. There are also American Depository Receipts listed on Nasdaq, with one of the most widely traded being L.M. Ericcson of Sweden.

www.syngenta.com

www.british-airways.com

www.sony.com

www.honda.com

An American depository receipt is created when the shares of a foreign company are purchased and put in trust in a foreign branch of a New York bank. The bank receives and can issue depository receipts to the American shareholders of the foreign firm. These ADRs allow foreign shares to be traded in the United States. Because many countries have securities priced higher or lower than the traditionally priced U.S. securities, each ADR may have a claim on more or less than one share of the foreign stock. For example, Switzerland is known for very high-priced shares, and each ADR of the pharmaceutical firm Syngenta is exchangeable for one-fifth of a share of the common stock. While in the United Kingdom (England), share prices are low and 1 ADR in British Airways, for example, is exchangeable into 10 shares of British Air. The New York Stock Exchange website allows you to check out the exchange ratio for each ADR listed on the NYSE.

When you call your broker and ask to purchase Sony Corporation or Honda Motor Company, Ltd. (which are represented by ADRs), you will notice virtually no difference between this transaction and buying shares of General Motors or Eastman Kodak. You can receive a certificate that looks very much like a U.S. stock certificate. You will receive your dividends in dollars and get your reports about the company in English. Generally, you will pay your normal commission rates.

Indirect Investments

The forms of indirect investments in the international securities include (*a*) purchasing shares of multinational corporations, (*b*) purchasing mutual funds or closed-end investment funds specializing in worldwide investments, (*c*) investing in exchange traded funds, and (*d*) engaging the services of a private firm specializing in foreign investment portfolio management.

Purchasing Shares of Multinational Corporations **Multinational corporations,** that is, firms with operations in a number of countries, represent an opportunity for international diversification. For example, the major oil companies have investments and operations throughout the world. The same can be said for large banking firms and mainframe computer manufacturers. When one buys ExxonMobil, to some extent one is buying exposure to the world economy (69.4 percent of sales are foreign for this firm). A list of the 20 largest U.S. multinational firms is presented in Table 19–9. Of particular interest is the third numerical column from the left, which represents foreign revenue as a percentage of total revenue, and the fourth column from the right, which represents foreign profit as a percentage of total profit.

www.exxon.com

Although buying shares in a U.S. multinational firm is an easy route to take to experience worldwide economic effects, some researchers maintain that multinationals do not provide the major *investment* benefits that are desired. Jacquillat and Solnik found that multinationals provide very little risk reduction

TABLE 19–9 Largest U.S. Multinational Firms (In millions of U.S. dollars)

2000 Rank	Company	Revenue Foreign	Revenue Total	Revenue Foreign as Percent of Total	Net Profits[a] Foreign	Net Profits[a] Total	Net Profits[a] Foreign as Percent of Total	Assets Foreign	Assets Total	Assets Foreign as Percent of Total
1	ExxonMobil	$143,044	$206,083	69.4%	$10,198[b]	$16,948[b]	60.2%	$56,742[c]	$89,829[c]	63.2%
2	Ford Motor	51,691	170,064	30.4	(599)	5,410	−11.1	19,874[d]	45,804[d]	43.4
3	IBM	51,180	88,396	57.9	3,914	8,093	48.4	14,348[c]	35,797[c]	40.1
4	General Motors	48,233	184,632	26.1	2,893	4,771[e]	60.6[e]	12,578[d]	35,376[d]	35.6
5	Texaco	43,146	60,220	71.6	1,007	2,542	39.6	7,879[c]	15,879[c]	49.6
6	General Electric	42,390	129,853	32.6	5,222	20,686[g]	25.2[g]	159,367	437,006	36.5
7	Citigroup	37,396	111,826	33.4	NA	13,519	NA	269,837[h]	741,114[h]	36.4
8	Wal-Mart Stores	32,100	191,329	16.8	650	6,424[e]	10.1[e]	25,742	78,130	32.9
9	Chevron	31,374	69,058	45.4	2,716	5,185	52.4	27,126	50,832	53.4
10	Hewlett-Packard	27,230	48,732	55.9	2,169	3,561	60.9	2,244[d]	4,500[d]	49.9
11	Compaq Computer	23,417	42,383	55.3	216	595	36.3	1,202[c]	3,431[c]	35.0
12	Enron	22,898	100,789	22.7	500	979	51.1	844[c]	11,743[c]	7.2
13	American Intl. Group	22,846	45,972	49.7	NA	5,636	NA	98,105[i]	306,577	32.0
14	JP Morgan Chase	21,338	60,065	35.5	2,963	5,727	51.7	NA	715,348	NA
15	Procter & Gamble	19,913	39,951	49.8	1,492	3,542	42.1	16,967	34,194	49.6
16	Intel	19,814	33,726	58.7	3,571	10,535	33.9	3,905[d]	15,013[d]	26.0
17	Motorola	19,720[E]	37,580	52.5	1,645	2,231[j]	73.7[i]	16,814	42,343	39.7
18	Philip Morris Cos.	19,280	63,276	30.5	3,105	8,510	36.5	7,425[c]	28,739[c]	25.8
19	Dow Chemical	14,145	23,008	61.5	1,149	1,578[e]	72.8	4,202[c]	9,190[c]	45.7
20	El du Pont de Nemours	13,759	28,268	48.7	1,218	2,375[e]	51.3[e]	5,295[d]	14,182[d]	37.3

[a] From continuing operations.
[b] Net income before corporate and financing activity and merger expense.
[c] Long-lived assets.
[d] Net property, plant and equipment.
[e] Net income before Identifiable assets.
[f] Includes proportionate interest in unconsolidated subsidiaries.
[g] Operating profit.
[h] Average assets.
[i] Excludes Canadian operations.
[E] Estimate.

Source: Reprinted by Permission of *Forbes* © 2004 Forbes Inc.

the real world of investing

The Growth of American Depository Receipts

After years of going unnoticed, the benefits that American depository receipts (ADRs) offer American investors are better understood. To avoid investor difficulties in collecting dividends, receipts were created that provided proof of ownership of the shares held abroad. This made it is less expensive and less troublesome for shareholders to collect dividends on their own.

Many companies from around the world are scrambling to get their stocks traded on American exchanges. This move to Wall Street allows foreign companies to expand their capital while filling the growing demand for ADRs by American investors. Although ADRs are considered to be more liquid, less expensive, and easier to trade than buying foreign companies' stock directly on that country's exchange, there are some drawbacks.

ADRs are treated like domestic stock on the American front and are traded in dollars, but they are still traded in their local currencies on their home markets. The gains or losses an investor can receive from changes in the currency exchange rate can also be offset by capital gains or losses on the investment itself. For those with short time horizons, this can be a serious problem, but for those with long-run interests, many experts argue that the dollar will usually even itself out, and high returns will win out.

There is still a lack of communication between companies and their shareholders abroad. It is difficult for individual investors to keep daily tabs on a foreign company without the aid of a broker.

Even though the SEC requires companies trading ADRs on American exchanges to use the U.S. standard of accounting, many "pink-sheet" ADRs not traded on an exchange are free from such restrictions. Pink sheets are price quotes for smaller or thinly traded over-the-counter companies. These companies are trying, however, to improve their accounting methods to catch the interests of foreign investors.

Politics can also be a disadvantage in ADRs. If a country is going through political turmoil, such unrest can send the stock price soaring or cause it to crash. The hefty taxes the foreign government takes out of the dividends can also be burdensome. To be reimbursed for the amount deducted, a U.S. investor has to request a credit by the Internal Revenue Service.

A final warning is to beware of management. History shows that in emerging economies, inexperienced companies often have tried to expand their business into markets in which they have little knowledge.

---

over and above purely domestic firms (perhaps only 10 percent).[5] The prices of multinational shares tend to move very closely with their own country's financial markets despite their worldwide investments. Thus, U.S. multinationals may not do well in a U.S. bear market even if they have investments in strong markets in other countries. This leaves us to turn to mutual funds and closed-end investment companies as potential international investments.

Mutual Funds and Closed-End Investment Companies As described in Chapter 18, mutual funds offer the investor an opportunity for diversification as well as professional management. Nowhere is the mutual fund concept more important than in the area of international investments. Those who organize the funds usually have extensive experience in investing overseas and are prepared to deal with the administrative problems. This, of course, does not necessarily lead to superior returns, but the likelihood for inexperienced blunders is reduced.

---

[5] Ibid.

One may also invest in closed-end investment companies specializing in international equity investments. As described in Chapter 18, a closed-end investment company has a fixed supply of shares outstanding and trades on a national exchange or over-the-counter, much as an individual company does. It may trade at a premium or discount from its net asset value. An example of an international closed-end fund is the Japan Fund.

Exchange Traded Funds Investors can use exchange traded funds (ETFs) to buy in international markets. The biggest market for exchange traded funds is found on the American Stock Exchange **www.amex.com**. It lists over 40 international funds that can be traded like common stocks.

According to the American Stock Exchange, each ETF is a basket of securities that is designed to generally track an index. The exchange traded fund mimics a major index such as the Financial Times 100 for the United Kingdom or the DAX for Germany. The ETF can track a broad stock index, a bond index, or an industry or sector index. The advantage is that it trades like an individual stock with all day trading and price tracking. Exchange traded funds generally have lower costs and better tax efficiency than mutual funds. Of course, the American Stock Exchange touts the ability to diversify using these funds.

www.jpmorgan.com

www.fidelity.com

Specialists in International Securities The large investor may consider the option of engaging the services of selected banks and investment counselors with specialized expertise in foreign equities. Major firms include Morgan Guaranty Trust Company, State Street Bank and Trust Company, Batterymarch Financial Management, and Fidelity Trust Company of New York. These firms provide a total range of advisory and management services. However, they often require a minimum investment well in excess of $100,000 and are tailored to the needs of the large institutional investor.

exploring the web

Website Address	Comments
www.adr.com	Provides screening and research services for American depository receipts
www.amex.com	Provides market for exchange traded funds
www.global-investor.com	Provides international news and information on foreign markets
cbs.marketwatch.com	Provides news on global markets
www.economist.com	Global magazine providing news on markets and economics
www.wsj.com	Provides information on global markets and economics
www.oecd.org	Provides international economic information and links to related sites
www.rubicon.com/passport/currency/currency.html	Provides currency rates and conversions

Summary

Investments in international securities allow the investor to diversify a portfolio beyond the normal alternatives. Because different foreign markets are influenced by varying and often contradictory factors, effective risk reduction can be provided. An example might be a sharp and unexpected increase in energy prices. The negative impact on oil importers will likely be offset by the positive impact on oil exporters.

Investments in selected foreign equity markets may also provide excellent return opportunities. A number of countries have had superior real GDP growth performance in comparison with the United States. They may also have greater savings rates and higher capital formation. Furthermore, a number of countries are becoming more competitive in traditional U.S. products such as automobiles, steel, and consumer electronics. Emerging countries may offer even greater return and risk-reduction benefits than investments in better established markets. However, many of the problems of international investments can surface in these less developed countries.

The impact of currency fluctuations on returns is an added dimension to international investments. Not only must the investor determine whether the security will provide a positive return, but he or she must also evaluate the possibility of the return being enhanced or diminished by changes in currency relationships with the U.S. dollar.

Key Words and Concepts

American depository receipts (ADRs) 548
correlation coefficient 533
currency fluctuations 541
diversification benefits 533
foreign currency effects 545
multinational corporations 549
World Index 539

Discussion Questions

1. Does an investor who achieves international diversification through foreign investments necessarily have to accept lower returns?
2. Why does Canada represent a relatively poor outlet for achieving risk reduction for U.S. investors? (Merely use your own judgment in answering this question.)
3. In discussing return potential in foreign markets, indicate why a number of foreign countries may have higher return possibilities than the United States.
4. According to researcher Bruno Solnik, how much larger would a pure U.S. portfolio have to be in relation to a well-diversified international portfolio to achieve the same risk-reduction benefits?
5. Explain how currency fluctuations affect the return on foreign investments.
6. Suggest two types of strategies to reduce or neutralize the impact of currency fluctuations on portfolio returns.
7. Suggest how foreign political risk may create a potential investment opportunity.
8. Are foreign markets likely to be more or less efficient than U.S.

markets? What effect does this have on bid-ask spreads and the ability to absorb large transactions?

9. Explain why high debt ratios in Japan may not be as great a problem as one might first assume.

10. What are some of the key problems in investing directly in foreign securities?

11. Explain the concept of an ADR.

12. Why did Jacquillat and Solnik indicate that multinational firms may provide very little risk-reduction benefits in comparison with domestic firms?

13. Why might mutual funds be particularly beneficial in the international area?

Problems

Foreign currency effects

1. Assume you invest in the German equity market and have a 15 percent return (quoted in euros).
   a. If during this period the euro appreciated by 10 percent against the dollar, what would be your actual return translated into U.S. dollars?
   b. If the euro declined by 10 percent against the dollar, what would your actual return be translated into dollars?
   c. Recompute the answer based on a 25 percent decline in the euro against the dollar.

Foreign currency effects

2. Assume you invest in the Japanese equity market and have a 10 percent decline (quoted in Japanese yen).
   a. If during this period the yen appreciated by 10 percent against the dollar, what would be your actual return translated into U.S. dollars?
   b. If during this period the yen appreciated by 25 percent against the dollar, what would be your actual return translated into U.S. dollars?
   c. Recompute the answer based on a 25 percent decline in the yen against the U.S. dollar.

Foreign currency effects

3. Assume you invest in the British equity market and have a 12 percent return (quoted in pounds). However, during the course of your investment, the pound declines versus the dollar. By what percent could the pound decline relative to the dollar before all your gain is eliminated?

Web Exercise

Assume you want to see how a foreign currency has performed against the dollar over a recent period of time and the implications for investments in companies that trade in that currency. Go to **www.x-rates.com**.

1. Click on "Currency calculator" under the menu along the left-hand margin.
2. You will then see "Convert" American dollar and "Into" American dollar in the middle of the page. Go to the first box (Convert American dollar) and follow the arrow down until you get to the Danish krone. Then click on "Calculate."
3. At the top of the page you will see the relationship between the Danish krone and the U.S. dollar. Write down this value. To better understand the meaning of the value you have just written down, if it is .168 USD, that means a Danish krone is only worth 16.8 percent of the dollar. Said another

way, $1.00 is worth 5.95 Danish krones (1 ÷ .168). If you were to purchase an item in Denmark that cost 11.90 Danish krones, that would cost $2.00 (2 × 5.95 = 11.90).

4. Now click the highlighted statement in the box below that says "Two currencies." You will see a graphic presentation of the krone versus the dollar over the last few months. Below the graph you will also see the lowest and highest value of the Danish krone versus the U.S. dollar.

5. Assume you bought a stock quoted in Danish krones at the lowest value of the krone to the dollar and sold it at the highest value of the krone to the dollar.* What would be the percentage gain if the stock price did not move? The only change in value would be the gain in the Danish krone to the dollar. Divide the highest value by the lowest value to get your answer.

6. Assume the same factors as before in regard to the krone versus dollar performance, but that the stock also went up by 20 percent. What would be your overall gain? (Multiply 1 plus the percentage gain computed in question number five times 1.20 and subtract 1.)

7. Once again assume the same factors as before in terms of the gain in the krone versus the dollar, but assume the stock went down by 20 percent. What would be your overall loss? (Multiply 1 plus the percentage gain computed in question five times .80 and subtract 1.)

*The assumption in this analysis is that the highest exchange rate follows the lowest exchange rate. While this is not always necessarily the case, the assumption is made to facilitate the analysis.

Note: From time to time, companies redesign their websites, and occasionally a topic we have listed may have been deleted, updated, or moved into a different location. Most websites have a "site map" or "site index" listed on a different page. If you click on the site map or site index, you will be introduced to a table of contents that should aid you in finding the topic you are looking for.

CFA Material

The following material contains a sample question and solution from a prior Level I CFA exam. While the terminology is slightly different from that in this text, you can still view the skills that are necessary for the CFA Exam.

CFA Exam Question
2. Unique risks are associated with international investing. Briefly describe *four* such risks. *(5 minutes)*

Solution: Question 2—Morning Section (5 points)
Four primary risks are:

1. *Currency fluctuations.* If the value of the investors' domestic currency strengthens after the purchase of foreign securities, the value of the investment declines.

2. *Availability of information.* Quality information about foreign companies may be less readily available to analysts than information about domestic companies. This results because of varying requirements for corporate disclosure, less exhaustive analysis conducted by the foreign financial community, and the use of accounting conventions that differ from those in the country of the investor.

3. *Liquidity.* Foreign equity issues may tend to be smaller (or larger) than those in the investor's country making the accumulation of substantial positions more (or less) difficult.
4. *Sovereign risks.* These risks include the potential for disruptive political, sociological, or psychological developments. Examples of political risk are the possibility of nationalization of local companies, expropriation of assets owned by foreign investors, punitive taxation, and restrictions on the withdrawal of capital.

Other unique risks that might be addressed are:

5. High transaction costs, including taxes.
6. Administrative cost/settlement problems.
7. Difficulty in assessing manager skill and high fee structure.

S&P Problems

www.mhhe.com/edumarketinsight

STANDARD & POOR'S

1. Log on to the McGraw-Hill website: **www.mhhe.com/edumarketinsight** (see page vi in the preface for instructions).
2. Click on Company, which is the first box below the Market Insight title.
3. Put the ticker symbol for Novartis (NVS) in the box, and click on go. Novartis is a competitor of Johnson & Johnson and is a Swiss pharmaceutical company listed on the New York Stock Exchange as American Depository Shares.
4. Go to the left margin and click on S&P Stock Reports, and after the list appears, click on Stock Report. Go to the footnotes at the bottom of the second page underneath the company's financial statements. What is the ratio of American depository shares relative to the price of an ordinary share listed in Switzerland?
5. Given the data in question 4, what price does a share of stock sell for in Switzerland (in U.S. $)? Does this price seem unusual?
6. Repeat this project with Ericsson (ERICY), a Swedish company. You will find the answer in the footnotes at the bottom of the company financials.
7. What is the ratio of American depository shares relative to the price of Class B ordinary shares? What is the price of Ericsson in U.S. dollars as it is traded in Sweden?
8. Compare the cultural differences between stock prices in Sweden and Switzerland based on these two examples.

The Wall Street Journal Project

There are many ADRs listed on the New York Stock Exchange in Section C of *The Wall Street Journal* under "New York Stock Exchange Composite Transactions." Find the closing price and dividend yield (%) for the ADRs representing four different countries:

TelMex (TMX)	Mexican
DaimlerChrysler (DCX)	German
Hanson (HAN)	British
Mitsubishi (MTF)	Japanese

Selected References

Risk and Return Considerations

Ammer, John, and Jianping Mei. "Measuring International Economic Linkages with Stock Market Data." *The Journal of Finance,* December 1996, pp. 1743–63.

Daniel, Kent; Sheridan Titman; and K. C. John Wei. "Explaining the Cross Section of Stock Returns in Japan: Factors or Characteristics?" *Journal of Finance,* April 2001, pp. 743–66.

Guyon, Janet. "Billion-Dollar Bets on Russia." *Fortune,* February 23, 2004, pp. 154–56.

Ibbotson, Roger G.; Richard C. Carr; and Anthony W. Robinson. "International Equity and Bond Returns." *Financial Analysts Journal,* July–August 1982, pp. 61–83.

Longin, Francois, and Bruno Solnik. "Extreme Correlation of International Equity Markets." *Journal of Finance,* April 2001, pp. 649–76.

Speidell, Lawrence S., and Ross Seppenfield. "Global Diversification in a Shrinking World." *Journal of Portfolio Management,* Fall 1992, pp. 57–67.

Emerging Markets

Barry, Christopher B.; Elizabeth Goldreyer; Larry Lockwood; and Mauricio Rodriquez, "Size and Book-to-Market Effects: Evidence from Emerging Equity Markets." Working Paper, Texas Christian University, October 1997.

Barry, Christopher B.; John W. Peavy III; and Mauricio Rodriquez. *Emerging Stock Markets: Risk, Return and Performance.* (Charlottesville, VA: Association for Investment Management and Research, 1997).

Domowitz, Ian; Jack Glen; and Ananth Madhavan. "Market Segmentation and Stock Prices: Evidence from an Emerging Market." *Journal of Finance,* July 1997, pp. 1059–85.

Mullin, John. "Emerging Equity Markets in the Global Economy." *FRBNY Quarterly Review,* Summer 1993, pp. 54–83.

Stone, Douglas. "The Emerging Markets and Strategic Asset Allocation." *Journal of Investing,* Summer 1992, pp. 40–45.

Currency Considerations

Bodmar, Gordon M., and M. H. Franco Wang. "Estimating Exchange Rate Exposures: Issues in Model Structures. *Financial Management,* Spring 2003, pp. 35–67.

Glen, Jack, and Philippe Jorion. "Currency Hedging for International Portfolios." *Journal of Finance,* December 1993, pp. 1865–86.

So, Raymond W. "Price and Volatility Spillovers between Interest Rate and Exchange Value of the U.S. Dollar." *Global Financial Journal,* Fall 2001, pp. 94–107.

chapter twenty

Investments in Real Assets

objectives

1. Understand the advantages and disadvantages of real assets.
2. Discuss the various forms of investments that real assets can take.
3. Explain the characteristics of investing in real estate.
4. Discuss the various forms of financing for real estate investments.
5. Explain the traditional appeal of precious metals as a form of investments.
6. Understand the factors that influence the value of collectibles.

Advantages and Disadvantages of Real Assets
Real Estate as an Investment
  Real Estate in the Last Decade and the Future Outlook
Valuation of Real Estate
  The Cost Approach
  Comparative Sales Value
  The Income Approach
  Combination of the Three Approaches
A More Comprehensive Analysis
Financing of Real Estate
  Types of Mortgages
Forms of Real Estate Ownership
  Individual or Regular Partnership
  Syndicate or Limited Partnership
  Real Estate Investment Trust
Gold and Silver
  Gold
  Silver
Precious Gems
Other Collectibles

In this chapter, we turn our attention to **real assets;** that is, tangible assets that may be seen, felt, held, or collected. Examples of such assets are real estate, gold, silver, diamonds, coins, stamps, and antiques. This is no small area from which to consider investments. For example, the total market value of all real estate holdings in the United States in the early 2000s was in excess of $10 trillion.

As further evidence of value, in the last decade, a Van Gogh painting sold for $40 million, and a 132-carat diamond earring set sold for $6.6 million. In 2000, a Honus Wagner baseball card sold for more than $1 million.

As was pointed out in Chapter 1, in inflationary environments, real assets have at times outperformed financial assets (such as stocks and bonds). With this in mind, the reader is advised to become familiar with these investment outlets—not only to take advantage of the investment opportunities but also to be well aware of the pitfalls. A money manager who is challenged by clients to include real assets in a portfolio (such as real estate or precious metals) must be conversant not only with the opportunities but also with the drawbacks.

Advantages and Disadvantages of Real Assets

As previously mentioned, real assets may offer an opportunity as an inflation hedge because inflation means higher replacement costs for real estate, precious metals, and other physical items. Real assets also serve as an investment hedge against the unknown and feared. When people become concerned about world events, gold and other precious metals may be perceived as the last safe haven for investments. While this has traditionally been the case, it did not prove so in the last decade. Neither the Persian Gulf War of 1991 nor international threats in the mid-1990s and the terrorist attack on September 11, 2001, have moved the price of precious metals to significantly higher levels. Even the Iraqi war of 2003–2004 had only a minor impact.

Real assets also may serve as an effective vehicle for portfolio diversification. Since financial and real assets at times move in opposite directions, some efficient diversification may occur. A study by Robichek, Cohn, and Pringle in the *Journal of Business* actually indicates that movements among various types of real and monetary assets are less positively correlated than are those for monetary assets alone.[1] The general findings indicate that enlarging the universe of investment alternatives would benefit the overall portfolio construction in terms of risk-return alternatives.

A final advantage of an investment in real assets is the psychic pleasure that may be provided. One can easily relate to a beautiful painting in the living room, a mint gold coin in a bank lockbox, or an attractive real estate development.

There are many disadvantages to consider as well. Perhaps the largest drawback is the absence of large, liquid, and relatively efficient markets. Whereas stocks or bonds can generally be sold in a few minutes at a value close to the latest quoted trade, such is not likely to be the case for real estate, diamonds, art, and other forms of real assets. It may take many months to get the desired price for a real asset, and even then, there is an air of uncertainty about the impending transaction until it is consummated.

Furthermore, there is the problem of dealer spread or middleman commission. Whereas in the trading of stocks and bonds where spreads or commissions are very small (usually 1 or 2 percent), dealer spreads for real assets can be as large as 20 to 25 percent or more. This is particularly true for small items that do not have great value. On more valuable items, such as rare paintings, valuable jewels, or mint gold coins, the dealer spread tends to be smaller (perhaps 5 to 10 percent) but still more than that on securities.

The investor in real assets generally receives no current income (with the possible exception of real estate) and may incur storage and insurance costs.

---

[1] Alexander A. Robichek, Richard A. Cohn, and John J. Pringle, "Return on Alternative Media and Implications for Portfolio Construction," *Journal of Business,* July 1972, pp. 427–43.

Furthermore, there may be the problem of high unit cost for investments. You cannot easily acquire multiple art masterpieces.

A final drawback or caveat in real assets is the hysteria or overreaction that tends to come into the marketplace from time to time. Gold, silver, diamonds, and coins may be temporarily bid out of all proportion to previously anticipated value. This happened in the late 1980s. The last buyer, who arrives too late, may end up owning a very unprofitable investment. The trick is to get into the recurring cycle early enough to take advantage of the capital gains opportunities that occur for real assets. Also, you should buy items of high enough quality so that you can ride out the setbacks if your timing is incorrect.

In the remainder of this chapter, we will examine real estate, gold, silver, diamonds, and other collectibles as investment outlets. Because real estate lends itself more directly to analytical techniques familiar to students of finance, it will receive a proportionately larger share of our attention.

Real Estate as an Investment

Approximately 60 percent of the households in the United States own real estate as a home or investment. Also, many firms in the brokerage and investment community have also moved into real estate. As an example, Merrill Lynch has acquired real estate affiliates to broker property, conduct mortgage banking activities, and package real estate syndications. Pension fund managers are also increasing the real estate component in their portfolios, going from virtually no representation two decades ago to almost 10 percent at present.

Some insight into changing real estate values may be gained from Figure 20–1 on the next page. We see the gain for a dollar invested in real estate in 1946 as compared with fixed-income investments and common stock.

Real estate investments may include such outlets as your own home, duplexes and apartment buildings, office buildings, shopping centers, industrial buildings, hotels and motels, as well as undeveloped land. The investor may participate as an individual, as part of a limited partnership real estate syndicate, or through a real estate investment trust.

Throughout the rest of the section, we will discuss real estate values in the recent past and relate it to the future outlook. We will also evaluate a typical real estate investment, consider new methods of real estate financing, and examine limited partner syndicates and real estate investment trusts.

Real Estate in the Last Decade and the Future Outlook

The mid-1980s started out as a bad time for real estate with the passage of the Tax Reform Act of 1986. As part of this legislation, the life over which a real estate investor could write off depreciation for tax purposes was extended from 19 years to 27.5 years for residential rental property and to 39 years for commercial property. This meant that an investor had to wait longer to take full advantage of tax deductions related to real estate. Also, real estate investors not actively involved in the management of property were severely restricted in writing off paper losses from real estate against other forms of income.

The effect of tax reform was to make real estate a less attractive investment. Because of the loss of many traditional tax benefits for real estate, some existing properties had less value, and new construction proceeded at a slower pace.

FIGURE 20-1 Growth in Value: 1946–2003 ($1 of investment)

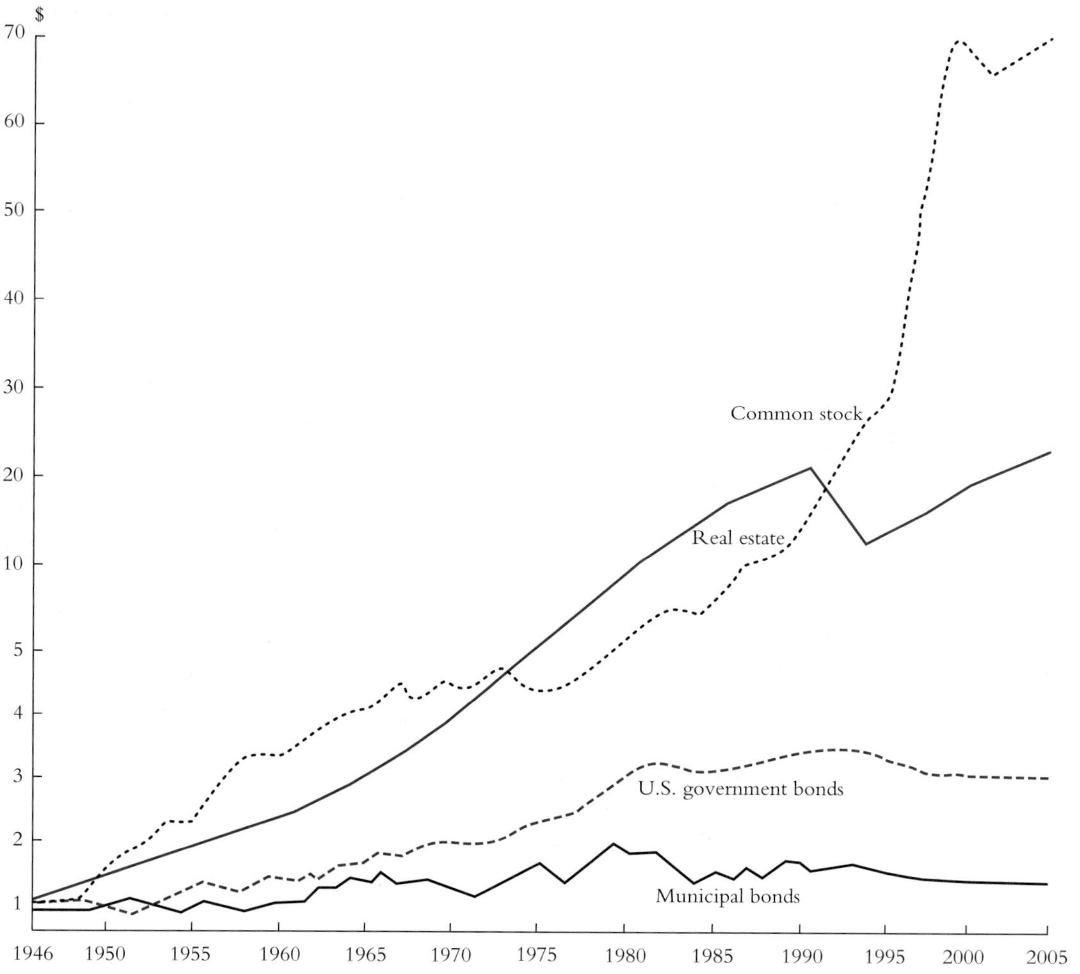

The initial negative impact of tax reform on real estate was also associated with declining economic conditions in various sections of the country during the late 1980s and early 1990s. First, the Southwest (and Texas in particular) was hit with a 70 percent plunge in oil prices in 1986. This meant office buildings, shopping centers, and homes built on an assumption of increasing energy prices to stimulate economic growth went begging for buyers. It was not unusual for a home that was purchased in Dallas, Oklahoma City, or Denver for $300,000 in 1986 to be sold at 50 to 60 percent of that amount five years later. Even as the Southwestern economy began to slowly recover in the early 1990s, real estate–related problems moved into the Northeast, with Massachusetts being hit particularly hard. The next area to suffer was the supposedly immune West Coast in the mid-1990s. Few thought it possible that the ever-growing state of California would see the real estate bubble burst in such dynamic areas as Los Angeles and the San Francisco Bay area.

Over the long term, however, real estate may still be a good investment. Why? With fewer new properties being developed as a result of tax reform and economic conditions, the glut in office space and apartments in certain sections of the country is beginning to disappear. Furthermore, with fewer new properties brought to the market, rents are going up on existing properties. The eventual effect of higher rents will be higher valuation. Evidence of "smart" money starting to flow into real estate markets can be seen in the Dallas–Fort Worth area, in Atlanta, and California markets. Historically, low interest rates have also contributed to this positive pattern.

Valuation of Real Estate

There are three primary approaches to determining the value of real estate.

The Cost Approach

The first is the **cost approach.** What better place to start than the cost to replace an asset at current prices? This is fairly easy to determine for relatively new property, where the components that went into the structure are easily identified and priced out. For older buildings, the challenge is somewhat greater because the building materials may no longer be in existence or may be currently prohibited (for example, asbestos). Some would assume a building is at least worth its replacement cost, but that it not always the case. A warehouse or apartment complex that is poorly located may be worth far less than the replacement cost. Also, when a certain part of the country is suffering from an economic setback, there may be no desire to replace the asset. Nevertheless, the cost basis serves as a useful estimate of value when used in conjunction with the other two approaches.

Comparative Sales Value

Many in the real estate industry look to the selling price of comparable real estate to determine value. If you are going to put a four-bedroom, three-bathroom house, with 2,500 square feet on the market, what better way to establish value than to look for recent sales prices for comparable property in the neighborhood? This approach is called the **comparative sales value.**

Of course, true comparables are difficult to find. While nearby property may appear to be similar, there can be differences in floor plans, landscape, traffic exposure, and so forth. Nevertheless, if a number of comparables can be identified, the differences may be averaged out or a grid established in which a base price is assigned and then modified for each different element.

Although the comparative sales approach is only a helpful guideline, it does have one indisputable value. *Actual sales* did take place at the recorded price.

The Income Approach

For income-producing property, the **income approach** may be applied. The basic question to be answered is this: "What is the potential annual operating income and at what level should it be valued (capitalized)?"

In its simplest form, this formula may be applied:

$$\frac{\text{Annual net operating income}}{\text{Capitalization rate (Cap rate)}} = \text{Value} \qquad (20\text{–}1)$$

The numerator is determined by an analysis of annual rentals, followed by a subtraction of expenses such as property taxes, insurance, etc. The numbers to be applied are future realistic numbers rather than current or historical values. Perhaps the current gross rentals are $35,000 per year but could easily be raised to $40,000 with a minimum of effort. It is this latter number that should be used. The same is true for expenses. If prior tax returns indicate that maintenance and upkeep expenses are too low to maintain the quality of the property, upward adjustments must be made.

The second component in Formula 20–1 on the previous page is the denominator, the capitalization rate. That is, the rate of return required by investors in similar-type investments. It is normally determined by examining the rate of return on recent transactions. It may be further modified by additional consideration of risk, changes in interest rates, etc.

Assume a property had a projected annual net operating income of $17,500 and a market capitalization rate of 10 percent. The value based on this approach would be $175,000:

$$\frac{\$17,500}{0.10} = \$175,000$$

While the approach is potentially helpful, it suffers somewhat from oversimplicity. For example, only one number is used for annual net operating income for the foreseeable future when it is quite likely to change over time. Also, different analysts may have difficulty in determining what the capitalization rate should be. At a cap rate of 9 percent, the property is worth $194,444, and at a cap rate of 11 percent, it is only worth $159,091.

Combination of the Three Approaches

In most cases, a final value will be determined by a combination of the three approaches—each imparts significant information, but each also has its shortfalls. While a one-third weighting of the value determined under each approach is appealing, in most cases (particularly those involving litigation), a different weighting approach is likely to be used. Perhaps comparable sales value will receive a 50 percent weighting, the income approach 35 percent, and the cost approach 15 percent.

A More Comprehensive Analysis

Application Example

In any valuation of an asset, the ultimate worth is based on the present value of future cash flows. This not only applies to stocks, bonds, oil wells, and new business ventures, but to real estate as well.

To determine cash flow variables, we will follow these six steps:

1. Determine the purchase price, the size of the mortgage, and the annual mortgage payment.
2. Compute the net operating income for each year of the anticipated holding period.
3. Translate this to annual cash flow during the holding period.
4. Project the selling price of the property after the holding period.
5. Discount the annual cash flows and the anticipated selling price after the holding period back to the present to determine the present value of the future benefits.

> 6. Compare the upfront cash commitment to the present value of future benefits to determine if the property provides a positive net present value.
>
> We will now discuss each of these steps.

1. Determine the Purchase Price and Financing Assume the Baily apartment complex (six units) can be purchased for $180,000. Discussion with a mortgage banker (lender) indicates a loan for 80 percent of the value would be available at 12 percent for 20 years. Thus, the loan would be for $144,000:

$$\$180{,}000 \times 80\% = \$144{,}000$$

The balance of the purchase price would be put up in cash ($36,000):

$$\$180{,}000 - \$144{,}000 = \$36{,}000$$

Next, we look up the annual mortgage payment. Examining Table 20–1 below, we see on the first line that the annual mortgage payment for 20 years at 12 percent is $19,280.

2. Determine the Net Operating Income for Each Year We will assume the buyer intends to hold the property for four years and then sell it. Thus, we determine the value each year in Table 20–2 on page 564. The values are assumed to slightly increase with the passage of time. Next we translate net operating income into cash flow.

3. Determine Annual Cash Flow Up until now we have only computed income from operations. The real issue is how much cash flow is being generated. Other nonoperating factors that must be considered are interest expense, depreciation, taxable income or losses (and related taxes or tax shield benefits), and repayment of the mortgage.

In Table 20–3 on page 564, we subtract depreciation and interest expense from net operating income to determine taxable income or loss for each year. But before we look at the bottom line in Table 20–3, let's briefly discuss depreciation and interest expense. **Straight-line depreciation** is based on a straight-line deduction of the value of the depreciable asset over a period for 27.5 years. This time period applies to rental residential property and is mandated under the Tax Reform Act of 1986.

You may recall the purchase price of the property was $180,000. We assume $40,000 of the purchase price represents land (which cannot be depreciated), so the amount of depreciable assets is $140,000. Assuming 27.5-year straight-line

TABLE 20–1 Annual Mortgage Payment for a 20-Year Loan (Principal Amount Equals $144,000)

	8%	10%	12%	14%	16%
Annual mortgage payment	$ 14,667	$ 16,913	$ 19,280	$ 21,742	$ 24,287
First-year interest expense	11,520	14,400	17,280	20,160	23,040
Total interest over the life of the loan	149,340	194,260	241,600	290,840	341,700

TABLE 20–2 Annual Net Operating Income

	Year 1	Year 2	Year 3	Year 4
Gross annual rental (6 units × $450 × 12 months in first year)	$32,400	$34,100	$36,400	$38,100
Less 5% vacancy rate	1,620	1,705	1,820	1,905
Net rental income	$30,780	$32,395	$34,580	$36,195
Less operating expenses				
Property taxes	$ 5,000	$ 5,100	$ 5,200	$ 5,300
Maintenance	1,500	1,550	1,650	1,710
Utilities	1,960	2,072	2,205	2,310
Insurance	2,200	2,240	2,290	2,340
Total operating expenses	$10,660	$10,962	$11,345	$11,660
Net operating income	$20,120	$21,433	$23,235	$24,535

TABLE 20–3 Taxable Income or Loss

	Year 1	Year 2	Year 3	Year 4
Net operating income	$20,120	$21,433	$23,235	$24,535
Less				
Depreciation	5,096	5,096	5,096	5,096
Interest expense	17,280	17,040	16,767	16,405
Taxable income (loss)	$ (2,256)	$ (703)	$ 1,372	$ 3,034

depreciation, 3.64 percent (1 ÷ 27.5 years) can be deducted each year. Based on $140,000 in depreciable assets, the annual write-off is $5,096 per year (line 3 in Table 20–3). Depreciation is a particularly valuable deduction because it reduces taxable income but does not represent an actual cash payment.

The deduction for interest expense is also important and changes from year to year as the loan balance becomes smaller. The interest expense is merely given in this case (line 4 of Table 20–3), but it can be easily computed through Internet amortization tables. As an example, in the first year the beginning loan balance is $144,000, and with 12 percent interest, interest owed in the first year is $17,280.

We now look to the bottom line of Table 20–3. The main observation is that there are taxable losses in the first two years and taxable income in the last two years. The losses in the first two years may potentially be used to offset income from other sources. To the extent the investor is actively involved with the property (it is not a passive investment under the terms of the Tax Reform Act of 1986), he or she will be able to use the losses as a tax shield (shelter) for other income.

Assuming the investor is in a 30 percent tax bracket, the taxable losses in Years 1 and 2 translate into the tax shield benefits shown in Table 20–4. Of course, the taxable income in Years 3 and 4 will require that taxes be paid.

We are now in a position to achieve our goal in step 3: determine annual cash flow. We have three forms of cash flow coming in. The first is net operat-

TABLE 20-4 Tax Shield Benefits or Taxes Owed

	Year 1	Year 2	Year 3	Year 4
Taxable income (or loss)	$(2,256)	$(703)	$1,372	$3,034
Tax rate	30%	30%	30%	30%
Tax shield benefits or taxes owed	$ 677	$ 211	$ (412)	$ (910)

TABLE 20-5 Annual Cash Flow

	Year 1	Year 2	Year 3	Year 4
Net operating income	$20,120	$21,433	$23,235	$24,535
Tax shield benefit or taxes owed	677	211	(412)	(910)
Annual mortgage payment	(19,280)	(19,280)	(19,280)	(19,280)
Cash flow	$ 1,517	$ 2,364	$ 3,543	$ 4,345

ing income (Table 20–2), and the second is annual tax shield benefits or taxes owed (Table 20–4). The third annual cash flow is the annual mortgage payment.[2] We can turn back to the circled item in Table 20–1 to easily determine this value. It will apply to each of the four years of the holding period.

The three sources of cash flow are brought together in Table 20–5 to determine the total annual value of cash flow.

We now move on to step 4. That is, after determining the annual cash flows during the four-year holding period, it is time to look at the potential sales price for the property after the holding period.

4. Project the Sales Price The investor initially paid $180,000 for the property, and we assume it increases in value by 6 percent per year over the four-year holding period. Using Appendix A for four periods at 6 percent, the compound sum factor is 1.262. This translates into a sales value of $227,160:

$180,000 Purchase price
× 1.262 Compound sum factor
$227,160 Value after 4 years

The investor, who is now the seller, will likely have to pay a real estate commission and other fees, which we will assume total 7 percent. The amount is $15,901 (7% × $227,160). This leaves the investor with a value of $211,259:

$227,160 Sales price
− 15,901 Commission and fees
$211,259 Net proceeds

---

[2] The interest component of the annual mortgage payment was deducted in computing taxable income or loss, but it was not subtracted out as a cash item. Therefore, it is appropriately included as part of the annual mortgage payment to determine cash flow.

To the extent the net proceeds exceed the book value of the property, a capital gains tax will also have to be paid. The book value of the property is equal to the initial purchase price minus depreciation to date. The purchase price was $180,000, and four years of depreciation at $5,096 per year have been taken (third line of Table 20–3 on page 564). Thus the book value is:

$180,000   Purchase price
− 20,384   4 years of depreciation (4 × $5,096)
$159,616[3]   Book value

The difference between the net proceeds from the sale and the book value is $51,643:

$211,259   Net proceeds
− 159,616   Book value
$ 51,643   Capital gain

The profit is categorized as a capital gain and it is subject to a maximum tax rate of 15 percent.[4] You will recall the investor paid a 30 percent tax on normal operating income, but investments held for over a year normally qualify for preferential capital gains treatment.

The capital gains tax in this case would be $7,746 (15% × $51,643). This would leave the investor with funds from the sale of $203,513:

$211,259   Net proceeds
− 7,746   Capital gains tax
$203,513   Funds from the sale

From this sum, the investor must pay off the mortgage balance that exists after four years as he or she closes out the ownership position. The mortgage banker informs us this is equal to $134,432.[5]

The cash flows from the sale minus the mortgage balance leaves the investor with net cash flow from the sale of $69,081:

$203,513   Funds from the sale
− 134,432   Payoff of mortgage
$ 69,081   Net cash flow (from sale)

5. Determine the Present Value of All Benefits   Because we have computed the annual cash flows from the four years of operations as well as the net cash flow from selling the property, we are now in a position to determine the

---

[3] This value is the same as taking depreciable assets of $140,000 minus depreciation to date of $20,384 and adding back $40,000 in original land value:

$140,000   Depreciable assets
− 20,384   Depreciation to date
$119,616
+ 40,000   Land
$159,616   Book value

[4] The recaptured depreciated amount could be taxed at 30 percent; however, we will disregard this complication.

[5] This value is computed by subtracting the repayment of principal each year from the initial mortgage.

TABLE 20–6 Present Value of the Cash Flows

Year	Cash Flow (Table 20–5)	Present Value Factor (12%)	Present Value
1	$ 1,517	0.893	$ 1,355
2	2,364	0.797	1,884
3	3,543	0.712	2,523
4	$73,426[a]	0.636	$46,699
		Total present value of cash flows	$52,461

[a] Fourth-year annual cash flow of $4,345 plus net cash flow from the sale of $69,081.

present value of the benefits. We assume the investor in this particular example has a required return of 12 percent on real estate investments, and we use that as the discount rate in Table 20–6. The present value of the future cash flows is $52,461.

6. Compare the Upfront Cash Payment to the Benefits The upfront cash investment was $36,000, and the present value of all future cash flows is $52,461. This indicates a net present value for the investment of $16,461:

$52,461   Present value of future cash flows
− 36,000   Upfront cash investment
$16,461   Net present value

Clearly, the project earns well in excess of the required return on the investment of 12 percent and is an acceptable investment. The actual yield or interest rate of return is slightly in excess of 22 percent. But keep in mind that real estate may be a very illiquid investment and almost all the return is based on a 6 percent annual increase in value. The annual operating gains are almost negligible. Nevertheless, this does appear to be an attractive investment.

Financing of Real Estate

One of the essential considerations in any real estate investment analysis is the cost of financing. In the prior example, we said a loan for $144,000 over 20 years at 12 percent interest would have yearly payments of $19,280. Note in Table 20–1 back on page 563 the effects of various interest rates on annual payments.

We see that the difference in annual payments ranges from $14,667 at 8 percent up to $24,287 at 16 percent. Even more dramatic is the increase in total interest paid over the life of the loan; it goes from $149,340 at 8 percent to $341,700 at 16 percent. (Keep in mind that the total loan was only $144,000.)

An investor who has the unlikely opportunity to shift out of the loan at 16 percent into one at 8 percent might be willing to pay as much as $94,446.16 for the privilege (tax effects are not specifically considered here):

16 percent interest − 8 percent interest = Dollar difference in annual payments
$24,287 − $14,667 = $9,620

The present value of $9,620 over 20 years assuming an 8 percent discount rate (see Appendix D) is:

$$\$9,620 \times 9,818 = \$94,449.16$$

Thus, it is easy to appreciate the role of interest rates in a real estate investment decision. No industry is more susceptible to the impact of changing interest rates than real estate. Each time the economy overheats and interest rates skyrocket, the real estate industry comes to a standstill. With the eventual easing of interest-rate pressures, the industry once again enjoys a recovery.

Types of Mortgages

In actuality, a whole set of mortgage arrangements is available as alternatives to the fixed-interest-rate mortgage (particularly for home mortgages). The borrower must now be prepared to consider such alternative lending arrangements as the **adjustable rate mortgage,** the **graduated payment mortgage,** and the **shared appreciation mortgage.**

Adjustable Rate Mortgage (ARM) Under this mortgage arrangement, the interest rate is adjusted regularly. If interest rates go up, borrowers may either increase their normal payments or extend the maturity date of the loan at the same fixed-payment level to fully compensate the lender. Similar downside adjustments can also be made if interest rates fall. Generally, adjustable rate mortgages are initially made at rates 1 to 2 percent below fixed-interest-rate mortgages because the lender enjoys the flexibility of changing interest rates and is willing to share the benefits with the borrower. Adjustable rate mortgages currently account for more than half of the residential mortgage market. Although adjustable rate mortgages usually have an upper boundary (such as 12 or 15 percent or a 6 percent lifetime adjustment over the original borrowing rate), there is a real possibility of default for many borrowers if interest rates reach high levels.

Graduated Payment Mortgage (GPM) Under this type of financial arrangement, the payments start out on a relatively low basis and increase over the life of the loan. This type of mortgage may be well suited to the young borrower who has an increasing repayment capability over the life of the loan. An example would be a 30-year, $60,000 loan at 9 percent that would normally require monthly payments of $583.99 under a standard fixed-payment mortgage. With a graduated payment mortgage, monthly payments might start out as $350 or $400 and eventually progress to more than $700. The GPM plan has been referred to by a few of its critics as the "gyp 'em" plan, in that early payments may not be large enough to cover interest, and therefore, later payments must cover not only the amortization of the loan but also interest on the accumulated, unpaid, early interest. This is not an altogether fair criticism but merely an interpretation of what the graduated payment stream represents.

Shared Appreciation Mortgage (SAM) Perhaps the newest and most innovative of the mortgage payment plans is the shared appreciation mortgage. This provides the lender with a hedge against inflation because he directly participates in any increase in value associated with the property being mortgaged.

The lender may enjoy as much as 30 to 40 percent of the appreciation in value over a specified time period, such as 10 years. The lender may take his return from the selling of the property or from the refinancing of the appreciated property value with a new lender. In return for this appreciation-potential privilege, the lender may advance funds at well below current market rates (perhaps at three-fourths of current rates). The shared appreciation mortgage is not yet legal in all states.

Other Forms of Mortgages Somewhat similar to the shared appreciation mortgage is the concept of equity participation that is popular in commercial real estate. Under an **equity participation** arrangement, the lender not only provides the borrowed capital but part of the equity or ownership funds as well. A major insurance company or savings and loan thus may acquire an equity interest of 10 to 25 percent (or more). This financing arrangement becomes popular each time inflation rears its head. Some lenders are simply unwilling to commit capital for long periods without a participation feature.

Borrowers may also look toward a *second mortgage* for financing. Here, a second lender provides additional financing beyond the first mortgage in return for a secondary claim or lien. The second mortgage is generally for a shorter period of time than the initial mortgage. Primary suppliers of second mortgages in recent times have been sellers of property. Often, to consummate a sale, it is necessary for the seller to supplement the financing provided by a financial institution. Sellers providing second mortgages generally advance the funds at rates below the first mortgage rate to facilitate the sale, whereas other second mortgage lenders (nonsellers) will ask for a few percentage points above the first mortgage rate to compensate for the extra risk of being in a secondary claim position.

In some cases, sellers may actually provide all the financing to the buyer. Usually the terms of the mortgage are for 20 to 30 years, but the seller has the right to call in the loan after three to five years if so desired. The assumption is that the buyer may have an easier time finding his own financing at that point in time. This may or may not be true.

Forms of Real Estate Ownership

Ownership of real estate may take many forms. The investor may participate as an individual, in a regular partnership, through a real estate syndicate (generally a limited partnership), or through a real estate investment trust (REIT).

Individual or Regular Partnership

Investing as an individual or with two or three others in a regular partnership offers the simplest way of getting into real estate from a legal viewpoint. The investors pretty much control their own destinies and can take advantage of personal knowledge of local markets and changing conditions to enhance their returns.

As is true with most smaller and less complicated business arrangements, there is a well-defined center of responsibility that often leads to quick corrective action. However, there may be a related problem of inability to pool adequate capital to engage in large-scale investments as well as the absence of expertise to develop a wide range of investments. Furthermore, there is unlimited liability to the investor(s).

Syndicate or Limited Partnership

To expand the potential for investor participation, a syndicate or limited partnership has traditionally been formed.[6] The **limited partnership** works as follows: A general partner forms the limited partnership and has unlimited liability for the partnership liabilities. The general partner then sells participation units to the limited partners whose liability is limited to the extent of their initial investment (such as $5,000 or $10,000). Limited liability is particularly important in real estate because mortgage debt obligations may exceed the net worth of the participants. The general partner is normally responsible for managing the property, while the limited partners are merely investors.

Although the restricted liability feature of the limited partnership remains attractive, the Tax Reform Act of 1986 generally restricted the use of limited partnerships as tax shelters. Historically, real estate limited partnerships generated large paper losses through accelerated depreciation (though not cash losses), and these paper losses were used to shelter other forms of income (such as a doctor's salary) from taxation. Under the Tax Reform Act of 1986, a taxpayer is no longer allowed to freely use passive losses to offset other sources of income such as salary or portfolio income. Such losses can only be used to offset income from other passive investments.

Real estate limited partnerships still exist but more for limited liability than for tax reasons. The successful partnerships stress strong cash flow generation and capital appreciation potential. In the earlier cash flow analysis in this chapter, a limited partnership was not involved, and the investor actively participated in managing the property. Some small tax write-offs were allowed, but note that the success of the project was much more dependent on cash flow and potential capital appreciation.

If you decide to invest in a limited partnership, you should follow certain guidelines. You must be particularly sensitive to the front-end fees and commissions the general partner might charge. These can vary anywhere from 5 to 10 percent to as large as 20 to 25 percent. The investor must also be sensitive to any double-dealing the general partner might be doing. An example would be selling property between different partnerships the general partner has formed and taking a commission each time. The inflated paper profits may prove quite deceptive and costly to the uninformed limited partner.

In assessing a general partner and his associated real estate deal, the investor should look at a number of items. First, he should review the prior record of performance of the general partner. Is this the 1st or 10th deal that the general partner has put together? The investor will also wish to be sensitive to any lawsuits against the general partner that might exist. The investor might also wish to ascertain whether he or she is investing in a **blind pool** arrangement where funds are provided to the general partner to ultimately select properties for investment or if specific projects have already been identified and analyzed.

---

[6] A syndicate may take the form of a corporation, but this is not common. The term *real estate syndicate* has become virtually synonymous with the limited partnership form of operation.

Finally, the investor may have to decide whether to invest in a limited partnership/syndication that is either *public* or *private* in nature. A public offering generally involves much larger total amounts and has gone through the complex and rigorous process of SEC registration. Of course, SEC registration only attempts to ensure that full disclosure has occurred—it does not judge the prudence of the venture. A private offering of a limited partnership syndication is usually local in scope and restricted to a maximum of 35 investors.

Secondary (resale) markets for both public and private limited partnerships exist, but the dealer spreads and commissions tend to be very high. The spreads on desirable property are perhaps 10 to 15 percent; on less desirable property, 20 to 30 percent or more. Really bad property may approach total illiquidity. As you might anticipate, a public limited partnership has much more resale potential than a private one.

Real Estate Investment Trust

Another form of real estate investment is the **real estate investment trust (REIT).** REITs are similar to mutual funds or investment companies and trade on organized exchanges or over-the-counter. They pool investor funds, along with borrowed funds, and invest them directly in real estate or use them to make construction or mortgage loans to investors.

The advantage to the investor of a REIT is that he or she can participate in the real estate market for as little as $10 to $20 per share. Furthermore, this is the most liquid type of real estate investment because of the large secondary market for the shares.

REITs were initiated under the Real Estate Investment Trust Act of 1960. Like other investment companies, they enjoy the privilege of single taxation of income (only the stockholder pays and not the trust). To qualify for the tax privilege of a REIT, a firm must receive at least 75 percent of its income from real estate (i.e., rents and interest on mortgage loans) and distribute at least 95 percent of its income as cash dividends.

REITs may take any of three different forms or combinations thereof. **Equity trusts** buy, operate, and sell real estate as an investment; **mortgage trusts** make long-term loans to real estate investors; and **hybrid trusts** engage in the activities of both equity and mortgage trusts. REITs are generally formed and advised by affiliates of commercial banks, insurance companies, mortgage bankers, and other financial institutions. Representative issues include Bank America Realty, and Connecticut General Mortgage.

www.cigna.com

www.reitnet.com

There are more than 400 REITs from which the investor may choose.[7] In Figure 20–2 on page 573, a *Value Line* data sheet is presented for Washington REIT, a typical industry participant. Many other REITs are also presented in *Value Line*.

Gold and Silver

We now examine a number of other forms of real asset investments. Precious metals represent the most volatile of the investment alternatives. Historically,

---

[7] Further information on REITs may be acquired from the National Association of Real Estate Investment Trusts, 1101 17th St., N.W., Washington, DC 20036.

the real world of investing

Are REITs Going through a Renaissance Period?

In an article in *Fortune* magazine, Ken Heebner, manager of the CGM funds in Boston, was quoted as saying, "When I buy REITs today, it reminds me of buying stocks in the 1970s, when the Dow was under 1,000. I think REITs represent the beginnings of a major new asset class for individuals."*

Actually, REITs have been around a long time but appear to be going through a current renaissance period. In the same article, Russell Platt, head of real estate securities at Morgan Stanley Asset Management (www.morganstanley.com), suggests that most office REITs have property priced $100 to $150 per square foot, but the equivalent replacement cost is $150 to $250 per square foot. This, of course, makes for an excellent investment opportunity.

REITs tend to specialize in various sectors of the real estate market such as apartments, hotels, health care facilities, shopping centers, and so on. The performance of a given sector tends to be derivative in nature; that is, if the hotel industry is in a boom period with high occupancy rates, hotel REITs will share the benefits in terms of market valuation.

If you invest in REITs you need to become familiar with the term *FFO*. FFO stands for *funds from operations* and represents net income plus depreciation and amortization charges (and excluding gains or losses from debt restructuring and sales of property). You do not need to be an expert in computing FFO to use it in your analysis; it is enough to know that it is the accepted measure of return in the REIT industry and is generally used in place of earnings per share. Thus, instead of talking about P/E (price-to-earnings) ratios, REIT analysts frequently refer to P/FFO (price-to-funds-from-operations) ratios. The P/FFO ratio is normally at a level of 50 to 70 percent of the P/E ratio for a REIT. In January 2004, the average REIT had a mean P/FFO ratio of 12× and a mean P/E ratio of 20×. As a further example, Weingarten Realty, a highly regarded shopping center REIT, had a P/E ratio of 21.5× and a P/FFO ratio of 11.1×. You would normally compare other shopping center REITs with the P/FFO of 11.1× of Weingarten Realty.

While REITs have generally performed well in the stock market during their recent recovery period, they are subject to the same ups and downs as other equity investments. They are particularly sensitive to interest rate changes because they borrow heavily and are frequently classified as high-yield securities, which means they go up in value when interest rates are going down and vice versa. If you are a potential REIT investor, make sure to study the outlook for interest rates before committing funds.

---

*Susan E. Kuhn, "Here Come the Good Years in Real Estate; From REITs to Vacation Condos, Good Deals Abound," *Fortune*, December 23, 1996, pp. 127–30.

---

gold and silver have tended to move up in troubled times and show a decline in value during stable, predictable periods.[8] Observe the movement in the price of gold between 1976 and 2003 in Figure 20–3 on page 574.

Gold

Major factors that tend to drive up gold prices are fear of war, political instability, and inflation (these were particularly evident in Figure 20–3 after 1979 with the takeover of U.S. embassies in Iran and double-digit inflation). Conversely, moderation in worldwide tensions and lower inflation cause a decline in gold prices.

www.kiplinger.com

Gold may be owned in many different forms, and a survey by *Kiplinger's Personal Finance Magazine* indicated that 30 percent of the U.S. population

---

[8] As previously pointed out, this pattern has not been evident in the 1990s but is still thought to carry long-term validity.

FIGURE 20-2 Data Sheet for REIT

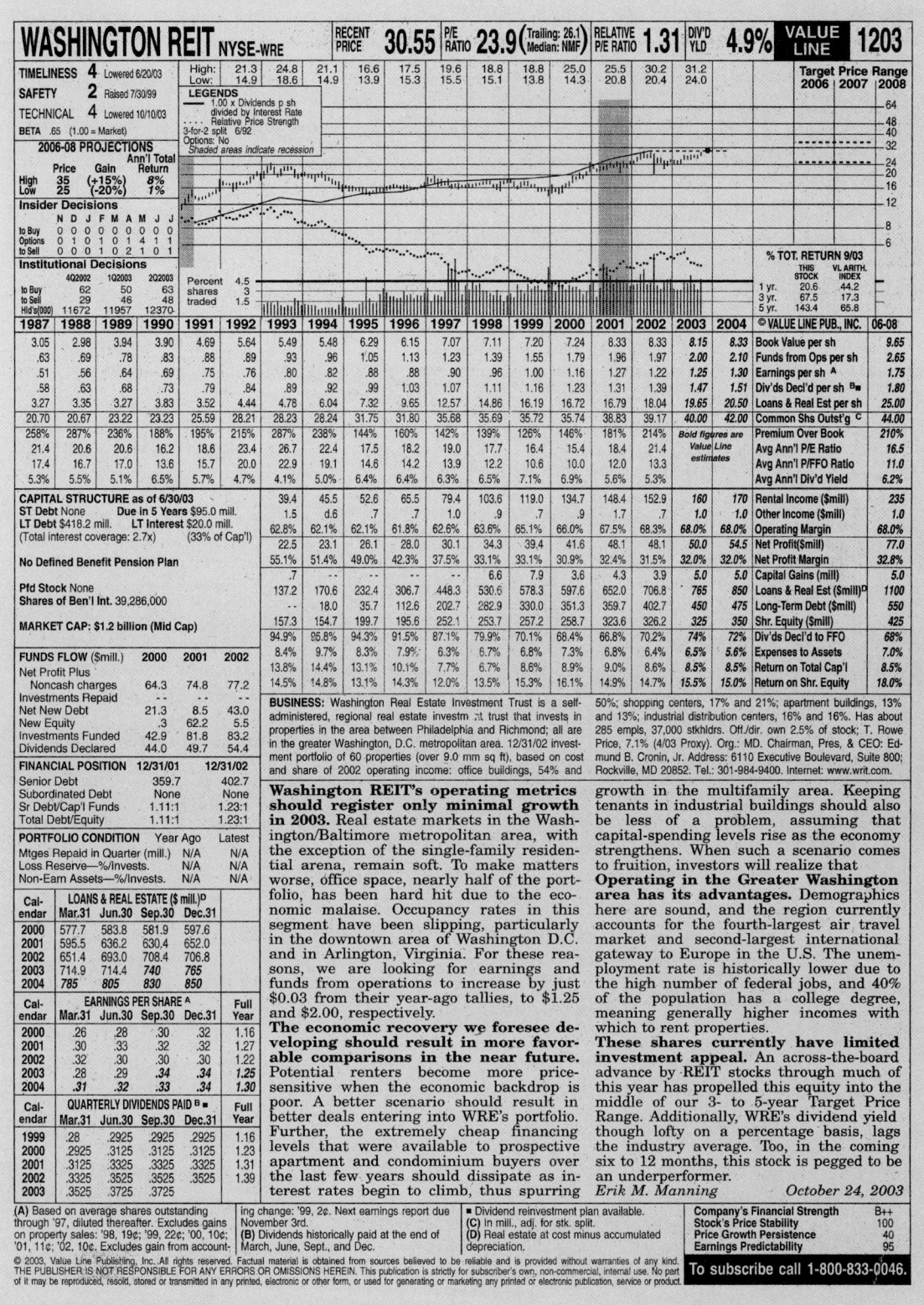

Source: Copyright 2003 by Value Line Publishing, Inc. Reprinted by permission. All Rights Reserved.

FIGURE 20-3 Movement in Gold Prices

London gold fixing

with incomes of more than $40,000 per year owned gold (directly or indirectly) or other forms of precious metals. Let's examine the different forms of gold ownership.

Gold Bullion Gold bullion includes gold bars or wafers. The investor may own anywhere from 1 troy ounce to 10,000 troy ounces (valued at approximately $4.1 million in 2004). Smaller bars generally trade at a 6 to 8 percent premium over pure gold bullion value, with larger bars trading at a 1 to 2 percent premium. Gold bullion may provide storage problems, and unless the gold bars remain in the custody of the bank or dealer who initially sells them, they must be reexamined before being sold.

Gold Coins Many of the storing and assaying costs associated with gold bullion can be avoided by investing directly in gold coins. There are three basic outlets for investing in gold coins. First, there are *gold bullion coins,* such as the South African Krugerrand, the Mexican 50 peso, and the Canadian Maple Leaf. These coins trade at a small premium of 2 to 3 percent over pure bullion value and afford the investor an excellent outlet for taking a position in the market. A second form is represented by *common date gold coins* that are no longer minted, such as the U.S. double eagle, the British sovereign, or the French Napoleon. These coins may trade at as much as 50 to 100 times their pure gold bullion value because of their value as collectibles. Finally, there are gold coins that are *old* and *rare* and that may trade at a numismatic value into the thousands or hundreds of thousands of dollars.

Gold Stocks In addition to gold bullion and gold coins, the investor may take a position in gold by simply buying common stocks that have heavy gold-mining positions. Examples of companies listed on U.S. exchanges include Newmont Mining (U.S. based), Placer Dome Inc. (Canada based), and ASA Limited (U.S. based). Because these securities often move in the opposite direction of the stock market as a whole, they may provide excellent portfolio diversification.

www.placerdome.com

www.barrick.com

Gold Futures Contracts Finally, the gold investor may consider trading in futures contracts. Gold futures are traded on five different U.S. exchanges and on many foreign exchanges.[9]

Silver

Silver has many of the same investment characteristics as gold in terms of being a hedge against inflation and a potential safe haven for investment during troubled times. Silver moved from $5 a troy ounce in 1976 to more than $50 an ounce in early 1980 and then back to $6 an ounce in 2004.

More so than gold, silver has heavy industrial and commercial applications. Areas of utilization include photography, electronic and electrical manufacturing, electroplating, dentistry, and silverware and jewelry. It is estimated that industrial uses of silver exceed annual production by 150 million ounces per year. Furthermore, the supply of silver does not necessarily increase with price because silver is a by-product of copper, lead, zinc, and gold. Because of the undersupply factor, many consider silver to be appropriate for long-term holding.

Investment in silver can also take many different forms. Some may choose to buy *silver bullion* in the form of silver bars. Because the price of silver generally is $\frac{1}{25}$ to $\frac{1}{75}$ the price of gold and larger bulk is involved for an equivalent dollar size investment, the storage and carrying costs can be quite high. Second, *silver coins* may be bought in large bags or as rare coins for their numismatic value. Keep in mind that dimes, quarters, and half-dollars minted during and before 1965 were 90 percent pure silver. As a third outlet, the investor may wish to consider *silver futures contracts*. Finally, the investor may purchase *stocks* of firms that have interests in silver mining, such as Hecla Mining or Echo Bay Mines.

www.hecla-mining.com

Precious Gems

Precious gems include diamonds, rubies, sapphires, and emeralds. Diamonds and other precious gems have appeal to investors because of their small size, easy concealment, and great durability. They are particularly popular in Europe because of a long-standing distrust of paper currencies as a store of value.

---

[9] There are also options on gold futures on the Comex.

the real world of investing

Baseball Cards as Collectibles

Although we most often associate baseball cards with the 10-year-old child who coaxes $2.00 from his parents to buy a pack of cards in the drugstore, there is actually a half-billion dollar a year industry out there. There are 100,000 serious baseball card collectors and millions of child arbitragers doing business on a daily basis.

Other forms of sports memorabilia have value as well. A baseball clearly autographed by Babe Ruth is worth about $7,000. An authentic Lou Gehrig game-worn uniform carries a $310,000 price tag. A truly enterprising collector went so far as to pay $500 for the dental records of Eddie Cicotte, a long-deceased pitcher for the infamous Chicago Black Sox of 1919.

Nevertheless, baseball cards and sports memorabilia have not fared particularly well since the last edition of this book was published. The fabled Mickey Mantle 1952 Topps baseball card has declined in value from $50,000 to $25,000 (it originally cost a penny), and the Nolan Ryan 1968 Topps rookie card has declined from $2,000 to $1,200. Overall, baseball cards have declined in value by 10 percent in the last four years.

Why the decline? Baseball cards, like other forms of collectibles and real assets, are viewed as a hedge against inflation, and there has been very little inflation against which it has been necessary to hedge. Also, the baseball players strike of the mid-1990s turned many fans against the game—not only at the turnstiles but in general enthusiasm for the game. This factor has translated into less devoted collectors of baseball cards as well. Also, the oversupply of baseball cards by an expanding group of card manufacturers is another negative.

There have been ups and downs in the baseball card market before, and the patient, contrarian investor may wish to view the current market as a buying opportunity for old, valuable cards in mint condition that are being sold by distressed owners.

There is an interesting exception to the current downturn in the market. In 2000, a 1910 Honus Wagner tobacco baseball card sold for more than $1 million. The previous high for the Wagner card was $640,000 in 1996. In 1985, it had changed hands at $110,000. Why all the upside momentum? Wagner did not approve of smoking, and when his card appeared in a tobacco-related set around 1910, he forced the American Tobacco Company to pull all but 100 off the market. Now, only 40 Wagner cards are thought to exist, and the law of supply and demand has clearly set in.

Also, other forms of baseball memorabilia (besides cards) have done extremely well in the last few years. It all started with the Sotheby's (www.sothebys.com) auction of the Barry Halper memorabilia collection in 2000. Mr. Halper, a multimillionaire and minority owner of the New York Yankees, had the largest memorabilia collection of items such as autographed baseballs (going back to the 1920s), players' uniforms, and Ty Cobb and Babe Ruth signed documents in existence. The auction brought in two and three times the anticipated value of cherished items and started a renewed interest in memorabilia. As evidence, Mastro Fine Sports (www.mastronet.com) of Oak Brook, Illinois, conducts memorabilia auctions over the Internet four or five times a year and normally grosses $10 to $12 million per auction. A 1927 Yankees autographed baseball, which was worth $5,000 a few years before, went for $70,000. An autographed copy of the 1948 *Babe Ruth Story* purchased by one of the authors for $1,100 in 1999 went for $4,000 in May 2001. The ill-fated Cubs' Bartman "fan-interference ball" sold for $106,600 in December 2003.

The reason diamonds are so valuable can be best understood by considering the production process. It is estimated that 50 to 200 *tons* of rock or sand is required to uncover one carat ($1/142$ of an ounce) of quality diamonds.

The distribution of diamonds is under virtual monopolistic control by De Beers Consolidated Mines of South Africa, Ltd. It controls the distribution of approximately 80 percent of the world's supply and has a stated policy of maintaining price control. Diamonds have generally enjoyed a steady, somewhat spectacular movement in price. For example, the price of a "D" color, one-carat, flawless, polished diamond increased more than tenfold between 1974 and 1980.

Of course, not all diamonds have done so well. Furthermore, there have been substantial breaks in the market, such as in 1974 and 1980–82 when diamond prices declined by one-fourth and more. Even with large increases in value, the diamond investor does not automatically come out ahead. Dealer markups may be anywhere from 10 to 100 percent so three to five years of steady gain may be necessary to show a substantial profit.

In no area of investment is product and market knowledge more important. Either you must be an expert yourself or know that you are dealing with an "honest" expert. Diamonds are judged on the basis of the four *c*'s (color, clarity, carat weight, and cut), and the assessment of any stone should be certified by a member of the Gemological Institute of America. As is true of most valuable items, the investor is well advised to purchase the highest quality possible. You are considerably better off using the same amount of money to buy a higher quality, smaller carat diamond than a lesser quality, high-carat diamond.

Other Collectibles

A listing of other collectibles for investment might include art, antiques, stamps, Chinese ceramics, rare books, and other items that appeal to various sectors of our society. Each offers psychic pleasure to the investor as well as the opportunity for profit.

Anyone investing in a collectible should have some understanding of current market conditions and of the factors that determine the inherent worth of the item. Otherwise, you may be buying someone else's undesirable holding at a premium price. It is important not to get swept away in a buying euphoria. The best time to buy art, antiques, or stamps is when the bloom is off the market and dealers are overburdened with inventory, not when there is a weekly story in *The Wall Street Journal* or *BusinessWeek* about overnight fortunes being made. There seems to be a pattern or cycle in the collectibles market the same as in other markets (arts, antiques, and stamps actually do move together).

As is true of other markets, the wise investor in the collectibles market must be sensitive to dealer spreads. A price guide that indicates a doubling in value every two or three years may be meaningless if the person with whom you are dealing sells for $100 and buys back for $50. The wise investor/collector can best maintain profits by dealing with other collectors or investors and eliminating the dealer or middleman from the transaction where possible.

www.money.com

www.coinworld.com

www.linns.com

Such periodicals as *Money* magazine and the *Collector/Investor* provide excellent articles on the collectibles market. Specialized periodicals, such as *American Arts and Antiques, Coin World, Linn's Stamp News, The Sports Collectors Digest,* and *Antique Monthly,* also are helpful. The interested reader can find books on almost any type of collectible in a public library or large bookstore.

exploring the web

Website Address	Comments
www.realtor.com	Has property search function, mortgage evaluation function
moneycentral.msn.com	Has property valuation function along with mortgage financing calculator
www.quicken.com	Provides mortgage financing information and payment calculator
www.nareit.com	Website for the industry trade group and provides information and data on REITs
www.hsh.com	Contains database of current residential mortgage rates
www.realestate.com	Provides information on property listings and mortgage financing and reports on property values and analysis
www.gmacrealestate.com	Provides property search, valuation calculation, and mortgage information
www.housevalues.com	Will estimate residential property values and provide report for homes in cities in its database

Summary

Investments in real assets must be considered in a total portfolio concept. They offer a measure of inflation protection, an opportunity for efficient diversification, and psychic pleasure to the investor.

A disadvantage is the absence of a large, liquid market such as that provided by the securities markets. There also may be a large dealer or middleman spread, and the investor may have to forgo current income.

The hysteria that grips these markets from time to time not only creates substantial opportunities for profit but also dictates that the investor must be particularly cautious about market timing. It can be quite expensive to be the last buyer in a gold or silver boom.

Real estate requires many of the analytical techniques that are utilized in valuing stocks and bonds. The basic methods for valuing real estate are the cost approach, comparable sales value, and the income approach. Often a weighted combination of the three is used to appraise real estate. A more sophisticated approach to valuing real estate is to do an in-depth cash flow/present value analysis as demonstrated in the chapter.

Gold and silver represent two highly volatile forms of real assets in which price movements often run counter to events in the economy and the world. Bad news is good news (and vice versa) for precious-metal investors. Gold and silver may generally be purchased in bullion or bulk form, as coins, in the commodities futures market, or indirectly through securities of firms specializing in gold or silver mining.

Precious gems and other collectibles, such as art, antiques, stamps, Chinese ceramics, and rare books, have caught the attention of investors in various time periods. Although there are many warning signs at

Key Words and Concepts

adjustable rate mortgage 568
blind pool 570
comparable sales value 561
cost approach 561
equity participation 569
equity trusts 571
graduated payment mortgage 568
hybrid trusts 571
income approach 561
limited partnership 570
mortgage trusts 571
real assets 557
real estate investment trust (REIT) 571
shared appreciation mortgage 568
straight-line depreciation 563

Discussion Questions

1. Why might real assets offer an opportunity as an inflation hedge?
2. Explain why real assets might add to effective portfolio diversification.
3. What are some disadvantages of investing in real estate?
4. What two factors have hurt real estate in recent times? Why might the future outlook be more positive?
5. What are the three primary approaches to real estate valuation? Should they be combined?
6. What is an adjustable rate mortgage?
7. For what type of borrower is the graduated payment mortgage best suited?
8. Explain a shared appreciation mortgage.
9. What is meant by a seller loan with a call privilege?
10. How is liability handled in a limited partnership?
11. What are REITs? What are the three types of REITs?
12. What are some factors that drive up the price of gold? What are factors that drive it down?
13. What are three different ways to invest in gold coins?
14. Suggest some commercial and industrial uses of silver. What forms can silver investments take?
15. Explain how the dealer spread can affect the rate of return on a collectible item.

Problems

Real estate financing

1. *a.* Using Table 20–1 on page 563, determine the annual savings on a 20-year, $144,000 mortgage by going from 12 percent interest to 8 percent interest.
   b. Using Appendix D with a discount rate of 8 percent, what is the present value of the annual savings over the next 20 years?

Real estate investment analysis

2. An investor is considering purchasing an apartment complex for $300,000. A loan for 20 years at 75 percent of the purchase price is available at 10 percent.
   a. Determine the size of the loan and the amount that will have to be put up in cash. Assume the annual mortgage payment is $26,427. (You will use this number later.)

b. The investor intends to hold the property for three years and then sell it. He is going to compute net operating income for the first year and then assume that amount will grow by 5 percent over the next two years.

Given the information below, compute net operating income for the first year (following the procedure in Table 20–2 on page 564). Then assume that amount will grow by 5 percent per year to determine net operating income in the second and third years.

First Year Data

Gross annual rental (10 units at $500 per month), 6% vacancy rate:

Property taxes	$8,250
Maintenance	2,375
Utilities	2,950
Insurance	3,250

c. Determine depreciation for each of the first three years. The building has a value of $238,000 (the remaining $62,000 is land value). Assume straight-line depreciation with a 27.5 year write-off.

d. Assume interest expense for the first three years is as follows:

Year 1	$22,500
Year 2	20,250
Year 3	18,225

Based on the information you computed in parts *b* and *c* and the data given in part *d*, compute taxable income (use a procedure similar to Table 20–3 on page 564).

e. Determine taxes owed for each of the three years. Use a procedure similar to the last two columns of Table 20–4 on page 565. Assume a tax rate of 33 percent.

f. Using net operating income from part *b*, taxes owed from part *d*, and annual mortgage payments for each of the three years of $26,427, compute cash flow for each of the three years. Use a procedure similar to Table 20–5 on page 565.

g. Assume the property increases in value by 7 percent per year over the next three years. Use Appendix A to determine how much the initial value of $300,000 will grow to after three years.

h. Deduct from the sales value computed in part *g*, 6 percent in commissions and fees to arrive at net proceeds.

i. Assume the property has a book value of $280,365. Subtract this value from net proceeds computed in part *h*. The difference represents capital gains.

j. Multiply the capital gains times 15 percent to get the capital gains tax.

k. Subtract the capital gains tax (part *j*) from the net proceeds (part *h*) to get funds from the sale.

l. Subtract the remaining mortgage of $206,694 from the funds from the sale (part *k*) to arrive at net cash flow from the sale.

m. Determine the present value of all the benefits at a discount rate of 10 percent from Appendix C. Set this up in a similar fashion to Table 20–6 on page 567. The cash flow in Years 1 and 2 can be found in part *f*. The cash flow for Year 3 is the sum of Year 3 from part *f* plus the value in part *m*.

n. Subtract the upfront cash investment of $75,000 ($300,000 purchase price minus $225,000 initial mortgage) from the total percent value of cash flows (part *m*) to determine the net present value. Should the property be purchased based on the net present value?

Web Exercise

Although the chapter covers many types of real assets, we will concentrate on real estate. The assumption is that you are interested in what property may be available in a given area. Go to **www.coldwellbanker.com**.

1. Click on "Find a Property" across the top of the screen.
2. On the first two white boxes, put in your home city and state (use two letters for the state). Click "Search."
3. When you see the Property List, click on the double arrows after the "Next" designation at the bottom until you get to a price range appropriate for your family (either your parents or yourself). Write down the price, the number of bedrooms (bd) and the number of bathrooms (bth).
4. Now click on the "Price" to then get more complete information on the right-hand portion of the screen. Write down the address and the number of square feet.
5. Click on "Neighborhood Info" across the top of the screen. Put in the address in the left portion of the screen and click on "Continue." Click on "Neighborhood" and write down four pieces of information about the neighborhood.
6. Click on "Mortgage Center" across the top, and write down the information about a 30-year fixed-rate mortgage under today's rates (top half).
7. This concludes the assignment. The intent was to show you how to get information on real estate. This procedure could apply to office buildings, apartments for sale, and other types of real estate.

Note: From time to time, companies redesign their websites, and occasionally a topic we have listed may have been deleted, updated, or moved into a different location. Most websites have a "site map" or "site index" listed on a different page. If you click on the site map or site index, you will be introduced to a table of contents that should aid you in finding the topic you are looking for.

S&P Problems

STANDARD &POOR'S

www.mhhe.com/edumarketinsight

1. Log on to the McGraw-Hill website: **www.mhhe.com/edumarketinsight** (see page vi in the preface for instructions).
2. Click on Industry, which is the third box below the Market Insight title. Under industry, there is a drop-down menu where you can select an industry. Click on the arrow to open the industry list. Scroll down the industry list to "Real Estate Investment Trusts" and click on go.

3. Under Compustat Reports in the left margin, click on GICS sub-industry profile, and expand the profile to a full page. What is the dividend yield for the real estate investment trusts compared to the S&P 500?

4. On the far right bottom corner, click on "constituents." A table will come up with the first 20 REITS. Above the alphabet, click on "all 214" and a list of real estate investment companies will appear.

5. S&P does not provide much information on Real Estate Investment Trusts at this time.

6. Go back to Company, and put JNJ into the box and click on go. Then go to Charting by Prophet, and click on the blue Charting by Prophet under the title. Once the graph appears, change the ticker symbol to MLS for Mills Corporation, a real estate investment trust that runs outlet shopping malls.

7. Examine the price performance for 1 year, 3 years, and 5 years by changing the time period. How has Mills performed? When interest rates started to rise in April of 2004, notice how the price dropped.

8. Go to Tools at the top of the page, click on the arrow and go to Studies, and then click on Comparison Chart. Scroll down the index in the box to the S&P 500. Highlight the S&P 500 Index, and click on "add." You will now have a five year comparison of Mills Corp. vs. the S&P. How does Mills compare?

9. How do you think your interest rate forecasts from Chapters 12 and 13 will impact the price of Mills Corp.?

The Wall Street Journal Project

Income-oriented investors often put their money in real estate investment trusts (REITs). To compare the yield on a REIT to current money market yields, go to the "Money Rates" table as listed in the index in Section C of *The Wall Street Journal*. Write down the yields on Treasury bills coming due in 13 and 26 weeks. Also record the yield on the Merrill Lynch Ready Assets Trust.

Now compare these yields to the dividend yield that can be earned on the following REITs:

    Federal Realty (FedRlty) (FRT)

    Health Care Property (HCP)

The dividend yields for the REITs can be found after the company's name in "The New York Stock Exchange Composite Transactions" part of Section C. The yield is located in the second column after the company's name. The column is labeled Div Yld %.

Are these two REITs providing a current yield higher than the money market rates you recorded? You also may want to keep in mind that the stock prices of REITs may go up or down.

Selected References

Portfolio Considerations with Real Assets

Milligan, Jack. "Alternate Investments Gain Wider Albeit Cautious Appeal." *CFA Magazine,* June–May 2003, pp. 46–47.

Investments in Real Estate

Badenhausen, Kurt. "The Buys, Holds and Sells of Real Estate." *Forbes,* March 1, 2004, pp. 94–96.

Corgel, John B., and Chris Djoganonpoules. "Equity REIT Beta Estimation." *Financial Analysts Journal,* January–February 2001, pp. 70–79.

Fitch, Stephane. "The Worst Reit." *Forbes,* March 1, 2004, p. 96.

Saderion, Zahra; Burton Smith; and Charles Smith. "An Integrated Approach to the Evaluation of Commercial Real Estate." *Journal of Real Estate Research,* Spring 1994, pp. 151–67.

Wilson, Susan; Ruijue Peng; and Oral Capps. "Modeling Office Returns at the Regional Level." *Journal of Portfolio Management,* Fall 2000, pp. 103–10.

Precious Metals and Precious Gems

Regular articles featured in: *Money, Personal Investor, Consumer Reports,* and *Changing Times.*

Tufano, Peter. "Who Manages Risk? An Empirical Examination of Risk Management Practices in the Gold Mining Industry." *Journal of Finance,* September 1996, pp. 1097–1137.

Collectibles

Flanagan, William G. "Collectors Masterpieces—or Master Ripoffs?" *Forbes,* March 24, 1997, p. 200.

Periodicals: *American Arts and Antiques, Antique Monthly, Coin World, Collector/Investor, Linn's Stamp News,* and *Sports Collectors Digest.*

part seven
Introduction to Portfolio Management

chapter 21
A BASIC LOOK AT PORTFOLIO MANAGEMENT AND CAPITAL MARKET THEORY

chapter 22
MEASURING RISKS AND RETURNS OF PORTFOLIO MANAGERS

MANY WOULD SAY

that portfolio management is much more important than picking individual stocks. In fact research shows that picking the right mix of asset classes is more important to long-run returns than picking the right stocks, that is, unless you are lucky enough to pick a Microsoft or Wal-Mart in their early days and hang on for the long ride up. Portfolio management is also the management of risk and tax effects, not just return. Eugene Sit, the founder, Chairman, and Chief Investment Officer of Sit Investment Associates (SIA), advisor to the Sit Mutual Funds, knows just how to balance these portfolio issues.

Sit Investment Associates, a Minneapolis-based company, was founded in July of 1981 with $1 million in working capital, and by its third year of operation, it had $1 billion in assets under management. In 1984, Sit formed an asset management subsidiary that specialized in fixed income securities and, in 1989, started an international division that manages assets globally with special emphasis on the Pacific Basin region. The international division serves as the sub-Advisor for the International Growth and Developing Markets Growth Funds. By the middle of 2004 Sit Mutual Funds had $1.5 billion and close to another $8 billion under management with Sit Investment Associates.

One of the major focuses of Sit Investment Advisors is the Sit Mutual Funds. There are 12 no-load funds in the Sit family of funds, covering most major asset classes but with an emphasis on growth. The funds are as follows: Small Cap Growth, Mid Cap Growth, Large Cap Growth, Science & Tech Growth, International Growth, Developing Markets Growth, Dividend Growth, Balanced, Tax-Free Income, Minnesota Tax-Free Income, Florida Tax-Free Income, Bond, U.S. Government Securities, and a Money Market fund. You can find these funds at **www.sitfunds.com**.

Gene Sit graduated from DePaul University in 1960 with a Bachelor of Science in Commerce and passed the CPA exam shortly after graduation. He got his investment experience working for American Express/IDS in Minneapolis and became the Chief Executive Officer and Chief Investment Officer of that firm before he founded Sit Investment Advisors. Sit also holds the CFA (Chartered Financial Analyst) designation and was a founding member of the Board of Governors of the Association for Investment Management and Research (AIMR). AIMR changed its name to the CFA Institute in 2003. Gene Sit has always been active in the financial community and served as chairman and trustee of the Research Foundation of the Institute of Chartered Financial Analysts. For his distinguished service to AIMR and the professional investment community, he was awarded the C. Steward Sheppard Award by the AIMR.

Gene has been an outstanding citizen of the local, regional, and national community. At the time of this writing, he serves as a trustee of Carleton College, the University of Minnesota's Carlson School's International Programs, and the Dean's Board of Visitors for The University of Minnesota Medical School, and as a director for several companies. He has previously been a trustee for TIAA/CREFF, The Minneapolis Institute of Arts, The Minnesota Historical Society, and the Minnesota Orchestral Association. Men like Gene Sit are few and far between and he believes in giving back to the community. Sit Investment Associates says, "The firm is dedicated to a single purpose: To be one of the premier investment management firms in the United States." This focus on excellence permeates all of Gene Sit's activities. We are pleased to feature him in this section.

Eugene Sit
Photo provided by Sit Investment Associates, Inc.

21

chapter twenty-one

A Basic Look at Portfolio Management and Capital Market Theory

objectives

1. Understand the basic statistical techniques for measuring risk and return.
2. Explain how the portfolio effect works to reduce the risk of an individual security.
3. Discuss the concept of an efficient portfolio.
4. Explain the importance of the capital asset pricing model.
5. Understand the concept of the beta coefficient.
6. Discuss the required return on an individual stock and how it relates to its beta.

Formal Measurement of Risk
    Expected Value
    Standard Deviation
Portfolio Effect
    Standard Deviation for a Two-Asset Portfolio
Developing an Efficient Portfolio
    Risk-Return Indifference Curves
    Optimum Portfolio
Capital Asset Pricing Model
    Capital Market Line
Return on an Individual Security
    Systematic and Unsystematic Risk
    Security Market Line
Assumptions of the Capital Asset Pricing Model
Appendix 21A: The Correlation Coefficient
Appendix 21B: Least Squares Regression Analysis
Appendix 21C: Derivation of the Security Market Line (SML)
Appendix 21D: Arbitrage Pricing Theory

www.fidelity.com

Assume it's 8:00 on Sunday evening, and you are watching a sporting event on ESPN. Commercials come on and, along with the latest shiny BMW and Lexus models, there is an ad about mutual funds.

We could take any mutual fund as an example, but in this particular case, we will use the Fidelity Blue Chip Growth Fund. The title of the fund is laden with upscale words. Fidelity is the best-known mutual fund company in the world (with scores of other funds besides this one). Blue chip implies high quality, and growth indicates the fund invests in companies that have strong possibilities to enhance their value. The ad for this fund in January 2004 indicated its value had gone up 21.64 percent over the last 12 months.

However, the real issue is how much risk or volatility the investor was exposed to in achieving this high return. There are two dimensions to any investment: risk and return, and this typical ad is only covering one: return. If the fund had to take an inordinately high amount of risk to achieve this result, it is certainly a less commendable performance. The truth is the fund did have a high degree of risk exposure, with 25.1 percent of its assets invested in technology stocks.

In this chapter, we develop a more complete understanding of how the investor perceives risk and demands compensation for it. We eventually build toward a theory of portfolio management that incorporates these concepts. While the use of mathematical terms is an essential ingredient to a basic understanding of portfolio theory, more involved or complicated concepts are treated in appendices at the end of the chapter.

As indicated in Chapter 1, risk is generally associated with uncertainty about future outcomes. The greater the dispersion of possible outcomes, the greater the risk. We also observed in Chapter 1 that most investors tend to be risk-averse; that is, all things being equal, investors prefer less risk to more risk and will increase their risk-taking position only if a premium for risk is involved. Each investor has a different attitude toward risk. The inducement necessary to cause a given investor to withdraw funds from a money market account to drill an oil well may be quite different from yours. For some, only a very small premium for risk is necessary, while others may not wish to participate unless there are exceptionally high rewards. We begin the chapter with a formal development of risk measures.

Formal Measurement of Risk

Having defined risk as uncertainty about future outcomes, how do we actually measure risk? The first task is to design a probability distribution of anticipated future outcomes. This is no small task. The possible outcomes and associated probabilities are likely to be based on economic projections, past experience, subjective judgments, and many other variables. For the most part, we are forcing ourselves to write down what already exists in our head. Having established the probability distribution, we then determine the expected value and the dispersion around that expected value. The greater the dispersion, the greater the risk.

Expected Value

Application Example

To determine the **expected value,** we multiply each possible outcome by its probability of occurrence. Assume we are considering two investment proposals where K represents a possible outcome and P represents the probability of that outcome based on the state of the economy. If we were dealing with stocks, K would represent the price appreciation potential plus the dividend yield (total return). Table 21–1 on the next page presents the data for two investments, i and j.

TABLE 21-1 Return and Probabilities for Investments *i* and *j*

Investment			Investment	
Return K_i	P_i (Probability of K_i Occurring)	Possible State of the Economy	Return K_j	P_j (Probability of K_j Occurring)
5%	0.20	Recession	20%	0.20
7	0.30	Slow growth	8	0.30
13	0.30	Moderate growth	8	0.30
15	0.20	Strong economy	6	0.20

We will say that $\overline{K}_i$ (the expected value of investment *i*) equals $\Sigma K_i P_i$. In this case, the answer would be 10.0 percent, as shown under Formula 21–1:

$$\overline{K}_i = \Sigma K_i P_i \qquad (21\text{-}1)$$

K_i	P_i	$K_i P_i$
5%	0.20	1.0%
7	0.30	2.1
13	0.30	3.9
15	0.20	3.0
		10.0% = $\Sigma K_i P_i$

Standard Deviation

Application Example

The commonly used measure of dispersion is the **standard deviation,** which is a measure of the spread of the outcomes around the expected value. The formula for the standard deviation is:

$$\sigma_i = \sqrt{\Sigma(K_i - \overline{K}_i)^2 P_i} \qquad (21\text{-}2)$$

Let's determine the standard deviation for investment *i* around the expected value ($\overline{K}_i$) of 10 percent.

K_i	$\overline{K}_i$	P_i	$(K_i - \overline{K}_i)$	$(K_i - \overline{K}_i)^2$	$(K_i - \overline{K}_i)^2 P_i$
5%	10%	0.20	−5%	25%	5.0%
7	10	0.30	−3	9	2.7
13	10	0.30	+3	9	2.7
15	10	0.20	+5	25	5.0
					15.4% = $\Sigma(K_i - \overline{K}_i)^2 P_i$

$$\sigma_i = \sqrt{\Sigma(K_i - \overline{K}_i)^2 P_i} = \sqrt{15.4\%} = 3.9\%$$

The standard deviation of investment *i* is 3.9 percent (rounded). To have some feel for the relative risk characteristics of this investment, we compare it with the second proposal, investment *j*.

We assume investment *j* is a countercyclical investment. It does well during a recession and poorly in a strong economy. Perhaps it represents a firm in the housing industry that is most profitable when the economy is sluggish and interest rates are low. Under these circumstances, people will avail themselves of low-cost financing to purchase a new home, and the stock of the firm will do well. In a booming economy, interest rates will advance rapidly, and the financing of housing will become expensive. Thus, we have a countercyclical investment. The outcomes and probabilities of outcomes for investment *j* are as follows:

The expected value for investment *j* is:

$$\overline{K}_j = \Sigma K_j P_j$$

K_j	P_j	$K_j P_j$
20%	0.20	4.0%
8	0.30	2.4
8	0.30	2.4
6	0.20	1.2
		$\overline{K}_j = 10.0\%$

The standard deviation for investment *j* is:

$$\sigma_j = \sqrt{\Sigma(K_j - \overline{K}_j)^2 P_j}$$

K_j	$\overline{K}_j$	P_j	$(K_j - \overline{K}_j)$	$(K_j - \overline{K}_j)^2$	$(K_j - \overline{K}_j)^2 P_j$
20%	10%	0.20	+10%	100%	20.0%
8	10	0.30	−2	4	1.2
8	10	0.30	−2	4	1.2
6	10	0.20	−4	16	3.2
					25.6% = $\Sigma(K_j - \overline{K}_j)^2 P_j$

$$\sigma_j = \sqrt{\Sigma(K_j - \overline{K}_j)^2 P_j} = \sqrt{25.6\%} = 5.1\% \text{ (rounded)}$$

We now see we have two investments, each with an expected value of 10 percent but with varying performances in different types of economies and different standard deviations (σ_i = 3.9 percent versus σ_j = 5.1 percent).[1]

Portfolio Effect

Application Example

An investor who is holding only investment *i* may wish to consider bringing investment *j* into the portfolio. If the stocks are weighted evenly, the new portfolio's expected value will be 10 percent. We define K_p as the expected value of the portfolio:

$$K_p = X_i \overline{K}_i + X_j \overline{K}_j \qquad (21\text{--}3)$$

---

[1] Actually, rather than use the standard deviation, we can also use its squared value, termed the *variance*, to describe risk. That is, we may use σ^2 (the standard deviation squared) to describe the risk in an individual security.

The X values represent the weights assigned by the investor to each component in the portfolio and are 50 percent for both investments in this example. The $\overline{K}_i$ and $\overline{K}_j$ values were previously determined to be 10 percent. Thus we have:

$$K_p = 0.5(10\%) + 0.5(10\%) = 5\% + 5\% = 10\%$$

What about the standard deviation for the combined portfolio (σ_p)? If a weighted average were taken of the two investments, the new standard deviation would be 4.5 percent:

$$X_i\sigma_i + X_j\sigma_j$$
$$0.5(3.9\%) + 0.5(5.1\%) = 1.95\% + 2.55\% = 4.5\%$$

The interesting element is that the investor in investment i would appear to be losing from the combined investment. His expected value remains at 10 percent, but his standard deviation has increased from 3.9 to 4.5 percent. Given that he is risk-averse, he appears to be getting more risk rather than less risk by expanding his portfolio.

There is one fallacy in the analysis. *The standard deviation of a portfolio is not based on the simple weighted average of the individual standard deviations (as the expected value is).* Rather, it considers significant interaction between the investments. If one investment does well during a given economic condition while the other does poorly and vice versa, there may be significant risk reduction from combining the two, and the standard deviation for the portfolio may be less than the standard deviation for either investment (this is the reason we do not simply take the weighted average of the two).

Note in Figure 21–1 the risk-reduction potential from combining the two investments under study. Investment i alone may produce outcomes anywhere from 5 to 15 percent, and investment j, from 6 to 20 percent. By combining the two, we narrow the range for investment (i, j) to from 7.5 to 12.5 percent. Thus, we have reduced the risk while keeping the expected value constant at 10 percent. We now examine the appropriate standard deviation formula for the two investments.

Standard Deviation for a Two-Asset Portfolio

The standard deviation for a two-asset portfolio is presented in Formula 21–4:[2]

$$\sigma_p = \sqrt{X_i^2\sigma_i^2 + X_j^2\sigma_j^2 + 2X_iX_jr_{ij}\sigma_i\sigma_j} \qquad (21\text{–}4)$$

The only new term in the expression is r_{ij}, the **correlation coefficient** or measurement of joint movement between the two variables. The value for r_{ij} can be from -1 to $+1$, although for most variables, the correlation coefficient falls somewhere in between these two values. Figure 21–2 demonstrates the concept

---

[2] For a multiple asset portfolio, the expression is written as:

$$\sigma_p = \sqrt{\sum_{i=1}^{N} X_i^2\sigma_i^2 + 2\sum_{i=1}^{N-1}\sum_{j=i+1}^{N} X_iX_jr_{ij}\sigma_i\sigma_j}$$

N is the number of securities in the portfolio.

Chapter 21 A Basic Look at Portfolio Management and Capital Market Theory 591

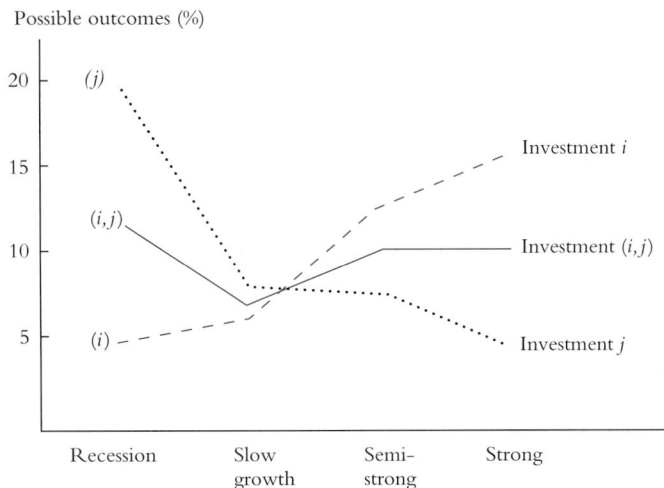

FIGURE 21-1 Investment Outcomes under Different Conditions

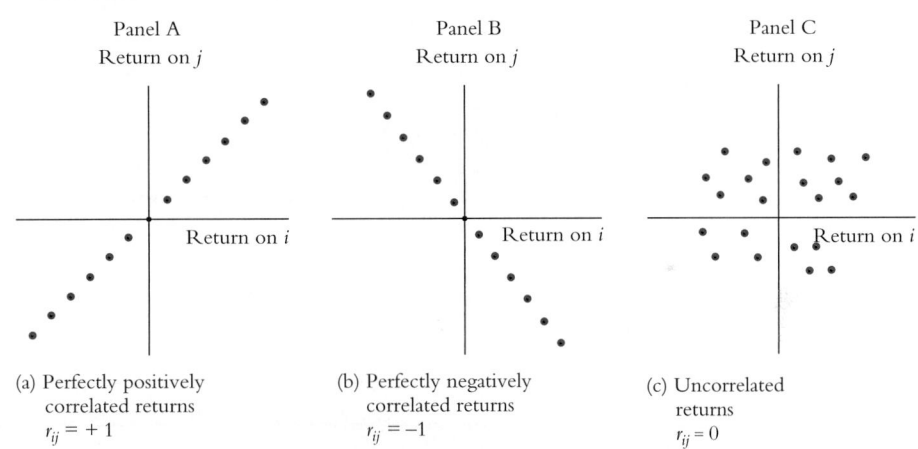

FIGURE 21-2 Correlation Analysis

of correlation. In Panel A, assets i and j are perfectly correlated, with r_{ij} equal to $+1$. As i increases in value, so does j in exact proportion to i. In Panel B, assets i and j exhibit a perfect negative correlation, with r_{ij} equal to -1. As i increases, j decreases in exact proportion to i. Panel C demonstrates assets i and j having no correlation at all, with r_{ij} equal to 0.

Application Example

The actual computation of the correlation coefficient for investments i and j is covered in Appendix 21A. It is not necessary to go through Appendix 21A before proceeding with our discussion, though some readers may wish to do so. As indicated in Appendix 21A, the correlation coefficient (r_{ij}) between our investment i and investment j is -0.70. This indicates the two investments show a high degree of negative correlation.

Plugging this value into Formula 21–4, along with other previously determined values, the standard deviation (σ_p) for the two-asset portfolio can be computed:[3]

$$\sigma_p = \sqrt{X_i^2\sigma_i^2 + X_j^2\sigma_j^2 + 2X_iX_jr_{ij}\sigma_i\sigma_j} \qquad (21\text{–}4)$$

where:

$X_i = 0.5, \sigma_i = 3.9$
$X_j = 0.5, \sigma_j = 5.1$
$r_{ij} = -0.70$

$$\begin{aligned}
\sigma_p &= \sqrt{(0.5)^2(3.9)^2 + (0.5)^2(5.1)^2 + 2(0.5)(0.5)(-0.7)(3.9)(5.1)} \\
&= \sqrt{(0.25)(15.4) + (0.25)(25.6) + 2(0.35)(-0.7)(19.9)} \\
&= \sqrt{3.85 + 6.4 + (0.5)(-13.93)} \\
&= \sqrt{3.85 + 6.4 - 6.97} \\
&= \sqrt{3.28} = 1.8\%
\end{aligned}$$

The standard deviation of the portfolio of 1.8 percent is less than the standard deviation of either investment i (3.9 percent) or j (5.1 percent). Any time two investments have a correlation coefficient (r_{ij}) less than +1 (perfect positive correlation), some risk reduction will be possible by combining the assets in a portfolio. In the real world, most items are positively correlated; the extent that we can still get risk reduction from positively correlated items gives extra meaning to portfolio management. Note the impact of various assumed correlation coefficients for the two investments previously described in terms of individual standard deviations:[4]

Correlation Coefficient (r_{ij})	Portfolio Standard Deviation (σ_p)
+1.0	4.5
+0.5	3.9
0.0	3.2
−0.5	2.3
−0.7	1.8
−1.0	0.0

The conclusion to be drawn from our portfolio analysis discussion is that the most significant risk factor associated with an individual investment may not be its own standard deviation but how it affects the standard deviation of a portfolio through correlation. As we shall later observe in this chapter, there is not considered to be a risk premium for the total risk or standard deviation of an individual security, but only for that risk component that cannot be eliminated by various portfolio diversification techniques.

---

[3] Note that the squared values, such as $(3.9)^2 = 15.4$, are the reverse of earlier computations. Previously, we found the square root of 15.4 to be 3.9 (see computation under Formula 21–2). The use of rounding introduces slight discrepancies where we square numbers for which we previously found the square root.

[4] Each is assumed to represent 50 percent of the portfolio.

Developing an Efficient Portfolio

We have seen how the combination of two investments has allowed us to maintain our return of 10 percent but reduce the portfolio standard deviation to 1.8 percent. We also saw in the preceding table that different coefficient correlations produce many different possibilities for portfolio standard deviations. A shrewd portfolio manager may wish to consider a large number of portfolios, each with a different expected value and standard deviation, based on the expected values and standard deviations of the individual securities and, more importantly, on the correlations between the individual securities. Though we have been discussing a two-asset portfolio case, our example may be expanded to cover 5-, 10-, or even 100-asset portfolios.[5] The major tenets of portfolio theory that we are currently examining were developed by Professor Harry Markowitz in the 1950s, and so we refer to them as the Markowitz portfolio theory. In 1990 Markowitz won the Nobel prize in economics for this work.

Assume we have identified the following risk-return possibilities for eight different portfolios (there may also be many more, but we will restrict ourselves to this set for now):

Portfolio	K_p	σ_p
A	10%	1.8%
B	10	2.1
C	12	3.0
D	13	4.2
E	13	5.0
F	14	5.0
G	14	5.8
H	15	7.2

In diagramming our various risk-return points in the table above, we show the values in Figure 21–3 on the next page.

Although we have only diagrammed eight possibilities, we see an efficient set of portfolios would lie along the ACFH line in Figure 21–3. This line is efficient because the portfolios on this line dominate all other attainable portfolios. This line is called the **efficient frontier** because the portfolios on the efficient frontier provide the best risk-return trade-off. That is, along this efficient frontier we can receive a maximum return for a given level of risk or a minimum risk for a given level of return. Portfolios do not exist above the efficient frontier, and portfolios below this line do not offer acceptable alternatives to points along the line. As an example of *maximum return* for a given level of risk, consider point F. Along the efficient frontier, we are receiving a 14 percent return for a 5 percent risk level, whereas directly below point F, portfolio E provides a 13 percent return for the same 5 percent standard deviation.

---

[5] The incremental benefit from reduction of the portfolio standard deviation through adding securities appears to diminish fairly sharply with a portfolio of 10 securities and is quite small with a portfolio as large as 20. A portfolio of 14 to 16 securities is generally thought to be of sufficient size to enjoy the majority of desirable portfolio effects. See W. H. Wagner and S. C. Lau, "The Effect of Diversification on Risk," *Financial Analysts Journal*, November–December 1971, pp. 48–53.

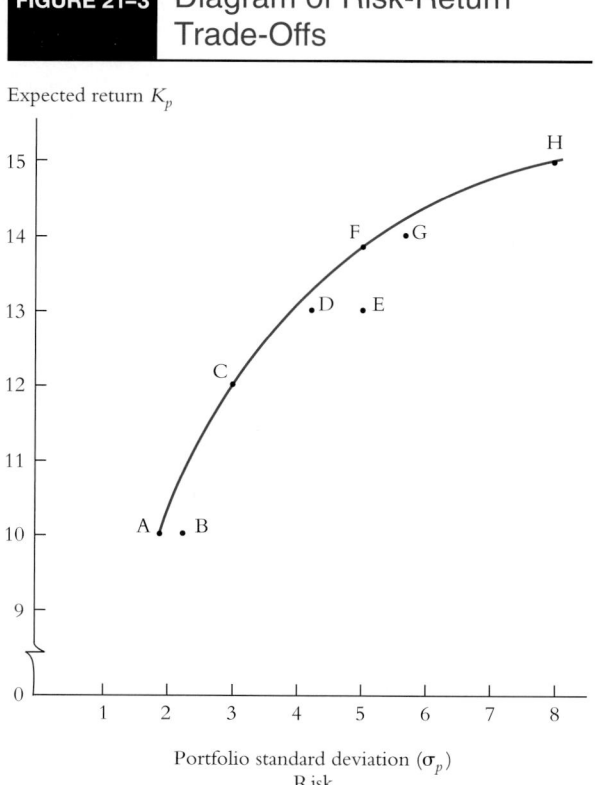

FIGURE 21-3 Diagram of Risk-Return Trade-Offs

To also demonstrate that we are getting *minimum* risk for a given return level, we can examine point A in which we receive a 10 percent return for a 1.8 percent risk level, whereas to the right of point A, we get the same 10 percent return from B, but a less desirable 2.1 percent risk level. One portfolio can consist of various proportions of two assets or two portfolios. For example, we can connect the points between A and C by generating portfolios that combine different percentages of portfolio A and portfolio C and so on between portfolios C and F and portfolios F and H. Although we have shown but eight points (portfolios), a fully developed efficient frontier may be based on a virtually unlimited number of observations as is presented in Figure 21-4.

In Figure 21-4, we once again view the efficient frontier in relationship to the feasible set and note that certain risk-return possibilities are not attainable (and should be disregarded). At this point in the analysis, we can stipulate that the various points along the efficient frontier are all considered potentially optimal and a given investor should choose the most appropriate single point based on individual risk-return trade-off desires. We would say that a low-risk-oriented investor might prefer point A in Figure 21-3, whereas a more-risk-oriented investor would prefer point F or H. At each of these points, the investor is getting the best risk-return trade-off for his or her own particular risk-taking propensity.

Risk-Return Indifference Curves

To actually pair an investor with an appropriate point along the efficient frontier, we look at his or her indifference curve as illustrated in Figure 21-5.

FIGURE 21-4 Expanded View of Efficient Frontier

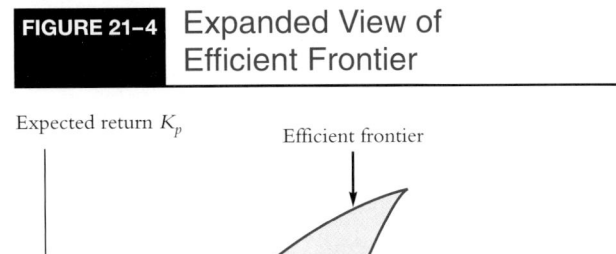

FIGURE 21-5 Risk-Return Indifference Curves

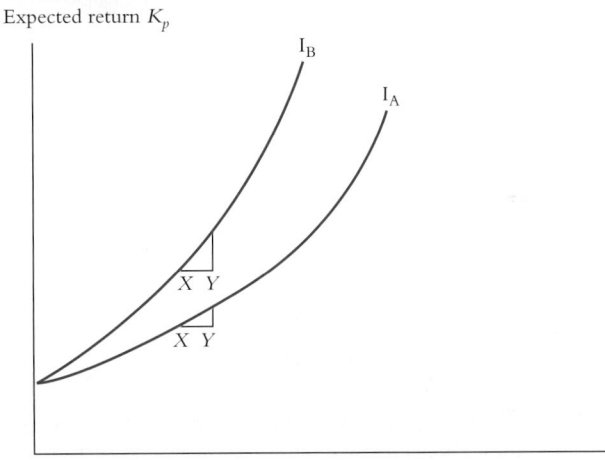

The **indifference curves** show the investor's trade-off between risk and return. The steeper the slope of the curve, the more risk-averse the investor is. For example, in the case of Investor B (I_B in Figure 21–5), the indifference curve has a steeper slope than for Investor A (I_A). This means Investor B will require more incremental return (more of a risk premium) for each additional unit of risk. Note that to take risks, Investor B requires approximately twice as much incremental return as Investor A between points X and Y. However, Investor A is still somewhat risk-averse and perhaps represents a typical investor in the capital markets.

Once the shape of an investor's indifference curve is determined, a second objective can be established—to attain the highest curve possible. For example, Investor A, initially shown in Figure 21–5, would have a whole set of similarly shaped indifference curves as presented in Figure 21–6.

While he is indifferent to any point along a given curve (such as I_{A4}), he is not indifferent to achieving the highest curve possible (I_{A4} is clearly superior to I_{A1}). I_{A4} provides more return at all given risk levels. The only limitation to achieving the highest possible indifference curve is the feasible set of investments available.

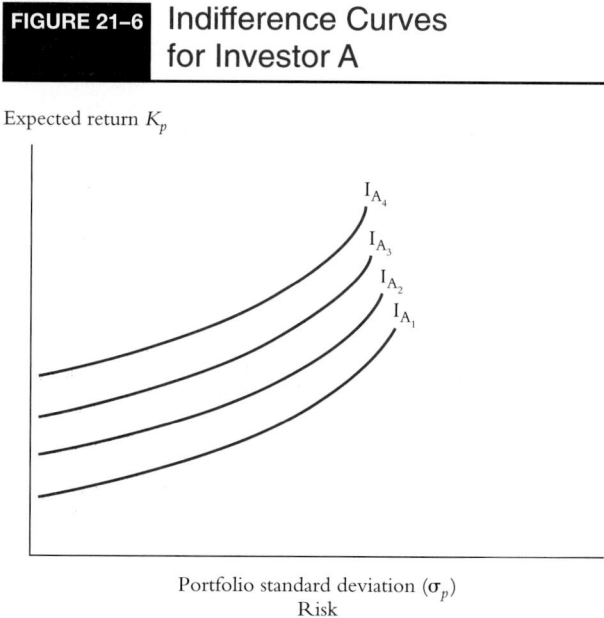

FIGURE 21–6 Indifference Curves for Investor A

Optimum Portfolio

The investor must theoretically match his own risk-return indifference curve with the best investments available in the market as represented by points on the efficient frontier. We see in Figure 21–7 that Investor A will achieve the highest possible indifference curve at point C along the efficient frontier.

This is the point of tangency between his own indifference curve (I_{A3}) and the efficient frontier. Both curves have the same slope or risk-return characteristics at this point. While a point along indifference curve (I_{A4}) might provide a higher level of utility, it is not attainable. Also, any other point along the efficient frontier would cross a lower level indifference curve and be inferior to point C. For example, points B and D cross I_{A2}, providing less return for a given level of risk than I_{A3}. Investors must relate the shape of their *own* risk-return indifference curves to the efficient frontier to determine that point of tangency providing maximum benefits.

Chapter 21 A Basic Look at Portfolio Management and Capital Market Theory 597

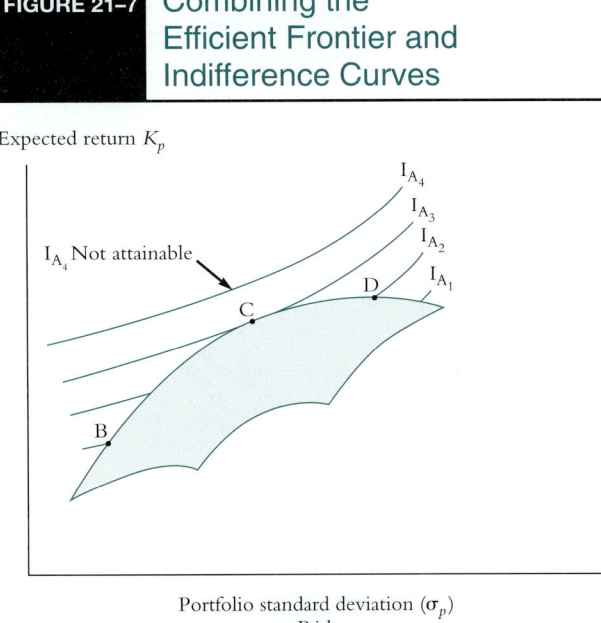

FIGURE 21–7 Combining the Efficient Frontier and Indifference Curves

Capital Asset Pricing Model

The development of the efficient frontier in the previous section gives insight into optimum portfolio mixes in an appropriate risk-return context. Nevertheless, the development of multiple portfolios is a rather difficult and tedious task. Professors Sharpe, Lintner, and others have allowed us to take the philosophy of efficient portfolios into a more generalized and meaningful context through the **capital asset pricing model.** Under this model, we examine the theoretical underpinnings through which assets are valued based on their risk characteristics.

The capital asset pricing model (CAPM) takes off where the efficient frontier concluded through the introduction of a new investment outlet, the risk-free asset (R_F). A risk-free asset has no risk of default and a standard deviation of 0 ($\sigma_{RF} = 0$) and is the lowest assumed safe return that can be earned. A U.S. Treasury bill or Treasury bond is often considered representative of a risk-free asset. Under the capital asset pricing model, we introduce the notion of combining the risk-free asset and the efficient frontier with the development of the R_FMZ line as indicated in Figure 21–8 on page 598.

The R_FMZ line opens up the possibility of a whole new set of superior investment opportunities. That is, by combining some portion of the risk-free asset as represented by (R_F) with M (a point along the efficient frontier), we create new investment opportunities that will allow us to reach higher indifference curves than would be possible simply along the efficient frontier. The only point along the efficient frontier that now has significance is point M, where the straight line from R_F is tangent to the old efficient frontier. Let us further examine the R_FMZ line.

We can reach points along the R_FMZ line in a number of different ways. To be at point R_F, we would simply buy a risk-free asset. To be at a point between R_F and M, we would buy a combination of R_F and the M portfolio along the

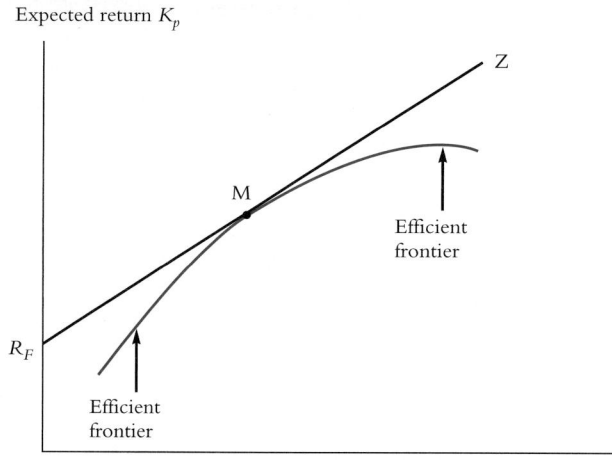

FIGURE 21-8 Basic Diagram of the Capital Asset Pricing Model

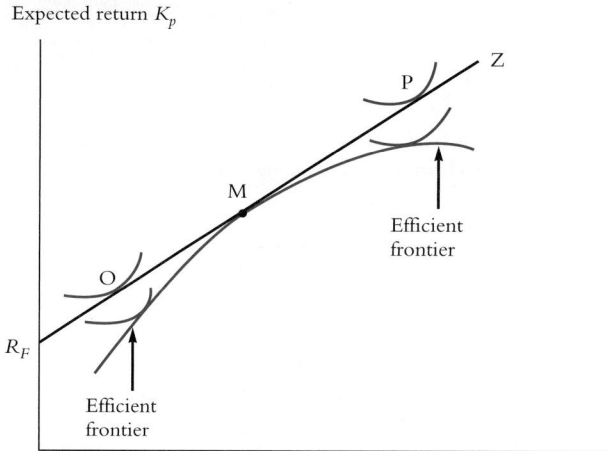

FIGURE 21-9 The CAPM and Indifference Curves

efficient frontier. To be at a point between M and Z, we buy M with our available funds and then borrow additional funds to further increase our purchase of the M portfolio (an example of this would be to be at point P in Figure 21–9). To the extent that M is higher than R_F and we can borrow at a rate equal to R_F or slightly higher, we can get larger returns with a combination of buying M and borrowing additional funds to buy M.

We also note that point M is considered the optimum "market basket" of investments available (although you may wish to combine this market basket with risk-free assets or borrowing). If you took all the possible investments that investors could acquire and determined the optimum basket of investments, you would come up with point M (because it is along the efficient frontier and tangent to the R_F line). Point M can be measured by the total return on the Standard & Poor's 500 Stock Average, the Dow Jones Industrial Average, the New York Stock Exchange Index, or similar measures. If point M or the market were not represented by the optimum risk-return portfolio for all investments at a point in time, then it is assumed there would be an instantaneous change, and the market measure (point M) would once again be in equilibrium (be optimal).

Capital Market Line

Application Example

The previously discussed $R_F MZ$ line is called the **capital market line (CML)** and is once again presented in Figure 21–10.

The formula for the capital market line in Figure 21–10 may be written as:

$$K_P = R_F + \left(\frac{K_M - R_F}{\sigma_M - 0}\right)\sigma_P$$

We indicate that the expected return on any portfolio (K_P) is equal to the risk-free rate of return (R_F) plus the slope of the line times a value along the horizontal axis (σ_P), indicating the amount of risk undertaken. We can relate the formula for the capital market line to the basic equation for a straight line as follows:

$$\text{Straight line } Y = a + bX$$

$$\text{Capital market line } K_P = R_F + \left(\frac{K_M - R_F}{\sigma_M}\right)\sigma_P \tag{21-5}$$

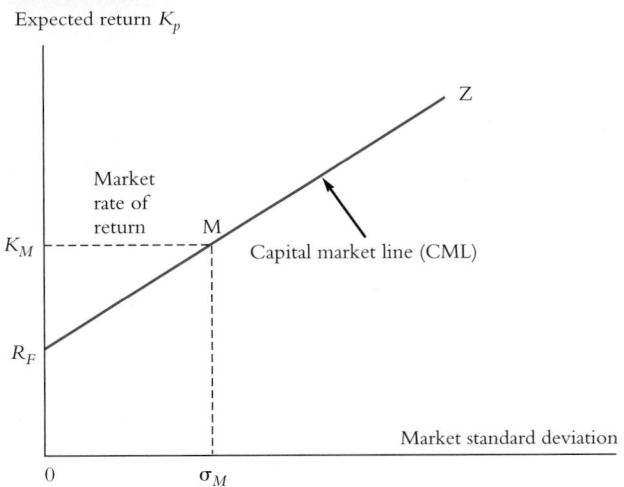

FIGURE 21–10 Illustration of the Capital Market Line

In using the capital market line, we start with a minimum rate of return of R_F and then say any additional return is a reward for risk. The reward for risk or risk premium is equal to the market rate of return (K_M) minus the risk-free rate (R_F) divided by the market standard deviation (σ_M). If the market rate of return (K_M) is 12 percent and the risk-free rate of return (R_F) is 6 percent, with a market standard deviation (σ_M) of 20 percent, there is a risk premium of 0.3:

$$\frac{K_M - R_F}{\sigma_M} = \frac{12\% - 6\%}{20\%} = \frac{6\%}{20\%} = 0.3$$

Then, if the standard deviation of our portfolio (σ_P) is 22 percent, we can expect a return of 12.6 percent along the CML computed as follows:

$$K_P = R_F + \left(\frac{K_M - R_F}{\sigma_M}\right)\sigma_P$$

$$K_P = 6\% + \left(\frac{12\% - 6\%}{20\%}\right)22\%$$

$$= 6\% + (0.3)22\%$$

$$= 6\% + 6.6\% = 12.6\%$$

The essence of the capital market line is that the way to get larger returns is to take increasingly higher risks. Thus, the only way to climb up the K_P *return* line in Figure 21–10 is to extend yourself out on the σ_P *risk* line. Portfolio managers who claim highly superior returns may have taken larger than normal risks and thus may not really be superior performers on a risk-adjusted basis. We shall see in the following chapter that the best way to measure a portfolio manager is to evaluate his returns relative to the risks taken. Average to slightly above average returns based on low risk may be superior to high returns based on high risk. One does not easily exceed market-dictated constraints for risk and return.

Return on an Individual Security

We have been examining return expectations for a portfolio; we now turn our attention to an individual security. Once again the return potential is closely tied to risk. However, when dealing with an individual security, the premium return for risk is not related to *all* the risk in the investment as measured by the standard deviation (σ). The reason for this is that the standard deviation includes two types of risk, but only one is accorded a premium return under the capital asset pricing model.

We now begin an analytical process that allows us to get at the two forms of risk in an individual security. The first form of risk is measured by the beta coefficient. While some of the concepts discussed below were briefly covered in Chapter 1, a much more comprehensive discussion is provided in this chapter.

Beta Coefficient In analyzing the performance of an individual security, it is first important to measure its relationship to the market through the **beta coefficient.** Let us lay the groundwork for understanding beta. In the case of a potential investment, stock *i,* we can observe its relationship to the market by tracing its total return performance relative to market total return over the last five years.[6]

Year	Stock i Return (K)	Market Return (K_M)
1	4.8%	6.5%
2	14.5	11.8
3	19.1	14.9
4	3.7	1.1
5	15.6	12.0

We see that stock i moves somewhat with the market. Plotting the values in Figure 21–11, we observe a line that is upward sloping at slightly above a 45-degree angle.

A straight line of best fit has been drawn through the various points representing the following formula:

$$K_i = a_i + b_i K_M + e_i \qquad (21\text{--}6)$$

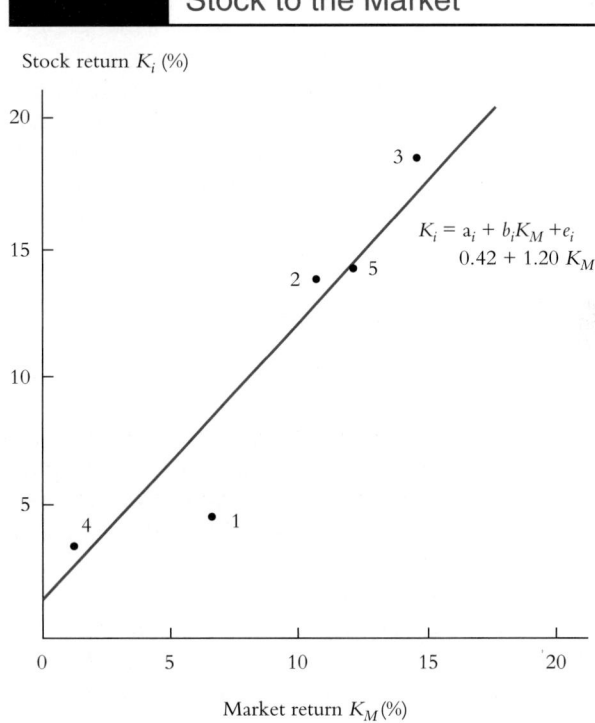

FIGURE 21–11 Relationship of Individual Stock to the Market

---

[6] Although monthly calculations are often used, we can satisfy the same basic learning objectives with annual data, and the analysis is easier to follow.

K_i represents the anticipated stock return based on Formula 21–6 where: a_i (alpha) is the point at which the line crosses the vertical axis; b_i (beta) is the slope of the line; K_M is the independent variable of market return; and e_i is the random error term. The $a_i + b_i K_M$ portion of the formula describes a straight line, and e_i represents deviations or random, nonrecurring movements away from the straight line. In the present example, the formula for the straight line is $K_i = 0.42 + 1.20\ K_M$ (indicating a beta or line slope of 1.2). These values can be approximated by drawing a line of best fit as indicated in Figure 21–11 or through the use of least squares regression analysis presented in Appendix 21B. Basically, the equation tells us how volatile our stock is relative to the market through the beta coefficient. In the present case, if the market moves up or down by a given percent, our stock is assumed to move 1.2 times that amount.

Because beta measures the correlation of a stock's total return to a market index, the beta of the market when regressed on itself will always be 1.0. With a beta of 1.2, our stock is considered to be 20 percent more volatile than the market and therefore riskier. A stock with average volatility would have a beta of 1.0, the same beta as the market. A stock having a beta of less than 1.0 would have less risk than the market.

Systematic and Unsystematic Risk

Previously, we mentioned the two major types of risk associated with a stock. One is the market movement or beta (b_i) risk. If the market moves up or down, a stock is assumed to change in value. This type of risk is referred to as **systematic risk.** The second type of risk is represented by the error term (e_i) and indicates changes in value not associated with market movement. It may represent the temporary influence of a competitor's new product, changes in raw material prices, or unusual economic and government influences on a given firm. These changes are peculiar to an individual security or industry at a given point and are not directly correlated with the market. This second type of risk is referred to as **unsystematic risk.**

Because unsystematic risk is associated with an individual company or industry, it may be diversified away in a large portfolio and is not a risk inherent in investing in common stocks. Thus, by picking stocks that are less than perfectly correlated, unsystematic risk may be eliminated. For example, the inherent risks of investing in cyclical semiconductor stocks may be diversified away by investing in countercyclical housing stocks. Researchers have indicated that all but 15 percent of unsystematic risk may be eliminated with a carefully selected portfolio of 10 stocks, and all but 11 percent, with the portfolio of 20 stocks.[7]

The systematic risk (beta) cannot be diversified away even in a large portfolio. Therefore, the market compensates an investor with a higher expected return when that investor buys securities with a high beta, or with a lower expected return than the market, when the investor buys securities with a beta less than the market. Using this method of risk adjustment, the capital asset pricing model creates a linear risk-return trade-off using the market as the reference point for risk and return.

---

[7] Wagner and Lau, "The Effect of Diversification on Risk."

FIGURE 21–12 Illustration of the Security Market Line

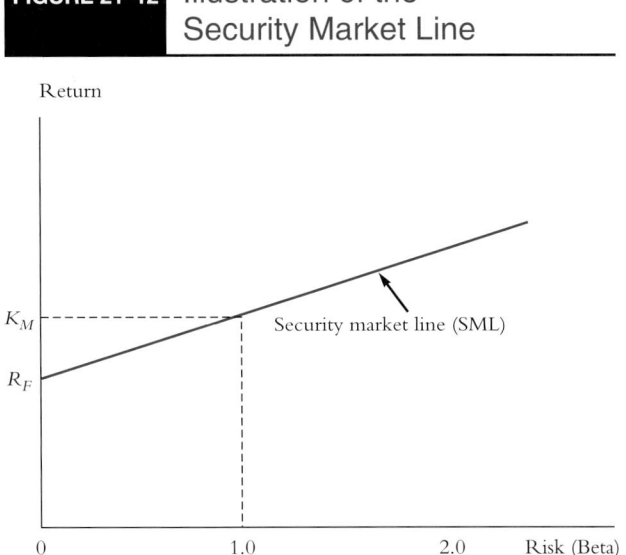

Because unsystematic risk can be diversified away, systematic risk (b_i) is the only relevant risk under the capital asset pricing model. Thus, even though we can describe total risk as:

Total risk = Systematic risk + Unsystematic risk

in a diversified portfolio, unsystematic risk approaches 0.

Security Market Line

We actually express the trade-off between risk and return for an *individual stock* through the **security market line (SML)** in Figure 21–12. Whereas in Figure 21–11, we graphed the relationship that allowed us to compute the beta (b_i) for a security, in Figure 21–12 we now take that beta and show what the anticipated or required return in the marketplace is for a stock with that characteristic. The security market line (SML) shows the risk-return trade-off for an individual stock in Figure 21–12 just as the capital market line (CML) accomplished that same objective for a portfolio in Figure 21–10 on page 599.

Once again, we stress that the return is not plotted against the total risk (σ) for the individual stock but only that part of the risk that cannot be diversified away, commonly referred to as the systematic or beta risk. The actual formula for the security market line (SML) is:

$$K_i = R_F + b_i(K_M - R_F) \tag{21-7}$$

Application Example

The mathematical derivation of the formula is presented in Appendix 21C. As we did with the capital market line for portfolio returns, with the security market line we start out with a basic rate of return for a risk-free asset (R_F) and add a premium for risk. In this case, the premium is equal to the beta on the stock times the difference between the market rate of return (K_M) and the risk-free rate of return (R_F). If R_F = 6 percent,

K_M = 12 percent, and the stock has a beta (b_i) of 1, the anticipated rate of return, using Formula 21–7, would be the same as that in the market, or 12 percent.

$$K_i = 6\% + 1(12\% - 6\%) = 6\% + 6\% = 12\%$$

Because the stock has the same degree of risk as the market in general, this would appear to be logical. If the stock has a beta of 1.5, the added systematic risk would call for a return of 15 percent, whereas a beta of 0.5 would indicate the return should be 9 percent. The calculations are indicated below:

Beta = 1.5
$$K_i = 6\% + 1.5(12\% - 6\%) = 6\% + 1.5(6\%) = 6\% + 9\% = 15\%$$
Beta = 0.5
$$K_i = 6\% + 0.5(12\% - 6\%) = 6\% + 0.5(6\%) = 6\% + 3\% = 9\%$$

Because the beta factor is deemed to be important in analyzing potential risk and return, much emphasis is placed on knowing the beta for a given security. Bloomberg, Value Line, Standard & Poor's, and various brokerage houses and investment services publish information on beta for a large number of securities. A representative list is presented in the table below:

Corporation	Beta (January 2004)
Merrill Lynch (www.ml.com)	1.70
American Express (www.americanexpress.com)	1.55
Disney (www.disney.com)	1.20
Southwest Airlines (www.iflyswa.com)	1.15
Du Pont (www.dupont.com)	1.00
Abbot Labs (www.abbottlabs.com)	.85
Coca-Cola (www.coca-cola.com)	.75
Piedmont Natural Gas (www.piedmontng.com)	.65

Assumptions of the Capital Pricing Model

Having evaluated some of the implications of the CAPM, it is important that the student be aware of some of the assumptions that go into the model.

1. All investors can borrow or lend an unlimited amount of funds at a given risk-free rate.
2. All investors have the same one-period time horizon.
3. All investors wish to maximize their expected utility over this time horizon and evaluate investments on the basis of means and standard deviations of portfolio returns.
4. All investors have the same expectations—that is, all investors estimate identical probability distributions for rates of return.
5. All assets are perfectly divisible—it is possible to buy fractional shares of any asset or portfolio.
6. There are no taxes or transactions costs.
7. The market is efficient and in equilibrium or quickly adjusting to equilibrium.

the real world of investing
Students as Portfolio Managers—The Number of Programs Continues to Grow

It started at the University of Wisconsin more than 35 years ago. Now students manage part of the university endowment in more than 100 colleges and universities. This is no simulation.

The largest such program is at Ohio State University, where the students are enrolled in courses that allow them to manage more than $10 million of the permanent endowment of the university. Other schools such as UCLA, Indiana University, the University of Southern California, Southern Methodist University, Notre Dame, Gannon College, Virginia Military Institute, DePaul University, and Texas Christian University have similar programs. Professor Edward C. Lawrence of the University of Missouri—St. Louis tracks all the programs across the country as to size, value, and source of funding. Some schools operate with as little as a few thousand dollars, while the typical program size is $150,000 to $200,000.

The authors are most familiar with the student-managed fund at Texas Christian University, where they have both served as faculty advisors. The students manage $1.5 million in stocks and bonds and have power to make their own investment decisions. The faculty advisors do not even have veto power (don't ask if they sweat a lot!). The students receive six hours of academic credit for their work and do intensive work to analyze securities and balance the portfolio. The students also have their own committees operating in such areas as economics and accounting.

As would be true of other professional money managers, they provide annual reports, in which they compare their performance with their own goals as well as with the popular market averages.

Listing these assumptions indicates some of the necessary conditions to create the CAPM. While at first they may appear to be severely limiting, they are similar to those often used in the standard economic theory of the firm and in other basic financial models.

The primary usefulness in examining this model or similar risk-return tradeoff models is to provide some reasonable basis for relating return opportunity with risk on the investment. Portfolio managers find risk-return models helpful in explaining their performance or the performance of their competitors to clients. A competitor's portfolio that has unusually high returns may have been developed primarily on the basis of high-risk assets. To the extent that this can be explained on the basis of capital market theory, the competitor's performance may look less like superior money management and more like a product of high risk taking. As we shall see in Chapter 22, many of the techniques for assessing portfolio performance on Wall Street are explicitly or implicitly related to the risk-return concepts discussed in this chapter.

Although empirical tests have somewhat supported the capital asset pricing model, a number of testing problems remain. To develop the SML in which stock returns (vertical axis) can be measured against beta (horizontal axis), an appropriate line must be drawn. Researchers have some disagreement about R_F. (Is it represented by short-term or long-term Treasury rates?) There is also debate about what is the approximate K_M, or market rate of return. Some suggest the market proxy variable will greatly influence the beta and that difficulties in dealing with this problem can bring the whole process under attack.[8]

---

[8] Richard Roll, "A Critique of the Asset Pricing Theory's Test," *Journal of Financial Economics,* March 1977, pp. 129–76. Also, "Ambiguity When Performance Is Measured by the Securities Market Line," *Journal of Finance,* September 1978, pp. 1051–69.

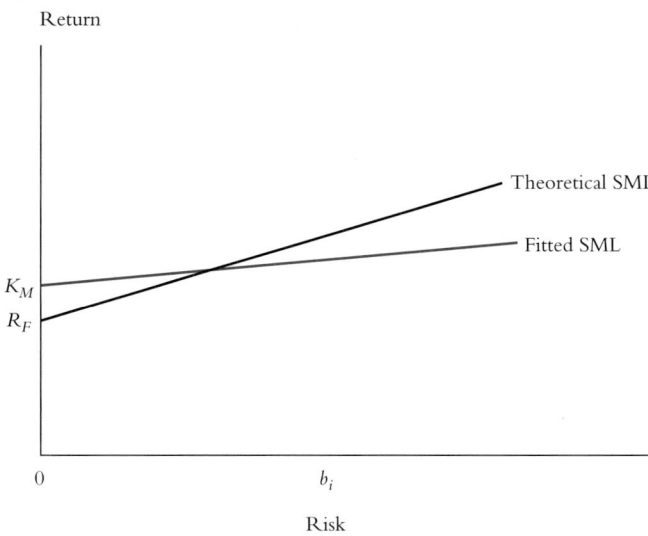

FIGURE 21–13 Test of the Security Market Line

When empirical data are compared with theoretical return expectations, there is some discrepancy in that the theoretical SML may have a greater slope than the actual line fitted on the basis of real-world data as shown in Figure 21–13.[9]

There may also be a possible problem in that betas for individual securities are not necessarily stable over time (rather than remaining relatively constant at 1.3 or perhaps 0.7, they tend to approach 1 over time). Thus, a beta based on past risk may not always reflect current risk.[10] Because the beta for a portfolio may be more stable than an individual stock's beta, portfolio betas are also used as a systematic risk variable. A portfolio beta is simply the weighted average of the betas of the individual stocks. We can say:

$$b_P(\text{portfolio beta}) = \sum_{i=1}^{n} x_i b_i \qquad (21\text{–}8)$$

and

$$K_P = R_F + b_P(K_M - R_F) \qquad (21\text{–}9)$$

By examining portfolio betas rather than individual stock betas, we overcome part of the criticism leveled at the instability of betas in the capital asset pricing model. Many of the other criticisms have also evoked new research that may provide different approaches or possible solutions to past deficiencies in the model. One such approach is the arbitrage pricing theory described in Appendix 21D.

---

[9] Franco Modigliani and Gerald A. Pogue, "An Introduction to Risk and Returns," *Financial Analysts Journal,* March–April 1974, pp. 68–86, and May–June 1974, pp. 69–86.

[10] Robert A. Levy, "On the Short-Term Stationary of Beta Coefficients," *Financial Analysts Journal,* November–December 1971, pp. 55–62. Also, Marshall E. Blume, "Betas and Their Regression Tendencies," *Journal of Finance,* June 1975, pp. 785–95.

Summary

The investor is basically risk-averse and therefore will demand a premium for incremental risk. In an efficient market context, the ability to achieve high returns may be more directly related to absorption of additional risk than superior ability in selecting stocks (this remains a debatable point that proponents of fundamental and technical analysis would argue).

Risk for an individual stock is measured in terms of the standard deviation (σ_i) around a given expected value ($\bar{K}_i$). The larger the standard deviation, the greater the risk. For a portfolio of stocks, the expected value (K_P) is the weighted average of the individual returns; but this is not true for the portfolio standard deviation (σ_P). The portfolio standard deviation is also influenced by the interaction between the stocks. To the extent the correlation coefficient (r_{ij}) is less than +1, there will be some reduction from the weighted average of the standard deviation of the individual stocks that we are combining. A negative correlation coefficient will provide substantial reduction in the portfolio standard deviation.

The CAPM supersedes some of the findings of classic portfolio theory with the introduction of the risk-free asset as represented by (R_F) into the analysis. The assumption is that an individual can choose an investment combining the return on the risk-free asset with the market rate of return, and this will provide superior returns to the efficient frontier at all points except M, where they are equal.

The capital asset pricing model also calls for an evaluation of individual assets (rather than portfolios). The security market line in Figure 21–12 on page 603 shows the same type of risk-return trade-off for individual securities as the capital market line does for portfolios. Investors in individual assets are only assumed to be rewarded for systematic, market-related risk, known as the beta (b_i) risk. All other risk is assumed to be susceptible to diversification.

A number of assumptions associated with the capital asset pricing model are subject to close review and challenge. However, it still remains the most widely used approach to risk management.

Key Words and Concepts

arbitrage pricing theory 615
beta coefficient 600
capital asset pricing model 597
capital market line (CML) 599
correlation coefficient 590
efficient frontier 593
expected value 587
indifference curves 595
security market line (SML) 603
standard deviation 588
systematic risk 602
unsystematic risk 602

Discussion Questions

1. Define risk.
2. What is an expected value?
3. What is the most commonly used measure of dispersion?
4. In a two-asset portfolio, is the portfolio standard deviation a weighted average of the two individual stocks' standard deviation? Explain.

5. What does the correlation coefficient (r_{ij}) measure? What are the two most extreme values it can take, and what do they indicate? In the real world, are more variables positively or negatively correlated?

6. What are the two characteristics of points along the efficient frontier? Do portfolios exist above the efficient frontier?

7. What does the steepness of the slope of the risk-return indifference curve indicate?

8. Describe the optimum portfolio for an investor in terms of indifference curves and the efficient frontier.

9. What new investment variable or outlet allowed market researchers to go from the Markowitz portfolio theory (including the efficient frontier) to the capital asset pricing model?

10. In examining the *capital market line* as part of the capital asset pricing model, to increase portfolio return (K_P) what other variable must you increase?

11. In terms of the capital asset pricing model:
    a. Indicate the two types of risks associated with an individual security.
    b. Which of these two is the beta risk?
    c. What risk is assumed not to be compensated for in the marketplace under the capital asset pricing model? Why?

12. What can be assumed in terms of volatility for a stock that has a beta of 1.2?

13. What does the security market line indicate? In general terms, how is it different from the capital market line?

14. In regard to the capital asset pricing model, comment on disagreements or debates related to R_F (the risk-free rate) and K_M (market rate of return).

15. Are betas of individual stocks necessarily stable (constant) over time?

Problems

Expected value

1. The Aaron Mutual Fund projects three possible outcomes for next year: weak performance (1 percent), good performance (12 percent), and outstanding performance (35 percent). The good performance has a 60 percent chance of happening and the other two outcomes each has a 20 percent probability. What is the expected value?

Expected value and standard deviation

2. An investment has the following range of outcomes and probabilities:

Outcomes	Probability of Outcomes
8%	0.25
12	0.50
20	0.25

Calculate the expected value and the standard deviation (round to two places after the decimal point where necessary).

Expected value and standard deviation (Problems 3 through 6 are a sequence.)

3. An investment has the following range of outcomes and probabilities.

Outcomes (Percent)	Probability of Outcomes
6%	0.30
9	0.40
12	0.30

Calculate the expected value and the standard deviation (round to two places after the decimal point where necessary).

Portfolio expected value and standard deviation

4. Given another investment with an expected value of 13 percent and a standard deviation of 3.1 percent that is countercyclical to the investment in problem 3, what is the expected value of the portfolio and its standard deviation if both are combined into a portfolio with 40 percent invested in the first investment and 60 percent in the second? Assume the correlation coefficient (r_{ij}) is $-.40$.

Portfolio standard deviation

5. What would be the portfolio standard deviation if the two investments in problem 4 had a correlation coefficient (r_{ij}) of $+.40$?

Portfolio standard deviation

6. If the two investments above were perfectly positively correlated ($r_{ij} = +1$), what would be the portfolio standard deviation?

Efficient frontier

7. Assume the following risk-return possibilities for 10 different portfolios. Plot the points in a manner similar to Figure 21–3 on page 594 and indicate the approximate shape of the efficient frontier.

Portfolio Number	K_P	σ_P
1	10%	1.5%
2	10	2.5
3	9	3.0
4	12	4.0
5	11	4.0
6	12	5.0
7	12	6.0
8	13.5	6.5
9	13	6.5
10	14	7.0

Efficient frontier

8. Referring to problem 7, if a new portfolio, no. 11, has a K_P value of 13.8 percent and a standard deviation (σ_P) of 7.1 percent, will it qualify for the efficient frontier?

Capital market line

9. Using the formula for the capital market line (Formula 21–5) on page 599, if the risk-free rate (R_F) is 7 percent, the market rate of return (K_M) is 12 percent, the market standard deviation (σ_M) is 10 percent, and the standard deviation of the portfolio (σ_P) is 13 percent, compute the anticipated return (K_P).

Capital market line

10. Recompute the answer to problem 9 based on a portfolio standard deviation of 16 percent. In terms of capital market theory, explain why K_P has increased.

Security market line

11. Using the formula for the security market line (Formula 21–7) on page 603, if the risk-free rate (R_F) is 7 percent, the beta (b_i) is 1.15, and the market rate of return (K_M) is 12 percent, compute the anticipated rate of return (K_i).

Beta consideration

12. If another security had a lower beta than indicated in problem 11, would K_i be lower or higher? What is the logic behind your answer in terms of risk?

Plotting best fit of data

13. Assume the following values for a stock's return and the market return.

Year	Stock i Return (K)	Market Return (K_M)
1	15.5%	14.9%
2	2.8	1.1
3	17.7	12.0
4	15.1	10.1
5	6.0	3.2

Rate of return

Plot the data and draw a line of best fit similar to that in Figure 21–11 on page 601.

14. Using the formulas in Appendix 21B, compute a least squares regression equation for problem 13. (Round beta and alpha to two places after the decimal point.)

Least squares regression analysis

15. Use the beta (b_i) from problem 14 and plug into the formula for the security market line (Formula 21–7 on page 603). Assume the risk-free rate (R_F) is 8 percent and the market rate of return (K_M) is 13.5 percent. What is the value of the anticipated rate of return (K_i)?

Web Exercise

In this web exercise, we will show how to determine the required rate of return for a stock using the capital asset pricing model.

1. The formula for the capital asset pricing model is:

$$K_i = R_F + b_i(K_M - R_F) \qquad (21\text{–}7)$$

K_i is the required rate of return that we are solving for; R_F is the risk-free rate; and we shall assume it is 4.6 percent; b_i is the systematic risk of a stock that we will estimate; $(K_M - R_F)$ is the equity risk premium or the amount the market is assumed to earn over the risk-free rate in the long term. We will use 6.4 percent in this example.

2. Now we are in a position to estimate the beta for a company and compute K_i, the required rate of return.
   While Value Line, Bloomberg, and other financial services provide estimates of beta, they are often very different. In this exercise, we are going to have you eyeball a value for beta. Go to **finance.yahoo.com**.

3. Enter Microsoft (MSFT) in the "Enter System" box and click "Go."

4. Along the left margin, click on "Basic Chart."

5. Then on the "Range" line, click on "5y max."

6. Then on the "Compare" line, select S&P and click "Compare."

Chapter 21 A Basic Look at Portfolio Management and Capital Market Theory

7. Eyeball the relative volatility of MSFT to the Standard and Poor Index (SPX) and estimate a beta (such as 1.1 or 1.3) based on the relative volatility of the stock versus the index.
8. Use this beta and the previously presented information on R_F and $(K_M - R_F)$ to compute K_i.
9. Follow this procedure for:
   a. Oracle (ORCL)
   b. IBM (IBM)
   c. Philip Morris (Mo)
10. What conclusion can you draw between the relationship of beta (b_i), a risk measure, and the required rate of return (K_i)?

Note: From time to time, companies redesign their websites, and occasionally a topic we have listed may have been deleted, updated, or moved into a different location. Most websites have a "site map" or "site index" listed on a different page. If you click on the site map or site index, you will be introduced to a table of contents that should aid you in finding the topic you are looking for.

The Wall Street Journal Projects

Assume you are asked to find the average price and average beta for a portfolio composed of the following seven stocks. The weights represent the percent of the portfolio invested in each stock.

Corporation	Weights
Citigroup	10%
Colgate-Palmolive	15
Hewlett-Packard	18
Merrill Lynch & Co.	20
Eastman Kodak	5
Pfizer	12
Texas Instruments	20
	100%

Each of the stocks is listed on the New York Stock Exchange, and its price can be found under "New York Stock Exchange Composite Transactions" in Section C of *The Wall Street Journal*. The betas can be looked up in *Value Line Investment Survey*.

1. To determine the average price for the portfolio, merely multiply each stock's price times its weight in the portfolio and sum.
2. To determine the average beta for the portfolio, follow the same general procedure. Does this appear to be a risky portfolio?

Selected References

Portfolio Considerations

Lin, Wenling. "Controlling Risk in Global Multimanager Portfolios." *Financial Analysts Journal,* January–February 2000, pp. 44–53.

Ravi, Jagannathan, and Tongshu Ma. "Risk Reduction in Large Portfolios: Why Imposing the Wrong Constraints Helps." *The Journal of Finance,* December 2003, pp. 1651–83.

Solnik, Bruno, and Jacques Roulet. "Dispersion as Cross-Section Correlation." *Financial Analysts Journal,* January–February 2000, pp. 54–61.

Capital Asset Pricing Model

Fama, Eugene F. "Efficient Capital Markets: II." *Journal of Finance,* December 1991, pp. 1575–1617.

Fama, Eugene F., and Kenneth R. French. "The CAPM Is Wanted Dead or Alive." *Journal of Finance,* December 1996, pp. 1947–58.

Jensen, Michael C., ed. *Studies in the Theory of Capital Markets.* New York: Praeger Publishers, 1972.

Roll, Richard. "Ambiguity When Performance Is Measured by the Securities Market Line." *Journal of Finance,* September 1978, pp. 1051–70.

Sharpe, William F. "Factor Models, CAPMs, and the APT." *Journal of Portfolio Management,* Fall 1984, pp. 21–25.

Uppal, Raman, and Tan Wang. "Model Misspecification and Underdiversification." *The Journal of Finance,* December 2003, pp. 2465–86.

Beta Measurement

Black, Fisher. "Return and Beta." *Journal of Portfolio Management,* Fall 1993, pp. 8–18.

Kim, Theodore. "Searching for Alpha Because You Can Never Go Beta Again." *CFA Magazine,* May–June 2003, pp. 40–43.

Miller, Edward M. "Why the Low Returns to Beta and Other Forms of Risk." *Journal of Portfolio Management,* Winter 2001, pp. 40–55.

Roll, Richard, and Steven A. Ross. "On the Cross-Sectional Relation between Expected Returns and Betas." *Journal of Finance,* March 1994, pp. 101–21.

Rosenberg, Barr. "Prediction of Common Stock Betas." *Journal of Portfolio Management,* Winter 1985, pp. 5–14.

Arbitrage Pricing Theory

Chen, Nai-fu. "Some Empirical Tests of the Theory of Arbitrage Pricing." *Journal of Finance,* December 1993, pp. 1393–1414.

Appendix 21A

THE CORRELATION COEFFICIENT

There are a number of formulas for the correlation coefficient. We shall use the statement:

$$r_{ij} = \frac{\text{cov}_{ij}}{\sigma_i \sigma_j} \qquad (21A\text{–}1)$$

Here, cov_{ij} (covariance) is an *absolute* measure of the extent to which two sets of variables move together over time. Once we have determined this value, we simply divide by $\sigma_i \sigma_j$ to get a relative measure of correlation (r_{ij}).

The formula for the covariance is:

$$\text{cov}_{ij} = \Sigma(K_i - \overline{K}_i)(K_j - \overline{K}_j)P \qquad (21A\text{–}2)$$

We take our K and P values from investment i and investment j in Chapter 21 on page 588 to compute the following:

K_i	$\bar{K}_i$	$(K_i - \bar{K}_i)$	K_j	$\bar{K}_j$	$(K_j - \bar{K}_j)$	$(K_i - \bar{K}_i)(K_j - \bar{K}_j)$	P	$(K_i - \bar{K}_i)(K_j - \bar{K}_j)P$
5%	10%	−5%	20%	10%	+10%	−50%	0.20	−10.0%
7	10	−3	8	10	−2	+6	0.30	+1.8
13	10	+3	8	10	−2	−6	0.30	−1.8
15	10	+5	6	10	−4	−20	0.20	−4.0
								−14.0%

$$\text{cov}_{ij} = \Sigma(K_i - \bar{K}_i)(K_j - \bar{K}_j)P = -14.0\%$$

Using the values in the chapter for σ_i equal to 3.9 and σ_j equal to 5.1, we determine:

$$r_{ij} = \frac{\text{cov}_{ij}}{\sigma_i \sigma_j} = \frac{-14.0}{(3.9)(5.1)} = \frac{-14.0}{19.9} = -0.70$$

Appendix 21B

LEAST SQUARES REGRESSION ANALYSIS

We will show how least squares regression analysis can be used to develop a linear equation to explain the relationship between the return on a stock and return in the market.

We will develop the terms in the expression:

$$K_i = a_i + b_i K_M + e_i$$

(e_i is the random error term and will not be quantified in our analysis.)

Using the data from the chapter on page 601,

Year	K_i	K_M
1	4.8%	6.5%
2	14.5	11.8
3	19.1	14.9
4	3.7	1.1
5	15.6	12.0

the mathematical equation to solve for b_i is:

$$b_i = \frac{N \Sigma K_i K_M - \Sigma K_i \Sigma K_M}{N \Sigma K_M^2 - (\Sigma K_M)^2} \qquad (21B-1)$$

For a_i, we use the following formula (which is dependent on a prior determination of b_i):

$$a_i = \frac{\Sigma K_i - b_i \Sigma K_M}{N} \qquad (21B-2)$$

We compute four columns of data and plug the values into our formulas.

K_i	K_M	$K_i K_M$	K_M^2
4.8	6.5	31.20	42.25
14.5	11.8	171.10	139.24
19.1	14.9	284.59	222.01
3.7	1.1	4.07	1.21
15.6	12.0	187.20	144.00
$\Sigma K_i = 57.7$	$\Sigma K_M = 46.3$	$\Sigma K_i K_M = 678.16$	$\Sigma K_M^2 = 548.71$

Also N(number of observations) = 5.

$$b_i = \frac{N\Sigma K_i K_M - \Sigma K_i \Sigma K_M}{N\Sigma K_M^2 - (\Sigma K_M)^2}$$

$$= \frac{5(678.16) - 57.7(46.3)}{5(548.71) - (46.3)^2}$$

$$= \frac{3390.80 - 2671.51}{2743.55 - 2143.69} = \frac{719.29}{599.86} = 1.20$$

Using our beta value, we now compute alpha:

$$a_i = \frac{\Sigma K_i - b_i \Sigma K_M}{N}$$

$$= \frac{57.7 - 1.2(46.3)}{5}$$

$$= \frac{57.7 - 55.6}{5} = \frac{2.1}{5} = 0.42$$

In summary:

$$K_i = a_i + b_i K_M$$
$$= 0.42 + 1.20\, K_M$$

Appendix 21C

DERIVATION OF THE SECURITY MARKET LINE (SML)

First, we graph the SML based on covariance (Figure 21C–1 on the next page.)[1]

Along the vertical axis we show return, and along the horizontal axis, covariance of return with the market.[2] We can describe our equation for the SML in terms of the slope of the line.

$$K_i = R_F + \frac{(K_M - R_F)}{(\sigma_M^2 - 0)} \text{cov}_{iM} \qquad (21C\text{–}1)$$

---

[1] The concept of covariance is described in Appendix 21A.

[2] Actually, σ_M^2 represents the covariance of the market with the market (a bit redundant). The cov_{MM} equals σ_M^2. The covariance of a variable with itself is equal to the variance.

FIGURE 21C–1 Derivation of the SML

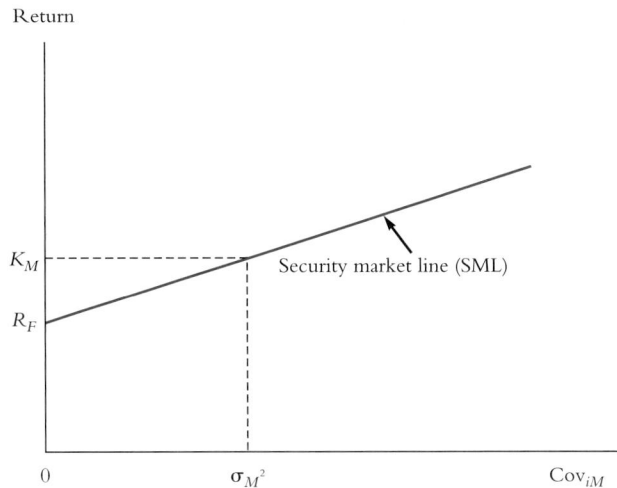

We then rearrange our terms:

$$K_i = R_F + \left(\frac{\text{cov}_{iM}}{\sigma_M^2}\right)(K_M - R_F) \qquad (21C-2)$$

The systematic risk of an individual asset is measured by its covariance with the market (cov_{iM}). We can convert this to a relative measure by dividing through by the market variance (σ_M^2). The *relative* systematic movement of an individual asset with the market is referred to as the beta regression coefficient. Thus, we show in Formula 21C–3:

$$b_i = \frac{\text{cov}_{iM}}{\sigma_M^2} \qquad (21C-3)$$

Substituting beta into Formula 21C–2, we show:

$$K_i = R_F + b_i(K_M - R_F) \qquad (21C-4)$$

Appendix 21D

ARBITRAGE PRICING THEORY

An alternative theory to the capital asset pricing model for explaining stock prices and stock returns is the arbitrage pricing theory (APT). This is a fairly sophisticated theory and will be of interest to those who wish to learn more about asset pricing.

Arbitrage pricing theory assumes a linear return generating model that makes the return on an investment a function of more than one factor. The capital asset pricing model also uses a linear return generating model but assumes that returns are a function of a stock's sensitivity to the equity risk premium. APT acknowledges that a stock's return may be a function of many factors. The arbitrage pricing model is a more generalized model than the CAPM and less restrictive in its assumptions; it does not assume equilibrium markets or make

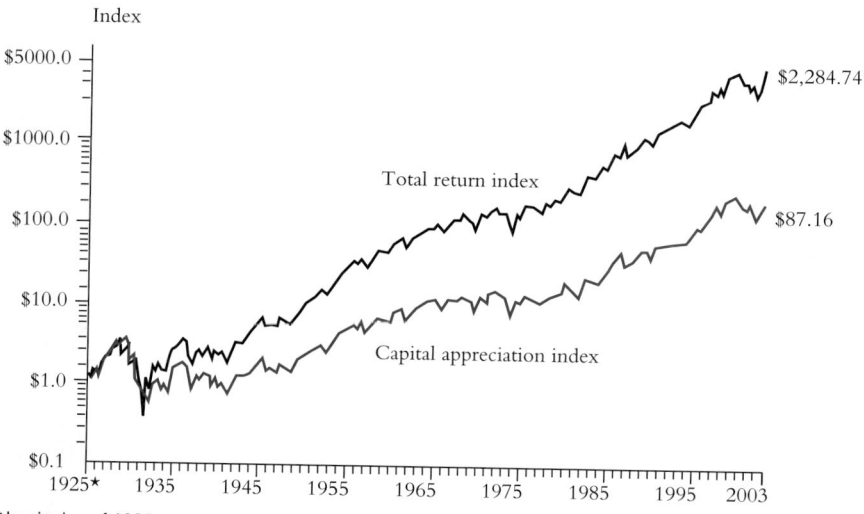

FIGURE 22-2 Large Company Stocks, Return Index from 1926–2003

Source: *Stocks, Bonds, Bills and Inflation® 2004 Yearbook*, © 2004 Ibbotson Associates, Inc. Based on copyrighted works by Ibbotson and Sinquefield. All rights reserved. Used with permissions.

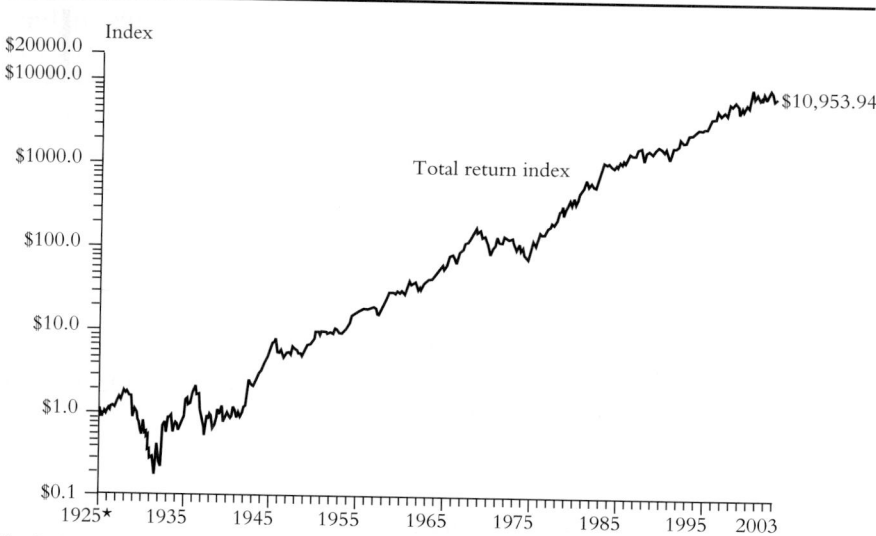

FIGURE 22-3 Small Company Stocks, Return Index from 1926–2003

Source: *Stocks, Bonds, Bills and Inflation® 2004 Yearbook*, © 2004 Ibbotson Associates, Inc. Based on copyrighted works by Ibbotson and Sinquefield. All rights reserved. Used with permissions.

But the beauty is, if you have a long-term perspective, mistakes can be overcome. Nowhere is that more apparent than in Table 22–1 in the first column. At the top of the table you see "Annual Returns." Let's go to the riskiest class, small company stocks. The worst year between 1926 and the present was 1937 with a loss of 58.01 percent (shown as minimum value return in the third and fourth

TABLE 22–1 Maximum and Minimum Values of Returns for 1-, 5-, 10-, 15-, and 20-Year Holding Periods (compound annual rates of return in percent)

Series Annual Returns	Maximum Value Return	Year(s)	Minimum Value Return	Year(s)	Times Positive (Out of 78 years)	Times Highest Returning Asset
Large Company Stocks	53.99	1933	−43.34	1931	55	16
Small Company Stocks	142.87	1933	−58.01	1937	54	34
Long-Term Corporate Bonds	42.56	1982	−8.09	1969	61	6
Long-Term Government Bonds	40.36	1982	−9.18	1967	57	8
Intermediate-Term Govt. Bonds	29.10	1982	−5.14	1994	70	2
U.S. Treasury Bills	14.71	1981	−0.02	1938	77	6
Inflation	18.16	1946	−10.30	1932	68	6

5-Year Rolling Period Returns	Maximum Value Return	Year(s)	Minimum Value Return	Year(s)	(Out of 74 overlapping 5-year periods)	Times Highest Returning Asset
Large Company Stocks	28.55	1995–99	−12.47	1928–32	65	23
Small Company Stocks	45.90	1941–45	−27.54	1928–32	65	38
Long-Term Corporate Bonds	22.51	1982–86	−2.22	1965–69	71	7
Long-Term Government Bonds	21.62	1982–86	−2.14	1965–69	68	2
Intermediate-Term Govt. Bonds	16.98	1982–86	0.96	1955–59	74	2
U.S. Treasury Bills	11.12	1979–83	0.07	1938–42	74	0
Inflation	10.06	1977–81	−5.42	1928–32	67	1

10-Year Rolling Period Returns	Maximum Value Return	Year(s)	Minimum Value Return	Year(s)	(Out of 69 overlapping 10-year periods)	Times Highest Returning Asset
Large Company Stocks	20.06	1949–58	−0.89	1929–38	67	20
Small Company Stocks	30.38	1975–84	−5.70	1929–38	67	39
Long-Term Corporate Bonds	16.32	1982–91	0.98	1947–56	69	6
Long-Term Government Bonds	15.56	1982–91	−0.07	1950–59	68	0
Intermediate-Term Govt. Bonds	13.13	1982–91	1.25	1947–56	69	2
U.S. Treasury Bills	9.17	1978–87	0.15	1933–42/1934–43	69	1
Inflation	8.67	1973–82	−2.57	1926–35	63	1

15-Year Rolling Period Returns	Maximum Value Return	Year(s)	Minimum Value Return	Year(s)	(Out of 64 overlapping 15-year periods)	Times Highest Returning Asset
Large Company Stocks	18.93	1985–99	0.64	1929–43	64	14
Small Company Stocks	23.33	1975–89	−1.30	1927–41	61	46
Long-Term Corporate Bonds	13.66	1982–96	1.02	1955–69	64	4
Long-Term Government Bonds	13.53	1981–95	0.40	1955–69	64	0
Intermediate-Term Govt. Bonds	11.27	1981–95	1.45	1945–59	64	0
U.S. Treasury Bills	8.32	1977–91	0.22	1933–47	64	0
Inflation	7.30	1968–82	−1.59	1926–40	61	0

20-Year Rolling Period Returns	Maximum Value Return	Year(s)	Minimum Value Return	Year(s)	(Out of 59 overlapping 20-year periods)	Times Highest Returning Asset
Large Company Stocks	17.87	1980–99	3.11	1929–48	59	9
Small Company Stocks	21.13	1942–61	5.74	1929–48	59	50
Long-Term Corporate Bonds	12.13	1982–01	1.34	1950–69	59	0
Long-Term Government Bonds	12.09	1982–01	0.69	1950–69	59	0
Intermediate-Term Govt. Bonds	9.97	1981–00	1.58	1940–59	59	0
U.S. Treasury Bills	7.72	1972–91	0.42	1931–50	59	0
Inflation	6.36	1966–85	0.07	1926–45	59	0

Source: *Stocks, Bonds, Bills and Inflation® 2004 Yearbook*, © 2004 Ibbotson Associates, Inc. Based on copyrighted works by Ibbotson and Sinquefield. All rights reserved. Used with permissions.

columns). The best year was 1933 with a gain of 142.57 percent (shown as maximum value return in the first and second columns). The difference between the best and worst is 200.58 percent (plus 142.57 percent to minus 58.01 percent). That's a large variance.

However, notice at the bottom of the table "20-Year Rolling Period Returns." These are returns for any and all 20-year periods between 1926 and the present. For small company stocks, the very best 20-year period (maximum value return) was 1942–1961 with an annual return of 21.13 percent. That's good news, but even better news is that the *worst* 20-year holding period (minimum value return) was 1929–1948 with a *positive* annual return of 5.74 percent. (Don't forget that period includes the market crash of 1929 and the aforementioned loss of 58.01 percent in 1937.) Thus over the long term, stocks are a relatively safe investment. You may also wish to examine other types of assets over other time periods (such as large company stocks over 10-year rolling periods).

All this information indicates a potentially bright future for individual investors with an appropriate time horizon, but what about professional money managers such as mutual funds, bank trust departments, and so on? Unfortunately, they are not accorded the luxury of a long-term time horizon. Their performance is not only measured annually, but quarterly as well. There is a large body of material related to measuring the performance of professional money managers and a discussion of some of that material follows.

Stated Objectives and Risk

A first question to be posed to a professional money manager is: Have you followed the basic objectives that were established? These objectives might call for maximum capital gains, a combination of growth plus income, or simply income (with many variations in between). The objectives should be set with an eye toward the capabilities of the money managers and the financial needs of the investors. The best way to measure adherence to these objectives is to evaluate the risk exposure the fund manager has accepted. Anyone who aspires to maximize capital gains must, by nature, absorb more risk. An income-oriented fund should have a minimum risk exposure.

A classic study by John McDonald published in the *Journal of Financial and Quantitative Analysis* indicates that mutual fund managers generally follow the objectives they initially set. As indicated in Figure 22–4, he measured the betas and standard deviations for 123 mutual funds and compared these with the funds' stated objectives. In Panel (a), we see the fund's beta dimension along the horizontal axis and the fund's stated objective along the vertical axis. Inside the panel, we see the association between the two. For example, funds with an objective of maximum capital gains had an average beta of 1.22, those with a growth objective had an average beta of 1.01, and so on all the way down to an average beta of 0.55 for income-oriented funds. In Panel (b) of Figure 22–4, a similar approach was used to compare the fund's objective with the portfolio standard deviation.

In both cases of using betas and portfolio standard deviations, we see that the risk absorption was carefully tailored to the fund's stated objectives. Funds with aggressive capital gains and growth objectives had high betas and portfolio standard deviations, while the opposite was true of balanced and income-

FIGURE 22-4 Risk and Fund Objectives for 123 Mutual Funds

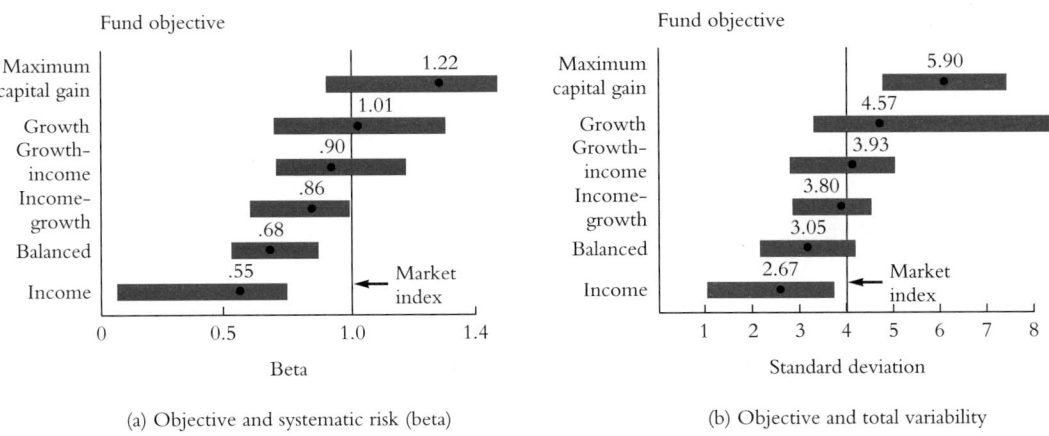

Source: John G. McDonald, "Objectives and Performance of Mutual Funds, 1960–1969," *Journal of Financial and Quantitative Analysis,* June 1974, p. 316.

oriented funds. Other studies have continually reaffirmed the position established in this seminal study by McDonald.

Adherence to objectives as measured by risk exposure is important in evaluating a fund manager because risk is one of the variables a money manager can directly control. While short-run return performance can be greatly influenced by unpredictable changes in the economy, the fund manager has almost total control in setting the risk level. He can be held accountable for doing what was specified or promised in regard to risk. Most lawsuits brought against money managers are not for inferior profit performance but for failure to adhere to stated risk objectives. Although it may be appropriate to shift the risk level in anticipation of changing market conditions (lower the beta at a perceived peak in the market), long-run adherence to risk objectives is advisable.

Measurement of Return in Relation to Risk

In examining the performance of fund managers, the return measure commonly used is excess returns. Though the term **excess returns** has many definitions, the one most commonly used is total return on a portfolio (capital appreciation plus dividends) minus the risk-free rate:

$$\text{Excess returns} = \text{Total portfolio return} - \text{Risk-free rate}$$

Thus, excess returns represent returns over and above what could be earned on a riskless asset. The rate on U.S. government Treasury bills is often used to represent the risk-free rate of return in the financial markets (though other definitions are possible). Thus, a fund that earns 12 percent when the Treasury bill rate is 6 percent has excess returns of 6 percent.

Once computed, excess returns are then compared with risk. We look at three different approaches to comparing excess returns to risk: the **Sharpe approach,** the **Treynor approach,** and the **Jensen approach.**

Sharpe Approach

Application Example

In the Sharpe approach,[5] the excess returns on a portfolio are compared with the portfolio standard deviation:

$$\text{Sharpe measure} = \frac{\text{Total portfolio return} - \text{Risk-free rate}}{\text{Portfolio standard deviation}} \quad (22\text{-}1)$$

The portfolio manager is thus able to view excess returns per unit of risk. If a portfolio has a return of 10 percent, the risk-free rate is 6 percent, and the portfolio standard deviation is 18 percent, the Sharpe measure is 0.22:

$$\text{Sharpe measure} = \frac{10\% - 6\%}{18\%} = \frac{4\%}{18\%} = 0.22$$

This measure can be compared with other portfolios or with the market in general to assess performance. If the market return per unit of risk is greater than 0.22, then the portfolio manager has turned in an inferior performance. Assume there is a 9 percent total market return, a 6 percent risk-free rate, and a market standard deviation of 12 percent. Then the Sharpe measure for the overall market is:

$$\frac{9\% - 6\%}{12\%} = \frac{3\%}{12\%} = 0.25$$

The portfolio measure of 0.22 is less than the market measure of 0.25 and represents an inferior performance. Of course, a portfolio measure above 0.25 would have represented a superior performance.

Treynor Approach

Application Example

The formula for the second approach for comparing excess returns with risk (developed by Treynor[6]) is:

$$\text{Treynor measure} = \frac{\text{Total portfolio return} - \text{Risk-free rate}}{\text{Portfolio beta}} \quad (22\text{-}2)$$

The only difference between the Sharpe and Treynor approaches is in the denominator. While Sharpe uses the portfolio standard deviation—Formula 22–1, Treynor uses the portfolio beta—Formula 22–2. Thus, one can say that Sharpe uses total risk, while Treynor uses only the systematic risk, or beta. Implicit in the Treynor approach is the assumption that portfolio managers can diversify away unsystematic risk, and only systematic risk remains.

If a portfolio has a total return of 10 percent, the risk-free rate is 6 percent, and the portfolio beta is 0.9, the Treynor measure would be:

$$\frac{10\% - 6\%}{0.9} = \frac{4\%}{0.9} = \frac{0.04}{0.9} = 0.044$$

This measure can be compared with other portfolios or with the market in general to determine whether there is a superior performance in terms of return per unit of risk.

---

[5] William F. Sharpe, "Mutual Fund Performance," *Journal of Business,* January 1966, pp. 119–38.

[6] Jack L. Treynor, "How to Rate Management of Investment Funds," *Harvard Business Review,* January–February 1965, pp. 63–74.

Assume the total market return is 9 percent, the risk-free rate is 6 percent, and the market beta (by definition) is 1; then the Treynor measure as applied to the market is 0.03:

$$\frac{9\% - 6\%}{1.0} = \frac{3\%}{1.0} = \frac{0.03}{1.0} = 0.030$$

This would imply the portfolio has turned in a superior return to the market (0.044 versus 0.030). Not only is the portfolio return higher than the market return (10 percent versus 9 percent), but the beta is less (0.9 versus 1.0). Clearly, there is more return per unit of risk.

Jensen Approach

Application Example

In the third approach, Jensen emphasizes using certain aspects of the capital asset pricing model to evaluate portfolio managers.[7] He compares their actual excess returns (total portfolio return − risk-free rate) with what should be required in the market, based on their portfolio beta.

The required rate of excess returns in the market for a given beta is shown in Figure 22–5 as the **market line.** If the beta is 0, the investor should expect to earn no more than the risk-free rate of return because there is no systematic risk. If the portfolio manager earns only the risk-free rate of return, the excess returns will be 0. Thus, with a beta of 0, the expected excess returns on the market line are 0. With a portfolio beta

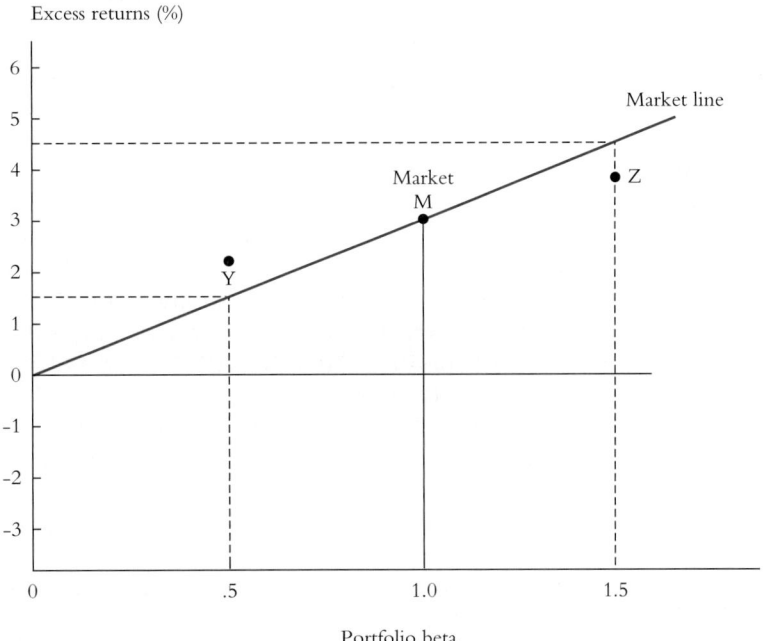

FIGURE 22–5 Risk-Adjusted Portfolio Returns

---

[7] Michael C. Jensen, "The Performance of Mutual Funds in the Period 1945–1964," *Journal of Finance,* May 1968, pp. 389–416.

of 1, the portfolio has a systematic risk equal to market, and the expected portfolio excess returns should be equal to market excess returns. If the market return (K_M) is 9 percent and the risk-free rate (R_F) is 6 percent, the market excess returns are 3 percent. A portfolio with a beta of 1 should expect to earn the market rate of excess returns ($K_M - R_F$), equal to 3 percent. Other excess returns expectations are shown for betas ranging from 0 to 1.5. For example, a portfolio with a beta of 1.5 should provide excess returns of 4.5.

Adequacy of Performance

Using the Jensen approach, the adequacy of a portfolio manager's performance can be judged against the market line. Did he or she fall above or below the line? While it would appear that portfolio manager Y in Figure 22–5 had inferior returns in comparison with portfolio manager Z (approximately 2.1 percent versus 3.9 percent), this notion is quickly dispelled when one considers risk. Actually, portfolio manager Y performed above risk-return expectations as indicated by the market line, while portfolio manager Z was below his risk-adjusted expected level. The vertical difference from a fund's performance point to the market line can be viewed as a measure of performance. This value, termed **alpha** or **average differential return,** indicates the difference between the return on the fund and a point on the market line that corresponds to a beta equal to the fund. In the case of fund Z, the beta of 1.5 indicated an excess return of 4.5 percent along the market line, and the actual excess return was only 3.9 percent. We thus have a negative alpha of 0.6 percent (3.9% − 4.5%). Clearly, a positive alpha indicates a superior performance, while a negative alpha leads to the opposite conclusion.

A key question for portfolio managers in general is: Can they consistently perform at positive alpha levels? That is, can they generate returns better than those available along the market line, which are theoretically available to anyone? The results of the classic study conducted by John McDonald on 123 mutual funds are presented in Figure 22–6.

The upward-sloping line is the market line, or anticipated level of performance based on risk. The small dots represent performance of the funds. About as many funds underperformed (negative alpha below the line) as overperformed (positive alpha above the line). Although a few high-beta funds had an unusually strong performance on a risk-adjusted basis, there is no consistent pattern of superior performance.

Around this same time period (the 1960s), the studies by Sharpe and Jensen[8] actually showed that mutual funds underperformed common stock indexes. Since then, there has been a raging debate about the adequacy of performance of mutual funds. In an excellent 1993 article in the *Financial Analysts Journal*, Richard Ippolito analyzed 21 major studies relating to mutual fund performance over the last four decades.[9] In examining the Ippolito material, we are left with the impression that mutual fund managers are not inferior performers; however, we would be hard pressed to say that investing in mutual funds will provide

---

[8] Sharpe, "Mutual Fund Performance"; Jensen, "The Performance of Mutual Funds in the Period 1945–1964."
[9] Richard A. Ippolito, "On Studies of Mutual Fund Performance, 1962–1991", *Financial Analysts Journal*, January–February 1993, pp. 42–50.

Chapter 22 Measuring Risks and Returns of Portfolio Managers 629

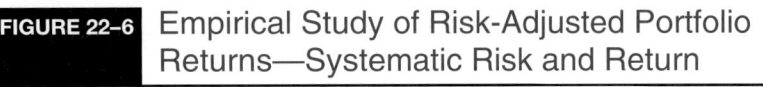

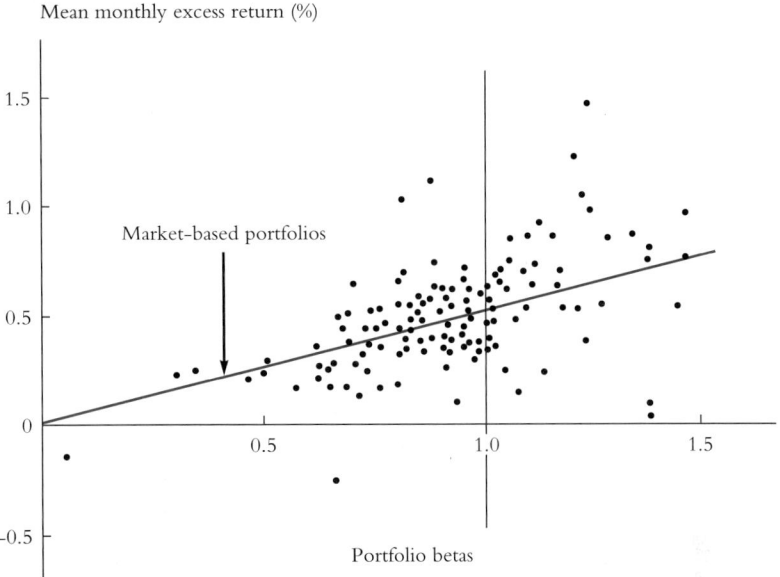

Source: John G. McDonald, "Objectives and Performance of Mutual Funds, 1960–1969," *Journal of Financial and Quantitative Analysis,* June 1974, p. 321.

returns that are higher than those reported in the popular common stock market indexes such as the Standard & Poor's 500 Index or New York Stock Exchange Index (after adjustment for the fund's risk).

What the Ippolito article suggests is that mutual funds are efficient gatherers of information and that, on average, they use the information well in their investment activities. However, there are costs associated with acquiring this information, and wise use of the information covers the cost of its acquisition.

Another recent study was done by Thomas Goodwin, in which he breaks down excess returns (in this case relative to the standard deviation) for various types of investment styles as shown in Figure 22–7 on page 630. The study is of 212 actively managed funds from 1986 to 1995 and uses the Frank Russell database. Risk-adjusted excess returns are shown on the x axis and the percent of time they occur is shown on the y axis. The important factor to note is that the plusses and minuses are pretty close to evening out. There is no statistically significant positive or negative excess returns for any of the six management styles.

Thus, we are left with the conclusion that after all factors are considered and after four decades of debate, mutual funds are neither superior nor inferior to the overall market in terms of risk-adjusted returns.[10] Studies of other types of money managers besides mutual funds, such as pension funds and endowment

www.russell.com

---

[10] For further confirmation of this point, see Mark M. Carhart, "On Persistence of Mutual Fund Performance," *Journal of Finance,* March, 1997, pp. 57–82. Carhart says successful funds cannot replicate good performance over the long term, but bad performing funds may persist in their poor performance.

630 Part 7 Introduction to Portfolio Management

FIGURE 22-7 Excess Returns: Based on Six Different Management Styles (1986–1995)

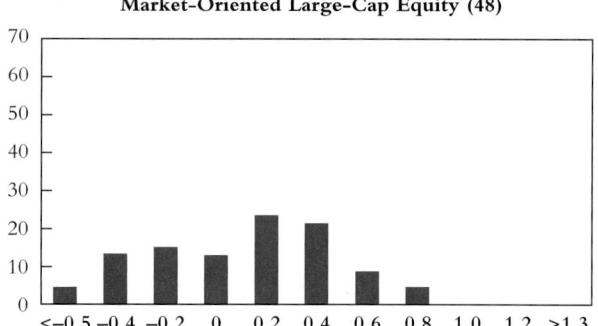
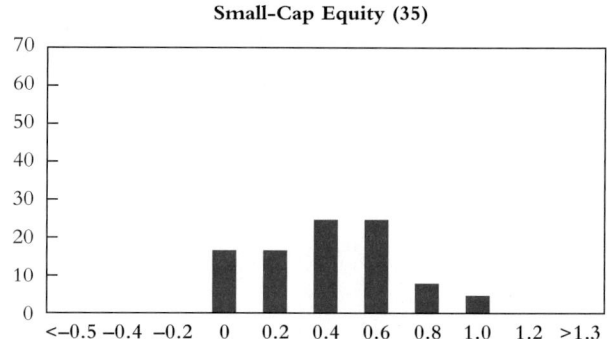
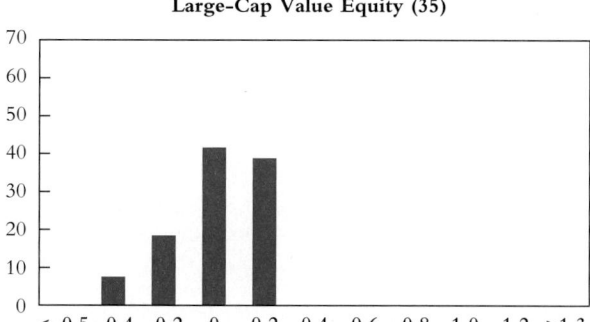
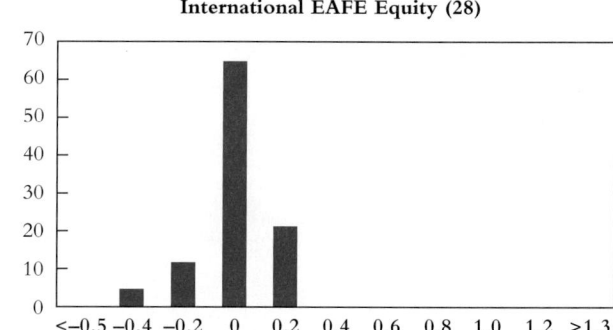
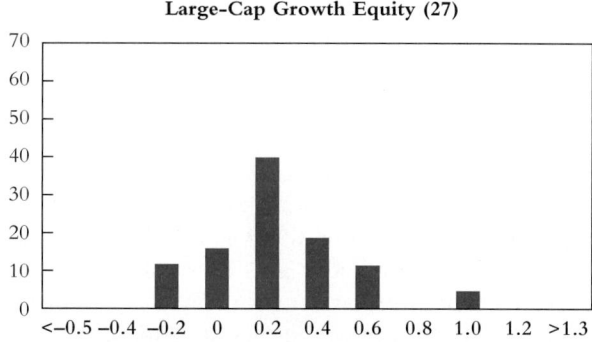
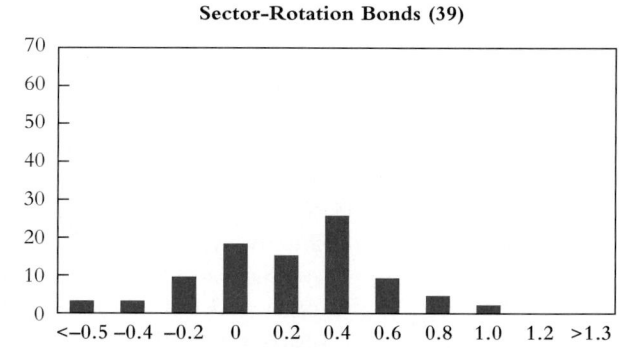

Note: Midpoints of ranges. Information ratios are on the *x* axes; relative frequencies, in percentages, are on the *y* axes. The number after the management style is the number of funds in that category.

Source: Thomas H. Goodwin, "The Information Ratio," ©1998, CFA Institute. Reproduced and republished from *Financial Analysts Journal* with permission from CFA Institute. All Rights Reserved.

funds, have reached similar conclusions.[11] Perhaps, it is not surprising that more investors are shifting their assets to **index funds,** in which fund managers

---

[11] Stephen A. Berkowitz, Louis D. Finney, and Dennis E. Logue, *The Investment Performance of Corporate Pension Plans,* New York: Quorum Books, 1988.

the real world of investing

Further Recent Evidence That Mutual Funds Have Difficulty Beating the Market

In early 2004, Standard & Poor's published the following data below comparing equity mutual fund performance to its S&P benchmark. The results cover a five-year period from 1999 to 2003.

While many groups did OK, for a mid cap equity mutual fund, the same could not be said. Mid cap growth, blend, and value funds all were beaten between 70 to 95 percent of the time.

Percentage of Funds in Each Mutual Fund Category Outperformed by the Comparable S&P Index

Fund Category	Comparison Index	Five Year
All domestic funds	S&P SuperComposite 1500	49.61%
All large capitalization funds	S&P 500	53.20
All Mid Capitalization Funds	S&P MidCap 400	81.70
All Small Capitalization Funds	S&P SmallCap 600	69.82
Large Capitalization Growth Funds	S&P/BARRA 500 Growth	45.22
Large Capitalization Blend Funds	S&P 500	54.61
Large Capitalization Value Funds	S&P/BARRA 500 Value	56.38
Mid Capitalization Growth Funds	S&P/BARRA MidCap 400 Growth	82.35
Mid Capitalization Blend Funds	S&P MidCap 400	74.32
Mid Capitalization Value Funds	S&P/BARRA MidCap 400 Value	94.92
Small Capitalization Growth Funds	S&P/BARRA 600 SmallCap Growth	72.05
Small Capitalization Blend Funds	S&P SmallCap 600	63.55
Small Capitalization Value Funds	S&P/BARRA 600 SmallCap Value	65.42

Source: Standard & Poor's Compustat® Data. For periods ending December 30, 2003.

merely attempt to produce the same results as those that could be attained from investing in a market index, such as the Standard & Poor's 500 Stock Index.

Diversification

An important service a money manager can provide is effective diversification of asset holdings. Once we at least partially accept the fact that superior performance on a risk-adjusted basis is a difficult achievement, we begin to look hard at other attributes money managers may possess. For example, we can ask: Are mutual fund managers effective diversifiers of their holdings?

As previously discussed in Chapter 21 and in this chapter, there are two measures of risk: systematic and unsystematic. Systematic risk is measured by the portfolio's (or individual stock's) beta. Under the capital asset pricing model, higher betas are rewarded with relatively high returns, and vice versa. As the market goes up 10 percent, our portfolio might go up 12 percent (beta of 1.2), and a similar phenomenon may occur on the downside. Unsystematic risk is random or nonmarket related and may be generally diversified away by the astute portfolio manager. Under the capital asset pricing model, there is no market reward for unsystematic risk since it can be eliminated through diversification.

The question for a portfolio manager then becomes: How effective have you been in diversifying away the nonrewarded, unsystematic risk? Put another way,

the real world of investing

If You Can't Beat Them, Join Them: The Growth of Index Funds

An index fund is one that attempts to replicate the performance of a popular market average such as the Standard & Poor's 500 Index (**www.standardandpoors.com**). The largest index fund is the Vanguard Index 500 (**www.vanguard.com**) (based on the S&P 500), which has tripled in the last decade.

Why all the growth? As pointed out in the chapter, it is somewhat difficult for mutual funds and other professional money managers to consistently beat the market averages. Between 1981 and 2003, the Standard & Poor's 500 Index went up at an 16 percent compound annual growth rate. A mutual fund, such as the Vanguard Index 500, that passively tracks that average is going to represent stiff competition for actively managed funds.

A passively managed stock fund invests in a portfolio that matches the S&P 500 Index on a daily basis. Thus if IBM's percent of the Index goes up on a given day as a result of a large price gain, and Procter & Gamble's percent goes down, IBM will be purchased and Procter & Gamble sold to match the percentage composition of the index at the end of the day.

The management fee and expenses for a passively managed fund is approximately 0.20 percent. This is quite low because of the absence of salaries for security analysts, portfolio managers, and so on. For actively managed funds, which do incur the above costs, the typical management fee is 0.75 to 1.25 percent.

Index funds have also spread to other areas such as Fidelity's (**www.fidelity.com**) funds that track the Wilshire 5000 Equity Index (**www.wilshire.com**), and the Morgan Stanley Capital Markets International Index (**www.morganstanley.com**).

While actively managed funds have experienced difficulty in beating the performance of index funds, many optimistic investors consider it almost un-American to accept the "average performance" of index funds. Thus, the hope for finding that one great fund will always continue. Ninety percent of mutual funds are still actively managed.

---

to what extent can a fund's movements be described as market related rather than random in nature? If we plot a fund's excess returns over an extended period against market excess returns, we can determine the joint movement between the two as indicated in Figure 22–8. In panel (a) we plot the fund's basic points. In panel (b) we draw a regression line through these points. Of importance to the present discussion is the extent to which our line fits the data. If the points of observation fall very close to the line, the independent variable (excess market returns) is largely responsible for describing the dependent variable (excess returns for fund X).

The degree of association between the independent and dependent variables is measured by R^2 **(coefficient of determination)**.[12] R^2 may take on a value anywhere between 0 and 1. A high degree of correlation between the independent and dependent variables will produce an R^2 of 0.7 or better. In panel (b) of Figure 22–8 it is assumed to be 0.90.

In Figure 22–9, the points do not fall consistently close to the regression line, and the R^2 value is assumed to be only 0.55. In this instance, we say the

---

[12] R^2 also represents the correlation coefficient squared. Thus, we can square Formula 21A–1 in Chapter 21. Another statement is:

$$R^2 = 1 - \frac{\Sigma(y''' y_c)^2/n}{\Sigma(y''' \bar{y})^2/n}$$

where y_c represents points along the regression line, and y is the average value of the independent variable.

Chapter 22 Measuring Risks and Returns of Portfolio Managers

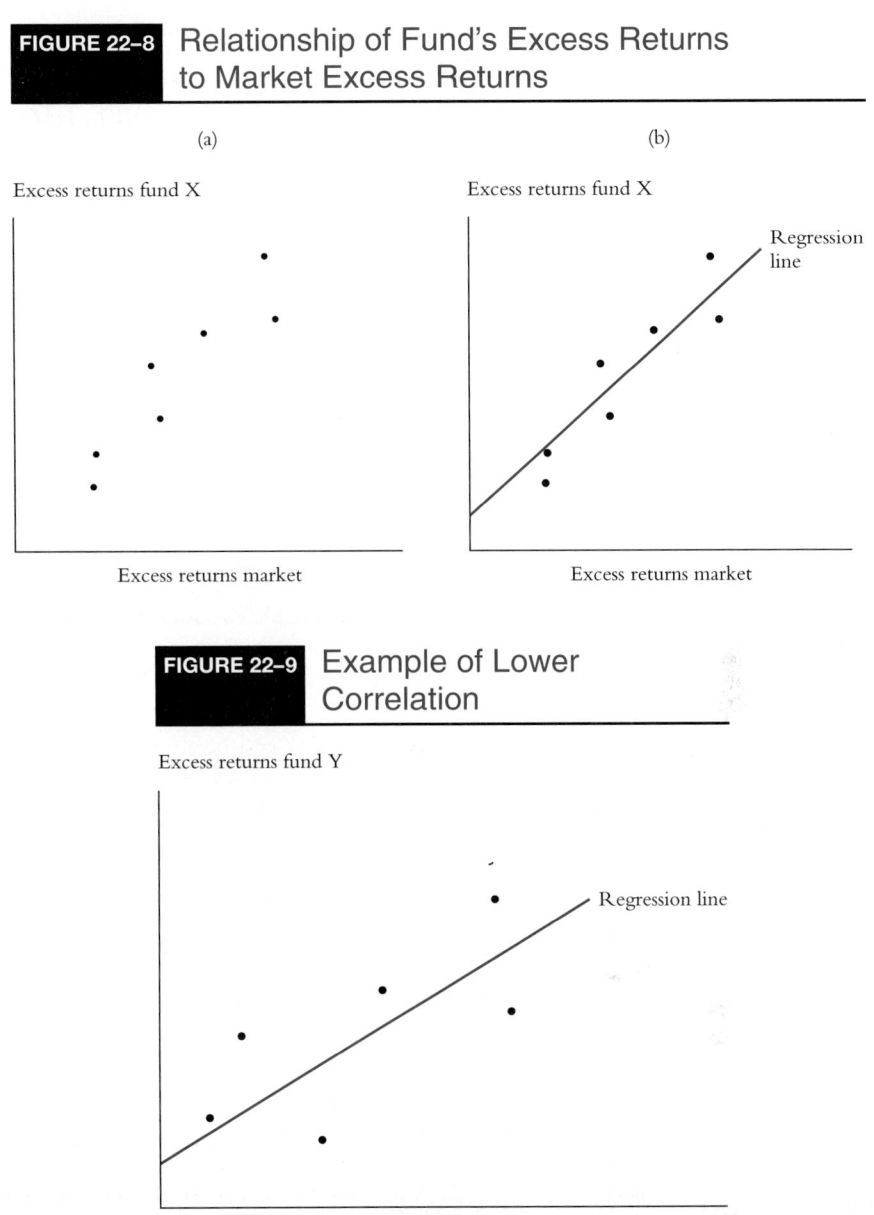

FIGURE 22-8 Relationship of Fund's Excess Returns to Market Excess Returns

FIGURE 22-9 Example of Lower Correlation

independent variable (excess market returns) was not the only major variable in explaining changes in the dependent variable (excess returns for fund Y).

The points in Figure 22–9 imply that the portfolio manager for fund Y may not have been particularly effective in his diversification efforts. Many other factors besides market returns appear to be affecting the portfolio returns of fund Y, and these could have been diversified away rather than allowed to influence returns. In this instance, we say there is a high degree of unsystematic, or non-market-related, risk. Because unsystematic risk is presumed to go unrewarded in the marketplace under the capital asset pricing model, there is evidence of inefficient portfolio diversification.

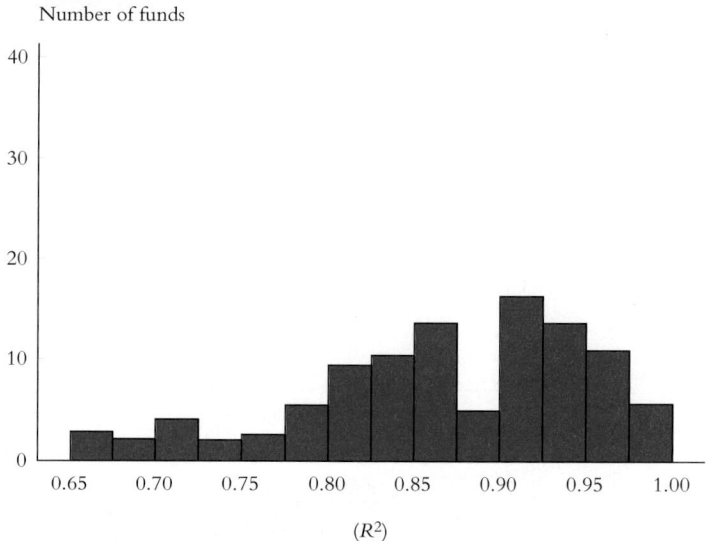

FIGURE 22–10 Quarterly Returns Attributable to Market Fluctuations: 100 Mutual Funds, 1970–1974

Source: Merrill Lynch, Pierce, Fenner & Smith, *Investment Performance Analysis, Comparative Survey,* 1974.

What does empirical data tell us about the effectiveness of portfolio managers in achieving diversification? How have they stacked up in terms of R^2 values for their portfolios? As indicated in Figure 22–10 above, their record is generally good.

The Merrill Lynch study of 100 mutual funds in Figure 22–10 shows an average R^2 value of approximately 0.90 with very few funds falling below 0.70. The actual range is between 0.66 and 0.98. Studies by McDonald, Jensen, and Gentry have led to similar conclusions.

Although many mutual funds invest in 80 to 100 securities to achieve effective diversification, this is often more than is necessary. A high degree of diversification can be achieved with between 10 and 20 efficiently selected stocks.

Other Assets As Well As Stocks

This chapter has dealt primarily with the ability to measure risk and return as it relates to portfolios of common stock. Most professionally managed funds have portfolios that are also diversified across asset classes. Brinson, Hood, and Beebower (BHB) examined 91 large corporate pension plans from 1974 to 1983 and found that the average plan included investments in stocks, bonds, T-bills, and real estate.[13] The combined asset mix makes performance evaluation more complex than the Sharpe, Treynor, and Jensen measures discussed earlier in the chapter, which can be applied only to the stock portion of the portfolio.

---

[13] Gary P. Brinson, Randolph Hood, and Gilbert L. Beebower, "Determinants of Portfolio Performance," *Financial Analysts Journal,* July–August 1986, pp. 39–44.

BHB suggest that performance of portfolios diversified across asset classes be compared with a portfolio that consists of the pension plan's normal percentage distribution between asset classes. BHB use the Standard & Poor's 500 Index, the Shearson Lehman Government/Corporate Bond Index, and 30-day Treasury bills as the measurement indicator for each of these asset classes. For an investment manager to generate superior performance, he or she would have to outperform a passively managed portfolio maintaining the plan's mix of asset classes.

Ignoring real estate and focusing on stocks, bonds, and T-bills, BHB found that, in general, the actual mean average total return on managed portfolios over the period was 9.01 percent versus 10.11 percent for the benchmark portfolio. In other words, active management cost the pension plans 1.10 percent per year. Of course, over other time periods the managed portfolios could reflect superior results. Stressed throughout the BHB analysis is also the fact that determining the appropriate asset allocation mix (stocks versus bonds versus T-bills) is much more important than simply picking winning or losing stocks.

Asset managers lose their jobs not so much because they picked stock A over stock B, but because they had a poorly allocated portfolio under a given market condition. For example, Table 22–2 shows a typical portfolio composition for large pension fund managers. Equities of all types make up 55 percent of the portfolio. If in a bull market, one is only 40 percent invested in equities, he or she could be in real trouble even if individual stock selection was great.

TABLE 22–2 Typical Weighted Portfolio for Money Managers

Asset Class	Weight
Equities:	
Domestic large capitalization	30% ⎤
Domestic small capitalization	15 ⎬ 55%
International	10 ⎦
Venture capital	5
Fixed income:	
Domestic bonds	15
International dollar bonds	4
Nondollar bonds	6
Real estate	15
Cash equivalents	0
	100%

Source: Gary Brinson, Jeffrey J. Diermeier, and Gary C. Schlarbaum, "A Composite Portfolio Benchmark for Pension Plans," ©1986, CFA Institute. Reproduced and republished from *Financial Analysts Journal* with permission from CFA Institute. All Rights Reserved.

A Specific Example—Asset Allocation

Suppose a portfolio manager is charged with the responsibility of overseeing the performance of a $100 million portfolio. At the end of each quarter, she must report her performance to the plan sponsor, which we shall assume is a pension fund committee for a large corporation.

TABLE 22–3 Comparison of Managed and Benchmark Portfolios

	Managed Portfolio			Benchmark Portfolio		
	(1) Asset Allocation	(2) Returns	(3) Weighted Returns	(4) Asset Allocation	(5) Returns	(6) Weighted Returns
Asset Class						
Equities:						
Domestic large capitalization	30%	9%	2.70%	30%	10%	3.00%
Domestic small capitalization	20	15	3.00	15	13	1.95
International	20	18	3.60	10	14	1.40
Total equities	70%		9.30%	55%		6.35%
Fixed income:						
Domestic bonds	11%	8%	0.88%	15%	9%	1.35%
Foreign bonds	8	10	0.80	10	12	1.20
Total fixed income	19%		1.68%	25%		2.55%
Real estate	7	10%	0.70	15	11%	1.65
Cash equivalents	4	4	0.16	5	4	0.20
Total portfolio	100%		11.84%	100%		10.75%

After intensive analysis of the economy using many of the approaches presented in Chapter 5, she decides to allocate her funds in the manner shown in column (1) of Table 22–3. The designation of funds into various categories of assets is called **asset allocation.** The second column represents her returns from each category during the course of the year. The third column shows the percentage invested (Column 1) times the returns (Column 2) and, in effect, represents her weighted return for each category and her total return for the year.

On the right side of the table, we see a representative benchmark portfolio that is the standard for measuring her performance. In Column 4, we observe the asset allocation; in Column 5, the return for each category; and in Column 6, the weighted returns for the benchmark portfolio.

For ease of presentation, we shall assume the risk associated with her portfolio is the same as that for the benchmark portfolio. Later we will consider the implications of different risk exposure.

In observing Table 22–3, note the overall results in Column 3 for the portfolio manager and those in Column 6 for the benchmark portfolio. The portfolio manager outperformed the benchmark portfolio by 1.09 percent; that is, her total return was 11.84 percent, while the benchmark portfolio had a 10.75 percent return.

The question is, How was this superior result achieved? In this particular case, she held a larger equity position (70 percent) than the benchmark portfolio (55 percent), which turned out to be fortunate because the stock market was moving up throughout the year (all categories of equities had strong positive returns).

We can further break down the performance of equities based on the three major categories of stock. Actually, for domestic, large capitalization stocks (those with $9 billion or more in market value), she slightly underperformed the market (9 percent versus 10 percent). An appropriate market measure for the benchmark portfolio of large capitalization stocks would be the Standard & Poor's 500 Index.[14] Notice that her performance on small capitalization stocks was 2 percent higher than the market portfolio (15 percent versus 13 percent). An appropriate market measure for the benchmark portfolio of small capitalization stocks would be the Russell 2000 Index.

Finally, she achieved a high rate of return on international equities, exceeding the benchmark return by a full 4 percent (18 percent versus 14 percent). The appropriate benchmark portfolio measure might be the Dow Jones World Index. We might even decide to break down our international equity investments and the benchmark comparisons by different areas of the world such as Mexico, Europe, Asia/Pacific, and so on. Further comparisons can be made among investments in established markets and emerging markets. The effect that the changing value of the dollar had on returns could also be considered.

In moving to fixed-income securities, our portfolio manager underperformed the benchmark portfolio, both domestically (8 percent versus 9 percent) and internationally (10 percent versus 12 percent). The same slight underperformance can be found in real estate (10 percent versus 11 percent). However, with only 19 percent of assets allocated to fixed income and 7 percent to real estate in the managed portfolio, this underperformance is not a problem.

In summary, our portfolio manager had a strong performance because of an equity position (70 percent) that was much higher than the benchmark portfolio (55 percent); that is, she benefited from superior asset allocation. She also gained from superior stock selection in the small capitalization and international equity areas; these factors more than overcame the slightly inferior performance in other categories.

Earlier in the chapter, we talked about risk considerations in measuring performance. Although we will not make a formal evaluation of risk in this case, certain factors are worthy of note. To the extent that the managed portfolio is riskier than the benchmark portfolio, the superior return would have to be partially discounted. Of course, if it is less risky than the market, the superior performance becomes even more meaningful.

While the higher equity component in the managed portfolio might imply greater risk, the large degree of international diversification could easily compensate for this factor. International securities may offset shocks in the U.S. market, and vice versa. Also, the managed portfolio appears to be more liquid than the benchmark portfolio, with real estate representing 7 percent of the holdings versus 15 percent for the benchmark portfolio. This is true in spite of a slightly lower cash position in the managed portfolio.

One last factor is worthy of note in discussing the performance of the portfolio manager. The results presented in Table 22–3 represent annual data. As mentioned earlier, the portfolio manager will not only need to present annual information for evaluation but normally reports quarterly to the investor as well. Because there is always strong pressure for performance, short-term swings in the market can test a portfolio manager's convictions. For example, when the stock market is going down, a portfolio manager with a large equity position (perhaps 70 percent or greater) may be under pressure to lighten up on stocks

---

[14] We could also add another category of MidCap stocks, but we have omitted it to shorten the presentation.

the real world of investing

My Sector Underperformed, But I Still Want a Raise

An important part of managing the stock component of a portfolio is the allocation of funds to the various sectors of the economy. A sector is a major grouping of companies in an area such as energy, technology, and so on. Obviously, a sector analyst wants his or her sector to perform well relative to a benchmark, such as the Standard and Poor's 500 Technology Index, but in the event he or she falls short in performance, the next best thing is to be underweighted (have a smaller percentage participation of the sector in your portfolio than that represented in the S&P 500 Index). Similarly, one might have cause for concern if he or she overperforms but is underweighted. All this comes back to the desire of portfolio managers to beat the overall S&P 500 Index. To understand these points, please observe the accompanying table.

The sectors listed are those used by Standard and Poor's (S&P) to break down the equity market into 10 different components. Column (1) shows your firm's asset allocation among the sectors. Column (2) indicates the S&P 500 weightings for the sectors at a given point in time, and Column (3) shows the difference in weights.

Next, the portfolio return is shown for each sector over a three-month holding period (Column 4), and in Column (5), the values are shown for the equivalent S&P 500 sectors. Then, in Column (6), the portfolio sector performance is shown relative to the comparable S&P sector. Column (7) is the all-important measure in which the difference in weights (Column 3) is multiplied by the sector over- or under-performance (Column 6). Thus, Column (7) indicates whether a positive or negative overall contribution is being made by each sector of the total equity return.

The math in Column (7) is a little tricky. When you multiple a percentage by a percentage, the answer tends to be very small. Look at industrials as an example (fourth line from the bottom). The value in Column (3) is 3.2 percent and the value in Column (6) is 5 percent. When the two percentages are multiplied by each other, the answer is 0.16 percent (0.032 × 0.05 = 0.0016).

Overall, the portfolio outperformed the S&P by 1.39 percent as shown at the bottom of Column (7). The largest positive contribution was energy (0.63 percent).

Assume you are in charge of information technology (third line from the top). You had the misfortune of underperforming by 3.2 percent (Column 6), but because you were underweighted by 9.8 percent (Column 3), you actually delivered a positive impact of 0.31 percent. A negative times a negative equals a positive. The question is: Do you ask for the raise?

Sector Return Analysis

Sector	(1) Portfolio Weighting	(2) S&P Weighting	(3) Difference in Weighting	(4) Portfolio Return	(5) S&P Return	(6) Sector Over- or Under-performance	(7) = (3) × (6) Sector Allocation Contribution
Telecommunications services	6.0%	5.6%	0.4%	2.0%	−3.0%	5.0%	0.02%
Utilities	3.1	3.9	−0.8	−2.0	4.0	−6.0	0.05
Information technology	8.0	17.8	−9.8	4.0	7.2	−3.2	0.31
Materials	3.3	2.8	0.5	5.0	4.2	0.8	0.01
Financials	15.6	17.6	−2.0	8.1	9.2	−1.1	0.02
Consumer discretionary	14.6	13.1	1.5	9.0	12.1	−3.1	−0.05
Industrials	14.7	11.5	3.2	9.0	4.0	5.0	0.16
Energy	14.3	7.0	7.3	18.0	9.4	8.6	0.63
Health care	17.0	13.3	3.7	14.9	10.7	4.2	0.16
Consumer staples	3.4	7.4	−4.0	6.8	8.8	−2.0	0.08
							1.39%

because of negative returns. However, down markets are normally the best time to buy, not to sell. This principle may be severely tested when a portfolio manager has to report a quarterly loss but, at the same time, suggests that unusually good buying opportunities now exist. While the stock market generally provides superior returns in comparison with other investments over the long term, such may not be the case over a short period of time. Well-informed portfolio managers, and those for whom they work, generally use a three- to five-year time horizon to determine whether performance is acceptable. However, in the world of money management, one or two bad quarters can sometimes mean the loss of an account.

The Makeup of Institutional Investors

Having discussed measurement and portfolio management techniques for institutional investors, we will now take a more specific look at the participants. **Institutional investors,** as opposed to individual investors, represent organizations that are responsible for bringing together large pools of capital for reinvestment. Our coverage will center on investment companies (including mutual funds), pension funds, life insurance companies, bank trust departments, and endowments and foundations.

Investment Companies (including Mutual Funds)

Investment companies take the proceeds of individual investors and reinvest them in other securities according to their specific objectives. Income and capital gains are generally distributed to stockholders and are subject to single taxation under Subchapter M of the Internal Revenue Code. Investment companies were discussed at some length in Chapter 18.

Other Institutional Investors

Other institutional investors (along with investment companies) and their extent of market participation are presented in Table 22–4 on page 640. Total institutional holdings are more than $10 trillion. We will briefly comment on pension funds, insurance companies, bank trust departments, and foundations and endowments.

Pension Funds Pension funds represent an important and growing sector of the institutional market and may be private or public. Private funds represent well over half of the pension fund market. The benefits that accrue under private pension funds may be insured or uninsured, with the latter arrangement occurring most frequently. Public pension funds are run for the benefit of federal, state, or local employees.

Insurance Companies Insurance companies may be categorized as either "life" or "property and casualty." Life insurance companies must earn a minimum rate of return assumed in calculating insurance premiums, and public policy emphasizes safety of assets. Part of life insurance company assets are in privately placed debt or mortgages, with the balance in bonds and stocks. Property and casualty insurance companies enjoy more lenient regulation of their

TABLE 22–4 Percentage of Institutional Market Held by Institutional Investors

		Percent
1.	Private noninsured pension funds	28.3%
2.	Open-end investment companies	16.1
3.	Other investment companies	1.9
4.	Life insurance companies	5.0
5.	Property-liability insurance companies	4.7
6.	Personal trust funds	26.4
7.	Common trust funds	1.6
8.	Mutual savings banks	0.9
9.	State and local retirement funds	4.8
10.	Foundations	7.5
11.	Educational endowments	2.8
		100%

Source: Compiled from a review of annual reports from the Securities and Exchange Commission and the New York Stock Exchange.

activities and generally have a larger percentage of their assets in bonds and stocks.

Bank Trust Departments The emphasis in bank trust departments is on managing other people's funds for a fee. Banks may administer individual trusts or commingled (combined) funds in a common trust fund. Often a bank will establish more than one common trust fund to serve varying needs and objectives. The overall performance of bank trust departments has been mixed, with the usual number of leaders and laggards. Bank trust management is highly concentrated with a relatively small number of trust departments holding the majority of funds. Out of approximately 3,000 bank trust departments, the top 10 hold one-third of all assets, and the largest 60 hold two-thirds.

Foundations and Endowments Foundations represent nonprofit organizations set up to accomplish social, educational, or charitable purposes. They are often established through the donation of a large block of stock in which the donor was one of the corporate founders. Examples include the Ford, Carnegie, and Rockefeller foundations. Endowments, on the other hand, represent permanent capital funds that are donated to universities, churches, or civic organizations. The management of endowment funds is often quite difficult because of the pressure for current income to maintain operations (perhaps the university library) while at the same time there is a demand for capital appreciation. Measurement of performance for foundations and endowments is moving more to a total-return basis (annual income plus capital appreciation) rather than the traditional interest-earned or dividend-received basis.

exploring the web

Website Address	Comments
www.morningstar.com	Provides analysis of mutual fund portfolios and modern portfolio theory statistics for mutual funds tracked by Morningstar and for personal portfolios; some analysis is fee-based.
www.financialengines.com	Provides portfolio analysis and information on personal financial planning
www.stockworm.com	Site will track and evaluate portfolios
finance.yahoo.com	Provides analysis of mutual funds using Morningstar data

Summary

The ability of portfolio managers to meet various goals and objectives is considered in this chapter. Many portfolio managers appear to demonstrate superior performances during market boom years. However, when this performance is adjusted for risk, any perceived superiority may quickly vanish.

Some concepts related to the capital asset pricing model may be used to evaluate the performance of money managers. Portfolio beta values are shown along the horizontal axis, while the market line indicates expected returns. Portfolio managers that are able to operate above the line (positive alphas) are thought to be superior managers, while the opposite would be true of those falling below the line. Research indicates that, on average, portfolio managers do not beat the popular averages or random portfolios on a risk-adjusted basis.

Nevertheless, mutual funds (or other managed portfolios) do have some desirable attributes. As indicated by a Merrill Lynch study (and others as well), mutual funds tend to be very efficient diversifiers. Their average correlation with the market (R^2) tends to be approximately 90 percent, indicating only 10 percent unsystematic, or nonrewarded, risk. In general, mutual fund managers also do a good job of constructing portfolios that are consistent with their initially stated objectives (that is, maximum capital gains, growth, income, etc.).

In a specific evaluation of a professional money manager, one may wish to judge how assets were allocated between stocks, bonds, real estate, cash equivalents, etc., and whether this was effective over a given time period. Furthermore, the performance within each asset classification can be compared with a benchmark portfolio's return. All of this analysis enables one to determine the overall adequacy of performance and how it was produced.

The market of institutional investors is made up of investment companies (closed-end and mutual funds), pension funds, insurance companies, foundations, endowments, and other participants. Although the great weight of empirical research has dealt with mutual funds, the same basic conclusions about risk-adjusted returns can be applied to other institutional investors.

Key Words and Concepts

alpha (average differential return) 628
asset allocation 636
excess returns 625
index funds 630
institutional investors 639
Jensen approach 625
market line 627
R^2 (coefficient of determination) 632
Sharpe approach 625
Treynor approach 625

Discussion Questions

1. What is a risk-adjusted return?
2. In evaluating a mutual fund manager, what would be the first point to analyze?
3. How can risk exposure be measured?
4. How are excess returns defined?
5. What is the Sharpe approach to measuring portfolio risk? If a portfolio has a higher Sharpe measure than the market in general under the Sharpe approach, what is the implication?
6. How does the Treynor approach differ from the Sharpe approach? Which of the two measures assumes unsystematic risk will be diversified away?
7. Under the Jensen approach, how is the market line related to the beta?
8. Explain alpha as a measure of performance.
9. What conclusions can be drawn from the empirical studies of portfolio (fund) managers' performances? Are they superior?
10. If investment companies do not offer returns that are, on average, any better than the market in general, why would someone invest in them?
11. What does a high R^2 (correlation) between a fund's excess returns and the market's excess returns indicate about the fund manager's ability to effectively diversify?
12. According to the Brinson, Hood, and Beebower (BHB) study, are asset allocation decisions (stocks versus bonds, etc.) more or less important than individual stock selection decisions?
13. What is meant by an institutional investor? Give some examples.

Problems

Sharpe approach to measuring performance

1. A firm that evaluates portfolios uses the Sharpe approach to measuring performance. How would it rank the following three portfolios?

	Portfolio Return	Risk-Free Rate	Portfolio Standard Deviation
Bowman Money Managers	11%	7%	20%
Donruss Group	15	7	25
Fleer Investment Company	10	7	14

Chapter 22 Measuring Risks and Returns of Portfolio Managers

Treynor approach to measuring performance

2. Assume a second firm that evaluates portfolios uses the Treynor approach to measuring performance. The firm is also evaluating the three portfolios in problem 1. The portfolio betas are as follows:

	Portfolio Beta
Bowman Money Managers	1.08
Donruss Group	1.20
Fleer Investment Company	1.10

  a. Using the Treynor approach, how would the second firm rank the three portfolios?
  b. Explain why any differences have taken place in the rankings between problems 1 and 2a.
  c. If the Treynor approach is utilized and the market return is 10 percent (with a risk-free rate of 7 percent), which of the portfolios outperformed the market?

Jensen approach to measuring performance

3. Assume the Jensen approach to portfolio valuation is being used.
  a. Draw a market line similar to that in Figure 22–2 on page 622 (i.e., show 0 excess returns at a 0 portfolio beta and 3 percent (10 percent − 7 percent) at a portfolio beta of 1).
  b. Now graph the three portfolios. Which portfolio(s) over- or underperformed the market?

Asset allocation

4. A portfolio manager has the following asset allocation and returns on his portfolio. Fill in the values in Column (3). Use Table 22–3 on page 636 as a guideline.

	(1) Portfolio Manager Asset Allocation	(2) Portfolio Manager Returns	(3) Portfolio Manager Weighted Returns
Asset Class			
Equities:			
Domestic large capitalization	31%	11%	
Domestic small capitalization	13	13	
International	4	22	
Total equities	48		
Fixed income:			
Domestic bonds	19%	8%	
Foreign bonds	9	9	
Total fixed income	28		
Real estate	5%	9%	
Cash equivalents	19%	5%	
Total portfolio	100%		

The benchmark portfolio with which he is being compared is shown as follows:

	(1) Benchmark Portfolio Asset Allocation	(2) Benchmark Portfolio Returns	(3) Benchmark Portfolio Weighted Returns
Asset Class			
Equities:			
Domestic large capitalization	30%	10%	3.00%
Domestic small capitalization	26	12	3.12
International	15	18	2.70
Total equities	71		8.82%
Fixed income:			
Domestic bonds	14	6%	.84%
Foreign bonds	5	8	.40
Total fixed income	19		1.24%
Real estate	5%	7%	.35%
Cash equivalents	5%	4%	.20
Total portfolio	100%		10.61%

   a. Explain why the portfolio manager under- or outperformed the benchmark portfolio.

   b. If cash equivalents had been reduced by the portfolio manager to 5 percent and had been invested in international equities at his indicated rate of return, would the portfolio manager have under- or outperformed the benchmark portfolio?

Web Exercise

1. For the following five stocks, you will write in their 1-year return following their beta.

   Home Depot (HD)
   American International Group (AIG)
   Harley Davidson (HDI)
   Consolidated Edison (ED)
   CISCO Systems (CSCO)

2. To get the 1-year return go to **www.bloomberg.com**. The 1-year return can be found by typing the ticker symbol after "Enter Symbol" and then hit "Enter." The 1-year return will show up at the end of the second line.

3. Fill in the table below:

Company	Beta	1-Year Return
Home Depot (HD)	1.30	
American International Group	.95	
Harley Davidson (HDI)	1.10	
Consolidated Edison (ED)	.65	
CISCO Systems (CSCO)	1.45	

4. Have the riskier companies provided higher returns as they are supposed to? Do not be surprised by your answer one way or the other.

Note: From time to time, companies redesign their websites, and occasionally a topic we have listed may have been deleted, updated, or moved into a different location. Most websites have a "site map" or "site index" listed on a different page. If you click on the site map or site index, you will be introduced to a table of contents that should aid you in finding the topic you are looking for.

S&P Problems

www.mhhe.com/edumarketinsight

STANDARD &POOR'S

1. Log on to the McGraw-Hill website: **www.mhhe.com/edumarketinsight** (see page vi in the preface for instructions).
2. Click on Company, which is the first box below the Market Insight title.
3. Put the ticker symbol for Johnson & Johnson (JNJ) in the box and click on go.
4. Click on S&P Stock Reports, and then click on stock report (in blue). You will find Johnson & Johnson's beta under Key Stock Statistics on the bottom left corner of page 1. Record the beta.
5. Now repeat this exercise for the following companies: Citigroup (C), Coca Cola (KO), Dell (DELL), Disney (DIS), Exxon Mobil (XOM), Ford (F), General Electric (GE), Harley Davidson (HDI), and McGraw-Hill (MHP).
6. Assume that you have invested $10,000 in each company for an equal-weighted portfolio. Combine these above nine companies with Johnson & Johnson, and compute the weighted portfolio beta.
7. What is the beta of the portfolio?
8. What is the range of betas between the high and low?
9. Is your portfolio risk equal to, less than, or greater than the market?
10. Are you surprised at the average beta given the presence of such a varied range of betas?
11. What conclusions can you draw from this exercise?

The Wall Street Journal Project

1. Assume you are responsible for evaluating the market over the last 12 months. Using the asset allocation in Column (1) on the next page, fill in Column (2) for market returns over the last 12 months and Column (3) for weighted returns (Column 1 × Column 2). Use *The Wall Street Journal* as your source of information.

	(1) Asset Allocation	(2) Market Returns YTD (% Change)	(3) Weighted Returns
Asset Class			
Equities:			
Large Capitalization[a]	25%		
Mid Capitalization[b]	15		
Small Capitalization[c]	20		
Fixed income:			
U.S. Treasury securities (intermediate)[d]		20%	
U.S. corporate debt issues (high yield)[d]		12	
Mortgage-backed securities (Ginnie Mae)[d]		8	
Total weighted returns			
(*Note:* These returns only include price changes—not dividends or interest.)			

[a] Use the S&P 500 Index found under the "Major Stock Indexes" in Section C of *The Wall Street Journal*.
[b] Use the S&P 500 Index found under the "Major Stock Indexes" in Section C of *The Wall Street Journal*.
[c] Use the Russell 2000 Index found under the "Major Stock Indexes" in Section C of *The Wall Street Journal*.
[d] Use "Major Bond Indexes" in Section C of *The Wall Street Journal*. It is usually on the same page as "Major Stock Indexes."

2. Generally speaking, did equities outperform fixed-income securities?
3. Which one of the three classes of equities performed best? Which performed worst?
4. Which of the three classes of fixed-income securities performed best? Which performed worst?
5. With 20-20 hindsight, describe some of the changes you would have made in your asset allocation 12 months ago given what you now know.

Selected References

Measuring Portfolio Performance

Akgun, Aydin, and Ranja Gibson. "Recovery Risk in Stock Returns." *Journal of Portfolio Management,* Winter 2001, pp. 22–31.

Carhart, Mark M. "On Persistence of Mutual Fund Performance." *Journal of Finance,* March 1997, pp. 57–82.

Coggin, T. Daniel; Frank J. Fabozzi; and Shafiqur Rahman. "The Investment Performance of U.S. Equity Pension Fund Managers: An Empirical Investigation." *Journal of Finance,* July 1993, pp. 1039–55.

Daniel, Kent; Mark Grinblett; Sheridan Titman; and Russ Wermers. "Measuring Mutual Fund Performance with Characteristic-Based Benchmarks." *Journal of Finance,* July 1997, pp. 1035–58.

Eraker, Bjorn; Michael Johannes; and Nicholas Polson. "The Impact of Jumps in Volatility and Returns." *The Journal of Finance,* June 2003, pp. 1269–1300.

Ippolito, Richard A. "On Studies of Mutual Fund Performance, 1962–1991." *Financial Analysts Journal,* January–February 1993, pp. 42–50.

Lazer, Ron; Beruch Lev; and Joshua Linvat. "Internet Traffic and Portfolio Returns." *Financial Analysts Journal,* May–June 2001, pp. 30–40.

Qian, Edward, and Stephen Gorman. "Conditional Distribution in Portfolio Theory." *Financial Analysts Journal,* March–April 2001, pp. 44–51.

Portfolio Strategy

Hartzell, Jay C., and Laura T. Starks. "Institutional Investors and Executive Compensation." *The Journal of Finance,* December 2003, pp. 2351–74.

Kandel, Samuel, and Robert F. Stambaugh. "On the Predictability of Stock Returns: An Asset-Allocation Perspective." *Journal of Finance,* June 1996, pp. 385–424.

Leibowitz, Martin L.; Stanley Kogelman; Lawrence N. Bader; and Ajay R. Dravid. "Interest Rate-Sensitive Asset Allocation." *Journal of Portfolio Management,* Spring 1994, pp. 8–15.

Lockwood, Larry J., and Scott C. Linn. "An Examination of Stock Market Volatility during Overnight and Intraday Periods, 1964–1989." *Journal of Finance,* June 1990, pp. 591–601.

APPENDIX A Compound Sum of $1

Period	1%	2%	3%	4%	5%	6%	7%	8%	9%	10%	11%
1	1.010	1.020	1.030	1.040	1.050	1.060	1.070	1.080	1.090	1.100	1.110
2	1.020	1.040	1.061	1.082	1.103	1.124	1.145	1.166	1.188	1.210	1.232
3	1.030	1.061	1.093	1.125	1.158	1.191	1.225	1.260	1.295	1.331	1.368
4	1.041	1.082	1.126	1.170	1.216	1.262	1.311	1.360	1.412	1.464	1.518
5	1.051	1.104	1.159	1.217	1.276	1.338	1.403	1.469	1.539	1.611	1.685
6	1.062	1.126	1.194	1.265	1.340	1.419	1.501	1.587	1.677	1.772	1.870
7	1.072	1.149	1.230	1.316	1.407	1.504	1.606	1.714	1.828	1.949	2.076
8	1.083	1.172	1.267	1.369	1.477	1.594	1.718	1.851	1.993	2.144	2.305
9	1.094	1.195	1.305	1.423	1.551	1.689	1.838	1.999	2.172	2.358	2.558
10	1.105	1.219	1.344	1.480	1.629	1.791	1.967	2.159	2.367	2.594	2.839
11	1.116	1.243	1.384	1.539	1.710	1.898	2.105	2.332	2.580	2.853	3.152
12	1.127	1.268	1.426	1.601	1.796	2.012	2.252	2.518	2.813	3.138	3.498
13	1.138	1.294	1.469	1.665	1.886	2.133	2.410	2.720	3.066	3.452	3.883
14	1.149	1.319	1.513	1.732	1.980	2.261	2.579	2.937	3.342	3.797	4.310
15	1.161	1.346	1.558	1.801	2.079	2.397	2.759	3.172	3.642	4.177	4.785
16	1.173	1.373	1.605	1.873	2.183	2.540	2.952	3.426	3.970	4.595	5.311
17	1.184	1.400	1.653	1.948	2.292	2.693	3.159	3.700	4.328	5.054	5.895
18	1.196	1.428	1.702	2.206	2.407	2.854	3.380	3.996	4.717	5.560	6.544
19	1.208	1.457	1.754	2.107	2.527	3.026	3.617	4.316	5.142	6.116	7.263
20	1.220	1.486	1.806	2.191	2.653	3.207	3.870	4.661	5.604	6.727	8.062
25	1.282	1.641	2.094	2.666	3.386	4.292	5.427	6.848	8.623	10.835	13.585
30	1.348	1.811	2.427	3.243	4.322	5.743	7.612	10.063	13.268	17.449	22.892
40	1.489	2.208	3.262	4.801	7.040	10.286	14.974	21.725	31.409	42.259	65.001
50	1.645	2.692	4.384	7.107	11.467	18.420	29.457	46.902	74.358	117.39	184.57

Appendix A Compound Sum of $1

APPENDIX A Compound Sum of $1 *(concluded)*

Period	12%	13%	14%	15%	16%	17%	18%	19%	20%	25%	30%
1	1.120	1.130	1.140	1.150	1.160	1.170	1.180	1.190	1.200	1.250	1.300
2	1.254	1.277	1.300	1.323	1.346	1.369	1.392	1.416	1.440	1.563	1.690
3	1.405	1.443	1.482	1.521	1.561	1.602	1.643	1.685	1.728	1.953	2.197
4	1.574	1.630	1.689	1.749	1.811	1.874	1.939	2.005	2.074	2.441	2.856
5	1.762	1.842	1.925	2.011	2.100	2.192	2.288	2.386	2.488	3.052	3.713
6	1.974	2.082	2.195	2.313	2.436	2.565	2.700	2.840	2.986	3.815	4.827
7	2.211	2.353	2.502	2.660	2.826	3.001	3.185	3.379	3.583	4.768	6.276
8	2.476	2.658	2.853	3.059	3.278	3.511	3.759	4.021	4.300	5.960	8.157
9	2.773	3.004	3.252	3.518	3.803	4.108	4.435	4.785	5.160	7.451	10.604
10	3.106	3.395	3.707	4.046	4.411	4.807	5.234	5.696	6.192	9.313	13.786
11	3.479	3.836	4.226	4.652	5.117	5.624	6.176	6.777	7.430	11.642	17.922
12	3.896	4.335	4.818	5.350	5.936	6.580	7.288	8.064	8.916	14.552	23.298
13	4.363	4.898	5.492	6.153	6.886	7.699	8.599	9.596	10.699	18.190	30.288
14	4.887	5.535	6.261	7.076	7.988	9.007	10.147	11.420	12.839	22.737	39.374
15	5.474	6.254	7.138	8.137	9.266	10.539	11.974	13.590	15.407	28.422	51.186
16	6.130	7.067	8.137	9.358	10.748	12.330	14.129	16.172	18.488	35.527	66.542
17	6.866	7.986	9.276	10.761	12.468	14.426	16.672	19.244	22.186	44.409	86.504
18	7.690	9.024	10.575	12.375	14.463	16.879	19.673	22.091	26.623	55.511	112.46
19	8.613	10.197	12.056	14.232	16.777	19.748	23.214	27.252	31.948	69.389	146.19
20	9.646	11.523	13.743	16.367	19.461	23.106	27.393	32.429	38.338	86.736	190.05
25	17.000	21.231	26.462	32.919	40.874	50.658	62.699	77.388	95.396	264.70	705.64
30	29.960	39.116	50.950	66.212	85.850	111.07	143.37	184.68	237.38	807.79	2,620.0
40	93.051	132.78	188.88	267.86	378.72	533.87	750.38	1,051.7	1,469.8	7,523.2	36,119.
50	289.00	450.74	700.23	1,083.7	1,670.7	2,566.2	3,927.4	5,988.9	9,100.4	70,065.	497,929.

Appendix B Compound Sum of an Annuity of $1

Period	1%	2%	3%	4%	5%	6%	7%	8%	9%	10%	11%
1	1.000	1.000	1.000	1.000	1.000	1.000	1.000	1.000	1.000	1.000	1.000
2	2.010	2.020	2.030	2.040	2.050	2.060	2.070	2.080	2.090	2.100	2.110
3	3.030	3.060	3.091	3.122	3.153	3.184	3.215	3.246	3.278	3.310	3.342
4	4.060	4.122	4.184	4.246	4.310	4.375	4.440	4.506	4.573	4.641	4.710
5	5.101	5.204	5.309	5.416	5.526	5.637	5.751	5.867	5.985	6.105	6.228
6	6.152	6.308	6.468	6.633	6.802	6.975	7.153	7.336	7.523	7.716	7.913
7	7.214	7.434	7.662	7.898	8.142	8.394	8.654	8.923	9.200	9.487	9.783
8	8.286	8.583	8.892	9.214	9.549	9.897	10.260	10.637	11.028	11.436	11.859
9	9.369	9.755	10.159	10.583	11.027	11.491	11.978	12.488	13.021	13.579	14.164
10	10.462	10.950	11.464	12.006	12.578	13.181	13.816	14.487	15.193	15.937	16.722
11	11.567	12.169	12.808	13.486	14.207	14.972	15.784	16.645	17.560	18.531	19.561
12	12.683	13.412	14.192	15.026	15.917	16.870	17.888	18.977	20.141	21.384	22.713
13	13.809	14.680	15.618	16.627	17.713	18.882	20.141	21.495	22.953	24.523	26.212
14	14.947	15.974	17.086	18.292	19.599	21.015	22.550	24.215	26.019	27.975	30.095
15	16.097	17.293	18.599	20.024	21.579	23.276	25.129	27.152	29.361	31.772	34.405
16	17.258	18.639	20.157	21.825	23.657	25.673	27.888	30.324	33.003	35.950	39.190
17	18.430	20.012	21.762	23.698	25.840	28.213	30.840	33.750	36.974	40.545	44.501
18	19.615	21.412	23.414	25.645	28.132	30.906	33.999	37.450	41.301	45.599	50.396
19	20.811	22.841	25.117	27.671	30.539	33.760	37.379	41.446	46.018	51.159	56.939
20	22.019	24.297	26.870	29.778	33.066	36.786	40.995	45.762	51.160	57.275	64.203
25	28.243	32.030	36.459	41.646	47.727	54.865	63.249	73.106	84.701	98.347	114.41
30	34.785	40.588	47.575	56.085	66.439	79.058	94.461	113.28	136.31	164.49	199.02
40	48.886	60.402	75.401	95.026	120.80	154.76	199.64	259.06	337.89	442.59	581.83
50	64.463	84.579	112.80	152.67	209.35	290.34	406.53	573.77	815.08	1,163.9	1,668.8

APPENDIX B Compound Sum of an Annuity of $1 (concluded)

Period	12%	13%	14%	15%	16%	17%	18%	19%	20%	25%	30%
1	1.000	1.000	1.000	1.000	1.000	1.000	1.000	1.000	1.000	1.000	1.000
2	2.120	2.130	2.140	2.150	2.160	2.170	2.180	2.190	2.200	2.250	2.300
3	3.374	3.407	3.440	3.473	3.506	3.539	3.572	3.606	3.640	3.813	3.990
4	4.779	4.850	4.921	4.993	5.066	5.141	5.215	5.291	5.368	5.766	6.187
5	6.353	6.480	6.610	6.742	6.877	7.014	7.154	7.297	7.442	8.207	9.043
6	8.115	8.323	8.536	9.754	8.977	9.207	9.442	9.683	9.930	11.259	12.756
7	10.089	10.405	10.730	11.067	11.414	11.772	12.142	12.523	12.916	15.073	17.583
8	12.300	12.757	13.233	13.727	14.240	14.773	15.327	15.902	16.499	19.842	23.858
9	14.776	15.416	16.085	16.786	17.519	18.285	19.086	19.923	20.799	25.802	32.015
10	17.549	18.420	19.337	20.304	21.321	22.393	23.521	24.701	25.959	33.253	42.619
11	20.655	21.814	23.045	24.349	25.733	27.200	28.755	30.404	32.150	42.566	56.405
12	24.133	25.650	27.271	29.002	30.850	32.824	34.931	37.180	39.581	54.208	74.327
13	28.029	29.985	32.089	34.352	36.786	39.404	42.219	45.244	48.497	68.760	97.625
14	32.393	34.883	37.581	40.505	43.672	47.103	50.818	54.841	59.196	86.949	127.91
15	37.280	40.417	43.842	47.580	51.660	56.110	60.965	66.261	72.035	109.69	167.29
16	42.753	46.672	50.980	55.717	60.925	66.649	72.939	79.850	87.442	138.11	218.47
17	48.884	53.739	59.118	65.075	71.673	78.979	87.068	96.022	105.93	173.64	285.01
18	55.750	61.725	68.394	75.836	84.141	93.406	103.74	115.27	128.12	218.05	371.52
19	63.440	70.749	78.969	88.212	98.603	110.29	123.41	138.17	154.74	273.56	483.97
20	72.052	80.947	91.025	102.44	115.38	130.03	146.63	165.42	186.69	342.95	630.17
25	133.33	155.62	181.87	212.79	249.21	292.11	342.60	402.04	471.98	1,054.8	2,348.80
30	241.33	293.20	356.79	434.75	530.31	647.44	790.95	966.7	1,181.9	3,227.2	8,730.0
40	767.09	1,013.7	1,342.0	1,779.1	2,360.8	3,134.5	4,163.21	5,529.8	7,343.9	30,089.	120,393.
50	2,400.0	3,459.5	4,994.5	7,217.7	10,436.	15,090.	21,813.	31,515.	45,497.	280,256.	1,659,731.

APPENDIX D — Present Value of an Annuity of $1

Period	1%	2%	3%	4%	5%	6%	7%	8%	9%	10%	11%	12%
1	0.990	0.980	0.971	0.962	0.952	0.943	0.935	0.926	0.917	0.909	0.901	0.893
2	1.970	1.942	1.913	1.886	1.859	1.833	1.808	1.783	1.759	1.736	1.713	1.690
3	2.941	2.884	2.829	2.775	2.723	2.673	2.624	2.577	2.531	2.487	2.444	2.402
4	3.902	3.808	3.717	3.630	3.546	3.465	3.387	3.312	3.240	3.170	3.102	3.037
5	4.853	4.715	4.580	4.452	4.329	4.212	4.100	3.993	3.890	3.791	3.696	3.605
6	5.795	5.601	5.417	5.242	5.076	4.917	4.767	4.623	4.486	4.355	4.231	4.111
7	6.728	6.472	6.230	6.002	5.786	5.582	5.389	5.206	5.033	4.868	4.712	4.564
8	7.652	7.325	7.020	6.733	6.463	6.210	5.971	5.747	5.535	5.335	5.146	4.968
9	8.566	8.162	7.786	7.435	7.108	6.802	6.515	6.247	5.995	5.759	5.537	5.328
10	9.471	8.983	8.530	8.111	7.722	7.360	7.024	6.710	6.418	6.145	5.889	5.650
11	10.368	9.787	9.253	8.760	8.306	7.887	7.499	7.139	6.805	6.495	6.207	5.938
12	11.255	10.575	9.954	9.385	8.863	8.384	7.943	7.536	7.161	6.814	6.492	6.194
13	12.134	11.348	10.635	9.986	9.394	8.853	8.358	7.904	7.487	7.103	6.750	6.424
14	13.004	12.106	11.296	10.563	9.899	9.295	8.745	8.244	7.786	7.367	6.982	6.628
15	13.865	12.849	11.939	11.118	10.380	9.712	9.108	8.559	8.061	7.606	7.191	6.811
16	14.718	13.578	12.561	11.652	10.838	10.106	9.447	8.851	8.313	7.824	7.379	6.974
17	15.562	14.292	13.166	12.166	11.274	10.477	9.763	9.122	8.544	8.022	7.549	7.102
18	16.398	14.992	13.754	12.659	11.690	10.828	10.059	9.372	8.756	8.201	7.702	7.250
19	17.226	15.678	14.324	13.134	12.085	11.158	10.336	9.604	8.950	8.365	7.839	7.366
20	18.046	16.351	14.877	13.590	12.462	11.470	10.594	9.818	9.129	8.514	7.963	7.469
25	22.023	19.523	17.413	15.622	14.094	12.783	11.654	10.675	9.823	9.077	8.422	7.843
30	25.808	22.396	19.600	17.292	15.372	13.765	12.409	11.258	10.274	9.427	8.694	8.055
40	32.835	27.355	23.115	19.793	17.160	15.046	13.332	11.925	10.757	9.779	8.951	8.244
50	39.196	31.424	25.730	21.482	18.256	15.762	13.801	12.233	10.962	9.915	9.042	8.304

APPENDIX D Present Value of an Annuity of $1 (concluded)

Period	13%	14%	15%	16%	17%	18%	19%	20%	25%	30%	35%	40%	50%
1	0.885	0.877	0.870	0.862	0.855	0.847	0.840	0.833	0.800	0.769	0.741	0.714	0.667
2	1.668	1.647	1.626	1.605	1.585	1.566	1.547	1.528	1.440	1.361	1.289	1.224	1.111
3	2.361	2.322	2.283	2.246	2.210	2.174	2.140	2.106	1.952	1.816	1.696	1.589	1.407
4	2.974	2.914	2.855	2.798	2.743	2.690	2.639	2.589	2.362	2.166	1.997	1.849	1.605
5	3.517	3.433	3.352	3.274	3.199	3.127	3.058	2.991	2.689	2.436	2.220	2.035	1.737
6	3.998	3.889	3.784	3.685	3.589	3.498	3.410	3.326	2.951	2.643	2.385	2.168	1.824
7	4.423	4.288	4.160	4.039	3.922	3.812	3.706	3.605	3.161	2.802	2.508	2.263	1.883
8	4.799	4.639	4.487	4.344	4.207	4.078	3.954	3.837	3.329	2.925	2.598	2.331	1.922
9	5.132	4.946	4.772	4.607	4.451	4.303	4.163	4.031	3.463	3.019	2.665	2.379	1.948
10	5.426	5.216	5.019	4.833	4.659	4.494	4.339	4.192	3.571	3.092	2.715	2.414	1.965
11	5.687	5.453	5.234	5.029	4.836	4.656	4.486	4.327	3.656	3.147	2.752	2.438	1.977
12	5.918	5.660	5.421	5.197	4.988	4.793	4.611	4.439	3.725	3.190	2.779	2.456	1.985
13	6.122	5.842	5.583	5.342	5.118	4.910	4.715	4.533	3.780	3.223	2.799	2.469	1.990
14	6.302	6.002	5.724	5.468	5.229	5.008	4.802	4.611	3.824	3.249	2.814	2.478	1.993
15	6.462	6.142	5.847	5.575	5.324	5.092	4.876	4.675	3.859	3.268	2.825	2.484	1.995
16	6.604	6.265	5.954	5.668	5.405	5.162	4.938	4.730	3.887	3.283	2.834	2.489	1.997
17	6.729	6.373	6.047	5.749	5.475	5.222	4.988	4.775	3.910	3.295	2.840	2.492	1.998
18	6.840	6.467	6.128	5.818	5.534	5.273	5.003	4.812	3.928	3.304	2.844	2.494	1.999
19	6.938	6.550	6.198	5.877	5.584	5.316	5.070	4.843	3.942	3.311	2.848	2.496	1.999
20	7.025	6.623	6.259	5.929	5.628	5.353	5.101	4.870	3.954	3.316	2.850	2.497	1.999
25	7.330	6.873	6.464	6.097	5.766	5.467	5.195	4.948	3.985	3.329	2.856	2.499	2.000
30	7.496	7.003	6.566	6.177	5.829	5.517	5.235	4.979	3.995	3.332	2.857	2.500	2.000
40	7.634	7.105	6.642	6.233	5.871	5.548	5.258	4.997	3.999	3.333	2.857	2.500	2.000
50	7.675	7.133	6.661	6.246	5.880	5.554	5.262	4.999	4.000	3.333	2.857	2.500	2.000

appendix E

Time Value of Money and Investment Applications

Overview

Many applications for the time value of money exist. Applications use either the compound sum (sometimes referred to as *future value*) or the present value. Additionally some cash flows are annuities. An **annuity** represents cash flows that are equally spaced in time and are constant dollar amounts. Car payments, mortgage payments, and bond interest payments are examples of annuities. Annuities can either be present value annuities or compound sum annuities. In the next section, we present the concept of compound sum and develop common applications related to investments.

Compound Sum

Compound Sum: Single Amount

In determining the **compound sum,** we measure the future value of an amount that is allowed to grow at a given rate over a period of time. Assume an investor buys an asset worth $1,000. This asset (gold, diamonds, art, real estate, etc.) is expected to increase in value by 10 percent per year, and the investor wants to know what it will be worth after the fourth year. At the end of the first year, the investor will have $1,000 × (1 + 0.10), or $1,100. By the end of year two, the $1,100 will have grown by another 10 percent to $1,210 ($1,100 × 1.10). The four-year pattern is indicated below:

$$1\text{st year: } \$1{,}000 \times 1.10 = \$1{,}100$$
$$2\text{nd year: } \$1{,}100 \times 1.10 = \$1{,}210$$
$$3\text{rd year: } \$1{,}210 \times 1.10 = \$1{,}331$$
$$4\text{th year: } \$1{,}331 \times 1.10 = \$1{,}464$$

Appendix E Time Value of Money and Investment Applications

After the fourth year, the investor has accumulated $1,464. Because compounding problems often cover a long time, a generalized formula is necessary to describe the compounding process. We shall let:

S = Compound sum
P = Principal or present value
i = Interest rate, growth rate, or rate of return
n = Number of periods compounded

The simple formula is:

$$S = P(1 + i)^n \qquad \text{(E–1)}$$

In the preceding example, the beginning amount, P, was equal to $1,000; the growth rate, i, equaled 10 percent; and the number of periods, n, equaled 4, so we get:

$$S = \$1,000(1.10)^4, \text{ or } \$1,000 \times 1.464 = \$1,464$$

The term $(1.10)^4$ is found to equal 1.464 by multiplying 1.10 four times itself. This mathematical calculation is called an exponential, where you take (1.10) to the fourth power. On your calculator, you would have an exponential key y^x where y represents (1.10) and x represents 4. For students with calculators, we have prepared Appendix F for both Hewlett-Packard and Texas Instruments calculators.

For those not proficient with calculators or who have calculators without financial functions, Table E–1 is a shortened version of the compound sum table found in Appendix A. It can be used easily. The table tells us the amount $1 would grow to if it were invested for any number of periods at a given rate of return. Using this table for our previous example, we find an interest factor for the compound sum in the row where $n = 4$ and the column where $i = 10$ percent. The factor is 1.464, the same as previously calculated. We multiply this factor times any beginning amount to determine the compound sum.

When using compound sum tables to calculate the compound sum, we shorten our formula from $S = P(1 + i)^n$ to:

$$S = P \times S_{IF} \qquad \text{(E–2)}$$

where S_{IF} equals the interest factor for the compound sum found in Table E–1 or Appendix A. Using a new example, assume $5,000 is invested for 20 years at

TABLE E–1 Compound Sum of $1 ($S_{IF}$)

Periods	1%	2%	3%	4%	6%	8%	10%
1	1.010	1.020	1.030	1.040	1.060	1.080	1.100
2	1.020	1.040	1.061	1.082	1.124	1.166	1.210
3	1.030	1.061	1.093	1.125	1.191	1.260	1.331
4	1.041	1.082	1.126	1.170	1.262	1.360	1.464
5	1.051	1.104	1.159	1.217	1.338	1.469	1.611
10	1.105	1.219	1.344	1.480	1.791	2.159	2.594
20	1.220	1.486	1.806	2.191	3.207	4.661	6.727
30	1.348	1.811	2.427	3.243	5.743	10.063	13.268

6 percent. Using Table E–1, the interest factor for the compound sum would be 3.207, and the total value would be:

$$S = P \times S_{IF}(n = 20, i = 6\%)$$
$$= \$5,000 \times 3.207$$
$$= \$16,035$$

Example—Compound Sum, Single Amount

Problem: Mike Donegan receives a bonus from his employer of $3,200. He will invest the money at a 12 percent rate of return for the next eight years. How much will he have after eight years?

Solution: Compound sum, single amount:

$$S = P \times S_{IF} \quad (n = 8, i = 12\%) \quad \text{Appendix A}$$
$$= \$3,200 \times 2.476 = \$7,923.20$$

Compound Sum: Annuity

Our previous example was a one-time single investment. Let us examine a **compound sum of an annuity** where constant payments are made at equally spaced periods and grow to a future value. The normal assumption for a compound sum of an annuity is that the payments are made at the end of each period, so the last payment does not compound or earn a rate of return.

Figure E–1 demonstrates the timing and compounding process when $1,000 per year is contributed to a fund for four consecutive years. The $1,000 for each

FIGURE E-1 Compounding Process for Annuity

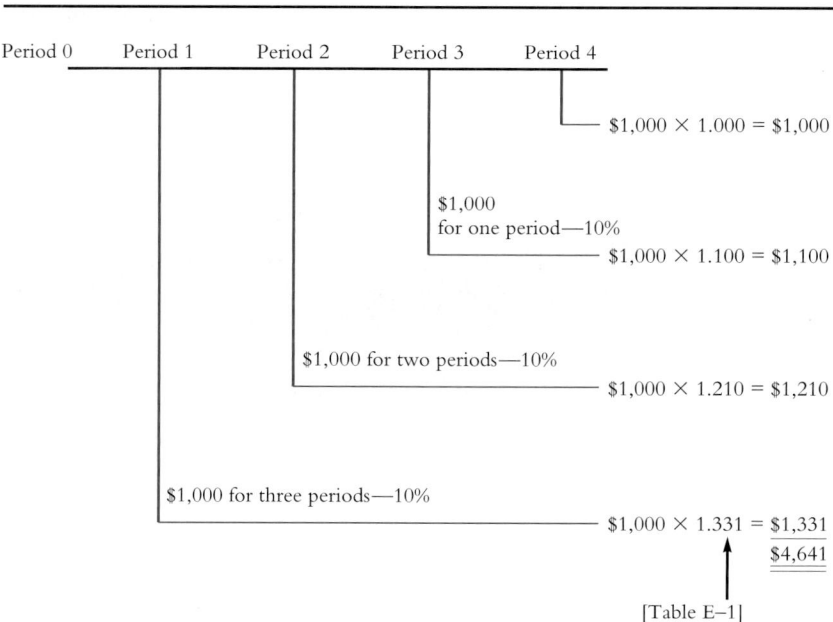

[Table E–1]

period is multiplied by the compound sum factors for the appropriate periods of compounding. The first $1,000 comes in at the end of the first period and has three periods to compound; the second $1,000 at the end of the second period, with two periods to compound; the third payment has one period to compound; and the last payment is multiplied by a factor of 1.00 showing no compounding at all.

Because compounding the individual values is tedious, compound sum of annuity tables can be used. These tables simply add up the interest factors from the compound sum tables for a single amount. Table E–2 is a shortened version of Appendix B, the compound sum of an annuity table showing the compound sum factors for a specified period and rate of return. Notice that all the way across the table, the factor in period one is 1.00. This reflects the fact that the last payment does not compound.

TABLE E–2 Compound Sum of an Annuity of $1 ($SA_{IF}$)

Periods	1%	2%	3%	4%	6%	8%	10%
1	1.000	1.000	1.000	1.000	1.000	1.000	1.000
2	2.010	2.020	2.030	2.040	2.060	2.080	2.100
3	3.030	3.060	3.091	3.122	3.184	3.246	3.310
4	4.060	4.122	4.184	4.246	4.375	4.506	4.641
5	5.101	5.204	5.309	5.416	5.637	5.867	6.105
10	10.462	10.950	11.464	12.006	13.181	14.487	15.937
20	22.019	24.297	26.870	29.778	36.786	45.762	57.275
30	34.785	40.588	47.575	56.085	79.058	113.280	164.490

One example of the compound sum of an annuity applies to the individual retirement account (IRA) and Keogh retirement plans. The IRA allows workers to invest $3,000 per year in a tax-free account and the Keogh allows a maximum of $40,000 per year to be invested in a retirement account for self-employed individuals.[1] Assume Dr. Piotrowski shelters $40,000 per year from age 35 to 65. If she makes 30 payments of $40,000 and earns a rate of return of 8 percent, her Keogh account at retirement would be more than $4 million.

$$S = R \times SA_{IF}(n = 30, i = 8\% \text{ return}) \quad \text{(E–3)}$$
$$= \$40,000 \times 113.280$$
$$= \$4,531,200$$

While this seems like a lot of money in today's world, we need to measure what it will buy 30 years from now after inflation is considered. One way to examine this is to calculate what the $40,000 payments would have to be if they only kept up with inflation. Let's assume inflation of 3 percent over the next 30 years and recalculate the sum of the annuity:

$$S = R \times SA_{IF}(n = 30, i = 3\% \text{ inflation})$$
$$= \$40,000 \times 47.575$$
$$= \$1,903,000$$

---

[1] The annual allowable deductibles are scheduled to increase between 2001 and 2011.

To maintain the purchasing power of each $40,000 contribution, Dr. Piotrowski needs to accumulate $1,903,000 at the estimated 3 percent rate of inflation. Since her rate of return of 8 percent is 5 percentage points higher than the inflation rate, she is adding additional purchasing power to her portfolio.

Example—Compound Sum, Annuity

Problem: Sonny Outlook invests $2,000 in an IRA at the end of each year for the next 40 years. With an anticipated rate of return of 11 percent, how much will the funds grow to after 40 years?

Solution: Compound sum, annuity:

$$S = R \times SA_{IF}(n = 40, i = 11\%) \quad \text{Appendix B}$$
$$= \$3,000 \times 581.83 = \$1,745,490$$

Present Value Concept

Present Value: Single Amount

The **present value** is the exact opposite of the compound sum. A future value is discounted to the present. For example, earlier we determined the compound sum of $1,000 for four periods at 10 percent was $1,464. We could reverse the process to state that $1,464 received four years from today is worth only $1,000 today if one can earn a 10 percent return on money during the four years. This $1,000 value is called its present value. The relationship is depicted in Figure E–2.

The formula for present value is derived from the original formula for the compound sum. As the following two formulas demonstrate, the present value is simply the inverse of the compound sum.

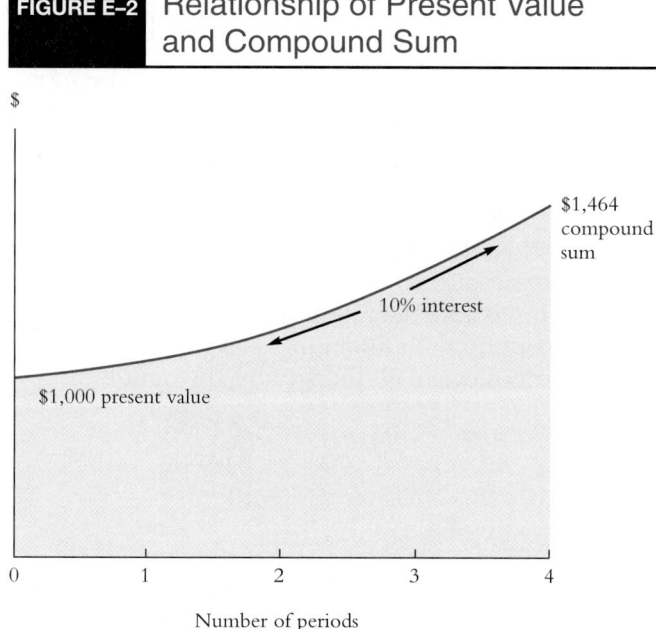

FIGURE E-2 Relationship of Present Value and Compound Sum

Appendix E Time Value of Money and Investment Applications

$$S = P(1 + i)^n \text{ Compound sum}$$
$$P = S \times 1/(1 + i)^n \text{ Present value}$$
(E–4)

The present value can be determined by solving for a mathematical solution to the above formula, or by using Table E–3, the Present Value of $1. When we use Table E–3, the present value interest factor $1/(1 + i)^n$ is found in the table and represented by PV_{IF}. We substitute it into the formula above:

$$P = S \times PV_{IF}$$
(E–5)

Let's demonstrate that the present value of $1,464, based on our assumptions, is worth $1,000 today:

$$P = S \times PV_{IF}(n = 4, i = 10\%) \quad \text{Table E–3 or Appendix C}$$
$$= \$1,464 \times 0.683$$
$$= \$1,000$$

TABLE E–3 Present Value of $1 ($PV_{IF}$)

Periods	1%	2%	3%	4%	6%	8%	10%
1	0.990	0.980	0.971	0.962	0.943	0.926	0.909
2	0.980	0.961	0.943	0.925	0.890	0.857	0.826
3	0.971	0.942	0.915	0.889	0.840	0.794	0.751
4	0.961	0.924	0.888	0.855	0.792	0.735	0.683
5	0.951	0.906	0.863	0.822	0.747	0.681	0.621
10	0.905	0.820	0.744	0.676	0.558	0.463	0.386
20	0.820	0.673	0.554	0.456	0.312	0.215	0.149
30	0.742	0.552	0.412	0.308	0.174	0.099	0.057

Present value becomes very important in determining the value of investments. Assume you think a certain piece of land will be worth $500,000 10 years from now. If you can earn a 10 percent rate of return on investments of similar risk, what would you be willing to pay for this land?

$$P = S \times PV_{IF}(n = 10, i = 10\%)$$
$$= \$500,000 \times 0.386$$
$$= \$193,000$$

This land's present value to you today would be $193,000. What would you have 10 years from today if you invested $193,000 at a 10 percent return? For this answer, we go to the compound sum factor from Table E–1 on page 659:

$$S = P \times S_{IF}(n = 10, i = 10\%)$$
$$= \$193,000 \times 2.594$$
$$= \$500,642$$

The compound sum would be $500,642. The two answers do not equal $500,000 because of the mathematical rounding used to construct tables with three decimal points. If we carry out the interest factors to four places, 0.386 becomes 0.3855 and 2.594 becomes 2.5937 and the two answers will be quite similar.

Near the end of the compound sum of an annuity section, we showed that Dr. Piotrowski could accumulate $3,398,400 by the time she retired in 30 years.

What would be the present value of this future sum if we brought it back to the present at the rate of inflation of 3 percent?

$$P = S \times PV_{IF}(n = 30, i = 3\%)$$
$$= \$3{,}398{,}400 \times 0.412$$
$$= \$1{,}400{,}141$$

The amount she will have accumulated will be worth $1,400,141 in today's dollars. If the rate of inflation averaged 6 percent over this time, the amount would fall to $591,322 ($3,398,400 × 0.174). Notice how sensitive the present value is to a 3 percentage point change in the inflation rate. Another concern is being able to forecast inflation correctly. These examples are simply meant to heighten your awareness that money has a time value and financial decisions require this to be considered.

Example—Present Value, Single Amount

Problem: Barbara Samuels received a trust fund at birth that will be paid out to her at age 18. If the fund will accumulate to $400,000 by then and the discount rate is 9 percent, what is the present value of her future accumulation?

Solution: Present value, single amount:

$$P = S \times PV_{IF}(n = 18, i = 9\%) \quad \text{Appendix C}$$
$$= \$400{,}000 \times 0.212 = \$84{,}800$$

Present Value: Annuity

To find the **present value of an annuity,** we are simply finding the present value of an equal cash flow for several periods instead of one single cash payment. The analysis is the same as taking the present value of several cash flows and adding them. Since we are dealing with an annuity (equal dollar amounts), we can save time by creating tables that add up the interest factors for the present value of single amounts and make present value annuity factors. We do this in Table E–4, a shortened version of Appendix D. Before using Table E–4, let's compute the present value of $1,000 to be received each year for five years at 6 percent. We could use the present value of five single amounts and Table E–3 on the previous page.

Period	Receipt	IF @ 6%	
1	$1,000 ×	0.943 =	$ 943
2	$1,000 ×	0.890 =	$ 890
3	$1,000 ×	0.840 =	$ 840
4	$1,000 ×	0.792 =	$ 792
5	$1,000 ×	0.747 =	$ 747
		4.212	$4,212 Present value

Another way to get the same value is to use Table E–4. The present value annuity factor under 6 percent and 5 periods is equal to 4.212, or the same value we got from adding the individual present value factors for a single amount. We can simply calculate the answer as follows:

where:

A = the present value of an annuity
R = the annuity amount
PVA_{IF} = the interest factor from Table E–4

Appendix E Time Value of Money and Investment Applications

TABLE E–4 Present Value of an Annuity of $1 ($PVA_{IF}$)

Periods	1%	2%	3%	4%	6%	8%	10%
1	0.990	0.980	0.971	0.962	0.943	0.926	0.909
2	1.970	1.942	1.913	1.886	1.833	1.783	1.736
3	2.941	2.884	2.829	2.775	2.673	2.577	2.487
4	3.902	3.808	3.717	3.630	3.465	3.312	3.170
5	4.853	4.713	4.580	4.452	4.212	3.993	3.791
8	7.652	7.325	7.020	6.773	6.210	5.747	5.335
10	9.471	8.983	8.530	8.111	7.360	6.710	6.145
20	18.046	16.351	14.877	13.590	11.470	9.818	8.514
30	25.808	22.396	19.600	17.292	13.765	11.258	9.427

$$A = R \times PVA_{IF}(n = 5, i = 6\%) \quad \text{(E–6)}$$
$$= \$1,000 \times 4.212$$
$$= \$4,212$$

Present value of annuities applies to many financial products such as mortgages, car payments, and retirement benefits. Some financial products such as bonds are a combination of an annuity and a single payment. Interest payments from bonds are annuities, and the principal repayment at maturity is a single payment. Both cash flows determine the present value of a bond.

Example—Present Value, Annuity

Problem: Ross "The Hoss" Sullivan has just renewed his contract with the Chicago Bears for an annual payment of $3 million per year for the next eight years. The newspapers report the deal is worth $24 million. If the discount rate is 14 percent, what is the true present value of the contract?

Solution: Present value, annuity:

$$A = R \times PVA_{IF}(n = 8, i = 14\%) \quad \text{Appendix D}$$
$$= \$3,000,000 \times 4.639 = \$13,917,000$$

Present Value: Uneven Cash Flow

Many investments are a series of uneven cash flows. For example, buying common stock generally implies an uneven cash flow from future dividends and the sale price. We hope to buy common stock in companies that are growing and have increasing dividends. Assume you want to purchase Caravan Motors common stock on January 1, 2004. You expect to hold the stock for five years and then sell it at $60 in December 2008. You also expect to receive dividends of $1.60, $2.00, $2.00, $2.50, and $3.00 during those five years.

What would you be willing to pay for the common stock if your required return on a stock of this risk is 14 percent. Let's set up a present value analysis for an uneven cash flow using Appendix C, the present value of a single amount. Since this is not an annuity, each cash flow must be evaluated separately. For simplicity, we assume all cash flows come at the end of the year. Also, the cash flow in year 2008 combines the $3.00 dividend and expected $60 sale price.

Year	Cash Flow	PV_{IF} 14%	Present Value
2004	$ 1.60	0.877	$ 1.40
2005	2.00	0.769	1.54
2006	2.00	0.675	1.35
2007	2.50	0.592	1.48
2008	63.00	0.519	32.70
Present value of Caravan Motors under these assumptions:			$38.47

If you were satisfied that your assumptions were reasonably accurate, you would be willing to buy Caravan at any price equal to or less than $38.47. This price will provide you with a 14 percent return if all your forecasts come true.

Example—Present Value, Uneven Cash Flow

Problem: Joann Zinke buys stock in Collins Publishing Company. She will receive dividends of $2.00, $2.40, $2.88, and $3.12 for the next four years. She assumes she can sell the stock for $50 after the last dividend payment (at the end of four years). If the discount rate is 12 percent, what is the present value of the future cash flows? (Round all values to two places to the right of the decimal point.) The present value of future cash flows is assumed to equal the value of the stock.

Solution: Present value, uneven cash flow:

Year	Cash Flow	PV_{IF} 12%	Present Value
1	$ 2.00	0.893	$ 1.79
2	2.40	0.797	1.91
3	2.88	0.712	2.05
4	53.12	0.636	33.78
			$39.53

The present value of the cash flows is $39.53.

Example—Present Value, Uneven Cash Flow

Problem: Sherman Lollar wins a malpractice suit against his accounting professor, and the judgment provides him with $3,000 a year for the next 40 years, plus a single lump-sum payment of $10,000 after 50 years. With a discount rate of 10 percent, what is the present value of his future benefits?

Solution: Present value, annuity plus a single amount:

Annuity

$$A = R \times PVA_{IF}(n = 40, i = 10\%) \quad \text{Appendix D}$$
$$= \$3{,}000 \times 9.779 = \$29{,}337$$

Single amount

$$P = S \times PV_{IF}(n = 50, i = 10\%) \quad \text{Appendix C}$$
$$= \$10{,}000 \times 0.009 = \$90$$

Total present value = $29,337 + $90 = $29,427

appendix F

Using Calculators for Financial Analysis

This appendix is designed to help you use either an algebraic calculator (Texas Instruments BA-35 Student Business Analyst) or the Hewlett-Packard 12C Financial Calculator. We realize that most calculators come with comprehensive instructions, and this appendix is only meant to provide basic instructions for commonly used financial calculations.

There are always two things to do before starting your calculations as indicated in the first table: clear the calculator, and set the decimal point. If you do not want to lose data stored in memory, do not perform steps 2 and 3 in the first box below.

Each step is listed vertically as a number followed by a decimal point. After each step you will find either a number or a calculator function denoted by a box ☐. Entering the number on your calculator is one step and entering the function is another. Notice that the HP 12C is color coded. When two boxes are found one after another, you may have an ☐ f ☐ or a ☐ g ☐ in the first box. An ☐ f ☐ is orange coded and refers to the orange functions above the keys. After typing the ☐ f ☐ function, you will automatically look for an orange-coded key to punch. For example, after ☐ f ☐ in the first Hewlett-Packard box (right-hand panel), you will punch in the orange-color-coded ☐ REG ☐. If the ☐ f ☐ function is not followed by another box, you merely type in ☐ f ☐ and the value indicated.

	Texas Instruments BA-35	Hewlett-Packard 12C
First clear the calculator.	1. ON/C ON/C	1. CLX Clears Screen
	2. 0	2. f
	3. STO Clears memory	3. REG Clears Memory
Set the decimal point. The TI BA-35 has two choices: 2 decimal points or variable decimal points. The screen will indicate Dec 2 or the decimal will be variable. The HP 12C allows you to choose the number of decimal points. If you are uncertain, just provide the indicated input exactly as shown on the right.	1. 2nd	1. f
	2. STO	2. 4 (# of decimals)

Appendix F Using Calculators for Financial Analysis

The [g] is coded blue and refers to the functions on the bottom of the function keys. After the [g] function key, you will automatically look for blue-coded keys. This first occurs on page 672 of this appendix.

Familiarize yourself with the keyboard before you start. In the more complicated calculations, keystrokes will be combined into one step.

In the first four calculations on this page and on page 669 we simply instruct you how to get the interest factors for Appendices A, B, C, and D. We have chosen to use examples as our method of instruction.

	Texas Instruments BA-35	**Hewlett-Packard 12C**
A. Appendix A Compound Sum of $1 $i = 9\%$ or 0.09; $n = 5$ years $S_{IF} = (1 + i)^n$ Sum = Present Value × S_{IF} $S = P \times S_{IF}$ Check the answer against the number in Appendix A. Numbers in the appendix are rounded. Try different rates and years.	To Find Interest Factor 1. 1 2. + 3. 0.09 (interest rate) 4. [=] 5. [y^x] 6. 5 (# of periods) 7. [=] answer 1.538624	To Find Interest Factor 1. 1 2. [enter] 3. 0.09 (interest rate) 4. [+] 5. 5 (# of periods) 6. [y^x] answer 1.5386
B. Appendix B Compound Sum of an Annuity of $1 $i = 9\%$ or 0.09; $n = 5$ years $SA_{IF} = \dfrac{(1 + i)^n - 1}{1}$ Sum = Receipt × SA_{IF} $S = R \times SA_{IF}$ Check your answer with Appendix B. Repeat example using different numbers and check your results with the number in Appendix B. Numbers in appendix are rounded.	To Find Interest Factor Repeat steps 1 through 7 in part A of this section. Continue with step 8. 8. [−] 9. 1 10. [−] 11. [÷] 12. 0.09 13. [=] answer 5.9847106	To Find Interest Factor Repeat steps 1 through 6 in part A of this section. Continue with step 7. 7. 1 8. [−] 9. 0.09 10. [÷] answer 5.9847

Appendix F Using Calculators for Financial Analysis

	Texas Instruments BA-35	Hewlett-Packard 12C
C. Appendix C Present Value of $1 $i = 9\%$ or 0.09; $n = 5$ years $PV_{IF} = (1 + i)^n$ Present Value = Sum × PV_{IF} $P = S \times PV_{IF}$ Check the answer against the number in Appendix C. Numbers in the appendix are rounded.	To Find Interest Factor Repeat steps 1 through 7 in part A of this section. Continue with step 8. 8. $\boxed{1/x}$ answer 0.6499314	To Find Interest Factor Repeat steps 1 through 6 in part A of this section. Continue with step 7. 7. $\boxed{1/x}$ answer 0.6499
D. Appendix D Present Value of an Annuity of $1 $i = 9\%$ or 0.09; $n = 5$ years $PV_{IF} = \dfrac{1 - [(1/(1+i)^n]}{i}$ Present Value = Annuity × PVA_{IF} $A = R \times PVA_{IF}$ Check your answer with Appendix D. Repeat example using different numbers and check your results with the number in Appendix D. Numbers in appendix are rounded.	To Find Interest Factor Repeat steps 1 through 8 in parts A and C. Continue with step 9. 9. $\boxed{-}$ 10. 1 11. $\boxed{}$ 12. $\boxed{+/-}$ 13. $\boxed{\div}$ 14. 0.09 15. $\boxed{=}$ answer 3.8896513	To Find Interest Factor Repeat steps 1 through 7 in parts A and C. Continue with step 8. 8. 1 9. $\boxed{-}$ 10. $\boxed{CH5}$ 11. 0.09 12. $\boxed{\div}$ answer 3.8897

On the following pages, you can determine bond valuation, yield to maturity, net present value of an annuity, net present value of an uneven cash flow, internal rate of return for an annuity, and internal rate of return for an uneven cash flow.

Bond Valuation Using Both the TI BA-35 and the HP 12C

Solve for V = Price of the bond, given:

C_t = $80 annual coupon payments or 8 percent coupon ($40 semiannually)
P_n = $1,000 principal (par value)
n = 10 years to maturity (20 periods semiannually)
i = 9.0 percent rate in the market (4.5 percent semiannually)

You may choose to refer to Chapter 12 for a complete discussion of bond valuation.

	Texas Instruments BA-35	Hewlett-Packard 12C
Bond Valuation	Set Finance Mode 2nd FIN	Clear Memory f REG
All steps begin with number 1. Numbers following each step are keystrokes followed by a box ☐. Each box represents a keystroke and indicates which calculator function is performed.	Set decimal to 2 places Decimal 2nd STO	Set decimal to 3 places f 3 1. 9.0 (yield to maturity)
The Texas Instruments calculator requires that data be adjusted for semiannual compounding; otherwise it assumes annual compounding.	1. 40 (semiannual coupon) 2. PMT 3. 4.5 (yield to maturity) semiannual basis	2. i 3. 8.0 (coupon in percent) 4. PMT
The Hewlett-Packard 12C internally assumes that semiannual compounding is used and requires annual data to be entered. The HP 12C is more detailed in that it requires the actual day, month, and year. If you want an answer for a problem that requires a given number of years (e.g., 10 years), simply start on a date of your choice and end on the same date 10 years later, as in the example.	4. %i 5. 1000 principal 6. FV 7. 20 (semiannual periods to maturity) 8. N 9. CPT 10. PV answer 934.96 Answer is given in dollars, rather than % of par value.	5. 1.092005 (today's date month-day-year)* 6. enter 7. 1.092015 (maturity date month-day-year)* 8. f 9. Price Answer 93.496 Answer is given as % of par value and equals $934.96. If Error message occurs, clear memory and start over. *See instructions in the third paragraph of the first column.

Yield to Maturity on Both the TI BA-35 and HP 12C

Solve for Y = Yield to maturity, given:

V = $895.50 price of bond
C_t = $80 annual coupon payments or 8 percent coupon ($40 semiannually)
P_n = $1,000 principal (par value)
n = 10 years to maturity (20 periods semiannually)

You may choose to refer to Chapter 12 for a complete discussion of yield to maturity.

	Texas Instruments BA-35	Hewlett-Packard 12C
Yield to Maturity	Set Finance Mode 2nd FIN	Clear Memory f REG
All steps are numbered. All numbers following each step are keystrokes followed by a box ☐. Each box represents a keystroke and indicates which calculator function is performed.	Set decimal to 2 places Decimal 2nd STO 1. 20 (semiannual periods)	Set decimal f 2 1. 89.55 (bond price as a percent of par) 2. PV 3. 8.0 (coupon in %)
The Texas Instruments BA-35 does not internally compute to a semiannual rate, so that data must be adjusted to reflect semiannual payments and periods. The answer received in step 10 is a semiannual rate, which must be multiplied by 2 to reflect an annual yield.	2. N 3. 1000 (par value) 4. FV 5. 40 (semiannual coupon)	4. PMT 5. 1.092005 (today's date)* 6. enter 7. 1.092015 (maturity date)*
The Hewlett-Packard 12C internally assumes that semiannual payments are made and, therefore, the answer in step 9 is the annual yield to maturity based on semiannual coupons. If you want an answer on the HP for a given number of years (e.g., 10 years), simply start on a date of your choice and end on the same date 10 years later, as in the example.	6. PMT 7. 895.50 (bond price) 8. PV 9. CPT 10. %i answer 4.83% 11. × 12. 2 13. = answer 9.65% (annual rate)	8. f 9. YTM answer 9.65% In case you receive an Error message, you have probably made a keystroke error. Clear the memory f REG and start over. *See instructions in the third paragraph of the first column.

Net Present Value of an Annuity on Both the TI BA-35 and the HP 12C

Solve for A = Present value of annuity, given:

n = 10 years (number of years cash flow will continue)
PMT = $5,000 per year (amount of the annuity)
i = 12 percent (cost of capital K_a)
Cost = $20,000

	Texas Instruments BA-35	Hewlett-Packard 12C
Net Present Value of an Annuity	Set Finance Mode 2nd FIN	Set decimal to 2 places
All steps are numbered and some steps include keystrokes. All numbers following each step are keystrokes followed by a box ⬚. Each box represents a keystroke and indicates which calculator function is performed on that number.	Set decimal to 2 places	f 2
	Decimal	f REG clears memory
	2nd STO	1. 20000 (cash outflow)
	1. 10 (years of cash flow)	2. CHS changes sign
The calculation for the present value of an annuity on the TI BA-35 requires that the project cost be subtracted from the present value of the cash inflows.	2. N	3. g
	3. 5000 (annual payments)	4. CFo
	4. PMT	5. 5000 (annual payments)
	5. 12 (cost of capital)	6. g CFj
The HP 12C could solve the problem exactly with the same keystrokes as the TI. However, since the HP uses a similar method to solve uneven cash flows, we elected to use the method that requires more keystrokes but which includes a negative cash outflow for the cost of the capital budgeting project.	6. %i	7. 10 g Nj (years)
	7. CPT	8. 12 i (cost of capital)
	8. PV	9. f NPV
	9. −	answer $8,251.12
	10. 20,000	If an Error message appears, start over by clearing the memory with
To conserve space, several keystrokes have been put into one step.	11. = answer $8,251.12	f REG

Net Present Value of an Uneven Cash Flow on Both the TI BA-35 and HP 12C

Solve for NPV = Net present value, given:

n = 5 years (number of years cash flow will continue)
PMT = $5,000 (yr. 1); 6,000 (yr. 2); 7,000 (yr. 3); 8,000 (yr. 4); 9,000 (yr. 5)
i = 12 percent (cost of capital K_a)
Cost = $25,000

Net Present Value of an Uneven Cash Flow

All steps are numbered and some steps include several keystrokes. All numbers following each step are keystrokes followed by a box ☐. Each box represents a keystroke and indicates which calculator function is performed on that number.

Because we are dealing with uneven cash flows, each number must be entered. The TI BA-35 requires that you make use of the memory. In step 2, you enter the future cash inflow in year 1, and in step 3, you determine its present value, which is stored in memory. After the first 1-year calculation, following year present values are calculated in the same way and added to the stored value using the SUM key. Finally, the recall key RCL is used to recall the present value of the total cash inflows.

The HP 12C requires each cash flow to be entered in order. The CFo key represents the cash flow in time period 0. The CFj key automatically counts the year of the cash flow in the order entered and so no years need to be entered. Finally, the cost of capital of 12% is entered and the f key and NPV key are used to complete the problem.

Texas Instruments BA-35

Clear memory ON/C 0 STO

Set decimal to 2 places

Decimal

2nd STO

Set finance mode

2nd FIN

1. 12 %i
2. 5000 FV
3. 1 N CPT PV SUM
4. 6000 FV
5. 2 N CPT PV SUM
6. 7000 FV
7. 3 N CPT PV SUM
8. 8000 FV
9. 4 N CPT PV SUM
10. 9000 FV
11. 5 N CPT PV SUM
12. RCL (answer 24420.90)
13. −
14. 25000 (cash outflow)
15. = answer −$579.10

Negative Net Present Value

Hewlett-Packard 12C

Set decimal to 2 places

f 2

f REG clears memory

1. 25000 (cash outflow)
2. CHS changes sign
3. g CFo
4. 5000 g CFj
5. 6000 g CFj
6. 7000 g CFj
7. 8000 g CFj
8. 9000 g CFj
9. 12 i
10. f NPV

answer −$579.10
Negative Net Present Value

If you receive an Error message, you have probably made a keystroke error. Clear memory with f REG

and start over with step 1.

Internal Rate of Return for an Annuity on Both the TI BA-35 and HP 12C

Solve for IRR = Internal rate of return, given:

n = 10 years (number of years cash flow will continue)
PMT = $10,000 per year (amount of the annuity)
Cost = $50,000 (this is the present value of the annuity)

	Texas Instruments BA-35	Hewlett-Packard 12C
Internal Rate of Return of an Annuity	Clear memory ON/C 0 STO	Set decimal to 2 places
	Set Finance Mode 2nd FIN	f 2
All steps are numbered and some steps include several keystrokes. All numbers following each step are keystrokes followed by a box ☐. Each box represents a keystroke and indicates which calculator function is performed on that number.	Decimal	f REG clears memory
	2nd STO	1. 5000 (cash outflow)
	1. 10 (years of cash flow)	2. CHS changes sign
	2. N	3. g
The calculation for the internal rate of return on an annuity using the TI BA-35 requires relatively few keystrokes.	3. 1000 (annual payments)	4. CFo
	4. PMT	5. 10000 (annual payments)
	5. 50000 (present value)	6. g Cfj
The HP 12C requires more keystrokes than the TI BA-35, because it needs to use the function keys f and g to enter data into the internal programs. The HP method requires that the cash outflow be expressed as a negative, while the TI BA-35 uses a positive number for the cash outflow.	6. PV	7. 10 g Nj (years)
	7. CPT	8. f IRR
	8. %i	answer is 15.10%
	answer is 15.10%	If an Error message appears, start over by clearing the memory with f REG
	At an internal rate of return of 15.10%, the present value of the $50,000 outflow is equal to the present value of $10,000 cash inflows over the next 10 years.	
To conserve space, several keystrokes have been put into one step.		

Internal Rate of Return with an Uneven Cash Flow on Both the TI BA-35 and HP 12C

Solve for IRR = Internal rate of return (return which causes present value of outflows to equal present value of the inflows), given:

n = 5 years (number of years cash flow will continue)
PMT = $5,000 (yr. 1); 6,000 (yr. 2); 7,000 (yr. 3); 8,000 (yr. 4); 9,000 (yr. 5)
Cost = $25,000

	Texas Instruments BA-35	Hewlett-Packard 12C
Internal Rate of an Uneven Cash Flow All steps are numbered and some steps include several keystrokes. All numbers following each step are keystrokes followed by a box ⬜. Each box represents a keystroke and indicates which calculator function is performed on that number. Because we are dealing with uneven cash flows, the mathematics of solving this problem with the TI BA-35 is not possible. A more advanced algebraic calculator would be required. However, for the student willing to use trial and error, the student can use the NPV method and try different discount rates until the NPV equals zero. Check Chapter 12 on methods for approximating the IRR. This will provide a start. The HP 12C requires each cash flow to be entered in order. The [CFo] key represents the cash flow in time period 0. The [CFj] key automatically counts the year of the cash flow in the order entered and so no years need to be entered. To find the internal rate of return, use the [f] [IRR] keys and complete the problem.	Clear memory [ON/C] 0 [STO] Set decimal to 2 places Decimal [2nd] [STO] Set finance mode [2nd] [FIN] 1. 12 [%i] (your IRR est.) 2. 5000 [FV] 3. 1 [N] [CPT] [PV] [STO] 4. 6000 [FV] 5. 2 [N] [CPT] [PV] [SUM] 6. 7000 [FV] 7. 3 [N] [CPT] [PV] [SUM] 8. 8000 [FV] 9. 4 [N] [CPT] [PV] [SUM] 10. 9000 [FV] 11. 5 [N] [CPT] [PV] [SUM] 12. [RCL] (answer 24,420.90) 13. [−] 14. 25000 (cash outflow) 15. [=] answer −$579.10 Negative NPV Start over with a lower discount rate (try 11.15). Answer is 24999.75. With a cash outflow of $25,000, the IRR would be 11.15%	Set decimal to 2 places [f] 2 [f] [REG] clears memory 1. 25000 (cash outflow) 2. [CHS] changes sign 3. [g] [CFo] 4. 5000 [g] [CFj] 5. 6000 [g] [CFj] 6. 7000 [g] [CFj] 7. 8000 [g] [CFj] 8. 9000 [g] [CFj] 9. [f] [IRR] answer 11.15% If you receive an Error message, you have probably made a keystroke error. Clear memory with [f] [REG] and start over with step 1.

glossary

A

abnormal return Gains beyond what the market would normally provide after adjustment for risk.

adjustable rate mortgage A mortgage in which the interest rate is adjusted regularly to current market conditions. It is sometimes referred to as a variable rate mortgage.

advances Increases in the prices of various stocks as measured between two points in time. Significant advances in a large number of stocks indicate a particular degree of market strength. *Also see* declines.

after-acquired property clause The stipulation in a mortgage bond indenture requiring all real property subsequently obtained by the issuing firm to serve as additional bond security.

aftermarket performance The price experience of new issues in the market.

alpha The value representing the difference between the return on a portfolio and a return on the market line that corresponds to a beta equal to the portfolio. A portfolio manager who performs at positive alpha levels would generate returns better than those available along the market line.

American depository receipts (ADRs) These securities represent the ownership interest in a foreign company's common stock. The process is as follows: The shares of the foreign company are purchased and put in trust in a foreign branch of a New York bank. The bank, in turn, receives and can issue depository receipts to the American shareholders of the foreign firm. These ADRs (depository receipts) allow foreign shares to be traded in the United States much like any other security. Through ADRs, one can purchase the stock of Sony Corporation, Honda Motor Co., Ltd., and hundreds of other foreign corporations.

annuities Cash flows that are equally spaced in time and are constant dollar amounts.

anomalies Deviations from the basic proposition that the market is efficient.

anticipated rate of inflation The expected rate of inflation that is included in the risk-free rate of return.

anticipated realized yield The return received on a bond held for a period other than that ending on the call date or the maturity date. In computing the anticipated realized yield, the investor considers both coupon payments and expected capital gains.

arbitrage An arbitrage is instituted when a simultaneous trade (a buy and a sale) occurs in two different markets and a profit is locked in.

arbitrage pricing theory A theory for explaining stock prices and stock returns. While the capital asset pricing model bases return solely on one form of systematic risk (market risk), arbitrage pricing theory can utilize several sources of risk (GDP, unemployment, etc.). Under this theory, it is assumed the investor will not be allowed to earn a return greater than that dictated by the various sensitivity factors affecting returns. To the extent that he does, arbitrageurs will eliminate the extra returns by selling the security and buying other comparable securities—thus the term *arbitrage pricing theory.* Unlike the capital asset pricing model, there is no necessity to define K_M (the market rate of return).

asset allocation The designation of assets in various categories for investment purposes. The typical allocation is between stock, bonds, and cash equivalents.

asset-utilization ratios Ratios that indicate the number of times per year that assets are turned over. They show the activity in the various asset accounts.

at-the-money An option on a stock that has a market value equal to the strike price.

automatic reinvestment plan A plan offered by a mutual fund in which the fund automatically reinvests all distributions to a shareholder account.

average differential return The alpha value that indicates the difference between the return on a portfolio or fund and a return on the market line that corresponds to a beta equal to the portfolio or fund.

B

back-end load An exit fee for selling a mutual fund.

balance sheet A financial statement that indicates, at a given point, what the firm owns and how these assets are financed in the form of liabilities and ownership interest.

balanced funds Mutual funds that combine investments in common stock, bonds, and preferred stock. Many balanced funds also invest in convertible securities as well. They try to provide income plus some capital appreciation.

banker's acceptance A short-term debt instrument usually issued in conjunction with a foreign trade transaction. The acceptance is a draft that is drawn on a bank for approval for future payment and is subsequently presented to the payer.

***Barron's* Confidence Index** An indicator utilized by technical analysts who follow smart money rules. Movements in the index measure the expectations of bond investors whom some technical analysts see as astute enough to foresee economic trends before the stock market has time to react.

basic earnings per share Earnings per share unadjusted for dilution.

basis The difference between the futures price and the value of the underlying item. Thus, on a stock index futures contract, basis represents the difference between the stock index futures price and the value of the underlying index. The basis may be either positive or negative, with the former indicating optimism and the latter signifying pessimism.

basis point One basis point is equal to 0.01 percent. It is used as a unit to measure changes in interest rates.

behavioral finance An offshoot of cognitive psychology which suggests that people are not consistent in how they view equivalent events if they are presented in different contexts. This behavior can lead to irrational investment decisions.

best efforts The issuing firm, rather than the investment banker, assumes the risk for a distribution. The investment banker merely agrees to provide his best effort to sell the securities.

beta A measurement of the volatility of a security with the market in general. A greater beta coefficient than 1 indicates systematic risk greater than the market, while a beta of less than 1 indicates systematic risk less than the market.

beta coefficient *See* beta.

beta-related hedge A stock index futures hedge in which the relative volatility of the portfolio to the market is considered in determining the number of contracts necessary to offset a given dollar level of exposure. If a portfolio has a beta greater than 1, then extra contracts may be necessary to compensate for high volatility.

beta stability The amount of consistency in beta values over time. Instability means prior beta values may not be reflective of future beta values.

Black-Scholes option pricing model A formal model used to determine the theoretical value of an option. Such factors as the riskless interest rate, the length of the option, and the volatility of the underlying security are considered. For a more complete discussion, see Appendix 15A.

blind pool A form of limited partnership for real estate investments in which funds are provided to the general partner to select properties for investment.

bond indenture A lengthy, complicated legal document that spells out the borrowing firm's responsibilities to the individual lenders in a bond issue.

bond mutual funds Mutual funds that specialize in bond investments and interest income.

bond price sensitivity The sensitivity of a change in bond prices to a change in interest rates. Bond price sensitivity is influenced by the duration of the bond in that the longer the duration of a bond, the greater the price sensitivity. A less sophisticated but acceptable approach is to tie price sensitivity to the maturity of the bond rather than the duration.

bond swaps The selling of a given bond position and immediately buying into another one with similar attributes in an attempt to improve overall portfolio return or performance.

bottom-up approach A method for choosing stocks that starts with picking *individual* companies and then looking at the industry and economy to see if there is any reason an investment in the company should not be made.

breadth of market indicators Overall market rules used by technical analysts in comparing broad market activity with trading activity in a few stocks. By comparing all advances and declines in NYSE-listed stocks, for example, with the Dow Jones Industrial Average, analysts attempt to judge when the market has changed directions.

bull spread An option strategy utilized when the expectation is that the stock price will rise. The opposite strategy is a bear spread.

business cycle Swings in economic activity encompassing expansionary and recessionary periods and, on average, occurring over four-year periods.

buying the spread A term indicating the cost from writing the call is more than the revenue of the short position. The opposite results in "selling the spread."

C

call option An option to buy 100 shares of common stock at a specified price for a given period.

call provision A mechanism for repaying funds advanced through a bond issue. A provision of the bond indenture allows the issuer to retire bonds before maturity by paying holders a premium above principal.

calls *See* call option.

capital appreciation A growth in the value of a stock or other investments as opposed to income from dividends or interest.

capital asset pricing model A model by which assets are valued based on their risk characteristics. The required return for an asset is related to its beta.

capital gain or loss Occurs when a stock held for investment purposes is sold at a gain or loss.

capital market line (CML) The graphic representation of the relationship of risks and returns with various portfolios of assets. The line is part of the capital asset pricing model.

cash or spot price The dollar value paid for the immediate transfer of a commodity.

cash settlement Closing out a futures or options contract for cash rather than calling for actual delivery of the underlying item specified in the contract—for example, pork bellies and T-bills. The stock index futures markets and stock index options markets are *purely* cash-settlement markets. There is never even the implied potential for future delivery of the S&P 500 Stock Index or other indexes.

CBOE Chicago Board Options Exchange, the first and largest exchange for options.

certificates of deposit Savings certificates that entitle the holder to the receipt of interest. These instruments are issued by commercial banks and savings and loans (or other thrift institutions).

certified financial planner (CFP) A financial planner who has been appropriately certified by the College for Financial Planning in Denver. He or she must demonstrate skills in risk management, tax planning, retirement and estate planning, and other similar areas.

chartered financial analyst (CFA) A security analyst or portfolio manager who has been appropriately certified through experience requirements and testing by the CFA Institute in Charlottesville, Virginia.

charting Use by technical analysts of charts and graphs to plot past stock price movements that are used to predict future prices.

circuit breakers Circuit breakers shut down the market for a period of time (usually 30 minutes) if there is a dramatic drop in stock prices.

closed-end fund A closed-end investment fund has a fixed number of shares, and purchasers and sellers of shares must deal directly with each other rather than with the fund. Closed-end funds trade on an exchange or over-the-counter.

coincident indicators Economic indicators that change direction at roughly the same time as the general economy.

combined earnings and dividend model A model combining earnings per share and an earnings multiplier with a finite dividend model. Value is derived from both the present value of dividends and the present value of the future price of the stock based on the earnings multiplier (P/E).

commercial paper A short-term credit instrument issued by large business corporations to the public. Commercial paper usually comes in minimum denominations of $25,000 and represents an unsecured promissory note.

commission broker An individual who represents a stock brokerage firm on the floor of an exchange and who executes sales and purchases stocks for the firm's clients across the nation.

commodities Such tangible items as livestock, farm produce, and precious metals. Users and producers of commodities hedge against future price fluctuations by transferring risks to speculators through futures contracts.

commodity futures A contract to buy or sell a commodity in the future at a given price.

comparable sales approach An approach to appraising real estate in which value is determined by the sales price for similar property.

compound sum The future value of an amount that is allowed to grow at a given interest rate over a period of time.

compound sum of an annuity Constant payments are made at equally spaced time periods and grow to a future value.

constant-dollar method Adjusting for inflation in the financial statements by using the consumer price index.

constant-growth model A dividend valuation model that assumes a constant growth rate for dividends.

construction and development trust A type of REIT that makes short-term loans to developers during their construction period.

Consumer Price Index An index used to measure the changes in the general price level.

contrary opinion rules Guidelines, based on such factors as the odd-lot or the short sales position, used by technical analysts who predict stock market activity on the assumption that such groups as small traders or short sellers are often wrong. *Also see* smart money rules.

conversion premium The amount, expressed as a dollar value or as a percentage, by which the price of the convertible security exceeds the current market value of the common stock into which it may be converted.

conversion price The face value of a convertible security divided by the conversion ratio gives the price of the underlying common stock at which the security is convertible. An investor would usually not convert the security into common stock unless the market price was greater than the conversion price.

conversion ratio The number of shares of common stock an investor receives when exchanging convertible bonds or shares of convertible preferred stock for shares of common stock.

conversion value The value of the underlying common stock represented by convertible bonds or convertible preferred stock. This dollar value is obtained by multiplying the conversion ratio by the per share market price of the common stock.

convertible security A corporate bond or a share of preferred stock that, at the option of the holder, can be converted into shares of common stock of the issuing corporation. Sometimes convertible securities can be exchanged for other assets or securities held by the issuing company.

correlation coefficient The measurement of joint movement between two variables.

cost approach An approach to appraising real estate (or other assets) in which value is determined by the cost to replace the asset at current prices.

coupon rate The stated, fixed rate of interest paid on a bond.

covered options The process of writing (selling) options on stock that is already owned.

covered writer A writer of an option who owns the stock on which the option is written. If the stock is not owned, the writer is deemed naked.

creditor claims Claims represented by debt instruments offered by financial institutions, industrial corporations, or the government.

cross hedge A hedging position in which one form of security is used to hedge another form of security (often because differences in maturity dates or quality characteristics make a perfect hedge difficult to establish).

currency fluctuations Changes in the relative value of one currency to another. For example, the French franc may advance or decline in relation to the dollar. To the extent a foreign currency appreciates relative to the dollar, returns on foreign investments will increase in terms of dollars. The opposite would be true for declining foreign currencies.

currency futures Futures contracts for speculation or hedging in different nations' currencies.

current-cost method Adjusting for inflation in the financial statements by revaluing assets at their current cost.

current ratio Current assets divided by current liabilities.

current yield The annual dollar amount of interest paid on a bond divided by the price at which the bond is currently trading in the market.

cyclical indicators Factors that economists can observe to measure the progress of economic cycles. Leading indicators move in a particular direction in advance of the movement of general business conditions, while lagging indicators change direction after general conditions, and coincident indicators move in unison with the economy.

cyclical industry An industry, such as automobiles, whose financial health is closely tied to the condition of the general economy. Such industries tend to make the type of products whose purchase can be postponed until the economy improves.

D

database A form of organized, stored data. It is usually fed into the computer for additional analysis.

debenture An unsecured corporate bond.

debt-utilization ratios Ratios that indicate how the firm is financed between debt (lenders) and equity (owners) and the firm's ability for meeting cash payments due on fixed obligations, such as interest, lease payments, licensing fees, or sinking-fund charges.

declines Decreases in the prices of various stocks as measured between two points in time. Significant declines in a large number of stocks indicate a particular degree of market weakness. *Also see* advances.

deep discount bond A bond that has a coupon rate far below rates currently available on investments and that consequently can be traded only at a significant discount from par value. It may offer an opportunity for capital appreciation.

deficit (government) The government spends more than it receives.

derivative products Securities that derive their existence from other items. Stock index futures and options are sometimes thought of as derivatives because they derive their existence from actual market indexes but have no intrinsic characteristics of their own.

diagonal spread A combination of a vertical and horizontal spread.

diluted earnings per share EPS adjusted for all potential dilution from the issuance of any new shares of common stock arising from convertible bonds, convertible preferred stock, warrants, or any other options outstanding.

dilution The reduction in earnings per share that occurs when earnings remain unchanged yet the number of shares outstanding increases, as in the conversion of convertible bonds or preferred stock into common stock.

direct equity claim Representation of ownership interests through common stock or other instruments to purchase common stock, such as warrants and options.

discount rate The interest rate at which future cash flows are discounted to a present value.

dispersion The distribution of values or outcomes around an expected value.

diversification Lack of concentration in any one item. A portfolio composed of many different securities is diversified.

diversification benefits Risk reduction through a diversification of investments. Investments that are negatively correlated or that have low positive correlation provide the best diversification benefits. Such benefits may be particularly evident in an internationally diversified portfolio.

dividend payout ratio Annual dividends per share divided by annual earnings per share.

dividend valuation model Any one of a number of stock valuation models based on the premise that the value of stock lies in the present value of its future dividend stream.

dividend yield Annual dividends per share divided by market price.

dollar-cost averaging The investor buys a fixed dollar's worth of a given security at regular intervals regardless of the security's price or the current market outlook. This provides a certain degree of discipline and also means more shares will be purchased at low prices rather than high prices since the amount of the regular investment is fixed and only the number of shares purchased varies.

dollar-denominated bonds Foreign bonds that are denominated (payable) in U.S. dollars.

Dow Jones Equity Market Index An index that includes 700 stocks in 82 industry groups. Unlike the Dow Jones Industrial Average, it includes stocks from the New York Stock Exchange, the American Stock Exchange, and the Nasdaq National Market System and is much more broadly based.

Dow Jones Industrial Average An index of stock market activity based on the price movements of 30 large corporations. The average is price-weighted, which means each stock is effectively weighted by the magnitude of its price.

Dow Jones World Industry Groups A table in *The Wall Street Journal* that shows the leading and lagging industries for a given day around the world. Specific price change information on more than 100 industries is also provided.

Dow Jones World Index An international stock index that covers 25 countries in three major sectors of the world. It shows this information individually and collectively.

Dow theory The theory, developed by Charles Dow in the late 1890s and still in use today, that the analysis of long-term (primary) stock market trends can yield accurate predictions for future price movements.

downside limit The lowest value a convertible bond should fall to based on its pure bond value (and an assumption that interest rates stay constant).

downside protection The protection that a convertible bond investor enjoys during a period of falling stock prices. While the underlying common stock and the convertible bond may both fall in value, the bond will fall only to a particular level because it has a fundamental, or pure, bond value based on its assured income stream.

downside risk The possibility that an asset, such as a security, may fall in value as a result of fundamental factors or external market forces. The limit of the downside risk for a convertible bond can be computed as the difference between the bond's market price and its pure bond value divided by the market price.

Du Pont analysis A system of analyzing return on assets through examining the profit margin and asset turnover. *Also*, the value of return on equity is analyzed through evaluating return on assets and the debt/total assets ratio.

duration The weighted average life of a bond. The weights are based on the present values of the individual cash flows relative to the present value of the total cash flows. Duration is a better measure than maturity when assessing the price sensitivity of bonds; that is, the impact of interest-rate changes on bond prices can be more directly correlated to duration than to maturity.

E

earnings per share The earnings available to holders of common stock divided by the number of common stock shares outstanding.

earnings valuation model Any one of a number of stock valuation models based on the premise that a stock's value is some appropriate multiple of earnings per share.

EBITDA Earnings before interest, taxes, depreciation, and amortization. It emphasizes operating income rather than the normally reported earnings after taxes.

Economic Growth and Tax Reconciliation Act of 2001 A tax act passed by the Bush administration that lowers marginal tax rates, phases out the estate tax, and provides a number of other tax benefits. It is scheduled to be rescinded in 2011 unless it is renewed.

effective diversification The diversification of a portfolio to remove unsystematic risk.

efficient frontier A set of investment portfolios in which the investor receives maximum return for a given level of risk or a minimum risk for a given level of return.

efficient hedge A hedge in which one side of the transaction effectively covers the exposed side in terms of movement.

efficient market The capacity of the market to react to new information, to avoid rapid price fluctuations, and to engage in increased or reduced trading volume without realizing significant price changes. In an efficient market environment, securities are assumed to be correctly priced at any point in time.

efficient market hypothesis (EMH) The concept that there are many participants in the securities markets who are profit maximizing and alert to information so that there is almost instant adjustment to new information. The weak form of this hypothesis suggests there is no relationship between past and future prices. The semistrong form maintains that all forms of public information are already reflected in the price of a security, so fundamental analysis cannot determine under- or overvaluation. The strong form suggests that all information, insider as well as public, is impounded in the value of a security.

efficient portfolio A portfolio that combines assets so as to minimize the risk for a given level of return.

Electronic Book The database system that covers all stocks listed on the New York Stock Exchange and keeps track of limit orders and market orders for the specialist.

electronic communication networks (ECNs) These are electronic trading systems that automatically match buy and sell orders at specified prices. ECNs are also known as alternative trading systems (ATSs) and have been given Security Exchange Commission approval to be more fully integrated into the national market system by choosing to either act as a broker-dealer or as an exchange.

emerging countries Foreign countries that have not fully developed their economic systems and productive capacity. Examples might include Chile, Jordan, Korea, Thailand, and Zimbabwe. A number of these emerging countries may represent good risk-reduction potential for U.S. investors because the factors that influence their economic welfare may be quite different from critical factors in the United States. Investments in these countries, at times, may also provide high returns.

equal-weighted index Each stock, regardless of total market value or price, is weighted equally. It is as if there were $100 invested in every stock in the index. The Value Line Index is a prime example of an equal-weighted index.

equipment trust certificate A secured debt instrument used by firms in the transportation industry that provides for bond proceeds to purchase new equipment, which in turn is collateral for the bond issue.

equity participation The lender also participates in an ownership interest in the property.

equity risk premium (ERP) An extra return that the stock market must provide over the rate on Treasury bills to compensate for market risk. It is defined as $(K_M - R_F)$ or the expected rate of return for common stocks in the market minus the risk-free rate.

equity trust A type of REIT that buys, operates, and sells real estate as an investment as opposed to mortgage trusts.

Eurodollar bonds Bonds that are denominated (payable) in dollars but that are issued and traded outside the United States.

excess returns Returns in excess of the risk-free rate or in excess of a market measure such as the S&P 500 Stock Index.

exchange listing A firm lists its shares on an exchange (such as the American or New York Stock Exchange).

exchange privilege A feature offered by a mutual fund sponsor in which a shareholder is able to move money between various funds under the management of the sponsor at a very minimal processing charge and without a commission.

exchange traded funds (ETFs) The American Stock Exchange created exchange traded funds that are similar to index mutual funds. Their structure is different than mutual funds but they allow an investor to buy an index such as the Standard and Poor's 500 on the AMEX just the same as buying common stock.

exercise price (warrant) The price at which the stock can be bought using the warrant.

expectations hypothesis The hypothesis that explains the term structure of interest rates, stating that a long-term interest rate is the average of expected short-term interest rates over the applicable time period. If, for example, long-term rates are higher than short-term rates, then according to the expectations hypothesis, investors must expect that short-term rates will be increasing in coming periods.

expected value The sum of possible outcomes times their probability of occurrence.

extraordinary gains and losses Gains or losses from the sale of corporate fixed assets, lawsuits, or similar events that would not be expected to occur often, if ever again.

F

Fed The Federal Reserve serves as the central banking authority for the United States. The Fed enacts monetary policy, and it plays a major role in regulating commercial banking operations and controlling the money supply.

federal deficit A situation in which the federal government spends more money than it receives through taxes and other revenue sources.

federal surplus A situation in which taxes and other government revenues provide more money than is needed to cover government expenditures.

FIFO A method of inventory valuation in which it is assumed that inventory purchased first is sold first (first-in, first-out).

financial asset A financial claim on an asset (rather than physical possession of a tangible asset) usually documented by a legal instrument, such as a stock certificate.

financial futures A contract to trade futures on interest rates, foreign exchange, and stock indexes.

financial hedging Reducing exposure to financial risks such as changes in interest rates, currency value or stock price. Hedging may entirely or partially eliminate negative effects of a market movement.

financial-service companies Firms that provide a broad range of financial services to diversify their consumer base. Services may include brokerage activities, insurance, banking, and so forth.

fiscal policy Government spending and taxing practices designed to promote or inhibit various economic activities.

floating-rate notes The coupon rate on the note or bond is fixed for only a short time and then varies with a stipulated short-term rate such as the rate on U.S. Treasury bills.

floor broker An independent stockbroker who is a member of a stock exchange and who executes trades, for a fee, for commission brokers experiencing excessive volumes of trading.

floor value A value that an income-producing security will not fall below because of the fundamental value attributable to its assured income stream.

flow-of-funds analysis Analysis of the pattern of financial payments between business, government, and households.

forced conversion When the company calls the convertible security knowing that the owners will take the stock and thus convert the debt to equity.

foreign currency effects To the extent a foreign currency appreciates relative to the dollar, returns on foreign investments will increase in terms of dollars. The opposite would be true for declining foreign currencies.

foreign funds Mutual funds that specialize in foreign markets and foreign securities.

foreign-pay bonds Bonds issued in a foreign country and payable in that country's currency. For example, a Japanese government bond payable in yen would represent a foreign-pay bond.

foreign political risks The risks associated with investing in firms operating in foreign countries. There is the danger of nationalization of foreign firms or the blockage of capital flows to investors. There also may be the danger of violent overthrow of the political party in power, with all the associated implications. Punitive legislation against foreign firms or investors is another political risk.

fourth market The direct trading between large institutional investors in blocks of listed stocks. The participants avoid paying brokerage commissions.

free cash flow After-tax earnings plus depreciation (and amortization) less necessary capital expenditures and anticipated dividend payments. Free cash flow emphasizes the amount of funds available to redeploy in the business or to be used for acquisitions.

fundamental analysis The valuation of stocks based on fundamental factors, such as company earnings, growth prospects, and so forth.

funded pension plan Current income is charged with pension liabilities in advance of the actual payment, and funds are set aside.

futures contract An agreement that provides for sale or purchase of a specific amount of a commodity at a designated time in the future at a given price.

futures contract on a stock market index A futures contract based on a market index, such as the Standard & Poor's 500 Stock Index or the NYSE Composite Index.

G

general obligation issue A municipal bond backed by the full faith, credit, and "taxing power" of the issuing unit rather than the revenue from a given project.

GNMA (Ginnie Mae) pass-through certificates Fixed-income securities that represent an undivided interest in a pool of federally insured mortgages. GNMA, the Government National Mortgage Association, buys a pool of securities from various lenders at a discount and then issues securities to the public against these mortgages.

going public Selling privately held shares to new investors in the over-the-counter market for the first time.

government securities Bonds issued by federal, state, or local governmental units or government agencies. Whereas corporate securities' returns are paid through company earnings, government securities are repaid through taxes or the revenues from projects financed by the bonds.

graduated payment mortgage A type of mortgage in which payments start out on a relatively low basis and increase over the life of the loan.

greed index A contrary opinion index that measures how "greedy" investors are. Greed is thought to be synonymous with bullish sentiment, or optimism. Under the assumptions of the greed index, the more greedy or optimistic investors are, the more likely the market is to fall and vice versa.

gross domestic product (GDP) A measure of output from United States factories and related consumption in the United States. It does not include products made by U.S. companies in foreign markets.

growth company A company that exhibits rising returns on assets each year and sales that are growing at an increasing rate (growth phase of the life-cycle curve). Growth companies may not be as well known as growth stocks.

growth funds Mutual funds with the primary objective of capital appreciation.

growth stock The stock of a firm generally growing faster than the economy or market norm.

growth-with-income funds Mutual funds that combine a strategy of capital appreciation with income generation.

H

hedge funds A generic name for funds that engage in a wide set of activities at one time in an attempt to generate a superior return. They normally are neither bullish nor bearish, but engage in buying, short selling, transacting in puts and calls, etc.

hedging A process for lessening or eliminating risk by taking a position in the market opposite to your original position. For example, someone who owns wheat can sell a futures contract to protect against future price declines.

hidden assets Assets that are not readily apparent to investors in a traditional sense, but add substantial value to the firm.

horizontal spread Buying and writing two options with the same strike price but maturing in different months.

hybrid trust A form of REIT that engages in the activities of both equity trusts and mortgage trusts.

I

Ibbotson study A study examining comparative returns on stocks and fixed-income securities from the mid-1920s to the present.

immunization Immunizing or protecting a bond portfolio against the effects of changing interest rates on the ending value of the portfolio. The process is usually tied to a time horizon. In the process, if interest rates go up, there will be a decline in the value of the portfolio, but a higher reinvestment rate opportunity for inflows. Conversely, if interest rates go down, there will be capital appreciation for the portfolio, but a lower reinvestment rate opportunity. By tying all the investment decisions to a specified duration period, the portfolio manager can take advantage of these counter forces to ensure a necessary outcome.

income bond A corporate debt instrument on which interest is paid only if funds are available from current income.

income approach An approach to appraising real estate by dividing annual net operating income by an appropriate capitalization rate, which is based on the required return by investors on similar-type property.

income statement A financial statement that shows the profitability of a firm over a given period.

income-statement method A method of forecasting earnings per share based on a projected income statement.

index fund A fund investing in a portfolio of corporate stocks, the composition of which is determined by the Standard & Poor's 500 Index or some other index.

indifference curves These curves show the investor's trade-off between risk and return. The steeper the slope of the curve, the more risk-averse the investor is.

indirect equity claim An indirect claim on common stock such as that achieved by placing funds in investment companies.

individual retirement account (IRA) An IRA allows a qualifying taxpayer to deduct $3,000 from taxable income and invest the funds at a bank, savings and loan, brokerage house, mutual fund, or other financial institution. The funds are normally placed in interest-bearing instruments, or perhaps in other securities, such as common stock. The income on the funds is allowed to grow tax-free until withdrawn at retirement. The annual allowable deduction is scheduled to increase to $5,000 over the decade.

industry factors The unique attributes that must be considered in analyzing a given industry or group of industries. Examples include industry structure, supply/demand of labor and materials, and government regulation.

industry life cycles Cycles that are created because of economic growth, competition, availability of resources, and the resultant market saturation of the particular goods and services offered. The stages are development, growth, expansion, maturity, and decline.

inflation A general increase in the prices of goods and services.

inflation-adjusted accounting Restating financial statements to show the effect of inflation on the balance sheet and income statement. This is supplemental to the normal presentation based on historical data.

inflationary expectations A value representing future expectations about the rate of inflation. This value, combined with the real rate of return, provides the risk-free required return for the investor.

initial public offering (IPO) The process of bringing private companies to the public market for the first time.

insider trading Trading by those who had special access to unpublished information. If the information is used to illegally make a profit, there may be large fines and possible jail sentences.

institutional investor A type of investor (as opposed to individual investors) representing organizations responsible for bringing together large pools of capital for investment. Institutional investors include investment companies, pension funds, life insurance companies, bank trust departments, and endowments and foundations.

in-the-money A term that indicates when the market price of a stock is above the striking price of the call option. When the strike price is above the market price, the call option is out of the money.

interest-rate futures Futures contracts involving Treasury bills, Treasury bonds, Treasury notes, commercial paper, certificates of deposit, and GNMA certificates.

interest-rate swaps The trading of interest rate exposure between two or more parties so that each participant may be able to rebalance his portfolio with less risk. Fixed-rate exposure and variable-rate exposure are normally exchanged.

international tax problems Many foreign countries impose a 7.5 to 15 percent withholding tax against the dividends or interest paid to nonresident holders of equity or debt securities. However, it is often possible for tax-exempt U.S. investors to secure an exemption or rebate on part or all of the withholding tax. *Also*, taxable U.S. investors can normally claim a U.S. tax credit for taxes paid in foreign countries. The problem is more likely to be one of inconvenience and paper shuffling rather than loss of funds.

internationally oriented funds Mutual funds and closed-end investment companies that invest in worldwide securities. Some funds specialize in Asian holdings, others in South African, and so on.

intrinsic value Value of a warrant or option equal to market price minus the strike (exercise) price.

inverse pyramiding A process of leveraging to control commodities contracts in which the profits from one contract are used to purchase another contract on margin, and profits on this contract are applied to a third, and so on.

investment The commitment of current funds in anticipation of the receipt of an increased return of funds at some point.

investment banker One who is primarily involved in the distribution of securities from the issuing corporation to the public. An investment banker also advises corporate clients on their financial strategy and may help to arrange mergers and acquisitions.

investment banking The underwriting and distribution of a new security issue in the primary market. The investment banker advises the issuing concern on price and other terms and normally guarantees sale while overseeing distribution of the securities through the selling brokerage houses.

investment companies A type of financial institution that takes proceeds of individual investors and reinvests them in securities according to their specific objectives. A popular type of investment company is the mutual fund.

J

Jensen measure of portfolio performance Jensen compares excess returns (total portfolio returns minus the risk-free rate) to what should be required in the market based on the portfolio beta. For example, if the portfolio beta is 1, the portfolio has a systematic risk equal to the market, and the expected portfolio excess returns should be equal to market excess returns (the market rate of return minus the risk-free rate). The question then becomes: Did the portfolio manager do better or worse than expected? The portfolio manager's excess returns can be compared to the market line of expected excess returns for any beta level.

junk bonds (high-yield bonds) High-risk, low-grade bonds rated below BBB. They often perform like common stock and may provide interesting investment opportunities.

K

K_e The term representing required rate of return based on the capital asset pricing model. It is the discount rate applied to future dividends and price.

key indicators Various market observations used by technical analysts to predict the direction of future market trends. Examples include the contrary opinion and smart money rules.

L

lagging indicators Economic indicators that usually change direction after business conditions have turned around.

leading indicators Economic indicators that change direction in advance of general business conditions.

least squares trend analysis A statistical methodology to make projections.

least squares trendline A trendline that minimizes the squared distance of the individual values from the line.

leveraged buyouts The management of the company or some other investor group borrows the needed cash to repurchase all the shares of an existing company. The balance sheet of the company serves as the collateral base to make the borrowing possible. After the leveraged buyout, the company may be taken private for a time in which unprofitable assets are sold and debt reduced. The intent is then to bring the company to the public market once again (or resell it to another company) at a large profit over the initial purchase price.

LIFO A method of inventory valuation in which it is assumed inventory purchased last is sold first (last-in, first-out).

limit order A condition placed on a transaction executed through a stockbroker to assure that securities will be sold only if a specified minimum price is received or purchased only if the price to be paid is no more than a given maximum.

limited partnership A business arrangement in which there is the limited liability protection of a corporation with the tax provisions of a regular partnership. All profits or losses are directly assigned to the partners. The general partner has unlimited liability.

Lipper Mutual Fund Investment Performance Averages Lipper publishes indexes for growth funds, growth-with-income funds, and balanced funds. Lipper also shows year-to-date and weekly performance for many other categories of funds.

liquidity The capacity of an investment to be retired for cash in a short period with a minimum capital loss.

liquidity preference theory A theory related to the term structure of interest rates. The theory states the term structure tends to be upward sloping more than any other pattern. This reflects a recognition of the fact that long maturity obligations are subject to greater price change movements than short maturity obligations when interest rates change. Because of increased risk of holding longer-term maturities, investors demand a higher return to hold such securities. Thus, they have a preference for short-term liquid obligations.

liquidity ratios Ratios that demonstrate the firm's ability to pay off short-term obligations as they come due.

load fund A mutual fund that charges a commission.

long position A market transaction in which an investor purchases securities with the expectation of holding the securities for cash income or for resale at a higher price in the future. *Also see* short position.

long-term anticipation securities (LEAPS) Longer-term options with expiration dates of up to two years.

Lorie and Fisher study A University of Chicago study indicating comparative returns on financial assets over half a decade. It is similar to the Ibbotson and Sinquefield study in many respects.

low-load fund The commission or load is only 2 to 3 percent instead of the normal 7.25 percent.

M

Macaulay duration The standard definition of duration of a bond, which is based on the weighted average life as represented by the present value of cash inflows.

margin account A trading account maintained with a brokerage firm on which the investor may borrow a percentage of the funds for the purchase of securities. The broker lends the funds at interest slightly above the prime rate.

margin maintenance requirement The amount of money that must be "deposited" to hold a margin position if losses reduce the initial margin that was put up.

margin requirements The amount of money that must be "deposited" to purchase a commodity contract or shares of stock on margin.

market A mechanism for facilitating the exchange of assets through buyer-seller communication. The communication, and not a central negotiating location, is the requisite condition for a market to exist, though some transactions (for example, trades at the various stock exchanges) do involve a direct meeting of buyers and sellers or their agents.

market capitalization The total market value of the firm. It is computed by multiplying shares outstanding times stock price.

market line On a graph, excess returns are shown on the vertical axis, the portfolio beta is shown on the horizontal axis, and the market line describes the relationship between the two.

market rate of interest The coupon rate of interest paid on bonds currently issued. Of course, a previously issued bond that is currently traded may be sold at a discount or a premium so that the buyer in effect receives the market rate even if the coupon rate on this older bond is substantially higher or lower than market rates. The market rate is also known as the yield to maturity.

market segmentation theory A theory related to the term structure of interest rates that focuses on the demand side of the market. There are several large institutional participants in the bond market, each with its own maturity preferences. Banks tend to prefer short-term liquid securities to match the nature of their deposits, whereas life insurance companies prefer long-term bonds to match their long-run obligations. The behavior of these two institutions and of savings and loans often creates pressure on short-term or long-term rates but very little on the intermediate market of five- to seven-year maturities. This theory helps to focus on the accumulation or liquidation of securities by institutions during the different phases of the business cycle and the resultant impact on the yield curve.

maturity date The date at which outstanding principal must be repaid to bondholders.

merger price premium The difference between the offering price per share and the market price per share of the merger candidate (before the impact of the offer).

modified duration Macaulay duration divided by one plus yield to maturity. It provides a better measure of bond price sensitivity to interest rate changes than does Macaulay duration.

monetarist An economic analyst who believes monetary policy tools, and not fiscal policy, can best provide a stable environment of sustained economic growth.

monetary policy Direct control of interest rates or the money supply undertaken by the Federal Reserve to achieve economic objectives. Used in some cases to augment or offset the use of fiscal policy.

money market account Accounts offered by financial institutions to compete with money market funds. The minimum deposit is $500 to $1,000, with a maximum of three checks drawn per month.

money market fund A type of mutual fund that invests in short-term government securities, commercial paper, and repurchase agreements. Most offer check-writing privileges.

money supply The level of funds available at a given time for conducting transactions in our economy. The Federal Reserve can influence the money supply through its monetary policy tools. There are many different definitions of the money supply. For example, M1 is currency in circulation plus private checking deposits, including those in interest-bearing NOW accounts. M2 adds in savings accounts and money market mutual funds, and so on.

monopolies Dominance of an industry by one company. Monopolies are not common in the United States due to antitrust laws, but they do exist by government permission in the area of public utilities.

mortgage A lien against real property.

mortgage trust A form of REIT in which long-term loans are made to real estate investors.

multinational corporations Firms that have operations in a number of countries. Multinationals are frequently found in such industries as oil, mainframe computers, and banking.

municipal bonds Tax-exempt debt securities issued by state and local governments (including special political subdivisions).

mutual fund A pooling of funds by investors for reinvestment. The funds are administered by professional managers. Technically, only an open-end (see definition) investment fund is considered to be a mutual fund.

mutual fund cash position An overall market rule that asserts that by examining the level of uncommitted funds held by large institutional investors, analysts can measure the potential demand for stocks and thereby anticipate market movements.

N

naked options The process of writing (selling) options on a stock that is not currently owned. It is highly speculative.

Nasdaq indexes Index measures for components of the over-the-counter market. The OTC Indexes are value-weighted.

Nasdaq Stock Market Nasdaq was formerly referred to as the National Association of Securities Dealers Automated Quotation system. This is where all over-the-counter stocks trade through electronic medium. Eventually the over-the-counter market became known as the Nasdaq Stock Market.

net asset value The net asset value (NAV) represents the current value of an investment fund. It is computed by taking the total value of the securities, subtracting out the liabilities, and dividing by the shares outstanding.

net debtor-creditor hypothesis Since inflation makes each dollar worth less, it is often argued that a person or firm that is a net debtor gains from inflation because payments of interest and return of principal are made with continually less valuable dollars. Conversely, a net creditor loses real capital because the loans are repaid in less valuable dollars.

net working capital Current assets minus current liabilities.

New York Stock Exchange Index A market value-weighted measure of stock market changes for all stocks listed on the NYSE.

no-load mutual fund A mutual fund on which no sales commission must be paid. The fund's shares are sold, not through brokers, but rather through the mail or other direct channels.

nominal GNP Gross national product expressed in current, noninflation-adjusted dollars.

nominal return A return that has not been adjusted for inflation.

nonconstant growth model Dividend valuation model that does not assume a constant growth rate for dividends.

O

odd-lot dealer A member of a stock exchange who maintains an inventory of a particular firm's stock in order to sell odd lots (trades of less than 100 shares) to customers of the exchange.

odd-lot theory The contrary opinion rule stating that small traders (who generally buy or sell odd lots) often misjudge market trends, selling just before upturns and buying before downturns. The theory has not been useful in predicting trends observed in recent years.

oligopolies Industries that have few competitors. Oligopolies are quite common in large, mature U.S. industries such as automobiles, steel, oil, airlines, and aluminum. The competition between companies in an oligopoly can be intense, and profitability can suffer as a result of price wars and battles over market share. Increasingly, obligopolistic industries are facing international competition, which has altered their competitive strategies.

online broker A brokerage firm that executes transactions on its Internet website at a minimum cost to the customer.

open-end fund An open-end investment fund stands ready at all times to sell or redeem shares from stockholders. There is no limit to the number of shares. Technically, a mutual fund is considered to be an open-end investment fund. *Also see* closed-end fund.

open-market operations The Federal Reserve's action of buying or selling government securities to expand or contract the amount of money in the economy.

operating margin Operating income divided by sales.

option The right acquired for a consideration to buy or sell something at a fixed price within a specified period.

option premium The intrinsic value plus a speculative premium.

option price The specified price at which the holder of a warrant may buy the shares to which the warrant entitles purchase.

Options Clearing Corporation Issues all options listed on the exchanges that trade in options.

options on industry indexes An option index contract tailored to a given industry. Thus, one who wishes to speculate on a given industry's performance or hedge against holdings in that industry can use industry index options (subindexes).

options to purchase stock index futures An option to purchase a stock index futures contract at a specified price over a given time. This security combines the options concept with the futures concept.

organized exchanges Institutions, such as the New York Stock Exchange, the American Stock Exchange, or any of the smaller regional exchanges, that provide a central location for the buying and selling of securities.

OTC National Market system A segment of the OTC stock market made up of stocks that have a diversified geographical stockholder base and relatively large activity in their securities. Stocks in the National Market system receive enhanced market activity reporting through the NASDAQ system.

out-of-the-money The strike price is above the market price of a stock on a call option or below the market price of a stock on a put option.

overall market rules Guidelines, such as breadth of market indicators or mutual fund cash positions, used by technical analysts who predict stock market activity based on past activity.

over-the-counter market Not a specific location but rather a communications network through which trades of bonds, nonlisted stocks, and other securities take place. Trading activity is overseen by the National Association of Securities Dealers (NASD).

P

par bonds Bonds that are selling at their par or maturity values rather than at premium or discounted prices. Par value on a corporate bond is generally $1,000.

par value (bond) The face value of a bond, generally $1,000 for corporate issues, with higher denominations for many government issues.

parity price The price to compensate for inflation exposure.

partial hedge A hedge position in which only part of the risk is eliminated or lessened.

peak The point in an economic cycle at which expansion ends and a recession begins.

perpetual bond A bond with no maturity date.

personal savings/personal disposable income The rate at which people are saving their disposable income. This has implications for the generation of funds to modernize plant and equipment and increase productivity.

portfolio The term applied to a collection of securities or investments.

portfolio effect The effect obtained when assets are combined into a portfolio. The interaction of the assets can provide risk reduction such that the portfolio standard deviation may be less than the standard deviation of any one asset in it.

portfolio insurance Protecting a large portfolio against a decline. A common strategy is to sell stock index futures contracts in anticipation of a decline.

portfolio manager One responsible for managing large pools of funds. Portfolio managers may be employed by insurance companies, mutual funds, bank trust departments, pension funds, and other institutional investors.

preferred stock A hybrid security that generally provides fixed returns. Preferred stockholders are paid returns after bondholder claims are satisfied but before any returns are paid to common stockholders. Though preferred stock returns are fixed in amount, they are classified as dividends (not interest) and are not tax deductible to the issuing firm.

present value The exact opposite of the compound sum. A future value is discounted to the present.

present value of an annuity The present value of an equal cash flow for several periods is determined.

price-earnings ratio The multiplier applied to earnings per share to determine current value. The P/E ratio is influenced by the earnings and sales growth of the firm, the risk or volatility of its performance, the debt-equity structure, and other factors.

price ratios Ratios that relate the internal performance of the firm to the external judgment of the marketplace in terms of value.

price-weighted average Each stock in the average is weighted by its price. The higher the price, the greater the relative weighting. The Dow Jones Industrial Average represents a price-weighted average.

primary market A market in which an investor purchases an asset (via an investment banker) from the issuer of that asset. The purchase of newly issued shares of corporate stock is an example of primary market activity. Subsequent transfers of the particular asset occur in the secondary market.

private placement The company sells its securities to private investors such as insurance companies, pension funds, and so on rather than through the public markets. Investment bankers may also aid in a private placement on a fee basis. Most private placements involve debt rather than common stock.

profitability ratios Ratios that allow the analyst to measure the ability of the firm to earn an adequate return on sales, total assets, and invested capital.

program trading Computer-based trigger points are established in which large volume trades are indicated. The technique is used by institutional investors.

prospectus A document that must accompany a new issue of securities. It contains the same information appearing in the registration statement, such as a list of directors and officers, financial reports certified by a CPA, the underwriters, the purpose and use for the funds, and other reasonable information that investors need to know.

public placement Public distribution of securities through the financial markets.

pure bond value The fundamental value of a bond that represents a floor price below which the bond's value should not fall. The pure bond value is computed as the present value of all future interest payments added to the present value of the bond principal.

pure competition Companies in pure competition do not have a differentiated product and they compete intensely.

pure pickup yield swap A bond swap where a bond owner thinks he or she can increase the yield to maturity by selling a bond and buying a different bond of equal risk. This implies market disequilibrium.

put An option to sell 100 shares of common stock at a specified price for a given period.

put provision This provision enables a bond investor to have an option to sell a long-term bond back to the corporation at par value after a relatively short period (such as three to five years). This privilege can be particularly valuable if interest rates have gone up and bond prices have gone down.

Q

quick ratio Current assets minus inventory (i.e., cash, marketable securities, and accounts receivables) divided by current liabilities.

R

R^2**—the coefficient of determination** It measures the degree of association between the independent variable(s) and the dependent variable. It may take on a value anywhere between 0 and 1.

real asset A tangible piece of property that may be seen, felt, held, or collected, such as real estate, gold, diamonds, and so on.

real estate investment trust (REIT) An organization similar to a mutual fund where investors pool funds that are invested in real estate or used to make construction or mortgage loans.

real GDP Gross domestic product expressed in dollars that have been adjusted for inflation.

real rate of return The return that investors require for allowing others to use their money for a given period. This is the value that investors demand for passing up immediate consumption and allowing others to use their savings until the funds are returned. Because the term *real* is employed, this means it is a value determined *before* inflation is added.

registered trader A member of a stock exchange who trades for his or her own account rather than for the client of a brokerage firm.

reinvestment assumption with bonds The assumed rate of reinvestment for inflows from a bond investment. It is normally assumed that inflows can be reinvested at the yield to maturity of the bond. This, however, may not be valid. Interest rates may go up or down as inflows from coupon payments come in and need to be reinvested. A more valid approach is to assign appropriate reinvestment rates to inflows and then determine how much the total investment will be worth at the end of a given period. This process is known as terminal wealth analysis.

reported income versus adjusted earnings Reported income is generally based on historical cost accounting, whereas adjusted earnings have been modified for inflation (on inventory and plant and equipment).

repurchase A purchase by a firm of its own shares in the marketplace.

required rate of return The total return required on an investment. For common stock, it is composed of the risk-free rate plus an equity risk premium. Once determined, it becomes the discount rate applied to future cash flows.

reserve requirements Percentages of bank deposit balances stipulated by the Federal Reserve as unavailable for lending. By increasing or reducing reserve requirements, the Fed can contract or expand the money supply.

resistance *See* resistance level.

resistance level The technical analyst's view that as long as a given long-term trend continues, prices of a particular stock or of the market as a whole will not rise above the upper end of the normal trading range (the resistance level) because at that point, investors sell in an attempt to get even or take a profit.

retention ratio The percent of earnings retained in the firm for investment purposes.

return on equity Net income divided by stockholder's equity.

revenue bond A municipal bond supported by the revenue from a specific project, such as a toll, road, bridge, or municipal coliseum.

risk Uncertainty concerning the outcome of an investment or other situation. It is often defined as variability of returns from an investment. The greater the range of possible outcomes, the greater the risk.

risk-adjusted return The amount of return after adjustment for the level of risk incurred to achieve the return.

risk-free rate The required rate of return before risk is explicitly considered. It is composed of the real rate of return plus a rate equivalent to inflationary expectations. It is referred to as R_F.

risk-free rate of return The rate of return demanded by an investor before consideration of risk. It is composed of the real rate of return plus an inflation premium.

risk premium A premium assumed to be paid to an investor for the risk inherent in an investment. It is added to the risk-free rate to get the overall required return on an investment.

rotational investing An investment strategy that refers to the practice of moving in and out of various industries over the business cycle. As the business cycle moves from a trough to a peak, different industries benefit from the economic changes that accompany the business cycle.

Roth IRA Works in the opposite fashion from a traditional IRA. You do not get a deduction for an initial contribution up to $3,000, but the money is allowed to accumulate tax free, and there is *no* tax at the time of withdrawal if certain conditions are met.

Russell 1000 Index The index includes the 1,000 largest firms out of the Russell 3000 Index. It is value-weighted.

Russell 2000 Index The index includes the 2,000 smallest firms out of the Russell 3000 Index. It is value-weighted.

Russell 3000 Index The index is composed of the 3,000 largest U.S. stocks as measured by market capitalization. It is value-weighted.

S

secondary market A market in which an investor purchases an asset from another investor rather than the issuing corporation. The activity of secondary markets sets prices and provides liquidity. *Also see* primary market.

sector funds Mutual funds that specialize in a given segment of the economy such as energy, medical technology, computer technology, and so forth. While they may offer the potential for high returns, they are clearly less diversified and more risky than a typical mutual fund.

secured bond A bond that is collateralized by the pledging of assets.

secured debt Debt that is backed by collateral.

Securities Act of 1933 Enacted by Congress to curtail abuses by securities issuers, the law requires full disclosure of pertinent investment information and provides for penalties to officers of firms that do not comply.

Securities Acts Amendments of 1975 Enacted to increase competition in the securities markets, this legislation prohibits fixed commissions on public offerings of securities and directs the Securities and Exchange Commission to develop a single, nationwide securities market.

Securities and Exchange Commission (SEC) The federal government agency created in 1934 to enforce securities laws. Issuers of securities must register detailed reports with the SEC, and the SEC polices such activities as insider trading, investor conspiracies, and the functionings of the securities exchanges.

Securities Exchange Act of 1934 Created the Securities and Exchange Commission to regulate the securities markets. The act further empowers the Board of Governors of the Federal Reserve System to control margin requirements.

Securities Investor Protection Corporation (SIPC) Created under the Securities Investor Protection Act of 1970, this agency oversees the liquidation of insolvent brokerage firms and provides insurance on investors' trading accounts.

security analyst One who studies various industries and companies and provides research reports and valuation studies.

security market line (SML) The graphic representation of risk (as measured by beta) and return for an individual security.

semistrong form of efficient market hypothesis The hypothesis states that all public information is already impounded into the value of a security, so fundamental analysis cannot determine under- or overvaluation.

serial payment A mechanism for repaying funds advanced through a bond issue. Regular payments systematically retire individual bonds with increasing maturities until, after many years, the entire series has been repaid.

settle price The term for the closing price on futures contracts.

shared appreciation mortgage A type of mortgage in which the lender participates in any increase in value associated with the property being mortgaged.

Sharpe measure of portfolio performance Total portfolio return minus the risk-free rate divided by the portfolio standard deviation. It allows the portfolio manager to view excess returns in relation to total risk. Comparisons between various portfolios can be made based on this relative risk measure.

shelf registration Large companies file one comprehensive registration statement that outlines the firm's plans for future long-term financing. Then, when market conditions seem appropriate, the firm can issue the securities through an investment banker without further SEC approval. Future issues are said to be sitting on the shelf, waiting for the most advantageous time to appear. An issue may sit on the shelf for up to two years.

short position (short sale) A market transaction in which an investor sells borrowed securities in anticipation of a price decline. The investor's expectation is that the securities can be repurchased (to replace the borrowed shares) at a lower price in the future. *Also see* long position.

short sales position theory The contrary opinion rule stating that large volumes of short sales can signal an impending market upturn because short sales must be covered and thereby create their own demand. *Also*, the average short seller is often thought to be wrong.

sinking-fund provision A mechanism for repaying funds advanced through a bond issue. The issuer makes periodic payments to the trustee, who retires part of the issue by purchasing the bonds in the open market.

small-firm effect A market theory that suggests small firms produce superior returns compared to larger firms on both an absolute and risk-adjusted basis.

smart money rules Guidelines, such as *Barron's* Confidence Index, used by technical analysts who predict stock market activity based on the assumption that sophisticated investors will correctly predict market trends and that their lead should be followed. *Also see* contrary opinion rules.

sold directly The least used method for distributing securities by a public corporation. The securities are sold directly to the public by the corporation without the assistance of an investment banker.

specialist or dealer hedge A specialist on an exchange or dealer in the over-the-counter market buys and sells stocks for his own inventory for temporary holding (as a part of his market-making function). At times, he may assume a larger temporary holding than desired with all the risks associated with that exposure. Stock index futures or options can reduce the market, or systematic, risk, although they cannot reduce the specific risk associated with a security.

specialty funds Mutual funds that have special purposes that do not neatly fit into another category. Examples include the Phoenix Fund, the Calvert Social Investment Fund, and the United States Gold Shares.

speculative premium The difference between an option or warrant's price and its intrinsic value. That an investor would pay something in excess of the intrinsic value indicates a speculative desire to hold the security in anticipation of future increases in the price of the underlying stock.

spot market The term applied to the cash price for immediate transfer of a commodity as opposed to the futures market where no physical transfer occurs immediately.

spreads A combination of options that consists of buying one option (going long) and writing an option (going short) on the same stock.

Standard & Poor's 100 Index An index composed of 100 blue-chip stocks on which the Chicago Board Options Exchange currently has individual option contracts.

Standard & Poor's 400 Industrial Index An index that measures price movements in the stocks of 400 large industrial corporations listed primarily on the New York Stock Exchange.

Standard & Poor's 400 MidCap Index An index composed of 400 middle-size firms that have total market values between $1.2 billion and $9 billion.

Standard & Poor's 500 Stock Index An index of 500 major U.S. corporations. In 2004 there were 373 industrial firms, 15 transportation firms, 47 utilities, and 65 financial firms. This index is value-weighted.

Standard & Poor's 600 SmallCap Index An index of the smallest capital stocks covered by Standard & Poor's. The stocks normally have a market capitalization of less than $1 billion (there is some overlap with the Standard & Poor's MidCap Index in terms of size).

Standard & Poor's 1500 Stock Index An index that combines the S&P 500, the S&P 400 MidCap, and the S&P SmallCap 600.

Standard & Poor's International Oil Index A value-weighted index of oil firms. Options on the

V

valuation The process of attributing a value to a security based on expectations of the future performance of the issuing concern, the relevant industry, and the economy as a whole.

valuation model A representation of the components that provide the value of an investment, such as a dividend valuation model used to determine the value of common stock.

Value Line Average The index represents 1,700 companies from the New York and American Stock Exchanges and the over-the-counter market. Many individual investors use the Value Line Index because it more closely corresponds to the variety of stocks the average investor may have in his or her portfolio. It is an equal-weighted index, which means each of the 1,700 stocks, regardless of market price or total market value, is weighted equally.

value-weighted index Each company in the index is weighted by its own total market value as a percentage of the total market value for all firms in the index. Most major indexes such as the S&P 500, S&P 400, and the NYSE Index, are value-weighted. With value-weighted indexes, large firms tend to be weighted more heavily than smaller firms.

variability The possible different outcomes of an event. As an example, an investment with many different levels of return would have great variability.

variable-rate mortgage A mortgage in which the interest rate is adjusted regularly.

variable-rate notes *See* floating-rate notes.

vertical spread Buying and writing two contracts at different striking prices with the same month of expiration.

vesting A legal term meaning pension benefits or rights cannot be taken away.

W

warrant A right or option to buy a stated number of shares of stock at a specified price over a given period. It is usually of longer duration than a call option.

warrant break-even The price movement in the underlying stock necessary for the warrant purchaser to break even, that is, recover the initial purchase price of the warrant.

weak form of efficient market hypothesis A hypothesis suggesting there is no relationship between past and future prices of securities.

weighted average life The weighted average time period over which the coupon payments and maturity payment on a bond are recovered.

white knight A firm that "rescues" another firm from an unfriendly takeover by a third firm.

Wiesenberger Financial Services An advisory service that provides important information on mutual funds.

Wilshire 5000 Equity Index A stock market measure comprising 5,000 equity securities. It includes all New York Stock Exchange and American Stock Exchange issues and the most active over-the-counter issues. The index represents the *total dollar value* of all 5,000 stocks. By measuring total dollar value, it is, in effect, a value-weighted measure.

World Index A value-weighted index of the performance in 19 major countries as compiled by Capital International, S.A., of Geneva, Switzerland.

Y

Yankee bonds Bond issued by foreign governments, foreign corporations, or major agencies that are traded in the United States and denominated (payable) in U.S. dollars.

yield curve A curve that shows interest rates at a specific point for all securities having equal risk but different maturity dates. Usually, government securities are used to construct such curves. The yield curve is also referred to as the term structure of interest rates.

yield spread The difference between the yields received on two different types of bonds, or bonds with different ratings. It is important to investment strategy because during periods of economic uncertainty, spreads increase because investors demand larger premiums on risky issues to compensate for the greater chance of default.

yield to call The interest yield that will be realized on a callable bond if it is held from a given purchase date until the date when it can be called by the issuer. The yield to call reflects the fact that lower overall returns may be realized if the issuer avoids some later payments by retiring the bonds early.

yield to maturity The internal rate of return or true yield on a bond. It is the interest rate (i) at which you can discount the future coupon payments (C_t) and maturity value (P_n) to arrive at the current value of a bond (v). It is synonymous with market rate of interest.

Ying, Lewellen, Schlarbaum, and Lease study A research study that indicates there may be an opportunity for abnormal returns on a risk-adjusted basis in the many weeks between announcement of the listing and actual listing of a security.

Z

zero-coupon bonds Bonds designed to pay no interest, in which the return to the investor is in the form of capital appreciation over the life of the issue.

index

A

A.G. Becker, 239
AAII. *See* American Association of Individual Investors
AAII Index, 250
Abbott Laboratories, 217–220, 222
ABN AMRO Rothschild LLC, 31
Abnormal returns, 268
Accounting. *See also* Financial Accounting Standards Board (FASB)
  accrual, 204
  historical-cost, 223
  inflation-adjusted, 223
  international standards, 289
  replacement-cost, 223
Accounts
  cash, 68
  margin, 68–70
  opening, 68
Accrual accounting, 204
Acquisition candidates, 268–270
Adjustable-rate mortgages (ARMs), 568
Adjustable-rate notes, 291
ADRs. *See* American depository receipts
After-acquired property clauses, 292
After-hours trading, 46
After-tax profit margin, 210
Agrawal, Anup, 270, 287
Agrawal, Deepak, 324
Airline industry, 148
Aked, Michael, 164
Akgun, Aydin, 646
Akhigbe, Aigbe, 164
Alcan Aluminum Ltd., 548
Alexander, Gordon J., 83
Alexander, Sidney S., 256
Alpha, 628
Alternative trading systems (ATSs). *See* Electronic communication networks (ECNs)
Altman, Edward I., 208, 209
Amazon.com, 137, 152
  convertible bonds, 381–388
  stock, 387–388
AMBAC. *See* American Municipal Bond Assurance Corporation
American Association of Individual Investors (AAII), 73
  "Individual Investor's Guide to Low-Load Mutual Funds," 503, 508, 509
  Index, 250
American Capital, 512
American depository receipts (ADRs), 548, 550
American Municipal Bond Assurance Corporation (AMBAC), 299
American Stock Exchange (AMEX), 37, 43, 53
  Composite Index, 64
  dual listing, 38
  exchange traded funds, 501, 551

American Stock Exchange (AMEX)—*Cont.*
  Market Value Index, 43
  options trading, 43, 412, 414, 458, 482
  warrant trading, 43
American Tobacco Company, 576
Ameritrade, 3, 47, 73
AMEX. *See* American Stock Exchange
Ammer, John, 556
Analysts. *See* Security analysts
Angel, James A., 83
Anheuser-Busch Cos., 308
Annual Economic Report of the President, 92
Annuities, 658
  compound sum, 652–653, 660–662
  present value, 656–657, 664–665
Anomalies, 259–260, 268
  January effect, 281
  surprise-earnings effect, 283
  Value Line ranking effect, 281, 282
  weekend effect, 281
Anticipated inflation factor, 14–15
Anticipated realized yield, 334
Apple Computer, 144–145, 272
Approximate yield to maturity, 332–333
APT. *See* Arbitrage pricing theory
Arbel, Avner, 279
Arbitrage, stock index, 479
Arbitrage pricing theory (APT), 615–618
Archibald, T. Ross, 259
ARM. *See* Adjustable-rate mortgages
Arnold Bernhard & Co., 94
ASA Limited, 575
Asset allocation, 634–637, 639
Asset utilization ratios, 212–213
Assets. *See also* Real assets
  fixed, 212
  hidden, 189
  intangible, 152
  risk-free, 597
  and stock valuation, 189
Association for Investment Management and Research (AIMR), 585. *See also* CFA Institute
AstraZeneca, 154
At the money, 415
AT&T, 9, 30, 41, 62, 71, 117, 178, 249, 256
ATSs (alternative trading systems). *See* Electronic communication networks (ECNs)
Automobile industry
  and business cycle, 135–136
  Japanese, 121, 152–153
  as mature industry, 147
  sales, 147
Aventis, 154, 217–220
Average differential return (alpha), 628

B

Bache Group, 396–397

Bacidore, Jeffrey M., 237
Back-end loads, 502
Badenhausen, Kurt, 582
Bader, Lawrence N., 647
Bailey, Warren, 237
Baker, H. Kent, 273
Baker, Malcomb, 287
Baks, Klaas, 524
Balance sheet
  analysis, 202–204
  inflation effects, 223–224
Balanced funds, 508
Ballalio, Robert H., 57
Bank America Realty, 571
Bank of America, 10, 92, 271
Bank One Corporation, 28, 33, 445
Bankers' acceptances, 315
Bankruptcy studies, 208–209
Banks. *See also* Financial institutions
  securities powers, 31–33
  trust departments, 640
Banz, Rolf W., 260, 277–278
Bar charts, 245–247
Barber, Brad M., 280
Barr Laboratories, 154
Barron's Business and Financial Weekly, 103–105
  bond information, 106
  closed-end funds, 498, 499
  Confidence Index, 251–253
  economic data, 92
  Market Laboratory-Economic Indicators, 250
  mutual fund performance data, 517
  odd-lot transactions, 248
Barry, Christopher B., 272, 287, 556
Baseball cards, 576
Basic earnings per share, 394
Basis, 473
Basis points, 332
Bass, Richard, 352
Basu, S., 259, 279
Batterymarch Financial Management, 551
Bauman, W. Scott, 199
Beaver, William H., 208–209
Beebower, Gilbert L., 287, 634–635
Behavioral finance, 255
Bekaert, Geert, 524
Benning, Carl J., 266
Berkin, Andrew L., 83
Berkowitz, Stephen A., 83, 630
Bernasek, Anna, 237
Bernstein, Peter L., 23
Best-efforts basis, 31
Beta coefficients, 170, 600–602
  of individual stocks, 13–14, 603–604, 631
  over time, 606
  portfolio, 606, 631
  and speculative premium, 418
Bethlehem Steel, 472

695

Bezos, Jeffrey, 137
Bhabra, Harjeet, 406
Bharadwaj, Anu, 490
Bierman, Harold, Jr., 199
Billingsley, Randall S., 406
Biotechnology industry, 144
Black, Fischer, 281, 431, 432, 612
Black-Scholes option pricing model, 432–438
Blind pools, 570
Bliss, Robert R., 431
Block, Stanley B., 268
Block trades, 47
Bloomberg Financial News, 107, 108, 604
Blue chip stocks, 59
Blume, Lawrence, 266
Blume, Marshall E., 257, 606
Bodnar, Gordon M., 431, 490, 556
Boeing, 335
Boesky, Ivan, 51, 261
Bond funds, 508–510
Bond markets, 45–46, 293
  efficiency, 312–313
  indexes, 66, 251–253
  indicators, 64–65
  and interest rates, 64, 335–336, 359, 362–363
  international, 313–314, 359
  investors, 302–303
  primary, 302, 303
  risk and return, 310–312
  secondary, 302
Bond swaps, 344
Bonds, 291. *See also* Convertible securities; Duration; Government securities
  call provisions, 292, 333–334
  corporate, 15–16, 300–302
  coupon rates, 363–364
  deep discount, 342
  dollar-denominated, 313–314
  Eurodollar, 314
  50-year, 335
  floating-rate, 291
  foreign-pay, 314
  income, 293
  indentures, 291
  information sources, 92, 93–94
  interest rates, 289, 291, 339–342
  investment-grade, 306
  issuing procedures, 303
  junk, 306–307, 510
  municipal, 46, 298–299
  par values, 291
  perpetual, 291
  price sensitivity, 335–336, 356, 359–361
  pricing rules, 341
  private placements, 31, 303
  public offerings, 31
  put provisions, 292
  quotes, 307–308
  rates of return
    anticipated realized yield, 334
    current yield, 329–330

Bonds—*Cont.*
  rates of return—*Cont.*
    reinvestment assumptions, 334–335, 367–368
    yield to call, 333–334
    yield to maturity, 330–333, 353
  ratings, 289, 299, 303–306
  repayment methods, 291–292
  risk premium, 15–16
  secured, 292–293
  sinking funds, 292
  trading, 45–46
  unsecured, 293
  valuation, 327–329, 355–356
  weighted average life, 356
  Yankee, 313–314
  yield spreads, 342–344
  zero-coupon, 291
Book value per share (BVPS), 183–184
Book value to market value effect, 280
Boorstein, Julia, 137
Boquist, John A., 237
Borde, Stephen F., 164
Bottom-up approach, 142
Boutchkova, Maria K., 56
Bowlin, Oswald D., 336
Boyle, Mathew, 137
Branch, Ben, 281
Brand names, 152
Braniff, 148
Breadth of market indicator, 253–254
Brennan, Michael J., 83, 266
Brenner, Michael, 431
Brick, Ivan E., 352
Brightman, Christopher, 164
Briley, James E., 466
Brinson, Gary P., 634–635
Bristol-Myers Squibb, 10
British Airways, 548
Brokerage houses, 25
  accounts with, 68–70
  careers in, 24–25
  commissions, 72–73
  discount, 3, 47, 72
  full-service, 72
  online trading, 47, 72–73
  research, 52, 98–99
  websites, 108
Brokers
  commission, 40
  on exchanges, 37, 40
  floor, 40, 71
Brown, Lawrence D., 287
Brush Engineering, 41
Buraschi, Andrea, 432
Burlington Northern, Inc., 458
Bush, George H. W., 117, 120
Bush, George W., 117–118, 121, 181
Business Cycle Indicators, 91, 128
Business cycles, 116, 126–128
  industry relationships, 135–137
  peaks, 128–129
  rotational investing, 160–162
  and specific industries, 160–162
  troughs, 128–129
BusinessWeek, 92, 100, 152

Buybacks. *See* Stock repurchases

C

Caccese, Michael S., 57
Calamos, John P., 407
Call options, 43, 411. *See also* Options
  buying, 420–423
  writing, 423–425
Call provisions, on bonds, 292, 333–334
CalPERS (California Public Employees Retirement System), 47
Calvert Social Investment Fund, 510
Campbell, Cynthia J., 407
Campbell, John Y., 352
Campbell Resources, Inc., 548
Campeau Corporation, 307
Canadian Fund, Inc., 510
Canadian Pacific Limited, 335
Cao, Melanie, 352
Capacity utilization, 135
Capital appreciation, 8, 12
Capital asset pricing model (CAPM), 597–600
  assumptions, 604–605
  risk in, 603
Capital gains. *See* Capital appreciation
Capital gains taxes, 9–10, 75–76, 513–514
Capital goods industries, 137
Capital market line (CML), 599–600
CAPM. *See* Capital asset pricing model
Capps, Oral, 583
Careers in investments, 24–26
Carhart, Mark M., 524, 629, 646
Carnegie Foundation, 640
Carr, Peter, 432
Carr, Richard C., 535, 556
Carter, Jimmy, 116–117, 181
Carter, Martha L., 57
Carter, Richard, 273, 287
Carty, Lea V., 237, 324
Cash accounts, 68
Cash flow analysis, of real estate, 562–567
Cash flow per share (CFPS), 183–184, 185
Cash flow, free, 185
Cash flows, statement of, 204–207
Cash prices, of commodities, 452
Castelino, Mark G., 490
Caster, Paul, 249
Caton, Gary L., 407
CATs, 365
Cavaglia, Stefano, 164
CBOE. *See* Chicago Board Options Exchange
CBOT. *See* Chicago Board of Trade
CD-ROMs, 105
CDs. *See* Certificates of deposit
Cellular Communications, 269
Center for Financial Research and Analysis, 227
Central banks, 535. *See also* Federal Reserve system
Certificates of deposit (CDs), 314–315
Certified financial planners (CFPs), 26

CFA Institute, 24, 105, 585
CFAs. *See* Chartered financial analysts
CFPs. *See* Certified financial planners
CFTC. *See* Commodity Futures Trading Commission
Chan, Louis K. C., 83
Charles Schwab Corporation, 3, 47, 72, 73
Chartered financial analysts (CFAs), 24, 26
Charts
  bar, 245–247
    Dow theory, 242–243
    point and figure, 247
    resistance levels, 243–244
    support levels, 243–244
    volume, 244
Chase Manhattan, 28, 34, 271. *See also* JP Morgan Chase
Chatterjea, Arkadev, 56
Chemical Bank, 268
Chen, Nai-fu, 612, 616
Cherian, Joseph A., 56
Chevron, 270
Chicago Board of Trade (CBOT), 43, 53
  commodity futures, 447, 452
  fees, 44
  financial futures, 453, 454
  options on futures, 458
  stock index futures, 469
Chicago Board Options Exchange (CBOE), 43, 411, 413
  options trading, 62, 414, 419, 458
  stock index options, 419, 479–480
  trading volume, 413
Chicago Mercantile Exchange (CME), 43, 44
  competitors, 44
  governance, 409
  International Monetary Market (IMM), 453, 454
  options on futures, 458
  program trading study, 469
  stock index futures, 469, 471
Chicago Stock Exchange (CHX), 37
Chicago Tribune, 108, 135
China, 118
  trade with U.S., 121
  WTO membership, 120
Cho, Doug W., 141
Choi, Frederick D. S., 237
Chordia, Tarun, 83
Christopher, Stephen E., 83
Chrysler, 209
CHX. *See* Chicago Stock Exchange
Cicotte, Eddie, 576
Circuit breakers, 51–53
CISCO Systems, 63, 137, 250, 255
Citicorp, 28, 92
Citigroup, 18, 28, 34, 35, 496
Citigroup Global Index, 539
Clark, Timothy, 353
Clinton, William, 117, 120, 181
Closed-end funds, 498–501, 502
  international, 550–551
CME. *See* Chicago Mercantile Exchange

CML. *See* Capital market line
CNN Financial, 108
Cobb, Ty, 576
Coca-Cola Company, 149, 178, 413
  brand recognition, 152
  foreign earnings, 226
  stock, 188
  website, 108
Coefficient of determination, 632–633
Coggin, T. Daniel, 646
Cognitive psychology, 255
Cohen, Marilyn, 141
Cohn, Richard A., 18, 558
Coincident indicators, 128–130
Coker, Daniel P., 266
Colby, Robert W., 247
Collectibles, 576, 577
College of Financial Planning, 26
Comára, António, 490
Combined earnings and dividend model, 176–177
Comcast, 47
Commercial and Financial Chronicle, 105
Commercial paper, 46, 315
Commission brokers, 40
Commissions
  in international markets, 546
  mutual funds, 502, 503
  options trading, 427
  for real asset purchases, 558
  regulation of, 50
  trading, 72–73
Commodities
  cash market, 452
  options on, 458
Commodities Futures Trading Commission, 409
Commodity futures, 6, 443–444
  categories, 445–446
  contracts, 447–448
  exchanges, 446–447
  gains and losses, 449
  on gold, 575
  hedging with, 444
  inverse pyramids, 449
  margin, 448, 449–450
  open interest, 452
  price movement limits, 450
  prices, 100, 102
  quotes, 451–452
  regulation of, 447
  on silver, 575
  speculating, 444–445
  trading, 447–450
Commodity Futures Trading Commission (CFTC), 447
Common stocks
  compared to convertibles, 387–388
  compared to options, 422, 425–426
  delisting, 40, 275
  exchange listings, 273–275
  foreign companies, 55, 548
  historical trends, 620–621
  information sources, 92, 93, 94, 98, 108

Common stocks—*Cont.*
  new issues, 271–272
  options on. *See* Options
  prices, 100, 101
  rate of return, 12, 620–621
  repurchases, 275–277
  risk premium, 15–18
  small firms, 45, 277–279
  technical analysis, 241
  valuation process, 115
Compaq Computers, 145, 227
Comparative sales value, 561
Competition
  among markets, 30
  in industries, 151–153
  pure, 150
Compound sum
  of annuity, 652–653, 660–662
  of single amount, 650–651, 658–660
Compustat, 105–107
Computer Associates, 283
Computer databases, 105–107
Computer industry, 144–145, 149. *See also* Technology companies
Computer systems. *See also* Electronic communication networks
  order routing, 42
Conference Board, 128
Connecticut General Mortgage, 571
Connell, Bradford, 199
Conrad, Jennifer, 257
Conrail, 335
Consolidated Rutile, 548
Consolidated tape, 37–38, 39
Constant growth model, 171–174
Constantinou, Constantina, 266
Consumer expectations, 125–126
Consumer price index (CPI), 124–125
Continental Airlines, 148
Contrary opinion rules, 248–251
Convertible securities, 380–381
  accounting considerations, 394–395
  call provisions, 391
  compared with common stock, 387–388
  conversion premiums, 384–385, 393
  conversion prices, 382, 391–392
  conversion ratios, 382
  conversion value, 382–384
  disadvantages, 391
  downside risks, 385, 391
  forced conversions, 387, 391
  investor's view of, 391–392
  issuer's view of, 392–393
  parity prices, 384
  popularity in 2000–2001, 393
  preferred stock, 6, 316–317, 388–391
  pure bond value, 382–384
  uses, 392, 399, 400
  yields, 391
  zero coupon, 393
Convexity, 378–379
Copeland, Laurence, 491
Corgel, John B., 583
Corporate bonds, 15–16, 300–302. *See also* Bonds

Corporations
   decision-making process, 178
   foreign, 55, 547
   going public, 35, 271–272
   growth companies, 149, 186–187, 188–189
   information sources, 93, 94, 98–99, 105–107
   management, 181
   multinational, 549–550
   reports to SEC, 50, 99–100
   websites, 100, 108
Correlation
   across equity markets, 533–536
   of stock prices over time, 256–257
   of two assets, 590–592
Correlation coefficient, 533–536, 590, 612–613
Corwin, Shane A., 287
Cost approach to real estate valuation, 561
Council of Economic Advisors, 116
   Economic Indicators, 92
Coupon rates, 291
Covered options, 423–425
Cowan, Arnold R., 407
Coy, Peter, 266
CPI. *See* Consumer price index
Crabbe, Leland, 325
Crack, F., 353
Crain, Susan J., 466
Credit Suisse First Boston, 31, 35, 296, 460
Creditor claims, 6
Cristea, Carrie, 237
Cross, Frank, 281
Cross-hedging, 458
CRSP database, 107
CSFB. *See* Credit Suisse First Boston
Cullity, John P., 141
Currency fluctuations, 493, 541–545. *See also* Exchange rates
Currency futures, 453–454
Currency options, 458
Current ratio, 213
Current yield, 329–330
Cyclical industries, 137, 186–187

D

Daimler-Chrysler, 209
Daniel, Kent, 525, 556, 646
Dann, Larry Y., 275, 276
Databases, 105–107
David W. Tice & Associates, 113
Day orders, 72
Day traders, 73–74
De Beers Consolidated Mines of South Africa, Ltd., 152, 577
Dealer hedges, 478
Dean Witter, 512
Debentures, 292
Debt-to-equity ratios, long-term, 214
Debt financing, 211–212, 400
Debt securities. *See* Bonds
Debt-utilization ratios, 214–215
Deep discount bonds, 342

Deficits
   federal, 117, 119–120
   trade, 121
Delisting, 40, 275
Dell Computer Corporation, 145, 181, 496
DeLong, Gayla L., 287
DeMark, Thomas R., 247, 266
Denis, David J., 237
Denis, Diane, 82
DePaul University, 239, 585, 605
Depreciation
   real estate, 563–564
   straight-line, 563–564
Der Horanesian, Mara, 199
Deregulation, 151
Derivatives, 409, 445, 468–469. *See also* Futures; Options; Swaps
Detamore-Rodman, Crystal, 524
Deutsche Telekom, 33
Developing countries. *See* Emerging markets
Devero, Amie, 237
Diagonal spreads, 438
Diamonds, 575–577
DIAMONDS (exchange-traded funds), 43, 469, 501
Dielman, Terry E., 276
Diermeier, Jeffrey J., 635
Diffusion indexes, 128
Digman, James H., 377
Dilution, 394–395, 400–401
Direct equity claims, 5
Direct investments, international, 548, 550
Direct offerings, 31
Discount brokers, 3, 47, 72
Discount rate, 122
Disney Corp., 47, 61, 188
Distribution of new issues, 31–34
Diversification
   benefits, 533–534
   international, 527–528, 532–536
   in mutual funds, 496–497, 512, 631–634
   of unsystematic risk, 602, 631–632
Dividend valuation models, 169, 171
   constant growth, 171–174
   general, 171
   nonconstant growth, 174–175
Dividends
   cumulative, 316–317
   in industry life cycles, 143–144, 145, 148–149
   payout ratio, 217
   per share (DPS), 183–184
   preferred stocks, 316–317
   taxes on, 9–10, 75, 316
   yields, 215, 216, 418
Dividends to price ratio, 215, 216
Djoganonpoules, Chris, 583
Dodd, Peter, 268
Dollar-cost averaging, 515–516
Dollar-denominated bonds, 313–314
Domowitz, Ian, 556
Donohue, Craig S., 409

Dortman, John R., 250
Doukas, John A., 199
Dow, Charles, 242
Dow Chemical, 413
Dow Jones & Company, 64, 100, 103, 242
Dow Jones Industrial Average (DJIA), 59–61
   advance-decline indicator, 253–254
   companies in, 472
   in Dow theory, 242–243
   effects of program trading, 469
   forecasts, 63, 113
   futures on, 468, 469
   Mini, 469
   options on, 43, 468, 479–480
   options on futures, 483
   performance, 28, 62
   reactions to bad news, 276
Dow Jones Industry Groups, 160, 161
Dow Jones Transportation Average, 60, 242
Dow Jones Utility Average, 60
Dow Jones World Index, 64, 637
Dow theory, 242–243
Downside limits, 385
Downside risks, 385, 391
Dravid, Ajay R., 647
Dreman, David, 165
Drexel Burnham Lambert, 307
Dreyfus Group, 501, 512
Driehaus, Richard, 239
Driehaus Capital Management, 239
Drug companies. *See* Pharmaceutical industry
Du Pont analysis, 211–212
Du Pont Company, 41, 211, 496
Dual trading, 37–38
Duff & Phelp, Inc., 304
Duke Energy, 9
Dun & Bradstreet
   Key Business Ratios, 98
   Million Dollar Directory, 98
Dunetz, Mark L., 377
Durable goods industries, 135
Duracell, 268, 271
Duration, 356–359
   convexity, 378–379
   and coupon rates, 363–364
   factors in, 364–365
   formula, 358
   Macaulay, 358
   and market rates, 362–363
   modified, 377–378
   and price sensitivity, 359–361
   uses of, 359, 366–367
   zero-coupon bonds, 365–366
Durham, J. Benson, 141

E

E*Trade, 3, 47, 73
Eales, J. S., 431
Earnings before interest, taxes, depreciation, and amortization (EBITDA), 185

Earnings per share (EPS), 165–167
  basic, 394
  forecasting, 185–188
  fully diluted, 394–395, 400–401
  primary, 394
Earnings surprises, 283
Earnings valuation models, 169, 175
  combined earnings and dividend, 176–177
  EBITDA, 185
  price-earnings ratio (P/E), 177–180
  short-term, 182
Easley, David, 266
Eastern Airlines, 148
Eastman Kodak, 458, 548
Easton, Stephen A., 431
EBay, 9
EBITDA (earnings before interest, taxes, depreciation, and amortization), 185
Echo Bay Mines, 575
ECNs. *See* Electronic communication networks
Economic activity, 124–126. *See also* Business cycles; Gross domestic product
  analysis of, 115–116
  industrial production, 133–135
Economic data, sources of, 84–91
Economic Growth and Tax Reconciliation Act of 2001, 11
Economic indicators, 128
  coincident, 128–130
  lagging, 128–130
  leading, 125–126, 128–130
Economic value added (EVA), 178
Ederington, Louis H., 407
EDGAR system, 50, 100, 200
Efficiency
  of bond markets, 312–313
  of international markets, 546
  of markets, 29
  of portfolios, 593–595
Efficient frontier, 593–594, 597
Efficient market hypothesis (EMH), 255–256
  semistrong form, 258–259, 275
  strong form, 260–261
  weak form, 256–258
8-K Reports, 99
Eisner, Michael, 47
El Paso, 283
Elan Corp., 391
Eldor, Rafi, 431
Electric utilities, 149, 300–301
Electronic Book, 42
Electronic communication networks (ECNs), 37, 46, 413
Eleling, Ashlea, 287
Eli Lilly, 70–71, 144, 178, 496
Ellis, Charles D., 275, 276
Elton, Edwin J., 324
Emerging markets
  comparative valuations, 542–543
  growth, 528
  market capitalizations, 528–531

Emerging markets—*Cont.*
  mutual funds, 493
  returns in, 536, 537
  trading in, 532
Emery, Douglas R., 407
EMH. *See* Efficient market hypothesis
Employee stock options, 289
Employment Act of 1946, 116, 122
Endowments, 640
Enron, 8, 227, 393, 409
EPS. *See* Earnings per share
Equal-weighted indexes, 63
Equipment trust certificates, 292
Equities. *See* Common stocks
Equity participation arrangements, 569
Equity risk premium (ERP), 170
Equity trusts, 571
Eraker, Bjorn, 377, 646
Ericsson, 548
ERP. *See* Equity risk premium
Estate planning
  hedges, 478
  and investments, 11–12
  taxes, 11
ETFs. *See* Exchange traded funds
Eurex, 44
Euro, 118, 121, 453, 535
Eurodollar bonds, 314
Eurodollar futures, 454
Euromarkets, 35. *See also* International securities markets
Euronext, 44
European Central Bank, 535
European Monetary Union, 535
European Union, 118
EVA. *See* Economic value added
Excess returns, 272, 625
Exchange listings, 273–275
Exchange rates. *See also* Currency futures; Foreign exchange
  effects on international investing, 541–545
  effects on trade, 121–122
Exchange traded funds (ETFs), 43, 501, 551
Exchanges, 37
  commodity futures, 446–447
  consolidated tape, 37–38, 39
  dual trading, 37–38
  foreign, 532
  futures, 43–44, 409, 453
  listing requirements, 38–40
  members, 40–42
  new listings, 273–275
  options, 43, 411–413
  regional, 37
  regulation, 48–53
  specialists, 41–42, 273
  stock index futures, 469
  stock index options, 479–480
  trading volumes, 38, 39
  websites, 107–108
Exercise prices, of options, 413
Expectations hypothesis, 337–338
Expected value, 587–588
Export-Import Bank, 297

Extraordinary gains and losses, 226
Exxon, 62, 275
ExxonMobil, 40, 63, 253, 496, 531, 549

F

Fabozzi, Frank J., 273, 466, 646
Fadiman, Mark, 500
Fall, Carol F., 18
Fallen angel bonds, 306–307
Fama, Eugene F., 256, 257, 258, 266, 280, 284, 287, 612
Families of funds, 512, 514–515
Fan, Rong, 466
Fanuc, 548
Farnsworth, Heber, 352
Farr, W. Ken, 165
FASB. *See* Financial Accounting Standards Board
FDA. *See* Food and Drug Administration
Federal agency securities, 46, 297–298
Federal Farm Credit Bank, 297
Federal funds, futures on, 454
Federal Home Loan Bank, 297
Federal Intermediate Credit Banks, 297
Federal National Mortgage Association, 46, 297
Federal Open Market Committee (FOMC), 122
Federal Reserve Bank of San Francisco, 86
Federal Reserve Bank of St. Louis
  FRED II database, 87
  International Economic Trends, 87
  Monetary Trends, 87
  National Economic Trends, 87–89, 90
  U.S. Financial Data, 87
  website, 87
Federal Reserve Bulletin, 85–86
Federal Reserve system
  Banks, 86
  Board of Governors, 50, 68, 85, 116
  economic data, 547
  monetary policy, 117, 122–124, 135, 136
  open-market operations, 122
  websites, 86–87
Federated Funds, 512
Feds Index, 283
Fergeson, Michael F., 377
Ferguson, Robert, 83, 199, 525
Ferri, Michael G., 83
Ferson, Wayne E., 525
FFO (funds from operations), 572
Fidelity, 501, 632
Fidelity Blue Chip Growth Fund, 586–587
Fidelity Contrafund, 513
Fidelity Investments, 47, 108, 307, 512
Fidelity Trust Company of New York, 551
FIFO (first-in, first-out), 224–226
Filler, R., 466
Filo, David, 137
Financial Accounting Standards Board (FASB), 152, 547
  chairman, 289

Financial Accounting Standards Board (FASB)—*Cont.*
  "Earnings per Share" statement, 394
  inflation-adjusted accounting, 223
Financial Analysis Journal, 105
Financial assets, 5
  and inflation, 18
  liquidity, 8–9
Financial futures, 445–446, 452–453
  currency futures, 453–454
  exchanges, 453
  interest-rate futures, 454–458
  options on, 458–459
Financial institutions. *See also* Banks
  economic data, 92
  mergers, 28, 33, 269, 271
  regulation of, 28, 31–33
  websites, 108
Financial planners, 26
Financial ratios, 208
  asset utilization, 212–213
  average tax rate, 217
  classification, 209–210
  debt-utilization, 214–215
  dividend payout, 217
  industry comparisons, 217–220
  liquidity, 213–214
  price, 215–216
  profitability, 210–212
  trend analysis, 220–222
  uses, 217–220
Financial statements, 200
  balance sheet, 202–204
  deficiencies, 223–227
  dilution and, 394–395
  extraordinary gains and losses, 226
  filed with SEC, 50, 99–100, 547
  foreign exchange transactions, 226
  of foreign firms, 55, 547
  income statement, 201–202
  inflation effects, 223–224
  inventory valuation, 224–226
  pension fund liabilities, 226, 227
  statement of cash flows, 204–207
Financial World, 92, 100
Finney, Louis D., 630
Finucane, Thomas J., 431
Fiscal policy, 118–122
Fisher, Kenneth L., 141
Fisher, Lawrence, 258, 366
Fitch, Duff & Phelps, 289, 304
Fitch, Stephanie, 583
Fixed-assets turnover, 212
Fixed-charge coverage, 214–215
Fixed-income securities. *See also* Bonds; Government securities
  bankers' acceptances, 315
  certificates of deposit (CDs), 314–315
  commercial paper, 46, 315
  money market accounts, 315–316
  money market funds, 315, 316, 506
Flanagan, William G., 583
Fleet Boston Financial, 271
Fleming, Jeff, 141
Floating-rate notes, 291
Floor brokers, 40, 71

Floor value, 383
Followill, Richard A., 491
FOMC. *See* Federal Open Market Committee
Food and Drug Administration (FDA), 154, 157, 220, 283
Forbes, 92, 100, 500
  mutual fund survey, 506
Forbes, William P., 266
Forced conversions, 387, 391
Ford Foundation, 640
Ford Motor, 335
Ford Motor Credit, 307
Forecasting
  earnings, 185–188
  interest rates, 359
Foreign currency effects, 545. *See also* Exchange rates
Foreign exchange, and financial statements, 226. *See also* Exchange rates
Foreign exchange futures. *See* Currency futures
Foreign funds, 510
Foreign-pay bonds, 314
Forest Oil, 396
Forest product companies, 189
Fortune, 92, 100, 137, 178
Foundations, 640
Fox, Justin, 23
Franchette, Darren L., 491
Francis, Jack C., 490
Frank Russell Company, 64, 629
Frankel, Micah, 237
Frankfurt Stock Exchange, 548
Franklin Templeton, 493
Free cash flow, 185
French, Kenneth R., 280, 281, 612
Friedman, Milton J., 131
Full-service brokers, 72
Fully diluted earnings per share, 394–395, 400–401
Fundamental analysis, 114, 200–201
  and efficient market hypothesis, 259–260
Funds from operations (FFO), 572
FundTrust, 511
Fung, Hung-Gay Fung, 491
Furst, Richard W., 273
Futures, 443–444. *See also* Commodity futures; Financial futures; Stock index futures
  basis, 473
  Eurodollar, 454
  exchanges, 43–44, 409, 453
  options on, 458–459, 468

G

Gannon College, 605
GAO. *See* Government Accounting Office
Garnett, Jeff, 224
Gastineau, Gary L., 57
Gates, Bill, 11
Gateway, 145
GDP. *See* Gross domestic product

Géczy, Christopher, 466
Gehrig, Lou, 576
Gemological Institute of America, 577
Gems, 575–577
Genentech, 144, 272
General dividend model, 171
General Electric, 62, 113, 253, 275, 411, 413, 531
General Motors, 10, 41, 69, 70, 117, 259, 496, 548
General obligation (GO) bonds, 299
Gentry, James A., 634
German bonds, 313
Gerstner, Lou, Jr., 244
Gibson, Ranja, 646
Gillette, 271
Ginnie Maes. *See* GNMA pass-through certificates
Glass-Steagall Act, 28, 31
GlaxoSmithKline, 154, 217–220, 222
Glen, Jack, 556
Global bond market, 313–314
Global funds, 510, 511
Global markets. *See* Emerging markets; International securities markets
GNMA pass-through certificates, 297–298
Goetzmann, William N., 525
Going public. *See* Initial public offerings (IPOs)
Gold, 572–575
  bullion, 574
  coins, 574–575
  futures, 575
  prices, 5, 571–572
  stocks, 575
Goldman Sachs, 35, 52, 108, 296, 327, 460
Goldreyer, Elizabeth, 556
Good till canceled (GTC) orders, 72
Goodman, David A., 279
Goodwin, Thomas H., 629, 630
Google, 108
Gorman, Stephen, 647
Goulet, Waldemar M., 273
Government Accounting Office (GAO), 76
Government National Mortgage Association (GNMA), 297–298
Government Printing Office, 91
Government securities, 293–294. *See also* Treasury securities
  federal agencies, 46, 297–298
  and Federal Reserve policy, 122
  of foreign governments, 543–544
  foreign investment in, 296, 303
  futures on, 454–456
  inflation-indexed, 295–296
  interest rates, 289
  options on, 458
  quotes, 309–310, 311
  retirement of, 117
  risk premium, 15
  trading, 45–46
  zero-coupon, 294–295

Graduated payment mortgages (GPMs), 568
Gramm-Leach-Bliley Act, 28, 31–33
Granville, Joseph, 251
Greenspan, Alan, 4, 122, 123, 135
Grinblatt, Mark, 525, 646
Gross domestic product (GDP), 124
　relationship to inflation, 125
　relationship to stock market performance, 132–133
Gross national product, 124
Gross profit margin, 210
Growth companies, 149, 186–187, 188–189
Growth funds, 508
Growth stocks, 188
Growth with income funds, 508
Gruber, Merlin J., 324
GTC. *See* Good till canceled (GTC) orders
Guaranteed price strategy, 423
Guarantees, for municipal bonds, 299
Guardian Life Insurance Company, 283
Gulf Oil, 270
Gupta, Anurag, 466
Gutfreund, John, 322
Gutner, Toddi, 352
Guyon, Janet, 556

H

Hagler, J. L., 407
Halper, Barry, 576
Hammond, Carl T., 273
Hardy, Donald J., 524
Harris, Jeffrey H., 287
Harris, Lawrence, 281
Harrisdirect, 3
Hartzell, Jay C., 647
Hauser, R. J., 431
Hauser, Shmuel, 431
Haushalter, David, 466
Hawawini, Gabriel A., 332
Hayt, Gregory S., 431, 490
Health care. *See* Pharmaceutical industry
HealthSouth, 283
Healy, Paul M., 271, 287
Healy, Thomas J., 524
Hecla Mining, 575
Hedge funds, 511
Hedges
　commodity futures, 444
　cross-, 458
　currency futures, 454
　dealer, 478
　estate, 478
　interest-rate futures, 456–458
　options, 426
　partial, 458
　retirement, 478
　specialist, 478
　stock index futures, 470, 471, 476–479
　stock index options, 482
　tax, 479
　underwriter, 478
Heebner, Ken, 572
Heineken, 149

Heinz (H. J.) Corporation, 72
Herz, Robert H., 289
Hesseldahl, Arik, 165
Hettenhouse, George W., 313
Hewlett-Packard, 145, 283, 472
Heynen, Ronald, 353
Hidden assets, 189
High-tech industry. *See* Technology companies
High-yield bonds. *See* Junk bonds
Hirschey, Mark, 266
Hirt, Geoffrey A., 181, 224
Historical-cost accounting, 223
Hite, Gailen, 325
Hoechst, 548
Hoffmeister, J. Ronald, 268
Hogarty, T., 271
Holden, Craig W., 491
Holding periods, 621–624
Holloway, Clark, 281
Home Depot, 9
Honda Motor Company, Ltd., 548
Hood, Randolph, 634–635
Horizontal spreads, 438
Horrigan, James O., 304
Household International, 393
Housing industry, 136. *See also* Real estate
Hovakimian, Armen, 406
Hughes, Patricia J., 266
Hutchins Corporation, 187–188
Hybrid trusts, 571

I

Ibbotson, Roger G., 18, 23, 63, 199, 272, 525, 535, 556
Ibbotson Associates, 17–18, 63
IBM, 63, 117, 137, 149, 256, 275, 413, 632
　financial reporting, 227
　personal computers, 144–145, 149
　stock price, 4–5, 7, 61, 243–244
IDS, 501
Ikenberry, David, 277
ImClone, 283
IMF. *See* International Monetary Fund
IMM. *See* International Monetary Market
Immunization, 366–367
In the money, 414
Income
　investing for, 8
　operating, 185
　in rate of return, 12
Income approach to real estate valuation, 561–562
Income bonds, 293
Income statement method, 187–188
Income statements
　analysis, 201–202
　inflation effects, 223–224
　inventory valuation, 224–226
Index arbitrage, 479
Index funds, 501, 508, 630–631, 632
Index of Bearish Sentiment, 250
Indexes. *See* Stock indexes

Indiana University, 605
Indifference curves, risk-return, 594–596, 597
Indirect equity, 5–6
Indirect investments, international, 548–551
"Individual Investor's Guide to Low-Load Mutual Funds," 503, 508, 509
Individual Retirement Accounts (IRAs), 12
Industrial production, 133–135
Industriscope, 105
Industry analysis, 142, 143
Industry groups, rotational investing, 160–162
Industry life cycles, 143–144
　decline, 148
　development, 144
　expansion, 145
　growth, 144–145, 188
　maturity, 146–148, 149
　pharmaceutical industry, 154
Industry structure, 149–153
Inflation, 11, 117
　anticipated, 14–15
　consumer price index, 124–125
　effects on financial statements, 223–224
　financial assets and, 18
　and price-earnings ratios, 178–180
　real assets and, 18
　relationship to gross domestic product, 125
Inflation-indexed Treasury securities, 295–296
Initial public offerings (IPOs), 35, 271–272
Insider trading
　illegal, 49, 51, 52, 261, 268–269
　profits, 261
　reports to SEC, 261
Institute for Supply Management (ISM) Index, 135
Institutional Investor, 24, 107
Institutional investors, 31, 47–48, 302, 639–640
Insurance companies, 639–640
Intangible assets, 152
Intel, 45, 63, 137, 244, 255, 283
InterActive Corp., 396
Interactive Data Corporation, 107
Interbrand Corp., 152
Interest-rate futures, 454–456
　hedging with, 456–458
　quotes, 454
　settle prices, 456
Interest-rate swaps, 459–460
Interest rates
　and bond markets, 64, 335–336, 359, 362–363
　and duration, 362–363
　forecasting, 135, 359
　mortgage, 136
　term structure, 336–339
　volatility, 339
Internal Revenue Service (IRS), 295, 298

International Monetary Fund (IMF), 528
International Monetary Market (IMM), 453, 454
International Paper, 189
International Securities Exchange (ISE), 413, 414
International securities markets, 528
   administrative problems, 546–547
   bonds, 313–314, 359
   commissions, 546
   company information, 547
   and currency fluctuations, 541–545
   developed countries, 528, 529
   differences, 539–541
   direct investments, 548, 550
   diversification benefits, 527–528, 532–536
   efficiency, 546
   emerging. *See* Emerging markets
   government bonds, 543–544
   indexes, 64, 516, 539, 540–541, 551
   indirect investments, 548–551
   interest rates and, 359
   mutual funds, 493, 510, 511, 550–551
   political risks, 546, 550
   portfolio managers, 551
   price-earnings ratios, 539–541
   quotes, 539
   returns in, 536–538, 541–545
   structures, 532
   trading in, 532, 546–548
   trading volumes, 45
   underwriters, 35–37
   withholding taxes, 546, 550
International trade, 120–122
Internet. *See also* Websites
   auctions, 576
   financial data on, 73, 107–109
   search engines, 108
   SEC reports on, 50, 99–100
   trading on, 47, 72–73
Interpolation, 332, 353
IntoSpace, 137
Intrinsic value
   of options, 415, 421
   of warrants, 397, 398–399
Inventory
   turnover, 212
   valuation, 224–226
Inverse pyramids, 449
Investment advisers, regulation of, 50
Investment Advisor Act of 1940, 50
Investment advisory recommendations, as contrary indicator, 250–251
Investment advisory services, 92
Investment bankers, 25–26. *See also* Underwriting
   competition, 34–37
   distribution process, 31–34
   fees, 34–35
   hedging by, 478
   performance, 272–273
   relationship with security analysts, 52, 113
   risks taken, 33
Investment companies, 639

Investment Companies Act of 1940, 50, 512
Investment Company Institute, 494, 501
Investment returns. *See* Returns
Investments, 5
   estate planning, 11–12
   forms of, 5–7
   interest rate considerations, 339–342
   liquidity, 8–9
   managing, 10–11
   market environment, 28–29
   objectives, 7–12
   retirement, 11–12
   risk. *See* Risk
   short-term and long-term, 9
   tax considerations, 9–10, 74–76
Investors
   in bond market, 302–303
   foreign, 296, 303
   individual, 47–48, 73–74, 248–249
   institutional, 31, 47–48, 302, 639–640
Investor's Business Daily, 105
Investors Management Science Company, 105
Ip, Greg, 472
IPOs. *See* Initial public offerings
Ippolito, Richard A., 261, 525, 628, 646
IRAs. *See* Individual Retirement Accounts
IRS. *See* Internal Revenue Service
ISE. *See* International Securities Exchange
Iskandar, Mai E., 407
ISM. *See* Institute for Supply Management
Italian bonds, 313

J

Jackworth, Jens, 432
Jacobs, Bruce L., 83
Jacquillat, Bertrand, 545, 549–550
Jaffe, Jeffrey F., 270, 287
Jagannathan, Murale, 287
Jain, Navaan, 137
January effect, 281
Japan. *See also* Nikkei 225 Stock Average
   automobile industry, 121, 152–153
   bonds, 313, 359
   stock market capitalization, 528
   Tokyo Stock Exchange, 548
   trade with U.S., 121
Jarrow, Robert A., 56, 57
Jennings, Robert H., 272, 287
Jensen, Michael C., 258, 612, 627, 628, 634
Jensen approach, 627–628
Jobman, Darrell, 466
Jobs, Steve, 144
Johannes, Michael, 377, 646
Johnson & Johnson
   asset utilization ratios, 212–213
   balance sheet, 202–204
   debt financing, 211–212
   debt-utilization ratios, 214–215
   dividends, 217

Johnson & Johnson—*Cont.*
   earnings, 176–177, 182–184
   income statement, 201–202
   industry comparisons, 217–220
   liquidity ratios, 213–214
   price ratios, 215–216
   price-earnings ratio, 177, 182
   profitability, 210–211
   reports on, 94, 95–97
   statement of cash flows, 205–207
   stock, 472
   tax rate, 217
   trend analysis, 220–222
Jones, Charles, 283
Jones, Charles P., 353
Jones, Sally-Ann, 491
Jorion, Philippe, 556
Journal of Finance, 105
Journal of Financial and Quantitative Analysis, 105
Journal of Financial Economics, 105
Journal of Financial Education, 105
The Journal of Portfolio Management, 105
JP Morgan, 28, 31, 33, 34, 35, 108
JP Morgan Chase, 28, 34, 92, 271, 460
JP Morgan Overseas Government Bond Index, 543–544
Junk bond funds, 307, 510
Junk bonds, 306–307

K

Kadlec, Gregory B., 56
Kandel, Samuel, 647
Kansas City Board of Trade, 467
Kao, Duen-Li, 324
Kaplan, Robert S., 259
Kaplan, Steven, 268
Kaplen, Paul D., 23
Karagiannis, Evangelos, 352
Katz, Steven, 313
Katzenberg, Jeffrey, 47
Kaul, Gantam, 257
Kealhofer, Stephen, 325
Keim, Donald B., 281
Kemna, Angelien, 353
Kerins, Francis J., Jr., 407
Kihn, John, 324
Kim, Charson, 199
Kim, S. H., 466
Kim, Theodore, 612
King, T. E., 407
Kirby, Chris, 141
Kirilenko, Andrei, 199
Kittrell, William, 181
Kogelman, Stanley, 199, 647
Koppenhaver, G. D., 466
Koretz, Gene, 141
Korkeamaki, Timo P., 407
Kuhn, Susan E., 324, 572
Kummer, Donald R., 268

L

L.M. Ericsson, 548
La Chapelle, Chris A., 273
Lagging indicators, 128–130

Lakonishok, Josef, 83, 277
Lam, Kim, 491
Lamont, Owen A., 23
Landsman, Wayne R., 199
Latane, Henry A., 283
Lau, C. S., 593, 602
Lawrence, Edward C., 605
Lazer, Ron, 646
Leading indicators, 125–126, 128–130
LEAPs. *See* Long-term equity anticipation securities
Lease, Ronald C., 274
Least squares regression analysis, 613–614
Least squares trend analysis, 186–187
Lee, Jae Ha, 466
Lehman Brothers, 35, 52
Leibowitz, Martin L., 199, 647
Leisikow, Dean, 83, 525
Leschhorn, Heiko, 377
Lev, Beruch, 646
Leverage strategy, 420–422
Levich, Richard M., 237
Levine, Dennis, 51
Levy, Kenneth N., 83
Levy, Robert A., 606
Lewellen, Wilbur G., 274
Lezner, Robert, 23
Li, Haitao, 237
LIFO (last-in, first-out), 224–226
Lim, Terrence, 141
Limit orders, 71–72
Limited partnerships, 570–571
Lin, Wenling, 611
Lindley, James T., 491
Linn, Scott C., 647
Linvat, Joshua, 646
Lipper Analytical Services, 65
Lipper Mutual and Investment Performance Averages, 65, 67, 517, 518
Liquidity, 8–9, 29
Liquidity effect, 132
Liquidity preference theory, 338
Liquidity ratios, 213–214
Lo, Andrew W., 266
Lo, Wai-Chung, 491
Load funds, 502, 503. *See also* Mutual funds
Lockheed, 209
Lockheed Martin, 209
Lockwood, Larry J., 556, 647
Logue, Dennis E., 83, 273, 630
London International Financial Futures Exchange, 44
London Stock Exchange, 107–108
Long positions, 70
Longin, Francois, 556
Longstaff, Francis A., 432
Long-Term Capital Management, 409
Long-term debt to equity ratio, 214
Long-term equity anticipation securities (LEAPs), 413
Loomis, Carol, 57
Lord, Richard A., 165
Losses, capital, 75–76

Low-load funds, 502. *See also* Mutual funds
Low P/E ratio effect, 279
Lynch, Anthony W., 525
Lyon, John D., 280

M

Ma, Christopher K., 466
Ma, Tongshu, 612
McAdams, Lloyd, 352
Macaulay, Frederick, 358
Macaulay duration, 358. *See also* Duration
McClean, Bethany, 283
McConnell, John J., 56, 82
MacDonald, Elizabeth, 237
McDonald, John G., 624–625, 628, 629, 634
McDonald's, 149, 152, 188, 458
McGee, Suzanne, 393
McGraw-Hill, Inc., 93, 94, 160, 303
McManus, Thomas, 472
Madhavan, Ananth, 556
Mahoney, James M., 377
Making markets, 31
Malkiel, Burton G., 23
Mam, Christopher, 324
Mamaysky, Harry, 266
Managed care, 160
Manaster, Steven, 273, 287
Mandelker, Gershon, 268, 270, 287
Mansi, Sattar A., 57
Mantle, Mickey, 576
Manufacturing, 133–135
Manville Corporation, 305
Mao, Connie X., 237
Marathon Oil, 270
Marchard, Patrick H., 491
Margin
 accounts, 68–70
 calls, 449–450
 commodity futures, 448, 449–450
 maintenance requirements, 448, 471
 minimum, 69
 requirements, 50, 68, 69
 and short sales, 70–71
 stock index futures, 471
Marginal tax rates, 75
Market capitalization, 277
Market line, 627
Market orders, 71
Market segmentation theory, 338–339
Market value added (MVA), 178
Market value, relationship to book value, 280
Markets, 29. *See also* Bond markets; Exchanges; International securities markets
 competition among, 30
 efficient, 29
 electronic communication networks, 37, 46
 functions, 29–30
 liquidity, 29
 making, 31
 over-the-counter, 37, 42, 44–46

Markets—*Cont.*
 primary, 30, 302, 303
 regulation, 48–53
 secondary, 30, 37, 302
Markowitz, Harry, 593
Markowitz portfolio theory, 593–594
Marshall, William J., 367, 377
Marston, Richard C., 431, 490
Martha Stewart Living Omnimedia, 283
Martin, John D., 336
Martin, Kenneth J., 271, 287
Mastro Fine Sports, 576
Masulis, R. W., 276
Mattel Inc., 63
Maturity dates, 291
Mayhew, Stewart, 431
Media General, 105
MedQuist Inc., 72
Meeks, Sue E., 273
Megginson, William L., 56
Mei, Jianping, 556
Merck, 8, 144, 217–220, 275
Mercury Finance, 113
Mergent, Inc. (Moody's), 92–93, 308
 Bond Record, 92, 308
 Bond Survey, 92
 Dividend Record, 92
 Handbook of Common Stock, 92
 Moody's Manuals, 92
Merger price premiums, 268–270
Mergers and acquisitions, 268–271
 cancellations, 270
 of financial institutions, 28, 33, 269, 271
 form of payment, 271
 performance of acquiring company, 270–271
 in pharmaceutical industry, 158, 269
 premiums for acquired companies, 268–270
 unfriendly, 270
 white knights, 270
Merjos, Anna, 275
Merrill Lynch, 178, 496
 accounts with, 68, 70
 bond trading, 46
 competitors, 3, 35
 fees, 72
 Martha Stewart case, 283
 mutual fund study, 634
 mutual funds, 307, 510, 512
 NYSE seats, 40
 odd-lot trading, 41
 online trading, 73
 real estate affiliate, 559
 research, 99
 security analysts, 52
 underwriting syndicates, 31
 website, 108
Merrill Lynch Pacific fund, 510
Mesa Petroleum, 270
Metrick, Andrew, 524
Meyers, Thomas A., 247
Microsoft, 137
 market capitalization, 61, 531
 MSN.com, 108

Microsoft—*Cont.*
  price/earnings ratio, 181
  stock, 30, 45, 63, 272, 283, 472, 585
MicroStrategy, 137
Mihov, Vissol, 431
Milbourn, Todd M., 237
Milken, Michael, 51, 52, 261, 307
Miller, Edward M., 612
Miller, Robert E., 199, 272
Milligan, Jack, 582
Milonas, Nikolaos, 432
Mingo, Kent A., 304
Mini Dow Jones Industrial Average, 469
Mini Nasdaq 100 Stock Index futures, 469, 474
Mini S&P 500 index futures, 474
Minimum maintenance standards, 69
Minkow, Barry, 232–233
Minton, Bernadette A., 466
Mirant, 393
Missouri Pacific, 342
Mitchell, George, 47
Mittelstaedt, H. Fred, 237
MMM, 250
Mobil, 270
Mobius, Mark, 493
Modified duration, 377–378
Modigliani, Franco, 23, 606
Modigliani, Leah, 23
Moeller, Thomas, 324
Molina, Carlos A., 324
Monetarism, 132
Monetary policy, 117, 122–124, 136
Money magazine, 76
Money managers. *See* Portfolio managers
Money market accounts, 315–316
Money market funds, 315, 316, 506
Money supply, 130–132
Monopolies, 150
Monroe, Robert J., 269
Monsanto, 178, 275
Moody's bond ratings, 289, 303–306, 547. *See also* Mergent
Moody's Investor Services, 303
Moore, Geoffrey H., 141
Moore, William T., 407
Morgan Guaranty Trust Company, 551
Morgan Stanley, 3, 72, 268–269, 393
Morgan Stanley Asset Management, 572
Morgan Stanley Capital International (MSCI), 539
Morgan Stanley Capital International Index, 632
Morgan, J. P. *See* JP Morgan
Morningstar
  Mutual Fund Survey, 503, 506, 516–517
  products, 98
  website, 98
Mortgage trusts, 571
Mortgages, 292, 568–569
  adjustable-rate (ARM), 568
  equity participation arrangements, 569
  GNMA pass-through certificates, 297–298

Mortgages—*Cont.*
  graduated payment (GPM), 568
  interest rates, 136
  second, 569
  shared appreciation (SAM), 568–569
Moses, O. Douglas, 199
Moster, James T., 491
Mott, Claudia E., 266
MSCI. *See* Morgan Stanley Capital International
Mullin, John, 556
Multinational corporations, 549–550
Municipal bond funds, 510
Municipal Bond Investors Assurance (MBIA), 299
Municipal bonds, 46, 298–299
  futures on, 454
  general obligation, 299
  guarantees, 299
  ratings, 299
  revenue, 299
  trading, 46
  in unit investment trusts (UITs), 525–526
  yields, 299, 300
Murphy, Austin, 466
Muscarella, Chris J., 272, 287
Musto, David K., 525
Mutual funds, 495–496
  advantages, 496–497
  advertising, 586–587
  automatic investments, 514
  averages, 65, 67, 68
  back-end loads, 502
  balanced, 508
  bond, 508–510
  capital gains taxes, 513–514
  cash positions, 254–255
  closed-end, 498–501, 502
  disadvantages, 497–498
  distributions, 513–514
  diversification, 496–497, 512, 631–634
  dollar-cost averaging, 515–516
  emerging markets, 493
  exchange privileges, 514–515
  exchange traded, 43, 501, 551
  families, 512, 514–515
  fees and expenses, 513, 632
  foreign, 510
  growth, 508
  growth with income, 508
  households owning, 494–495
  index, 501, 508, 630–631, 632
  information sources, 98, 506
  international, 493, 510, 511, 550–551
  junk bond, 307, 510
  load, 502, 503
  low-load, 502
  managers, 261, 493, 624–625
  money market, 315, 316, 506
  municipal bond, 510
  net asset values (NAV), 500, 501
  no-load, 502–505
  objectives, 506–511, 512, 624–625
  performance
    advertising, 586–587

Mutual funds—*Cont.*
  performance—*Cont.*
    compared to market indexes, 261, 628–629, 631
    evaluating, 516–519
    McDonald study, 624–625, 628
    returns, 517–519
  prospectuses, 512–513
  purchasing, 515
  quotes, 503, 504
  regulation of, 50, 512
  reinvestment, 514
  sector, 510
  selecting, 511–512
  shareholder services, 514–515
  specialty, 510–511
  taxation of, 513–514
  tax-exempt, 510
  turnover rates, 513
MVA. *See* Market value added

N

Naik, Vasanttilak, 431
Naked options, 423–425
Nantell, Timothy J., 276
NASD. *See* National Association of Securities Dealers
Nasdaq Stock Market, 44–45, 53
  American depository receipts, 548
  indexes, 28, 59, 63, 469, 474
  national market issues, 45
  100 Stock Index, 63
    futures on, 468, 469, 474
    Mini, 469, 474
    options on, 411, 479–480
  small cap issues, 45
  trading volume, 45
National Association of Securities Dealers (NASD), 44, 50
National Bureau of Economic Research (NBER), 118, 126, 135
National Council on Economic Education (NCEE), 409
National Endowment for Financial Education, 26
Natural gas pipeline companies, 189
Natural resources, as assets, 189
NatWest Securities, 472
NAV. *See* Net asset values
Nawalkha, Sanjay K., 353, 377
Nayar, Nandkumar, 407
NBER. *See* National Bureau of Economic Research
NCEE. *See* National Council on Economic Education
Negative news, stock market reactions, 276
Nesbitt, Stephen L., 466
Net asset values (NAV), 500, 501
Net working capital to total assets ratio, 213, 214
Netscape, 272
Neuberger, Brian M., 273
New York Board of Trade, 28
New York Cotton Exchange, 447
New York Futures Exchange, 454

Index

New York Stock Exchange (NYSE)
  advance-decline indicator, 253–254
  after-hours trading, 46
  American depository receipts (ADRs) listed on, 548, 550
  circuit breakers, 51–53
  delisting, 40, 275
  dual listing, 38
  effects of terrorist attacks, 28, 37
  electronic communication networks and, 46
  foreign companies listed, 55, 548
  indexes, 63. See also Dow Jones Industrial Average
  listing requirements, 38–39
  market share, 38
  members, 40–42
  new listings, 273
  order execution, 71
  program trading on, 51–53
  Rule 390, 46
  short sales, 249
  specialists, 41–42
  Super Dot system, 42
  trading volume, 28, 38, 45, 244
The New York Times, 100, 108
Newmont Mining, 575
Newspapers, 100–105, 108
NexGen, 272
Niederhoffer, Victor, 473
Nike, Inc., 149
Nikkei 225 Stock Average, 64, 528
  futures on, 471, 474
Nocera, Joseph, 165
No-load funds, 502–505. See also Mutual funds
Nonconstant growth model, 174–175
Norgaard, Connie, 275
Norgaard, Richard, 275
Norton, Rob, 165
Notre Dame University, 605
Novartis, 154, 217–220, 222
Novell, 250
Nuclear utilities, 301
Nuveen, Inc., 525–526
NYSE. See New York Stock Exchange

O

OARS (Opening Automated Report Service), 42
O'Bryne, Stephen F., 199
Odd-lot dealers, 41
Odd-lot theory, 248–249
O'Hara, Maureen, 266
Ohio State University, 605
Oil companies, 189
Olde, 72
Oligopolies, 150
O'Neal, Edward S., 525
Online brokers, 72–73
Online trading, 47, 72–73
Opdyke, Jeff D., 52
Open-end funds, 498, 501
Open interest, 452
Open-market operations, 122
Opler, Tim, 406

Oppenheimer, Henry R., 268
Oppenheimer Special Fund, 513
Optimum portfolios, 596
Option prices, on warrants, 397
Options, 5, 410–411. See also Stock index options
  at the money, 415
  Black-Scholes option pricing model, 432–438
  buying calls, 420–423
  buying puts, 425–426
  call, 43, 411
  commissions, 427
  on commodities, 458
  covered, 423–425
  on currencies, 458
  employee stock options, 289
  exchanges, 43, 411–413
  exercise prices, 413–414
  expiration dates, 413–414
  on financial instruments, 458
  on futures, 458–459, 468
  hedging with, 426
  in the money, 414
  intrinsic values, 415, 421
  naked, 423–425
  orders, 414
  out of the money, 414–415
  premiums, 414–415, 416–419
  put, 43, 411
  speculative premium, 416–419
  spreads, 426, 438–441
  on stock index futures, 482–484
  straddles, 426
  strategies, 419
    as alternative to stocks, 422, 425–426
    guaranteed price, 423
    leverage, 420–422
    protecting short positions, 422–423
  tax treatments, 426–427
  trading, 411, 414
  trading cycles, 413
  trading volumes, 412, 419
  writers, 414
  writing calls, 423–425
Options Clearing Corporation, 412–413, 414
Oracle, 45, 63, 137, 185
Orders, 71
  day, 72
  good till canceled, 72
  limit, 71–72
  market, 71
  for options, 414
  placement and execution, 71
  stop, 72
  stop-loss, 72
Organized exchanges, 37, 43–44. See also Exchanges
Ortegren, A. K., 407
Ostdiek, Barbara, 141
Out of the money, 414–415
Over-the-counter markets, 37, 44–46. See also Nasdaq Stock Market
  bonds, 45–46

Over-the-counter markets—Cont.
  commercial paper, 46
Overall market rules, 253–255
Ovtchinnikov, Alexei V., 82
Oxelheim, Lars, 57

P

P/E. See Price-earnings ratios
P/FFO. See Price/funds from operations ratios
Pacific Coast Exchange (PSE), 413, 414
Paleps, Krisha G., 271, 287
Pan Am, 148
Panigirtzoglou, Nikolaos, 431
Pantzalis, Christos, 199
Par value, 291
Paré, Terrence P., 23
Parity prices, 384
Park, Cheol, 324
Partial hedges, 458
Partnerships, real estate, 569–571
Passive losses, 570
Pastor, Lubos, 199
Patel, Ajay, 406
Patents, pharmaceutical, 159
Paterson, James D., 275
Peavy, John W., III, 279, 556
Peers, Alexandra, 261
Peng, Ruijue, 583
Penn-Central, 208
Pension funds
  as investors, 639
  liabilities for, 226
  valuation, 227
Pepsi, 149
Periodicals
  business, 100, 181
  journals, 105
  newspapers, 100–105, 108
Perpetual bonds, 291
Personal computers
  databases, 105
  industry, 144–145, 149, 227
Peters, Edgar E., 83
Peterson, James D., 287
Peterson, John E., 491
Pfizer, 8, 153–154, 157, 158, 217–220
Pharmaceutical industry
  comparative company analysis, 155–156
  demographic influences, 159–160
  financial ratios, 217–220
  generic drugs, 159
  global, 153–154
  growth rates, 154
  ImClone, 283
  leading companies, 153–154
  life-cycle analysis, 154
  mergers, 158, 269
  net income, 154
  operating revenues, 154
  patents, 159
  product diversity, 158–159
  regulation, 154
  research and development, 157–158
Pharmacia, 153–154

Philadelphia Exchange (PHLX), options trading, 412, 414, 458, 482
Phoenix Fund, 510
Pillsbury, 269
Pinches, George E., 257, 304, 313
Pipeline.com, 137
Placer Dome Inc., 575
Platt, Russell, 572
Pogue, Gerald A., 606
Pogue, Thomas F., 304
Point and figure charts, 247
Political risks in international markets, 546, 550
Polson, Nicholas, 377, 646
Pomerantz, Carrie Schwab, 3
Porter, Michael E., 151, 165
Portfolio effect, 589–592
Portfolio insurance, 478
Portfolio managers
  asset allocation, 634–637, 639
  careers, 24–25
  diversification by, 631–634
  international specialists, 551
  objectives, 624–625
  performance, 619–620, 624, 628–629
  risk exposure, 624–625
  students, 605
Portfolios, 5
  betas, 606, 631
  efficient, 593–595
  efficient frontier, 593–594, 597
  optimum, 596
  sector allocation, 638
  two-asset, 590–592
Post, Mitchell A., 325
Poterba, James M., 83
Potter, Roger, 181
Precious gems, 575–577
Precious metals. *See* Gold; Silver
Preferred stocks, 6, 316–317. *See also* Convertible securities
  callable, 316
  convertible, 316, 388–391
  dividends, 316–317
  quotes, 317
Prell, Michael J., 336
Premiums. *See also* Risk premium; Speculative premium
  option, 414–415, 416–419
Present value. *See also* Duration
  of annuity, 656–657, 664–665
  of single amount, 654–655, 662–664
  of uneven cash flow, 665–666
Price-to-book value model, 183–184
Price to book value ratio, 215, 216
Price-to-cash flow model, 183–184
Price-to-dividend model, 183–184
Price-earnings ratios (P/E), 177–180, 215
  individual firms, 215–216
  individual stocks, 180–183
  industry, 181
  in international markets, 539–541
  low, 279
  market, 179–180
  relative, 182–183

Price/funds from operations ratios (P/FFO), 572
Price ratios, 215–216
Price-to-sales model, 183–184
Price-weighted averages, 61
PriceWaterhouseCoopers, 289
Primary earnings per share, 394
Primary markets, 30, 302, 303. *See also* Underwriting
Pringle, John J., 18, 558
Private placements, 31, 303
Procter & Gamble, 445, 632
Productivity, 135
Profitability ratios, 210–212
Program trading, 51–53, 469
Prospectuses
  mutual funds, 512–513
  new issue, 33, 49, 55, 99
Proxy procedures, 50
Proxy statements, 99
Prudent Bear Fund, 113
Prudential Securities, 99, 108, 396
Psychology, cognitive, 255
Public offerings. *See also* Initial public offerings (IPOs); Underwriting
  distribution, 31–34
  prospectuses, 33, 49, 55, 99
Public Service of Indiana, 301
Public utilities, 149, 150–151, 300–301
Pure bond value, 382–384
Pure competition, 150
Pure pickup yield swaps, 344
Put and Call Dealers Association, 411
Put-call ratio, 251
Put options, 43, 411, 425–426. *See also* Options
Put provisions, on bonds, 292

Q

Qian, Edward, 647
QQQs, 469
Quaker Oats, 268
Quest, 283
Quick & Reilly, 72
Quick ratio, 213

R

R^2, 632–633
Rahman, Shafiqur, 646
Rajan, Raghuram, 287
Rapid-American Corporation, 307
Rate of return, 12
  anticipated inflation factor, 14–15
  real, 14
  required, 12–13, 169–171
  risk-free, 15, 169–170
  risk premium, 15–18
Ratings, bond, 289, 303–306
Ratio analysis, 207–208. *See also* Financial ratios
Ravi, Jagannathan, 612
Ravid, S. Abraham, 352
Reagan, Ronald, 41, 117, 120, 181
Real assets, 5, 557. *See also* Gold; Real estate
  advantages, 558

Real assets—*Cont.*
  collectibles, 576, 577
  commissions, 558
  disadvantages, 558–559
  gems, 575–577
  and inflation, 18
  silver, 5, 575
Real estate, 559–561
  depreciation, 563–564
  financing, 567–569
  mortgages, 568–569
  ownership forms, 569–571
  partnerships, 569–571
  passive losses, 570
  price appreciation, 565–566
  syndicates, 570–571
  taxes and, 559–560
  valuation
    cash flow analysis, 562–567
    comparative sales value, 561
    cost approach, 561
    income approach, 561–562
  volatility, 5
Real Estate Investment Trust Act of 1960, 571
Real estate investment trusts (REITs), 571, 572, 573
Real rate of return, 14
Receivables turnover, 212
Recessions, 117, 118, 121, 126, 133, 136
Red herrings, 49
Redback Networks, 395
Reeb, David M., 57
Regional exchanges, 37
Registered traders, 40–41
Registration trading statements, 55, 99
Regulation
  of commodity exchanges, 447
  of financial institutions, 28, 31–33
  of industries, 150–151
  Investment Advisor Act of 1940, 50
  Investment Companies Act of 1940, 50, 512
  of pharmaceutical industry, 154
  Real Estate Investment Trust Act of 1960, 571
  Securities Act of 1933, 48–49, 52, 55
  Securities Acts Amendments of 1975, 48, 50
  Securities Exchange Act of 1934, 48, 49–50, 51, 52, 55, 99
  Securities Investor Protection Act of 1970, 50–51
Reilly, Frank K., 272
Reinganum, Marc R., 260, 278, 279
Reinvestment assumptions, 334–335, 367–368
  terminal wealth analysis, 368–370
REITs. *See* Real estate investment trusts
Rendleman, Richard, 283
Renshaw, Edward, 23, 141
Replacement-cost accounting, 223
Repurchases, 275–277. *See also* Stock repurchases
Required rate of return, 12–13, 169–171
Reserve requirements, 122

Resistance levels, 243–244
Resorts International, 307
Retention ratio, 166
Retirement
  hedges, 478
  investing for, 11–12
Return on assets, 210, 211
Return on equity (ROE), 165–167, 211
Returns
  abnormal, 268
  arbitrage pricing theory, 615–618
  average differential (alpha), 628
  beta coefficients, 170, 418, 600–602
  capital asset pricing model, 597–600
  excess, 272, 625
  expected value, 587–588
  historical trends, 620–621
  on individual securities, 600–604, 605–606
  in international markets, 536–538, 541–545
  long-term, 621–624
  market line, 627
  on mutual funds, 517–519
  rates of, 12
  required, 12–13, 169–171
  risk and, 15–18, 594–596, 625
  by sector, 638
  small-firm effect, 277–279
Revco, 307
Revell, Janice, 23
Revenue bonds, 299
Rexford, Bradley, 227
Rhim, Johg-Chul, 407
Rhoades Corporation, 224–226
Richardson, Vernon J., 266
Riepe, Mark, 23, 199
Risk
  capital asset pricing model, 597–600
  investment objectives and, 7–8
  measures, 12–14, 587–589
  political, 546, 550
  portfolio effect, 589–592
  and returns, 15–18
    in bond market, 310–312
    excess returns, 272, 625
    holding periods, 621–624
    indifference curves, 594–596, 597
    Jensen approach, 627–628
    Sharpe approach, 626
    Treynor approach, 626–627
  in special situations, 284
  standard deviation, 588–589
  systematic, 14, 602, 631
  unsystematic, 602, 631–632
Risk-free assets, 597
Risk-free rate of return, 15, 169–170
Risk premium, 15–18
Ritchen, Peter, 466
Ritter, Jay R., 272, 287
RMA Annual Statement Studies, 98
Robert Morris Associates, 98
Robichek, Alexander A., 18, 558
Robinson, Anthony W., 535, 556
Rockefeller Foundation, 640
Rodriguez, Alex, 255

Rodriguez, Mauricio, 556
ROE. *See* Return on equity
Roll, Richard, 57, 258, 259, 278–279, 281, 336, 533, 605, 612, 616
Root, Charley, 63
Rosenberg, Barr, 612
Ross, Stephen A., 612, 616
Rotational investing, 160–162
Roulet, Jacques, 612
Rozeff, Michael S., 261
Ruback, Richard S., 271, 287
Rubinstein, Mark, 266
Rukeyser, Louis, 248
Rule 390, 46
Russell 1000 Index, 64
Russell 2000 Index
  as benchmark, 59, 637
  companies included, 64
  futures on, 471
  options on, 479–480
Russell 3000 Index, 64
Ruth, Babe, 63, 576
Ruth, Simon, 524
Ryan, J., 281
Ryan, Nolan, 576
Rzadkowski, Grzegorz, 377

S

S&P. *See* Standard & Poor's Corporation
Saderion, Zahra, 583
Sales forecasts, 187–188
Sales per share (SPS), 183–184
Salomon Brothers, 18, 322, 365
Salomon Smith Barney, Inc., 28, 33, 99, 108, 393, 512
Salomon, R. S., 23
SAM. *See* Shared appreciation mortgages
Sanger, Gary C., 56, 275, 287
Santa-Clara, Pedro, 141, 353
Sarin, Atulya, 237
Sartoris, William S., 313
Saunders, Edward M., 266
Saylor, Michael, 137
SBC, 496
Scandals, corporate, 283, 289
Schadt, Rudi W., 525
Schlarbaum, Gary G., 274, 635
Schmidt, Klause M., 406
Scholes, Myron S., 431, 432
Schrand, Catherine, 466
Schwab, Charles, 3
Schwartz, Anna J., 131
Schwartz, Eduardo S., 432
Scottrade, 3
SEC. *See* Securities and Exchange Commission
Second mortgages, 569
Secondary markets, 30, 37, 302. *See also* Exchanges
Sector funds, 510
Sector returns, 638
Secured debt, 292–293
Securities. *See also* Bonds; Common stocks
  delisting, 40, 275
  direct offerings, 31

Securities—*Cont.*
  exchange listings, 38–40
  issuing methods, 31
  public offerings, 31–34
  registration, 49, 55
Securities Act of 1933, 48–49, 52, 55
Securities Acts Amendments of 1975, 48, 50
Securities and Exchange Commission (SEC), 33, 48
  circuit breakers and, 51–53
  EDGAR system, 50, 100, 200
  8-K Reports, 99
  investigations of companies, 283
  powers, 49, 99
  reporting to, 50, 55, 99–100, 261, 547
  Rule 12b-1, 513
  shelf registration, 33–34, 303
  study of securities markets, 260–261
  10-K Reports, 50, 99
  10-Q Statements, 99
  website, 99–100, 200
Securities Exchange Act of 1934, 48, 49–50, 51, 52, 55, 99
Securities Industry Association, 24
Securities Investor Protection Act of 1970, 50–51
Securities Investor Protection Corporation (SIPC), 50–51
Security analysts, 24–25, 52, 113
Security market line (SML), 603–604, 605–606, 614–615
Sellers, Patricia, 165
Seppenfield, Ross, 556
September 11, 2001, terrorist attacks, 28–29, 37, 118, 120, 533
Serial payments, 291–292
Servaes, Henri, 287
Service industries, 137
Settle prices, 456
SFAS. *See* Statement of Financial Accounting Standards
Shared appreciation mortgages (SAM), 568–569
Sharpe, William F., 612, 626, 628
Sharpe approach, 626
Shefrin, Hersh, 466
Shelf registration, 33–34, 303
Shell Canada, 305
Shockley, Richard L., 377
Short interest ratio, 249
Short positions, 70–71, 422–423
Short sales, 70–71, 249
  motives, 113
  ratio, 249
  by specialists, 253
Short sales position theory, 249–250
Short squeezes, 472
Short-term earnings model, 182
Siegel, Lawrence B., 18
Silver, 5, 575
Simkowitz, Michael A., 269
Simon, David P., 491
Simons, John, 165
Sindelar, J., 272
Singh, Ajai K., 407

Singleton, Clay, 313
Sinking funds, 292
Sinquefield, Rex, 63
SIPC. *See* Securities Investor Protection Corporation
Sit, Eugene, 585
Sit Investment Associates, 585
Sit Mutual Funds, 585
Skeratt, Len, 266
Small-firm effect, 277–279
Smart money rules, 251–253
Smith Barney, 3, 68
Smith, Burton, 583
Smith, Charles, 583
Smith, David M., 406
Smith, Randall, 365
SML. *See* Security market line
So, Raymond W., 556
Soldofsky, Robert M., 304
Solnik, Bruno H., 535, 545, 549–550, 556, 612
Sony Corporation, 149, 548
Sotheby's, 576
SoundView Capital Markets, 3
Southern Methodist University, 605
Special situations, 284. *See also* Mergers and acquisitions
  anomalies, 281–283
  bad news, 276
  exchange listings, 273–275
  federal investigations, 283
  new issues, 271–273
  small firms, 277–279
  stock repurchases, 275–277
Specialists, 41–42, 273
  hedging, 478
  performance, 260–261
  short sales by, 253
Specialty funds, 510–511
Speculative premium
  on options, 416–419
  on warrants, 397–398
Speidell, Lawrence S., 556
Sports memorabilia, 576
Spot prices, of commodities, 452
Spreads
  options, 426, 438–441
  yields, 342–344
Sprint Capital Corporation, 31, 33
Sprint Corporation, 31, 33, 35
Stambaugh, Robert F., 647
Standard & Poor's Corporation, 93, 604
  100 Stock Index, 61–62, 419
  400 MidCap Index, 61, 474
  500 Stock Index, 61, 152
    as benchmark, 59, 635, 637, 638
    companies included, 472
    futures on, 468, 469, 471, 474, 475
    growth rates of companies, 146–147
    index funds, 501, 508, 632
    options on, 43, 411, 419, 468, 481–482
    options on futures, 483

Standard & Poor's Corporation—*Cont.*
  500 Stock Index—*Cont.*
    relationship to economic activity, 132–133
  600 SmallCap Index, 61
  1500 Stock Index, 61
  Bond Guide, 93–94, 308
  bond ratings, 289, 303–306, 547
  Compustat, 105–107
  Corporation Records, 93
  Global Stock Markets Factbook, 539
  Industry Survey, 160
  mutual fund performance, 631
  NetAdvantage, 94
  Security Owner's Stock Guide, 317
  Stock Guide, 93
  Stock Reports, 94, 95–96
  Trendline, 246
  website, 93
Standard deviation, 588–589
  two-asset portfolio, 590–592
Standard Oil of California, 270
Starks, Laura T., 647
State and local government securities. *See* Municipal bonds
State Street Bank and Trust Company, 551
Statement of Financial Accounting Standards (SFAS) No. 95, 204
Statement of Financial Accounting Standards (SFAS) No. 128, 394
Statman, Meir, 466
Stephens, Clifford, 287
Stern Stewart & Co., 178
Stevens, Donald J., 269
Stewart, Martha, 283
Stickel, Scott E., 281, 287
Stock exchanges. *See* Exchanges
Stock index arbitrage, 479
Stock index futures, 467–468
  arbitrage with, 479
  basis, 473
  cash settlement, 472
  exchanges, 469
  features, 474
  hedging with, 470, 471, 476–479
  leverage, 475
  margin requirements, 471
  options on, 482–484
  speculation with, 474–476
  trading, 469–471
  trading cycle, 471
  volatility, 475
Stock index options, 43, 411, 467–468, 479
  exchanges, 479–480
  hedging with, 482
  on industry indexes, 482
  trading, 419, 481
Stock indexes
  as benchmarks, 58–59
  equal-weighted, 63
  international, 64, 516, 539, 540–541, 551
  as leading indicators, 130
  mini, 469

Stock indexes—*Cont.*
  mutual funds based on, 501, 630–631, 632
  price-weighted, 61
  relationship to economic activity, 132–135
  uses, 68
  value-weighted, 62
Stock pickers, 113, 142
Stock repurchases, 275–277
Stockbrokers, 24. *See also* Brokers
Stockholder's equity 214. *See also* Return on equity (ROE)
Stocks. *See* Common stocks; Preferred stocks
Stoll, H. A., 279
Stone, Douglas, 556
Stop-loss orders, 72
Stop orders, 72
Straddles, 426
Straight-line depreciation, 563–564
Strauss, Thomas, 322
Strebel, Paul, 279
Strike prices, of options, 413–414
Stripped Treasury securities, 294–295, 310, 312
Students, as portfolio managers, 605
Sun Microsystems, 45, 108, 137
Sunbeam, 113
Sunder, Shyam, 259
Super Dot system, 42
Support levels, 243–244
Surpluses, federal, 120
Surprise-earnings effect, 283
Survey of Current Business, 89–91
Sustainable growth model, 165–167
Swaps
  bond, 344
  interest-rate, 459–460
  pure pickup yield, 344
Sweeney, Richard J., 324
Sydney Stock Exchange, 548
Symbol Technologies, 283, 380–381
Syndicates
  real estate, 570–571
  underwriting, 31–34
Synergy, 271
Syngenta, 548
Systematic risk, 14, 602, 631

T

T. Rowe Price European Stock Fund, 506, 507, 516–517
T. Rowe Price Funds, 501, 512
Takslar, Glen B., 352
Tandon, Kishore, 56
Tariffs, 120
Tarun, Chordia, 57
Taubman, Beth W., 141
Tax Act of 2001, 11
Tax Reform Act of 1986, 559–560, 564, 570
Tax Relief Act of 2003, 9–10, 74–75, 316
Taxes
  average rate, 217
  and bond swaps, 344

Taxes—*Cont.*
 on capital gains, 9–10, 75–76, 513–514
 cheating, 76
 cuts, 117, 120
 on dividend income, 9–10, 75, 316
 estate, 11
 exemption for municipal bond income, 298, 510
 fiscal policy, 118–122
 and hedging, 479
 increases, 117, 120
 in international markets, 546, 550
 and investment objectives, 9–10, 74–76
 and January effect, 281
 loss carryovers, 74–75
 marginal rates, 298
 and municipal bond funds, 510
 and mutual funds, 513–514
 and options trading, 426–427
 rates, 74–75
 and real estate investments, 559–560, 564, 570
 on zero-coupon bonds, 295
Technical analysis, 241
 chart types, 244–247
 contrary opinion rules, 248–251
 Dow theory, 242–243
 and efficient market hypothesis, 257–258
 key indicators, 248
 overall market rules, 253–255
 smart money rules, 251–253
Technology companies, 188, 472
 personal computer industry, 144–145, 149, 227
 stock prices, 137
 stocks listed on Nasdaq, 45, 63
 valuation, 185
Telephone companies, 151
Templeton, 501
Templeton Asset Management Ltd., 493
Templeton Emerging Markets Fund Incorporated, 493
Templeton World Fund, 510
10-K Reports, 50, 99
10-Q Statements, 99
Term structure of interest rates, 336–339
Terminal wealth analysis, 368–370
Terminal wealth table, 368–370
Terrorist attacks, 28–29, 37, 118, 120, 533
Texaco, 472
Texas Christian University, 605
Texas Instruments, 496
Thakor, Anjan V., 237
Thomadakis, Stavros B., 432
Thomas, P. B., 407
Thomson Financial, Inc., 98
Tice, David, 113
Time value. *See* Present value; Speculative premium
Time Warner, 41, 269
Times interest earned, 214
TIPS. *See* Treasury Inflation Protection Securities

Titman, Sheridan, 406, 525, 556, 646
Tokyo Stock Exchange, 548. *See also* Nikkei 225 Stock Average
Tombstone advertisements, 31, 32, 33
Top-down approach, 142–143
Toshiba, 548
Total asset turnover, 212
Total debt to total assets ratio, 214
Total return, on mutual funds, 517–519
Trade deficits, 121
Traders, 9
 day, 73–74
 institutional, 47–48
 registered, 40–41
Trading ranges, 243–244
Transaction costs, 8
Transworld Airways. *See* TWA
Travelers Group, 472
Travelers Insurance, 28, 33
Treasury Inflation Protection Securities (TIPS), 295–296
Treasury securities. *See also* Government securities
 bills, 15, 293–294, 310
 bonds, 293–294, 309
 inflation-indexed, 295–296
 notes, 293–294, 309–310
 quotes, 309–310, 311
 stripped, 294–295, 310, 312
 zero-coupon, 294–295, 310
Trend analysis, 220–222
Treynor, Jack L., 57, 626
Treynor approach, 626–627
Trezevant, Robert, 237
TRW, 117
Tufano, Peter, 583
Turner Broadcasting, 268
TVA, 335
TWA, 148
Tyco, 113, 283

U

UBS, 35, 68, 72, 99, 304
UBS Warburg, 31
UCLA, 605
UITs. *See* Unit investment trusts
Ulan, Michael, 141
Underwriting, 31, 272–273
 fees, 34–35, 393
 hedges, 478
 in international markets, 35–37
 leading institutions, 34–37
 syndicates, 31–34
Unfriendly takeovers, 270
Unger, Laura, 52
Unisys, 227
Unit investment trusts (UITs), 525–526
United Banks of Switzerland. *See* UBS
United Kingdom
 bonds, 313
 London Stock Exchange, 107–108
United Services Gold Shares, 510
U.S. Census Bureau, 91
U.S. government. *See also* Federal Reserve system; Government securities

U.S. government—*Cont.*
 budget, 118
 Council of Economic Advisors, 92, 116
 Department of Commerce, 547
  Bureau of Economic Analysis, 86, 89, 91
  Survey of Current Business, 89–91
 economic policy, 116–118
 Government Accounting Office (GAO), 76
 and international trade, 120–121
 investigations of companies, 283
 Web portal, 91
U.S. Steel, 270
U.S. Treasury. *See* Treasury securities
U.S. Trust Corporation, 3
University of Chicago, Center for Research in Security Prices, 107
University of Michigan, 125–126
University of Missouri—St. Louis, 605
University of Southern California, 605
University of Wisconsin, 605
Unsecured debt, 293
Unsystematic risk, 602, 631–632
Uppal, Raman, 612
Urias, Michael S., 524
Usmen, Nilufer, 466
Utilities. *See* Public utilities

V

Valkanov, Rossen, 141
Valuation. *See also* Dividend valuation models; Earnings valuation models
 of bonds, 327–329, 355–356
 of common stocks, 115, 168, 189
 economic value added (EVA), 178
 of warrants, 397–399
Value investors, 113, 493
Value Line, 604
 ranking effect, 281, 282
 ratings, 547
 REIT information, 571, 573
Value Line Average, 59, 63
Value Line Convertibles, 94
Value Line Index, 467
Value Line Investment Survey, 94, 97, 281, 282
Value Line Options, 94
Value-weighted averages, 62
Van Horne, James C., 273
Vanguard Group, 501, 512
Vanguard Index 500 fund, 508, 509, 632
Variable-rate notes, 291
Varikooty, A. P., 287
Venture capital, 400
Vermaelen, Theo, 276, 277
Verones, Pietro, 199
Vertical spreads, 438
 bear, 441
 bull, 439–441
Vetsuypens, Michael R., 272, 287
Virginia Military Institute, 605
Volatility
 of interest rates, 339
 of investments, 5
 of stock index futures, 475

Vora, Ashok, 332
Vorst, Tom, 353
Vu, Joseph, 249

W

Wachovia Bank Corp., 269
Wachter, Jessica, 524
Wagner, Honus, 576
Wagner, W. H., 593, 602
Waksal, Sam, 283
Walker, Jay, 137
The Wall Street Journal, 52, 100–103, 242
  bond indexes, 64, 66
  bond quotes, 307
  commodity futures prices, 100, 102, 451–452
  international markets, 64, 65
  mutual fund tables, 503, 504
  preferred stock quotes, 317
  short sales figures, 249
  stock prices, 45, 100, 101
Wall Street Transcript, 105
Wall Street Week, 248
Wal-Mart, 152, 472, 585
Wang, Jiang, 266
Wang, M. H. Franco, 556
Wang, Tan, 612
Warga, Arthur D., 324, 325
Warrants, 5, 395–397
  accounting considerations, 400–401
  exchanges, 43
  intrinsic value, 397, 398–399
  option prices, 397
  speculative premiums, 397–398
  uses of, 399, 400
  valuation, 397–399
Warshawsky, Mark J., 237
Washington REIT, 571, 573
Washington State Power Authority, 301
Webb, Gwendolyn, 56
Websites. *See also* Internet
  class project, 109–110
  corporate, 100, 108

Websites—*Cont.*
  economic data, 91
  Federal Reserve bank, 86–87
  Securities and Exchange Commission (SEC), 99–100, 200
  stock price charts, 108
  U.S. government, 91
Weekend effect, 281
Wei, Jason, 352
Wei, K. C. John, 556
Weighted average life, 356
Weil, Roman L., 366
Weingarten Realty, 572
Weisbenner, Scott J., 83
Wendy's International, 63
Wermers, Russ, 525, 646
Westinghouse Electric, 472
Weyerhaeuser, 189
Whaley, R. E., 279
White, Barry C., 199
White knights, 270
Whyte, Ann Marie, 164
Wiggins, James B., 490
Wiggins, Roy A., III, 491
Wilshire 5000 Equity Index, 64, 632
Wilson, Jack W., 353
Wilson, Susan, 583
Winters, Drew, 324
Withholding taxes, 546, 550
Wolf, Avner, 490
Woolworth, 472
World Bank, 314
World equity markets. *See* International securities markets
World Index, 539
World Trade Center, 28, 37, 533
World Trade Organization (WTO), 120–121
World Wide Web. *See* Websites
WorldCom, 185
Wright, Roger L., 276
Writing call options, 423–425
WTO. *See* World Trade Organization

Wu, Liuren, 432
Wurgler, Jeffrey, 287
Wyeth, 154

X

Xerox, 152, 188
Xu, Yexiao, 23

Y

Yahoo, 108, 137, 152
Yankee bonds, 313–314
Yawitz, Jess B., 367, 377
Ye, Jia, 83
Yield curves, 336–339
Yields
  anticipated realized, 334
  to call, 333–334
  on convertible bonds, 391
  current, 329–330
  dividend, 215, 216, 418
  to maturity, 330–333, 353
  spreads, 342–344
Ying, Lewellen, Schlarbaum, and Lease study, 274–275
Ying, Louis K. W., 274
Young, Allen E., 275, 276
Yu, Yun, 82

Z

Z scores, 209
Zaman, Mir A., 261
Zaremba, Lester S., 377
Zeckhauser, Richard, 473
Zero-coupon bonds, 291
  convertible, 393
  duration of, 365–366
  terminal wealth analysis, 370
  Treasury issues, 294–295, 310
Zeta Services Inc., 209
Zhong, Rui, 237
Zhou, Chunsheng, 406
Zwecher, Michael J., 83
ZZZZ Best Co., 232–233